The Art and Science of
Social Research

The Art and Science of
Social Research

Deborah Carr
Boston University

Elizabeth Heger Boyle
University of Minnesota

Benjamin Cornwell
Cornell University

Shelley Correll
Stanford University

Robert Crosnoe
University of Texas at Austin

Jeremy Freese
Stanford University

Mary C. Waters
Harvard University

W. W. NORTON & COMPANY, INC.
New York • London

W. W. NORTON & COMPANY has been independent since its founding in 1923, when Wiliam Warder Norton and Mary D. Herter Norton first published lectures delivered at the People's Institute, the adult education division of New York City's Cooper Union. The firm soon expanded its program beyond the Institute, publishing books by celebrated academics from America and abroad. By midcentury, the two major pillars of Norton's publishing program—trade books and college texts—were firmly established. In the 1950s, the Norton family transferred control of the company to its employees, and today—with a staff of four hundred and a comparable number of trade, college, and professional titles published each year—W. W. Norton & Company stands as the largest and oldest publishing house owned wholly by its employees.

Copyright © 2018 by W. W. Norton & Company, Inc.

Printed in Canada

First Edition

Editor: Sasha Levitt
Assistant Editor: Miranda Schonbrun
Project Editor: Diane Cipollone
Managing Editor, College: Marian Johnson
Managing Editor, College Digital Media: Kim Yi
Production Manager: Eric Pier-Hocking
Media Editor: Eileen Connell
Associate Media Editor: Mary Williams
Media Project Editor: Danielle Belfiore
Digital Production: Lizz Thabet, Mateus Teixeira
Marketing Manager, Sociology: Julia Hall
Design Director: Lissi Sigillo
Designer: Anna Reich
Photo Editor: Agnieszka Czapski
Permissions Manager: Megan Schindel
Composition: Graphic World
Manufacturing: Transcontinental Interglobe

ISBN: **978-0-393-91158-9 (pbk.)**

W. W. Norton & Company, Inc., 500 Fifth Avenue, New York, N.Y. 10110
wwnorton.com
W. W. Norton & Company Ltd., 15 Carlisle Street, London W1D 3BS
1 2 3 4 5 6 7 8 9 0

Brief Contents

Contents

Part 1
CONCEPTUAL ISSUES IN RESEARCH

Part 3
RESEARCH APPROACHES

Part 4
ANALYZING AND PRESENTING RESULTS

Preface

Doing sociological research requires a deep understanding of the steps and mechanics of the scientific process, such as selecting a research topic, developing a theoretical framework, setting forth hypotheses, operationalizing key concepts, and designing a study that can convincingly and rigorously answer compelling questions. Yet social science research is also an art; human beings are not as predictable as molecules. As a result, strict and formulaic adherence to the classic scientific method is not always the best (or most realistic) approach.

In *The Art and Science of Social Research*, a team of internationally renowned sociologists—experts in surveys, experiments, evaluation research, in-depth interviewing, ethnography, materials-based methods, and social network analysis—introduce students to the core concepts and procedures of social science research. The authors also share insights into how sociologists uphold methodological rigor while also realistically addressing the challenges that arise when investigating the unpredictable topic of social behavior. Our hope is that readers will become captivated by social research methods and will be inspired to carry out original research of their own, or will become savvy and thoughtful consumers of research studies carried out by others. In this era of information overload, when dozens of studies about health, self-esteem, dating behavior, political attitudes, unemployment trends, and climate change fly across our radar (or smartphone screen) on a daily basis, it is more important than ever to understand what research findings mean, how they were discovered, and whether we should believe them.

How the First Edition of *The Art and Science of Social Research* Was Born

This book was conceived roughly a decade ago. I was having a working lunch with my then-editor Karl Bakeman (now editorial director for digital media), to discuss our latest ideas for updating my co-authored textbook *Introduction to Sociology* (Giddens, Duneier, Appelbaum, and Carr, 2018), also published by W. W. Norton. Our conversation turned to the topic of research methods, and we talked animatedly about how wonderful it would be for students to learn not just the "nuts and bolts" of social research and abstract rules like the scientific method, but to also learn about the ways that research is *really* done. We wanted to share real-life insights into the challenges, surprises, and, yes, even mistakes, that researchers encounter when carrying out their work. We wanted to show that researchers can re-strategize, change course, and innovate to carry out compelling, rigorous, and influential scholarship—even when things don't go as originally planned.

Karl then asked, "Who would be the best person to write this kind of book? Is there a sociologist who is known for being 'the best' methodologist?" I thought for a moment and replied that there was not a single person who would be "best" because sociologists tend to specialize in different methods. Even though nearly all professional sociologists have a general knowledge of surveys, fieldwork, experiments, and so on, often based on our graduate training and the books we read, we have deep and hard-won knowledge only of those methods that we use day in and day out in our own research. Wouldn't it be an amazing educational experience for students to learn about experiments from someone like Shelley Correll, who is internationally recognized for her path-breaking and policy-shaping experimental research showing why working mothers suffer a wage penalty in the labor market? Or qualitative methods from a world-renowned scholar like Mary Waters, who has authored 11 influential books, including the classic *Ethnic Options* (1990), which vividly revealed how European Americans think and talk about ethnicity? We continued to talk about some of the nation's leading sociologists who were doing high-impact research that exemplified what different research methods can (and cannot) do.

To cut to the chase, W. W. Norton agreed to support the publication of such a book. I was delighted when each and every person on my "dream team" of scholars agreed to write about a particular set of research methods and concepts. What's remarkable is that all of the authors not only shared my vision for the book, but also knew exactly how to clearly and vividly convey their ideas, experiences, and expansive knowledge of research methods, gleaned from teaching and mentoring their own undergraduate and graduate students. Although the book technically was authored by seven individuals, it shares one unified voice.

Shelley Correll (Stanford University) authored the chapters on experimental and evaluation research, while Mary Waters (Harvard University) wrote about ethics, in-depth interviewing, ethnography, and analysis of qualitative data. Elizabeth (Liz) Heger Boyle (University of Minnesota) is widely known for her research on laws and legal systems across history and social contexts, including the regulation of abortion, female genital cutting, and nuclear power. Her research methods are unified by her innovative use of materials, including public and historical records, legal documents, media, and secondary data sets. Her passion for historical and comparative research led her to create IPUMS-Demographic and Health Surveys, an online system that unlocks access to critically important data on women and children's health for all researchers around the world. Liz conveys her deep knowledge and experience in her chapter on materials-based methods.

Benjamin (Ben) Cornwell (Cornell University), one of the nation's leading scholars and teachers of social network methods, has written a clear and engaging chapter on this rapidly evolving approach, making *The Art and Science of Social Research* one of (if not the only) undergraduate methods textbooks with an entire chapter dedicated to network data and analysis. Ben has creatively applied network methods to such intriguing topics as drug sales and risky sexual practices. His expertise in designing and collecting social network data for the large National Social Life, Health, and Aging Project (NSHAP), as well as analyzing social network data, makes him the ideal author.

Robert (Rob) Crosnoe (University of Texas at Austin) is a rare and prolific scholar who has used both qualitative and quantitative methods to study the lives of adolescents, and the ways that schools, parents, and peers shape one's health, well-being, and future opportunities. He has not only conducted in-depth interviews with American youth, but also serves as a co-investigator of the NICHD Study of Early Child Care and Youth Development. Rob has written our foundational chapters focused on theory, concepts, reliability, validity, and other critical building blocks of social research.

Jeremy Freese (Stanford University) is an innovative methodologist who creatively applies statistical methods to both core and cutting-edge questions in sociology, including social inequalities in health and gene-environment interactions. Jeremy also is a leader in developing new data resources and building on existing ones, in his roles as principal investigator on the Time-sharing Experiments for the Social Sciences (TESS) and the General Social Survey (GSS). He has written chapters on some of the most difficult topics in research methods, including sampling and quantitative data analysis, with clarity, insight, and even good humor.

I drew on my experiences as a long-time instructor of introduction to sociology when writing the book's opening chapter, which provides a brief overview of the field of sociology. And in the survey research chapter, I share my experiences and insights as a co-investigator on large surveys such as the Wisconsin Longitudinal Study (WLS) and Midlife in the United States (MIDUS) and principal investigator of the National Longitudinal Study of Youth 1979 (NLSY79). One of my personal passions is writing about social science, whether in academic journals read by professional sociologists, textbooks read by students, or blogs and trade books read by anyone who is curious about human lives. My experiences as an editor, author, and reader have taught me tricks of the trade, which I share in the final chapter on communicating research results.

Major Themes

Three overarching themes run throughout our book. First, as our title conveys, we believe that *social research is both an art and a science.* Good social science rests on foundations like objectivity, rigorous design, and careful adherence to scientific procedures, but it also requires creativity, thoughtful interpretation, nimble problem-solving, a critical eye (often cast on our own work), and the recognition that human beings often are not rational and predictable creatures.

Second, we firmly believe that *no single method is "best."* Rather, each is ideally suited for addressing different types of research goals, with some topics requiring multiple methods to answer a researcher's questions most effectively. We describe the strengths and limitations, possibilities and pitfalls of each method so that readers can make informed decisions when designing their own work.

Third, we convey that *a solid grasp of social research methods is critical for both producing and consuming knowledge.* The skills one learns in the course can help in myriad professions—from market research, to business, to law, to medicine, to education. Just as importantly, a solid knowledge of research methods is critical to being an informed citizen who can examine, challenge, and make sense of the countless research sound-bites we encounter every day. How do we know to heed a newscaster's warning that "doing more than two hours of Facebook a day may make you depressed" or "eating breakfast can raise your school grades"? Understanding key concepts such as causal ordering and social selection and knowing how to scrutinize the nuts and bolts of research studies can help us make wise and well-informed decisions.

Organization

The book's 17 chapters are arranged in three parts. Part I (Chapters 1–3) focuses on conceptual issues in social science research. Chapter 1 introduces readers to the types of puzzles investigated by sociologists and the philosophies and goals underlying social research. Chapter 2 describes what theory is, how theory is used in the research process, and the different theoretical frameworks that sociologists draw on to motivate their research questions. Chapter 3 describes the hallmarks of ethical research practices, highlights some of the most infamous examples of unethical research, and explains how these cases informed the creation of explicit rules and guidelines for ethical research.

Part 2 (Chapters 4–6) focuses on what we refer to as the building blocks of empirical social science research: hypotheses, measurement, reliability, validity, and sampling. Chapter 4 describes how researchers develop and test hypotheses, and underscores the importance of measurement when testing theory. Chapter 5 characterizes two of the main criteria used when evaluating the quality and rigor of a study: reliability and validity. Chapter 6 describes sampling strategies, the strengths and weaknesses of these different sampling approaches, and practical strategies for mitigating against those weaknesses.

Part 3 (Chapters 7–13) arguably contains the most exciting material in this book, showcasing the strengths, limitations, and applications of seven research approaches: survey research (Chapter 7), experimental research (Chapter 8), evaluation and translational research (Chapter 9), ethnography (Chapter 10), in-depth interviewing (Chapter 11), materials-based methods, including historical-comparative methods, content analysis, and secondary data analysis (Chapter 12), and social network analysis (Chapter 13).

The final section, Part 4 (Chapters 14–17), provides practical guidance for analyzing and presenting results from one's research. Chapters 14 and 15 focus on the analysis of quantitative data; Chapter 14 covers descriptive and bivariate analyses, and Chapter 15 focuses on more advanced multivariate methods. Chapter 16 provides a step-by-step guide for analyzing qualitative data, including data collected through in-depth interviews, participant observation research, and focus groups. Chapter 17 provides tips on communicating social science research results to diverse audiences.

Pedagogical Goals and Tools

Our pedagogical features were designed with several goals in mind: *clarifying key concepts* through repetition, marginal definitions of key terms, Concept Check questions, and end-of-chapter summaries; *sparking student enthusiasm for research* and an appreciation of the ways that research methods can be applied to contemporary social questions through active-learning exercises, vivid visual examples of research documents and tools, and examples of social science in the mass media; and *demonstrating that social science is both an art and a science* by providing a glimpse into individual researchers' trials and tribulations in the field.

The first page of each chapter includes a roadmap of the chapter's content in an easy-to-read text box. This outline identifies the chapter's major sections and subsections. Readers are eased into each chapter with examples of real-world research questions or a contemporary social problem to demonstrate the breadth and depth of social research. Concept Check questions at the end of every major section ask readers to define, compare and contrast, or provide examples of important concepts and topics to ensure mastery of the material and promote active reading. The text provides clear definitions and illustrations of the bold-faced key terms; these terms also are defined in the margins for easy reference. The key terms are listed once again in the end-of-chapter spread, with page numbers showing readers precisely where they can find the original definition. The end-of-chapter review recaps the main themes discussed in each of the chapter's subsections. But we want readers to do more than memorize concepts; we want you to get your hands dirty and do real research. To that end, each chapter includes an active learning assignment that involves carrying out key steps of the research process, whether selecting a sampling frame for a survey, doing a mini-ethnography at a campus sporting event, or diagramming and analyzing one's own social networks.

The book is rich with artwork and photographs that enliven the text and clarify key terms. Consistent with the belief that a picture is worth a thousand words, the book includes images of early Census data records, historical archives, geocoded maps, social network diagrams, technologies used in survey research labs, research field sites, and other components of the research process to bring abstract ideas to life. Each chapter also includes detailed charts, graphs, tables, and heuristic diagrams to illustrate and clarify the concepts, strategies, and results described in the text.

We also bring research to life through our "Conversations from the Front Lines" boxes in each chapter. These boxes feature sociologists talking about their research, the challenges they've faced, and innovative ways they have carried out their studies. The featured researchers represent highly diverse topics, methods, and career histories. For instance, Hollie Nyseth Brehm is an early career scholar doing influential work on genocide in Rwanda and the Sudan, while Tom Smith is an eminent senior scholar who has directed the General Social Survey (GSS) for nearly four decades.

Finally, "From the Field to the Front Page" features show how social science has an impact beyond the academy. These breakout boxes feature a recent study that captured the national imagination and was reported widely in the mass media. We provide insights into why particular studies are captivating to the general public, but we also urge readers to look beyond the "clickbait" headlines and to delve carefully into the study, to understand precisely what the researchers discovered and the methods they used to arrive at their conclusions.

In addition to the book itself, W. W. Norton provides extensive support materials for instructors and students. The Interactive Instructor's Guide includes helpful and detailed chapter outlines, discussion questions, suggested readings, and class activities. A coursepack for Blackboard and other learning management systems includes chapter quizzes, flashcards, podcast exercises, and more. Lecture PowerPoint slides with lecture notes as well as a Test Bank are also available. A big thank you to media editor Eileen Connell and associate media editor Mary Williams for overseeing the creation of this innovative support package.

Acknowledgments

The publication of a first edition textbook is an exciting milestone, and one that we could not have reached without the creativity, hard work, thoughtful insights, and constructive advice of a community of scholars, editors, teachers, students, and publishing professionals. First and foremost, we are indebted to our editor Sasha Levitt, who has done an extraordinary job in shepherding our book through the writing, editing, and production process. Sasha read every word (more than once), and provided invaluable advice in helping to ensure that our content was complete and comprehensive, that the text could be easily understood by undergraduates, and that the examples we used were timely, compelling, and relevant. Sasha has the rare ability to keep one eye on the "big picture" and the other on the essential details, right down to dotting the i's and crossing the t's. Her contributions are immeasurable. We also are grateful to Karl Bakeman, whose ingenuity, wisdom, and persistence guided the original conceptualization, scope, and author team of this book. Developmental editor Steven Rigolosi did a superb job in making sure our text was concise, clear, snappy, well-organized, and of a single editorial voice. A sincere thank you to the rest of the team at W. W. Norton, including project editor Diane Cipollone, production manager Eric Pier-Hocking, assistant editor Miranda Schonbrun, design director Lissi Sigillo, designer Anna Reich, and photo editor Agnieszka Czapski.

Finally, we are tremendously grateful to the many scholars and instructors who provided detailed and constructive feedback on our chapters. We have heeded their advice and believe that the reviewers have helped us write a book that instructors will genuinely want to use in class and students will genuinely learn from and, ideally, enjoy reading. Our "class testers," who assigned early chapters of the book in their own methods classes, were especially helpful. Their students are fortunate to have such engaged and pro-active teachers, and our readers will benefit from the thought, time, and care they have dedicated to strengthening our book.

William P. Anderson, Grove City College

Jennifer Barber, University of Michigan

Christie Batson, University of Nevada, Las Vegas

Alison Bianchi, University of Iowa

Matthew Brashears, University of South Carolina

Ashley Brooke Barr, University at Buffalo, SUNY

Wendy Cadge, Brandeis University

Victor Chen, Virginia Commonwealth University

Madhavi Cherian, New York University

Ashley Daily, Florida State University

Jonathan Daw, Pennsylvania State University

Joan Ferrante, Northern Kentucky University

Samantha Friedman, University at Albany, SUNY

Stacy George, Whitworth University

David Gibson, University of Notre Dame

Carol Glasser, Minnesota State University, Mankato

Neha Gondal, Boston University

Kyle Green, Utica College

Mark Gunty, University of Notre Dame

Kristin Haltinner, University of Idaho

David Harding, University of California, Berkeley

Orestes Patterson Hastings, Colorado State University

Terrence D. Hill, University of Arizona

Jonathan Horowitz, University of North Carolina, Chapel Hill

Mosi Ifatunji, University of North Carolina at Chapel Hill

Jeehoon Kim, Idaho State University

Pam Hunt Kirk, University of West Georgia

Julie Kmec, Washington State University

Kelsy Kretschmer, Oregon State University

Anne-Kathrin Kronberg, Frankfurt University

Laszlo Kulcsar, Kansas State University

Martin Kunović, University of Wisconsin–Madison

Samantha Kwan, University of Houston

Catherine Lee, Rutgers University

Carolyn Liebler, University of Minnesota

Amy Lucas, University of Houston–Clear Lake

Scott M. Lynch, Duke University

Kimberly Mahaffy, Millersville University

Christopher Steven Marcum, National Institutes of Health

Andrew Martin, Ohio State University

Ruby Mendenhall, University of Illinois at Urbana-Champaign

Denise Obinna, Mount St. Mary's University

Paolo Parigi, Stanford University

Laura Pecenco, San Diego Miramar College

Becky Pettit, University of Texas at Austin

Ann Rotchford, University of North Carolina at Wilmington

Katrina Running, Idaho State University

Frank L. Samson, University of Miami

Markus Schafer, University of Toronto

Solee Shin, National University of Singapore

Karrie Ann Snyder, Northwestern University

Caleb Southworth, University of Oregon

Trent Steidley, University of Denver

Judith Stepan-Norris, University of California, Irvine

Elizangela Storelli, George Mason University

Jaclyn Tabor, Indiana University Bloomington

Lisa Wade, Occidental College

Russell E. Ward, University at Albany, SUNY

Andrew Whitehead, Clemson University

Deborah Carr
Boston University

About the Authors

Deborah Carr is Professor of Sociology at Boston University. She previously held faculty positions at Rutgers University, the University of Michigan, and the University of Wisconsin–Madison. Dr. Carr studies health, aging, and families over the life course. She has written about the ways that older adults cope with loss, how body weight affects our psychosocial well-being, and generational differences in work-family choices. She has published more than 100 articles and chapters and several books, including *Worried Sick: How Stress Hurts Us and How to Bounce Back*. She is editor-in-chief of *Journal of Gerontology: Social Sciences* and principal investigator of the National Longitudinal Study of Youth 1979.

Elizabeth Heger Boyle is Professor of Sociology and Law at the University of Minnesota. She studies the role of international laws on women and children's health around the world. Her current research focuses on abortion policies. She has also written extensively on the impetus for and impact of laws related to female genital cutting. Professor Boyle is currently the principal investigator on two projects (IPUMS-DHS and IPUMS-PMA) that make comparative and historical data on women and children's health accessible to all researchers through the Internet.

Benjamin Cornwell is Associate Professor of Sociology and Director of Graduate Studies at Cornell University, where he teaches social network analysis, sequence analysis, graduate sociological theory, and sociology of disasters. His research focuses on the implications of socially networked and sequenced social processes for individuals and organizations—and, in particular, how such processes shape social stratification. He has documented the role of social network structure in a wide variety of processes, including the sale of drugs, risky sexual practices, health, and access to valuable resources like credit and expertise. His research on the dynamic nature of social networks in later life has been covered in dozens of media outlets.

Shelley Correll is Professor of Sociology and Organizational Behavior at Stanford University, where she is also the director of the Clayman Institute for Gender Research. Her expertise is in the areas of gender, workplace dynamics, and organizational culture, with an emphasis on gender and technical work. She has received numerous national awards for her research on the "motherhood penalty," research that demonstrates how motherhood influences the workplace evaluations, pay, and job opportunities of mothers. She is currently conducting research in Silicon Valley tech companies to understand how gender stereotypes and organizational practices affect the advancement and retention of women in technical jobs.

Robert Crosnoe is the C.B. Smith, Sr. Centennial Chair #4 at the University of Texas at Austin, where he is chair of the department of sociology and a faculty member in the Population Research Center. He is a life course sociologist who conducts mixed-methods research on the connections among the health, social development, and education of children, adolescents, and young adults and the contributions of these connections to socioeconomic and immigration-related inequalities in American society. Some specific topics of interest include high school social cultures, parenting, early childhood education, and teen substance use.

Jeremy Freese is Professor of Sociology at Stanford University. Much of his research concerns interactions of social, psychological, and biological processes, especially in terms of how social advantages turn into stronger skills and better health. He is co-leader of the Health Disparities Working Group for the Stanford Center of Population Health Sciences, and he is co-principal investigator of the General Social Survey and the Time-Sharing Experiments for the Social Sciences.

Mary C. Waters is the John L. Loeb Professor of Sociology at Harvard University, where she has taught introduction to research methods to thousands of undergraduates over the last 30 years. Her work has focused on the integration of immigrants and their children, immigration policy, the transition to adulthood, the impact of natural disasters, and the measurement and meaning of racial and ethnic identity. The author or co-author of 11 books and over 100 articles, she is an elected member of the National Academy of Sciences and a fellow of the American Academy of Arts and Sciences and the American Philosophical Society.

The Art and Science of
Social Research

The social world is complex and human beings are unpredictable, making sociological research both a science and an art.

THE ART AND SCIENCE OF SOCIAL RESEARCH
An Introduction

Sociological Perspectives: An Overview
Agency versus Structure
Adopting a Sociological Imagination
Attention to Differences and Hierarchies
How Does Sociology Resemble—and Differ from—Other Social Sciences?

Types of Social Science Research
Basic versus Applied Research
Qualitative versus Quantitative Research

Cross-Sectional versus Longitudinal Study Designs
Unit of Analysis

Starting the Research Process: Choosing a Question and Setting Goals
Asking Questions
Research Goals: Description, Exploration, and Explanation

Overview of This Book

You have probably spent long and lively evenings discussing and debating questions about the human condition such as the following:

- Why are some teenagers bullies, while others are victims of bullying?
- What traits do we look for in a potential romantic partner?
- What makes someone a political liberal or conservative?
- Why are some historical periods marked by protest and social unrest, while others appear to be calm and placid?

Even if not phrased in such lofty philosophical terms, most of us are hungry to understand our own behavior as well as the behaviors, beliefs, and feelings of those people who are most important to us. Why do some of our classmates succeed in school and work, while others struggle? Why are so many college graduates today delaying marriage and childbearing until their thirties? Are blacks more likely than whites to suffer violence at the hands of police officers, and if so, why? Why are some corporate workplaces pleasant and enjoyable places to work, while others are tense and competitive? Some of the questions we debate transcend our own lives and focus on the world around us: Why do men and (to a lesser extent) women join violent and often radical organizations like ISIS or the National Alliance, a neo-Nazi group? Why do some time periods and geographic regions see particularly high rates of suicide, hate crimes, drug addiction, and other social problems? Why is women's sexuality punished in some cultures and celebrated in others?

Answering questions like these is the core mission of sociology. **Sociology** is the scientific study of the social lives of individuals, groups, and societies. It is a far-ranging, diverse, and exciting field of study, encompassing a seemingly endless number of topics. Sociologists explore both macro- and micro-level issues. **Macrosociology** focuses on large-scale social systems such as the political system or the economy, whereas **microsociology** focuses on personal concerns and interpersonal interactions such as doctor-patient relationships, how spouses negotiate housework and child-care arrangements, and the ways that one's peers might encourage law-abiding versus delinquent behavior. Yet macrosocial and microsocial phenomena are inextricably linked, where systems of economic and social inequalities affect even our most private decisions and feelings.

Students who are new to sociology sometimes think that it is the study of *everything*. But as we shall soon see, sociology is guided by several defining themes that distinguish it from other social sciences such as anthropology, psychology, and history. One of the most important themes is the **sociological imagination**, a distinctive viewpoint recognizing that our personal experiences are powerfully shaped by macrosocial and historical forces (Mills, 1959). Using the sociological imagination helps us to step back from our taken-for-granted assumptions about everyday life, especially the common assumption that our lives are shaped by our personal choices alone and that we are the masters of our own destinies.

Sociology is also a science, or the rigorous and systematic study of individuals, groups, and social institutions. Sociologists answer questions by collecting and analyzing high-quality and verifiable data. Precisely how we carry out our research varies according to the questions we ask, the theories guiding our work, the types of populations we are interested in studying, and practical concerns such as the financial costs of carrying out research or ability to gain access to the people, corporations, subcultures, or nations we would like to study. As we will show throughout this book, sociologists have many methods and tools for carrying out their research. These research methods fall into two broad categories: quantitative and qualitative.

Quantitative research encompasses the collection and analysis of numerical data, often obtained from surveys or social network information. Qualitative methods emphasize interpretation and observation, using approaches such as open-ended interviews or rich descriptions of social settings and groups. A third

sociology The scientific study of the social lives of individuals, groups, and societies.

macrosociology The study of large-scale social systems and processes such as the political system or the economy.

microsociology The study of personal concerns and interpersonal interactions.

sociological imagination A distinctive viewpoint, originated by C. Wright Mills, recognizing that our personal experiences are powerfully shaped by macrosocial and historical forces.

category, mixed methods, combines quantitative and qualitative approaches, with the goal of providing richer insights than would have been achieved using only one of the two approaches (Small, 2011).

You will learn much more about the distinctive characteristics, strengths, and weaknesses of quantitative and qualitative methods in Part 3 of this book. Much of this book focuses on describing precisely what methods sociologists use, offering a step-by-step guide so that you can carry out your own research study. To get a sense of the diversity of methods used by sociologists, consider that some researchers conduct surveys of literally thousands of high school seniors in the United States each year (Miech et al., 2016a), while others observe at close hand a specific group of people, such as sex workers in Southeast Asia (Hoang, 2015). Some sociologists conduct experiments to understand how a new workplace policy will affect employees' productivity and job satisfaction (Moen et al., 2016), while others dig deep into historical archives to identify the social and political conditions that enable charismatic leaders to rise to power (Skocpol, 1979).

At first blush, these four examples of sociological research couldn't be more different from one another, yet they share two very important characteristics: They rely on high-quality data and use systematic approaches to answer their questions. These two characteristics distinguish sociology from casual, or "armchair," observations. Our casual observations of the world may be insightful, and they may pique our interest enough to explore a particular research topic more deeply. However, our casual observations typically focus on our friends, families, or the neighborhoods in which we live and work; as such, they are not typically **generalizable**, meaning they do not characterize the human condition far beyond our immediate social world.

As you learn about research methods and the real-life experiences of sociologists, it will become clear that sociological research is both an art and a science. Sociology is clearly a science, with well-established guidelines for carrying out rigorous research on social behavior. As you'll learn in Chapter 4, sociologists take measurement seriously and work hard to develop effective measures even of seemingly fuzzy or subjective phenomena such as loneliness or beauty. Yet social research is a challenging scientific enterprise because people are not as predictable as cells or molecules. As a result, our research methods must take into account the fact that countless (and ever-changing) factors shape human social life. For this reason, sociological research is also an art form, requiring creativity, thoughtful interpretation, nimble problem-solving, a critical eye (often cast on our own work), and the recognition that human beings often are not rational and predictable creatures. But this is precisely what makes social science research so intriguing.

We begin this chapter by providing a brief overview of sociology and its guiding themes, as well as a discussion of how sociology differs from other social sciences such as anthropology or psychology. We then provide a glimpse into the broad approaches that sociologists use: basic and applied research, qualitative and quantitative methods, and studies that collect data at a single point in time

generalizable The extent to which results or conclusions based on one population can be applied to others.

and those that collect data at multiple time points. We offer a brief sketch of the research process, its goals, and the factors that researchers must consider before embarking on a research project. We conclude with an overview of the chapters that follow. We hope that this brief introduction whets your appetite for social research and sparks ideas for the kinds of questions you might explore as part of your social research methods course.

SOCIOLOGICAL PERSPECTIVES: AN OVERVIEW

Sociological perspectives encourage us to identify and understand the complex interconnections between the behavior of individuals and the structures of the societies in which they live. As we strive to understand the complex interplay between microsocial and macrosocial phenomena, three themes may orient our thinking. First, sociology emphasizes the importance of both agency and structure in shaping human behavior. Second, adopting a sociological imagination helps us understand that many seemingly "personal troubles" are actually symptoms of more sweeping "public issues" (Mills, 1959). Third, sociologists recognize that personal characteristics, such as race, social class, and gender, expose us to different structural opportunities as well as constraints. We describe how and why these three orienting themes are such an integral part of sociology relative to other social science disciplines, including anthropology, psychology, and history.

Agency versus Structure

agency Our capacity to make our own choices and act autonomously.

social structures The patterned social arrangements that may constrain (or facilitate) our choices and opportunities.

Our everyday lives are shaped by both agency and structure. **Agency** is our capacity to make our own choices and act independently. We may believe that we freely choose where to attend college, whom to fall in love with, what career path to pursue, and whether to live a healthy or unhealthy lifestyle. Yet sociologists recognize that these personal choices are influenced by **social structures**, the patterned social arrangements that may constrain (or facilitate) our choices and opportunities (McIntyre, 2013). For instance, your decision of where to go to college was likely influenced by your (or your parents') ability to pay tuition. You can't fall in love with someone you've never met, and most of the people we meet live in our neighborhoods and attend our schools. Even those people we "meet" through Internet dating sites and apps like Tinder tend to come from social backgrounds similar to our own. The jobs we take depend on our educational credentials and the extent to which a career counselor encourages or dissuades us from entering a particular field. The choice to adopt a healthy lifestyle is much easier for people who can afford gym memberships and nutritious low-calorie meals. Sociological research helps demonstrate the ways that individuals make and carry out their choices within the constraints of social structures.

Adopting a Sociological Imagination

The notion that individual lives are powerfully shaped by forces outside of ourselves, such as economic or historical factors, is a guiding theme of C. Wright Mills's (1959) classic writings on the sociological imagination. According to Mills, "The sociological imagination enables its possessor to understand the larger historical scene in terms of its meaning for the inner life and external career of a variety of individuals" (Mills,

1959, p. 7). That means we cannot understand human behavior merely by viewing individual actors as free agents who are disconnected from larger sociohistorical contexts. Rather, our biographies are a product of personal experiences and historical forces. Viewing the world through the lens of the sociological imagination can be challenging because people in Western societies like the United States are socialized to view the world in terms of individual achievement and failure. For instance, we don't often consider that a "self-made millionaire" might have benefited from things like a thriving postwar economy or entitlement programs like the GI Bill that provided free college for veterans returning home from World War II. Conversely, we have a tendency to view people's problems as the result of their own individual shortcomings such as laziness or bad luck (Zuckerman, 1979).

The sociological imagination teaches us that what we may think of as "personal troubles," such as marital problems, substance abuse, difficulty paying for college tuition or maintaining a work-life balance, may instead be "public issues," or widespread problems that have social roots and are shared by many others (Mills, 1959). These roots are often related to the structure of society and the changes happening within it. To apply the sociological imagination to a real-world example, let's revisit a trend noted in this chapter's introduction: the rising age of first marriage in the United States. As Figure 1.1 shows, the median age at which Americans marry has risen steadily over the past 50 years. In 1960, the median age at which women and men married for the first time was 20 and 23, respectively. By 2016, these ages had climbed steadily up to 27 and nearly 30. Some observers may sneer that young people today are too immature, selfish, or unfocused to settle down. Millennials, the generation born between 1980 and 2000, have been derided as the "Me, me, me generation" who refuse to "grow up" (Stein, 2013).

By applying the sociological imagination to this question—Why are young people postponing marriage?—we may start to recognize that seemingly personal choices are deeply intertwined with larger social and historical forces. Most people want to wait until they are "financially ready" to marry, meaning they want to have a good job and a stable place to live. But securing a good job today often requires a bachelor's or even a master's degree, which means staying in school longer than prior generations did. And rising housing costs mean that young people often need to work for several years after graduation to scrape together a down payment. The urge to marry young also has faded in recent years for cultural reasons, including greater acceptance of premarital sex and nonmarital cohabitation. Sixty years ago, a young couple who was passionately in love might make a quick dash to the altar so that they could have sex as a married couple, lest they be considered immoral. Today, couples feel little pressure to "wait for marriage," so they can enjoy sexual intimacy without rushing into marriage. Many couples live together, enjoying all the benefits of marriage without having to bear the high costs of a wedding. In short, sociologists recognize that even the most private and personal

FIGURE 1.1 Median Age at First Marriage, 1956–2016

The median age at first marriage in the United States increased steadily for men and women between 1956 and 2016.

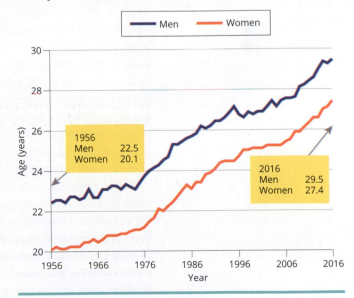

1956
Men   22.5
Women 20.1

2016
Men   29.5
Women 27.4

Source: U.S. Census Bureau, 2017.

In the mid-1950s, the average bride was just 20 years old and her groom 22 years old.

intersectionality A theoretical tradition emphasizing that our overlapping identities and group memberships are critical to our life experiences.

choices about love and marriage are shaped by the far less romantic forces of economy and history.

Mills further observed that if seemingly "personal choices" are happening in large numbers or in patterned ways, then we are likely witnessing a public issue rather than a personal trouble. If a handful of Millennials are delaying marriage, that may be an indication of a personal decision or preference, but if large proportions are doing so, that alerts us to the fact that this is a major social issue rather than the idiosyncratic choice of a few. Using the sociological imagination as a lens through which to observe the world may help empower individuals to transform their personal dissatisfaction or self-blame into public concerns in order to facilitate social change.

Attention to Differences and Hierarchies

The sociological imagination emphasizes the role of historical contexts in shaping our lives, while other sociological approaches focus more broadly on other macrosocial or structural factors that affect our lives. One of the most important areas of inquiry in sociology is understanding the ways that social hierarchies of race, class, gender, age, and other axes of inequality affect our lives. For instance, research done in the traditions of feminist theory and critical race theory, which we describe in Chapter 2, emphasize how gender and race hierarchies affect nearly every aspect of individuals' lives, while conflict theories emphasize the centrality of social class. Other scholars work in a tradition called **intersectionality**, which emphasizes that our overlapping identities and group memberships, such as being a middle-class black woman or working-class white man, are critical to our life experiences (Crenshaw, 1991). As we shall see throughout the book, researchers working in nearly every sociological tradition consider at least some dimensions of social difference in their research and design their studies to enable comparisons of these different groups.

HOW SOCIAL SCIENCE RESEARCH CAN SHED LIGHT ON SOCIAL DIFFERENCES

Considering simultaneously the themes of the sociological imagination and differences helps us gain important insights into how social change may unfold differently on the basis of one's social location. To give one example, let's revisit the question of marriage timing: Why are young adults today delaying marriage until their late-twenties and thirties? We noted earlier that this seemingly personal choice is shaped by macrosocial trends, including an economy that favors those with college or advanced degrees, rising housing costs, and shifting cultural beliefs about nonmarital sex and cohabitation (Arnett, 2014; Furstenberg, 2016). Yet when we consider the marital choices of particular subpopulations, especially African American women, we see that many other issues are at play.

Social scientists have observed that black women are not merely delaying marriage; rather, a considerable proportion may not marry at all. The U.S. Census examined the proportion of women in the United States who had not yet married and compared these proportions on the basis of whether a woman was white, black, Latino, or Asian (Figure 1.2). Although most women had married by the time they reached age 50, black women were far less likely to have married than women of other races. Fewer than 10% of white women were still single by age 50, compared to 25% of black women. These analyses are based on relatively older adults, who have already reached their 50th birthdays (U.S. Census Bureau, 2011). However, researchers have also used sophisticated statistical methods to project how many Generation X and Millennial women will stay single for life: they estimate that more than 80% of white women born in 1980 will marry, yet just half of black women born in 1980 will do so (Martin, Astone, & Peters, 2014).

Understanding the reasons for and implications of these patterns requires the skills and insights of both quantitative and qualitative researchers. Quantitative analysts have focused on identifying explanations for these trends and point to the shortage of "marriageable" black men: Sociologist William Julius Wilson has argued that high rates of imprisonment and premature death are removing men from the communities where they would otherwise marry. High rates of unemployment, especially in urban areas with few job prospects, mean that large numbers of black men may be viewed as not "marriageable" in the eyes of women (Wilson, 2012). Other researchers point out that black women are more likely than black men to earn a college degree and take a professional job, so the economic incentive to marry—the notion that two paychecks are better than one—is less relevant for women of color (Martin, Astone, & Peters, 2014).

Qualitative researchers, by contrast, delve deeply into what these patterns may mean for black women's daily lives. Sociologist Averil Clarke (2011) conducted open-ended interviews with more than 50 middle-class heterosexual black women and found that singlehood was not due to personal choice or the decision to privilege career over romance. Rather, it reflected persistent social inequalities, similar to those noted by the quantitative researchers. Clarke detailed how singlehood and bleak romantic prospects could take a personal toll: Some women repeatedly returned to incompatible partners, while others lost hope of ever finding "Mr. Right." Many rejected the prospect of becoming single mothers, not wanting to affirm a negative stereotype of black women's sexuality—a stereotype that was inconsistent with their personal and professional identities. As we shall see in the chapters that follow, researchers working in all methodological traditions can help untangle the complex interrelations among macrosocial factors, such as history, the economy, and systems of inequality, and micro-level phenomena, such as health, family formation, criminal behavior, work experiences, and the like.

How Does Sociology Resemble—and Differ from—Other Social Sciences?

Sociology is such a broad and inclusive field of study that many of the topics investigated by sociologists also are of great interest to social scientists working in other disciplines, including anthropology, psychology, and history. Each of these academic disciplines is also methodologically and substantively rich, and it would be a disservice

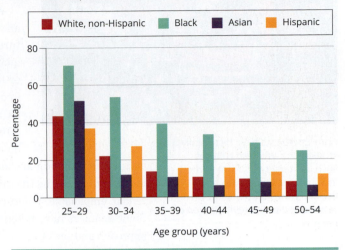

FIGURE 1.2 Percentage of Women Never Married by Age, Race, and Hispanic Origin, 2009

The proportion of U.S. women who have never married is consistently higher among black women compared to white, Asian, and Hispanic women.

Source: U.S. Census Bureau, 2011.

Anthropologists have historically studied non-Western cultures such as immigrants from Fuzhou in Southeast China, who have flooded New York's Chinatown and contributed to the revitalization of the area.

anthropology The study of societies and cultures, often non-Western.

cultural relativism The principle whereby scholars refrain from making judgments about practices they observe and instead adopt the viewpoint of the communities being studied.

psychology The study of individual behavior, attitudes, and emotions, and their causes.

history The study of past events, presidencies, social movements, or cultural patterns.

to describe them in excessively simplistic terms. Still, we provide just a few brief points of contrast to show the main themes and methods used by these related fields. We illustrate these contrasts by showing how each discipline might help us understand the social context and meaning of body weight.

Anthropology, like sociology, is the study of individual and group behavior. Anthropologists dig deeply into the cultures they study and use methods that are similar to those of qualitative sociologists, often doing observation, fieldwork, or in-depth interviews. Some anthropologists are interested in cultures and communities that no longer exist, so they rely on archaeological methods to obtain data (Haviland et al., 2010). Historically, anthropologists tended to focus more on non-Western cultures while sociologists focused on Western cultures, but that divide has blurred. Likewise, anthropologists have been characterized as emphasizing the influence of culture on social behavior, whereas sociologists tend to emphasize structure, although that boundary also has blurred in recent years. Some scholars have noted that sociologists tend to take more of a problem-focused approach and seek to remedy those things they deem problematic, whereas anthropologists tend to uphold the principle of **cultural relativism** and therefore refrain from making judgments about what they observe and instead try to adopt the viewpoint of the communities they are studying (Boas, 1887).

Psychology, by contrast, is the study of individual behavior, attitudes, emotions, and their causes (Gleitman, Gross, & Reisberg, 2010). Most psychologists focus on contemporary populations and concerns. In recent decades, growing numbers of psychologists have focused on biological and neurological influences on behavior, although a subgroup specializing in social psychology pays close attention to social context and group memberships. Most psychologists use experimental methods and examine whether exposure to a particular treatment affects what people do, think, or feel, but social psychologists, because they place a greater emphasis on social group membership than do biologically oriented psychologists, often use large survey data sets. In general, psychologists tend to be less interested in social structures than sociologists are. As such, they pay less attention to the role of social class or race differences in the phenomena they study and instead focus on what they call *individual differences*, such as personality, intelligence, or motivation, as influences on social behaviors. For psychologists, the individual is almost always the focus, although some specialize in the interactions of very small groups. Sociologists, by contrast, are interested in groups and societies as well as individuals.

History refers to the study of past events, such as wars, presidencies, social movements, or pop culture trends (Cole & Symes, 2015). Because most historians study the quite distant past and therefore cannot collect data from living respondents, most tend to use materials-based approaches, such as those described in Chapter 12. These materials include historical records, letters, maps, death and birth certificates, and photographs and other documents that can be used to reconstruct, describe, and analyze the past. Historians who study more recent events may conduct in-depth interviews with witnesses, such as Holocaust survivors or leaders of the civil rights movement. While the research that historians and historical sociologists conduct is similar in many ways, their analytic and theoretical approaches differ. Sociologists tend to approach history through a theoretical lens in an effort to draw broad conclusions about human behavior, whereas historians seek to understand and document the particular details of an event or sequence of events.

Using the theories and tools of their trades, sociologists, anthropologists, psychologists, and historians would each cast a different, although equally valuable, lens on a topic such as body weight. Quantitative sociologists might document the proportion of Americans who are overweight or obese and examine how these patterns vary on the basis of sociodemographic factors such as race or income. For instance, one reason why African Americans are more likely than whites to be obese is that they are more likely to live in poor neighborhoods that lack full-service grocery stores and safe places to exercise. At the same time, these neighborhoods are home to a disproportionate number of fast-food restaurants that serve inexpensive yet high-fat "supersized" meals (Boardman et al., 2005). Qualitative sociologists, by contrast, might conduct in-depth interviews with low-income persons to understand how they make choices about diet and exercise and how they feel about their bodies. One interview study of 28 overweight and obese women living in a poor rural area found that many lived from paycheck to paycheck and would eat (or even overeat) because they worried about running out of food. As one woman admitted: "I don't like to waste food, so sometimes I'll find myself eating what the kids left over on their plates." Others turned to "emotional eating" to cope with the stress of financial strain, seeking solace in ice cream, cookies, chips, and other fattening foods. As one husband said of his overweight wife, "She gets in those moods where she just wants to eat everything. . . . She seems like she's eating all day" (Bove & Olson, 2006).

Historians might explore the ways that eating patterns or cultural portrayals of "ideal" body types have changed over time. Historian Joan Jacobs Brumberg's (2000) fascinating book *Fasting Girls: The History of Anorexia Nervosa* showed that young girls' desire to starve themselves is not, in fact, a contemporary phenomenon. Brumberg documents that "female self-denial," as she calls it, dates back as far as the thirteenth century medieval era, when young women used starvation to demonstrate religious devotion and achieve martyrdom. Today, anorexia is generally believed to be triggered by a desire for a very slender physique and a need to assert control over one's body. In the 1920s, the birth of the "silver screen" prompted movie stars to practice very strict "slimming" regimens, which inspired generations to lose weight (in often unhealthy ways). Using meticulous historical records, including religious documents, medical records, and photographs, Brumberg provides an in-depth account of how the motivations and strategies for attaining a very slender physique have shifted throughout history.

Adopting a cultural view of body practices, anthropologists might conduct in-depth explorations of particular societies to understand their conceptualizations of beauty and health. Although Western cultures

African Americans experience higher levels of obesity in part because they are more likely to live in food deserts—areas without full-service grocery stores.

view a slender physique as the cultural ideal for women, several cultures in Africa equate women's beauty and health with very large bodies. In Mauritania and among the nomadic Moors of the Sahara, for example, girls are force-fed camel milk, goat meat, mullet, porridge, and other fattening foods from the time they are very young. Anthropologist Rebecca Popenoe (2004) conducted intense fieldwork in an Arab village near Niger and discovered that force-feeding is viewed as good for children, as fatness is equated with happiness and a bright future. Obese young women are considered more sexually desirable and are more likely to get married. Once they're married, their husbands do all they can to keep their wives obese. A very large wife is a status symbol, a sign that a man is prosperous enough to feed her well. These cultural practices partly reflect the fact that nomadic cultures often survive periods of poverty and scarcity, and fatness is viewed as a source of protection against starvation. Taken together, these studies of body weight reveal the distinctive contributions of research conducted in different academic disciplines with different research methodologies.

CONCEPT CHECKS

1   Contrast agency versus structure.

2   Contrast macrosocial versus microsocial phenomena.

3   Define intersectionality.

4   Name one way that sociology differs from psychology.

TYPES OF SOCIAL SCIENCE RESEARCH

Social science research has many purposes: Some researchers want to understand theoretical questions about human behavior, whereas others want to do research that can directly affect the lives of those they study. Sociological research also differs with respect to the kind of data and methods used: Some sociologists use statistical approaches to document trends and patterns, whereas other sociologists seek to provide deep description. We spend much of this book describing when, why, and how a researcher would choose to use a quantitative versus qualitative approach. Additionally, some sociologists study people at one point in time, whereas others are able to revisit their subjects or study sites multiple times to explore change over time. In this section, we provide a thumbnail sketch of basic and applied research, quantitative and qualitative research, cross-sectional versus longitudinal study designs, and units of analysis. We underscore that no one approach is better or worse, more or less valuable than the other. Rather, each is simply suited for a different type of research goal.

Basic versus Applied Research

basic research A form of research that seeks to answer theoretically informed questions or to resolve a fundamental intellectual puzzle about social behavior.

Sociological research can be either basic or applied; which approach an investigator takes is closely tied to his or her research goals and intended audience. (We will say much more about communicating results to the appropriate audience in Chapter 17.) **Basic research** does not necessarily have an applied or immediate goal, such as reducing rates of depression among college students by the year 2020. Rather, basic research seeks to answer theoretically rich questions or to resolve a fundamental intellectual puzzle about social behavior. For this reason, most basic research takes place in academia, conducted by professors who are interested in the pursuit of knowledge. By stimulating new ways of thinking about a social issue, these pursuits may ultimately revolutionize how practitioners think about—and confront—a social problem. Basic research in sociology uses whichever method the investigator believes will best address his or her inquiry, encompassing everything from surveys to ethnography, experiments to materials-based methods.

Applied research, by contrast, seeks to answer a question in the real world or to address a concrete problem. Whereas the goals of basic research may be theoretical development and testing, the goals of applied research are entirely practical, such as evaluating the effectiveness of a particular program, policy, or intervention. Applied researchers can use a range of methods. Evaluations of educational interventions or new public policies tend to use experimental designs because they are particularly well suited to identifying whether the program has effected a meaningful change. Market researchers might use a survey to understand the characteristics of those people who say they plan to buy a new car in the upcoming year. Some applied research is carried out by professors at universities, but it is more often designed and carried out by researchers working in policy organizations, think tanks, or even the institutional research arm within the organization being studied. For instance, a public school system may employ a social scientist to carry out research exploring whether a new curriculum is linked to students' improved performance on standardized tests. A corporation's research department might conduct a focus group in order to understand consumers' views toward a new product the corporation is rolling out.

To illustrate the differences between basic and applied research, let's focus on a question that is of great interest to policy makers: high school graduation rates. Social scientists, parents, and educators alike are interested in identifying factors that promote students' school performance, especially high school graduation rates. An applied study might evaluate the impact on high school graduation rates of a very specific program, such as the Becoming a Man (BAM) intervention study (Heller et al., 2016). As part of this program, young African American men in Chicago schools were randomly assigned to one of two groups: One was exposed to the "usual" school curriculum, while others participated in a weekly after-school program where they learned skills to help them respond calmly and thoughtfully to risky situations, like threats from classmates or altercations with police. The students assigned to this program went on to have high school graduation rates that were nearly 20% higher than those of their peers who did not participate in the program. The applied researchers' primary concern was to evaluate whether programs like BAM, designed specifically to facilitate calm decision-making, were helping or hurting teenagers' educational outcomes, as these results could inform the development and widespread use of such programs.

applied research A form of research that seeks to answer a question or concrete problem in the real world or to evaluate a policy or program.

Teens involved in the "Becoming a Man" program had fewer arrests, earned higher grades, and had better attendance.

THE AUTHORS OF *THE ART AND SCIENCE OF SOCIAL RESEARCH*

Deborah Carr (Debby) is a professor of sociology at Boston University and before that was on the faculty at Rutgers University for 14 years. She is a life course sociologist who uses large survey data sets to explore the ways that social factors, including family relationships and stress, affect health in later life.

Why did you become a sociologist? Was there a particular class, person, or event that put you on this career path?

My original career goal was to be a journalist, but I majored in sociology simply because I found the topic fascinating, from my very first day as a student in introduction to sociology. I hadn't realized that all the issues I felt passionately about—social-class inequalities, sexism, racism, and so on—were an academic field I could study! After college, I did work as a travel magazine writer for several years but then returned to graduate school for a PhD in sociology so that I could ultimately study and write about issues I cared about deeply.

Describe one major finding from your research and how you came to this discovery. How does this work illustrate the core principles of sociology?

I'm interested in how social relationships affect our well-being, so I used data from a large survey of older married couples to explore whether happiness is shaped not only by our own experiences in the marriage, but our spouse's as well. I discovered a finding that the media liked to report as "happy wife, happy life." Even if men were disappointed in their marriages, they reported high levels of happiness if their wives were satisfied in the marriage. Happy wives, especially those raised in the 1940s and 1950s, might provide sufficient care for their husbands so that they are generally happy, even if not enamored with their wives and marriages. Women's happiness was relatively unaffected by their husbands' marital satisfaction, perhaps because men would not communicate their feelings about the marriage to their wives, reflecting gender differences in how we talk about (or avoid talking about) relationships. This study is sociological because it reveals the complex ways that historically situated gender roles affect even the most micro-level outcome of happiness.

Elizabeth Heger Boyle (Liz), professor of sociology and law at the University of Minnesota, studies law and globalization, especially related to women's and children's human rights. Most of her research uses historical records and data sets with information on multiple time periods and countries. Her goal is to better understand when and why countries adopt laws designed to improve life for women or children and what makes those laws more or less effective in creating social change.

Why did you become a sociologist? Was there a particular class, person, or event that put you on this career path?

I loved sociology from the first social problems lecture (in Marvin Krohn's class at the University of Iowa), and switched from an accounting major to a sociology major at that time. Sociology continued to be my passion, leading me to change careers from a securities lawyer to a sociology professor later in life.

Describe one major finding from your research and how you came to this discovery. How does this work illustrate the core principles of sociology?

Why do countries pass laws? Typically, we think laws reflect the will of the people within a country. I was not so sure; I thought lawmakers, especially in poor countries, might be more influenced by powerful international organizations than by their local population. To answer this question, I studied laws regarding female circumcision (a practice carried out on girls that can be harmful to their health) in countries where most women were circumcised. For me, female circumcision laws were an example of democratic representation within countries.

To find out what laws existed and how and why they had been passed, I used U.S. Human Rights Reports, scholarly articles, news articles, United Nations publications, and other sources. I also conducted interviews with local politicians and activists from the countries where female circumcision was common. I found that in every one of these countries where most women are circumcised, if it had a government, it had passed a law or decree that *banned* female circumcision. This supported my hypothesis that laws in this case reflected international pressure more than local citizen desires. The laws gave women more power to reject a practice harmful to their health but at the same time took democratic authority away from (mostly poor) countries.

My results challenged the assumption that laws are the will of the people. If they were, then I should have found laws that *required* female circumcision or perhaps regulated the practice to make it safer in countries where most women are circumcised. Although I used methods that often are used by historians, my study was truly sociological because, for me, female circumcision laws represented the broader concept of democratic representation. I was less interested in female circumcision itself than in what the practice could tell me about international power relations.

Benjamin Cornwell, *associate professor of sociology at Cornell University, is a sociological methodologist who studies social network structures, the life course, social inequality, and health. He applies social network and sequence analysis techniques to examine questions such as "How does one's position within a complex web of ever-changing social ties affect one's health and health-related behavior?"*

Why did you become a sociologist? Was there a particular class, person, or event that put you on this career path?

I started my undergraduate education as a philosophy student. I am indebted to that field for giving me a deep appreciation for perennially important questions like "Why does social inequality exist?" It became clear to me early on that philosophy wouldn't satisfy my desire to look at such issues empirically, to see how they occur in the real world. I credit my father—who was also a sociology major back in the 1960s—with convincing me that sociology provides a more satisfying set of tools for understanding the intricacies of social life. He was the director of a hospital social work department and dealt every day with emergency cases involving abused children or long-neglected older adults. I became a sociologist in part because I wanted to help develop new ways to study and understand such important social problems.

Describe one major finding from your research and how you came to this discovery. How does this work illustrate the core principles of sociology?

One interesting finding from my recent research is that socially disadvantaged older adults—especially racial minorities and people who have lower levels of formal education—experience higher rates of turnover within their personal social networks than do more advantaged older adults. For example, members of these disadvantaged groups lose more network members due to things like network members' residential instability and network members' deaths. Furthermore, disadvantaged older adults have more trouble than others with "replacing" their ties once they are lost. I discovered this through a detailed analysis of changes in social networks that were reported by thousands of respondents in a large, nationally representative, longitudinal survey of older Americans.

Many network analysts focus on developing objective mathematical measures and sophisticated analytic techniques. But my work is clearly sociological because it highlights how social networks are infused with social context and meaning. It becomes clear very quickly that in the context of social networks, advanced analytic concepts like network dynamics and clustering map onto sociological concepts like bereavement and segregation, respectively. Much of my work attempts to expose the connections that exist between these sociological and analytic concepts.

In sharp contrast, a basic study might explore a broad range of factors linked to high school graduation. For instance, Astone and McLanahan (1991) used data from the High School and Beyond study, a large, long-running survey of high school students. They found that high school sophomores who received more encouragement from their parents and more help with their homework went on to have higher graduation rates than those of their peers who received less parental support. Although the study's focus was on teens' high school graduation rates, the researchers' larger theoretical aim was to understand the importance of social support and integration and to show how these strong ties may be linked to beneficial outcomes for young people. This study is an example of basic research because its findings help us understand how social integration, a concept dating back to Émile Durkheim, might enhance the life chances of young people.

We are drawing a distinction between basic and applied research to demonstrate the breadth and multiple uses of sociological research; however, we caution strongly against the belief that one is better or more useful than the other. As social scientist Keith Stanovich (2007, p. 107) has observed, "It is probably a mistake to view the basic-versus-applied distinction solely in terms of whether a study has practical applications, because this difference often simply boils down to a matter of time. Applied findings are of use immediately. However, there is nothing so practical as a general and accurate theory."

Qualitative versus Quantitative Research

We have already defined and touched on qualitative and quantitative methods and will continue to highlight this distinction throughout the book. Here we provide just a few brief points of distinction to give a sense of their breadth and compatibility.

Qualitative methods typically collect and analyze data that enable rich description in words or images. The most common qualitative method in sociology is field research, including ethnography and in-depth interviewing. Textual analysis of historical documents, letters, and films also is a form of qualitative research. **Quantitative methods**, by contrast, rely on data that can be represented by and summarized into numbers. Survey research is the most widely used quantitative method in sociology, but social network analysis and experimental methods also generate numerical or statistical data that researchers can analyze. Even some data collected by qualitative researchers can be quantified, such as the number of times a particular topic is discussed in an open-ended interview or the number of times a particular action or interaction is observed in a field study. In the chapters that follow, we will discuss in depth the uses and relative strengths and weaknesses of these two broad classes of research. For now, we will simply note that qualitative methods are well suited to gaining an in-depth understanding of a relatively small number of cases, whereas quantitative methods offer less detail on a particular case but more breadth because they typically focus on a much larger number of cases.

Social scientists sometimes characterize these two methods or research communities as in opposition to one another, referring to "quals versus quants." This characterization is both incorrect and foolish. It is true that most researchers specialize in one approach versus the other, but this is simply a function of training and experience, rather than the value of one method versus the other. As we will underscore throughout the book, these two broad methodological approaches complement rather than

qualitative methods
Research methods that collect and analyze data that enable rich description in words or images.

quantitative methods
Research methods that rely on data that can be represented by and summarized into numbers.

compete with one another. In fact, the value of one approach is often bolstered by the other through the process of mixed-methods research.

A **mixed-methods approach**, or multimethod approach, is exactly what the phrase suggests: Researchers use more than one method in a single study, as they believe that two different types or sources of information will reveal insights that would not have been uncovered using only one approach. The use of multiple methods to study a single research question is also referred to as **triangulation**, meaning that a researcher can obtain a more detailed and clear understanding of his or her study topic by examining it from several different methodological perspectives. This process is valuable because the limitations of one approach may be counterbalanced by the strengths of the other (Olson, 2004).

For example, sociologist Vincent Roscigno and colleagues (2007) were interested in understanding discrimination against older employees in the workplace. They obtained data on more than 2,000 verified cases of age discrimination filed against employers in Ohio between 1988 and 2003. They used these data to conduct a quantitative analysis of the factors that predicted whether a worker would be fired "without just cause." Their statistical analysis found that the first spike of age discrimination claims occurred around age 50, when workers are entering their prime earning years and their salaries are increasing the most. The other spike comes when workers are just about ready to retire and may be eligible for pensions.

The researchers also were interested in the personal testimonies and experiences of the workers. They drew a random sample of 120 cases and closely examined statements from the employees and the employers about what happened. These personal testimonies revealed how blatant some companies were in discriminating against older workers and how painful this was to employees. In one case, a former manager testified that he was pressured by upper management to "get rid of those old men" at his retail store. In another case, a 64-year-old director of finance was let go after being told she was "un-trainable" and too old to learn the new computer skills needed for her job. As this fascinating study reveals, quantitative analyses can tell us what is happening and why, whereas qualitative data can reveal the complex interactions and dynamic processes that underlie such statistical patterns.

Cross-Sectional versus Longitudinal Study Designs

Just as research varies on the basis of whether the information obtained is largely quantitative or qualitative, approaches vary on the basis of timing. We can collect or use data obtained at one point in time, an approach referred to as a **cross-sectional study design** (Figure 1.3). This approach provides a snapshot of a particular population at a particular historical moment. For instance, a cross-sectional survey might tell us that in the year 2017, 62% of adults in the United States approved of same-sex marriage (Masci, Brown, & Kiley, 2017).

However, that single-point-in-time observation would not be sufficiently informative if we wanted to understand social and historical change. Researchers can track social change by using a second approach, called a **repeated cross-sectional study design**, or *trend design*; by definition, this involves conducting a cross-sectional study at multiple points in time, where each snapshot captures a different cross section of people in, say, 1980, 2000, and 2020. The overall population of interest may be the

mixed-methods approach A general research approach that uses more than one method in a single study.

triangulation The use of multiple research methods to study the same general research question and determine if different types of evidence and approaches lead to consistent findings.

cross-sectional study design A study in which data are collected at only one time point.

repeated cross-sectional study design A type of longitudinal study in which data are collected at multiple time points but from different subjects at each time point.

FIGURE 1.3 Three Types of Research Designs

Three commonly used research designs are cross-sectional study designs, repeated cross-sectional study designs, and panel designs.

1. Cross-Sectional Design

Time 1

A single sample drawn at a single point in time.

2. Repeated Cross-Sectional Design

Time 1   Time 2

Two or more distinctive samples drawn at two or more distinctive time points (longitudinal).

3. Panel Design

Time 1   Time 2

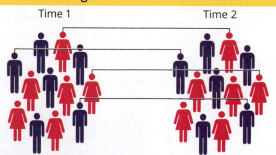

A single sample drawn at two or more distinctive time points (longitudinal).

same, such as "American adults," but the specific people drawn from the population to participate in the study are different at each time point. For example, as Figure 1.4 shows, data from repeated cross-sectional surveys tell us that the proportion of Americans who support same-sex marriage has climbed steadily from just 35% in 2001 to a clear majority of 62% in 2017 (Masci, Brown, & Kiley, 2017). In 2014, for the first time ever, a majority of U.S. adults (52%) said they supported same-sex marriage. Documenting trends like these is a critical goal of sociology, as it provides insights into how and why social change happens.

While repeated cross-sectional data can tell us whether aggregate- or societal-level change is happening, it cannot tell us whether a particular individual changed his or her views over time. Studying within-person change would require a third approach, called a **panel design**. These designs observe the same individuals at multiple points, such as interviewing a group of high school seniors in 2000 and then recontacting them in 2005, 2010, 2015, and so on. Both repeated cross-sectional designs and panel designs are examples of **longitudinal study designs**, in which data are collected at multiple points in time. A panel design tracks the *same individuals* at multiple points in time, whereas a repeated cross-sectional design typically captures *different individuals* at multiple points in time. Each of these approaches can be used to address different kinds of questions, and each has its own strengths and weaknesses.

Cross-sectional studies are the simplest and most straightforward research approach. Many researchers use this single-snapshot approach because it is relatively inexpensive and does not require the challenge of locating and recontacting all the people in their study at a later point in time. For instance, if you collect your own data for your research methods course paper or your senior thesis, you would not likely have the time or resources to contact your subjects more than once during the semester. A cross-sectional design also has the benefit of being nimble; it can be implemented quickly to assess a new or hot-button issue. For instance, a one-time survey could be quickly administered to evaluate students' attitudes toward a new university policy on campus drinking.

Yet cross-sectional studies have several important weaknesses. First, they cannot ascertain causal ordering, meaning that they cannot tell us whether X affects Y or Y affects X. For example, let's say that a researcher distributes a questionnaire in your research methods class today, with questions such as "What is your GPA this semester?" and "On how many days in the past week did you have more than three alcoholic drinks?" The researcher might find that students who report more drinking also report poorer grade point averages. But can we really conclude that drinking too much *causes* students to do poorly in school? Might it be just as plausible that poor academic performance caused a stressed-out student to drink heavily? Students with low GPAs may seek to drown their sorrows in alcohol.

By observing people at just one point in time, a cross-sectional design cannot ascertain the presence of a cause-and-effect relationship. Establishing **causality** requires that the purported cause *precede* the purported effect. In this case, if we want to make claims that drinking causes poor academic performance, we would need to ascertain that the drinking problem preceded rather than followed a student's poor academic performance. Documenting cause and effect is one of the most vexing challenges that social scientists face; for this reason, we will revisit this theme of causality throughout the book and will show how researchers working in different methods—from surveys to experiments to in-depth interviewing—strive to untangle this puzzle. (For another example of the challenges involved in establishing causality, see the "From Field to the Front Page" feature.)

Data sets that track individuals at multiple points in time are much better suited than a single cross-sectional design for ascertaining cause and effect. Sometimes, panel studies capture a large swath of the population spanning a full age range; other times, these studies focus on one clearly defined group, such as a group of people all born in a single year or who entered college in a particular year. These latter studies are referred to as **cohort designs**, because they explicitly trace the experiences of a particular cohort. A longitudinal cohort design would be a particularly effective approach for investigating whether drinking causes poor academic performance among college students. Such a design would enable a researcher to follow a group of freshmen across four years of college. A researcher could then examine whether drinking behavior during the first semester of freshman year predicts GPA during the second semester or whether freshman year drinking is associated with graduating on time. This would enable the researcher to effectively establish causal ordering. This approach is also referred to as a **prospective design**, in that it follows individuals forward or prospectively over time. This approach is quite different than asking seniors to retrospectively recall their freshman-year drinking, as they may not accurately recall that information or may misreport it in an effort to maintain a positive self-concept.

Yet longitudinal data, specifically data from panel studies, also have important limitations. The most serious drawback is that some panel members may drop out between the waves of the study. This is referred to as **attrition**. The first time point of a panel study is typically referred to as Time 1. If the people who drop out between Time 1 and Time 2 are different from those who remain in the study, then our results may be misleading. To revisit our drinking and GPA example, let's say that students who drink most heavily during their first semester of college are most likely to fail out of school. If

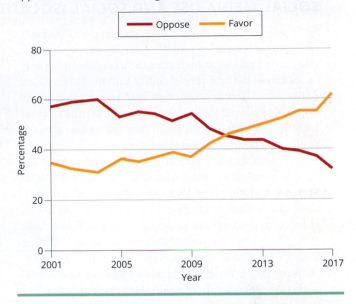

FIGURE 1.4 Changing Attitudes on Gay Marriage

Data from repeated cross-sectional surveys show how Americans' approval of same-sex marriage increased from 2001 through 2017.

Source: Masci, Brown, & Kiley, 2017.

panel design A type of longitudinal study in which data are collected on the same subjects at multiple time points.

longitudinal study design A study in which data are collected at multiple time points.

causality A relationship where one factor or variable is dependent on another factor or variable.

cohort design A type of longitudinal study design in which data are collected from a particular cohort at multiple time points.

prospective design A study that follows individuals forward over time.

attrition The loss of sample members over time, usually to death or dropout.

SOCIAL MEDIA USE AND SOCIAL ISOLATION AMONG YOUNG ADULTS

If you are like most college students, you probably spend at least a few minutes each day on social media, sharing photos on Instagram or "liking" friends' posts on Facebook. But how do these online activities affect young adults' social lives beyond the screen? Are people spending time cozied up with their iPhone instead of getting together with their friends? Or do social networking ties actually keep us updated on the next great party?

News headlines in March 2017 offered a somewhat bleak view of social networking. *Mashable* warned that "Social Media Use Might Leave Us Feeling #ForeverAlone" (Gallucci, 2017) while *Huffington Post* told us "Social Media Is Increasing Loneliness among Adults" (Huff Post Lifestyle, 2017). Even the venerable NPR announced, "Feeling Lonely? Too Much Time on Social Media May Be Why" (Hobson, 2017). Yet, if we dig more deeply into the actual study that generated these headlines (Primack et al., 2017), we cannot necessarily conclude that social media use *causes* loneliness. In fact, the reverse could be equally true. Lonelier young adults could seek solace in social media.

What exactly did the researchers find, and how did they find it? In 2014, Primack and colleagues administered questionnaires to a sample of 1,787 U.S. young adults and asked them whether and how often they used social media. They also measured feelings of social isolation using a tool called the Patient-Reported Outcomes Measurement Information System (PROMIS). Participants were asked to report how many days in the past week they felt each of the following ways: I feel left out; I feel that people barely know me; I feel isolated from others; I feel that people are around me but not with me. The investigators also obtained detailed information on race, sex, education, income, and marital status. They controlled or "held constant" these factors to help ensure that the observed association between social networking and loneliness did not reflect these other factors. For instance, unemployed people may have more time to spend on Facebook, yet might also be more isolated because they don't have a workplace.

The researchers classified people on the basis of how often they used social media, and then examined whether people in each of these categories differed with respect to their social isolation scores. People were categorized into four groups of roughly equal size on the basis of their social media use. People in the top quartile used social media more than two hours a day; they were twice as likely to report feeling socially isolated compared to their peers in the lowest quartile, who spent less than half an hour on social media each day. Study participants who visited social media platforms 58 or more times per week were three times as likely

Social scientists debate whether social media strengthens or undermines young adults' social well-being.

to feel socially isolated compared to those who visited fewer than nine times per week.

So are social networking sites a potential threat to our nation's emotional health? The researchers are quick to point out that we should not jump to that conclusion. The study was based on cross-sectional data, so the researchers cannot ascertain causal ordering. As study coauthor Elizabeth Miller told reporters, "We do not yet know which came first—the social media use or the perceived social isolation. It's possible that young adults who initially felt socially isolated turned to social media" (Hobson, 2017).

The research team suggests plausible reasons why social networking might increase loneliness. Social media may be taking the place of more "authentic" social experiences. Social networking sites also present idealized snapshots of our peers' lives; these carefully constructed photos might trigger feelings of envy and the distorted belief that everyone else is living a happier and more successful life than we are.

This study exemplifies important lessons. First, correlation, or an association between two phenomena such as social networking use and social isolation, is not causation; from a single cross-sectional study, we cannot ascertain which came first. Second, it reveals the importance of measurement. Although concepts like "loneliness" may seem too emotional or private to measure scientifically, social scientists can assess loneliness levels using tools such as the PROMIS. Finally, it shows that most studies fulfill at least some of the goals of both basic and applied research. The study investigators were broadly interested in theoretical questions regarding social integration, a topic of inquiry dating back to Durkheim. They were also interested in the concrete question of exactly how much social networking is too much.

those students who drink most heavily and who have the poorest GPAs drop out of our study, then those remaining at Time 2 will be very different, perhaps including those who can drink heavily yet manage to excel in school. Losing panel members to drop-out is an important source of bias; in subsequent chapters, we will show the strategies researchers can use to address this potential pitfall.

A further limitation is that the costs of doing panel studies are high. It takes a lot of time, effort, energy, and money to keep track of people in a research study, to locate them at later time points, and to entice them to participate in the study once again. Some people do not want to continue to participate in a study because they have become bored or tired of participation, a phenomenon called subject fatigue (Lavrakas, 2008). Despite these limitations, most sociologists agree that using a study design that tracks subjects over multiple points in time is more illuminating than a single snapshot.

Unit of Analysis

Because of the breadth of topics sociologists study, research designs may focus on different units of analysis. A **unit of analysis** is simply the entity being studied. The most common is people, with researchers focusing on individual thoughts, feelings, and behaviors. Other units of analysis might be families, high schools, corporations, non-profit organizations, religious congregations, cults, governments, and even nations. A researcher's selection of a unit of analysis is tightly tied to his or her research question. Any given topic may be plausibly studied at any level of analysis, ranging from the most micro (the individual) to the most macro (a nation). However, some research methods are better for studying micro- versus macro-level units of analysis. For instance, we can easily ask questions of individuals and observe their behavior at close range using methods such as surveys, in-depth interviews, or experiments. However, researchers may rely on very different techniques to study the functioning of a corporation or a state government; they may examine archival documents or observe the everyday workplace dynamics within a specific corporate setting.

No particular unit of analysis is better or more informative than others. The selection of a unit of analysis is determined by the research question under exploration. For instance, let's say that a research team decides to revisit the classic question explored by pioneering sociologist Émile Durkheim (1897) in his book *Suicide*. Durkheim examined whether social integration, and particularly one's religious denomination, was a predictor of suicide. A contemporary researcher interested in linkages among religion, social integration, and suicide might consider an individual, organization, or nation as the unit of analysis. An individual-focused study might use data from a large national survey and explore whether an individual's self-reported religious denomination or frequency of religious attendance is linked to whether one has thought about or attempted suicide in the past year (Rasic et al., 2009).

Another researcher might use geographic regions as the unit of analysis, exploring whether area-level suicide rates are associated with religious characteristics of that region. Pescosolido and Georgianna (1989) obtained data on counties in the United States, including county-level suicide rates, and religious information such as the proportion of Catholics, Jews, and Evangelical Protestants in each county. They found that counties that had greater proportions of Catholics had lower suicide rates, whereas a higher proportion of Episcopalians in a region was linked to higher suicide

unit of analysis The level of social life about which we want to generalize.

rates. Building on Durkheim's work, Pescosolido and Georgianna (1989) argue that the religious composition of an area may be linked to levels of social support and the presence of networks that are more or less protective during times of distress.

Some studies may focus on a unit of analysis that is larger than an individual person but smaller than a county, state, or nation. Such approaches would focus on an organization, such as a religious congregation. Researchers who focus on the group or organization as their unit of analysis cannot interview a house of worship, per se, but they can obtain information about the overall congregation from one designated representative, such as a clergy person or congregation president. For instance, the National Congregations Survey collects data from a sample of congregational leaders representing more than 3,800 churches, synagogues, mosques, and other places of worship. A researcher interested in congregations could explore questions such as: Do larger congregations have more community and social outreach programs than smaller congregations? Do more ethnically diverse congregations have a greater commitment to socially inclusive policies (Chaves & Eagle, 2015)?

Researchers must be mindful of mismatches between units of analysis, or using data from one type of unit to draw conclusions about another type of unit. Most often, a researcher will incorrectly conclude that "ecological" or contextual factors directly influence individual-level experiences, where group-level data are used to make claims about individual-level processes. To avoid making this mistake, called the **ecological fallacy**, researchers should follow a simple rule: Data or observations from one level of analysis should be used to draw conclusions about that level of analysis only. For example, although Durkheim's work showed that nations that are largely Catholic had lower suicide rates than nations that are largely Protestant, we cannot conclude that a Catholic individual is less likely than a Protestant individual to commit suicide.

ecological fallacy A mistake that researchers make by drawing conclusions about the micro level based on some macro-level analysis.

CONCEPT CHECKS

1 How do basic and applied research differ?

2 What are the benefits of doing mixed-methods research?

3 Describe at least one weakness each of cross-sectional and longitudinal approaches.

4 What is the ecological fallacy?

STARTING THE RESEARCH PROCESS: CHOOSING A QUESTION AND SETTING GOALS

Whether you are taking a course in sociology, psychology, biology, or physics, you will likely learn about the scientific method. The **scientific method** is the systematic process of asking questions and carrying out rigorous research to answer those questions. The process generally follows five steps:

1. Identify an important question that needs an answer.

2. Construct a hypothesis, or prediction, about the answer to this question.

scientific method The systematic process of asking and answering questions in a rigorous and unbiased way.

3. Gather data that allow the researcher to assess the accuracy of this prediction.

4. Analyze the data to determine whether the prediction is accurate.

5. Draw and report conclusions.

In the chapters that follow, we describe in great detail how to carry out steps 2 through 5. We also underscore the importance of following a clear, rigorous, and well-defined approach. Doing so provides other researchers with the opportunity to replicate the study, or carry it out in a different setting using the exact same methods, to determine if the basic findings of the original study can be generalized to other participants and circumstances. In this section, we will provide some brief guidelines for taking the important first step in the scientific process: identifying a research question (you will learn more about this process in Chapter 2). We then describe the broad analytic goals that researchers may set forth when they pose their research questions: description, exploration, and explanation.

Asking Questions

The first and arguably most important step of the research process is asking a good question, or posing an important sociological puzzle. Three general conditions guide a social scientist's formulation of his or her question: its social importance, scientific relevance, and feasibility (King, Keohane, & Verba, 1994). Social importance refers to whether answering the research question will make a difference in the world. Will these findings lead to discoveries that might inform public policy or social practices or help humankind? Scientific relevance refers to whether the study will resolve an important puzzle in sociology, whether practical or theoretical. Will the results help to adjudicate between two theoretical perspectives on a single question? Finally, feasibility refers to whether the researcher can effectively carry out a rigorous and well-designed study that answers the research question in a timely and cost-effective way.

Researchers should think critically about how well their question stacks up alongside each criterion before embarking on their project. Social importance is probably the easiest to ascertain. We might evaluate importance by documenting how common a particular social phenomenon is, showing whether the number of people experiencing a particular problem has increased over time, or demonstrating that a particular social phenomenon causes harm. For instance, between 2000 and 2014, the rate of deaths in the United States from drug overdoses involving opioids (opioid pain relievers and heroin) increased by a remarkable 200%, as shown in Figure 1.5 (Rudd, 2016). In the late 2010s, obituaries in small-town newspapers all too frequently reported the deaths of young people who succumbed to their addictions (*New York Times*, 2017). Questions such as "How do young adults get access to opioids?" or "What are the risk

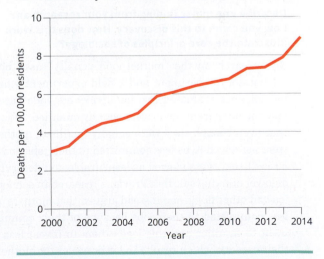

FIGURE 1.5 Drug Overdose Deaths Involving Opioids

Deaths in the United States due to overdoses of opioids rose dramatically between 2000 and 2014.

Source: Rudd, 2016.

THE AUTHORS OF *THE ART AND SCIENCE OF SOCIAL RESEARCH*

Shelley Correll, professor of sociology at Stanford University, is a sociologist of gender who studies how gender stereotypes affect men and women's experiences in the workplace. She uses experiments and observations in workplaces to explore how gender inequality persists in modern workplaces, and she develops and evaluates interventions to reduce workplace inequalities.

Why did you become a sociologist? Was there a particular class, person, or event that put you on this career path?

The summer after my sophomore year in college I had an internship at a chemical company in Texas. The first day on the job my supervisor warned me that the chemical industry was no place for a woman. I was stunned: This was the late 1980s and I believed that our society was well on the path toward gender equality. I had taken one sociology class, on race and ethnicity, and I loved it. The insights from that class helped me understand my experiences at the chemical company, and those experiences inspired me to go to graduate school in sociology and study gender inequality in the workplace.

Describe one major finding from your research and how you came to this discovery. How does this work illustrate the core principles of sociology?

My research on the "motherhood penalty" used both a laboratory experiment and a field experiment where participants evaluated two job applicants—one parent and one nonparent—who were equally qualified. I found that even though they were equally qualified, mothers were perceived to be less committed to their jobs and as a result they were viewed as less hirable and deserving of lower starting salaries. Previous research in economics and other fields had instead argued that mothers *are* less committed to their jobs because of their commitment to families and this leads them to invest less in their careers, which results in lower wages for mothers. My work shows that even when mothers have the same commitment to work and the same level of investment in their careers, they are still disadvantaged because

of the way stereotypes about mothers affect employers' *perceptions* of their workplace commitment.

Robert Crosnoe (Rob), professor and chair of sociology at the University of Texas at Austin, is a life course sociologist who studies the development of children, adolescents, and young adults in the context of families and schools. His research has three strands: (1) the interplay of the academic and social lives of girls and boys from adolescence into young adulthood; (2) socioeconomic differences in how parents manage the educational opportunities of children and adolescents; and (3) the early education of children from Mexican immigrant families. He carries out his research by mixing statistical analysis of quantitative data with qualitative analysis of interview and observational data.

Why did you become a sociologist? Was there a particular class, person, or event that put you on this career path?

In my junior year of college, well on my way to law school because I could think of nothing better to do with my life, I enrolled in a sociology class on gender that opened my eyes to the often invisible structure of society that shapes people's lives. My professor suggested that I think about going to graduate school in sociology, and I decided to give it a try. Sometimes, our life's work can depend on almost accidental events, such as enrolling in a sociology class.

Describe one major finding from your research and how you came to this discovery. How does this work illustrate the core principles of sociology?

In my study of how adolescents navigate the social ups and downs of high school, both quantitative and qualitative analyses showed that students who do not fit in socially in their high schools—whether they are bullied, isolated, or simply disconnected—are less likely to go to college after high school. In this way, what happens in high school has long-term effects on life. As in developmental psychology, my research tracks the unfolding maturation of young people within their interpersonal relations. It is sociological, however, in how it links different stages of life within complex institutional contexts (for example, high schools) and broader social and historical changes such as the growth of the adolescent population or the rise of social media.

Jeremy Freese, *professor of sociology at Stanford University, studies social inequality and works to draw connections among biological, psychological, and social levels of analysis. His work includes research on inequalities in education, health, jobs, and technology skills. He teaches courses on statistical methods for social research, on social science genomics, and on the social dynamics of sports and other competitions.*

Why did you become a sociologist? Was there a particular class, person, or event that put you on this career path?

I took a sociology course my first semester at college, and alongside that I also got involved in a research project run by a sociology professor. So I did not have any big epiphany that led me to choose sociology; I just stayed. What has been great for me about sociology, though, is that I have worked on all sorts of different topics using different approaches over the years, and sociology has always been a platform for me to engage with work in other disciplines without ever making me feel fenced in by my discipline.

Describe one major finding from your research and how you came to this discovery. How does this work illustrate the core principles of sociology?

I have contributed to what is called the "fundamental cause" perspective on health inequalities. The key idea is that the same technology advances that improve health often create inequalities because people of higher socioeconomic status benefit more from innovations than people of lower status. For type 1 diabetes, for example, there was effectively no inequality before the advent of insulin treatment, because everyone died within 10 or so years. Insulin treatments have been a major lifesaving triumph, but, at the same time, now we do have inequalities where poorer individuals with type 1 diabetes tend to have health complications sooner, mostly for a very large number of reasons connected to the day-to-day management of the demands of the disease.

Mary C. Waters, *professor of sociology at Harvard University, uses both demographic and qualitative methods to study racial and ethnic identity, the integration of immigrants and their children into American society, the transition to adulthood, and the consequences of natural disasters for people over time. She teaches courses on research methods, immigration, racial and ethnic relations, and sports and society.*

Why did you become a sociologist? Was there a particular class, person, or event that put you on this career path?

I was a philosophy major as an undergraduate, but in my sophomore year I got a work-study job working for sociology professors doing educational research in elementary schools. I learned about designing a project, collecting data, entering the data, and analyzing it using statistics. The excitement of doing research convinced me to apply to graduate school so I could do my own projects.

Describe one major finding from your research and how you came to this discovery. How does this work illustrate the core principles of sociology?

In graduate school I was working with my advisor Stanley Lieberson analyzing a new question on ancestry in the 1980 Census. The question was, "What is this person's ancestry?" It was open-ended, and the census coded up to three responses per individual. We were examining patterns of intermarriage, residence, occupations, and educational outcomes. But we kept wondering what it meant for people to say they were Irish and Italian or just English or German, when their ancestors may have immigrated to the United States many generations back. I decided to ask a sample of whites the census ancestry question in order to understand the meaning of these ethnic labels. I eventually published this study as a book, *Ethnic Options*, which argued that white ethnicity, which had been tied to discrimination and hardship in the immigrant generation, was now something optional, enjoyable, and freely chosen by whites in the United States. This work contributed to a core area of sociological study—the assimilation of immigrants and their descendants over time as they become Americans.

Social researchers might base a research question on a pressing social problem, such as the rising rate of opioid overdoses in the United States.

value-free The goal of being objective and not biased by personal ideologies.

factors for opioid addiction?" would register very high in social importance.

To evaluate the scientific relevance of a question, a sociologist must dig deeply into prior studies written on the topic; this process is referred to as a *literature review*, which you will learn how to do in the next chapter. If another study examines the exact same question, in the exact same way, it is not clear how the proposed research will contribute to science. Yet sometimes two studies might appear to explore a similar question, but each is scientifically relevant either because they are testing different theoretical frames or because they are exploring different cultural contexts that might lead to very different outcomes.

Feasibility is another important consideration when planning a research study. Researchers need to consider how difficult it will be to access subjects, sites, or populations, how much money is required to obtain supplies needed for the study, such as printing costs for surveys or recoding equipment for ethnography, and so on. They also should consider how much time it will take to carry out the study sufficiently to answer the research question.

One other subtle consideration should guide a researcher's choice of a research question: the goal of being **value-free**, or objective, in how the question is framed. Researchers take great care to be objective when they carry out their work. As we shall soon learn, social scientists take many precautions to ensure that their research is unbiased, precise, subject to critical review, and free from any prejudices on the part of the investigator or members of the research team. But sometimes subtle biases can seep in very early in the project by the way that social scientists ask and frame their research questions. It is inevitable that our personal interests and passions may guide our choice of a research question, but sociologists need to be mindful so that their personal values do not lead them to pose their research questions in a biased manner (Gunnel, 2010). Most experts agree it is virtually impossible for researchers to be completely value-free in their work. That being said, researchers should still aim to minimize those biases.

Research Goals: Description, Exploration, and Explanation

descriptive research Research that documents or describes trends, variations, and patterns of social phenomena.

Sociologists have diverse goals when they embark on their research. Research studies may be descriptive, exploratory, or explanatory. We will reintroduce these three categories again in Chapter 2, when we define theory and show the different purposes of sociological theory. **Descriptive research** documents or describes trends, variations, and patterns of social phenomena. Description should be the first step a researcher takes when starting a project and generating questions. We must first understand *what* is happening before we can ask questions about *why* and *how* it is happening. For instance, a researcher would not want to develop complex research questions about unemployment without first addressing the simple descriptive question, "What is the unemployment rate in the United States?"

Quantitative and qualitative research methods are both well suited to describing social phenomena. How exactly researchers answer descriptive questions depends on the specific method they use. For example, some qualitative sociologists observe people in their natural environments and describe precisely what they see. They might describe what a typical day is like at a zoo (Grazian, 2015) or what goes on at meetings of white nationalist groups (Hughey, 2012). Researchers who conduct content analysis, or the analysis of materials such as media, might ask: What proportion of prime-time television characters belong to ethnic or racial minority groups? (Harwood and Anderson, 2002). Survey researchers might ask: What proportion of American adults support the legalization of medical marijuana? Answers to these questions may be quite simple (for instance, 93% of U.S. adults support the legalization of marijuana for medical purposes if prescribed by a doctor; Quinnipiac Poll, 2017) or they may be rich and detailed. "Thick description" is a goal of many ethnographic studies (Geertz, 1973).

Exploratory research, by contrast, tends to answer questions of *how*, with the goal of documenting precisely how particular processes and dynamics unfold. Qualitative approaches are very well suited to exploratory questions. Exploratory research might examine the ways that people interact in a particular setting, how they interpret their surroundings, and how they try to change or adapt to those surroundings. For instance, sociologist Phaedra Daipha (2015) was interested in how weather forecasters make their predictions. How do they know whether it's going to snow tomorrow? How do they know whether it will be 1 inch or 2 feet of snow? She observed at close hand the daily interactions among scientists at the National Weather Service and found that while they relied heavily on their complex meteorological data, they sometimes just got up from their computer screens, walked outside, and looked up at the sky to figure out what was going on. Rich descriptions like these help sociologists understand how groups function, how decisions are made, how cultural norms are established, and other questions focused on social processes.

Explanatory research is considered the highest and most sophisticated type of research. Explanatory research documents the causes and effects of social phenomena, thus addressing questions of *why*. These questions might be: Why do women earn less than men even when they work in the same profession? or Why do some couples divorce while others stay married? At the core of *why* questions is the goal of comparison, or trying to understand why two or more groups differ from one another along some outcome, such as earnings. For this reason, *why* questions often develop directly out of the answers obtained from *what* questions.

For example, before we can address the question of why some high school students go on to college while others do not, we first must understand underlying descriptive and comparative patterns. We might begin our research by answering the basic question, "What proportion of all high school students go on to college?" We might then ask a comparative question, such as "What proportion of high school students from high-versus low-income families go to college?" The latest data from the National Center for Education Statistics (2016a) tell us that 82% of high school seniors from high-income families go on to college, compared with just 52% of seniors from lower-income homes. The answer to our *what* question demonstrates that there is indeed a considerable

exploratory research
Research that tends to answer questions of how, with the goal of documenting precisely how particular processes and dynamics unfold.

explanatory research
Research that documents the causes and effects of social phenomena, thus addressing questions of why.

gap in who gets to attend college, so that would likely motivate us to do explanatory research to determine *why* lower-income high school students are less likely to attend college.

OVERVIEW OF THIS BOOK

We provide a brief road map of the chapters that follow in order to give a preview of the breadth and depth of social science methods. Chapter 2 introduces readers to sociological **theory**, describing what theories are, how theory is used in the research process, and the different theoretical frameworks that sociologists draw on to motivate their research questions. Theories can be abstract and difficult to grasp, so we illustrate how different theoretical perspectives might explain one important social trend: the skyrocketing number of students enrolled in U.S. colleges and universities. This number has increased 10-fold from roughly 2 million in 1950 to more than 20 million today. Understanding the value and application of social theory is essential to sociological research, regardless of the specific method one employs.

Chapter 3 delves into ethical issues in social science research. **Ethics** refers to the moral system that determines whether actions are right or wrong, good or bad. Just as these concerns guide our personal choices, they also guide our research. The chapter explores a few of the most infamous examples of unethical research and explains how these ethical lapses informed the creation of explicit rules and guidelines for scientific research, including the requirement of voluntary informed consent and the establishment of institutional review boards. The chapter also describes the strategies that contemporary researchers use to protect their research subjects' confidentiality, rights, and dignity.

The next three chapters introduce what we refer to as the building blocks of empirical social science research: hypotheses, measurement, reliability, validity, and sampling. How we define and how much importance we place on each of these building blocks varies on the basis of whether one is doing quantitative or qualitative work, yet a fundamental understanding of each foundational concept is necessary as one begins to design a study. Chapter 4 describes how researchers develop and test hypotheses and underscores the importance of measurement when testing theory. Chapter 5 describes two of the main criteria used when evaluating the quality and rigor of a study: reliability and validity. **Reliability** refers to whether a measure produces consistent results each time it is used, whereas **validity** refers to whether a measure accurately captures the concept it is meant to measure. These are two of the most challenging topics in research methods, so we illustrate them using the concrete example of poverty in the United States.

Chapter 6 then describes **sampling** strategies, a critical concern for all researchers. Even the most ambitious researcher cannot study every member of the population of

theory A sequential argument consisting of a series of logically related statements put forward to illuminate some element of social life.

ethics The moral system that determines whether actions are right or wrong, good or bad.

reliability A quality of a measure concerning how dependable it is.

validity A quality of a measure concerning how accurate it is.

sampling The process of deciding what or whom to observe when you cannot observe and analyze everything or everyone.

interest, such as *all* college students in the United States or *all* sex workers in Southeast Asia. Rather, they must strategically select a sample or subset of people in the population of interest. There are many ways to sample, with the precise strategy adopted varying widely across research approaches. We describe the strengths and weaknesses of these different sampling approaches, along with strategies for mitigating against those weaknesses.

Chapters 7 through 13 contain the most exciting material in this book, showcasing the strengths, weaknesses, and applications of seven distinct methodological approaches: *survey research* (Chapter 7), *experimental research* (Chapter 8), *evaluation and translational research* (Chapter 9), *ethnography* (Chapter 10), *in-depth interviewing* (Chapter 11), *materials-based methods*, including historical-comparative methods, content analysis, and quantitative data analysis (Chapter 12), and *social network analysis*, including the analysis of "big data" (Chapter 13). In practice, very few sociologists use all seven approaches in their work; most are experts or specialists in just two or three methods. (See the "Conversations from the Front Lines" feature to learn about the authors' different methodological specializations.) Still, it is important to understand what each method can and cannot do, enabling you to select a method best suited to your research goals.

Our research doesn't stop after we collect our data. After we come back from the field or archive or carry out our survey, we must analyze that data. Data analysis is every bit as exciting and enlightening as data collection, as this is the stage of the research process where we test our hypotheses and start to uncover answers to our specific research questions. Researchers have many data-analysis techniques at their disposal. You can do a straightforward bivariate analysis that compares the self-esteem levels of high school girls and boys or a more sophisticated multivariate analysis that explores simultaneously the many factors that might shape boys' and girls' self-esteem. We recognize that most readers of this book will embark on basic analyses, whereas a smaller number of students may delve into more complex methods. We provide an in-depth discussion of beginner, intermediate, and advanced data-analysis techniques so that you can focus on precisely the tools you need. Chapters 14 and 15 focus on **quantitative data analysis**: Chapter 14 covers descriptive and bivariate analyses, whereas Chapter 15 focuses on more advanced multivariate techniques. Chapter 16 provides a step-by-step guide for **qualitative data analysis**, including data collected through in-depth interviews, ethnographic observations, and focus groups.

Our final chapter, Chapter 17, provides helpful tips on communicating research results to an audience. As you will see, precisely how you communicate your findings depends on your intended audience. Sociologists may carefully choose their language, how they present their work in text, tables, and figures, and how much they focus on theoretical versus applied issues on the basis of who their audience is. Sociologists most often communicate with other sociologists, but many also hope to share their findings with journalists, policy makers, and the general public and must carefully choose language that conveys their complex work in straightforward and engaging terms. Communicating our work clearly and persuasively is a necessary step toward influencing sociological thought and, ideally, generating new knowledge that may enhance the well-being of those people, institutions, and nations we've studied.

quantitative data analysis The process by which substantive findings are drawn from numerical data.

qualitative data analysis The process by which researchers draw substantive findings from qualitative data such as text, audio, video, and photographs.

Summary

Sociology is the rigorous and systematic study of individuals, groups, and social institutions. There are a wide variety of methods, both quantitative and qualitative, that sociologists can use to investigate their research questions. All social research methods rely on high-quality data and use systematic approaches to draw generalizable conclusions about the social world.

Sociological Perspectives: An Overview

- Sociologists understand that while individuals have agency, or the ability to make their own choices, social structure can constrain or facilitate these choices.
- The sociological imagination helps us see that what we often think of as personal troubles may be public issues, or problems rooted in social contexts and historical forces that affect large groups.
- Almost all sociological research considers the ways in which experiences and opportunities are shaped by race, class, gender, age, and other axes of inequality.
- Anthropologists, like sociologists, study individual and group behavior and use methods similar to qualitative sociologists, including interviews and fieldwork. Historically, anthropology has focused more on non-Western cultures.
- Psychology is the study of individual behavior, attitudes, and emotions. Rather than focusing on social groups, psychologists almost always focus on the individual and often consider biological and neurological influences on behavior.
- Historians attempt to document and understand past events, typically with materials-based approaches. Unlike sociologists, historians typically do not attempt to make broader conclusions about human behavior.

Types of Social Science Research

- Basic research aims to explore theoretically rich questions and solve intellectual puzzles, with the goal of contributing to generalizable knowledge about the social world. By contrast, applied research aims to solve a specific and concrete problem in the real world.
- Qualitative methods collect and analyze data that enable rich description in words or images, while quantitative methods collect and analyze numerical data. Some researchers will use a mixed-methods approach in which they use more than one method to analyze the same research question.
- A cross-sectional study design collects data at one point in time, while longitudinal study designs collect data at multiple time points.
- Repeated cross-sectional study designs and panel studies are the two main types of longitudinal designs. Panel studies collect data from the same group of people at multiple points in time, while repeated cross-sectional designs collect data from different individuals over time. While longitudinal designs are ideal for studying social change and establishing causal ordering, they are costlier for researchers to conduct and may involve problems like subject fatigue and attrition.
- Most research questions can be investigated with multiple units of analysis, so researchers must choose whether to use individuals or larger groupings of individuals, such as cities or countries.

Starting the Research Process: Choosing a Question and Setting Goals

- Sociologists use the scientific method to identify research questions, make hypotheses, and collect and analyze data.

- Identifying a research question is arguably the most important step of the research process. Sociologists aim to develop questions that are socially important, scientifically relevant, and feasible to study.

- While it may be inevitable for the personal values and passions of sociologists to guide their research questions, they must strive to be value-free and minimize the influence of their biases on their research.

- Social research questions may be descriptive, exploratory, or explanatory. Descriptive research questions describe trends, patterns, and variations of social phenomena. Exploratory questions explore how social phenomena occur through detailed attention to the processes and dynamics of social behavior. Explanatory research questions explain why social phenomena occur by identifying cause-and-effect relationships.

Key Terms

agency, **6**

anthropology, **10**

applied research, **13**

attrition, **19**

basic research, **12**

causality, **19**

cohort design, **19**

cross-sectional study design, **17**

cultural relativism, **10**

descriptive research, **26**

ecological fallacy, **22**

ethics, **28**

explanatory research, **27**

exploratory research, **27**

generalizable, **5**

history, **10**

intersectionality, **8**

longitudinal study design, **18**

macrosociology, **4**

microsociology, **4**

mixed-methods approach, **17**

panel design, **18**

prospective design, **19**

psychology, **10**

qualitative data analysis, **29**

quantitative data analysis, **29**

qualitative methods, **16**

quantitative methods, **16**

reliability, **28**

repeated cross-sectional study design, **17**

sampling, **28**

scientific method, **22**

social structures, **6**

sociological imagination, **4**

sociology, **4**

theory, **28**

triangulation, **17**

unit of analysis, **21**

validity, **28**

value-free, **26**

Exercise

State a research question that you would like to answer.

- Defend your question on the grounds of social importance.

- Why is your question scientifically relevant? What practical or theoretical puzzle will answers to your question resolve?

- Is it feasible that you will be able to answer your question? Why or why not?

Theory allows us to move from many observations and pieces of information to an abstract understanding of a single larger phenomenon.

RESEARCH FOUNDATIONS
Linking Sociological Theory to Research

The idea that talents and skills are recognized and rewarded in school, work, and other societal institutions is firmly ingrained in American culture. All around us, however, are signs that meritocracy might not be alive and well in everyday life. Consider that . . .

- Social class organizes jury deliberations, with wealthier, more highly educated individuals given more influence because they are viewed as more capable (York & Cornwell, 2006).

- In college classrooms, students strongly weight instructors' physical attractiveness in evaluating their effectiveness as teachers (Hamermesh, 2011).

- White athletes perform better when they think that performance on an athletic task is more indicative of innate sports intelligence than of innate physical ability, while black athletes show the opposite pattern (Stone et al., 1999).

- Mothers are less likely to be hired than otherwise similar women because they are viewed as less competent workers (Correll, Benard, & Paik, 2007).

These examples reveal that something is going on besides meritocracy and that it cuts across diverse settings and contexts. Theory allows us to see these seemingly separate social realities as a cohesive whole, as different manifestations of the same underlying processes. Social scientists can draw on a range of theories to understand the general phenomenon resulting in these four specific social patterns. For example, *status characteristics theory* (a subset of the broader *expectation states theory*) argues that in group settings, external markers of status—such as one's race, gender, social class, or physical attractiveness—are used to sort people by calling on ideas about worth and esteem that set performance expectations. These expectations then shape who takes the lead and who is marginalized (Berger, Wagner, & Webster, 2014). Thus, in all four social patterns, a personal characteristic that has no real connection to the activity at hand sorts group members into different roles. Other perspectives, like *schema theory*, focus on the connection between the human need to categorize and the cultural ideas and stereotypes that can be invoked in categorization (Bem, 1981). The basic insights of feminist and critical race theories, which we discuss later in this chapter, are also useful for making sense of these social patterns.

The point is that sociological theories allow us to move from many concrete observations and pieces of accumulated information to an abstract understanding of a single larger phenomenon or a broad range of social phenomena. This goal is at the very heart of the sociological imagination described in Chapter 1. In this chapter, we discuss the role of theory in the general process of social research. Because this textbook is for methods coursework, this chapter is not about theory per se but instead about how theory is used in the research process. In this spirit, we begin with a general overview of theory as a concept and then focus on how theory is applied within research studies.

THEORY WITHIN THE SCIENTIFIC METHOD

In everyday conversation, people use the word *theory* to connote a hunch, guess, or simple generalization that they develop to explain their own experiences; for example, a theory about why they don't get many dates or about what kinds of alcohol get them drunkest. Yet, scientists are referencing a far more elaborate and systematic process when they talk about theory. A basic scientific definition of

theory is *a sequential argument consisting of a series of logically related statements put forward to illuminate some element of social life.* In this definition, a theory is a well-articulated and well-reasoned supposition about a social phenomenon that moves logically and systematically from one point to related points and to a conclusion or expectation.

For example, the opening of this chapter provided a succinct summary of status characteristics theory. This theory, however, is actually made up of multiple statements, conditions, and rules that are linked together. Arriving at the final theory—that status characteristics stratify groups through the assignment of power and prestige within the group—first requires that all these different pieces of the theory hold.

In social research, theory is explanation, developing a logical story for social phenomena. **Empiricism** refers to the idea that the world can be subjected to observation, or the use of the senses to gather data about social phenomena. Theory and empiricism are the key ingredients of the **scientific method**, which is the systematic process of asking and answering questions in a rigorous and unbiased way. It has five basic steps:

1. Identify an important question that needs an answer.

2. Construct expectations about the answer to this question.

3. Gather data that allow researchers to assess the accuracy of these expectations.

4. Analyze the data to determine whether the expectations are accurate.

5. Draw and report conclusions.

The first two steps fall into the general category of theory, and the third and fourth steps fall into the general category of empiricism. The fifth step represents the integration of the two (Figure 2.1).

In practice, theory and empiricism cannot be separated. Social research cannot stand on one or the other. Theory without empirical evidence is just speculation in search of proof. At the same time, empiricism unguided by theory—often called *dust-bowl empiricism*—is just a fishing expedition. As the five steps of the scientific method illustrate, scientists draw conclusions by combining theory and empiricism. The steps in the scientific method are bidirectional; that is, the interplay between theory and empiricism can and usually does run both ways.

As an illustration of this bidirectional process, consider the *looking-glass self*, a classic theoretical perspective in sociological social psychology. Its central tenet is that we draw conclusions about our value and self-worth by looking at how we are treated by others (Cooley, 1902). The reactions we elicit in social situations create a mirror in which we see ourselves. For example, if we perceive that others view us as smart or funny, we then view ourselves as such. Over time, mixed empirical evidence has led to reformulations of this classic theory. One refinement suggests that individuals take action to bring others around to their own views of themselves, rather than passively accepting what others think of them. For example, a student who sees herself as very intelligent may regularly answer questions

theory A sequential argument consisting of a series of logically related statements put forward to illuminate some element of social life.

empiricism The idea that the world can be subjected to observation, or the use of the senses to gather data about social phenomena.

scientific method The systematic process of asking and answering questions in a rigorous and unbiased way.

FIGURE 2.1 The Steps of the Scientific Method

Theory and empiricism are the key ingredients of the scientific method.

1. Identify an important question that needs an answer.
2. Construct expectations about the answer to this question.
3. Gather data that allow researchers to assess the accuracy of these expectations.
4. Analyze the data to determine whether the expectations are accurate.
5. Draw and report conclusions.

Theory

Empiricism

Theory + empiricism

Cooley's (1902) theory of the looking-glass self proposes that we evaluate our self-worth based on our perceptions of how others see us.

in class in an effort to ensure that her classmates also view her as very intelligent. Empirical evidence from research supports this refinement of the theory (Yeung & Martin, 2003).

Thus, theory begets empirical tests, which refine theory, which then is retested; this is what we mean when we say that the steps in the scientific method are bidirectional. Because so much of this textbook revolves around the empirical portion of this two-way process, the remainder of this chapter focuses on the theoretical portion, both in terms of what it entails and how it is used in practical ways.

Purposes of Theory

Different kinds of theory are useful for different reasons. In this section, we describe various ways that theory is used and the different forms it takes. In general, scientists use theory for three purposes: to *describe*, to *explain*, and to *explore*. We discuss these three different purposes of theory in turn, using examples from both quantitative and qualitative research.

1. To describe. Theory can capture the general elements of a complicated social phenomenon as a means of promoting understanding of how and why it occurs. This kind of theory is characterized by the great amount of detail it introduces in trying to explain something from the inside out and the concise way it organizes that detail into basic insights and principles. Thus, descriptive theory often arises from research studies (an inductive process, which we will describe shortly) and is not typically used to guide research studies. Often, although not always, descriptive theory centers on the *social construction of reality*, the idea that documenting objective reality—the "truth"—is less important than understanding the subjective realities that people develop within specific contexts. Such descriptive theory may be concerned with how a context works in the eyes of people within that context, including the researcher.

Interpretivist research is a common form of qualitative research that illustrates descriptive theory. Many interpretivists are interested in how culture is produced and reproduced. For example, William Corsaro (2003) has extensively studied children's play through close observation. He has generated highly detailed descriptions of many specific aspects of the patterns he has observed, including how children learn to playfully insult one another. These focused descriptions have built over time into a general conception that children actively create their own culture (for example, rituals, myths, values) rather than passively absorb cultural traditions from parents, teachers, and the media. Corsaro and other interpretivists argue that many sociologists have failed to detect this phenomenon because they have been studying children from an adult perspective.

Importantly, the term *description* does not refer to a cursory accounting—a researcher simply listing things that happen or what people are doing. The interpretivist tradition, for example, is anything but cursory and goes well beyond a simple accounting of specific actions in specific settings. Instead, it offers "thick" description that firmly embeds an understanding of behavior within social contexts in ways that provide general knowledge of both the behavior and the context to outsiders (see Geertz, 1973).

Although descriptive theory is most often associated with qualitative research, thinking that it is solely confined to qualitative research would be a mistake. Demography—or, the study of the changing characteristics of populations, which is one of the most quantitative fields within the social sciences—has often been advanced by more descriptive theoretical practices. For example, one of the key theoretical models in demography is the *demographic transition*, which centers on the rapid decline of both birthrates and death rates during industrial development. This model describes a major population trend in ways that speak to the effects of modernization on human life (Johnson-Hanks, 2008).

2. To explain. Theory can articulate the processes through which a particular social phenomenon unfolds in order to pose hypotheses that can then be empirically tested. Thus, it guides research studies (in a deductive process that we will explain later in the chapter). This explanatory label is somewhat misleading because, truthfully, most theories explain something—thick description, after all, also explains what is happening within some social context. As a result, some social scientists—especially quantitative researchers—refer to the explanatory function of theory as *prediction* instead. In their view, a hypothesis is a prediction about how one variable will affect another. We will use the term *explanatory theory* here to be more inclusive.

A good illustration of explanatory theory comes from criminology. Many theories have been developed to explain criminal behavior, and studies are often organized around tests of the hypotheses put forth by these theories. The *general theory of crime* is one example. According to this explanatory theory, poor-quality or lax socialization in childhood affects a person's level of self-control, which then determines whether he or she will engage in crime when the opportunity or motivation is there (see Britt & Gottfredson, 2011). This straightforward hypothesis has been tested in many different ways in a variety of contexts. Most of this criminological research has been quantitative, but it need not be.

Indeed, although explanatory theory is generally associated with quantitative methods, many qualitative researchers also engage in hypothesis testing. One example comes from Christine Williams's (2006) research in two national chains of toy stores. Drawing on theoretical frameworks from organizational sociology, she posed hypotheses about how the racial composition of the workforce in stores and the setting of stores would influence labor organizing within them. Williams used intensive ethnographic methods—while actually working in the stories as a cashier and in other positions—to test these hypotheses.

3. To explore. Theory can serve as a guide, helping researchers study social problems in a targeted way. Rather than directly generating or testing specific hypotheses, theory can point researchers to more specific questions that need answers or angles that need to be considered. These answers and considerations can then

Sociologist William Corsaro uses theory to describe the ways children actively create their own culture through play.

Life course perspectives focus on the transitions we make, such as the transition from middle school to high school student. As the film *Mean Girls* vividly captured, the transition to high school can be fraught, as students learn about their school's culture and social hierarchy.

be woven together to arrive at some more general explanation. In these ways, exploratory theory narrows down the numerous avenues of inquiry to a manageable focus and then helps to interpret the results.

The *life course perspective* guides exploration by asserting that human lives are best understood as dynamic trajectories that are embedded in social contexts and frequently altered and redirected by key transitions, such as getting married or exiting the workforce (Elder, Shanahan, & Jennings, 2015). Scientists working from a life course perspective approach a topic by asking questions related to this orienting theory: Does it evolve over time, vary across contexts, or change during transition periods?

For example, research in multiple disciplines has drawn on the life course perspective to study a key transition of the early life course: moving from middle school to high school. These years of adolescence tend to be turbulent, marked by often sudden and sharp changes in social and educational trajectories. Following principles of the life course perspective, quantitative studies began to focus on the role of this abrupt transition from one school to another, paying ample attention to the larger social context in which this transition occurs (for example, peer contexts). Indeed, many of the negative changes in behaviors and attitudes during early adolescence are attributable to the social disruption of school transitions—disconnecting from old friends, having to meet new people, navigating a much larger and heterogeneous peer world. Yet, whether these changes are good or bad depends on the combination of how students were doing in middle school and how many of their middle school peers are in their new high schools. Students who were doing great socially in middle school and transitioned to a new high school with many of their middle school classmates did really well, but so did students who were doing poorly in middle school and transitioned into a new high school with few of their middle school classmates (Benner & Graham, 2009; Langenkamp, 2009; Schiller, 1999).

Importantly, qualitative studies following students across this transition have shown how students use the transition to reinvent themselves, adopt new identities, and change their course in purposeful ways. One study vividly described how headbangers can become hippies and nerds can become normals (Kinney, 1999; see also Benner, 2011, for a review of the literature). Collectively, this body of quantitative and qualitative research uses exploratory theory to gain new insights into a key social phenomenon; specifically, that school transitions can be disruptive, but that disruption is not always problematic.

Level of Abstraction in Theory

Because sociological inquiry targets multiple levels of social life, theory—for description, explanation, or exploration—is often constructed and used in relation to different levels of specificity versus abstraction. As Figure 2.2 shows, *level* refers to different points along the continuum between the individual and society.

The **macro level** is the "big picture"—the structure, composition, and processes of society. Thus, macro-oriented theory focuses on the largest collective units that make up society (for instance, societal institutions such as the educational system) or on societies and cultures as a whole. For example, *institutional theory* attempts to describe and explain variations among nations, states, or other large political entities, arguing that these entities change over time because they are striving to gain legitimacy among other entities, less so because of the actual value of the change (Meyer, 2010). A country might offer free schooling to children for no other reason than the fear of appearing "backward" on the global stage if it does not. Macro-oriented theories are common in social science fields interested in macro-level processes, such as demography and political sociology.

At the opposite end of the continuum is the **micro level**, which encompasses face-to-face interaction and small-group processes; it is all about what happens among people in intimate settings such as families or dating relationships. Micro-oriented theory typically focuses on interaction, communication, and relationships, and it tends to bridge social experiences with psychological and cognitive processes. *Social comparison* is a micro-level theory; it deals with the ways that individuals evaluate their abilities and personal qualities by using those around them as benchmarks of comparison. How they see themselves therefore depends on who surrounds them (Suls & Wheeler, 2012). For some, social comparison results in a fairly accurate appraisal of one's own abilities and qualities, but the process poses risks to others. For example, children of high academic ability often have less positive academic self-concepts if they are in classrooms with high-achieving and competitive peers than if they are in lower-performing classrooms. Although the child's ability is the same in both settings, the standard of comparison in the former is much higher than in the latter (Marsh & Hau, 2003). Because social psychology—which bridges sociology and psychology—is a field concerned with micro-level processes, it is organized by many micro-oriented theories.

In the middle is the **meso level**. Much more focused than the macro level but on a broader scale than the micro level, the meso level encompasses what happens in physical settings and organizations (such as communities, churches, and the workplace) that link individuals to the larger society. For example, *neighborhood collective efficacy* refers to the capacity for people in a community to come together to pursue commonly shared goals (Browning, Leventhal, & Brooks-Gunn, 2005). The tendency for individual adolescents in socioeconomically disadvantaged neighborhoods to engage in riskier behavior is in part explained by the fact that poverty interferes with the collective efficacy among neighbors that can monitor and control young people. As another example, the *family process model* posits that the effects of macro-level economic upheavals such as the Great Depression on children's well-being are filtered through disruptions in family and community networks (Conger, Conger, & Martin, 2010; Elder et al., 2015). In other words, the effects of the macro on the micro are very often channeled through the meso.

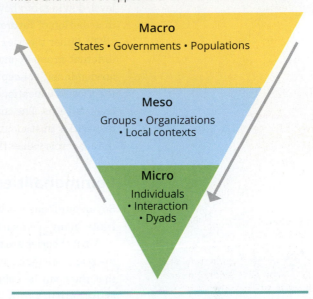

FIGURE 2.2 Three Levels of Social Life

The three levels of abstraction represent a continuum, with micro and macro at opposite ends and meso in the middle.

Macro
States • Governments • Populations

Meso
Groups • Organizations • Local contexts

Micro
Individuals • Interaction • Dyads

macro level The broadest way of thinking about social life, focusing on the structure, composition, and processes of society.

micro level The most intimate way of thinking about social life, focusing on face-to-face interaction and small-group processes.

meso level The middle ground way of thinking about social life, focusing on the physical settings and organizations that link individuals to the larger society.

Almost any sociological topic can be approached from a macro-, meso-, or micro-level perspective. Each level provides distinctive insights. Consider the issue of educational inequality. Some theories attempting to explain educational inequality are macro level, delving into how the educational system sorts students in ways that ensure the distribution of future workers to high- and low-status occupations (Bowles & Gintis, 1976). Other theories target the micro level, trying to explain how young people from different groups compare themselves to others in their classrooms as they develop academic self-concepts that drive future academic progress (Marsh & Hau, 2003). Most theories of educational inequality, however, target the meso level, especially school-level patterns. The controversial *oppositional culture thesis*, for example, suggests that disparities in students' school performance are rooted in racial/ethnic differences in the academic values that develop within peer crowds in diverse schools (Ogbu, 1997).

Commonalities among Theories

So far, our focus has been on different kinds of theories. Theories also share common traits, many of which define the very nature of theory.

Most theories are testable (that is, they can be qualitatively or quantitatively examined) and falsifiable (that is, they can be proved wrong). They have value to the extent that they can be subjected to rigorous empirical inquiry that informs them and/or assesses their worth. These two characteristics of theory are both relevant to the debate about teaching evolution versus intelligent design in schools. Evolution is a scientific theory in part because it generates hypotheses that can be empirically tested. Intelligent design, however, is not falsifiable in that the existence of God or some other "intelligent designer" of the universe can never be proved or disproved. It is a matter of faith.

Most theories are also generalizable, meaning they can be applied to general classes of events rather than to only one event. Their goal is to explain and make predictions about recurring phenomena. For example, theories for why the American Revolution happened (one specific event) are less common than theories about the political and economic conditions that make some countries riper for revolution than others (see Skocpol, 1979, for a famous example). A theory will not explain why Mary suffers depression, but it *will* attempt to explain why certain groups, such as women, are more likely to suffer depression than others.

Finally, theories should be probabilistic. They describe, predict, or point to what is likely to happen rather than what will certainly happen. They are all about the odds. Think about it this way: If you are a bettor, how do you make a decision that increases your chances of winning? Your decision is probably based on data, such as a basketball team's prior record or a racehorse's lineage. Researchers look for or create data that help them assess the odds. For instance, social scientists have developed theories to explain why women suffer from depression more than men do, recognizing that there will, of course, be some male-female pairs that defy this general trend. Consider that victimization (for example, physical or sexual abuse) and chronic strains (for example, harassment, economic hardship) both increase the likelihood that someone will suffer from depression, but that women are much more likely to suffer victimization or chronic strains than men (Nolen-Hoeksema, 2001). Women, therefore, will likely experience more depression than men, even if any one woman in your life may be less depressed than a man you know.

Use of Theory in Research

When discussing the various purposes of theory, we mentioned that theory arises from empirical research or guides empirical research, as discussed in the "Conversations from the Front Lines" feature. This distinction touches on the two basic ways that researchers use theory in relation to their empirical analyses.

INDUCTIVE APPROACH

An **inductive approach** refers to the process by which scientists draw a general understanding of some social phenomenon through specific empirical observations. Working from loosely defined ideas that are based on past studies, inductive theorists begin collecting data—usually through direct observational methods such as ethnography—with a broad conceptual blueprint in mind. Over time, they see basic patterns emerging from their observations, and they try to explain these patterns. The goal is to build up to an explanation.

The work of Annette Lareau (2004), who spent nearly 10 years observing the inner workings of American families, offers an excellent example of the inductive approach. She did not begin her research with specific predictions of what she would find, but she was guided by two things: (1) the sociological concept of *cultural capital*, which refers to the nonmonetary assets that someone can use to get ahead (for example, knowledge of art, music, and literature), and (2) past empirical findings about social class differences in parents' involvement in their children's education. Lareau spent hundreds of hours observing parents and school-age children in their own homes, and she gradually detected a distinct class pattern in parents' approaches to raising children. Middle- and upper-class parents engaged in a process she called "concerted cultivation"; they explicitly treated their children as projects to be invested in and managed. In contrast, working-class parents took a "natural growth" approach that emphasized letting children be children and find their own way.

Although the inductive approach to theory and empirical analyses is most often associated with qualitative research (and descriptive or exploratory theory), it is also well suited to quantitative research. For example, certain quantitative techniques can be used to examine which survey responses tend to hang together (that is, if you answer X to one survey item, you will likely respond Y to the next item). Using such techniques, you could look at the most common ways different parenting techniques tend to go together across levels of parental education. Let's say you find that all parents tend to spend a lot of time watching television with their children, but that this shared television time tends to go along with many educational activities (reading together) and cultural activities (visiting museums) among the most-educated parents and with more entertainment and leisure activities (sports and play) among the less-educated parents. These data could then help you construct a theoretical model about social class differences in family time use and how parents use time to fulfill specific goals that they have for their children (see Crosnoe & Trinitapoli, 2008).

> **inductive approach** The process by which scientists draw a general understanding of some social phenomenon through specific empirical observations.

Annette Lareau used an inductive approach to study social class differences in childrearing. She observed up close how working- and middle-class parents interacted with their children, and then developed theories regarding the "natural growth" and "concerted cultivation" approaches to childrearing.

BARBARA SCHNEIDER, ELIZA PAVALKO, AND GARY ALAN FINE

Ever heard the phrase "publish or perish"? It refers to the pressures on social scientists (and really all college professors) to publish their studies in academic journals. Prestige, pay, and even employment depend on such publications. Scientists who do not publish may not actually perish, but they may lose their jobs. Consequently, the editors of major journals have great power. They are the gatekeepers to publication in that they oversee the peer-review process. In this capacity, they also tend to have a good grasp of what is going on in their fields. These gatekeepers therefore can provide a great deal of insight into how the concepts discussed in this chapter play out in the real world.

The American Sociological Association publishes several peer-reviewed journals that highlight new research in some of the subfields of sociology. Sociologists who served terms as editors of three of these journals agreed to share their thoughts on the link between theory and empiricism today. They were asked a simple question—How do the scientists who submit manuscripts to your journal and get articles published in your journal tend to use theory?—and to reflect on what their answers said about the state of their fields today.

Barbara Schneider, *Sociology of Education*

The field of sociology of education and its namesake journal originated from an interest to improve society through changes in education. Early theoretical work focused primarily on how individual and social systems influence individuals' educational and occupational choices. Today the theoretical field has broadened considerably, and scholars are continually developing new principles to explain how and why social inequities continue to exist in educational institutions in and outside the U.S. The journal almost exclusively publishes empirical work that tests assumptions grounded in existing theories. Oftentimes, scholars will use existing theories for purposes of "shooting them down" to craft and test new insights into the operation of social systems, including but not limited to families, peer groups, and school and neighborhood communities. Such new theoretical insights are bringing new vitality and interest into the field and the journal, as researchers seek to understand how educational opportunities are distributed across social systems and how they can become more equitable.

Eliza Pavalko, *Journal of Health and Social Behavior*

One of the unique criteria for *Journal of Health and Social Behavior* and part of the journal's mission statement is that articles must be grounded in important theoretical issues in medical sociology. This means

DEDUCTIVE APPROACH

deductive approach The translation of general theory into specific empirical analysis.

A **deductive approach** refers to the translation of general theory into specific empirical analysis. Working from a deductive perspective, researchers take what is already known about a social phenomenon and integrate it into a coherent argument that attempts to explain or make a prediction about that phenomenon in a way that can be tested empirically. The goal of a deductive approach is to eventually organize and guide empirical activities.

Status characteristics theory, mentioned earlier in this chapter, is an example of a deductive theory used in experiments. Status characteristics theory has generated

theory is a very important part of our review of articles, and reviewers take this very seriously. How that is done varies considerably across articles. Probably most either test hypotheses from a specific explanatory theory or draw upon and add to a general orienting framework, but others engage in theory building. As in sociology in general, we have learned much in medical sociology from both deductive and inductive approaches. While the journal encourages submissions of both types, we get many more papers submitted that use a deductive approach or a combination of deductive and inductive. I think in part this reflects the difficulty of reporting quality inductive research in the short length of a journal article.

Among articles we do review, the most common problem I see is that theory is tacked on, or what I think of as a "coat closet" approach to theory. Authors know they need theory, so they open the closet and find the best fit and stick it on the front and back of the paper. This is also one of the most common reasons for a paper to be rejected because attention to the theory helps answer the "so what?" question. Theory helps the reader understand why this empirical test is important and what it tells us about health.

Gary Alan Fine, *Social Psychology Quarterly*

This journal publishes such a wide variety of methodologies and theoretical approaches—experimental research, historical research, ethnographic research, survey research, and conversation analysis. Each one has different standards, and there is no one primary use of theory in this field.

> " This means theory is a very important part of our review of articles, and reviewers take this very seriously. "

numerous statements about how, where, and when general status characteristics (such as race) and specific status characteristics (such as athletic ability) will organize performance in groups. These statements, grounded in the knowledge accumulated over time from past studies, offer predictions that can be, and have been, tested through laboratory experiments (Berger et al., 2014). The theory guides action.

Outside the lab, quantitative researchers use deductive approaches when working with survey data. Let's go back to another major explanatory theory of crime. *Differential association theory* posits that young people learn to be criminals when they are surrounded by people who adopt positive attitudes about deviant behavior more

TABLE 2.1 The Differences between Inductive and Deductive Uses of Theory

Type	Goal	Direction			Example
Inductive	Observe patterns and build up to an explanation.	Specific ⟶ General Concrete ⟶ Abstract Bottom ⟶ Up			An analyst finds married people are healthier and then develops a theory of social support and health.
Deductive	Create an argument to organize and guide empirical activities.	General ⟶ Specific Abstract ⟶ Concrete Top ⟶ Down			A sociologist reads Durkheim's theories about social relationships and designs a study to test these ideas.

than they adopt negative ones. This theory has led to hypotheses that young people's delinquent activity will increase as the number of delinquent peers in their schools and communities increase and that marriage leads to a reduction in criminal activity by breaking men's contact with their criminally oriented peers (Osgood et al., 2013; Sutherland, Cressey, & Luckenbill, 1995; Warr, 2002). One could also take a qualitative approach with this theory by using interviews and observational techniques to illuminate how people make sense of the balance of positive and negative attitudes about criminality within their social groups or which positive or negative attitudes tend to have the most influence on crime.

Inductive and deductive approaches are not separate from each other. Instead, they often work together. To illustrate how they might converge, we can revisit Lareau's concerted cultivation model of parenting, which was formulated through an inductive approach. This model was used by quantitative researchers to generate hypotheses about social class, parenting, and children's achievement that they then tested with national survey data. This hypothesis testing confirmed many of the tenets of Lareau's model but also expanded it by showing how race/ethnicity and social class often magnify each other's effects on parents and children (Bodovski & Farkas, 2008; Cheadle, 2008). Empirical action led to theory that guided empirical action in a very productive loop.

The point here is that the scientific method might appear to be unidirectional but, in both reality and practice, it involves more than a single way of linking theory to observation. As Table 2.1 shows, deductive theory is a top-down approach, and inductive theory is a bottom-up approach.

CONCEPT CHECKS

1   Briefly define descriptive, explanatory, and exploratory theories.

2   Abortion is a divisive issue in the United States. How might a macro-oriented sociologist explain current debates about the acceptability of abortion?

3   Contrast inductive reasoning with deductive reasoning.

SOCIAL SCIENCE THEORY

Having explained what theories are and what forms they take, we can now take a step back and think more broadly about where theories come from and how they are constructed and used.

Paradigms

One of the major influences on the development and use of theory is the **paradigm**, which is *a broad set of taken-for-granted and often unacknowledged assumptions about how social reality is to be defined.* At first, the idea of defining reality may seem odd because we think of reality as being objective and not debatable, something that just is. Yet, as anyone who has traveled away from home knows, people from different societies often misunderstand one another, and not just because of language differences. They have different subjective realities because different peoples have different ideologies, values, and views that powerfully shape how they see the world—the basic idea behind the social construction of reality that was mentioned earlier in this chapter. One need not leave the United States, however, to encounter others with different subjective realities. Such factors as gender, race, religion, and urbanicity can lead to such differences even in the same society.

A common illustration of subjective reality concerns differences between Western countries and Asian countries in their identification of the fundamental units of society. In the United States, the fundamental unit is the individual. Americans view society as a collection of individuals and, as a result, resist anything that infringes on individual rights. In contrast, the Japanese view society as a collection of groups, especially families, more than as a collection of individuals. Consequently, they are likely to support the idea of giving up some individual rights to serve group interests. Thus, a Japanese person and an American may define the world differently without necessarily recognizing that their definitions are socially constructed ideas, not naturally occurring facts. Media coverage of Olympic events illustrates these basic differences, with American media fixating on individual effort and Japanese media paying more attention to the social contexts that produced that effort (Markus et al., 2006). Americans watching Japanese coverage, and vice versa, might be confused because the same objective event is being subjectively defined in a way that is different from their own subjective definition, which they think is objective. Two paradigms clash.

Even though the United States is an individualistic society overall, people in the United States often differ in just how individualistically they see the world. For example, Republicans in the United States are more likely to see poverty as an issue of personal responsibility, and Democrats are more likely to see it as a societal failure. With these very different worldviews, the fact that these two groups of people within the same individualistic society have different views of the

paradigm A broad set of taken-for-granted and often unacknowledged assumptions about how social reality is to be defined.

Michael Phelps has won 28 Olympic medals, the most of any athlete in history. While U.S. media coverage focuses on individual achievement, Japanese media coverage of the Olympics focuses on the role of community and context in shaping its athletes.

welfare system—the former negative, the latter more supportive—is not surprising (Moffitt, 2015; Murray, 2016).

In science, paradigms can point to how issues should be studied and what questions should be asked. The philosopher Thomas Kuhn (1962) introduced the ideas of paradigms and paradigm shifts, both of which have entered the popular lexicon. He argued that scientists internalize paradigms to such a degree that they often do not think about them, question them, or understand how strongly paradigms guide scientific inquiry. As a result, paradigms are hard to change without some powerful event or discovery.

In sum, paradigms organize the theories to which scientists are introduced and predisposed to like. They give insight into how theories are developed and then put into action empirically. Scientists working from different paradigms will not use theory in the same way. The "From the Field to the Front Page" feature discusses an example of such a difference.

Scientific Paradigms

Social scientists are guided by many different paradigms. Before describing some of these paradigms, a basic paradigmatic difference within social science (and between social and natural sciences) needs to be discussed, one dealing with the relative emphasis on uncovering objective versus subjective "truths."

The paradigm on which the scientific method was originally based is positivism, an approach grounded in systematic and unbiased scientific inquiry. **Positivism** holds that all knowledge can be confirmed or refuted through empirical observations. Auguste Comte, a nineteenth century French philosopher, viewed social science as a positivist endeavor akin to natural science. According to Comte, social life has patterns that can be objectively understood by following a sequence of logical analysis and preventing personal values and cultural ideologies from entering the inquiry. If biologists can study infections this way, Comte believed, then sociologists can study social integration this way, too. Positivism remains a powerful theme in social science today. It is especially strong in quantitative research, although it is by no means exclusive to this kind of scientific inquiry.

Over time, competing paradigms have developed on the basis of the argument that the social sciences differ from the natural sciences and therefore cannot be modeled after them. According to this perspective, society is very "messy," and the scientists studying society are human. Values and biases can seep in even as we try to guard against them. Different people can see the same thing in very different ways. As a result, objective research on objective truths is difficult. **Postmodernism**—a paradigm characterized by significant skepticism of claims about general truths, facts, or principles—and other non-positivist paradigms therefore try to explain how humans arrive at subjective truths, including how the investigator's background and ideology factor into his or her study of these subjective truths.

Positivism and postmodernism represent opposite poles of social research. In general, most frameworks lean toward one side or the other but do not represent an ideal form of either.

positivism The paradigm holding that all knowledge can be confirmed or refuted through empirical observation.

postmodernism A paradigm characterized by significant skepticism of claims about general truths, facts, or principles.

WHEN PARADIGMS CLASH: THE RISING AGE AT FIRST MARRIAGE

In 2009, two sociologists, Mark Regnerus and Andrew Cherlin, engaged in a heated debate in the *Washington Post* about age at first marriage in the United States. This debate, which generated thousands of comments from readers online, sheds light on the interplay among theoretical frameworks, scientific evidence, and media coverage.

The average age at first marriage in the United States is now 28 for men and 26 for women, a dramatic increase from the twentieth century (the average ages were 25 and 21, respectively, in 1900). Especially noteworthy, according to the two sociologists, is the shrinking gender gap in age at first marriage. Regnerus bemoaned this trend. He argued that as a woman ages, she has greater difficulty finding a suitable mate and less time to have children. Cherlin dismissed this argument as misguided, claiming that Regnerus had ignored the reasons for women's delayed marriage and diverted attention away from more pressing social problems, such as out-of-wedlock childbearing.

In reading these essays back to back, *underlying paradigmatic differences* emerge. Both arguments share some common assumptions. They both convey the idea that marriage is functional, either explicitly (Regnerus) or implicitly (Cherlin). Moreover, they are both positivist—data tell the story. Regnerus, however, takes a micro-level interactional view, discussing emotions, personal choice, and negotiation—and concludes that marrying late complicates women's lives. Cherlin takes a more macro-level stance, discussing the link between economic structure and marriage trends as well as the societal constraints on personal choice. In earlier decades, people married young because they completed little formal schooling and because they needed children to help support the family. Today, societal conditions are greatly improved. As a result, young people can stay in school, pursue fulfilling careers, find a spouse with whom they share interests and values, and have fewer children— but they invest more time, money, and energy in their children than past generations did. Thus, two sociologists have different takes on the same issue, in part because of how they approached it. Different approaches lead to different questions, which lead to different answers.

This debate also speaks to the *uneasy relationship between science and media*. Regnerus defended his argument by saying that it is based on the "best" research. What "best" means, however, is unclear. An online commenter accused Regnerus of perpetrating "junk science," but, again, how is *junk science* defined, and on what basis was that accusation made? Most stories in the popular media provide no information about the theoretical and methodological

Sociologists Andrew Cherlin and Mark Regnerus offer vastly different perspectives on the state of marriage in the United States.

details that would allow readers to assess what is the "best" research and what is "junk science." Under these constraints, readers are likely to agree with one argument or the other on the basis of prior opinions about the topic rather than an accurate assessment of scientific merit.

Regnerus used many anecdotes (personal stories that may not be representative of a larger population's experiences) in his essay—about how his own early marriage made him more economically thrifty and about a young student getting married to her friends' horror. Anecdotes are very common in media reports because they personalize abstract issues and attach human faces to statistics. They are what readers engage with and then remember, so that actual evidence is ignored or taken lightly. The problem is that anyone can come up with an anecdote to fit any argument, which is why anecdotes are virtually absent from scientific journals. Qualitative findings, often based on inductive research, provide that human voice in scientific findings, but they are *not* anecdotes. Instead, they are examples derived from a systematic process of data collection and analysis. Scientists will not use a personal story unless it is indicative of some observed pattern. Jesse Streib (2013), for example, used qualitative research to sketch out some general ways that socioeconomic status shapes how people view marriage and then used quotes from couples of different socioeconomic strata as specific illustrations of each general pattern. In the media, however, the same rule does not apply, and a striking anecdote can turn a debate.

Dueling interpretations of the same data and trends make for exciting viewing on television news and active debate on social media. The coverage usually does not provide the full context of the dueling perspectives, however, so viewers and readers cannot make a fully informed judgment about the merits of each interpretation.

Selected Sociological Paradigms

Although an exhaustive review of paradigms and associated theories in sociology is beyond the scope of this book, here we highlight a few that have been influential. They are ordered by level, moving from the more macro toward the more micro. Although most of the theories discussed so far in this chapter might be thought of as mid-range or meso level, in that each has a more limited focus, these theoretical frameworks are often thought of as all-inclusive theories that attempt to provide an explanation for the fundamental nature of social life. As such, they are often referred to as grand theories. Table 2.2 summarizes these four frameworks.

STRUCTURAL FUNCTIONALISM

According to the macro-level framework of structural functionalism often associated with Talcott Parsons, society must be viewed as a collection of interrelated parts, each with a unique role, that come together to form a whole. The goals are the stability and survival of the social system, and so each part can be understood in terms of what it contributes to that enterprise. If something stabilizes the system, it is functional. If it destabilizes the system, it is dysfunctional (note this is the origin of the term *dysfunctional family* heard so often on daytime talk shows). Functional things persist, and dysfunctional things eventually die. The structural-functionalist perspective flourished in the 1950s and 1960s, and some scholars have observed that the emphasis on stability is consistent with the conservative cultural environment of mid-twentieth century America.

To explain some phenomenon, then, structural functionalism starts with the question: How does it promote the stability of society? For example, functionalists may interpret the continued strength of marriage as a legal and social institution in the United States as reflecting the role that marriage plays in child-rearing, which is necessary to the survival of any group.

TABLE 2.2 Four Selected Sociological Paradigms

Framework	Primary Level	Basic Question about a Social Phenomenon	Sample Theories
Structural functionalism	Macro	Does it promote stability of society?	Functional role theory
Conflict	Macro	Does it give some groups advantages over others?	Critical race theory
Rational choice	Macro/meso/micro	Does it maximize benefits relative to costs?	Time allocation
Symbolic interactionism	Micro	How does it play out in face-to-face interaction?	Looking-glass self

One of the major benefits of structural functionalism is that it is simple and straightforward. By viewing social life through the single lens of functionality, this paradigm allows for the comparison of seemingly diverse social phenomena in concrete ways. Yet, that simplicity can also be dissatisfying by not allowing for different phenomena to arise for different reasons. Moreover, structural functionalism often forces uncomfortable reflections about social ills. Because crime rates are highly stable, structural functionalists must consider how crime is functional—that is, how it contributes to the stability and persistence of society.

CONFLICT

The macro-level conflict perspective associated with Karl Marx contends that the struggle between the powerful and the less powerful is the key element in understanding society. If society is a collection of competing interests, then understanding how social groups coerce and dominate one another to serve their own interests is essential. In this struggle, those who achieve power are motivated to use it in ways that maintain their own advantages.

Understanding some aspect of society, then, requires answering a key question: How does it help one group put or keep down another group? Going back to the topics of marriage and crime, conflict theorists might focus on the ways in which many traditional family forms keep the young subordinate to the old or on how the criminal justice system perpetuates racial inequality through different arrest, conviction, and incarceration rates.

Rooted in the conflict tradition are feminist theories and critical race theories, which view gender and race as fundamental organizers of society that invariably create "haves" and "have-nots." Such theories catalog how gender and race are infused in groups, organizations, and institutions in ways that oppress some and empower others. For example, feminist theories of the family stress that men and women (and boys and girls) have competing interests in their families, so that what is good for one might be bad (or at least less good) for the other. This dynamic sparks uses of power that reinforce the position of men and weaken the position of women in and out of the home. Such a dynamic can be clearly seen not only in cases of physical abuse of women by their male partners but also in how men and women divide household tasks in ways that diminish women's earning prospects relative to men's in the labor force (Ferree, 2010).

As another example, critical race theories argue that the histories, actions, and customs of the educational system in the United States can only be understood through the prism of white supremacy and the power of whiteness as a property that non-white students can never have. Consequently, white students benefit more than non-white students from a system that was meant to help them all. As such, an institution with an official mission of promoting equality unofficially exacerbates inequality (Gillborn, 2005; Ladson-Billings & Tate, 1995).

Although substantively different than structural functionalism, the conflict paradigm shares many of the same major benefits and drawbacks in that its simplicity is both valuable and limiting. Also like structural functionalism, the conflict paradigm can lose sight of individual people. Yet, it is often praised for bringing the issues of power and dominance into discussions of social dynamics, especially in relation to race/ethnicity, gender, wealth, and other major stratification systems.

RATIONAL CHOICE

Targeting the macro and micro levels as well as the meso level that connects them, the rational choice paradigm adapts economic principles to social life. It sees people as logical and informed beings making decisions to maximize self-interest—weighing potential costs and benefits and acting accordingly. Consequently, the rational choice approach to understanding some aspect of society involves a consideration of the benefits it brings to the individual or society. A starting question might be: Is it a good proposition?

Rational choice underlies inquiry in many fields, including organizational behavior and demography. It is intuitively appealing to many researchers because it gives humans agency and posits that their life trajectories are under their control and that social institutions can be trusted to behave in predictable ways. Like the other paradigms, however, it has its critics. Non-economists have pointed out that not all people have equal access to the information needed to make rational decisions or to the very ability to make decisions in the first place, suggesting that a consideration of power dynamics is missing from the perspective. In particular, sociologists have argued that this paradigm is "undersocialized" (Coleman & Fararo, 1992; Goode, 1997).

For example, according to the rational choice–based perspective of Gary Becker (1965) on the household division of labor, an increase in one spouse's relative market efficiency should result in a decrease in that spouse's share of housework. In other words, if spouse A gets a raise, then spouse B should take on more of the housework so that each spouse can specialize in the area in which he or she brings the most value. Given that women earn less than their husbands in most American families, rational choice theory would predict that women would do more housework. Women are essentially exchanging housework for financial support, and men are exchanging their earnings for a well-maintained home.

Scholars outside of the rational choice perspective vigorously challenge this interpretation. Adherents of conflict theory in general, and feminist theories more specifically, argue that rational choice perspectives assume equal status among actors—an assumption they find questionable given well-documented gender differences in economic and social power throughout history. Other scholars critique rational choice perspectives for ignoring the social meaning of housework. In particular, critics argue that housework often is equated with femininity, while being a successful breadwinner is associated with masculinity. In fact, research shows that men who are economically dependent on their wives do less housework as a way to assert their masculinity (Brines, 1994; Yavorsky, Kamp-Dush, & Schoppe-Sullivan, 2015). Thus, cultural values can disrupt rational decision-making. An awareness of how social meanings factor into the perceived costs and rewards that drive rational choice is therefore warranted.

SYMBOLIC INTERACTIONISM

Symbolic interactionism is a micro-level paradigm that encompasses many social psychological theories, such as the looking-glass self. It is based on the idea that the substance of society plays out in face-to-face interactions. According to theorists associated with this framework, including George Herbert Mead, humans communicate through symbolic exchange, or spoken and unspoken communication. Words and gestures mean nothing in and of themselves but instead derive meaning from the fact that we have designated them as representing something. In other words, social context provides meaning. For example, a handshake is nothing more than two pieces of skin touching, but it takes on much greater importance because humans in some cultures designate it as a greeting. The word *love* is a sound made by our vocal cords, but it means much more because of the idea designated by that sound. The symbols used in a society reveal what that society values. Thus, understanding society requires an understanding of the exchange of symbols that occurs in small groups, both reflecting and shaping what occurs across the society. After all, even though everyone in a society might shake hands, that custom had to start off between two people at some point and then spread from there.

Symbolic interactionism is a micro-level paradigm focused on face-to-face interaction, including nonverbal forms of communication such as hand gestures.

Unlike the other frameworks, symbolic interactionism is not geared at explaining society as a whole but instead at elucidating the ways in which societal issues play out among individuals. When looking at some social issue, then, a starting question might be: How is it interpersonally produced, molded, and experienced? For example, Peggy Giordano and her colleagues have used symbolic interactionism to theorize about both marriage and crime. They have explored the ways in which men and women attach differing meanings to their relationships. For example, young men become more dependent on and more strongly influenced by their romantic partners because, unlike young women, they view their partners as the main source of social support in their lives. Giordano and her colleagues have also explored how the interplay between personal choice and the constraints imposed by relationships factors into men's turning away from crime. Echoing other research on marriage and crime alluded to earlier in this chapter, this research highlights how marriage leads to fundamental shifts in men's identities that lessen the value that they attach to the rewards of crime (Giordano, Cernkovich, & Rudolph, 2002; Giordano, Longmore, & Manning, 2006).

If structural functionalism and conflict paradigms are criticized for ignoring individuals, symbolic interactionism often elicits criticisms that it is too focused on individual behaviors and interactions and obscures the larger social structures and processes (for example, power and inequality) that shape our everyday lives. In gleaning important information about the micro level that could easily be missed, it might overlook other important insights about the macro level. Thus, like the other paradigms we've discussed, symbolic interactionism has both advantages and disadvantages.

Different Paradigms, Different Insights: Higher Education

One way to see the strengths and weaknesses of various paradigms is to consider how someone working with each might approach the study of a particular social issue.

Sociologists often study higher education, which is an important and policy-relevant topic in the world today. The United States has the largest higher-education system in the world, and the increase in the number of Americans going to college was one of the most dramatic population trends of the past century (Figure 2.3). The number of students enrolled at U.S. colleges and universities increased roughly fivefold in just 25 years, climbing from around 2 million in 1950 to 11 million in 1975. Since 1975, the pace of increase has been steady, yet slightly slower, with more than 20 million students enrolled in 2015. What insights might each of the four frameworks offer?

A structural functionalist would interpret the higher enrollments as a sign that increasing the population's educational attainment is functional because a more educated population will be healthier and more economically productive. A conflict theorist

FIGURE 2.3 Total Enrollment in Degree-Granting Colleges in the United States

The number of Americans going to college has risen dramatically since the middle of the last century, jumping from just 2 million in 1950 to more than 20 million in 2015.

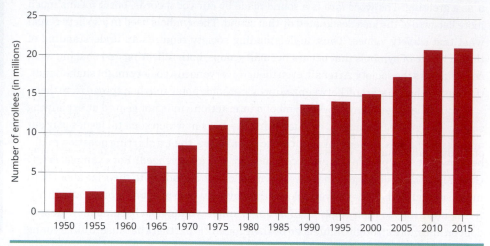

Source: National Center for Education Statistics, 2016b.

would seek to understand how increasing college enrollments are helping the powerful stay powerful. For example, the value placed on higher education may promote credentialism, in which people are differentiated by the diplomas they have (and can afford) rather than by a comparison of their skills. From a rational choice perspective, the increased productivity of an educated population is key, as is the rising economic premium that comes with a college degree, which brings in more money than a high-school degree over the long haul. On both the societal and individual levels, therefore, the rise in college enrollments would be explained as a good investment. Finally, symbolic interactionists would think about how higher education plays out on the micro level, likely focusing on the college classrooms in which symbols are learned and produced.

Thinking through paradigms in this way reveals how even people from the same societies, cultures, and contexts can disagree about the world because they look at it from different vantage points. More important, it suggests that society is so complex that it cannot be fully understood from any one vantage point. Each framework offers key insights but cannot provide a complete explanation of any social phenomenon. Consequently, integrating the insights offered by each framework is key.

CONCEPT CHECKS

1 Are paradigms evolutionary or do they change more radically in narrower windows of time? Explain.

2 Positivism attempts to make the social sciences more like the natural sciences. Is positivism a worthy goal for the social sciences? Does it work?

3 What are some of the key characteristics that differentiate symbolic interactionism from the other frameworks?

THE ELEMENTS OF THEORY

Paradigms are about the grand themes that influence the construction and use of theories. Looking more closely at theories takes us into the nuts and bolts of social research, linking paradigms to actual empirical analyses. We provide a brief overview here and revisit each in much greater detail in Chapter 4.

Concepts

Just like molecules come together to form water, plants, or steel, concepts are assembled together to make a theory. A **concept** is *an idea that can be named, defined, and eventually measured in some way.* Poverty and love are concepts. They are not concrete or unambiguously observable, like a car or a body. They are abstract—existing in the mind and in the world of symbols more than in the natural world. So, a stack of gold is a concrete resource, but wealth is an abstract concept about the accumulation of resources. Sexual intercourse is a concrete behavior, but sexual attraction is an abstract feeling. When dealing with abstractions, straightforward and precise definitions are of the utmost importance. Paradigms help determine which concepts are under study and how those concepts are defined and measured

Essentially, theories are sets of concepts that have been systematically linked together. In the general theory of crime, for example, the key concepts are socialization, self-control, and crime. The theory links these concepts in an explanatory chain of relations (socialization influences the development of self-control, which reduces engagement in criminal activities). In the next section, we explore these relations among concepts.

> **concept** An idea that can be named, defined, and eventually measured in some way.

Relations among Concepts

As in the general theory of crime, theory is usually about the relations among concepts, not just the concepts themselves. Those relationships take five general forms (Figure 2.4). One key distinction is whether relations are positive or negative.

When two concepts are positively (or directly) related, an increase in one goes along with an increase in the other—they move in the same direction, as signified by the positive sign in Figure 2.4. As educational attainment increases, a theory might attest, income will increase. When concepts are negatively (or inversely) related, an increase in one goes along with a decrease in the other—they are expected to move in opposite directions, as signified by the negative sign in Figure 2.4. As educational attainment increases, a theory might attest, health problems will decrease.

The positivity/negativity of relations is often associated with statistics, such as positive or negative correlations, so one might assume that they are strictly useful for quantitative (and especially deductive) research. The same basic principles apply to theory that is based on qualitative research, including inductive approaches. For example, let's go back to the theoretical model of concerted cultivation that Lareau developed on the basis of her years of ethnographic research with families. Although she does not use the terms *positive relations* or *negative relations*, they still apply. Social class is positively related to intensive educational involvement and investment among parents (as social class goes up, those parenting behaviors become more frequent), and

mediation The expected relation between two concepts is channeled through a third concept that links them to each other.

moderation The strength of the association between two variables is made weaker or stronger by a third variable.

intensive involvement and investment among parents is positively related to children's achievement in school (again, as one goes up, so does the other).

A theory might posit that three or more concepts relate to one another in different ways. Again, these types of relations are often associated with quantitative research, but qualitative research draws on them, too. Whether theory is used in quantitative or qualitative research or whether theory is guiding a statistical analysis or arising from a qualitative analysis, there are very common ways to think about how multiple concepts are linked together.

In **mediation**, the expected relation between two concepts is channeled through a third concept that links them to each other. In the example from Lareau's ethnographic work, parents' intensive educational involvement and investment links social class to children's achievement in school in her theoretical model. Social class is expected to affect parenting, and parenting then affects children's achievement. Recall the family process model, a theoretical perspective described earlier in the chapter about child development in the context of macro-level changes that create family hardship. In that theoretical model, the relation between families' economic hardship and their children's socioemotional problems is mediated by harsh discipline—economic struggles (concept 1) make parents act more harshly toward their children (linking concept), which leads children to act out (concept 2).

In **moderation**, the strength of the relationship between two variables is conditioned (made weaker or stronger) by a third variable. That third concept could make those two concepts appear to be very closely related or not related at all. Because their relation is conditional on the third concept, that concept might be called a *conditioning concept*. Williams's ethnography of toy stores, mentioned earlier in the chapter, is an example of moderation. She went into the study with a theory-based expectation that the link between workers' experiences and their labor organization would depend on the setting of the store. The family process model is also a theoretical perspective with a moderation component. The relation between economic hardship and children's socioemotional problems is moderated by parental support—children living in family hardship (concept 1) generally do worse socioemotionally (concept 2), but this general relation does not hold when parents remain supportive of children despite economic hardship (conditioning factor). Parental support turns that relation up or down.

In **spuriousness**, the relation between two concepts is complicated by a **confound**, or a third variable that is linked to two concepts in a way that makes them appear to be related even when they are not. In other words, the relation between two variables seems to exist but actually does not—it is a mirage (as signified by the "X" in Figure 2.4). Spuriousness is unlikely to be a part of a theory and more likely to come up when testing

FIGURE 2.4 Categories of Relations within a Theory

Relations among concepts take five general forms.

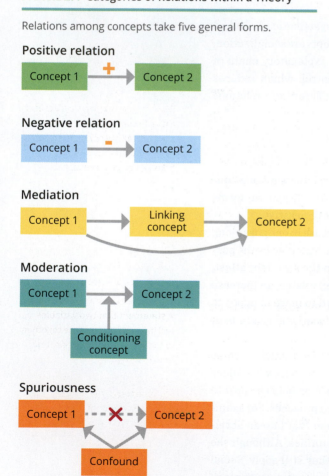

Positive relation

Concept 1 → + → Concept 2

Negative relation

Concept 1 → − → Concept 2

Mediation

Concept 1 → Linking concept → Concept 2

Moderation

Concept 1 → Concept 2

Conditioning concept

Spuriousness

Concept 1 - - ✕ - - Concept 2

Confound

a theory, so it is less important to consider in this chapter. An example of spuriousness in this sense is the potential for the links posited in the family process model to be spurious, a concern that would guide tests of this theoretical model. The key relation in this theoretical model—between families' economic hardship and children's socioemotional problems—may have a confound, such as parents' educational attainment, which affects the likelihood of both economic troubles and children's socioemotional development at the same time. Failure to account for that confound in a test of this relation, therefore, would lead to misleading results.

Goals, Hypotheses, and Questions

Theory gives scholars goals for their empirical research. Those goals can take the concrete form of specifying actual relations to test or can be more exploratory or descriptive, suggesting avenues to follow or questions to ask.

Relations among hypotheses are specified in a **hypothesis**, which is a *testable statement of a relationship*. The hypothesis guides actual research in the deductive process, and tests of hypotheses are common in quantitative studies such as experiments or survey research; but as we noted earlier with the toy store example, hypotheses can also guide qualitative studies. For example, the family process model generates numerous hypotheses about the relationships among its key concepts. One testable hypothesis is that parents' loss of income during a recession will increase their adolescent children's engagement in delinquent activities.

Hypotheses cannot be proved, only disproved; this process is known as falsification, as discussed earlier in this chapter. What scientists really aim to do is disprove the **null hypothesis**, which predicts that concepts are completely unrelated. In testing the validity of the family process model, the null hypothesis would hold that parental income and adolescent delinquency are not related to each other. If a test of the null hypothesis reveals that adolescents whose parents lose income are more delinquent than those teens whose parents do not lose income, then those results are evidence that the null hypothesis does not hold. We can reject it.

There are several types of hypotheses. One important thing to know about hypotheses is that they are always written as statements, not questions.

1. A **hypothesis of difference** makes a testable statement about group differences. "Race differentiates people on alcohol consumption, such that whites drink more than non-whites" is an example of a hypothesis of difference.

2. A **hypothesis of association** deals with variables that increase or decrease together, without an explicit specification of cause and effect. It covers both direct and inverse relations. A hypothesis of association (which is another way of saying *related*) is often stated with an "if-then" structure: "If religiosity goes up, then health problems go down." Like a hypothesis of difference, this kind of hypothesis captures a simple association between concepts. While a hypothesis of difference is about the comparison of two or more distinct groups of people, a hypothesis of association is about the comparison of people who differ in degree in some way (for example, more or less money rather than black vs. white).

3. A **causal hypothesis** is a prediction about cause and effect within an association of difference. For example, the hypothesis about religion and health suggests that religiosity and physical health problems tend to move together, but it does not

spuriousness When an apparent relation between two concepts is actually the result of some third concept (confound) influencing both of them.

confound A third variable that is linked to two concepts in a way that makes them appear to be related even when they are not.

hypothesis A testable statement of a relationship between two concepts.

null hypothesis A hypothesis that no relationship between concepts exists or no difference in the dependent variable between groups exists.

hypothesis of difference A testable statement about group differences in some concept.

hypothesis of association A statement that two variables will increase or decrease together, without an explicit specification of cause and effect.

causal hypothesis A statement that the relationship between two concepts is the result of cause and effect.

specify the cause. Does being more religious reduce health problems, do health problems distract people from participation in religious life, or is it some combination of the two? A causal hypothesis would be: "Religiosity prevents health problems" or "Health complications prevent participation in religious life." Similarly, the hypothesis about race and alcohol use suggests that alcohol use differs across racial groups without saying that race itself leads to different drinking behaviors.

Theories often focus on causes, and so causal hypotheses are common outcomes of theories. As you will read in later chapters, however, definitively establishing causality is difficult outside of experiments. Survey research and qualitative studies have more trouble clearly delineating cause and effect because of spuriousness, although researchers can take steps to improve **causal inference**—the degree of confidence that an observation based on the test of a hypothesis is truly causal. Researchers should instead focus on hypotheses of association or at least be quite forthright about any threats that they face in trying to test a causal hypothesis.

Although hypothesis testing is a way of linking theory to empirical inquiry that can be found in both quantitative and qualitative research, it is indicative of the deductive approach to using theory rather than the inductive approach. In the inductive approach, theory is usually the result of the empirical inquiry rather than the organizer of the empirical inquiry. Still, many of the same principles of theory and empirical research apply to the inductive process, even if hypothesis testing does not. Instead of hypotheses, scholars use past research and existing theories to craft questions that they want to ask or lines of inquiry that they want to pursue. The empirical research that they conduct is then used to construct new theories, which, of course, can then be used for hypothesis testing.

Whether the result of the deductive use of theory in hypothesis testing or the inductive process of generating theory, the repeated use of descriptive, explanatory, or exploratory theory can lead to patterns of evidence that strongly confirm the basic tenets of a theory. In such cases, scientists can become increasingly sure that a theory is correct and, as a result, put forth a proposition, or a *statement of a solid conclusion about some general relationship or pattern*. What if almost every experiment testing hypotheses from status characteristics theory shows that male gender leads to greater perceptions of competence from others in group activities? We might propose that, yes, this role of gender in small groups is a proposition now, not a hypothesis. An even stronger statement about a theory is a law, essentially an acceptance of a proposition as a fact. If there is a law, it must always hold under the same circumstances. Although laws are put forward in the natural sciences (for example, the law of gravity), they are rare in the social sciences. You may have heard of the law of supply and demand in economics, but whether it is a proposition (very consistent) or a law (always occurring) is arguable in a way that many laws of natural science are not. Regardless of whether propositions or laws are the ultimate outcomes, the work of translating theory into empirical observation in social science is to accumulate knowledge about social patterns.

Measurement of the Elements of Theory

Concepts—and their relations—are fundamental components of theory. For theory to be used in empirical research (either deductively or inductively), those concepts need to be measured in some concrete way. Measurement translates theory into action.

causal inference The degree of confidence that an observation based on the test of a hypothesis is truly causal.

This two-way translation is about **conceptualization** (how variables are defined by or for theory) and **operationalization** (how variables are measured for observation or through observation), which are the subject of Chapter 4. For now, we focus on conceptualization because it is such a large part of the theory side of this translation.

Concepts need to be defined in some way, and variables do that. **Variables** are *representations that capture the different dimensions, categories, or levels of a concept*. They recognize that concepts *vary* in the forms that they take. As already noted, crime is a popular subject of theory. The general theory of crime suggests that socialization and self-control lead to criminal behavior. Crime is a concept that many people have an intuitive understanding of, but how do we actually define that intuitive understanding? One way would be a person's engagement in activities that are illegal in some context, which can be measured in a relatively straightforward way. A survey might ask respondents to report how many illegal activities they had engaged in during the past year. An observational study might record instances of illegal behaviors during an ethnographic window. With these variables, scientists can test the hypotheses from the general theory of crime.

In an inductive process, theory does not specify hypotheses about crime. Instead, scientists examine data (that they have collected or that are already available) to look for patterns and then conceptualize what those patterns mean. Over time, the data might suggest to them that some set of behaviors is the best way to define the concept of crime, and they could then look at how such a variable is related to other themes in their data.

In Chapter 4, you will learn about different types of variables, about dimensions, and about different ways to measure variables. They are introduced here only as a means of better understanding some key first steps in the exchange between theory and empiricism.

conceptualization The process of precisely defining ideas and turning them into variables.

operationalization The process of linking the conceptualized variables to a set of procedures for measuring them.

variables Representations that capture the different dimensions, categories, or levels of a concept.

CONCEPT CHECKS

1 | Give an example of an abstract concept. Suggest three different variables that might be used to capture this concept.

2 | Contrast mediation, moderation, and spuriousness.

3 | A researcher observes a correlation between body weight and self-esteem, where heavier persons have lower self-esteem. What is a possible confound that may account for this association?

FROM THEORY TO EMPIRICAL STUDY AND BACK

With the background provided and terms defined, we can focus on the steps that researchers take to move from theory to empirical observation. In the discussions in the following sections, each step is based primarily on the steps of the scientific method outlined at the start of this chapter. As such, it is more aligned with the deductive, positivist approach, which is useful for both quantitative and qualitative research but is more common in the former. As we go through the steps, this discussion will be supplemented with information about how this process might unfold differently in an inductive approach, which is more common in qualitative research.

Identifying an Important Question That Needs an Answer

A key question is the main spark of a research project, but from where does this question come? The first step in asking a question is selecting a topic. The most powerful factor in selecting a topic is simply what researchers find interesting. Another consideration is what researchers deem important to study—as evidenced by major public debates (such as the debate about immigration), or by controversial policy agendas (such as welfare reform), or by other issues in the public eye. For example, autism has attracted such enormous public attention that sociologists have begun to study it, with some researchers documenting how autism diagnoses are "contagious" within communities (Liu, King, & Bearman, 2010).

Assessments of what is currently known or unknown also guide scientists in selecting a topic. Researchers may decide not to study a topic because it has already been thoroughly studied; other topics provide an open field because they are so little understood. Researchers often look for holes or gaps in the general knowledge base. For example, genome mapping spurred sociological research on the ways in which environmental influences can reinforce or counterbalance genetic predispositions to certain behaviors (Guo, Roettger, & Cai, 2008).

Some practical considerations in research include money, access, and ethical and/or legal restrictions. The costs of tracking families across national borders might prohibit a researcher from studying international migration, and getting access from the military to study decision-making during battle will be difficult. Exploring the roots of murder can be tricky because the researcher has an ethical and legal responsibility to report crime. These practical considerations affect whether studying a topic, even one of great interest and import, is "doable."

Thus, researchers choose topics that interest them and others, that they can potentially illuminate in a new way, and that they can study without overly burdensome constraints. With a topic chosen, asking a question about that topic is next. After all, a topic is often only as good as the questions that can be asked about it. In general, scientists ask questions that maximize their potential to make a unique contribution to knowledge about the topic.

If you read a research article about a study, whether it is the result of a deductive or inductive approach, the introductory material, or front end, is usually all about the question, why it should be asked, and what the possible or expected answers will be. The rest of the article is about the empirical procedures that the scientists used to attempt to answer the question, what they found, and what they concluded about these findings. In this chapter, we focus on the front end.

REVIEWING THE LITERATURE

Perhaps the most important activity in figuring out a question to ask is the literature review. The literature is *the body of writings and reports on a topic that has been accumulated over time*. It is the existing knowledge base. A **literature review**, then, is a *systematic reading of the body of theory and evidence to determine what has been done (and how) and what needs to be done*. It provides information about how the topic is usually studied, the theories often associated with it, the general pattern of findings, and the common challenges that researchers in this area face. The literature

Research questions are often inspired by major public debates.

literature review A systematic reading of the body of theory and evidence to determine what has been done (and how) and what needs to be done.

review is a critical step in identifying "holes": Although a topic may have been studied in depth, particular aspects of this topic may be unexplored or relatively unexplored territory.

Resources for Conducting a Literature Review In the past, literature reviews were conducted in libraries using card catalogs and hard-copy texts. Today, they are done primarily online. The Internet has made literature reviews easier to do, but it has also raised the risk that they will be low quality. For many, a literature review simply entails Googling a topic or searching Wikipedia. These searches provide a vast amount of information, but much of it is untrustworthy or misleading. For the most part, there is no way to know if the contents of a webpage have been vetted (checked by experts).

The web can be valuable if used cautiously. Most universities have academic search engines that allow researchers to scan titles related to some topic—based on a keyword, a title word, or some other criterion—and then read **abstracts** (brief descriptions of content). Some search engines are general (for example, Web of Science), and some are much more discipline-specific; for example, Sociological Abstracts is devoted to sociology texts, PsychInfo to psychology texts, and Medline to medical texts. Google has Google Scholar, a special search engine dedicated to academic writings, including scientific studies.

abstract A brief description of the content of a scientific report.

Most scientific reports are published in journals, which are often the main focus of literature reviews. Typically, the journals are peer-reviewed, which means that every article was read, critiqued, and approved by other experts in the field before it was published. However, journals vary greatly in their standards. Thus, being critical of journals is important. Rankings of journal impact—a gauge of how widely read and cited the articles in the journal are—are available and should be considered.

Many disciplinary organizations sponsor their own journals. For example, the American Sociological Association publishes a general journal, *American Sociological Review*, as well as journals for various subfields, including *Sociology of Education* and *Sociological Theory*. Articles in these journals often reference articles in other journals that can then be tracked down. Some journals, such as the *Annual Reviews* (for example, *Annual Review of Sociology*), feature articles that synthesize the state of the field on some topic. Such articles, which do not report the results of a single study but try to draw general statements about patterns of results across studies, provide an excellent first read on a topic as well as a guide to other key sources.

Other periodicals, such as general-interest newspapers and magazines, provide useful context for a topic. Because of their target audiences, however, these periodicals simplify complex debates, provide little detail about how evidence was produced, and can misstate scientific findings. Thus, a *New York Times* article might provide a useful timeline of changes in immigration law but would not be helpful for figuring out important theoretical and methodological issues in the study of the consequences of immigration.

Books can be excellent sources for literature reviews. Unfortunately, books do not show up on many scholarly search engines. Moreover, judging a book's quality may be difficult because of a lack of information about peer review and other standards of scientific rigor. One strategy is to look for the books that are cited most often in other scholarly texts, especially those that are mentioned as important or seminal.

Many governmental agencies produce reports on various topics, providing statistics, describing historical trends, or compiling relevant information. The Census Bureau (U.S. Department of Commerce) is a good example; so are the National Center for Education Statistics (U.S. Department of Education) and the Bureau of Labor Statistics (U.S. Department of Labor). Nongovernmental organizations, such as the Pew Charitable Trusts, also produce reports that provide good background information.

DEVELOPING SEARCH PARAMETERS AND COMPILING AN ANNOTATED BIBLIOGRAPHY

For most topics, the volume of information available may be daunting. Consequently, researchers should develop some basic parameters for their searches, decide where they will focus, commit to a timeline, and specify the kinds of sources they will target. Many literature searches start big and then become increasingly specific. For example, initial search words might be quite general, but after skimming more texts or examining them in detail, the researcher begins to steer toward subsets of the broad topic that allow for a more tailored search. In this way, literature reviews are path dependent. At the start of the journey, many paths can be taken, but with each step the options for the next step decrease until a single path is clear.

When reading the compiled texts, simply writing notes in the margins of the texts will not be sufficient. Instead, researchers should keep a running file of notes on texts, answering the same set of questions (for example, what are the general paradigms and theories? The key theoretical questions? The hypotheses or aims?) for each text. The set of notes for each text should be accompanied by the complete citation information for that text. Various documentation styles are used in the social sciences, such as Chicago style and American Psychological Association (APA) style. All styles require the same basic information: author, date, title, and source. Having a note file for each topic or subtopic is a good idea. A note file may take the form of, but is not limited to, an **annotated bibliography**, which is a *list of texts with an accompanying brief description of the content of each text and of the reader's reaction to or thoughts on each text.*

annotated bibliography
A list of cites with a short description of the content of the text as well as the reader's thoughts on the text.

ORGANIZING AND ANALYZING YOUR NOTES

The final step in preparing your literature review is organizing and analyzing your notes. The goal is to identify key recurring themes, especially those related to general patterns of findings or to open questions. You can then group themes together by the similarities or connections among them. Drawing a "map" of identified themes—including thematic clusters and the links among themes and clusters—helps make sense of the literature.

Although hard work, a literature review is valuable because it allows you to define key concepts, identify variables, and look for links. The potential relations that emerge from a literature review point to questions that need to be asked. For example, if the topic is religious extremism, a literature review might lead you to become interested in the causes of religious violence, and the associated theories might suggest that you focus on economic inequality as one possible cause. The question you pursue would then be: Does economic inequality lead to religious extremism? That question lends itself to hypothesis testing in a deductive process. Or, perhaps this review shows you that there is a lack of clear understanding about these causes, leading you to pose a more open-ended question (What are the causes of religious extremism?) that will guide research to develop a theory in an inductive process. Your question, regardless of how specific or open-ended, forms the basis for your study.

Constructing a Hypothesis about the Answer to the Question at Hand

A theory-driven question motivates research. In the case of deductive research, that question lends itself to a testable hypothesis. How do you transform a question into a hypothesis?

First, concepts must be defined (or conceptualized) as variables. The abstract concept of religious extremism needs to be distilled into something more concrete that varies in observable ways; for example, violence perpetrated by members of one group against another.

Second, very general concepts need to be further specified. For example, the researcher needs to specify historical time frame and unit of analysis (for example, the person, school, or state, as we will discuss in Chapter 4). Is the point to understand what happens over time, across societies, within societies, or some combination of the three? Is the variable state-level, group-level, or interpersonal? These kinds of specifications narrow the goals of the research in practical ways that facilitate empirical inquiry.

Third, the different concepts need to be arranged within an expected relation (Figure 2.5). In a causal hypothesis, the concept purported to be the cause is the **independent variable**; it is the variable that leads to or affects another variable. The **dependent variable** is the variable that is acted upon. These terms are also used in other kinds of hypotheses, such as hypotheses of association, out of convention, even if they are not strictly about cause-and-effect relations.

Fourth, concepts need to be linked together. Making a statement about the direction of the link (positive, inverse) is a starting point, with more complicated arrangements (mediation, moderation) possibly built into the statement. The resulting statement of the relation between the concepts is the hypothesis. Note that it is written as a statement ("Economic inequality leads to religious extremism") that can then be tested, rather than as a question ("Does economic inequality lead to religious extremism?").

As you now know, inductive research does not use theory to pose hypotheses for empirical research. Instead, it uses empirical research to craft theory. Still, this exploration is guided by past research or existing theories. As such, the questions will remain questions, or goals to help organize the research, and are not crafted into hypotheses. They are the building blocks of theory rather than the result.

Gathering Data, Analyzing Data, and Drawing Conclusions

With the concepts defined and the relations between concepts hypothesized, the next step in linking theory to observation is operationalization, which involves decisions about how to

independent variable In a causal hypothesis, the concept purported to be the cause; the variable on which values of the dependent variable may depend.

dependent variable In a causal hypothesis, the variable that is acted upon; the outcome we are seeking to understand.

FIGURE 2.5 Relations between Variables in a Causal Hypothesis

Independent variable	Dependent variable
• Predictor	• Outcome
• Cause	• Effect
• Actor	• Acted upon

measure each variable in the hypothesis and, ultimately, how to analyze the relation between these variables. We provide an in-depth discussion of operationalization and other building blocks of research in Chapters 4 and 5, and the remaining chapters delve into the various methods of analyses that follow operationalization.

Going through the Steps

Following the evolution of a general topic into a specific hypothesis, question, or goal provides greater understanding of the process as a whole. To that end, consider the topic of intimate partner violence (IPV) within the deductive research process. IPV is frequently in the news and generates a lot of debate and discussion. In 2014, for example, fans of Baltimore Ravens running back Ray Rice were stunned when a video emerged of the star football player knocking out his then-girlfriend (whom he later married) in the elevator of an Atlantic City hotel. She is one of the more than 1 million women physically injured by a romantic partner each year. Although studying partner violence can be difficult because of ethical constraints and access limitations, it is a legitimate scientific activity.

A literature review will narrow the focus from this broad topic. In a search, use of various phrases related to IPV will be helpful; for example, "domestic violence," "spousal abuse," "partner violence," and so on. Doing so would reveal a review in *Annual Review of Sociology* (Jackman, 2002) on violence in social relations, several relevant studies over the past 20 years (including one in the prestigious *American Sociological Review*: Berk, et al., 1992), and an entire journal (*Journal of Interpersonal Violence*) devoted to these topics. The literature review will also provide insights into the theoretical frameworks that organize research on this topic, the levels of society targeted by that research, and the predictors and outcomes that have been linked to spousal abuse. It will also highlight theories that may be useful for posing questions. These theories may not be about partner violence per se but touch on relevant topics (violence in general, gender inequality, marital relations, and so on).

The information gleaned from the literature review can then be used to ask an informed question. For example, much of the work on intimate partner violence is focused on the meso or micro level, exploring what happens between couples within families and in communities. The review is likely to highlight a pattern of intergenerational transmission, in which many abusive men had fathers who were abusive of their own spouses or intimate partners. In the course of the review, the researcher might also come across theories, such as social cognitive theory (Bandura, 2001), which suggests that people engage in violent behavior because they come to see that it rewards them. Synthesizing these elements could lead to several questions about IPV, including "Is violence learned within families?"

To convert this question into a testable hypothesis, we need to define what learning and partner violence are. According to accepted theory, learning is mostly about observation and then imitation. Thus, the concept of observation can become a variable: observation of violent acts between intimate partners. IPV encompasses, but is not limited to, verbal, physical, and sexual assaults, and it can refer to legal marriage and/or more informal romantic partnerships. Given that the question focuses on violence, and given evidence from the literature review that legal marriage may foster abuse, the concept of IPV can become a variable: engagement in violent acts against a wife or husband (legal partners specifically rather than the more general category of intimate partners). As for specification, the unit of analysis is the individual, with observation of IPV occurring during childhood and spousal abuse occurring in adulthood. The goal is to compare, within some population, how individuals differ on adult behavior because of earlier experience. Observation of IPV as a child is the independent variable, and spousal abuse is the dependent variable. The relationship is direct and causal.

The resulting hypothesis, therefore, is that witnessing acts of abuse between parents as a child will lead to greater levels of abuse perpetrated against one's spouse as an adult. Based on theory, this hypothesis can be extended to include an **mediating variable**. In that mediational hypothesis, witnessing acts of abuse between parents as a child will lead young people to internalize the idea that violence is a means of achieving what they want, which in turn will lead to greater levels of abuse perpetrated against one's spouse as an adult.

This hypothesis is testable and falsifiable. Although many practical considerations must be taken into account, including the obvious ethical complexity of this line of inquiry, this hypothesis can be tested empirically to produce evidence that confirms or disproves it. One can see how these steps might also apply to inductive research, in which scientists could use past research to construct a more in-depth study of IPV (or spousal abuse more specifically) that is not constrained by any specific hypotheses.

mediating variable
The variable that links the independent variable to the dependent variable.

CONCEPT CHECKS

1 | Two studies report different findings on some issue. Would looking at whether one, both, or neither is peer-reviewed be a way to determine which text is correct? Why or why not?

2 | "Do girls have more fun than boys?" is a question. Convert this question into a hypothesis with an independent variable and a dependent variable.

3 | On the basis of a theory of cognitive load, a scientist hypothesizes that distracting doctors in hospital emergency rooms will lead to greater rates of HIV contamination. What are the challenges of testing this hypothesis?

CONCLUSION

Theory and empiricism are the two key ingredients of the scientific method. Consequently, scientists can only draw sound conclusions about some social phenomenon by combining the two, but how they go about this combination varies widely. For some, theory arises from empirical research (inductive approach). For others, theory guides empirical research (deductive approach). Still others mix these two approaches, as we saw in the case of Lareau's study of social class differences in parenting. Worth stressing here is that the similarities between these various approaches to theory and empirical research are greater than the differences, the most important similarity being careful conceptualization and operationalization. Before we take a deeper dive into both conceptualization and operationalization in Chapter 4, we first consider the ethics of conducting social research.

Summary

Theory is a critical component of sociological inquiry. Theory allows researchers to pose new questions about the social world, develop methods to test assumptions, and make sense of empirical observations.

Theory within the Scientific Method

- Social research uses the scientific method, which is based on theory and empiricism, to ask and answer questions.
- Scientists use theory for three purposes: to describe, to explain, or to explore social phenomena. Descriptive theories seek to explain how and why phenomena occur, explanatory theories make predictions about the relationships between phenomena, and exploratory theories specify the particular aspect of a phenomenon that will be studied.
- Theories often target a specific level of social life, with macro and micro at opposite ends and meso in the middle.
- Theories share common traits: Most are testable, falsifiable, generalizable, and probabilistic.
- Theory is used in research in two main ways: In an inductive approach, theory arises from empirical observations. In a deductive approach, theory guides empirical analysis.

Social Science Theory

- Social science theories are situated within paradigms, or broad taken-for-granted assumptions about how the world works. Paradigms are subjective interpretations of reality; they vary widely across cultures and population subgroups.
- Macro-level sociological paradigms include structural functionalism and the conflict perspective. Symbolic interactionism is a micro-level paradigm. Rational choice theory targets the macro and micro levels as well as the meso.

The Elements of Theory

- Social research theories are built by linking concepts together in systematic ways. Two concepts can be positively (or directly) or negatively (or inversely) related. Mediation, moderation, and spuriousness are ways of characterizing expected relationships between three or more concepts.
- Social researchers use theories to develop testable hypotheses, which can be supported or falsified through empirical investigations. A hypothesis can test for differences, associations, or causal relationships between variables.
- Many of the concepts social researchers study are abstract, and must be more precisely defined through the process of conceptualization in order to be studied.

From Theory to Empirical Study and Back

- In addition to personal interest and practical considerations like time and access, researchers must consider what has already been studied when choosing a research topic.

- The Internet is a valuable tool for conducting a literature review, but care must be taken to ensure that the sources are credible. Peer-reviewed journal articles are typically the focus of a literature review.
- In order to transform a research question into a hypothesis, general concepts need to be defined as variables, and time frame and unit of analysis specified. The concepts then need to be arranged within an expected relation.

Key Terms

abstract, 59
annotated bibliography, 60
causal hypothesis, 55
causal inference, 56
concept, 53
conceptualization, 57
confound, 54
deductive approach, 42
dependent variable, 61
empiricism, 35
hypothesis, 55

hypothesis of association, 55
hypothesis of difference, 55
independent variable, 61
inductive approach, 41
literature review, 58
macro level, 39
mediating variable, 63
mediation, 54
meso level, 39

micro level, 39
moderation, 54
null hypothesis, 55
operationalization, 57
paradigm, 45
positivism, 46
postmodernism, 46
scientific method, 35
spuriousness, 54
theory, 35
variables, 57

Exercise

Historically, female college students were less likely than their male counterparts to enter medical school. Because of dramatic changes in gender role socialization, norms about female employment, and increased educational opportunities for girls, this gender gap has nearly closed. Yet, despite going to medical school at rates nearly equal to men, women still make up a distinct minority of all physicians in the United States today, and they are especially underrepresented in high-paying, high-prestige fields, such as surgery. Sociologists have long been interested in these and other forms of gender segregation. Yet, they often disagree about the underlying causes, in part because they do not share the same assumptions and interests.

To better understand how these differences arise, consider the four theoretical frameworks described in this chapter (structural functionalism, conflict, rational choice, symbolic interactionism) and complete the following tasks:

- Explain how a person working from each framework would account for the underrepresentation of women in prestigious, high-paying medical specialties such as surgery and cardiology. What basic question would that person ask, and what kinds of answers might that person give?
- Using Sociological Abstracts, Google Scholar, or some other academic search engine, find an article about sex segregation in the workforce (whether about the medical field or another field) published in a peer-reviewed journal. Which framework does this article reflect? How can you tell?

All sociologists, regardless of research question or method, face difficult ethical choices when carrying out their studies.

ETHICAL ISSUES IN SOCIAL SCIENCE RESEARCH

Research is a social process that always involves ethical choices—how you frame your study, whom you sample, how you collect data, how you analyze it, how you store your data after you analyze it, how you present your results, and how your results are used in the real world. Every step in the research process and every research method has ethical implications. We discuss ethical standards throughout the book, but in this chapter we focus on the baseline expectations for ethical social research.

We begin by highlighting three studies that raise some important questions about right and wrong decisions. We then describe the principles underlying all ethical research. Next, we review the history of ethical lapses in research that gave rise to the systems currently in place, including the role of informed consent in protecting human subjects. We conclude with a discussion of the challenges that social scientists face when they believe that deceiving subjects is necessary for their research and when they confront conflicts of interest.

THREE ETHICAL DILEMMAS

Sociologists tackling any question, and using any method, face difficult ethical choices when carrying out their studies. As the next three dilemmas convey, researchers studying topics as far-ranging as friendship networks on Facebook, drug dealers, and military conflict in the Persian Gulf region all must be mindful of the ethical challenges they face.

A Facebook Study: Accessing Friends' Data without Permission

In 2006, sociologists at Harvard University received permission from Facebook and Harvard University to download the Facebook profiles of an entire class of students. The researchers wanted to use these profiles to build a social network database to study how people's friendship networks change over time and how friends influence people's tastes in music and books. Research assistants recorded each student's gender; home state; college major; political views; favorite music, movies, and television programs; network of friends; and romantic tastes. They also recorded who was tagged in each student's online photos, and each student's friends were coded for characteristics such as race and gender. The resulting database followed all the Harvard students who were on Facebook from their freshman year until graduation. The research assistants doing the coding were Harvard undergraduates, who could access the profiles of students who had set their privacy settings so that only people at Harvard or only friends of friends could access their profiles. None of the study's subjects was informed about the study.

In the final published study, the data set was identified as coming from an "anonymous northeastern American university." After the researchers took steps to protect the privacy of the students whose data were collected, they made the data set available to other researchers, a condition of the funding that comes from the National Science Foundation, a federal organization that provides funding for American researchers to conduct their research (Lewis et al., 2008). In 2011, a reporter asked the opinion of one of the students

Researchers at Harvard University received permission from their university and Facebook to download students' profiles for research purposes. What ethical concerns might this raise?

whose data were analyzed without her permission. She was not bothered: "Anything that's put on Facebook somehow will make it out into the general public, no matter what you attempt to do . . . so I never have anything on my Facebook profile that I wouldn't want employers, my grandmother, like anyone in the world to be able to see" (Parry, 2011). Would you feel the same way? Is it ethical to study people who believe that only their friends and the friends of their friends can see their information? How would you decide?

Gang Leader for a Day: Lying to Drug Dealers

One of the best-selling sociology books of the past decade is Sudhir Venkatesh's *Gang Leader for a Day* (2008). Venkatesh, a sociology professor at Columbia University, wrote the book about his experiences as a graduate student conducting an ethnography in the notorious Robert Taylor Homes. (An *ethnography* is a scientific description of the customs of individual peoples and cultures; we discuss ethnographic research in detail in Chapter 10.) This high-rise public housing project on the south side of Chicago was home to 20,000 poor people, and Venkatesh studied the gangs and drug dealers who lived and worked there. A review of the book in *Newsweek* magazine noted that it "renders a window into a way of life that few Americans understand." But at what price?

Sudhir Venkatesh's ethnography *Gang Leader for a Day* raised ethical concerns regarding the researcher's role when he becomes aware of potentially illegal or dangerous behavior.

To be accepted by a gang of drug dealers, Venkatesh had to convince them that he would not report their activities to the police. But what should he have done when he saw them beating someone up or heard them plan a drive-by shooting? Venkatesh decided to do nothing so as to maintain his position in the field. He also deceived the people he studied about his true purposes. While he did tell his subjects that he was a student and was there to study them, he led the gang leader, J.T., to believe he was writing a biography of J.T. By playing on J.T.'s sense of self-importance, Venkatesh gained entry into a world of criminal behavior and an underground economy that is often hidden from outsiders.

While *Gang Leader for a Day* has been enormously successful, it has also sparked controversy. One review of the book said it was "evil" (Cowen, 2008) because Venkatesh encouraged and fed a drug dealer's ego. Other scholars worried that he caused harm to his research subjects when he shared information about them with the gang leader, and that it was unethical to silently stand by when people were hurt and when the gang planned crimes. Was this research ethical? How would you decide?

Human Terrain System: Military Studies of Local People

In 2007, the U.S. military launched a controversial social science program aimed at increasing the military's understanding of local populations and applying this new cultural understanding to the military decision-making process. Known as the Human Terrain System, the program embedded social scientists in combat units to study the local people and explain cultural and social practices, beliefs, and behaviors—the "human terrain"—to military leaders. The five-member Human Terrain teams created a database of local and regional leaders and tribes, social problems, economic issues, and political disputes. For instance, as the military moved into an area

The Human Terrain System employed social scientists to help the U.S. Army better understand the beliefs, values, and behaviors of local residents in Afghanistan and Iraq.

in Afghanistan, one of the embedded anthropologists identified a local village with a high concentration of widows. She explained that these women had no financial support, which led many of their sons to consider joining the well-paid insurgents fighting with the Taliban. The military responded by developing a job-training program for the widows (Rohde, 2007).

Nonetheless, the program, which was shut down in 2014, was controversial. The American Anthropological Association passed a resolution against the Human Terrain System, arguing that the program violated their code of ethics because the U.S. military could use the information gathered on local people to harm them (Glenn, 2007, 2009). A debate in the pages of the *American Anthropologist* was heated, with some arguing that the Human Terrain System represented the militarization of anthropology and put all anthropologists at risk because people would suspect them of being spies or of working for the U.S. government (Gonzalez, 2007).

This is not a new debate. One of the most famous American anthropologists, Margaret Mead, helped the Office of Strategic Services (OSS), a precursor of the Central Intelligence Agency (CIA), develop psychological warfare units during World War II. Ruth Benedict, another prominent anthropologist, wrote a book in 1944 analyzing Japanese culture and habits of thought and emotion to help the American war effort against Japan.

Is it ethical for social scientists to study civilians in wartime and provide that information to the military? How would you decide?

DEFINING RESEARCH ETHICS

Whenever you conduct research with human subjects, you must consider whether your research is ethical. **Ethics** refers to the moral system that determines whether actions are right or wrong, good or bad. One does not have to be a bad or evil person to perform unethical research. On the contrary, many instances of unethical research are the result of well-meaning researchers who have not fully thought through the ways in which their research could harm people.

Although many people derive their sense of right and wrong from their religious or spiritual beliefs, scientists rely on three ethical principles to guide their research. These three principles were described in the *Belmont Report* of 1979. The report was issued by the National Commission for the Protection of Human Subjects of Biomedical and Behavioral Research (1979), which was established by Congress when it passed the National Research Act of 1974. The *Belmont Report* forms the foundation of our national system designed to protect humans who take part in medical or social science research.

The three principles outlined in the *Belmont Report* are respect, beneficence, and justice.

1. **Respect** means that people are to be treated as autonomous agents. They have a right to decide whether they will take part in a research study. Respect also means that individuals with diminished autonomy—children, people with mental disabilities or suffering from diminished decision-making capacity (for example, Alzheimer's patients)—receive protection in the decision-making process.

2. **Beneficence** refers to the responsibility to do good—to maximize benefits for science, for humanity, and for research subjects, and to prevent research subjects from suffering any harm as a result of the research.

3. **Justice** requires that the risks and potential benefits of the research be distributed equally among subjects. Research must be conducted in a fair and nonexploitative manner, and no one who might benefit from being part of the research should be systematically excluded. Similarly, powerless and vulnerable people should not be targeted as research subjects and bear the risks of the study simply because they are more likely to take part or because they are more accessible to the researcher.

These three ethical principles guide the establishment of norms and legal requirements for conducting research that all social scientists must follow. The main mechanism for ensuring these protections is the requirement of voluntary **informed consent**. Individuals must have the freedom to say yes or no to being part of a research project, and they must have all the possible benefits and risks of participation explained to them before they consent to participate. In most social science research, the risks are most likely to be social or psychological rather than physical. Social harms include embarrassment, shame, negative self-knowledge, emotional upset, and loss of privacy. Informed consent can be given by signing a form or by agreeing orally.

Informed consent also means that no one can be coerced or forced to take part in a research project. Bosses cannot require employees, teachers cannot require students, and jailers cannot force prisoners to take part in research. In the case of **vulnerable populations** who cannot give informed consent due to age or diminished mental capacity (for example, senility or an intellectual disability), special protections must be put in place. For instance, parents must give informed consent for their children to be part of a research study.

The respect principle leads to a requirement that researchers protect individuals' privacy and confidentiality. **Privacy** refers to control over the extent, timing, and circumstances of sharing oneself (behaviorally, physically, or intellectually) with others. Research subjects should control the information they share with others, and if they do share information because they trust a researcher, then the researcher must keep that information private and not release it to the public.

In the United States, **institutional review boards (IRBs)** ensure that research adheres to all these principles. IRBs are committees located at institutions where research is conducted, such as universities and colleges, hospitals, and survey research firms. Any institution that receives research money from the federal government, through organizations such as the National Science Foundation (NSF) or National Institutes of Health (NIH), must have an institutional review board. This board is

respect The principle that people are to be treated as autonomous agents in research studies and that those with diminished autonomy receive protection.

beneficence The principle that refers to the responsibility to do good and to protect subjects from harm in a research study.

justice The principle that research must be conducted in a fair manner with the potential risks and benefits distributed equally among participants.

informed consent The freedom to say yes or no to participating in a research study once all the possible risks and benefits have been properly explained.

vulnerable population A group of people who cannot give informed consent, including those who are underage or have diminished mental capacity.

privacy Control over the extent, timing, and circumstances of sharing oneself with others.

institutional review board (IRB) A committee located at an institution where research is done that is responsible for reviewing all research involving human subjects, with the goal of protecting the human subjects and preventing ethical violations in the research.

responsible for a thorough review of *all* research conducted at the institution, not just federally funded research. Researchers must receive approval from these boards before they begin their research. The story of how this system arose begins with some notorious cases of unethical research.

A BRIEF HISTORY OF ETHICAL PROBLEMS IN RESEARCH

Researchers and IRBs today are vigilant about maintaining the highest possible ethical standards in research to help ensure that atrocities are never again committed in the name of science. We briefly review six of the most infamous ethical breaches and the important lessons learned.

Experiments and Torture at Nazi Concentration Camps

During World War II, the Nazis conducted horrible experiments on prisoners in concentration camps. Denying the humanity of the prisoners, doctors deliberately inflicted pain, suffering, disease, and death on people in gruesome scientific experiments. Many doctors directed these experiments, some of which involved vaccines, pregnancy, and organ transplants. One Nazi doctor, Sigmund Rascher, conducted "freezing experiments" with 300 prisoners at the Dachau concentration camp in order to learn the most effective ways to treat German pilots suffering from hypothermia. Some prisoners were submerged in tubs of ice water for up to five hours while others were taken outside and strapped down naked. Rascher then monitored their heart rate, muscle control, core temperature, and when they lost consciousness. Eighty prisoners died in the experiment (Palmer, 2010). After the war ended, many of those conducting experiments at the concentration camps were prosecuted as war criminals at trials in Nuremberg, Germany.

Nuremberg Code A set of ethical principles for human subjects research, including the requirement of informed consent, developed in the wake of the Nuremberg Trials following World War II.

risk versus benefit analysis An assessment in which the potential harms to research subjects are weighed against the potential benefits of the research.

The revelations in these trials led to the development of the **Nuremberg Code** in 1947. This code established the principle that experiments should never be designed to harm participants, and that people must consent to take part in experiments and have the right to withdraw whenever they choose and without penalty. It also established the principle of **risk versus benefit analysis** to determine whether an experiment should be allowed. In short, the potential harms to research subjects must be weighed against the potential benefits of the research. While the Nuremberg Code applied only to *experiments* done with human beings, it laid the groundwork for the later rules that would govern all research methods involving human beings. (Experiments, explained in detail in Chapter 8, are just one of several social science research methodologies.)

The Tuskegee Syphilis Experiment: Deliberate Harm

Several other unethical biomedical experiments came to light in the postwar period. Perhaps the most notorious is the Tuskegee syphilis experiment. The U.S. Public Health Service conducted a long-running study of syphilis among poor African

American men in Tuskegee, Alabama, beginning in 1932. Nearly 400 men with advanced syphilis were recruited for the study, along with a comparison group of 201 non-infected men. When the study began, there was no cure for syphilis, and the purpose of the study was to watch the disease unfold "until autopsy" (Jones, 1993, p. 32).

In the 1940s, antibiotics were discovered that could cure the disease, but none of the men was informed about or treated with the drugs. The men were not told that they had syphilis; instead, they were told they had "bad blood." They were deliberately deceived about the nature of the study, and they were subjected to painful procedures such as spinal taps. To prevent the subjects from being treated, the researchers worked with the local draft board to ensure that they were not drafted during World War II, because the military would have diagnosed the condition. The researchers also arranged with local physicians to withhold treatment from the men. The study continued through 1972, when national media attention caused the Public Health Service to end the study and offer treatment to the few surviving men (Jones, 1993).

From 1932 to 1972, the U.S. Public Health Service conducted a study of syphilis among poor black men in Tuskegee, Alabama, that involved deceiving the subjects about their condition and withholding lifesaving treatment.

While the Tuskegee syphilis experiment involved withholding lifesaving medicine from subjects in order to study the natural course of disease, two other high-profile medical studies involved deliberately infecting people with disease. In the Willowbrook hepatitis study in the early 1950s, children residing in a state facility who had been classified as "mentally retarded" were infected with hepatitis by doctors by feeding them the feces of people who had the disease. In the Jewish Chronic Disease Hospital study in the 1960s, senile elderly patients were deliberately injected with live cancer cells in order to study whether they contracted the disease. All of these cases involved deliberate harm to vulnerable populations: the illiterate poor men in Tuskegee, children with diminished mental capacity in Willowbrook, and older adults with dementia in the Jewish Chronic Disease Hospital (Amdur & Bankert, 2007).

The 1950s to 1970s: Four Controversial Studies

From the 1950s to the 1970s, four high-profile social science studies led to public outcry and captured the attention of Congress.

THE WICHITA JURY STUDY

In 1955, University of Chicago researchers conducted the Wichita jury study. Concerned that showmanship by lawyers might unduly influence jurors, the researchers conducted a study in which they secretly taped jury deliberations in Wichita, Kansas. They presented their findings to academic audiences, and gradually the local and national press found out. The public outcry led to congressional hearings. If jurors could not be sure that their deliberations were private, the argument went, no defendant in the United States could ever be guaranteed a fair trial. Congress eventually passed a law barring the recording of jury deliberations.

THE MILGRAM OBEDIENCE EXPERIMENT

The Milgram obedience experiment also raised ethical issues. Stanley Milgram was a psychology professor at Yale University. In the 1950s, Milgram wondered how ordinary people could have taken part in Nazi atrocities. He wanted to understand how people could follow the orders of authority figures even when they thought what they were doing was wrong. Milgram designed a laboratory study that involved deception. Subjects were told that the study was about the effects of punishment (in this case, electric shocks) on learning. The subjects were to be the "teachers," and they would have to administer electric shocks to "learners" who did not answer questions correctly. Unbeknownst to the subjects, the learners were laboratory personnel who were pretending to be study participants. The subjects believed they were actually administering shocks of higher and higher voltage each time the learner answered incorrectly. They could not see the learners but heard their screams of pain and their pleas that the experiment end.

Many of the subjects became very distressed and tried to stop administering shocks, but the experimenter told them in a calm yet very authoritative voice that "the experiment must continue." Surprisingly, more than half the research subjects administered shocks they thought were high intensity and potentially lethal to the learners. After the experiment was completed, the subjects were told that they had not hurt anyone and that they had been deceived about the study's real purpose (Milgram, 1977).

There is a great deal of debate about whether Milgram's study crossed ethical boundaries. Subjects who participated may have had to live with the knowledge that they could have harmed or even killed people. Milgram conducted a 12-month follow-up study of participants, and less than 1% reported that they regretted taking part in the study (Milgram, 1977). Nevertheless, most scholars agree that no IRB would approve Milgram's study today.

ZIMBARDO'S STANFORD PRISON EXPERIMENT

Another widely known psychological experiment is Philip Zimbardo's Stanford prison experiment. This 1971 experiment involved 24 male undergraduates recruited through an advertisement in a campus newspaper. Zimbardo built a simulated prison in the basement of Stanford University's psychology building and assigned half the subjects to be "prisoners" and the other half to be "guards." The prisoners were picked up at their homes by police, handcuffed, and brought to the prison. The guards wore uniforms and were given minimal instructions about how to run the prison. Participants knew they were taking part in a simulation, and they signed informed consent forms warning them that some of their basic civil rights would be violated if they were selected to be prisoners. (To see the consent form that the volunteer participants signed, refer to Figure 3.1.)

The research quickly spiraled out of control. The guards became increasingly arbitrary, cruel, and sadistic toward the prisoners, and the prisoners became increasingly passive, depressed, and hopeless. Five student prisoners were released early because they developed emotional problems. The experiment was called off before it was due to

The now infamous Zimbardo Stanford prison experiment demonstrated how simulated experiments can spiral out of control, and how researchers' subjectivity and investment in the study can cause them to lose sight of their participants' well-being.

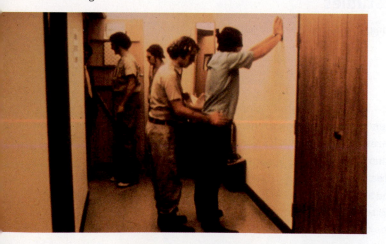

FIGURE 3.1 Stanford Prison Experiment Consent Form

Prison Life Study
Dr. Zimbardo
August 1971

_____   _____
       (date)   (name of volunteer)

I, _____, the undersigned, hereby consent to participate as a volunteer in a prison life study research project to be conducted by the Stanford University Psychology Department.

The nature of the research project has been fully explained to me, including, without limitation, the fact that paid volunteers will be randomly assigned to the roles of either "prisoners" or "guards" for the duration of the study. I understand that participation in the research project will involve a loss of privacy, that I will be expected to participate for the full duration of the study, that I will only be released from participation for reasons of health deemed adequate by the medical advisers to the research project or for other reasons deemed appropriate by Dr. Philip Zimbardo, Principal Investigator of the project, and that I will be expected to follow directions from staff members of the project or from other participants in the research project.

I am submitting myself for participation in this research project with full knowledge and understanding of the nature of the research project and of what will be expected of me. I specifically release the Principal Investigator and the staff members of the research project, Stanford University, its agents and employees, and the Federal Government, its agents and employees, from any liability to me arising in any way out of my participation in the project.

Witness: _____   _____
                                                (signature of volunteer)

If volunteer is a minor:

Witness: _____   _____
                                      (signature of person authorized to
                                           consent for volunteer)

_____
                                        (relationship to volunteer)

Source: Stanford University Libraries, 2011.

conclude because a visiting psychologist intervened. Zimbardo later admitted that the research was "unethical because people suffered and others were allowed to inflict pain and humiliation" and that he had become so involved in the experiment that he did not recognize the harm happening to the students. He concluded that he made a mistake and should have stopped the experiment earlier (Zimbardo, Maslach, & Haney, 1999).

The findings of this study—that anyone randomly assigned to be a guard with little direction and a lot of power over prisoners could become sadistic and cruel in that situation—had implications long after the experiment was called off. Zimbardo served as an expert witness in the trial of the soldiers accused in the Abu Ghraib torture scandal that occurred in Iraq in 2004. Zimbardo published a book in 2007, *The Lucifer Effect*, explaining the connection between the Stanford prison experiment and the behavior of the National Guard members who engaged in the torture of Iraqi prisoners 40 years later.

TEAROOM TRADE

The most notorious sociological study to raise serious ethical issues is Laud Humphreys's *Tearoom Trade* study (1970), which Humphreys conducted in 1966–1967 when he was a graduate student in sociology at Washington University in St. Louis. The study began as an inquiry into homosexual behaviors in public spaces. Some public bathrooms—called "tearooms"—were known as places where men could go to engage in sexual encounters with other men. Humphreys spent time observing these encounters by assuming the role of "watchqueen," a man who looks out for the police while enjoying watching the men in the tearoom. This part of the study is not controversial because the tearoom was a public place and the men knew they were being watched, although they did not know they were being studied.

But Humphreys took the research a major step further. He followed many of the men to their cars and surreptitiously wrote down their license plate numbers. He then told some "friendly policemen" that he was a salesman who needed to reach these men, and the police provided him with the names and addresses that corresponded to the license plate numbers. A year later, Humphreys disguised his appearance, went to the men's homes, and told them they were chosen to take part in a random-sample public health survey. As part of the survey, he asked the men many questions about their private lives without revealing that he knew about their behaviors in the tearoom. He found that 55% of the men were married and lived with their wives. They did not think of themselves as either bisexual or homosexual. Only 14% of the sample were members of the gay community and interested primarily in same-sex sexual relationships (Sieber, 1992).

In 1970, Humphreys published a book about his study, *Tearoom Trade: A Study of Homosexual Encounters in Public Places*, to a very mixed reaction. On the positive side, it had some public policy effects. Tearoom arrests at that time accounted for the majority of arrests for homosexuality in the United States, and as a result of the book, some police departments ceased their raids of public restrooms (Sieber, 1992, p. 8). The book was awarded the prestigious C. Wright Mills Award by the Society for the Study of Social Problems, but it also was roundly criticized for its deceptive methods. Some faculty members even went so far as to try to rescind Humphreys's PhD, and one eminent sociologist, Alvin Gouldner, hit Humphreys in the head in anger about the study, leading Humphreys to be hospitalized (Galliher, Brekhus, & Keys, 2004).

All of these studies raise ethical questions about whether they ever should have occurred in the first place. Nobody defends the Nazi experiments, which caused suffering and death. Yet there is still much debate within the medical community about whether the results of these experiments should be used, given their origins in horrible human suffering and murder. The results of the experiment on submersion in ice water have been quoted in many medical journals and have played a role in the development of thermal suits and warming treatments for hypothermia patients (Palmer, 2010).

The ethics of many of the studies described earlier are more ambiguous. The studies conducted by Milgram, Zimbardo, and Humphreys raise serious issues about possible harm to research subjects and about privacy, respect, and deception. But these studies did not cause lasting harm to their subjects and did contribute to our knowledge of human behavior. Most of these studies would not have been approved if the current IRB system had reviewed them and if the researchers had present-day monitoring and training. In the next section, we discuss how that system works in practice.

THE INSTITUTIONAL REVIEW BOARD SYSTEM

Congressional hearings on the ethical concerns of medical and social science studies culminated in the National Research Act of 1974, which established the modern IRB system. The IRB reviews and approves all research involving human subjects before the research begins, with the goal of protecting the human subjects and preventing ethical violations in the research. Any institution that receives federal money for research must have an IRB, and it is not unusual for large universities to have IRB offices that employ 10 or more people.

Institutional review board committees include scientists from the institution, usually representing a broad range of expertise. At least one committee member must come from the community; that is, a citizen not affiliated with the institution. This "community member" may represent ethnic or socioeconomic groups that could be subjects in the research but are not represented among the IRB's scientist members. The community member's role is to ask questions that the scientists on the board might not think of and to read the documents that will be presented to subjects from a layperson's perspective.

One key question is: What constitutes research with human subjects? Ethnographic research or in-depth interviewing would most certainly need review, but what about a historian conducting an oral history or a sociologist working with census data or other surveys that have been de-identified and released to the public? (*De-identified data* do not include subjects' names or any other information that could reveal their identities.) This question is a matter of some debate, and rules have changed over time. The legal definition of **human subjects research** is any study of persons that is a systematic investigation designed to develop or contribute to generalizable knowledge.

In 2003, the Oral History Association issued a policy statement that oral histories are not designed to contribute to generalizable knowledge. Rather, they describe

human subjects research
Any study of persons that is a systematic investigation designed to develop or contribute to generalizable knowledge.

Members of the Irish Republican Army who participated in an oral history project conducted by Boston College experienced backlash from the Belfast community.

individual lives and thus should be exempt from review. Oral histories are quite similar to in-depth interviews (discussed in Chapter 11). The key distinction for the IRB is whether the interviews are done for research (designed to result in generalizable knowledge) or for preservation of an individual history (defined as not constituting research). The federal Office for Human Research Protections (OHRP) has stated that some oral history projects probably do need review and that local IRBs should make the decision on a case-by-case basis.

A cautionary tale of an oral history project that raised serious ethical issues is the Boston College Belfast Project, an oral history of the Northern Ireland conflict that was conducted with members of the Irish Republican Army (IRA) and the Ulster Volunteer Force. The project, which began in 2001, produced 46 interviews that detailed numerous illegal activities by forces on both sides of the conflict. Participants were told that their interviews would remain confidential until after they died, and the study was not reviewed by an IRB or by Boston College's legal team. The British government then requested the tapes in order to investigate a murder committed by the IRA and discussed in the interviews. This request resulted in the U.S. Department of Justice issuing a subpoena for the interviews and Boston College releasing portions of seven interviews. Gerry Adams, the leader of the Sinn Fein political party in Ireland, was arrested in relation to a 1972 murder of a mother of 10 children whom the IRA accused of being an informer. Adams was subsequently released, and Boston College decided to return the interviews to the research subjects and close the archives of the oral histories because they could not protect the interviews from legal proceedings (Schworm, 2014).

How the IRB Works

Proposed research is reviewed either by the full IRB or by a subset of staff members. The full IRB reviews all research that involves any risk, vulnerable populations, or deception. Researchers submit a **research protocol**, which includes the intended research methods and procedures, a description of the people who will be asked to take part in the research and how they will be recruited, a description of all the possible risks and benefits to participants, the steps that will be taken to minimize risk and to support subjects if there are any adverse consequences, and the major research questions addressed by the study. The protocol also must describe the method that the researchers will use to obtain informed consent. Usually this involves describing the research to participants, outlining what will happen to them, what the possible risks and benefits are, and what the researcher will offer the participants to deal with any adverse effects. The informed consent also needs to tell the subjects that they can withdraw from the study at any time with no penalty, and it must provide the name and phone number of an IRB representative whom the subject can call for more information about the study and to verify that it has been approved. Some researchers also

research protocol A description from the researcher of the intended methods and procedures, target population and recruitment methods, possible risks and benefits of the study, and major research questions.

provide a list of phone numbers of counselors or websites where study participants can get help if the research questions trigger a negative emotional response. The consent form must be written in jargon-free language to ensure that all subjects can understand it. Figure 3.2 reproduces a sample consent form.

In some cases, the research protocol can be approved without a complete committee discussion. Expedited review is possible when the research does not include vulnerable populations, the data are already collected and de-identified, the research does not touch on sensitive subjects that might cause psychological or physical harm to subjects, and the informed consent process is straightforward and well designed. In such cases, staff members can green-light the research.

Assessing Risks and Benefits

One of the most challenging parts of the IRB review process is assessing possible risks. Very rarely will social science research lead to physical harm of the subject. The possible harms are much more likely to be emotional or psychological turmoil; economic or social harm resulting from loss of privacy if the confidentiality of data is compromised; or legal risk if research uncovers or documents illegal activities. Emotional upset can occur in interview studies or surveys that ask about traumatic or sad events. For example, Harvard sociologist Mary Waters conducted a study of survivors of Hurricane Katrina, surveying people who had been trapped in New Orleans when it flooded. People told the researchers about wading through floodwater containing dead bodies. One woman was trapped on a roof for several days as she waited for rescue and had a miscarriage in the 26th week of her pregnancy. Others described not knowing whether their family members were dead or alive. More than half of the sample suffered from post-traumatic stress disorder (PTSD). When researchers asked study participants about their experiences during and after the hurricane, they took the risk that talking about what happened might trigger psychological distress (Rhodes et al., 2010). Before Waters and her collaborators began their study, they identified many risks and took steps to minimize them. They trained their interviewers to recognize distress during the interviews and prepared a list of local mental health resources and crisis lines that would provide counseling for people who became upset. The IRB required the researchers to give this list to everyone they interviewed, even if interviewees did not seem upset during the interview.

The risks of this research were counterbalanced by the benefits—both to the people interviewed and to the wider community. Far from feeling that the study was too intrusive, the interviewees thanked the researchers for listening to them. Most felt that talking with the interviewers helped the respondents make sense of and process their experiences. Interview respondents were also eager for the world to hear their stories and were hopeful that Waters's research, and other studies like it, would keep the plight of Katrina survivors alive for public policy makers and fellow citizens whose attention would be drawn to the next news headline long before the Katrina survivors had rebuilt their lives. Similar risks and benefits were outlined in the research protocol of a group of sociologists who studied school shootings. Katherine S. Newman and her colleagues interviewed teachers and parents whose memories of the death and destruction they witnessed were still powerful and at times overwhelming (Newman, 2004). Yet the interviewees also hoped that the benefits of a study of school shooting

FIGURE 3.2 Sample Consent Form

You are invited to participate in a research study that is being conducted by _____ [**please complete**], who is a _____ [**e.g., student, professor, etc.**] in the _____ [**Department, School, Unit**] at [**Name of University**]. The purpose of this research is to determine _____ [**please complete**].

Approximately __ [***please complete #***] subjects will participate in the study, and each individual's participation will last approximately _____ [***please complete with an accurate duration of participant's time***].

The study procedures include: _____ [***State the complete study procedures for each participant, preferably in chronological order. For example, "Participation in this study will involve the following:"***].

This research is confidential. Confidential means that the research records will include some information about you and this information will be stored in such a manner that some linkage between your identity and the response in the research exists. Some of the information collected about you includes [***SPELL OUT SOME OF THE ELEMENTS***]. Please note that we will keep this information confidential by limiting individual's access to the research data and keeping it in a secure location [***SPELL OUT ANY OTHER SECURE STORAGE/MAINTENANCE OF THE DATA, e.g., password-protected computers, encryption methods etc.***].

The research team and the Institutional Review Board at [**Name of University**] are the only parties [***please modify if others will have access to the data***] that will be allowed to see the data, except as may be required by law. If a report of this study is published, or the results are presented at a professional conference, only group results will be stated. All study data will be kept for _____ [***indicate the length of time data will be retained, e.g., destroyed upon completion of the study procedures; destroyed upon publication of study results; retained indefinitely, as stated in study protocol. Per federal regulations it must be at least three years***].

The risks of participation include: [***Describe any foreseeable risks or possible discomforts, or state "There are no foreseeable risks to participation in this study"***].

You have been told that the benefits of taking part in this study may be: [***please list possible benefits***]. However, you may receive no direct benefit from taking part in this study. You will receive _____ [***please fill in or remove statement if subjects are not compensated/paid or given RU points***] for completing the entire study.

Participation in this study is voluntary. You may choose not to participate, and you may withdraw at any time during the study procedures without any penalty to you. In addition, you may choose not to answer any questions with which you are not comfortable.

FIGURE 3.2—Sample Consent Form

If you have any questions about the study or study procedures, you may contact myself at [*please provide your full contact information*].

If you have any questions about your rights as a research subject, please contact an IRB Administrator at [Name of University IRB]:

Institutional Review Board
[Name of University]
[Street Address]
[City, State ZIP code]
[Phone Number]
[E-mail address]

You will be given a copy of this consent form for your records.

Sign below if you agree to participate in this research study:

Subject (Print) _____

Subject Signature _____ Date _____

Principal Investigator Signature _____ Date _____

sites would uncover patterns and causes that might help prevent future tragedies. You can find the consent form used in the Newman study in Appendix A.

Sometimes we can understand the potential risks and benefits of research only in retrospect. Consider the *Tearoom Trade* study. Humphreys believed that he was protecting the people he interviewed by making sure they could not be identified when the results were published. However, he did keep their names, addresses, and license plate numbers for more than a year before he showed up at their homes and interviewed them. He thought the benefits of his research were (1) to make clear that not every man who engages in same-sex sexual relations thinks of himself as "homosexual," and (2) to describe the relationship between social class and homosexual behaviors (Humphreys, 1970).

Humphreys conducted his research before the onset of the AIDS epidemic. When AIDS first hit the United States, it was considered a "gay disease" because it primarily infected gay men during the first years of the epidemic in the 1980s. Imagine if the AIDS epidemic had hit right when Humphreys published his study. The data that he gathered informed the research community that many men who have sex with men are married to women and do not consider themselves gay. Humphreys's research therefore suggested that the disease could easily travel into the heterosexual community and that public health campaigns should not target only people who identified as gay or bisexual. No one could have easily foreseen these benefits of the research.

Similarly, nobody could have predicted the risks to the men whom Humphreys studied. Imagine the pressure Humphreys would have been under to identify the men if the public had become aware of the AIDS epidemic soon after he completed his study. The wives who had no idea what their husbands were doing in public restrooms on their way home from work would have been at risk of contracting a deadly disease. Humphreys would likely have been pressured to release information to public health professionals, and if he had chosen to withhold that data, he could have been accused of putting the women at great risk.

Controversy over IRBs

In recent years there has been a growing debate about whether IRBs have overstepped their bounds and are suppressing social science research. Jack Katz (2007) has argued that IRBs are "nationwide instruments for implementing censorship." He argues that since IRBs were first created in the 1970s, they have expanded their reach into areas that do not need oversight, such as the humanities and even the arts. Katz also claims that in reaction to harms that occurred in biomedical research in the 1990s, IRBs have needlessly tightened their control over social science research, which has not seen severe ethical breaches in recent years.

Katz argues that there is an inherent contradiction in the IRB's role with respect to reviewing what he calls "muckraking research"—studies designed to uncover the abuse of power or the deliberate infliction of harm on others in the real world. If the IRB is supposed to protect research subjects from harm, then what about research that seeks to identify people who perhaps *should* be exposed and prevented from harming those with less power? Suppose a study of police officers identifies systematic racist behavior by several of the officers who participate in the study. The study does not identify the officers, but its results trigger an investigation that leads to those police officers losing their jobs. Is this outcome something that the researchers should hope for? Or protect against? Katz argues that muckraking studies are actually trying to damage subjects—"if not as named individuals or companies, then as representatives of a type of abhorrent social practice" (Katz, 2007, p. 803).

Katz discusses the work of Harvard sociologist Devah Pager (2003), described in detail in Chapter 8. Pager's study documented discrimination in hiring decisions against blacks and people with a criminal record. Her research was targeted by a government official who attempted to rescind her previously approved National Institute of Justice (NIJ) grant because she would be deliberately deceiving the employers she was studying. Although Pager's study was ultimately approved, a similar study by a different researcher at a different university was blocked by an IRB for the same reason (Katz, 2007, p. 802). Katz argues that IRBs should not review ethnographic studies before they go forward, not only because good research may be prevented, but also because it is impossible for an ethnographer to anticipate all risks. He argues that rather than reviewing studies before they are conducted, IRBs should conduct their reviews after the work is completed and before it is published, when the ethical issues can be confronted in detail and concretely.

IRB review can be criticized on other grounds, too. Some believe that IRB review legalizes and bureaucratizes ethical behavior in a way that may trick researchers and subjects into thinking that ethical behavior is "taken care of" before the research begins. While getting consent from study participants is important at the outset, consent is actually an ongoing process. Ethnographers, for instance, become accepted in the field and develop real relationships with the people they study. It is important that researchers constantly make sure that people are still willing to be part of a study, even years into the fieldwork, when the people may forget that everything they say and do is fodder for a research project. In this sense, then, "consent" is not completed by an agreement at the beginning of the research but is an ongoing process that must constantly be renegotiated.

In short, researchers should never fall into the trap of believing that because they obtained permission to undertake a particular study, they don't have to continue to make ethical decisions about their research. In the end, researchers are human beings, and studying other human beings will always bring up unanticipated issues and dilemmas. It is important that researchers make ethical decisions, not just legally defined, IRB-sanctioned permissible decisions.

CONCEPT CHECKS

1 | What are the advantages and disadvantages of the IRB system?

2 | Describe an unethical study that could have been prevented by the existence of an IRB. Which studies that might have been prevented by the IRB system have yielded important knowledge?

3 | What is the definition of *human subjects research*? What kinds of studies would be exempt from review by a full IRB committee? What kind of studies would need review by the full IRB committee?

4 | What aspects of the *Tearoom Trade* study would an IRB find unacceptable? What ethical principles did this study violate?

PROFESSIONAL CODES OF ETHICS

In addition to institutional review boards, professional organizations of researchers have developed codes of ethics that govern their members' behavior. For example, the American Sociological Association (ASA) Code of Ethics (included in Appendix B) covers many of the topics reviewed in this chapter. It specifies sociologists' many professional responsibilities to act ethically in terms of their relations with one another and with the public and in their responsibilities as teachers and supervisors of graduate students. In addition to straightforward issues such as prohibiting plagiarism, discrimination, and harassment of coworkers, the code specifies particular issues that sociologists must be aware of. These issues include conflicts of interest in the funding of social science research and the scientists' obligations to truthfully convey their research findings to other scientists and the general public, even if those findings go against the scientists' own beliefs or political opinions.

Privacy and Confidentiality

The loss of privacy because of personal data being compromised is a major concern for social science research. Data gathered in a study can either be held anonymously or confidentially.

anonymity When no identifying information can be linked to respondents and even the researcher cannot identify them.

Anonymity means that the researcher retains no identifying information, including names, addresses, Social Security numbers, or license plate numbers. When data are anonymous, researchers cannot link the information they gathered about an individual to that individual. If a researcher promises anonymity when you take part in a study, it will be impossible for the researcher to connect you to your data.

Although anonymous data collection is the ideal, often it is not possible to gather data anonymously. For example, in a longitudinal study where the respondents will be recontacted over time, it is necessary to retain their names and addresses and to connect the next wave of data to the past one. Ethnographers are often so enmeshed in their fieldwork that they come to know the people they study very well. Even if they use code names in their field notes, they are often able to reconnect those code names to individual people by memory or through descriptions that would allow anyone familiar with the small town, office, or school being studied to identify the individuals by name. In such cases, anonymity cannot be maintained, and the researcher has an ethical responsibility to guarantee the confidentiality of the data.

confidentiality When participants' identifying information is only accessible to the research team.

Confidentiality means that the researcher can link the data to the individual's identity but promises not to release the data and to keep the data private. But can promises of confidentiality always be kept? Researchers face a number of challenges in keeping data private.

First, in some instances the ethical requirement, and often the legal requirement, is *not* to maintain confidentiality. Laws vary from state to state, but in many places the law requires researchers to alert the authorities if they learn about a child who is suffering abuse or if the subjects they are studying threaten to harm themselves or others. Thus, researchers cannot give subjects a consent form that promises complete confidentiality. Instead, they must tell research subjects that if they learn specific types of information in the course of the study, they are required to report it.

Second, unlike priests and lawyers, researchers do not have the legal right to refuse to cooperate with law enforcement in order to protect their research subjects. Suppose a researcher learns about illegal behavior during the course of a study. A court of law can subpoena that information, and law enforcement can seize it with a warrant.

Third, social scientists can be called to testify in criminal or civil cases. So, if researchers learn about the sale or use of illegal drugs, a person's status as an undocumented immigrant, or other illegal activities or behaviors, they risk contempt of court and jail time if they refuse the legal system's requests for the data. Steven Picou, a sociologist who studies disasters, did a study from 1989 to 1992 on the impact of the *Exxon Valdez* oil spill on small Alaskan villages. Lawyers for Exxon subpoenaed his files. Picou had to persuade the court to allow Exxon access only to files that had been used for publication purposes, and the court arranged for the files to be released only to an Exxon sociologist, whom the court prohibited from releasing data that would identify individuals. This arrangement allowed Picou to protect the people to whom he had promised confidentiality and to avoid being held in contempt of court and facing jail time or fines (Israel and Hay, 2006).

Rik Scarce, a sociology graduate student at Washington State University, was not so fortunate. He spent 159 days in jail for contempt of court because he refused to share details of his research on radical animal rights organizations with a grand jury (Scarce, 1999). Roberto Gonzales, a sociologist at Harvard University, has to think about legal risks a lot; his work has involved interviewing young undocumented immigrants at risk of deportation (see "Conversations from the Front Lines").

This threat of legal action is a big problem for researchers studying deviant behavior, because they are very likely to gather data that could put their participants at risk for legal action. In 1988, Congress recognized this danger and passed a law allowing the Department of Health and Human Services to issue a **certificate of confidentiality**. This certificate allows researchers to protect their participants from future requests for data disclosure, but it must be issued *before* the research begins. Researchers who study undocumented immigrants or who ask people about possible illegal activities in surveys or in qualitative research should obtain a certificate of confidentiality, which legally protects the confidentiality of their research subjects. The language of the law is very far reaching; it states that if a certificate is issued, then researchers "may not be compelled in any Federal, State or local civil, criminal, legislative or other proceedings to identify such individuals" (Public Health Service Act §301[d], 42 U.S.C. §241[d]).

certificate of confidentiality
A certificate issued by the National Institutes of Health that allows researchers to protect participants from future requests for data disclosure.

The Challenges of Digital Data

The news is filled with stories of banks and retailers notifying customers that their credit card data or Social Security numbers have been stolen or compromised. Identity theft is a major crime that is often linked to stolen Social Security numbers that thieves use to apply for credit in their victims' names. Researchers must be aware of the digital security of the data they gather. When they retain identifying information on people (perhaps because they are conducting longitudinal studies), they must

Conversations from the Front Lines

ROBERTO GONZALES

Roberto Gonzales is an assistant professor of education at Harvard University and the author of Lives in Limbo: Undocumented and Coming of Age in America *(2015). The book is based on 12 years of fieldwork with 150 undocumented youth in Los Angeles as they graduate from high school and face barriers to further education and work because of their undocumented status. Undocumented youth represent a vulnerable population. They are at risk of deportation if immigration authorities become aware of their status, and they are often understandably reluctant to talk with researchers. We spoke with Professor Gonzales to understand how he protects his research subjects and how he navigates the difficult issues associated with studying a group of people who cannot be open about who they are.*

What special precautions do you take as you do research with undocumented young people?

Given my respondents' immigration status, I go to great lengths to gain trust and ensure confidentiality. My previous work as a youth worker in Chicago taught me that gaining rapport takes time and intentionality. There, I met many young people who had been let down by adults who had broken promises. I had also witnessed young people provide teachers, researchers, and others with the answers they thought they wanted to hear in order to send them on their way.

When I started my research with undocumented young adults, I wanted to make sure that I was viewed as someone who was giving at least as much as I was asking. I wanted to be seen as a regular and consistent fixture in the community. And I wanted to make sure that I had built close enough rapport with individuals to elicit authentic responses to questions. (I also wanted to be around long enough to be able to triangulate my observations with what they told me.)

In my Los Angeles study, for example, in order to gain access and rapport, I began by volunteering at local organizations and schools. I also attended community meetings. Over time, as I started meeting potential respondents, I started spending more time with individuals. I accompanied respondents to work, home, and school. I met their friends and talked to their teachers and mentors.

> **I have gone to great lengths to ensure the confidentiality of all research subjects and made that explicitly clear in my human subjects research applications.**

Having gone through a thorough human subjects review process, I took several measures to ensure confidentiality. I made sure to eliminate any potential identifiers in the data I collected. I petitioned to bypass the requirement of asking for written consent from respondents. I didn't want to leave any kind of a paper trail, and having their signature on a consent form would directly

be careful not to keep Social Security numbers, addresses, and names on computers connected to the Internet (which can be hacked) or on laptops (which can be lost or stolen). Increasingly, universities are requiring researchers to keep sensitive data not only in password-protected files but also on encrypted discs that prevent unauthorized persons from accessing information.

link them. All respondents, instead, consented verbally after being read a pre-prepared script. I also gave pseudonyms to respondents at the time of the initial meeting (from then forward—in field notes, the interview transcript, and any other document listing names—I referred to them by their pseudonym), and I never collected home addresses. After each interview was conducted, I deleted all e-mail correspondence. And after each interview was transcribed, I deleted and destroyed audiotapes and files. Throughout the study, all data were either on a password-protected computer or in a locked file cabinet.

Have any of the people you interviewed been deported?

To my knowledge, only one of my respondents (out of 150) was deported while I was still in the field. I met him very early in my study at one of my field sites, and he was among my first interviews. Three years later, I met and interviewed his brother, who informed me he had been arrested and would be deported. Apparently, he was in the passenger seat of a coworker's car when they were pulled over. The police found a pipe bomb in the car, and both were charged with felonies.

Were you worried at all that your research would put people at risk?

I have tried to be very responsible with my research. None of the data in my possession contain any identifiers (names, addresses, places of work). But I think one always has those worries. While I have certainly written about ways in which respondents have broken the law (by working or driving), I have tried to minimize the risk by focusing on general trends rather than individual acts.

How was the process of getting IRB approval?

I have received IRB approval for two separate projects related to undocumented status and am seeking it for a third. So far, I have not experienced much difficulty along the way. Both projects were approved without much delay. As mentioned before, I have gone to great lengths to ensure the confidentiality of all research subjects and made that explicitly clear in my human subjects research applications.

What have been your experiences with presenting your work to policy makers?

I have been invited to participate in a number of policy forums in Washington, D.C., and around the country. My work has also been presented on the floor of Congress. Working with policy makers has been an education, to say the least. But I have always felt supported.

Finally, I know you must get hate mail (everyone who writes on undocumented immigrants gets a lot). Have you ever felt worried about your own safety?

I certainly have received a fair amount of angry e-mails. I understand that immigration is a deeply contentious subject, and people have strong opinions. I've written op-eds and have had some of my research findings reported in the press. These tend to reach wider audiences and elicit a range of opinions from people around the country. But I have also spoken publicly in various settings, and I haven't yet been confronted by someone who caused me to fear for my own safety. I appreciate that my work compels people to debate. I hope it also helps them to think about migration in ways they had not thought about before.

In addition, researchers must be very careful about using e-mail to recruit or communicate with research subjects. E-mail is not secure or private. A survey conducted by the American Management Association (2007) found that 52% of companies monitored their employees' e-mail use. Additionally, research surveys are increasingly being conducted online. When someone agrees to take part in a web-based survey or experiment, the researcher cannot know for sure whether some participants are actually under the age of 18 (and therefore need parental consent). It is also much more difficult for researchers to know whether the subject has understood the informed consent materials when the process occurs online.

Researchers using web-based surveys must be particularly careful with data security issues. They must protect sensitive data when moving it from computer to computer, and they should use the Secure Sockets Layer (SSL) protocol that encrypts the data during transmission in the same way that online stores protect credit card data. If secure transmission is not provided for the data, research subjects need to be told that "transfer of information across the Internet is not secure and could be observed by a third party." If people are taking surveys on shared computers, they must be reminded to clear the data and log out of the computer so that their private information is not available to the next person who uses the computer.

Increasingly, foundations and government agencies such as the National Institutes of Health and the National Science Foundation are asking researchers to make data whose collection they have sponsored available to the social science community so that other researchers can use it. Researchers must be careful to de-identify these data before disseminating them. Of course, de-identifying data requires deleting names and addresses, but it also means preventing **deductive disclosure**—using unique combinations of variables to identify individuals—by taking steps to make sure that no one can reconstruct a person's identity. (We discuss variables in depth in Chapter 4.)

For example, Add Health is a large longitudinal study of adolescents in the United States. In this data set, which began as a school-based study, the cross-tabulation of just five variables would allow someone to identify a single respondent among the 90,000 cases. Therefore, anyone who uses the Add Health data must sign a contract promising to take a number of stringent precautions in using the data:

- Copying the original data set only once and storing the original CD-ROM in a locked drawer or file cabinet

- Saving the computer programs used to construct analysis data files, but not the data files themselves

- Retrieving paper printouts immediately upon output

- Shredding printouts no longer in use

- Password protecting Add Health data

- Signing pledges of confidentiality

- Agreeing to use the data solely for statistical reporting and analysis

The danger of deductive disclosure is exacerbated by the growing movement in social science research to share data sets across researchers. The Facebook study mentioned at the beginning of the chapter shows how difficult it can be to de-identify a data set. That study was funded by the National Science Foundation, which required that the data be made available to other researchers. The data were described as coming from a study of a "northeastern American university." Soon after the data were released, however, a privacy scholar at the University of Wisconsin–Milwaukee was able to identify the university as Harvard and the people studied as

deductive disclosure The use of unique combinations of variables to identify specific individuals in data sets.

the class of 2009 (Zimmer, 2010). Because the data set included each student's hometown, college major, and ethnicity, it was easy to identify individual students once it was known that the group studied was the Harvard class of 2009. For instance, the class contained only one student each from the states of Delaware, Louisiana, Mississippi, Montana, and Wyoming. Zimmer also pointed out that only one student each identified as Albanian, Hungarian, Iranian, Malaysian, Nepali, Filipino, and Romanian, so it would be very easy to identify those individuals. When all of this information came to light in 2011, the data set was removed from public access, and the researchers began working on creating a data set that scholars could use, but not to identify individuals.

The Census and Confidentiality

Nobody is required to participate in surveys or research conducted by scholars or polling firms. However, people living in the United States do not have a choice about answering the questions in the decennial census, administered by the federal government's Census Bureau. They are required by law to provide answers. This law covers both the U.S. census, which is conducted every 10 years, and the American Community Survey (ACS), which is in the field continually and provides detailed data about people. Both ask questions about data that many people see as private, such as race and ethnic ancestry, income, occupation, and birthplace. The Census Bureau does guarantee to the public that their data will be kept safe. For example, people answering questions from the Census Bureau can expect that their answers—their income, their marital status, whether they own or rent their home—will not be available to anyone who can manipulate data files. Title 13 of the United States Code prohibits the Census Bureau from publishing results that would reveal an individual's or a business's data.

The law that gives the Census Bureau the authority to collect data about people and businesses also makes wrongful disclosure of confidential census information a crime. Penalties are up to 5 years in prison and up to $250,000 in fines. Everyone who works at the Census Bureau and has access to data takes a sworn lifetime oath to protect the confidentiality of the data: "I will not disclose any information contained in the schedules, lists, or statements obtained for or prepared by the Census Bureau to any person or persons either during or after employment" (U.S. Census Bureau, 2009).

The Census Bureau also promises that it will "use every technology, statistical methodology, and physical security procedure at our disposal to protect your information." A disclosure review board at the Census Bureau meets to discuss every data release, including "microdata" (de-identified individual-level data) as well as aggregated data in tables and reports. Every data release in any form is reviewed and discussed to ensure that it does not allow anyone to identify personal information about an individual.

Let us give you an example of what the Census Bureau protects. When Mary Waters, one of the authors of this textbook, was a graduate student in the early 1980s, she worked on a project that involved analyzing the 5% Public Use Microdata file of the census of 1980. At that time, the census had two versions: a "short form" capturing basic demographic data such as age, race, and sex, which was administered to the entire U.S. population, and a "long form" capturing much richer social and economic data, which was administered to 5% of the U.S. population. The 5% sample was a de-identified data set of individuals that included all of their long-form responses. The microdata were organized by state, with some large cities identified on the records.

As a curious young sociologist, Waters wondered whether she could find people she knew in the data. She knew that "sociologist" was a coded occupation, so she selected all of the sociologists in a particular state, and then she looked at the women. She knew some women sociologists, and she knew their ages and how many children they had. She set about trying to find a particular person—searching, for instance, for a 43-year-old married female sociologist who lived in North Carolina and had five children. Fortunately, she was not able to find anyone she knew. This was a good outcome, because what she was doing was not ethical. She thought she was conducting a harmless test of her research skills, akin to a data treasure hunt, but if she had been able to find people she knew, she would have invaded their privacy. Waters later learned that the Census Bureau had protected the data against this kind of use. It is precisely this kind of data snooping that disclosure avoidance techniques are designed to thwart.

The Census Bureau uses a variety of statistical techniques to prevent people from finding published information on identifiable individuals, families, or businesses. Two of these techniques are suppression and data swapping. Both are used in the release of microdata, tables, and reports. In **suppression**, data are simply not shown. In cases where tables created with census data would have only a few individuals or businesses in a cell, those cells are not shown; other cells might also be hidden if it would be possible to estimate information on individuals or businesses by subtracting the suppressed cells from the totals. Suppression was first used with the 1980 census results and is now used with a variety of data released from the census and other government surveys. You might notice that data has been suppressed if you look at race data, such as black-white, at the block level. If there is only one black or white individual on the block, the individual's data might be suppressed to protect his or her identity.

Data swapping is usually done at the neighborhood level. A sample of households is selected and matched on a set of key variables with nearby households that have similar characteristics (such as the same number of adults and the same number of children). The data on these families are swapped across blocks. Those using the data sets will not be able to identify individual families at the lowest geographic level of data release, but at a more aggregated level the counts of people are accurate. For instance, if there are very few Asian families in a local area, the data on two Asian families might be swapped across blocks. You would therefore not be able to find the single Asian family with three children living on Maple Street, because in reality they live on Oak Street; in the data set, their data have been swapped with the Asian family with five children who do live on Maple Street. However, researchers would still have an accurate portrayal of the overall ethnic composition of the geographic region.

Genetic Material and Confidentiality

A new trend in social science research is the addition of biological data to large social surveys, such as the Fragile Families study and the Add Health study (see Chapter 7).

suppression A technique for ensuring confidentiality in which data are simply not shown.

data swapping A statistical technique for ensuring confidentiality in which data on households that have been matched on a set of key variables are swapped across blocks.

ETHICAL BREACHES AT THE U.S. CENSUS BUREAU

In the weeks leading up to both the 2000 census and the 2010 census, a small but vocal group of public figures, bloggers, and talk-radio hosts exhorted Americans not to answer the census. Many of these people, including then–Republican Rep. Michele Bachmann of Minnesota, cited the behavior of the Census Bureau during World War II as a reason for boycotting the census. During the war, in one of the more shameful episodes in our national history, more than 100,000 Japanese Americans were rounded up and interned in prison camps. The Census Bureau played a role in that internment, providing the War Department with data on where Japanese Americans lived. Using the results of the 1930 and 1940 censuses, the bureau provided the War Department with detailed counts of Japanese American families by neighborhood in California, Arizona, Wyoming, Colorado, Utah, Idaho, and Arkansas so that they could be rounded up and sent to internment camps. In 1943, in response to a threat against President Franklin D. Roosevelt, the bureau provided the Treasury Department with lists of Japanese Americans, including name, address, age, sex, occupation, and citizenship status (Minkel, 2007). While the actions were legal as a result of the War Powers Act in effect at that time, they violated the long-standing Census Bureau rules in effect before and after the war of never sharing private information about people, even with law enforcement and other government agencies.

At the time of the 2000 census, Kenneth Prewitt, then director of the census, issued an apology for the bureau's actions during World War II and strongly argued that laws in effect today would prevent anything like that from happening again. The Census Bureau website tells the public that the law now protects their data: No other government agency, including the Internal Revenue Service (IRS), Department of Homeland Security, FBI, and CIA, can get any individual person's census information for 72 years. The Department of Justice has also issued a ruling that no other law—including the Patriot Act—overrides census rules on confidentiality.

Even though the Census Bureau has gone to great lengths to assure citizens that their data will remain private, a recent data release catapulted this issue to the front pages again. In 2004, the news came out that in 2002 and 2003, the Census Bureau had provided detailed data on Arab Americans by ZIP code to the Department of Homeland Security. The data included breakdowns by country of origin, categorizing individuals as Egyptian, Iraqi, Jordanian, Lebanese, Moroccan, Palestinian, Syrian, and two general

Data from the 1930 and 1940 censuses were used to round up Japanese Americans so they could be sent to internment camps.

categories, Arab/Arabic and Other Arab. When the news broke, Department of Homeland Security officials said they had requested the data to determine at which airports they should make information available in Arabic. This explanation did not satisfy a lot of people, especially because the detailed breakdown by country of origin would not be necessary to determine how many people spoke Arabic.

The Census Bureau did not technically break any laws or violate its own privacy rules in complying with the Department of Homeland Security's request, as these data are public and available to anyone who knows how to create a table on the Census Bureau website. However, the incident did contribute to the worries people have about the safety of their information, reminding them of how the data on Japanese Americans were used. As James Zogby, president of the Arab American Institute, told the *New York Times*, "The data sharing was particularly harmful at a time when the Census Bureau is struggling to build trust within Arab American communities. As this gets out, any effort to encourage people to full compliance with the census is down the tubes. How can you get people to comply when they believe that by complying they put at risk their personal and family security?" (Clemetson, 2004).

In this case, the Census Bureau's past unethical decisions to share data cast a long shadow on its recent, more ethically ambiguous decision to produce data for Homeland Security. As this case reveals, a research decision may technically comply with an organization's ethical code, yet at the same time may put some individuals at risk.

These and other studies gather self-reported survey data on risky behaviors such as drug use, multiple sexual partners, risk-taking, and juvenile delinquency, and they also gather blood and saliva samples to examine biological indicators such as hormones and genetics. Gene-environment studies are becoming very common today, and a wide range of factors—from political party preference to friendship choices to sexual behavior to depression—is being linked to genetic markers. These studies pose special ethical issues in terms of informed consent, rights to privacy, and the researcher's responsibility to provide research results to the subjects. As Gail Henderson (2008) points out, the meaning of genetic information in gene-environment studies is probabilistic and complex, making it difficult to describe in informed consent documents.

Great care must be taken to explain to the research subjects that the study of these biomarkers will not generate information about the role of specific genes in people's health or lives. A gene might be associated with risk of depression, for instance, but having that genetic marker does not necessarily mean that a person will become depressed. Researchers must also protect against violations of confidentiality; studies show that people are highly concerned about the privacy and protection of their genetic data.

There is much controversy about whether genetic material should be kept for reanalysis in the future and whether doing so poses a risk for individuals. Henry Greely (1998, pp. 483–484) speculates about worst-case scenarios that could develop in the future: "Could preventive action be taken against someone carrying a 'violence gene,' could health coverage be denied for infants born after prenatal diagnoses associated with medical conditions, or could genetic evidence of low intelligence or learning disabilities be used to limit government-funded educational opportunities for certain children?"

Henderson (2008, p. 268) notes that new knowledge might lead to situations in which the genetic material that is donated now could be relevant for an individual's health in the future in ways we cannot know today. She cautions, "For now, researchers should consider whether and how participants who donate biological specimens could be recontacted if information that is relevant to their individual health is obtained."

CONCEPT CHECKS

1 What is the difference between anonymity and confidentiality? Can a researcher promise absolute confidentiality to research subjects? Why or why not?

2 Why is deductive disclosure a growing problem in social science research? What are two methods the Census Bureau uses to prevent such disclosure?

3 What ethical issues does genetic material pose for social science research? What are some methods of dealing with those issues?

DECEPTION IN RESEARCH

Deception of research subjects is one of the most hotly contested ethical areas in social science research. Some eminent social scientists, such as Kai Erikson, former president of the American Sociological Association, take an absolute position and believe that deception is never justified. However, some scholars argue that many research questions cannot be adequately studied without some degree of deception. Many researchers and IRBs thus struggle with the question of when it is permissible to deceive the people you are studying about your identity or about the real purposes of your research.

The issue of deception is relevant to many research methods, but it appears most often in ethnographic and experimental research. It is also an important emerging issue in Internet research. Recall that Venkatesh gained full access to a group of some-times violent, drug-dealing gang members, in part by deceiving the gang's leader into thinking that Venkatesh was planning to write a biography about him.

Venkatesh told the gang members he was a sociologist and that he was study-ing them, but some ethnographers keep their identities totally hidden and pass as "natives" (we discuss the different roles an ethnographer can take in Chapter 10). Political scientist Ric Pfeffer studied a Baltimore factory in the 1970s (Pfeffer, 1979). Although he had a law degree and PhD from Harvard University, he created a fake résumé for himself during a yearlong sabbatical, listing only his high school degree. He was hired to work on the shop floor and was quickly accepted as "one of the guys." But his argumentative nature, along with his considerable skills as a negotiator, were not lost on his coworkers, who asked him to run for shop steward in the union election and to negotiate with management over their next contract. He won the elec-tion and went to work as the union representative. While the people in the factory got the benefit of a Harvard-educated lawyer negotiating on their behalf, they also had someone representing them who did not have to live with the consequences of the union-management fight. Unbeknownst to Pfeffer's coworkers, he would be leaving the factory in September to return to his teaching job at Johns Hopkins University. Even though he was thoughtful about the ethical dilemmas he was facing, he was ultimately representing people whose fate he did not share.

While Pfeffer probably had a choice about whether to tell his coworkers that he was an academic, ethnographers sometimes argue that they would never get access to research sites unless they pretend to be insiders or, at a minimum, lie about the real nature of their research. Studies of right-wing social movements, drug cultures, cults, and other movements suspicious of outsiders are often undertaken with some degree of subterfuge. This is especially true of studies of antisocial behaviors such as racial discrimination and domestic violence, where people usually do not want their behavior known.

One of the best known and most cited studies in sociology is Erving Goffman's *Asylums*, a study of Saint Elizabeth's Hospital, a mental institution in Washington, D.C. Goffman (1961) studied the experience of the asylum's inmates by posing as the assistant to the athletic director for a year. He argued that he could not have com-pleted the study if everyone at the hospital had known his true identity. Similarly, Laud Humphreys argued that he had to deceive the people he studied when he showed up at their houses with a survey; they didn't identify as gay or bisexual and they would never have answered his questions about their lives if they had known he had observed them in the tearoom.

Experiments are another method where researchers often deceive subjects. We have already discussed Pager's field experiment in which she deceived employers

"On the Internet, nobody knows you're a dog."

into believing that people were applying for jobs. In the laboratory, subjects often are not told the true nature of the experiment because knowing the real purpose of the experiment would contaminate the results. When subjects know a study's hypothesis, they will often behave in a way that confirms that hypothesis, out of a desire to be a "good" research subject. This process, called **demand characteristics**, biases the study findings. For example, the results of studies of the way stereotypes affect behavior could be biased if subjects were told, "We are studying whether you do less well on tests if we remind you of your race or gender before the test."

How does one design an ethical study if it involves deception? How can people give informed consent if they do not know the true nature of the study? The American Sociological Association Code of Ethics allows deception only if there is no alternative way to do the study, and only if the research involves no more than minimal risk to the research subjects. The American Psychological Association tells its members that psychologists should never deceive research participants about significant aspects of the study that would affect their willingness to participate. The informed consent document must never be part of the deception, so it should not include anything that is untrue. Usually, the experiment or study is described in such general terms that it does not give away the true purpose of the study—describing a study of "interpersonal relations," for instance, rather than racial discrimination.

When a research study involves deception, subjects must be debriefed at the end of the experiment. In **debriefing**, participants are told the true nature of the study and the reason for the deception.

Internet research provides many opportunities for deception. Online chatrooms, discussion forums, dating sites, and even social networking sites like Facebook provide opportunities for people to pretend to be someone they are not. A researcher working online can join a closed group or observe interactions among people in discussion boards very easily without being noticed or telling people they are being studied. The ethical rule is that researchers cannot study behavior that people reasonably expect to be private. While no one can claim that talking in public on a street corner is private, many people implicitly believe that what they post in an online support group or forum is intended to be read only by others in the group and should not be fodder for a research study.

CONFLICTS OF INTEREST

Scientists are supposed to objectively work to discover the truth. They have a **conflict of interest** if their interests or loyalties compromise the way they design, conduct, or report their research. The Human Terrain System project, which we described earlier in this chapter, raised several ethical issues with respect to research objectivity and

demand characteristics
The process whereby research subjects, when they become aware of a study's hypothesis, behave in a way that confirms that hypothesis.

debriefing The process of interviewing participants after the study and then informing them of the actual purpose of the experiment.

conflict of interest If researchers' interests or loyalties compromise the way they design, conduct, or report their research.

independence. The social scientists who studied the people of Afghanistan and Iraq did so in service of the military, which sponsored their research and was also at war. If during the course of their work the Human Terrain scientists learned something that could harm a research subject (by being shared) or American military personnel or innocent civilians (by not being shared), how would the scientists decide what to do? What happened to the research they provided to the military? Could it be used to target the subjects the scientists were studying if those subjects posed a threat to the mission or military personnel? These are all ethical issues that plague research that is funded by third parties.

When social scientists receive their funding from the National Science Foundation or other government agencies, they are explicitly told to publish and disseminate their data and their findings no matter what those findings are. But what happens when a right- or left-wing foundation with a political agenda funds the research? Should a social scientist take money from such a foundation if there is subtle (or not-so-subtle) pressure to find a particular conclusion?

One controversial study brings up the ethical issues associated with bias. Sociologist Mark Regnerus accepted research funding from two conservative institutions, the Witherspoon Institute and the Bradley Foundation, to study how children raised by gay couples compared to those raised by heterosexual couples (Oppenheimer, 2012). The president of the Witherspoon Institute, which has been active in opposing same-sex marriage, told Regnerus (before he began the study) that he wanted the study to be finished before the Supreme Court ruled on same-sex marriage. Regnerus found that the children raised by parents who reported ever having a same-sex relationship had worse outcomes than those raised by parents who were in intact heterosexual relationships (Regnerus, 2012a).

The study, which had a number of methodological flaws, has since been widely discredited because of the researcher's decisions about how to define "same-sex couples" and "heterosexual couples." In effect, Regnerus restricted the heterosexual families to parents who had not separated or divorced. But he included in the gay families any parent reporting any gay relationship, even if the parents were no longer together. Those decisions biased the comparison groups in a way that led to the conclusion that the funders wanted—that children do not do as well growing up with gay parents. Further analysis of the same data by other researchers shows that parents' sexual orientation has no effect on children's developmental outcomes, as long as you compare children who grow up in intact two-parent stable households, regardless of the parents' gender (Cheung & Powell, 2015). Did Regnerus's strong personal religious and political beliefs influence his analyses? Did the foundations that funded him influence how he coded his data? Independent investigations of his work have not led to findings of fraud, but both the American Sociological Association and the American Psychological Association have criticized the study for its methodological flaws.

Social scientists should avoid all conflicts of interest, even perceived conflicts of interest. They should never conduct research where their compensation depends on the outcome of the research. They should also avoid any financial arrangement that a reasonable observer would see as compromising their research independence. In general, this means that the researchers and their families should not have financial interests in companies sponsoring their research.

Harder to enforce and to detect are the subtle biases of researchers' political ideologies. If the researchers are pro-immigrant, for instance, are they less likely to design a study in which they might find high costs from immigration to society as a whole? If they are fans of the free market, are they likely to omit variables that may lead to results that point to the need for market regulation? Unconscious bias is probably more of a risk in these cases than willful and intentional misconduct.

Personal bias also affects the reporting of research results. For example, a liberal researcher might be tempted not to publish a paper that shows negative effects on children who grow up in a single-parent household. A conservative scholar might not want to publish a study showing that the children of gay parents fare just as well as the children of heterosexual parents. Max Weber called these types of findings "inconvenient facts" and stressed that researchers not only shouldn't suppress them but also should seek them out. If you have strong political or moral beliefs, as a researcher you must face facts that are inconvenient or uncomfortable for you and don't mesh with your preconceived ideas. Social science is a science because we do not let our political beliefs dictate the answers to our research questions; we test hypotheses with empirical research, and we do not suppress or downplay any results that we do not like.

Professional codes of conduct emphasize that researchers should be transparent about the sponsors of their study and any conflicts of interest that might exist so that consumers of the research can draw their own conclusions about the possible influences on the research. In addition, researchers should be very clear about when they are reporting results that they believe to be objective and fair and when they are expressing their own political or ideological positions.

CONCEPT CHECKS

1   What is debriefing, and why is it important when a study has used deception?

2   Is it ethically permissible to study online communities without informed consent from the participants? Why or why not?

3   If you were on an IRB reviewing the Human Terrain System project, what aspect(s) of it would you be most concerned about? What steps could be taken to make the study more acceptable from an ethical point of view?

CONCLUSION

The history of ethical lapses in social science research has led to the development of an institutional system to safeguard research subjects and to enforce the principles of respect, beneficence, and justice. Institutional review boards do a great deal to enforce ethical standards, and these boards review almost all social science research. The system also relies on the ethical behavior of scientists to overcome their own biases, adhere to their professional codes of conduct, and honestly carry out and report their research. The system is complex, because human beings are both conducting the research and being studied as subjects of the research, and there are many gray areas that do not lend themselves to clear and rigid rules. While many social scientists grumble about the paperwork and bureaucracy involved in human subjects review, it is clear that the current system prevents repeats of many of the worst abuses that occurred before the safeguards were put in place. It is also clear that there will always be new methods and situations that raise thorny ethical dilemmas for researchers.

End-of-Chapter Review

Summary

Research with human beings always involves ethical choices and dilemmas. In an effort to prevent future ethical lapses and abuse, a national system has been established to protect humans who participate in research, including the requirement of voluntary informed consent.

Defining Research Ethics

- The Belmont Report outlines three principles for conducting ethical research: respect, beneficence, and justice.
- Researchers can ensure that these ethical principles are met by obtaining informed consent from their research subjects. Additional protections are required for vulnerable populations, including those who cannot give consent due to age or diminished mental capacity.

A Brief History of Ethical Problems in Research

- Nazi experiments on concentration camp prisoners during World War II led to the development of the 1947 Nuremberg Code, which laid the groundwork for modern ethical standards in human subjects research.
- Conducted by the U.S. Public Health Service, the Tuskegee Syphilis Experiment involved deceiving subjects about their health status and withholding lifesaving medication.
- Famous studies by Milgram, Zimbardo, and Humphreys would most likely not be approved by the modern IRB system. Although these studies produced useful information, they also raise serious ethical issues concerning deception, privacy violations, and psychological harm.

The Institutional Review Board (IRB) System

- The Institutional Review Board (IRB) system was established by the National Research Act of 1974 to protect human subjects against ethical violations in research.
- The rules about what constitutes human subjects research have changed over time. The current legal definition is a systematic investigation of people that develops or contributes to generalizable knowledge.
- One of the biggest challenges for an IRB is assessing whether the risks posed to human subjects will be counterbalanced by the potential benefits.

Professional Codes of Ethics

- In addition to IRBs, professional organizations of researchers, such as the American Sociological Association (ASA), also maintain codes of ethics for their members.
- Social science researchers can collect data anonymously or confidentially to protect the privacy of their research subjects. However, the promise of confidentiality can sometimes conflict with the legal system, especially for researchers studying deviant behavior.
- The reliance on digital technology to collect, store, and share data creates additional concerns about confidentiality for human research subjects.

Deception in Research

- Social scientists disagree on whether deception should ever be permitted in research. Deception is more common in ethnographic and experimental research.
- When research involves deception, subjects must be debriefed at the end of the study.

Conflicts of Interest

- Researchers should avoid all conflicts of interest that can bias how they design, conduct, or report their research. They should also be transparent about any conflicts of interest.
- Researchers should not allow personal biases to seep into their research but rather should confront "inconvenient facts."

Key Terms

anonymity, 84

beneficence, 71

certificate of
   confidentiality, 85

confidentiality, 84

conflict of interest, 94

data swapping, 90

debriefing, 94

deductive disclosure, 88

demand characteristics, 94

ethics, 70

human subjects
   research, 77

informed consent, 71

institutional review board
   (IRB), 71

justice, 71

Nuremberg Code, 72

privacy, 71

research protocol, 78

respect, 71

risk versus benefit
   analysis, 72

suppression, 90

vulnerable population, 71

Exercise

In 1971, Philip Zimbardo conducted the Stanford prison experiment, described earlier in this chapter. In 2000, Katherine Newman conducted a study of school shootings. In the almost 30 years separating the studies, IRB requirements regarding informed consent became much more elaborate. Compare the informed consent forms for people taking part in the two studies (shown in Figure 3.1 and Appendix A).

- What elements missing from the Zimbardo consent form are present in the Newman form?
- In what ways are these forms helpful to people deciding whether to take part in the research projects?
- What would you add or subtract from the Zimbardo form? Why?
- What would you add or subtract from the Newman form? Why?

When studying social phenomena like poverty, sociologists have a multitude of choices and styles for carrying out their research, which makes defining key concepts and clarifying measurement processes all the more critical.

FROM CONCEPTS TO MODELS
Hypotheses, Operationalization, and Measurement

In Chapter 2, we discussed how theory can spark questions and generate hypotheses and expectations about findings. In this chapter, we describe how theories give rise to empirical studies. The translation of broad theories into concrete studies has two key components, which we briefly introduced in Chapter 2: The first, conceptualization, is the process of precisely defining ideas and turning them into variables; the second, operationalization, is the process of linking the conceptualized variables to a set of procedures for measuring them.

conceptualization The process of precisely defining ideas and turning them into variables.

operationalization The process of linking the conceptualized variables to a set of procedures for measuring them.

Conceptualization and **operationalization** are all about what you want to study and how you will study it—how you move from thinking to doing and become more specific and explicit along the way. Both processes require the utmost care to ensure trustworthy results. This chapter sets forth the steps of each process, laying a foundation for the later chapters on specific research methods (for example, surveys, ethnography, and network analysis). We start by discussing a major sociological topic, poverty, to illustrate the importance of thinking through and articulating conceptualization and operationalization.

DEFINING AND MEASURING POVERTY: AN INTRODUCTION TO CONCEPTUALIZATION AND OPERATIONALIZATION

Many sociologists are committed to understanding social problems—the persistent ills of society, such as crime, war, and racism—because they believe that the only way to eliminate them is to identify and eradicate their causes. One important social problem that sociologists study is poverty, which is part of the broader issue of inequality.

Through their research, social scientists have shed a great deal of light on poverty. For example, we know that poverty can have harmful effects on child development (Conger, Conger, & Martin, 2010; Duncan et al., 2012). We also know that poverty tends to be more intermittent than stable, with only a small minority of U.S. families experiencing poverty for more than 5 years in a row (Ratcliffe & McKernan, 2010). Pushing beyond the individualist mindset of many Americans, William Julius Wilson (1987) has demonstrated how macro-level trends, such as the historical movement of jobs from urban areas to suburbs, have isolated the poor in inner cities and eliminated opportunities for social mobility (see also Desmond, 2016; Sharkey, 2013). Yet, social science research has also identified factors that mitigate the harmful effects of poverty. For example, we have learned that involved parents can protect children from the risks of poverty and that strong social networks—whether friendships or extended families—can arise within poor communities as people assume responsibility for one another (Brody et al., 2013; Furstenberg et al., 1999; Stack, 1974).

The media report sociological research findings such as these because of the public's interest in poverty. Indeed, most readers of this textbook probably have some familiarity with the topic of poverty. Why, then, is it so hard for the average person to answer the question: *What exactly is poverty?*

Conceptualizing and Operationalizing Poverty

For most Americans, the answer to "What exactly is poverty?" is "I know it when I see it." Sociologists have to be more precise and explicit. Would it surprise you to learn that the seemingly simple concept of poverty has been defined and measured in hundreds of different ways? The studies referenced earlier, for example, tend to have different conceptualizations and operationalizations of poverty, even though they all focus on the same general idea.

Let's think about the conceptualization of poverty, or defining the term. Sociologists face a range of options for defining poverty. We can define it with an *absolute standard*; that is, a specific quantitative assessment of income or assets that applies to all people regardless of context. For example, we can define the poor as people who lack basic necessities, such as shelter and food. Or we can define poverty with a *relative standard*, identifying the poor by how deprived they are relative to the rest of a society. In this approach, someone is labeled poor if she has much less than those around her, regardless of how much she has overall. You can see that relative standards can get tricky. The assets of the average poor person in North America would likely make him comfortable in many countries in sub-Saharan Africa, but most Americans are concerned with what counts as poverty in the United States, not with the relative poverty levels of North America and Africa.

Now let's turn to operationalization, or measuring poverty in the way that the federal government has chosen to define it. The U.S. government sets the federal poverty line (FPL) at the annual cost of an adequate diet for a family of a given size multiplied by 3. As Figure 4.1 shows, the FPL for a family of four was just over $22,000 in 2010. In 2015, it was $24,250, meaning that any family with a total annual household income below this threshold would be counted as poor (U.S. Department of Health and Human Services, 2016).

This absolute standard for measuring poverty is certainly precise, but some consider it too precise. Social scientists, including many who have used the measure in their own research, have heavily criticized the FPL. Surely, they argue, the definition of poverty should include wealth—one's material possessions, including homes, cars, savings, and investments—because some very wealthy Americans actually have zero income. Moreover, the same amount of money does not mean the same thing in different parts of the country, which may have very different costs of living (Chien & Mistry, 2013; Conley, 1999). For example, living in San Francisco is much more expensive than living in Kansas City. An alternative to the FPL, the supplemental poverty measure, offers an arguably more accurate take by combining information on income with data on context-specific expenses (Johnson & Smeeding, 2012), but it is used less commonly than the FPL, in part because it is more complicated.

The choice of operationalization also depends on the level of social life about which we want to generalize, or our **unit of analysis**. For example, are we interested in individuals? Neighborhoods? Entire nations? Counting up the number of economic stressors that a person has faced in the past year (for example, trouble paying bills, getting behind on rent)

unit of analysis The level of social life about which we want to generalize.

FIGURE 4.1 U.S. Federal Poverty Line, 1980–2015

The U.S. government defines poverty with an absolute standard known as the federal poverty line, which is based on total annual household income.

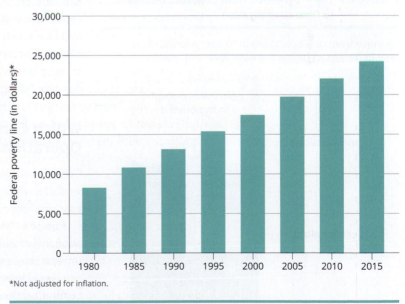

*Not adjusted for inflation.

Source: U.S. Health and Human Services, 2016.

would be appropriate for categorizing individual people but not neighborhoods. Neighborhood poverty is generally assessed through summary factors that can be more directly and comparably measured across large numbers of people, such as average income. One can try to identify the unit of analysis in a study by asking whether the researchers are trying to compare people to each other or neighborhoods to each other.

Social context also matters. Measures that are appropriate for studying the United States may not work for other parts of the world. For example, the World Bank defines the poor in developing countries as those people living on less than $1.90 per day (Ferreira, 2015). Similarly, perspective is important, as poverty can be a subjective experience. Some people feel poor, regardless of whether some "objective" measure of income suggests that they are. To the degree to which these subjective appraisals affect the way people look at the world, behave, and structure their lives, they matter. Emphasizing that poverty can be a subjective experience also points out the problems of using clear dividing lines to categorize the poor and nonpoor, as many people are in an ambiguous state around those lines. In such states, whether they think of themselves as poor may be more important than where they fall on some blunt measure. Indeed, qualitative researchers have long eschewed such measures and instead let people say whether they are poor or not (Halpern-Meekin et al., 2015; Yoshikawa, Aber, & Beardslee, 2012).

Lastly, many strategies for measuring poverty raise ethical concerns. For example, what are the potential pitfalls of using tax returns in research? Is it ethical to study poverty using an experimental design, which is considered the gold standard of social science research?

The range of possibilities for conceptualizing and operationalizing poverty seems infinite, which may be frustrating for scholars or policy makers seeking concrete answers. In general, there is usually no single correct way to define or measure a concept. Accepting this basic truth gives social scientists freedom when conducting studies but also makes it much easier for them to get lost in the process. The goal of this chapter is to help you keep your definitions and measurements focused and to help you make well-informed decisions along the way.

Which Comes First, Conceptualization or Operationalization?

Conceptualization and operationalization go together; one would be worthless without the other. We can think of the two concepts broadly.

Figure 4.2 shows the process of conceptualization and operationalization for quantitative research. At first, basic issues of interest may seem clear-cut, but attempting to measure them can reveal how fuzzy they are. Researchers must define (conceptualize) these issues in some meaningful way so that they and their audiences are thinking and talking about the same

FIGURE 4.2 The Progression from Conceptualization to Operationalization

To move from conceptualization to operationalization, researchers must define the basic issues of interest.

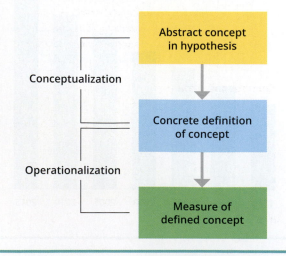

things. Once a definition is in place, the challenge is to come up with a systematic plan for observing or measuring that issue as it has been defined.

Definition, therefore, bridges the abstract art of thinking and the concrete art of doing. Returning to the topic of poverty, consider a widely cited 1998 study in *American Sociological Review*. An interdisciplinary team from economics, sociology, and psychology (Duncan et al., 1998) was interested in quantitatively evaluating the hypothesis that the timing and duration of poverty in childhood influences individual well-being into adulthood. This project linked two straightforward, familiar concepts that are almost too broad to be useful for research: poverty and well-being.

The first challenge for the investigators was to define what poverty and individual well-being meant in their research, knowing that neither concept has a single "right" definition. Given their interest in policy and the income-based ways that the U.S. government attempts to alleviate poverty and help families, the investigators defined poverty in terms of a lack of income. Because they were interested in the timing and duration of poverty, they examined family income at various stages of children's lives: ages 0–5, 6–10, and 11–15. The researchers were interested in the long-term effects of early poverty, so they chose to conceptualize individual well-being in terms of schooling, because schooling occurs across the early stages of the life course and has powerful effects on earnings, health, the odds of marrying, and other aspects of life into and through adulthood. Because schooling can encompass various educational factors (enrollment, grades, test scores, coursework), the researchers chose to define schooling in terms of persistence, or how far students progress through the various grades and levels of the system. Such a definition is concrete enough to be compared across different schools and locales.

After establishing these definitions, the investigators turned to measurement, or getting data to assess their hypothesis. Because they wanted a national picture, they used a publicly available national data set called the Panel Study of Income Dynamics (PSID; we will learn more about national surveys such as the PSID in Chapters 6 and 7). Using data from the PSID, the investigators chose specific ways to measure the key variables. Income was measured by parents' pretax earnings, averaged within and across the three age ranges of childhood and broken into four categories: $15,000–$24,999, $25,000–$34,999, $35,000–$49,999, and $50,000+. Schooling persistence was measured by years of school completed by age 15.

Figure 4.3 summarizes this case of conceptualization and operationalization. In this study and more generally, disagreement is possible but confusion should not be. In other words, other researchers reading this study might disagree with the choices made regarding definitions and measurement, but they will not be unsure about what choices were made. Everyone who reads the study knows exactly what the researchers did and can thus interpret the findings correctly.

FIGURE 4.3 **The Progression from Conceptualization and Operationalization in a Specific Study of Poverty**

For this study, researchers conceptualized poverty as lack of income and well-being in terms of schooling.

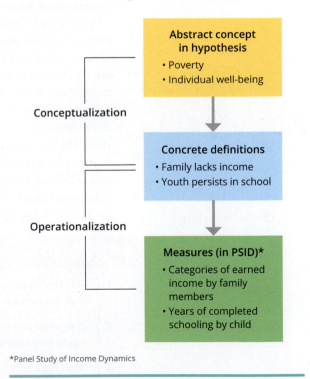

*Panel Study of Income Dynamics

Source: Duncan et al., 1998.

Sociologist Kathryn Edin conducted ethnographic fieldwork to develop a definition of poverty that fully encompassed the experience of poor single moms.

The PSID study involved statistical analysis of surveys (we will learn more about this approach in Chapters 14 and 15). Many studies of poverty follow this quantitative approach, but certainly not all of them. For example, qualitative studies by Kathryn Edin (Edin & Lein, 1997; Edin & Nelson, 2013; Halpern-Meekin et al., 2015) have involved extensive interviewing with and observations of low-income parents (especially mothers) raising children. Such qualitative work follows a different approach to conceptualization and operationalization. To recap a key discussion from Chapter 2, in quantitative research, conceptualization and operationalization occur before data collection and analysis. Quantitative research is largely *deductive*, meaning it involves the translation of general theory into specific empirical analysis. Qualitative research, in contrast, is more *inductive*, drawing general understanding from specific empirical observations. That difference is a reason why many qualitative researchers use the term *expected findings* rather than *hypotheses*. They are not testing some predetermined hypothesis, although they likely have some assumptions about what they might find.

For these reasons, conceptualization and operationalization cannot always be classified neatly. Researchers generally start with highly abstract concepts such as poverty. Qualitative research, however, does not necessarily flow from these abstract concepts into definition and measurement. Qualitative researchers start collecting data, perhaps through fieldwork or open-ended interviews, and then let definition and measurement decisions arise from the data they obtain. For example, Edin did not embark on her ethnographic work with a clear definition of poverty. Instead, she developed a list of basic questions that she wanted to explore, and then she went to the homes of poor families with this list of questions, adding new questions as the interviews progressed. On the basis of these interviews, she and her collaborators created a conceptual definition of poverty that went far beyond income or even money. Indeed, she has helped to define poor women as living in marginalized segments of society, isolated from the economy and from social networks that could help them improve their situation. For these women, poverty went beyond not having a job (and, therefore, income) at any one time to encompass the ways in which their family responsibilities and their lack of skills cut them off from the possibility of getting a job to support their children. While Duncan's team conceptualized and operationalized before starting to analyze the PSID, Edin analyzed data as a means of conceptualizing and operationalizing.

CONCEPT CHECKS

1   Give three possible definitions of poverty. How are these definitions less abstract than the concept of poverty?

2   In what ways might qualitative researchers operationalize poverty differently than would quantitative researchers?

3   What problems might arise if public debates about poverty relied on evidence from studies with different conceptualizations or operationalizations of it?

CONCEPTUALIZATION

Conceptualization means defining terms and concepts clearly and precisely. As Figure 4.4 shows, the conceptualization process moves from the abstract and general to the concrete and specific. The last step of this process marks the transition into operationalization (measurement), which we discuss later in this chapter.

To make our discussions of conceptualization and operationalization more specific, we will use three topics that social scientists often study:

1. **Onset of puberty.** The age at which young people begin to go through puberty affects their lives. For example, early maturing youth, especially girls, are more likely to have socioemotional and academic problems than peers who go through the transition "on time." Why? One explanation is that others treat those who start puberty early as being older than their actual maturity level. As a result, they get put into situations that they are not adequately equipped to deal with (Cavanagh, 2004; Haynie, 2003; Moore, Harden, & Mendle, 2014).

2. **Parental monitoring.** Young people often engage in risky behaviors such as smoking, drinking, or drug use. Involved and caring parenting can protect young people from taking such risks. Specifically, when parents keep track of whom their children know, what they do, and where they go, adolescents are less likely to engage in troubling behaviors. An equally plausible process is that well-behaved youth keep their parents in the loop (Fletcher, Steinberg, & Williams-Wheeler, 2004; Ragan, Osgood, & Feinberg, 2014; Stattin & Kerr, 2000).

3. **School quality.** As a result of No Child Left Behind policies in the early 2000s and increased competition for admission to prestigious universities in recent years, the notion of "good" high schools has become a major source of public debate and social research. One well-known ranking of U.S. high schools, published by the magazine *Newsweek*, uses the number of students who took Advanced Placement (AP) exams to rank schools. Every year, people howled in protest about the narrow definition of school quality, with many arguing that any high school ranking should take into account other academic factors, as well as nonacademic indicators of quality such as social support (Crosnoe, 2011; Lawrence-Lightfoot, 1983).

We will revisit these topics throughout this chapter.

FIGURE 4.4 Levels of Conceptualization

The process of conceptualization moves from the general to the specific, starting with abstract concepts and ending with concrete indicators.

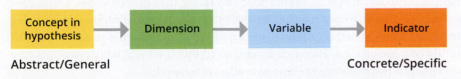

Abstract/General   Concrete/Specific

Concepts and Variables

concept An idea that can be named, defined, and eventually measured in some way.

Concepts are highly abstract ideas that summarize social phenomena and are linked together within hypotheses (or expected findings). The faulty assumption that each concept has one accepted definition is a major source of miscommunication and misunderstanding—we think that we are all talking about the same thing when in fact we are not!

Going back to our three examples listed earlier, consider the onset of puberty. The "onset of puberty" concept makes it seem as though puberty is a discrete event that happens at some point in time. Puberty, however, is a gradual process, which makes the onset of puberty hard to define. The concepts of "parental monitoring" and "school quality" are equally slippery. We might think there is a general agreement about what these concepts entail, but that general agreement likely encompasses a great deal of variation. That variation is a product of the abstract quality of concepts; they are difficult to pin down.

Rigorous empirical social science is about pinning things down, and so the process of turning abstract concepts into something more concrete begins with translating concepts into variables. **Variables** are representations that capture the presence or absence of a concept (for example, "Are you in love? Yes or no?") as well as the level of a concept (for example, "How much would you say you love your partner?"). By definition, variables have to vary. To study love, researchers must convert the concept of "love" from an ethereal idea about human connection into something concrete that someone can have more or less of than someone else. In this way, variables break down concepts into data points that can be compared.

variables Representations that capture the different dimensions, categories, or levels of a concept.

For example, in 1986 psychologist Robert Sternberg put forward a classic conceptualization of love on the basis of the combination of different feelings (Sternberg, 1986). This conceptualization differentiated romantic love (the combination of high levels of intimacy and passion with weak expectations of future commitment, as is often found in new romances) from companionate love (the combination of high levels of intimacy and commitment with a lower level of passion, as is often found in long-term marriages). In both of these concepts, the variables of intimacy, passion, and commitment can vary from low to high.

How might we translate our three illustrative concepts into variables?

- Onset of puberty: early, on time, late

- Parental monitoring: a range from infrequent to frequent monitoring

- School quality: a continuum from low to high quality

In each example, the variable listed represents a single approach to translating a concept into something measurable. For example, the parental monitoring variable captures the quantity of monitoring but says nothing about the quality. One parent may engage in many monitoring behaviors but without any skill, while another parent might be very adept at monitoring but do so only rarely. In both approaches, a more precise variable that captures one distinct aspect of the concept of parental monitoring gives researchers something useful to work with but also eliminates something meaningful about the concept. Research cannot avoid this trade-off, which explains why conceptualization decisions are crucial to all good research.

Units of Analysis

Earlier in this chapter, we mentioned how the conceptualization and operationalization of poverty might differ depending on whether the researcher is interested in individual poor people or poor neighborhoods. This distinction reveals the importance of specifying units of analysis, or the level of social life about which we want to generalize. What is a study trying to explain? Is it something about people or the groups that they form? Is it something about institutions or the organizations and people within them? Or is it something about society itself?

Units of analysis include the *individual* (for example, adolescents), *group* (for example, friendship cliques), *organization or institution* (for example, schools), and *society* (for example, the United States), each of which can be broken down into subunits. Another unit of analysis, **social artifacts**, encompasses aspects of social life that can be counted. Some social artifacts are concrete things, such as newspaper articles, tombstones, or text messages. For example, one interesting study conducted in the wake of the deadly Columbine High School shootings in 1999 counted newspaper articles about the massacre and about congressional debates on school safety to examine the link between media coverage and legislative activity (Lawrence & Birkland, 2004). Other artifacts are acts, such as handshakes or sexual activities.

A single concept can be studied with different units of analysis. Consider the onset of puberty, which seems like the perfect example of an individual-level variable. Puberty is about intimate changes to *your* body. Indeed, most studies approach the onset of puberty as a characteristic that differentiates one person from another. Such research seeks to identify the causes of individual differences in the onset of puberty ("Why did your friend finish puberty by eighth grade while you were still waiting for it

> **social artifacts** Concrete aspects of social life that can be counted, such as newspaper articles, tombstones, or text messages.

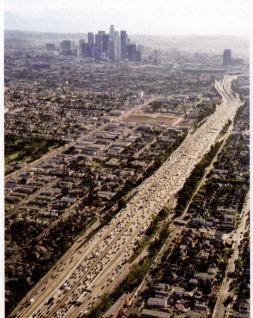

Individuals, peer groups, schools, and cities are all examples of units of analysis.

in ninth grade?") or the effects of puberty onset on some aspect of life ("Does the early onset of puberty explain why your friend went through several relationships before you had your first date?"). At the individual unit of analysis, evidence suggests that the presence of a stepfather in the home can accelerate girls' transitions through puberty, and the link between the onset of puberty and early loss of virginity seems to be completely explained by hormones for boys but by peer influences for girls (Belsky et al., 2007; Udry, 1988). Although these two studies asked different questions and looked at different mechanisms (social or biological), both examined puberty as an individual-level factor.

The onset of puberty can also be studied at a more macro level of analysis. For example, different groups can be characterized by their average rate of puberty onset; there is evidence suggesting that puberty begins much earlier in African Americans than in other groups (Cavanagh, 2004). (Of course, in any randomly selected pair composed of an African American girl and a white girl, the former may go through puberty earlier or later than the latter.) At this level of analysis, what matters is not what happens to individual girls but rather what is characteristic of their groups, which can be important to public health interventions. As another example, the average age of puberty today can be compared to that of other eras (Euling et al., 2008). Doing so would reveal that Americans tend to go through puberty earlier today than they did a century ago, information important for understanding adolescence and developing health and educational programs to serve the adolescent population.

Conceptualization at different levels of analysis is not difficult, but measuring at different levels of analysis can be tricky because individual-level data are often added together (aggregated) to capture individual concepts at the group level. A discussion of historical change in the onset of puberty in the United States occurs at a national level of analysis. Yet, researchers measure that national level by getting data on puberty from individuals and then calculating an average across the group. A country's average age of puberty is a national-level concept, and its measurement is based on the **aggregation** of individual-level data.

aggregation The process of counting or averaging individual-level data in some context to capture individual-level concepts at the group level.

To use another of our examples, one measure of high school quality is the percentage of seniors who enroll in college. This school-level concept is a standard of comparison among schools. The principal of each high school could be asked to estimate the percentage of college-bound seniors so as to generate a report for each individual school. Alternatively, all seniors in a high school could be surveyed about their plans for attending college, and then the number of college-bound students could be counted as a percentage of the senior class. In this case, the individual data of many students are aggregated into a single variable. Whether individual- or school-level data are used, the concept and its final variable are school level. In this case, you could determine the unit of analysis by asking yourself, "Does every student in the school have to have the same value on this school variable or can one student differ from another?" In the former case, you would be looking at a school-level variable; in the latter, it is individual level.

Dimensions

dimensions Components of a concept that represent its different manifestations, angles, or units.

General concepts often encompass multiple **dimensions**, or components that represent different manifestations, angles, or units of the concept. A concept might have many dimensions, which is fine for discussion but impractical for research. Because designing and implementing studies requires a more focused approach, a researcher must determine which dimension of the concept is of greatest relevance to the study.

Let's go back to school quality. We all understand, in general, what this concept means, but it is so abstract that it is practically meaningless. Does school quality refer to the ability of a school to facilitate a student's acquisition of academic skills? Does it refer to the degree to which schools provide a safe, healthy place for young people to develop? Or does it refer to some other dimension? Because school quality is a multi-dimensional concept, any study has to be precise about which dimensions of school quality are being researched. As No Child Left Behind makes clear, federal and local governments prioritize academic dimensions of school quality. Parents selecting schools for their children are often concerned with the socioemotional dimensions of school quality. Research has focused on each of these dimensions, making discussions of the general concept of school quality more difficult.

Dimensions are about conceptualization. A discussion of dimensions touches on different ways to slice a concept, different ways of conceptually defining it. Dimensions are not about measurement, at least not at the start of a research study, but they then need to be captured by variables as the study progresses. Figure 4.5 captures this gradual transition from the abstract to the concrete as researchers slice a concept into dimensions and then create variables to represent those dimensions. The concept in this figure is parental discipline, which comes in different forms that can be represented in different ways, but this exercise can be done for any concept that researchers want to study.

Types of Variables

Once the unit of analysis and dimension are specified, we can think more concretely about constructing variables. Variables take many forms, mostly concerning the various ways that categories can be compared to each other. For example, income is a common variable that can go up or down, but not all variables are numbers. Person A can have higher or lower income than Person B. But one cannot think sensibly of race (another common variable) going up or down or Person A being of a higher or lower race than Person B. The racial categories cannot be ranked quantitatively—they

FIGURE 4.5 From Concepts to Variables

The process of conceptualization involves first slicing a concept into dimensions and then creating variables to represent those dimensions.

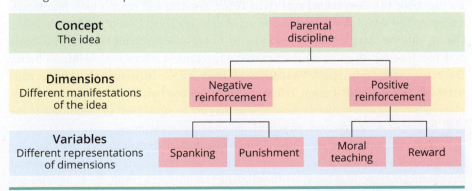

are parallel. To go further, we can think of Person A having twice as much income as Person B, but we cannot think of Person A having twice as much race as Person B.

Because the type of a variable determines how it is measured and analyzed, understanding variable type is an important part of linking conceptualization to operationalization. There are four main types of variables. Table 4.1 breaks down the various types of variables and provides examples of each. We use the issue of school quality to provide a more detailed illustration of these types and the differences among them.

The first two types of variables are **categorical**. They have a finite set of possible values that are fixed and distinct from one another. Differences between categories in categorical variables can never be known. The second two types of variables are **continuous**. Theoretically, they have an infinite set of possible values. The values exist on a continuum from low to high, and the differences between points on the continuum are meaningful and identifiable.

1. A **nominal variable** catalogs states or statuses that are parallel and cannot be ranked or ordered. Race is a nominal variable. Even though social values and cultural norms may assign more prestige to one race or another, races themselves do not represent quantitative categories that are ranked as greater or less than one another.

For example, a long line of research has revealed that one basic way to designate school quality is by school sector, with private schools in the United States, especially Catholic schools, consistently outperforming public schools in overall academic achievement (Morgan, 2001). School sector is a nominal variable. We can create categories for private and public and even refine these categories by splitting private into Catholic, non-Catholic religious, and independent categories and public into urban, suburban, and rural categories. Each category represents a different kind of school that can be compared to other kinds of schools, but we cannot think of going up or down in terms of school sector or of one school having more sector than another.

2. **Ordinal variables** have categories that can be ordered in some way. Although their categories can be ranked from low to high, the difference or distance between ranks cannot be known. In other words, some value judgment can be made about whether one category is greater or less than another, but we cannot know by how much.

For example, the No Child Left Behind legislation mandated standardized testing in all public schools and the public release of the testing results, both overall and for targeted groups such as low-income students and English-language learners (U.S. Department of Education, 2001). As a result, many states created designations for schools on the basis of test performance, developing categories to provide an easy way for the public to assess school quality. In Texas, districts and schools have four labels: exemplary, recognized, acceptable, and unacceptable (Texas Education Agency, 2011). Clearly, an exemplary school is better than an unacceptable school, but we do not know how much better. We also cannot say that a recognized school is three times better than an unacceptable school. The categories themselves are meaningful, but the gaps between the categories are not. After all, the difference in quality between an exemplary school and a recognized school may or may not be equivalent in magnitude to the quality gap between a recognized school and an acceptable school.

3. **Interval variables** have a continuum of values with meaningful distances (or intervals) between them but no true zero (a value of zero on the variable does not represent the absence of something being captured by the variable). As a result, the categories can

THE FAB FIVE AND THE ACTING WHITE THEORY

In the early 1990s, the University of Michigan's basketball team, led by five freshmen starters, made an improbable run in the NCAA Tournament. The team was dubbed the "Fab Five." In an ESPN documentary about the team, one Fab Five player, Jalen Rose, made controversial remarks about the Duke University basketball team: "I hated everything I felt Duke stood for. Schools like Duke didn't recruit players like me. I felt like they only recruited black players that were Uncle Toms." Here, "Uncle Tom," a reference to the anti-slavery novel *Uncle Tom's Cabin*, is a pejorative term for African Americans perceived as being too subservient to whites. Rose was implying that African American men who attended prestigious universities like Duke were "less black" than those who attended state schools, many of whom grew up in poor or disadvantaged homes. Grant Hill, a former Duke and NBA star, responded in the *New York Times* that being raised in a stable two-parent home, doing well in school, and being well-behaved did not make him any less black.

This heated exchange between Rose and Hill dominated the media for several days. This media firestorm mirrors a major controversy in the social sciences. At issue is "the burden of acting white," a concept that some researchers have used to explain the lower average levels of academic achievement among black students when compared to white students. This concept comes from the cultural ecological perspective, which holds that the historical subjugation of African Americans has led some black youth to equate conventional achievement with their oppressors and to develop an "oppositional" culture. Peer groups reject conventional achievement, such as good grades and proper grammar, as whiteness and penalize high-achieving black youth by ridiculing and isolating them (Ogbu, 1997). Initial studies articulated the theory and supported it with preliminary evidence. Yet, the theory remained controversial and generated numerous studies that effectively countered its basic claims.

Quantitative research has revealed that black youth value academic success and are actually more popular with peers when they do well in school (Ainsworth-Darnell & Downey, 1998; Harris, 2006). Qualitative research has revealed that the "acting white" phenomenon does occur but that it is caused by schools' negative reaction to African American culture and, more generally, that it is a resistance of assimilation rather than achievement (Carter, 2006; Tyson, Darity, & Castellino, 2005). Despite this ample counterevidence, the "acting white" thesis is still discussed regularly in the media and social science. This continued controversy could reflect problems in the link between conceptualization and operationalization.

A former member of the "Fab Five" incited controversy when he accused the black players on a rival team of "acting white."

First, some concepts in the acting white theory are not clearly specified. As a result, they can be conceptualized differently across studies, producing measures that are difficult to compare. For example, opposition and resistance have been conceptually and operationally defined in many different ways. Because the audience may not be sufficiently aware of these differences, the contradictory findings across studies may be very confusing.

Second, operational definitions have not always matched conceptual definitions. Conceptually, oppositional culture concerns the ways that peers penalize one another for achievement. Thus, to evaluate the oppositional culture thesis, operational definitions must include some social consequences, but such consequences are rarely measured. When they are (for example, loss of friends), they often reveal little evidence of a penalty for achievement.

Third, other aspects of the theory have been conceptualized too narrowly. Oppositional culture is defined primarily in a racialized way ("acting white") when the idea is not inherently racial. Qualitative research has revealed oppositional culture in diverse groups of youth. It comes out in different ways across groups that amount to the same thing. For example, white youth have oppositional culture, but they equate conventional achievement with acting stuck up, not acting white. Thus, oppositional culture is about power and status, not race.

A tight and transparent connection between conceptualization and operationalization, therefore, provides a more coherent sense of evidence for or against a controversial idea. The confusion over "acting white" in the media reflects, at least partly, confusion among social scientists about definitions and measurement.

TABLE 4.1 Four Types of Variables

Variable Type	Class	Key Characteristic	Example
Nominal	Categorical	Has parallel categories	Hair color
Ordinal	Categorical	Has ranked categories	School quality
Interval	Continuous	Continuum with no true zero	Time of day (12-hour clock)
Ratio	Continuous	Continuum with true zero	Body weight

be compared explicitly rather than simply noting that one is greater or less than another, but, because of the lack of a true zero, we cannot think of them in terms of proportions or other complex mathematical operations. The temperature scale is often used to illustrate this type of variable. If the average winter temperature is 20 degrees in one community and 40 degrees in another, we can say that the former community is 20 degrees colder than the latter. Yet, because 0 degrees on the temperature scale does not mean that there is no temperature (and because negative temperatures are still temperatures), we cannot say that the former community is twice as cold as the latter.

One measure of high school quality might be seniors' average scores on the SAT. Because of its unique scoring system, a score of zero is not possible on the SAT—even if a student gets every single question on the test wrong! To see why this test characteristic is important, compare a school with an average SAT score of 1,400 to one with an average score of 700. One could conclude that the first school had an average score 700 points higher than the second, and that conclusion would be sound. Further concluding that the first school had an average SAT score twice as high as the second school might be tempting, but that conclusion would be false. If the SAT score scale does not start with zero, then expressing one school's average score as a proportion of another school's is not possible (or at least not correct).

4. **Ratio variables** are interval variables that do have a true zero. As a result, values can be compared and contrasted with the most detail. Differences can be expressed in terms of the distance between values (as with interval variables) but also in terms of one value being some proportion or percentage of another.

In recent years, the Bill & Melinda Gates Foundation has spent billions of dollars to improve the quality of public schools in the United States. One initial priority concerned school size. Believing that smaller schools provide better learning environments and reduce the likelihood of students falling through the cracks, the foundation advocated reducing school size, especially in urban schools serving racial and ethnic minorities (Fouts et al., 2006). School size is a good example of a ratio variable. Theoretically at least, a school's enrollment could fall to zero (prompting a closing, one would assume) or it could grow to as big a student body as the building will allow. Thus, a school with 2,400 students is bigger than a school with 800 students (a distinction possible with an ordinal variable), has 1,600 more students than that other school (a distinction possible with an interval variable), and has a student body three times the size of the other school (a distinction possible only with a ratio variable).

ratio variables Variables with a continuum of values with meaningful distances (or intervals) between them and a true zero.

Indicators

Understanding the dimensions of a concept and the types of variables that can be used to capture those dimensions moves the conceptualization process closer to measurement. Choosing indicators is a final step. **Indicators** are the values assigned to a variable. They are part of the plan that researchers develop to sort the variable into various categories. Identifying an indicator is a conceptual procedure that provides the blueprint for measurement.

The onset of puberty is a dimension of the larger concept of puberty, which itself is a dimension of the even larger concept of physical maturation. As noted earlier, the most common unit of analysis for research on puberty onset is the individual level. Because the onset of puberty refers to a duration of some length, the variable that is derived from the dimension of puberty onset will likely be continuous. One way of conceptualizing the variable is the length of time between birth and the start of puberty.

To create the indicators, researchers must define the length of time between birth and puberty. Time can be measured many ways. Years are a common approach. Yet, as any teenager will testify, meaningful differences in the onset of puberty can exist within the same year. Months, then, are a better indicator of the length of time between birth and the beginning of puberty. Puberty itself is so complex that there is no single indicator of puberty and no single event that signifies its start. This case is one in which hard choices must be made. For girls, the situation is somewhat easier, as girls' pubertal development does have a major discrete event that is easily identifiable: the onset of menstruation. For boys, identifying an event that marks the onset of puberty is more difficult. The equivalent to menarche—semenarche, or the production of sperm—is not so easily detectable. As a result, researchers often use the first appearance of adult physical characteristics, such as body hair. Therefore, if the researchers want to use the same indicator across genders, the number of months between birth and the growth of body hair would be a useful indicator of puberty onset.

With indicators identified, we have traveled through the conceptualization process. With a concrete conceptual definition in hand, the next step is to determine the measurement that follows from that definition.

> **indicators** The values assigned to a variable.

CONCEPT CHECKS

1. The hypothesis that academic achievement reduces problematic behaviors can be conceptualized on multiple levels of analysis. How might the hypothesis be conceptualized for an individual-level unit of analysis? How about a school-level unit of analysis?

2. Which type of variable has categories that cannot be ranked? Which type of variable allows for the most detailed kinds of comparisons? Explain.

3. Conceptualization is a process that gradually moves research from the abstract to the concrete. Which is more abstract and which is more concrete—dimensions or indicators? Pick a dimension for the concept of school quality and provide an example of a possible indicator for the dimension.

OPERATIONALIZATION

Once each component of a hypothesis (or statement of expected findings) has a conceptual definition, those definitions need to be measured through observation. Operationalization identifies a plan for the concrete and systematic measurement of a variable. As Figure 4.6 shows, operationalization involves two steps: (1) converting a conceptual definition into an operational definition that sets the parameters for measurement, and (2) using the operational definition to collect data.

Just as there are many conceptual definitions for a variable, there are many operations for observing it—from literally observing with the eye to creating survey items or experimental conditions, among other possibilities. Researchers must explain their decision-making process so that the audience will know exactly what they have done and why.

Continuing with the onset of puberty, our detailed definition of a variable for this concept has a specified indicator: the number of months between birth and the appearance of body hair. This definition and its accompanying indicator are narrow enough to leave a lot out of the concept of puberty onset but also precise enough to translate into accurate measurement. Still, some difficult choices about measurement remain. How exactly will we check the hair growth? One way would be to collect a sample of preteens and give them body checks every day. This approach, of course, is rife with ethical issues. A more practical and realistic strategy—one used by the long-running National Institute of Child Health and Human Development (NICHD) Study of Early Child Care and Youth Development (Belsky et al., 2007; NICHD Early Child Care Research Network, 2005)—is to have preteens checked regularly by nurse practitioners using the Tanner stage procedure, an observational protocol for identifying stages of puberty (Marshall & Tanner, 1969). Youths and their parents are more willing to submit to this kind of measurement in a formal medical context. The problem is that this procedure is time-intensive and costly.

To the extent that a large sample is being targeted, these costs would likely be prohibitive. Thus, for large samples, researchers might have to rely on self-reports. This protocol was used by the National Longitudinal Study of Adolescent to Adult Health (Add Health), a survey of 20,000 teenagers from across the United States. One question asked of all boys was, "How much hair is under your arms now—which sentence best describes you?" The boys then had to choose from a set of categories ranging from "I have no hair at all" to "I have a whole lot of hair that is very thick, as much hair as a grown man." Such self-reports might involve many biases compared to the medical data—including the possibility that youth "speed up" their development when asked about it—but offer benefits in terms of ease and accessibility of measurement. This approach can be extrapolated to qualitative studies of puberty, in which researchers rely on what subjects say to gauge onset, whatever the indicator being used.

Any decision about measurement likely comes with difficult trade-offs between potential benefits and costs. Researchers must weigh these trade-offs when designing studies. Operationalization is a

FIGURE 4.6 Steps of Operationalization

Operationalization can be broken down into two steps: First, the conceptual definition is converted into an operational definition. Second, this operational definition is used to collect data.

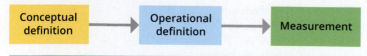

choice, and researchers must justify their choice so that everyone knows how to assess the study and compare the findings to the results of other studies. Often, researchers decide to use a "tried and true" operationalization from other related studies so that they can compare their results with prior studies. When tried and true measures are found to be problematic, researchers may design their own operationalization and clearly convey the choices and rationale behind their procedures.

Field of Study

One factor driving operationalization is field of study, which can guide the researcher's approach. Researchers bring a background to a study, and that background—which encapsulates their experience and expertise—naturally contributes to decisions about measurement.

The difference between quantitative and qualitative research is important to understanding the process of operationalization. Quantitative researchers typically view operationalization as an end result of the conceptualization process. Qualitative researchers do not follow this same linear path. Rather, they start with a more open conceptualization process and use observation to refine the process and come up with conceptual definitions. As a result, data collection procedures are established and followed (operationalized) earlier.

Even within the general quantitative and qualitative areas, decisions about procedures vary greatly. Quantitative researchers might design surveys or experiments. As we shall see in Chapter 7, in surveys, operationalization is about the development of questions. Likewise, as we will see in Chapter 8, in experiments, operationalization is about defining the treatment effect—how people in the experimental group will be exposed to something that those in the control group will not. For example, the experimental group may watch a violent film clip, while the control group does not, as a way to test whether exposure to violence affects some outcome, such as aggression, on an experimental task (Hasan et al., 2013).

Another quantitative approach is content analysis (Chapter 12), in which written materials are analyzed, and operationalization involves instructing readers on what to code. In one good example that was mentioned earlier in the chapter, scholars reviewed articles in newspapers (tapping into public debates) and the *Congressional Record* (tapping into policy discussions) in the aftermath of the mass shooting at Columbine High School and coded them according to the type of primary explanation of the event that was featured. Although both public forms highlighted gun-related explanations, media paid more attention to popular cultural explanations (for example, violent movies and video games; Birkland & Lawrence, 2009).

Qualitative researchers, in contrast, often use in-depth interviews (Chapter 11), in which operationalization involves identifying the questions to be asked. Another common method is ethnography (Chapter 10), in which operationalization involves determining the settings to be observed and what researchers will look for in those settings.

For example, parental monitoring is likely to be studied differently by researchers with different orientations, even though all those researchers share the same basic definition of the concept. Ethnographers from the interpretivist tradition are unlikely to approach the expected findings thinking about surveys and scales, and a statistically adept criminologist is unlikely to consider doing participant observation to test the hypothesis. Field of study, therefore, is usually a first filter in the operationalization process, narrowing down the range of options.

Mismatches between Units of Analysis: Ecological Fallacies and Reductionism

Confusion about units of analysis is a common problem that, if not corrected, can invalidate the conclusions drawn from data. This problem involves a mismatch between units of analysis; it occurs when what happens on one unit of analysis does not necessarily translate to another.

One problem is the **ecological fallacy**, when conclusions are made about the micro level on the basis of some macro-level analysis. Assume that a researcher is interested in the question of whether parental monitoring reduces juvenile delinquency. In an attempt to answer this question, she might ask parents to complete a survey in which they report on their monitoring behaviors but not on any corresponding data for their adolescent children. As a solution, she could draw on the rates of juvenile arrests in various ZIP codes published by the local police department. This approach would be sound methodologically, but it could also create an ecological fallacy if the researcher does not shift her original unit of analysis (individual families) to the new unit of analysis (whole neighborhoods). To have both the independent variable (monitoring behaviors) and the dependent variable (juvenile delinquency) on the same unit of analysis, she would have to aggregate the parent surveys by ZIP code to produce an average level of parental monitoring in each ZIP code that could then be analyzed with the arrest rates. In other words, she needs to shift her focus to understand that she is not studying parenting and delinquency within individual families but rather the levels of parental monitoring and juvenile delinquency in whole neighborhoods.

What conclusions might the researcher draw from an inverse correlation between average parental monitoring in a ZIP code and the ZIP code arrest rate? You might be tempted to conclude that the data support her hypothesis. Her data, however, would show only that monitoring and arrest rates correlate on the ZIP code level; that is, in ZIP codes in which parental monitoring is on average high, arrest rates tend be low. The researcher could not use these data to assess whether specific parents who engage in frequent monitoring have teenage children who engage in less delinquency. Why not? Perhaps adolescents rebel against high-monitoring parents when they live in communities with low overall levels of monitoring, and their delinquent behavior is what increases delinquency rates in their communities. This scenario, whether true or not, is difficult to rule out. If it is not ruled out, no reasonable claims about the effect of parental monitoring on juvenile delinquency can be made.

Another problem, the reverse of the ecological fallacy, is **reductionism**, which occurs when conclusions are made about the macro-level unit on the basis of analyses of micro-level data. Reductionism reduces something quite complex into too-simple terms or simplifies societal or group phenomena into individualist explanations. Suppose that a researcher surveyed families in a city, asking parents to report on their monitoring behaviors and youth to report on their engagement in delinquent activities.

ecological fallacy A mistake that researchers make by drawing conclusions about the micro level based on some macro-level analysis.

reductionism A mistake that researchers make by drawing conclusions about the macro-level unit based on analyses of micro-level data.

If the researcher finds an inverse correlation in these individual-level data—higher monitoring is associated with lower rates of delinquency—he might be tempted to think that his results can be useful in city debates about crime prevention. On the basis of his data, he might claim that the best way to spend money is to create community programs to teach parents how to monitor their children's behavior. Although he may be correct in that assertion, he is likely reducing the complex issue of crime to an individualist explanation about "good" and "bad" parents when in fact many macro-level structures and trends could be at work, including a lack of work opportunities for teenagers due to bad economic times and low-quality schooling due to lack of state investment.

Problems with units of analysis have long plagued social research. In fact, the ecological fallacy is present in one of the foundational studies of sociology: Émile Durkheim's *Suicide* (1897). Durkheim drew conclusions about the links among religion, social integration, and suicide on the basis of district-level data about religious affiliation and suicide in France (see Denney et al., 2015). This research has been criticized because Durkheim used findings that rates of suicide were higher in Protestant areas to conclude that Protestants were more likely to commit suicide than Catholics. Ultimately, one of the most important questions a researcher can ask is: At what level of analysis do I want to focus the discussion (conceptualization), and do I have the data to do that successfully (operationalization)?

Measurement

The process of empirical observation and measurement varies with individual project goals. Nevertheless, we can identify four basic forms of measurement: reports, observation, artifact counts/assessments, and manipulation.

REPORTS

Reports are direct feedback, written or verbal, from people. The most common type is *self-report*, when the subject of a study provides information to the researcher. In *other-report*, someone besides the subject, such as a parent, teacher, or physician, provides information about that subject.

For example, the previously mentioned NICHD Study of Early Child Care and Youth Development relied on parent and teacher reports about children's health and learning when children were young but switched to self-reports when the children reached adolescence and were mature enough to provide their own reports. Reports were collected in face-to-face interviews, with interviewers recording subject responses, or in written surveys in which subjects filled in bubbles like on a standardized test. When the subject matter was sensitive, interviewers gave subjects a small personal computer loaded with a response-gathering program. Subjects would read the survey questions and type in their responses without the interviewer seeing them. Although telephone and face-to-face interviews have historically been common ways of collecting data, the widespread use of e-mail and social networking sites has led to web-based surveys in recent years. We discuss surveys and the different modes of administration in depth in Chapter 7.

The use of reports is common in quantitative methodologies, especially surveys. Reports are also used widely in experiments, with researchers using surveys or

reports Direct feedback, written or verbal, from people.

KATHRYN EDIN & PEGGY C. GIORDANO

Historically, most social scientists conducted either quantitative or qualitative research. Doing both kinds of research or collaborating across this methodological divide was uncommon for reasons that are practical (each method requires extensive training) and more complicated (quantitative and qualitative researchers may have different worldviews of objective reality). Increasingly, however, research that mixes quantitative and qualitative methods has begun to bridge this false divide (see Axinn & Pearce, 2006; Creswell & Clark, 2007). Here, we highlight two researchers involved in mixed-methods research.

Kathryn Edin, a sociologist at Johns Hopkins University, is a qualitative researcher who often partners with quantitative researchers on large studies. For example, she was on the team behind Moving to Opportunity (MTO), a large-scale experiment that gave low-income families vouchers to relocate to middle-class neighborhoods. The quantitative team established the experiment's effects on families and youth, and the qualitative researchers attempted to understand why these effects occurred (or not) (Clampet-Lundquist et al., 2006; Kling, Liebman, & Katz, 2007).

Peggy C. Giordano, a sociologist at Bowling Green State University, conducts both quantitative and qualitative research. For example, in the Toledo Adolescent Relationships Study (TARP), Giordano and her colleagues conducted a survey of 1,300 teenagers and then did in-depth interviews with 100 within this sample to understand the development of young people's romantic lives (Giordano, Longmore, & Manning, 2006).

Mixed-methods research is far less common than either solely quantitative or solely qualitative research. Why do you think that is? What are the major challenges to mixed-methods research?

Edin: There are three flavors of mixed-methods studies. One uses qualitative data as grounding for a survey.

A second deploys the qualitative study to generate hypotheses about unanswered questions generated by a prior survey. Sometimes, they can be explored systematically in a subsequent survey wave, so the qualitative study is a first step in the subsequent iteration. Third, qualitative data are used to measure things that surveys can't get, usually because the information sought is sensitive or nuanced.

One challenge is that qualitative researchers often think about sampling—events versus people, for example—in ways that differ from quantitative researchers, which is why interviews, and not true ethnography (which favors direct observations of behavior), are usually deployed in mixed-methods research—the logic of sampling is easier to import. Another challenge is power. Qualitative researchers often feel their work is devalued by quantitative researchers, and by the social science enterprise more generally. Thus, many are hesitant to take part in mixed-methods research.

The link between theory and data often differs between quantitative and qualitative research. Do these differences make partnerships between quantitative and qualitative researchers (or a researcher doing both) difficult? How do you work through these obstacles?

Edin: Inductive approaches [inferring generalities from specifics] are critically important for providing qualitative grounding for all types of research and for hypothesis generation and theory construction. But mixed-methods research is often not well set up for this function. Ideally, mixed-methods research should be grounded in extensive pilot work that is ethnographic—sampling places and events via observation—and relies on some sort of systematic in-person interviewing, as only certain types of people show up at the places and events. For example, the MTO survey was designed based on insights from a preliminary qualitative study that suggested including mental and physical health, which turned out to be the only big impacts. MTO also had qualitative data collections during and after the quantitative data collection for validation of the measures and approaches and to explore why the experiment worked or not. What's cool about MTO is the iterative nature of the qualitative and quantitative.

> ## "
> Ideally, a mixed-methods approach will provide a more multilayered perspective on a given phenomenon, but it is important to fully confront and then integrate emerging findings from the two types of methods as the research unfolds. "

Giordano: Working together with scholars who have the training/background in each way of knowing is a great way around this dilemma. However, quantitative and qualitative researchers have such different approaches to this link. Quantitative analyses usually begin with an existing theory that is tested, while qualitative researchers typically derive theoretical insights from their analyses of the data themselves. Ideally, a mixed-methods approach will provide a more multilayered perspective on a given phenomenon, but it is important to fully confront and then integrate emerging findings from the two types of methods as the research unfolds.

As a researcher who has done more quantitative studies, when do you typically bring qualitative data into the mix?

Giordano: Qualitative methods are very useful at the beginning of projects, as observations and intensive interviews provide a window on the perspectives and natural language of individuals navigating the aspect of social life you are interested in investigating. But a true mixed-methods approach will rely on the qualitative side of things throughout the entire process. So, we collected in-depth relationship history narratives from a subset of those participating in our longitudinal study. These narrative data have been useful as we have sought to interpret results of quantitative analyses, delve further into our understanding of mechanisms underlying a statistical association (for example, why

and how is poverty linked to risk for dating violence?), identify specific beliefs and emotions that are associated with a given set of behaviors, and specify sequences of action and reaction. Even late in the game, we have uncovered new domains of interest through analyses of qualitative data that could then be examined with the larger sample group.

In a recent study of how people move away from involvement in criminal activity, for example, many narratives mentioned spirituality as an important catalyst for change. However, when we actually examined the association over the full time span of the study (over 20 years), spirituality was not systematically related to "desistance" from crime across the sample as a whole. The qualitative data were critical in pointing out the heavy reliance on religion and spirituality, and the quantitative results provide a sobering counterpoint about how this actually plays out across a large sample group and a significant span of the life course. More fine-grained analyses of the qualitative data identified specific difficulties of relying on spirituality absent any economic and social supports to bolster the hoped-for changes in life direction.

The concept of measurement is quite different in quantitative and qualitative research. Do you think of measurement differently when working with mixed methods than when working with either quantitative or qualitative alone?

Edin: One huge benefit of qualitative research is to get a survey to ask the right questions and improve the quality of the measures. Qualitative researchers have a healthy skepticism of survey questions, and this "emperor has no clothes" function can prove hugely helpful to survey researchers and experimentalists. Sadly, the quantitative folks don't often turn to qualitative folks for this kind of vital help. Similarly, lots of qualitative folks wipe their hands of surveys, judging this approach as worthless. We can't really move forward with these kinds of attitudes. I think that in order to improve and increase mixed-methods research, we have to radically change how we train graduate students. And not just by exposing students to different methods—they need to be exposed to the language and logic and literature of sister disciplines.

interviews to gather information from subjects before and after the experiment as a means of assessing how subjects change as a result of the experimental treatment. Reports, including interviews, are also a core activity of qualitative research.

Reports can also be categorized by the types of questions asked, and the types of answers allowed, in the research.

1. In **open-ended questions**, subjects are free to say as much or as little as they want and to provide answers in their own words. Open-ended questions are the norm in interview-style qualitative studies. Their purpose is to get subjects speaking freely, and interviewers can follow up with more questions. Quantitative researchers also use open-ended questions. For example, the Add Health study included some questions that had no preset response categories. Instead, teenagers were allowed to write in responses in sentence form; one question was "What makes [your] school different from other schools?"

2. **Closed-ended questions** allow for only specific responses. In some cases, closed-ended questions have no preset responses but, by virtue of the question, constrain responses. For example, an interviewer may ask "Are you currently legally married?" or a survey may start with the question "How old are you?" Even if response categories are not given, subjects can realistically respond only yes or no to the first question and give a number in response to the second question.

3. More commonly, closed-ended questions have **response categories**. Table 4.2 summarizes six types of response categories as well as an example from the research on parental monitoring.

The process of designing questions and responses often is guided by the question: How much variation is needed to adequately measure the variable? Researchers can aim for precise measures that capture great detail or they can be blunt and sort subjects into basic categories. Going back to our poverty example, income questions can be closed-ended but without response categories, asking respondents to write in how much money they earned from work or other sources in the past year. They can also have response categories, but the range of response categories varies across studies. Some studies might have response categories at $1,000 intervals ($0–$1,000, $1,001–$2,000, and so forth), $10,000 intervals ($0–$10,000, $10,001–$20,000, and so forth), or smaller or larger intervals. The level of detail (granularity) that researchers will go to depends on the goals of the study, costs, and other considerations (for example, how much space is available on a survey). Aiming for more precision is usually advisable during data collection, because researchers can easily collapse a large number of categories into a smaller number during data analysis, but they cannot divide a small number of categories into more detailed categories.

Closed-ended measures must provide response categories that are **exhaustive**, meaning all respondents must have at least one accurate response available to them—they must be able to fit in somewhere and somehow. A race measure with only white and African American would not be exhaustive, but a race measure with white and non-white would be. In the former, an Asian respondent would not have an available response, but he or she would fit in the latter (non-white). Response categories should also be **mutually exclusive**, meaning respondents should be able to respond accurately in only one way. In the race measures just mentioned, mutual exclusivity is problematic,

open-ended question A broad interview question to which subjects are allowed to respond in their own words rather than in preset ways.

closed-ended question A focused interview question to which subjects can respond only in preset ways.

response categories The preset answers to questions on a survey.

exhaustive Preset response categories that give all subjects at least one accurate response.

mutually exclusive Preset response categories that do not overlap with one another, ensuring that respondents select the single category that best captures their views.

TABLE 4.2 Types of Response Categories

Type	Description	Example from Parental Monitoring study
Binary or dichotomous	Questions with the most basic responses possible.	Do you set a curfew for your teenager? *Yes, No*
Non-ordered categories	Questions that require sorting into nominal categories that cannot be ranked.	What types of after-school activities have you signed your teenager up for in the past year? *None, Organized Sports, Youth Club, Religious Group, Other*
Frequency (ordinal)	Questions that require an assessment of timing or duration in ranked categories.	How often do you talk to the parents of your teenager's friends? *Never, Rarely, Occasionally, Often*
Frequency (interval/ratio)	Questions that require an assessment of timing or duration in terms of units of time.	How many days of the week do you talk to the parents of your teenager's friends? *0, 1, 2, 3, 4, 5, 6, 7*
Degree	Questions that require an assessment of the extent to which something is true or of the magnitude of something.	How important do you think it is to monitor your teenager's comings and goings? *Not at All, A Little, Somewhat, Very Much*
Agreement	Questions that require subjects to assess how true or untrue some statement about their lives or the world is (often referred to as Likert scales).	How much do you agree with this statement— parents who do not set rules for what time their teenagers have to be home on a weekend night are bad parents? *Strongly Disagree, Disagree, Neither Disagree nor Agree, Agree, Strongly Agree*

given that many people can claim to be both white and non-white at the same time— just ask former president Barack Obama.

Thus, high-quality measures typically allow subjects to fit into exactly one category. For example, a measure asking girls to self-report whether they started menstruating early (age 11 or younger), on time (ages 12–14), or late (age 15 or older) would be exhaustive and mutually exclusive. With the rare exception of girls with chromosomal disorders that prevent menstruation, everyone starts menstruating at some age and only that one age. This measure might have other problems (for example, the blunt categories mask meaningful variation), but all respondents will be able to respond in one of the preset response categories. If the on-time category was eliminated without adjusting the age ranges, then the measure would not be exhaustive— how would girls who started menstruating after age 11 and before age 15 respond? Perhaps the measure could be changed to be about the onset of puberty more generally. If the response categories were early menstruation (age 11 or younger), on-time menstruation (ages 12–14), late menstruation (age 15 or older), early genital hair growth (age 11 or younger), on-time genital hair growth (ages 12–14), or late genital

→ NOTE: Please answer BOTH Question 8 about Hispanic origin and Question 9 about race. For this census, Hispanic origins are not races.

8. Is Person 1 of Hispanic, Latino, or Spanish origin?

☐ **No,** not of Hispanic, Latino, or Spanish origin
☐ Yes, Mexican, Mexican Am., Chicano
☐ Yes, Puerto Rican
☐ Yes, Cuban
☐ Yes, another Hispanic, Latino, or Spanish origin — *Print origin, for example, Argentinean, Colombian, Dominican, Nicaraguan, Salvadoran, Spaniard, and so on.* ⬧

`[                                    ]`

9. What is Person 1's race? *Mark ☒ one or more boxes.*

☐ White
☐ Black, African Am., or Negro
☐ American Indian or Alaska Native — *Print name of enrolled or principal tribe.* ⬧

`[                                    ]`

☐ Asian Indian   ☐ Japanese   ☐ Native Hawaiian
☐ Chinese   ☐ Korean   ☐ Guamanian or Chamorro
☐ Filipino   ☐ Vietnamese   ☐ Samoan
☐ Other Asian — *Print race, for example, Hmong, Laotian, Thai, Pakistani, Cambodian, and so on.* ⬧   ☐ Other Pacific Islander — *Print race, for example, Fijian, Tongan, and so on.* ⬧

`[                                    ]`

☐ Some other race — *Print race.* ⬧

`[                                    ]`

The U.S. Census question on race is exhaustive because everyone can check or write in something, but it is not mutually exclusive because people can check or write in more than one race.

observation The process of seeing, recording, and assessing social phenomena.

hair growth (age 15 or older), then the categories would not be mutually exclusive. A girl could be early on one of the measures and late on the other.

An easy way to achieve exhaustiveness is to include a catch-all category in the responses, one that "catches" those persons who do not fit into the preset categories. This category might be labeled "other" or "don't know." The point is to make sure that every subject gets assigned a value, even if that value is not all that meaningful.

Worth noting is that exclusivity is not always desirable. Many studies now allow respondents to identify themselves as belonging to multiple races, reflecting the multicultural nature of American society. The data can then be used to create new variables for people who identify as a member of a single race and those who identify as a member of more than one race. Another example is a survey in which respondents select all of the factors that apply to them. Perhaps teenagers are asked to check off which, if any, markers of pubertal development (change in voice, genital hair growth, genital growth) they have experienced. The goal might be to identify who is further along in the process. The point is that although exhaustiveness is always a must, exclusivity is not, but departures from exclusivity need to be made consciously and for a specific reason.

OBSERVATION

Observation is the process of seeing, recording, and assessing social phenomena. Observation is commonly used in qualitative studies. In Chapter 2, we discussed the ethnographic work of Annette Lareau (2003), who spent months living with a set of families to come up with a theory about social-class differences in parenting. She observed what was happening generally but did not count or rate anything per se. Observation is also common in quantitative studies, although the end result is different. An example is the Home Observation for Measurement of the Environment (HOME) procedure, which has been used in national studies for decades (Bradley & Caldwell, 1979). In the HOME, interviewers study families' homes, record different information (for example, number of books), and make more general assessments of various qualities that are then converted into concrete ratings. The HOME, therefore, is a quantitative measure that is based on observation.

Observational measurement generally focuses on two dimensions: *degree* and *amount/frequency*. These observational approaches have been used in the study of school quality. The research that Sara Lawrence-Lightfoot (1983) summarized in *The Good High School* used observation in the form of ethnography. Lawrence-Lightfoot spent time in schools, observed classes and interactions among adults and students, and then made general statements about what worked and what did not work across several dimensions of organization, socioemotional quality, and instruction. By contrast, the Classroom Assessment Scoring System (CLASS) produces 7-point ratings (low to high) of numerous classroom dimensions (for example, positive climate, instructional support) on the basis of observers' ratings of what they witness across multiple timed observational periods (Pianta, La Paro, & Hamre, 2007). These numerical ratings can be analyzed statistically to examine the potential causes and consequences of school quality. Both *The Good High School* and CLASS are examples of observational measurement, but they serve different purposes and are aligned with different theoretical and methodological traditions.

ARTIFACT COUNTS/ASSESSMENTS

Artifact counts/assessments are tied to content analysis and similar materials-based methodologies (Chapter 12). An artifact count involves the cataloging of social artifacts and objects, qualitatively or quantitatively. For example, suppose that someone wants to study how the results of international math tests—which generally have shown that U.S. teenagers score below their peers in many other developed countries—have generated public concern about school quality in the United States. The researcher could conduct this study by analyzing media coverage, such as newspaper articles. He could count the number of articles concerning school quality published in the months before and after the release of test results. This measurement would be quantitative. Going deeper, independent raters could evaluate the content of each article and assess whether an article reflected concern about school quality or something else. Such an assessment would be inherently qualitative, although it could be converted into some quantitative scale (for example, no concern, some concern, great concern).

Observational approaches can be used to assess the quality of home and school environments. The Home Observation for Measurement of the Environment (HOME) procedure is an example of a quantitative measure based on observation.

MANIPULATION

Manipulation is usually paired with other forms of measurement during experiments. Rather than independently counting or evaluating reports, observations, or artifacts, experimenters need to "do something" to subjects and observe the results. For example, they might attempt to change attitudes, behaviors, or knowledge by asking subjects to read something, having them interact with others in a controlled setting, teaching them some skill, or exposing them to some event. That manipulation is a measurement in the sense that it represents one level of the independent variable; the other level of the independent variable typically is "no exposure" to a manipulation (that is, the control group).

The manipulation must be paired with some other assessment of the subject before and after the manipulation to determine how much a person changed on some factor as a result of the manipulation. That assessment could be a survey, interview, test, or something else. For example, in stereotype threat experiments, members of the **control group** and **experimental group** each take standardized tests, but each member of the experimental group (and not the control group) must mark his or her race on the test sheet first. The manipulation is that they have been cued to think about race,

artifact count/assessment The process of cataloging social artifacts and objects, qualitatively or quantitatively.

manipulation Something that is done to some subjects of an experiment but not others so that the outcomes of the two groups can be compared.

experimental group The group that is exposed to the experimental manipulation.

control group The group that is not exposed to the manipulation of the independent variable.

which can create racial disparities in test performance. Such research has been used to design interventions in schools and colleges to reduce the achievement gap (Cohen et al., 2006).

Assessing Measurement: Reliability and Validity

Because conceptualization and operationalization are so closely linked, assessments of the quality and effectiveness of a measure cannot be limited to the properties of the measure alone. They must also touch on the degree to which the variable's conceptual and operational definitions are aligned. A measure can have strong properties (for example, straightforward with exhaustive and mutually exclusive responses) but not do a great job of capturing the variable as it is conceptualized, and vice versa.

Two standards are crucial to understanding the match between conceptual and operational definitions: reliability and validity. In brief, **reliability** refers to how dependable a measure is. When a measure is reliable, it will consistently yield the same results no matter how many times it is given to the same samples. For example, in representative samples of families, a reliable measure of parental monitoring will show a similar minority of parents in the low-monitoring category every time it is administered. **Validity** refers to the accuracy or truthfulness of a measure. When a measure is valid, it adequately captures the conceptualization of some variable. Validity has numerous dimensions, which we cover in Chapter 5.

These two standards—reliability and validity—go hand in hand. The ideal measure is both reliable and valid, and the worst-case scenario is a measure that is unreliable and invalid. In between these extremes are cases in which a measure is reliable but not valid (it yields bad information in a highly consistent way) or it is valid but not reliable (it has the potential to inconsistently yield good information). We discuss reliability and validity in much more detail in the next chapter.

Time Span

Up to this point, we have approached measurement in terms of *how* to measure variables. Another question is *when* to measure some variable. We can answer this question in two basic ways that apply equally well to quantitative and qualitative studies. The first involves **cross-sectional study designs**, in which data are collected at only one time point. The second involves **longitudinal study designs**, in which data are collected at multiple time points. Longitudinal study designs come in many forms. Two of the most common are a repeated cross-sectional study design and a panel design.

With a **repeated cross-sectional study design**, data are collected at multiple points but from different people at each time—a new sample at each stage. These data can show, for example, whether attitudes toward same-sex marriage have become more favorable over time, but they cannot tell us whether a particular individual changes his or her mind between the two time points. With a **panel design**, data are collected multiple times from the same people—the same sample at each stage. These data allow us to document within-person changes.

For example, Monitoring the Future is a repeated cross-sectional survey of high school students conducted every year. A similar survey is given to new groups of

reliability A quality of a measure concerning how dependable it is.

validity A quality of a measure concerning how accurate it is.

cross-sectional study design A study in which data are collected at only one time point.

longitudinal study design A study in which data are collected at multiple time points.

repeated cross-sectional study design A type of longitudinal study in which data are collected at multiple time points but from different subjects at each time point.

panel design A type of longitudinal study in which data are collected on the same subjects at multiple time points.

FIGURE 4.7 Historical Trend in Adolescent Alcohol Use from Monitoring the Future

Data from Monitoring the Future, a repeated cross-sectional survey of high school students conducted every year, shows us that the proportion of U.S. high school seniors who consume alcohol has been steadily declining since the early 1990s.

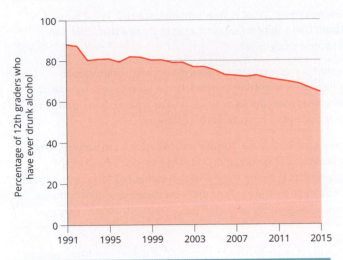

Source: Miech et al., 2016b.

FIGURE 4.8 Life Course Trend in Adolescent Alcohol Use from Add Health

Data from Add Health, a panel survey of middle and high school students, shows us that alcohol use sharply increases, then peaks and plateaus as U.S. youth move from adolescence into adulthood.

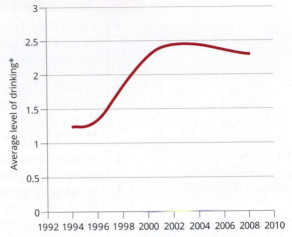

*Note: Level of drinking measured on a scale from 1 (no drinking in the past year) to 7 (drinking nearly every day in the past year).

Source: Author calculations.

youth each year as they move into the appropriate grades. These repeated cross-sections allow researchers to track continuity and change in adolescent attitudes and behaviors across time and generation, but they do not allow any consideration of what happens to youth in the sample in the years after they take the survey. The sample is constantly turned over, with new participants each year (Miech et al., 2016b). Drawing on data from repeated cross-sections in Monitoring the Future, Figure 4.7 shows that the proportion of U.S. 12th graders who drink alcoholic beverages has slowly but steadily declined from the late twentieth century through the early twenty-first.

In contrast, the Add Health study that we mentioned earlier has a panel design. It followed a group of middle and high school students from the early 1990s through the first decade of the twenty-first century. The surveys changed at each time point to reflect the participants' changing lives as they aged, left their parents' homes, and entered adulthood. This panel design allows researchers to gauge the basic pathways that youth take as they move from adolescence into adulthood, but it does not allow any historical comparison of this youth cohort to those who came before or after (Harris et al., 2009). Figure 4.8 uses Add Health data to show that, on average, alcohol use sharply increases, peaks, and then plateaus as participants move from their teen years into their late twenties and early thirties.

Longitudinal studies, especially those with panel designs, have advantages and disadvantages. They provide more power to help researchers detect causal effects than cross-sectional studies do, but they are plagued by attrition problems.

attrition The loss of sample members over time, usually to death or dropout.

Attrition happens when members of a sample drop out over time, thereby changing the composition of the sample, perhaps by altering its racial or socioeconomic composition.

CONCEPT CHECKS

1   Consider this interview question: "What is your romantic status?" What type of measure is this question? Can you come up with a set of three exhaustive and mutually exclusive response categories?

2   A researcher is interested in the association between women's educational attainment and their likelihood of getting married. Come up with an example of a study of this association that commits an ecological fallacy. Also come up with an example of a study that commits a mistake of reductionism.

3   Keeping with the same example of the association between women's educational attainment and their likelihood of getting married in question 2, what kind of knowledge might be gained from a longitudinal design compared to a cross-sectional design? Would that knowledge be the same or different depending on whether a repeated cross-sectional design or panel design was employed? Why or why not?

COMPLETING THE RESEARCH PROCESS

Conceptualization and operationalization are about study design. Study execution comes next. The research process continues after the creation of operational definitions to guide measurement and involves the collection, analysis, and interpretation of data.

The steps of this empirical portion of the research process can vary considerably across studies depending on a number of factors, and researchers will also pursue and complete even the same steps in highly diverse ways. Still, there are some generalities.

Sampling. Most researchers determine whom or what to collect data on, but one sample may include people, another corporations, still another interpersonal interactions, and so forth. An ethnography of a school involves sampling, even if that just means picking a school to study.

Data collection. Many researchers gather data from their samples, but one may do so by having respondents complete a survey on the web, another by conducting an experiment in a lab, still another by observing people on the street, and so forth.

Data processing and analysis. Most researchers review the data that they have collected, identify any problems or gaps, come up with a final set of data for study, and then apply techniques to identify themes in the data. One researcher may do so by running a statistical program on quantitative data, another by looking for recurring patterns in qualitative data, still another by using software to identify recurring patterns in qualitative data, and so forth.

Interpretation of data. Most researchers draw conclusions on the basis of the data that they have analyzed, but one may do so by reporting significant findings from a statistical model, another by assessing whether the impact of an experiment is of sufficient magnitude to matter, and another by weighing the meaning of various themes emerging from a qualitative study.

Each one of these steps requires much more detail, description, and illustration, all of which will be provided in subsequent chapters. They are brought up here simply to give a preliminary idea of how the conceptualization and operationalization of a study then translates into actual action. We will get into each one of the steps in the subsequent chapters devoted to the specific methods available to social researchers, highlighting how these steps are undertaken in different ways for researchers coming from different traditions and taking different approaches.

CONCLUSION

The translation of broad theories into concrete studies has two key components: conceptualization and operationalization. Conceptualization refers to the process of precisely defining ideas and translating them into variables, moving from the abstract and general to the concrete and specific. Through operationalization, we then link those conceptualized variables to a set of procedures for measuring them. In other words, operationalization involves converting the conceptual definition into an operational definition that can be measured. Two standards are crucial to understanding the match between conceptual and operational definitions: reliability and validity. And like conceptualization and operationalization, these two standards go hand in hand. In the next chapter, we return to the example of poverty to provide an in-depth look at reliability and validity.

Summary

The processes of conceptualization and operationalization allow researchers to translate theories into concrete studies. Both are critical to the production of accurate and trustworthy data about the social world.

Defining and Measuring Poverty: An Introduction to Conceptualization and Operationalization

- Conceptualization involves defining ideas and turning them into variables. Operationalization is the process of linking those variables to a set of procedures for measuring them. The U.S. government conceptualizes poverty using an absolute standard of income and operationalizes this standard as the annual cost of an adequate diet for a family of a given size multiplied by three.
- Researchers must consider the units of analysis for a study, the social context of the phenomena being studied, and ethics when making operationalization choices.
- Conceptualization and operationalization go hand in hand. While quantitative researchers typically move from conceptual definitions to more precise operational definitions that form the basis of their study design, qualitative researchers allow concepts and measures to arise from the data they collect.

Conceptualization

- Conceptualization involves translating a concept into something measurable.
- Concepts can often be studied with different units of analysis, or levels of social life, as well as with different dimensions, or components of the concept.
- After breaking down the concept into its different dimensions, the next step in the conceptualization process is to create variables to represent those dimensions. Variables are representations that capture the presence or absence as well as the level of a concept.
- The last step of the process involves assigning indicators—or values—to the variables.

Operationalization

- Operationalization is the process of identifying a plan for measurement and often involves making trade-offs between the potential benefits of using "tried and true" measures and developing novel ways to measure variables.
- Quantitative researchers typically see operationalization as the end of the conceptualization process, while qualitative researchers view operationalization as a more open process that emerges from data collection and analysis.
- Mismatches in the units of analysis occur when researchers incorrectly translate findings for one unit of analysis into findings for another.
- Social researchers use four basic forms of measurement for empirical data: reports, observation, artifact counts, and manipulation.
- Reliability and validity are standards for assessing the degree to which a variable's conceptual and operational definitions are aligned.
- Social research can measure data using a cross-sectional study design, in which data are collected at a single point in time, or a longitudinal study design, in which data are collected at multiple time points. Two common types of longitudinal study designs are a repeated cross-sectional study design and a panel design.

Completing the Research Process

- After conceptualization and operationalization comes study execution, which typically involves sampling, collecting and processing data, and analyzing the data.

Key Terms

aggregation, **110**

artifact count/ assessment, **125**

attrition, **128**

categorical variables, **112**

closed-ended question, **122**

concept, **108**

conceptualization, **102**

continuous variables, **112**

control group, **125**

cross-sectional study design, **126**

dimensions, **110**

ecological fallacy, **118**

exhaustive, **122**

experimental group, **125**

indicators, **115**

interval variables, **112**

longitudinal study design, **126**

manipulation, **125**

mutually exclusive, **122**

nominal variables, **112**

observation, **124**

open-ended question, **122**

operationalization, **102**

ordinal variables, **112**

panel design, **126**

ratio variables, **114**

reductionism, **118**

reliability, **126**

repeated cross-sectional study design, **126**

reports, **119**

response categories, **122**

social artifacts, **109**

unit of analysis, **103**

validity, **126**

variables, **108**

Exercise

The mortality rate is the number of deaths per 1,000 persons in a population in a given year. This rate is a useful way of comparing different societies and tracking historical changes within societies. Many factors are related to the mortality rate. Sociologists have been particularly interested in the link between educational attainment and mortality on both the individual and population levels. An enormous social science literature focuses on this topic, documenting that more highly educated persons live longer and that more educated societies have lower mortality rates. Yet, even though educational attainment and mortality appear to be fairly straightforward concepts, the literature encompasses a great deal of variation in the conceptualization and operationalization of these topics.

To better understand such variation and the challenges it presents to researchers, use Sociological Abstracts to locate three peer-reviewed articles (by different authors) that focus on this link. After reading these articles, answer the following questions on your own or in a group:

- What dimensions of educational attainment (for example, quantity, quality) are considered in each of the studies, and what are the indicators selected for these dimensions?
- How are the various indicators measured in each study?
- Do the studies target different levels of analysis (individual level, population level)? If so, explain what these levels are and how the conceptualization and operationalization of educational attainment and mortality differ across them.
- What are the advantages and disadvantages of each approach to the conceptualization and operationalization of educational attainment and mortality? Is there a study in which these trade-offs are less substantial than in the others and, if so, why?

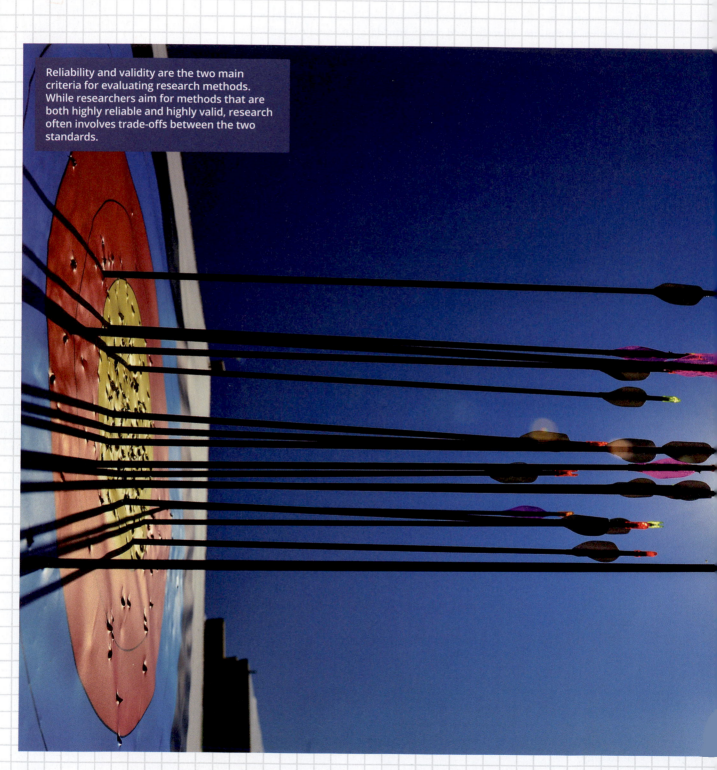

Reliability and validity are the two main criteria for evaluating research methods. While researchers aim for methods that are both highly reliable and highly valid, research often involves trade-offs between the two standards.

EVALUATING RESEARCH
Reliability and Validity

In Chapter 4, we introduced two of the main criteria for evaluating research methods: reliability (dependability, or how consistently the same operation yields the same results) and validity (truth or accuracy). Reliability and validity center on the link between conceptualization and operationalization. When research results are reliable and valid, there is a strong link between the definition of a variable and its measurement.

In this chapter, we look more closely at these two standards, discussing them in terms of general approaches (for example, quantitative and qualitative methods) and specific methodological approaches (for example, surveys and experiments). As in Chapter 4, we start with an illustrative example—poverty—to set the stage.

THINKING ABOUT RELIABILITY AND VALIDITY: MEASURING AND TRACKING POVERTY

Recall our discussion of the conceptualization (definition) and operationalization (measurement) of poverty in Chapter 4. There we described how the federal poverty line (FPL) is calculated in the United States. The FPL is used to determine the proportion of the U.S. population that is poor—the poverty rate—and to track how this rate changes over time and across different areas and groups.

Social scientists have widely criticized the calculation of the FPL—basically, the dollar amount of an adequate food budget for a family of a given size in a given year multiplied by 3. They point to several problems:

1. The FPL does not take regional variation in cost of living into account.

2. What constitutes an adequate diet is highly subjective.

3. The motivation for multiplying by 3 is weak and hard to justify.

4. The FPL does not take into account other kinds of expenses (for example, housing and child care).

Generally, these problems with the FPL lead the poor in the United States to be undercounted. In other words, many Americans who are economically disadvantaged are not counted as poor when they should be (Edin & Kissane, 2010; Citro & Michael, 1995; Moffitt, 2015; Ruggles, 1997). This problem prevents us from understanding the full scope of poverty in the United States and limits our ability to do something about it. Importantly, though, the undercount is problematic in any given year but less of a problem when looking at poverty trends over time. To see why, look at Table 5.1. If there is a fairly stable error rate in the FPL, then each year the estimate of the poverty rate will be too low. If the error rate is 7 percentage points every year, then our assessment of poverty will always be way off, but it will be consistently wrong by the same amount.

Look at the "Estimated Rate" column in Table 5.1. Using the FPL as our measure of poverty, we see an increase of 4 percentage points between 1973 and 2010. (We chose these dates because 1973 was the tail end of the War on Poverty, a large-scale government program begun in the 1960s to reduce the U.S. poverty rate, and 2010 was the height of the severe economic downturn of the 2000s.) If we use a hypothetical "real" poverty line (that is, a true estimate of the poverty rate that compensates for some of the problems with the FPL that its critics have raised), the estimated change in poverty between 1973 and 2010 is the same: 4 percentage points. Thus, even though we are wrong about the poverty rate in any given year, we are right about the change in the poverty rate across years. It is reliable over time without being very accurate at any one time.

In response to widespread criticism of the FPL, the National Academy of Sciences (NAS) convened a panel to suggest a way to calculate the U.S. poverty rate more accurately. The panel proposed that the new poverty line—the supplemental line mentioned in Chapter 4—be based on annual household budgets in four categories: (1) food (as in the FPL), (2) clothing, (3) shelter, and (4) other needs, including child care, transportation, and utilities (for example, the electric

TABLE 5.1 The Calculated and Hypothetical Poverty Rates by Year

Year[*]	Estimated Rate[†]	"Real" Rate[‡]
1973	11.1	18.1
2010	15.1	22.1

[*]The year 1973 is chosen as the tail end of the War on Poverty, and the year 2010 is chosen as the height of and beginning of the recovery from the Great Recession.
[†]Rate according to the federal poverty line (U.S. Department of Health and Human Services, 2011).
[‡]Hypothetical rate based on stable 4 percentage point error.

bill). Like the FPL, this new poverty line would be updated yearly, but, unlike the FPL, it would be calculated separately by geographic area (Citro & Michael, 1995).

The NAS poverty line corrects many of the problems of the traditional FPL that produce inaccurate estimates of the poverty rate. It also takes steps to improve the tracking of the poverty rate over time. As a result, it gives a new (and more positive) picture of poverty in the United States; specifically, it tells us that poverty has declined in recent decades more than is recognized and that government efforts to reduce poverty have been more effective than previously believed (Fox et al., 2015).

However, the increase in detail and precision that comes with the NAS poverty line does create some complications for comparison over time. Consider the budget categories. What would happen if public transportation expands to the extent that families spend less on transportation costs? What would happen if the government begins offering child-care subsidies that make child care less expensive? The Internet is now so important to work, school, and life in the United States that Internet access may be considered a necessity, not a luxury item. The NAS poverty line could take such changes into account in any given year, but how would they affect the comparison of poverty over time? So while this new poverty line is accurate, and research suggests that it is reliable, there are some threats to its reliability that need to be addressed.

These challenges to conducting research on poverty in the United States point to thorny issues concerning reliability and validity. To improve on one standard, we may have to give up something on another. In such cases, do we prioritize one over the other? As we try to answer this question, we see another example of a recurring theme in this textbook: Even things that seem simple and straightforward are usually much more complex than they first appear.

Defining Reliability and Validity

Reliability refers to dependability, consistency, and predictability, or how consistently the same operation yields the same results. A highly relevant measure or method reveals similar information no matter how many times it is applied to collect or code data, as long as the basic circumstances and conditions are the same. Reliability is not necessarily about being correct but instead about being stable and predictable.

Validity is about the truth or accuracy of results. Is the operation accurately capturing something in the real world? A highly valid measure or method gets to the heart of the concept being measured. Validity is about being correct, not about stability. Because definitions of *correct* and *incorrect* are more elusive than definitions of *consistency* or *stability*, validity is much trickier to assess than reliability.

The classic way to illustrate the differences between reliability and validity is to use a bullseye (Figure 5.1). Person 1 is valid but not reliable. She has gotten close to the bullseye but not in a consistent way. Person 2 is reliable but not valid. All of his shots cluster tightly together but are not near the bullseye. Person 3 is valid and reliable.

Researchers want to be like Person 3—consistently hitting the bullseye. Of course, they rarely are, and so they must grapple with both reliability and validity and the occasional

reliability A quality of a measure concerning how dependable it is.

validity A quality of a measure concerning how accurate it is.

FIGURE 5.1 Bullseye Depictions of Reliability and Validity

Researchers aim to be like Person 3, both valid and reliable; however, this is rarely possible in practice, and researchers often have to make trade-offs.

Person 1:
Valid

Person 2:
Reliable

Person 3:
Valid and
reliable

trade-offs between the two. Consider a topic that many find fascinating: physical attractiveness. Generally, the literature shows that attractive people (male and female, young and old) have better outcomes in school, work, and other areas (Hamermesh, 2011; Langlois et al., 2000). One study might have an observer rate every subject on attractiveness. This method would be highly reliable in the sense that the observer will use the same standard in every rating. To the extent that the rater has idiosyncratic ideas about what is and is not attractive, however, his or her ratings could diverge sharply from general norms in society. Using multiple raters (especially from diverse groups) can increase validity, but if raters disagree over some physical features, the results may be less reliable. In other words, using multiple raters might lead to greater validity but lower reliability.

With these examples, we do not mean to imply that reliability and validity are mutually exclusive, or parts of a zero-sum game in which gains in one always come with losses in the other. Rather, we want to drive home the important fact that reliability and validity are independently important standards for evaluating the link between conceptualization and operationalization.

Before we move on to a closer examination of reliability and validity, a consideration of quantitative and qualitative methods is in order. The terms *reliability* and *validity* are much more common in quantitative research than in qualitative research. Because qualitative methods involve much back-and-forth between researcher and subjects, with researchers constantly revising and adjusting their methods and approach as they learn more about the topic in a particular setting, issues of reliability and validity become much more ambiguous and fluid. Lincoln and Guba (1985) argue that instead of validity and reliability, qualitative research should instead be judged based on *credibility* and *dependability*.

Credibility can be assessed with the question: Do the respondents agree with how the researcher is presenting and interpreting their words? According to Lincoln and Guba, qualitative researchers are presenting the subjective experiences of the respondents, so the work should be partly judged based on the credibility of the account to the respondents themselves. Dependability refers to whether the findings are consistent, and whether the same findings would be repeated given the *same* circumstances or context. This is slightly different from reliability, where the same findings would be expected from a *different* context or investigator, as is the case with a survey. Given these considerations, qualitative researchers tend to see reliability and validity as far less clear-cut concepts than quantitative researchers do. Consequently, the following sections focus primarily on quantitative methodologies, especially survey methods.

CONCEPT CHECKS

1 What is the basic difference between reliability and validity?

2 Which of the two poverty lines discussed in this section, the FPL or the NAS poverty line, is preferable? Explain why in terms of reliability and validity.

3 Come up with two measures of obesity, one that may be accurate (valid) but not reliable, and one that may be reliable but not valid.

RELIABILITY

To achieve reliable results, researchers make sure that their measures are capturing a concept in ways that allow for comparison across data collections. To illustrate the dimensions of reliability, we draw on three sets of examples: the quality of homes and schools, mental health, and parent education.

Widely used observational protocols (official procedures) for measuring the quality of schools and homes are good examples of the steps that researchers take to increase reliability. You may recall the Classroom Assessment Scoring System (CLASS; Pianta, LaParo, & Hamre, 2007) and the Home Observation for Measurement of the Environment (HOME; Caldwell & Bradley, 2003) from Chapter 4, which are used to measure the quality of the classroom and home environments, respectively. Their developers believed that measuring key aspects of classrooms and homes is best done by independent observers rather than the parents, teachers, and children who live, work, or learn in that environment. Yet, the researchers also realized that different observers can look at the same settings in different ways, prioritizing some things over others in their overall assessments and attending to some aspects more than others. Thus, both the CLASS and HOME protocols are highly systematic, providing explicit, detailed instructions regarding what observers are to look for (and when) and how to interpret what they see. Moreover, all observers must first code sample videotapes of classrooms and homes and then compare the results to general averages. The goal is to demonstrate that their codings and final assessments generally agree with the norm.

These steps increase the reliability of CLASS and HOME, both of which are widely considered to be valid measurement systems. This reliability means that researchers can compare CLASS scores across the country to assess regional variation in the classroom quality of preschools and elementary schools (Pianta et al., 2007). The HOME can be included in national samples as a means of studying the degree to which quality of the home environment explains racial/ethnic or socioeconomic disparities in child outcomes (NICHD Early Child Care Research Network, 2005).

Researchers have developed reliable methods for observing and rating the quality of preschool and elementary classrooms.

Calculating Reliability

Some common statistical calculations are useful for illustrating what reliability is and why it matters. **Cronbach's alpha (α)** is a straightforward calculation that measures a specific kind of reliability for a **composite variable** (Cronbach, 1951); that is, a variable that averages a set of items (typically from a survey) to measure some concept. **Internal reliability** concerns the degree to which the various items lead to a consistent response and, therefore, are tapping into the same concept. The higher the alpha, the more internally reliable the composite is, meaning that people respond to the various items in a consistent way.

Cronbach's alpha (α) A calculation that measures a specific kind of reliability for a composite variable.

composite variable A variable that averages a set of items (typically from a survey) to measure some concept.

internal reliability The degree to which the various items in a composite variable lead to a consistent response and, therefore, are tapping into the same concept.

For example, let's say that there is a set of items about how often people go on online dating services, go on dates, and have romantic relationships. If the scale is internally reliable, how you respond to the first item will strongly predict how you respond to the second item, and both of those responses will strongly predict how you respond to the third. In other words, if you say you frequently go on eHarmony, we would expect you to also report going on lots of dates and having boyfriends/girlfriends. As a result, we could average those three items together into a variable called "romantic activity" and be sure that the variable was capturing something meaningful rather than simply a collection of different behaviors. If the scale is internally unreliable, your response on one of these items would not do much to tell us how you would respond to the others. We would keep those three items separate because they are capturing different things.

A Cronbach's alpha score of 1 is perfect reliability. The convention in the field is that scores above 0.7 are considered internally reliable, and scores below 0.6 are considered unreliable, with scores between 0.6 and 0.7 somewhere in between. A common measure of mental health is the Center for Epidemiologic Studies Depression scale, or CES-D (see Radloff & Locke, 1986), which averages scores on 20 items about feelings in the past week (Figure 5.2). The CES-D will be discussed in greater detail in our "Conversations from the Front Lines" feature in this chapter. The alpha score for the CES-D in the National Longitudinal Study of Adolescent to Adult Health (Add Health), a nationally representative survey of American teenagers, is 0.87. This alpha indicates that the CES-D is a reliable composite variable in general, as it is capturing a consistent pattern of depressed feelings and, therefore, can tell us something meaningful about depression. If the CES-D had an alpha of 0.35, then it would not be a reliable measure. A low alpha means that the items in the composite are not tapping into a common phenomenon because people do not respond to the items in a consistent way. That is, people's response on one item does little to predict their response on another item, so we would be better off just looking at each item on its own rather than averaging them together.

When multiple observers or coders are used in data collection, it is important to report measures of **intercoder reliability**. For example, as mentioned earlier, CLASS coders have to be in agreement with the "gold standard" coding norm 80% of the time. Intercoder reliability, which can be calculated in several ways, reveals how much different coders or observers agree with one another when looking at the same data. The more agreement among coders, the more reliable the coding protocol is, making comparison and contrasts easier. Recall the research discussed in Chapter 4 about content-coding of newspapers and the *Congressional Record* for explanations of the Columbine High School shootings. In that research, the intercoder reliability of coders familiar and unfamiliar with the overall hypotheses of the study was 0.93, suggesting that the materials were coded quite consistently even in different conditions. Readers can have more confidence in the results (Birkland & Lawrence, 2009; Lawrence & Birkland, 2004). See Chapter 12, which covers materials-based methods, for more on content analyses of newspapers.

Worth stressing here is that increasing intercoder reliability does not necessarily promote accuracy. In the case of CLASS, for example, the reliable measure will be accurate only to the extent that the "gold standard" codings used for comparison are accurate.

intercoder reliability A type of reliability that reveals how much different coders or observers agree with one another when looking at the same data.

FIGURE 5.2 Center for Epidemiologic Studies Depression Scale (CES-D)

Below is a list of some of the ways you may have felt or behaved. Please indicate how often you've felt this way during the **past week**. Respond to all items.

Place a check mark (✓) in the appropriate column. During the past week...	Rarely or none of the time (less than 1 day)	Some or a little of the time (1–2 days)	Occasionally or a moderate amount of time (3–4 days)	All of the time (5–7 days)
1. I was bothered by things that usually don't bother me.				
2. I did not feel like eating; my appetite was poor.				
3. I felt that I could not shake off the blues even with help from my family.				
4. I felt that I was just as good as other people.				
5. I had trouble keeping my mind on what I was doing.				
6. I felt depressed.				
7. I felt that everything I did was an effort.				
8. I felt hopeful about the future.				
9. I thought my life had been a failure.				
10. I felt fearful.				
11. My sleep was restless.				
12. I was happy.				
13. I talked less than usual.				
14. I felt lonely.				
15. People were unfriendly.				
16. I enjoyed life.				
17. I had crying spells.				
18. I felt sad.				
19. I felt that people disliked me.				
20. I could not "get going."				

Source: Radloff & Locke, 1986.

Reliability in Design

The most effective method for increasing the reliability of a research method is to do a very careful job of conceptualization, conscientiously working through each step of conceptualization outlined in Chapter 4 (see, specifically, Figure 4.2) to ensure a clear translation between conceptualization and operationalization. By building a solid conceptual foundation and then clearly defining a set of operations (measurement, data collection) on the basis of this foundation, researchers leave less room for error.

KRISTA PERREIRA

Looking at population-level trends in depression (for example, Which groups in society are most depressed? Is depression increasing across history?) is challenging because the best way to identify depression—having a clinician diagnose it—would be too time-consuming and expensive on a national scale. Thus, survey researchers have had to come up with scales of depressive symptoms to gauge depression, usually by counting the number of symptoms of depression people have. This survey measurement offers an opportunity to discuss issues of reliability and validity, which we do here by highlighting the work of a team of social scientists who measured depression across race/ethnicity. They analyzed the widely used Center for Epidemiologic Studies Depression Scale (CES-D; see Figure 5.2) and reported that although the CES-D was reliable and valid in general, it was far less so for certain U.S. racial/ethnic groups. We talked with the leader of this team—Dr. Krista Perreira of the University of North Carolina—about what these findings suggest about biases in population-level analyses of depression.

What was the motivation for conducting this study?

The growth in the population of immigrants in the United States has fueled interest in understanding health disparities. Yet, the measurement of these disparities in surveys can be sensitive to systematic cultural and linguistic differences in the wording and interpretation of survey questions. Many measures of health, education, and social well-being were originally developed for use with primarily European American and English-speaking populations. They have not been thoroughly evaluated for measurement biases that may reduce the validity of cross-cultural comparisons and make common statistical procedures (for example, comparing means) inappropriate. Thus, measurement equivalence is essential in health disparities research.

Given how long the CES-D has been around, why did it take so long for someone to ask these questions?

The CES-D was first developed in 1976. Initial evaluations did explore simple differences in factor structures [how items go together] between white, African American, and Hispanic population groups. Our research went beyond this by taking a more in-depth statistical approach and by examining measurement equivalence not only by race/ethnicity but also by immigrant generation. In earlier decades, researchers may not have asked questions about cross-cultural equivalence in measurement because there was less cultural diversity. In the 1970s and 1980s, less than 5% of the U.S. population was foreign-born. By 2000, more than 10% was foreign-born. As the population has become increasingly diverse, both researchers and funders of research have become more willing to reexamine fundamental assumptions related to conducting cross-cultural research. In addition, researchers may not undertake new psychometric

For example, the CLASS protocol is based on a well-defined conceptualization of pre-K and elementary classroom quality (Table 5.2), one that covers 10 subdimensions within three general dimensions: emotional support, classroom organization, and instructional support. Observers are trained on how to look for and interpret these dimensions and subdimensions, and they do so in carefully and explicitly prescribed time units that alternate between observation and recording. The CLASS protocol involves a lot of work and coordination, but it is not confusing. Rather, observers

> **As the population has become increasingly diverse, both researchers and funders of research have become more willing to reexamine fundamental assumptions related to conducting cross-cultural research.**

evaluations of commonly used instruments because of their entrenched popularity and because of limited funding streams for this research to improve health and social science measures. Popular measures, such as the CES-D, which have been utilized for so long, become part of the fabric of social science research. They are so deeply woven into the repertoire for research in health disparities that no one thinks to question them.

Based on the findings of this study, what is your assessment of the CES-D in terms of reliability and validity?

In answering this question, I think it's important to emphasize that the CES-D does not provide a diagnosis of depression. Instead, it is intended to indicate the prevalence of symptoms of depression. It is also important to consider the type of study to be conducted; in this case, a study of adolescents. Based on our results, the 20-item CES-D is not likely to produce consistent results across youth from diverse groups. Asian American youth will respond to some items in quite a different way from Hispanic youth, and these measurement differences will be reflected in statistical results and undermine their validity. Within a particular population group (for example, first-generation Hispanic youth), the CES-D can provide reliable measures, but the mixture of effect and cause indicators (that is, sometimes symptoms are signs of depression or outcomes of it) in the CES-D undermines its validity even in studies of particular population groups.

What are the lessons to be learned from this study in terms of creating new measures and using old measures?

As researchers, we are always building upon the work of our predecessors. Sometimes to move forward with greater confidence and alacrity, we must reexamine our foundations. Many well-regarded and frequently utilized measures were developed in an age where an understanding of cross-cultural differences was in its infancy. Thus, it is essential that we revisit these instruments and develop new ones that will be more appropriate for cross-cultural or cross-ethnic comparisons.

See: Perreira, Deeb-Sossa, Harris, & Bollen, 2005

have a clear plan for what they need to do that is based on the underlying theory of classroom processes.

Let's look at another construct that is studied extensively by social scientists: educational attainment. An individual's educational attainment is a primary component of the *status attainment process*—how individuals enter into and secure a position in the nation's class hierarchy. Parents' educational attainment is a crucial measure of the advantages on which children can draw to get ahead in life (Attewell & Lavin,

TABLE 5.2 Conceptualization of Classroom Quality

Concept	General Dimensions	Subdimensions
Classroom quality	Emotional support	Positive climate
		Negative climate
		Teacher sensitivity
		Regard for student perspectives
	Classroom organization	Behavior management
		Productivity
		Instructional learning formats
	Instructional support	Concept development
		Quality of feedback
		Language modeling

Source: From the Classroom Assessment Scoring System (CLASS); see Pianta et al., 2007.

2007; Goldin & Katz, 2008). Educational attainment can be measured in many different ways: years of schooling, degrees obtained, or some marker of quality, such as selectivity of the schools attended or achievement outcomes. Because educational attainment can be measured in so many different ways, a clear conceptualization of what educational attainment entails for any given project is important. In studies of the link between educational attainment and health, what matters is exposure to the educational system, and so years of schooling is a reliable measure (Mirowsky & Ross, 2003a). When looking at labor market outcomes (what education buys you), degree status is important, because two people with the same number of years of education have different work prospects if one graduated from college and one did not (Goldin & Katz, 2008).

In sum: Conceptualization that is both thorough and sound will generally point to the most reliable operationalization.

Precision in Design

precision A quality of measurement referring to how detailed and specific it is.

Precision is a key element of measurement that supports reliability. The more detailed and precise the measures are, the more reliable they tend to be. Again, the key is leaving little room for error. The CLASS and HOME protocols are highly precise; they cover a wide range of potential events that can be observed in classrooms or homes, and they give observers systematic guidance on how to categorize those events. The HOME is broken up into numerous dimensions (for example, cognitive stimulation), which, in turn, are broken up into numerous components (presence of play materials, parental involvement, and variety of stimulation available). As a result, observers conducting the HOME are not tasked with making some generic summary judgment of the home environment. Instead, they break up this broad construct into smaller and smaller pieces so that they can make more focused assessments and then combine the information to arrive at a final assessment. This precision helps ensure higher levels of reliability among many different observers in a variety of settings.

Parent education is a good example of the importance of precision in survey methodology. In general, the more categories, the better. Consider a common measure of educational attainment, which includes categories for less than high school diploma, high school diploma, some college, college degree, some postgraduate education, and postgraduate degree. This categorical scheme seems fairly precise, and it is. Still, it could be even more precise. Might someone who went to trade school after high school be confused about which box to choose? Does attending a trade school count as "some college" or would it be more accurate to choose "high school diploma"? Any such confusion is a threat to reliability, because different people may respond to that confusion in different ways.

Another straightforward way to increase precision is to use multiple indicators to measure any one construct. For example, "child mental-health problems" represents a very broad construct, so broad that any single piece of information is unlikely to reliably identify it. The more information that can be gathered, the more researchers can agree on what mental-health problems look like and which children suffer from them. The Child Behavior Checklist (CBCL) is a survey instrument used to assess different kinds of mental-health problems in young children (Achenbach, 1991). One of the most common problems that the CBCL is used to identify is the degree to which children appear to internalize emotional distress (suppressing it and keeping it inside). Because different children may internalize distress in different ways, inclusion of a large number of symptoms is important. The CBCL, therefore, gives internalizing scores to children on the basis of parent, teacher, or other adult observations of 32 different symptoms of withdrawal (for example, child would rather be alone), somatic issues (child has aches and pains), and anxiety (child appears to fear that something bad will happen). These 32 data points provide a breadth of coverage that allows researchers to identify a problem that can look very different depending on the child and the setting.

One reason why the CBCL, HOME, and CLASS are used so often is that they have been *vetted*, or carefully examined by experts. They are *established measures*. Past research has demonstrated the reliability of these measures, so current researchers can use them with some confidence that data are being collected or something is being measured in a dependable way.

Testing Robustness

Clear and precise conceptualization is perhaps the best way to improve reliability in data collection and measurement, regardless of the method used. Another strategy to improve reliability is to assess **robustness**; that is, how well the operational protocol is working. This strategy aims to gauge the robustness of some operational approach in the early stages of a study so that the researchers can address any reliability problems before the study is fully under way.

The **split-half method** is appropriate when dealing with a measure consisting of multiple items, as in the CBCL and CES-D. The researcher randomly splits the set of items for a measure into two sets to create two separate measures instead of one. These

robustness A quality of an operational protocol referring to how well it works.

split-half method A method of testing robustness in which the similarity of results is assessed after administering one subset of an item to a sample and then another subset.

two measures are then tested in a sample of individuals—the *same* people respond to each of the items in the first measure and then respond to each of the items in the second. Comparing how the same people respond to the two measures gives some idea of how reliable the overall measure would be. A reliable measure would mean that the average scores for each measure were similar.

We can go back to the CES-D as an example. Recall that it has 20 items all tapping into what are supposed to be symptoms of depression. A researcher can divide these 20 items into two sets of 10, gather a sample of people to respond to the items in each of the two measures, and then compare how the people responded to each measure. If the overall CES-D is reliable, then the two measures will produce similar scores. Even though the two measures contain different items, they are both measuring symptoms of depression (see Makambi et al., 2009, for an example). A split-half coefficient then gauges how reliable the overall CES-D measure is by demonstrating how consistently people respond to a set of items about depressive symptoms, no matter which depressive symptoms are included.

There are other variations on the split-half method. An alternative to splitting the measures in two and then administering them to the same sample is splitting the sample in two and administering the same measure to each one. As an illustration, consider the two ways that we might evaluate the reliability of a test that includes 30 vocabulary words from the SAT. One approach would be to randomly have everyone in the class take a test with the 15 even-numbered items and then take another test with the 15 odd-numbered items. If the test is a reliable assessment, the people in the class will tend to score the same on the test with the even-numbered items as they do on the test with the odd-numbered items. Another approach would be to randomly assign everyone in the class to two separate groups and then have each group take the same test with the full 30 items. If the test is a reliable assessment, the two groups will score very similarly when taking the same test.

test-retest method A method of testing robustness in which the similarity of results is assessed after administering a measure to the same sample at two different times.

An approach similar to the split-half method is the **test-retest method**, in which the same measure is administered to a sample and then re-administered to the same sample later. Again, survey items provide a good example of how this method works. Consider an assessment in which parents are asked about the involvement in their children's school activities in the past year. The full set of items on this assessment could be administered to a group of parents at one time point and then again a few weeks later. Presumably, because the questions ask the parents about the past year, the respondents should report very similar responses to the items across the two time points. If they do, then that survey measure could be deemed reliable.

One problem with the test-retest method is that other factors, such as recent changes in their children's academic progress, could change parents' responses in ways that have nothing to do with reliability per se. Perhaps a decrease in academic performance between the two time points causes parents to get more involved at school, creating a difference in their responses to the measurement that is unrelated to reliability. Despite such limitations, the test-retest method is a common way to assess reliability and revise a measurement strategy accordingly. This method can reveal some surprising results when applied to seemingly straightforward measures that are considered highly reliable. For example, an analysis of responses in a widely used national study revealed that young people's responses to questions about their race—whether they reported being white or black—frequently changed from year to year (Penner & Saperstein, 2008). Race would seem to be a stable characteristic, but the test-retest method revealed that the race measure was not very reliable!

Lastly, **pilot testing** involves administering some version of a measurement protocol (a survey, an experiment, an interview) to a small preliminary sample of subjects as a means of assessing how well the measure works and whether it presents any problems that need to be fixed. After the pilot test, researchers can make any necessary corrections before "officially" administering the measure to a large sample.

Researchers often pilot test a survey with a small preliminary sample of subjects before embarking on a large-scale research project.

Pilot testing is a key feature of many large-scale data collections. Let's say that we are planning to do a national data collection in which we interview, face to face, 10,000 Americans about their educational experiences and health behaviors. Before expending the tremendous amounts of time and money involved in such an enterprise, we want to make very sure that our measures of core constructs are reliable. As a first step, we might convene a random sample of 100 Americans to test out the measures we plan to use so that we can get all the bugs out. When large-scale projects are proposed to the National Institutes of Health for funding, the proposal includes a section on preliminary studies in which researchers describe the pilot testing they have done to ensure reliability.

pilot testing The process of administering some measurement protocol to a small preliminary sample of subjects as a means of assessing how well the measure works.

Reliability and the Possibility of Error

Improving reliability can certainly improve the accuracy of measurement, but reliability and accuracy do not overlap completely. They are not equivalent. Reliability is a goal in its own right because it is fundamental to good comparison. Any measurement involves some error. That error might be *random*; for example, there will always be some people who do not understand a certain item in ways that are hard to predict. Error could also be *systematic*; for example, some interview or test item might be consistently biased against certain cultural groups, a charge often leveled at the SAT. The point is to be aware of the possibility of error, to aim to minimize it, and to be honest and clear about it so that sound comparisons can be made from the results.

CONCEPT CHECKS

1 The term *reliability* is used in different ways. What are the differences and similarities between the reliability of an experimental method and the internal reliability of a composite variable?

2 In terms of measurement, what does *precision* mean and how can it be increased?

3 What is the basic principle underlying the split-half and test-retest methods? Which method would you prefer to use and why?

VALIDITY

To many researchers, validity is the most important assessment. We want to know how close our method is getting to the truth. Of course, this goal is very ambitious, because truth and objective reality can be quite slippery at times—a core tenet of sociology is the social construction of shared reality. For this reason, validity is much harder to assess than reliability. There is no statistical tool for measuring validity according to some quantitative standard—no Cronbach's alpha. In addition, there are no set standards or conventions for assessing validity. Nonetheless, we can discuss the kinds of validity that scientists consider when trying to gauge the validity of their research.

Internal Validity

internal validity of a study The degree to which a study establishes a causal effect of the independent variable on the dependent variable.

internal validity of a measure The degree to which a measure truly and accurately measures the defined concepts.

face validity A dimension of validity concerning whether a measure looks valid.

Like reliability, validity is a term that is most often used in quantitative research. Shortly, we will get to the issue of external validity, which refers to how generalizable the results of a study are, but we start with internal validity. There are two ways to think about internal validity. The first, **internal validity of a study**, refers to the degree to which a study establishes a causal effect of the independent variable on the dependent variable. As you will read about in Chapter 8, experimental designs tend to be the most internally valid method, as their primary advantage over other methods is that they can establish causality.

Our focus here is on internal validity related to measurement. **Internal validity of a measure** refers to the degree to which a measure truly and accurately measures the defined concepts. This kind of internal validity is highest when conceptualization is strongly linked to operationalization. Table 5.3 provides an overview of various dimensions of internal validity of measurement. We discuss each dimension in turn.

The most basic and simple dimension of internal validity is **face validity**: literally, whether something looks valid on the face of it. What is its face value? Does it look right and sound right? Mental-health problems, including depression, are commonly conceptualized in terms of moods and feelings, and so a survey that asks respondents to report on their moods and feelings seems right, and one that does not include such items seems wrong. A home-based observational protocol of the quality of a home environment that involves parents and children has face validity, whereas a teacher assessment of the quality of a home environment does not. Face validity is the first, and most shallow, assessment of validity that a researcher can make. It works best when it leads to more rigorous assessments of more complex dimensions of validity.

criterion-related validity A dimension of validity concerning how closely a measure is associated with some other factor.

concurrent validity A dimension of validity concerning how strongly a measure correlates with some preexisting measure of the construct that has already been deemed valid.

Criterion-related validity assesses the validity of a measure according to how closely it is associated with some other factor. Essentially, we gain confidence in the validity of a measure when it is related to things to which it is supposed to be related and when it is unrelated to things to which it should not be related. A temperature gauge would seem to be invalid if people started wearing heavy coats when readings on the gauge are high; it would seem more valid if people instead started wearing T-shirts when readings on the gauge are high.

Criterion-related validity can be broken down into two different but closely connected subsets: concurrent validity and predictive validity. A measure with **concurrent validity** will correlate strongly with some preexisting measure of the

TABLE 5.3 Dimensions of Internal Validity of Measures

Dimension		Key Question
Face		Does it seem appropriate and sensible?
Criterion	Concurrent	Does it correlate with a well-established measure of the same concept?
	Predictive	Does it correlate with a measure that it should predict?
Content		Does it cover all of the different meanings of a concept?
Construct		Do the items in a measure connect to the underlying concept?

construct that has already been deemed valid. For example, if you were to develop a new system for evaluating a home's level of cognitive stimulation for children, you would definitely want it to correlate at a high level with the cognitive-stimulation component of the widely used HOME protocol. If it doesn't, you will need to go back to the drawing board because your measure is most likely not tapping what you want it to tap. In other words, the operationalization needs to be reworked to better capture the conceptualization.

When a measure has **predictive validity**, it will correlate strongly with a measure that it should predict. If the concept in question is supposed to cause some event to happen, then a measure of that concept should be correlated with a measure of that event. Your new measure of cognitive stimulation in the home should predict higher scores on children's achievement tests. If it does not, your measure has a problem. To achieve both concurrent and predictive validity, you need to assess whether your measure or method is behaving, or producing results, as it should and is therefore accurately tapping into the concept that you want to capture.

Content validity is all about coverage, or how well a measure is encompassing the many different meanings of a single concept. Does the measure represent all of the facets of the concept? A multidimensional concept is a major challenge to valid measurement. A measure may capture one or several dimensions well but not tap into all dimensions and, therefore, be less valid than one that captures all dimensions.

The assessment of classroom quality is a good example for illustrating content validity. Typically, conceptualizations of classroom (and school) quality focus on academic dimensions—how academically challenging the classroom is, or the extent to which cognitive and academic skills are being actively and effectively developed. Yet, especially when dealing with elementary schools, classroom quality cannot be conceptualized solely in terms of academic dimensions (a similar point about school quality was made in Chapter 4). The overall sense of socioemotional supportiveness is also a key factor in conceptualizations of what makes a classroom good or bad (Crosnoe et al., 2010). A measure of classroom quality that focuses only on academic dimensions or socioemotional dimensions, therefore, would be less valid than one that combines both. The CLASS observational protocol integrates assessments of socioemotional climate, classroom organization, and instructional activity (refer

predictive validity A dimension of validity concerning how strongly a measure correlates with a measure that it should predict.

content validity A dimension of validity concerning how well a measure encompasses the many different meanings of a single concept.

construct validity A dimension of validity concerning how well multiple indicators are connected to some underlying factor.

back to Table 5.2), which increases its validity. It covers all of the dimensions equally (Pianta et al., 2007).

A final standard of internal validity, **construct validity**, refers to how well multiple indicators are connected to some underlying factor. This type of validity is important because some phenomena are not directly observable and can only be identified by cataloging their observable symptoms. If a patient has a brain tumor, the doctor can look at a brain image and point directly to the tumor. If a patient is an alcoholic, the doctor cannot point to a single concrete thing that indicates alcoholism. That is because alcoholism is a psychological, behavioral, and physical disorder that is characterized by a diverse array of symptoms. You can only see the symptoms, and, at some point, you can say that those symptoms add up to alcoholism.

Let's say that we want to create a measure for alcoholism. We would likely create multiple items capturing different observable symptoms of alcoholism and then combine them. Trouble quitting drinking might be one, and physical discomfort from withdrawal would be another. We could probably come up with dozens. These items would be single, concrete hypothesized symptoms of the underlying condition of alcoholism that we cannot see or measure directly as a whole but only in parts (in this case, the symptoms). If our proposed measure of alcoholism is high in construct validity, then all of the items will correlate with a marker of alcoholism if there were indeed some way to measure it directly. Various statistical procedures test construct validity by determining how well the items correlate. The "Conversations from the Front Lines" feature earlier in the chapter, which focuses on the measurement of depression across racial/ethnic groups, offers a good example of construct validity and how it is assessed.

External Validity

external validity A dimension of validity concerning the degree to which the results of a study can generalize beyond the study.

Another type of validity worth considering is **external validity**, or the degree to which the results of a study can generalize beyond the study. It involves two basic questions.

1. *How representative is the group being studied?* If only men are included in a survey-based study on the effects of mental health on parenting behavior, then the experiment would seem to be low in external validity. We cannot be sure whether the results are about parenting or about fathering. If we are interested in the effects of parenting, then the focus on fathers is likely to be problematic—we will have a hard time convincing others that the results of our experiment are generalizable. If an ethnographic study of black schooling experiences focused only on the experiences of low-income children, then the external validity would be low because the study excluded middle-class or affluent black children. Narrowing the goals of each study—informing understanding of fathers rather than parents, of low-income black children rather than black children more generally—would increase external validity.

2. *How "real" is the study?* This question is most commonly asked about experiments, which tend to maximize the internal validity of the study (establishing cause and effect) but are vulnerable to issues of external validity. Because recruiting people to come into labs is difficult, due in part to the time commitment involved, experiments typically do not have the large samples often used in survey research. Thus, finding a representative sample is challenging. At

the same time, some experiments might seem contrived to subjects—would people act in the lab the same way that they do in the real world? People might be self-conscious knowing that they are being observed or simply think that the whole situation seems artificial. In these cases, experiments lose external validity because we do not know if the same results would emerge outside the lab.

As an old saying among social scientists goes, "Can you really simulate war in a laboratory?" If the subjects separate what they are doing in the experiment from "real life," then the results of the experiment—which we hope to generalize to real life—may be misleading. The "From the Field to the Front Page" feature, which focuses on experimental tests of obedience and conformity, captures the issue of external validity.

Worth stressing here is that experiments are not the only method vulnerable to questions of external validity. For example, surveys often include **vignettes**—hypothetical situations that people are asked to put themselves in or consider other people in—and then ask questions about how they would respond. A vignette might involve imagining yourself in a violent marriage in which you are abused and then ask questions about what you would do in that situation. The degree to which you can realistically consider that possibility could affect how you respond to the question and, therefore, affect the conclusions that the researchers might glean from the survey. As another example, people in ethnographic studies might be affected by the very act of being observed so that they behave differently in the study than they would in real life.

Of these two issues related to external validity, the first (representativeness) is easier to address than the second (reality). Scientists can take specific, concrete steps to ensure that the participants are representative of the population being studied. Questions about the reality of studies are much more challenging. Within the realm of ethical treatment, there is likely no experiment or study that is as real as real life, and, therefore, we always give up some external validity when we conduct research, experimental or not. The key is to be critical and honest about this issue when designing the study (for example, by debriefing subjects afterward about their experiences) and when reporting the results.

Linking Internal and External Validity

At this point, you might be wondering about the connection between internal and external validity as well as how exactly they differ. We use an example of an experiment testing the link between having a verbally abusive boss and work stress to illustrate both internal and external validity.

In the experiment, the **manipulation** (what you "do" to the subjects) is exposure to a violent boss. We measure it by bringing subjects from an undergraduate research methods class into the lab, randomly splitting them into an experimental group and a control group. We have the experimental group work on a project with a team leader who is verbally abusive; the control group has a team leader who is impersonal but professional. Afterward, we measure the outcome using a short survey with nine questions aimed at capturing workplace stress, such as "How upset are you while working?" "How difficult is it to cope with problems while working?" We take the responses on these nine items (measured on a five-point scale), average them, and compare scores across the two groups. The results show that the level of work stress was higher in the experimental group than in the control group. Because people were randomly assigned

vignette A short description of characters or situations that is presented to respondents in order to elicit a response.

manipulation Something that is done to some subjects of an experiment but not others so that the outcomes of the two groups can be compared.

MILGRAM IN THE AGE OF REALITY TV

In 2010, a French documentary titled *The Game of Death* sparked outrage for reimagining a famous psychological experiment as a reality TV show. In the documentary, unwitting participants are led to believe that they are contestants on a game show pilot titled *The Xtreme Zone*—complete with famous host and live audience. Participants are directed to deliver electric shocks to an actor posing as a fellow contestant when he answers their questions incorrectly. By repackaging an infamous study from the 1960s, the documentary renewed debates about the ethics of social research in general and, more specifically, about human beings' tendency to underestimate their own susceptibility to social influence. For social scientists, the film also provides a useful starting point for a discussion of validity.

First, let's go back to 1960 and the original Milgram experiment. Subjects thought that they were participating in a study about learning. They were assigned to be teachers, and the learners were all *confederates*, meaning they knew the study's real purpose and were following a script. The teachers were instructed to give increasingly powerful electric shocks to the learners every time the latter answered a question incorrectly. No one was really being shocked, but the teachers didn't know that. Fully 65 percent of the teachers went all the way to the highest shock level, despite the (fake) screams of the learners. Occasionally, teachers resisted or showed reluctance, but after a scientist in a white lab coat told them to continue, they generally continued administering the shocks.

Second, let's return to the present day. Subjects have signed up to be contestants on a reality TV program. The setup was essentially the same as the Milgram experiment, except that everything was done in front of a live audience. The authority figure was a TV host, not a scientist in a white coat. The purpose was not to make sense of how people can do things they find repugnant simply because they are following orders. Instead, it was to examine the degree to which television and the possibility of fame can erode free will. This time around, the rate of people going all the way to the extreme (delivering the greatest shock to the learner/contestant) was even higher than in the Milgram experiment: 81%.

Although the issues of free will, conformity, and obedience are interesting in their own right, we can also move beyond the substantive findings of this film/social science hybrid to consider how it relates to the evaluative standards discussed in this chapter. How well does *The Xtreme Zone* hold up to an analysis of its method, ethical concerns notwithstanding? The methods in question seem to be reliable in that they turned up consistent results despite the different circumstances between the laboratory experiment and the

A participant in the original Milgram study helps apply fake electrodes to the confederate learner.

fake TV show. They also seem to be internally valid in that they appear to represent a good match between conceptualization and operationalization. They certainly pass the face validity test.

More open to debate is the external validity of the exercise, whether in the lab or on TV. One component of external validity is generalizability—how well the results apply in the real world. In Milgram's study, the subjects were fairly homogenous in terms of race/ethnicity. Moreover, they were drawn from areas around Yale University, suggesting that the subjects could have been slightly more attuned to the authority of Yale personnel and more likely to go along with their orders. For *The Xtreme Zone,* all the subjects signed up to be on a reality show. That is a specific group, certainly not representative of the general public. Perhaps they might have been more likely to go along with just about anything as long as they were on TV. Selecting a random sample with no knowledge of the study's official or unofficial aims is ideal.

Another component of external validity is how "real" the study is. On some level, the participants in the Yale study had to know that they would not have been allowed to kill people, and the same is true for the TV game show. Murder and torture are against the law, and they certainly would not be televised! If these exercises had happened in more natural settings without being sanctioned by a university or a film crew, the results might have been very different.

As this update of classic social science attests, external validity is difficult to assess and address. Coming up with concrete remedies for threats to external validity is a challenge. How do you make something more real? Can a study ever truly be real, or is some artificiality always involved? These challenges get at a theme of this chapter and of social science research in general: There is no perfect approach, and there are always unknowns.

to the two groups, meaning assignments were based on chance and everyone had an equal chance of being in either the experimental group or the control group, any differences in their outcomes should be attributable to the treatment.

This experiment seems to capture a causal effect. In that way, the study has internal validity overall. Yet, the internal validity of the measurement needs a closer look. Our critics wonder how valid our measure of work stress is. We respond by saying that the items certainly appear to be capturing stress (face validity), and there are nine items that tap different symptoms, which means we have broad coverage of the concept of stress (content validity). Further, we show that the measure is highly correlated with reports of wanting to resign, which is an established correlate of workplace stress in other studies and, therefore, evidence of predictive validity.

We seem to have a good case, but our critics take us down in three ways. First, they run a new study in which they administer the measure to a new group of subjects and also collect cortisol samples from them. Cortisol is the stress hormone, so elevated levels are a physical sign that someone is under stress, including workplace stress (see Almeida et al., 2016). Lo and behold, there is no difference in cortisol levels between people who score high on the measure and people who score low on our measure. It has low construct validity.

Second, the critics argue that there is no way that having a hypothetical team leader be verbally abusive to someone in a short lab activity could successfully re-create the experience of having an abusive boss at work (especially given that ethics prevented us from having the team leaders be *really* abusive), suggesting that external validity is low.

Third, the critics point out that a group of 18- and 19-year-old college students might not be the best sample with which to study workplace dynamics, another problem with external validity.

Thus, our experiment had some good qualities, but it ultimately was weaker than we had hoped in terms of internal and external validity. That does not mean the experiment was worthless. After all, it put forward a possible association that future studies can examine in a more rigorous way. It is a step in the process, and future studies will improve on it.

Statistical Validity

A third type of validity, statistical validity, also should be discussed before closing this chapter. A major consideration in quantitative research, **statistical validity** refers to the degree to which a study's statistical operations are in line with basic statistical laws and guidelines. Assessments of statistical validity encompass many different dimensions, including questions about whether the right operational definitions were used, whether the methods designed and implemented truly follow from operational definitions, and whether the methods have been properly applied.

Ordinary least squares (OLS) regression is one of the most common statistical procedures used by social scientists to evaluate the associations between variables. The OLS technique estimates how well changes in the independent variable predict changes in the dependent variable. If educational attainment (the independent variable) has a coefficient of −0.50 in an equation with depression as the dependent variable,

statistical validity A dimension of validity concerning the degree to which a study's statistical operations are in line with basic statistical laws and guidelines.

ordinary least squares (OLS) regression A statistical procedure that estimates how well changes in the independent variable predict changes in the dependent variable.

FIGURE 5.3 Illustration of a Bell Curve

A normal distribution takes the shape of a bell curve, with most values in the middle and a few values at the ends.

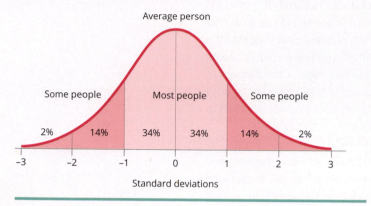

normal distribution The random distribution of values in a bell-shaped curve.

then we can conclude that every year of schooling a person has relative to others is associated with a half-point decrease on the depression scale. Many of the research findings that are reported in the media, journals, and textbooks are based on OLS regression (Gordon, 2010).

Although OLS results are straightforward, this statistical method is based on a number of assumptions that lower statistical validity. OLS assumes a **normal distribution**, meaning that values in a sample follow the familiar bell curve pattern in which most people will score in the middle with few people scoring at the low or high ends (Figure 5.3).

In the example of educational attainment and depression, the assumption of a normal distribution is problematic because depression rarely is normally distributed in a sample. Most people have few symptoms, and only a small number of people will have many symptoms. Thus, cases will be bunched up on the low end of the distribution rather than in the middle.

Ordinary least squares also assumes that cases are "independent" from one another, meaning that they represent random drawings from the population. In practice, this assumption frequently does not hold because of the need to sample within specific units of social life. For example, many national studies of children and adolescents are school based. They target a random sample of schools and then take a random sample of students within each school. This practice greatly eases many of the logistical barriers to large-scale data collection, but it also violates assumptions of independence. Why? Two youth randomly selected from the same school in the same community are very likely to be more similar to each other than two youth randomly sampled from the population at large. Fortunately, statistical procedures are available to offset many threats to statistical validity.

CONCEPT CHECKS

1 A scientist comes up with a ranking of the best high school algebra classes in your school district based on one criterion for assessing classroom success: the proportion of students in the class who get A's on their final exam. How would you assess this measurement approach in terms of face validity and content validity?

2 If you create a measure of physical attractiveness, how would you try to assess its criterion-related validity? What criteria would you use for assessments of both concurrent and predictive validity?

3 Consider an experiment on the effects of physical attractiveness on success in getting dates. In what ways could you design this experiment to increase external validity?

CONCLUSION

Reliability and validity are two of the main criteria for evaluating research methods. Reliability is concerned with dependability and consistency of measurement, and validity is concerned with the truth and accuracy of measurement. These criteria are often discussed separately, but they are not mutually exclusive. Indeed, the best measures are both reliable and valid, meaning that the definition of a variable and how it is measured are strongly linked to each other. Of course, sometimes researchers have trouble measuring variables in ways that are both reliable and valid and have to make trade-offs. They might have to give up some reliability to achieve validity, or vice versa. The important thing to remember is that researchers have to consider both when designing studies and that the consumers of their studies need to think about both to evaluate the conceptualization and operationalization of them.

Summary

Validity and reliability are standards that social researchers use to assess the link between the definition of a variable and its measurement. These standards help ensure that variables are measured in ways that are effective for gaining knowledge about the social world.

Thinking about Reliability and Validity: Measuring and Tracking Poverty

- Problems with the FPL lead to an undercount of the poor. The supplemental poverty line corrects many of these issues, but it also poses new challenges that underscore the give-and-take researchers often face when trying to maximize validity and reliability.

- Reliability refers to an operational definition's ability to yield consistent results, while validity is an assessment of how accurately an operational definition captures something "real." Researchers aim to maximize both of these standards in their measures.

- Reliability and validity do not necessarily go hand-in-hand. A measure can be reliable but not valid, or vice versa.

Reliability

- Statistical tests can help researchers assess the reliability of their measures. Cronbach's alpha is a statistic that measures the internal reliability of a composite variable, or the degree to which the items that make up a composite variable lead to a consistent response. When multiple researchers are responsible for collecting data for a study, intercoder reliability refers to the consistency of the coders' observations.

- An effective way to ensure reliability is to develop precise conceptualizations of the phenomena being studied. Researchers can increase precision by using multiple indicators to measure a single construct. Researchers may also choose to use established measures of their concepts to maximize reliability.

- Researchers can assess their operational protocol early in a study to address any issues going forward. The split-half method, test-retest method, and pilot tests are all ways to test the robustness of a measure.

- A reliable measure is not necessarily an accurate measure. Both random and systematic errors are still possible in studies with reliable measures.

Validity

- Because validity is about capturing the truth, it's much harder to assess than reliability.

- Internal validity is a concept that can refer to both studies and measures. The internal validity of a study refers to the extent to which a study establishes a causal effect of an independent variable on a dependent variable. The internal validity of a measure refers to the degree to which a measure accurately captures a real-world concept.

- Internal validity has many dimensions, including face validity, criterion-related validity, content validity, and construct validity (Table 5.3).

- External validity is the extent to which the results of a study can be generalized, or applied, beyond the study. Considerations of external validity should include how representative the group being studied is in relation to the population of interest and how well the behavior of research subjects during the study reflects behavior in the real world.

- Statistical validity compares a study's statistical procedures to basic statistical guidelines and laws. OLS regression, a common statistical method used to evaluate associations between variables, is based on assumptions that lower statistical validity. For example, OLS assumes a normal distribution and that cases are "independent" of one another.

Key Terms

composite variable, **137**

concurrent validity, **146**

construct validity, **148**

content validity, **147**

criterion-related validity, **146**

Cronbach's alpha (α), **137**

external validity, **148**

face validity, **146**

intercoder reliability, **138**

internal reliability, **137**

internal validity of a measure, **146**

internal validity of a study, **146**

manipulation, **149**

normal distribution, **152**

ordinary least squares (OLS) regression, **151**

pilot testing, **145**

precision, **142**

predictive validity, **147**

reliability, **135**

robustness, **143**

split-half method, **143**

statistical validity, **151**

test-retest method, **144**

validity, **135**

vignette, **149**

Exercise

In the twenty-first century, much attention has been paid to what is widely perceived as a growing and solidifying partisan divide between conservatives and liberals in the United States. Discussion of this divide in the mass media gives the impression that Americans fall squarely into one of two camps with little to no overlap between the two. Yet, political ideology is best thought of as a continuum from the most purely conservative to the most liberal, with most Americans falling somewhere in between. To plan a research study in which your goal is to assess the average American's score on the conservative-liberal continuum (and think about reliability in the process), come up with a set of five questions to determine how conservative or liberal respondents are. For example, you could ask: "Should the government play an active role in reducing racial/ethnic differences in income?" Responses should be on a Likert scale (a scale of agreement with attitudes); for example, strongly disagree, disagree, neither disagree nor agree, agree, strongly agree.

- Administer this five-question scale to 10 different people. Try to get a diverse sample when doing so.
- Hypothetically, your scale has a Cronbach's alpha of 0.8. What does that mean? What if it were 0.4?
- Tinker with your scale by dropping some items. Can you improve the internal reliability score?

When deciding what or whom to study—a process known as sampling—it is important for researchers to be strategic and methodical.

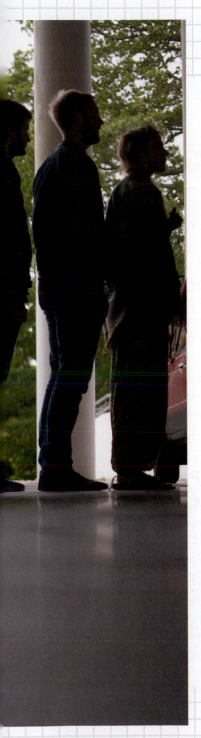

SAMPLING STRATEGIES

Try entering the phrase "percent of Americans" into Google. Here are some of the first hits you might see:

- "62 *percent of Americans* say the country is headed in the wrong direction."
- "33 *percent of Americans* are overweight and an additional 34 percent are obese."
- "70 *percent of Americans* oppose new energy taxes."
- "13.2 *percent of Americans* live at or below the poverty line."
- "32 *percent of Americans* describe themselves as 'extremely patriotic.'"

The authors of this book all live in the United States, and nobody asked us if we think the country is headed in the wrong direction. Did anyone ask you? How can a news story say that 62% of Americans think the country is headed in the wrong direction without asking all of our opinions?

All of these numbers are based on polls in which less than a thousand people were interviewed. There are roughly 320 million adults in the United States today. Can a pollster accurately summarize the opinions of 320 million people by talking to fewer than a thousand of them?

The answer is yes, if "accuracy" means getting answers that are within a few percentage points of what we would learn if we asked every adult in the United States. However, interviewing a **sample**, or subset, of all Americans will yield accurate results only if we use an appropriate method of selecting people to contact. If we use an inappropriate method, we can ask millions of people and get dramatically misleading results.

Sampling is the process of deciding what or whom to observe when we cannot observe and analyze everything or everyone we want to. The most important point about sampling is this: *When we cannot observe everything, being strategic and methodical about what we observe is better than simply collecting the most information we can.*

In this chapter, we will see that the best sampling strategy depends on the research question and available resources, including money, time, and personnel. In the most common case, researchers are trying to describe some feature of a population, such as the percentage of Americans who support the legalization of marijuana or live below the poverty line. Researchers use a range of strategies for ensuring that their estimates are as accurate as possible. Most sampling strategies involve randomly selecting people from a population to participate in a study. However, for some research questions and some methodologies, drawing a representative sample—that is, a sample that most accurately mirrors the overall population—may be counterproductive. As we will see, it is sometimes better to collect in-depth information about a few cases—or even only one case—rather than less detailed information about a larger number of cases.

USING SAMPLES TO DESCRIBE POPULATIONS

When you were young, your parents or teachers may have tried to change your behavior by telling you cautionary tales about the mistakes they made in their younger years. The counterpart for students of sampling is the infamous *Literary Digest* poll of 1936.

A Cautionary Tale: The *Literary Digest* Poll

Literary Digest was one of the most popular magazines of its day, and in 1920 it began a feature in which it sent postcards to a sample of Americans asking whom they planned to vote for in the presidential election later that year. At the time, there were no national polling organizations, and the results of the *Literary Digest* poll were eagerly received, partly because the poll had correctly predicted who would be elected president in 1920 (Warren Harding), 1924 (Calvin Coolidge), 1928 (Herbert Hoover), and 1932 (Franklin D. Roosevelt).

sample A subset of a population selected for a study.

sampling The process of deciding what or whom to observe when you cannot observe and analyze everything or everyone.

The 1936 election pitted incumbent president Franklin D. Roosevelt against Kansas governor Alf Landon. By then, the poll was a lucrative venture for *Literary Digest*, so the magazine conducted its most ambitious poll yet. It sent out 10 million postcards, which at the time was more than a fourth of all registered voters in the United States. More than 2 million postcards were completed and returned.

The *Literary Digest* poll took place long before computers, so you can imagine the effort required to send out all those postcards and count the results. When the data were tallied, the results were clear: Landon was going to be the next president. He received 57% of the votes in the poll, compared to only 43% for Roosevelt.

Then came the actual election. Not only did Roosevelt win; he won with the largest share of the vote of almost any presidential election in history. *Literary Digest* predicted Landon would win 31 states. He won two. The poll had Landon winning California with 52% of the vote; instead, he got 31%. Within 2 years, *Literary Digest* was out of business.

What went wrong? There were two major problems (see Blumenthal, 2010). First, the magazine obtained addresses from lists of people who owned automobiles and telephones, which at that time were still luxuries for many Americans. Roosevelt's support was much stronger among poorer Americans than among wealthier Americans. Second, people who were unhappy with Roosevelt's presidency were likely more motivated to send back their postcards than were people who were satisfied.

As political pollsters do today, *Literary Digest* tried to use a sample of people to predict the political preferences of the entire population. However, the *Literary Digest* pollsters believed that the more people who responded to their survey, the more accurate their estimate would be. We still talk about the *Literary Digest* poll 80 years later because of how spectacularly wrong this assumption is.

More than 10 years after the *Literary Digest* polling debacle, the *Chicago Tribune* incorrectly picked Governor Thomas Dewey of New York to win the 1948 election against incumbent President Harry S. Truman based on data from polls.

Probability Samples and Random Choice

When the goal of sampling is to describe a population, there should be no systematic differences between the people who are selected for the sample and the people who are *not* selected for the sample. A research disaster ensued in the *Literary Digest* poll because the people in the sample were wealthier and more dissatisfied with President Roosevelt than the people not in the sample. Because the pollsters' basic method of sampling people was flawed, getting postcards from 2 million people did them no good.

How do you select a group of people who are the most comparable to the people you do not select? Although we have focused on the *Literary Digest* poll, we will see the same challenge come up in experiments (Chapter 8), where researchers need to divide people into two groups that are as comparable as possible. In both surveys and experiments, the solution is the same: *Choose randomly*. But what exactly does *random* mean?

The type of car someone drives is not random. The last digit of his or her Social Security number is random. You can probably imagine a variety of potential differences between people who drive a Toyota Prius and people who drive a Ford F-150 pickup truck. But there are no systematic differences between people whose Social Security number ends in a 3 versus a 7.

In the same way, when we use random selection to determine the members of our sample, there is no systematic difference between the sample and the population from which it is drawn. Any differences are strictly due to random chance alone. Because statisticians understand random chance very well—after all, the entire casino industry is based on it—we can be very precise about how large these random chances might be and how we can minimize them.

Samples that are based on random selection are called probability samples. More precisely, a **probability sample** is one in which (a) random chance is used to select participants for the sample, and (b) each individual has a probability of being selected that can be calculated. (As we will see, sometimes in probability samples individuals all have the same probability of being selected, but this doesn't have to be the case.) Before we explain why probability samples are desirable when we are trying to describe populations, and how probability sampling is done in practice today, we need to clarify what we mean by *population* and why researchers end up using samples in the first place.

Target Populations, Parameters, and Censuses

A **target population** is a group about which social scientists attempt to make generalizations. For instance, in the case of a poll result about how many American adults support the legalization of marijuana, the target population is all American adults. In a study of binge drinking among first-year students at a particular college or university, the target population is all first-year students at that school.

Target populations do not necessarily refer to groups of individuals. They may refer to groups of nations, corporations, or even written documents or legal cases. As an example of the latter, sociologist Laura Beth Nielsen and her colleagues were interested in understanding which workplace discrimination cases filed with the Equal Employment Opportunity Commission resulted in a judgment in favor of the plaintiff (Nielsen, Nelson, & Lancaster, 2010). They found that one in five plaintiffs in discrimination suits acts as his or her own lawyer, for instance. These people are three times more likely to have their cases dismissed. In this study, the target population was all employment discrimination lawsuits filed in federal court from 1988 to 2003.

Usually, researchers would achieve more precise results if they could study the entire target population instead of sampling it. A **census** is a study that includes data on every member of a population. Censuses are more common in social research when the population in question is not composed of people. For example, sociologist Edwin Amenta and his colleagues were interested in why some social movements received more coverage in the *New York Times* than others. To conduct their study, they searched for mentions of an extensive list of social movement organizations in all the issues of the *New York Times* published in the twentieth century (Amenta et al., 2009).

In the *New York Times* study, researchers found that the AFL-CIO labor union was the most covered social movement organization in the twentieth century, mentioned in

---

probability sample A sample in which (a) random chance is used to select participants for the sample, and (b) each individual has a probability of being selected that can be calculated.

target population A group about which social scientists attempt to make generalizations.

census A study that includes data on every member of a population, as opposed to only a sample.

an average of 41.7 stories annually. That number—41.7 stories per year—is an example of a **population parameter**, a number that characterizes some quantitative aspect of a population. You can think of the population parameter as the "true value" or "true measurement" of some aspect of the population.

Censuses have a great advantage in that they assess population parameters directly. If researchers had used a probability sample of *New York Times* articles from the twentieth century, they still could have estimated how many times the newspaper mentioned the AFL-CIO in an average year. This estimate would probably be close to, but not exactly, 41.7. We could then calculate statistics that allow us to speak precisely about how large the difference might be between the estimate and the correct number. Whenever we use a sample to estimate the characteristics of a target population, there is always uncertainty about how close our estimates come to the parameter. A true census is not plagued by this uncertainty.

Censuses of people are rare because they are often not feasible. Even when they are possible, they often do not offer enough of a practical advantage to be worth the extra cost of data collection compared to a sample. An exorbitant amount of money and an army of interviewers would be required to contact each and every person in the United States. However, a census is possible when researchers can obtain data on populations of individuals without contacting them directly. For example, political scientists often study voting patterns for members of Congress; data are readily available for every member for every vote. By contrast, imagine how difficult it would be to contact all 100 senators and 435 representatives and ask them to accurately report on every vote they have ever made during their term! The rise of "big data" is due in part to social scientists obtaining permission to study public administration records, which can include information on whole populations. For example, by linking data from birth certificates and school records for all children born over an entire decade in Florida, a group of economists found that low birth weight has a negative effect on academic performance (Figlio et al., 2014).

A census is also possible when the list of individuals in the target population is relatively modest and readily obtained. For example, a university conducting a study of first-year students might be able to administer a survey to all freshmen.

In the case of national populations, the only censuses that are based on collecting data directly from individuals are conducted by governments. The U.S. government conducts a census every 10 years, with the goal of compiling very basic demographic and housing information. From a purely social science perspective, it is not clear that conducting a national census is the most effective approach to gathering this information. Despite its considerable expense, the U.S. Census does not succeed in including everyone in the country. Poor people, urban residents, and people who move frequently—and especially the homeless—are often missed or undercounted. For this reason, many social scientists believe that the U.S. Census achieves lower-quality results than it would if it

The U.S. government conducts a census every 10 years. Among other things, data from the census are used to determine the number of congressional districts each state gets.

relied on estimates calculated with a highly sophisticated probability sampling technique. (Legally, this point is moot. In 1999, the U.S. Supreme Court ruled that sampling cannot be used to determine the number of congressional districts each state gets, which is the constitutional reason for conducting the census.)

As this example suggests, even when censuses are possible, samples may still result in better-quality data. Consider the study of employment discrimination cases by Laura Beth Nielsen, mentioned earlier. Some basic, even key, information on all cases is available. However, the researchers were also interested in analyzing more in-depth information that they could collect only by looking at materials from the case. It would have been too costly and time consuming to analyze every case, so the research team focused on a probability sample of cases, allowing them to collect data that would help them answer some of their questions. The benefits of the probability sample were more than enough to offset the uncertainty that is introduced when a sample is used instead of a census.

Advantages of Probability Sampling

As noted earlier, a probability sample is based on random selection: Whether or not individuals are selected for the sample is strictly a matter of chance. To give a simple example, say a sociologist wants to know the prevalence of binge drinking among first-year students at her university. The university has 2,000 first-year students, and the sociologist decides to survey a probability sample of 200 of them. She might use a computer to assign every student a random number, and then select the students with the lowest 200 numbers for the survey. In that case, each student has a 0.1 probability (200 out of 2,000, so 1 in 10) of being selected to participate in the survey, and whether or not they are part of the selected 10% is determined purely by chance.

Let's contrast this example with a **nonprobability sample**. Say that instead of choosing 200 first-year students randomly, the sociologist noticed that 200 first-year students were taking sociology courses. Rather than go to the trouble of collecting a random sample, she simply administers the survey to the 200 first-year sociology students. This type of sample, where a researcher selects the sample that requires the least time or effort, is called a **convenience sample**.

The key issue is representativeness: how well the sample mirrors the population. Would a survey of only first-year sociology students provide an accurate representation of binge drinking among all first-year students? Not if sociology students binge-drink more or less than other students. (You may have your own hypotheses as to whether this may be the case.) Even if we can't think of any reasons why sociology and nonsociology students would differ in their drinking behavior, we cannot be sure that their behavior does *not* differ, which would undermine our confidence in the results.

A probability sample has two key advantages over a nonprobability sample:

1. Estimates based on a probability sample are **unbiased**. That is, to whatever extent estimates differ from the true population parameter, they are equally likely to overestimate it as they are to underestimate it. For example, if sociology students are less likely to binge-drink than other freshmen, a convenience sample of first-year sociology students will systematically underestimate the

nonprobability sample A sample that is not drawn using a method of random selection.

convenience sample A sample that selects observations based on what is cheapest or easiest.

unbiased A sample estimate that is the same as the population parameter except for the difference caused by random chance.

true prevalence of binge drinking among all first-year students. In other words, convenience samples may be systematically nonrepresentative. Probability samples do not have this problem.

2. In a probability sample, the only difference between the estimates and the true parameter is due to chance. This difference is called **sampling error**. When sampling error alone is responsible for differences between sample estimates and population parameters, we can make precise statements about our uncertainty. (We will talk more about uncertainty later in this chapter.)

In contrast, with a nonprobability sample, there may be systematic differences between our sample and the target population. The *Literary Digest* poll was a nonprobability sample because it systematically overrepresented wealthier Americans by relying on automobile and telephone records. This overrepresentation did not occur by chance; it was a **systematic error**, or a flaw built into the design of the study. Typically, in nonprobability samples, we have no way of knowing the size of the bias introduced by systematic error, and so we have no way of speaking precisely about the uncertainty in our estimates.

As we write this, the homepage of one of our favorite news sites features a "Quick Poll" asking readers if they approve of how the president is handling the economy. Would the results of this nonprobability sample accurately estimate the result we would get if we asked every adult in the U.S. population this question? Would the results even accurately estimate the sentiments of the population of people who read this news site?

We can imagine various ways that people who answer these polls may be different from those who do not. For instance, people who are inclined to answer the poll probably have stronger opinions. That means the "Quick Poll" will yield results that are biased by systematic error. And with nonprobability sampling, we have no way of clearly evaluating the size of the difference between the sample estimate and the population parameter.

Margin of Error

Gallup publishes poll results about presidential approval ratings on a daily basis. In March 2017, Gallup reported that "43 percent of American adults approve of the job the president is doing, with a margin of error of 3 percentage points." When a poll is unbiased, the true percentage of presidential approval is equally likely to be greater than 43% as it is to be less than 43%. The **margin of error** allows us to talk about how confident we can be that the true value of the parameter is close to 43%.

The margin of error is often relegated to the fine print or a footnote, if it is reported at all. But it is vital to interpreting results from probability samples and to understanding why probability samples are better than nonprobability samples. To explain why, let's use a computer to simulate an election between a Democratic candidate and a Republican candidate. Let's assume a population of a million people, and the race is exactly tied, with each candidate enjoying exactly 50% support. If we could conduct a complete census of every voting adult, we would find the race to be exactly tied. If we draw a probability sample of people, the estimate will likely not be exactly 50% for each candidate, but we want our estimate to be close.

sampling error The difference between the estimates from a sample and the true parameter that arise due to random chance.

systematic error A flaw built into the design of the study that causes a sample estimate to diverge from the population parameter.

margin of error The amount of uncertainty in an estimate; equal to the distance between the estimate and the boundary of the confidence interval.

FIGURE 6.1 Results from 10,000 Simulated Polls of Size 500 when the True Parameter is 50.0%

Dark red indicates the 50% of all results closest to the true parameter, and dark and light red together indicate the 95% of all results closest to the true parameter. (Each bar in the histogram is two-tenths of a percentage point.)

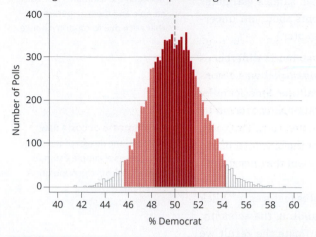

sampling distribution A set of estimates that would be observed from a large number of independent samples that are all the same size and drawn using the same method.

confidence level The probability that a confidence interval includes the population parameter.

confidence interval A range of possible estimates in which researchers can have a specific degree of confidence; includes the population parameter.

To show what happens, let's take 10,000 different samples with 500 people each, all selected purely at random. Figure 6.1 shows a graph of the estimates we get from all these different samples. This is an example of a **sampling distribution**—a set of estimates that would be observed from a large number of independent samples that are all the same size and drawn using the same method. In practice, sampling distributions are only theoretical, because we only have the one sample that we are working with, but the advantage of a simulation is we can draw as many samples as we please.

Two things are noteworthy. First, even though particular samples overestimate or underestimate the true parameter of 50%, the average over all the samples is almost exactly 50%. In other words, the estimates from this properly executed probability sample are unbiased. Second, even though the estimates of those who will vote Democratic range all the way from 43% to more than 56%, smaller errors are more likely than larger errors. In the example shown in Figure 6.1, half of the estimates are between 48.4% and 51.6%, or only 1.6% different from the true parameter of 50%. Ninety-five percent are between 45.6% and 54.4%, or only 4.4% off. Put a different way, if we had conducted only one poll, there is a 95% chance that the sampling error from that poll would be 4.4% or less.

This value of 4.4% that we just generated is the margin of error. That is, when a poll reports a margin of error, we can be 95% confident that the difference between the poll result and the true parameter is no greater than that amount. The "95%" here is called the **confidence level** of our estimate of the margin of error. It does not have to be 95%, but 95% has come to be by far the most common value that is used in practice.

In the case of the Gallup poll of presidential approval, the report of 43% approval with a 3% margin of error means that we can be 95% confident that the true level of presidential approval within the target population is between 40% and 46%. This range implied by the margin of error is sometimes called the **confidence interval**, so one might say that the boundaries of the 95% confidence interval for our estimate of presidential approval are 40% and 46%.

Two things need to be emphasized about margin of error:

1. Margin of error pertains only to sampling error. If a study has systematic error in addition to sampling error, then all bets are off. The techniques we just described tell us nothing about the possible size of systematic error. Because we have no way of ruling out systematic error in a nonprobability sample, margin of error applies only to probability samples.

   Remember: In real life, we don't know the population parameter—this is why we are taking a sample. Sampling error is the error inherent in estimating population parameters from samples. In practice, we never know what the sample error is in any particular case, but probability samples give us the leverage we need to quantify its likely range.

2. Margin of error has a specific relationship with sample size. As sample size gets larger, the sampling error gets smaller, and so does the margin of error. Again, though, this rule applies only with sampling error. The problem with the *Literary Digest* poll was systematic error, and that is why surveying 2 million people didn't predict the correct outcome of the presidential election.

In probability samples, increasing sample size decreases the margin of error, but there are diminishing returns, meaning that the improvement gained by adding another person to the sample decreases as our sample size gets larger. Margin of error is proportional to the *square root* of sample size. Say Gallup wanted to decrease the margin of error from 3 percentage points to 1 percentage point (that is, by a factor of 3). You might think that Gallup would have to interview three times as many people. In actuality, however, they would need to interview *nine* times as many people (because 9 is the square of 3). To go from 3 percentage points to half a percentage point (a factor of 6) requires interviewing *36* times as many people. Because decreasing the margin of error comes at an ever-increasing cost, researchers have to weigh how much sampling error is acceptable against other demands of their budgets.

PROBABILITY SAMPLING IN PRACTICE

So far we have discussed the simplest version of probability sampling, which is equivalent to drawing names from a hat. In practice, much social research that uses probability sampling is more complicated because two key techniques, *clustering* and *stratification*, often allow researchers to get even better results at a lower cost. These techniques require researchers to weight their sample so that some people "count" more than others. This section describes clustering, stratification, and weighting in detail. First, however, we present the simplest method of sampling a bit more formally.

Simple Random Sampling

Sociologists Ronald Weitzer and Charis Kubrin wanted to study lyrics that demean women in popular hip-hop music (Weitzer & Kubrin, 2009). If the researchers relied on their own music collections or listened only to songs suggested by their friends and students, their sample might have inaccurately represented the overall population of hip-hop songs. For example, people might suggest songs to them because they remembered the songs as having misogynistic (anti-woman) lyrics. This result would be a sample that overstated the misogyny in hip-hop songs. Or, hip-hop fans who wanted to prove that their favorite musical genre was pro-women might suggest songs by empowered female artists such as Beyoncé or Nicki Minaj.

To prevent bias from creeping into their sample, Weitzer and Kubrin made a list of every song on a platinum-selling hip-hop album between 1992 and 2000, about 2,000 songs in all. (A platinum album is one that has sold at least a million copies.) This list of songs is called a **sampling frame**, a list of population members from which a probability sample is drawn. Then they used a computer to choose 400 songs completely at random from this list. Each song on the list was equally likely to be selected into the sample. Moreover, if one song on a particular album was selected, another song on that same album was no more or less likely to be selected than any other song on the list. Consequently, each possible combination of 400 songs was equally likely to be selected for the study.

Weitzer and Kubrin's sample is an example of a **simple random sample**, the most straightforward type of probability sample. A simple random sample has two key features. First, each individual has the same probability of being selected into the sample. Second—and this is the tricky part—each *pair* of individuals has the same probability of being selected. In a simple random sample, everyone's chance of being selected into the sample is completely independent of everyone else's. A simple random sample truly is like drawing names out of a hat at random.

Contrast a simple random sample with another straightforward probability sampling technique, the **systematic sample**. In the simplest case, if you want to use a systematic sample to draw a sample that is $1/n$ the size of the total population, you first select one of the first n individuals on the list of members of your sampling frame, and then every nth member on the list after that. So, you could start with an alphabetized list of all 2,000 songs. To draw a sample of 400 songs—one-fifth of the population—you would randomly select one of the first five songs on the list and then every fifth song thereafter. So, if you selected the third song at random, the 8th, 13th, and 18th songs would also be in the sample, and so on until the 1,998th song.

As in a simple random sample, every member of the population in a systematic sample has an equal probability of being selected. But not all pairs are equally likely. For example, if systematic sampling is used, it is impossible for two consecutive songs on the list to be selected into the same sample.

sampling frame A list of population members from which a probability sample is drawn.

simple random sample A type of probability sample in which each individual has the same probability of being selected and in which each pair of individuals has the same probability of being selected.

systematic sample A probability sampling strategy in which sample members are selected by using a fixed interval, such as taking every fifth person on a list of everyone in the population.

UCI sociologist Charis Kubrin studies public perceptions of rap music and has served as an expert witness in court cases in which rap lyrics were used as criminal evidence.

In practice, it is just as easy to select 400 names at random using a spreadsheet as it is to select every fifth song, and a researcher conducting a study like Weitzer and Kubrin's would probably opt for a simple random sample because it is easier to explain. However, the logic of the systematic sample is very important in political exit polls, where researchers try to interview people after they have finished voting and are exiting their polling place. Researchers do not have a sampling frame—after all, there is no way of knowing in advance who exactly will vote—so they cannot draw a simple random sample in advance. Yet it is extremely important that they use a probability sampling method, because the people who are most eager to tell others how they voted can be a very biased sample of all voters. As a result, one common method is that interviewers are instructed to keep track of the order in which individuals leave the polling place and to approach only every nth person about the survey.

Systematic samples are a type of probability sample often used for political exit polls.

Cluster Sampling

The National Center for Education Statistics (NCES) conducts a number of studies that involve not just surveying individual students but also getting information from their parents, teachers, and school administrators. Because NCES surveys are conducted in classrooms and in person, traveling to and establishing logistics with each school involved in a study can require significant time and expense. For this reason, surveying 20 students at the same school is much cheaper than surveying 20 students from 20 different schools. Sending an interviewer to one school is much more efficient than sending interviewers to 20 different schools that may be located in 20 different states!

In addition, the U.S. government does not maintain a master list of all students in a particular grade, so it would be impossible to conduct a simple random sample of all kindergarteners or eighth graders. However, lists of schools do exist, and schools have lists of their own students.

In **cluster sampling**, the target population is first divided into groups, called *clusters*. Some of these clusters are selected at random. Then, some individuals are selected at random from within each selected cluster. This sample is still a probability sample because everyone in the population has some probability of being selected. Because schools are different sizes, not every student has the same probability of being selected. We can address that issue with weighting, as we describe later in this chapter.

The NCES examples illustrate the two main advantages of cluster sampling. First, especially when studies are conducted in person and travel is involved, cluster samples allow researchers to conduct many more surveys at a much lower cost than they would incur with simple random sampling. Second, cluster sampling allows researchers to take probability samples when a sampling frame—a list of all the members of the population—doesn't exist.

To give another example, Demographic and Health Surveys (DHS) are conducted in dozens of developing countries to obtain vital information, such as the proportion

cluster sampling A probability sampling strategy in which researchers divide up the target population into groups, or "clusters," first selecting clusters randomly and then selecting individuals within those clusters.

of a nation's adults who are HIV-positive. No central roster of the populations of these nations exists, so researchers cannot possibly select a simple random sample. Yet, even if such a list did exist, it would not be cost-effective to send interview teams to 20 different remote areas to interview only one person in each area, which could happen if the researchers were using a simple random sample. Given the expense of travel, it makes more sense to conduct multiple interviews in a given area.

To do cluster sampling, the DHS researchers typically divide a nation into a large number of geographic areas (clusters) and then select some of these areas randomly. Next, they subdivide each geographic area further (creating another layer of clusters) and then choose some subareas randomly. The research teams then list every household within the selected subareas, and finally, they randomly choose households within each of the selected subareas to participate in the study. Cluster sampling allows teams of DHS researchers to interview many more people than they otherwise could at the same cost, while still maintaining all the key benefits of probability sampling.

Stratified Sampling

Sociologists Alexandra Kalev, Frank Dobbin, and Erin Kelly wanted to study the effectiveness of diversity training, mentoring programs, and other practices for encouraging diversity in the workplace (Kalev, Dobbin, & Kelly, 2006). To conduct their study, they combined government records with their own surveys to take a sample of 700 businesses. To identify the population of businesses from which to sample, they took advantage of the fact that all U.S. employers with more than 100 employees (and fewer in many cases) must file reports with the federal Equal Employment Opportunity Commission (EEOC). They used these reports to compile a roster of companies, which served as their sampling frame.

The researchers could have taken a simple random sample of this roster. Yet, consider that a single company with 100,000 workers employs the same number of people as 1,000 companies that employ 100 workers each. A simple random sample would be dominated by small companies, and giant companies could be left out of the sample entirely, even though many Americans work for big companies (Walmart alone employs more than 1.5 million people in the United States; Malcolm & Davidson, 2015).

To address this issue, the researchers divided employers into two groups: (1) those who employed more than 500 workers and (2) those who employed fewer than 500 workers. There are more small employers than large employers in the United States. Yet, the researchers selected about twice as many companies from the group of large employers than from the group of small employers so that the proportions of companies selected better reflected the proportions of all Americans who work for them.

This strategy is an example of **stratified sampling**. In stratified sampling, the population is divided into groups (called **strata**), and the researcher selects some members of every group. In Figure 6.2(b), the same proportion from each group was selected, but this need not be the case. In the study of employers, researchers selected more large employers than they would have obtained under simple random sampling. This is still a probability sample, in that all employers on the EEOC list had some probability of being selected, but (as a result of the researchers' decisions) large employers had a higher probability of being selected than small employers.

stratified sampling A probability sampling strategy in which the population is divided into groups, or strata, and sample members are selected in strategic proportions from each group.

strata Subgroups that a population is divided into for the purposes of drawing a sample. Individuals are drawn from each stratum.

Stratified samples are used for two main reasons that may seem contradictory, but each makes sense in its own research context:

1. Stratifying can allow researchers to **oversample** some groups so that the researchers have more data on those groups than they would if they had used simple random sampling. For example, the medical data set CARDIA was explicitly designed to study differences in cardiovascular (heart) health between white and black Americans. There are about five times as many whites as blacks in the United States, but the study would not be well served if it did not include enough black participants to make precise comparisons. CARDIA instead stratifies the sample by race and selects equal numbers of blacks and whites as participants.

2. Stratifying can prevent pure chance from causing samples to be nonrepresentative. Say researchers are drawing a sample of first-year students at a university, and they know that 10% of the students at that university are black. If the researchers want their sample to represent the population as accurately as possible, they could stratify the sample by race and select 10% of the sample from the black group. Using this sampling method, the researchers do not have to worry that they will get an unusual random sample in which the proportion of blacks differs substantially from the proportion of blacks in the university's general population.

It is important to understand the difference between clustering and stratification (Figure 6.2). In both cases, the sampling is done in stages, and the population is divided into groups. In cluster sampling, some clusters are selected at random, and the entire sample is drawn only from selected clusters. In stratified sampling, the sample includes some individuals from every stratum, but researchers have made a strategic decision about what proportion of their sample should be drawn from each stratum.

Stratified sampling and cluster sampling are often used together. As we discussed, NCES studies often use cluster sampling: First a group of schools is randomly selected, and then students are randomly sampled within each school. When NCES draws a random sample of schools, it does not want to draw a disproportionate number of private schools, rural schools, or schools from a particular region of the country. So it divides the schools into strata on the basis of these and other characteristics, and then it randomly selects schools within each stratum in the appropriate proportions. Likewise, NCES might want to make sure it does not get an unusual number of boys versus girls in a particular school. Therefore, it may divide the students at each school into separate strata of girls and boys and then select equal numbers of each.

Weighting

Imagine an election study in which blacks are oversampled in twice their proportion to the U.S. population as a whole. The goal might be to increase the number of blacks that researchers have in their sample. Blacks make up only 12% of the U.S. population, so a random sample survey of 500 Americans

oversample A group that is deliberately sampled at a rate higher than its frequency in the population.

FIGURE 6.2 Three Different Ways of Drawing a Probability Sample of 12 from 6-Person Groups

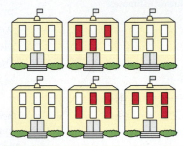

(a) **Cluster Sampling:** Some groups selected at random. Some persons selected at random from each selected group.

(b) **Stratified Sampling:** Some people selected at random from each group so that every group is sure to have some people selected.

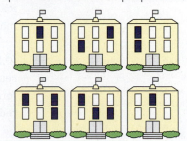

(c) **Simple Random Sampling:** People selected randomly without reference to what group they belong to.

would likely include only 60 blacks. However, 60 cases may not be sufficient to do a thorough and accurate analysis of the political preferences of blacks. Thus, to increase the absolute number of blacks in a sample, researchers may design a study where blacks make up 24% rather than 12% of their sample.

The sample is still a probability sample, but the sample is no longer representative of the overall U.S. population. For example, blacks are far more likely to support Democratic candidates than is any other major ethnic group, so any sample in which blacks are overrepresented will overrepresent support for Democrats. Given this, why doesn't oversampling lead to results that are as problematic as the catastrophic *Literary Digest* poll?

The short answer is that oversampling would lead to exactly the same problems *if* no correction were made. If a probability sample is conducted in such a way that different people have different probabilities of being selected, then the results must be **weighted** for estimates to be accurate.

When a sample is weighted, some observations count more than others. The basic principle is this: The more a particular group is overrepresented in the sample, the less weight each individual from that group should receive. For example, if a poll oversampled blacks at twice their proportion in the U.S. population, then each black person in the sample would have only half (1/2) the weight of other respondents when researchers calculated estimates for the population as a whole.

In probability sampling, it is not a problem if some individuals have a higher likelihood of being in the sample than others, *as long as we know what those probabilities are*. If Person A is x times more likely to be in our sample than Person B, then we give Person A $1/x$ times as much weight as Person B when computing our estimates.

Weighting to adjust for clustering and stratification can get very complicated, but the basic principle is not controversial. More controversial is the idea that weights can address systematic error in surveys. In **postsurvey weighting**, we weight our sample to match known characteristics of the population from which it is drawn.

Consider a scenario in which a researcher follows all the rules in drawing a good probability sample, but then many people refuse to participate in the study. If some people are more likely to refuse than others, this can lead to a sample that is unlike the population in easily detectable ways. For example, perhaps 27% of our sample is over 65 years old, but the 2010 U.S. Census indicates that only 18% of adults are over age 65. If we do not adjust our results, sample estimates will be biased for any characteristic on which older adults and younger adults differ. Older adults are more likely to oppose marijuana legalization, for example, so a sample in which older adults are systematically overrepresented could lead a researcher to overstate the level of opposition to marijuana legalization in the population.

In our study, people over age 65 are overrepresented by a factor of approximately 1.5 (0.27/0.18). In postsurvey weighting, we would apply the basic rule that overrepresented groups should receive less weight. People over age 65 in our sample would therefore count only 0.67 (1/1.5) as much as people under age 65. This adjustment should reduce or eliminate the bias in our estimates of opposition to legalizing marijuana.

What makes postsurvey weighting controversial is the fact that researchers can also use it with nonprobability samples. Some companies recruit people to participate in surveys through advertisements and then weight whatever volunteers they get to match demographic characteristics from the U.S. Census. Does this technique work? Could it have saved the *Literary Digest* poll?

weighted Samples in which some cases should be counted more or less than others in producing estimates.

postsurvey weighting When a sample is weighted to match known characteristics of the population from which it is drawn.

Recall that one of the problems with the *Literary Digest* poll was that wealthier people were both overrepresented in the poll and less likely to support Roosevelt. If the postcards had also asked questions about wealth and the magazine staff had information about the distribution of wealth in the population, they could have given less weight to the wealthier respondents in their sample. This adjustment would have brought the results of the poll closer to the truth. However, recall that another problem with the *Literary Digest* poll was that people unhappy with Roosevelt were more likely to fill out the survey. Postsurvey weighting would not have fixed this problem, so some bias would have remained.

Here is the bottom line: There is no reason to think that nonprobability samples with postsurvey weights are a suitable substitute for probability samples (Yeager et al., 2011). In probability samples, postsurvey weighting likely yields better estimates in most circumstances than not weighting. At the same time, postsurvey weighting is not a substitute for selecting a proper sample and securing participation from as many of the people selected for the sample as possible.

CONCEPT CHECKS

1 | The General Social Survey canvasses about 2,000 people a year using state-of-the-art sampling techniques. Quite often, the survey will have zero respondents from Nebraska, even though this outcome would be unlikely with simple random sampling. Is this outcome due to clustering or stratification? Explain.

2 | The Pew Research Center conducts surveys on religion in American life. These surveys often oversample individuals who are Jewish, Mormon, atheist, or agnostic. Why? In generating population statistics based on samples that include oversampling, should the oversampled individuals be given more weight or less weight than Protestants and Catholics?

WHEN NONREPRESENTATIVE SAMPLES ARE USEFUL

As we've learned, testing hypotheses is an important part of the scientific method. What kinds of samples are best for testing hypotheses? Is it essential to use only randomly selected, representative probability samples to test hypotheses? Not necessarily.

To explain why, let's start with an example from medical research. When toxicologists hypothesize that exposure to a potentially dangerous chemical may cause cancer in humans, they often begin by examining the effect of that particular chemical on mice. Conducting the same experiments on humans would be unethical, so studying mice is considered a reasonable first step in trying to determine the chemical's possible effects on people.

These scientists do not select representative samples of mice. Nor do they simply use whatever mice are most convenient. Instead, scientists use mice that are as similar to one another as possible. Some scientists even use special mice that are genetically identical to one another. Why? To consider the possibility that exposure to a chemical might be harmful, researchers want everything else in the study to be as controlled and comparable as possible, which makes the effects of the chemical exposure clearer. This is what researchers mean when they say they "hold constant" all other variables or that "all else is equal" other than the test variable, in this case chemical exposure.

In social science research, representative samples are usually ideal—and often indispensable—because of their power to accurately describe populations. If you want to estimate how a nation feels about legalizing marijuana or raising taxes, you want a sample that accurately reflects the population. However, the virtues of representative samples that make them ideal for descriptive questions make them less than ideal for other kinds of questions. Specifically, representative samples are often not ideal for testing hypotheses about cause-and-effect relationships.

The Benefits of Nonrepresentative Samples

Highly nonrepresentative samples are often better for initial tests of hypotheses than representative samples. To see why, consider an example from research on Alzheimer's disease, which is the sixth most common cause of death in the United States and is becoming more prevalent. The number of Alzheimer's cases has increased in recent years because the U.S. population is becoming older, and Alzheimer's disease typically strikes adults in their seventies and older. In the past, an important question was posed in Alzheimer's research: Is the disease due to brain changes occurring later in life or rather do the causes of Alzheimer's disease affect the brain over a much longer period even though the disease usually manifests itself very late in a person's life?

In the 1980s, epidemiologist David Snowdon wanted to know whether traits that individuals exhibit early in life could be linked to the development of Alzheimer's disease in old age. Rather than choosing a representative study of all Americans for his study, however, Snowdon and colleagues followed a sample of 678 Catholic nuns from the School Sisters of Notre Dame (now called "The Nun Study"). Using nuns as his subjects, he was able to learn things about Alzheimer's disease that he would not have learned if he had used a representative sample of 700 adults.

Why nuns? First, nuns are much older than the average American woman, because becoming a nun was a much more common choice for young women in the past than it is today. Nuns typically have healthier lifestyles as well—few nuns smoke, for instance—and so they are more likely to survive to very old age, giving them a greater risk of Alzheimer's disease simply due to their advanced age. Second, nuns have much more similar lifestyles to one another than do members of a group of randomly chosen individuals. Nuns live together and thus share a diet, a physical environment, and a range of other factors that could plausibly be linked to risk of Alzheimer's disease.

Also, by choosing a group that lived together and shared the same career, the researchers were able to gather higher-quality information in a comparable format than they would have otherwise. For example, upon joining the sisterhood, usually in their late teens and early twenties, each nun was required to write an essay.

In order to learn about the development of Alzheimer's disease, David Snowdon used a nonrepresentative sample of 678 nuns from the School Sisters of Notre Dame.

These essays provided the data for one of the most valuable findings from Snowdon's study. The more complex the sentences used in a nun's essay when she was a young adult, the less likely she was to develop Alzheimer's disease five or six decades later (Snowdon et al., 1996). Snowdon's research offered strong support for the hypothesis that Alzheimer's disease is a condition that develops over the course of people's lives, even though the symptoms of severe dementia typically appear only in old age. The Nun Study helped inspire work on whether mental exercise, like doing crossword puzzles, might delay the onset of Alzheimer's disease, although evidence so far on this point has been mixed at best.

From this example, we can draw two broad lessons about why it may be more effective to test hypotheses in nonrepresentative samples.

1. *The diversity of representative samples makes detecting cause-and-effect relationships more difficult.* It is easier to identify a cause when the cases we study are very similar to one another. When cases differ in ways that influence an outcome, we need a larger sample to distinguish the effects of our hypothesized cause, if any, from the effects of these other influences. For example, if we find that junior-high students who spend more time playing violent video games are more likely to get into fights at school, we cannot necessarily conclude that playing violent video games causes kids to fight. Perhaps students who frequently play violent video games live in homes with little parental supervision or have violent parents, and these family factors rather than the video games trigger aggression at school. If, instead, we focused on a sample of children with similar family lives rather than a sample of all children, we could better isolate the distinctive effect (if any) of playing violent video games on children's behavior.

2. *We can often gather more or better information on nonrepresentative samples than we can on representative samples.* Perhaps the most valuable long-running study for understanding the effects of lifestyle differences such as diet or smoking on women's health has been the Nurses' Health Study (Colditz, Manson, & Hankinson, 1997). Why focus on nurses? The researchers anticipated that nurses would be better able to answer sometimes fairly technical questions about their health and that nurses would be more motivated to participate in a health study than would women who worked in other professions. When the study moved from mail questionnaires to the more time-intensive and intrusive collection of blood and urine specimens, the investigators were pleased to find participation rates much higher than one would expect from a probability sample. One reason is that the average nurse is less squeamish about giving blood than the average person.

Nonrepresentative Samples and Generalizability

Most published experiments in psychology are conducted on groups of college undergraduates. College students certainly are not representative of all adults. Among other things, they are much younger on average than adults overall. College students are not even representative of all persons of their age, as those who attend college have more affluent family backgrounds than those who do not attend college. Also, students at a particular college are a much less diverse population than all American adults.

Why, then, do so many studies use college students as research subjects? College students are the easiest group for psychologists to study, making them a quintessential convenience sample. They often participate in studies for course credit or very small cash incentives. Researchers would have to spend much more time, energy, and money trying to recruit subjects who live far from campus, hold full-time jobs, or are too busy with work and family obligations to participate in a study.

Nonetheless, experiments on college students typically allow researchers to detect effects with a sample size smaller than a representative sample of the U.S. population. If a hypothesis holds true throughout all subgroups of a target population, then we would expect any finding we observe in a representative sample to also hold in whatever nonrepresentative sample we might use. When psychologists are studying basic cognitive or perceptual processes that they believe to be fairly universal across time, place, and subpopulations, why not focus on people they can study most cheaply?

The hitch here is that we cannot conclude that a hypothesis holds true in the same way throughout all subgroups of a population until we test that hypothesis across the range of subgroups. This is the issue of *generalizability* that we discussed in Chapter 5.

One strategy for establishing robust, generalizable conclusions is to first test whether evidence for a hypothesis can be established using a nonrepresentative sample such as undergraduates. If it can, then subsequent research can consider whether the same hypothesis also holds in a representative sample of a more general population. For example, sociologists Trenton Mize and Bianca Manago (ms) proposed that public perceptions of men's and women's sexuality differed in a way that men's heterosexuality could be understood as more "precarious." Specifically, they presented people with scenarios in which a person who had dated exclusively members of the opposite sex in the past had a recent sexual encounter with someone of the same sex. Mize and Manago hypothesized that a single sexual encounter would be perceived as calling into question whether someone was heterosexual more when it was a man having sex with another man than a woman having sex with another woman.

Mize and Manago first conducted their experiment using a nonprobability sample recruited using an online site in which people do small tasks for payment. Results supported their hypothesis, but the people who participate in experiments on these sites are not a representative sample: They are younger, have higher levels of education, and are more politically liberal, which raises the question of whether Mize and Manago's hypothesis only holds among certain groups. As their next step, the researchers replicated their study on a probability sample of all U.S. adults. The two experiments yielded similar results, making the case for their hypothesis much stronger.

Sociologists have traditionally been quite skeptical about the extent to which cause-and-effect findings based on college students can be generalized to the population at large. College students differ from the general public in many ways: On average, for example, they are younger, come from more affluent backgrounds, and hold more liberal attitudes on many social issues. Further, experiments often take place in laboratory settings that do not approximate "real life" in many respects. (We will discuss these issues further in Chapter 8.) Despite these important concerns, experiments that have been done both on college students and on representative samples have found consistent results more often than they have found differences (Druckman & Kam, 2011).

At the same time, evidence from sociology also shows that seemingly well-established cause-and-effect patterns may vary widely across groups in previously

"DO CHILDREN OF SAME-SEX PARENTS REALLY FARE WORSE?"

So read a *Time* magazine headline amid the media firestorm that followed the publication of an extremely controversial study by sociologist Mark Regnerus (2012a). Some journalists interpreted the study as showing that being raised by same-sex parents led to a host of negative outcomes, including lower educational attainment, being unemployed, having psychological problems, and getting arrested.

Regnerus's study was criticized by many social scientists. His study compared two groups of people selected from a probability sample of adults aged 18 through 39. The first group comprised respondents who reported having been raised by both their biological father and biological mother from when they were born to age 18. The second group comprised respondents who met two criteria. First, they were not part of the first group; that is, they reported that they had not been continually raised by both biological parents to age 18. Second, they said yes to a question asking if one of their parents had ever been involved in a romantic relationship with someone of the same sex. Regnerus's study showed that the members of the second group had worse outcomes than members of the first group.

The problem with interpreting the Regnerus study as a legitimate study of same-sex parenting is that a person in the second group wasn't necessarily raised by two parents of the same sex. In fact, the overwhelming majority of people in the second group were not. Of the 175 respondents who answered yes regarding their mother's relationship with a same-sex partner, only 6 reported having lived with their mother and a female partner for 10 years or more, and only 18 reported doing so for 5 years or more (Regnerus, 2012b). In fact, for most of the 175 cases, there is no reason to believe that the women in the relationship with the mothers had ever lived with the mother at all. The study was interpreted as though it had implications for same-sex couples raising children, and yet the vast majority of people in the key group were not raised by a same-sex couple for any significant length of time, if at all.

Sociologists have long known that divorce and other instability in households are associated with many negative outcomes for children. Most of the people in the key comparison of the Regnerus group very likely experienced either a divorce or a long period being raised by a single parent (or both). Comparing these people to respondents who had been raised continually by both parents likely just replicates what is already known about the effects of family instability and says nothing about whether gays and lesbians make better (or worse) parents than straight people.

What if we compared children who were raised by stable same-sex couples to children raised by stable opposite-sex

Protesters against same-sex marriage often invoke a "for the sake of the children" defense.

couples? Here is where sampling comes in. One key virtue of the Regnerus study might seem to be that it was based on a representative sample of the U.S. population. Yet same-sex couples raising children are statistically rare today, and they were even rarer when the respondents in Regnerus's sample were growing up. It took interviews with 15,000 people just to yield the six cases in which respondents had been raised by their mother and a female partner for more than 10 years. This is obviously not a large enough sample on which to base conclusions about whether children in some sorts of families do better or worse than their peers.

Sociologist Michael Rosenfeld (2010) was also interested in same-sex parenting, but he used data derived from a special random sample from the U.S. Census. The sample allowed him to study more than 3,000 children in grades 1–8 who were raised by same-sex couples. The problem here is that the census collects very limited information, so Rosenfeld's study looked only at whether there are differences in the likelihood of children having been held back a grade in school. His study found no differences between married heterosexual couples and same-sex couples once parents' education and family income were taken into account.

The Regnerus study had many outcome measures and a representative sample, but the comparison groups were not valid, and the most valid comparison would have had far too few people raised by same-sex couples. The Rosenfeld study had enough people to make stronger comparisons, but it could study only a narrow outcome of children's well-being.

Overwhelmingly, published studies have found no evidence that being raised by same-sex couples has negative consequences for childern. This conclusion has been endorsed by courts that have considered the available scientific evidence (Adams & Light, 2015).

unanticipated ways. For example, social scientists have known for a long time that women commit far fewer violent crimes than men. However, recent work by sociologists Gregory Zimmerman and Steven Messner shows that the size of the gender gap varies across neighborhoods (Zimmerman & Messner, 2010). The gender gap in violent crime is narrowest among people who live in the most disadvantaged neighborhoods. How do they explain this pattern? They found that people living in disadvantaged neighborhoods are exposed to more violence, and the relationship between exposure to peer violence and being violent oneself is stronger among women than among men.

When studying cause-and-effect relationships, how well the group we are studying represents a population is often a secondary concern. During the first stage of research, it is often more important simply to find evidence that a cause-and-effect relationship might exist. After this possibility is established, it becomes important to understand how broadly the effect exists, its average size in the population, and whether the effect is larger among some groups of people than others.

CONCEPT CHECKS

1   One of the most important ongoing studies of cardiovascular health in the United States has been based on thousands of adults from the small city of Framingham, Massachusetts. What do you think is an advantage of conducting a health study in a small city? What would be a disadvantage?

2   A team of researchers wants to study whether a newly developed pre-kindergarten education program improves children's readiness for school. Apart from any cost or logistic issue, what might be an advantage of focusing the study on a sample of children from poor families rather than a representative sample of children from all families?

SAMPLING IN CASE-ORIENTED RESEARCH

As we will see in later chapters, there is a basic distinction in social research between *case-oriented* research projects and *variable-oriented* research projects. (Mixed-methods projects may have both case- and variable-oriented aspects.) Most of this chapter has focused on variable-oriented research. In **variable-oriented research**, researchers study a large number of cases, such as undergraduates or employment discrimination lawsuits, but they have only a modest amount of information on each case. A survey might collect data from thousands of respondents but on only a few dozen questions.

In **case-oriented research**, by contrast, researchers immerse themselves in an enormous amount of detail about a small number of cases (maybe even only one case). Ethnographic research (Chapter 10) is case oriented in that research will typically be conducted in a small number of field sites, and materials-based research (Chapter 12) is typically case oriented in that researchers focus intensely on a small number of historical examples.

Choosing a single case to study intensely is still sampling. The researchers need a rationale for why they are studying that case instead of something or someone else

variable-oriented research Research in which social scientists study a large number of cases, such as undergraduates or employment discrimination lawsuits, but only with information organized into variables about each case.

case-oriented research Research in which social scientists immerse themselves in an enormous amount of detail about a small number of cases, or even just a single case.

and why insights from that case contribute to our understanding of social life. Also, focusing on a single case does not mean that a researcher can learn everything there is to know or talk to everyone who might have something worthwhile to say about it. Even in case-oriented studies, researchers still need to make strategic decisions about what to observe.

In this section, we discuss the two key ways that sampling for case-oriented projects is different from sampling for variable-oriented projects. First, we discuss some of the reasons why case-oriented researchers select the cases they do. Second, we discuss the sequential nature of case-oriented research.

Selecting Cases

Selecting cases to study intensely determines how researchers will spend months or years of their working lives. How do they decide which cases to study?

When making their choice of cases, researchers need to keep one key principle in mind: *In selecting a small number of cases for intensive study, random sampling is usually a bad idea.* Why? Researchers may invest months or years in a case and hence are able to study very few of them. Consequently, case selection is too important to leave to chance. Instead, for the type of research for which case studies work best, purposive sampling will almost always be more informative than choosing cases randomly. In **purposive sampling**, cases are deliberately selected on the basis of features that distinguish them from other cases. The researchers choose the case on the basis of the features that they believe make the case especially informative.

In the following sections, we briefly describe some of the reasons why social researchers choose particular cases and the kinds of questions those cases can answer. These reasons include access to and quality of data, typicality, extremity, importance, deviant cases, contrasting outcomes, key differences, and past experience and intuition. In the end, social researchers' choice of cases may be based on a combination of these reasons as well as others not listed here.

purposive sampling A sampling strategy in which cases are deliberately selected on the basis of features that distinguish them from other cases.

ACCESS TO AND QUALITY OF DATA

Sociologist Shamus Khan (2011) was interested in the privileges afforded to social "elites" and how children of often wealthy elites experienced privilege in their everyday lives. To study this phenomenon, he spent a year teaching and observing students at one of the most elite boarding schools in the United States. Many schools might have fit this bill, but Khan chose St. Paul's School, in New Hampshire, in part because he had attended the school himself, and he knew that his personal history would make it easier for him to get access to the school and its students. Without this personal connection, he might not have been able to conduct his study at all. Khan's history as a student also provided him with valuable background knowledge about the school and its decision makers.

For his study of how privilege is experienced in the everyday lives of children of "elites," Shamus Khan chose St. Paul's School as his research site, partly because his status as a former student helped facilitate access.

As Chapter 10 explains, access is a vital part of ethnographic research. Researchers must gain permission from gatekeepers to observe the sites they wish to study, and of course they need willing participants to interview. Even when many potential cases or sites are available, the ease and depth of access that the researcher can expect to attain may vary considerably. As a result, researchers may choose the cases that offer the most promising and efficient prospects for access and the participation of key informants.

TYPICALITY

A famous work of early American sociology provided an in-depth look at one American town, "Middletown," in the 1920s. The researchers' goal was to provide a comprehensive picture of cultural life in the small and rapidly growing American cities that were a vital part of the westward spread of industrialism across the United States. "Middletown" was really Muncie, Indiana, and like many such cities, it was booming: Its population tripled between 1890 and 1920. Robert and Helen Lynd (1929) focused on documenting the changes afoot in Muncie with the ambition of anthropologists tasked with documenting the culture of a primitive society for the first time. The study was especially important for showing how the growth of Muncie was accompanied by increasing division of the town into working and business classes and how this divide revealed itself in economic, cultural, and lifestyle differences.

typical When a case's features are similar in as many respects as possible to the average of the population it is supposed to represent, and when nothing makes it stand out as unusual.

Why focus so much attention on just one small town in Indiana? The Lynds were able to amass an array of records, interviews, and other information about Muncie that would not have been possible without the years they spent in the town. As such, *Middletown: A Study in Modern American Culture* draws together and documents many different changes happening simultaneously. A study based on more superficial information from a sample of dozens of cities could not have achieved this same depth.

Robert and Helen Lynd chose to study the city of Muncie, Indiana—which they referred to as "Middletown"—because it was a typical American city.

Nevertheless, why Muncie? The key thing to keep in mind is that sociologists were not interested in Muncie specifically. Rather, Muncie was important because many of the changes happening in Muncie were also occurring in other towns of similar size. Consequently, the value of studying Muncie was justified because it represented a "typical" city of that size. A case is **typical** when its features are similar in as many respects as possible to the average of the population it is supposed to represent, and when nothing makes it stand out as unusual. The ideal case in such a study is precisely the one that seems to have nothing special about it.

EXTREMITY

In the 1970s, Berkeley sociologist Arlie Hochschild was interested in service workers whose jobs often required them to display a particular emotion, regardless of how they felt. For instance, flight attendants were (and still are) expected to display a calm, cool, smiling demeanor at all times, even if they were frightened of turbulence or angered by a surly passenger (Hochschild, 1983). Hochschild argued that service-sector workers, such as waitstaff, receptionists, and salespeople, sell not only their labor but also their ability to project a desired demeanor. Hochschild wished to document specifically how people in certain professions do this and the emotional toll it might take on them.

To do so, she focused on two occupations, which she chose not for their typicality but because they were jobs in which people worked under particularly strong pressure to display specific emotions. The first group was composed of flight attendants. Keep in mind that this was an era in which flight attendants were still called "steward-esses," business travelers were much more likely to be male, and female workers were expected to cheerfully tolerate boorish male behavior. As one attendant described it, "You have married men getting on the plane and suddenly they feel anything goes. It's like they leave that reality behind, and you fit into their fantasy as some geisha girl" (Hochschild, 1983, p. 93).

For her study of "emotion work," Arlie Hochschild focused on two extreme cases: flight attendants and bill collectors.

The second job was bill collectors. Whereas flight attendants were expected to remain sunny throughout long flights, delayed departures, and unruly passengers, bill collectors were expected to be firm, suspicious, and intimidating even while hearing stories from people who could not pay their bills because of heartbreaking circumstances. "If you're too nice . . . they [the bosses] give you a hard time," one bill collector told Hochschild (p. 140).

Focusing on extreme cases provided particularly vivid examples of the phenomenon Hochschild was interested in—emotional displays as part of one's job. This allowed Hochschild to show that jobs involving "emotional labor" were not only often experienced as stressful by workers but also often left them feeling estranged from their own feelings.

IMPORTANCE

Jerome Karabel's *The Chosen* (2005) is a history of the admissions process to elite universities. He describes how ideas of academic "merit" have changed and how barriers to admission for groups such as Jews and Asian Americans were enforced and eventually dismantled. Understanding admissions to elite colleges is important because a degree from these schools is a path to subsequent success, which is a big reason why students work so hard to get into prestigious schools.

Karabel's study is based on extensive archival research regarding admissions at three universities. Karabel did not make a list of all elite universities and choose three at random, nor did he choose three schools because he regarded them as most typical. Instead, he selected the "Big Three"—the three schools conventionally regarded as the most elite and most important for developing the political and economic leaders of the next generation: Harvard, Yale, and Princeton. Whereas *Middletown* studied Muncie because it was unexceptional among booming small cities of the 1920s, *The Chosen* justified its focus on Harvard, Yale, and Princeton because of their presumed importance and elite status.

Ashley Mears's (2011) book *Pricing Beauty: The Making of a Fashion Model* is an extensive ethnographic investigation of fashion modeling, based on Mears's own work as a model (while also a graduate student in sociology). She interviewed many other models and others working at different jobs in the fashion industry. Her work focuses on models in two cities: New York City and London. Models work in many cities, and New York and London are not typical of cities in which models work. They are, however, two of the most important cities for the fashion industry, and they provide an important contrast insofar as London is more focused on the artistic side of the fashion business, and New York is more focused on the commercial side. In studying two of the most important cities in the business, Mears's goal was not to show us a day in the life of an "average" fashion model. Rather, she provides insights into the especially competitive and culturally influential world of fashion in its leading locations.

DEVIANT CASE

deviant case A case that is unusual, unexpected, or hard to explain given what we currently understand.

A **deviant case** is one that does not fit a usual pattern or common understanding of how the world works. Such cases are also sometimes called *anomalies* or *outliers*. Deviant cases are puzzles. By trying to understand why they are different, researchers may gain a more general understanding of what they are studying.

One classic example of this approach comes from organizational sociology. A very old idea about organizations is called the "iron law of oligarchy" (Michels, 1915). In an *oligarchy*, relatively few people wield an enormous amount of power. The idea is that while truly democratic organizations sound great in principle, in reality they are not sustainable. Instead, inevitably, they evolve into bureaucracies run by relatively small groups of elites who are often as interested in preserving their power as they are in serving the larger purpose of the organization.

For something to be known as an "iron law," it must seem to be universal. Consider the case of labor unions, which often begin with great enthusiasm for democracy. Yet, looking at labor unions in the 1940s and 1950s, we can see many labor unions that served as obvious examples of the iron law in action. However, one did not: the International Typographical Union (ITU), composed of people who worked in printing. For example, while union presidents often consolidate power and win reelection by wide margins, ITU presidents were often defeated when they ran for reelection.

To understand why this one union was so different, sociologist Seymour Martin Lipset and his colleagues conducted a detailed analysis of it, interviewing hundreds of members (Lipset, Trow, & Coleman, 1956). They found that a number of unusual features about the ITU came together to promote democracy rather than oligarchy. Typographers were relatively well educated compared to most people in union jobs at the time. Typography involved irregular hours that resulted in workers spending an unusual number of hours together both at work and outside of it. The ITU also had an unusual history of being founded as a confederation of local unions that already had a strong sense of autonomy, which they were not interested in giving over to centralized elites. By intensely studying the ITU, Lipset and his colleagues had hoped they would learn lessons that would help make new unions stay as truly democratic as the ITU was. Instead, their book is quite pessimistic, because it concludes that the ITU's democracy resulted from special circumstances that new organizations could not easily copy.

CONTRASTING OUTCOMES

Sometimes researchers choose a pair of cases that together form a puzzle. Following well-publicized news stories about medical errors committed by exhausted interns and medical students at major hospitals, organizational sociologist Katherine Kellogg (2009) studied the impact of new regulations intended to shorten the workweek of surgical interns to "only" 80 hours per week. The two hospitals she chose to study provide a puzzle because their response to the new regulations was very different. In one hospital, the new regulations were largely successful at producing change, whereas at the other they largely failed to change the number of hours worked by interns. Adding to the mystery was the fact that the two hospitals were very similar on a range of characteristics considered important for how organizations change. Both hospitals also had some "reformers" who supported change and some "defenders" who were against it.

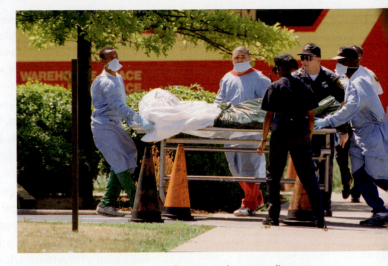

By comparing two adjacent lower-income neighborhoods sociologist Eric Klinenberg was able to discover the social causes of the striking differences in death rates during the Chicago heat wave of 1995.

So what accounted for the jarring difference in responses? Kellogg's study highlighted differences in how the two hospitals conducted their afternoon rounds. The afternoon rounds at one of the hospitals provided what Kellogg called a "relational space" that enabled reformers to work together toward building support for change, without fear of belittlement or retaliation. The other hospital did not provide this relational space during afternoon rounds. Without the opportunity for reformers to work together, resistance to change prevailed.

As another example, sociologist Eric Klinenberg (2002) wanted to better understand why 750 adults died during the sweltering heat wave that struck Chicago in 1995. He was particularly interested in two adjacent lower-income neighborhoods, North and South Lawndale, that had striking differences in death rates. North Lawndale had 10 times more deaths per capita than South Lawndale, even though both neighborhoods were equally poor.

Comparing the two neighborhoods, Klinenberg showed that crime in North Lawndale discouraged people from leaving their homes to receive relief and help from others. In addition, a weaker organization of churches and block clubs meant that North Lawndale organizations had less capacity to reach out to vulnerable people during the heat wave. These findings helped Klinenberg understand why the most socially isolated persons—those who lived alone—suffered the worst consequences of the heat wave.

KEY DIFFERENCES

In their research, Kellogg and Klinenberg chose their cases in order to understand why, despite their similarities, the cases had very different outcomes. In other situations, a researcher is interested in the range of consequences that might follow from a key difference between two cases.

Some researchers choose cases that are as similar as possible except for a specific difference whose consequences the researcher wishes to document. For example, Daniyal Zuberi (2006) was interested in how differences in health care and workplace policies affect the lives of working-class people. Of course, "working class" encompasses a vast range of different jobs and industries. But Zuberi was not interested in different jobs; he was interested in different policies. So, consistent with our earlier discussion about sampling to understand cause-and-effect relationships, he focused on a single industry: hotels. In fact, all the people he interviewed worked the same jobs within four different hotels that were all owned by the same company.

The first key difference in his study was that two of the hotels were in Seattle, Washington, and two were in Vancouver, British Columbia, Canada. Canada has much more generous social welfare policies than the United States. The second key difference was that, in each city, Zuberi studied one unionized hotel and one non-unionized hotel. Union jobs typically have more generous benefits, and the policies surrounding union protections are quite different in the United States and Canada. Using this design, Zuberi was able to show how more generous social policies, especially in tandem with unionization, have a wide range of positive effects on the lives of working-class employees.

PAST EXPERIENCE AND INTUITION

The examples above all presume that researchers have a reasonably clear idea of their research questions when they select their case for study. In practice, researchers do not always start with a set of specific questions. Rather, they might begin fieldwork with little more than a gut feeling that interesting insights can be gained in the site they have chosen to study. Or they may begin what turns out to be fieldwork as an actual participant, rather than as a researcher.

For example, sociologist Matthew Desmond (2007) begins his ethnographic study of wildland firefighters by saying, "I began fighting fire because someone asked me to." As a college student, he had taken a summer job as a firefighter. He did not know he would become a sociologist, would return to the firefighting job after starting graduate school, and end up writing a book about firefighting.

One of the most unfair criticisms of ethnographic research is that researchers often end up "studying themselves" (sometimes snidely referred to as "*me*-search"). This criticism is unfair because the social settings in which individuals spend their lives often do, in fact, have fascinating aspects with very general implications. In other words, our workplaces and hobbies in many cases serve as an excellent case study of something, but it might require an ingenious ethnographer to figure out what. Desmond's work on firefighting takes up general sociological questions: Why do people seek out dangerous jobs when safer jobs with similar pay are available? How do organizations train these people to understand and manage the risks in their jobs?

In other words, ethnographers may start fieldwork with only an intuition that the setting provides larger insights about social life, and only through their fieldwork do they figure out what those insights are. Over the course of the project, the researchers may develop research questions that fit the site so well that the site ends up seeming like the perfect choice. If not for the introduction in Desmond's book about how he started firefighting, readers might have imagined that he had started with his research questions, surveyed a range of possible occupations he could study in detail, and then decided that being a wildland firefighter was the most suitable case.

The important point here is that there is nothing wrong with developing research questions in the course of doing research or starting with vague questions that become sharper as researchers learn more about their cases. What matters ultimately is how well the insights and evidence advance our understanding of the research questions. Of course, being vigilant about one's objectivity is especially important when studying sites with which you have a personal history. At the same time, studying cases you are already familiar with offers significant advantages: You already have considerable background information about the setting and connections with people you can interview.

Sequential Sampling

Compared to survey-based projects, fieldwork and materials-based research projects allow researchers greater flexibility to engage in **sequential sampling**. This strategy allows researchers to make decisions about what additional data to collect on the basis of their findings from ongoing analyses of data already collected (Small, 2009). Insights gained from an initial case study can guide later choices about what may serve as ideal cases for comparison. Or, after completing a single case study, researchers may become interested in how their observations contrast with what they would have observed elsewhere, leading them to embark on a comparative project.

For example, Jeffrey Sallaz (2009) studied casino work by serving as a dealer in a Las Vegas casino and interviewing many other casino workers. This work led him to become interested in how casino work differs in parts of the world that are trying to mimic the Las Vegas experience under very different economic, political, and historical conditions. He decided to look at the casino industry in South Africa, and he discovered a casino there that was built as a replica of the Las Vegas casino where he had worked. He went to South Africa and got a job as a dealer in that casino.

Sallaz discovered that the conditions of employment were very different in Las Vegas and South Africa. For example, in Las Vegas, dealers have a fair amount of "entrepreneurial" autonomy at tables in order to boost the income they receive from tips. In South Africa, however, dealers are monitored very closely and forbidden from accepting tips. Sallaz interpreted the difference in terms of how South Africa integrates a "modern" industry like casino gambling with a long-standing culture of employment in which workers are distrusted and personal initiative is discouraged.

Sequential sampling can be applied to individuals, as well as to sites, within a fieldwork study. However, this strategy would not be sensible in most survey research. In a large-scale survey, researchers typically decide up front the number of people to be interviewed, how they will be selected, and what they will be asked. Typically, a question would not be altered in the middle of conducting a survey unless a very serious problem is discovered. For instance, if interviewers report that many

sequential sampling A flexible sampling strategy used in case-based research in which researchers make decisions about what additional data to collect based on their findings from data they've already collected.

ESZTER HARGITTAI

Eszter Hargittai is a professor in the Institute for Mass Communication and Media Research at the University of Zurich, where she directs the "Web Use Project." She is a leading authority on differences in how people use the Internet. She received her PhD in sociology from Princeton University.

Why is digital inequality important?

Digital media have relevance for every part of people's lives: from education to entertainment, from travel to trade, from well-being to work. Knowing who uses technologies in beneficial versus potentially harmful ways is essential to understanding whether digital media are helping to level the playing field across the population, or whether they are contributing to increased inequality. Internet skills in particular are an important focus of research, because developing interventions to improve people's web-use skills is less expensive and daunting than other types of interventions to decrease digital inequality. Research shows that Internet skills are related to many types of beneficial online behavior and that those from more privileged socioeconomic backgrounds tend to have higher Internet skills. Accordingly, the already advantaged are reaping more benefits from their digital media uses with the potential to contribute to increased social inequality. Interventions to improve people's Internet skills can help counter this.

What do you think is the biggest misconception that many people have about young people's Internet use?

Public rhetoric often suggests that young people who grew up with the Internet are automatically savvy with digital media, and that they are innately more skilled than those older than them. Plenty of scientific evidence shows these are myths. The assumptions are harmful because they can rob young people of the opportunity to learn how to be thoughtful, critical, and efficient users of technology. When teachers assume too much about

young people's Internet skills, they do not incorporate related lessons into the curriculum. When students think they know more than adults do, they do not ask questions or seek support in ways that can improve their skills.

You have studied how college students use the Internet. How did you draw the sample for this study? Why did you choose to study students at the University of Illinois, Chicago?

Due to the problematic assumptions about young people's digital savvy that I mentioned, I found it important to focus some of my research on young adults who have grown up with technology, to gather data on their Internet skills. For several reasons, I collected my data on students at the University of Illinois, Chicago (UIC), even though it was not the most convenient, as I had no affiliation with the university. UIC's undergraduate curriculum includes a required first-year writing program. This is helpful because it sidesteps problems about representativeness that may emerge if one sampled students through elective courses or courses required through specific field specializations. The program's director was willing to work with me to survey students in the classroom. This had two significant advantages.

First, and most importantly, it was essential that I not use an online method for collecting responses because then participation in my study might itself depend on web-use skills. Collecting data that way could have biased the sample against those with lower skills, not to mention those with fewer Internet access options or a lower likelihood of having the type of privacy ideal for answering questionnaires. The sample could have been skewed toward participants who were savvier and more active users. Second, being able to administer the survey in the classroom helped avoid such complications as securing people's postal addresses, something unlikely to have been possible through the university due to privacy laws. Also, sending out over a thousand surveys in postal mail comes with considerable logistics and financial cost.

Worth noting is that I wanted to leave myself the option of following up with the study participants in the future. This required two important steps up front. First, I had to include a question on the consent form approved by the institutional review board about students agreeing to be recontacted. Second, I had to ask for contact information. I used a sheet separate from the survey on which people could write their name, their postal address, and their e-mail address. These sheets were paired with the surveys with the same study ID number so we would be able to match them up without compromising the survey form's confidentiality. As students handed back the material, we separated the surveys from the information sheets immediately. These were kept separate from the surveys at all time, under lock and key.

> " It was essential that I not use an online method for collecting responses because then participation in my study might itself depend on web-use skills. "

How easy has it been to get [people/students] to respond to your survey? Do you do anything extra?

In the first wave, administering the survey in class helped with reaching high levels of participation (even though no one was required to take part). The toughest part was getting into all the classes, which were taught by several dozen instructors whom I had to contact individually to ask permission for a visit. In the subsequent waves, reaching participants was harder for multiple reasons. First, young adults move around frequently and many of the addresses we had collected in the first wave were no longer valid. We obtained updated mailing records and monitored bounced envelopes to see if we could resend the instrument to updated addresses. Also, the cost of postal mailings is considerable, especially when multiple contacts are necessary since only a small portion of people return the survey after the first mailing.

To encourage participation, I offered financial incentives. Before sending out the survey, I sent a letter reminding people that they had participated in this study, and let them know that they would be receiving a survey soon. This letter included a $1 bill to signal that they could trust our intentions regarding the payment. In the survey mailing, I included a $2 bill with the questionnaire, the self-addressed stamped return envelope, and letter with instructions. This again signaled our seriousness about the study and the hope was that the wow-factor accompanying a $2 bill (many people have never seen one) would encourage participation.

Both letters explained that, if participants returned the completed survey, we would send a gift card ($25 in the second wave, $40 in the third wave). In the second wave, we learned that sending the payment electronically using e-cards led to many of the gift cards ending up in people's spam folders, which caused considerable follow-up correspondence to sort out. In the third wave, we decided to send all gift cards in postal mail, which may have been more costly financially but preempted logistical problems later. In the second and third waves, we also let participants know that we would be holding a drawing for one of two iPods/iPads.

respondents are misunderstanding a question, the researcher may alter it. But this decision would make the responses to the revised question incomparable with the responses to the original question, so the earlier data would likely be wasted. In most cases, researchers do not begin to analyze the data from a survey until all data have been collected.

In contrast, in a fieldwork study that involves interviewing key informants, researchers routinely ask questions that probe and test ideas that were developed on the basis of earlier interviews. **Key informants** are people whom a researcher interviews intensively, typically multiple times, over the course of a fieldwork project. Researchers often select key informants on the basis of emerging insights, and sometimes new informants are recommended by other informants. This technique—known as snowball sampling—can be used to learn about hidden populations such as computer hackers or intravenous drug users. We discuss snowball sampling in more depth in the next section.

Sociologist Mario Small (2009) suggests that people who conduct in-depth interview projects (Chapter 11) should approach each interview with the same purposiveness that they would apply to selecting field sites. He also recommends that researchers try to think of hypotheses that are suggested by each interview. Then, researchers should select new interview subjects that will allow the researchers to test and refine these hypotheses.

The example Small gives is an interview with a black respondent about immigration. The respondent's answers cause the researcher to speculate that perhaps blacks who have been discriminated against by Latinos are more likely to favor immigration reform. Small offers three possibilities regarding whom to interview next. First, the researcher might interview other blacks who have been discriminated against by Latinos to see if they also favor immigration reform. Second, the researcher might interview other blacks who have not experienced discrimination by Latinos to see if they are less supportive of immigration reform. Third, the researcher might interview blacks who have been discriminated against by Russian immigrants, for example, to see if discrimination by other ethnic groups in general might reflect larger generalizations about how experiences of discrimination shape attitudes about immigration reform. In each case, the researcher reconsiders his or her research question after each interview, developing and refining ideas to be pursued in the next interview.

When conducting in-depth interview projects, researchers often focus on **sampling for range** across the key dimensions of the project (see Small, 2009). In other words, someone doing an interview study of an organization may try to interview people who occupy a wide range of different roles within the organization, from security guard to CEO, regardless of how common each of the roles is in the organization. To determine when an adequate number of cases has been interviewed, researchers on fieldwork projects often evaluate **saturation**, the extent to which new interviews continue to generate new insights about the project. Early in an in-depth interview project, researchers will often be learning a great deal and getting many new ideas from each interview they conduct. As the project goes on, the interviews become less informative and begin confirming insights more than generating new ones.

key informant A person who is usually quite central or popular in the research setting and who shares his or her knowledge with the researcher or a person with professional or special knowledge about the social setting.

sampling for range A purposive sampling strategy in which researchers try to maximize respondents' range of experiences with the phenomena under study.

saturation When new materials (interviews, observations, survey responses) fail to yield new insights and simply reinforce what the researcher already knows.

Researchers use the diminishing returns from new interviews to determine when a sample may be regarded as complete.

SAMPLING HIDDEN POPULATIONS

Some populations are difficult to study because they are based on characteristics of individuals that are not openly known and that individuals might not want to discuss. Imagine, for instance, a researcher who wants to study what motivates computer hackers (Turgeman-Goldschmidt, 2005). Computer hackers are rare, and very few publicly acknowledge that they are hackers.

Putting up an advertisement to recruit computer hackers as study subjects would likely yield very few volunteers. Worse, those hackers who would respond to an advertisement are probably not representative of computer hackers as a whole. However, many hackers do know one another and likely trust one another more than they would a stranger who says he or she is doing a study. If one can successfully interview a few hackers, perhaps those hackers can also put the researcher in touch with other hackers who would otherwise be unknown to the researcher or unwilling to participate.

A **snowball sample** is a type of sequential sample in which researchers ask participants in a study to use their social networks to help recruit new participants. If each participant introduces the researcher to a few new participants, the size of the sample can grow—that is, "snowball"—quickly.

Snowball samples have been used to study populations we would otherwise know little about, such as female gang members (Schalet, Hunt, & Joe-Laidler, 2003) or drag queens (Berkowitz & Belgrave, 2010). At the same time, snowball samples are often criticized because researchers often cannot ascertain how "representative" their samples are. For example, in the study involving computers hackers, the researcher found that almost none of the people she talked to said they were motivated by money, but instead for the fun and thrill-seeking. This is plausible, but one might worry that, instead, financially motivated hackers are less likely to be friends with the hackers who served as the original group of volunteers for the study.

In recent years there have been efforts to develop more formal methods of snowball sampling that allow one to evaluate the representativeness of samples (Mouw & Verdery, 2012; Salganik & Heckathorn, 2004). Some of these methods were originally developed in the context of trying to describe characteristics of undocumented immigrants and intravenous drug users, which is a matter of particular public health importance because of the spread of HIV and hepatitis.

We can see the core idea of these more formal methods if we think about drawing a sample from an individual's Facebook friends. The sample would not be a very good sample of the overall population of Facebook users; for example, a college student presumably has a much larger

snowball sampling A sampling strategy in which the researcher starts with one respondent who meets the requirement for inclusion and asks him or her to recommend another person to contact (who also meets the requirement for inclusion).

Snowball samples involve drawing on respondents' social networks in order to access hidden populations such as drag queens or computer hackers.

proportion of college students among their Facebook friends than the real percentage of Facebook users who are college students.

If we took a sample of the friends of an individual's friends, however, the sample would be closer to representative. And the friends of the friends of someone's friends would be more representative still. In other words, as we venture farther out into the social networks of the original members of our snowball sample, the resulting sample is less biased and more representative. The new methods of snowball sampling use information about the referral networks that led individuals to be contacted for the study in order to make inferences about the representativeness of the resulting sample.

CONCEPT CHECKS

1   Why is random sampling a good idea when trying to describe populations but a bad idea when selecting one case for intensive study?

2   Do you think your college or university would make a good case for a sociologist who wanted to get a sense of college life in your country? In what ways is your school typical? In what ways is it *not* typical? If the researcher was going to study your school and another school, what type of school would provide a good second case?

3   Suppose a researcher is trying to understand why some start-up companies succeed while others fail. She looks at two examples of each that had seemed very similar when they were founded. Which rationale(s) has she used to select her cases?

CONCLUSION

The best type of sampling to use in a study depends on the type of study being conducted. If the goal of the research project is to provide an accurate description of a target population, there is no good substitute for probability sampling. Although simple random samples are often easy to understand, in practice researchers can often get better results for the same cost by using clustering or stratification instead.

When researchers are interested in studying cause-and-effect relationships, having a representative sample of a population is not important, at least not at first. It might be easier to determine that a cause-and-effect relationship exists among a specific subpopulation, as in our examples of nurses and nuns. After showing that a cause-and-effect relationship exists for some people, researchers can then tackle the question of whether the relationship operates across the entire population.

In case-oriented research, the selection of a case is too crucial to be left to chance. Researchers may use a variety of different criteria to choose cases, including access to and quality of data, typicality, extremity, importance, deviance from the norm, contrasting outcomes, key differences, and past experience and intuition. Sampling in case-oriented research is often sequential; that is, researchers generate ideas on the basis of the information they have collected and then determine what information they should collect next.

Ultimately, sampling addresses the problem that we almost never have sufficient time, money, and access to collect all possibly useful information for the questions we want to answer. These constraints on resources are not a problem only for social researchers. They occur in any profession where part of the job is gathering information, drawing conclusions, or making decisions. In all cases, the project leaders need to decide which strategy will get them the most useful information with their limited resources. As this chapter has explained, success in gathering information and drawing conclusions is not simply a matter of getting as much data as possible. Rather, it is a matter of being strategic so that the data gathered fit the question being asked and do so in a way that minimizes how much the limitations of the data collection ultimately distort the conclusions.

End-of-Chapter Review

Summary

Sampling is the process of determining what and whom to study. Most sampling strategies involve random selection, which ensures the sample is representative; however, when testing hypotheses, nonrepresentative samples can be useful. Ultimately, the choice of sampling strategy should be guided by the research question and available resources.

Using Sampling to Describe Populations

- Probability sampling strategies use random choice to select subjects for a research study, meaning every person in a population has some chance of being selected. Random selection ensures there are no systematic differences between those who are selected for the sample and those who are *not* selected.

- Probability samples have two key advantages over nonprobability samples: They are unbiased and we can make precise estimates about the differences between sample estimates and the true parameter.

- A margin of error expresses how confident researchers are that the results of a study based on a sample population reflect the parameters of the target population. As sample size increases, the margin of error decreases.

Probability Sampling in Practice

- A simple random sample, which is equivalent to picking names out of a hat, is the most straightforward type of probability sample.

- Cluster sampling is a strategy that allows researchers to develop a probability sample when either a sampling frame is not available or when a simple random sample would be too time consuming or costly. This strategy involves randomly selecting from among groups of individuals (or clusters), such as U.S. states, and then randomly selecting individuals within those clusters.

- Stratified sampling involves dividing the population into groups and then selecting a predetermined proportion of each group into the sample. Stratified sampling allows researchers to obtain more data on certain subgroups of a population than they might otherwise be able to with a random sample.

- When a probability sample is constructed in such a way that some subgroups have different probabilities of being selected compared to others, researchers must use weighting in order to ensure that their results are accurate.

When Nonrepresentative Samples Are Useful

- Nonrepresentative samples are often more useful for initial tests of hypotheses than probability samples for two reasons. First, it is easier to deduce cause-and-effect relationships between variables with a sample of individuals who are very similar to one another. Second, researchers can often obtain more or better information from a nonrepresentative sample than they would from a larger, representative sample.

- Despite the benefits of nonrepresentative samples for hypothesis testing, they do not allow researchers to make arguments about the generalizability of their findings.

Sampling in Case-Oriented Research

- In case-oriented research, random sampling is not a good idea. Instead, researchers use purposive sampling, in which cases are deliberately selected on the basis of features that make them especially informative.

- Researchers doing case-oriented research choose their cases for many different reasons, including access to and quality of data, typicality or extremity, importance, deviance, contrasting outcomes, key differences, and past experience.
- Sequential sampling allows researchers to make decisions about their sample based on their initial findings. Snowball samples are a type of sequential sample used to study hidden populations such as hackers.

Key Terms

case-oriented research, 176
census, 160
cluster sampling, 167
confidence interval, 164
confidence level, 164
convenience sample, 162
deviant case, 180
key informant, 186
margin of error, 163
nonprobability sample, 162
oversample, 169
population parameter, 161

postsurvey weighting, 170
probability sample, 160
purposive sampling, 177
sample, 158
sampling, 158
sampling distribution, 164
sampling error, 163
sampling for range, 186
sampling frame, 166
saturation, 186
sequential sampling, 183
simple random sample, 166

snowball sampling, 187
strata, 168
stratified sampling, 168
systematic error, 163
systematic sample, 166
target population, 160
typical, 178
unbiased, 162
variable-oriented research, 176
weighted, 170

Exercise

In this exercise, you will generate a random sample of 10 moments throughout your day.

- First, you need to generate your sample. The Random.org website has a "Random Clock Time Generator" (https://www.random.org/clock-times/) that you can use to generate random times. You want to have it generate 10 random numbers at any time of the day (that is, between midnight and 11:59 p.m.). Generate the 10 numbers (don't worry about the seconds) and record them.
- Second, for the day in question, record what you were doing at the various times. Do not wait until the end of the day to record your activities. For your waking hours, setting an alarm on your phone can be a good reminder.
- Third, imagine if the only information someone had about your day was the 10 observations in your sample. Do you think the 10 observations provide a good representation of that day? What would you say is the biggest difference between that full day and what somebody would conclude just from looking at the sample?
- Fourth, do you think the 10 observations provide a good representation of how you typically spend your time? How would the data differ if you gathered 1,000 random observations of your time over an entire year, as opposed to the 10 observations from just that day?

Surveys are widely used in sociological research because they can provide detailed information on nearly all aspects of social and political life.

SURVEY RESEARCH

How do you and your friends meet potential dates? While parties, classes, and mutual friends were once the main ways for young adults to meet a romantic partner, technology plays a major role today. According to a recent survey by Pew Research Center (Smith, 2016), 27% of Americans ages 18–24 have used an online dating site or mobile dating app, and 57% know someone who met his or her partner this way. Although your parents' generation might have been wary of online dating, Americans today believe it's just fine. In fact, the Pew survey found that nearly two-thirds agree that "online dating is a good way to meet people."

A survey, like the Pew survey of online dating, is a social research method in which researchers ask a sample of individuals to answer a series of questions. Surveys provide an exciting opportunity to answer new and unexplored sociological questions. Political pollsters, market research firms, federal statistics organizations, health-care systems, and academic researchers alike use surveys to obtain detailed information on nearly all aspects of social and political life. We can learn about buying habits, political and social attitudes and identities, health behaviors, sexual activity, favorite television shows, and crime victimization from surveys. Surveys are one of the most widely used research methods in sociology, accounting for roughly one-third of all published studies (O'Leary, 2003).

In short, surveys allow us to describe patterns, test hypotheses, explore subgroup differences, document patterns of stability and change over time, and develop theories of human behavior. We begin this chapter by describing what surveys are, highlighting their strengths and weaknesses. Next we describe the different ways that surveys can be administered, along with the challenges researchers encounter when asking people deeply personal questions. We then highlight the characteristics of high-quality and low-quality surveys, showing how some questions are better than others at eliciting valid answers. After providing a basic overview of designing and carrying out your own survey, we conclude by discussing ethical issues that survey researchers must consider.

WHAT ARE SURVEYS AND WHAT CAN THEY DO?

survey A social research method in which researchers ask a sample of individuals to answer a series of questions.

primary data collection When social scientists design and carry out their own data collection.

secondary data source A resource collected by someone else.

key informant A person who is usually quite central or popular in the research setting and who shares his or her knowledge with the researcher or a person with professional or special knowledge about the social setting.

Some social scientists design and carry out their own **surveys**; this is called **primary data collection**. Most sociologists, however, use and analyze data from large surveys carried out by the federal government, major universities, professional survey research organizations, or market research firms. For researchers who use rather than design surveys, survey data are a **secondary data source**, or a resource collected by someone else. Visit the website of a survey data depository such as the Inter-university Consortium for Political and Social Research (ICPSR; www.icpsr. umich.edu), and you will find hundreds of surveys whose data are available for you to explore.

Respondents and Key Informants

Survey researchers ask members of a sample to answer a series of questions. The individuals who answer survey questions are the respondents. Most surveys are concerned with individuals' lives, thoughts, and behaviors and ask respondents to answer questions about themselves. For example, if researchers wanted to know how often the average American attends religious services, they might ask: "Aside from weddings and funerals, how often do you attend religious services—at least once a week, a few times a month, or less often than that?"

Surveys also can be used to learn about the characteristics and practices of social institutions such as schools, corporations, or religious organizations. For example, a researcher might be interested in documenting the average size of churches, synagogues, or mosques in the United States or she might want to know how racially diverse these houses of worship are. The National Congregations Study focuses on more than 3,000 congregations throughout the United States (Chaves & Anderson, 2014). Researchers studying social institutions identify a **key informant** to serve as their respondent. This is a single knowledgeable person at each site—in the case of religious congregations, perhaps a minister, priest, rabbi, or other staff person. The key informant provides answers on behalf of the organization to broad survey questions, such as "How many adults would you say regularly participate in the religious life of your congregation?"

To understand the structure of houses of worship, a survey researcher might speak with one key informant such as a clergyperson.

Survey Formats

Surveys can take several different forms. A researcher may administer the survey in person or by telephone. Surveys also may be completed directly by respondents, either by filling out a **self-administered questionnaire (SAQ)** distributed by mail or by answering questions online. Each of these approaches, referred to as **modes of administration**, has distinctive strengths and weaknesses, yet they all share similar properties (Groves et al., 2011).

All surveys are highly structured, meaning that researchers define nearly all questions on the survey in advance, so there is little room for free-flowing conversation. Most survey questions are **closed-ended**; respondents choose an answer from a list of preset **response categories** provided by the researcher. Closed-ended questions allow researchers to easily compare responses across different populations and time periods. The closed-ended approach is different from in-depth interviewing (Chapter 11), in which an interviewer asks very broad, **open-ended questions**, such as, "How do you get along with your parents these days?"

In contrast, a structured survey interview might ask a respondent: "Do you agree or disagree with the following statement? Overall, I am satisfied with my relationship with my mother." Possible answers are limited to (say) six categories ranging from "agree strongly" to "disagree strongly." The follow-up question would typically be another structured question with fixed response options, such as "How much does your mother make you feel loved and cared for? A lot, somewhat, a little, or not at all?" These closed-ended categories might seem limiting or sound robotic, but you will soon understand why fixed categories are so essential to survey research.

Timing of Surveys

Surveys may be administered at a single point in time, capturing a snapshot of social life at one historical moment. These single-observation surveys are called **cross-sectional surveys**. Cross-sectional surveys are well suited for comparing the experiences of subgroups at one point in time; they can answer questions such as "Do men and women hold different beliefs regarding gun control in 2017?" In contrast,

self-administered questionnaire (SAQ) A survey completed directly by respondents through the mail or online.

mode of administration The way the survey is administered, such as face to face, by phone or mail, or online.

closed-ended question A focused interview question to which subjects can respond only in preset ways.

response categories The preset answers to questions on a survey.

open-ended question A broad interview question to which subjects are allowed to respond in their own words rather than in preset ways.

cross-sectional survey A survey in which data are collected at only one time point.

longitudinal survey A survey in which data are collected at multiple time points.

repeated cross-sectional survey A type of longitudinal survey in which data are collected at multiple time points but from different subjects at each time point.

panel survey A type of longitudinal survey in which data are collected from the same subjects at multiple time points.

longitudinal surveys involve collecting survey data at multiple points in time. As you learned in Chapter 4, there are two main types of longitudinal study designs: repeated cross-sectional studies (also called *trend studies*) and panel studies. For **repeated cross-sectional surveys**, researchers interview different samples of individuals at multiple time points. As a result, repeated cross-sectional surveys are excellent for documenting historical trends. For example, each year for the past 50 years, first-year college students have been surveyed about their attitudes, plans, and behaviors. Thus, researchers can document the ways that college students' majors, career goals, drug use, and ability to pay for college change from year to year, with each year representing data from a different cohort of freshmen (Eagan et al., 2016).

The second type of longitudinal survey is the **panel survey**, which involves interviewing the same sample of individuals at multiple points in time. Panel surveys can answer questions such as "Do individuals' attitudes toward gun control change as they age?" Panel surveys are ideal for exploring how people change over time, and they are particularly valuable to life-course sociologists, who study how early life experiences affect later-life outcomes. For instance, panel surveys such as the National Longitudinal Study of Adolescent to Adult Health (Add Health)—a survey that first interviewed students in grades 7–12 and then followed up with four additional interviews with the same students through their twenties and thirties—allow us to explore how parental involvement in childhood affects teens' chances of going on to college and ultimately securing rewarding jobs (Gordon & Cui, 2012).

Each approach has strengths and weaknesses, and researchers select the approach that best matches their research aims (Table 7.1). The main limitation of cross-sectional surveys is that researchers cannot easily determine cause and effect: Because all measures are obtained at a single point in time, we can document associations but not causation. For instance, a cross-sectional survey may find that unpopular

TABLE 7.1 Characteristics of Cross-Sectional Surveys versus Panel Surveys

Characteristic	Cross-Sectional Surveys	Panel Surveys
Cost	Relatively low, as respondents are contacted only once	Relatively high, as respondents must be "traced," retained, and reinterviewed over time
Ease of administration	Relatively easy, as participants are interviewed only once	Difficult, includes following up and locating subjects, long wait times between waves
Causal inference	Cannot ascertain causal ordering, as all measures are obtained at the same time	Excellent, because measures at one wave can be used to predict outcomes at subsequent waves
Sources of bias	Coverage and samples typically exclude those who are difficult to reach	Same biases as cross-sectional survey, with addition of selective attrition, or "loss to follow-up"
Ability to document change	Cannot assess within-person change	Well suited to assess within-person change over time
Attention to social history	Cannot disentangle age, period, and cohort effects	Panel studies focused on a single cohort cannot differentiate age versus period effect. Multicohort longitudinal studies cannot differentiate age versus cohort effect.

high-school students have low self-esteem; however, the survey cannot tell us whether being unpopular hurts the students' self-esteem, or whether their low self-esteem prevents them from socializing and establishing friendships. The main limitation of panel studies is sample **attrition**, which occurs when people drop out of the study. Attrition tends not to occur at random, so it may bias study results. Because the people who participate and continue in panel studies tend to have more education and better health than those who do not, panel studies run the risk of providing an overly positive view of their sample members' lives (Groves et al., 2011).

Strengths of Surveys

A survey based on a high-quality random sample can provide accurate estimates of the characteristics, behaviors, and attitudes of an entire population, even if the survey sample includes just 1,000 to 2,000 people. Surveys also enable researchers to explore a broad range of topics, compare population subgroups, track social change over time, and study very large populations (Groves et al., 2011).

BREADTH OF TOPICS

Surveys vary widely in their breadth, depth, and length. Nearly all surveys obtain basic demographic data such as age, race, sex, marital status, and perhaps socioeconomic status characteristics such as educational attainment. Demographic data are an essential component of most surveys because social scientists are interested in documenting inequalities on the basis of race, age, sex, and other factors. Federally funded surveys in the United States, such as the U.S. Census, are required by law to collect data on race because it is a critical factor in making policy decisions, particularly for civil rights (Office of Management and Budget, 1995). States also use data about race to meet legislative redistricting requirements, evaluate equal employment opportunities, and assess racial disparities in health (Turner & LaMacchia, 1999).

Beyond demographic data, surveys vary widely in the number and breadth of questions they ask. Some are focused on a single topic and administered for a very specific purpose. For example, a market research firm may ask just a few questions, such as your age, sex, the kind of car you drive, and whether you plan to purchase a new car in the next 6 months. The information obtained in these very brief surveys is not used to test hypotheses. Rather, the results serve a specific purpose, such as helping an auto manufacturer estimate the number of people in the United States who plan to buy a Honda in the next 6 months or helping the Democratic National Committee predict the proportion of 18- to 24-year-old voters who plan to vote Democratic, Republican, or Independent in an upcoming election. A very brief single-topic survey is often called a **poll**. A poll typically includes just one or a few questions, and these questions often require only simple yes/no answers (Traugott, 2008).

Other surveys cover a broad range of topics, such as attitudes toward social issues (for example, legalization of marijuana) or reports of health behaviors (for example, whether one smoked e-cigarettes in the past year). These comprehensive surveys are sometimes called *omnibus surveys* because they cover multiple topics and can be used by researchers with diverse research interests. The General Social Survey (GSS) and the National Survey of Midlife Development in the United States (MIDUS) are examples of omnibus surveys. MIDUS asks 3,000 randomly selected Americans to answer dozens of questions about their health, family, neighborhood, ethnic background, and sexual relationships. This breadth of questions gives researchers great latitude in generating hypotheses about the associations among these measures. Researchers using the MIDUS data have explored whether married people are healthier than single people (Donoho et al., 2015), whether overweight and obese individuals are more likely than slender people to report workplace discrimination (Carr & Friedman, 2005), and whether people become more or less happy as they grow older (Mroczek & Kolarz, 1998).

Although the designers of omnibus surveys want rich, detailed, and varied content, they do not want to demand too much of their respondents' time. Depending on the mode of administration, designers of omnibus surveys hope to take no more than 30–45 minutes of their respondents' time. If respondents become bored and stop answering questions midstream, the quality of the survey data will be compromised.

One way to limit the length of a survey while maximizing the number and breadth of questions is to use a **split-ballot design**. With this strategy, a randomly selected subset of respondents, typically 50% of those persons selected to participate in the survey, receives one topical ballot, or module, while the other 50% receives a different topical ballot (Petersen, 2008). For instance, a randomly chosen subset of 1,500 GSS participants (50% of the 3,000 respondents) may be asked a series of questions about their attitudes toward physician-assisted suicide, while the other 1,500 are asked about their attitudes toward gun control. This design cuts down on total survey time by sparing respondents from answering both modules yet also provides researchers with information on two important and controversial issues.

> **split-ballot design** A survey in which a randomly selected subset of respondents, typically 50% of those persons selected to participate in the survey, receives one topical module while the other 50% receives a different topical ballot.

COMPARISONS ACROSS GROUPS AND OVER TIME

As we learned in Chapter 1, sociologists are interested in the ways that our race, class, and gender shape our experiences, as well as the ways that history shapes these personal experiences. Surveys are particularly good at exploring subgroup differences and historical trends because of the consistency of their measures: All respondents answer the same questions, with the exact same wording and exact same response categories. There are minor exceptions to this rule, including split-ballot approaches and skip patterns (which we discuss later in the chapter). In general, though, consistency of measurement is an essential component of most surveys. This uniformity allows us to compare responses across subgroups and track how responses change over time.

For these reasons, surveys allow us to explore core sociological questions, such as "Are college graduates more politically liberal than people who did not go to college?" (comparing subgroups) or "Have political attitudes become more liberal or conservative over time?" (tracking change over time). To answer these questions effectively, we need fixed questions and response categories. A survey can ascertain the respondent's level of education with a question such as "What is the highest educational degree that you have completed: a graduate degree or higher; a 4-year college degree;

a 2-year college degree; a high school diploma; or less than a high school diploma?" This question classifies each respondent into one education category, allowing researchers to compare people across categories. It would be difficult, perhaps even impossible, to classify people according to their educational level if we asked an open-ended question, such as "How much schooling do you have?" Imagine the difficulties researchers would face if respondents offered up creative answers like "Not enough" or "Just the school of hard knocks!" They could not compare people easily, especially if they were working with a sample of thousands of individuals, generating hundreds of different responses.

Likewise, fixed response options allow us to compare subjective phenomena such as political inclinations. Although the fixed categories may not perfectly capture every respondent's views, they are developed so that they capture a nearly full range of responses, and every respondent can find an answer that approximates his or her view. For instance, we can measure underlying political views with this question: "We hear a lot of talk these days about liberals and conservatives. Consider a 7-point scale on which the political views that people might hold are arranged from extremely liberal (1) to extremely conservative (7). Where would you place yourself on this scale or haven't you thought much about this?" Respondents can then place themselves into one of seven categories—(1) extremely liberal, (2) liberal, (3) slightly liberal, (4) moderate/middle of the road, (5) slightly conservative, (6) conservative, or (7) extremely conservative—or they can indicate that they "haven't thought much about this question." Researchers can then compare the average response to this question with the responses of persons in each of the educational categories described earlier.

For example, if we see that the average response among high school dropouts is 6 (conservative) and the average score of college graduates is 1.5 (somewhere between extremely liberal and liberal), we could conclude that higher education is associated with holding more liberal political views.

Likewise, if we ask a particular question with the exact same wording every time we administer the survey, we can track trends over time. These historical analyses are very important to sociologists, who are interested in documenting and explaining social change (Marsden, 2012). If we know that a question has been consistently administered every year for 40 years, we can conclude with a great deal of certainty that population-level changes in attitudes reflect a real sociohistorical trend, rather than a change in how the question was worded. For example, the GSS has asked the political orientation question nearly every year of its more than 40-year history, revealing trend data like that shown in Figure 7.1. As the graph reveals, while the proportion of Americans

FIGURE 7.1 Political Views in the U.S. from 1974–2014

For the past 40 years, the GSS has asked respondents about their political orientation. This chart shows the proportion each year who identify as liberal, moderate, or conservative. How do fixed questions and categories such as these help us understand stability and change in social trends over time?

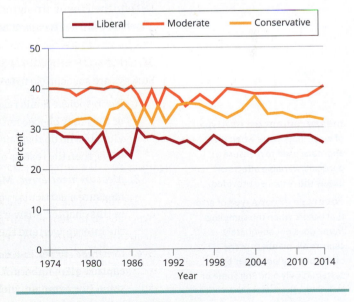

Source: General Social Survey, 1974–2014.

who identify as liberal, conservative, or moderate wavers slightly from year to year, we see that 40% say they are moderate and roughly 30% each identify as liberal or conservative consistently across the four-decade period.

GENERALIZABILITY

Surveys tend to have better external validity than other methods, such as experiments, ethnographies, or case studies. Recall from Chapter 5 that the quality of a research project is assessed in part by its external validity, or the degree to which the results of a study can generalize beyond the study. Surveys based on random samples have excellent external validity. As you learned in Chapter 6, some samples are randomly selected from well-defined populations, such as all high school students in the United States. Others are convenience samples, such as fellow students in your introduction to sociology class. The results from studying the former could be generalized to characterize the experiences of all U.S. high school students, while the results of studying the latter would likely be representative only of sociology students at your university. For these reasons, survey researchers strive to collect data from random samples of their populations of interest (Kalaian & Kasim, 2008).

Because the GSS is focused on the U.S. population, it is based on a probability sample of U.S. adults ages 18–90 (Marsden, 2012). By contrast, a survey such as the National Survey of Family Growth (NSFG) is focused on women's childbearing behavior, so for most of its 40-year history, the survey has focused on women ages 15–44 (Boslaugh, 2008). Although the GSS has just 3,000 respondents and the NSFG had roughly 5,000 respondents in its latest wave, both of these data sets can be generalized to describe the experiences of all Americans and women of reproductive age, respectively.

Challenges of Survey Research

Despite their many strengths, surveys have important limitations. Two general points of concern are sources of error and response rates.

SOURCES OF ERROR IN SURVEYS

Surveys are susceptible to four main types of errors (Groves et al., 2011):

1. *Nonresponse.* Some respondents may choose not to participate in a survey at all or they may choose not to respond to particular questions on the survey. If individuals who do respond and individuals who do not respond differ in systematic ways, then the results of the study may be biased.

2. *Measurement error.* **Measurement error** occurs when the approach used to measure a particular variable affects the response provided. As we discuss later in this chapter, answers may be influenced by factors such as the survey design, the interviewer, and the setting.

3. *Coverage errors.* In a **coverage error**, the sampling frame does not adequately capture all members of the target population, either by systematically omitting some (for example, those without phones cannot complete a phone survey) or by including others more than once (those with two phones).

measurement error A type of error that occurs when the approach used to measure a particular variable affects or biases the response provided.

coverage error A type of error that occurs when the sampling frame does not adequately capture all members of the target population, either by systematically omitting some or including others more than once.

4. *Sampling error.* **Sampling error** refers to any differences between the characteristics of the survey sample and the characteristics of the population from which the sample is drawn.

sampling error The difference between the estimates from a sample and the true parameter that arise due to random chance.

It is important to consider potential sources of error when designing a survey, as these considerations help researchers decide which mode of administration to use, how to word questions, and how to encourage participation in the survey (Groves et al., 2011). Later in the chapter, we explore the strategies that survey researchers use to minimize these errors.

RESPONSE RATES

One of the most serious challenges in survey research is achieving a high response rate. According to the American Association for Public Opinion Research (2015), the *response rate* (or *completion rate*) equals the total number of completed surveys from reporting units divided by the total number of units in the sample. *Reporting units* are typically individuals, but they could also be key informants representing a corporation, school, or house of worship.

Say you randomly select 1,000 full-time students from your college's listing of all full-time students, and 780 students complete the survey you send them. Your response rate is 78% (780/1,000). That is a very good response rate. While researchers would love to have 100% response rates, that is a rare, almost impossible, feat. In reality, response rates may range from 20% to 80% depending on the survey and mode of administration.

You may have noticed that we calculated a response rate on the basis of "completed" surveys. This is a fairly strict definition because respondents do not always *complete* their surveys. Sometimes people get bored when completing long self-administered surveys, and they quit before answering all the questions in their booklets. Other times, they may be in the middle of a telephone interview when they are interrupted by their child's temper tantrum. Others, still, may become upset by some of the questions and refuse to participate further; a question about childhood abuse, for example, may bring back sad or troubling memories. Recall from Chapter 3 that study participants have the right to end their participation in a study at any time. For this reason, the American Association for Public Opinion Research offers an alternative version of response rate in which the numerator includes both complete *and* partial interviews. A partial interview is one in which the respondent does not complete the full survey. Although a partial interview is better than a refusal to participate, it is not as useful to a researcher as a completed interview (American Association for Public Opinion Research, 2015).

CONCEPT CHECKS

1 Name two common characteristics of surveys.

2 Contrast a respondent with a key informant.

3 How can a survey be used to track social change?

4 What are the main sources of error in surveys? Explain each one.

TYPES OF SURVEYS: MODES OF ADMINISTRATION

Surveys can be administered in many different ways, with new modes and strategies always in development. Historically, three approaches, or *modes*, have been used most widely: (1) face-to-face interviews, (2) telephone surveys, and (3) mail surveys, or self-administered modes. In the past decade, however, researchers have relied more heavily on Internet-based surveys.

Researchers might choose one mode over the others for many reasons, and each approach has its own distinctive strengths and weakness (Bowling, 2005). Researchers also may use mixed modes (two or more modes on a single project). Some of the main criteria for deciding which mode to use are cost, response rate, researcher control over the data-collection process, and the potential for interviewer effects. **Interviewer effects** refers to the possibility that the mere presence of an interviewer, or that interviewer's personal characteristics, may lead a respondent to answer questions in a particular way, potentially biasing the survey responses (Dillman, Smyth, & Christian, 2014).

Face-to-Face Interviews

A face-to-face interview (or personal interview) is one in which the interviewer meets in person with the respondent and asks a series of questions from the **interview schedule**, which is the full set of questions that the interviewer asks the respondent (Dillman, Smyth, & Christian, 2014). The interview may take place in the respondent's home or at a public place of the respondent's choosing, such as a coffee shop. Some surveys, such as the GSS, make every effort to interview respondents in their own homes, where the interviewer also assesses features of the home that may affect the respondent's answers. These features include the noise level in the household, how well the respondent understood the questions, and whether another family member was present. Interviewer observations are a type of **paradata**, or data about the process by which the survey data were collected. Data analysts may find these observations useful when trying to understand the ways that people answer survey questions (Couper & Lyberg, 2005).

Sometimes surveys yield higher-quality data if the interview happens in a setting away from the home. For instance, if a woman is being asked questions about spousal abuse when her aggressive husband is sitting in the next room or if an LGBT child is answering questions about sexual identity while his or her socially conservative parents are within earshot, the respondent may be afraid to provide truthful answers.

Historically, the interviewer would ask questions and record the respondent's answers in a preprinted copy of the survey booklet. This handwritten approach is known as a **paper-and-pencil interview (PAPI)**. After completing the face-to-face interview, the interviewer would return the survey booklet to the research organization, where a data-entry assistant would enter all of the respondents' answers

FIGURE 7.2 Example of a Survey Showcard

During a face-to-face survey, an interviewer may present the respondent with a showcard that reminds them of the question's response options.

Questions 17, 23, 66, 114a–f

CARD 5

Agree strongly

Agree

Neither Agree nor Disagree

Disagree

Disagree Strongly

into a database. This manual data-entry process could introduce error if the clerk mistyped a respondent's answer. The process also had the added cost of the data-entry clerk's wages.

Today, the face-to-face interview process is much more efficient. Interviewers typically do a **computer-assisted personal interview (CAPI)**. The interviewer uses a laptop or tablet computer that is preprogrammed with all of the survey questions and response categories (Olsen & Sheets, 2008). The interviewer reads the questions and response categories aloud, entering the respondent's answers. If a question has many response categories, it may be hard for respondents to remember them, so the interviewer will often hand the respondent a **showcard** (Figure 7.2), a preprinted card that reminds the respondent of all the response options for a particular question (Flizik, 2008). For example, many survey questions have as their possible response categories "agree strongly, agree, neither agree nor disagree, disagree, disagree strongly." Respondents might forget these categories or they may get annoyed if they have to listen to the interviewer repeat them throughout the interview. It is easier to simply hand respondents the showcard so that they can respond with their answer.

In contemporary survey research, sophisticated computer programming occurs prior to the start of the interview. The CAPI software is programmed to ensure that the interviewer does not skip any questions. If the interviewer tries to move on to a new question without completing a prior question, a beep will indicate that the skipped question must be answered. The software also ensures that the responses entered fall within the allowable range of values.

The CAPI software also helps interviewers and respondents successfully navigate the survey's skip patterns. A **skip pattern** refers to a question or series of questions associated with a conditional response to a prior question. Although all respondents can answer some questions (for example, "How old are you?"), other questions can be answered only by a subset of persons. As such, a skip pattern begins with a **screener question** (or *filter question*) that serves as a gateway to or detour around a follow-up question.

Figure 7.3 is an example of a skip pattern from the Changing Lives of Older Couples, a study that explored older widows' and widowers' adjustment to the loss of their spouse. The researchers were interested in the romantic lives of older widows and widowers, but they feared it would be insensitive to ask a recently widowed 75-year-old woman, "How often do you go out on dates?" A more appropriate approach would be to first delicately ask whether she had any interest in dating (screener question S18) and, if she indicated that she was interested, proceed to the follow-up questions.

computer-assisted personal interview (CAPI) A face-to-face interview in which the researcher uses a laptop or tablet computer that is pre-programmed with all of the survey questions and response categories.

showcard A preprinted card that reminds the respondent of all the response options for a particular question or questions

skip pattern A question or series of questions associated with a conditional response to a prior question.

screener question A question that serves as a gateway to (or detour around) a follow-up question; also called a *filter question*.

FIGURE 7.3 Example of a Skip Pattern

The designers of the Changing Lives of Older Couples study wanted to ask widows and widowers about their current dating behavior. S18 is the "screener" to gauge one's interest in dating. Respondents who indicate that they are not interested in dating then skip out of this section of questions.

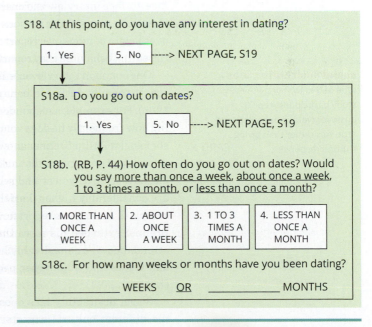

S18. At this point, do you have any interest in dating?

1. Yes   5. No ----> NEXT PAGE, S19

S18a. Do you go out on dates?

1. Yes   5. No ----> NEXT PAGE, S19

S18b. (RB, P. 44) How often do you go out on dates? Would you say more than once a week, about once a week, 1 to 3 times a month, or less than once a month?

| 1. MORE THAN ONCE A WEEK | 2. ABOUT ONCE A WEEK | 3. 1 TO 3 TIMES A MONTH | 4. LESS THAN ONCE A MONTH |

S18c. For how many weeks or months have you been dating?

_____ WEEKS   OR   _____ MONTHS

STRENGTHS OF FACE-TO-FACE INTERVIEWS

Face-to-face interviews are considered the "gold standard" of survey research because the presence of a skilled interviewer helps ensure that respondents understand the survey questions and do not skip any questions that are sensitive or troubling (Dillman, Smyth, & Christian, 2014). Interviewers can also help to clarify questions and response categories. For example, as part of the Wisconsin Longitudinal Study (WLS), a survey of more than 10,000 men and women now in their seventies, researchers were interested in the types of financial preparations that older adults make, such as wills. Respondents were asked: "Do you have a signed and witnessed will?" Most people know what a will is, so respondents could easily answer the question. The next question asked about a financial tool that is less common: "Do you have a revocable trust?" If survey respondents said they did not understand the term or that they weren't sure whether they had one, the interviewer would then read the following explanation from the CAPI screen: "Revocable trusts designate who will get property in that trust after their death." Interviewers must read these explanatory remarks verbatim so as not to bias respondents' answers.

LIMITATIONS OF FACE-TO-FACE INTERVIEWS

As noted earlier, the presence of an interviewer may lead a respondent to answer questions in a way that is not entirely accurate. For instance, studies have shown that people report more open-minded attitudes toward gender issues when interviewed by a woman (Kane & Macaulay, 1993). One fascinating study showed that the interviewer's physique may affect how people answer survey questions. Researchers in the Netherlands asked respondents in a face-to-face interview about their eating behaviors, and followed up with a brief mail questionnaire that the respondents answered privately in their homes (Eisinga et al., 2011). Respondents who had been interviewed by persons with an average body weight reported the same eating behaviors during the face-to-face interview and on the follow-up mail questionnaire. However, those interviewed by very slender persons underreported their eating and those interviewed by overweight persons overreported their eating in the face-to-face interview, relative to the eating behaviors they reported privately on the mailed questionnaire.

One common interviewer effect is a **social desirability bias**, in which respondents report socially desirable behaviors and attitudes in the survey setting (Nederhof, 1985). For example, a respondent might try to impress an interviewer by overreporting how frequently he does volunteer work or attends religious services. Research by sociologist Philip Brenner shows that Americans report quite high levels of religious attendance on surveys that ask questions such as "Aside from weddings and funerals, how often do you attend religious services?" However, these self-reported levels are considerably higher than those detected using a daily diary method, in which a sample of Americans report how they spent every hour in the past 24 hours. Notably, Brenner extended his research to 14 nations and found that overreporting church attendance was considerably higher in the United States, highlighting how culture and values may guide what people see as a socially acceptable answer on a survey (Brenner, 2011).

Social desirability bias does not operate the same way for all people; it reflects the different cultural expectations that individuals face. Case in point: It is well

social desirability bias A type of bias that occurs when study participants report positively valued behaviors and attitudes rather than giving truthful responses.

documented that women tend to underreport the number of sexual partners they've ever had, whereas men overreport their number (Fisher, 2009). These biases reflect a culture in which sexually experienced women are stigmatized while their male counterparts are celebrated (Kreager & Staff, 2009).

Just as people are motivated to overreport positively valued behaviors, they may try to hide socially undesirable behaviors or attitudes. Others may try to conceal beliefs that could be hurtful or insulting to the interviewer. For example, a white respondent who holds racist attitudes may not fully divulge his or her views, especially if the interviewer belongs to an ethnic or racial minority (Davis, 1997).

Although some survey researchers try to match the interviewer and respondent on personal traits such as age or race to help minimize interviewer effects, this matching is often very difficult to accomplish (Schaeffer, 1980). It would be challenging, perhaps even impossible, to match interviewer and respondent along all the dimensions that may matter for a face-to-face interview. For most survey research organizations, the key concern is using a skilled interviewer who works in the region close to the respondent's home.

Survey researchers have made great strides in addressing another potential source of bias in face-to-face interviews: Respondents may be reluctant to report a behavior that is stigmatized (for example, having an abortion) or a behavior that is illegal (for example, illicit drug use). To make the face-to-face interview setting more comfortable when discussing sensitive topics, an interviewer may hand the laptop or tablet computer to the respondent and allow her to read questions directly off the screen or listen to a recording of the questions and then enter her answers into the computer. **Audio computer-assisted self-interview (ACASI)** is an innovative technology designed to facilitate this self-administered component of the face-to-face interview.

audio computer-assisted self-interview (ACASI)
An interview in which the respondent uses a laptop or tablet to listen to and answer prerecorded questions.

The federal government's National Center of Health Statistics has for many years carried out the National Survey of Family Growth (NSFG), which asks women about sensitive topics, including whether they've had an unwanted pregnancy or abortion. In 1995, for the first time, researchers used ACASI so that women could privately answer questions regarding their abortion history. Women would answer these questions on the computer while the interviewer left the room. Studies have found that women are more likely to report having had an abortion when the survey question is administered via ACASI rather than via a face-to-face interview (Fu et al., 1998).

Telephone Surveys

A telephone survey is a structured interview that is administered over the telephone, whether a landline, cell phone, or smartphone. Respondents for telephone surveys are commonly identified through random-digit dialing (RDD), where telephone numbers are generated at random. RDD ensures that all people who own a phone can be contacted, including those who might be unlisted in their local phone directory. Researchers interested in a particular geographic region may select an area code for that region and then generate random numbers for the next seven digits.

In the mid- and late-twentieth century, survey researchers were at risk of missing those people who did not own phones. Also, they occasionally made the error of calling the same person twice if that person had two separate phone lines. These coverage errors imposed some bias on the findings of early telephone surveys, because telephone owners were typically older and more financially and residentially stable than those who did not own phones. Likewise, those who owned multiple phones were considerably better off financially than those who owned one phone or no phone. In the 2010s, however, concerns about excluding those with no phone are minor, as more than 95% of the U.S. population has either a landline or cell phone (McGeeney, Kennedy, & Weisel, 2015).

STRENGTHS OF TELEPHONE SURVEYS

Telephone surveys have many of the strengths of face-to-face interviews. A skilled interviewer guides the respondent through the survey questions, ensuring that no questions are skipped and offering explanations for terms or phrases that the respondent does not understand. Just as face-to-face interviewers are assisted by CAPI technology, telephone interviewers use the similar **computer-assisted telephone interview (CATI)** technology. This technology helps ensure that the interviewer and respondent follow the survey's skip patterns correctly and that the respondent receives only pertinent questions. CATI technology can be combined with voice recognition software so that the computer "asks" the questions and then records and codes the answers provided by the respondent (Kelly, 2008).

Telephone surveys have several additional strengths. First, the cost is substantially lower. Some researchers have estimated that a phone survey costs roughly 10% to 20% less per question than a face-to-face survey (Groves et al., 2011). Second, phone interviews typically are conducted in a central location, such as a survey organization's calling center, where multiple interviewers sit at their computers in cubicles. These call centers typically have a supervisor on duty at all times who can monitor the interviewers' work and answer questions as needed. This supervision helps ensure that the data collected are of high quality.

Unlike face-to-face interviews, telephone interviews can be conducted with relatively little advance planning. Whereas a face-to-face survey requires scheduling and traveling to the interview, and a mail survey requires printing and mailing the document, a telephone survey can be conducted as soon as the research team has drafted its survey instrument. Often, standard survey questions that have been used many times before are sufficient, so researchers can launch their telephone survey immediately. For example, immediately after a presidential debate, survey research organizations conduct telephone polls to measure whether Americans' views of a particular candidate are more favorable or less favorable than they were prior to the debate.

Telephone surveys can also gauge national sentiment on hot-button issues. For example, in May 2016, President Barack Obama issued an executive order directing public schools to allow transgender students to use the bathroom that matches their gender identity. At that time, the schools faced a possible

computer-assisted telephone interview (CATI) A telephone interview in which the researcher uses a laptop or tablet computer that is preprogrammed with all of the survey questions and response categories.

Telephone interviews are often carried out at a survey organization's call center.

loss of federal funding if they did not follow the guidelines of the executive order. Immediately after the announcement, a CBS/*New York Times* telephone poll reached out to a random sample of 1,300 Americans to assess their attitudes (Neidig, 2016). The poll showed very divided views: 46% agreed with state laws that require transgender people to use the bathroom that corresponds to their biological sex, and a slightly smaller proportion (41%) agreed that transgender individuals should use the bathroom of the gender with which they identify (see "From the Field to the Front Page" feature).

LIMITATIONS OF TELEPHONE SURVEYS

Telephone surveys have several important limitations, some of which are similar to those of face-to-face interviews. Some people are reluctant to discuss personal matters over the phone, while others offer positively biased accounts of their attitudes and behaviors. Interviewer effects also are possible. Even though respondents cannot see the interviewer, they may still glean his or her gender, age, or ethnicity on the basis of voice. Some studies show that telephone survey respondents report more optimistic attitudes about the economy when interviewed by a male (Groves & Fultz, 1985), while others show that respondents are more likely to report that they will vote for a black candidate in an upcoming political election when interviewed by an African American (Finkel, Guterbock, & Borg, 1991).

Telephone interviews also have limitations that differ from those of face-to-face interviews. First, many people do not want to be bothered in their homes. The explosion of telemarketing and "robocalls" poses a considerable threat to legitimate survey organizations. Many people see an unfamiliar incoming number and choose not to answer. If those who choose to answer their phones differ significantly from those who do not, sample bias will result. Older adults, those with more spare time, those with a more trusting nature, or those who are lonely are more likely to answer a call from an unfamiliar phone number.

Survey researchers have devised strategies to address this problem, but these innovations add cost to the survey (Dillman, Smyth, & Christian, 2014). One approach is to send potential respondents an advance letter (Figure 7.4) that describes the study and shows that the survey organization is reputable. The letter should clearly state the name of the organization sponsoring the survey, including the name of the main contact person. It should also briefly describe the goals of the study, specifying the survey's general topic and providing a sentence about the value of the study, such as its contribution to our understanding of Americans' health or economic well-being. The letter also must convey that participation is completely voluntary (with one exception: Participation in the U.S. Census is required by law). Potential respondents also should be informed as to whether their participation is confidential or anonymous. Finally, the letter should thank the respondent and provide a telephone number, website, or e-mail address where the prospective respondent can go for further information (Dillman, Smyth, & Christian, 2014).

If the telephone survey is being administered as part of a panel study, the advance letter might remind respondents of their participation in earlier waves of data collection. The advance letter also may tell respondents when they will receive their interview call. If respondents are notified that they will be receiving a call from the

FIGURE 7.4 Example of an Advance Letter

An advance letter is sent to potential respondents prior to the start of a survey. It is often personalized with specific information, which would appear in the brackets.

<<printdate>>

<<fnam>> <<lnam>> <<suffix>>
<<addr>>
<<city>>, <<state>> <<zip>>
Phone: <<phone1_formatted>>

Dear <<fnam>> <<lnam>>,

We are sorry to have learned of the loss of your late <<relatetxt>>, <<decedent_fname>> <<decent_lnam>>. <<decedent_fnam>> <<decedent_lname>> was a valued member of a large group of Wisconsin high school students and siblings who participated in the long-running Wisconsin Longitudinal Study. In 1957, high school seniors completed a questionnaire about their high school experiences and plans for the future. The graduate and one of their siblings later participated in surveys about life experiences after high school. By participating in this study, your late <<relatetxt>> and others have helped scholars and policy makers learn a great deal about education, work, health, and family over the life course.

Now we are seeking your participation in a follow-up interview about your late <<relatetxt>>. We are interested in learning about your <<relatetxt>>'s experiences at the end of life, such as the quality of medical care <<heshe>> received, and in learning about your experiences at that time and more recently. This information will help us to understand how end-of-life health care may be improved. We appreciate your <<relatetxt>>'s participation in the Wisconsin Longitudinal Study. However, your participation in the study remains strictly voluntary. You are free to decide to participate or not, and you may choose not to answer any questions with which you are uncomfortable. We understand that talking about the death of a loved one can be difficult; however, many people have found the interview to be both enjoyable and helpful, and found it rewarding to contribute their experiences to this study—the only study in the United States that has followed a large number of high school graduates and their families across 50 years of their lives. The study is conducted by the University of Wisconsin–Madison and is supported by the National Institute on Aging, an agency of the federal government's National Institutes of Health.

Throughout this study we have maintained our promise to everyone we speak with never to reveal to anyone any personal information about individuals or their families. We will continue to strictly follow this policy.

You may call the University of Wisconsin Survey Center toll free at 1-800-123-XXXX to arrange a convenient time for your interview. If you have questions, you may call <<fnam>> at the UW Survey Center, at 1-800-123-XXXX, fname@university.edu. Otherwise, the UW Survey Center will contact you within a few days. If you are contacted at an inconvenient time, please tell the interviewer and he or she will be happy to make an appointment with you.

You may learn more about the study by calling the UW Survey Center, or on the Internet at www.wisls.org/WISTFL/WISTFL.htm. We appreciate your participation in this important study.

Sincerely,

Deborah Carr
Faculty Affiliate, Center for Demography of Health and Aging
University of Wisconsin–Madison

National Opinion Research Center at the University of Chicago, they may be more inclined to answer their phone when they see an unfamiliar incoming call on the target interview date. Another strategy is to call homes during those times of day when people are not likely eating dinner or preparing to leave for a day of work. Random-digit calls at 7:30 p.m. on a Wednesday are generally more effective than those at 7:30 a.m. on a Sunday (Dillman, Smyth, & Christian, 2014).

Respondent fatigue is an additional concern; most respondents do not want to stay on the phone for long periods of time. Respondents who become bored by the survey, fatigued by the interview process, or distracted by the goings-on in their homes may break off the interview midstream, leaving the researcher with incomplete data. Additionally, the questions administered in telephone interviews must be very simple and straightforward. Interviewers can report the response categories over the phone, but they are unable to hand respondents a showcard to remind them of the response options (Dillman, Smyth, & Christian, 2014). Telephone interviews also do not allow researchers to capture some types of paradata, including the quality of the housing, whether a family member was present during the interview, or other observable factors that provide important information about the respondent. However, telephone interviews can still provide key information, such as how well the respondent understood the questions (West, 2013).

A relatively new limitation of telephone surveys is that a respondent's cell phone number does not necessarily correspond to where the respondent lives. For this reason, when researchers use random-digit dialing, they must ask the respondent about his or her location, especially if they are conducting a survey that is targeted to persons living in a particular geographic region (Steeh & Piekarski, 2007).

Mail Surveys

Many respondents think, "I don't want to report my income (or how many sex partners I've ever had) to a complete stranger who is talking to me on the phone or sitting across from me at my parents' kitchen table." Survey researchers recognize that face-to-face and telephone interviews might lead some participants either not to answer a question or to answer in such a way as to appear good, honest, or admirable to the interviewer. Self-administered questionnaires (SAQs) are an important corrective because respondents complete these questionnaires on their own, away from the interviewer's watchful eye. At the same time, however, the lack of an in-person or telephone interviewer increases the chances that respondents will misunderstand or skip important questions.

Self-administered questionnaires are typically distributed via postal mail. A *questionnaire*, which is a highly structured series of questions presented in a booklet form, is mailed to a random sample of respondents. In some cases, such as the MIDUS study, participants first complete a telephone interview and then receive a 48-page questionnaire booklet in the mail, along with a stamped envelope so that they can easily return their completed questionnaire. Researchers typically ask respondents to complete and return their questionnaires within a particular time frame, such as 2 weeks. This time frame ensures that respondents have time to ponder the survey questions. The deadline is also sufficiently tight so that respondents do not procrastinate or forget to complete and return their questionnaires.

STRENGTHS OF MAIL SURVEYS

Mail surveys are less susceptible to the interviewer effects that may bias face-to-face and (to a lesser extent) telephone interviews. In a mail survey, people are more likely to report unhealthy or undesirable behaviors and less likely to inflate

RESEARCHERS USE SURVEY METHODS TO COUNT TRANSGENDER YOUTH

One of the first things President Trump did upon taking office in January 2017 was rescind the guidelines issued by the Obama administration that directed schools to allow transgender students to use the bathroom that corresponds to their gender identity. Conservative politicians and parents, who feared men would enter women's restrooms and prey on innocent young girls, supported this reversal. Others despaired, noting that these accommodations are necessary to ensure vulnerable children feel safe and secure. Transgender children are often teased, victimized, and worse, with many experiencing depression and suicidal thoughts (Haas, Rodgers, & Herman, 2014).

Social scientists are committed to understanding just how many youth would be affected by "bathroom bills"—legislation that forces all people to use the bathroom that aligns with the sex assigned to them at birth. It is difficult to know because the United States does not have an official count or estimate of the number of children (or adults) who identify as transgender. There are no nationally representative surveys that ask young people detailed questions about their gender identity. Yet, as described in the May 2016 *New York Times* article "As Attention Grows, Transgender Children's Numbers Are Elusive" (Hoffman, 2016), survey researchers are pioneering efforts to count transgender youth using small, local, and nonrepresentative surveys.

For example, in 2015 the Dane County Youth Assessment survey asked roughly 18,500 Wisconsin students in grades 7–12 questions about their health, family life, and friends. The survey found that 1.5% of students self-identified as transgender, while three times as many students (4.6%) reported that they weren't sure what *transgender* means. A very similar pattern was found in the 2006 Boston Youth Survey of 1,000 public high-school students. When asked "Are you transgender?" 1.6% of students indicated "yes," while 6.3% answered "don't know" and another 5.7% skipped the question (Almeida et al., 2009).

Although 1.5% is a very small proportion, it eclipses the proportion of adults who report that they are transgender. The handful of surveys that ask adults about transgender identity typically find that fewer than 0.5% of adults identify as such. For example, the Massachusetts Behavioral Risk Factor Surveillance Survey, suggests that 0.5% of adults aged 18–64 identify as transgender (Conron et al., 2012), while a comparable survey in California puts the rate at 0.1% (Gates, 2011).

Experts in survey research point out several reasons why we should be skeptical of these estimates. First, the mode of interview matters. A face-to-face interview can ensure that

A 2015 survey found that 1.5% of students identify as transgender—far more than the proportion of adults.

respondents understand the meaning of transgender. At the same time, a respondent might not feel comfortable identifying as transgender in a face-to-face interview. A young person, in particular, might fear being judged by the interviewer or, worse yet, may worry that his or her conservative parents might overhear.

Second, response categories may matter. In the case of gender identity, many surveys have relied on this question: "Do you identify as: (a) male, (b) female, or (c) transgender?" Children and teens, in particular, might feel that two or three categories apply to them. For instance, a child may recognize that she was born male (a), but identify and dress as a female (b) and, as a result, may be transgender (c).

The case of transgender children and teens vividly reveals some of the limitations of survey research, especially when studying topics that are poorly understood, stigmatized, or new to the public's consciousness. However, survey researchers are making steady progress in their efforts to understand transgender youth. In 2019, the Centers for Disease Control and Prevention (CDC) plans to measure transgender identity for the first time in its Youth Risk Behavior Survey (YRBS), which is based on a nationally representative sample of grades 9–12 in all public and private schools.

Survey researchers are optimistic about the possibility of collecting and examining these new data, but they also recognize that understanding the daily lives of transgender youth also may require using in-depth interviews and other methods that can supplement and expand on the findings yielded by surveys.

their reports of positive attributes because they do not feel the social pressure of an interviewer's presence.

There are some intriguing exceptions to this rule, however, as well as instances in which the freedom to answer mail surveys in private may bias the responses. Some researchers have found that respondents offer more accurate reports of their body weight and smoking in face-to-face interviews than in mailed questionnaires. Why? It is difficult for a respondent to claim that he is a nonsmoker if the interviewer sees an ashtray on the coffee table and clearly dishonest to report that one weighs 150 pounds if the interviewer can see that the respondent weighs considerably more or less (Christensen et al., 2014).

Another strength of mail surveys is their relatively low cost. Whereas face-to-face surveys sometimes require skilled interviewers to travel long distances, self-administered mail surveys cost far less. The main costs are printing, copying, and assembling the survey document; designing the sample; mailing the advance letter and survey; providing self-addressed stamped envelopes and entering the survey responses into the study database. This low cost is related to another strength of mail surveys: The research team can more easily reach a large and geographically diverse sample because the per-head cost of collecting data is lower than it is for face-to-face interviews, and a survey can be mailed anywhere.

LIMITATIONS OF MAIL SURVEYS

While mail surveys are popular, they also have important limitations. Because an interviewer is not present to explain confusing questions or guide the respondent through the survey, mail surveys are susceptible to missing data or more frequent "don't know" responses. Researchers also cannot ensure that the survey is completed by the intended respondent. A survey might be sent to an older adult, and his or her adult child may instead answer the questions, potentially biasing the results (Dillman & Parsons, 2008).

Perhaps the most significant limitation of mail surveys is low response rate, often ranging from just 20% to 40% (Dillman & Parsons, 2008). It is easy to toss a printed questionnaire into the recycling bin, especially when no interviewer is present to urge the respondent to complete the survey. This low response rate is a potential threat to the survey's generalizability because those who complete their mail surveys tend to be significantly different from those who do not. They tend to be literate and well educated, with the free time necessary to fill out the survey, or they may feel a greater sense of social obligation than those who do not complete their surveys (Dillman, Smyth, & Christian, 2014). If those who complete and return their surveys differ from those who do not, the results of the survey may be biased accordingly.

Survey researchers have developed strategies to help boost mail survey response rates. They may follow up with several telephone calls, send a reminder postcard, or send a personalized letter encouraging the potential respondent to participate. These reminders may be followed by a second (or even third) copy of the questionnaire and prestamped return envelope. Occasionally, the researchers might include a small amount of cash, such as a crisp $5 bill taped inside the questionnaire booklet, as a way to increase participation rates. However, these techniques increase the cost of the survey and have only modest rates of success (Church, 1993; Dillman, Smyth, & Christian, 2014).

Internet-Based Surveys

One of the most rapidly evolving survey modes is online or Internet surveys. Internet surveys use computerized self-administered questionnaires on the web, where respondents read and answer each question on a computer, tablet, or smartphone screen. Web-based and e-mail–based surveys have long been used in market research, often for very short surveys. In recent years, however, academic and government researchers are increasingly using these platforms. The research organization typically e-mails a unique link to a potential respondent, who then clicks on the link and completes the survey online. The respondent proceeds through a series of questions, either typing in the correct answer, clicking on the appropriate response category, or using a dropdown menu and selecting the preferred response option (Couper & Miller, 2008).

Internet-based surveys are easy to design and administer and can reach a very large number of respondents at relatively little cost.

STRENGTHS OF INTERNET-BASED SURVEYS

Online surveys have many advantages. First, they cost relatively little. Online surveys do not require paying interviewers to travel to respondents' homes. They also eliminate the need to print, mail, and return hard-copy surveys. Once the survey is programmed, there is no added cost for each person who completes it. Additionally, researchers do not need to pay data-entry clerks to enter respondents' answers into a database. This direct process also minimizes the risk of data-entry errors (Dillman, Smyth, & Christian, 2014).

Second, online surveys are relatively easy to design and administer. Many software programs like SurveyMonkey or Zoomerang are available to users at no or low cost, and they provide a variety of templates that researchers can modify to meet their needs (Couper & Miller, 2008). Researchers can quickly design and disseminate their surveys without the delay of scheduling an interview or relying on the postal service. Platforms like Amazon's Mechanical Turk (MTurk) allow researchers to post their surveys online, yielding quick and high-quality responses (Buhrmester, Kwang, & Gosling, 2011).

Third, respondents can easily navigate the questions, including the skip patterns, because the survey is preprogrammed. Web surveys can be designed with graphics, sound, and animation to combat respondent boredom and fatigue. They also tend to have fewer missing responses than mail surveys because the online survey is programmed such that respondents cannot proceed until they complete all the questions on each screen. Respondents typically complete and return web-based surveys more quickly than mail surveys, as they simply need to click and enter their answers (Couper & Miller, 2008).

Online surveys also can reach potential respondents throughout large geographic areas. Some would even argue that online surveys may reach nearly anyone in the world, and all that's required is a valid e-mail address. For researchers focused primarily on wealthy developed nations such as the United States, Canada, or Japan, concerns about coverage errors are modest, because e-mail and Internet access is widespread.

For example, in the United States, 84% of the population had Internet access in 2015. However, this access is not equal among all subpopulations. As such, older adults and those with lower levels of education, as well as ethnic minorities and persons living in rural areas, are more likely to be excluded from the potential pool of Internet survey respondents (Perrin & Duggan, 2015).

When we adopt a more global view, these disparities are even more pronounced. While 89% of people in North America have regular Internet access, the same can be said of just 27% of people in Africa and 45% of people in Asia (Internet World Stats, 2016). Thus, the results of global Internet surveys may be biased just as telephone survey results were biased in the mid-twentieth century—because the most economically disadvantaged are systematically excluded.

Internet surveys are roughly comparable to mail surveys with respect to response rates (Couper & Miller, 2008). As with mail surveys, the research team often needs to send e-mail reminders or offer incentives to persuade potential respondents to complete their surveys, such as the chance to be entered into a raffle for a gift card. Researchers can increase the response rate by e-mailing potential participants an advance letter that describes the goals and importance of the study (Kaplowitz, Hadlock, & Levine, 2004).

LIMITATIONS OF INTERNET-BASED SURVEYS

The primary limitation of online surveys is that the participants may be biased toward younger people and those with more resources. Age and socioeconomic status correlate with political and social attitudes; younger people and more highly educated people tend to be more politically liberal than older people and less educated people (Desilver, 2014; Pew Research Center, 2016). Thus, the results of online surveys may be biased accordingly.

Additionally, while it may be easy to reach a very large number of potential respondents via e-mail, the surveys will not reach people whose e-mail addresses have changed. Some people might also unwittingly (or purposely) delete the e-mail message. Just as people's "snail mailboxes" are full of junk mail, our e-mail boxes are full of spam, and some people are wary of opening a message from an unfamiliar address.

Mixed-Mode Approaches

We have described face-to-face, telephone, mail, and web-based surveys as if they are alternatives to one another. In practice, researchers may use more than one mode. The use of mixed modes is motivated by the recognition that every mode has limitations (Table 7.2), and a study using two or more modes may help compensate for the limitations of each mode used (De Leeuw, 2005).

Researchers use mixed-mode approaches for several reasons. The first is to obtain new or different types of information from a single respondent. For example, long lists of attitudinal or symptom items are administered more easily in SAQs. Second, mixed modes allow researchers to assess the quality of their data and potential sources of bias. For instance, we previously noted that people reported very different eating behaviors on self-administered versus face-to-face surveys. These sources of bias would not have been detected if only an SAQ had been used (Christensen et al., 2014).

TABLE 7.2   Strengths and Weaknesses of Four Major Modes of Survey Administration

Attribute	Face-to-Face Interview	Mail or SAQ	Telephone Interview	Web-Based Survey
Cost	High	Low	Moderate	Low
Response rate	High	Low	High	Moderate
Researcher control over interview	High	Low	Moderate	Moderate
Interviewer effects	High	Low	Moderate	Low

Third, some potential study participants might not want or be able to participate in a survey via a particular mode (De Leeuw, 2005). For example, a person without access to an Internet-enabled device like a laptop, tablet, or smartphone could not participate in an Internet survey, so researchers may choose to conduct a telephone interview with this person. Finally, a mixed-modes approach may help increase response rates. If a potential mail survey participant refuses to complete and return the questionnaire, the research team may telephone the person and persuade him to answer the survey questions over the phone.

The use of mixed modes is an important strategy for minimizing coverage and nonresponse errors, increasing response rates, and reducing bias in the study results. However, researchers using mixed modes should not simply combine their data and treat all of it the same way. Because the mode of administration affects how people answer survey questions, data analysts often use sophisticated statistical techniques to take into account **mode effects**, the ways that the mode of administration might affect respondents' answers (David, 2005).

mode effects The ways that the mode of administration might affect respondents' answers.

CONCEPT CHECKS

1   Name the four modes of survey administration and a main strength of each.

2   How might social desirability bias affect face-to-face and telephone interviews?

3   Describe the main limitation of mail surveys.

4   Why might a researcher use mixed modes in survey research?

SURVEY CONTENT: WHAT DO WE ASK AND HOW DO WE ASK IT?

survey instrument The types of questions asked, the response categories provided, and guidelines that help survey designers organize their questions.

By now, you should have a strong grasp of what surveys are and the kinds of information they can obtain. We now dig more deeply into the nuts and bolts of the **survey instrument** itself: the types of questions asked, the response categories provided, and guidelines that help survey designers organize their questions. These decisions draw heavily on scientific studies showing that a seemingly simple word choice or the decision to place a question at the beginning versus the end of a survey may shape how respondents answer that question (Wright & Marsden, 2010).

Types of Questions

Some survey questions obtain factual information, such as age, race, ethnicity, or employment status, while others capture subjective experiences, such as satisfaction with one's job, happiness in one's romantic relationship, or beliefs regarding topics such as abortion or stem cell research. However, nearly all survey questions share the same structure: The **stem** poses the question, and the response categories provide the preset answers that respondents may select. Most survey questions are closed-ended, with specific answer choices, but some surveys include open-ended questions, where respondents provide their own answer to the question.

CLOSED-ENDED QUESTIONS

The most basic closed-ended question provides a **dichotomous outcome** category, meaning that only two options are available, such as "yes" or "no." However, most closed-ended questions provide multiple response categories. These categories may reflect the statuses one possesses, the frequency with which one engages in a particular behavior, or the intensity with which a person endorses a particular view. For example, a survey might assess marital status with this question: "What is your marital status? Are you currently married, divorced, separated, widowed, or have you never been married?" Response categories should be both mutually exclusive and exhaustive. **Mutually exclusive** means that the categories do not overlap with one another: This ensures that respondents select the single category that best captures their views. In order for a response set to be **exhaustive**, respondents must have at least one accurate response available to them.

Closed-ended questions are often used to measure the frequency of behaviors, such as attending religious services, exercising, or arguing with one's parents. One common way to measure frequency is to ask the number of times in the past day, week, month, or year that someone did or felt something. For example, depressive symptoms are commonly measured with questions such as "How many days in the past week did you feel sad, blue, depressed, or lonely?" Another way to measure frequency is with broad descriptive categories such as "always," "sometimes," "rarely," or "never," but these categories are not ideal because different people define subjective frequencies differently. Thus, it is better to use a more precise set of categories, such as "several times a week," "at least once a week," "a few times a month," or "less than once a week." This level of specificity helps minimize the impact of different personal standards for what constitutes "frequent" versus "infrequent."

Most closed-ended questions use a **rating scale**, where respondents choose one option among a series of ordered categories. For example, you might receive a survey from your favorite restaurant asking you to indicate "how important" service is. You would rate each attribute of service using one of the following categories: not at all important, slightly important, important, and very important.

One of the most widely used rating scales is the **Likert scale**, which captures the respondent's level of agreement or disagreement with a particular statement,

stem The part of the survey question that presents the issue about which the question is asking.

dichotomous outcome When only two options are available to a question, such as "yes" or "no."

mutually exclusive Preset response categories that do not overlap with one another, ensuring that respondents select the single category that best captures their views.

exhaustive Preset response categories that give all subjects at least one accurate response.

rating scale A series of ordered categories.

Likert scale A type of rating scale that captures the respondent's level of agreement or disagreement with a particular statement.

such as "It would be a good thing if women were allowed to be ordained as priests" or "I see myself as someone who tends to find fault with others." The most basic Likert scale includes four options: (1) agree strongly, (2) agree, (3) disagree, and (4) disagree strongly. However, some researchers prefer more nuanced gradations, such as (1) agree strongly, (2) agree somewhat, (3) agree a little, (4) disagree a little, (5) disagree somewhat, and (6) disagree strongly (Figure 7.5). Other researchers provide a midpoint category for those who do not have strong feelings, such as "neither agree nor disagree."

Survey researchers generally agree that more nuanced categories more precisely capture respondents' feelings and that data analysts could combine categories (for example, "somewhat" and "a little") if they want a simpler snapshot of attitudes. The "neither agree nor disagree" option is controversial. Some researchers believe that survey questions should not offer this option; instead, respondents should make a **forced choice** to indicate their general leanings toward either agreement or disagreement. By contrast, other researchers believe that "neither agree nor disagree" is a legitimate response for people who are either uninformed about the topic or who genuinely hold ambivalent views (Allen & Seaman, 2007).

Some survey research experts believe that agree-disagree categories are subject to **acquiescence bias**, in which some respondents answer "agree" to attitudinal questions. Some researchers have found that respondents who have lower levels of education and who are less informed on a particular topic are particularly susceptible to acquiescence bias and are more likely to agree with any statement read to them. As a result, some researchers encourage the use of forced-choice questions instead of agree-disagree type questions.

forced choice Survey questions that do not offer choices like "neither agree nor disagree," therefore forcing the respondent to indicate their general leanings toward either agreement or disagreement.

acquiescence bias The tendency for respondents to answer "agree" to closed-ended attitudinal questions.

FIGURE 7.5 Example of a Rating Scale

Rating scales such as this Likert scale ask respondents to indicate their level of disagreement or agreement with a statement or attitude.

Circle the ONE number that best describes your agreement or disagreement with each statement.

I see myself as someone who...	Agree Strongly	Agree Moderately	Agree Slightly	Disagree Slightly	Disagree Moderately	Disagree Strongly
a. is talkative.	1	2	3	4	5	6
b. tends to find fault with others.	1	2	3	4	5	6
c. does a thorough job.	1	2	3	4	5	6
d. is reserved.	1	2	3	4	5	6
e. prefers the conventional, traditional.	1	2	3	4	5	6
f. is full of energy.	1	2	3	4	5	6
g. prefers work that is routine and simple.	1	2	3	4	5	6
h. is a reliable worker.	1	2	3	4	5	6
i. can be tense.	1	2	3	4	5	6
j. tends to be quiet.	1	2	3	4	5	6
k. values artistic, aesthetic experiences.	1	2	3	4	5	6
l. tends to be disorganized.	1	2	3	4	5	6

Source: John, Naumann, & Soto, 2008.

For example, researchers at the Pew Research Center have compared responses on two different types of questions assessing attitudes toward world peace. In one scenario, they ask respondents their level of agreement or disagreement with the statement, "The best way to ensure peace is through military strength." They found that 55% of people agreed, 42% disagreed, and the remaining 3% did not know. By contrast, when respondents were given the forced choice of endorsing only one of two possible attitudes, just 33% chose the position, "The best way to ensure peace is through military strength." Fully 55% endorsed the competing statement, "Diplomacy is the best way to ensure peace." This experiment showed that providing two contrasting options may be an effective way to avoid acquiescence bias.

Another type of closed-ended question asks respondents to rank-order their priorities or preferences. Whereas rating questions ask people to evaluate each particular attitude or object on its own, **ranking items** ask respondents to directly compare different objects or entities to one another. For example, market researchers may ask people to indicate the first, second, and third most important attribute that they consider when purchasing a new car. The three attributes of fuel efficiency, quality, and safety consistently rise to the top (Consumers Union, 2012).

> **ranking items** A type of closed-ended question that asks respondents to rank-order their priorities or preferences.

You might be tempted to think that most people can easily answer survey questions. However, survey researchers recognize that some questions are difficult to answer or require a "best guess" rather than a definitive answer. This is often the case when the questions ask about income and personal finances. In such cases, survey researchers may use a specific type of closed-ended question called an **unfolding question** (or *unfolding brackets*). If respondents cannot easily answer the question "What is your annual household income from all sources?" they are asked a follow-up question such as "Is your annual household income from all sources less than $50,000?" with response options of "yes" and "no." If they answer "yes," they are asked if their income is less than $40,000. If they answer "no," they are asked if their income is less than $60,000. This unfolding series of questions continues until the researcher determines that the person's household income is, for instance, between $60,000 and $70,000. Questions regarding household finances are more likely than nearly any other survey question (including sex life questions!) to elicit answers of "don't know" or even a refusal to answer, so methods like the unfolding brackets approach are an important innovation (Pleis, Dahlhamer, & Meyer, 2007).

> **unfolding question** A sequence of questions intended to elicit respondent estimates about topics such as income when respondents are uncertain of the answer; also called *unfolding brackets*.

OPEN-ENDED AND SEMI-STRUCTURED QUESTIONS

While most survey questions are closed-ended, surveys also may include a small number of open-ended or semi-structured questions in which respondents are free to provide their own responses. Typically, these open-ended questions require only a brief answer, unlike the lengthy and complicated answers often provided in an in-depth interview. Open-ended questions are typically executed in one of two ways:

1. First, an open-ended question might be embedded in a closed-ended question through a response category referred to as "other, specify." Here, respondents have a set of plausible response options, but some individuals might believe that the preset categories do not capture their experience. Thus, they would answer "other" and provide their more detailed answer.

2. Second, a question might be purely open-ended, with no preset response categories. In this case, respondents simply provide an answer in their own words.

For example, Carr (2012) conducted a face-to-face survey of 300 older adults to understand how they plan for their end-of-life medical care. The survey included closed-ended questions asking respondents whether they had a living will. Carr was also interested in the reasons people might engage in (or avoid) end-of-life planning. Respondents who reported not having a living will were asked: "Can you tell us why you do not have a living will?" Preset responses included "I don't need one. I'm in good health" and "I don't need one. My family knows my preferences" along with a final response category, "other, specify." These open-ended responses provided new insights that the survey designers had not considered when drafting their survey. For example, one person responded, "I don't need one, because my health is in God's hands."

Researchers typically present data from their open-ended survey questions in two ways. First, they may use selected open-ended answers as illustrative quotes to bring life to the statistical patterns detected in the closed-ended data (Carr, 2012). Second, they may transform open-ended responses into closed-ended categories. For example, Carr and her colleagues noticed that many people avoided end-of-life planning because they did not want to think or talk about death. Open-ended answers such as "It's bad

FIGURE 7.6 Adverse Childhood Experiences Index

The Behavioral Risk Factor Surveillance System is an annual state-based RDD survey that collects data from U.S. adults regarding their health conditions and risk factors such as their experiences of early adversity. The ACE index is constructed by summing the number of adverse experiences one had in the first 18 years of life.

Prologue: I'd like to ask you some questions about events that happened during your childhood. This information will allow us to better understand problems that may occur early in life, and may help others in the future. This is a sensitive topic and some people may feel uncomfortable with these questions. At the end of this section, I will give you a phone number for an organization that can provide information and referral for these issues. Please keep in mind that you can ask me to skip any question you do not want to answer. All questions refer to the time period before you were 18 years of age. Now, looking back before you were 18 years of age—.

1) Did you live with anyone who was depressed, mentally ill, or suicidal?

2) Did you live with anyone who was a problem drinker or alcoholic?

3) Did you live with anyone who used illegal street drugs or who abused prescription medications?

4) Did you live with anyone who served time or was sentenced to serve time in a prison, jail, or other correctional facility?

5) Were your parents separated or divorced?

6) How often did your parents or adults in your home ever slap, hit, kick, punch or beat each other up?

7) Before age 18, how often did a parent or adult in your home ever hit, beat, kick, or physically hurt you in any way? Do not include spanking.

8) How often did a parent or adult in your home ever swear at you, insult you, or put you down?

9) How often did anyone at least 5 years older than you or an adult, ever touch you sexually?

10) How often did anyone at least 5 years older than you or an adult, try to make you touch sexually?

11) How often did anyone at least 5 years older than you or an adult, force you to have sex?

Source: CDC, 2016.

luck to talk about being sick," "I don't want to think about dying," or "It's too scary to think about" could then be bundled into a single category: "avoidance/don't want to think about end-of-life issues."

How do survey researchers decide whether to use a closed-ended or open-ended question on a particular topic? Paul Lazarsfeld (1944), one of the founding fathers of survey research, provided four general criteria that remain helpful today: (1) the goals of the survey, (2) the respondent's knowledge about the topic, (3) how much thought a respondent has given to a particular topic, and (4) the respondent's motivation to answer the question. In general, closed-ended questions are preferable when the researcher wants to document the frequency of a behavior, factual information about the respondent, or the respondent's level of agreement with an attitude. If researchers believe that respondents will not want to speak at length about a difficult topic, such as death or family conflict, they should use closed-ended questions because selecting a fixed response might be less threatening. However, if researchers are interested in the question of "why," such as why an individual might be opposed to medical marijuana, they should use an open-ended question. Open-ended questions also are useful if the respondent is unfamiliar with the topic, doesn't have an opinion, or simply hasn't thought about the topic.

SINGLE ITEM VERSUS COMPOSITE

Many of the survey questions we have discussed so far are single items, meaning a single question that captures relevant information. For example, one question about marital status is sufficient to establish whether a respondent is married. Yet some concepts are best measured with a composite of several questions. Developing **composite measures** is a complex process, often requiring a sophisticated knowledge of statistics. Here we provide a brief overview to help you understand how to interpret the two main types of composite measures: an index and a scale. Although these two terms are often used interchangeably, they differ in important ways.

An **index** sums responses to survey items capturing key elements of a particular concept being measured, such as the total number of health symptoms one has or the number of fundamentalist religious beliefs that one endorses. One widely used index is the Adverse Childhood Experiences (ACE) measure, which asks respondents if they experienced each of 11 adverse experiences before age 18, including emotional, physical, and sexual abuse (Felitti et al., 1998). Although some researchers are interested in whether a particular form of childhood adversity has long-term consequences, others are interested in whether the total number of adversities matters. This is where an index proves useful. Mounting research shows that the more adverse childhood experiences one had (regardless of what the particular experiences were), the greater one's risk of substance use, illness, and even premature death. Figure 7.6 reproduces items that form the ACE index, and Figure 7.7 portrays the results from a study linking these index scores with the risk of alcohol abuse (Felitti et al., 1998).

composite measure A measure that combines multiple items, whether as a scale or an index, to create a single value that captures a multifaceted concept.

index A composite measure that sums responses to survey items capturing key elements of a particular concept being measured.

FIGURE 7.7 ACE Index Score and Risk of Alcoholism

This chart shows that with each additional adverse experience in childhood, one's risk of alcoholism in adulthood increases.

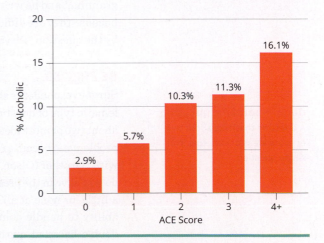

Source: Felitti et al., 1998.

scale A composite measure that averages responses to a series of related items that capture a single concept or trait, such as depressive symptoms or self-esteem.

Unlike an index, a **scale** averages responses to a series of related items that capture a single concept or trait, such as depressive symptoms or self-esteem. Thus, a scale score summarizes one's responses to related items, and it reliably captures the overall strength or intensity of one's views or experiences. These overall scale scores are considered more reliable measures than a single item. Even if an individual makes an error when completing one scale item or answers one item in a non-characteristic way, these idiosyncratic variations are averaged out when the scale is constructed (Furr, 2011). By contrast, the components of an index may not necessarily be statistically related. Looking back at the ACE measure, a person may have divorced parents but no other risk factors.

A scale also may include more specific subscales that capture even more fine-grained concepts. For example, as you learned in Chapter 5, a widely used measure of depressive symptoms is the Center for Epidemiologic Studies Depression (CES-D) Scale (Radloff, 1977). If you average one person's responses to all the items on the CES-D scale, you will have a reliable and valid summary of that person's depressive symptoms. Yet you may notice that the symptoms capture different types of experiences. The CES-D encompasses subscales such as depressed mood, captured with items such as "feel sad" and "feel depressed," and social isolation, measured with items such as "feel that people were unfriendly" and "feel lonely."

Characteristics of High-Quality Questions

When designing a survey, you should strive for questions that are clear, valid, and reliable. Here we briefly describe guidelines for developing survey questions.

USE CLEAR AND SIMPLE LANGUAGE

All questions and response options should be brief, clear, and concise. Words should be simple to ensure that people of all educational levels can understand them. For example, using words like "work" rather than "employment" or "most important" rather than "top priority" will ensure that respondents understand the question's focus (Dillman, Smyth, & Christian, 2014). Questions should be brief, use proper grammar, and be written in complete sentences. Double-negatives should be avoided, because they are difficult to understand. For example, respondents might be confused by the question "Do you favor or oppose not legalizing physician-assisted suicide?"

BE PRECISE

double-barreled question A question that asks about two or more ideas or concepts in a single question.

Survey respondents should understand precisely what a question is asking. One problematic type of question is a **double-barreled question**, which is a question that asks about two or more ideas or concepts in a single question. Double-barreled questions are problematic because respondents may agree with one part of the question but disagree with the other (Olson, 2008). For example, a survey might ask "How much confidence do you have in the president's ability to handle domestic and foreign policy: a lot, some, a little, or none at all?" A respondent might have great confidence in the president's ability to handle domestic issues but less confidence regarding foreign policy. The double-barreled question does not allow respondents to differentiate their views toward the two separate concepts in the question.

You can use a few simple methods to achieve precision. First, define abbreviations the first time they are used. Second, briefly define concepts that people do not readily recognize or understand, such as a "revocable trust" or "Affordable Care Act." Third, do not presume prior knowledge on the part of the respondent, especially when asking questions about complex political issues, medications, or financial issues. Finally, make the response categories as precise as possible. Providing specific time units, such as "once a week," is preferable to vague units such as "sometimes."

EXERCISE CAUTION WHEN DEALING WITH SENSITIVE TOPICS

When asking questions about sensitive topics such as child abuse, drug abuse, or sexuality, it is important to use neutral language that does not stigmatize the behavior of interest (Lee, 1993). Questions should avoid emotionally laden words that might upset respondents. For example, rather than asking "Have you ever been raped?" a survey question might ask "Have you ever been forced to have sexual relations against your will?"

Wording that upsets respondents could have several negative implications for your survey (Lee, 1993). First, the respondent may drop out of the study. Second, a strong emotional reaction may bias a respondent's answers to subsequent questions. A respondent upset by memories of an early life trauma may carry that mood throughout the survey and therefore may offer excessively negative responses to questions on matters such as life satisfaction. Third, sensitive or troubling questions may pose psychological harm to respondents, an ethical issue we discuss later in this chapter.

AVOID LEADING QUESTIONS

Survey questions should be as fair and evenhanded as possible. Although academic and government surveys typically achieve this goal, surveys conducted by organizations with a particular political or economic agenda may ask leading questions. Leading questions are phrased to "lead" or guide respondents to a particular answer, yielding results that support the organization's goals. Common leading strategies include question stems that suggest what "most people" think or feel, implicitly pressuring respondents to answer in the same way (Fowler, 2014). For example, an employer might attempt to gauge employee satisfaction with a question such as "People working at Acme Corporation love their jobs. How do you feel about your job here at Acme?" Respondents may feel that they, too, should love their jobs lest they be considered a poor employee. A more appropriate question would be "On a scale from 1 to 5, with 1 being very dissatisfied and 5 being very satisfied, how satisfied are you with your position at Acme Corporation?"

Leading questions may include a morally charged word that pushes respondents toward or away from a particular answer. For example, the question "Should responsible parents use child car seats?" implies that those who answer "no" are not responsible parents. A more evenhanded alternative would be "Do you agree or disagree with the following statement: 'The law should require special car seats for infant passengers'?" When reading the results of surveys, whether consumer-satisfaction surveys or political polls, it is wise to research the wording of the questions and determine if they were written in a leading way.

"Tried and True" Questions versus Designing New Questions

Researchers must decide whether to use "tried and true" questions from existing surveys or to develop new questions. Survey researchers often use preexisting questions, or measures, provided that they have high validity and reliability (Dillman, Smyth, & Christian, 2014). Literally thousands of these questions are available to researchers, with the precise question wording and response options available through data depositories such as the ICPSR. Many of the surveys that we've discussed in this chapter, such as the GSS, MIDUS, and WLS, make their survey instruments publicly available via their websites.

Table 7.3 lists the websites of several widely used survey data sets so that you can browse their survey instruments and see the broad range of questions available. You can also see the *frequencies* (information on how many survey respondents answered these questions) by exploring the study codebooks. A **codebook** lists all the questions used in a survey along with their response categories. In some cases, the codebook also provides the number and/or proportion of persons in each response category.

One important reason survey researchers use preexisting measures is to compare their own results with the results obtained from different samples or populations. In particular, researchers administering their own survey to a small nonrepresentative sample may want to compare their results with those obtained in a nationally

codebook A system of organizing information about a dataset, including the variables it contains, the possible values for each variable, coding schemes, and decision rules.

TABLE 7.3   Examples of Widely Used Survey Data Sets

Data Set	Website
Changing Lives of Older Couples (CLOC)	http://cloc.isr.umich.edu/
General Social Survey (GSS)	www.gss.norc.org/
Longitudinal Study of Generations (LSOG)	www.icpsr.umich.edu/icpsrweb/ICPSR/studies/22100
Midlife in the United States (MIDUS)	http://midus.wisc.edu/
National Longitudinal Study of Adolescent to Adult Health (Add Health)	www.cpc.unc.edu/projects/addhealth
National Longitudinal Studies of Youth	www.bls.gov/nls/
National Social Life, Health, and Aging Project (NSHAP)	www.norc.org/Research/Projects/Pages/national-social-life-health-and-aging-project.aspx
Panel Study of Income Dynamics (PSID)	http://psidonline.isr.umich.edu/
Wisconsin Longitudinal Study (WLS)	www.ssc.wisc.edu/wlsresearch/

representative sample. For example, let's say you are interested in the financial burden of attending college, and you decide to conduct a survey of first-year students on your campus. Rather than writing a new question about financial stress, you choose to include a preexisting question from the American Freshman survey, a nationally representative survey that has been administered to first-year students at 1,900 colleges and universities annually for more than 50 years. This survey includes the question "Do you have any concern about your ability to finance your college education?" Response categories include "None, I am confident that I will have sufficient funds," "Some, but I probably will have enough funds," and "Major, not sure I will have enough funds to complete college." If you administered this question to your sample, you could assess whether financial strain on your campus is higher or lower than the national average (Eagan et al., 2016).

You are more likely to develop original questions if you are studying a new topic for which preexisting questions either are not available or do not adequately capture your topic of interest. For example, sociologist Kristen Springer is interested in the ways that masculinity beliefs affect men's health. She hypothesized that men who feel strong pressure to comply with gender-typed expectations such as "men should not ask for help" might have poor health because they avoid getting regular checkups or engage in risky behaviors like drinking and driving too fast. After reviewing the sociological literature on masculinity and health, Springer discovered that survey researchers had not yet developed relatively short, valid, and reliable measures of masculinity beliefs (Springer & Mouzon, 2011). Springer subsequently designed her own masculinity belief measures, which were included on the mail questionnaire administered as part of the WLS.

Springer developed her own survey questions in order to study how masculinity beliefs affect men's health. She found that men with strong masculinity beliefs are half as likely as other men to engage in preventative health care, such as getting a flu shot.

Writing new survey questions requires a deep understanding of the relevant theoretical literature. For instance, Springer read theoretical writings on cultural beliefs about masculinity before drafting her survey items. She then operationalized core aspects of these theories by writing survey questions that captured distinctive aspects of masculinity beliefs. Her ideas were based on the writings of Robert Brannon (1976), who proposed that contemporary masculinity comprises four dimensions: success, toughness, independence, and concealing emotions. Springer wrote eight survey questions capturing these four dimensions. She assessed concealing emotions with items such as "When a man is feeling pain, he should not let it show" and toughness with items such as "In some kinds of situations, a man should be ready to use his fists." Response options were the Likert agree-disagree categories. The process Springer followed closely mirrors the lessons conveyed in Chapter 2 and Chapter 4: A researcher begins with a theory, such as theories of gender relations, then develops specific concepts related to these theories, such as the concepts of hegemonic masculinity. The researcher then defines—or conceptualizes—masculinity by breaking it down into four dimensions. The final stage—operationalization—involves developing survey items that capture these four dimensions of masculinity so that the researcher can measure it.

Placement of Questions

The layout of a survey is critically important. Researchers pay careful attention to the order in which questions appear and the types of questions that follow one another. Three important scientific factors guide question placement: establishing trust and rapport early in the survey, avoiding monotony and response set, and avoiding order effects.

ESTABLISH TRUST AND RAPPORT EARLY IN THE SURVEY

Imagine you're on a blind date, and the first words your date utters are "What's your GPA?" Or, worse yet, "Tell me about your ex." You might be tempted to walk away on the spot. A survey, like a first date, is a delicate social interaction, so survey interviewers need to establish trust and rapport immediately. The first question on a survey should be easy to answer, straightforward, and focused on a pleasant or interesting topic (Dillman, Smyth, & Christian, 2014). A difficult, off-putting, or complex question may scare off a respondent, just as intrusive questions might scare off a suitor. Pleasant opening questions help the interviewer build rapport with the respondent or, in the case of an SAQ, help increase the respondent's sense of commitment to the research project.

Basic demographic data are typically collected toward the end of the survey, with one exception. Demographic factors often are the screener questions for skip patterns that follow. A survey will need to establish early on whether a respondent is male or female if it needs to branch respondents into (or around) subsequent questions about menstrual history or other topics that are applicable only to one sex. Likewise, a marital status question must come before questions on marital quality.

AVOID MONOTONY AND RESPONSE SET

Survey designers are concerned with minimizing boredom to prevent respondents from quitting partway through the survey. One technique is to follow a lengthy and dry module (for example, questions about income) with a brief section on a more fun or pleasant topic such as hobbies. To keep the respondent engaged, factual questions about age, sex, race, and education might be followed by subjective questions about job satisfaction. These questions typically have the same set of response options, such as a 6-point Likert scale. To facilitate completion of these items, survey designers often place them in a matrix or grid, which clearly shows the statements and response categories (see Figures 7.5 and 7.8 for examples). However, some respondents fall into a behavior called **response set**, the tendency to select the same answer to several sequential questions, perhaps out of boredom or a desire to quickly finish the survey (Fowler, 2014).

Survey designers have two main strategies for avoiding response set. (These strategies also are effective in addressing acquiescence bias.) The first is to change the response categories after several items to keep respondents alert. For example, the first three items might have response categories ranging from "agree strongly" to "disagree

response set The tendency to select the same answer to several sequential questions, perhaps out of boredom or a desire to quickly finish the survey.

FIGURE 7.8 The Rosenberg Self-Esteem Scale

To avoid response set, researchers will often word some questions positively and others negatively. Response set is the tendency to select the same answer to a series of questions.

	Questions	Agree Strongly	Agree	Disagree	Disagree Strongly
1.	On the whole I am satisfied with myself.				
2.*	At times I think that I am no good at all.				
3.	I feel that I have a number of good qualities.				
4.	I am able to do things as well as most other people.				
5.*	I feel I do not have much to be proud of.				
6.*	I certainly feel useless at times.				
7.	I feel that I am a person of worth, at least the equal of others.				
8.*	I wish I could have more respect for myself.				
9.*	All in all, I am inclined to feel that I am a failure.				
10.	I take a positive attitude toward myself.				

Source: Rosenberg, 1965.

strongly," while the following three items might have response categories ranging from "very true" to "not at all true."

The second, and more common, approach is to word some questions positively and others negatively so that responses on the agree-disagree continuum have different meanings for different items. For example, some of the self-esteem items in Figure 7.8 are worded as positive descriptions, while those denoted with asterisks are worded as negative descriptions (Rosenberg, 1986). As you can see, a response of "agree strongly" means something very different for item 1 ("On the whole I am satisfied with myself") than for item 2 ("At times I think that I am no good at all"). This technique encourages respondents to read and answer items carefully and precisely. It also provides important information for data analysts, who can use sophisticated statistical techniques to discern whether some items were answered incorrectly (Fowler, 2014).

AVOID ORDER EFFECTS

The order in which questions appear may bias the responses. Because of **order effects**, responses to a survey question might be influenced by questions that appeared earlier on the survey (Bishop, 2004). For example, survey researchers have found that respondents strive to look consistent in their responses. If a respondent answers the question "How religious are you?" with "very religious," he might not feel comfortable giving the honest response of "never" to a subsequent question about how often he attends religious services. Therefore, he might offer the less truthful response of "sometimes" in an attempt to appear consistent in his behaviors and identity.

One strategy for avoiding order effects is to randomize the order of questions (Zaller & Feldman, 1992). A researcher might use a split-ballot design where a random half of the sample receives the religious identity question first, while the other random half receives the religious identity question later in the module. This technique allows

order effects When the order in which questions appear biases the responses.

priming effects A type of order effects in which exposure to a particular image, word, or feeling shapes how respondents think and feel in the immediate aftermath.

researchers to detect whether answers about specific religious behaviors are biased when they appear before or after a question about general religiosity.

A specific type of order effects is **priming effects**, where exposure to a particular image, word, or feeling shapes how we think and feel in the immediate aftermath (Oldendick, 2008). Thus, the order in which questions are asked may bias answers either positively or negatively. One fascinating study found that when survey respondents were asked to recall the names of politicians recently involved in political scandals, they subsequently indicated very low levels of trust when asked about their current elected officials. By contrast, respondents indicated considerably higher levels of trust when the trust questions did not follow the question about recent political scandals (Schwarz & Bless, 1992). When "primed" to think about dishonest politicians engaged in scandals, respondents subsequently carried a distrustful feeling to their assessments of elected officials.

CONCEPT CHECKS

1 List and explain three characteristics of high-quality survey questions.

2 Why might a researcher design new questions rather than use tried-and-true measures?

3 Name two principles that guide the layout and design of surveys.

CONDUCTING THE SURVEY

You now know the characteristics of high-quality survey questions and the guidelines researchers follow when assembling those questions into a survey. You must now complete several additional steps before you start data collection. The most important is the pretest.

Pretesting the Survey

A pretest is a trial run in which researchers administer the survey to people who are similar to those in the target sample (Dillman, Smyth, & Christian, 2014). For instance, if you plan to administer your survey to a random sample of all undergraduates at your college, you could first test the initial draft on people who live in your dorm, taking care to include men and women, as well as first-year students, sophomores, juniors, and seniors. (Importantly, pretest respondents should not participate in the official fielding of the survey, because their prior knowledge of the survey may bias their responses.) The pretest identifies problems with the survey, including confusing questions, problematic skip patterns, or questions that might turn off potential respondents. The pretest also provides information on the survey's duration and pacing; it may reveal parts of the questionnaire that feel long and tedious to respondents (Dillman, Smyth, & Christian, 2014).

The pretest should be conducted in precisely the same way you intend to conduct your final survey. The mode must be the same, the pretest sample should be as similar to the target sample as possible, and the conditions under which the survey is conducted should be as similar as possible. After conducting the pretest and discovering which aspects of the survey are problematic, researchers make changes to fix those problems. Any substantial changes must then be pretested.

The pretest stage may include a **cognitive interview** (or a *cognitive pretest*). This procedure shows how survey respondents interpret particular questions, and it can be especially helpful when developing new measures (Willis, 2015). One part of a cognitive interview is a "thinking out loud" activity where pretest participants share their thoughts about the question—whether it was clear or confusing, what they think the question was trying to measure, and why they answered as they did.

For example, in 2011 the GSS developed new measures to capture attitudes about climate change (Smith, 2011). Participants were asked which of three statements best matched their views: (1) climate change is caused mainly by human activities; (2) climate change is caused mainly by natural forces; and (3) climate change is not happening now. When participants explained their answers, many who indicated the "natural forces" belief elaborated that the natural forces were in response to human activity, with comments like "Mother Nature is angry" or "climate change is an act of God." This information helped the researchers refine their items and response categories.

Conducting Preliminary Data Analysis

How do you know whether the pretest was a success and the survey is ready to enter the field? Researchers can use both "soft" impressionistic data and "hard" quantitative data to identify and fix problems revealed during the pretest.

"Soft" data might be complaints from respondents that the survey is too long or comments such as "I don't understand the question." "Hard" data include preliminary statistical analyses of the survey responses: These analyses begin by looking at **frequency distributions**, which reveal the number and proportion of respondents in each response category for each question. (We will revisit frequency distributions in Chapter 14.) If a relatively high proportion of respondents says "don't know" or refuses to answer a question, then the question needs refinement. Survey experts generally agree that if data are missing for more than 10% of cases on a single question, your data may be biased because those who refuse to answer a question are often significantly different from those who do answer (Dong & Peng, 2013). Some people will say "don't know" because they do not want to divulge their true answer; for instance, very overweight and obese people are more likely than slender people to answer "don't know" when asked their body weight (Carr, Jaffe, & Friedman, 2008). At other times, respondents genuinely do not know how to answer the question because it is on a topic they know nothing about and do not have an opinion. Philip Converse (1970), a founding father of survey research, described this as a "non-attitude."

Frequency distributions also reveal whether the respondents are dispersed across all categories or clustered in just one or two; the latter suggests that you may need more fine-grained categories to capture the nuance in respondents' experiences (Rea & Parker, 2014). For example, if 98% of respondents answer "yes" and 2% say "no" to the question "Are you happy with your current romantic partner?" researchers might revise the question to read "How happy are you with your current romantic partner? Would you say very happy, somewhat happy, not very happy,

Conversations from the Front Lines

PAMELA HERD

Pamela Herd is professor of sociology and public affairs at the University of Wisconsin–Madison. She is an expert in survey research, health, aging, and health policy and is the coauthor of the award-winning book Market Friendly or Family Friendly? The State and Gender Inequality in Old Age *(Harrington Meyer & Herd, 2007). In 2010, she became the director of the Wisconsin Longitudinal Study (WLS), a long-running survey of more than 10,000 men and women who graduated from Wisconsin high schools in 1957. Dr. Herd is the third director of the WLS, following in the footsteps of study founder and former University of Wisconsin chancellor William H. Sewell, who directed the study from 1962 until the 1970s, at which time Professor Robert M. Hauser took over the study and directed it for nearly 40 years until his retirement in 2010. Professor Herd tells us about her experiences running this one-of-a-kind study.*

Can you tell us a bit about the Wisconsin Longitudinal Study (WLS)?

The WLS is based on a random sample of all 1957 Wisconsin high school graduates. We also conducted parallel interviews with one sibling of each graduate to help us understand similarities and differences in families. When they were high school seniors, the main WLS participants completed a self-administered questionnaire at school. They then completed a telephone interview at age 36 (in 1975), and completed both telephone and mail-back SAQs at ages 53 (1992), 65 (2004) and 72 (2011). Response rates are high, consistently topping 80%. The content of WLS surveys has changed over time to reflect the respondents' changing lives. In 1957, we asked questions about college and work plans, high school friends, and grades. The survey content was then expanded to cover marriage, family, childbearing, and jobs when the respondents reached young- and mid-adulthood. The most recent waves focused on major concerns among older adults, including health, cognitive functioning, psychological well-being, retirement, caregiving, bereavement, social support, and end-of-life preparations.

In 2011, we expanded the study in a major way. When we conducted in-person interviews with the then 72-year-old graduates, we also obtained detailed biological assessments. This included saliva samples, which we use to generate genetic data, as well as measures of their height, weight, and waist/hip circumference. We also conducted physical tests just as would be conducted at a doctor's office. These included measures of hand grip strength, lung function, walking (gait) speed, the capacity to get up and out of a chair, and many other measures that capture their memory and cognitive skills.

The WLS is unique because we can merge in with the survey data a rich array of administrative and supplemental data. For example, we have data on the IQ tests they were given in high school. We also used yearbook photos and text to obtain information on their high school activities, attractiveness, and even a measure of body weight. Because we are interested in the early-life factors that are associated with how long a person lives, we also linked the survey data to an official data source called the National Death Index (NDI), which has death certificate information for those participants who have since died. To understand economic well-being, we can link our survey data with social security earnings and benefits records. And we can understand health-care use of older adults by linking their survey data with Medicare claims data. Of course, we obtain permission from our participants before obtaining their social security or Medicare records.

Increasingly, WLS has not only focused on aging and health but become a data resource that can be used by researchers across many disciplines, from biomedical sciences and evolutionary biology to economics, political science, psychology, and sociology.

What kinds of questions can researchers answer with longitudinal studies like the WLS that they wouldn't be able to answer with cross-sectional data? Likewise, are there novel things you've learned from the telephone, mail, or face-to-face components of the study?

The kinds of research questions that can be explored in the WLS are quite vast. The National Research Council (a prestigious nonprofit organization that guides scientific research in the United States) has continually pointed to the WLS as one of the best life-course longitudinal studies of aging. Some of the study's novel strengths are its long history, the sibling design, the depth and breadth of the data, and its innovative measurement and use of biological data.

Because we have tracked people over their entire lives, the WLS is uniquely positioned to understand how things that people experience early in their life influence their well-being, from their health to their finances, across their lives and into old age. For example, there is a lot of evidence that being socially active—such as having friends, going out socially, or volunteering—in later life protects people from the onset of dementia. But because existing studies don't have data on social engagement from earlier in peoples' lives, we don't know whether it's being socially engaged in later life per se that reduces one's risk or whether it's about being socially engaged across one's entire life that's protective. Because the WLS has data on the level of people's social engagement in high school, as well as across the remainder of their life, we can better understand these relationships.

> "
> **The WLS is uniquely positioned to understand how things that people experience early in their life influence their well-being, from their health to their finances, across their lives and into old age.**
> "

In terms of the mode of data collection, our experience with the face-to-face interviews in 2011 and a recent pilot study conducted in 2014 made it clear how in-person interviews allow for novel types of data collection. This is especially true for a sample where we focus extensively on aging and health. We were able to collect very precise physical functioning data, such as a gait speed test, which is one of the best predictors of mortality. We were also able to collect biomedical data, including saliva samples, which allowed us to generate genetic data on our participants, as well as fecal samples, which allowed us to generate data on the gut microbiome. The gut microbiome is composed of the trillions of microbes that inhabit your gut; it plays a significant role in shaping health, especially obesity-related health conditions. There is growing evidence that the environment—from where you live to who you interact with—can influence the composition of your gut microbiome. Finally, more precise measures of cognition are much more feasible in person; this is important for understanding aging-related changes like early dementia symptoms.

What have been some of the toughest challenges or biggest surprises you've faced with the study?

There are many challenges when running a study at the scale of the WLS. I've found the comparison to running a small business to be apt. Everything from maintaining study funding to negotiating with the administrators at the university and the businesses that supply us with the computers and supplies we need to run the study is a part of your obligation as a principal investigator (PI).

The scientific challenges, for me, have been one of the surprising joys of running the WLS. Some of these challenges involve broad questions, such as how can a study like the WLS be used to help us understand how social relationships influence basic biological factors that influence our health? We already know that social isolation increases the risk for everything from dementia to mortality, but we don't understand how social relationships "get under the skin" to influence these outcomes. Other challenges have focused on more nitty-gritty questions, like, how do you convince people to provide you with a saliva sample? We require them to fill a fairly large test-tube with saliva, which can be difficult to do, and for some even unpleasant. We need the saliva sample so that we can test whether social relationships help offset the genetic risk for dementia. Generally, we have found that our participants are more open to doing these things if they understand what we might learn that will help advance science.

What do you believe are some of the greatest innovations in survey research we've seen over the past decade?

I think that some of the greatest survey research innovations have involved the improved collection and measurement of health data. This has required significant technological innovation—such as the ability to use saliva to provide information on participants' genetic makeup as well as an actual saliva kit that can be deployed in the field for thousands of our participants.

or not at all happy?" This rewording allows gradations that are not captured in the simpler version of the question.

Going into the Field

After you have identified your sample and pretested, revised, and refined your survey, you are ready to go into the field, or administer your survey. Research teams often provide advance notice to potential respondents via an advance letter. This letter should arrive in the potential respondent's mailbox or e-mail inbox roughly 1 week before the research team contacts him or her (Dillman, Smyth, & Christian, 2014).

You are now ready to carry out your survey. Regardless of the mode you choose, the initial contact with the respondent—whether during the face-to-face visit, the first few moments of the telephone call, or on the introductory page or screen of the mail or Internet survey—should briefly introduce the survey's purpose and convey respect and gratitude to the respondent. The survey researcher will also obtain informed consent from the respondent at this point, informing the respondent of the potential benefits and risks of participation. The researcher also informs respondents that they are free to skip any questions or cease participation if they wish. The process of carrying out a survey requires time, money, energy, persistence, and attention to detail, but it also yields fascinating data that can uncover exciting discoveries about our lives.

CONCEPT CHECKS

1   What is the main purpose of a pretest?

2   What information can a cognitive interview provide?

3   Why do researchers examine frequency distributions of their study measures after the pretest?

ETHICAL CONCERNS IN SURVEY RESEARCH

Researchers must "do no harm" to their participants. They must inform research subjects of any potential sources of harm, and they must make their best efforts to protect the respondents' confidentiality and anonymity. These concerns guide all researchers, but survey researchers have several specific strategies for upholding this ethical code.

The first is to protect the **confidentiality** of a survey participant's responses. Surveys obtain highly personal and sensitive information, such as income, HIV status, or illicit drug use. If this information is made public, it could be a source of harm to respondents. Researchers must work to ensure that all survey responses are kept strictly confidential, meaning only members of the research team have access to the respondents' information. Researchers can protect the confidentiality of respondents by assigning each respondent an ID number: This number is the only identifying information on the survey. A document linking the names of respondents to their identifying numbers is kept in a separate, secure, private location that is accessible only to key members of the research team. For Internet and electronic surveys, the research team

confidentiality When participants' identifying information is only accessible to the research team.

must use appropriate encryption technologies to ensure that information provided over the Internet is safe and secure (Fowler, 2014).

It is unrealistic and impractical for survey researchers to promise anonymity to respondents. **Anonymity** means that no identifying information can be linked to respondents or their survey answers. Anonymity may not be desirable from the researcher's perspective: If a respondent's survey record has no identifying information, then researchers cannot conduct follow-up interviews as part of a panel survey or as part of a mixed-mode approach (Dillman, Smyth, & Christian, 2014). For these reasons, it is much more realistic for survey researchers to promise their respondents confidentiality rather than anonymity. It is exceedingly rare today that a survey respondent's identity is betrayed, given the many rules and constraints in place.

Survey researchers also must be mindful that their questions may cause respondents minor psychological distress. For example, when Carr carried out a telephone survey asking older adults about the deaths of loved ones as part of the Wisconsin Study of Families and Loss (WISTFL), she warned them at the beginning of the survey that some questions might be difficult to answer. If respondents were troubled or saddened by a question, Carr provided a list of counseling resources, hotlines, and websites. She also reminded them that they were free to skip any question that made them uncomfortable. In practice, many survey respondents welcome rather than avoid discussing difficult topics such as death and dying, because the survey context provides a safe and private space to discuss such topics. Still, researchers must take precautions to treat every survey respondent with respect, beneficence, and justice.

anonymity When no identifying information can be linked to respondents and even the researcher cannot identify them.

CONCEPT CHECKS

1   Compare confidentiality and anonymity.

2   Why is it difficult to ensure anonymity in survey research?

3   How might researchers protect respondents troubled by difficult survey questions?

CONCLUSION

Survey research is one of the most widely used methods in the social sciences because it allows for the exploration of myriad topics, including subgroup and historical variations in attitudes, behaviors, and personal characteristics. Surveys are relatively inexpensive to carry out, and researchers can obtain rich and detailed information from large, diverse, and geographically dispersed samples. It takes a great deal of care and expertise to carry out a survey effectively. Researchers must understand the strengths and weaknesses of the four main modes of administration, and they must carefully construct their survey questions and design. The quality of survey data are potentially weakened by nonresponse, measurement, coverage, and sampling errors, so researchers are continually innovating to address and minimize the impact of such errors. Given the abundance of survey data collected by academic and governmental researchers, including omnibus surveys such as the GSS and MIDUS, even emerging scholars can begin to analyze these data, test hypotheses, and contribute to our understanding of contemporary social and political life.

End-of-Chapter Review

Summary

Surveys are one of the most widely used methods in social research. They allow researchers to collect a wide variety of information about large populations, test causal hypotheses, and document patterns of social change.

What Are Surveys and What Can They Do?

- All surveys are highly structured, meaning they ask respondents prewritten, closed-ended questions with fixed response options.
- Cross-sectional surveys collect data at a single point in time, whereas longitudinal surveys collect data at multiple points in time.
- Advantages of surveys include their ability to collect a wide breadth of information from large groups of people and to assess changes in populations over time, as well as their high level of external validity.
- Surveys are subject to multiple sources of error, including nonresponse, measurement error, coverage error, and sampling error.

Types of Surveys: Modes of Administration

- Face-to-face interviews are often seen as the "gold standard," as the interviewer can ensure the respondent understands the survey and does not skip questions.
- Telephone surveys, like face-to-face surveys, benefit from the guidance of an interviewer. They are also more cost effective and require less advance planning.
- Mail surveys are cost effective and generally do not suffer from social desirability biases. However, they tend to garner low response rates.
- Online surveys are becoming increasingly common because they're cost effective, easy to administer, convenient, and can target large, representative samples. However, participation may be biased toward younger people and those with more resources.

Survey Content: What Do We Ask and How Do We Ask It?

- Most survey questions are closed-ended with fixed response categories. Response categories should be mutually exclusive and exhaustive.
- Many concepts that social researchers study may be best captured with a composite measure. Indexes and scales are two types of composite measures.
- High-quality surveys use clear, neutral language, strive for precision, and avoid double-barreled and leading questions. The placement of questions can help researchers establish rapport with respondents, reduce monotony, and limit order effects.

Conducting the Survey

- Before conducting the survey, researchers often do a pretest with a group of people who are similar to the target sample.
- To analyze the pretest, researchers can use both "soft" data, such as comments from respondents, as well as "hard" data, such as preliminary statistical analyses.

Ethical Concerns in Survey Research

- Survey researchers must take care to protect respondents' confidentiality. It is unrealistic and impractical for researchers to promise anonymity to their respondents.
- Researchers should be sensitive to survey questions that may cause respondents to experience psychological distress.

Key Terms

Exercise

Suppose that your college or university is considering becoming a "dry campus." That means that alcoholic beverages would be completely banned from campus. The university will proceed with this plan if it believes there is widespread support among current students. You are tasked with conducting a rigorous and reliable survey to gauge attitudes toward having a dry campus. University administrators also are interested in knowing whether particular student subpopulations differ in their views.

- Describe your sampling frame. Who will you interview and why? How will participants be chosen? What safeguards will you take to ensure that your sample is not biased?

- What mode(s) of administration will you use and why? What are the relative strengths and weaknesses of this mode?

- Construct a brief scale (no more than four items) to measure attitudes toward a dry campus. Please provide complete question wordings and response categories.

- Construct a brief set of questions (no more than eight) on social, demographic, or other background characteristics you would want to know about in order to understand different subgroup views toward the campus alcohol policy.

- Describe one hypothesis you have regarding subgroup differences in views on becoming a dry campus. Be sure that your hypothesis uses only variables available in your survey.

Job hunters mill about at a job fair in Durham, North Carolina, for workers with a criminal record. A recent experiment found that a criminal record has a more damaging effect on black job applicants than their white counterparts.

EXPERIMENTAL RESEARCH

Consider the following questions:

- Does a criminal record harm a black man more than it does a white man when they apply for jobs?

- Does thinking about death increase our belief in God?

- Do racial stereotypes cause black people to perform worse on aptitude tests than white people?

- Do employers discriminate against mothers in hiring decisions?

- Does threatening a man's sense of his masculinity make him more likely to sexually harass a female coworker?

- Is a product, idea, or contribution judged more positively when it is presented by a higher-status (versus a lower-status) person?

Researchers have used experimental methods to answer these and many other questions. As mentioned in earlier chapters, experiments are the best method for establishing cause-effect relationships, or **causality**. That is, compared with other research methods, experiments most effectively evaluate whether a change in an independent variable causes a change in the dependent variable. (For a review of dependent and independent variables and of causal hypotheses, see Chapter 2.)

In this chapter, we describe the experimental method in detail, highlighting the unique strengths of experiments as a research method. We compare the strengths and limitations of four different types of experiments: laboratory, field, survey, and natural experiments. Next, we describe the steps in designing a laboratory experiment, the most common type of experiment. Because all research methods have strengths and weaknesses, we end the chapter by discussing the limits of the experimental method and the unique ethical issues that experimental methods often raise.

KEY FEATURES OF EXPERIMENTS

An **experiment** is a research method where the researcher manipulates one or more **independent variables** to determine the effect(s) on a **dependent variable**. Experiments share three key features: (1) manipulation of the independent variable, (2) random assignment of participants to experimental and control conditions, and (3) experimental control of other factors that could influence the outcome of the experiment.

Manipulation of the Independent Variable

Manipulation of the independent variable is the defining feature of an experiment. When an independent variable is manipulated, researchers actively change the level of the independent variable and observe the effects of that change. In other quantitative research methods, researchers observe natural variation of the independent variable rather than actively change it. For example, if a researcher is interested in whether children from lower-income families perform worse at school than those from higher-income families, the researcher would observe the natural variation in the income levels of children's families.

Experimenters, by contrast, intentionally manipulate the independent variable. For example, in an experiment designed to assess the effects of threats to masculinity (independent variable) on sexual harassment (dependent variable), researchers varied whether male participants had their masculinity threatened (Maass et al., 2003, experiment 2).

causality A relationship where one factor or variable is dependent on another factor or variable.

experiment A research method where the researcher manipulates one or more independent variable(s) to determine the effect(s) on a dependent variable.

independent variable In a causal hypothesis, the concept purported to be the cause; the variable on which values of the dependent variable may depend.

dependent variable In a causal hypothesis, the variable that is acted upon; the outcome we are seeking to understand.

FIGURE 8.1 Relationship between the Independent and Dependent Variable in an Experiment

In the masculinity-threat experiment, threats to masculinity were the independent variable and sexually harassing behaviors were the dependent variable.

Independent variable ⟶ Dependent variable

Threats to masculinity ⟶ Sexually harassing behaviors

To carry out this manipulation, the researchers first had participants complete a gender self-concept survey. Regardless of how participants answered the survey, the researchers gave one group of men feedback that they had scored in the normal range of masculinity, while the other group of men was given feedback that they had scored in the feminine range. By manipulating the feedback the two groups of men received, the researchers created two conditions: *a masculinity threat* condition and a *gender-affirming* condition. The masculinity threat condition was the **experimental condition**, and the gender-affirming condition was the **control condition**. The researchers could then compare the results for men in the two conditions to see if the threatened group engaged in more sexually harassing behavior (Figure 8.1).

Another example will help solidify your understanding of experimental conditions. Let's say a researcher is interested in studying whether negative racial stereotypes affect the performance of African American students on aptitude tests. To test this relationship, the researcher would manipulate the independent variable (negative racial stereotypes) to create two conditions: one where African American students are exposed to a negative racial stereotype and a second where they are not. By subjecting participants to different conditions, researchers can determine whether exposure to negative racial stereotypes (the independent variable) caused changes in test performance (the dependent variable).

experimental condition
A condition in an experiment where the independent variable is manipulated.

control condition A condition where the independent variable is not manipulated.

random assignment
A process that ensures that participants have an equal likelihood of being assigned to experimental or control conditions in order to ensure that individual characteristics are randomly distributed across conditions.

experimental group The group that is exposed to the experimental manipulation.

control group The group that is not exposed to the manipulation of the independent variable.

Random Assignment of Participants to Experimental and Control Conditions

The second key feature of an experiment is **random assignment** of participants to experimental and control conditions. Random assignment ensures that individual characteristics such as personality traits, biological traits, family background, and attitudes are randomly distributed across conditions. Acting as the great equalizer, random assignment distributes individual differences among participants to each condition. Because these individual differences are equally distributed across conditions, they cannot influence experimental results. In short, random assignment ensures that the *only* difference between the **experimental group** and the **control group** is the independent variable.

Researchers use a number of techniques for randomly assigning participants to each condition. For example, the researcher could have participants draw a number from 1 to 99. Participants who draw odd numbers are assigned to one condition, and those who draw even numbers are assigned to another. Other times, researchers might use a computer program to generate a random number. Let's say the random number generated is 3. The researcher would then select every third name on the list of all study participants (the sampling frame) for assignment to the experimental condition, cycling back to the top of the list and selecting every third name until capturing 50% of all persons on the list. Those in the 50% not randomly chosen for the experimental condition would be assigned to the control condition.

Experiments have been conducted to determine whether exposure to negative racial stereotypes (independent variable) affects test performance (dependent variable) among African American students.

To determine whether negative racial stereotypes cause African Americans to perform poorly on aptitude tests, the researcher must be sure that the African American participants in the negative-stereotype condition (experimental condition) do not differ from those in the no-stereotype condition (control condition), except for their exposure to a stereotype. For example, results might be skewed if the researcher assigned participants in the experiment's morning sessions to the negative-stereotype condition and participants in the afternoon sessions to the no-stereotype condition. Participants in the morning sessions might perform worse on the aptitude test simply because they are more tired than those in the afternoon session, not because the stereotype caused them to perform worse.

If, after randomly assigning participants to a condition, the researchers find that participants in the negative-stereotype condition perform worse on an aptitude test than those in the no-stereotype condition, they can be much more confident that the negative stereotype, and not some other factor, caused lower test performance. As this example shows, random assignment is essential for establishing causality.

Experimental Control of Other Factors

The third key feature of experiments is the amount of control the researcher has over other factors that might affect the relationship between the independent variable and the dependent variable. For example, if researchers are interested in whether people judge products created by men more favorably than those of identical quality created by women, they could have participants in one condition read an essay with a man's name given as the author while participants in another condition read the same essay with a woman's name shown as the author. Participants would then rate the quality of the essay, and the researchers would compare the ratings of the male-authored essay to those of the female-authored essay.

If the author's gender does not affect ratings, the two essays should receive the same ratings because participants in the two conditions read the exact same essay. If the researchers instead find that the male author's essay received higher ratings, they have uncovered strong evidence that the author's gender caused a bias in ratings. Experimental studies similar to the essay study just described have found a small but consistent tendency to rate identical products created by men more favorably than those created by women (Swim et al., 1989). A similar experiment found that résumés with men's names were evaluated more positively than identical résumés bearing women's names (Steinpreis, Anders, & Ritzke, 1999). By using identical products or résumés, the researcher maintains considerable control over other factors that could affect ratings, which is essential for establishing that gender—and not some other factor—caused the differences in ratings.

Returning to our example of racial stereotypes and test performance, experimental studies of *stereotype threat* have consistently found that African Americans randomly assigned to a condition where they are led to think about negative racial stereotypes perform worse on aptitude tests than African Americans assigned to a no-stereotype condition (Steele, Spencer, & Aronson, 2002). Experimental control is essential for making this claim. For example, the researchers must give all participants the same aptitude test, thereby controlling for test difficulty. They must also ensure that participants in each condition are exposed to the same testing environment—a quiet room with good lighting and no other people present. Only after taking such precautions can researchers ensure that stereotype threat, rather than numerous other factors, caused lower test performance.

CONCEPT CHECKS

1 What are the three key features of experiments?

2 In the essay study described in this section, identify the independent variable and the dependent variable. How could a researcher manipulate the independent variable?

3 Why is random assignment necessary?

ADVANTAGES OF EXPERIMENTS

Experiments have three key advantages as a research method:

1. Experiments are the best research method to establish causality; for example, assessing whether threatening a man's masculinity *causes* him to be more likely to sexually harass a coworker.

2. Experiments can uncover mechanisms that produce an outcome, establishing not only *if* employers discriminate against mothers, but also *why*.

3. Experiments can be used to evaluate abstract theories about the workings of the social world.

We now turn to examples that illustrate the strengths of the experimental method.

Establishing Causality

In earlier chapters, we learned that experiments are the best method for assessing causality. Manipulating the independent variable while experimentally holding constant other factors that could influence the dependent variable allows us to feel confident that changes in the independent variable caused changes in the dependent variable. To establish that one variable causes changes in the other variable, three conditions must be met: (1) the two variables must be correlated, or co-vary, meaning an increase (or decrease) in one variable is associated with an increase (or decrease) in the other; (2) the cause (independent variable) must precede the effect (the dependent variable); and (3) the relationship between the independent variable and dependent variable must not be spurious, or caused by some other factor.

In practice, researchers have little trouble meeting the first two conditions, but the problem of **spuriousness** is more challenging. Recall from Chapter 2 that a relationship between the independent and dependent variables is spurious when it is complicated by a confound, or a third concept that is linked to the two variables in a way that makes them appear to be related even when they are not. Experiments uniquely solve the problem of spuriousness. By experimentally holding other factors constant and

spuriousness When an apparent relation between two concepts is actually the result of some third concept (confound) influencing both of them.

RECENTLY I'VE BECOME FASCINATED WITH 19TH-CENTURY HOOP DRESSES.

Concerned that she would be passed over for a promotion if management knew she was pregnant, Donna concealed the fact.

varying only the independent variable, we are assured that the relationship between the independent variable and the dependent variable is not spurious.

The existence of the "motherhood penalty" illustrates why experiments are good at detecting bias and discrimination. Using survey data on U.S. workers, researchers compared the hourly wages of mothers and childless women who were otherwise very similar—all the subjects had the same level of education, the same type of job, the same amount of work experience, and the same marital status, and they were also similar on a host of other dimensions. Holding all of these factors constant, the researchers found that mothers earn approximately 5% lower wages, per child, than childless women do (Budig & England, 2001).

But can we conclude that discrimination against mothers *causes* mothers' lower wages? Although survey data allow us to compare highly similar mothers and non-mothers, researchers cannot control for the infinite potential differences between the two groups. This inability to control for all possible variations between mothers and non-mothers means we cannot know for sure whether the motherhood penalty occurs because mothers differ from childless women in some way that legitimately affects their pay or because employers discriminate against mothers. This is where an experiment can be useful. With an experiment, we can compare how individuals evaluate mothers and non-mothers who have the same qualifications, allowing us to more fully control for differences in quality.

In a motherhood penalty experiment conducted by one of this book's authors, participants rated two equally qualified female job applicants (Correll, Benard, & Paik, 2007). Pretesting of the applicants' résumés and other supporting materials established that the two applicants were equally qualified. Having established that the two applicants were equally qualified, researchers added a line to one of the résumés describing the applicant as an officer in an elementary school PTA, thereby identifying her as a mother. The second applicant's résumé listed her involvement as an officer in her neighborhood association. Does adding this very small bit of information about being a mother change the ratings of the two applicants, who were previously judged as equally qualified? If so, we can conclude that motherhood causes a bias in the evaluations.

In fact, that was exactly the researchers' conclusion. Mothers were offered starting salaries that were $11,000 lower than those offered to childless women with equivalent résumés; in addition, mothers were 90% less likely to be recommended for hire than childless women with equivalent résumés. In another condition of the experiment, men's names were put on the very same résumés, and a different set of participants rated these fathers and childless men. While participants were biased against mothers in the first condition, they were biased *in favor* of fathers in the second. Because researchers were able to carefully control the quality of the applicants, we can feel confident claiming that evaluators were biased against mothers (but not against fathers), leading to the negative outcomes experienced by mothers.

Uncovering Mechanisms That Produce Discrimination

Experiments are also good for identifying the mechanisms that produce discrimination, showing us *why* and *how* discrimination occurs. For example, studies have shown that when hiring criteria are ambiguous, evaluators will pay more attention to the criteria that favor advantaged groups, such as men or whites. In one interesting experiment, Uhlmann and Cohen (2005) had participants evaluate either a male or female job applicant for a police chief position. Each applicant was strong on one criterion and weak on another. In one condition, the applicant was presented as well educated but lacking experience on the street. In a second condition, the applicant had good street experience but lacked formal education. Participants then rated the importance of each criterion (education and street experience) and said how likely they would be to hire each applicant.

Researchers have found that delineating clear hiring criteria reduces bias in hiring decisions.

The study found that participants constructed their criteria to give an advantage to the male applicant. When the male applicant had more education, participants rated education as significantly more important for the job. But when he had more street experience, street experience was rated as more important. Because participants shifted which criterion was more important to their decision, the male applicant was significantly more likely to be recommended for hire regardless of whether he had a strong educational background but lacked street experience or had strong street experience but lacked formal education.

In the next phase of the study, the authors had a different set of participants rate the importance of education versus experience *before* evaluating applicants. This exercise eliminated the bias that had previously favored the male applicant and demonstrated that clearly stated criteria can lead to fairer hiring decisions. Studies like this one have been cited in gender-discrimination lawsuits (see "Conversations from the Front Lines").

Testing Abstract Theories: How Do Status Beliefs Form?

Experiments are often conducted in highly artificial settings where the researcher exposes participants to a specific situation while intentionally removing other features that occur in real-life situations. For example, a researcher who is interested in the effects of gender on some outcome might have a participant interact with a partner of a different gender who is otherwise exactly equal to the participant on other dimensions, such as race, physical attractiveness, and problem-solving ability. Because people typically differ from one another in many ways, the setup is artificial, but it allows the researcher to study the unique effects of gender. Similarly, because of their artificiality, experiments are well suited for testing abstract theories about how the social world works.

For example, sociologist Cecilia Ridgeway and colleagues were interested in how people form beliefs that one particular category of people is more highly esteemed

WILLIAM T. BIELBY

William T. Bielby is a sociology professor at the University of Illinois at Chicago and former president of the American Sociological Association. His research specialties are in the areas of organizational behavior, gender and racial inequality, and research methods. Bielby has frequently served as an expert witness in gender- and race-discrimination cases.

How did you become interested in studying gender discrimination? What are the challenges of this topic of research?

Early on in my career I began studying the ways in which organizational policies and practices create socioeconomic inequality. That led to an interest in explaining job segregation by sex: Why do men and women so often end up in different kinds of jobs and have different career paths in organizations?

The biggest challenge in doing this research is gaining access to data at the organizational level. Organizations, especially private companies, are very reluctant to give outside researchers access to information about the gender and racial composition of jobs. As a result, most research on gender and racial segregation in employment relies on national surveys and analyzes gender and race segregation at the occupational level, aggregated across organizations. Those kinds of studies miss the substantial amount of segregation that occurs within occupations—for example, when men and women do similar work in the same company but in different job titles, with different career paths.

You've testified in numerous class-action employment-discrimination cases, including high-profile gender-discrimination cases against Walmart and a large race-discrimination case against Merrill Lynch. How did you become involved in these cases? What role did experimental research play in the cases?

Back in 1990 some attorneys in California brought a large class-action gender-discrimination lawsuit against Lucky Stores on behalf of women in hourly jobs in the grocery store chain. At the time, Lucky Stores was almost completely gender segregated. Men and women rarely worked in the same jobs in a store: Men were in jobs that had a path to management while women were in dead-end jobs. No official company policy formally reserved some jobs for men and others for women, so it was important for the attorneys to understand whether and how company practices created and sustained gender segregation, and to explain this to the judge in the case. The attorneys discovered that my colleague James Baron and I had published a series of studies on workplace gender segregation, and they hired me to do a case study of Lucky Stores and to testify at trial about my findings regarding the organizational factors that contributed to gender segregation in the company's California stores.

> **Some of the most reliable and valid studies of gender stereotypes are based on experimental research. Part of my role as an expert in the case was to describe those studies to the judge.**

After studying segregation patterns in the stores, the company's written policies, and testimony from company managers about how they made decisions about job assignments and promotions, I concluded that in the absence of formal procedures and guidelines for making employment decisions, managers' decisions were heavily influenced by gender stereotypes. Managers shared an implicit understanding that some jobs in the stores were "men's work" and others were "women's work," because they subscribed to stereotypical beliefs that women's family demands limited their availability for and interest in jobs that led to management careers and that men were uniquely qualified for these jobs.

Some of the most reliable and valid studies of gender stereotypes are based on experimental research. Part of my role as an expert in the case was to describe those studies to the judge and to explain why they allow us to better understand how the practices of Lucky Stores contributed to gender-based job segregation.

The Lucky Stores case was the first of its kind to go to trial, and the judge relied heavily on my expert testimony in her lengthy written opinion finding the company legally liable for discriminating against its female employees. The Lucky Stores case established a precedent, and it soon became common for plaintiffs in class-action discrimination cases to offer expert testimony of a sociologist who does an organizational case study and testifies about the relevance of social science research to the matters before the court. In the years that followed, I testified in dozens of cases with issues like those raised in the Lucky Stores case, including the nationwide class-action gender-discrimination case filed against Walmart, the largest employment class-action lawsuit ever.

The American Sociological Association issued a brief in defense of your conclusions in the Walmart case. Why was your testimony so controversial?

Well, to me and to the governing board of the American Sociological Association it was not controversial, but attorneys for Walmart argued vociferously that it was. It is not unusual for corporate defendants in class-action discrimination lawsuits to argue: (1) that social science testimony offered by plaintiffs' experts should be inadmissible because the science is unreliable and invalid (it is "junk science"); or (2) that it should be discounted because the science does not apply to the organization whose practices are being challenged (the science lacks external validity). Walmart's lawyers made both arguments. In its brief, the American Sociological Association described the reliability and internal validity of the methods used in scientific studies I relied upon in my case study of Walmart, explained how the case-study method can be used to draw valid inferences about the causal impact of organizational policies and practices in a new setting (one that was not studied in extant research), and explained the scientific basis for the assertion that employment practices like those alleged to be in place at Walmart can lead to discriminatory employment outcomes.

You've noted that experimental research complements data from other research methods such as surveys, ethnographies, and case studies of organizations, helping to "connect the dots." Can you explain what you mean by this and provide an example?

From quantitative surveys, first-hand qualitative observation and interviews, and analysis of organizational documents we can gain rich insights into organizational dynamics, especially as they pertain to employment discrimination. But rarely can we intervene and systematically *manipulate* organizational contexts and practices in "real world" businesses and then gauge the impact on employment outcomes. Usually, from those methods alone we can only draw inferences about causal mechanisms. Experimental research, conducted in an environment under the researcher's control, allows us to do precisely that. Accountability studies provide a good example. These modify the classic studies of stereotyping and cognitive bias by also experimentally manipulating whether subjects are held accountable for their decisions—for example, by requiring that they explain their decision-making rationale to a third party versus having no such obligation. Such studies typically show that being subject to accountability substantially reduces cognitive bias, and because accountability is experimentally manipulated with random assignment, we can be confident that the moderating effect on bias is due to accountability per se and not due to other features of the decision-making context.

You teach research methods regularly. What do you hope your students will take away from the course?

In my classes students are expected to learn the strengths and weaknesses of each method we cover, and which methods are best suited for specific kinds of research questions and social contexts. But for important research questions with "real world" implications, I hope students develop a capacity to draw upon research studies using a wide range of methods, and use that work to gain a more holistic understanding of the social phenomena that motivated their research. In my work providing expert testimony, I have benefited from being placed in situations in which it is part of my job to achieve that kind of understanding for myself and then communicate it effectively to others.

than another (Ridgeway et al., 1998). How, for example, did the differences between men and women become associated with beliefs that men are generally more highly esteemed than women, more natural leaders, and deserving of higher pay? Why isn't gender instead like eye color, where differences in eye color do not signal higher or lower status?

Ridgeway developed a theory about how distinctions such as race and gender come to be associated with beliefs about differences in status (Ridgeway, 1991; Ridgeway et al., 1998). One hypothesis is that a distinction will become associated with status beliefs if (1) one category of the distinction (such as men in the case of gender) has greater resources, on average, than the other category, and (2) the two groups interact with each other in situations where they must work together to achieve shared goals. According to the theory, as group members interact with one another in these settings, they will observe the average differences in resources and come to believe that the "richer" group has higher status than the "poorer" group. For example, we might assume that people who occupy nicer offices in an office building are more important or have higher status than those with smaller, less desirable offices. If the people who have the fancier offices are more frequently members of one group and not another, observers might form a general belief that the group with the better offices has higher status.

To evaluate her theory, Ridgeway first had to create a distinction that had no preexisting status value attached to it. To do so, she had participants rate a series of paintings by two artists and then told them that their painting preferences determined their "personal response style," a distinction that they were led to believe was a stable part of their personality. Participants then engaged in two rounds of interactions with two different partners, both of whom, they were told, were from the other response-style group. Before beginning the interactions, participants were randomly assigned to either a condition where they learned that they were being paid more than their partners or a condition where they learned that their partners were being paid more. This procedure created an average resource difference between people from the two different response-style groups. After the two rounds of interaction, participants were asked to rate their own group and the other group in terms of each group's status. Would people form status beliefs—seeing one group as higher status than the other—after just two brief interactions?

The answer was yes. By the end of the second round of interactions, participants who had more resources than their partners had formed beliefs that their group was more leader-like, more powerful, and higher in status than the other group. More surprisingly, participants who were paid less than their partners formed beliefs that the *other* group had higher status than their own group. This result is quite surprising given the tendency toward *in-group bias*, a well-documented phenomenon that refers to our tendency to rate groups to which we belong as superior to other groups.

More generally, Ridgeway's experiment showed one way that a distinction that initially has no status value ("personal response style") can acquire status value. If resources are even slightly skewed to favor one group—for whatever reason—and if members of the groups interact with one another to accomplish shared goals, they will come to believe that the group with more resources has higher status. This conclusion can help us understand how race or gender may have acquired status value in our society over time. By using a highly artificial setting where participants differed on a specific distinction and level of pay but were otherwise equal, Ridgeway was able to evaluate her theory about how status beliefs form.

TYPES OF EXPERIMENTS

So far, all of the examples we have described have been laboratory experiments. Laboratory experiments are the most pure form of an experiment because they allow the researcher to easily manipulate the independent variables, randomize participants into conditions, and control features of the experimental setting. However, other types of experiments also have their advantages. Next we compare four types of experiments: laboratory experiments, field experiments, population-based survey experiments, and natural experiments.

Laboratory Experiments

As their name implies, **laboratory experiments** take place in laboratories. The laboratory setting gives researchers the maximum amount of control over the environment in which the experiment is conducted. During a laboratory experiment, the experimenter goes through the experimental procedures with the participants, observing and giving instructions. In doing so, the experimenter ensures that participants notice the manipulation of the independent variable and that other factors that might interfere with the results are controlled. In the sexual harassment study, for example, the researchers could ensure that some participants had their masculinity threatened while others had their masculinity affirmed. They did this by having the experimenter show participants their score on a (fake) "masculinity survey" and by commenting verbally on whether the participant was "normally masculine" or had scored in the feminine range. Outside of the laboratory, such clear manipulation would be difficult to achieve.

STRENGTHS AND WEAKNESSES OF LABORATORY EXPERIMENTS

Because of the high degree of experimenter control, laboratory experiments have a high degree of internal validity. High **internal validity** means that a study is well suited to evaluate claims involving causal relationships. **External validity** refers to

laboratory experiment An experiment that takes place in a laboratory.

internal validity The degree to which a study establishes a causal effect of the independent variable on the dependent variable.

external validity A dimension of validity concerning the degree to which the results of a study can generalize beyond the study.

Students participate in a laboratory experiment. This setting allows for a high degree of experimental control, as the researcher can ensure that participants notice the manipulation of the independent variable.

the extent to which the conclusions drawn from a study generalize to a larger population or to a different setting. The majority of laboratory experiments rely on nonrandom samples of college students for participants, which reduces their external validity. Later in the chapter, we discuss how researchers can increase the external validity of experimental findings. (For a further review of issues surrounding validity, see Chapter 5.)

As noted earlier, laboratory experiments occur in highly artificial settings. These settings can be an advantage when testing abstract theories, because the artificial setting allows us to disentangle the complexity of a social phenomenon that occurs in the natural world. For example, in the status-belief study discussed earlier, Ridgeway and colleagues (1998) used the lab setting to isolate the effect of resources from the effect of all the other factors that influence the formation of status beliefs. If we are interested in more applied questions, however, such as whether employers exhibit bias against a particular group of people, a more realistic experimental setting would be desirable.

We have seen many examples of laboratory experiments in this chapter. Let's examine one more to illustrate the strengths and weaknesses of laboratory experiments. Sociologist Robb Willer (2009) was interested in whether there is a motivational basis for religious ideology. We know that political ideology can be self-serving, with individuals more strongly endorsing political ideologies or beliefs that benefit them personally. But is religious ideology also self-serving? Does the intensity of our religious beliefs increase, for example, in times when we are personally motivated to believe in God, such as when we contemplate dying?

To investigate, Willer manipulated his independent variable—contemplation of death—by randomly assigning participants to one condition of the experiment in which they wrote an essay about their feelings and emotions when they contemplate their own death. Those randomly assigned to a second condition wrote essays on a neutral topic (feelings evoked while watching television). The researchers then asked participants, who were college students, "How likely do you think it is that there is life after death?" As hypothesized, participants who wrote essays about their own death (and therefore were more motivated to believe in an afterlife) reported a significantly stronger belief in the afterlife than those who wrote essays about watching television.

Willer's experiment has several methodological strengths. First, Willer cleanly manipulated the independent variable—contemplation of death—in a manner that was salient to participants. **Salience** means that the manipulation made participants aware of the independent variable. Second, by randomly assigning participants to conditions, participants' prior beliefs about the afterlife were equally distributed across the two conditions. Random assignment also equally distributed other factors that might have affected the results, such as whether a relative had recently died.

However, the lab setting is highly artificial. People (especially 20-year-old college students) do not usually spend their days in a small cubicle writing essays about death. And because the study relied on a sample of college students, we do not know if older

salience When participants notice the experimental manipulation, such as noticing that a job applicant is female (or male).

adults or non-college students would behave as the college students did. Nonetheless, this study allows us to evaluate an abstract prediction about the motivational basis of religious beliefs. The ability to isolate and cleanly manipulate the independent variable makes us confident that motivation to believe in God *causes* an increase in the intensity of religious beliefs. As is common with experimental studies, Willer's study has a high degree of internal validity but a lower degree of external validity. That is, the data provide strong evidence in support of the hypothesis that contemplation of death increases belief in God, but the data leave us less certain about whether the findings generalize to other settings or populations.

Field Experiments

Field experiments overcome some of the limits of laboratory experiments by taking the experiment out of the lab and into a more natural or "real world" setting. As in laboratory experiments, researchers conducting field experiments manipulate the independent variable and randomly assign participants to conditions. Unlike laboratory experiments, however, field experiments take place in natural environments with participants who are normally found in those settings. The natural setting makes field experiments well suited for evaluating more applied questions but less well suited for exploring more abstract social processes.

Field experiments are often used to evaluate the success of interventions to improve educational and health outcomes. For example, Blackwell and colleagues conducted an experiment to assess whether teaching students that intelligence was a *malleable* rather than a *fixed* trait could improve students' classroom motivation and mathematical performance (Blackwell, Trzesniewski, & Dweck, 2007). The independent variable in this experiment is "intelligence theory," and there are two conditions: (1) fixed, where intelligence is believed to be more or less unchangeable; and (2) malleable, where intelligence is believed to be a quality that can be developed.

Participants were 99 seventh-grade students at a school in New York City. Students at this school had previously been randomly assigned to an "advisory class" at their school. The researchers then assigned advisory classes to receive either the *fixed* or *malleable* intervention. During their advisory class, the research team taught the students in the "malleable condition" that "you can grow your intelligence" and "learning makes you smarter," while students in the "fixed" condition were taught memory tricks and other lessons about academic successes and failures. The researchers hypothesized that students who learned that intelligence was malleable would show increased academic motivation and improved mathematical performance compared to those who learned that intelligence was fixed.

Importantly, students and their teachers were blind to condition, meaning they did not know that they were receiving the fixed or malleable intervention. The researchers delivering the intervention were not blind to condition; they obviously knew which intervention they were delivering. In some experiments, researchers *and* participants are blind to condition. For example, if an intervention is given to participants in a sealed envelope and researchers do not know which intervention is in which envelope, the study would be **double blind**, meaning neither researcher nor participant is aware of which condition the participant is in. Double-blind experiments are an important

field experiment An experiment that takes place in a natural or "real world" setting.

double-blind study A study where neither the researcher nor the participant is aware of which condition the participant is in.

defense against experimenter effects. **Experimenter effects** occur when a researcher subtly or unconsciously affects the performance of a study participant. Both verbal and nonverbal cues, such as nodding or an encouraging tone of voice, may nudge the participant into behaving in such a way as to confirm the study's hypothesis. The researcher not knowing whether a subject is in the experimental or control group is an important safeguard against the potential biases imposed via experimenter effects.

Consistent with the researchers' hypothesis, students in the malleable condition showed a positive change in academic motivation over time compared to those in the fixed condition. Further, students in the malleable condition experienced improvements in their math grades, while students in the fixed condition experienced a decline in math grades over the same period. This experiment shows how a simple intervention can improve student motivation and performance. Further, because the experiment was conducted in an actual school and not a laboratory, we can be more confident that teaching students that intelligence is malleable can foster positive educational outcomes.

AUDIT STUDIES

Work by sociologist Devah Pager (2003) on criminal status, race, and hiring is an excellent example of a special type of field experiment called an **audit study**. Audit studies are used to assess whether characteristics such as gender, race, and sexual orientation lead to discrimination in real labor and housing markets. Pager was interested in whether having a criminal record would be more detrimental to black job applicants than to their white peers. That is, while we might realistically expect that those with a criminal record would have more difficulty getting a job than those without a criminal record, would the stigma of a criminal record be more damaging for black men than for white men?

Pager's study had two independent variables—race and whether a man had a criminal record. A **factorial design experiment** is an experiment that has two or more independent variables. To manipulate race, Pager hired young black men and white men as "auditors" or "testers." She trained these testers to be as similar to each other as possible in their style of presentation, dress, and speech. The black and white testers then went out to apply for low-wage jobs in person. To identify their criminal status, the testers checked either "yes" or "no" on a box on the job application that asked if they had ever been convicted of a crime. To control for other factors that could affect how employers reacted to the testers, black and white testers presented themselves as equally qualified, with similar job histories and experience. Pager then measured whether the testers received a callback from employers. To measure whether the testers were called back, Pager set up a voicemail box for each tester. She could then tally the number of calls from prospective employers of the black versus white applicants.

Pager found that having a criminal record was more of a disadvantage for black job applicants than for white job applicants. Employers called back black men with a

An experiment by sociologist Devah Pager found that the stigma of a criminal record is more damaging for black job candidates than white job candidates.

criminal record only 5% of the time, but they called back white men with a criminal record at the significantly higher rate of 17%. In addition, a white man with a criminal record was just as likely to be offered a job or called back for an interview as a black man with a clean history (Figure 8.2)!

STRENGTHS AND WEAKNESSES OF FIELD EXPERIMENTS

The key advantage of a field experiment over a laboratory experiment is probably clear from Pager's study. By having her testers apply for actual jobs and then measuring how real employers responded to them, Pager could be certain that a criminal background harms black men more than it does white men in a real job market. If Pager had conducted her study in a laboratory setting with college students evaluating the job candidates, we would be less confident about generalizing from the findings.

In general, field experiments are better at assessing whether an outcome occurs than at evaluating the process that produces the outcome. So, for example, while field experiments are excellent for assessing whether a group is discriminated against, they are less helpful for figuring out *why* the discrimination occurs. Another disadvantage of field experiments is that researchers have less control over other features of the setting. For example, in the educational intervention study, students were randomly assigned to their advisory classes by the school. The researchers did not have control over that randomization. In Pager's study, the white testers and the black testers were trained to be as similar as possible and were selected to be similar in terms of age, appearance, and other characteristics. However, people's appearance differs in all kinds of ways that the researcher cannot control.

Finally, while field experiments occur in more realistic and consequential settings, of necessity they, like laboratory experiments, frequently rely on nonrandom samples. The educational intervention was conducted in one school in New York City. Similarly, Pager could not realistically have her testers apply to a random sample of jobs from all over the country. Out of necessity, she chose a specific location—Milwaukee, Wisconsin—in which to conduct her study. Would we find similar results in other parts of the country? Pager and her colleagues replicated the original study in New York and found similar results (Pager, Western, & Bonikowski, 2009), which increases our confidence in the generalizability of the results.

Population-Based Survey Experiments

A **population-based survey experiment** is an experiment conducted on a random sample of the population of interest. These experiments are called "survey" experiments because researchers rely on survey methods to recruit a sample of participants

FIGURE 8.2 Impact of a Criminal Record on Job Callbacks for Blacks and Whites

In her audit study, Devah Pager found that employers were significantly more likely to call back a white man with a criminal record than a black man with a criminal record.

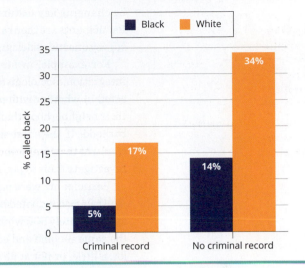

Source: Pager, 2003.

population-based survey experiment An experiment that relies on survey methods and is conducted on a representative sample of the population of interest.

that is representative of some population. As we learned in Chapter 7, surveys are ideally administered to a random sample of persons in the appropriate sampling frame.

In a survey experiment, participants often read a description of a scenario and then answer questions about how they would react to the given situation. What makes a survey experiment an "experiment" is that researchers vary the independent variable by changing key features of the scenario, thus creating the experimental conditions. Participants are then randomly assigned to read one version of the scenario and answer survey questions designed to measure the dependent variable.

For example, in studying the attitudes of white Americans toward residential integration, sociologists Howard Schuman and Lawrence Bobo (1988) were interested in whether whites would be more resistant to having a black family move into their neighborhood than to having a Japanese American family move into their neighborhood. If they had simply asked people this question, it is doubtful that anyone would have openly admitted preferring Japanese neighbors to black neighbors. So, to investigate their hypothesis, Schuman and Bobo conducted a survey experiment.

Participants were part of a larger national telephone survey of a random sample of Americans conducted by the University of Michigan Survey Research Center. Half of approximately 300 white participants were asked the question, "If a black family with the same income and education as you moved in next door to you, would you mind a lot, a little, or not at all?" The other half of the sample was asked the same question, except "Japanese American family" was substituted for "black family." Participants were randomly assigned to either the "black family" or "Japanese American family" condition, and the dependent variable was their degree of resistance to having either a black or Japanese American neighbor.

Schuman and Bobo found significantly more objections to having a black neighbor than to having a Japanese American neighbor. While 18.6% of the participants said they would mind having a black neighbor, only 2.7% of the participants indicated that they would mind having a Japanese American neighbor. Because the data from this experiment came from a random sample of whites in the U.S. population, we can feel confident that the higher resistance to black neighbors found in the sample would generalize to the larger population of whites in the United States. In other words, the external validity is high.

Survey experiments are increasingly becoming web-based. For example, the Time-sharing Experiments for the Social Sciences (TESS) program allows social science researchers to run experiments online using a nationally representative panel of participants, providing "researchers the opportunity to capture the internal validity of experiments while also realizing the benefits of working with a large, diverse population of research participants" (www.tessexperiments.org/index.html). With support from TESS, Doan, Hoehr, and Miller (2014) conducted an experiment with a nationally representative sample to assess factors affecting individuals' attitudes toward gay and lesbian couples. Participants were randomly assigned to read a scenario about a couple that was presented as either a heterosexual, gay, or lesbian couple. Members of the heterosexual couple were described as Brad and Jennifer, the lesbian couple were called Heather and Jennifer, and the gay couple were described as Brad and Matt. All other features of the scenario were the same except for the sexual orientation of the couple (the independent variable).

AUDIT STUDY REVEALS HIRING DISCRIMINATION AGAINST MUSLIMS

In the nearly two decades since 9/11, discrimination and hate crimes against Muslims have increased dramatically. Women wearing headscarves or *hijabs*, a symbol of one's Muslim faith, have reported harassment as they walk down the street, ride on public transportation, and wait in line at their local stores. Others allege that they have not been hired for jobs, even if qualified, because of their Arabic-sounding name or headscarves. Case in point: In October 2016, Zahraa-Imani Ali, a Muslim woman living in Chicago, sued a security company for employment discrimination, alleging that the firm rejected her because of her faith and her hijab.

A year earlier, Ali, a former correctional officer, had applied for a job with Securitas Security Services. During her phone interview, Ali asked whether wearing a hijab would create issues at work. The company's recruiter assured Ali it would not. Yet in a series of e-mails, a Securitas regional compliance manager recommended against further pursuing Ali as a candidate. The Council on American-Islamic Relations filed a federal lawsuit on behalf of Ali, alleging that the firm's decision was based "at least in part, but likely entirely, on the fact that Ms. Ali wears the hijab as part of her adherence to the Islamic faith," according to her lawyer Robert West (Patrick, 2016).

Discrimination cases are notoriously hard to prove. Yet experimental research can help us understand whether hiring decisions are affected by prejudice. Just as sociologist Devah Pager and colleagues did in the United States to understand discrimination against felons, Austrian social scientist Doris Weichselbaumer carried out an audit study to learn whether employers in Germany would discriminate against potential job applicants who were Muslim.

Weichselbaumer chose to carry out her study in Germany for two important reasons. First, unlike in the United States or other European nations, job seekers in Germany typically attach their photograph to their résumé. This allowed the research team to include a visual image of a woman wearing a headscarf, a personal detail that would not be evident in a standard job application. Second, Germany—like the United States—has been beset by rising reports of anti-Muslim discrimination. Observers fear that these aggressions will only grow as Germany opens it borders to rising numbers of Muslim refugees (Dearden, 2016).

The research team created résumés for three fictitious female characters with identical qualifications. One applicant had a German name (Sandra Bauer), one a Turkish name (Meryem Öztürk) and was dressed in Western clothing,

At 17, Samantha Elauf was denied a job at Abercrombie & Fitch because of her headscarf. She brought her case to the Supreme Court, which ultimately ruled in her favor.

and one had that same Turkish name but was also wearing a headscarf in her photo. All three applications featured photos of the same person, although the names differed and one was wearing a modern-style headscarf, intended to signal that the applicant was a young modern woman who could easily work in a secular environment. The researchers sent out roughly 1,500 applications. The results showed strong evidence of hiring discrimination against practicing Muslims, but the study also found discrimination against the applicant of Turkish versus German ethnicity, even when the Turkish applicant was wearing Western garb.

When Meryem Öztürk wore a headscarf, she had to send 4.5 as many applications as Sandra Bauer to receive the same number of callbacks for interviews. When Meryem was pictured without a headscarf, she still had to send 1.4 as many applications as Sandra Bauer. Dr. Weichelsbaumer's findings are important because they were based on an experimental design, considered the "gold standard" for ascertaining causal inference. Because the applications were identical, the study essentially "held constant" educational attainment, employment history, and physical attractiveness—known correlates of hiring decisions.

The results demonstrate that religious discrimination is pervasive. As Dr. Weichelsbaumer explained to reporters, "One obvious suggestion is for companies to stop encouraging applicants to attach photographs to their résumés. … But that will not address the deep well of suspicion and resentment many Muslims face in Western countries. … Achieving greater social acceptance for minorities is going to be a long process—and will not just be an economic question, but a political struggle as well" (Carmichael, 2017).

Participants were then asked a series of questions about the couple that were designed to reveal whether they believed the couple should have formal rights, such as the right to hospital visitations and insurance benefits, and whether the couple should have informal privileges, such as the right to hold hands or kiss in public. One key finding from this study is that heterosexual participants who were randomly assigned to read about a gay or lesbian couple were just as likely to grant formal rights to the couple as were those assigned to read about a heterosexual couple. However, they were less likely to support informal privileges for gay and lesbian couples.

STRENGTHS AND WEAKNESSES OF SURVEY EXPERIMENTS

Because survey experiments are conducted on a random sample of the population, they have a higher degree of external validity than laboratory or field experiments, but their internal validity tends to be lower due to less control over other features of the experimental setting. Because participants are drawn from a large, diverse population, they are often spread out geographically. Consequently, the experimenter cannot be present to ensure that the manipulation of the independent variable was salient, or clear, to all participants. Other factors in the environment, such as a television playing in the background, could influence the participants' attention to the experimental manipulation. If the independent variable is not salient to participants, we are less confident that it is the cause of the change in the dependent variable.

Further, survey experiments rely on self-reports of how people believe they would behave or feel, which does not always correspond to actual behavior or feelings (Fazio, 1990). For example, Pager and Quillian (2005) followed up Pager's 2003 audit study described earlier with a survey of the same employers from that study. They found that employers' self-reports about whether they would hire a black or white applicant with a criminal record were only weakly correlated with how they had actually behaved in the audit study (Figure 8.3).

As with all methods, we see a trade-off between external and internal validity in survey experiments. By relying on a random sample of the population, we are more confident that our results generalize to a larger population. At the same time, we are less confident that we have accurately assessed the causal relationship that the study was designed to evaluate. Social scientists are increasingly researching how to better integrate experimental and survey research methods in order to maximize both internal and external validity (Mutz, 2011).

Natural Experiments

In a **natural experiment**, the independent variable is manipulated by "nature," not by the experimenter. (This method is sometimes called a *naturally occurring experiment*.) For example, a researcher might be interested in

FIGURE 8.3 Employers' Self-Reports vs. Behavior in Audit Study

Pager and Quillian found that 62 percent of employers reported in a survey that they were "very likely" (bottom portion of bars) or "somewhat likely" (solid portion of bars) to hire blacks with a criminal record. In their audit study of the same employers, however, only 5% called back black candidates with criminal records.

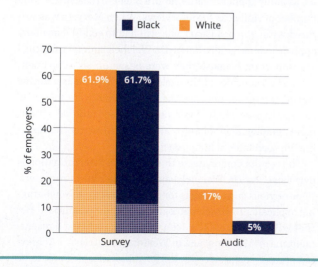

Source: Pager and Quillian, 2005.

the effect of a naturally occurring independent variable such as an economic recession, a natural disaster, or the implementation of a new school testing program. Participants in natural experiments are assigned to conditions by natural forces and not by experimental procedures. Because they lack random assignment, and because experimenters cannot manipulate the independent variable, natural experiments are more of an observational study than a true experiment. Researchers often rely on natural experiments when conducting a controlled laboratory experiment would not be possible. Because natural experiments are set in motion by natural changes that manipulate the independent variable of interest, researchers must stay attuned to the world around them, waiting for a natural experiment to happen.

natural experiment
An experiment in which the independent variable is manipulated by "nature," not by the experimenter.

An interesting example of a natural experiment comes from Goldin and Rouse's (2000) study of gender discrimination in the hiring of orchestra musicians. Professional orchestras historically have been highly male-dominated, with men holding approximately 88% of the positions in the "Big Five" orchestras, such as the New York Philharmonic and the Boston Symphony Orchestra, until about 1980. Given this large disparity, some researchers have hypothesized that the low percentage of women in orchestras was due to a bias against women musicians. For example the conductor of the New York Philharmonic from 1978 to 1990 is credited with saying, "I just don't think women should be in an orchestra" (Goldin & Rouse, 2000, p. 719).

How could we evaluate whether the people making hiring decisions were biased against women or whether the women who applied were simply less talented or proficient than the male applicants? Despite its ability to expose discrimination, a field experiment was not possible in this case because of the small number of orchestra job openings each year. A laboratory experiment would also be impractical because it would be virtually impossible to get world-renowned conductors to come to the laboratory to evaluate male and female musicians whose talent the experimenter could hold constant. Luckily for researchers, a natural manipulation of the independent variable occurred.

Starting in the 1970s and 1980s, orchestras gradually begin switching to blind auditions. Previously, male and female musicians auditioned in front of a team of evaluators, but they now began to audition behind a screen, which prevented the evaluators from seeing the musician. The introduction of the screen created a natural manipulation of the independent variable, which created two conditions: a condition where the gender of the musician was known (before the introduction of blind auditions) and a condition where the gender of the musician was unknown (after the introduction of blind auditions). This natural experiment allowed researchers to assess whether women are more likely to be hired when their gender is unknown. Using data from the top five orchestras in the United States, the researchers found that 25% more women were hired after orchestras switched to gender-blind auditions. In short, the data support the finding that orchestras were prejudiced against women musicians in the period before the introduction of blind auditions.

Orchestras today typically conduct blind auditions, where the musicians perform behind a screen.

STRENGTHS AND WEAKNESSES OF NATURAL EXPERIMENTS

The key strength of a natural experiment is that it occurs in a very realistic and consequential setting. However, natural experiments are often so realistic that the results are relevant only to the setting in which the study was conducted. That is, we can be very confident that non-blind auditions were detrimental to women musicians, but does this pattern extend to other types of jobs or is it unique to orchestras? As with field experiments, the realistic setting is better for assessing whether an outcome occurs than for uncovering the mechanism that produces the outcome.

Another disadvantage of a natural experiment is that the researcher cannot randomly assign participants to the conditions. In our orchestra example, the researcher obviously could not assign some women and men to audition in the earlier historical period when their gender was known and others to the later period when screens were introduced. We must therefore ask what else was different in the period when non-blind auditions were common. Might other historical differences have produced the change rather than the blind-audition procedure? Goldin and Rouse creatively control for the effects of historical period in their analysis, but random assignment, if possible, would have increased their (and our) confidence that gender bias caused fewer women to be hired in the era before blind auditions.

Summary

The four types of experiments we have discussed differ in terms of (1) the amount of control the researcher has over the setting, (2) the extent to which the researcher can cleanly manipulate the independent variable, (3) the ease with which participants can be randomly assigned to condition, (4) the nature of the sample, and (5) the extent to which the setting is artificial versus realistic (Table 8.1). In general, experiments where researchers can cleanly manipulate the independent variable while holding other factors constant and randomly assign participants to conditions have the highest internal validity. That is, they will produce data that can most convincingly evaluate whether changes in the independent variable *cause* changes in the dependent variable. However, this high degree of internal validity—often associated with laboratory experiments—comes at the expense of external validity. To achieve the kind of control desired in a laboratory experiment, researchers often create highly artificial settings and rely on nonrandom, nondiverse samples of participants (or *convenience samples*), such as college student volunteers.

By contrast, experiments that rely on random samples, such as many survey experiments, have higher external validity. We gain confidence that the conclusions drawn in these settings would generalize to a larger population. However, this high degree of external validity often comes at the expense of internal validity. To conduct a survey experiment on a random sample of the U.S. population, researchers have to recruit participants who are located all over the United States. Thus, the researcher loses a great deal of control over the setting and, importantly, has a more difficult time effectively manipulating the independent variable while holding other factors constant. Consequently, internal validity is reduced.

Finally, the extent to which an experimental setting is artificial versus realistic affects whether the claims researchers make are more specific and tied to a particular place and time or are instead more abstract and general. Highly realistic settings,

TABLE 8.1 Strengths and Weaknesses of the Four Types of Experiments

Experimental Method	Strengths	Weaknesses	Validity
Laboratory experiments	Researcher has maximum control over the experimental setting and can ensure that the manipulation of the independent variable was salient to all participants. The artificial setting allows researchers to test more abstract theories and to disentangle complex social phenomenon.	Most laboratory experiments rely on non-random samples, so researchers are less confident that results are generalizable. Because the laboratory environment is highly artificial, lab experiments are less effective for exploring more applied, "real world" questions.	Higher internal validity Lower external validity
Field experiments	Because field experiments take place in a real-world setting, they are better at evaluating more applied questions and for assessing whether an outcome occurs. The real-world setting gives researchers greater confidence that the results are generalizable.	Researchers have less control over the experimental setting and frequently rely on nonrandom samples. Less suited for evaluating the processes that produce an outcome and less useful for testing abstract theories.	Lower internal validity Higher external validity
Survey experiments	Survey experiments often use random samples, so researchers can be more confident that results are generalizable.	The researcher has less control over the experimental setting and cannot ensure that the manipulation of the independent variable was salient to all participants or that participants were not influenced by environmental factors. Surveys rely on self-reports, which do not always correspond to actual behavior.	Lower internal validity Higher external validity
Natural experiments	Realistic setting allows researchers to draw strong conclusions about specific settings. Good for assessing whether an outcome occurs.	Often so realistic that the results are relevant only to the setting in which the study was conducted. The researcher has no control over the experimental setting and cannot randomly assign participants to the condition. Less suited for evaluating the processes that produce an outcome.	Lower internal validity Higher external validity

such as those used in Pager's field experiment on race, criminal record, and hiring and Goldin and Rouse's natural experiment on gender and orchestra hiring, allow us to draw strong conclusions about particular settings. For example, we can feel confident that gender biased the evaluations of women orchestra musicians in the United States and that blacks with a criminal record are especially disadvantaged when applying for low-wage jobs in the United States.

While these studies convincingly document bias and discrimination, they do not uncover the more abstract and general processes by which bias emerges. More artificial settings, such as those found in laboratory experiments, intentionally remove many of the features of "real life," thereby exposing social processes that are otherwise hard to see. As such, artificial settings are often better for evaluating abstract social psychological processes. For example, Willer (2009) was able to show that holding all else constant, self-serving motivations to believe in God increase the intensity of religious beliefs. This conclusion is less tied to specific time and place and is instead a statement of an abstract social psychological process by which self-serving motivations increase the intensity of our beliefs.

In sum, different types of experiments have distinctive strengths and weaknesses, making them well suited for different purposes. Is the goal to document a specific type of outcome, such as whether discrimination against some group occurs? Or is the goal instead to test an abstract theory or evaluate some social psychological process? In the next section, we describe in more detail how laboratory experiments are conducted. We focus on a laboratory experiment because it is the most pure type of experiment.

CONCEPT CHECKS

1   Compare a laboratory experiment to a field experiment in terms of internal validity and external validity.

2   Compare a laboratory experiment to a natural experiment in terms of their artificiality. Which is better for testing abstract theories? Which is better for assessing concrete outcomes? Explain.

3   What are the advantages and disadvantages of a survey experiment compared with a laboratory experiment?

DESIGNING A LABORATORY EXPERIMENT

Many decisions must be made at each stage of a laboratory experiment if the experiment is going to effectively assess whether a change in the independent variable causes a change in the dependent variable. In general, a laboratory experiment progresses in four stages:

1. First, the researcher creates a setting that is engaging and makes sense to the participant.

2. Second, the researcher manipulates the independent variable while holding other factors constant.

3. Third, the researcher devises a valid and reliable measure of the dependent variable.

4. Finally, the researcher assesses the quality of the experiment and works to ensure the participant's well-being.

We describe each of these stages in the sections that follow.

Creating the Setting

For an experiment to be successful, participants must be actively engaged in the experiment. They need to follow experimental procedures and pay attention to what is being asked of them. They should be comfortable and not distracted by factors unrelated to the experiment. Finally, they should not be suspicious about the study's hypothesis; suspicion can cause participants to behave in artificial ways and thus bias the study results.

Keeping participants engaged and focused requires giving them a sense of purpose. If participants don't understand why they are being asked to participate, they may become distracted or not take the experiment seriously. However, it is often unwise to tell participants the experiment's true purpose. Consider what might have happened if researchers had said to participants in the motherhood study, "We are going to have you evaluate job applicants to see if you discriminate against mothers." The amount of discrimination observed would almost certainly be less than if the researcher had not divulged the experiment's true purpose. In other instances, revealing the exact purpose of the experiment can make participants react in ways that are artificially consistent with the study hypotheses. This occurs because many participants come to the laboratory wanting to be helpful to the researcher. Either way, if participants change their behavior as a result of learning the true purpose of the experiment, the researcher will not be able to determine the true causal relationship (if any) between the independent and dependent variables.

To keep participants engaged without revealing the study's true purpose, researchers often create a **cover story**, which is a false reason for participation. For example, in the motherhood study, researchers told participants that a company specializing in high-tech communication devices was hiring someone to lead a new marketing division, and the company was interested in obtaining input from younger adults about the quality of its applicants. Researchers then asked participants to rate two applicants, one parent and one nonparent. Importantly, the researchers did not tell participants that they were interested in how parenthood affected the applicants' ratings. Notice that the cover story told participants what they would be doing—rating job applicants— and explained why college students were being asked for their input. It gave participants a sense of purpose without revealing the study hypothesis.

Likewise, in the sexual harassment study, the researchers could not simply tell their male participants, "We are going to threaten your masculinity and then observe whether you sexually harass women." Instead, they created a cover story, telling participants that they were going to engage in a visual memory task in which they would exchange images with a partner via computer. The partner, who always had a female name, was actually a computer program, and the researchers encouraged participants to chat with "her" electronically as they exchanged images. One file of images was labeled "porno," while other files contained neutral images. Using the chat line, the partner indicated that she found the pornographic images offensive and did not wish to receive them. Therefore, if a participant sends pornographic images to the partner after hearing that she finds the images offensive, he would be engaging in a mild form of sexual harassment.

This cover story was effective for several reasons. First, it is plausible that researchers would involve college students in a study of visual memory. Second, participants are likely to be engaged in the task because they are actively sending images and interacting over a chat line with a partner. Finally, it cleverly disguises the study's true purpose.

At this point, you may be concerned that researchers are deceiving participants. Is it ethical to lie to people about a study in which they have agreed to participate? As we discussed in Chapter 3, deception—if carried too far—can be harmful to research subjects and is a major ethical violation. We discuss this issue in more detail later in this chapter.

cover story A false reason for participation in an experiment.

Manipulating the Independent Variable

To be effective, the manipulation of the independent variable in a laboratory experiment needs to be strong enough that participants are aware of it, yet not so strong that participants guess the study's hypothesis. In the motherhood study, if participants had not noticed that one of the applicants was a mother, the researchers would not have been able to assess the effects of motherhood on the applicants' ratings. However, if the researchers had strongly emphasized that one of the applicants was a mother, this would likely have affected participants' behavior in unrealistic ways.

There are many ways to manipulate the independent variable. In the essay example, the author's gender was manipulated by altering the author's first name from a common woman's name to a common man's name. In the motherhood study, researchers manipulated parental status by making one applicant's résumé indicate that she was an officer in an elementary school PTA and making the nonparent's résumé indicate that she was an officer in a neighborhood association. In the sexual harassment study, the researchers manipulated their independent variable by having male participants take a survey designed to assess their masculinity. Regardless of how the men actually answered the survey, half randomly received feedback that their score was "absolutely normal," while the other half were shown a graph depicting their score in the "feminine range." To ensure that participants noticed the manipulation, the experimenters also described the feedback to participants verbally.

confederates Individuals who pretend to be study participants but who are instead trained to play a role in the experiment.

THE USE OF CONFEDERATES

Sometimes researchers rely on confederates to help manipulate the independent variable. **Confederates** are individuals who interact with participants in the experiment while pretending to be participants themselves. In reality, they are part of the research team, trained to enact certain roles or behaviors.

Psychologist Solomon Asch (1955, 1956) used confederates in his classic studies of conformity. Asch was interested in the ways that groups influence their members. In a series of experiments, Asch brought participants to the lab and told them that they were taking part in a visual acuity test. Researchers showed male participants, who were seated in a semicircle, a standard line. The researchers then asked them to look at another set of lines and select the line that was the same length as the standard line. As you can see in Figure 8.4, the correct answer was obvious: One line was clearly the same length as the standard line, while two other lines were clearly of different lengths. Going around the semicircle, each man stated his answer, in turn, out loud.

However, all of the men in the group were confederates except for one real participant. Asch designed the study so that the confederates announced their answers before the real study participant. In the first two trials of the experiment, the confederates gave the correct answer, as did the real

FIGURE 8.4 Asch Experiment

In Soloman Asch's experiment, participants were shown a line (left) and then asked to look at a set of lines (right) and pick out the one that is the same length as the line on the left. As you can see, the answer was obvious. But when confederates all gave the wrong answer, three out of four study participants conformed to group pressure and also gave an incorrect answer in at least one of the trials.

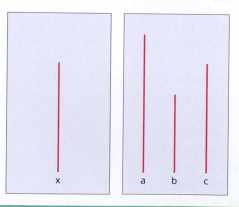

participant. But in the third and many subsequent trials, all of the confederates gave the same obviously wrong answer. What would the real participant do? Would he state the obviously correct answer or would he instead conform to group pressure and state the unanimous wrong answer? Seventy-five percent of the participants in this study went along with the group and gave the wrong answer on at least one of the trials.

The use of confederates was essential to this study because Asch was interested in conformity to group norms and thus needed to create a situation in which participants faced an overwhelming amount of disagreement, much more than Asch could have obtained with real study participants. In subsequent experiments, Asch altered the number of confederates who gave incorrect answers, thereby manipulating the amount of conformity pressure.

BETWEEN-SUBJECT VERSUS WITHIN-SUBJECT MANIPULATIONS

Researchers must decide whether to manipulate the independent variable on a *between-subject* basis or a *within-subject* basis. In a **between-subject design**, participants are randomly assigned to different levels of the independent variable. For example, in the sexual harassment study, the independent variable was masculinity threat. Some participants were assigned to one level of the independent variable, where their masculinity was threatened, while other participants were assigned to the other level of the independent variable, where their masculinity was affirmed. Likewise, in Willer's (2009) study about how motivations to believe in an afterlife affect intensity of religious belief, some participants wrote essays about death, while others wrote about a neutral topic.

In contrast, all of the participants in a **within-subject design** receive all levels of the independent variable. For example, in the study on motherhood and hiring, Correll and colleagues (2007) had participants evaluate two job applicants, one parent and one nonparent. Thus, all participants received both levels of the independent variable—parent and nonparent. Likewise, in Pager's (2003) experiment, one tester with a criminal record and one without both applied for the same job, so each employer received both levels of the criminal-status independent variable (criminal and noncriminal).

Researchers generally prefer within-subject designs because they require fewer participants and because they give the researcher more control over unrelated factors. In the motherhood study, if the researchers wanted to have 20 evaluations of mothers and 20 of non-mothers, only 20 participants total would be required, because each participant rates both a mother and a non-mother. If the study had instead used a between-subject design, one set of participants would be randomly assigned to evaluate a mother and another set would evaluate a non-mother. This design would therefore require 20 participants for each condition—mother and non-mother—or a total of 40 participants. Experiments that rely on fewer participants cost less money and require less time to complete. Additionally, if the study had used a between-subject design, participants would have been evaluating only a mother *or* a non-mother. When evaluating only one applicant, participants often make implicit comparisons to others whom they imagine would be applying for a job, which can bring a host of unrelated factors into their decision making. When participants are instead comparing two applicants, as in the within-subject design, they focus on the comparison between two

between-subject design
A study design in which participants are randomly assigned to different levels of the independent variable, such as viewing résumés for a male or a female job applicant.

within-subject design
A study design in which participants receive all levels of the independent variable, such as viewing résumés for both male and female job applicants.

FIGURE 8.5 Design of Motherhood Experiment

The motherhood penalty experiment used a mixture of within-subject and between-subject designs. Parental status was manipulated within subjects while gender of applicant was manipulated between subjects.

actual applicants, which brings fewer extra factors into their decision making.

Unfortunately, within-subject designs are not always possible. For example, in the sexual harassment experiment, participants could not be assigned to both levels of the independent variable—masculinity threatened and masculinity affirmed. It would make no sense to first tell a participant that his masculinity level was normal and then later tell him that he scored abnormally in the feminine range.

In some studies, researchers use a mixture of within-subject and between-subject designs (Figure 8.5). In the motherhood study, for example, participants in one condition evaluated two female applicants (a mother and a non-mother), while participants randomly assigned to a second condition evaluated two male applicants (a father and a non-father). Parental status was manipulated within subjects: All subjects evaluated both levels of the parental-status variable—a parent and a nonparent. Gender of applicant was manipulated between subjects: Half of the participants evaluated male applicants, and the other half evaluated female applicants. The researchers could have instead used a completely within-subject design, with each participant evaluating both levels of the parental-status and gender variables. With this design, they would evaluate four equivalently qualified applicants—a mother, a childless woman, a father, and a childless man. This design would have required fewer participants than the design used by the researchers.

In fact, the researchers considered using a fully within-subject design, but they were concerned that the design would make participants suspicious about the study hypothesis because it would require them to evaluate four highly qualified applicants who differed in very systematic ways (two were parents, two were not, two were women, and two were men). Because of this concern, the researchers decided to manipulate parental status within-subject and to manipulate gender between-subject. As this example shows, and as we have emphasized throughout this book, researchers often have to balance competing goals, sometimes sacrificing a bit of control and efficiency for a design that will be believable and make sense to the participants.

Measuring the Dependent Variable

The next step in creating an effective laboratory experiment is coming up with a valid and reliable measure, or operationalization, of the dependent variable. As you learned in Chapter 5, *valid* measures adequately measure the concept of interest. For example, a survey question that asks participants how happy they are would *not* be a valid measure of self-esteem. Happiness and self-esteem are related, but they are not the same concept. *Reliable* measures produce consistent values under the same circumstances when applied to the same object or person. For example, a yardstick produces a reliable measure of length because it produces the same length measurement each time it is used to measure the length of the same object.

Three main types of dependent measures are commonly used in experimental research: behavioral, attitudinal, and physiological measures. We discuss each in turn.

BEHAVIORAL MEASURES

Behavioral measures rely on observation of overt and observable actions by a study participant. For example, if a researcher wanted to measure how much participants like their partner in an experiment, she could develop a behavioral measure of "liking." The researcher might have a confederate ask the participant for help with a tedious task after the experiment is over. The logic behind this measure is that participants should be more likely to help a person with a tedious task if they like that person.

As an example, let's return to the research on stereotype threat. Behavioral measures are commonly used to measure whether stereotypes have a negative effect. After researchers manipulate the independent variable—the presence or absence of a negative stereotype—participants take an aptitude test. A participant's score on the test is a behavioral measure of how that individual responds to stereotypes. We have also seen several other examples of behavioral measures. In the sexual harassment study, Maass and colleagues (2003) measured sexual harassment by measuring how frequently participants sent pornographic images to their partners. In her field experiment, Pager (2003) measured whether employers called job applicants back.

In another experiment that involves an especially clever behavioral measure, researchers were interested in evaluating the hypothesis that those in powerful positions are less able than those in less powerful positions to take the perspective of others (Galinsky et al., 2006). The logic is that those in powerful positions are concerned primarily with their own well-being and are therefore less able to imagine the motivations or perspectives of others.

To evaluate this hypothesis, the researchers randomly assigned participants to either a high-power or low-power condition. Those in the high-power condition wrote an essay about a time when they had power over another individual, and those in the low-power condition wrote about a time when someone else had power over them. To measure the dependent variable—taking the perspective of others—they later had participants draw the letter *E* on their foreheads with a marker (Figure 8.6). Although it sounds simple, there are two ways to complete this task. Participants could draw the *E* as though they are reading it themselves, which leads to an *E* that is backwards from the perspective of others. Or they could draw the *E* as though another person were reading it. As predicted, those in the high-power condition were less likely to take the perspective of others. Behaviorally, this meant they were more likely to draw the letter *E* as if they were reading it themselves. In contrast, those in the low-power position were more likely to draw the *E* as if others were reading it.

ATTITUDINAL MEASURES

Attitudinal measures are self-reports in which participants respond to questions about their attitudes, opinions, emotions, and beliefs. For instance, the researcher might ask subjects, "How much did you like your partner today?" The subjects might respond using a series of set

FIGURE 8.6 Perspective-Taking Experiment

Researchers used a clever behavioral measure—asking participants to draw the letter *E* on their foreheads—to get at whether people in powerful positions are less able to take the perspective of others.

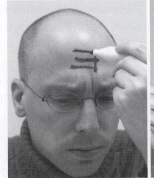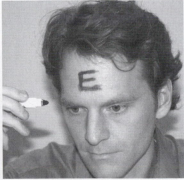

Source: Galinsky et al., 2006.

categories such as "a lot," "somewhat," "a little," and "not at all." Attitudinal measures are sometimes collected when behavioral measures are inconvenient or impossible to collect. For example, in the survey experiment discussed earlier in this chapter (Schuman & Bobo, 1988), researchers asked white participants how they would feel about a black or Japanese American neighbor moving in next door. Obviously, it would have been impractical for the researchers to behaviorally measure how whites actually react when a black or Japanese American person moves in next door. People do not move frequently enough to make such a study feasible.

When using attitudinal measures, researchers are often assuming that participants' responses are good proxies (stand-ins) for actual behavior. However, as you learned in Chapter 7, attitudinal measures are susceptible to **social desirability bias**, where participants answer questions in socially desirable ways rather than giving truthful responses. For example, a person might mind having a black neighbor more than she would admit on a survey. An employer might respond more positively to an attitudinal measure about his willingness to hire a person with a criminal record compared to what he would do if the actual situation presented itself, as found by Pager and Quillian (2005).

While the type of measure preferred is influenced by the concept being studied, experimental researchers generally prefer behavioral measures to attitudinal measures. This preference reflects the desire of social scientists to understand how people actually treat one another and respond to the social world rather than how people respond to self-report questions about their attitudes and behaviors.

However, researchers prefer attitudinal measures when they are interested in understanding *why* an outcome occurs, such as why a group is discriminated against or why someone's religious beliefs might be strengthened. In the motherhood penalty lab experiment, the researchers not only asked participants whom they would recommend for hire but also asked them to rate the applicants on a variety of dimensions, including how competent they seemed and how much they thought they would like the applicants. These attitudinal measures allowed the researchers to disentangle the mechanism that produced the discriminatory outcome: Mothers were less likely to be recommended for hire than equally qualified non-mothers *because* participants viewed mothers as less competent than non-mothers, not because they liked the mothers less.

PHYSIOLOGICAL MEASURES

Physiological measures are biological responses to stimuli. They include heart rate, blood pressure, brain activation patterns, vocal patterns, and hormone levels. Often, there is no single physiological response that is a precise measure of the dependent variable being studied. For example, it would be hard to find a single physiological measure to determine how much participants like their partners. However, some dependent variables, such as stress, can be measured quite effectively with physiological measures. Like attitudinal measures, physiological measures are good at uncovering processes that produce social outcomes. One advantage physiological measures have over attitudinal measures is that it is harder for people to control physiological responses, making physiological measures less susceptible to social desirability biases.

An interesting use of physiological measures comes from the stereotype threat literature. In addition to being used to study race, stereotype threat research has also

social desirability bias
A form of bias that occurs when study participants report positively valued behaviors and attitudes rather than giving truthful responses.

physiological measures
Biological responses to stimuli.

been used to study gender issues. Experimental studies have found that women who are exposed to negative gender stereotypes perform worse on tests of math and spatial abilities (Spencer, Steele, & Quinn, 1999). Recently, researchers have been using a technique called *functional magnetic resonance imaging* (*fMRI*) to produce images of the brain that show which regions are being used as individuals engage in various tasks, such as solving math or spatial problems. In one study, researchers randomly assigned women college students to one of three conditions: a negative-stereotype condition, a positive-stereotype condition, or a neutral control condition (Wraga et al., 2006). In the negative-stereotype condition, participants read on their computer screens that men perform better on image-rotation tasks because men have greater spatial reasoning. In the positive-stereotype condition, participants read that women perform better on image-rotation tasks because women are better at taking the perspective of others. In the control condition, participants received neutral information. The researchers then had participants summarize the information on their computer screens to ensure that the experimental manipulation had been successful.

The researchers measured the effect of the stereotype using behavioral, attitudinal, and physiological measures. The behavioral measure assessed participants' performance on an image-rotation task similar to that found in the video game *Tetris*. Using this measure, the scientists found that women exposed to the negative stereotype made significantly more errors on the task than those in the control condition, while those in the positive-stereotype condition made significantly fewer errors than those in the control group. Because the women had been randomly assigned to condition, we can be confident that these differences in performance were caused by exposure to different types of stereotypes.

This behavioral measure allows us to detect differences in an outcome. But *why* does this difference occur? *How* do stereotypes affect performance? To answer these questions, the researchers relied on a physiological measure, using fMRI to examine the women's brain activation patterns in the three conditions. The researchers found that women in the negative-stereotype condition had higher activation in the brain region associated with increased emotional load. This extra mental focus created an additional burden on women in this condition as they attempted to solve the mental-rotation problems. By contrast, women in the positive-stereotype condition had increased activation in visual processing and memory areas, which are well-established assets for performing this sort of task. The researchers concluded that stereotypes influence test performance by affecting the efficiency with which the brain processes information.

Finally, the researchers attempted to measure the effect of the stereotype using an attitudinal measure, asking the women if the stereotype had affected their test performance. More than 90% said no, even though the images of their brains clearly showed that the stereotype had affected them. In short, the physiological measure (the fMRI scans) helped to uncover social processes when the individual participants were unaware of the effects.

Unfortunately, it can be difficult and expensive to collect physiological measures in the laboratory. For example, most researchers do not have access to the expensive equipment required for fMRI. Hormones, by contrast, are relatively less expensive to

TABLE 8.2 The Three Main Types of Dependent Measures Used in Experiments

Type of Dependent Measure	Examples
Behavioral measures	An observable action by a participant, such as performance on an aptitude test or whether an employer calls back a job candidate.
Attitudinal measures	Self-reports of attitudes, emotions, and behaviors, such as answers to questions like, "How would you feel about a black or Japanese American neighbor moving in next door?"
Physiological measures	Biological responses to stimuli, including heart rate, blood pressure, brain activation patterns, and hormone levels.

collect. The hormone cortisol, for example, can be collected via saliva samples. Cortisol, which is often called the "stress hormone" because it responds to environmental threats, including fear, stressful situations, or threats to social status, is increasingly of interest to social scientists (Dickerson & Kemeny, 2004). However, collecting reliable measures of cortisol response requires considerable time in the laboratory, and measures are affected by time of day, birth-control pills, food consumption, and many other factors. Other physiological measures, such as heart rate, are easy and cheap to collect but are affected by a whole host of factors beyond those of interest to the experiment. Still, techniques for collecting physiological measures are improving, and they show great promise for the future.

Wrapping Up the Experiment

The final step in conducting a laboratory experiment occurs after the independent variable is manipulated and the dependent measure collected. The researcher needs to assess the overall quality of the experiment and ensure that participation in the study has not harmed the participant. To accomplish these tasks, researchers interview participants after the study and then inform them of the actual purpose of the experiment, a process known as **debriefing** (which we described in Chapter 3).

ASSESSING THE QUALITY OF THE EXPERIMENT

Even when an experiment is well designed, it is possible that participants did not understand the directions they were given or did not notice the experimental manipulation. Or they may have become suspicious about the study hypothesis, which could have caused them to behave in nonrealistic ways. By interviewing participants after the experiment is complete, researchers can determine if the experiment occurred as planned.

Generally, researchers begin by asking the participant if he or she has any questions or thoughts about the study, which gives participants the chance to voice any suspicions or concerns. Next, the researcher follows up with more specific questions, asking participants about the experimental manipulation. For example, in the motherhood study, researchers asked participants what they noticed about the applicants. If the participant did not mention that one of the applicants was a parent, the researcher followed up by asking if the participant noticed that either applicant had children.

debriefing The process of interviewing participants after the study and then informing them of the actual purpose of the experiment.

Finally, researchers should ask participants if they had difficulty completing any part of the study, which could alert the researchers to problems in the study design.

DEBRIEFING THE PARTICIPANT

When participants have been given a false rationale for the study, it is important to *debrief* them, or tell them the true purpose of the study, before they leave the laboratory. Debriefing should be done with great sensitivity, as participants may understandably be upset upon learning that they have been deceived. Experimenters should look for signs that a participant is upset and have a set of procedures for dealing with upset participants, including where to refer them for further help.

It often helps to tell participants that the goal was not to deceive them but to learn about an important social process. For example, with discrimination experiments, it is quite effective to explain the importance of understanding how and why discrimination occurs. The researchers should also explain why they deceived the participant in the first place. The researchers might mention that telling the participants the true purpose of the study would likely have caused them to behave unrealistically or in such a way as to aid the researchers in confirming their hypothesis. Participants generally understand and accept this explanation.

Some participants become upset by their own behavior, especially if they engaged in a discriminatory or selfish way. This response can occur even when a study does not involve deception. For example, some experiments involve placing people in various social dilemmas and measuring whether they share resources or hoard them. Participants who kept resources for themselves might later feel bad about this behavior.

In experiments where participants were given false feedback about themselves, such as the sexual harassment study, the researchers must be certain that participants understand that the feedback was not real. They may ask participants to repeat back to them a statement like "I understand that the score on the masculinity survey did not in any way reflect my true masculinity."

Finally, telling participants the study's true purpose can help them gain a valuable educational experience from their participation. As you may know from your own experience, some introductory psychology and sociology courses require students to participate as subjects in experimental studies on campus to gain first-hand knowledge of the research process. Researchers have found that participants are often interested in learning about how the study they just participated in was conducted. In fact, some participants ask if they can participate in other studies or take classes where studies like the one in which they just participated are discussed.

CONCEPT CHECKS

1   What is the purpose of a cover story in an experiment?

2   What is the difference between a between-subject and a within-subject manipulation of the independent variable? Give an example of each.

3   What is the difference between a behavioral measure and an attitudinal measure? Give an example of each.

THE EXPERIMENTAL METHOD: ETHICAL ISSUES AND LIMITATIONS

Every research method has its unique strengths and weaknesses. While experiments are associated with a high degree of internal validity, they often lack external validity, or the ability to produce findings that can generalize to a larger population or different setting. We describe some ways that researchers have attempted to increase external validity without sacrificing internal validity, but first we discuss some of the special ethical issues that often arise during experiments.

Ethical Issues Involving Experiments

Not all research questions can or should be studied with experimental methods. For example, it would be highly unethical to manipulate the income levels of children's families, placing some in poverty, just to observe how poverty affects children's school performance. This is a clear-cut case of a proposed research study that would be unethical.

As noted earlier in this chapter, many laboratory experiments involve deception, with researchers providing participants with a false rationale for the study. While deceiving participants allows researchers to more accurately evaluate their study hypothesis, it nonetheless raises ethical issues about lying to participants. How should researchers decide when it is ethically acceptable to deceive participants and when it is not?

To answer this question, researchers must consider whether the costs of participating in a study are outweighed by its benefits, or the gains in knowledge that the study produces. Because researchers have a deep interest in their own work, they are not always able to examine the cost-benefit question objectively. As you may recall from Chapter 3, an impartial oversight board, called an institutional review board (IRB), carefully considers the costs and benefits and decides whether a study should be approved. If costs to participants are low and the importance of the knowledge obtained is high, the IRB will likely approve the study.

In discrimination studies, the deception of subjects is relatively minor, and it allows us to better understand the circumstances that lead to discrimination—knowledge that is important to a society concerned with equality. The sexual harassment study involved a higher level of deception. Researchers gave participants not only a false rationale for the study but also false information about their masculinity levels. The researcher's IRB approved the study (including the deception) because understanding the causes of sexual harassment is important, and it is hard to imagine gaining the knowledge this study produced with any less deception or with any other research method. That is, the IRB decided that the benefits to society offset the cost to participants. However, the IRB required a more elaborate debriefing of participants to ensure that they left the study knowing that the masculinity feedback they received was bogus (Maas et al., 2003, p. 864). The IRB believed it would be too costly to participants if they were to leave the study believing that they were insufficiently masculine.

Some field experiments raise their own unique set of ethical issues. Sometimes participants are not aware that they are participating in a study and therefore have not given their consent. For example, in Pager's (2003) field experiment, her testers applied for actual jobs, which brought them into contact with real employers who were making real hiring decisions. These employers did not know they were part of a study. IRBs almost always insist that participants consent to being part of a study. So why did the IRB approve this field experiment, and why did it not insist that employers give their consent? First, the members of the IRB likely judged the importance of the knowledge to be obtained to be quite high. This study was very well designed to measure whether race and a past criminal conviction lead to discrimination—knowledge that is important if we wish to reintegrate former felons into society.

The expected benefit was high, but what about the cost? The cost came in the form of taking up some of the employers' time as they considered hiring the testers—people who obviously are not going to end up taking the job even if it is offered to them. Because the amount of time wasted by any employer was low, and the importance of the knowledge was quite high, the IRB approved the study. Of course, given the importance of protecting the anonymity of research participants, the IRB required Pager to keep confidential the names of all employers contacted as part of her study.

While experiments often raise unique ethical concerns, all studies involving human participants have some cost. Even a short survey takes up time that a participant could have used for some other purpose. No knowledge is free. It is important that researchers and oversight boards carefully consider whether the value of the knowledge obtained in a particular study offsets the costs to participants.

Limitations of the Experimental Method

As noted earlier in this chapter, the biggest limitation of experiments, especially laboratory experiments, is their lack of external validity. Experimental researchers often attempt to increase the external validity of their study by (1) replicating the experiment across different samples of participants, (2) replicating the study with a different kind of experiment, or (3) evaluating the hypothesis with a nonexperimental research method.

REPLICATING THE EXPERIMENT ACROSS DIFFERENT SAMPLES

One example of replication across different samples comes from the work of Joshua Correll and colleagues on police shooting bias (Correll et al., 2002). The question that motivated their study was: Does the race of a target affect a police officer's decision to shoot? In particular, are police quicker to shoot black targets? To answer these questions, participants played a video game where they saw images of a target person who was either black or white. During a series of trials, the black and white targets were holding an object that was sometimes a gun and sometimes a neutral object, such as a camera. The targets were presented against complex backgrounds so that participants had to look at the target, assess whether he was holding a gun or a harmless object, and then quickly decide to press either a "shoot" or "non-shoot" button.

The study found that participants were quicker to make the correct decision to shoot an armed target if the target was black than if he was white. But they were quicker to make the correct decision *not* to shoot an unarmed target if he was white. These results could be important for understanding how race affects police officers' decisions to shoot, a topic of great importance to policy makers in the wake of several high-visibility cases of police shootings of black men in recent years. However, the initial experiment was conducted on a nonrandom sample of college students, most of whom were white, thereby limiting the generalizability of the results.

Stills from the video game used in the police shooting bias experiment show black and white targets holding either a gun or a neutral object. Participants more quickly made the correct decision to shoot if the target was black.

To increase the external validity of their findings, the researchers replicated the study on a sample of older adults whom they recruited from bus stations, malls, and food courts. They also recruited a more racially diverse sample, with almost 50% of the participants being black. They found the same results with the more diverse sample. Because Correll and colleagues replicated their study using a more diverse sample, we can feel more confident that their original findings generalize beyond college students. Of course, it would be most relevant to recruit a sample of police officers to participate in the study, but it would likely be difficult to find a police department that would be willing to participate.

REPLICATING THE STUDY WITH A DIFFERENT KIND OF EXPERIMENT

In the motherhood study, the researchers attempted to increase the external validity of their results by following up the laboratory experiment with a field experiment (Correll, Benard, & Paik, 2007). The laboratory experiment found that undergraduate participants were almost twice as likely to recommend a non-mother for hire than they were to recommend an equally qualified mother. The experiment also uncovered the mechanism that produced this effect: Mothers were less likely to be hired because participants saw them as less competent. Would real employers also show a bias against mothers?

To answer this question, the researchers sent résumés similar to those from their laboratory experiment to employers who had advertised a job in a wide-circulation newspaper. The researchers sent two résumés in response to each advertisement—one from a parent and one from a nonparent. This field experiment found that employers were indeed biased against mothers: Non-mothers received more than twice as many callbacks from employers as equally qualified mothers received. Not only did both samples—college students and employers—show a bias against mothers, but the amount of bias was very similar across the two samples. However, the field experiment was not able to uncover the mechanism that produced the bias. As we have emphasized, field experiments are better at evaluating whether an outcome, such as discrimination, occurs. By contrast, laboratory experiments are better at uncovering mechanisms that lead to an outcome.

EVALUATING THE HYPOTHESIS WITH A NONEXPERIMENTAL RESEARCH METHOD

Another way to increase external validity is to use different types of research methods to study the same general research question, a practice called **triangulation**. For example, if we consider the results of the motherhood penalty experiment alongside other research on this topic, we feel even more confident in making the general claim that mothers are discriminated against in the paid labor market. Earlier in the chapter, we described a study that used survey data on a random sample of the U.S. population and found that mothers earned lower wages than non-mothers in the same kinds of jobs even though both sets of women had equal job experience and equal educational levels (Budig & England, 2001). Qualitative data from interviews with employers shows evidence that employers discriminate against mothers. If we consider all these studies together—data from laboratory experiments, field experiments, a survey of a random sample of the population, and qualitative interviews—we consistently find that mothers experience disadvantages in the workplace and that discrimination contributes to this disadvantage. When so many different types of research methods find similar results, our confidence in the generalizability of the conclusions increases.

> **triangulation** The use of multiple research methods to study the same general research question and determine if different types of evidence and approaches lead to consistent findings.

CONCEPT CHECKS

1 What two criteria do IRBs use to decide whether to approve a study that involves deceiving participants?

2 Laboratory experiments are often criticized for their lack of external validity. Describe two ways that experimental researchers seek to increase external validity.

CONCLUSION

Among the methods available to social researchers, experiments are the most effective for establishing causality. They are also well suited for identifying the mechanisms that produce discrimination, such as against mothers or blacks in the workforce, as well as for testing abstract theories about how the social world works, such as how we form beliefs about status in our everyday lives. As with all methods, experiments often involve trade-offs between internal and external validity. While laboratory experiments afford the highest degree of experimental control and thus high internal validity, the reliance on nonrandom samples reduces the study's external validity, or the ability to directly generalize from the results to real-world settings. Consequently, researchers will often attempt to replicate their findings with different samples and with different types of experiments or even a different type of method. Even so, experiments—with their unique ability to get to the heart of cause-and-effect relationships—are a powerful tool at social researchers' disposal. In the next chapter, we explore how experiments, among other research methods, can be used to assess the efficacy of social interventions.

End-of-Chapter Review

Summary

Experiments are the most effective method for establishing causality, meaning they are best able to evaluate whether a change in an independent variable causes a change in a dependent variable. Experimental methods are particularly well suited for identifying the mechanisms that produce discrimination as well as testing abstract theories.

Key Features of Experiments

- Manipulation of the independent variable is the key feature of an experiment. Researchers actively change the level of an independent variable and then measure any resulting effects in a dependent variable.

- Random assignment of participants to experimental and control conditions ensures that participants' individual differences are randomly distributed across groups so that the only difference between the two groups is the independent variable.

- Researchers have a high degree of experimental control, allowing them to state with confidence that changes in the independent variable—and not other factors—caused changes in the dependent variable.

Advantages of Experiments

- Experiments are the best method for evaluating causal relationships because they allow researchers to manipulate the independent variable while experimentally holding constant other factors that could affect the dependent variable.

- Experiments are also useful for uncovering the mechanisms that produce discrimination.

- Experiments allow researchers to test abstract theories in controlled environments.

Types of Experiments

- Laboratory experiments are the most pure form of experiment. The lab setting gives the researcher a high degree of control.

- Field experiments take place in natural settings, making them well suited for evaluating more applied questions. The researcher has less control, but the real-world setting allows researchers to be more confident about generalizing from the findings.

- Population-based survey experiments involve asking a representative sample of some population to respond to a given scenario.

- Natural experiments rely on processes that are already occurring, such as a recession, to assess the effects of an independent variable on a dependent variable.

Designing a Laboratory Experiment

- The first step is to create an engaging setting that makes sense to participants. Researchers often create a cover story, or a false reason for the study.

- The second step is to manipulate the independent variable while holding other factors constant. It's important that the manipulation be strong enough that participants are aware of it, but not so strong as to give away the study's hypothesis.

- The third step is to devise a valid and reliable measure of the dependent variable. There are three main types of dependent measures: behavioral, attitudinal, and physiological measures.

- The final step is to assess the quality of the experiment by interviewing the study participants to ensure they understood the directions and noticed the experimental manipulation. Participants given a cover story must be debriefed.

The Experimental Method: Ethical Issues and Limitations

- Deception may sometimes be used in experiments when revealing the study's true purpose could cause participants to behave in artificial ways.
- The biggest limitation of experimental methods is their lack of external validity. To increase an experiment's external validity, researchers can conduct the same experiment with a different population, replicate the study with a different type of experiment, or evaluate the hypothesis with a nonexperimental method.

Key Terms

attitudinal measures, 261

audit study, 248

behavioral measures, 261

between-subject design, 259

causality, 236

confederates, 258

control condition, 237

control group, 237

cover story, 257

debriefing, 264

dependent variable, 236

double-blind study, 247

experiment, 236

experimental condition, 237

experimental group, 237

experimenter effects, 248

external validity, 245

factorial design experiment, 248

field experiment, 247

independent variable, 236

internal validity, 245

laboratory experiment, 245

natural experiment, 252

physiological measures, 262

population-based survey experiment, 249

random assignment, 237

salience, 246

social desirability bias, 262

spuriousness, 239

triangulation, 269

within-subject design, 259

Exercise

Select one of the two research questions below and describe a laboratory experiment you could design to answer the question. In your answer:

- Describe your setting, including any cover story you might use.
- Identify your independent and dependent variables.
- Describe how you would manipulate your independent variable.
- Describe how you would measure your dependent variable, and explain whether the measure is an attitudinal, behavioral, or physiologic measure.

Research Question 1: Are groups less likely to take advice from experts who are women than from experts who are men?

Research Question 2: Does fear increase risk-taking behavior?

Evaluation research is designed to assess whether a social intervention such as Head Start, which provides early-childhood education to low-income families, is producing its desired effect.

09

EVALUATION RESEARCH

Researchers, government agencies, politicians, businesses, and the general public are often interested in whether social programs are effective in changing behaviors or attitudes. For example:

- Does reducing class size improve student learning?

- Do abstinence-only sex education programs reduce teen pregnancy?

- Does a workplace program that allows employees control over when and where they work increase employee satisfaction?

- Do urban housing assistance programs reduce homelessness?

- Do community programs designed to promote marriage improve relationship quality?

Consider the first question. We might expect that smaller class sizes would allow teachers to spend more time with each student, and, consequently, students would learn more. But is our hunch correct? And if it *is* correct, what costs are involved in making this change? To decrease the size of classes, school districts must hire more teachers, which is quite costly. Systematically evaluating whether smaller classes improve learning—and by how much—helps school districts and states make informed decisions about how to allocate funds and staff schools.

This research about class size is an example of *evaluation research*. In the first section of the chapter, we define evaluation research and discuss some of its challenges. Then, we describe the steps necessary to conduct high-quality evaluation research, providing two examples of large-scale evaluation research projects. Because one of the main goals of evaluation research is **translation**, or the process of implementing the components of an evaluation research project on a larger scale, we conclude the chapter with a discussion of how political factors, logistical issues, and ethical concerns affect the implementation of evaluation research and its translation into social programs.

WHAT IS EVALUATION RESEARCH?

Evaluation research is not a specific research method. Instead, evaluation research can use many of the research methods discussed in Part 3 of this book, including experiments, surveys, and interviews. What sets evaluation research apart is the *purpose* of the study. **Evaluation research** is designed to determine whether a social intervention, such as reducing class size or implementing a new workplace program, produces its intended effects. A **social intervention** is a policy implementation or change, such as introducing a new urban housing program, that is intended to modify the outcomes or behaviors of individuals or groups. While many evaluation researchers are university faculty, more than half of all evaluation researchers work in settings other than universities, including private businesses, nonprofit organizations, and agencies of federal, state, and local governments (Rossi, Lipsey, & Freeman, 2004, p. 28).

Evaluation research seeks to answer specific questions that are important to diverse **stakeholders**, who are the various parties with interests in the outcomes of the evaluation. As an example, consider a community proposal to reduce government spending by replacing some trained police officers with less expensive community officers. The stakeholders include trained police officers, who do not want to lose their jobs; community members, who are concerned with neighborhood safety; and homeowners, who do not want their property taxes to increase. Each of these stakeholder groups might be concerned with different aspects of the research. Those concerned with costs want the evaluation to measure cost savings; those concerned with safety want crime statistics compared.

Evaluation research faces several distinct challenges:

1. **Politically charged contexts**. Evaluation research and decisions about whether to implement proposed interventions often take place in politically charged social contexts. Suppose that our community policing research found that community officers save money and produced no decrease in community

safety. The police officers' union, which would likely lose some of its jobs if trained police officers were replaced with community officers, might challenge and object to the study's results. In the case of an abstinence-only sex education program, those who support more comprehensive forms of sex education are likely to be suspicious of findings that support abstinence-only programs, while those who support abstinence-only programs will likely challenge any results showing that such programs are ineffective.

2. **Logistical challenges**. Interventions often present considerable logistical challenges. For example, to determine whether smaller class sizes improve student learning, many new teachers need to be hired. Large numbers of students need to be assigned to small classes so that researchers can compare them to students in larger classes. To study an intervention aimed at helping the homeless, the researchers must locate large numbers of homeless people and involve them in the study. To assess whether community programs designed to promote the benefits of marriage help communities, large numbers of citizens from different communities need to participate in the intervention. These are not easy tasks.

3. **Ethical concerns**. Finally, evaluation research often raises serious ethical concerns. Evaluating whether an intervention, such as abstinence-only sex education, is effective requires some individuals to participate in the intervention. What if the intervention is not effective? What if it is not only ineffective but also harmful? These concerns are magnified if the participants are children or others who usually do not make the decision to participate in a study.

Despite these challenges, evaluation research is becoming increasingly common. Government agencies want to know which social interventions produce the best results so that tax dollars are spent on programs that work. When done well, evaluation research can help organizations evaluate the effectiveness of programs designed to improve the lives of the people they serve. While no evaluation is perfect, high-quality evaluation research provides the best information possible about the effectiveness of an intervention within a given set of real-world constraints (Berk & Rossi, 1999).

CONCEPT CHECKS

1 | What is a stakeholder? What groups might be stakeholders in an intervention to reduce class sizes in an elementary school?

2 | What are the three major challenges of evaluation research?

CONDUCTING EVALUATION RESEARCH

Evaluation research generally proceeds in three steps:

1. Formulating the evaluation question

2. Measuring the desired outcome

3. Implementing the intervention and assessing its effects

Let's consider each step in detail.

Formulating the Evaluation Question

The crucial first step in undertaking evaluation research is specifying the question that the evaluation is designed to answer. Good evaluation questions focus the research on areas of greatest concern. Therefore, researchers should develop their questions in consultation with key stakeholders to ensure agreement about the study's purposes and how the results will be assessed and used.

Good evaluation questions should be both *reasonable in scope* and *answerable* (Rossi et al., 2004).

1. **Reasonable scope**. Although the research may be motivated by a major social concern, such as the effectiveness of public education in the twenty-first century, researchers must narrow a broad inquiry into a very precise question that the study can answer. Because most interventions are designed to produce important but modest effects, grandiose questions are often unreasonable (that is, their scope is much too large). For example, it would be unreasonable to ask whether an urban housing program would completely eliminate homelessness.

2. **Answerability**. The research question must be stated with enough precision that researchers can collect data that measures the outcome of interest. A classic example of a question that lacks precision is whether a given program is "successful." How is success to be measured? Different stakeholders likely have very different interpretations of success. If the evaluation is to produce usable results, the researcher must make the effort to specify the evaluation question more precisely before designing the intervention.

One of the evaluation questions at the start of this chapter—"Do abstinence-only sex education classes reduce teen pregnancy?"—is both reasonable and answerable. It is reasonable to expect that a sex education program would affect sexually related outcomes such as pregnancy. And a change in the rate of teen pregnancy is measurable. By framing the question around teen pregnancy, the evaluation focuses on an issue that interests diverse stakeholders, such as parents, school districts, and teenagers.

Measuring the Desired Outcome

reliability A quality of a measure concerning how dependable it is.

validity A quality of a measure concerning how accurate it is.

Researchers must be able to effectively measure the outcome of interest. Researchers must also ensure that their outcome measures are reliable and valid. (For a review of **reliability** and **validity**, see Chapter 5.) *Valid* measures ensure that researchers are measuring what they intend to measure and not some other factor. In general, more precise measures produce higher validity. For example, if we tried to measure employee job satisfaction by asking employees "How happy are you?" our measure would lack validity because many factors besides job satisfaction influence a person's sense of happiness. It would be better to ask employees more precise questions about how satisfied they are with specific components of their job—for example, their coworkers, their supervisor, and their schedule.

Reliable measures produce consistent values under the same circumstances when applied to the same object or person. A bathroom scale reliably measures weight if a person whose weight has not changed receives the same weight reading each time she or he steps on the scale. Reliability is crucial if we are measuring whether an intervention produces a change in some outcome. For example, if we were interested in evaluating whether a particular diet produces weight loss, we might weigh program participants before they begin the diet and again after they've been on the diet for some amount of time. If the program is effective, one thing we would expect to see is participants' weight decrease over time. However, to confidently conclude that the diet is effective, we need to be certain that our scale is reliable. If it isn't, the lower weight readings might be the result of scale errors, not the diet.

Generally, self-reported measures are less reliable than performance measures (such as grades or test scores) or behavioral measures (such as observations of students' classroom behavior). If we are interested in measuring a person's generosity, it is better to observe whether he places money in a donation box rather than asking him, "How generous are you?" Self-reported measures are sensitive to participants' moods and to **social desirability bias**, which are study participants' desires to present themselves in a positive light. However, self-reported measures are sometimes useful when the research question is concerned with participants' specific attitudes and beliefs. For example, if we want to know if a new workplace program increases employee satisfaction, it makes sense to simply ask employees how satisfied they are with their workplace.

social desirability bias A type of bias that occurs when study participants report positively valued behaviors and attitudes rather than giving truthful responses.

Implementing the Intervention and Assessing Its Effects

The main goal of evaluation research is to assess whether a social intervention produces its intended effect. To achieve this goal, researchers must first decide which research method is best suited to implementing and evaluating the intervention. We start with an example of an evaluation that uses a method known as a *randomized experiment*. However, because randomized experiments are not always possible, researchers frequently rely on what are called *quasi-experimental methods*. We define and discuss randomized experiments, quasi-experimental methods, and qualitative methods in the next section.

In our class-size example, researchers conducted an experiment where some students were randomly assigned to smaller classes, and other students were randomly assigned to larger classes. In other words, researchers gave the small-class-size intervention to one group of individuals (the **treatment group**) and withheld the intervention from another group (the **control group**). Treatment groups are sometimes referred to as "experimental groups." When the treatment and control groups are equivalent except for the intervention, we can be confident that any difference in the outcome between the two groups is due to the intervention and not some other factor. For example, if a group of students who were placed in small classes (the treatment group) has higher test scores than a group of students who were not placed in small classes (the control group), and the two groups were otherwise equivalent, we would feel confident claiming that the small-class intervention caused the higher test scores.

treatment group The group that receives the intervention.

control group The group that is not exposed to the manipulation of the independent variable.

If, however, the two groups were different in ways other than the intervention, we would be less confident that a smaller class size caused the improvement in test scores. For example, if a late afternoon class was the treatment group and an early morning class was the control group, time of day and not class size might be responsible for the higher scores. That is, members of the treatment group might score higher simply because they took their tests later in the day when they were less tired and not because they were in small classes.

When assessing our results, we are concerned with both internal validity and external validity. As you learned in Chapter 5, **internal validity** is concerned with

internal validity The degree to which a study establishes a causal effect of the independent variable on the dependent variable.

causality. In evaluation research, internal validity means that the intervention (and not some other factor) caused a change in the outcome of interest. Suppose that researchers are studying whether a new urban housing assistance program reduced homelessness. While the study was being conducted, developers flooded the market with new affordable apartments, causing rents in the area to fall. With so many low-cost options, many homeless people can now afford housing and are no longer homeless. The increase in new housing compromised the study's internal validity because we cannot be certain that our housing assistance program caused the lower rate of homelessness. Instead, the increase in affordable apartments might have been the cause.

External validity is concerned with generalizability, whether findings from one evaluation study generalize to other instances where we might wish to apply the same intervention. For example, if a school district implements a program that successfully increases student learning among a group of third graders, the district might wish to implement the program again next year with the new class of third graders. Likewise, if a program designed to reduce homelessness was effective in one city, other cities might want to implement the same program.

Can we expect to achieve the successful results of an initial intervention when we implement the intervention in a new location or at a different time? Several factors may threaten external validity. First, the participants might differ from one setting to the next, and the intervention might affect the new groups differently. A program designed to increase learning among students in rural areas might be less effective in urban schools, for example. Second, the intervention might be applied or implemented differently in different settings. Third, the new settings might differ in ways that enhance or detract from the effect of the intervention. In the police example described earlier, one community might have well-established neighborhood groups, which helps the community successfully replace police officers with community officers. A different community that lacks well-developed neighborhood groups might find that implementing the community officer program does not produce the same results.

> **external validity** A dimension of validity concerning the degree to which the results of a study can generalize beyond the study.

CONCEPT CHECKS

1   What is the difference between a treatment group and a control group? Imagine that a researcher is evaluating whether a new diet program leads to weight loss. Describe the treatment group and the control group.

2   Why is it important that treatment groups and control groups be equivalent at the start of an evaluation?

3   What do we mean by "internal validity" in evaluation research? Why is internal validity important?

RESEARCH METHODS USED IN EVALUATION RESEARCH

Two key factors affect the choice of research method in evaluation research. First, as noted earlier, the control and treatment groups should be as equivalent as possible. Randomized field experiments are the preferred choice for achieving this equivalence.

When random assignment is not possible, evaluation research often relies on quasi-experimental methods.

A second factor that influences the choice of research method is the purpose or goal of the evaluation. Most evaluation research is concerned with finding out whether an intervention achieved its intended effect and how large the effect was. In these cases, researchers most frequently turn to quantitative methods such as randomized field experiments or quasi-experiments. Sometimes researchers are interested in *why* an intervention has an effect or *how* the intervention is experienced. "How" and "why" questions are better answered with qualitative research methods, including interviews and observation.

Randomized Field Experiments

There are several approaches for ensuring that treatment groups and control groups are equivalent, but the method that produces the most internally valid results is the **randomized field experiment**. Unlike controlled laboratory experiments, which take place in a laboratory, randomized field experiments take place in the field, or natural settings such as schools or workplaces. In randomized field experiments, participants are randomly assigned to either the **treatment condition** or the **control condition**. Random assignment does not mean haphazard assignment. Rather, researchers must design the random-assignment procedure to ensure that individual differences among participants do not affect whether they are placed in the treatment or control group.

As we discussed in Chapter 8, there are many techniques for randomly assigning participants to a condition. For example, the researcher could have participants draw a number from 1 to 99. Participants who draw odd numbers could be assigned to the treatment condition, and those who draw even numbers could be assigned to the control condition. With random assignment, differences among individuals, such as their gender, their family background, and their attitudes and motivations, are equally distributed across the treatment and control groups, thereby not affecting the outcome of interest.

On purely methodological grounds, randomized field experiments are considered the "gold standard" of evaluation research. They are preferred over other methods because they produce results that are not biased by differences between treatment and control groups. However, as we will see later in the chapter, randomized field experiments are costly and are often difficult to carry out. Further, they often raise ethical concerns about randomization. Is it ethical, for example, to randomly assign some students to regular-size classes if we have strong reasons to believe that students learn better in smaller classes? The decision to employ a randomized field experiment or some other method therefore involves trade-offs between what is best methodologically and what is feasible, affordable, and ethical. Later in the chapter, we discuss two examples of randomized field experiments—one that examines whether small class size increases student learning and a second that evaluates whether abstinence-only sex education affects adolescent sexual behavior and knowledge.

Quasi-Experimental Methods

When random assignment is not feasible or ethical or when random assignment would be too costly, researchers often turn to **quasi-experimental methods**. These methods still attempt to compare the effect of the treatment to a control, but they lack random

randomized field experiment An experiment that takes place in a natural setting and where participants are randomly assigned to the treatment or control condition.

treatment condition A condition in an experiment where the independent variable is manipulated.

control condition A condition where the independent variable is not manipulated.

quasi-experimental methods Experimental methods that lack random assignment of individuals to treatment and control groups.

biased When results either overstate or understate the true effect of an intervention.

assignment of individuals to treatment and control groups. As we have stressed, the advantage of random assignment is that we can assume the groups are equivalent. Without random assignment, the assumption of equivalence is questionable. If treatment and control groups are nonequivalent, we run the risk of producing biased results. When results are **biased**, they either overstate or understate the true effect of the intervention.

One especially problematic procedure for assigning individuals to treatment or control groups is simply to allow individuals to volunteer to be in the treatment condition. Returning to the class-size example, imagine if researchers had allowed parents to volunteer to have their children placed in smaller classes. Parents who were more involved in the school would be more likely to hear about the study and, consequently, more likely to volunteer their children for the smaller classes. Parents who were less involved would be less likely to hear about the study and, consequently, less likely to volunteer their children. As a result, the children of the less involved parents would be placed in the control condition—the larger class size. If children in the small classes ended up with higher test scores, would we feel confident claiming that their success was due solely to being in a small class? Or might the higher test scores have come about because those in the treatment group had more involved parents than those in the control group? That is, parental involvement, not smaller class size, might have produced the increase in test scores. In all likelihood, both factors—smaller classes and more involved parents—improved the test scores. If we were to claim that the small-class-size intervention was the sole cause of the higher test scores, we would be overestimating the effect of the intervention.

The type of bias that is introduced when control and treatment groups differ in some way that affects the outcome of interest is called **selection bias**. In our example, the treatment group and control group differed with respect to the involvement of their parents—a difference that likely affected test scores. Because differences in treatment and control groups can bias the results, researchers who rely on quasi-experimental methods use several approaches to ensure that the treatment and control groups are as equivalent as possible.

When treatment and control groups are formed by a procedure other than randomization, the procedures are said to use a **nonequivalent comparison design**. We now review several of these procedures, including matching, the use of statistical controls, and the use of reflexive controls, providing an example of each.

selection bias A form of bias that occurs when certain types of people are "selected" into particular situations based on their personal characteristics; in experiments, selection bias occurs when the control and treatment groups differ on some characteristic prior to the intervention that affects the outcome of interest.

nonequivalent comparison design A study design in which treatment and control groups are formed by a procedure other than randomization.

matching procedure A method of ensuring that treatment and control groups are as equivalent as possible. Researchers select pairs of participants who are identical on specific characteristics and split them up to form the treatment and control groups.

MATCHING

Researchers using quasi-experimental methods often attempt to ensure that treatment and control groups are equivalent by using a **matching procedure**. After selecting participants for the treatment group, the researchers assemble a control group by selecting individuals who are identical, or "matched," on specific characteristics. In our class-size example, a researcher might construct the control group by selecting students who have similar past academic performance and share the same gender, race/ethnicity, and socioeconomic status as the treatment group. The tricky part of matching is deciding which characteristics should be used for matching and which can be safely ignored. With our class-size example, it might be safe to ignore differences in students' height because it is unlikely that height affects test scores, but we would not want to ignore differences in students' prior school performance.

A recent evaluation of the Community Healthy Marriage Initiative provides a good example of matching (Bir et al., 2012). This initiative invited communities in the United States to apply for federal grants to fund programs to "support healthy marriages community wide" (Bir et al., 2012, p. ES-1). This funding was motivated by the belief that promoting healthy marriages leads to positive benefits for children, adults, and their communities. Three cities—Dallas, Texas; St. Louis, Missouri; and Milwaukee, Wisconsin—were selected to receive funding ranging from $5 million to $11 million per city. While each city was allowed to customize its intervention, all were required to follow the same model, which had both a community component and an interpersonal component. The community component included promotion of media messages that touted the advantages of marriage, and the interpersonal component involved classes on relationship skills and referrals to other services.

The evaluation team specified a number of outcomes that were of primary interest, including interest and participation in classes and services, relationship status, self-reported measures of the quality of individuals' relationships, self-reported measures of parenting skills, attitudes toward marriage, and whether individuals were aware of media messages about the advantages of marriage. If the intervention was successful, we would expect to see improvements on these measures after the implementation of the intervention. That is, people in these communities should have been more likely to attend a class on relationship skills, be more aware of pro-marriage media messages, and have more positive attitudes toward marriage after the intervention than before.

However, would we feel confident claiming that the intervention was responsible for any improvements on these measures? What if other changes, such as changes in the economy or increases in similar services by local churches, were instead responsible for the changes found? Without a control group, we cannot know whether any changes found in the cities that received grants were due to the grant funding or were instead due to other factors.

To be able to more confidently assess the effectiveness of the intervention, researchers used a matching procedure to create control groups. For each treatment city (Dallas, St. Louis, and Milwaukee), researchers identified a comparison community by matching them on several dimensions, including marriage rates, single-parent households, race, ethnicity, poverty rates, unemployment rates, and educational levels. They also attempted to match the intervention city with a comparison city in the same general geographic area. The comparison city for Dallas was Fort Worth, Texas; the comparison city for St. Louis was Kansas City, Missouri; and the comparison city for Milwaukee was Cleveland, Ohio.

To assess the impact of the federal grants, researchers first measured whether there were improvements on the outcome measures after the interventions in Dallas, St. Louis, and Milwaukee. They then asked whether the improvements in the intervention cities (the treatment group) were greater than those found in the comparison communities that had not received federal grants (the control group). Because the communities were well matched, if researchers found greater improvements in the intervention communities, they would feel confident claiming that the intervention produced its intended effects.

This was not what the researchers found. While the intervention communities were able to effectively roll out the intervention—for example, the cities funded media campaigns on the advantages of marriage and held classes on relationship skills—these communities experienced no greater gains than the comparison communities on the outcome measures, such as relationship quality or attitudes toward marriage.

STATISTICAL CONTROLS

With matching procedures, researchers match treatment and control groups on factors that they believe might otherwise affect the outcome of interest. However, because it is rarely possible to know with certainty what factors will affect evaluation outcomes, there is always some risk of selection bias even with the most carefully designed matching procedure. For this reason, researchers tend to also collect data on many other characteristics of those in the treatment and control groups. When their research is complete, they can use statistical techniques to assess the effects of these characteristics on the outcome of interest. (We discuss these methods in Chapter 15.)

In the Healthy Marriage Initiative evaluation, researchers collected data on various community characteristics, such as the average age of the population, the racial and ethnic composition, marital composition, employment status, and average income. Researchers then controlled for these effects statistically to ensure they were not biasing the results. When researchers control for the effects of additional variables to ensure the treatment and control groups are equivalent, they are using **statistical controls**. However, it is impossible to collect information on every possible characteristic of individuals, so the risk that the control and treatment groups differ in some important way always remains.

REFLEXIVE CONTROLS

Perhaps the simplest method for ensuring that treatment and control groups are equivalent is to have participants serve as their own controls. When researchers compare measures of an outcome variable on participants before and after an intervention, they are using **reflexive controls**. The simplest type of reflexive control is the pre-post design. With a **pre-post design**, researchers measure the outcome of interest once before the intervention, introduce the intervention, and then measure the outcome again.

For example, if a researcher wants to know if a new educational program improves students' math achievement levels, they could measure the math achievement levels of a group of students, implement the new program, and then measure the students' math achievement levels at some point after the intervention. If students' math scores increase after the intervention, we might conclude that the intervention produced the increase. However, this claim might seem dubious to you because we would expect students' math achievement levels to go up over the course of the school year even without the new program because of normal student learning. If we claim that the new program was solely responsible for the increase in math scores, we would likely be overestimating the effect of the program. As this example shows, simple pre-post studies will produce biased estimates if other factors that also change over the intervention period affect the intervention outcomes. For this reason, simple pre-post designs should only be used for short-term evaluation studies to assess outcomes that are unlikely to change on their own.

statistical controls A statistical technique that adjusts for the effects of additional variables that may differ between treatment and control groups.

reflexive controls A method for ensuring treatment and control groups are equivalent in which researchers compare measures of an outcome variable on participants before and after an intervention.

pre-post design A type of reflexive control design in which the researcher measures the outcome of interest once before the intervention, introduces the intervention, and then measures the outcome again.

A stronger reflexive control design is a **time-series design**, which takes multiple measures of the outcome of interest over time. Returning to our math achievement example, with a time-series design, researchers would collect data on students' math achievement levels at multiple points prior to and after the introduction of the intervention. If the intervention was rolled out at the start of the seventh grade, for example, researchers might examine students' math scores from the fifth and sixth grades, before the intervention, and then look at their math scores again in the seventh and eighth grades, after the intervention. Researchers might find that scores go up each year because of normal learning that occurs during the school year. If the intervention is successful in improving math achievement levels, however, scores would increase more during the seventh-grade year, when the intervention occurred, than during the fifth-grade and sixth-grade years.

Even more sophisticated are **multiple time-series designs**, which compare the effect of an intervention over multiple locations. The orchestra study described in Chapter 8 provides a good example (Goldin & Rouse, 2000). As you recall, the "Big Five" orchestras in the United States introduced a blind audition process where musicians who were being considered for hire auditioned behind a screen so that their gender was not visible to the judges. The screen intervention was designed to ensure that any gender biases on the part of the judges did not affect their hiring decisions. The evaluation question was straightforward: Did the introduction of the blind audition process lead the orchestras to hire more women?

The researchers conducting the study gathered yearly data on the female share of new hires for four of the Big Five orchestras from 1950 to the 1990s. As Figure 9.1 shows, the general trend is that the proportion of new hires that is female increases

time-series design A type of reflexive control design in which the researcher takes multiple measures of the outcome of interest over time.

multiple time-series design A type of reflexive control design in which the researcher compares the effect of an intervention over multiple times and locations.

FIGURE 9.1 Proportion of New Hires Who Are Female at Four Major Orchestras

Using a multiple time-series design, Goldin and Rouse were able to determine that the switch to blind auditions accounted for 30% of the increase in the percentage of female new hires from 1970 to 1996.

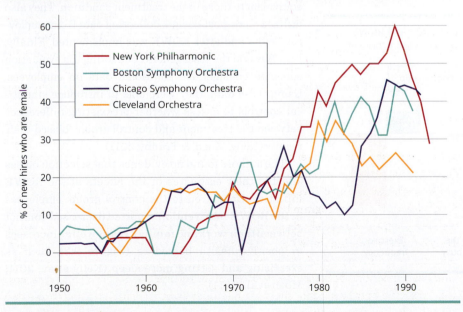

Source: Goldin and Rouse, 2000.

over time. But is this increase due to the introduction of the screen? During the same period, the most selective music schools were also admitting more female students. This means that the increase in female hires by the Big Five orchestras might instead have been caused by the increase in the number of female graduates from top music schools, and not by the introduction of the blind audition process.

It is important to note that screens were not introduced by all of the orchestras at the same time. Instead, the screens were introduced over the period from the early 1970s to the late 1980s. This allowed researchers to compare at different points in time the orchestras that had already adopted screens with those orchestras that had not yet introduced screens. If the screen causes orchestras to hire more women, we would expect the share of female hires to go up earlier for orchestras that introduced the screen earlier. In fact, this is what researchers found. Overall, they found that the switch to blind auditions explains 30% of the increase in the percentage of female new hires over the period from 1970 to 1996. This is an impressive increase for such a simple intervention.

ROWE: AN APPLICATION OF QUASI-EXPERIMENTAL DESIGN

The implementation and evaluation of an intervention called the Results-Only Work Environment (ROWE), instituted by the Best Buy Corporation at its corporate headquarters, is an example of a well-executed evaluation research study that relied on a quasi-experimental design (see "Conversations from the Front Lines"). The intervention was designed to give employees at the consumer electronics chain more control over their schedules in order to reduce work-family conflict. The intervention allowed employees in the treatment condition to work whenever and wherever they wanted, while those in the control condition continued to work a standard schedule in the office.

Teams of employees were selected for the treatment condition, and the researchers used a matching procedure to ensure that those in the control condition were equivalent to those in the treatment condition. They also utilized a pre-post design, collecting data from employees before and after ROWE was implemented. Finally, Best Buy and the researchers conducting the evaluation collected considerable additional data on employees. Using these data, they were able to introduce statistical controls to assess whether preexisting differences between the treatment and control groups biased their results (Kelly, Moen, & Tranby, 2011).

The authors found no evidence that selection biases affected their estimates of the effects of the ROWE initiative. Compared to the control group, employees in the ROWE intervention reported decreased conflict between their work and family lives as well as increases in positive health behaviors (Figure 9.2), such as exercising and getting more sleep (Kelly et al., 2011; Moen et al., 2011).

FIGURE 9.2 Changes in Health Care Behaviors Caused by ROWE Intervention

Researchers surveyed Best Buy employees before the ROWE intervention and again six months after ROWE was introduced.

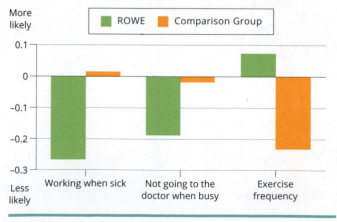

Source: Moen et al., 2011.

Qualitative and Quantitative Approaches

In the 1970s, qualitative evaluation methods emerged as alternatives to quantitative randomized field experiments. Today, qualitative and quantitative methods are more commonly viewed as complementary (McDavid & Hawthorn, 2006). By combining both types of methods, researchers can answer a broader set of questions than either approach could achieve on its own.

- *Qualitative* evaluation research uses many of the qualitative methods described elsewhere in this book, such as interviews, focus groups, and observation (see Chapters 10 and 11). With qualitative approaches, the goal is often to uncover *how* an intervention is being experienced by individuals so that researchers can understand *why* an intervention is working—or not working. Researchers can then use this knowledge to modify interventions and maximize their success.

- *Quantitative* approaches seek to determine *whether* an intervention achieved its intended effect, and if so, *how large* the effect was.

Qualitative methods can be used at multiple stages of the evaluation process. Researchers often conduct interviews or focus groups with key stakeholders before beginning an evaluation. The goals are to help focus the intervention and come up with a workable evaluation question. When researchers collect qualitative data to help them design effective questions for their survey instrument, this is called **formative research**. During the course of the project, researchers can use participant observation to better understand how the intervention is being delivered and how participants are experiencing it.

McDavid and Hawthorn (2006) describe a large body of evaluation research that has attempted to assess the effectiveness of nurse home-visitation programs; that is, programs where nurses visit first-time mothers with the goal of improving health outcomes for newborns and their mothers. Some of this research used randomized field experiments to determine whether nurse visits had their intended effects. While nurse visits were generally found to have positive effects on mothers and infants, some of the experiments found no effects.

Why would the nurse-visit intervention be successful in some settings and not others? Qualitative evaluation methods can help answer this question. In the case of nurse home visits, we need an in-depth study that looks at what actually happens during the home visits. In one such study (described by McDavid & Hawthorn, 2006), researchers conducted an 8-month observational study of 53 home visits by one nurse (see Byrd, 1999). A researcher accompanied this nurse on each of her visits and collected detailed data on her interactions with mothers. What the researcher found was that the nurse validated some mothers' caregiving abilities but raised doubts about the caregiving abilities of other mothers. Often, the nurse expressed doubts or confidence in a mother *before* her visit when examining the screening forms provided by the health department.

For example, learning that a mother was very young or uneducated caused the nurse to become concerned, and this concern affected how she interacted with the mother. When mothers sensed that the nurse lacked confidence in their caregiving

formative research A type of research where researchers collect qualitative data to help them design effective questions for their survey instrument.

Conversations from the Front Lines

ERIN KELLY

Erin Kelly is a professor of work and organization studies at the Massachusetts Institute of Technology's Sloan School of Management. As an organizational sociologist, Kelly studies the impact of work-family and antidiscrimination policies in American workplaces. She's also a member of the Work, Family & Health Network, an interdisciplinary team of researchers brought together by the National Institutes of Health and the Centers for Disease Control and Prevention to study workplace policies in an effort to improve the health of workers and their families.

You were part of a research team that was invited by Best Buy to evaluate an intervention called ROWE, or Results-Only Work Environment. How did you come to work with Best Buy?

Our research partnership with Best Buy was the result of both scholarly preparation and good luck. Phyllis Moen [a sociology professor at the University of Minnesota] and I had recently applied for a grant to be part of the Work, Family & Health Network, which was tasked with investigating how work organizations might address work-life conflicts in order to improve the health and well-being of workers, families, and our society more generally. We had argued in our application that scholars should focus on employees' control over when and where they do their work but also pointed out that most companies set up flexible work arrangements (if they allowed them at all) in a way that did not help employees feel more control over how their work came together with the rest of their lives.

Phyllis and I sometimes attended an informal "think tank" of local Minneapolis-area managers who met over lunch to discuss work-life issues and share new policies or programs that their organizations were implementing. At one of those sessions, the pioneers of ROWE, Cali Ressler and Jody Thompson, explained how they were beginning to try to change Best Buy's culture at the corporate headquarters. They said their new approach allowed employees to do "whatever they want, whenever they want, as long as the work gets done." Phyllis and I looked at each other across the room, excited because this sounded like an approach that could shift schedule control to employees, which was the strategy we had just proposed pursuing in our grant application. We then met with Jody, Cali, and other managers at Best Buy to discuss how we might study ROWE. The firm was interested in an outside evaluation of this new initiative, and we saw this as an opportunity to study a real innovation in how workplaces approach flexibility, work effectiveness, and work-life concerns.

Your team was responsible for evaluating the effectiveness of ROWE. What were your main findings?

We compared employees in departments that started ROWE with employees in departments that continued working under existing company policies; for each group, we collected two waves of survey data so we could compare the changes experienced by those moving into ROWE with changes experienced by their peers. Those comparisons show that ROWE reduced work-life conflicts and improved employees' sense that their work fit with the rest of their lives and that they had enough time for family connections. We found that employees' sense of control was an important mediator, meaning the changes in work-life conflict and fit occurred in part due to the changes in perceived schedule control.

We also found that ROWE employees saw improved sleep quality, energy levels, and self-reported health, while reporting less "burnout" and psychological distress. Employees in ROWE began to manage their health differently: They are less likely to feel obligated to work when sick and more likely to go to a doctor when necessary, even when busy with work. Finally, we found benefits for the company. Employees in ROWE were less likely to leave the firm than their counterparts (6.1% vs. 11.1% leaving in the study period).

Why was it important to use both qualitative and quantitative methods in your evaluation of ROWE?

The qualitative component was crucial for learning more about the concerns of the people we were studying, so we could capture as much of their perspective in the survey as possible, but also important for investigating how ROWE worked (or didn't work) in specific contexts. We try to start our projects with qualitative research, and, in this case, two graduate students (Samantha Ammons and Kelly Chermack) were "adopted" by teams at Best Buy so we could understand the workers' experiences before and during ROWE. Those early observations revealed that employees felt pressured to come into work when they were sick (Kelly et al., 2010, p. 290), and so we added a survey question to see if that changed with ROWE.

> **Evaluation research usually has the goal of deciding whether something 'works,' but it is important to understand what the current situation is—from the perspective of people living it—before studying whether the policy or program is creating a change.**

We also observed many ROWE training sessions. That helped us identify sources of resistance to ROWE, such as one senior manager's belief that employees needed to work in the office because "the world is run by those who show up" (qtd. in Kelly et al., 2010, p. 297). The qualitative data allowed us to compare how teams implemented ROWE, which was important for understanding how employees and managers responded to the freedom that ROWE offers. We saw that teams made more significant changes when they collectively discussed what they would like to change and when team managers had deeper knowledge of the employees' everyday work tasks. That task-specific knowledge made managers more comfortable stepping back and "trusting" employees to work when, where, and how they chose (Chermack et al., 2015).

The decision about what method to use during evaluation research often involves trade-offs between what is best methodologically and what is feasible, affordable, and ethical. Can you speak to a time when you had to make this trade-off?

In this study, we were not able to randomly assign teams to go through ROWE or continue working under the existing company policies. Thompson and Ressler, who were leading the ROWE program at Best Buy at the time, believed that these changes would be more effective if departments chose to move into ROWE (a "pull" strategy) rather than being told they needed to do so (a "push" strategy). While that is sensible for implementing organizational change, it raised the question of whether the ROWE groups were different than other groups—even before they began ROWE. We worked with the Best Buy team to identify departments that were as similar as possible to the groups moving into ROWE so we could use those as our control groups. That meant identifying control group departments with similar workforces, similar work tasks, and managers who seemed to be similarly supportive of work-life concerns as those that were about to start ROWE. We also gathered detailed information on these control groups so we could identify any differences at the outset and adjust for them in our analyses.

Do you have any advice to give to a student who is conducting his or her first evaluation research project?

I would recommend they start by spending time with the people who will be affected by the new policy or program. Evaluation research usually has the goal of deciding whether something "works," but it is important to understand what the current situation is—from the perspective of people living it—before studying whether the policy or program is creating a change. This strategy also helps the researcher think about what would constitute a meaningful change for different stakeholders and what would count as success for each group. That is especially important for sociologists doing research in workplaces or schools, where there is a clear hierarchy and a real possibility that evaluation research will reflect what those at the top see as important or valuable rather than capture the perspective of all of the people in that setting.

Using qualitative evaluation methods (an in-depth observational approach), researchers were able to evaluate why nurse intervention programs were successful in some settings and not others.

abilities, they became more reluctant to share information with the nurse. As a result, the interactions between mother and nurse were less productive and led to fewer positive outcomes. When the nurse instead validated a mother's caregiving abilities, both mother and child experienced positive outcomes: The mother became more confident in her caregiving abilities, the newborn received better nutrition, and abnormal health conditions were prevented.

The researcher had intended to collect data from several nurses, but due to the time-consuming nature of the study (it takes a great deal of time to carefully observe 53 visits that are occurring over a large geographic area), the study was limited to observing one nurse. As we have emphasized throughout this book, research often involves trade-offs. In this case, the researcher sacrificed the breadth of data that would have been possible with fewer observations of many nurses for the in-depth data that could be collected from one nurse. This data can be used to inform future interventions by suggesting how to better structure nurse visits.

CONCEPT CHECKS

1   How is a randomized field experiment different from a quasi-experiment?

2   What is selection bias?

3   What are the main advantages of qualitative methods in evaluation research?

TRANSLATING EVALUATION RESEARCH INTO LARGE SOCIAL PROGRAMS

Evaluation research typically assesses the effectiveness of an intervention in a small, highly controlled environment with the goal of implementing the intervention more broadly if it is found to be effective. For example, if an urban program designed to reduce homelessness in one neighborhood is found to reduce homelessness, city officials might wish to expand the program into a larger citywide program. Other cities may also want to adopt the program. If the program is not found to be successful, it is doubtful that the program would be expanded.

When an intervention is successful, policy makers still have to decide whether the intervention is worth the cost of implementing it more broadly. Cost becomes even more of a concern when the intervention produces only a small effect. Small effects are not necessarily bad. If the intervention is addressing an important social problem, such as reducing teen pregnancy, even small effects might be very important. To assess whether the value of an intervention is large enough to justify broad implementation, researchers may conduct a **cost-benefit analysis** where they compare the estimated value of the intervention to the cost of the intervention. Note that the monetary value of an intervention often has to be *estimated*. For example, what is the dollar value associated with a small increase in student learning or the prevention of a teen pregnancy? Even though such estimates are often tricky, they are important for making decisions about whether to continue allocating funds to the program.

Even when an intervention is clearly successful, translating the results from a small, controlled setting to a larger environment can be challenging. In more complex environments, many factors can affect whether the intervention will be successful. Another challenge is attempting to apply the findings from an evaluation study to environments that are substantially different from the environment where the initial study was conducted. If smaller class sizes were found to increase student learning in Tennessee, would we expect the same effect in California? If a Results-Only Work Environment intervention is successful at Best Buy, a U.S.-based, multinational consumer electronics retailer, would this intervention work at other companies? Researchers cannot know the answer to these questions with certainty, but they can assess the similarities between the new environment and the one that was evaluated. The more similar the environments, the greater the likelihood that the intervention will work in the new environment.

Another issue in applying an intervention more broadly is whether it will be implemented in the same way that it was in the original study. If the intervention is implemented under very different conditions, we cannot be certain that it will produce its intended effect. As we will see shortly, when California attempted to reduce class size in its schools, it implemented the intervention in a different way than the intervention was implemented in Tennessee (the site of the original study). These differences undermined the intervention's effectiveness.

The more important or pressing the social problem, the more political the terrain in which decisions are made. For example, evaluation research clearly showed that smaller classes increased students' test scores in Tennessee, and that this improvement endured as students progressed through higher grades. Yet, even with compelling results from a well-designed randomized field experiment, smaller class sizes were not uniformly adopted across the United States. Why? Policy makers in different states had to consider how much student learning had increased because of smaller classes and whether these gains were worth the substantial costs of hiring more teachers. Different stakeholders likely have different perspectives on the cost-benefit analysis. For example, while parents and teachers might favor reducing class sizes, people who are childless might be reluctant to have their tax dollars pay for the small learning gains enjoyed by other people's children.

The abstinence-only sex education evaluation research, mentioned earlier in this chapter, found very little evidence that abstinence-only education changed youths' sexual behavior or knowledge. However, abstinence education programs were not canceled, and the U.S. government continued to support these programs financially. In the

cost-benefit analysis
The process of comparing the estimated value of the intervention to the cost of the intervention.

next section, we provide a more detailed discussion of these two studies to illustrate the steps in evaluation research and its unique challenges.

CONCEPT CHECKS

1 What factors affect whether a social intervention is implemented more broadly?

2 What is a cost-benefit analysis, and why is it challenging to conduct?

TWO EXAMPLES OF EVALUATION RESEARCH

In this section, we discuss in depth two well-known examples of evaluation research. Both relied on randomized experimental designs. The first evaluated whether smaller classes increase student learning, and the second evaluated whether abstinence-only sex education affects the sexual behavior of youth.

Tennessee Class-Size Experiment

In 1985, the Tennessee state legislature authorized and funded a randomized experimental study to examine the effects of class size on student learning in early primary grades (kindergarten through third grade). The legislature allocated $3 million to fund the first year of what was to be a 4-year study. As one representative explained, it was important for the state to conduct a well-designed study of class size before investing in a costly new program (Word et al., 1990). The Tennessee study was named Project STAR (Student/Teacher Achievement Ratio).

The STAR study is considered one of the most important educational investigations ever undertaken (Mosteller, 1995). Approximately 11,600 students and 1,300 teachers in 79 schools and 42 school districts in Tennessee took part in the study. For each participating school, students in grades K–3 were randomly assigned to one of three classroom types: (1) regular-size classes of 22 to 26 students, (2) regular-size classes that also included a teacher's aide, or (3) small classes of 13–17 students. The regular-size classroom was the control group, and there were two interventions—the small classroom and the regular-size classroom with a teacher's aide. Teachers were also randomly assigned to teach in one of the three types of classrooms.

Researchers from several Tennessee universities partnered with the Tennessee Department of Education to design the study and to conduct the evaluation. The central evaluation question was whether smaller classes increase student learning. By including an intervention in which a teacher's aide was added to a regular-size classroom, the study could also determine whether a teacher's aide would increase student learning without a decrease in class size. Teacher's aides are less expensive than teachers, so if they produce equivalent gains, adding aides to regular-size classrooms would be a less costly intervention than decreasing class size.

Project STAR was a randomized experimental study of the effects of class size on learning.

The key measures of "student learning" were gains in students' reading and math scores on two different types of standardized tests. These performance measures are well validated in educational research. If smaller classes improve student learning, we would expect to see greater test-score gains for students in the smaller classes than for students in the regular-size classes. Because students were randomly assigned to one of the three types of classrooms, preexisting differences among students in terms of their ability, work habits, and other factors were equally distributed across the different types of classrooms. And because teachers were also randomly assigned to one of the three types of classrooms, differences in teachers' teaching ability were also equally distributed across classroom type.

With random assignment of both teachers and students, we can be confident that any gains in student learning were due to smaller class size. As one set of researchers writing about the STAR study commented, "The basic premise of experimentation—choosing groups of subjects through randomization or preselection such that the only difference between them is the variable of interest—remains the ideal method of building social science knowledge" (Grissmer et al., 2000). The "variable of interest" in the STAR study is class size, and by using a randomized field experiment, the study attempted to make class size the only difference between the groups of students being studied. The project's leaders also ensured that students from various types of schools—inner city, suburban, rural—were included so that the results would have greater external validity.

In addition to test scores, researchers also tracked student progress on other measures, such as the grades students earned in their classes and whether students were ever retained in a grade (that is, "held back"). They also collected data on teaching practices.

What did we learn from this large-scale experiment? First, small classes led to significantly and substantially greater improvements in reading and mathematics test scores than regular classes did. For example, first-grade students assigned to small classes scored in the 64th percentile on the reading test, on average, while students in regular-size first-grade classes scored only in the 53rd percentile, a difference of 11 percentage points. The regular classes with teacher's aides showed some improvements over regular classes without aides, but the improvements were smaller and less consistent than the gains in the small classes. In other words, placing an aide in the classroom does not have the same effect on learning as reducing overall class size. Second, the positive effects of smaller class sizes were greater for minority students and students attending inner-city schools than for white students and those attending suburban schools. As Figure 9.3 shows, while all students benefited from smaller classes, the gains were larger for minority students in both the first and second grades. This finding is important because educational researchers and school districts want to reduce gaps in educational achievement among various social groups.

FIGURE 9.3 Benefits of Small Classes on Achievement in Reading for White and Minority Students

The small-class-size intervention led to significant improvements in reading scores, particularly for minority students in first and second grades.

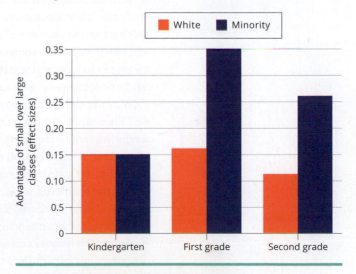

Source: American Educational Research Association, 2003.

The gains in learning also persisted over time. All students were placed in regular-size classes by the fourth grade, but students who had been in small classes in K–3 continued to outperform their counterparts who had been in regular-size classes in the early primary years. The most recent follow-up study found that students who had been in small classes in K–3 were more likely to pursue college than those who had been in regular-size classes. This positive effect was especially notable for black students. Small classes also led to higher high school graduation rates.

TRANSLATING THE RESULTS OF THE STAR STUDY

If evaluation research finds that an intervention is effective, policy makers are often interested in how the results of the study might be applied more broadly or in new settings. Because of the widely publicized success of the STAR program, in 1996 California decided to immediately reduce class sizes in all of its K–3 classrooms. The California Department of Education hired a consortium of research institutes, including the RAND Corporation and the American Institutes for Research, to evaluate the effects of class-size reduction (CSR) on achievement and other factors.

California's experience illustrates the difficulties of implementing an intervention that has been successful elsewhere. In a report written in 2002, researchers concluded that the effect of CSR on student achievement in California schools was inconclusive. Test scores had increased since the implementation of CSR, but the gains were small, and it was not clear that the reduction in class size caused the increases. For example, in reduced-size classes, 34% of third-grade students scored above the national median in reading, compared with 32% of third graders in regular-size classes—a difference of only 2 percentage points. By 2001, almost all schools had implemented CSR, which meant that there were no longer any regular-size classes to serve as control groups. With no control groups, it was no longer possible to compare test scores between students in regular-size classes and students in reduced-size classes.

The California study did find that teachers in reduced-size classes were more likely than those in larger classes to say that they (1) know what each student knows, (2) provide individual attention to students, and (3) are able to meet the needs of all students. They also reported fewer behavioral problems in their classrooms than teachers in regular-size classes. The program was also very popular with parents and teachers. While these self-reported measures were encouraging, self-reported measures are generally less reliable than other measures. The results of the main outcome of interest—gains in academic achievement—were inconclusive.

Why did California not experience the same gains in test scores that Tennessee did? There are many possible explanations. First, reducing class sizes for all K–3 classrooms in a large state such as California required an enormous increase in the number of teachers. Almost 30,000 new teachers had to be hired. Many of them lacked proper credentials or training, leading the evaluation researchers to conclude that "CSR was associated with declines in teacher qualifications and more inequitable distribution of credentialed teachers" (Bohrnstedt & Stecher, 2002, p. 6). The new, less-qualified teachers were more likely to teach in schools with larger numbers of poor and minority students. The heavier concentration of less-qualified teachers in poorer schools was, of course, not part of the study design. Instead, teaching jobs in poorer schools are likely less desirable, meaning that more-qualified teachers probably avoid these positions. Second, while the Tennessee study had established that small class sizes of

15–16 students improved learning over classes that had 22–24 students, many of California's "small" classes had closer to 20 students. By Tennessee's standards, California's reduced class sizes were actually "moderate" rather than "small."

California's experience drives home a few key lessons when translating evaluation research. First, adequate resources must be in place before launching a large-scale social intervention. While California had the financial resources at the time to implement CSR, the human resources—a large number of well-qualified teachers—were not available. In hindsight, it would have been better to implement the program incrementally, perhaps starting with students or school districts most in need. Second, it is important to rely on the specific scientific knowledge that has been established in prior evaluation research. The STAR study provided compelling evidence that K–3 classes with 13–17 students show greater achievement than regular-sized classes of 22–24 students. The STAR results did not show that *any* reduction in class size leads to improved learning. Recognizing that the California class sizes may not have been small enough to produce the desired results, the CSR research consortium recommended in its 2002 report that on the basis of the evidence of the STAR study, California should conduct carefully controlled experiments to "assess what difference moving to a class size of 15 or fewer would make, beginning with those schools that serve the largest number of low-income and minority students" (Bohrnstedt & Stecher, 2002, p. 10).

Title V, Section 510 Abstinence Education Program

In 1996, the U.S. Congress allocated $50 million per year to fund education programs that would teach abstinence from sexuality outside of marriage. These programs were implemented across the United States in public high schools, middle schools, and the higher grades of elementary schools. While the programs varied from region to region, they all included an intervention where youth were taught about the risks associated with sexual activity and the values of abstaining from sexual activity prior to marriage. The goal of the intervention was to decrease sexual activity and increase sexual knowledge. One year later, Congress authorized a scientific evaluation of what were called "Title V, Section 510 Abstinence Education Programs." The U.S. Department of Health and Human Services hired Mathematica Policy Research to evaluate four of these abstinence education interventions (Trenholm et al., 2007).

The evaluation used an experimental design where eligible youth in participating communities were randomly assigned to either the treatment group that received the abstinence intervention or to the control group that did not receive the intervention. Four different programs were evaluated. Two were in urban communities (Milwaukee, Wisconsin, and Miami, Florida), and two were in rural areas (Powhatan, Virginia, and Clarksdale, Mississippi). In three of the communities, the youth were primarily African American or Hispanic and from poor single-parent families. In Powhatan, the youth were mostly non-Hispanic whites from working-class

Researchers used an experimental design to evaluate the effectiveness of abstinence-only sex education programs.

and middle-class two-parent families. The youth were all either in middle school or upper elementary grades, and the interventions occurred in school settings. In all cases, the interventions consisted of teaching youth about abstinence using the definition laid out by the federal government. Students were taught that sexual activity outside of marriage is likely to have harmful psychological and physical effects. They were also taught how to reject sexual advances and cautioned that drug use increases their vulnerability to sexual advances.

To evaluate whether these programs were successful, the researchers first had to formulate an evaluation question. The question they posed was whether sexual abstinence education reduced sexual behavior and increased sexual knowledge. Next, the researchers had to decide how to measure "sexual behavior" and "sexual knowledge." To measure sexual behavior, they surveyed youth about whether they'd had sexual intercourse, whether their sexual activity was "unprotected," the number of sexual partners they'd had, their expectations about abstaining from sex in the future, and their reported rates of pregnancy, births, and sexually transmitted diseases (STDs). Notice that these measures of sexual behavior are all self-reported.

While researchers generally prefer observational measures, in this case observational measures would have been virtually impossible to collect because researchers cannot follow youth around and observe their sexual behavior. Nonetheless, we might worry about whether youth would lie about their sexual activity when asked about it. To the extent that youth in the treatment condition felt more pressure to report not having sex (even if they were) than those in the control condition, differences in rates of sexual behavior between the groups could be due to differences in what students *reported* about their sexual activity rather than true differences in sexual behavior. To measure their sexual knowledge, youth were quizzed about their knowledge of STDs and risks of pregnancy, as well as their perceptions about the effectiveness of various birth-control methods.

By comparing youth who were randomly assigned to receive the abstinence education program with those youth who did not receive the intervention, researchers could evaluate whether the program produced its intended effects. If the program was successful, we would expect youth in the treatment condition to be more likely to abstain from premarital sex, have fewer sexual partners, and have more knowledge about risky sexual behaviors than their counterparts in the control condition. And, because youth were randomly assigned to either the treatment or control condition, we should feel confident that any differences between the treatment and control groups were caused by the intervention. The design has high internal validity. In a report summarizing the results, the researchers wrote, "The rigor of the experimental design derives from the fact that, with random assignment, youth in both the program and control groups were similar in all respects except for their access to the abstinence education program services" (Trenholm et al., 2007, p. xvi).

FIGURE 9.4 Impact of Abstinence Education Programs on Sexual Behaviors

An evaluation study of federally funded abstinence education programs found that students who received the abstinence education intervention (treatment group) were no more likely than students in the control group to remain abstinent.

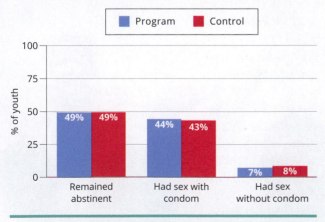

Source: Trenholm et al., 2007.

What did the study reveal? Youth who received the abstinence education program were no more likely than those in the control group to abstain from sex. As Figure 9.4 shows, 49% of both groups reported being "always abstinent." The two groups also did not significantly differ in their rates of unprotected sex, age at first intercourse, or number of sexual partners. The program did produce an increase in youths' ability to identify STDs, but the program had no impact on the other measures of sexual knowledge, including the effectiveness of various forms of birth control and the knowledge of risks associated with unprotected sex. The study authors concluded that the evaluation "highlights the challenges faced by programs aimed to reduce adolescent sexual activity and its consequences" (Trenholm et al., 2007, p. 61). They also note that abstinence education did not *increase* STD risks, which some critics of abstinence education had suggested might occur. However, the most important finding was that there were almost no differences between the treatment group and control group, suggesting that the abstinence education program had no effect on sexual behavior and very little effect on sexual knowledge.

CONCEPT CHECKS

1   Why did the results from the Tennessee STAR experiment not translate into similar results for California?

2   Summarize the results of the abstinence education program. Why were the results controversial?

THE CHALLENGES OF EVALUATION RESEARCH: ETHICAL, LOGISTICAL, AND POLITICAL CONCERNS

Researchers have to balance the demands of doing what is best from a scientific standpoint with what is possible given ethical concerns as well as logistical, financial, and political constraints. As we have stressed, randomized field experiments are preferred because they have high internal validity. However, randomized field experiments are not possible in many, or even most, situations.

Two factors that limit the use of randomized field experiments are their high cost and time-consuming nature, as we saw with the Tennessee STAR experiment. Because of these financial and time demands, randomized experiments tend to be used only when the evaluation question is very important and when there is enough time to carry out the experiment. If policy makers must make a decision quickly (which is often the case), randomized experiments will not be useful.

For example, the main portion of the Tennessee STAR experiment took 4 years to complete. If the Tennessee legislature needed a quick answer about whether reduced class sizes increase learning, the STAR experiment would have been of little use to them. The original experiment took 4 years because students had to be in small classes for a sufficient amount of time for the small classes to have an effect. Plus, researchers wanted to see if the gains associated with small classes persisted, so they had to monitor students over a long period of time as the students transitioned to higher grades. The STAR experiment was also expensive, costing $3 million to fund just the first year of the study. Given the importance of childhood education and of closing the achievement gap among different groups in society, Tennessee decided to fund the experiment.

Ethical Concerns

Another barrier to the use of randomized field experiments is the belief by some that it is unethical to randomly assign individuals to the control group. For example, if there are strong reasons to believe that small classes will benefit students, are we arbitrarily denying some students the best chance to succeed in school by randomly assigning them to the control condition where they are placed in regular-size classes? Importantly, in the Tennessee experiment, students in the control group experienced the same size of classes that existed prior to the study. They were not assigned to larger classes. Thus, the study compared current practices (regular-size classes) to the new program of small classes. (In medical studies, the control group is called the *standard treatment*, meaning the treatment the participants would normally receive outside of the study and not some lesser treatment.)

Now that the STAR experiment is complete, we have convincing evidence that smaller classes do improve student achievement. So, it is true that those in the control group were denied a benefit that those in the treatment group received. Those randomly assigned to regular-size classes had smaller test-score gains, were more likely to drop out of high school, and were less likely to attend college. However, without random assignment, we would not have compelling, internally valid evidence that smaller classes produce educational advantages. (For another example of the ethical issues surrounding random assignment, see the "From the Field to the Front Page" feature, which describes a controversial experimental program to assess the effectiveness of a program designed to help those at risk of becoming homeless.)

Logistical Issues

Logistical issues add another layer of complexity to evaluation research. One important issue is *differential attrition rates* (study dropout rates) between those in the treatment and control groups. If treatment groups are receiving a benefit, such as a service of some sort, they might be more likely to remain in the study than those in the control group. If we lose access to members of the control group, we can no longer collect data on them, which means we can no longer compare them to the treatment group. Without data from the control group, we cannot assess the effectiveness of the intervention.

Another issue is that some populations at whom an intervention is targeted are difficult to find and hard to follow over time. Interventions aimed at helping homeless people often face this problem. Finally, individuals may not comply with the intervention. Imagine a weight-loss intervention that requires individuals to exercise several times per week so that researchers can compare them with a control group that did not exercise. Randomly assigning individuals to groups will do no good if individuals in the treatment condition, unbeknownst to the researcher, do not exercise.

While the STAR experiment was successful, it also illustrates the logistical difficulties of carrying out a truly randomized field experiment. One problem that quickly arose in the study was the coming and going of students during the school year. Some students who were initially randomly assigned to one of the three types of classrooms left the school, while other students who were not initially in the study enrolled in the

IS IT ETHICAL TO DENY PEOPLE A HOME BASE?

Many communities have programs designed to help families or individuals who are homeless or at risk of becoming homeless. These include short-term financial subsidies, temporary shelters, and programs that assist with the job-search process. Do these programs work? Are people who participate in them more likely to find housing or stay in their housing? Is one type of program more effective than another? To answer these questions, New York City decided to undertake a randomized field experiment to evaluate its $23 million Home-Base program. HomeBase, which began in 2004, offers job training, counseling services, and emergency money to help people stay in their homes.

When the media reported that the New York City Homeless Services Department was planning to commission an experimental study of HomeBase, public reaction was swift and highly critical. An article in the *New York Times* quoted Scott Stringer, the Manhattan borough president, as saying, "They should immediately stop this experiment. The city shouldn't be making guinea pigs out of the most vulnerable" (qtd. in Buckley, 2010). One city councilwoman vowed to hold hearings on the study, calling it "inhumane" to deny 200 of New York's most vulnerable citizens the services they need (Moore, 2010).

The controversy was over randomization into the control group. The study design involved collecting data over a 2-year period from 400 families who came to HomeBase for help. All of these families were behind on their rent and in danger of being evicted. Researchers wanted to know if participation in HomeBase kept them from becoming homeless. The researchers decided to compare the rate of becoming homeless for those who received HomeBase support (treatment group) with the rate for those who did not receive support but were otherwise equivalent (control group).

How did HomeBase randomize individuals into the treatment and control groups? When families contacted HomeBase, their names were placed into a computer database, and the computer then randomly assigned them to receive HomeBase services or to deny them help. Those denied help were given the names of other agencies. Because the assignment was random, researchers were able to effectively assess whether participation in HomeBase, and not some other factor, reduces the incidence of homelessness. But is it ethical to deny individuals services they need?

Then-mayor Michael Bloomberg defended the study by saying, "In the end, we are only going to spend money on things that work, so we have to find out what works" (qtd. in Moore, 2010). Defenders of the study also noted that

many people are routinely denied help anyway. The study, they claimed, merely organized the denial of benefits in a way that allowed the program to be evaluated.

The HomeBase study illustrates several themes discussed in this chapter. First, random assignment of individuals to treatment and control groups allows for the best evaluation of an intervention. Second, evaluation research is often conducted in politically and ethically charged environments. Third, conducting an effective randomized field experiment is often challenging because of logistical issues. To assess the effectiveness of the program, the researchers need to collect data over the 2-year period for those in the treatment group and the control group. Collecting data on the control group certainly presents challenges because they were denied services—how will researchers track them?

Whether the HomeBase study produces high-quality results depends on how successful the researchers are in solving these logistical issues. Also, whether the study continues and whether its results are translated into future programs largely depends on who carries more weight in public debate and decision making—those who argue that a randomized field experiment is necessary to assess whether HomeBase is having the desired effect or those who argue that denying services to people who are most in need is inhumane.

school. While it is not uncommon for students to move from one school to another, this movement did introduce logistical problems for the evaluation study. New students had to be randomly assigned to a classroom type and, because they joined the class later than their peers, they had less exposure to the treatment (the small class size). Subsequent statistical analysis confirmed that leaving and entering students did not affect the overall conclusion that small classes increase learning (Grissmer et al., 2000). However, in an ideal experiment, researchers would prefer to have a consistent group of students throughout the whole study. The real world is rarely so accommodating!

A second problem was that the state of Tennessee did not believe it could require school systems to participate in the study. So, while all Tennessee school systems were invited to participate, each school system decided whether to take part in the study. As a result, the characteristics of the students participating in the STAR experiment were different from those of the average Tennessee student. The STAR sample had a higher concentration of minority students and students from less-advantaged socioeconomic backgrounds. The sample was also quite different from students nationwide in the United States. Because the STAR sample was not representative of U.S. students, some questioned whether the findings from the STAR experiment would generalize to other parts of the country. One encouraging piece of evidence is that a very similar study, carried out in Wisconsin, found similar results. The Wisconsin sample had a much higher concentration of white students and found that small class sizes increased learning. The study also found that the positive effect of smaller classes was greater for low-income students.

Politics

Politics often plays a frustrating role in evaluation research. What is important to policy makers today often changes as new officials are elected and public opinion changes. When this happens, policy makers may lose interest in a program before the evaluation is complete. For example, in the 1970s, randomized field experiments were under way in several states to evaluate whether providing financial support to felons recently released from prison might lower the chances that they would commit crimes again in the future (Rossi et al., 2004). Felons who were recently released from prison in Texas and Georgia were randomly assigned to experimental groups, where they received some financial support upon release, or control groups, where they received no financial support. Researchers then tracked the former prisoners for 1 year to measure whether they had been rearrested and whether they had obtained a job.

Researchers found that former prisoners who received financial support had a lower level of rearrest than that of former prisoners who did not receive support. The former prisoners who received financial support were also able to obtain better jobs, although it took them longer to find jobs than those prisoners who received no financial support (Rossi, Berk, & Lenihan, 1980). Even though the evaluation showed benefits to providing former prisoners with short-term financial support, by the time the results were available in some states, political winds had shifted, and policy makers were no longer interested in financial assistance programs for former felons. Consequently, the results of the experiments had no chance to influence policy decisions.

Finally, stakeholders often intervene in the interpretation of results and influence whether the intervention is implemented on a larger scale. The abstinence-only sex education evaluation discussed earlier is a good example. As might be expected, the report's findings were controversial, and responses to it were swift and polarized.

On the basis of the study results, critics of abstinence education insisted that the government stop allocating large sums of money to these programs. Rather than accept the findings, proponents of abstinence education attacked the study design, questioning the study's external validity and arguing that the results of the study could not be generalized to the larger U.S. youth population. The youth who had participated in the study, they noted, were disproportionately from minority communities or single-parent families, leading them to speculate that abstinence education might be effective for nonminority and/or middle-class students. As this example shows, decisions about future implementations of social interventions are rarely straightforward, even when evaluation research is well designed and well funded.

While we would hope that important policy decisions would be made using the best available scientific evidence, we should not bemoan the fact that evaluation research takes place in a political context. As we have emphasized, evaluation research is intended to provide evidence that can help policy makers and organizations make important decisions in an informed way. Important decisions are important precisely because large numbers of people care about them and because the decisions affect groups differently. Decisions with important social consequences should be made by the large numbers of people who have stakes in the outcomes of the decision.

Shifting political winds can prevent evaluation research, such as field experiments evaluating the benefits of financial-assistance programs for former felons, from influencing policy decisions.

CONCEPT CHECKS

1 | What factors limit the use of randomized field experiments?

2 | Sometimes stakeholders fail to act on the results of an evaluation study, either by failing to continue a successful intervention or continuing an intervention that failed to produce its intended effects. Why?

CONCLUSION

Evaluation research is useful because it provides the best information possible about the effectiveness of an intervention within a given set of real-world constraints (Berk & Rossi, 1999). Without scientific evidence, our decisions would be based solely on gut feeling, opinion, or guesswork. Effective evaluation research begins with a good evaluation question: one that is reasonable in scope and answerable. This question then informs the choice of research method. Because the treatment and control groups need to be as equivalent as possible, randomized field experiments are optimal. When random assignment isn't possible, researchers often turn to quasi-experimental methods. The STAR study, which used a randomized field experiment, provided compelling evidence of the benefits of smaller classes on student learning, most notably for minority students. Because of its focus on assessing social programs, evaluation research is often conducted outside the world of academia. In the future, you may be called upon to conduct an evaluation research project as an employee of a private business, nonprofit organization, or a federal, state, or local government agency.

End-of-Chapter Review

Summary

Evaluation research is designed to determine whether a social intervention produces its intended effect. The main goal of evaluation research is translation, or the implementation of the social intervention on a larger scale.

What Is Evaluation Research?
- Evaluation research does not refer to a particular method but rather to research intended to assess the impact of a social intervention.
- Evaluation research brings together diverse stakeholders and often is conducted in politically charged contexts. There are also logistical challenges and ethical concerns.

Conducting Evaluation Research
- The first step is formulating an evaluation question that is both reasonable in scope and answerable.
- The outcome of evaluation research must be measurable, and the outcome measures must be both valid and reliable. Behavioral measures are often preferred.
- Researchers must decide which method is best suited to implementing and evaluating the intervention. Assessing the effects of an evaluation project involves considering the internal and external validity of the results.

Research Methods Used in Evaluation Research
- Randomized field experiments are considered the gold standard of evaluation research because they are based on random assignment.
- When a randomized experiment is not possible, researchers often use quasi-experimental methods. With these methods, experimental and control groups are formed using a procedure other than randomization, such as matching or the use of statistical controls or reflexive controls.
- Evaluation research often combines both quantitative and qualitative methods in an effort to answer a broader set of questions. Qualitative research can be used to help design effective survey questions, known as formative research, or to better understand how an intervention is being delivered and experienced.

Translating Evaluation Research into Large Social Programs
- The goal of evaluation research is to take evidence from a successful intervention and translate those findings into larger social programs.
- Several factors affect whether an intervention will be implemented more broadly, including cost, the generalizability of the findings, and whether the intervention can be implemented in the same way as the original intervention.

Two Examples of Evaluation Research
- Project STAR was a randomized experimental study of the impact of class size on student learning.
- An evaluation study of federally funded abstinence education programs used a randomized field experiment to determine whether the programs reduced sexual activity and increased sexual knowledge.

The Challenges of Evaluation Research: Ethical, Logistical, and Political Concerns

- Randomized field experiments raise ethical concerns because it can mean denying important benefits to participants in the control group.
- Logistical problems that can arise in evaluation research include differential attrition and difficulties with tracking participants over time.
- Politics can affect whether evaluation research is implemented on a larger scale. Stakeholders may also intervene, especially if the findings are controversial.

Key Terms

biased, 280
control group, 277
control condition, 279
cost-benefit
    analysis, 289
evaluation
    research, 274
external validity, 278
formative research, 285
internal validity, 277
matching procedure, 280

multiple time-series
    design, 283
nonequivalent
    comparison design, 280
pre-post design, 282
quasi-experimental
    method, 279
randomized field
    experiment, 279
reflexive controls, 282
reliability, 276

selection bias, 280
social desirability
    bias, 277
social intervention, 274
stakeholder, 274
statistical controls, 282
time-series design, 283
translation, 274
treatment condition, 279
treatment group, 277
validity, 276

Exercise

Suppose that a university is concerned about the amount of alcohol its students are consuming and decides to implement a new education program on the dangers of binge drinking. The university believes that this program will reduce the amount of alcohol students consume during the school year. To evaluate the effectiveness of the new program, the university plans to use a randomized field experiment.

- Write an evaluation question that is precise and realistic. Use the examples at the beginning of the chapter as a guide. Your question should mention the intervention and state what outcome you expect to produce if the intervention is effective.
- What might be the stakeholders' concerns? What is at stake for administrators? What about students? Are there other stakeholders?
- How might the university assign students to treatment and control groups?
- How should researchers measure the outcome of interest? When should they measure the outcome?
- How will the university know whether the intervention achieved its intended effect?
- How could qualitative methods be added to the study? What could we learn from them?

Ethnographers immerse themselves in the lives and social worlds of the people they hope to understand. Participant observation research has been used to understand the experiences of people dealing with eviction and homelessness.

ETHNOGRAPHY

Can you answer the following questions on the basis of your personal experiences?

- Why do people join gangs? What is a typical "day in the life" of a gang member?

- Do poor people have the same values as middle-class people or do the two groups care about very different things?

- Why do people join cults, and what are their experiences inside the cult?

- What is it like to be a female Marine?

- What do college students do in their dorms, and why do they behave that way?
- What happens when a surgeon makes a mistake in surgery? How do their supervisors let them make enough mistakes to learn while ensuring no patients die as a result?

Participant observation, or **ethnography**, is a research method designed to answer these questions and others like them. Researchers immerse themselves in the lives and social worlds of the people they want to understand. One of the most widely read practitioners of this method, Elliot Liebow (1993), describes the basics of the method in very simple terms: "In participant observation, the researcher tries to participate as fully as possible in the life of the people being studied.... One simply goes where they go, gets to know them over time as best one can, and tries very hard to see the world from their perspective" (p. vii). Bronislaw Malinowski, who studied the people of Papua New Guinea in the early 1900s, noted that the goal of ethnography is to "grasp the native's point of view, his relation to life, to realize his version of the world" (Altheide & Johnson, p. 287).

In this chapter, we review the historical roots of ethnography, the different roles an ethnographer can take in the field, and the range of topics and questions that ethnographers address. We stress that ethnography is different than mere description or journalism because in addition to telling a story, an ethnography is creating or testing a social science theory and contributing to the scientific study of society. We then take you through the steps of conducting an ethnography, from choosing a question to writing up the results. Finally, we review new developments in this classic research method as it adapts to twenty-first-century questions.

Margaret Mead conducts an ethnography in the Admiralty Islands, part of Papua New Guinea, in 1953. Her classic study *Sex and Temperament in Three Primitive Societies* found that gender roles there differed dramatically from those in the United States.

ETHNOGRAPHY: HISTORICAL ROOTS

Ethnography is the principal tool of anthropology. Like sociologists, anthropologists study human beings, often through fieldwork in far-off locales with people who have not been extensively studied. In the mid-twentieth century, early anthropologists such as Margaret Mead and Clifford Geertz traveled to remote areas to study village life and culture. These trailblazing anthropologists spent long periods of time in remote places, such as islands, mountains, or jungles, learning and describing the intricate rules and customs that govern everyday life. In the Americas, the early ethnographers often studied Native Americans, and sympathetic accounts of life on Indian reservations helped to combat some of the widespread anti–Native American sentiment of the early twentieth century (Kroeber, 1925).

In the early twentieth century, when both sociology and anthropology were establishing themselves as social sciences, the division of labor was fairly clear-cut. Sociologists studied aspects of their own society, and anthropologists went abroad—studying the "other," the non-Westerner, the native. Anthropologists studied people from different cultures, while sociologists studied subcultures within their own culture. A **subculture** is a group within a larger culture, a subset of people with beliefs and behaviors that differ from those of the larger culture. Early sociological participant observation studies therefore focused on immigrant communities, poor urban neighborhoods, and "deviant" groups that were defined as different from mainstream culture. For instance, early sociological studies of urban life in Chicago include vivid descriptive field studies of homeless people, gangs, and immigrant groups. Robert Park, who headed the sociology department at the University of Chicago (the "Chicago school") in the early twentieth century, encouraged his students to get out into the city and study people as they went about their everyday lives. Park (1950) believed that "what sociologists most need to know is what goes on behind the faces of men, what it is that makes life for each of us either dull or thrilling" (pp. vi–vii).

Over time, this stark division of labor broke down. Anthropologists began to study their own societies, and sociologists began conducting studies across the globe. For example, anthropologist Laurence Ralph (featured in Chapter 16) studied the effects of gun violence on a poor African American neighborhood in Chicago (Ralph, 2014). Meanwhile, sociologist Javier Auyero studied gun violence in a neighborhood in Buenos Aires, Argentina (Auyero & Berti, 2016). Both ethnographies are very similar in that they elucidate the connections between the neighborhoods the researchers studied and the cities, nations, and global networks that serve to perpetuate poverty and violence.

As technological advances spread throughout the world, cultures were no longer isolated, and their people became fully capable of speaking for themselves. The idea of a white, Western, middle-class anthropologist living among the natives and then "explaining" the culture of an isolated tribe to folks back home was very unsettling to anthropologists, who did not want to exploit the native people they respected and admired. In addition, **globalization**, or the development of worldwide social and economic relationships, means that there are now few places on Earth where the native people are not already fully aware of and participating in the world beyond their village or town. Now, anthropology and sociology are not differentiated by where they do fieldwork but rather by their different tools and the foci of their studies.

Historical differences in the focus and kind of fieldwork that anthropologists and sociologists do is responsible for the different associations of the terms *ethnography* and *participant observation*. Vestiges of the different theoretical approaches of both disciplines remain. Ethnography was the primary method of

subculture A group within a larger culture; a subset of people with beliefs and behaviors that differ from those of the larger culture.

globalization The development of worldwide social and economic relationships.

With the rise of globalization, the boundaries between sociology and anthropology became less about geographic location and more about the tools used and foci of their studies.

anthropologists and emphasized a cultural understanding of the people being studied. Sociologists see culture as just one among a number of variables that influence the people they study, along with economics, psychology, organizations, and politics. To describe their process, the early American sociologists of the Chicago school adopted the term *participant observation*. Everett Hughes, one of Park's students, taught the method at the University of Chicago to some of the most influential researchers in the discipline, including Erving Goffman, Howard Becker, Herbert Gans, and Anselm Strauss. While the Chicago school has long been credited with the development of this methodology, recent scholarship suggests that W. E. B. Du Bois developed these methods earlier, but as an African American scholar—the first to receive a PhD in sociology—was not given credit because of the systemic racism of the time (Morris, 2015). Meanwhile, *ethnography* has developed into a contested term, with some arguing it should be used only to describe the way anthropologists do long-term, complete immersion in a culture.

In the past, researchers drew fine-grained distinctions among the terms *participant observation*, *ethnography*, and *fieldwork*, but today we use the terms more or less interchangeably to describe the work of social scientists who spend time with people in their everyday lives in order to understand their circumstances, worldviews, ideas, and behaviors. Robert Emerson (1983) describes the goal of fieldwork as *interpretive understanding*—something that is "acquired through regular and intimate involvement, maintained over time and under a variety of diverse circumstances, in the worlds of others" (p. 15).

In the twenty-first century, research methods have expanded to include virtual field methods; for example, studying people's behavior on the Internet by observing them virtually or observing neighborhoods virtually through Google Street View and satellite imagery. So, in effect, those doing virtual fieldwork might encounter the "field" via a computer screen in the comfort of their own homes. In this chapter, however, we restrict the method to empirical work in which the researcher is physically present—fieldwork involves learning about other people in their worlds, not just theorizing about them from behind a desk.

CONCEPT CHECKS

1   How did sociology and anthropology differ when they first emerged as social science disciplines?

2   How has globalization affected fieldwork and ethnography?

THE DIVERSE ROLES OF THE ETHNOGRAPHER

Researchers vary widely in how they balance the tasks of participation and observation. Studies also vary in the degree to which people know they are being observed and studied. A researcher can adopt one of four roles when doing fieldwork. These range from the complete participant to the participant observer, the observer, and the covert observer (Junker, 1960; Gold, 1958). The appropriate role depends on the research question and the circumstances of the research.

Complete Participant

Fieldworkers who become **complete participants** in effect "go undercover," immersing themselves in a fieldwork site and keeping their identities as researchers a secret. The fieldworker does not tell the subjects that they are being studied and pretends to be a native. The complete participant role is difficult for researchers because they must pretend to be someone they are not—and they must constantly conceal their true identity and their true purpose. This practice raises a number of ethical issues because it involves deceiving the research subjects. In fact, it is prohibited by the Code of Ethics of the American Anthropological Association (AAA) and is only permitted by the American Sociological Association (ASA) if there is no other way to conduct the study.

Complete participation is not the most common role adopted by fieldworkers. Rather, most ethnographers tell the people they are studying who they really are. Nonetheless, a few very famous ethnographers have engaged in complete participation. Perhaps the most famous example is Erving Goffman (1961), who worked as a state hospital assistant while researching the book *Asylums* (rumored to be the basis for the movie *One Flew Over the Cuckoo's Nest*). Goffman humanized the patients in the mental hospital and showed how mental hospitals are similar to other "total institutions"—a term he coined to refer to institutions that contain people and regiment every aspect of their lives, such as prisons, army training camps, nursing homes, and boarding schools. Goffman explains how the patients' erratic behavior was often not due to their illnesses but to the effects of socialization into the institution, with patients adopting the "roles" they are expected—and indeed required—to play.

Researchers who decide to deceive their research subjects face many challenges. They live with the constant anxiety that their true identities will be discovered. They are always "performing" and must be very careful lest a small slip betray them. Their deception may cause them uneasiness or discomfort. Deception becomes harder the longer they are in the field, as they get to know people better, develop friendships, and begin to care about the people they are studying.

An example of these strains is Randy Alfred's (1976) study of Satanists in San Francisco. Alfred was interested in studying a cult of Satanists, and he did such a good job of showing interest and dedication to the group that they made him the church historian. His new responsibilities were very useful for his research because he got access to a lot of information, but as he began to regard his subjects sympathetically, he started to feel bad about deceiving them. Ultimately, he confessed his deception to the leader of the church. Perhaps fortuitously, lying was seen as a Satanic thing to do, and the church did not hold it against him.

How would you feel about being studied without knowing it? Cathy Small, an anthropologist at Northern Arizona University, was interested in understanding the lives of college students. So at age 52, in the early 2000s, she applied to college, moved into the freshman dorm,

> **complete participant** One of the four roles a researcher can adopt when doing fieldwork; as complete participants, fieldworkers "go undercover," immersing themselves in a fieldwork site and keeping their identities as researchers a secret.

In order to study a cult of Satanists, Randy Alfred went undercover as a complete participant and even became the church historian.

and enrolled in a full load of classes. She never told the other students that she was studying them or that she was a professor. At the end of the year, she went back to work as a professor and wrote a book about what she learned, *My Freshman Year: What a Professor Learned by Becoming a Student*. Even though she published the book under a pseudonym, Rebekah Nathan (2006), it did not take commentators and reviewers much time to root out and publish her true identity. The steps Small had taken to protect the identities of her subjects were thus compromised, and their sometimes illegal and unethical behaviors (underage drinking, cheating on exams and homework) were exposed.

Notably, the ethical issues surrounding Small's choice to deceive her subjects elicited the strongest reaction. Anthropologists were very critical of Small's decision to deceive the students she studied, citing the AAA's Code of Ethics. Small wrote that after the fieldwork was over and she became a professor again, she ran into one of the students she studied on campus, who told Small that she felt "fooled." Small wrote, "I imagine that there are a few other fellow students who might feel the same way and with whom I will never have the opportunity to speak" (Nathan, 2005, p.168). This suggests that Small did not make a concerted effort to find and "debrief" all the students she deceived, which is a requirement of the ASA Code of Ethics. As we mentioned earlier, the ASA allows deception in research under certain circumstances but requires that researchers tell subjects the truth at the end of the study.

Another issue facing complete participants is the fear of **going native**. Most researchers begin to see the world differently when they immerse themselves in the field—which is the point of the method. While all fieldworkers go a little bit "native" in terms of seeing the world as their subjects see it, a real danger for those who completely immerse themselves is that they will lose their original identity. Graduate students arriving at the University of California, Berkeley, in 1979 (including Mary Waters, a coauthor of this textbook) heard a cautionary tale of a graduate student who was "lost" a year earlier. The student had decided to study the "Moonies," members of the Unification Church headed by Rev. Sun Myung Moon. The Moonies demanded cult-like separation from one's previous friends and social world. The student went off to study the cult and its members but did not return. She became a church member, dropped out of school, and cut off all contact with her family, friends, and professors. Her parents had to fly out to Berkeley and convince her to leave the cult. She had "gone native" in a way that frightened all the sociologists. For years afterward, graduate students were warned to choose field sites for their first-year projects that were much less intense. Never fear, other researchers have successfully studied the Moonies without losing themselves (Barker, 1984; Lofland & Stark, 1965).

Sometimes, complete participation leads to insights that make major contributions to the discipline. In 1954, a woman named Marian Keech stated that supernatural beings were visiting Earth in flying saucers and sending messages to her. Predicting that the world would end by

going native The threat that fieldworkers who completely immerse themselves in the world of their subjects will lose their original identity and forget they are researchers.

Graduate students at UC Berkeley were told the cautionary tale of a student who went native while studying the cult-like Unification Church. Church members participate in a mass wedding in South Korea.

flood on December 21, 1954, she called on people to join her group, give up their jobs and money, and gather at a designated house, where a flying saucer would pick them up and save them from certain death. As Keech began to attract followers, social psychologists Leon Festinger, Henry Riecken, and Stanley Schachter (1956) saw her prophecy as a perfect way to study a question they had been pondering: How would people react when a strong belief was proved untrue? The researchers hired students to join the movement, study the true believers, and examine how they reacted to the failure of the prophecy on the night in question.

To gain entry to the group, the student researchers told stories of their own experiences of strange supernatural occurrences. The students' deception not only got them accepted into the group, but it also bolstered the group's beliefs in supernatural occurrences. This is an example of **reactivity**, whereby the presence and actions of the researcher change the behaviors and beliefs of the research subjects. With ethnography, the researcher cannot help but influence the situation in myriad ways just by being present and interacting with others. This is similar to the issue of experimenter effects, explored in Chapter 8, whereby the researcher subtly or unconsciously affects the performance of a study participant.

The student researchers successfully joined two different groups of followers—one in town, and one more isolated. When the end of the world did not occur on the appointed day, the participants were sad and surprised, but by the next morning Keech announced that she had received another message: Because so many people had demonstrated their belief by gathering at the house to be rescued, God had decided to save Earth from destruction!

While many followers subsequently abandoned the cult, the more isolated group did not. The failure of the prophecy led these believers to renew their commitment to the group and to Keech. They began to recruit new members even more aggressively. From this research emerged the theory of cognitive dissonance, which has become very influential in psychology and sociology. **Cognitive dissonance** refers to the unpleasant or distressing feeling we experience when we hold two discrepant beliefs or when we engage in a behavior that violates our beliefs. For instance, we might feel conflicted if we learn that our new boyfriend or girlfriend holds political beliefs very different from our own or if we are an outspoken vegetarian who, in a moment of weakness, eats a hamburger. The theory predicts that we act to reduce the dissonance (disconnect) we feel when we need to balance contradictory beliefs that we hold simultaneously. When the world did not end—an event clearly at odds with the cult members' strongly held beliefs—the members experienced cognitive dissonance. However, accepting Keech's new (albeit implausible) explanation eliminated the cognitive dissonance and allowed the cult members to hold onto their original beliefs.

While some researchers have succeeded in doing good work as complete participants, it is much less common than any of the other roles and is more ethically worrisome and carries many risks. Beginning researchers will often use an undercover approach because they assume they will be rejected if they identify themselves as researchers. However, even private organizations can sometimes be convinced to grant researchers access. Very often, being honest can win over people and allow research to proceed without deception.

Participant Observer

participant observer One of the four roles a researcher can adopt when doing fieldwork; as a participant observer, the researcher tells at least some of the people being studied about his or her real identity as a researcher.

When acting as a **participant observer**, the researcher tells at least some of the people being studied about his or her real identity as a researcher. The researcher participates fully in the social life of the setting, trying to blend in as much as possible and experience the world the way the research subjects do. This is probably the most common role adopted in fieldwork today.

Often, researchers will reveal their identity as social scientists to some people and keep it a secret from others. Christine Williams (2006), who studied retail workers by working in two different toy stores, told her employers that she was a professor looking for an extra part-time job, but she kept her identity a secret from her coworkers and the customers in the store:

> My friends and colleagues who knew about my venture into the toy stores were curious about what my coworkers thought of me. Wasn't it obvious that I really wasn't a salesclerk? Didn't my PhD make me stand out? What was it like to be undercover? But the fact is, I was never undercover. When I was working at these stores I really was a salesclerk. No one knew that I was also a professor (except the personnel managers who hired me), no one asked, and I'm pretty sure that no one cared. My coworkers had their own problems. I quickly learned that it was considered rude to ask about a coworker's background, since it was understood that no one intentionally sought a low-wage retail job. To the question "Why do you work here?" most would answer "Because IKEA never called back." It is a middle-class conceit to think that where you work is a reflection of your interests, values and aptitudes. In the world of low-wage retail work, no one assumes that people choose their occupations or that their jobs reflect who they really are. (pp. 18–19)

Another good example of participant observation is the book *Paying for the Party* (Armstrong & Hamilton, 2013). In this case, the researchers informed all their subjects that they were being studied. Elizabeth Armstrong (a professor in her late thirties) and Laura Hamilton (a graduate student in her late twenties) moved into a dormitory at a state university in order to study social class and gender dynamics among undergraduates. In contrast to "Rebekah Nathan," who deceived her subjects, Armstrong and Hamilton told their subjects about their study. The researchers lived in a women's dormitory, "interacting with participants as they did with each other—watching television, eating meals, helping them dress for parties, sitting in as they studied, and attending floor meetings. [They] let the women guide [the] conversations, which often turned to 'boys,' relationships, and hooking up" (p. 596). Armstrong and Hamilton focused on hookup culture on college campuses, and their research made front-page headlines for its descriptions of the ways in which class and gender shape experiences on college campuses.

informed consent The freedom to say yes or no to participating in a research study once all the possible risks and benefits have been properly explained.

The lack of deception means that people know they are being studied. This is a double-edged sword. On the one hand, the researcher is free to ask questions and to take notes in public, although most researchers try not to constantly remind people that they are being studied. The ethical quandary is less of a concern (or even nonexistent) because subjects' **informed consent** can be assumed by their acceptance of the researcher's presence in their world. That is, subjects can choose to stay in or exit the study once they know that the researcher is observing them.

THE DARK SIDE OF A PARTY CULTURE

Are colleges dangerous for women? Are men being falsely accused of rape on college campuses nationwide? Does the raucous "party culture" of Greek life contribute to binge drinking and sexual assaults on college campuses? Recent media reports would certainly have us think so. A widely read *New York Times* article in July 2014 profiled a young woman who alleged she was raped at a frat house party at Hobart and William Smith College in upstate New York, and that the college mishandled her sexual assault complaint (Bogdanich, 2014). At Stanford University, a male student was found guilty of sexually assaulting an intoxicated and unconscious woman behind a dumpster outside of a fraternity party in January 2015. The trial received a great deal of coverage and a statement from the victim describing her suffering went viral. Turner was given a six-month jail sentence (he was released after serving just three), which prompted public outcry.

What is happening on college campuses? In 2015, the Association of American Universities conducted a large survey about sexual assault and sexual misconduct on college campuses. It received a total of 150,072 responses from students on 27 different campuses. Of the female respondents, 23 percent said they had experienced some form of unwanted sexual contact; nearly 11 percent said they experienced unwanted penetration or oral sex. Heavy drinking is one of the most significant precursors of sexual assault, which has led many to question the party culture that characterizes college life. Sociologists Elizabeth Armstrong and Laura Hamilton spent five years at a large Midwestern state university studying a group of women from freshman through senior year in a "party dorm" on campus. Their 2013 book *Paying for the Party: How College Maintains Inequality* has provided some answers to a curious public.

The book's main argument is that the campus "party pathway" of hard drinking, parties, and sexual hookups, anchored in the Greek system of fraternities and sororities and supported by the administration, affects all students and sets the tone for both academic life and social life on campus. Armstrong and Hamilton document social-class differences in the effects of the party culture. While affluent students make their way through school, graduate, and go on to work and form families, poorer students often get sidelined by the party culture in ways that lead them not to graduate and often leave them saddled with debt. *Paying for the Party* describes the campus party scene, along with the pressure that women feel to drink and to dress in sexy outfits to go to parties. Students whose parents have been to college often give them advice about staying safe in these situations, using a buddy system, and

A 2015 survey found that nearly one in four female college students has experienced nonconsensual sexual contact.

avoiding being alone at a party. But the working-class students, whose parents did not attend college, did not have the benefit of that advice, and particularly during freshman year they often found themselves in dangerous situations. These women described being pressured to drink by men at parties and a "high-stakes status competition that fuels drinking" (p. 92).

Armstrong and Hamilton's sociological analysis provides a nuanced understanding of the party scene that is missing from many of the media accounts. They show how working-class women are at greater risk of sexual assault at college fraternity parties because they don't have extensive networks of other women friends, and they haven't been warned by parents who are knowledgeable about college life and the dangers of the fraternity system.

They also describe in detail how central the party scene is to the college experience, and how difficult it would be to outlaw or ban fraternities and sororities. In fact, they argue, the party scene is not incidental to college life but has become a central factor in college finances, relations between students and faculty, and the reasons affluent parents pay for their children to attend college. They tie the party scene to macrosocial factors like the decline in state support for universities, which leads to a competition among state and private universities for "full pay" students with limited interest in academics. These students and their parents pay for a party atmosphere that provides a good time, while their futures are assured through parental wealth and connections that will find them jobs after graduation. Working-class students who do not have these cushions and connections either do not finish school or finish with limited job possibilities and great debt. The systemic roots of this party culture on campus mean that it is difficult, if not impossible, for any one university campus to reverse these trends.

Hawthorne effect Named after a study of factory workers, the phenomenon whereby merely being observed changes subjects' behavior.

On the other hand, the researcher's presence may change the way people behave. When people know they are being observed, they may be on their best behavior—hiding their true beliefs and behaviors in order to make the best impression. The **Hawthorne effect**, named after a famous study of workers at Hawthorne Works, a factory in the Midwest, refers to the fact that merely being observed often changes subjects' behavior. Most ethnographers report that the Hawthorne effect fades quickly. If the researcher is present for a sustained period of time and is fully engaged in social life, subjects begin to forget about the research and to act naturally around the researcher. Researchers can also use their newness to the situation to their advantage, asking people to explain the social world to them as they go through their everyday activities.

Observer

observer One of the four roles a researcher can adopt when doing fieldwork; as an observer, the researcher tells people they are being observed but does not take part in the subjects' activities and lives.

In the **observer** role, the researcher tells people they are being observed but does not take part in the subjects' activities and lives. Many newspaper reporters who spend time in the field adopt the observer role. They attend meetings, listen to conversations, and take notes on what happens, but they do not participate at all. While a participant observer studying migrant workers would pick the crops along with the workers, a researcher adopting the observer role might go out to the fields and spend the day there, but he or she would not do a farmworker's job. An observer in a school setting might sit in a classroom and document the dynamics among students and between teachers and students, perhaps counting how many times students are asked questions or how many times teachers praise or criticize their students. In both these cases, the researchers gain valuable information about people in their natural settings, but by not participating they may miss the "feel" of the life they are studying. They don't experience the emotions of being angry with or afraid of the boss, or the bone-chilling cold or searing heat of outdoor work, or the numbing repetitiveness of working on an assembly line.

Given these limitations, why would a researcher choose just to be an observer and not a participant as well? Sometimes, being solely an observer is the price of admittance to a field site or the observer simply cannot do what his or her subjects are doing. Don Chambliss (1989) studied elite swimmers and how they perfect their craft. He could not have kept up with them in the pool even if he'd tried—it was better for him

Ethnographers have adopted the observer role in order to study elite athletes or people in occupations such as medicine or law, which can't be practiced without a license.

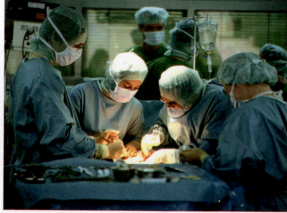

to observe the workouts and the interactions between the players and their coaches. By doing so, he was able to learn how the swimmers perceive the training and how the pursuit of excellence varies across levels of competition.

Similarly, in many studies of occupations, a researcher cannot actually practice the craft. Sociologists cannot practice medicine or law without a license, so if a researcher wants to understand how doctors interact with their patients or how big law firms are organized, the researcher has to be an observer rather than a participant (Bosk, 1979; Pierce, 1996). Charles Bosk adopted the role of observer in order to study the training of young surgeons in a teaching hospital and learn how both the interns and the more senior doctors dealt with medical mistakes.

Covert Observer

A researcher can sometimes observe people who do not know they are being observed or studied. In this case, the researcher is completely *covert*. Covert observation happens most often in public situations where many people are present and the researcher can fade into the crowd. While **covert observers** pose the least danger of altering the dynamics of the world they are studying, they also run the greatest risk of misunderstanding the situation. As outsiders watching events unfold, the researchers have limited or no insights into how the participants understand the situation and why they act as they do. Covert observers can eavesdrop, but they often miss the richness of the subjective understandings that true participants have.

Covert observer studies are frequently the first stage of what will become a participant observation study. The researcher observes the situation from the outside. Researchers often begin neighborhood studies by driving or walking the streets or observing interactions in city parks and other areas where people come together.

Systematic observation is a method of covert observation in which the researcher follows a checklist and timeline for observing phenomena. Social scientists Robert Sampson and Stephen Raudenbush developed a method for studying neighborhoods using a van that traveled Chicago streets with video cameras recording the stores, houses, and neighborhood life. (This study was conducted before Google Street View was developed, but the images and method of filming were quite similar.) A team of coders then viewed the images of the streets and systematically coded them using a checklist, including items on physical disorder (cigarettes on the street, empty beer bottles, graffiti, abandoned cars) and social disorder (adults loitering, people drinking alcohol, prostitutes walking the street, people selling drugs). The coding yielded a summary measure of neighborhood disorder that was objective and reliable across coders. Sampson and Raudenbush (1999) were then able to compare this measure with residents' subjective perceptions of disorder, as well as with other variables such as crime and income. This method can now be applied to many neighborhoods across the country using Google Street View (Hwang & Sampson, 2014). Such virtual neighborhood observation can be either a prelude to a more sustained and interactive participation in the life of the neighborhood or it can be a small study unto itself.

Table 10.1 summarizes the four roles available to the ethnographer.

covert observer One of the four roles a researcher can adopt when doing fieldwork; as a covert observer, the researcher observes people who do not know they are being observed or studied.

systematic observation A method of observation in which the researcher follows a checklist and timeline for observing phenomena.

TABLE 10.1 The Four Roles of the Ethnographer

Role Type	Description
Complete participant	Fieldworkers "go undercover" and immerse themselves in a fieldwork site, keeping their identities as researchers a secret from their subjects.
Participant observer	Fieldworkers tell subjects that they are being studied. Researchers participate as fully as possible in the field site.
Observer	Fieldworkers tell subjects that they are being studied. Researchers do not actually participate in life in the field; rather, they observe and interact as little as possible.
Covert observer	Fieldworkers do not tell subjects they are being studied. Researchers do not participate in life in the field; rather, they observe what is going on in a way that does not let people know they are being observed.

CONCEPT CHECKS

1   What four different roles can a fieldworker choose from when conducting a field research project?

2   Give two reasons why a researcher would decide not to reveal his or her identity to people they are studying in the field.

3   What are the advantages and disadvantages of the covert observer role? The complete participant role?

WHAT TOPICS DO ETHNOGRAPHERS STUDY?

community studies
Studies most related to the way anthropologists study whole villages, tribes, or towns or the way sociologists study neighborhoods or towns.

While ethnographers can study almost anything, there are a few favored topics. **Community studies** are most directly related to the way anthropologists study whole villages, tribes, or towns. Sociologists have studied small-town America, but neighborhood studies within big cities have been more numerous. W. E. B. Du Bois (2010/1899) wrote an early urban ethnography titled *The Philadelphia Negro*. He lived in the Seventh Ward of Philadelphia, a largely black neighborhood in that segregated city, in the late 1890s. Du Bois discussed the interactions between the working class and middle class in the neighborhood and how members of the middle class resisted being lumped together with the poor.

While the early ethnographies focused on Chicago's immigrant neighborhoods, other cities have featured prominently in ethnographies. In the late 1930s, William Foote Whyte (1943/1955) studied an Italian neighborhood, Boston's North End, for his book *Street Corner Society*. For a long time, his methods appendix has served as a "bible" of sorts for novice fieldworkers. Whyte was one of the first sociologists to apply the anthropological methods of fieldwork to the modern urban community. He wrote honestly and at length about the challenges he confronted (including the lack of written information about how to conduct fieldwork), the ways he made contact with the people he studied, and the dilemmas he faced in the field. For instance, Whyte wrote about how he struggled with how much he should influence the lives of the men he was hanging out with: Should he act like a friend and help them out or was that changing the lives he was trying to study? He wrote that he helped the men write letters to apply for jobs, which he didn't think was cause for concern, but he also loaned the men money occasionally. That felt much more problematic because he knew that the money meant more to them than to him, and that it would cause financial problems if he insisted on repayment but feelings of obligation and indebtedness if he wrote off the loan (Whyte 1943/1955, p. 304).

The West End was an Italian American working-class neighborhood that was demolished for urban renewal. Herbert Gans's ethnography of the neighborhood was conducted shortly before the residents were forcibly removed.

Twenty years later, from 1957 to 1958, Herbert Gans (1962) studied the West End, another Italian neighborhood in Boston, although this one was not destined to survive. It was demolished for urban renewal, replaced with modern high-rise apartment buildings. The second-generation Italian American families that Gans studied relocated to towns surrounding Boston, but even now, more than 50 years later, they have reunions and lament the loss of their neighborhood. In fact, obituaries in the *Boston Globe* still list people as former residents of the West End.

Both Gans and Whyte studied communities that outsiders perceived as dangerous "slums" and showed that they were in fact vibrant, beloved communities—places where people belonged and where neighbors interacted with one another and put down roots. Where outsiders, including the Boston Housing Authority, saw blight, Gans and his subjects saw a village. From these early beginnings, a very robust field of urban ethnography has developed (Duneier, Kasinitz, & Murphy, 2014), studying gentrification, race and ethnic relations, and relations in shops and parks and in union halls and political parties. When the postwar suburban housing boom led families to leave cities in the 1950s, sociologists followed the flow, writing a number of important studies of the new suburban towns, including Levittown, Pennsylvania (Gans, 1967).

Fieldwork has not been limited to the study of cities and suburbs. In fact, fieldwork has been conducted on many different topics, settings, and social groups. Ethnographers have researched institutions and organizations intensively. Goffman's (1961) classic book *Asylums*, mentioned earlier, analyzed mental hospitals from the perspectives of their workers and their patients. Hundreds of researchers have studied schools, including sociologist Paul Willis, who wrote the classic British study *Learning to Labour* (Willis, 1977) (see also Pascoe, 2007; Thorne, 1993).

Ethnographers have also written about deviant subgroups and behaviors. Early Chicago school ethnographers studied dance hall girls who were paid to dance with lonely men (Cressey, 2008/1932). Many ethnographers have studied gangs (Horowitz, 1983; Venkatesh, 2008). Drug dealers, drug users, and the drug trade have been examined in depth (Adler, 1985; Bourgeois, 1995; Contreras, 2012). Howard Becker (1953) wrote a classic account of how one becomes a marijuana user. Homelessness is another common topic—beginning with the classic study of the "hobo" (Anderson, 1961), through more recent analyses by sociologists Elliot Liebow (1993), Gwendolyn Dordick (1997), David Snow and Leon Anderson (1993), and Mitchell Duneier (1999).

Like many social scientists, ethnographers are often drawn to studying people who are suffering or lack power. Liebow's (1967) study of unemployed black men on the street corner, Burawoy's (1979) study of factory workers, Desmond's (2016) study of people who have been evicted from their homes, and Bourgeois's (1995) study of drug dealers in East Harlem all provide windows into the lives of people suffering deprivation. These lives are often very different from the lives of the mostly middle-class and upper-class college students and graduates who will read these ethnographies.

There are a more limited number of ethnographies that study "up" rather than studying "down." The novelist F. Scott Fitzgerald (1928/1989) once wrote: "Let me tell you about the very rich. They are different from you and me." Some sociologists are interested in learning *just how* the super-rich are different. In order to study the elite and soon-to-be elite, Shamus Khan (2011) got access to St. Paul's, a highly selective boarding school attended by the children of the very rich. A graduate of the school, Khan returned as a teacher and spent a year studying how these high school students learn class solidarity and how to justify the privilege they will enjoy because of their membership in that social class.

Other social scientists have gotten access to the upper class through workplace ethnographies. Karen Ho (2009) studied investment bankers by becoming one for a year, getting recruited by Bankers Trust while a graduate student at Princeton University. Lauren Rivera (2015) studied how elite students from Ivy League schools are recruited and hired by investment banks, management consulting firms, and law firms by becoming a "recruitment intern" at one firm and observing on-campus recruitment information sessions.

Studies that focus on the upper class at work are a subset of a wider tradition of ethnographers studying work and occupations of all sorts. Researchers have studied why factory workers don't slack off (Burawoy, 1979; Roy, 1952); how female Marines and male nurses are treated in gender-atypical occupations (Williams, 1991); and what it's like to work at McDonald's (Leidner, 1993). Police work is a popular topic among ethnographers (Glaeser, 1999; Hunt, 2010; Moskos, 2008; Van Maanen, 1978). Ethnographers have studied the work of doctors (Bosk, 1979), lawyers (Pierce, 1996), jazz musicians (Becker, 1963), wildland firefighters (Desmond, 2007), casino workers (Sallaz, 2009), fashion models (Mears, 2011), air-traffic controllers (Vaughan, 2005), and doormen (Bearman, 2005). Several important studies have looked at scientists and how they work in their laboratories (Knorr-Cetina, 1999). Social scientists have even studied other social scientists (Kurzman, 1991). These studies all explore the on-the-job socialization that occurs in these occupations, the unspoken rules that govern life at work, the contradictions and ethical dilemmas people experience, and the ways in which larger sociological forces—power, sex roles, racial prejudice, and discrimination—govern life on the job.

CONCEPT CHECKS

1 | What can be learned from a neighborhood study? Give an example of a neighborhood study and a key finding from the study.

2 | Why would an ethnographer be more likely to study a deviant or underprivileged group than an upper-class group?

THEORY AND RESEARCH IN ETHNOGRAPHY

As we discussed in Chapter 2, one of the most contentious issues in social research is the role of theory. Should theory *guide* field research or should theory *emerge from* fieldwork? Two related questions are: What topics or sites are appropriate for fieldwork, and where do research questions and designs come from? Researchers who are drawn to the participant-observation method may choose a setting and study it, hoping for a sociological angle to emerge. At the opposite extreme, a researcher may read about a theory, such as the false consciousness of the working class as described by Karl Marx, and set out to test the theory. Which is the correct approach? The answer depends on the researcher's primary goals. In this section, we look closely at two specific approaches to ethnography, also considering issues of validity and reliability in ethnographic research.

Approaches to Theory in Ethnography

When using the **grounded theory** approach, the researcher does not begin with a theory but rather develops a theory on the basis of experiences and observations in the field. According to Kathy Charmaz (2006), the grounded theory approach consists of "systematic yet flexible guidelines for collecting and analyzing qualitative data to construct theories 'grounded' in the data themselves" (p. 2). Elijah Anderson (2006) has written several important ethnographies using this approach. His first, an account of "street corner" men who hung out at a bar called Jelly's on Chicago's South Side, began with no research question at all. Anderson wrote an account of his fieldwork in 2006, noting that when he started the project he had "no explicit sociological problem or question" (p. 449). He thought that starting with a question would have led him to focus too early, closing off areas of inquiry that could later prove valuable.

On the other side of this debate is Michael Burawoy, an ethnographer who advocates for an **extended case study approach**. In this approach, the researcher starts with an established theory and chooses a field site, or *case*, to improve upon or modify the existing theory. For Burawoy and others who take this approach, the site of the fieldwork—the *micro context*—is best understood through theories that try to explain the *macro context*, such as commodification or male domination. The extended case study approach tells researchers to search for theories "that highlight some aspect of the situation under study as being anomalous and then proceed to rebuild (rather than reject) that theory by reference to the wider forces at work, be they the state, the economy, or even the world system" (Burawoy et al., 1991, p. 6). In other words, researchers should start with a theory that would predict that the situation they are studying would be different and then seek to explain why the reality differs.

An example is Burawoy's own work on factory workers. A Marxist theory would predict strong class consciousness among the working class and an antagonistic attitude toward factory work. Instead, Burawoy found that the factory employees worked especially hard and did not have the political orientation Marxism would predict. He took what he found in the factory and extended and revised the Marxist theory to explain why the factory workers behaved as they did.

While these two approaches represent extremes along a continuum, most ethnographers agree that fieldwork must do more than just describe the world they are

grounded theory A systematic, inductive approach to qualitative research that suggests that researchers should extrapolate conceptual relationships from data rather than formulate testable hypotheses from existing theory.

extended case study approach An approach to theory in qualitative research in which the researcher starts with an established theory and chooses a field site or case to improve upon or modify the existing theory.

studying. Journalists also do field observations and interviews, but sociologists who do participant observation bring a theoretically guided sociological perspective to the field. Sociologists must constantly evaluate their observations and perceptions of the world they are studying against existing theories of the social world, other research findings on the topic, and their own sense of what the situation and its people can teach us about society. This "dual citizenship"—being in the world *and* thinking about it as a social scientist—means that ethnographers are always changing how they see the situation, trying out explanations, and exploring new interpretations of what is happening. For example, when typing up field notes, an ethnographer may come up with a possible explanation about how people see the world and then test this explanation at the fieldwork site the next day. This iterative process continues throughout the fieldwork and into the writing stage as ethnographers work to make sense of their findings.

Howard Becker (2009) argues that this back-and-forth between data at the initial observation, possible interpretations and hypotheses about what is going on, and new data at a later time leads researchers down roads they could not have envisioned before they began their fieldwork. According to Becker, successful field researchers

> interpret data as they get it, over periods of months or years, not waiting . . . until they have it all in to start seeing what it means. They make preliminary interpretations, raise the questions those interpretations suggest as crucial tests of those ideas, and return to the field to gather the data that will make those tests possible. . . . Doing research that way is a systematic, rigorous, theoretically informed investigative procedure. But researchers can't know ahead of time all the questions they will want to investigate, what theories they will ultimately find relevant to discoveries made during the research, or what methods will produce the information needed to solve the newly discovered problems.

This approach, however, makes it difficult for ethnographers to meet some of the bureaucratic requirements of doing research. It is tough to write a grant proposal specifying the hypotheses to be tested if these hypotheses will emerge or change after the fieldwork begins. And it is hard to begin the fieldwork if funding organizations won't award grants before they know what hypotheses will be tested! It is also quite challenging for ethnographers to fill out standard applications for institutional review boards (see Chapter 3). They can't obtain informed consent from all the people they observe because they don't know their subjects ahead of time or how they will interact with the people being studied. In some cases, they can't even specify in advance the questions they will be asking in the field because the questions change as they learn new things. This flexibility is a key strength of participant observation, but it is also a weakness. How do ethnographers know they are asking the right questions? How do they know when they have answered the question and can go home? Would other researchers reach the same conclusion?

Validity and Reliability in Ethnographic Research

How do we evaluate whether an ethnography is any good? Because participant observation relies heavily on researchers' perceptions and interpretations, reliability is not its strong suit. Different researchers may see and interpret very different things at the same research site. However, ethnography promises greater validity; ethnography can get closer to the truth of a specific situation or event. Because the researcher becomes so close to the people being studied and is so deeply immersed in their world, the ethnographer gains a deeper understanding of the situation.

Recall that *external validity* refers to the extent to which research results can be generalized beyond one case. While ethnography focuses on getting deep into one setting and providing great detail about it, most ethnographers believe that their research has something to say beyond the one particular place or group they studied. Matthew Desmond (2016) wrote an ethnography about homelessness and eviction in Milwaukee, Wisconsin, but in his book he made conclusions about the process of eviction throughout the United States. So, too, while Armstrong and Hamilton (2013) studied just one American state university, the subtitle of their book is *How College Maintains Inequality*. They describe the specifics of their study site, but they use their work to understand college life across the United States. Most ethnographers do not choose their research site because they believe it is representative, but after they have studied it in depth they try to apply what they have learned to other, similar situations. Doing so involves discussing the aspects of the ethnography that are likely to be similar across cases.

How can researchers guard against allowing their biases to influence the story they tell to the reader? Howard Becker (1998) quotes advice provided by his mentor, Everett Hughes. Hughes told Becker to "identify the case that is likely to upset your thinking and look for it" (p. 87). Becker advises ethnographers to imagine that anything is possible and to pay close attention to anything weird or unusual. Maintaining this mindset helps the fieldworker imagine how things could have turned out differently and encourages the ethnographer to search for unlikely events and causes.

Duneier (2011) offers another way to guard against bias. He imagines that his ethnography is going to be put on trial for ethnographic malpractice:

> The trial will be held at a courtroom near the site of study, and witnesses who know about my subject will be called. The important thing about these witnesses is that they will be the ones I most fear hearing from because what they know is least convenient for the impressions I have given the reader. They may also have been the least convenient for me to get to know. (p. 2)

In addition, Duneier suggests that ethnographers construct an "inconvenience sample"—a sample of events and people that would call into question the ethnographer's own interpretations of what happened in the field:

> Ethnographers well into their studies could, as a matter of course, ask a few simple questions: Are there people or perspectives or observations outside the sample whose existence is likely to have implications for the argument I am making? Are there people or perspectives or phenomena within the sample that, when brought before the jury, would feel they were caricatured in the service of the ethnographer's theory or line of argument? Answers to questions of this kind can help the investigator to create an "inconvenience sample." (p. 8)

It is quite hard for a reader to judge the validity of an ethnographic account. Nonetheless, many ethnographies have stood the test of time, providing generations of students and social scientists with unique insights into the lives of people very different from themselves. Ethnographies have opened new worlds for readers, helping them to understand how people live under conditions very different from those of their own experiences. This is a key strength and contribution of ethnography.

CONDUCTING AN ETHNOGRAPHIC FIELD STUDY

Although there is great variation in the topics ethnographers study, there are clear steps to follow when conducting an ethnographic field study. First, the researcher must choose a topic and a site for the research. Second is the important process of negotiating access to the site and forming relationships with subjects. Third, the researcher must spend time in the field and take field notes. Fourth is deciding when and how to leave the field. Finally, there is the work of writing up the results of the study.

Choosing a Topic

It can be difficult, especially for a beginning researcher, to choose a topic that will have a clear payoff in terms of producing a worthwhile ethnography. Although many topics are potentially interesting, they may not provide information that is particularly innovative, that contributes to our understanding of existing theory, or that generates a new theory. An experienced sociologist can help new researchers see what is sociologically interesting in their field site.

A common problem arises when researchers immerse themselves in a field site with no real question, hoping that something interesting will emerge in the course of the fieldwork. Many field sites do not "pay off" in terms of advancing our understanding of the site and its people. However, sometimes patience is required. When you read ethnographies, you will notice that researchers often encounter blind alleys before the real ethnography takes off.

Consider Alice Goffman's (2014) ethnography of inner-city men living in the shadow of the police (see "Conversations from the Front Lines"). Her first idea—to study a highbrow video rental shop and the interactions of its workers and employees—went nowhere. She then started working in a cafeteria on her college campus, where she got to know some of the workers. Realizing that some of the workers couldn't read, she volunteered to tutor the relatives of one coworker. The tutoring sessions introduced her into a neighborhood and web of friends and family, all inner-city black people in Philadelphia. For a long while, she thought she was studying mothers and teens. Eventually, she made a connection between her field site and the important trend of the mass incarceration of young black men in U.S. society, which became the basis of her book *On the Run*.

The most difficult and hard-to-predict aspect of fieldwork is the path from a broad topic or site to a research question and then to an answer. It is best to begin with a practical or theoretical question about the subject you want to study. It may not be the question on which you ultimately focus, but you should be able to specify some reason why you think your field site is worth studying. A site where people face pressing challenges or hardships can be fertile ground for discovering a research focus. For example, homeless shelters, shelters for those fleeing domestic violence, or organizations for people who are unemployed will expose the researcher to the struggles and social worlds that theories in sociology are very much concerned with.

While some ethnographers choose a promising site and then discover their question, others start with a question or topic and must then choose a site to investigate it. In Chapter 6, we discussed sampling in case-oriented research. When selecting cases to study, researchers rarely choose randomly. Rather, researchers engage in **purposive sampling**, whereby cases are deliberately selected on the basis of features that distinguish them from other cases. Researchers may choose a site for study because it is accessible, typical, extreme, important, or deviant. Sometimes ethnographers choose two or more sites in order to be able to contrast them. For instance, Monica McDermott (2006) worked as a convenience store worker in order to observe race relations between blacks and whites. She chose one store in Boston and one in Atlanta so she could compare two cities with very different histories of race relations. When a researcher chooses a site to answer a specific research question, it is important to explain the logic of that choice and the trade-offs involved.

purposive sampling A sampling strategy in which cases are deliberately selected on the basis of features that distinguish them from other cases.

Negotiating Access, or "Getting In"

To study a site and its people, researchers must find a way to gain access to the site. Because ethnography often involves developing close relationships with the people being studied, negotiating access can be difficult. While the goal of ethnography is to immerse oneself in the lives and social worlds of the people being studied, researchers can't just show up and expect to immediately become a part of this new world, especially when the researcher is an outsider. Power dynamics are also at play in who is more amenable to being studied. Often, a college-educated ethnographer is seeking to study a marginalized group, and this power differential works in the ethnographer's favor because it is harder for people with less power to say no. Members of more elite groups are more likely to protect their privacy and exclude outsiders.

INSIDERS AND OUTSIDERS

Researchers often choose sites on the basis of their own "insider status" or "outsider status." Some researchers are already part of the life in a site and begin to think about studying it. They are insiders who realize they are in a very sociologically interesting world. They then begin to study the site systematically, transforming themselves from mere participants into participant observers. Many successful ethnographies have

ALICE GOFFMAN

The United States imprisons a far greater percentage of its people than any other nation; currently, 6.9 million people live under police supervision. Alice Goffman, a sociology professor at the University of Wisconsin–Madison, spent 6 years in Philadelphia study- ing poor black families whose lives have been affected by prison and intensive policing. In her book On the Run: Fugitive Life in an American City *(2014), she chronicles the lives of a group of young men who are in and out of jail and police control. Goffman's work has gotten a lot of attention—both positive and negative—in the press and within the discipline of sociol- ogy. Many have praised her work for putting a human face on the injustices faced by young black men at the hands of the police. Critics have questioned Goffman's field meth- ods, including whether she did enough to protect her sub- jects' identities, whether all the events in her book occurred exactly as she described them (she destroyed her field notes in order to protect her subjects), and whether she did enough to stop the violence she described witnessing. We talked with Goffman about her study, which began as an ethnography assignment for an undergraduate sociology class, developed into her senior thesis, became her doctoral dissertation, and ultimately inspired the book and a TED talk.*

In your study of young men in Philadelphia who are on the run from the police, how did you first gain access to people so different from you?

I began by studying a cafeteria on the campus of the Uni- versity of Pennsylvania when I was an undergraduate. I wanted to understand how the workers managed their interactions with the students. So I got a job in the cafete- ria. I made peanut butter sandwiches. And the first thing I learned is that the cafeteria workers were not talking and thinking about what the students said or thought.

They were not thinking about the students much at all. The cafeteria was undergoing a change. It was being de-unionized and they were hiring new young African Americans who would work for less pay and fewer

benefits. The women were very worried about this change and upset about training these new workers. That was what was on their minds. So I learned the first lesson of fieldwork—be willing to toss aside your original question and pay attention to what is really happening in the field.

After some time working in the cafeteria, I got interested in literacy. One day, one of the women who reg- ularly worked there was out sick with kidney stones, so there was a reshuffling of who did what work. I realized that there were some sandwiches that were mislabeled. As I watched the process, I understood that a system had been set up so that the labels were in separate folders. This allowed you to label the sandwiches without having to read the labels. Some of the workers could not read! Mrs. Dean had set up a system so she could manage peo- ple who could not read. This protected the dignity of the women who could not read.

> " **When you are doing an ethnography, you have to really believe in the mission of it, because it is so hard to actually do it.** "

In my freshman year of college, I got to know the family of one of my coworkers by offering to tutor. I met Aisha and her cousin. In my sophomore year, I moved to the neighborhood they lived in and everything began to develop over time. It was not until I got to Princeton [for graduate school] that I learned about mass incarcera- tion, and I realized that the level of policing on the guys I was with was related to that larger theme.

There is a lot of anxiety writing about people who are so different from you. The strain of being where you do not belong, with people whom you would not normally meet or hang out with. It is never easy to overcome the divide between black and white people. I was constantly dealing with my own racial position and my position as a writer and as a friend to the people in the field. It has been interesting to me to get to know ethnographers of color because these divides don't just happen when you are an outsider. When you are an insider, there is the danger of not having enough distance and also the pressure on you to not air your dirty laundry. So ethnography is ethically fraught no matter what side you may be on. When you are doing an ethnography, you have to really believe in the mission of it, because it is so hard to actually do it. There are a lot of research methods and topics that are less ethically and personally challenging and a lot safer.

How much do you help the people you study? Did you loan them money? Drive them places? Do you think your presence in their lives changed them at all?

This is one of the reasons why it is easier to do ethnography when you are young. When you are poorer, you don't have to ask yourself if you should help because you can't. I did bail people out of prison. There were times when I asked my parents for money to help people. But that was not good. I learned that you can't fix people's problems. Who am I to know what people should do? They are often between a rock and a hard place. How do you tell them what to do? Bail money was a question because the family wants them home, but there are a lot of ethical issues. Bail money is $200, $300, $400. What if you say no and don't help, and that person gets stabbed in jail? That's on your head. Or, on the other hand, what if you contribute the money and the guy comes home? What if he gets shot? What if he gets in trouble for something else and gets locked up?

I began to think of help as gestures of friendship. Anytime you have friendships where people are in unequal circumstances, then it is a tough thing. In every part of life, it's always tough. I did not take the attitude that it was an experiment. I acknowledged that I can't change the outcomes of events. You do your best for people as you would for anyone in your life. I got job contacts for people. I brought people to Penn and Princeton. The relationships I had with people in the field were real and important in themselves.

What advice would you give a young ethnographer beginning his or her first study?

I think the most important thing is to have respect for other people. You as a writer and as an observer should approach your role with a humility and a respect for people who are letting you into their lives. You should be open about what you don't know. Find a topic that is really important to you, that you really care about, that is meaningful to you. Write the way you want to read. Think about the books that you love and try to emulate that. Cornel West has said that ethnography has the capacity to show people having dignity and strength despite all that is thrown at them. You are given a freedom in the university to choose to work on things that matter in the world, to choose topics with moral urgency. You should take that freedom seriously.

Since your book has come out, there have been some harsh reviews of it and criticisms. What do you think about these arguments?

One critique of the book is that it has been reproducing and promoting stereotypes of black criminality—the last thing we need to see is black people doing drugs; in the context of these stereotypes, we don't need another book showing criminality—and that my book is fueling the policies that we are trying to change. When you are writing about poor, stigmatized people, that is something to take seriously. When I first read those reviewers, I got convinced I had done a bad thing. But since then, I have heard from people who have made me think differently. I got an e-mail from a man who said, "I sit in my Silicon Valley office, holding back tears. I want to tell you that you have hit a painful chord of frustration and anger I feel from the police. Thank you for being passionate about a topic that people in the U.S. don't want to think about."

I have heard from people who are the targets of the police, who are poor and in the underground economy. People who are dealing with addiction and violence. People who live with the reality of the experiment we are conducting in mass incarceration. And I think we need to honor that reality. We need to recognize the systems pulling people away from each other.

been written by insiders. Howard Becker was a jazz musician, paying his way through graduate school by playing in a band. He used his insider status to begin studying the world he was at home in, eventually publishing an article exploring the relationship between musicians and their audiences and the pressures that musicians felt to be "artistic" or to "sell out" (Becker, 1951).

Randol Contreras is another insider-ethnographer. Contreras grew up in the South Bronx, a poor neighborhood in New York City, where he was surrounded by drug dealers. He got involved in the drug trade as a teen but abandoned it to focus on his studies. After working his way through community college and earning his BA, Contreras attended graduate school to study sociology. For his dissertation, he decided to go back to his old neighborhood and study the drug dealers. His insider knowledge—paired with his new sociological perspective—generated an award-winning book, *The Stickup Kids: Race, Drugs, Violence, and the American Dream* (Contreras, 2012).

One of the best-selling ethnographies of all time began as an undergraduate senior thesis. In his junior year at Harvard University, Jay MacLeod began doing community service in a nearby housing project. Working with school-age boys, he began to notice how they had very low aspirations for their eventual careers. MacLeod worked in the community for more than a year before he determined that the question of how teenagers develop their future aspirations was a good topic for his thesis. He moved out of his college dorm and into a run-down apartment across the street from the housing project to begin his fieldwork, but he was already a familiar face in the neighborhood and had already developed relationships with the families he would eventually write about. In his powerful ethnography *Ain't No Makin' It*, MacLeod (1995) vividly showed how two groups of teenaged boys—the mostly black "Brothers" and the mostly white "Hallway Hangers"—had very different goals for their schooling and work.

Nearly two decades later, Matthew Desmond worked as a wildland firefighter in Arizona during the summers to support himself through college. Only in his fourth year on the job did he decide to study the firefighters. He was steeped in the firefighters' culture by then, yet when a man in his crew died and his fellow firefighters accepted the death with little or no emotion, Desmond was puzzled. He decided he wanted to understand how the firefighters learned to accept the possibility of death seemingly without fear. The methods appendix of his book *On the Fireline: Living and Dying with Wildland Firefighters* (Desmond, 2007) is titled "Between Native and Alien." In this appendix, he argues that his insider status gave him unparalleled access to his subjects, noting that "to the men at Elk River I was primarily a firefighter and secondarily an ethnographer." His task as an ethnographer was to transform himself from a "native" to an outsider, to question the thoughts and behaviors he had accepted as normal and unproblematic, "to convert my home into an alien land" (p. 4).

Other researchers enter their field sites as true outsiders. Sudhir Venkatesh was hired as an interviewer for a research project at the University of Chicago in his first

A cross that says "Drugs crucify" was erected on a light pole in the Bronx, New York, in the aftermath of drug-related violence in the area. Randol Contreras returned to his South Bronx neighborhood to do participant observation research of the drug trade for his book *The Stickup Kids*.

year of graduate school. He was sent to conduct surveys in a housing project. On his first visit, he was stopped by a gang that held him overnight until the members could decide how to deal with him for trespassing on their "turf." He was eventually accepted by the gang leader, prompting Venkatesh to conduct a long-term study of the gang and its members (Venkatesh, 2008).

Some researchers choose their sites for theoretical reasons. A Marxist scholar, Michael Burawoy (1979), whom we learned about earlier, was interested in studying working-class people and understanding the lives of factory workers. Kimberly Hoang (2015) was interested in gender theory, globalization, and the ways in which paying for sex brings together rich Westerners and poor women from developing countries. She thought the literature on sex work focused too much on the workers and not enough on the male clients. She went to Vietnam and worked in a number of different bars where connections were made between men seeking to pay for sex and women sex workers.

These two different paths into fieldwork—studying what you already know, and breaking into a new social situation—present researchers with different challenges and opportunities. In a classic article, Robert Merton (1972) described these trade-offs as the *insider-outsider problem*. Writing during the turbulent late 1960s, Merton addressed the question of who should study whom, asking whether certain groups have a monopoly on knowledge about themselves. For instance, could white people really understand and write about what it's like to grow up in a poor black inner-city neighborhood? Or is that subject better suited to a black sociologist? Merton pointed out that insiders and outsiders bring different strengths and weaknesses to studying subgroups within a society. Neither approach is "better," but in each case the researcher should be aware of how his or her status influences understandings and access to the group.

GAINING ACCESS THROUGH GATEKEEPERS

At the beginning of the fieldwork, the researcher who is already established in the field faces the task of making all that is familiar unfamiliar. If you are studying a world you already know well, the task of the researcher is to make explicit all the understandings and interpretations that those who are part of the world already take for granted. The researcher has to change focus and examine the field site as an outsider in order to understand and explain the social situation.

Researchers who enter a brand new site as outsiders must first gain access to the site or the group. Often, "getting in" means persuading gatekeepers to allow the researcher to enter the field. **Gatekeepers** are the people with the authority to allow outsiders into (or ban them from) the setting—an employer, the head of a gang, a union boss, a college admissions officer. Some gatekeepers have formal authority, such as an elementary school principal who decides whether researchers will be allowed into the school building, whom they can talk to, and which parts of the school are off-limits. Other gatekeepers have informal authority, such as the most popular kid in the peer group who decides whether an outsider can hang out with the group or the homeless person who has assumed authority in the bus station and enforces rules about who sleeps where. Researchers who are not keeping their identities secret must convince gatekeepers that the research will not harm them, their group, or their institution.

gatekeeper A person with the authority to allow outsiders into (or ban them from) a research setting.

Interacting with Subjects

Once you are in your site, your interactions with other people become a major source of knowledge and data, as well as a source of potential ethical dilemmas. As Desmond (2007) notes, when you are an ethnographer, you become a research instrument. How people react to you, what they tell you, and how you feel in a variety of different situations are all sources of information about the social world you are studying.

EARLY INTERACTIONS

Many ethnographers have noted that whom you talk to and who accepts you in the first few days of your fieldwork can have long-term implications. If there is a feud among factions in the site, you may inadvertently close off contact with one faction merely because the first few people who were friendly to you are part of the other faction. Making contact with a high-status person first can be advantageous because you may get faster access to the whole site, but it may also associate you with those in control and make those at the bottom of the hierarchy suspicious of you. Astute fieldworkers don't worry too much about who does the initial outreach, but they do understand that the way they get into the group will yield a particular type of information and connection at the beginning of the fieldwork. They also work to recognize the biases created by their early experiences in the field, and they seek to go beyond the initial social ties they created at the field site.

Most ethnographers who enter a new site report that the first few days, weeks, and months are very challenging. In effect, the researcher is being re-socialized into a new culture and way of life. All of this socialization is happening to an adult, not to a child. (Usually, we socialize children into our culture and ways of life; adults who are unsocialized are often viewed suspiciously.) Your instincts about how to behave, how to dress, and how to interact with people in the field site may all be wrong, and your task is to learn how to behave as a native would. Alice Goffman offers a poignant example. Months after she entered the field, she agreed to be set up on a date with a young, attractive man from the neighborhood. The date was a disaster as a romance, but it led to a breakthrough in the fieldwork when the young man, Mike, took pity on Goffman and explained all the ways she was not behaving as a proper young woman. In his estimation, she dressed wrong, she acted wrong, she looked wrong, and she behaved like a man, not like a woman. He took her under his wing as his "little sister" and began to school her about how things worked in his world.

Rosalie Wax (1971) notes that during the early days in the field, a researcher is likely to feel "insecurity, anxiety, loneliness, frustration and confusion" (p. 20). The point is not to run away from these feelings (as much as you might want to) but to figure out what triggers them. What does everyone else seem to know that you don't? Why do the people around you think you are behaving stupidly or rudely, when you think your behavior is normal? Feeling out of your element is a sign that you are becoming immersed in a new world. Although it might not feel good, it is normal and a sign of progress.

RELATIONSHIPS BETWEEN RESEARCHER AND SUBJECTS

Not surprisingly, ethnographers hold different views regarding the nature of their relationships with people in the field. Herbert Gans strongly advises researchers to be friendly but not friends with the people they study. He believes that researchers should establish and maintain a neutral and objective position in the field, which means not developing deep relationships with subjects. Remaining neutral helps the researcher behave as an objective scientist in the field.

Other ethnographers argue that researchers cannot help but become emotionally involved with the people they are studying, and that it is common for researchers to become friends and develop strong relationships with their subjects. Describing the homeless women he studied in a soup kitchen, Elliot Liebow (1993) writes, "I think of Betty and Louise and many of the other women as friends. As a friend I owe them friendship. Perhaps I also owe them something because I have so much and they have so little, but I do not feel under any special obligation to them as 'research subjects.' Indeed, I do not think of them as 'research subjects'" (p. xvi).

The differing approaches of Gans and Liebow to friendship and other relationships in the field reflect larger issues in ethnography and its relationship to sociology as a science. The Gans model emphasizes the importance of objectivity and the scientist as a neutral observer who should not influence the social world but rather objectively measure and describe it. This approach is in line with the positivist model of natural science research and its use of the scientific method (see Chapter 2).

Yet, when Matthew Desmond writes that ethnographers become research instruments, he is underscoring the ways in which ethnography departs from the model of the neutral scientific observer. It is in a researcher's own experiences of the stigma of homelessness, the fear of violence in the neighborhood, or the complex thinking that goes into running a drug trade that the researcher begins to truly understand the people he or she is studying. This approach harkens back to Max Weber's idea of the goal of sociology as **verstehen**—a German word best translated as "empathetic understanding." These two approaches to knowledge coexist in social science research, with ethnography aligning more closely with the more subjective Weberian view.

verstehen A German word best translated as "empathetic understanding."

BUILDING RAPPORT

Regardless of whether you develop lasting friendships in the field, you do need to develop rapport with the people you are studying. **Rapport** is a close and harmonious relationship that allows people to understand one another and communicate well. Developing rapport in the field is very similar to making friends in your personal life, but in fieldwork it often involves limiting the "real you" from coming out in your interactions. Your political and personal opinions may be very different from those of your research subjects, and you cannot risk alienating your subjects by being completely yourself. In "real life," we don't necessarily need or want to understand and be in close communication with people who are very different from us, but that is often the goal of fieldwork.

It is important to note that there are ethical implications of limiting the "real you." Even when you are upfront about your identify as a researcher, your research subjects may feel betrayed after the fact, when the study is published. The anthropologist Nancy Scheper-Hughes did fieldwork in a tight-knit town in rural Ireland in 1974. She moved there with her husband and young children and never deceived the people she studied about the fact that she was an anthropologist. She became close to many people who then shared some of their deepest secrets with her. But when her book was published and the town she had given the pseudonym Ballybran was identified as An Clochán, the people she studied felt betrayed. In *Saints, Scholars, and Schizophrenics*, Scheper-Hughes

rapport A close and harmonious relationship that allows people to understand one another and communicate effectively.

wrote about her subjects' sexual repression, the way in which they did not hug or kiss their children and show them affection, and the high incidence of schizophrenia.

In the twentieth anniversary edition of her book, Scheper-Hughes (2001) writes about returning to Ireland to visit her former friends. One of the women she had been close to told her, "There is quite a difference between whispering something beside a fire or across a counter and seeing it printed for the world to see. It becomes a public shame" (p. xviii). Her return visit, 20 years after the initial fieldwork, was cut short when the townspeople decided to banish her, asking her to leave. So, even when you are not a covert participant and are open about your status as a researcher, there is still the possibility that your subjects will ultimately feel used and deceived.

KEY INFORMANTS

key informant A person who is usually quite central or popular in the research setting and who shares his or her knowledge with the researcher or a person with professional or special knowledge about the social setting.

Most fieldworkers report that their research is aided by a relationship they develop with a key informant in the field. A **key informant** is a person who is usually quite central or popular in the setting and who shares his or her knowledge with the fieldworker, becoming a trusted teacher and sometimes rising to the level of a collaborator in the research. These people are central characters in the written ethnographies that result from the fieldwork, and the value of their knowledge and their sponsorship cannot be underestimated.

William Foote Whyte's key informant in Boston's North End was named Doc. Doc took the young researcher under his wing, introducing him around and explaining who was who, as well as the dynamics between the "corner boys" and the "college boys." While Whyte acknowledges his debts to Doc at length in the book, later critics have noted that Whyte's reliance on Doc might have biased his findings, as Whyte adopted Doc's perspective without enough critical distance or skepticism.

Another well-known key informant is Tally in Elliot Liebow's (1967) classic *Tally's Corner.* When Liebow set out to study the lives of lower-class black men, he narrowed his study down to a manageable size by focusing on Tally's friends, who all hung out on the same corner in Washington, D.C. In *Gang Leader for a Day,* Venkatesh's key informant was J.T., the leader of the gang. J.T. was not only the gatekeeper who granted Venkatesh access to the gang but also the lead character of the ethnography, even allowing Venkatesh to take on the role of gang leader for a day—leading a criminal gang and facing the day-to-day decisions that a gang leader must make. Mitchell Duneier (1999) studied a group of poor men who sold books on the streets of Greenwich Village in New York City, and his book on the study, *Sidewalk,* includes an afterword by Hakim Hasan, Duneier's key informant. Hasan tells the story of his encounters with Duneier from his own perspective and chronicles his reactions to the arguments put forth in the book. Unfortunately, there is no magic formula for how to find the key informant. Finding that person is often a mixture of luck and being an astute researcher who is open to following any opportunity that presents itself.

Producing Data: Field Notes

field notes The data produced by a fieldworker, including observations, dialogue, and thoughts about what is experienced in the field.

Field notes are the data produced by a fieldworker. Researchers produce these notes whenever they can—usually at the end of the day or in stolen moments throughout the day. They are the raw materials of the research that will eventually be transformed into a written report published as a journal article or a book.

Especially in the early stages of research, fieldworkers try to pay attention to everything they can because they don't know what will be important when they narrow their focus and produce their analysis later on. Erving Goffman (1989) once told young researchers, "There is a freshness cycle when moving into the field. The first day you'll see more than you will ever see again. And you'll see things that you will never see again. So the first day you should take notes all the time" (p. 130). Over time, you will begin observing the same thing over and over in the field, so your volume of notes will go down. Nonetheless, field notes are a major commitment. One estimate holds that writing up good field notes takes twice as long as the time spent in the field. So, if you are in the field for 4 hours during the day, expect to spend 8 hours that night writing it up.

Field notes are both (1) descriptive accounts of what has happened in the field and (2) analytic notes where the researcher relates field experiences to theory and the research literature. Because fieldwork is a constant dialogue between concepts and theory on the one hand, and the empirical (real) world on the other, it is important that the field notes accurately reflect what happens in the field, which even after a few hours may be difficult for the researcher to remember or re-create. For this reason, you should always try to write your field notes the same day, when your recollections are fresh, even if you are very tired.

What should go into field notes? First, you should include your *direct observations*:

- A chronological account of your observations and experiences

- Episodes—an account of a conversation, an event, or an occurrence that has a beginning and an end

- Physical descriptions—of people, locations, and streets

All of these direct observations should be as detailed and concrete as possible and arranged by date and time. Your field notes should be as specific as possible so that your written ethnography "shows" rather than "tells." A note saying "The speaker's hand shook as he drank a glass of water, his face glistened with sweat, and he anxiously looked at the clock several times" is much more effective than a note saying "Speaker was nervous." Specific details allow the reader to imagine the situation much more clearly than vague descriptions do.

Second, you should note your *inferences* and ideas about what is going on, but you should separate these from the descriptions. You can put these notes in a different Word file or in a different section of your notebook. Some people use a different-color pen or font to distinguish these. However you handle it, it's important to be clear when your notes contain direct objective observations of what is happening and when you are making inferences or conjectures about what you observe. For example, you might describe a classroom interaction between teachers and students in great detail, but then in the inferences that accompany your description of that interaction you might

Field notes, like those shown here from Matthew Desmond's participant observation study of wildland firefighters, should include direct observations such as an account of a conversation.

write your conclusions about the situation. You might note your belief that the teacher was trying to "guilt" certain students into paying attention or that one student didn't raise her hand because she was scared of the teacher. These inferences may be important later when you go back to your notes to understand your thinking at the time.

Ethnography is an excellent method for studying behavior, but it is difficult to accurately record subjects' emotions, thoughts, or attitudes unless you have done direct interviews with the subjects. It is one of the trade-offs of choosing a research method. An interview study can give you direct access to how an individual thinks or feels about a situation or behavior, but you do not get direct observation of how they actually behave. An ethnographer gets to see behaviors with his or her own eyes but does not have the same access to the research subject's thinking or emotions.

Third, you should report your own *feelings* and *reactions* during the day. Were you angry that a student was afraid of the teacher? Did you feel that students were hoping you would come to their aid? Did you remember what it was like to be 16 and bored in a high school math class? Did the teacher remind you of your own ninth-grade teacher? If so, in what ways?

Finally, you should record your *sociological analysis* of the situation. Does it fit with any theories you know about; for example, racial domination or symbolic interactionism? Does it remind you of a passage from a particular book or journal article? These analyses can be as short as a phrase or sentence or as long as a multipage, detailed entry in your notebook. They will be the building blocks of your analysis and a guide to what's important in your study.

Sometimes a researcher is able to take notes during the events themselves; for instance, in a study of classroom dynamics. But often, there is no time or place to take notes; for example, if you are working in a fast-food restaurant or hanging out with a gang on the streets. In those cases, you can jot down reminders of what is important to remember and then spend the night trying to re-create the conversations and your other observations. Of course, ethnographers can work any time of day, and many study people at night. David Grazian (2003, 2008) studied blues bars in Chicago and nightclubs in Philadelphia, writing up his field notes when he could, often the next morning.

Conversations are a major part of ethnographies, and getting them right is a big job. Unless you have recorded people (which you cannot do without their permission), you must re-create the conversations from memory in your field notes. Such conversations typically are presented in the final ethnography as verbatim, but they are almost never direct transcripts (Fine, 1993).

It is not unusual to have thousands of pages of notes at the end of your fieldwork. These notes are the raw data that you must analyze and make sense of, just as quantitative analysts try to make sense of data collected in very large surveys. Increasingly, researchers use qualitative data analysis software (covered in Chapter 16) to bring order to their field notes.

Leaving the Field

While much has been written about getting into the field, far less has been written about leaving the field. Eventually, the time comes for what Lofland (1971) calls the "agony of betrayal"—leaving the field and returning to your everyday life. How do you know it is time? The most widely accepted answer is: when you stop learning anything new—when you've reached **saturation**. This is when your observations are not yielding new insights or anomalies, and your explanation is fitting your findings. Many ethnographers argue that an abrupt end to learning does not happen often. Even after years in a situation, something new and unanticipated can occur.

Nevertheless, the fieldwork must come to an end. Sometimes there is a natural end to a study—the school year ends and the class you have been following moves onto another grade; a social protest ends and the sit-in or movement disbands. Often, there is no natural end point. A researcher might simply conclude that he has learned all he can from the field. The research might have to end because the student must turn in her research paper or the professor's sabbatical is over and she must go back to teaching.

Leaving the field raises a number of practical and ethical questions. If the researcher has deceived the participants and they do not know that they've been studied, how does the researcher explain the departure? Does the researcher come clean and explain what he has been doing? Does the researcher have a cover story for why she is leaving? Often, people feel betrayed when they learn that they've been the subjects of a study and find out that their relationship with the researcher was based on a lie. Carolyn Ellis (1986) spent years studying a group called Guineamen without telling them she was studying them. When she published a book about them, *Fisher Folk*, they felt enraged and betrayed, sharing their outrage with journalists who interviewed them (Allen, 1997).

Even researchers who did not deceive their subjects find it hard to transform their relationships when they leave the field. Sometimes, the subjects feel exploited because the researcher might make money from a book that is published as a result of the research. Jay MacLeod reports that the boys he studied asked him how much money he made, and he felt some guilt about it. Sudhir Venkatesh (2002) writes about the ethnographer as a type of hustler—the gang members thought of him that way because he was using their lives to get ahead in his career and to make money.

Most ethnographers report that even when they developed very strong relationships in the field, it is hard to maintain those relationships after the fieldwork is over and they return to their "real" lives. However, it is very important for researchers to keep their promises to the people they studied. Often, this entails giving them a copy of the report or book that results from the research. Sometimes, as in the case of Mitchell Duneier (1999), the researcher promises the research subjects the right to read and approve of how they are portrayed before the ethnography is published. While this promise may seem noble and generous, it is difficult to fulfill. There is often a long lead time between the end of the research and the production of the book or article. Also, researchers may honestly believe that their own interpretation of events and people is more correct than the subjects' interpretations.

If a researcher allows the people in the ethnography to approve their portrayal, it also opens the ethnography to questions of bias. People will want to be portrayed in the best way possible and will naturally try to cut out any details they think present them in an unflattering light. These revisions can undermine the validity of the study. The most important requirement of science is that it be accurate and unbiased. The practice of giving veto power to people who appear in the ethnography can undermine the reader's faith that the researcher has been true to what he or she witnessed in the field. It can also severely constrain the researcher, so it is not a promise to be made lightly.

> **saturation** When new materials (interviews, observations, survey responses) fail to yield new insights and simply reinforce what the researcher already knows.

Writing the Ethnography

Books that result from participant observation, or ethnography, differ in style and form. They can vary by the intended audience (academic or mainstream), the amount of objective reporting and author's subjective experiences included, and the degree to which they try to be scientific and objective rather than polarizing or opinionated. Van Maanen (2011) and Adler and Adler (2008) have developed typologies that organize ethnographic books according to these differences. We describe here three types of ethnographic writing: realist tales, confessional tales, and advocacy tales.

The most common type of ethnographic writing is what Van Maanen calls **realist tales** and what Adler and Adler call *classical* or *mainstream ethnography*. These ethnographies are often written objectively, in the third person, with most discussion of methods and the ethnographer's role placed in the introduction or the appendix. These accounts confidently describe a "real world" situation, explaining the lives and understandings of the people in their pages. Examples of this type of ethnography include such classics as *Tally's Corner* (Liebow, 1967) and *The Urban Villagers* (Gans, 1962). The first book that Sudhir Venkatesh (2000) wrote on his fieldwork with gangs in Chicago, *American Project: The Rise and Fall of a Modern Ghetto*, was written in this style.

The second type of ethnographic writing reflects what has been called the *reflexive turn* in scholarship. In a reflexive approach, researchers reflect on their own role in the ethnography, recognizing the fact that by their very presence they have probably changed what they are observing. Van Maanen calls the books in this category **confessional tales**, and Adler and Adler call them *postmodern ethnographies*. In this style of writing, the account of the field is very personalized. It incorporates the researcher's thoughts and feelings throughout, and it is almost always written in the first person. Venkatesh's (2008) second book on his fieldwork in Chicago, *Gang Leader for a Day*, was written for a wide audience and puts Venkatesh himself front and center.

The third type of ethnographic writing is what Van Maanen calls **advocacy tales**, or *critical ethnographies*. These go beyond reporting and observing to documenting a wrong and advocating for political change. Tanya Golash-Boza has spent several years studying immigrants who are deported from the United States back to Latin America and the Caribbean. Most of the deportees are men who were either undocumented or who had legal residence but were convicted of a crime that led to deportation. Golash-Boza (2015) begins her book *Deported: Immigrant Policing, Disposable Labor, and Global Capitalism* with her firm belief that these deportations are a cruel way for the country to control the labor supply; that is, by disciplining people in the United States and expelling surplus labor to their native countries. She uses her ethnographic observations to highlight the deportees' misery and make a compelling argument that deportation is harmful and should be stopped.

Desmond (2016) used his ethnographic work on the process and ramifications of eviction to argue that the United States should develop a new housing policy. While the bulk of his book *Evicted: Poverty and Profit in the American City* is a realist tale that documents the eviction experiences of eight extremely poor families in Milwaukee, Desmond uses the last chapter of his book, as well as the results of a survey on eviction that he conducted alongside his ethnography, to argue that the United States should provide housing vouchers for families in the same way it supplies food assistance and emergency medical care.

realist tale A type of ethnographic writing, also known as classical or mainstream ethnography, often written objectively, in the third person, with most discussion of methods and the ethnographer's role placed in the introduction or the appendix.

confessional tale A type of ethnographic writing, also known as postmodern ethnography, in which the account of the field is very personalized and incorporates the researcher's thoughts and feelings throughout; often written in the first person.

advocacy tale A type of ethnographic writing, also known as critical ethnography, that goes beyond reporting and observing to documenting a wrong and advocating for political change.

After publishing his book, he developed a website (justshelter.org) that provides community housing activists with a place to archive eviction stories and to access organizations devoted to changing U.S. housing policies.

CONCEPT CHECKS

1   What role do key informants play in the field?

2   What are the four major elements of field notes?

3   What is the relationship between theory and data in field research, and what role do field notes play in this relationship?

4   How is the researcher portrayed differently in a mainstream/classical ethnography as opposed to a confessional/postmodern ethnography?

CONTEMPORARY DEVELOPMENTS IN ETHNOGRAPHY

In this section, we discuss four recent developments in ethnography—the use of ethnography in business, visual ethnography, team ethnography, and cyberethnography.

Ethnography in Business

Ethnographic methods are increasingly being used in business research. Major technology companies such as Google, Microsoft, Intel, and Facebook all employ social scientists who are experts in qualitative research and ethnography to help the companies understand their customers, explore new product ideas, and monitor how people use their products. At Intel, for example, a team of 20 social scientists, headed by an anthropologist, designed a low-cost, child-friendly notebook computer based in part on ethnographic research on families, children, and schools, and how children interact with computers in different ways than adults (Business Think, 2011).

Google has conducted deep research on mobile phone use. The company designed studies to understand how and why people use their mobile phones. Researchers shadowed people at home and at work, conducted long interviews, watched closely how people interact with their phones in different situations, and examined people's emotional connections with their phones. Who *loved* their phones and could not live without them, and why (Experiencia, 2011)?

One of the aims of ethnography in market research is to understand the cultural meanings people attach to products. How do people come to associate positive or negative meanings with logos, brand names, or specific stores? Why do young people suddenly seem to find a particular style or brand attractive or unattractive? Microsoft employs ethnographers to understand unmet needs that might lead to new products and ways the company can improve its existing products. As one of their researchers described it, Microsoft's mantra is that "technology should conform to people's lives, supporting their existing needs and behaviors, rather than people's lives having to conform to technology, changing their needs and behaviors" (Moisander & Valtonen, 2012, p. 8).

High-tech companies are not the only businesses using ethnography. Many other companies, from Harley-Davidson to General Mills, are studying consumer behavior with ethnographic research. Marriott Corporation hired a team to assess how it could redesign its hotel lobbies to better attract young business travelers. The research team went to 12 different cities and observed how people used the lobbies, bars, and cafés in the hotels. The researchers observed that hotel lobbies tended to be dark, with seating set up for conversations but not for work. They saw a need for small meeting spaces where people could meet with coworkers and discuss business but also relax (Ante & Edwards, 2006).

The federal government has also used ethnographic methods to determine where it is falling short in providing a good experience to people in their quest for government services. The researchers labeled their study the Federal Front Door, and they studied everyone from college students to retirees to understand how people experienced the process of applying for benefits, seeking information, or trying to contact a federal bureaucracy (Chronister et al., 2016).

A new occupation has developed from ethnographic studies of people and products in the computer field. *Usability experts* study how consumers engage with websites and technology to help engineers and software developers design better platforms and improve user experience. The researchers use ethnographic techniques to understand how people experience the products. Their purpose is not to gain a deep understanding of cultural values, motivations, beliefs, and emotions, but rather to improve the machine-human interface.

Visual Ethnography

visual ethnography A form of ethnography that involves taking photos of and filming people in their everyday lives.

Visual ethnography involves taking photographs of and filming people in their everyday lives. Reality television provides many examples of what it feels like to be filmed during everyday life. Shows such as *Survivor,* which puts people in extreme situations with strangers and then films them night and day, exist alongside shows such as *Big Brother* or *Naked and Afraid*, which also assemble groups of strangers and follow them over time. While such shows are not about social research but rather about entertainment, they have normalized the idea of constant surveillance.

Researchers are increasingly using similar techniques to study people in their natural habitats. A team of anthropologists from the University of California, Los Angeles, filmed 32 dual-earner, middle-class families between 2002 and 2005, amassing 1,540 hours of videotape. The researchers were then able to analyze questions such as: How much time do the wife and husband spend on housework? What are the sources of conflict in the home? How do parents interact with their children? A researcher roamed the houses of the volunteer families and filmed at 10-minute intervals. Families told journalists that they became used to the cameras and felt like they acted as normally as possible while they were being taped (Carey, 2010).

Thomas Espenshade, a sociologist at Princeton University, is also directing a video ethnography project. He is planning to install "baby cams" in a sample of family homes, stratified by race and class, to collect video and audio data on these families' strategies for raising children. Scholars know that the achievement gap in educational outcomes by race and class has been stubbornly persistent. Children from different social classes start school with very different levels of vocabulary and behaviors. Middle-class children have a head start, and working-class and poor kids often never catch up. Espenshade and his team will be using video cameras to try to understand how child-rearing varies by social class, not by asking people what they do but by analyzing how parents behave with and talk to their children. These video ethnographies open up private lives to social science scrutiny in ways ethnographers could not accomplish in person.

Team Ethnography

While ethnographers are sometimes represented as loners who march to a different drummer, there have always been **team ethnographies**, which are conducted by two or more scholars working together. The study that led to the publication of *When Prophecy Fails* (Festinger, Riecken, & Schacter, 1956) could not have been accomplished by one researcher alone; a team was necessary to cover the two sites where the cult's members were gathering for news from the supernatural beings. Another classic ethnography, *Boys in White*, a study of medical students, was conducted by a team of ethnographers who studied different aspects of the medical school experience (Becker et al., 1961).

In recent years, teams of ethnographers have been embedded in larger studies, providing ethnographic insights into questions that are also addressed by surveys, field experiments, and in-depth interviews. Mary Waters was part of a study of second-generation Americans living in New York City: The full study involved a telephone survey of a probability sample of young adults whose parents had immigrated to the United States, in-depth interviews with a subsample of respondents, and eight ethnographies in different parts of the city. The ethnographies explored some of the same issues on which the survey and the interviews focused—identification as an American or with their parents' native country, encounters with racism and exclusion, language use, and preferences for ethnic or American food and music. The surveys and the interviews focused on individuals, while the ethnographies examined communities and how people from different backgrounds interact with one another.

The ethnographers chose sites throughout the city for their fieldwork and met with the leaders of the overall study (Kasinitz et al., 2008) every week for more than a year. In this way, the ethnographies were informed by the survey results that were just being analyzed, and the in-depth interviewers were sensitized to issues that came up in the surveys and the ethnographies. The ethnographers studied community colleges, unions, retail stores, churches, and political parties (Kasinitz, Mollenkopf, & Waters, 2004). This kind of ongoing back-and-forth between ethnography and other methods can enrich findings across different approaches and is a good example of **triangulation**.

Cyberethnography

The study of online life is called **cyberethnography**, or **netnography** (Kozinets, 2015). As we spend more and more of our lives online, the study of how we behave in online communities has matured. Serious ethnographers have begun to examine the online world. Eiko Ikegami (2013) has been studying how people with autism are able to experience a different social reality through avatars—or online personalities who live and interact in "virtual worlds." The question of the extent to which the study of online life is the same as the study of "real life" remains unresolved (Wilson & Peterson, 2002).

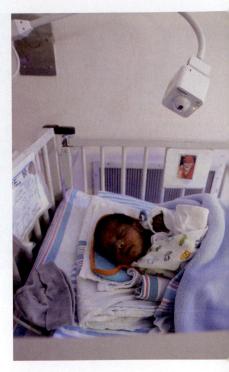

Visual ethnography is being used to study how families interact with and talk to their children in their private homes.

team ethnography An ethnography conducted by two or more scholars working together.

triangulation The use of multiple research methods to study the same general research question and determine if different types of evidence and approaches lead to consistent findings.

cyberethnography, or netnography A form of ethnography focused on the study of online life.

Cyberethnographies study online life, such as the interactions and culture found in the online video game *World of Warcraft*.

Communities form online through chat rooms and discussion boards. Followers of blogs interact with one another, as do players of online video games such as *Second Life* or *World of Warcraft*. Distinctive cultures develop around online behavior. Communicating IN ALL CAPS is seen as rude, lurking (reading comments and posts without participating or introducing oneself) is frowned upon in some venues, and online communities often have moderators who enforce the rules. How do these rules develop and become accepted? How do online communities deal with disruptive participants—or "trolls"—who do not follow the rules? Under what circumstances do online relationships become offline ones?

In an online community, the data are the online postings, and the researcher takes field notes on what he or she observes, connecting those observations to analytic interpretations. Issues of sampling are quite important because Internet communities can self-segregate, and there are so many online forums that it is hard to know whether one has covered the most important or influential ones. While ethnographies do not strive for representativeness the way that a survey does, it is important for researchers to determine whether they are observing a rare phenomenon or a common phenomenon. (This is a critical question in all ethnography.) In addition, because the online researcher has access only to the communications posted online, he or she does not know whether people are being honest about who they are and what they believe.

Lurking or analyzing online behavior without telling people they are being studied presents an ethical quandary for researchers. Most online communities are open; anyone can become a member, post comments, and take part in conversations. Nevertheless, people who are involved in ongoing discussions in communities that are based on shared circumstances, such as bereavement communities or support groups for people diagnosed with serious illnesses, often assume that others will not repeat their comments. They also may believe that they are posting or participating anonymously. If they disclose their identities, they may expect others to respect their confidentiality. But these are just assumptions. Sometimes people inadvertently leave clues about their identities in online discussion groups. And sometimes others will "out" them, violating their confidentiality. Are researchers violating people's privacy by studying these interactions? Should researchers seek permission from anonymous Internet users to quote them in a research study? These issues are far from settled.

CONCLUSION

Ethnography was one of the very first methods adopted by sociologists and is still a strong tool in the social scientist's toolbox. It may be closer to the *art* than the *science* of research in that it is a highly personal method—depending in great part on the people skills of the researcher and on the ability of the researcher through his or her writing to bring the reader into a different world. Yet, ethnographers, as we have shown in this chapter, follow important methodological steps in order to contribute to a scientific understanding of the social world. In that way, good ethnography is very different from journalistic description. When done well, ethnography can provide the reader with an empathetic understanding of other human beings and their social worlds—providing a window into lives and situations that lie beyond a reader's own experiences. Because it can be so accessible, ethnography is often the method used in the sociological texts that become best sellers and that bring new students into the study of sociology. Today's *Gang Leader for a Day* and *On the Run* join yesterday's *Tally's Corner* and *Street Corner Society* in bringing a sociological analysis and a sharp lens to the study of the social world. As a technique that is accessible to a beginning researcher, ethnography is also a tool that students can practice as they learn a sociological approach to society.

End-of-Chapter Review

Summary

Ethnographers fully immerse themselves in the lives and social worlds of their subjects. While ethnography is a highly personal method, researchers follow important methodological steps in order to contribute to a scientific understanding of the social world.

Ethnography: Historical Roots

- Ethnography has its roots in anthropology. Historically, anthropologists studied other cultures, whereas sociologists focused on understanding their own cultures.
- This stark division of labor has since faded, partly due to globalization. Today, these fields are less differentiated by location than by the tools and foci of their work.

The Diverse Roles of the Ethnographer

- Researchers can adopt one of four roles when conducting fieldwork: complete participant, participant observer, observer, and covert observer.
- As a complete participant, researchers fully immerse themselves in their field sites and do not reveal their identity as researchers to the people they are studying.
- The most common role is participant observer. Researchers reveal their identity to most of their subjects while still fully immersing themselves in the setting.
- In the role of observer, a researcher tells people they are being studied but doesn't participate in their lives.
- Covert observers do not tell the research subjects that they are being observed.

What Topics Do Ethnographers Study?

- Community and neighborhood studies, especially of large urban areas, are common topics. They explain how communities develop and change, and how neighbors interact.
- Ethnography is also used to study organizations, deviant subcultures, and marginalized groups.

Theory and Research in Ethnography

- Researchers don't agree on the role theory should play in ethnography. Some argue that theories should emerge from fieldwork (grounded theory approach), while others say that ethnographic research should begin with a theory that can then be explored in the field (extended case study approach).
- While reliability is not a strength of ethnography, it has strong external validity.

Conducting an Ethnographic Field Study

- When conducting an ethnographic field study, there are six main steps: choosing a topic, negotiating access, interacting with subjects, producing data, leaving the field, and writing the ethnography.
- Some researchers choose a promising site and then develop a question, while others start with a question and then find a site to investigate it. The process of gaining access is dependent on whether the researcher is an insider or an outsider.
- The people with whom an ethnographer interacts during the early days of fieldwork can have long-term implications. Most fieldworkers get help from key informants.
- Field notes are the raw material that will become the ethnography. They should include direct observations, inferences, feelings and reactions, and analyses.
- Ethnographies can take different forms, including realist tales, confessional tales, and advocacy tales.

Contemporary Developments in Ethnography

- Ethnography is increasingly being used in business research to help companies learn about their customers and how they use existing products as well as to develop new products.
- Visual ethnography uses photos and film to study people in their natural habitats.
- Cyberethnography is the study of online life.

Key Terms

advocacy tale, 332

cognitive dissonance, 309

community studies, 314

complete participant, 307

confessional tale, 332

covert observer, 313

cyberethnography, or netnography, 335

extended case study approach, 317

field notes, 328

gatekeeper, 325

globalization, 305

going native, 308

grounded theory, 317

Hawthorne effect, 312

informed consent, 310

key informant, 328

observer, 312

participant observation, or ethnography, 304

participant observer, 310

purposive sampling, 321

rapport, 327

reactivity, 309

realist tale, 332

saturation, 331

subculture, 305

systematic observation, 313

team ethnography, 335

triangulation, 335

verstehen, 327

visual ethnography, 334

Exercise

Attend a college or youth sports event as a participant observer. Pay attention to the team, the venue, the interactions among the players and coaches, and the fans and people working or volunteering at the game. Take field notes while you are observing (and afterwards) and then write a three-page analysis of the game from a sociological perspective.

Observing

- Examine this game and the rituals surrounding it with fresh eyes, as if you have never seen a game like this before. Who is there? What unwritten and unspoken assumptions does everyone share? What kind of rules do people know to follow, and what happens when someone breaks a rule? (For instance, do people know where to sit or stand, when to cheer, and what to say when they cheer? How do they know those things?) Look for meanings and shared beliefs that seem to matter to people.

- Take notes that allow you to show, not tell. What does the game sound like? Smell like? Jot down these details so that your readers will be able to visualize the scene.

- Can you surmise anything about the gender, race, age, and social-class dynamics at play at the game? Are power relations on display? Do the seating patterns, the kinds of cheers, or the directions on the field suggest who has more power in this situation?

- How does this exercise affect you? Does taking notes make you feel different than you normally would? What is puzzling to you?

Writing

- Summarize your experience. What did you see? Do any themes emerge from your observations? Provide specific examples from your notes to support your answer.

- What strengths and weaknesses did you perceive with ethnography as your research method? Do you think your presence affected people's behavior? What would you have wanted to ask people if you were interviewing them about their behaviors at the game?

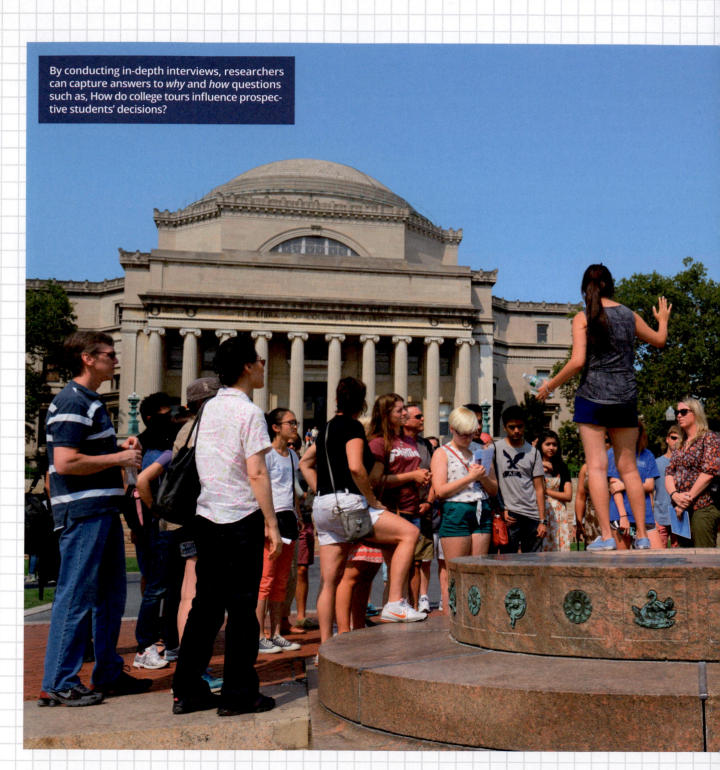

By conducting in-depth interviews, researchers can capture answers to *why* and *how* questions such as, How do college tours influence prospective students' decisions?

IN-DEPTH INTERVIEWING

In the United States, college is not only a rite of passage but also big business. You may wonder:

- How do millions of high school seniors sort themselves into the 4,168 colleges and universities in the United States?

- What factors influence a young person to choose one college over another?

- At what point in high school do teens start thinking about their college decision?

- How much do practical concerns such as tuition costs or proximity to one's home or job drive students' school choices?

- How do all of the brochures, websites, visiting days, information sessions, and college tours shape prospective students' decisions?

- What role do parents, guidance counselors, friends, siblings, and teachers play in the decision-making process?

Many stakeholders want answers to these questions. For example, colleges want to know how to spend their marketing dollars, how to train their campus tour guides, and how to structure and pitch to prospective students. Teachers and guidance counselors want information that will help them advise their students. An industry of college search specialists works with families (for a large fee) to help their children decide which colleges to apply to.

Sociologists are very interested in how young people sort themselves into different colleges. The social class, gender, ethnic, religious, and academic ability profiles of colleges differ a great deal, and they also can change over time. Colleges such as Skidmore that started out as women's colleges and then became coeducational struggle with how to increase enrollment of young men when their reputations have not caught up with their realities. Skidmore began admitting men in 1971, but in 2016 the college still enrolled more women than men (61% compared to 39%). How do the individual choices of millions of 17- and 18-year-olds combine to create these social patterns? This question is well suited to qualitative interviewing and focus groups. These research methods allow researchers to study social processes over time, helping them understand the decision makers' subjective feelings and beliefs.

In-depth interviewing is a qualitative method in which the researcher asks open-ended questions to elicit as much detail as possible about the interviewee's experiences, understandings, thoughts, feelings, and beliefs. Usually, the interview is then transcribed and analyzed. In a **focus group**, people are interviewed in a group. The interviewer or moderator poses questions or topics, and the group of respondents discusses the topic in detail.

We begin this chapter with a discussion of the kinds of questions in-depth interviews can answer and then outline the three main types of in-depth interviews. After providing an overview of the steps involved in an in-depth interview study, we address issues surrounding validity and reliability. We conclude with a brief discussion of focus groups.

in-depth interviewing A qualitative method in which the researcher asks open-ended questions to elicit as much detail as possible about the interviewee's experiences, understandings, thoughts, feelings, and beliefs.

focus group A group interview, led by a moderator, on a specific topic.

WHAT TOPICS DO INTERVIEWERS STUDY?

As with all methods, it is important to match the method with the research question. In-depth interviews cannot answer questions about how prevalent or widespread an attitude, belief, or behavior is. For instance, interviews are not well suited to answering the question "How many working-class high school students versus middle-class students apply to selective colleges?" or "How many students apply to colleges outside their home states?" In-depth interviews are not generally based on probability samples and so researchers cannot generalize from the sample to the population.

However, in-depth interviewing is a good method to answer *how* or *why* questions, such as:

- How does a working-class student learn about colleges, and how does he or she determine which schools to apply to?

- Why do some students refuse to consider colleges outside of their home states while other students welcome the chance to apply to faraway schools?

- How do students learn about colleges, and do different kinds of students pursue some sources of information (website discussion forums) and disregard others (glossy brochures)?

- Are applicants attracted to a school because of winning athletic teams, the food in the dining hall, or the average class size?

Researchers have used in-depth interviews to study many different topics beyond college-choice decisions. These topics include family life and social roles in marriage (Hochschild, 1997; Komarovsky, 1967); how people learn to smoke marijuana (Becker, 1953); how women choose work or family (Gerson, 1986, 2011); how parents raise their children (Lareau, 2003); how poor families live on welfare (Edin & Lein, 1997); why women have babies when they are not married (Edin & Kefalas, 2011); what it's like to grow up in rural America (Carr & Kefalas, 2009); the meanings of racial and ethnic identities (Jimenez, 2010; Lacy, 2007; Roth, 2012; Waters, 1999); how organizational disasters such as the space shuttle *Challenger* tragedy unfold (Vaughan, 1996); how criminals come to stop engaging in crime (Sampson & Laub, 1993); how losing a parent affects adult children (Umberson, 2003); and why doctors are reluctant to tell terminally ill patients how long they have left to live (Christakis, 1999).

Businesses and nonprofit organizations also use in-depth interviews in their research. Businesses such as Google have large internal research divisions, and in-depth interviews are one of the tools they use to study how people use computers and mobile devices. They have interviewed people about sharing mobile phones, their knowledge of and attitudes about online security issues, and their online education and research skills (DeLuca et al., 2016; Matthews et al., 2016; Russell, 2015). Frame-Works Institute is an independent nonprofit organization that does in-depth interview research to identify the most effective ways to frame social and scientific issues. For instance, FrameWorks discovered through their research that people are more likely to think climate change is an important issue if they hear about its possible effects on their own health rather than the effects on the environment. They also learned that framing the issue of immigration in terms of families is more effective than appeals to justice for different racial and ethnic groups (O'Neil, Kendall-Taylor, & Nall Bales, 2014).

Using in-depth and cognitive interviews, FrameWorks studies the metaphors and frames that people use to interpret the world and advises policy makers, scientists, and nonprofit leaders about how best to communicate their work to the public and key stakeholders.

TYPES OF IN-DEPTH INTERVIEWS

While it is often said that survey research and survey questionnaires involve "interviews" and "interviewers," they are quite different from qualitative interviews. Surveys (see Chapter 7) are highly structured with prepared multiple-choice answers or short-answer questions. For this reason, surveys are sometimes called *structured interviews.* Survey interviewers ask questions in exactly the same way with all respondents, and the respondent is asked to answer succinctly even with open-ended questions.

In-depth interviews, by contrast, are much more flexible. There are two main types of in-depth interviews, which differ in how flexible or structured they are.

- In a **semi-structured interview**, the interviewer has a prepared list of questions and follow-up prompts, or probes. This list of questions is called the **interview schedule** (Figure 11.1). In a semi-structured interview, the interviewer is free to ask the questions out of order, ask follow-up questions that are not on the schedule, and allow the conversation to develop naturally and organically.

- In an **unstructured interview**, the interviewer has a list of general topics he or she would like to cover, but the questions and the unfolding of the interview are very flexible and may differ from interviewee to interviewee. There are no preset questions at all, just a list of topics to guide the conversation.

A survey about college choice might ask: "How many colleges did you visit before you decided on a school? How important were those visits to your choice of college (very important, somewhat important, not very important, not at all important, not applicable)?" A semi-structured interview might have a series of initial questions and follow-up probes. The initial questions might be, "Did you visit any colleges? Think about the first time you visited a college; what was that like?" Follow-up probes might include: "Whom did you go with? How far away was the college from your home? Did you go on a tour or attend an information session?"

Note that the question "What was that like?" might elicit a very long response. Interviewees might describe going with their parents, driving a long distance, staying overnight, attending a class, going on a tour, or attending a college party. They might describe how that first campus visit was different from looking at websites or reading brochures. Or they might say that the visit did nothing to change their existing opinion of the college. All of these comments, especially the details about how the interviewees thought and felt, would be food for later analysis. An unstructured interview might just have a list saying "college visit" and would leave to the interviewer the best way to work that topic into the conversation (Table 11.1).

TABLE 11.1 Three Types of Interviews

Interview Format	Example of Questions
Structured interview (survey)	Did you visit the college you decided to attend before making your decision? (Yes, No)
Semi-structured interview	Tell me about your first college visit. What was it like? Follow-up probes: Did you go on a tour or attend an information session? What were you most interested in learning about? Did you like the tour guide?
Unstructured interview	College decision making—visits?

FIGURE 11.1 Example of a Semi-Structured Interview Schedule

This is an abridged version of an interview schedule used to study young adulthood in San Diego, New York, Minneapolis, and Iowa.

Introduction: Today we would like to talk about your life as a young adult.

I. CURRENT HOUSEHOLD/LIVING ARRANGEMENT

1. Please tell me about your present living situation.
   - How long have you lived here? Who lives with you here? (number of persons and relationships)

2. Since you left high school, where have you lived and with whom? (when: approximate years?)

3. Tell me about your community/neighborhood *(or principal place where you live, if group quarters)*.
   - What is it like to live here (best/worst things)?
   - How did you come to live here? Why did you choose this place/neighborhood?
   - What are the people like? Are you close to your neighbors? Can you count on them?
   - Are you near family? Who?
   - Do you feel safe? Is crime a problem? Is alcohol or drug abuse a problem?
   - Do you make use of schools, churches, recreation, entertainment, medical facilities, shopping, child care, or other services in the area? Can people your age find affordable housing?
   - How would you compare your community/neighborhood to others nearby?
   - Is your community/neighborhood getting better or worse? How?

4. Did you grow up here? If not, can you describe where you grew up? How is it different or similar?
   - What were the best/worst things about where you grew up?
   - Why did you leave the community/neighborhood you grew up in? Do you ever want to move back home/to your old neighborhood? Why?
   - What place feels most like "home" to you?

Source: Waters et al., 2011.

In addition to semi-structured and unstructured interviews, the qualitative interviewing method has several variations, including oral histories, life history interviews, and cognitive interviews.

Oral Histories

An **oral history** is an unstructured or semi-structured interview in which people are asked to recall their experiences in a specific historical era or during a particular historical event. Oral histories provide eyewitness testimonies and are generally presented as edited stories with very little additional analysis. Chicago writer and radio broadcaster Studs Terkel published two blockbuster books of oral histories, *Hard Times: An Oral History of the Great Depression* and the Pulitzer Prize–winning *The Good War: An Oral History of World War II* about the experiences of ordinary Americans during these two important historical events (Terkel 1970, 1984). Oral histories have also been used to document popular culture; for instance, a video-taped oral history series of major rock musicians such as Chuck Berry, Grace Slick, and Art Garfunkel conducted by the Rock and Roll Hall of Fame, as well as oral histories of iconic television shows such as *Saturday Night Live* and *The Daily Show* (Smith, 2016).

Oral histories tend to be more informal and more open-ended than in-depth qualitative interviews. Oral histories are not collected to develop social science theory or to test or generate hypotheses about a social phenomenon. Rather, their

oral history An unstructured or semi-structured interview in which people are asked to recall their experiences in a specific historical era or during a particular historical event.

goal is to preserve the stories of individual people. Historians or other researchers may or may not analyze these stories. One limitation of an oral history is the possibility of recall bias. Just as there is retrospective recall bias in surveys, where people either do not remember the past or reconstruct the past in such a way that confirms their current self-beliefs, oral histories are also shaped by memory. This can be a problem if the researcher is relying on the oral histories to provide a factual account of an event or experience. However, these biases and subjective understandings can also be a resource in the hands of a skilled analyst. While an older veteran's recall of his heroism in war may or may not be accurate, the account is still a valuable source of information about the kinds of behaviors soldiers value and praise.

Since 2003, oral histories do not require review by campus institutional review boards (IRBs; see Chapter 3). The ruling by the Office for Human Research Protections established that oral histories are not designed to contribute to "generalizable knowledge" in the way that other in-depth interviews are. Instead, they focus on preserving an individual account of history and are thus exempt from review by an IRB.

A number of online repositories house oral history interviews, some of them conducted by historians, but many conducted by family members, friends, volunteers, and the interviewed individuals themselves. The American Folklife Center of the Library of Congress is an excellent repository of oral histories, including the Civil Rights History Project and the Veterans History Project. For the Civil Rights History Project, more than 100 video interviews were conducted between 2000 and 2013. Many of them are available online. The Veterans History Project has collected firsthand accounts of U.S. veterans from World War I up through the wars in Afghanistan and Iraq. More than 100,000 veterans and civilians who served in a support role to the armed services have been interviewed, and collection is ongoing.

StoryCorps is another ongoing collection of interviews, but it is not focused on a particular experience or historical period. Founded in 2003, this independent nonprofit organization has collected more than 45,000 interviews with nearly 90,000 people. Its stated mission is "to remind one another of our shared humanity, strengthen and build the connections between people, teach the value of listening, and weave into the fabric of our culture the understanding that every life matters. At the same time, we will create an invaluable archive of American voices and wisdom for future generations." StoryCorps is not trying to do research per se, but rather to preserve the stories that Americans currently find important. Story themes include friendship, growing up, identity, gay and lesbian life, life in the military, work, teachers, memory loss, wisdom, and struggle.

Another well-known oral history archive is the USC Shoah Foundation Institute for Visual History and Education. This site archives 54,000 audiovisual testimonies of victims and witnesses to the Holocaust as well as the 1994 Rwandan genocide and the 1937–1938 Nanjing Massacre in China.

The goal of oral history interviews, such as those collected by StoryCorps, is to preserve the stories of individual people.

Life History Interviews

Life history interviews are designed for research purposes, not just for preserving the past. They are used to understand the **life course**—how lives unfold over time, or the timing and sequencing of important life events such as leaving home, marriage, the death of a parent, becoming a parent, occupational choice, retirement, and other turning points in individual lives.

Two excellent examples of life history interviews are Glen Elder's (1974) *Children of the Great Depression* and Robert Sampson and John Laub's (1993) *Crime in the Making*. Elder wanted to study the lifelong effects of growing up during the Great Depression and how early economic adversity affects people during their youth, middle age, and old age. He began his longitudinal study of 167 youths in Oakland, California, in 1931 and conducted more than 12 hours of in-depth interviews at different points in each participant's life cycle to understand how growing up during the Great Depression affected people in both the short and long term. Although many were impoverished as children, most of the men served in World War II, and the men and women raised their children in the growing affluence of postwar America. His main finding was the incredible resilience of this generation. Despite experiencing great deprivation, many of the youth from poor families were driven to overcome their poverty and successfully achieved socioeconomic stability and affluence by midlife. This generation came to be known as the "Greatest Generation" because of their sacrifices during World War II and their postwar prosperity. Elder's work identifies the roots of that greatness in their childhood and adolescent responses to adversity.

Sampson and Laub (1993) took over a panel study that began tracking subjects during their childhoods in the late 1930s. The original study, led by the husband-wife research team of Sheldon and Eleanor Glueck, tracked 1,000 disadvantaged boys, half of whom were already juvenile delinquents, and the other half at risk of delinquency (Glueck & Glueck, 1950, 1968). The Gluecks interviewed the boys at ages 14, 25, and 32. They also conducted interviews with family members, teachers, neighbors, and employers, and they obtained detailed notes from psychiatric and physical assessments and agency records. (Today, an IRB would require the researchers to obtain the respondents' permission to access all of these records.)

After finding all these research materials in boxes at the Harvard Library, Sampson and Laub digitized them and analyzed them using modern statistical techniques. Their 1993 book *Crime in the Making* challenged earlier theories that viewed deviance as inherent, and instead found that criminal behavior changes over the life course in response to one's social roles and relationships. For instance, marriage and steady employment helped many of the formerly delinquent men quit criminal behavior as they moved into adulthood. Sampson and Laub continued the original study by locating and conducting in-depth interviews with 52 of the original study participants,

life history interview An in-depth interview used to understand how lives unfold over time, the timing and sequencing of important life events, and other turning points in individual lives.

life course The study of human development over the life span, taking into account how individual lives are socially patterned and affected by historical change.

Glen Elder conducted life history interviews with people who grew up during the Great Depression in order to better understand the short-term and long-term effects of economic adversity.

who were now elderly men in their seventies (Laub & Sampson, 2003). These life history interviews covering 50 years of the men's lives provided a rich understanding of the mechanisms by which some men were able to leave crime behind and become responsible members of the community. They found "turning points" that moved the men away from a life of crime—marriage, military service, school, work, and residential change. This research is now recognized as one of the most important studies of how people move in and out of crime over time.

Cognitive Interviews

Used primarily to design or make sense of survey questions, **cognitive interviews** ask people to reflect out loud on their thinking as they answer a survey question. The researcher can ask probes or follow-up questions to identify any confusion or inconsistencies in the responses. Cognitive interviews can also uncover new responses that researchers did not think of when designing multiple-choice response categories. Through cognitive interviews, people who design, analyze, or interpret survey questions can better understand whether respondents are answering the question the way the researchers had intended. As mentioned in Chapter 7, cognitive interviewing can be very helpful in pretesting a survey, but it can also be used as a stand-alone technique to uncover how respondents think about particular questions or concepts.

The U.S. Census Bureau has used cognitive interviews to learn how people will understand and respond to questions on the census. The Census Bureau asked same-sex couples how they would answer a relationship question on the census. Many wanted the term *spouse* to be an option, rather than *husband* or *wife*. The researchers also used cognitive interviewing to test a combined race and ethnicity question that allowed respondents to select multiple categories if they identify as "multiracial or multiethnic." The researchers wanted to learn whether people who identify as multiethnic or multiracial would in fact select multiple category boxes. One respondent who was both Chilean and Peruvian helped researchers understand why the terms *multiracial* and *multiethnic* are potentially problematic. When given the opportunity to choose Hispanic as well as other racial categories, this respondent only selected Hispanic. He explained his thinking: "The instruction said that I could pick multiple boxes if I was multiethnic or multiracial. I'm not. My ethnicity is Hispanic, and my race is white." He then explained that he chose Hispanic over white because he identifies more as a Hispanic and "wants the Census to know we're here" (Smirnova & Scanlon, 2013, pp. 19–20). Notably, the term *Hispanic* was actually invented by the Census Bureau for the census of 1970, and it has taken a while for people to fully identify with it. Many people prefer *Latino* because it is a Spanish term. The census was subsequently revised in order to give people the choice of "Hispanic or Latino."

CONCEPT CHECKS

1   What are two main differences between semi-structured and unstructured interviews?

2   How is an oral history interview different from a life history interview?

3   How does a cognitive interview help a survey researcher design a closed-ended survey?

HOW TO CONDUCT AN INTERVIEW STUDY

Successful interviewing encompasses several important steps:

1. Deciding whom to interview and how many people to interview.
2. Writing and pretesting the interview schedule.
3. Conducting the interviews.
4. Recording and transcribing the interviews.
5. Coding the responses.
6. Analyzing and writing the results.

We discuss the first four steps in this section and the final two steps in Chapter 16.

Sampling: Deciding Whom to Interview

The first step in conducting in-depth interviews is deciding whether you are seeking *informants* or *respondents*. **Informants** are people who have special knowledge about a research question because of their social or professional position. **Respondents** are ordinary people you are seeking to learn from.

For example, in a study of immigrants in a small town, the researcher might have two or three very different samples. The first would be people who are in a position to provide specialized information; for example, the mayor, leaders of immigrant organizations, the principal of the local high school, the director of a health-care agency that provides care to immigrants, and local religious leaders. Because these people have either a specialized or a bird's-eye view of how immigrants integrate into the larger community, they are sometimes called *elite interviews*. (However, this term may be a misnomer, as the interviewees may not be "elite" in the ordinary sense of the term.) Another term that is sometimes used is *expert sample*, because the interviewees are people with expertise in the issues being studied.

The researcher would also want to speak with a sample of immigrants, and perhaps also a sample of native-born local residents, to understand how the immigrants are received in the town. The interviewer chooses these respondents because they fit into the categories of people the researcher is interested in understanding. In most cases, the researcher chooses a sample designed to provide a range of experiences and background characteristics.

CASE STUDY LOGIC

The "holy grail" of most research is a statistically representative probability sample. If every respondent has a known chance of being selected, the sample will be representative of the population, and we can use statistics to infer knowledge about the population from what we learn about the sample (see Chapter 6). However, few samples for in-depth interviews are randomly chosen, and few samples are large enough to be statistically representative of the population. Like ethnography, in-depth interviewing is a form of case-oriented research. And as you learned in Chapter 6, when selecting cases to study, random sampling is not a good idea. Instead, with case-oriented research, it is more effective to use **purposive sampling**, where cases are selected on

informant A person who has special knowledge about a research question based on the person's social or professional position.

respondent The person who is interviewed. Also called an *interviewee*.

purposive sampling A sampling strategy in which cases are deliberately selected on the basis of features that distinguish them from other cases.

the basis of features that distinguish them from other cases. Cases can be drawn for various theoretical reasons. The researcher may draw cases that are typical, important, extreme, or deviant.

Sampling for in-depth interviews requires great thought and care—choosing cases that will help the researcher understand the thinking and behaviors of the people interviewed (Goertz & Mahoney, 2012; Matthews, 2005; Weiss, 1994). Indeed, Small (2009) recommends that researchers think about their interviewees not as a sample of 35 people but as a set of 35 individual cases to be analyzed. **Case study logic** means that each person or case is teaching you something, and your goal is to understand the case or person in detail, not as a representation of a wider population (Yin, 2002).

Remember that in-depth interviews are best suited to answering *why* and *how* questions not *how many* or *how often* questions. For example, we cannot use in-depth interviews to answer the question, "How many high school students will choose their college on the basis of the tour they receive on campus?" However, we *can* use the interviews to understand why some students decide whether they can see themselves fitting into a particular campus on the basis of the tour they took.

Therefore, the best way to choose a sample for an interview study is to **sample for range**—to try to maximize interviewees' *range* of experiences with the phenomena you are investigating. In our college choice example, it would be important to think about what characteristics might influence how high school students decide on a college. Perhaps you think that students with high GPAs and test scores are courted by more colleges and therefore bring more of a "buyer's" mentality to the task, while those with low GPAs and poor test scores take more of a "seller's" mentality. To test your hypothesis, you will want to select a sample of students with a wide range of academic abilities so that you can examine the differences among them. You would also refer to published studies to identify other important characteristics of your sample that might influence their range of experiences.

For example, in a study on race and ethnic identities among West Indian immigrants to the United States conducted by one of this book's authors, sociologist Mary Waters (1999) hypothesized that social class shaped the identities adopted by immigrants. Waters interviewed teachers and cafeteria workers about their experiences with immigration and race in the United States. She built a range of social-class backgrounds into the sample so that she could explore whether class differences in identities emerged. Waters asked whether working-class and middle-class immigrants had different experiences with American race relations that might in turn influence their racial and ethnic identities. This approach allowed her to explore some of the social and psychological mechanisms through which social class affects racial identities. She found that working-class and poor West Indian immigrants were more likely to identify as "African Americans" or just "black Americans" whereas middle-class immigrants reject this label and instead identify as "Jamaican Americans" or "West Indian Americans" in order to signal their differences from what they perceived as lower-class African Americans.

A similar approach was used to study gender identity. Sociologist Christine Williams (1989) was interested in the factors that shape our gender identities—the taken-for-granted things we do and say that make us feel feminine or masculine

case study logic An approach to research in which the goal is to understand the case or person in depth, not as a representation of a wider population.

sampling for range A purposive sampling strategy in which researchers try to maximize respondents' range of experiences with the phenomena under study.

(see "Conversations from the Front Lines"). She wanted to explore how people identify the parts of themselves that they associate with femininity or masculinity and how they convey their gender identity to others. Her ingenious sampling strategy was to sample on extremes—to interview people working in gender-nontraditional occupations to see how they maintained their gender identities in situations where one would not expect to see "typical" men or women. She interviewed female Marines and male nurses; at that time, roughly 96% of Marines were male, and 97% of nurses in the United States were female. The people she interviewed are not "representative" of all men and women, but they are people whose jobs have made them think about their gender identities in ways that most of us do not have to. Male nurses had to figure out how to be

"masculine" yet nurturing and caring at work. Female Marines had to figure out how to be "feminine" yet aggressive, strong, and tough on the job. For example, women Marines were required to take courses on cosmetics and had to wear makeup for some events. Male nurses would emphasize their masculinity on the job by highlighting their physical strength, such as their ability to lift patients on their own.

By interviewing female marines and male nurses, Williams was able to gain valuable insights into gender identity and presentation that she may not have discovered if she had used a sample that was representative of all men and women.

SNOWBALL SAMPLING

The most common method of choosing a sample for in-depth interviews is **snowball sampling** (discussed in detail in Chapter 6). This method involves starting with one respondent who meets your requirement for inclusion and asking him or her to recommend another person to contact (who also meets your requirement for inclusion). The researcher follows the chain of recommendations, always making sure to take only one suggestion for a research subject to contact from each person (Biernacki & Waldorf, 1981). For example, sociologist Karen Jaffe (2008) was interested in how personal identity and body image change after a person experiences a very large weight gain or weight loss (for example, through the use of bariatric surgery). After she found an appropriate respondent, she asked whether the respondent knew another person who also experienced a major change in body weight. The great advantage of snowball sampling is that you are not cold-calling potential respondents, but rather calling them on the recommendation of someone they know and presumably trust, which makes them more likely to consider your request thoughtfully rather than rejecting you immediately.

snowball sampling A sampling strategy in which the researcher starts with one respondent who meets the requirement for inclusion and then asks him or her to recommend another person to contact (who also meets the requirement for inclusion).

As you learned in Chapter 6, snowball sampling is a particularly useful technique when studying hard-to-identify populations such as drug users or gang members. As with all nonprobability samples, the drawbacks of snowball sampling are that you do not know the actual distribution of people in the population and how representative they are. Oversampling people from one social network may also introduce bias, so it is very important to only take one referral of a respondent from each person you talk to in order to maximize variation in the social networks you are sampling from.

CHRISTINE L. WILLIAMS

Dr. Christine L. Williams studies gender, class, and race inequalities in the workplace. She is a professor and former chair of the sociology department at the University of Texas at Austin and is the author and editor of many books and articles, including Gender Differences at Work: Women and Men in Nontraditional Occupations *(1989),* Still a Man's World: Men Who Do Women's Work *(1995), and* Inside Toyland: Working, Shopping, and Social Inequality *(2006). She uses both ethnography and in-depth interviews in her work.*

Williams is well known for the concept of the "glass escalator," which she developed when she studied male nurses, librarians, and elementary-school teachers. Women are often described as facing a "glass ceiling" at work, which means that they can rise only so far in their professions before they get stuck. While there are many female lawyers, the top ranks of partners at prestigious law firms are still overwhelmingly male. In contrast, men make up a small percentage of the workers in female-dominated professions, but they rise quickly in their careers and are overrepresented in the top ranks of these professions. Because of the "glass escalator," men in these professions just seem to get promotion after promotion, even when they are not trying to rise in their careers.

What was your first-ever study and how did you choose a method?

It was a study of women ballet dancers that I did for my master's degree. I chose in-depth interviewing because I wanted to understand the dancers' motivations for participating in this highly demanding art form. Mastering ballet is elusive, extremely time consuming, physically and emotionally taxing, and expensive. A number of books at the time documented the harsh conditions of the ballet world, including the rampant eating disorders among dancers. Given this context, I wanted to understand its attractions from an insider's point of view. I found out that women are drawn to ballet because it provides discipline, structure, and social connections that they felt were otherwise lacking in their lives. I realized that these positive aspects could contribute to the exploitation and hardship that others were documenting. The dancers I talked to were very self-critical, isolated from "outsiders," and emotionally vulnerable—a dangerous situation that was ripe for abuse.

What problems did you encounter?

One of the ballet dancers I interviewed was 15 years old, and I recall that interviewing her was like pulling teeth. She seemed very shy. That made me think that in-depth interviewing may not be a good method to use with adolescents (or else maybe I just wasn't a skilled-enough interviewer at the time).

What is your favorite study that you have done? Why?

I like all of them! I'm the kind of person who talks to strangers on the bus. I'm always curious about what other people are thinking, especially those who have had utterly different experiences than me. In-depth interviewing gives me the opportunity to see the world from another point of view.

What was the worst problem you ever encountered in an interview? How did you resolve it?

My worst experience happened when I was interviewing noncustodial divorced fathers about their relationships to their children. We were trying to understand why many men lose contact with their children following divorce. One divorced dad started crying during the interview. I should have been prepared for that, but I wasn't, and I hurriedly changed the subject. Afterward, I consulted with a colleague with training in social work, and she taught me how to deal with these kinds of situations: Stop the interview, acknowledge the emotion, be sympathetic, offer the person a tissue, don't change the subject, resume only if and when the person is ready.

What advice would you give to students doing their first interview study?

The biggest mistake that first-time interviewers make is to ask respondents to do their sociology for them. Interviews should focus on what is important to respondents. Presumably they've been selected because they have unique experiences and insights. That should be the focus of the interview questions. Applying a sociological framework comes afterward, during the process of analysis, interpretation, and writing.

> " The biggest mistake that first-time interviewers make is to ask respondents to do their sociology for them. "

For example, I would never ask a nurse, "How does your gender impact your experiences in the nursing profession?" That is asking the respondent to be a sociologist. It is my job to figure out how a particular profession or organization promotes or excludes people on the basis of their gender. So I ask instead, "How did you get interested in the nursing profession? What was going on in your life at the time?" Then I interpret their answers through a sociological lens.

What is your reply to the argument some make that you can't trust what people say in interviews; that you have to see what they do, not what they say, because people won't tell the truth?

In-depth interviews are not the best method to record what people do. It's better to use indirect and observational methods for that. If you want to know how much beer people drink, it is far more accurate to count the number of beer bottles in their recycling bins than to ask them directly how much beer they drink. In-depth interviews are the best method for understanding a person's worldview. If you want to know what beer drinking means to people, the only way to find out is to ask them.

Paradoxically, when in-depth interviews are done well, they are filled with contradictions, tension, and ambivalence. Far from distracting lies or untruths, these moments reveal the essence of social life, as individuals struggle to align their experiences with their values and beliefs. In contrast, the pat response is often a misleading response. I always probe those.

But what if people intentionally lie? There are some tell-tale signs. If respondents are evasive, refuse to look me in the eyes, act annoyed, or speak in truisms, they are probably not telling the truth. In these instances, I try to understand why. Maybe they don't trust me because of who I am. As a sociologist, I know that race, class, and gender differences can result in distorted communication, so a good study should always reflect on how the researcher's social location impacted the interview experience—how who you are shaped what you learned. People also may lie because they worry about how their information will be used. Even with the promise of confidentiality, respondents may be worried about protecting their privacy—an important point to consider when interpreting their remarks.

DETERMINING THE NUMBER OF INTERVIEWS

As Small (2009) notes, the most common question a researcher asks in designing such a study is "How many cases do I need?" Most seasoned qualitative researchers believe that you need to keep interviewing until you stop learning new things from each additional respondent, a situation called **saturation** (Glaser & Strauss, 1967). Until you reach saturation, every new interview is teaching you something about the phenomenon you are studying, and with each new interview you either replicate that knowledge or discover new information that you can pursue further. Patrick Carr and Maria Kefalas (2009) designed a study to understand what it is like to grow up in rural America. Carr and Kefalas's study involved interviewing young adults who graduated from high school in Ellis, a small town in Iowa (a purposive sample). They interviewed people 5 years and 10 years after graduation, when the interviewees were approximately 23 and 28 years old. Carr and Kefalas hypothesized that the transition to adulthood would be different for those who stayed in their rural hometowns and those who left, so they made sure to talk with both "stayers" and "leavers."

As they began interviewing people, they learned that there was a third type of person—"returners." These were people who had left Ellis to try living in a different place, but who decided for various reasons that they would be better off back in Ellis. Carr and Kefalas further discovered that the leavers could be grouped into two types: the "achievers" and the "seekers." The achievers were the young people who left Ellis to attend college and who did not return, as they believed they could achieve their best potential elsewhere. For many of the achievers, leaving their hometown was not something they necessarily wanted to do, but rather was a means to an end—being successful and achieving their destiny. If they could have been a successful brain surgeon or actor or lawyer in Ellis, they might have stayed. In contrast, the seekers were eager to leave Ellis behind and experience the wider world. For them, leaving was an end in itself.

Carr and Kefalas realized the distinction between achievers and seekers as they were conducting their interviews. They had designed their study to include leavers and stayers, but they never thought about returners or differentiating the leavers into seekers or achievers until the interviews turned up these categories. They were open to the idea that there might be even more categories, but after 104 interviews they reached saturation. So, at first they sampled for a range of geographic locations, but they later revised their sampling strategy to ensure they interviewed enough stayers, returners, achievers, and seekers. In their book *Hollowing Out the Middle: The Rural Brain Drain and What It Means for America* (Carr & Kefalas, 2009), they traced the different life trajectories of these four types of people in their transition to adulthood. At the beginning of their project, they learned a great deal from each incremental interview. By the end, they had reached saturation and were confirming the typology and theoretical explanations they had developed.

Before researchers begin their study, they often need to budget for the number of interviews they will conduct. In IRB applications as well as in grant proposals,

For their study of rural America, Carr and Kefalas interviewed four different types of young adults: stayers, achievers, seekers, and returners.

researchers often have to specify the number of interviews they plan to conduct, which leads us back to the question of how many cases you need for an interview study. One key consideration is the scope and type of comparisons that will be made when analyzing the interviews. As Glaser and Strauss (1967) point out, "The possibilities of multiple comparisons are infinite, and so groups must be chosen according to theoretical criteria" (p. 47).

To return to the question of how students choose colleges, one could imagine a college conducting a simple study to compare students who visited and had an interview with students who visited and did not have an interview. The college might then examine whether the students' perceptions of their campus visits differed on the basis of whether they had an interview. The comparisons that the college wants to make determines the sample size. For example, if GPA is important, the college would want the sample to include a range of academic backgrounds. If gender is important, then the college would want to have roughly equal numbers of men and women in the sample, and it would need to ensure that the sample includes men with high GPAs, men with low GPAs, women with high GPAs, and women with low GPAs. If the college does not believe that gender makes a difference, the researcher would need fewer students in the sample because the college would be examining fewer subgroups.

Many researchers use a general rule of having at least 30–35 interviews, with 10–15 in each subcategory (Warren, 2002). This is not a scientific principle but one that experienced qualitative interviewers have learned over time. Many researchers reach saturation after about 30 interviews. Some researchers also argue in favor of setting a maximum number of interviews. Gerson and Horowitz (2002) recommend no fewer than 60 interviews and no more than 150, arguing that 150 interviews lead to too much information. Many qualitative researchers believe that the strength of the method is in getting to know your respondents really well and analyzing themes within—rather than across—cases. Many researchers also believe that as the number of interviewees becomes too large, it becomes impossible to really know each of the interviewees and his or her story in great depth (Lareau, 2012). However, this stance is controversial. Especially with team projects, some researchers are collecting and analyzing hundreds of in-depth interviews (Clampet-Lundquist et al., 2011; Kasinitz et al., 2008).

MIXED-METHODS SAMPLES

More and more researchers are designing studies that combine different types of research methods. For instance, some embed in-depth interviews within a larger representative sample survey. At the end of the survey, the researchers may ask individuals if they would be willing to talk in greater detail about their experiences. An in-depth interviewer then contacts the people who said "yes" to schedule an in-person interview.

For instance, Kasinitz and colleagues (2008) used a survey of 3,000 young adults to examine patterns of assimilation and social mobility among young adults who were the children of immigrants living in New York City and its suburbs. The researchers were interested in the educational, career, and financial outcomes of second-generation Americans across a range of ethnic groups and regions. They found that the Chinese second generation, or those young adults who were born in the United States to Chinese-born parents, had the highest educational attainment and incomes, followed by native-born white Americans. The next-highest-achieving groups were second-generation Russians, followed by second-generation South Americans, West Indians, and Dominicans. Native-born African Americans and native-born Puerto Ricans had the lowest levels of education and earnings.

Although these rank-orderings provided a springboard for understanding the prospects of young adults, the researchers also were interested in many other questions that were better suited to in-depth interviewing. For example, did second-generation youth identify as Americans or with their parents' ethnic origins? The researchers recontacted 300 of their original survey respondents and administered a semi-structured in-depth interview that allowed them to learn more about their respondents.

In the first few in-depth interviews, the researchers asked a lot of questions about educational and occupational success. The researchers soon realized that interviewees from different groups assessed their lives in different ways. So the researchers devised a new question: "How would you define *success* for someone your age?" Responses varied widely by ethnic origin. The Chinese and Russians defined success like the researchers did—in terms of education, occupation, and income. African Americans mentioned education, money, fun, material goods, stability, and being their own boss as signs of success. Neither the Chinese nor African Americans mentioned having children or being married as signs of success, but the young adults whose parents emigrated from South America mentioned these frequently and often linked them to the idea of stability. This new open-ended question was a gold mine, yielding important new insights the authors had not previously imagined. This method has since been repeated in a study in Los Angeles (Lee & Zhou, 2014).

CONCEPT CHECKS

1 What is the difference between an informant and a respondent?

2 What is case study logic, and how does it differ from the logic of probability sampling?

3 Why do in-depth interviewers often decide on a sample size after they've begun their interviewing?

4 What does *saturation* mean? How do researchers know when they've reached saturation?

Writing an Interview Schedule

A good interview feels a lot like a conversation between interviewer and interviewee. The interviewer needs to participate enough in the give-and-take of the discussion to make it feel like a conversation to the respondent, but the interviewer also must focus on guiding the respondent to provide information that meets the interviewer's agenda.

The key to an effective interview is a good interview schedule. Unlike a survey, which cannot be changed once it is in the field, an interview guide is designed to be flexible. Often, researchers change the interview guide as they learn more about the research topic through early interviews.

Writing the initial interview guide can be a challenge because researchers have so many questions and might not be able to anticipate how they will flow together. Most researchers begin by getting all their questions down on paper (or more likely on a computer screen) in whatever order occurs to them. Kristin Luker (2008) suggests putting the questions on index cards (or scraps of paper) to make it easier to physically rearrange them.

GETTING STARTED: WHAT DO YOU WANT TO KNOW?

Before you write the interview questions, your first step is to articulate all you want to know from the people you will be interviewing. You will have questions at many levels of abstraction and specificity, and you may find that you write down your overall research question in several different ways. You will likely have a mix of complex questions, *leading questions* (which lead respondents toward a particular response—"How do you feel about the illegal and dangerous activities of the nearby gangs?") and *argumentative questions* (which use inflammatory language or adopt positions that might upset some respondents—"Don't you think only Communists would join an organization like Occupy Wall Street?"). Other questions might be stated in theoretical terms or academic jargon. That is okay; it's all part of starting the process, and you can go back and fix the poorly worded questions later.

In general, you will want to identify leading or argumentative questions and rephrase them to be more neutral. However, sometimes interviewers will use questions that are deliberately provocative in order to get respondents to talk about difficult or highly controversial subjects. In her study of black immigrants, Waters used a quote from another respondent in order to give people permission to talk about racism: "Some people have told me they think African Americans see racism even when it does not exist, what do you think?" While this was a leading quote, it allowed people to talk about a controversial topic they might have avoided otherwise.

ARRANGING QUESTIONS BY TOPIC

The next step is to arrange the questions by topic or subject area. Group all the questions about a particular topic together, thinking about how they might flow in a conversation. How would you introduce the topic? Which question would you need to ask first? Which topic naturally flows from that answer? Because you will likely have several different topics or subjects, you will need to provide what Luker calls "turn signals," or transition markers, to steer the conversation in a new direction. An example is an interview in which you first ask about a respondent's job. As you transition to asking about his or her neighborhood, you would say something like, "Now I have some questions about your neighborhood. How long have you lived here?"

In general, interviews should not begin with very specific questions. Rather, the flow works best if you introduce topics and subtopics with broad questions. For example, you could begin an interview on neighborhoods by asking, "What is it like to live in this neighborhood?" Some respondents will talk for a long time with just that one question.

EDITING THE QUESTIONS

Once your questions are in a logical order with the transitions noted, you can edit the questions. Remember that you are the analyst and the respondent is not a social scientist. Your questions should not use academic jargon or assume a level of knowledge that the respondent will not have. For example, you should not ask if the respondent's neighborhood is characterized by "social solidarity" or "collective efficacy." Instead, you would ask if there was ever a time when neighbors got together to try to improve the city or if neighbors ever accept packages for each other or look after elderly neighbors. You can ask what the respondent would do if he or she saw a teen spray-painting graffiti in the neighborhood. The answers will allow you, the analyst, to decide if the neighborhood has a high level or low level of social capital among neighbors.

GUIDELINES FOR QUESTION DESIGN: GETTING INTERVIEWEES TO TALK

Howard Becker (1998) has a cardinal rule for designing questions: Ask *how*, not *why* (p. 58). For example, you may want to know why high school students are strongly influenced by their tour guide when they visit college campuses, even though they know that the tour guide is only one of thousands of students. But as Becker and many other qualitative researchers have pointed out, "why" questions often invoke a defensive reaction from respondents.

In his famous study "Becoming a Marijuana User," Becker (1953) started by asking people *why* they smoked marijuana. This question provoked defensive justifications for doing something that the respondents knew was illegal. When Becker instead asked "*How* did you first start smoking grass [weed]?" he eliminated the defensive, guilty reactions. Instead, he got the detailed stories he wanted. Asking students *how* they decided whether they might fit in at a college might lead them to tell you about their tour guides, how they related to some and not to others, and how they began to think about the whole college as a result.

Overall, the questions you ask should be open-ended and should elicit stories, not simple answers. They should reveal the complex circumstances and sometimes contradictory thoughts and feelings that people have about the experience. A good question tells interviewees that there is no right or wrong answer. For example, if you are interviewing an immigrant, you might start with the question, "How did you come to move to the United States for the first time?" Or, interviewing someone about their experience in a social movement, you might ask how they came to attend their first political meeting.

In his study of marijuana users, Becker realized that his respondents were more open and forthcoming when he asked *how* they started smoking rather than *why* they smoke.

Kevin Delaney (2012) was interested in how different kinds of jobs led people to think differently about money. His hypothesis was that the kinds of work we do influence the way we view money. He interviewed professional poker players, hedge fund managers, salespeople working on commission, fundraisers, debt counselors, investment advisers, and clergy members. He notes that his research question would not resonate with the people he interviewed:

> It did not take me long to find out that you cannot sit down with someone and begin by saying "So how do you think about money here at your work?" The most likely response to this question is, "Well, what do you mean by that?" (p. 215)

Instead, he had to figure out how to elicit details about the interviewees' work and their relationship to money in a way that felt natural and would get them talking about a topic that Americans are notorious for avoiding:

> After much experimenting, I found success with a pair of opening questions that I would use to get the ball rolling. The first was this: "If you were talking to a third- or fourth-grade class as part of a career day at their school, how would you describe what you do in your job?" This helped respondents give a very clear, concise, and somewhat simplified explanation of what they do for a living.... The second question I would ask was, "Now what does that simplified description of your job leave out?" This question would elicit more complicated and detailed aspects of their job. Often these two questions were enough to begin a very long conversation about money and work. (pp. 215–216)

Another excellent way to get people to talk is to ask for their opinions as experts. Here, the interviewers present themselves as naïve or uninformed. (Of course, very often the interviewer is genuinely naïve or uninformed; that's why he or she is doing the research—to learn!) Nothing will silence interviewees faster than the idea that experts are interviewing them and they might give a "wrong" answer. Judith Levine (2013) studied mothers on welfare and how welfare reform changed their benefits and work requirements. She downplayed her knowledge of the welfare system to get her interviewees to talk at length about their own understanding of the system:

> I played dumb. I pretended I had little understanding of welfare rules and asked participants to explain them to me. After doing so, if they did not mention a particular rule that was important, I began to ask more specific questions about the rule to ascertain whether they were aware of it and what their understanding of it was. This approach both produced a more accurate sense of their impressions of various rules and aided rapport, since it did not seem as if I was the authority testing them on their knowledge. (p. 221)

In a survey questionnaire, the questions need to be neutral, but the questions in an in-depth interview can be much more varied. Interviewers should never be judgmental or try to get interviewees to agree with them, but interviewers can push respondents to resolve contradictions in what they are saying or even to react to others' opinions. When Waters (1999) interviewed whites about African Americans, some interviewees occasionally made racist and derogatory comments. She nodded and probed to get them to talk more even though she did not agree with them. In everyday life, she would have strongly disagreed and disputed the assertions, but in an interview situation she wanted people to open up and say what they really thought. So she led those interviewees to believe that she was not offended by their comments.

Sometimes interviewers dig for more information by asking respondents to respond to another person's opinion. One technique is to refer to fictional interviewees. For example, if a respondent is asked whether the neighborhood has any problems and the respondent does not mention any, the interviewer can say something like, "Other people I have interviewed in this neighborhood say that there is a crime problem in the neighborhood. Have you ever heard that?" Then the respondent is free to agree or disagree with the opinion.

Another option is to play devil's advocate. If a respondent says that he has never cheated on his taxes, the researcher can say, "Everyone cheats on their taxes; maybe you just don't remember the small changes that you might have made." The interviewer's comment may lead respondents to share a corner they cut in preparing their taxes or the respondent may hold fast to the idea that he would never cheat on his taxes. In either case, by pushing against a surface answer and challenging the respondent, researchers get more information.

TRIAL AND ERROR

Trial and error is a big part of figuring out which questions elicit the necessary detail and get respondents to reflect in the way the researcher needs them to. Waters (1999) wanted to understand how American race relations affected West Indian immigrants in the United States. How did people who grew up in a society where the vast majority of people are black adjust to life in a place where blacks are a minority and are often discriminated against? Asking this question directly did not work. Waters adjusted her strategy. She began asking, "When you first arrived in the United States, what most surprised you?" While some West Indian interviewees talked about seeing skyscrapers or even escalators for the first time, a large number of them began talking about being a racial minority and America's obsession with race. Respondents reported their surprise that so many forms—when they applied for a job or registered their children for school—asked about their race. They were not accustomed to being asked for an official race category. This response often led to discussions about precisely the experiences Waters was interested in—how did West Indian people come to see themselves as "black" immigrants in America?

The question also led to a completely unanticipated response that Waters pursued in interviews and ended up writing about extensively. Many interviewees told her they were most surprised by the fact that Americans are not allowed to hit their children when they misbehave. Established West Indian immigrants often told new immigrants about this "rule" during their first days in the United States. The community was very concerned that teenagers would call the Department of Social Services to report their own parents and that teachers would turn in parents to the authorities, who would then charge the parents with child abuse for behaviors they considered necessary to raising decent, obedient children (Waters & Sykes, 2009). Ultimately, Waters found that West Indian immigrants needed to change their parenting techniques to "fit in" in America. She argued that this change in behavior was a powerful part of their assimilation to American life. Waters's simple interview question led her in a direction she had not anticipated before she began her research.

PROBING WITH FOLLOW-UP QUESTIONS AND KEEPING THE INTERVIEW ON TRACK

Probes, or follow-up questions, are very important. Probes should always pursue concrete incidents rather than general states or opinions. For example, if someone responds to a general question about the neighborhood by mentioning crime, follow-up questions might ask what kinds of crime are prevalent in the neighborhood and whether the interviewee or someone she knows has been the victim of a crime; that is, enough follow-up questions to elicit as many details as possible about crime and the many reactions to it by the victim, the neighbors, the police, and the city.

When the interviewee goes off on a tangent, the interviewer must find a way to redirect the conversation back to the main themes and questions. Redirecting a conversation requires skill; the respondent should not feel cut off or disrespected, but at the same time, the interviewer should not waste valuable time and energy (and transcribing costs) on long digressions not relevant to the study. Sometimes redirection can be accomplished easily by asking the next question on the schedule. Other times the interviewer might need to say something like, "Let's get back to talking about this neighborhood and how you interact with your neighbors," which politely makes it clear that the conversation has gone off topic.

USING VIGNETTES AND PHOTOS

In-depth interviews can also make use of **vignettes**, which are short descriptions of characters or situations that are presented to respondents in order to elicit a response. For example, a researcher could present a moral or professional dilemma to a respondent and ask how he would respond. Or, in a study of identity, the researcher could describe people who vary by gender, race, ethnicity, and social class and ask the respondent who is most like him or her. The researcher could then ask the respondent to discuss why he chose a particular person as most like himself. This technique should be used when it is very difficult to make a concept concrete enough to ask questions about it. In such cases, a small story or description can help greatly.

Vignettes can also be used to approach sensitive topics that are difficult for respondents to talk about. In a study of how to prevent mother-to-child transmission of HIV, researchers conducting qualitative interviews and focus groups used a vignette that described the actions of a mother with HIV in order to get respondents, who were HIV positive themselves, to talk freely about the choices such a mother would make (Gourlay et al., 2014).

Photos can be very useful for the same reasons. A picture, it is said, is worth a thousand words. In the world of interviewing, a picture can sometimes elicit thousands of words from interviewees. One approach is to ask respondents to share their own photo collections with the researcher. Family pictures can serve as a jumping-off point for talking about childhood experiences. Sibling rivalries, parental tensions, and supportive extended families are often captured in old pictures, and they may trigger a conversation between the researcher and the respondent about the everyday and extraordinary experiences of childhood and adolescence.

Wendy Roth (2012) used photos to understand the racial categories that Puerto Ricans and Dominicans use to identify people. She interviewed people who had never left Puerto Rico or the Dominican Republic and migrants in New York from the two sending societies. She began by showing respondents people with varying skin color, hair texture, and facial characteristics. Roth wanted to determine whether Puerto Ricans and Dominicans used a North American racial classification, which is more binary (black or white), or a Latin American one, which sees many different intermediate categories. The photos, reproduced in Figure 11.2, allowed interviewees to explain how something they did automatically was actually very complicated and nuanced. A respondent named Ines from Santo Domingo in the Dominican Republic describes the complex thoughts she has as she classifies people into different racial categories:

(1) The race, more or less finer, the race is less negro . . . it's a mix. He's not blanco. Mulatto [or] more blanco than mulatto. (2) Mulatto. (3) Negra. (4) More or less

vignette A short description of characters or situations that is presented to respondents in order to elicit a response.

FIGURE 11.2 Photographs of Different People of Latino Origin

Roth used photos in her interviews with Puerto Ricans and Dominicans to help respondents articulate their thoughts about race.

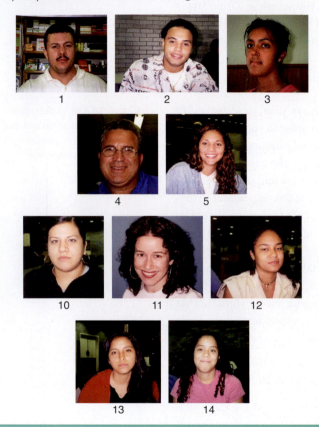

Source: Roth, 2012.

blanco. (5) She's not blanca, she's like india, these people that are neither blanca nor negra. Her nose is very ordinary. She has blue eyes, but she's not blanca, she's not fine. (11) This one is more blanca than fine, than the one with the light eyes (10). You know why? Because of the features, right?

Q: Which features?

[She's] Triguena, more or less. . . . She has curly hair, she has "good" hair, right? . . . Triguena. (12) She's not blanca. This one is negra. (13) India, india. . . . (14) This one is very pretty but she has "bad" hair . . . negra. (p. 21)

Roth was able to use the photographs to get her respondents to verbalize how they classify people differently than native-born Americans. Americans generally classify by skin color into white, black, and Hispanic. But Roth's Latin American respondents used photographs to show her how they used hair, the shape of facial features (such as the nose), and eye color to classify people according to many different Latin American racial categories.

PRETESTING THE INTERVIEW SCHEDULE

Once you have an interview schedule, the next step is to pretest it. You cannot know which questions will lead respondents to speak at length about the themes you are interested in until you try them out on a few people. Some questions will work really well and others will not. You may need to rearrange the order of the questions to get a good flow. Ideally, you will want to pretest the interview with someone who is similar to the respondents you will be interviewing as part of your actual study. But you will probably not want to use a "real" respondent for the pretest. Someone you know well can be a good candidate for the pretest, as they will truthfully tell you when your questions do not make sense.

CONCEPT CHECKS

1 | How are an in-depth interview and a normal conversation similar, and how are they different?

2 | Why are in-depth interviews better suited to "how" questions than to "why" questions?

3 | Name two strategies to get a respondent to open up and talk freely in an interview.

Conducting the Interview

Like an actor learning lines in rehearsals, the interviewer will learn the questions better as he or she conducts more interviews. However, the interviewer should know the schedule very well even before embarking on the first interview; many interviewers memorize it completely so they never have to look at the list of questions. Even if you cannot completely memorize the questions, you should know them so well that a quick glance at the schedule tells you what to ask next.

The first few real, as opposed to pretest, interviews that you conduct will be some of the most difficult but also the most rewarding. They are difficult because interviewing is hard work. You must follow an interview schedule but appear as if you are having a natural conversation. You must actively listen and think about follow-up questions but appear at ease and interested in everything your interviewee is saying. It is in the first few interviews that you really begin to learn about the topic you are studying. You will likely be surprised by some of the answers, and you will probably sense how rewarding your respondents find the interview. Most respondents enjoy in-depth interviews because they get to share their experiences and opinions with a smart, empathetic, and interested person.

RECORDING THE INTERVIEW

If at all possible, you should audio record every interview. Most people are wary of audio recording in the first 5 or 10 minutes, but they usually adjust quickly and stop being self-conscious about how they sound. Recording allows you to concentrate on the conversation rather than on taking notes, and it allows you to transcribe quotes verbatim when you do your analysis (as we will describe in Chapter 16). It is essential that you ask interviewees for permission to record the interview. In addition, IRBs require you to tell the respondent that you will turn off the recorder upon his or her request. Requests to stop the recording usually come when the interviewees want to reveal sensitive information. For example, immigrants may reveal that they are undocumented, spouses may reveal that they have been unfaithful, or women may reveal that they have had an abortion. The best course of action is to turn off the recorder, discuss the sensitive topic, and then turn the recorder back on and resume the interview. Afterward, you can re-create the details in your notes.

Ideally, you should conduct the interview in a quiet place where you will not be interrupted, such as an office or conference room. Sometimes, it is possible to meet in the respondent's home or office, but interviews are conducted in many different places—from outdoor park benches to coffee shops, restaurants, and waiting rooms.

It is wise to invest in a clip-on directional microphone. You clip it on your respondent (perhaps on a shirt or jacket), and it picks up his or her voice even when there is a lot of background noise. Without it, you may find it difficult, even impossible, to hear the respondent when you are listening to the recording. However, if you use a directional microphone and there is a lot of background noise, your own voice will not be as clear in the recording. You may then need to review the interview soon after you've completed it, filling in the questions or any comments you made while you can still remember the interview in great detail.

Every interviewer will have technical difficulties at some point. If you do enough interviews, it will happen. The following tips will help you prevent—or deal with—mishaps.

1. If your recorder has batteries, check them before every interview and bring spare batteries or a charger cord with you to every interview.

2. Do a sound check before the interview begins to ensure that the respondent's voice is recorded properly.

3. After the interview, before you do anything else—before you eat dinner or take a shower or talk to your friends or family—check the beginning, middle, and end of the recording to make sure the entire interview was recorded. If it was, then all you need to do is record your impressions of the interview and other information that might be important for the analysis. You might record what your respondent looked like, how nervous or comfortable he or she seemed, and what the house and neighborhood were like, if that is where you met. You also might jot down notes about improvements to the existing interview questions, potential new questions, or questions that you might want to drop because they are not working well.

4. If you discover that your interview was not recorded properly (and, in our experience, it is always the terrific interviews that experience the technical glitches), then you can usually reproduce a great deal of the interview if you do so immediately afterward. If the conversation is fresh in your mind, you can use the interview schedule to remember and record much of what your interviewee said. If you wait too long, you may forget the details and lose important information.

Often, after the interview seems to be over and the interviewer has turned off the recorder, the respondent may continue talking. The very act of turning off the recorder seems to free people to remember things they wanted to mention in the interview or allows them to discuss a sensitive topic that they did not want recorded. This is another time to engage and listen carefully, and then immediately afterward record or write down every detail you can remember.

PAYING RESPONDENTS

In recent years, it has become increasingly common for interviewers to pay respondents for interviews. Student researchers can rarely afford to pay their respondents, but if a research grant is funding the project, the budget may allocate money for small payments or gift cards to interviewees. Researchers typically provide this payment to respondents at the end of the interview; however, according to IRB rules, subjects still receive their compensation even if they do not complete the interview. If payment were contingent on answering each and every question, subjects might feel coerced into answering questions they are uncomfortable with, for fear of losing their payment. These stipends are not paying people for their time, per se, but rather to cover the expenses incurred by participating in the study, such as transportation or child care. In fact, many IRBs prohibit a stipend that is too high because of the concern that a high fee could be coercive, enticing people to agree to an interview because they cannot turn down a large sum of money. In addition, some respondents, such as prisoners, cannot be paid for taking part in an interview because of institutional rules.

After the Interview: Writing Field Notes and Transcribing

Once each interview is completed, the interviewer needs to take two additional steps: writing field notes and transcribing the interview.

WRITING FIELD NOTES

After each interview, the researcher should write up field notes to capture his or her observations and experiences in the field (Figure 11.3). Field notes for interviews generally include descriptions of the person who was interviewed, the location of the interview, and anyone else who was present when the interview took place; the respondent's demeanor, body language, and facial expressions; how the researcher felt about the interview; and any thoughts about the interview's theoretical importance or how it fits with the overall research questions.

TRANSCRIBING THE INTERVIEWS

After you have recorded the interview and written your field notes, the interview recordings need to be transcribed. *Transcribing*, or typing up the interview conversation

FIGURE 11.3 Field Notes from an In-Depth Interview with a Hurricane Katrina Survivor

Katrina Survivor

R [The Respondent] is a married 22 year old security guard and mother of two who lives with her husband. He is not the father of her boys and she does not plan to have more children because she felt that could get in the way of finishing her nursing school. R had evacuated to Mississippi but has since returned to Small Town, LA.

I interviewed R outside of Starbucks in Small Town from about 8 pm to 10 pm. Originally, we were supposed to talk at 2:30 pm but she was called into work. She went out of her way to meet me in the evening, perhaps because she felt bad about canceling without notice earlier.

R was dressed in her security guard uniform. She works for FEMA guarding FEMA trailers parked at Six Flags. She seems proud of how much money she is making there. She made frequent references to the fact that she makes $17 an hour and how she is saving it and trying to invest in CDs and college funds. This stood out because nobody else I've spoken with has talked about investing in this way. Also, she comes from a low-income background. She was raised by her grandparents after her mother gave her up in favor of being "in the world," which meant partying and going to clubs.

This respondent did not consider herself to be from New Orleans. Having grown up in a suburb, she saw herself as different from New Orleans residents in terms of language and dress. She was also critical of those who received money during the hurricane recovery and did not use it appropriately. She felt that some had literally gambled it away, when they could have used it as an opportunity to better themselves, for example by putting a down payment on a house. Her sentiments resonated with those of [another interviewee] in this regard.

Foremost among her life goals is to finish nursing school. She felt that the only thing that could get in the way was having another child. She was strongly opposed to this despite the will of her husband to have more children. She already has two boys from another man who is not in her life at all. She coupled with her current husband when she was pregnant with the second child. She was pregnant during the hurricane and attributes the stress associated with the hurricane with causing her to go into premature labor.

Although the hurricane had an impact in her life, a major car accident that her husband was in was in some ways more impactful. After surviving an accident which involved his car plummeting off of a bridge, their relationship grew much closer. She now goes to him for advice and to talk. This is a change from earlier in their relationship. For instance, following the hurricane, he tried to talk to her about it and she refused. She felt this may have been in part due to post-partum emotions.

word for word, can be very time consuming if you do it yourself or expensive if you pay someone to do it. As a general rule, every 1 hour of interview time takes 5 to 6 hours to transcribe. A transcribing machine (designed for digital or analog recordings) is very useful if you are doing more than a few interviews. The machine has a foot pedal that reverses the recording by a variable amount of time that you can set. You press the foot pedal to listen as you type, and when you take your foot off the pedal, the machine backs up anywhere from a few words to a few sentences, enabling you to catch up.

Some researchers have opted to use voice-recognition software, which automatically types the voices that it "hears" on the recording (a method known as speech to text, or STT). One limitation of voice-recognition software is that it needs to be "trained" to recognize the speaker's voice. During an interview, two people are talking, and by the time you have trained the software to understand the voice, accent, or speaking style of a particular respondent, you are moving on to the next interviewee (along with his or her vocal idiosyncrasies). Fortunately, there is a way around this constraint. You can train the software to recognize your voice, and then you can listen to your interviews using headphones and speak aloud the interviewee's words you are hearing verbatim, which should be recognized by the voice-recognition software. So instead of typing the interviewee's words, you are speaking them in your voice, and the software types out the text. This technique is also time consuming, but it allows researchers who are not good typists to get all their interviews into written form.

Many experts highly recommend transcribing your own interviews, even if you are not a fast or skilled typist, because the transcribing process brings researchers closer to their data. Experienced researchers also advocate keeping ongoing notes about what you are thinking and observing as you transcribe. We will further discuss techniques of qualitative data analysis in Chapter 16; for now, it is important to recognize that interviewing and data analysis should not be separate processes. They are best done at the same time. While transcribing might seem to be a mindless task, it is not. To the contrary, you may achieve many important insights as you transcribe. After listening to, transcribing, and/or reading aloud a few interviews, the researcher is closer to the material and can suggest new questions, new probes, and possibly new types of people who should be interviewed.

CONCEPT CHECKS

1 What do IRBs require researchers to do when recording interviews?

2 What are a few steps you can take to prevent mishaps when recording interviews?

3 What kinds of observations should you include in your field notes?

VALIDITY AND RELIABILITY IN IN-DEPTH INTERVIEWS

reliability A quality of a measure concerning how dependable it is.

In Chapter 5, we described validity and reliability as two benchmarks that researchers often use to assess the quality of their study, including the measures and sample used. **Reliability** refers to how dependable the measure is—whether you get the same result if different researchers conduct the study again. **Validity** refers to the accuracy or truthfulness of a measure. It measures whether you are accurately measuring what you are studying. Recall from Chapter 5 that researchers differ with respect to the importance they place on traditional measures of validity and reliability, with some arguing that qualitative and quantitative research be judged according to different standards.

Qualitative in-depth interviews are very much influenced by the interviewer. No two interviewers will have exactly the same interview. The hope, however, is that the interviews will achieve high validity. To maximize validity, in-depth interviewers probe respondents with follow-up questions to fully understand their answers. The premise of the method is that the human connection and sustained communication between interviewer and interviewee will produce high-quality, valid data.

However, open-ended interviews can be critiqued on a number of grounds. Researchers who come from a survey research background often criticize the nonrepresentative samples, the ways in which the interviewer's identity and behavior can affect the study participants' responses, and the lack of reliability in that different interviewers could probably elicit different responses from the same respondent. Sociologist Stephen Vaisey (2009, 2014) has argued that surveys are much better than in-depth interviews at uncovering cultural beliefs and values, such as attitudes about infidelity or personal moral standards. Borrowing from advances in cognitive neuroscience, Vaisey argues that there are two distinct levels of cultural motivations and beliefs in people: a conscious level and an intuitive, often unconscious level. Vaisey argues that multiple-choice survey questions are better able to measure people's intuitive, unconscious values and beliefs than an in-depth interview that asks them to think about and discuss their motivations for their actions:

> If talking about our mental processes with an interviewer is like describing a criminal suspect to a sketch artist, then answering survey questions is like picking the suspect out of a lineup. The latter is much less cognitively demanding and potentially much more accurate, provided the right choices are in the lineup. (Vaisey, 2009, p. 1689)

Vaisey suggests that you can better understand people's moral decisions with a survey question than you can with a more open-ended in-depth interview. For example, Vaisey asked teens how they would decide whether to do something their parents would disapprove of. The choices on his closed-ended survey question included statements like "I would do what makes me feel happy" or "I would do what God or the scripture says is right." Vaisey argues that these forced choices between a utilitarian morality (do what makes you happy) and a religious morality (do what God wants you to do) are better windows into moral decision making than open-ended questions in qualitative interviews, such as "How do you normally know what is good or bad, right or wrong?"—a question that teens often have no idea how to answer.

Interviews have also been harshly criticized for their supposed inferiority to ethnography. Critics suggest that in-depth interviews may provide surface comments or rationalizations for behavior rather than a deep understanding of people's beliefs and motivations. Jerolmack and Khan (2014) summarize this criticism when they argue that "what people say is often a bad predictor of what they do" (p. 1). They worry that interview studies assume a consistency between attitudes and behaviors, when in

validity A quality of a measure concerning how accurate it is.

reality people often behave in ways that are the direct opposite of what they say they will do or what they say people should do.

Sociologist Annette Lareau provides a clear illustration in her book *Unequal Childhoods*. Lareau (2003) intensely observed working-class and middle-class parents and children over a period of time. She also interviewed them. While working-class and middle-class parents expressed the same beliefs in "intensive mothering," their behaviors differed starkly. The middle-class parents packed their children's daily schedules with lessons and activities (see "From the Field to the Front Page"), while the working-class parents encouraged their children to structure their own lives and gave them a great deal of independence. Lareau argues that these approaches to parenting were so ingrained, and so taken for granted, that parents could not articulate them in interviews. Instead, she had to learn about them by observing them.

In-depth interviewers have responded to these criticisms by pointing to the ways they assess the validity of their methods. In the interview itself it is important to be attentive to body language, tone of voice, and inconsistencies and contradictions across the interview. If respondents do not make eye contact, answer in generalities, or give contradictory answers, those are clues that they may not be answering truthfully or, at the very least, are unsure of their answers. Interviewers can indicate in their field notes when they think respondents might be giving answers that are not truthful.

In-depth interviewers also point out that the research question itself determines whether the method is useful or not. Different research questions require different methods. Pugh (2013, 2014) defends the use of in-depth interviews to study culture, arguing that a skillful interviewer picks up on nonverbal cues, emotions, and the ways in which the interaction between the interviewer and the interviewee contributes to understanding. Pugh interviewed parents about how they coped with financial instability. One woman who had been laid off told Pugh during the interview that she was okay with being laid off because she had decided to move on and try to find a new job anyway. Yet Pugh heard and saw the anger the respondent felt, and she concluded that the interviewee's surface words were masking a much more complex set of feelings.

The best social science research carefully fits the method with the question being asked. Ethnographers can best describe people's behaviors and whether those behaviors match what those people say. Survey researchers can best describe the prevalence of attitudes, beliefs, and behaviors in a population. In-depth interviews can help us understand how people see and understand the world and the ways in which they think about and process the social world. When the research question and the interviews are well matched, in-depth interviews are a powerful and useful method for social scientists.

CONCEPT CHECKS

1 | What do interviewers gain by transcribing or listening carefully to their interviews?

2 | What are some of the criticisms of in-depth interviewing?

3 | What are some of the major threats to the validity of in-depth interviewing?

HELPFUL OR HURTFUL? PUSHING KIDS TO DEVELOP COMPETITIVE CAPITAL

Are kids over-scheduled? Are youth sports too competitive? The question of whether elementary-school children are too involved in after-school activities is a hotly debated issue. One concerned mom, Lenore Skenazy, founded a movement called Free-Range Kids after she wrote an essay about letting her 9-year-old son take the New York City subway home by himself. She was attacked as the "world's worst mom" on NBC's *Today Show* (Skenazy, 2015), but she later parlayed the moniker into a gig hosting a television show with that title on the Discovery Channel. Other parents and experts argue that kids need activities to keep them active, healthy, and involved with other kids; to help them develop interests and skills for lifelong enjoyment; and to build a résumé for admission to selective colleges.

Hilary Levey Friedman conducted nearly 200 in-depth interviews with parents, kids, and coaches when studying whether kids are overworked from being involved in too many extracurricular activities.

Hilary Levey Friedman's work on children's activities has been widely cited in these debates. Friedman, the author of *Playing to Win: Raising Children in a Competitive Culture* (2013), studied children's youth soccer, competitive dance, and competitive chess to understand why middle-class parents invest so much time and energy in getting their kids to and from these activities. She argues that parents want their kids to develop "competitive kid capital." In a world of economic anxiety, middle-class parents understand that they cannot pass all their advantages on to their kids. They see success in higher education and the labor market as something their children will need to win for themselves. As a result, they think that teaching kids to be competitive and to strive to win at sports, dance, chess, or other areas of life will help them maintain their class position in their adult lives. In effect, Friedman links middle-class parents' attention to their kids' extracurricular activities with income inequality and the precarious nature of the middle class.

Friedman's work has been featured in newspapers and magazines across the country, including the *New York Times, Washington Post, Psychology Today, Slate,* the *Atlantic,* and many others. Friedman spent 16 months following parents and kids to soccer games, chess tournaments, and dance competitions. She also conducted nearly 200 in-depth interviews with parents, kids, and coaches. She determined that parents wanted their sons and daughters to learn five lessons from these activities: the importance of winning and being competitive, the need to persevere after losing, the need to perform under time pressures, the need to be adaptable, and the need to perform while others are watching.

The debate over youth activities became even more inflamed with recent discoveries of the harm that concussions can cause to the human brain. Some experts, including the concussion expert Dr. Robert Cantu, have advocated banning all tackle football for children under age 14 on the basis of studies of NFL players that show that greater cognitive decline is associated with starting to play football at a younger age (Diamond, 2015). While Friedman does not support the ban, she has written that she will not allow her two young sons to play football.

Friedman argues that sports and other after-school activities are generally good for children—to a point. The danger comes when parents become too competitive and drive their children too hard. In one article, Friedman argues that these activities are really a form of "children's work." She points out that child labor laws prohibit children from working 35 hours a week. But some very young gymnasts train more than that. Should the government regulate the number of hours that child athletes can practice each week? Friedman concludes that "just as we protect the safety of children who work on newspaper routes and in the entertainment and agricultural fields, we should consider protecting the safety of children in activities" (Friedman, 2009, p. 211).

FOCUS GROUPS

People do not form opinions and beliefs in a vacuum. Rather, people powerfully influence one another through social interaction. Focus groups are group interviews on a specific topic. They allow the researcher to observe and record the interactions among people and how their opinions or beliefs are constructed through interactions. The method was developed in the 1930s and 1940s by two Columbia University sociologists, Paul Lazersfeld and Robert K. Merton. Lazersfeld pioneered the method during World War II, when he studied American soldiers (Merton & Kendall, 1946).

Since then, social scientists have used focus groups to study a wide variety of topics. Shively (1992) examined how Native Americans and European Americans responded to cowboy movies. Knodel, Chamratrithirong, and Debavalya (1987) studied family planning and contraceptive use in Thailand. Elder and colleagues (2007) studied why people decided not to evacuate from New Orleans prior to Hurricane Katrina. Calvo, Rojas, and Waters (2014) studied attitudes among native-born Spaniards toward immigrants' use of social services.

Focus groups are used often not only in social science research but also in market and political research. Politicians and their advisers use focus groups to identify the arguments or positions that voters will find persuasive; lawyers also use focus groups to test their arguments before they present them to a jury. Advertisers and product developers often run focus groups to understand how people will react to a new product or ad. For example, Disney runs focus groups with preschoolers when developing a new movie or television program. Disney spent 5 years developing a new animated children's program with a hero named Sofia the First. Disney has agreements with Los Angeles–area preschools that allow their researchers to show an episode to the children (ages 2–5) and then to record how they talk about the plot and the characters with each other and the researchers.

At a test of one episode, the researchers learned that the children did not understand the term "slumber party," so Disney changed the phrase to "big sleepover." One girl told the group that Sofia's stepsister was her favorite because "She's kinda mean but kinda nice." The researchers summarize the children's reactions for the writers back at Disney Studios. In this case, they told the writers to make the moral clearer for the youngest children, who did not quite get it. The school got $100 from Disney for allowing the focus group. The kids got Disney stickers (Rosman, 2013).

Two elements of focus groups set them apart from in-depth interviews.

1. Focus groups are intended to capture interaction. Consequently, they are designed so that the people taking part will ask each other questions and discuss topics. Watching people interact allows researchers to see whether the participants have stable ideas or whether they can be persuaded to change their minds. In a one-on-one interview, a respondent might assert a very strong opinion, but that opinion might be very unstable and easily changed if other

Advertising agencies have long used focus groups for market research in order to create the most effective advertisements.

people challenge it. A focus group will usually produce a give-and-take among participants that separates strongly held opinions from lightly held ones.

2. Focus groups tend to focus more narrowly than in-depth interviews—discussing specific issues or topics in great detail rather than trying to cover a range of topics.

A focus group is led by a **moderator**, who guides the discussion. Sometimes, researchers hire a professionally trained person to serve as the moderator. Other times, the researcher serves as the moderator. The moderator's primary job is to ask the questions that the researcher has designed, keep the participants on topic, make sure all participants take part, and ensure that no participant dominates the discussion. The moderator can ask follow-up probes, redirect the conversation, and try to control the flow of the discussion. If the researcher is not moderating, he or she will sometimes observe the discussion through a one-way window (which appears to be a mirror to the people in the focus group room). Focus group members sign a consent form granting the researcher permission to observe or record them.

moderator A professionally trained person who leads the discussion in a focus group.

Sampling for Focus Groups

Sampling principles for focus groups are similar to those for in-depth interviewing. Purposive sampling makes the most sense—the researchers should think about the characteristics that are most important to the topic they will be examining and choose a range of people with those characteristics. For example, if the researcher thinks that gender and religion might influence opinions on abortion, the focus group sample should include men and women, as well as adherents to the major religions, atheists, and agnostics. Researchers usually find people to take part in focus groups through advertisements, snowball samples, or convenience samples (see Chapter 6).

Once the researcher has a pool of potential participants, constructing the groups takes care and effort. Focus groups should be designed to put people at ease and get them talking freely. The principle of **homogeneity** means that you should avoid putting people of very different social statuses or backgrounds together. Researchers should be particularly attuned to the power dynamics among participants. It is best to group people of equal power relations together and avoid mixing supervisors and subordinates, where those with less power would be less likely to speak their minds. Thus, if you are studying a school, you would put together groups of teachers and would then create separate focus groups for students. If you are studying a military group, you would put together groups of officers and separate groups of enlisted personnel. However, as Morgan and Krueger (1993, p. 36) note, "The goal is homogeneity in background and not homogeneity in attitudes. If all the participants share virtually identical perspectives on a topic, this can lead to a flat, unproductive discussion."

homogeneity The principle that states that you should put people of similar social statuses or backgrounds together when constructing a focus group.

Running and Analyzing the Focus Group

The optimum size of a focus group is about 6–10 people—large enough to keep the conversation lively but small enough to ensure everyone can take part in the discussion. Researchers usually have 8–12 questions for the moderator to cover and aim for 1–2 hours of discussion. If possible, participants should be strangers who come together solely for the purpose of the focus group. This rule is followed most closely in election and market-research situations. In contrast, social science researchers are often studying people in real-life situations; for example, people who work together, live in the same neighborhood, or belong to the same organization. In many cases, the participants know one another outside of the focus group, which means they might behave differently than if they were coming together for the first time at the focus group.

One ethical issue to be aware of: Sometimes the group dynamic can lead people to disclose sensitive or private information (Morgan & Krueger, 1993). Researchers cannot guarantee anonymity or confidentiality in a group setting, although they can emphasize that individuals should not repeat anything said in the group setting. Researchers must disclose their inability to control information shared in the group in the informed consent form that they ask participants to sign before taking part in the focus group. The researcher should be aware of confidentiality issues when designing the study questions; some topics might be too sensitive to be studied with focus groups. For instance, answers to questions about criminal activity could put participants at legal risk.

It is very difficult to take notes on a focus group as it is happening, because the researcher needs to keep track not only of what was said but also who said it. Videotaping can be very useful here; a videotape allows you to identify who is speaking—essential for matching a participant with his or her words. Transcribing a focus group takes more time and is more expensive than transcribing a one-person interview. People interrupt one another and talk over one another, making it difficult to keep track of who is speaking at any given time. It is important to transcribe as closely as possible because the researcher will want to look at patterns of interaction in the analysis of the data.

CONCEPT CHECKS

1   In what other contexts besides social science research are focus groups used?

2   Explain two ways in which focus groups differ from in-depth interviews.

3   Why is it important for the members of a focus group to be homogenous? If you were conducting a study of how parents of young children use day care, how would you organize the participants into effective focus groups?

CONCLUSION

In-depth qualitative interviewing is a very common method in the social sciences—not only as the sole method in use but also in mixed-methods studies, in which it is combined with ethnography or survey research. On the surface, it is deceptively simple. It involves a conversation on a topic—the researcher asks open-ended questions and the respondent answers. But as this chapter has shown, there is also an art to in-depth interviewing. It involves establishing rapport with respondents, directing the interview while still making it seem like a normal conversation.

Like all of the methods covered in this book, in-depth interviewing involves trade-offs between validity and reliability. Unlike a survey, where the answers to the questions are presented to the research subject, the open-ended questions in an interview allow respondents to give answers the researcher might not have imagined. The give-and-take between interviewer and interviewee means that there is less opportunity for misunderstanding or miscommunication. Interviewees have the time and the freedom to say what they really feel and believe, creating opportunities for greater validity because the interviewer can fully understand what the interviewees are saying. However, the best in-depth interviews may be the least reliable across interviewers because they are truly open-ended. The interviewer's personality and behaviors can influence the respondent. One interviewer might follow up on something that the respondent said, while another interviewer might skip over that detail.

In-depth interviews are very useful in discovering new themes that can then be tested with large sample surveys or pursued further with ethnographies. Often, though, they can answer important questions on their own. They tell us how people are thinking about events and relationships. As such, they are a key tool in the social scientist's toolbox.

End-of-Chapter Review

Summary

In-depth interviewing is a qualitative method that involves using open-ended questions to elicit as much detail as possible about people's experiences, thoughts, feelings, and beliefs, allowing researchers to understand the world as their research subjects see it. In-depth interviewing is often combined with survey research or ethnography, but it can also produce useful knowledge about the social world on its own.

What Topics Do Interviewers Study?

- In-depth interviews are useful for answering questions about how and why events occur, such as how students make decisions about where to attend college.
- Unlike survey methods, which typically use large representative samples, in-depth interviews cannot necessarily explain how widespread a phenomenon is.

Types of In-Depth Interviews

- Unlike surveys, which are highly structured interviews with predetermined questions and response options, in-depth interviews are more flexible. Researchers can ask follow-up questions and let the interview flow naturally based on participants' responses.

- A semi-structured interview uses an interview schedule, or a prepared list of questions. An unstructured interview does not use any preset questions, though the researcher will come to the interview with a list of topics to guide the conversation.
- Oral histories are an informal type of in-depth interview that aims to record respondents' experiences of a particular historical event.
- Like oral histories, life history interviews record events that happen over the course of an individual's life. Life history interviews contribute to social theory and can be used to test hypotheses about how peoples' lives change over time.
- Cognitive interviews are used primarily to pretest survey questions.

How to Conduct an Interview Study

- In-depth interviewers use purposive sampling, selecting cases on the basis of certain features. Researchers aim to understand each case in detail, called "case study logic."
- Saturation point is a rule of thumb used by researchers to decide when they have learned all they can from an interview study. Researchers must also consider the study's budget and whether they have equal representation from all subgroups of the target population when deciding how many interviews to conduct.
- Researchers prepare an interview schedule by designing open-ended questions that will allow respondents to give in-depth, conversational responses, and then organizing the questions to ensure a good flow.
- Techniques for getting participants to talk include asking for respondents' opinions as experts, prompting them with stories of fictional interviewees, playing devil's advocate, and using photos or vignettes.
- It is typically best to record an in-depth interview, but this can only be done with respondents' permission. After an interview is complete, the researcher should write field notes to capture his or her experiences and observations.

Validity and Reliability in In-Depth Interviews

- In-depth interviews usually have high validity because the interviewer can probe the respondent with follow-up questions to get a thorough understanding of their thoughts. Interviews typically have lower reliability because different interviewers may elicit different responses from the same respondent.
- Some researchers have critiqued the validity of in-depth interviews on the basis of their use of nonrepresentative samples. Others have argued that they are less useful than surveys for uncovering honest cultural attitudes, and less able to uncover deep motivations for behavior than ethnographies.
- Qualitative researchers have responded to these criticisms by explaining the ways that they assess validity, including paying attention to participants' tone of voice and body language.

Focus Groups

- Focus groups are interviews conducted in a group setting. Researchers who run focus groups recognize that opinions are constructed through social interaction.
- Like in-depth interviews, focus groups use nonrepresentative samples that are constructed using purposive sampling. Researchers typically aim for homogeneity in background by grouping people of similar status together.

Key Terms

case study logic, **350**

cognitive interview, **348**

focus group, **342**

homogeneity, **371**

in-depth interviewing, **342**

informant, **349**

interview schedule, **344**

life course, **347**

life history interview, **347**

moderator, **371**

oral history, **345**

purposive sampling, **349**

reliability, **366**

respondent, **349**

sampling for range, **350**

saturation, **354**

semi-structured interview, **344**

snowball sampling, **351**

unstructured interview, **344**

validity, **367**

vignette, **361**

Exercise

Members of every generation experience historic events that shape their worldviews, political opinions, and outlook on life. Glen Elder wrote about the lifelong effects of growing up during the Great Depression. Later generations have been shaped by the assassination of President John F. Kennedy, the Moon landing, the Vietnam War, the explosion of the *Challenger* space shuttle, and the 9/11 terrorist attacks. What historical events have shaped your age cohort? What effect might these events have on your lives going forward? Find someone to interview about the most important historical events he or she has experienced.

Suggested Questions

Tell me a little about yourself.

- How old are you?
- Where did you grow up?
- Have you moved around a lot?

What do you think is the most important historic event that has happened in your lifetime? This is an event that you think has had the greatest impact on the United States.

- PROBE: This could be one specific event, a series of related events, or any other change that had an important impact on the nation.

How old were you when this happened?

Do you remember how you heard about it?

- PROBE: Were you alone or with family or friends? Did you watch it on television, seek news online, or find out some other way?

How did you feel about it?

- PROBE: Were you scared, happy, proud, worried, excited?

Why do you think this event was important to you?

Why is it important to the nation?

Do you think of it as something you might tell your children and grandchildren?

Materials-based research involves analyzing existing materials such as records in order to explore questions that can't be answered by observing or talking to people.

12

MATERIALS-BASED METHODS

Consider the following important questions:

- What sparks riots and revolutions?
- What interventions are most effective at slowing the pace of mass killings in a genocide?

- Do environmental laws really reduce carbon emissions?
- How do perceptions of beauty change across generations?

These questions are challenging because we cannot answer them easily through direct conversations with or observations of people. Rather, we need other sources of information, such as government records, legal codes, measures of the environment, and popular media. This chapter focuses on **materials-based methods**, which are sociological methods that involve analyzing existing materials rather than interviewing, surveying, or observing people. **Materials**, as we use the term, include expert analyses, reports, records, news media, other media, written accounts of events, physical materials, maps, and preexisting data sets.

Materials-based methods do not directly engage with human research subjects. For this reason, these types of methods are sometimes called **unobtrusive methods**. Many sociologists find this term problematic, however, because it incorrectly implies that other types of sociological methods are intrusive and unwelcome. Furthermore, it defines materials-based methods by what they are *not* rather than what they are. That is why we are introducing the new term *materials-based methods*.

We begin this chapter by explaining why some sociologists choose to use materials-based methods. Next, we discuss the range of materials that sociologists use, the differences between primary and secondary information, and some key sources for finding materials. We also identify the best places to acquire these materials, including how to make a Freedom of Information Act (FOIA) request for materials from the government. In the last half of the chapter, we explain three types of materials-based analyses and how to conduct them. These include historical and comparative analyses, content analyses, and quantitative analyses using secondary data sets. We conclude the chapter with a discussion of the limitations of materials-based methods.

WHY USE MATERIALS RATHER THAN PEOPLE TO ANSWER SOCIOLOGICAL QUESTIONS?

A fact of human existence is that people leave traces of themselves behind. We know about early human societies because we have physical evidence of their tools, weapons, drawings, religious icons, and other artifacts. Contemporary societies have these same items and many others, such as landfills, cemeteries, and interstate highways. When humans started writing things down, they began preserving information in a whole new way. The inventions of audio and video transmission and recording introduced radio, television, movies, and podcasts into everyday life. Access to collections of materials skyrocketed with the development of the Internet. History is now memorialized in everything from news archives to the Cartoon Network. Profound or trivial, these societal traces can provide answers to important questions about how societies work—answers that sociologists might not uncover by observing or interviewing people.

---

materials-based methods
Sociological methods that involve analyzing existing materials rather than interviewing, surveying, or observing people.

materials Preexisting information, such as expert analyses, reports, records, news media, other media, written accounts of events, maps, and preexisting data sets, or physical objects used as the basis for materials based research.

unobtrusive methods Term used to describe materials-based methods.

Sociologists turn to collections of records or materials rather than directly to individual research subjects for four main reasons.

1. First, individuals are not the best sources of information about **macro-social phenomena**; that is, social patterns or trends that are bigger than any individual. As we learned in Chapter 2, macro-level studies look at societal composition, structures, and processes. Societal *structures* are the stable patterns of social relationships and institutions that compose any society. For example, people do not interact randomly in any way that strikes them at the moment; rather, their actions and personal exchanges are influenced by the *social roles* they hold (such as parent, child, boss, employee, instructor, student) and the *institutions* to which they belong (such as families, the capitalist economy, higher education). These roles and institutions "structure" what people think they should do and how they should do it.

   For example, under most circumstances, killing someone is considered one of the worst crimes possible. However, if a person in the role of "soldier" kills another person considered "the enemy" during the institutional context of "war," the killing is considered appropriate or even necessary. Sociologists therefore cannot simply ask the broad question "Why do people kill?" Instead, they need to ask "When do societies approve of killing?" or "When, why, and how do societies engage in war?" Surveys with random samples of individuals can tell us what the average American thinks about war, and interviews with soldiers can tell us how members of the military experience war and combat, but neither of these methods can reveal the larger social, historical, and economic forces that give rise to war.

   Because macro-oriented theories focus on the largest collective units that make up society, studies developing these theories often rely on preexisting expert analyses, government reports, media, and other records. Drawing on these materials, sociologists can assess the advantages and disadvantages of different structures or they can synthesize what is happening or happened to many different people simultaneously. For example, Theda Skocpol (1979) wanted to know why revolutions had occurred in some countries but not in others. Skocpol assembled a rich collection of books and articles that had been written about French, Russian, and Chinese history. After analyzing these materials, Skocpol rejected the idea that charismatic revolutionaries lead others to violently overthrow governments. Rather, she argued that revolutions coincided with political crises only when farmworkers were relatively powerful while landowners were not. Skocpol determined that these two conditions existed in France and Russia when those countries experienced revolutions, in 1789 and 1917, respectively. In China, in contrast, a weak peasantry and powerful

macro-social phenomena
Social patterns or trends that are bigger than any individual, such as societal composition, structures, and processes.

Theda Skocpol used materials related to the 1917 Russian Revolution to understand the causes of violent revolts.

landlords prevented revolutionary action when the Qing dynasty collapsed in 1911. Skocpol's analysis is important for understanding the circumstances in which individual actions can lead to major social change. Interviewing farmworkers and landowners would not have given her the bird's-eye view of history that was the key to her macro-level argument.

2. The second reason to use materials rather than human respondents is that the answers to some questions do not exist in living memory. People don't live forever. If some or all of the things you want to study happened in the past, memories of the events may have faded or the individuals who experienced the events may have died. For example, even if Skocpol had wanted to conduct interviews to help answer her research question, the peasants and landlords who witnessed the French and Russian revolutions were no longer alive.

3. The third reason to use materials is that people are not always the best sources of information—even about themselves. People want to put their best faces forward, so they will sometimes revise or misreport their behavior or attitudes when they know they are being studied. (Recall the discussion of social desirability in Chapter 7.) Because individuals are immersed in their own historical era, geographic location, and particular culture, they are not very good at answering questions about how or why they do certain things. If the present is all they know, they also cannot explain why or how they are different from people in other times and places. They may also romanticize the past in a way that is more consistent with fiction than fact. People are socialized to presume that certain things are true, and these beliefs can persist even when the facts contradict them. This is the problem of **societal blind spots**.

societal blind spots A tendency of individuals to romanticize the past or to presume that certain things are true, even when the facts contradict them.

For example, many Americans think that families used to be more stable in the past and that marital dissolution and single parenting are recent phenomena. Family historian Stephanie Coontz challenged this widespread belief in a "golden era" in her influential book *The Way We Never Were: Families and*

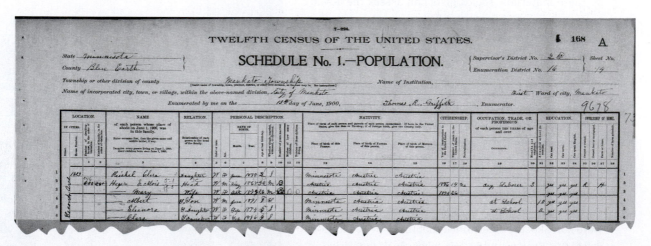

This page from the 1900 U.S. Census for Mankato, Minnesota, shows children Albert (age 9), Eleanor (age 6), and Clara (age 4) living with their grandparents, E. Alois and Mary Heger. Census data is one source that Coontz used to determine that family instability is not a new thing.

the Nostalgia Trap (1992). Using government statistics and reports over many decades, Coontz found that the typical American family of yesteryear was actually quite different from what people today call the "traditional" family. In the 1800s, the age of sexual consent was less than 10 years old in some states, and marriages in those days were on average shorter than they are now because of husbands abandoning their wives or one spouse dying prematurely. In short, it is not true that children in the nineteenth century lived in more stable home environments than they do today. Historical government records, including U.S. Census household rosters, were crucial for helping Coontz understand how the American family has changed over time.

Furthermore, people may not recognize how certain individuals or groups have more privilege than others; such differences seem "normal" to them. For example, whites often fail to notice racism against racial and ethnic minorities (Feagin & Hernan, 2000; O'Brien et al., 2009). As an illustration, in 2016 Paul Sorvino, a white actor famous for playing a mobster in the classic film *Goodfellas*, noted that throughout his long and distinguished Hollywood career, he had witnessed almost no racism (Papapostolou, 2016). However, Sorvino's observation might be based on the fact that he rarely worked with racial and ethnic minorities.

The facts suggest that Hollywood does indeed exclude racial and ethnic minorities from key roles. Sociologists Darnell Hunt and Ana-Christina Ramón (2015) used information about movies and television shows from 2012 and 2013 that they gleaned from the Internet Movie Database (IMDb) and other sources to document the presence (or absence) of racial and ethnic minorities in Hollywood. They found that minority groups were underrepresented 2 to 1 among film leads (see "From the Field to the Front Page"). In cases like this one, gathering and analyzing objective facts about the study question will yield more accurate results than soliciting subjective opinions and recollections through interviews or surveys.

Materials-based methods sometimes capture genuine behavior more accurately than individuals' accounts of events, which are subject to social desirability bias, societal blind spots, memory lapses, and attempts at impression management. Of course, some materials, such as diaries and journals, can contain the same types of biases, so not all materials-based methods will avoid these problems.

4. The fourth reason to use materials rather than human respondents is that materials facilitate studies otherwise difficult or impossible to carry out. Materials-based methods take advantage of rich materials that already exist. For example, most researchers do not have the skills or resources to conduct multiple nationally representative surveys, but the National Health Interview Surveys, General Social Surveys, and other such resources make these types of data accessible to everyone. Likewise, it would be extremely difficult for a team of researchers to conduct interviews related to human rights every year in every country in the world. The U.S. Department of State and Amnesty International, however, have established networks that allow them to conduct such research, and they prepare annual human rights country reports that researchers and others can use.

BLACKS IN HOLLYWOOD: "ARE WE MAKING SURE THAT EVERYONE IS GETTING A FAIR SHOT?"

On January 14, 2016, the 2015 Oscar nominees were announced, and a firestorm of criticism ensued. The world learned that, for the second year in a row, *all* the nominees in the lead and supporting actor categories were white, despite the fact that actors such as O'Shea Jackson Jr. in *Straight Out of Compton*, Idris Elba in *Beasts of No Nation*, John Boyega in *Star Wars: The Force Awakens*, and other black actors had received critical and popular acclaim. The hashtag #Oscarssowhite caught fire. Director Spike Lee, who received an honorary Oscar, explained in his acceptance speech, "I see no black folks except for the man who's the security guard who checks my name off the list as I got into the studio.... We need to have a serious conversation about diversity and get some flavor up in this" (Grow, 2015). Even then-President Obama weighed in, saying the Oscars debate was the expression of a broader concern (Child, 2016): "Are we making sure that everybody is getting a fair shot?"

The materials-based research of Prof. Darnell Hunt and colleagues (Hunt & Ramón, 2015; Hunt, Ramón, & Price, 2014) answered this question in the Hollywood context and became an important part of the discussion (France, 2016). Hunt and his colleagues used materials-based methods to avoid two key problems that can arise with interviews or surveys on such a sensitive topic: societal blind spots and social desirability bias. Hunt and Ramón (2015) found that although racial and ethnic minorities constituted 37% of the U.S. population in 2013, they remained underrepresented in films and television shows in both acting and other types of roles. Whites outnumbered minorities by 2 to 1 as leading actors in films, 2 to 1 in directing films, 3 to 1 among film writers, and 6 to 1 among leading actors in broadcast television shows.

Hunt and Ramón's analysis was based on 347 films released in 2012 and 2013 and on 1,105 television shows airing on broadcast and cable television during the 2012–2013 season. Their research team compiled data from many Hollywood industry sources, including the Studio System, which compiles budget and box office data for movies; Variety Insight, which tracks people, projects, and companies across television, film, and digital entertainment; Nielsen, which identifies who is watching what on television; the Internet Movie Database (IMDb); and Box Office Mojo, an online box-office reporting service owned by IMDb.

Hunt and Ramón (2015) found that television shows that model inclusive societies, such as *New Girl*, have plot lines that avoid racial and ethnic stereotyping.

Hunt and Ramón's research team also conducted a content analysis of popular broadcast and cable television shows that modeled an inclusive society (at least three of the first eight credited actors had to be members of ethnic or racial minority groups). Applying these criteria yielded a total of 16 shows, including *Chicago Fire* (NBC), *Dexter* (Showtime), and *New Girl* (Fox). For each show, researchers reviewed four episodes: the season premiere or pilot, the season finale, and two randomly selected episodes from the season. To maximize intercoder reliability, researchers watched segments of the shows together and agreed on a coding scheme and how to apply it. Hunt and Ramón found that minority leads had more screen time in comedies while white leads had more screen time in dramas. Common racial and gender stereotypes were not typical features of the 64 episodes examined, suggesting the value of these diverse shows for reducing prejudice.

Another aspect of Hunt and Ramón's work dispels the idea that racism in Hollywood is driven by profit—that whites dominate films because of audience preferences. Their analysis showed that films with relatively diverse principal actors—between 30% and 50% minorities—had the greatest median box office receipts and the highest median return on investment. For example, *Fast & Furious 6* was a tremendous box office success.

The need for materials-based analysis often emerges from a combination of these four reasons. For example, many macro-social phenomena, such as revolutions and genocides, occur over very long periods of time or occur infrequently. Few individuals (fortunately) will be exposed to significant numbers of these events. Because these events are so momentous, they frequently prompt analysis and reports that can be archived for later generations. Furthermore, roles and institutions—that is, macro phenomena—often operate invisibly to shape attitudes and behaviors, leading to societal blind spots. In sum: For some research questions, it is better to review materials than to interact with individuals.

CONCEPT CHECKS

1 Why do some sociologists find the term *unobtrusive methods* problematic?

2 What are four main reasons that researchers use materials-based methods?

3 Give an example of a behavior that is acceptable or necessary in one institutional context but not in another. Explain how the behavior is perceived in the two different contexts.

MATERIALS USED IN MATERIALS-BASED METHODS

As societies develop, they leave behind materials that provide clues about their members' activities and values. These materials provide a treasure trove of information for the imaginative and enterprising researcher. This section introduces the broad array of materials that sociologists use in their research. Materials-based researchers often use several types of materials to find answers to their key questions.

Expert Analyses

Expert analyses in the form of books and articles on the topic of interest—for example, U.S. families for Stephanie Coontz (1992) or the French and Russian revolutions for Theda Skocpol (1979)—are a boon to sociologists conducting research. Academic books and articles are the most valuable because they have typically undergone a rigorous peer-review process. The point of the review process is to ensure the quality of the publication: that the evidence is adequate and supports the conclusions; that the reasoning is sound and not slanted. (Chapter 2 offers guidance on how to determine if your sources have gone through the peer-review process.)

Through your school's library, you may have access to online search engines such as Sociological Abstracts, an excellent tool for finding expert analyses related to your topic. You will also want to use search engines outside of sociology, such as Historical Abstracts or Oxford Bibliographies. Once you have found several books or articles that are particularly relevant to your question, carefully review their bibliographies for other promising sources and recently conducted studies. You can usually use search engines to determine who has cited these relevant books and articles. You can also contact the author of a book or article to ask his or her advice on other promising sources.

Be cautious about using Google or Google Scholar to find expert analyses; not all of the articles in Google Scholar have been peer-reviewed for quality. Be even more wary of websites or documents created by those with no clear qualifications. These authors may accidentally or purposely alter history. For example, the website www.martinlutherking.org purports to provide a "true historical examination" of Dr. Martin Luther King Jr., but it is actually a fraudulent site sponsored by Stormfront, a white supremacist group. The website uses invalid and incomplete "evidence" to promote a particular view of history. Always click the "About Us" link on websites and read the statement of expertise with a critical eye. If it says the authors are "experts," what criteria are used to define an "expert"? If none are listed, be skeptical. Be even more skeptical if the website provides no information about the authors at all. If you're unsure about how reputable a source is, consult with your professor or campus librarian.

Reports

Sociologists often supplement expert analyses with reports and records. *Reports* are syntheses of information, typically created by governments or organizations as part of a review process. For example, the U.S. Department of State prepares annual Country Reports on Human Rights Practices for each country in the world (except the United States itself). The reports (commonly referred to as Human Rights Reports), which include stories that illustrate a nation's respect for human rights, are based on interviews, observations by U.S. embassy personnel, and other sources, such as news reports. The 2014 report for Mexico described the torture and murder of three student protesters and the disappearance of 43 other students in Iguala, Guerrero, Mexico. According to the report, the mayor of Iguala, Jose Luis Abarca, personally requested that a criminal gang carry out the atrocities. The 2015 report for Mexico noted that the bodies of the 43 missing students had yet to be found. Social scientists use these reports to answer questions about which countries violate human rights and under what circumstances (see, for example, Abouharb & Cingranelli, 2006; Cingranelli, Richards, & Clay, 2014). These analyses make it possible for policy makers to better ensure that human rights are protected.

The best ways to find original reports is to visit government agency websites, an approach that we will describe in detail later in this chapter. International governmental organizations such as the United Nations (UN), the World Health Organization (WHO), and the International Labor Organization (ILO) also routinely prepare high-quality reports, which are available on their websites. Private organizations—both for-profit and not-for-profit—also sometimes produce reports. For example, Amnesty International publishes annual human rights reports for all countries.

As with expert analyses, researchers need to be cautious about using reports that come from questionable or partisan sources. Some reports are based on careful

The disappearance and presumed murder of 46 students in Mexico in 2013 prompted massive protests and was highlighted in U.S. State Department reports.

research; others have no factual basis or "cherry pick" facts to support a particular view. Reputable reports will explain their underlying methodology, often in a detailed appendix. If the reports are used extensively in social science research already (as is true of the Country Reports on Human Rights Practices), that is a good indication that they are respected sources of evidence.

Records

Records are documents that memorialize events or characteristics at a particular moment in time. Records include a very broad category of information, including, for instance, censuses, vital statistics (that is, birth, marriage, and death dates), statutes and legal opinions, treaties, historical temperature measures, an organization's press releases, and documentation of the cast of actors in movies. Social scientists can use records to answer important questions such as why certain types of individuals live longer than others. Answering this question requires information on a sample of people who have already died, so it lends itself to a materials-based research method.

Inwood, Oxley, and Roberts (2016) took up this question in New Zealand to better understand the difference in life spans between whites and the indigenous Māori in that country. They used World War I and II military enlistment records to identify men's ethnicities and physical stature, and then matched military records with death records. Analyzing men who survived the wars, they found that the indigenous Māori were significantly more likely to die at younger ages than men descended from European settlers and that the disparity widened at precisely the time when New Zealand was transitioning to a modern health-care system. The implication is that whites benefited more than the Māori from twentieth century improvements in health care.

Governments tend to keep thorough records, including records of their own activities. For instance, through the U.S. Holocaust Memorial Museum website, you can find records relating to the German construction and administration of concentration camps during World War II. Governments also hold many records related to individuals. These records are often kept confidential for as long as the individuals are still alive to protect their privacy, so researchers cannot always access them. Many researchers visit state or local government archives to physically review hard copies of government records that are not available online.

News Media

The news media is a unique and relatively comprehensive source of information on everything from memorable events (the first airplane flight across the Atlantic) to daily living ("best" brownie recipe). Researchers sometimes use news media to

Military enlistment records helped researchers understand why the indigenous Māori of New Zealand were dying at younger ages than their white counterparts.

determine the facts related to certain events or topics. For example, Susan Olzak and Suzanne Shanahan (2003) reviewed newspaper articles to document when and where racial and ethnic minorities had engaged in collective action in the United States. At other times, news coverage itself is analyzed to uncover biases regarding who and what are the topics of news stories.

Search engines on news websites provide one way to find the news on a particular topic. Lexis/Nexis, which you may have access to through your library, is an excellent source for news coverage of events over the past few decades. Lexis/Nexis allows you to run complex Boolean searches (searches with "and" and "or"). It also allows you to search multiple newspapers simultaneously; this search function is particularly important if you are conducting a cross-national project. However, because newspapers often copy stories from one another or pull stories from wire services such as the Associated Press (AP) and United Press International (UPI), it is a good idea to select only a limited number of newspapers to search. Otherwise, you will end up with many copies of the same article. In addition, be sure to check the date ranges for the newspapers you are searching to ensure that they extend back to the time period that is relevant to your project. Researchers can also find microfilm copies of older or more obscure newspapers at local history libraries.

Other Media

media Artifacts of popular culture, including paintings, novels, songs, television shows, movies, magazines, comic books, and blogs.

Media other than news refers to artifacts of popular culture, including paintings, novels, songs, television shows, movies, magazines, comic books, and blogs. Unlike news, other forms of media are rarely presumed to be evidence of facts; rather, they are treated as representations of beliefs and attitudes. A recent study using media is Love and Park's (2013) content analysis of photographs from 23 introductory criminal justice and criminology textbooks. Women were infrequently the central focus of photos, and photos of women and men interacting rarely made it into the books at all. The texts reflected the social stereotype that criminal justice is a male sphere, perhaps subtly suggesting to female students that they should not pursue criminal justice careers.

Like the selection of a research method, the selection of a particular type of media depends on the particular type of materials or information needed to answer the research question. In general, researchers tap the same sources that consumers seeking entertainment use: Netflix, Amazon, Apple Music, Spotify, cable television services, and so on. Written and published materials, such as novels, magazines, and comic books, can be found in libraries and new and used bookstores. Love and Park obtained their textbooks from publishers, but they could likely have found many of them in the libraries at their universities. For artwork, such as paintings, sculptures, posters, and photographs, researchers might turn to the U.S. National Archives online or to museums, art programs, or private collections (if they can get access).

Television shows like *The Wire* portray criminal justice as a male sphere. Love and Park (2013) found the same is true for recent criminal justice textbooks.

Most forms of media are protected by copyright, which prevents individuals from distributing copyrighted material for profit, but this does not impose a major impediment for using media in research. Sociological analyses of media involve describing materials and making inferences from them—not sharing the original material—so these analyses are generally outside copyright concerns. However, researchers who wish to include material in its original form in a published paper should first obtain reprint permission from the copyright holder.

Individual Accounts of Events

First-person accounts, such as diaries, letters, journals, video blogs, or Facebook posts, can provide valuable evidence on many topics. If you are interested in material from the Internet age or from a famous person (such as Richard Nixon), the material will likely be easy to find. As noted in Chapter 11, many oral history interviews (for example, those conducted by the Civil Rights History Project and the Veterans History Project) are now available online. These interviews provide information on "ordinary" people who were witnesses to extraordinary historical events or periods.

The first step in assessing the quality of first-person accounts is the distance in time and space of the person from the events he or she recorded. Is the person writing about something he or she experienced personally? In general, direct observations are better than secondhand information. Even direct observers, however, may have reasons to misreport; for example, to cover up their own bad behavior or to make themselves look more noble or important. For instance, if someone in your neighborhood goes on to become a famous movie star, you might be tempted to exaggerate how well you know that person.

In general, first-person accounts are a good source of primary evidence on how people are thinking about a topic or how someone experienced a particular event. However, as with media, researchers are cautious about using first-person accounts as accurate evidence of historical facts.

> **first-person account**
> Primary evidence of what a person experienced, gleaned from interviews, diaries, or similar sources.

Physical Materials

Most of the materials we've mentioned in this chapter are written or digitized, but social scientists can use other physical materials beyond the written page. For example, they might examine boys' and girls' toys to assess differences in gender socialization. They might review water or soil samples to determine exposure to health risks. The Massachusetts Department of Public Health, in conjunction with the Silent Spring Institute (2016), for example, gathered data on private and public water supplies, septic and sewer systems, and land use on Cape Cod to determine which (if any) environmental factors affected rates of breast cancer in different locations. The Florida Healthy Beaches Program (Florida Department of Health, 2016) monitors beaches weekly for bacteria and fecal matter, which, in high concentrations, can cause gastrointestinal illness, infections, or rashes for swimmers or waders. Students in an environmental justice class might use the reports from these water-quality samples to determine if individuals using beaches near poor neighborhoods are exposed to more waste than those using beaches in wealthy neighborhoods.

Maps

Social scientists use *maps,* or representations of the whole or a part of a space or area, to determine how things are related spatially. Maps are an excellent source of information on societal traces, such as the placement of hazardous waste facilities or freeways, spatial differences in crime rates or levels of air pollution, or the concentration of grocery stores versus liquor stores in a neighborhood. Wolch, Wilson, and Fehrenbach (2005) used maps to assess racial inequality in access to parks in Los Angeles (Figure 12.1). Hollie Nyseth Brehm (2014), who is the subject of this chapter's "Conversations from the Front Lines" feature, used maps to determine which Sudanese cities have been bombed during the genocide there.

FIGURE 12.1 Racial Inequality in Access to Parks in Los Angeles

The map on the left shows park acres per 1,000 children in white-dominated census tracts in Los Angeles. The darkest patches indicate more park area. The map on the right is the same measure in Latino-dominated census tracts. By comparing these maps, it is clear that the typical white child in Los Angeles will have more access to parks than the typical Latino child.

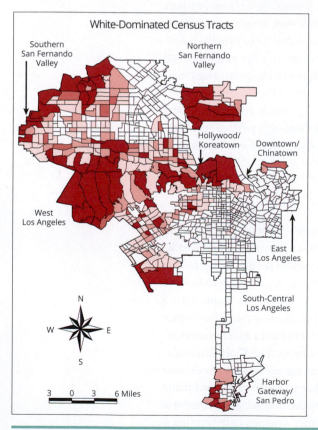

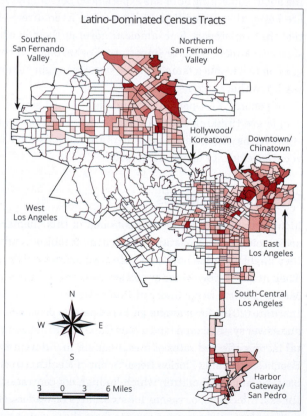

Population data based on 2000 Census PL 94-171.

Source: Wolch, Wilson, & Fehrenbach, 2005.

The U.S. Census Bureau is an excellent source of current and historical maps of areas in the United States. Google Maps and Google Earth provide access to contemporary maps for all parts of the world. For more sophisticated analyses with maps, researchers turn to a **geographic information system (GIS)**, which takes many bits of quantitative data and associates them with locations on maps to create visual images of how social phenomena are unfolding. The GADM database of global administrative areas, created by Robert Hijmans (2015), includes high-resolution country administrative areas (such as provinces or counties) and is suitable for use with GIS software. Hijmans's database precisely delineates the borders of 294,430 current and historical administrative areas.

Currently, use of a GIS to analyze data requires extensive training. However, promising data resources in development will make it easier to integrate geography and social characteristics in future sociological analyses. For example, the Terra Populus website allows researchers to integrate population and environmental data from censuses, surveys, land-cover information (for example, the location of deserts or forests), and climate records. Many researchers find the visual aspect of geographic information systems appealing because it introduces a unique way to explore data.

geographic information systems (GIS) Statistical software that takes many bits of quantitative data and associates them with locations on maps to create visual images of how social phenomena are unfolding.

Data Sets

Data sets include materials that have been converted into quantitative data and preserved in files suitable for analysis with statistical software. Nearly every type of material mentioned in this chapter can be quantified and converted into a data set, but data sets are most commonly created from survey responses, reports, records, or media. These data sets can usually be accessed through government and academic websites.

As noted earlier, the information in the State Department's Country Reports on Human Rights Practices assesses how well countries are supporting human rights. Cingranelli et al. (2014) quantified these assessments. For example, they developed an ordinal measure of the extent to which countries refrained from "political or extrajudicial killings": (0) practiced frequently, (1) practiced occasionally, and (2) have not occurred/unreported. In a codebook, they describe at length how they determine the political or extrajudicial killings rating for each country. When government officials are responsible for 50 or more extrajudicial killings within a year—as was the case for Mexico in 2014—the country is assigned a zero for this variable. The numerical scales of Cingranelli et al. (2014) are called the CIRI Human Rights Data, and they are widely used by sociologists and political scientists.

Researchers often share the data sets they have constructed to answer particular questions or operationalize particular concepts. Many of these data sets are accessible through the University of Michigan's Inter-university Consortium for Political and Social Research (ICPSR), one of the largest academic data repositories in the United States. The data sets vary in breadth, quality, and ease of use. It is often a good idea to contact the researchers who constructed a data set to get their insights before you use the data set.

Increasingly, businesses and the government use electronic traces of people's activities (such as websites visited or cell phone usage) to gather information

big data Data sets with information on millions of individuals and their preferences, behaviors, or networks, often drawn from electronic traces.

about millions of individuals and their preferences, behaviors, and networks. This information is then deposited into data sets. These **big data** can be used to study many things, from spending behavior to potential terrorist networks. The data sets are often tightly controlled for profit, national security, or privacy reasons, so they can be difficult for social science researchers to access. In recent years, social scientists have begun to create their own big data sets, such as Benjamin Schmidt's (2015) searchable online data set of more than 14 million Rate My Professor reviews. These data might be used to explore whether student evaluations of professors vary on the basis of the professor's gender, the course topic, or even whether the course was taught in the spring or fall semester (Figure 12.2).

In sum: Social scientists have access to a vast and diverse pool of materials, ranging from first-person accounts to official reports, maps to media, and physical materials to surveys. By thinking creatively and rigorously examining these materials, social

---

FIGURE 12.2 "Helpful" and "Unhelpful" RateMyProfessor.com Graphs

Two figures from Benjamin Schmidt's website show how often the words *helpful* and *unhelpful* appear on RateMyProfessor.com. In general, students of female instructors (orange dots) use both of these words more than students of male instructors (blue dots). The figures show that students in computer science classes are the most likely to use either of these terms in their online evaluations. Together, the charts suggest that helpfulness is something students are more likely to expect from women than from men.

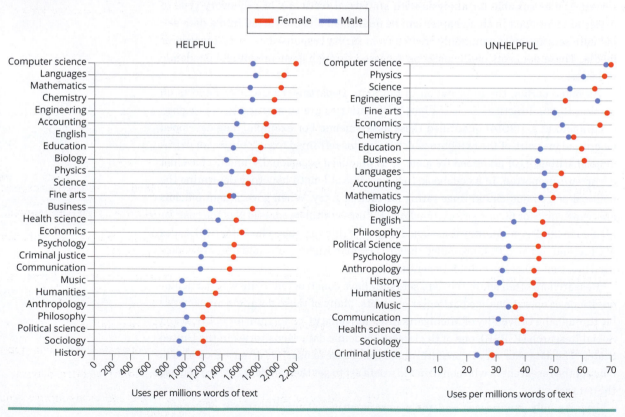

Source: Schmidt, 2015.

scientists are able to draw important conclusions about individuals, organizations, and nations.

CONCEPT CHECKS

1 What steps should researchers take to determine if information and analyses provided on private websites are trustworthy?

2 Pick one of the questions from the very beginning of this chapter and describe a type of material that could help answer it. Explain why this would be a good source of information.

3 Pick one type of material mentioned in this section and think of a research question you could answer with it.

PRIMARY VERSUS SECONDARY INFORMATION

In materials-based research, sociologists distinguish between **primary information**, which is firsthand evidence in its original, unaltered form, and **secondary information**, which is gathered, reported, and sometimes altered by another (Table 12.1). Primary information includes researchers' direct observations, such as a count of the number of books in a section of the local public library, and original first-person accounts, such as a doctor's report of a person's cause of death on a death certificate. Secondary information is indirect evidence of something; it comes through at least one other person. For example, when researchers use the CIRI database, mentioned

primary information
Researchers' direct observations.

secondary information
Indirect evidence of something; the researchers learn of it through at least one other person.

TABLE 12.1 Primary versus Secondary Information

Examples of Primary Information		
Direct observation...	...is primary evidence of...	...whatever was observed.
An interview...	...is primary evidence of...	...topics within the interviewee's experience.
Diary entries...	...are primary evidence of...	...the diarist's feelings and experiences.
A birth certificate...	...is primary evidence of...	...a person's date and place of birth, name, sex, and parents.
The *Congressional Record*...	...is primary evidence of...	...bills considered by the U.S. Congress.
Examples of Secondary Information		
A *New York Times* article...	...is secondary evidence of...	...the events reported on.
General Social Survey data...	...are secondary evidence of...	...U.S. residents' attitudes on many topics.
A death certificate...	...is secondary evidence of...	...the deceased person's date of birth.
U.S. Department of State Human Rights Reports...	...are secondary evidence of...	...human rights abuses in countries around the world.

earlier, they are relying on the researchers' accuracy in converting words into numbers. The place of birth on a death certificate is another example of secondary information. Doctors typically don't know the deceased's place of birth; they have to get this detail from family members who may or may not have accurate information. Thus, the place of birth on death certificates is often based on family stories rather than doctors' firsthand knowledge.

The researcher cannot control the quality or content of secondary information because it has already been collected. It is therefore especially important for the researcher to carefully evaluate quality by considering whether the information came from a reputable, expert source and whether the collection techniques were appropriate and well executed. In addition, because someone else assembled the secondary information, it rarely contains all the information the researcher wants in precisely the way the researcher wants it. This can lead to problems in the **validity** of some measures. Measures are valid when they clearly measure the concept of interest.

When a researcher collects data on her own for the explicit purpose of answering her particular research question, she can make sure that the data are a good representation of her core concepts. This is more difficult when someone else collected the data. For example, if a researcher is interested in whether healthy people have more progressive attitudes, she might use existing attitude survey data, such as the World Values Survey (WVS), for her study. The WVS only asks one question about health, however: "How would you describe your state of health these days? Would you say it is very good, good, fair, or poor?" How people answer this question may be affected by their personalities and their moods on the day the question was asked. Health status measured through this type of self-reporting is therefore less valid than assessments based on physical exams. Researchers sometimes have to accept measures that are less valid than they would prefer when using secondary information.

Note that the same material can constitute primary or secondary evidence, depending on how it is used. Take, for example, newspaper articles. Ye Wang and Shelly Rodgers (2014) used news articles as primary information on news coverage. They compared news reporting on health issues across Hispanic, black, and mainstream newspapers in California (five newspapers in each category). They found that Hispanic newspapers were the most thorough in reporting local health issues. More news stories in Hispanic newspapers did not mean that Hispanics were experiencing more health problems than other groups; it was not primary evidence of community health. Rather, it meant that the Hispanic newspapers provided more extensive coverage of health issues.

Other times, researchers use news stories as secondary evidence of particular facts. For example, sociologist Susan Olzak (McAdam et al., 2009) has conducted numerous studies to examine whether and when ethnic collective action leads to violence. She could not possibly be present to witness every case of ethnic-based collective action in the United States. Instead, she relied on the reports of journalists. To document the occurrence of ethnic collective action, she and her team reviewed thousands of articles published in the *New York Times*. They first selected new stories that were associated with 14 *New York Times* index headings, such as "Race Relations." They then read those articles and coded whether they contained news of violent collective action, public disruptions, strikes, or a nonevent. On the basis of the news stories, they

validity A quality of a measure concerning how accurate it is.

constructed a data set of when and where ethnic collective action has occurred in the United States. Olzak's team used secondary evidence, that is, journalists' reports, of the occurrence of ethnic collective-action events.

<table>
<tr><td colspan="2">CONCEPT CHECKS</td></tr>
<tr><td>1</td><td>Give an example of primary information and an example of secondary information. What is the key difference between the two types of information?</td></tr>
<tr><td>2</td><td>What are some concerns with using secondary data in sociological research?</td></tr>
<tr><td>3</td><td>A researcher wants to use paintings in a museum to assess how conceptions of beauty have changed over time. How does the researcher's purpose differ from the purpose of the museum curators, and how might this difference affect the researcher's findings?</td></tr>
</table>

WHERE DO RESEARCHERS FIND MATERIALS FOR ANALYSES?

An **archive** is a place where materials are brought together, organized by theme, preserved, and made available for inspection by scholars (Wright, 2010). At one time, archives were associated with particular places, but today many archives can be at least partially accessed on the Internet.

Governments, organizations, or individuals (including you) can construct and maintain archives of materials. In this section, we discuss each of these sources of material.

> **archive** A physical or web location where materials are brought together, organized by theme, preserved, and made available for inspection by scholars.

Governments

For millennia, states have maintained records of the people they govern. For example, governments often use a *census* to count the people within their borders and learn important facts about them, such as where they live and their occupations. Governments still conduct censuses today, and they also collect and preserve data in a broad range of other areas, including criminal justice, public health, pollution, education, and finance. Governments make much of this information available to the public, although the ease of access and the level of detail vary.

Reports, records, and data sets are often archived by government agencies that are responsible for the oversight and administration of policies and law in particular areas, such as the U.S. Department of Education or the U.S. Environmental Protection Agency. If you visit the websites of these agencies, you'll be able to view and download material in the form of reports, records, maps, charts, and tables.

The U.S. Census Bureau is a particularly important source of information because its primary purpose is recording the size and characteristics of the U.S. population at particular moments in time. The U.S. Bureau of Justice Statistics is a popular source of information on court systems, criminal activity, and crime victims. Both of these agencies allow you to download data sets or view tables of information online, such as criminal court caseloads by state. The Census Bureau website also allows visitors to view many types of information with maps (datamapper.geo.census.gov/map.html). For example, anyone can easily see how U.S. states and counties vary on many different characteristics (such as the percentage of people over 65 or the percentage of adults with a college degree). The president's cabinet includes the heads of 15 major federal agencies; each of these entities is a source of valuable archived material and data.

When a government has information about individuals who are still alive today, it may release some of its data in **aggregate** form; that is, as summary statistics describing people or organizations of a particular type or in a particular location. For example, at factfinder.census.gov, you can find the aggregate number of people in your ZIP code whose incomes exceed $200,000 per year, but you cannot find out if your next-door neighbor belongs to that group. Similarly, the STATcompiler tool of the Demographic and Health Surveys Program provides statistics, tables, and figures at the country level for low- and middle-income countries. As we learned in Chapter 3, aggregation helps protect the privacy of individuals included in the data. Often, researchers conducting archival analyses are most interested in aggregated data because such data make it easy to identify differences across places or changes over time. Other times, as in the analysis of New Zealand death records by Inwood et al. (2016), research questions require access to **micro data**, or individual-level data.

For some information, governments may determine that privacy is not a major concern and make individual information public. This is the case in most U.S. states with respect to criminal justice. Convictions and sometimes even arrest records are publicly available in newspapers, at courthouses, and on the Internet. Although it is difficult to learn your next-door neighbor's income from government records, it is relatively easy to find out whether he or she has ever been convicted of a crime.

Policies like the Freedom of Information Act (FOIA) in the United States expand the amount of government information available to researchers. The FOIA allows almost any individual to request information from the government (see foia.gov). Jasmine Ha, a graduate student at the University of Minnesota, wanted to know which countries were sending the most young people to study in the United States, where those students were going within the United States, and what they were studying. First, she had to identify the agency that could provide records about international student visas by contacting different government agencies as well as researchers who had used similar data. She determined that U.S. Immigration and Customs Enforcement (ICE), an office within the U.S. Department of Homeland Security, was the most likely source of the information she needed.

Next, she carefully reviewed earlier FOIA requests and found several requests similar to hers that had been partially or fully granted. She then tailored her own request to look as much like those as possible. For example, she found that a request for "the entire foreign student visa system" was not granted, whereas requests for information about clearly defined visa types (such as F-1, M-1) were typically more successful. Lastly, she filed a request for a fee waiver. While the government charges a nominal amount ($25 or less) for a FOIA request, what it calls the "printing fee" can be exorbitant. This fee is typically $0.10 per page, and Ha knew she was asking for records on millions of individuals—which could lead to thousands of dollars in printing fees. The government is required to respond to most FOIA requests within 20–30 business days. After 4 weeks, Ha received a response that (1) her

---

aggregate data Summary statistics, such as a group mean, describing people or organizations of a particular type or in a particular location.

micro data Individual-level data.

fee-waiver request was granted and that (2) ICE-FOIA would deliver the information she had requested.

The *Open Government Initiative* focuses on transforming government records into quantitative data sets and making them available in electronic form. Since the Open Government Initiative was launched in 2009, many U.S. federal agencies have started to compile frequently requested information, which they disseminate online through a FOIA Library page on their website. If researchers can find the information they need in an agency-specific FOIA Library, they will save the time and effort of filing their own FOIA requests. Additionally, after a FOIA request is granted, the information is considered public. FOIA "Logbooks" for government agencies provide the names of previous requesters and the information they received. Researchers can contact the previous requester(s) to obtain a copy of that material.

The website www.usa.gov provides a complete list of all federal agencies and many state agencies. At www.data.gov, a researcher can browse topics or conduct key-word searches to find government information that has been stored as quantitative data. The data are mostly from the U.S. federal government, but some data have been provided by other countries or by U.S. state, county, and city governments. Searching through these sites is one promising way to find useful archived governmental information. However, the sheer amount of archived government material can make the task overwhelming. Researchers therefore tend to look at what archives and data other scholars in their research areas have used in the past. Taking clues from earlier studies allows researchers to more quickly find the information they need.

Organizations

In addition to the government, for-profit and not-for-profit organizations also archive material and keep records of their activities, their employees and clients, and sometimes their industries. Material that is required by law, such as the financial reports of public corporations with shareholders, is typically accurate and accessible. It may not be comparable over time, however, because legal reforms can change what and how information is reported. Other types of organizational records, such as employees' performance evaluations or the minutes from boards of directors meetings, may be archived, but they are typically private and therefore difficult to access.

Certain types of organizations are more likely to create public archives than others. Large, older organizations are more likely to have archives than smaller, newer organizations. For example, the Ford Motor Company has 13,000 boxes of company records that are available to researchers, and the company is in the process of digitizing all of its historic Ford and Lincoln automobile advertising images (Ford Media Center, 2013). Some organizations, such as churches or small businesses, are particularly *unlikely* to make their records public because they have neither the interest nor the financial or personnel resources to do so.

Nonprofit associations that are promoting policy change also tend to be eager to make information public. For example, the Global Initiative to End All Corporal Punishment of Children, a nongovernmental organization that seeks to end the violent

The Global Initiative to End Corporal Punishment, a nongovernmental organization, published this map on its website to shame states into paying more attention to violent discipline.

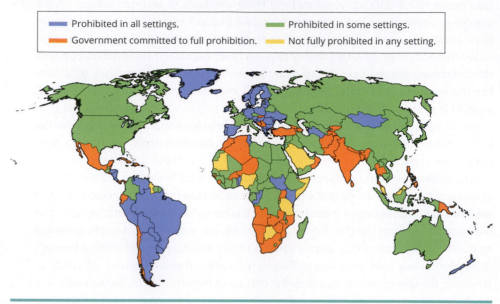

Legend:
- Prohibited in all settings.
- Government committed to full prohibition.
- Prohibited in some settings.
- Not fully prohibited in any setting.

Source: Global Initiative to End All Corporal Punishment of Children, www.endcorporalpunishment.org, April 2017.

discipline of children, maintains a website with data on all countries' corporal punishment policies over time (www.endcorporalpunishment.org). This organization wants to shame countries into passing anti–corporal punishment policies, so it has an incentive to accurately document laws (Figure 12.3).

As we saw earlier in this chapter, some organizations provide false or biased information. For this reason, researchers must approach private websites with caution, carefully evaluating the material for bias and accuracy.

Individuals

Finally, researchers, industry professionals, moral crusaders, and even hobbyists who have done the difficult work of collecting information in a particular area often make their data available to others. Research ethics dictates that researchers share not only their findings but also the original data they collected and organized if someone requests it. For example, Prof. Pamela Paxton has spent much of her career considering what makes women go into politics and how having more female politicians affects government policies. To answer these questions, she and her research team (Paxton, Green, & Hughes, 2008) did extensive cross-national research to find out how many women have served as legislators or members of parliament in nearly every country in the world since 1945. Assembling these data was a monumental task that required scouring historical records in dozens of different languages. Fortunately, future researchers won't have to repeat this effort because Paxton and her collaborators have made the data available on the Data Sharing for Demographic Research website.

Data sets like Paxton's are an invaluable resource for new researchers, allowing them to take on big topics that would otherwise be completely out of reach. Kristopher Robison (2010) used Paxton's data to study whether women's political empowerment affects a country's risk of terrorism. Using yearly counts of terrorist attacks across 154 countries from 1976 to 2000, Robison found that more women in parliament was negatively associated with terrorism. Robison (2010, p. 751) suggests that women "are set within social arrangements in modern societies that empower them to attenuate violence as a solution to major social problems." The more power women have, not only in politics but also in the workplace, his study finds, the less terrorist attacks a country experiences.

When you are using information archived by individuals, take care to review the individual's qualifications and the specific methods he or she used to collect it. Especially when individuals are not academics, be attuned to potential biases and shortcomings in the data-collection process.

After researchers have found the particular materials that interest them and assessed their quality, they can use several methods to analyze them: (1) historical-comparative methods, (2) content analysis, or (3) quantitative data analysis. Often, they will use some combination of these. We describe these methods in the following sections.

CONCEPT CHECKS

1 What types of data can be accessed through the U.S. government?

2 What steps should researchers requesting information through FOIA take to help ensure their request is granted?

3 Consider an organization to which you belong. What type of organization is it? Does it make any information publicly available on its website? How might that information be used in a sociological setting?

HISTORICAL AND COMPARATIVE METHODS

Researchers can often better understand macro processes and reveal the blind spots of contemporary societies by examining how societies are organized in other time periods or places. **Historical research methods** contribute to sociological knowledge and theory by examining change *over time* to answer questions about how and why social processes unfold in particular ways. **Comparative research methods** examine variation *across locations* for the same purpose. Although historical methods focus on time and comparative methods focus on space or geographic location, both approaches use mostly records, reports, and preexisting academic literature or expert accounts as evidence of events. Because of the similarities in these two approaches, sociologists often group historical and comparative methods into a single category. For example, the American Sociological Association has a section dedicated to "Comparative and Historical Sociology."

Sociologist Ari Adut's (2005) case study of Oscar Wilde, a popular British writer in the late 1800s, provides an example of historical methods. Wilde is best remembered

historical research methods Examining change over time to answer questions about how and why social processes unfold in particular ways.

comparative research methods Using materials to examine change across locations to answer questions about how and why social processes unfold in particular ways.

For her case study on Oscar Wilde, Ari Adut used historical research methods to better understand under what conditions something develops into a public scandal.

for his plays, such as *The Importance of Being Earnest*, and novels, such as *The Picture of Dorian Gray*. He is equally well known for having been sentenced to 2 years of hard labor for "gross indecency." In nineteenth century Victorian England, this vague law was used to criminalize gay men's sexual behavior. Adut viewed Wilde's experience as a case of public scandal and asked whether a "scandalous" person's *behavior* is the primary reason why he or she is targeted. At the center of Adut's analysis is the puzzle of why Wilde was not prosecuted for "indecency" much earlier in his life; his sexual liaisons with men were well known to members of his social network long before his criminal trial. This anomaly drove Adut's analysis.

Adut used newspaper stories, legal records, and the historical accounts of individuals to reconstruct the public humiliation that Wilde suffered when his sexual relationships with other men became the center of a legal firestorm. He found that Wilde's lifestyle became scandalous only when it threatened the position of the elites around him. One of Wilde's romantic partners, Lord Alfred Douglas, was the son of Scottish nobleman John Douglas, the ninth Marquess of Queensberry. Queensberry insisted that action be taken against Wilde and threatened to call into question the reputations of other elites who did not support him. Adut's study suggests that the public exposure of bad behavior is not necessarily triggered when the behavior shocks the conscience of a community, but rather when the behavior threatens to damage powerful peoples' reputations in the process.

Adut's general conclusion based on Wilde's specific case has important implications for understanding current scandals. It helps us understand, for example, why sports organizations such as the NFL for years helped to cover up domestic violence situations involving their players but are suddenly now at the forefront of condemning such abuse after the high-visibility case of former Baltimore Ravens running back Ray Rice. Historical analyses such as Adut's use historical events to better understand how general social processes unfold.

History versus Historical Sociology

How do historical case studies in sociology differ from the research that historians do? The main difference lies in sociologists' explicit theoretical orientation. Recall from Chapter 2 that sociologists may draw on diverse theories ranging from conflict theories to rational choice perspectives. The goal of historians, in contrast, is to provide precisely accurate accounts of history on the basis of detailed empirical evidence.

Two recent historical case studies of Abraham Lincoln illustrate the difference. These books draw extensively on historical accounts and original records from Lincoln's lifetime. The goal of historian Doris Kearns Goodwin's (2009) *Team of Rivals: The Political Genius of Abraham Lincoln* is—as its title suggests—to illuminate Lincoln's political genius. Goodwin examines individual personalities, hidden agendas, grandstanding, and backroom politics. Her central focus is Lincoln's decision to invite political rivals into his administration as cabinet members and his ability to turn them into allies through his political savvy and profound intellect. Her goal is to shed new light on an important story. She wants her readers to know Lincoln and know him well.

Sociologist Barry Schwartz's (2003) *Abraham Lincoln and the Forge of National Memory* is very different. It begins with a question: What sociological concept does

Abraham Lincoln embody? While there are many possible answers to this question, Schwartz decided to focus on Lincoln as a case of memory. No one living today has ever met Abraham Lincoln, and yet most of us "remember" things about him—he grew up in a log cabin, he was the president during the American Civil War, and he was assassinated by John Wilkes Booth. Perhaps most important, we think of Abraham Lincoln as a national hero because he ended slavery. This last memory was of great interest to Schwartz as he developed his study. The historical data told him that Lincoln's reputation had changed over time, from the man "who saved the Union" to the man "who freed the slaves." Schwartz hypothesized that while the facts of Lincoln's life mattered in how the president was remembered, interest groups and politics long after Lincoln's death were equally important in shaping and reshaping the country's "collective memory" of him.

Once Schwartz had decided that Lincoln was a good case to develop the concept of collective memory and test his hypotheses, he focused on the historical facts that were relevant to memorializing Lincoln. Beyond expert accounts and original records from Lincoln's era, he also drew on newspaper articles, paintings, statues, sermons, and speeches about Lincoln in the years after the president's assassination. These materials revealed how Lincoln was discussed in public discourse and the turning points in that discourse. They provided primary evidence of how Lincoln was remembered, but not necessarily accurate evidence of what happened during Lincoln's life. Unlike a historian, who wants to understand a particular aspect of a case in great detail, Schwartz wanted to better understand how societies work. He was not interested in Abraham Lincoln *per se*, but rather in what Lincoln reveals about the social construction of collective memories and how they change over time.

Thus, sociologists approach history through a theoretical lens, using historical cases to formulate and test theories. They develop general concepts, such as "scandal" and "collective memory," that provide links across historical events and contemporary societies. In contrast, historians tend to study history more for its intrinsic merit and to ensure the accuracy of the historical record. A historian's main goal is to understand the particular details of a sequence of events. Neither a sociological nor a historical approach is better than the other; they have different goals, and they are not interchangeable.

Steps in the Historical-Comparative Research Process

A historical-comparative study begins when a researcher identifies a case or cases that are noteworthy in some way. Next, the researcher identifies a range of hypotheses, finds and organizes material related to the cases, reviews and interprets that material, and writes up the analysis. We discuss each of these steps in turn.

SELECTING CASES

Like ethnography (Chapter 10) and in-depth interviewing (Chapter 11), historical-comparative research is a form of case-oriented research. Researchers who wish to conduct a historical-comparative analysis begin by carefully choosing one or several cases that will help them understand the relationships between the concepts that interest them. Small-case comparisons typically work best with two to four cases, but

purposive sampling A sampling strategy in which cases are deliberately selected on the basis of features that distinguish them from other cases.

sometimes more cases are used. For the method to work, the researcher has to know each case in depth. That gets more difficult as the number of cases increases.

Selecting the case or cases involves **purposive sampling**, whereby cases are deliberately selected on the basis of features that distinguish them from other cases (see Chapter 6). When choosing their sample, researchers may use several different criteria. Researchers may select a case because it is *important*, as in Schwartz's historical analysis of Abraham Lincoln. Historical-comparative sociologists may also choose *typical* cases, beginning with a topic that seems familiar, such as families in the United States (recall Coontz's study). In studies based on typical cases, researchers use data to reveal societal blind spots, hidden assumptions, and inaccuracies in how people understand the phenomenon being analyzed. *Deviant cases*, or anomalies, involve situations where the outcome is unexpected, such as Oscar Wilde's delayed arrest, prosecution, and conviction. They help researchers understand the mechanisms that are necessary for an outcome to occur. Cases can also be selected on the basis of *contrasting outcomes* or *key differences*. These types of case selection are often called *Mill's methods*, after John Stuart Mill, who described them in the mid-nineteenth century.

counterfactuals A thought exercise of imagining what might have happened but did not, which can be useful in case selection.

Almost all cases in historical-comparative methods involve a surprise or a counterintuitive puzzle. One way to think about whether you have selected noteworthy cases is to think in terms of **counterfactuals**. Counterfactuals involve thinking about what might have happened but did not or what might have happened if the focal event or condition had not occurred. If one traveled back in time to a point before an event occurred, what would sociological theories predict would happen and what did people at the time expect to happen? If a different outcome would have been likely, that is a promising case.

Choosing an interesting case and figuring out what is interesting about it can be challenging for the novice researcher. It is a good idea to consult with your instructor about good cases that relate to a research question that interests you. Case selection is intimately tied to the research question; the two often develop together, which explains why purposive sampling is appropriate in historical-comparative analysis.

DEVELOPING CONCEPTS AND HYPOTHESES

The next step in historical-comparative research involves developing an extensive series of hypotheses about how your concepts might be linked. These hypotheses should be based on sociological theory, a commonsense understanding of the world, and your own knowledge of both your topic and prior research on the topic. Why did your case turn out the way it did?

Researchers engaged in historical-comparative methods tend to have strong hunches about the answers to their questions before they delve extensively into their analysis of the materials. Their goal is to determine whether there is sufficient evidence to support their hunches. The quest for answers sometimes raises a problem: Researchers may get locked into one view of the historical record and fail to recognize other possible or likely explanations. This may have been a problem for Michael Bellesiles (2000) when he conducted the analysis for his book *Arming America: The Origins of a National Gun Culture*. In his research, he veered away from expert reports and other materials to claim that most Americans did not own guns until after the Civil War. This conclusion is untrue, and a panel of prominent historians declared his book an unprofessional and misleading work, as they explained in the conclusion of an official review (Investigative Committee, 2002):

> When Professor Bellesiles collected this data, he was only incidentally interested in the question of gun data. His data sheets have categories for many other things, but not for guns, which come in only as he happens to note them, sometimes in the margins of other entries. . . . Unfortunately, this seemingly randomly gathered information later took on a life of its own. He appears carelessly to have assumed that his counts were complete, and moved forward with a larger project on the basis of this unsystematic research that appears to have involved dipping into rather than seriously sampling the records. (p. 17)

The historians concluded that Bellesiles was not guilty of fraud but rather of "sloppy scholarship" that led to misleading results. Bellesiles's experience is a cautionary tale: It exemplifies why an early and comprehensive theoretical framework that provides a range of alternative connections and explanations is important in the process of conducting historical-comparative research.

Soldiers in the U.S. Civil War continued to own their guns after the war ended, contrary to the suggestion of Bellesiles (2000).

FINDING AND ORGANIZING INFORMATION

The next step is finding high-quality, unbiased, and complete information on your cases. These materials should be related to the concepts that you have identified. Expert analyses by historians and others are often particularly important or useful.

The goal of gathering data is to learn as much as possible about your cases with respect to the particular angle you are exploring. At the same time, you must necessarily limit the scope of your analysis. For example, if you are examining education policy, be sure to identify the particular time period on which you will focus—perhaps the period leading up to a major reform, such as compulsory schooling laws in the nineteenth century or the implementation of Common Core in the twenty-first century. As noted in Chapter 2, if you do not set a clear scope for your analysis, it can become unwieldy.

Take extensive notes as you read and review. Your notes should summarize the content and identify links between the content and your hypotheses. You can take three steps to determine when you have gathered sufficient materials:

1. First, approach your sources systematically, recognizing and eliminating gaps in your knowledge. For example, if you are studying U.S. health policy since the beginning of the twenty-first century, make certain you have reviewed the legislative history for every year since 2000 to learn systematically about all new health-law proposals. If you study only the years in which you know that legislation was proposed, there will be gaps in your knowledge, and you may miss important facts.

2. Second, closely consider the contradictions you encounter. If one source tells one story and another source tells a different story (even a slightly different story),

you should seek additional information to resolve the contradiction. Discrepancies may lead you to the conclusion that one source is simply wrong, but more often they signal some complexity or nuance.

3. Third, try to reach saturation, which signals that you are becoming sufficiently informed about your cases. **Saturation** occurs when new materials reinforce what the researcher already knows and provide no new information. When saturation occurs, you can be confident that you thoroughly understand your cases.

saturation When new materials (interviews, observations, survey responses) fail to yield new insights and simply reinforce what the researcher already knows.

Time is crucial in unpacking how and why things happened. If a protest occurred after a law was passed, then you know that the protest did not lead to the law. Time is important not only because it establishes what happened first, but also because it reveals the length of time between events, the duration of events, and whether similar patterns of events repeated themselves (Aminzade, 1992). Although information on time and chronology doesn't prove causation, it does provide important clues about how change came about.

In addition, sorting by time period, such as month or year, allows you to integrate the different stories in your material. For example, one of the authors of this book analyzed nuclear-power policies in four countries (Boyle, 1998). She found many single-country accounts of protests over nuclear policies but few accounts that compared protests across countries. When she arranged the separate country stories in chronological order, she discovered that Germany's announcement that it would discontinue its nuclear-power program came only days after French police shot and killed an anti–nuclear power protester. Creating a timeline allowed her to see a transnational connection that would have otherwise remained hidden.

As you might imagine, compiling detailed historical timelines by hand, using multiple data sources, can be highly complicated and time consuming, perhaps even overwhelming. To create timelines, some researchers use software designed for qualitative data analysis (for example, ATLAS.ti, which we will learn about in Chapter 16). A more basic but effective option is to put the text or notes from each source on its own page in a word-processing program such as Microsoft Word or in its own row in Microsoft Excel. Insert your own intuitive *sorting keys*, such as the date of the event and important people, organizations, and places, at the top of each page or in an Excel column. You can then electronically or manually sort and re-sort the material to answer your questions. Make sure you include source information, such as the web link or publication information of the book or journal article you cited, including the page number, on each page or in each column.

ANALYZING THE DATA

After you have gathered and organized your information, it is time to begin the analysis. One of your most important tasks at this stage is affirming or refuting the different possible

Protests, such as this Belgian anti-nuclear protest, may be prompted by events occurring in other countries. A timeline that combines events in different countries is one way to find out.

explanations that you identified on the basis of sociological theories. For case study analyses, sociologists do not try to find one causal factor that led to a particular outcome. Instead, they embrace the complexities of their cases and try to unpack complete processes that led to their outcomes of interest.

Your final step is to write up your findings. First, introduce the cases and the puzzle that drew you to them. Next, lay out your concepts and theory-based expectations, explaining the key findings in the existing literature and describing how they influenced your concepts and hypotheses. You might also point out limitations or gaps in the literature, to set the stage for your study's unique contribution. Next, move into the details of your cases and explain how specific facts support or refute your hypotheses. Do not simply tell the reader your conclusions; rather, lay out your evidence and explain your reasoning in linking it to your hypotheses. Finally, conclude with an assessment of the implications of your analysis for theory development around your key concept. In some cases, you may want to speculate about the implications of your work for social policy or practice.

CONCEPT CHECKS

1   What is the difference between historical-comparative methods in sociology and historical analysis in history?

2   Using the Abraham Lincoln case studies, provide an example of how different evidence is relevant for different research questions, even when they relate to the same historical figure.

3   What three criteria do historical-comparative sociologists use to determine whether they have gathered sufficient material?

CONTENT ANALYSIS

Content analysis of materials, which focuses on the text or images found in the materials, is another common sociological method. Content analysis seeks to uncover evidence of bias, with the idea that successful writers, journalists, artists, and producers create a world that represents what they think is true or appealing, reflecting in turn societal blind spots or the hidden biases of the public. In **quantitative content analysis**, researchers systematically review some kind of material (for example, legal opinions, news stories, novels, movies, or blogs) to test hypotheses. **Critical content analysis** is more inductive, focusing on a single piece of material (such as a speech) or a small number of items and analyzing the material in great depth. Frequently, content analysis involves looking at materials over time. For that reason, the method is sometimes part of a broader historical analysis.

Quantitative Content Analysis

One example of quantitative content analysis is a study conducted by Janice McCabe and her colleagues (McCabe et al., 2011), which systematically reviewed 101 years of children's books. The researchers were interested in whether levels of feminist

quantitative content analysis Testing hypotheses through the systematic review of materials that have been converted into a quantitative data set.

critical content analysis An interpretive analysis of media designed to uncover societal blind spots.

Janice McCabe found that books such as *About Harriet*, which featured girl characters, were more common in the early twentieth century than in the mid-twentieth century.

activism affected the portrayal of girls and boys in children's literature. They found books primarily through the *Children's Catalog*, a robust annual review of U.S. children's literature.

In all, McCabe and her colleagues reviewed more than 5,000 books. They first classified book titles as containing a male name or pronoun (such as "George" or "he"), a female name or pronoun (such as "Harriet" or "her"), both, neither, or nonidentifiable. They also identified central characters in the books as male, female, both, neither, or nonidentifiable. They found that boys appeared in titles twice as often as girls, and that primary characters were 1.6 times more likely to be male than female. In terms of their research question, they found that the 1930s to the 1960s—the period between the women's suffrage movement of the 1920s and the women's movement of the late 1960s—had the greatest overrepresentation of boys. This finding supported their hypothesis: When feminist mobilization waned, so, too, did the presence of girls in children's literature.

There are a certain number of boys and girls in the United States—that is an objective reality. McCabe's content analysis highlights the subjective or perceived aspects of reality. The notion that boys are more interesting than girls or that boys are more appropriate protagonists in stories is subjective. Researchers who conduct culture-based content analyses believe subjective perceptions are important. In the case of children's books, they shape how boys and girls see themselves and experience the world. Subjective perceptions have real consequences.

Similar quantitative content analyses have considered gender differences in the portrayal of male and female athletes in *Sports Illustrated* (Fink & Kensicki, 2002), overrepresentation of African Americans as lawbreakers on television news (Dixon & Linz, 2000), and changes in representations of gays and lesbians in *New York Times* advertisements (Ragusa, 2005). These and other studies share the goal of uncovering the social construction of difference, which maintains inequities on the basis of gender, race, sexual orientation, or other personal characteristics.

STEPS IN QUANTITATIVE CONTENT ANALYSIS

The core elements of quantitative content analysis are identifying the research question, selecting the media to analyze and obtaining access to it, drawing a random sample of cases, developing concepts and related hypotheses, reviewing the media according to rules that operationalize core concepts, incorporating other data if necessary, assessing the data in light of the hypotheses, and writing up the conclusions. Table 12.2 provides an example of these processes for two different research questions.

Sampling Quantitative content analysis involves both purposive and representative random sampling. Researchers first select the material to analyze through purposive sampling. For example, they may pick materials, such as Supreme Court opinions, because they are *important*, which is one basis for purposive sampling.

McCabe and her colleagues likely chose to study children's books because those books are a *typical* example of media that is influential in shaping how young people understand the world. If you are interested in uncovering societal blind spots, such as subtle differences in the treatment of men and women, it is best to review material

TABLE 12.2   Examples of Components of Quantitative Content Analysis for Two Research Questions

Research Question: *Do levels of feminist activism affect the portrayal of gender in children's literature (McCabe et al., 2011)?*			
Sampling	**Concepts**	**Operationalization**	**Spreadsheet Entries**
Award-winning and most popular children's books, 1900–2000, drawn from *Children's Catalog*	Gender in children's literature over time	Dependent variables: • Gender of names in book titles • Gender of main characters	Each row is a book; columns include publication year, gender in title and gender of main character
	Feminist activism over time	Independent variable: • Year or era	

Research Question: *Do black and Hispanic newspapers have more localized health stories relative to mainstream newspapers (Wang & Rodgers, 2014)?*			
Sampling	**Concepts**	**Operationalization**	**Spreadsheet Entries**
Newspapers: 15 newspapers representing five regions in California; within each region, one black newspaper, one Hispanic newspaper, one mainstream newspaper News articles: all articles related to health in the 15 newspapers on the basis of key-word searches; articles published between Oct. 2007 and Feb. 2008	Localized health coverage	Dependent variables: • News that features a local health or medical event, such as a flu outbreak • News that features a local expert • News that features local services, such as free mammograms at a local clinic	Each row is a health-related news story; columns include region, newspaper, whether the newspaper has primarily black, Hispanic, or white subscribers, date, local event or not, local expert or not, local services or not
	Communications received by individuals in different ethnic and racial communities	Independent variable: • Whether news story appears in black, Hispanic, or mainstream newspaper	

that is typical rather than explicitly related to your topic. One key benefit of materials-based methods is that they can capture genuine human behavior. When forms of media are constructed with an explicit and overt bias, that natural quality is lost. It is better to study material that is a slice of ordinary life or is at least unrelated to the particular prejudices you wish to uncover. This is why McCabe chose to study all children's books rather than, say, children's books about girls' empowerment. The latter would likely consciously avoid gender bias even if that is not a typical behavior among those who write and publish children's books.

Key differences are another basis for sampling in quantitative content analysis. For example, Wang and Rodgers, mentioned earlier, chose three sets of newspapers—those with mostly white subscribers, those with mostly black subscribers, and those with mostly Hispanic subscribers—to determine how this key difference affected coverage of health-related issues. Although this selection method focuses on dissimilarity across units, for it to work the cases cannot be *too* different. If two cases are vastly different, then there are too many different factors that could potentially affect the outcome of interest. For example, it would be inappropriate to compare a newspaper with mostly black subscribers to a television station with mostly Hispanic viewers and a website visited by mostly white Internet users. In this case, a researcher could not sort out the most important factors related to any observed outcomes. Even when cases are selected on the basis of key differences, they must have some shared features.

Once you've identified the material to analyze, you may be confronted with a very large number of cases (for example, many hours of a television show or thousands of newspaper articles), so set limits on how much you will analyze. Draw a random sample of items or segments. For example, if you find N articles on ethnic protests in newspapers, you may want to draw a random sample of n, a number that you determine to be large enough to be representative of the articles collected but not so numerous as to overwhelm you as a researcher.

Operationalizing concepts Recall from Chapter 4 that **operationalization** is the process of linking the conceptualized variables to a set of procedures for measuring them. In content analysis, researchers operationalize their key concepts into variables through coding. **Coding** is the process of translating written or visual material into standardized categories suitable for quantitative analysis. The categories can be counts, such as the number of times violence occurs in a 30-minute television show. For ordinal variables (such as a five-category rating of schools) or nominal variables (such as race), researchers create a **coding scheme**, which lists all the possible categories and outlines specific rules for how to apply those categories to the material. Researchers typically assign a number to each ordinal or nominal variable category to facilitate statistical analyses of the data. For example, McCabe and colleagues operationalized the concept "gender in children's literature" through gender in book titles. The possible categories for gender in book titles were "male name or pronoun" (1), "female name or pronoun" (2), "both" (3), "neither" (4), or "nonidentifiable" (5). These categories are *mutually exclusive*—only one applies to any particular book title—and they are *exhaustive* in that they describe every possible type of book title.

Record your coding in a spreadsheet computer program like Microsoft Excel. An example is provided in Figure 12.4. Each row is one unit of content, such as one episode of a television show or one news article. Columns provide an ID, date, source, and values for your variables of interest. Make certain that your coding scheme includes all possible variables of interest, including independent variables that might influence the content. For example, if you are coding text from books and you expect the author's nationality to influence that content, your spreadsheet should include a column for author nationality. McCabe and colleagues operationalized their independent variable (feminist activism) using time, so each row in their spreadsheet had to include a book's publication year as well as information on its title and main character.

Coding schemes can be much more complex than McCabe's. For example, it took Cingranelli and his colleagues (2014) four pages to spell out the rules for coding "religious freedom" on the basis of the Human Rights Reports. Two factors drive the complexity of coding. The first is the ambiguity of the concept of interest. People have a

FIGURE 12.4 Recording Data on Children's Books in the Twentieth Century

Researchers conducting quantitative content analysis create numerical categories for each variable and then enter those variables into a spreadsheet so that they can be analyzed statistically. Each row is one piece of material, such as a children's book. Each column is a variable.

	A	B	C	D	E	F	G
			Little Golden Book 0 = No 1 = Yes	Caldecott Winner 0 = No 1 = Yes	Gender in Title 1 = Male name or pronoun 2 = Female name or pronoun 3 = Both 4 = Neither 5 = Nonidentifiable	Gender Main Character 1 = Male name or pronoun 2 = Female name or pronoun 3 = Both 4 = Neither 5 = Nonidentifiable	Main Character Age 0 = Child 1 = Adult
1	Book ID	Year of Publication					
2	10001	1900	0	0	1	1	0
3	10002	1925	0	0	1	1	0
4	10003	1927	0	1	2	2	0
5	10004	1943	0	1	4	1	1
6	10005	1955	1	1	1	2	0
7	10006	1995	1	0	5	5	0
8							

widely shared understanding of what is meant by "girl" or "boy," but they may disagree on what is meant by "religious freedom." The CIRI coders had to precisely spell out what actions represented infringements of religious freedom.

The second factor driving the complexity of coding schemes is the length and complexity of the material being coded. In contrast to book titles, which are only several words long, the religious freedom section of each Human Rights Report runs from a couple of paragraphs to several pages. Furthermore, Cingranelli and colleagues were not simply counting the occurrence of particular words and phrases; they were evaluating the meaning of the reports. Regardless of the complexity of the source material, it is best to limit the number of categories for each variable and keep them simple. Cingranelli and his colleagues' religious freedom variable has only three categories: government restrictions on religious practices are "severe and widespread" (0), "moderate" (1), or "practically absent" (2).

Creating a coding scheme can be tricky. The best plan is to review some of the material you plan to code before creating your coding scheme. Once you have a sense of the material, then create a preliminary coding scheme and apply it to a small sample of your material. Chances are, you will come across some material that doesn't fit easily into your categories. When this happens you can either create a **decision rule**, which is a rule for categorizing difficult material, or you can create a new category. For example, if McCabe and colleagues were conducting their research today, they might find some transgender characters. They could create a decision rule to always code these characters' gender as "both," "neither," or "nonidentifiable" or they might instead create a new category for these characters. Continue to modify your coding scheme until you are satisfied that it is adequately capturing the key aspects of your concept. Importantly, once it is finalized, go back and reevaluate your earlier coding. Recall Bellesiles's

decision rule Used in quantitative content analysis, a rule that clearly distinguishes mutually exclusive categories of a variable.

incorrect assessment of gun ownership, which arose because he changed his coding scheme midway through his analysis and didn't go back to review all the material he had already coded.

For all but the simplest coding projects, it is useful to maintain a separate **codebook**. Codebooks, which are also used in survey research (Chapter 7), can be created in either a spreadsheet program, like Excel, or a word-processing program, like Word. They list the variables in order and provide information about each variable. They contain the name of each variable, the different categories that are possible for that variable, and the corresponding number for each category. For example, the Cingranelli and colleagues (2014) codebook includes the variable "Country," which has 202 possible categories from Afghanistan to Zimbabwe. Each country is assigned its own number: Brazil is 170; the United States is 662. You can understand why the codebook is essential—no one can keep that many numbers in his or her head. The codebook should also include for each variable a clear description of your decision rules, followed by some specific examples from the coded texts. Keeping a codebook that explains how you constructed your data set will allow you or others to add more material to the data set later.

Analyzing your data and writing up your findings After you enter all your material into a spreadsheet, you can begin to analyze it and to evaluate whether your hypotheses are supported. (You will learn more about data analysis techniques in Chapters 14 and 15.) Cross tabulations and charts that show how the content of your material changes over time or across categories are usually the most effective way to present your data. As you write up your analysis, be sure to highlight examples of your media content throughout, providing rich, revealing quotes or images. These examples help make your paper more interesting and visually appealing.

NEW TRENDS IN QUANTITATIVE CONTENT ANALYSIS

The idea of doing coding by hand may sound daunting. Fortunately, new technologies can automate the coding process by searching for words or word combinations in digital files and constructing a data set on the basis of the search. For example, through a technique known as "data scraping," the AidData project (Anon, 2016) scanned foreign-aid documents from many organizations and government agencies over many decades, collecting the characteristics of financial flows, such as the amounts of money transferred and the purposes for which aid was given. This new data allowed researchers for the first time to make a systematic comparison of when and why Arab countries gave aid compared to other countries and organizations. Shushan and Marcoux (2011) found that aid from Arab countries declined during the wars in Iraq and Afghanistan when U.S. and British aid to Middle Eastern countries increased.

Automated coding has the advantages of being efficient and able to handle huge numbers of digital files. However, because no human is evaluating the output, automated programs will make some mistakes. These programs will include some instances that are not good representations of your concept, and they will miss others. Spot checking (that is, manually reviewing) some of the work produced will help you

> **codebook** A system of organizing information about a data set, including the variables it contains, the possible values for each variable, coding schemes, and decision rules.

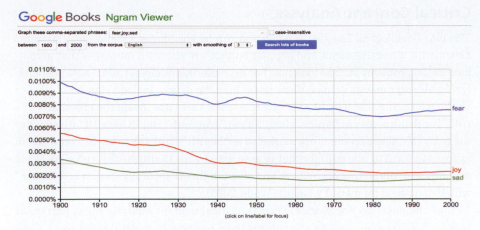

(click on line/label for focus)

This Ngram shows that the word *fear* appears more frequently in books than it did in 1980, while the appearance of the words *joy* and *sad* haven't changed much across the same period. Acerbi et al. (2013) used counts of synonyms of these words in their content analysis.

refine the link between your concept and your computer output. For example, if you are interested in the practice of female circumcision and told the system to search newspapers for "female circumcision," "female genital mutilation," and "FGM," you would get a lot of basketball articles because FGM is also an abbreviation for "field goals made."

Some content analysis tools are now available online. They are not as effective as conducting your own analysis, and they do not offer as many options as the sophisticated software packages, but they are fast. Google's Ngram Viewer allows you to assess how many times particular words appeared in books. You choose your language, the time period, and the word you want counted, and the Ngram Viewer will produce a chart showing the word's frequencies over time. Alberto Acerbi and his colleagues (Acerbi et al., 2013) used Ngram as a measure of how the mention of emotions has changed in English-language texts over time. They began with lists of synonyms for emotion words, including *anger, fear, joy, sadness, disgust,* and *surprise.* The authors found in general that use of emotion words declined over the course of the twentieth century. We are less expressive about our emotions in texts today than we were 100 years ago, with one notable exception—fear. Use of *fear* and synonyms for *fear* started to increase in the 1980s and has continued to do so.

Another useful tool for content analysis is Tagxedo, which will create word clouds from any content you put into it. For example, you could compare how the words appearing in your college's course catalog in 1990 (if you can get a digital copy) compare to those in the current course catalog. You could compare the words in the speeches given in 2016 by Hillary Clinton and Donald Trump at their respective national conventions. Word clouds are quantitative because they are based on counts, but the images produced lend themselves to more inductive assessment of the material.

Critical Content Analysis

The blog Sociological Images, founded and run by sociologist Lisa Wade, illustrates how media, advertisements, and popular culture are rife with messages that perpetuate social problems such as violence. For example, in a Sociological Images post analyzing Monster energy drinks, Wade noted how the drinks include simulated slashes on the packaging that look like vicious scratches; these are inside the crosshairs of a rifle. The drink comes in flavors called "Sniper," "Assault," and "Khaos." The blog notes the irony that these products are marketed as "health" drinks even as they promote an aggressive form of masculinity that is associated with taking health risks. As Wade explains, the "marketing normalizes and makes light of a lot of aggression and danger," which "isn't good for men or women" (Wade, 2015).

Like the posts on Sociological Images, critical content analysis takes particular images from popular media and analyzes them to uncover societal blind spots. Generally, researchers using this approach will evaluate a small number of items, such as President George W. Bush's State of the Union addresses (Sowińska, 2013), selected using purposive sampling techniques. Indeed, sociologists working in the critical theory tradition, including feminists and critical race scholars, may **deconstruct** a single cultural artifact; that is, take apart the content and suggest hidden or alternative meanings. These scholars believe that certain ways of thinking are so pervasive in societies that they can be found in virtually any representation of reality.

deconstruction A critical interpretive approach to research that involves dissecting the content of some type of media to uncover hidden or alternative meanings.

A critical perspective is useful for uncovering rules that are so taken for granted that we don't even realize that they shape the world. For example, the first chapter of Michel Foucault's *The Order of Things* (1970) is an extensive analysis of Diego Velázquez's painting *Las Meninas*. At first glance, the painting appears to be a portrait of a young princess bathed in light and standing in the foreground. Upon closer inspection, you see that the painter himself is in the portrait off to the left, and you imagine that he is painting the princess. He is not looking at the princess, however; he and most everyone else in the painting are looking at someone or something that is not visible. What? The answer is in the mirror in the center of the portrait, which shows a reflection of King Philip IV and his wife—the princess's parents. The point of Foucault's analysis is that Velázquez has broken a rule so taken for granted that we didn't even realize it was a rule: Paintings are supposed to be about the images they feature.

Is the princess being painted in this famous portrait? If you think yes, take a closer look.

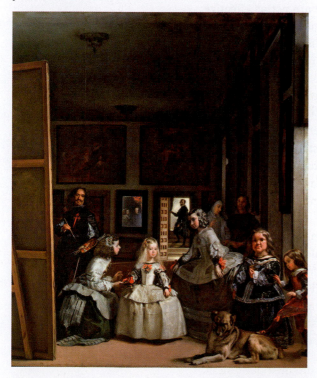

A quantitative approach that involves counting and coding will miss these hidden rules and expectations. In fact, a useful exercise for thinking critically about media is learning to see what is *not* there. For example, for years the highly popular *Thomas the Tank Engine* television show and books had only two female characters. Poor Annie and Clarabel, who appeared only rarely, were coaches that were pulled by the male engines. Meanwhile, Thomas, Percy, Gordon, Henry, James, Edward, and Sir Topham Hatt got to do all the fun stuff. Sociologists who do critical content analysis are attuned to these peculiar—and revealing—representations of communities.

Critical content analysis operates on a different set of methods than most sociological work. It is based on interpretation (via certain interpretive rules) rather than evidence. For example, in written texts, critical scholars will look for particular linguistic features, such as metaphors used to describe a dominant group and its values versus a marginalized out-group and its values. Because critical content analysis is so different from evidence-based methodologies, we do not have space to describe the technique in detail. For our purposes, critical content analysis and related tools, like Sociological Images, are most useful for generating ideas about research questions and interesting cases.

CONCEPT CHECKS

1 What kinds of sampling are involved in quantitative content analyses: purposive, random, or both? Explain.

2 What is a codebook, and why is it useful?

3 How are the methods of critical content analysis different from other sociological methods?

QUANTITATIVE DATA ANALYSIS IN MATERIALS-BASED RESEARCH

Quantitative data analysis involves converting materials into numerical data and then analyzing the data to investigate relationships and test hypotheses. Hollie Nyseth Brehm (2014), a sociologist at the Ohio State University, used quantitative data analysis to study how genocides unfold (see "Conversations from the Front Lines"). To answer her research question, Brehm studied the genocides in Rwanda, Bosnia, and the Sudan. She traveled to Rwanda and Bosnia to get access to archived materials that were available only in those countries—in Rwanda, a nationwide survey about when and where people had died and a book (created by a survivors' organization) with the names of people killed; in Bosnia, a nongovernmental organization's list of people killed in Bosnia compared against records from an international court that attempted to prosecute killers. Data on Sudan were drawn from U.S. government records and data collected by an individual scholar regarding bombings in the country. Brehm assembled this material into three separate data sets, one for each country. (She was unable to integrate the information into a single data set because the measures were not comparable. For example, she had data on bombings for Sudan but not for Bosnia.)

Brehm found that the way genocides unfold depends very much on whether and to what extent there are preexisting groups created by the state to carry out violence. In Bosnia-Herzegovina and Darfur (a region of Sudan), previously organized armies and militias generally committed the violence. Strategic concerns dictated patterns of

> **quantitative data analysis**
> The process by which substantive findings are drawn from numerical data.

HOLLIE NYSETH BREHM

Hollie Nyseth Brehm is an assistant professor of sociology at the Ohio State University. Her work focuses primarily on the causes and processes of mass violence. She conceptualizes genocidal violence as a series of unfolding events rather than a single event. This innovative approach allows her to suggest important new explanations for mass killings, which may ultimately lead to more effective prevention and intervention strategies. Her work is having a profound impact on academics, the public, and policy makers.

What inspired you to tackle a topic as complex as genocide in your research?

I became inspired to study genocide during my first year of graduate school. The director of Genocide Watch was a guest speaker in my public health and human rights course. Prior to his lecture, I knew about the Holocaust but did not realize that genocide had continued to occur with such alarming frequency. I was shocked to learn that genocide had killed more people than all international wars of the twentieth century combined.

After the lecture, I searched for sociologists who study genocide. While I found several, it was also clear that the discipline of sociology has largely neglected the topic. This surprised me, as genocide is a multifaceted, dynamic social phenomenon that discriminates against people because of their perceived membership in a socially constructed group.

What data did you use, and why were they originally created? How much did you have to supplement your data set with other sources of information?

I examined information for three recent genocides—Rwanda (1994), Bosnia-Herzegovina (1992–1995), and the Darfur region of Sudan, a genocide that is still ongoing. To assess why some parts of each country saw comparatively more violence, I needed data on genocidal violence that was available at local levels. We typically think of genocide in terms of a total death count—for instance, up to 1 million people were killed in Rwanda—but I needed information about where those people died.

This kind of information cannot be found online or in any U.S. archive. Instead, I actually had to travel to each country in order to obtain data. Before traveling, I conducted research to assess what types of data may exist. In Rwanda, a university had collaborated with a government ministry to conduct a nationwide survey about when and where people had died. This was the only measure available across the entire country, so I contacted the government commission that kept the survey and requested permission to use it. As no data are perfect, I checked these data against other sources. For example, a survivors' organization had created a book of the names of people who were killed in a certain region, and comparing the survey data from that region to the book of names helped me assess the validity of the survey.

In Bosnia, a nongovernmental organization (NGO) had collected the only comprehensive list of people who had died. As this list also included the location of death, I contacted the organization and requested access. As in Rwanda, I needed to meet with them in person in order to obtain the data, and I was granted permission. I then used records from the International Criminal Tribunal for Yugoslavia—which tried major perpetrators of the violence—to assess the validity of these data.

Data for Darfur were harder to obtain, as the violence was (and is) still ongoing. Ultimately, I learned that the U.S. government has tracked villages in Darfur that were bombed by the Sudanese government, which is perpetrating the genocide, and I used that information for my analysis.

Although I used archived materials to conduct my statistical analysis, traveling to Rwanda and Bosnia and requesting data in person meant that I was also able to learn about each genocide from people who witnessed the violence. I conducted 110 interviews with witnesses in different parts of the countries. I also traveled to Uganda to interview refugees from different parts of Darfur to learn more about how the violence unfolded. This allowed me to learn more about the dynamics of the violence—something I could not ascertain from the data sets.

What were your greatest challenges in finding and using data on genocides?

I would be lying if I said there were not many challenges in finding and analyzing data on genocide. First, data on genocide are political. For instance, the number of people who were killed in the genocide in Rwanda has become very politicized, and many people have a vested interest in this figure. Some people suggest that 500,000 were killed, and others suggest 800,000 were killed. Yet, the government of Rwanda maintains that more than 1 million people were killed, and some government officials even suggest that citing lower estimates is genocide denial.

> " The key is that the data have to be collected in a manner that you think is scientifically sound, valid, and reliable. "

Beyond this, obtaining accurate data on any type of violence during genocide is difficult. Data on most forms of crime can be problematic to collect under everyday circumstances, but when a country is embroiled in turmoil, they typically are not worried about collecting data. Data collection thus takes place after the violence has ended—sometimes years afterward. In Bosnia, for instance, the nongovernmental organization used as many secondary sources as possible to try to collect the names of everyone who died. They even published the lists publicly and encouraged people to submit the names of people who were missing from the list. But, if an entire family had fled or had been wiped out, we cannot be certain that their names were submitted to the list.

Lastly, there is some aversion to quantifying violence. Aggregate numbers are necessary to share the broader stories of the genocides, analyze the patterns of violence, and better understand why and how genocide occurs. Such numbers are powerful, though they are reductive. For example, to understand what factors influence how many people are killed in each community, individual deaths are combined into single quantities collapsed over many units of space and time. Numbers like these certainly do not privilege the individual's story, though they in no way mean to diminish it. Instead, I believe these statistics show a different side of the story—how an individual's experience can be contextualized in broader patterns.

How are you using your research findings to help people who may experience genocide?

I am motivated to better understand how genocides unfold in order to inform responses to genocide. The United Nations as well as the U.S. government and numerous other governments and think tanks constantly monitor situations in which genocide may be likely. While deciding *who* intervenes in genocide is quite political, we first have to know more about how genocides unfold in order to know how best to respond to such violence.

In line with this, I was asked to join a government task force that forecasts atrocity worldwide. They use data much like the data I collected to try to understand where violence may be likely and how it may unfold. The task force is composed of scholars and policy makers, so it is a great opportunity to bring social scientific work to policy makers who may not otherwise find it. Likewise, the task force affords me the opportunity to learn from policy makers' experiences and to better understand what social scientific research would be most useful for policy.

What do you see as the benefits of conducting quantitative analyses using existing data sets?

Personally, I did not have any other options! Violence in Rwanda and violence in Bosnia had occurred two decades prior to when I was engaged in research, so simultaneously studying the violence was impossible. Furthermore, the difficulties of entering the Darfur region in Sudan meant that this was also impossible for the case of Darfur.

Beyond difficulties in collecting certain types of data, I think that scholars trying to decide between using existing data sets or collecting their own data should first assess what has been done. In each of my cases, institutions had previously collected data that could be used to answer my questions, and I thought these data had been collected using sound scientific methodology and with the benefit of many more resources than I had at my disposal as a graduate student. Thus, rather than reinvent the wheel, it seemed wise to rely upon these existing data sets. The key is that the data have to be collected in a manner that you think is scientifically sound, valid, and reliable. In line with this, the data-collection procedures must be documented clearly so that you can realistically assess them.

violence. In contrast, in Rwanda, community members who were not part of previously organized formal groups participated in the violence. In the case of Rwanda, community factors (not strategic concerns) explained variation in the intensity of the violence and how it spread. Specifically, communities with younger, unmarried, unemployed people (those whom sociologists have shown are more likely to commit crimes) experienced more intense violence. The United Nations Special Adviser on the Prevention of Genocide requested Brehm's findings, which may be used to revise the framework the United Nations applies to identify countries at risk of genocide.

Steps in Materials-Based Research with Secondary Quantitative Data Sets

As you have seen throughout this text, many sociological methods, including surveys, experiments, and sometimes interviews, use quantitative data analysis. The same is true of some types of materials-based research. Quantitative data analysis techniques are covered in detail in Chapters 14 and 15. In this section, we focus on issues that are important for quantitative analysis using *secondary data sets*; that is, preexisting data sets rather than data sets constructed by the researcher.

USING PREEXISTING DATA SETS TO HELP CONSTRUCT A RESEARCH QUESTION

Potential research topics are often wide open for quantitative analyses because of the large number and range of excellent data sets available via depositories such as ICPSR or www.data.gov. Such depositories hold data resources that extend far beyond surveys. When you are using historical-comparative methods and conducting content analysis, it is best to develop your research topic simultaneously with the selection of your cases or media content, but this is less of a concern for quantitative analyses of secondary data. That said, it is a good idea to come up with several possible questions within your research topic, because preexisting data are not necessarily available or able to answer every potential question. Many preexisting data sets will include items that are relevant to your research question, but they may be missing other key items of interest.

FAMILIARIZING YOURSELF WITH THE DATA AND DATA-COLLECTION PROCESS

Preexisting data sets look very polished and ready to use, but they can still contain errors and biases. Furthermore, even if the data set is perfect in every way, you are likely to misuse it if you are unfamiliar with its background. Therefore, before you begin your analysis, find out more about the data you are about to use. You can access important contextual information by reading the frequently asked questions (FAQ) section that accompanies most data sets. You may also want to read published research studies or working papers based on the data.

Once you've reviewed any FAQ and previous studies, assess the data structure. Are the data for a single time period, cross-sectional from several time periods, or longitudinal? The next step is determining the unit of analysis, such as individuals, schools, or countries (as described in Chapter 4). These steps will help you determine the data set's usefulness for answering your research question.

Assuming that the data-set structure and unit of analysis match your research questions, the next step is reviewing the sampling frame for the data set. The key question regarding sampling is whether you need to apply **sampling weights** when you conduct your analysis (refer to Chapter 6 for a detailed explanation). For example, you may recall that some surveys oversample particular groups of individuals. The data set will contain weights that you can apply to the data to ensure an overall representative sample. This is also a good time to see whether the data have been manipulated to protect respondents' privacy.

The next step is reviewing the codebook or codebooks to determine which questions interest you. Preexisting data sets include so much information on so many topics! The codebook introduces you to the information included in a particular data set, listing all the variables available in a survey, the value labels and codes for each, and the frequency distribution of responses. It also provides information on whether a survey question that particularly interests you was asked in multiple years or only once. If you are using Integrated Public Use Microdata Series (IPUMS) data, it is particularly easy to access this piece of information. IPUMS projects allow you to link to information from the codebook and other sources directly through each variable name.

sampling weights Values that are assigned to each case so that researchers can construct an overall representative sample; often found in secondary data sets.

MERGING MATERIALS INTO A SINGLE DATA SET

Like Brehm, researchers doing quantitative data analysis often merge multiple sources of data into a single data file. It is possible to combine data sets when the data have matching units of analysis, such as U.S. states or countries around the world. If one data source contains the unemployment rate for Alabama, and another includes the percentage of people in Alabama with college degrees (for roughly the same time period), then the two pieces of information can be combined into one data set.

There are some rules to keep in mind when attempting to merge data files across different units of analysis (Figure 12.5). Units of analysis range from the micro level (individuals) to the macro level (corporations, countries). You can assign macro information directly to micro units. For example, say you have individual-level survey data on family size that includes the country in which each person lives, and you want to know whether having more women in parliament is associated with individuals wanting to have fewer children. You can add the percentage of women in parliament from the relevant country to each individual's record to help answer this question. This data-merging strategy helps avoid ecological fallacies, that is, assuming everyone within a group has the average characteristics for that group (see Chapter 4), because it allows the researcher to assess the independent effects of individual characteristics (preferred number of children) and group characteristics (living in a country with a high percentage of women in parliament) at the same time.

FIGURE 12.5 Merging Data Across Units of Analysis

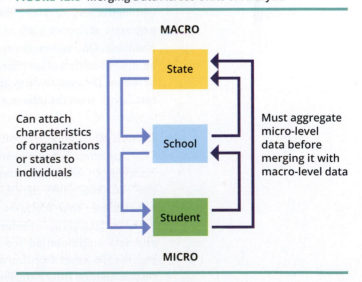

MACRO

State

School

Student

MICRO

Can attach characteristics of organizations or states to individuals

Must aggregate micro-level data before merging it with macro-level data

To merge in the other direction—applying micro data to macro records—you need to aggregate the micro data first. If you think individual attitudes toward gun ownership influence gun deaths by state, for example, you could merge individual survey data of attitudes toward guns with a data set of gun deaths by state. To do this, you would first use the micro data to calculate the percentage of individuals supportive of gun ownership by state. You would then add the percentage for each state to the state-level data set.

Combining two or more data sets in which individuals are the unit of analysis is difficult or impossible. These data sets typically do not include individuals' names or other identifying information, nor do they include information on the same individuals, so there is no way to match them. Even if existing data sets do identify individuals, there is relatively little systematic public information on individuals that could be attached to them. Occasionally, as with Inwood and colleagues' (2016) research using military and death records of New Zealanders, there is enough information to combine individuals' records. Even then, it is a painstaking process. More commonly, researchers aggregate and merge data sets of individuals across years or samples in order to conduct comparative analysis. For example, researchers frequently combine multiple years of the General Social Survey or multiple country samples of the Demographic and Health Surveys (DHS) to conduct their analyses.

CHECKING YOUR ANALYSIS AGAINST PREVIOUSLY PUBLISHED REPORTS

When you use preexisting data sets, it is best to begin with descriptive statistics, such as frequency tables, on your key variables of interest. Others will have used the data previously; you should compare your results with theirs to see if they match. For example, the DHS and IPUMS-DHS data sets include country reports that summarize the data for each country; you can use these reports to check the accuracy of your results. The descriptive tables in published articles also provide a basis for comparisons. If your results are different from published results, you may have forgotten to weight your data, you may be missing certain variables, or you may be coding values incorrectly.

Some secondary data sets, such as IPUMS-USA, IPUMS-International, and DHS (through STATcompiler), now have online tabulators. These provide summary or aggregate statistics, such as the percentage of households in Zimbabwe with indoor plumbing. Online tabulators sometimes allow for more sophisticated multivariable analyses, and they often offer different options for displaying the results, such as charts or tables. Depending on your research questions, you may be able to use the online tabulators to get the information you need without having to download any data files.

CITING AND DESCRIBING THE DATA SETS

The final step in the research process is writing up your results. Chapter 17 will walk you through each step of this process. For now, remember that you must cite your secondary data set, just as you would any book or article that you are referencing. Your methods section should list and describe potential problems with the data, if those problems are relevant to your analysis. It should also explain any data manipulation you performed, such as weighting the data. Make sure to provide the exact wording of each survey question you use if the data are survey responses, and fully describe your variables.

LIMITATIONS OF MATERIALS-BASED METHODS

Materials-based methods are very well suited to studies of macro phenomena. They can often avoid some of the pitfalls of methods that require interviewing people directly, such as social desirability bias. They can also use rich data resources to explore questions that might otherwise be impossible to research. Despite its many advantages, however, materials-based research has two key limitations. First, researchers may encounter barriers to accessing materials. Second, the materials themselves may have shortcomings.

Barriers to Access

As you search for material, you may encounter some barriers. One is cost. While a lot of information is freely available, you must pay for some types of information. As a general rule, if advertisers would be interested in a question similar to your research question, then there is probably a fee for the information you want. For example, it is very costly to access detailed Nielsen ratings data, which provide information on how many people watch different television shows. Some countries, such as China, charge for access to their data, if they are willing to provide the data at all.

You may also encounter barriers if you wish to access the private records of organizations. The only way to access these sources (ethically) is to create a connection with the organization and ask for access. If you plan to do so, prepare a clear, short report that explains the importance of your question, the ways in which you will protect the anonymity of the organization and its employees and customers, and precisely what data or information you need. You are more likely to be successful if you have already established a relationship with the organization and the question you are investigating is one that also interests the organization's management.

Sometimes, even if you can access information, it can be difficult to use. For example, the material might be in a language you do not understand. It might be the case that a data set can be read only by a computer program you do not own or use. When you encounter barriers, assess whether the value of the data outweighs the difficulty of overcoming the barrier to access. If it doesn't, then try to find a different source, even if that means revising your research question. Researchers will rarely find "perfect" materials that meet every single one of their needs or that include information on every possible concept they are interested in measuring. The key is to find high-quality information that you can readily access and that meets at least most of the criteria on your wish list.

Potential Shortcomings in Materials

Because researchers using materials are removed from actual events, people, and places, they may miss some important nuances of the social world they are studying. Researchers using secondary data are also removed from the data-gathering process, which makes it difficult for them to detect errors in the data and makes misuse of the data more likely.

Furthermore, materials from some historical eras may lack information on women, ethnic and racial minorities, and other groups. For example, the 1810 U.S. Census includes only the names of "heads of households," who were defined as men unless there were no men in the household. This means there is no way to use U.S. Census data to track the movement of most women from one household to another between 1810 and 1820 and beyond.

Finally, materials are rarely tailored to the researcher's particular question. The material may have been created for a purpose completely unrelated to the research. Even if the materials were created for research purposes, the specific research questions they were created to answer will likely be different from the current researcher's questions. The best way to address these shortcomings is to combine materials-based methods with other types of research methods whenever possible, a practice called **triangulation**. Researchers will rarely find the "perfect" material that meets all of their needs and which includes data on every possible measure of interest. By combining methods, you are more likely to find the information you need.

triangulation The use of multiple research methods to study the same general research question and determine if different types of evidence and approaches lead to consistent findings.

CONCEPT CHECKS

1 What two barriers may you confront when trying to access materials for sociological research?

2 What strategy should you use if you need to get access to the private records of an organization?

3 What are two potential shortcomings associated with materials-based research? Provide examples of each.

CONCLUSION

Materials-based research, which relies on materials and preexisting information, is uniquely valuable for answering certain types of research questions. A huge range of materials is available to researchers, including books and articles, reports, records, media, newspapers, firsthand accounts, and data sets. The government is a particularly rich source for much of this information. Materials-based methods can use primary evidence, but researchers also utilize secondary evidence, which they must assess in terms of quality and representativeness. Materials-based analysis can take the form of historical-comparative analysis (which explores change across time and across locations) or content analysis (which focuses on the text or images in materials). It can also involve the statistical analysis of preexisting data. While materials-based analysis is a valuable tool for sociologists, it does have some weaknesses: Researchers may encounter barriers to access, and the materials themselves may have shortcomings. Careful researchers are aware of these limitations and take steps to minimize them.

Summary

Materials-based methods study the social world through reports, records, media, and other materials. These methods offer unique advantages for exploring research questions about macro-level social phenomena and historical events and also allow for cross-cultural comparisons. Social researchers using materials-based methods have a variety of options for data analysis, including historical-comparative methods, content analysis, and quantitative analyses.

Why Use Materials Rather Than People to Answer Sociological Questions?

- Talking with individuals is usually not the best way to learn about macro-level social phenomena, or the large patterns and institutions that make up a social structure.
- Second, materials-based methods allow social researchers to study questions whose answers do not exist in living memory.
- People may not always be the best resource for studying what is happening in their society. Individuals may be influenced by social desirability bias, societal blind spots, or memory lapses.

Materials Used in Materials-Based Methods

- The main types of materials used in materials-based research include expert analyses, reports, records, news media and other media, individual accounts of events, physical materials, maps, and data sets.
- Researchers will often use multiple resources to investigate a single research question.

Primary versus Secondary Information

- Primary information is unaltered, firsthand evidence, while secondary information is collected by someone other than the researcher.
- Researchers cannot control the quality or content of secondary data. As such, they must consider the reputation of the source and the data-collection techniques.

Where Do Researchers Find Materials for Analyses?

- An archive is a place where materials are compiled to be studied. While many archives are physical locations run by organizations, today archives also include digital databases.
- Archives are often compiled by governments and corporations, though researchers, activists, and hobbyists also create archives. Policies like the Freedom of Information Act have expanded the types of government data that can be requested by the public.

Historical and Comparative Methods

- Historical methods measure how societies change over time, while comparative methods study differences across places at a given point in time.
- When conducting historical-comparative research, researchers select case(s) using purposive sampling. Researchers may choose cases that are important or typical or on the basis of contrasting outcomes or key differences.
- To get high-quality information on their cases, researchers should assess sources systematically, consider contradictions between sources, and try to reach saturation.
- When analyzing the data, researchers should affirm or refute the possible explanations identified on the basis of sociological theories.

Content Analysis

- Content analyses are materials-based methods that analyze the text or images embedded in materials.
- In quantitative content analysis, researchers must operationalize their key concepts into variables. This is accomplished through coding, in which written or visual material is translated into standardized categories for quantitative analysis.
- Critical content analyses can help reveal the hidden meanings or rules that guide daily life. Unlike other research methods, critical content analysis is based on interpretation rather than evidence.

Quantitative Data Analysis in Materials-Based Research

- When conducting quantitative data analysis of preexisting data sets, researchers should consider what type of previous studies have used the data, the data-collection methods, and whether the time frame and units of analysis are appropriate for their research questions.
- Researchers who want to merge two or more secondary data sets must be attentive to the units of analysis in each.

Limitations of Materials-Based Methods

- Researchers may face barriers to accessing the data, including cost or privacy issues.
- Materials-based methods also have methodological limitations. Researchers using secondary data are removed both from the actual events, people, and places being studied as well as the data-gathering process. Also, researchers will rarely find a data source that is perfectly suited for their research question.

Key Terms

aggregate data, 394

archive, 393

big data, 390

codebook, 408

coding, 406

coding scheme, 406

comparative research methods, 397

counterfactuals, 400

critical content analysis, 403

decision rule, 407

deconstruction, 410

first-person account, 387

geographic information systems (GIS), 389

historical research methods, 397

macro-social phenomena, 379

materials, 378

materials-based methods, 378

media, 386

micro data, 394

operationalization, 406

primary information, 391

purposive sampling, 400

quantitative content analysis, 403

quantitative data analysis, 411

sampling weights, 415

saturation, 402

secondary information, 391

societal blind spots, 380

triangulation, 418

unobtrusive methods, 378

validity, 392

Exercise

Conduct a quantitative content analysis using magazine covers. The goals of the exercise are to practice selecting cases, formulating hypotheses, setting up a coding scheme, coding material to create quantitative data, analyzing the data, and reporting results.

- Select two magazines that vary on some important dimension but are otherwise similar. For example, *GQ* and *Vogue* are similar because they are both fashion magazines read predominantly by white people, but men tend to subscribe to the former while women tend to subscribe to the latter. Briefly explain the key similarities and differences in the two magazines you selected.

- Use the Internet or a library archive to find a good number of examples of your magazines' covers. If you cannot find a systematic archive of your magazines' covers, a reasonable approach is to search Google Images. If none of your search options produces a good selection of magazine covers, you will have to select different magazines.

- Develop a set of hypotheses relevant to your magazine comparison. Begin by thinking about the key dimension of difference. For *GQ* and *Vogue*, one key dimension of difference is the gender of the readers, so the hypotheses might relate to why and how women and men want to see different representations of fashion and beauty. Depending on the magazines you choose, other key differences could be the race, age, or social class of the readers or the topics covered by the magazines (for example, *Good Housekeeping* versus *Working Woman*). Time period can also be a dimension of difference.

- Use your hypotheses as the basis for creating a coding scheme. Make sure you are measuring something (or multiple things) for *each* hypothesis. Each hypothesis should have its own unique evidence to allow you to assess whether it is supported. In other words, your coding scheme should correspond to your hypotheses.

- Determine the population of covers you want to review. Is it useful to consider all years of your magazines or only older or more recent years? Specify a particular time period. Then devise a sampling strategy to select the covers you will review.

- Code the magazine covers in your sample. Figure 12.6 provides an example of an Excel spreadsheet like the one you will create. Each column is a variable, and each line represents one magazine cover. The spreadsheet uses numbers rather than words to make analysis easier. Create a codebook related to the spreadsheet that explains each variable and the decision rules for assigning categories. For example, for the "Exposed" variable, the codebook might explain that "scantily clothed" means that genitals, butt, or (for women) nipples are visible, although the model is wearing some clothing.

- Analyze your data. How do the percentages in each category differ across your magazines? Create charts to illustrate the differences. Which of your hypotheses were supported? Which were not supported? Explain the implications.

FIGURE 12.6 Example of Quantitative Content Analysis Data Entries

	A	B	C	D	E	F	G
1	Magazine 0 = GQ 1 = Vogue	Year	Gender 0 = Male 1 = Female 2 = Both 3 = Indeterminate	Race 0 = White 1 = Black 2 = Asian 3 = Hispanic White 4 = Multi-racial 5 = Other 6 = Indeterminate	Exposed 0 = Naked 1 = Partially naked 2 = Scantily clothed 3 = Fully clothed	Age 1 = Child 2 = Teenager 3 = Young adult 4 = Older adult 5 = Elderly	Weight 0 = Below average 1 = Average 2 = Above average
2	1	1958	0	0	3	3	2
3	1	1968	0	0	3	3	2
4	1	1978	1	0	2	2	1
5	1	1988	0	1	3	4	1
6							

We are all connected to one another through a vast web of social relationships. Social network analysis can help us understand how everything from job opportunities to disease to new ideas spread through society.

SOCIAL NETWORK ANALYSIS

If you were to choose one person in the world at random, chances are that you have at least a friend of a friend of a friend of a friend of a friend in common with that person. This "six degrees of separation" finding, first reported by Stanley Milgram in 1967, was confirmed in a 2003 follow-up study using e-mail chains

(Dodds, Muhamad, & Watts, 2003) and yet again in a 2012 study of Facebook contacts (Backstrom et al., 2012).

This social connectedness affects all aspects of our lives. For example, in 2007 a study concluded that obesity is "socially contagious." The researchers found that your chance of becoming obese increases by more than 50% if one of your friends is obese. Even electronic (as opposed to face-to-face) social connections can greatly influence people's lives. In July 2014, a controversial Facebook study, in which the company experimentally manipulated friends' newsfeeds, found that Facebook friends' moods are contagious. For instance, when a Facebook user's friends posted material that contained more negative emotional content (for example, sadness), that user would subsequently post more negatively charged content also (Kramer, Guillory, & Hancock, 2014).

Given these findings, it is apparent that the vast web, or network, of social relations in which we are all connected has important consequences for our everyday lives. The systematic study of the structure of this web of social connections is called **social network analysis**. In recent years, few methods have grown as rapidly as social network analysis. It has helped researchers explain a wide variety of phenomena, ranging from labor-market outcomes (Franzen & Hangartner, 2006) and individual health (Smith & Christakis, 2008) to community-level outcomes such as collective action (Centola & Macy, 2007) and crime (Morenoff, Sampson, & Raudenbush, 2001).

Social network analysis is not a single research method but rather a family of methods that are used to systematically identify, measure, and visualize the structure of social relationships. These methods, which have both qualitative and quantitative aspects, vary greatly in character and application, and they are easily used in combination with other methods. For example, network methods are often used to derive measures of a given individual's position within a particular community, which can then be used as variables in other analyses.

The breadth and variety of network analysis techniques makes it difficult to cover every dimension of this framework. This chapter is a primer on key network terminology and concepts. It explains how social network data are collected, methodological innovations, and some recent developments.

WHAT IS A SOCIAL NETWORK?

It is thought that the term *social network* was first used scientifically in the mid-1950s to describe the patterns of social ties that existed in a small Norwegian community (Barnes, 1954). A **social network** is a "set or sets of actors and the relation or relations" that link them together (Wasserman & Faust, 1994,

social network analysis
The systematic study of the web of relationships that link actors in a given setting.

social network A set (or sets) of actors and the relations that link them together.

SIX PEDIGREES OF SEPARATION

"...AND THAT HOUND WENT TO OBEDIENCE SCHOOL WITH A SPANIEL WHO STAYED AT A KENNEL WITH A COLLIE WHO LIVES NEXT DOOR TO KEVIN BACON'S MUTT!..."

p. 20). **Social actors** may include individuals, families, organizations (such as firms), and other social entities.

Social networks are not restricted to electronic social networks like Instagram, Twitter, and Facebook. Rather, social networks are predominantly composed of many kinds of off-line or "real world" social relationships, including everyday ties to family members, neighbors, teachers, and many others—even passing contact between two people who do not know but may recognize each other (for example, at a bus stop). People also form ties with larger associations and organizations; for example, when they attend a religious service or make a purchase at a local store. Social network analysis makes it possible to systematically visualize and analyze the numerous connections among all types of individual and collective social actors, including individuals, businesses, voluntary associations, and committees, as well as cities, states, and nations.

Some key aspects of social networks are easiest to understand with the aid of visual diagrams. To that end, Figure 13.1 depicts a real social network. This network represents the social ties that existed within a retirement community in the United States in 2009. Specifically, this diagram shows which members of that community engaged in discussions with each other (first reported in Schafer, 2011). We will return to this figure throughout the chapter to explain key features of social network analysis.

The social network approach views individuals or other actors as **nodes** in a larger social structure. The network shown in Figure 13.1 includes 105 retirees. These people are the nodes, which are represented as circles. The other key ingredients of a social network are the **ties**, or links, that connect the nodes. These links are typically the social relationships that exist between the actors in the social setting that is being examined. The ties may reflect friendship, social support, social exchange, contracts, conflict, kinship, and many other relationships. To identify the retiree network in Figure 13.1, for example, Schafer (2011) recorded ties wherever a given resident reported that he or she talked to another resident about "important issues." The diagram shows these reported connections. For example, resident A indicated that she talked to residents B, C, D, E, and F about important issues.

The nature of the social ties being examined depends on the types of social actors being studied. For example, some studies of networks among firms use the existence of formal business contracts between firms as evidence of ties in the network. Other researchers have constructed a network of Hollywood movie actors by using movie credits to determine which actors have worked with each other (e.g., see Rossman, Esparaza, & Bonacich, 2010).

SOCIAL NETWORK CONCEPTS

Several features of social networks are noteworthy. We can break these down into three general classes of concepts: (1) those that refer to the overall structure of a network, (2) those that refer to the actors in the network, and (3) those that refer to the ties that compose the network.

social actors The social network analysis term for individuals, families, organizations (such as firms), and other social entities.

nodes The social network analysis term for the actors who appear in a network structure, especially when diagrammed.

ties The links that connect the nodes in a social network.

The Oracle of Bacon draws on the concept of "six degrees of separation," a social network phenomenon that was famously demonstrated by Stanley Milgram. In a 1967 study, he showed that any two strangers tend to be connected by just a few friends in common. The Oracle of Bacon demonstrates this by showing that all Hollywood actors are linked to each other through just a few steps in the vast network of movies.

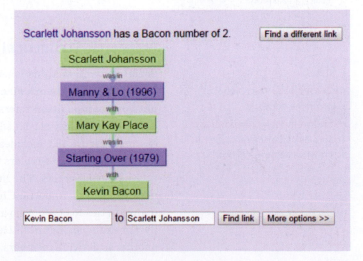

This network diagram is arranged such that nodes (that is, the social actors being represented in the network as circles) that are linked to each other (represented using directed arrows) appear close together, whereas nodes that are not connected to each other are placed far apart from each other. Green circles represent men, and orange circles represent women.

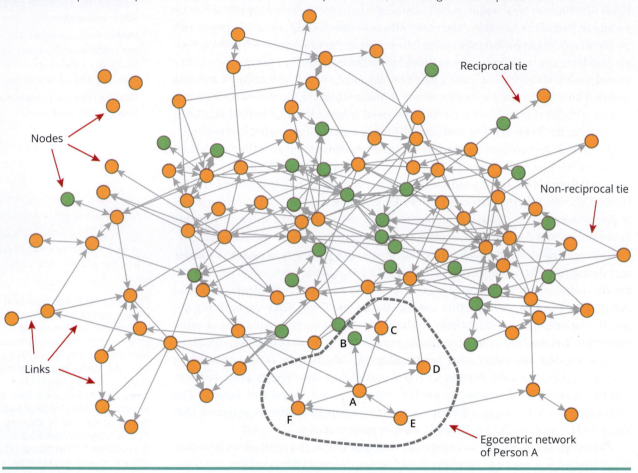

Source: Schafer, 2011.

Network-Structural Characteristics

Social network analysis is useful for characterizing the overall structure of a given social setting. **Network size** refers to the number of actors in the network. **Social network composition** refers to the types of actors who compose the network. The actors are typically classified on the basis of some attribute, such as race or sex. For example, Figure 13.1 includes 77 women (orange circles) and 28 men (green circles). *Network heterogeneity* refers to the extent to which a network is made up of different types of social actors. The more types of social actors, the more heterogeneous the network is. It is important to note that actors have a strong tendency to form and maintain ties to others who are similar in some way; this tendency is called homophily. For example, Figure 13.1 shows a tendency for people of the same sex to name one another as network members.

network size The number of actors in the network.

social network composition The profile of the different types of actors who compose a network.

Network researchers are often interested in the extent to which actors within a network are interconnected. A foundational concept is the **triad**, which refers to a set of three nodes and the links that may or may not exist among them (Simmel, 1950). Consider the case of the triad consisting of residents A, D, and E in Figure 13.1. Persons A and E are linked, as are A and D. However, D and E are not directly connected to each other. We refer to this situation as an *open* or *empty* triad, because all of the possible connections in this triad are not realized. If D and E had a social relationship with each other, then actors A, D, and E would constitute a *closed* triad.

The extent to which a given person's network members are connected to one another has major implications for how that network functions and the opportunities it presents to individuals. For example, Coleman (1988) pointed out that closed triads make it possible for two members of the group to coordinate with each other, to compare information, and to exercise social control over the third member. Furthermore, a closed triad has *redundant* connections: If any one of the three members is incapacitated for some reason, a channel still exists between the other two. A network that has a large number of closed triads is called a **dense network**.

DIRECTED AND NONDIRECTED NETWORK TIES

Network ties can be either directed or nondirected. A **directed network tie** is one that specifies relations between two actors that may or may not be mutual. The ties in Figure 13.1 are directed. While person A said that she discussed important things with person B, notice that B did not say the same thing about A. This lack of mutual relations is a feature in many social relationships. For example, in an exchange relationship, the fact that A "sends" something to B—whether money, material goods, or information—does not mean that B sends something back to A. Emotions and feelings often work the same way. The fact that A feels a certain way about B does not mean that B will feel the same way about A.

Knowing even this simple piece of information provides important insight into the structure of a network and how it can act to diffuse and channel social phenomena. **Reciprocity** refers to the tendency for actors to give and receive emotions, information, support, and resources in generally equal and balanced ways (Gouldner, 1960). Research suggests that two people are more strongly attracted to and influenced by each other when their relationship is characterized by reciprocity. One study (Fujimoto & Valente, 2012) found that adolescents were most likely to mirror the drinking behavior of those adolescents whom they listed as friends *and* who also named them as friends in return.

Researchers are often concerned with whether two people have a social relationship that is inherently mutual and exists whether or not both actors report it. **Nondirected network ties** occur when a relationship exists regardless of a given individual actor's perspective. For example, for researchers studying sexual networks, the question is whether two people have had sex with each other. Likewise, epidemiologists are often interested in whether two people had contact or were physically exposed to each other in some way. In such cases, the issue of "directionality" is irrelevant. Nondirected networks such as these are as common as directed networks. There are large bodies of research on contact networks—which are crucial for understanding the spread of some diseases—as well as neighbor networks, sexual networks, and networks formed by mutual involvement in an organization or group.

triad A set of three nodes that are at least indirectly connected to each other.

dense network A network that has a large number of ties.

directed network tie A link between two actors in a network that may or may not be mutual.

reciprocity The extent to which pairs of actors give and receive mutual emotions, information, support, and resources in generally equal and balanced ways.

nondirected network tie A link between two actors that is by definition mutual, such as the link between siblings, or co-members of the same club.

cohesion The degree to which actors in a network are highly interconnected.

network density The extent to which network members are connected to one another, quantified in terms of the proportion of possible connections in the set that are actually realized.

clique A subset of at least three actors who are all directly connected to one another.

geodesic distance The fewest number of steps a given actor must take to "reach" another actor in the network. Also known as *path length*.

diffusion The communication or dissemination of information or resources among social actors through network ties over a period of time.

Cliques—subsets of at least three actors who are all connected to one another— are more likely to form when network members are similar in such social characteristics as age, gender, class, race, or ethnicity.

COHESION, NETWORK DENSITY, AND GEODESIC DISTANCE

Network researchers are especially interested in how the relationships that exist between specific pairs of actors combine to form larger network structures. Network data are often used to assess the extent to which a given set of actors experiences **cohesion**, or the degree to which actors are highly interconnected. The level of cohesion provides clues about the capacity for coordination, consensus, and social control within a particular setting. A common measure of cohesion is **network density**, the extent to which network members are connected to one another, which can be measured in terms of the proportion of possible connections in the set that are actually realized. For example, in the circled part of the network in the lower-right portion of Figure 13.1, there are six people (A through F). In total, $n^2 - n$ links are possible in a given network, where n = the number of network members. In this case, there are 36 − 6, or 30, possible ties. Within this set, 8 directed ties are actually observed (for example, A chooses E, E chooses A). Thus, the density of this subnetwork is 8/30 = 0.27. That is, 27% of the links that could have existed in this subgroup are actually present. Note that this level of density is relatively low for a personal social network. For example, the density of off-line adolescent friendship networks is upwards of 40% (Haynie, 2001).

Cohesion also exists wherever there are tight-knit subsets or clusters within a network. For example, you are probably familiar with the term *clique*, which may conjure up a group of high school students who banded together and excluded others from their group. Your impression of a clique is similar to the formal definition used by social network analysts, whereby a **clique** is a subset of at least three actors who are all connected to one another. Network analysts use software that can quickly identify small or large cliques within a given network. One commonly used measure of the extent of cohesion in a network is the *clustering coefficient,* or the proportion of triads in the network that are closed triads (Watts & Strogatz, 1998).

A high level of cohesion also occurs when there is a short geodesic distance between any given pair of actors in the network. **Geodesic distance**, also known as *path length*, refers to the fewest number of steps any given actor must take to "reach" another actor in the network. For example, you would be three steps away from your college roommate's mother's best friend. To return to our example in Figure 13.1, actor D is only two steps away from actor E, with A serving as an intermediary. In other words, the path length, or geodesic distance, between D and E is 2. Actors that are directly connected to each other (for example, A and D) have a distance of 1, whereas actors who have no direct or indirect pathways to each other in the network technically have an undefined distance. Networks that have shorter average path lengths are more cohesive, and they have greater capacity for **diffusion**; that is, the communication or dissemination of information or resources among social actors will occur over a shorter period of time (Rogers, 1995). To return to the example at the beginning of this chapter, Stanley Milgram found that, on average, a given pair of people are connected by just six degrees of separation, or a path length of 6 (Milgram, 1967).

STRUCTURAL HOLES AND EQUIVALENCE

In contrast to cohesion, some network settings are characterized by a lack of connectedness between different regions or clusters. The gaps that exist among sets of actors within a network are called **structural holes** (Burt, 1992). For example, if there are two cliques of students within a school and the members of clique A never speak to the members of clique B, then there is a structural hole between the two cliques. Structural holes may be spanned by way of a *bridge*; that is, a tie that exists between actors who are connected to different, otherwise poorly connected regions of the network. For example, in Figure 13.1, actor A sits on **bridges** that connect actors B-D with actors E-F in the retirement community. In the example of the two school cliques, bridging can happen when a member of clique A is a neighbor or past friend of a member of clique B. Through that tenuous connection, those two people might be able to prevent conflict between the two cliques.

Equivalence refers to similarities between social actors with respect to the ties they maintain with other actors in the network (Lorrain & White, 1971). Some network members share exactly the same patterns of ties with other network members, making them structurally equivalent to each other. Equivalence often characterizes people who belong to the same groups in the same community; for example, two friends from the same hometown who enroll in the same college and pledge the same sorority or fraternity. They are equivalent—that is, they know all the same old and new friends, the same parents, and the same teachers, and thus are in some ways interchangeable—until they eventually form new friendships with different people.

Network Actor Characteristics

The positions that actors occupy within a social network have important implications for them. One important concept is **centrality**, or the extent to which an actor can access a larger number of other actors in the network through relatively few intermediaries (Freeman, 1979). Centrality generally reflects greater social status, as well as more exposure to and influence over the flow of information and resources within a network. It signals that the actor is highly embedded in the community rather than sitting on the outskirts. When we refer to someone as "well connected," we are intuitively thinking about the concept of centrality.

Let's return to Figure 13.1 to examine centrality in more detail. Resident C occupies a more central position in the overall retirement community network than resident A does. Resident C was named as a discussion partner by three community residents, whereas resident A was named by only two. This captures a simple but important dimension of connectedness known as degree centrality. **Degree centrality** refers to the number of ties a given actor has.

The number of ties an actor has is consequential, but so is the manner in which those ties link the actor up to a larger web of network connections. **Closeness centrality** is the average number of steps it takes for a given actor to "reach" or access the other members of the network, or the average length of the shortest paths to each

structural holes The gaps that exist between (sets of) actors who are poorly connected or unconnected within a network.

bridge A tie that connects two (sets of) otherwise poorly connected (or unconnected) actors in a network. Bridges span structural holes.

equivalence Similarity between social actors with respect to the profile of ties they maintain with other actors in the network.

centrality The extent to which an actor plays an important role in connecting a large number of other actors in a network.

degree centrality The number of ties a given actor has.

closeness centrality The degree to which an actor can "reach" or access the other members of the network in a small number of steps.

of the other network members (Freeman, 1979). Resident C has relatively high closeness centrality, because she can contact other community residents through relatively few intermediaries. Most other actors—such as residents E and F—are less central in the network.

The closely related concepts of *betweenness* and *bridging* focus on the extent to which a given actor connects other network members who would otherwise be unconnected or connected only through a longer, more roundabout chain of contacts. An actor who has high **betweenness centrality** is one who is positioned on the shortest paths between other pairs of actors (Freeman, 1979). *Bridging* refers to a situation where an actor is connected to two larger sets of actors that are otherwise poorly connected to each other in the network.

Betweenness and bridging confer great advantages upon individuals in terms of gatekeeping, brokerage, and other strategic opportunities, and in terms of influencing larger diffusion processes (e.g., Burt, 1992; Gould & Fernandez, 1989). For example, a woman who frequently travels back and forth between two countries implicitly sits on a bridge between the friends she maintains in both of those places. Thus, she can take ideas, innovations, jokes, information, and anything else that she encounters in one place and present them to her friends in the other place.

betweenness centrality
The extent to which an actor serves as an intermediary on the shortest paths between other pairs of actors in the network.

tie strength The extent to which a given tie is characterized by emotional closeness or intensity, frequent interaction, and durability or stability.

Network Tie Characteristics

To understand how a social network functions, information about its social ties is crucial. One important concept is **tie strength**, which reflects the extent to which a given tie is characterized by emotional closeness or intensity (for example, how much two people like each other), frequency of interaction, and durability or stability (how long the connection has existed).

Strong ties are associated with wide-ranging and unconditional social support, because closer, long-standing social relationships allow people to develop trust and reliable expectations regarding each other's behavior. *Weak ties*, in contrast, entail relatively few social obligations or expectations. They do, however, give people access to more social networks (Granovetter, 1973). For example, two people who have not known each other for very long likely do not know each other's family and friends, which means that they can introduce each other to large numbers of new contacts and provide new opportunities for social interaction. Research shows that people who have access to weak ties get more information about job opportunities that their other friends might not know about (Granovetter, 1973; Yakubovich, 2005). Figure 13.2 shows two examples of hypothetical network structures in which weak ties serve as "bridges" between otherwise poorly connected regions of a network. This means that people who maintain weak ties tend to have access to more distant regions of a network. Strong ties rarely serve this function, as they

FIGURE 13.2 Strength of Weak Ties

Two hypothetical networks from Granovetter's (1973) original paper about weak ties. Weak ties between people are denoted as dashed lines, strong ties as solid lines. Notice that the weak ties serve as bridges between groups.

(a)
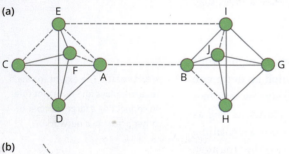

(b)
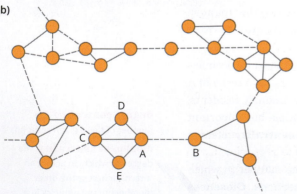

Source: Granovetter, 1973.

tend to exist in more densely connected subgroups. All things considered, people who maintain a mixture of strong and weak ties in their social networks are better off, because they have access to social support *and* access to unique and diverse social ties (see Burt, 2005).

Tie strength is closely related to other network tie characteristics. One relevant concept is **tie valence**, or the extent to which a tie is characterized by positive or negative relations. Stronger, more enduring ties tend to be characterized by more positive relations. For example, you may not want to maintain social ties with your high school rival, but you have regular and ongoing contact with your dearest friend from high school. (However, this does not mean that passionate negative feelings, like anger, are not common in strong relationships.) Another important feature of ties is their extent of *multiplexity*, or the number of different ways in which a given pair of actors are connected to each other (Verbrugge, 1979). For example, if two people are friends as well as coworkers and roommates, they are bound to each other in multiple ways, thus allowing a wider range of social interactions. Multiplexity can provide interesting insight into the complexities of social relationships. The sociologist Georg Simmel (1922/1971) noticed that the closest positive emotional relationships—for example, ties between husbands and wives—also tend to invoke the strongest negative ties (for example, conflict and disagreement). In short, close ties tend to be the most multiplex of all and can involve both positively and negatively valenced relations.

> **tie valence** The extent to which a tie is characterized by positive or negative sentiments or relations.

CONCEPT CHECKS

1. What is the difference between a node and a tie?
2. What is one measure of the level of cohesion in a social network? Define and explain the measure.
3. What is the distinction between centrality and bridging?
4. What are some characteristics of tie strength?

SOCIAL NETWORK STUDY DESIGN ISSUES

How do researchers collect the data that are necessary to study networks? In this section, we examine some of the key issues that face researchers who attempt to collect primary social network data. We begin by addressing the questions that researchers wrestle with when they start collecting information about social networks.

Boundary Specification

The most fundamental question facing a researcher when designing a social network study is: "What is the relevant set of actors and social connections to be studied in the setting?" As Stanley Milgram discovered in his study of small-world networks, social actors are all connected to one another in some way. So, if a researcher wants to study a particular social network, the researcher first needs to specify the boundaries of the most relevant part of the larger global network (Laumann, Marsden, & Prensky, 1983).

To specify boundaries, the researcher often declares which (types of) social actors and which (types of) social ties will be studied. For example, you might hypothesize that students' abilities to find a good job after college depends on how well-connected the people at their university are to companies that are hiring. Here, the goal would be to examine the networks of university employees. The question is where to limit the boundaries of these networks. Are you interested only in the network ties of current students, faculty, and staff at that university or should alumni also be included? Are you interested only in these people's professional contacts (for example, the ties they maintain on the professional networking site LinkedIn) or are you also interested in their informal social ties (for example, the ties they maintain on Facebook)?

In practice, specifying boundaries means identifying a sampling frame and deciding which types of social actors and network ties are most relevant to the research question at hand. Boundary specification often boils down to deciding (1) between an *egocentric* (individual-focused) versus a *whole-network* (community-focused) design, and (2) which and how many types of social actors and ties should be examined. Egocentric designs start with the set of actors of interest—which may be a mere sample of actors within the study's scope—and examine only the social network contacts to which those actors are (or report to be) directly connected. Whole-network designs, in contrast, attempt to collect data from all of the people who fall within the network's boundaries.

Sociocentric and Egocentric Designs

Two key data-collection and analytic issues in social network studies are (1) the scope of the network data to be collected, and (2) from whose perspective the network is observed. In most cases, analysts are interested in the large, overarching social structure that exists in a given setting; that is, an entire network structure that includes numerous actors who may or may not be directly connected to one another. Such studies are called **sociocentric network designs**, or *whole-network designs*. The network in Figure 13.1 is a whole network; it represents the structure of an entire community. The research scope in Figure 13.1 extends beyond any one actor and instead considers the actor as just one node in the larger social structure.

Many social scientists are concerned with individual-level outcomes, such as health or educational attainment. Therefore, they often conceptualize networks from the perspective of individual actors within the setting. Doing so involves identifying a given individual—or **ego**—within a population, as well as the set of other people—called **alters**—to whom ego is connected. This **egocentric network approach** is appropriate when individual actors are the ultimate units of analysis and when the analyst is interested only in the *local network* that surrounds a given actor; that is, the part of the network to which the actor is directly connected, and not the network as a whole.

For example, the General Social Survey (GSS), a nationally representative survey of American adults, asks each respondent to provide the names of up to five people with whom they discuss "important matters." Respondents also provide some information about those alters' attributes, indicating which of the alters are connected to one another. However, the alters are not interviewed. Thus, while researchers have no way

sociocentric network design A study that is interested in an entire network structure that includes numerous actors who may or may not be directly connected to one another. Also called *whole-network design*.

ego A given individual in a network in whose perspective on a network a researcher is interested.

alters The other actors to whom one is connected within a given network.

egocentric network approach The study of a network from the perspective of individual actors within the setting.

to analyze the entire, community-wide network in which a given ego is embedded, they can at least observe ego's most immediate social contacts. Even this basic information about ego's network can be useful in determining the social influences, behaviors, and resources to which a person is exposed. For example, GSS data have shown that people tend to maintain social ties with those who are similar to them in terms of race and socioeconomic status, but this tendency has declined since these data were first gathered in the mid-1980s. In other words, our social networks are becoming more diverse (Smith, McPherson, & Smith-Lovin, 2014).

As another example, refer back to Figure 13.1. The egocentric social network of resident A is circled and shown with the node borders of her network contacts in bold. The egocentric network includes only those actors to whom A is directly connected. An egocentric network "circle" like this one could be identified for each of the 105 individuals in the network. Note that resident A's egocentric network includes information about any links that exist among the alters. It does not include anyone whom ego did not name, even if those people named ego. This egocentric information is sufficient to assess the size, composition, and density of ego's personal network, as well as the strengths of her network ties. Even if we did not have the data on the whole network that is shown in this figure, we could get a basic sense of ego's network connectedness via the data that are available within the circle, which ego could provide herself.

Egocentric studies typically proceed by first identifying the key actors to be studied, then collecting information about those actors' network alters. The most common approach is to identify a set of survey respondents, and then ask them to identify the members of their network. The network members themselves are not interviewed. Rather, the researcher relies on the respondent to provide any information the researcher wants to know about the alters, including their attributes, behaviors, and relationships with one another.

Egocentric and sociocentric studies use different data-collection strategies, have different advantages and disadvantages, and make different types of analyses possible. Egocentric designs are more practical in settings in which the actors are not likely to know one another, as in large population-based surveys that include people from different regions. Studies that use the GSS data are good examples of egocentric studies. Egocentric design requires a sacrifice in the breadth and quality of the network data because this design is entirely dependent on respondent recall, comprehensiveness, and accuracy. Nonetheless, egocentric network data can be used to study a wide variety of network features. Researchers have used egocentric network data to determine the extent to which individuals are connected to people from different racial groups (e.g., Smith et al., 2014); the extent to which individuals' network members know one another (Burt, 1992) and how that level of connectedness affects their ability to coordinate social support and social control on their own behalf (e.g., Coleman, 1988; Haines, Hurlbert, & Beggs, 1996); and whether people are connected to high-status others who can give them access to valuable resources (e.g., York Cornwell & Cornwell, 2008).

In sociocentric network designs, researchers have information about all of the actors in the network, which makes it possible to directly measure the attributes and relationships of each actor's network members. This information is particularly important if there is some concern that respondents in egocentric network studies misperceive or misreport their network members' attributes or behaviors. In addition, whole networks provide more accurate measures of individual actors' structural positions; for example, each actor's closeness centrality and the extent to which he or she is equivalent to another actor in the network. Whole networks also make it possible to examine network-level properties, such as the extent to which the network is populated with clusters of actors, and whether any structural holes separate regions of the network. For instance, analyses of global network data from e-mail communications and social networking sites like Facebook are providing support for the theory that we are all connected in a "small world" social network; that is, a system in which you are only a few steps from any other randomly chosen person elsewhere in the world (Backstrom et al., 2012; Dodds, Muhamad, & Watts, 2003).

Data Organization

matrix A rectangular array of rows and columns (as in a spreadsheet) in which the actors in a network are listed in the headings and the ties between them are recorded in the corresponding cells.

Social network data are usually recorded and arranged in matrices. A **matrix** is a rectangular collection of cells in which the actors in the network are arranged along the row and column headings and the information about their ties to each other is recorded in the corresponding cells where pairs of actors intersect. For example, if we wish to map the social ties that exist among a group of students who live in the same dormitory, we can begin by creating a spreadsheet in which each resident's name appears once in a row heading and once in a column heading. Then we enter information into each of the cells at the intersection of the two residents in the corresponding row and column.

In many cases, network analysts simply record whether a tie exists between the actors in question. If a tie exists, "1" appears in the corresponding cell. Otherwise, a "0" appears. The matrix that results from this procedure is called an *adjacency matrix*. Such a matrix can distinguish between situations in which two actors, A and B, "send" ties to each other (for example, they both name each other as friends) from situations in which one of those actors names the other but that connection is not reciprocated (for example, A names B as a friend but B does not name A as a friend).

Figure 13.3 shows the adjacency matrix that records the directed network information for resident A in Figure 13.1. With egocentric networks, which typically include 3 to 10 people, these matrices are easy to complete. Whole-network designs require more data entry because they include many more people. The size of a network matrix increases geometrically as the number of actors being studied increases. This aspect of social network analysis hampered the collection and analysis of large social networks for decades, until computer technology made the storage and analysis of network matrices easier and less costly (see "Conversations from the Front Lines" interview). The collection and analysis of whole-network data has also been made easier by the advent of large electronic networks such as Facebook (Lewis et al., 2008). These sites make it possible to study how entire groups of people are interconnected.

FIGURE 13.3 Adjacency Matrix Showing the Egocentric Social Network of Resident A

This matrix refers to the egocentric network that is circled in Figure 13.1. Matrices such as this provide all the information one needs to construct a social network.

	A	B	C	D	E	F
A	—	1	1	1	1	1
B	0	—	0	1	0	0
C	0	0	—	0	0	0
D	0	0	0	—	0	0
E	1	0	0	0	—	1
F	0	0	0	0	0	—

One- and Two-Mode Designs

Some aspects of collecting and organizing network data are complicated by the fact that so many different types of social actors are networked. Researchers typically construct social networks by analyzing the relationships that exist within a set that is composed of a given type of actor. Examples include networks of acquaintance-ship among students in a dormitory, networks of kinship among residents of a village, and networks of sexual relations among people in a city. These networks are called **one-mode networks**, because they include just one type of actor. In some cases, however, researchers may want to examine the relationships that exist between one type of actor (for example, individuals) and another type of actor (for example, local businesses). In such cases, research-ers consider connections that exist between two modes of social actors, or **two-mode networks** (see Borgatti & Halgin, 2011; Breiger, 1974). For example, the researcher may record individuals' connections to specific events, meetings, workplaces, voluntary associations, or other social elements within a given setting. In doing so, the researcher constructs what are called *affiliation networks* (see Borgatti & Everett, 1997; Wasserman & Faust, 1994).

One of the earliest studies of two-mode networks analyzed Southern women's connections to informal social events in the 1930s. They found that which events women attended was highly patterned by their social class, reinforcing a structural gap between the lower and upper strata of Southern society.

The earliest example of a two-mode network study was conducted during the Great Depression by Davis, Gardner, and Gardner (1941). These social anthropologists wanted to examine the social network of 18 women in a small U.S. town—Natchez, Mississippi. They argued that their research would make it possible to glimpse the under-lying class structure that socially segregated people in the town. They believed differ-ent class groups would show up as different clusters or cliques in the network. To reveal the network, they collected data from various sources to determine which of the town's 14 key social events each woman attended. They used the degree of overlap in the events a given pair of women attended to measure the extent of similarity in the women's social classes in the community. The results provided additional support for the theory that social class is reproduced within the community on a daily basis via the patterns of informal events that people attend (Warner & Lunt, 1941). Two-mode networks are very common in organizational research, where scholars track the extent to which companies' boards of directors overlap with one another.

one-mode network A network that includes just one type of actor.

two-mode network A network that includes two different types of actors.

CONCEPT CHECKS

1   What is boundary specification?

2   What is the difference between egocentric and sociocentric (or whole) social network data?

3   What is an adjacency matrix?

4   Provide an example of a one-mode social network and of a two-mode social network.

COLLECTING SOCIAL NETWORK DATA

A great deal of social network data have already been collected and archived. Thus, it is possible for researchers to access these data sets and conduct network analyses with them. For example, the GSS makes available multiple years of nationally representative egocentric network data on Americans. Network data are also available online and in other published sources (e.g., Wasserman & Faust, 1994) and data repositories such as the Inter-university Consortium for Political and Social Research (ICPSR) and the University of California at Irvine network data repository. Nonetheless, there are many cases in which existing data will not suffice to answer the particular question that a researcher wants to study. For example, suppose a researcher wants to study the friendship networks that form among new students in a given school or the informal advice networks that emerge among executives in Silicon Valley. In such cases, it would be necessary to collect primary (original) social network data. This section provides guidance to researchers who want to collect network data that no one else has collected.

Direct Observation

Social network data can be collected in many ways. Perhaps the earliest approach involved direct observation of social interaction. Social network analysis grew out of early ethnographies and small-group research, which focused on patterns of interaction within families and among people in small groups, villages, and towns (e.g., Barnes, 1954). The researchers often conducted their research by observing the actors within a given bounded setting, recording the presence and frequency of some form of interaction (for example, talking) among them. A famous example is a study of African factory workers (Kapferer, 1972), in which a researcher recorded observable interactions—for example, conversations, joking, and job assistance—among 23 employees over several months to map their informal social network. The observed interaction structure helped explain how sides formed when disputes arose between two workers. Direct observation is not feasible in larger populations and can be difficult to accomplish without multiple coders and real-time recording equipment. Because of the difficulties associated with recording and organizing such complex data, direct observation is rarely used to collect social network data.

Archival Data

Archival data are often used to examine social networks. Some researchers have used individuals' private directories containing the names and phone numbers of their acquaintances and colleagues, as well as personnel files, news reports, old study records, or biographical records, to reconstruct social networks (e.g., see Burt, 1992; Christakis & Fowler, 2007; Galaskiewicz, 1985; Padgett & Ansell, 1993). Social network data can also be collected with contact diaries. In this approach, respondents are asked to record their contacts in retrospect for a given period of time (usually a single day), and researchers review these records to develop a profile of respondents' networks (Fu, 2005).

Not all social network analyses involve the study of people. Therefore, it is not always necessary to use observational research or contact diaries to collect data.

For example, researchers who are interested in long-term linkages that exist among firms might study these connections by analyzing official records regarding exchange contracts between firms. Researchers who are interested in the theoretical or methodological approaches that scientists have in common could analyze records regarding which scholars cite each other in their published research. Online databases make it relatively easy to collect such data.

Surveys

Perhaps the most common data-collection approach involves using survey methods, usually in-person interviews (see Chapter 7). Respondents typically answer a series of questions that are designed to elicit the names of their network members, information about the attributes of their network members, and the nature of their relationships with those members. Because of the large volume of information that is typically generated by these questions, this approach usually (but not always) involves computer-assisted personal interview (CAPI) systems. Only rarely are network studies conducted via paper-and-pencil interviews (PAPI).

Self-reported data obtained via survey methods are immensely useful for learning about the types of social network connections that people maintain, their perceptions of network members' attitudes and behaviors, and their understanding of the larger social webs to which they are connected. Such data have been used in thousands of scientific studies to answer such questions as: How many friendships do people typically maintain? How much, and what types of, social support do people in different social groups have access to? To what extent do the behaviors of one's network members affect one's own behaviors? For instance, Kreager and Haynie (2011) used network data to explore influences on teenagers' binge drinking. They were especially interested in the ways that one's romantic partner linked a teen to new peer groups. Surprisingly, they found that drinking by friends of partners had stronger effects than one's own friends' drinking.

Some researchers have turned to mobile devices—especially smartphones—to gather data. For example, some researchers equip respondents with mobile devices that have preloaded survey apps. They can then "ping" subjects remotely several times during a short period of time and administer survey questions that respondents answer using their device's touch-screen function. This approach, which is called *ecological momentary assessment* (EMA), can be used to generate real-time data with questions such as "Who are you with right now?" (see Shiffman, 2009; Shiffman, Stone, & Hufford, 2008). EMA provides an important alternative to retrospective time-diary approaches to identifying real-time social contact networks. Using this technology, researchers can get less biased information about what people do, with whom, and where, at different times of the day. For example, one study (Scharf et al., 2013) used EMA to ask adolescents about the extent and nature of their exposure to media that involved smoking and/or alcohol-related content—information that may be difficult to remember in a retrospective diary.

Events like the one pictured here have several network implications. For one, network analysts might use information about who attends such events to identify cliques and other cohesive subgroups. In addition, network analysis helps researchers identify which individuals are the most likely to engage in risky behaviors at these events, such as binge drinking.

Smartphones can also obtain highly detailed data that can be used to link respondents to one another in real time. For example, researchers have designed apps that automatically record when the people carrying them are within a certain distance of their network members or even what they are saying to those people and/or feeling at that time (see Eagle, Pentland, & Lazer, 2009). These data provide insight into not only the nature of real-time social interaction (which can be useful for understanding how networks are enacted on a daily basis), but also how those interactions relate to other real-time phenomena, such as one's location, neighborhood context, or emotional or physical activity. One study of American undergraduates (Oloritun et al., 2013) found that the students with whom their subjects interacted on weekend nights were more likely to be considered close friends than those with whom their subjects did not interact on weekend nights, controlling for contact at other times and other predictors of friendship (for example, gender and race).

One disadvantage of the EMA approach is that it increases respondent burden, reduces respondent privacy, and severely limits the number of questions that can be asked at a given time. To address the last of these issues, EMA studies often include a longer initial and/or exit interview that is conducted using traditional survey methods. To address issues relating to respondent privacy, researchers who use EMA must provide extra assurances of data confidentiality and privacy during the institutional review board (IRB) process. (For a more detailed discussion of ethical issues in social research, see Chapter 3.)

Online Social Networks

Often, when people hear the term *social network*, they immediately think of social networking sites (SNSs) such as Facebook, Instagram, Twitter, and LinkedIn (Ellison & Boyd, 2013). Other online or electronic networks, such as those maintained via mobile phone communications, also leap to mind. But by now it should be clear that the term *social network* includes a much broader set of social ties, actors, and contexts. For example, everyday face-to-face interaction does not fall under the umbrella of online or electronic networks. Indeed, much of the social action that composes everyday life—talking to people, attending classes, going to parties, having sex, working, eating, playing sports—happens outside of online networks. Thus, online networks capture only a unique portion of the broader array of networks in which social actors are embedded.

Nonetheless, online networks have been playing an important role in social network analysis since the dawn of the twenty-first century. Online networks provide contexts for social interaction that differ markedly from those of face-to-face interactions. For instance, many of the nontextual features of social interaction (for example, emotion, visual cues, vocal tone, the potential and capacity for physical contact) are absent from or severely limited in online contexts. For this reason, the relationships that make up online networks are enacted and maintained through a different set of interaction devices, such as emoticons, written text, photographs, and links to websites. Physical proximity is less of a factor in the emergence and maintenance of online network ties, resulting in networks that are less constrained by geography and the social norms of the local community in which people reside

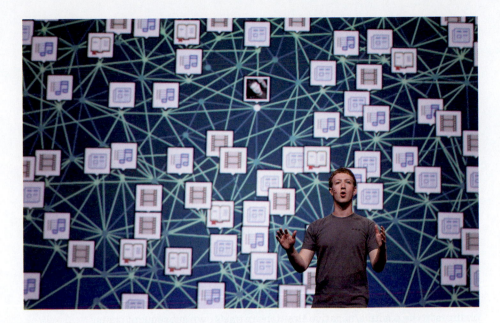

Online social networking sites such as Facebook have changed the way people communicate their social connections and have indeed changed the meaning of the term *social network*. Among other things, these online sites give rise to a unique web of connections that is intertwined with other offline social networks. Even though online networks often mirror these other networks, they also provide new channels of social influence and diffusion.

(see Wellman, 2001; Wellman et al., 1996). However, recent research shows that two actors are more likely to form online network ties when they live in the same general area (Hristova, Musolesi, & Mascolo, 2014; Takhteyev, Gruzd, & Wellman, 2012).

Online social networks not only represent a unique type of social network—that is, networks that are maintained via computer-mediated communication—they also constitute a new forum for the collection and analysis of social network data. The growing popularity of social networking sites has produced unprecedented quantities of network data that are relatively easy and inexpensive to collect. The collection of such vast amounts of data is part of the so-called data science or big data movement (see Lazer et al., 2009). Among other things, this movement involves a massive change in scope. Some scientists have shifted from collecting and analyzing information about several hundred or several thousand subjects to collecting and analyzing information about hundreds of thousands or millions of subjects at a time. They may collect and analyze information about individuals' social networks, their web-surfing habits, credit card usage, consumption patterns, and other contexts in which huge reams of data are stored electronically. For example, one study of links on Flickr (an online community that revolves around posted images that are often embedded in social media) crawled the Internet to obtain publicly accessible data on more than 950,000 Flickr users and the more than 9 million links they maintained with one another (Mislove et al., 2008).

This rise of big data raises challenges for the interpretation and generalizability of findings from social network studies. The advantages and disadvantages of using online network data depend on the purpose and context of the study. Some researchers use online social networks to bypass the more conventional survey approach to network data collection. A sociologist can gather data by observing a given subject's Facebook page and by browsing her friends' pages or by looking at newsfeed history, tweets, or other activities. This approach allows researchers to observe subjects' networks directly, rather than forcing them to collect costly self-reports. Furthermore, researchers can automate the data collection so that it is constantly updated and does not require any direct interaction with subjects. This method also reduces respondent burden. Some social scientists have made significant headway in accessing data from online social networking sites such as Facebook (e.g., Burke, Kraut, & Marlow, 2011; Cha et al., 2010; Hitsch, Hortacsu, & Ariely, 2010; Kwak et al., 2010; Lewis, Gonzalez, & Kaufman, 2012; Lewis et al., 2008; Wimmer & Lewis, 2010).

Yet, major analytical challenges remain in the analysis and interpretation of online social network data. One of the biggest challenges is structuring data-collection processes to adequately address concerns about subjects' and their network members' consent and privacy. In June 2014, a controversy erupted over an experiment conducted by Facebook and academic researchers, who manipulated the content on the pages of 689,003 Facebook users to determine whether (perceived) moods were "contagious." The researchers filtered the information these users received about their network members' photos, comments, and other posted content so that it contained either more positive content or more negative content than usual. They found that (perceived) changes in the content of one's network members led to parallel changes in the positive/negative emotions in one's own subsequent posts.

Perhaps the biggest limitation of online social network data is this: The data tend to be relevant to only a subset of the general population and therefore are not highly generalizable. For example, people who use online networking sites tend to be from privileged backgrounds, better educated, and younger than those who do not use online networking sites (Boyd & Crawford, 2012; Hargittai, 2010; White & Selwyn, 2013). These findings reflect the so-called digital divide, which refers to the fact that people from lower social strata (for example, those who live in poorer or more isolated neighborhoods) have less access to online social networks, wireless service, smartphones, and other electronic networking technology (Friemel, 2016; Haight, Quan-Haase, & Corbett, 2014; Lee, Park, & Hwang, 2015). Social scientists are still struggling with these limitations.

Network Analysis Software

As discussed earlier, complex data matrices underlie social networks of all types, from those that exist online to those that exist off-line in "real" face-to-face relationships. The larger the network, the more difficult it is to do social network analysis, and to organize social network data, by hand. Until the second half of the twentieth century, researchers had no choice but to use slow general-purpose computer language to analyze network data.

Fortunately, several programs designed specifically for the rapid analysis of networks are now widely available. The most popular are Ucinet (Borgatti, Everett, & Freeman, 2002), Pajek (Batagelj & Mrvar, 1998), and the "statnet" package in R. There are many others, too, some of which are free and available online. Many of these programs combine network-analytic tools (for example, the calculation of network centrality measures) with the capacity to create visually appealing network diagrams to aid in the interpretation of network structure. Partly because network analysis also uses other analytic approaches (for example, regression analysis), larger statistical analysis packages, including Stata and SAS, have begun to integrate network analysis and diagramming capabilities.

CONCEPT CHECKS

1   Provide an example of network data that can be studied using archival data.

2   What is ecological momentary assessment?

3   What are some drawbacks of collecting social network data via electronic networks?

RESPONDENTS AS SOCIAL NETWORK INFORMANTS

Most social network research concerns nonelectronic social network ties; for example, discussion networks or friendship networks that may or may not be maintained online. When the goal is to gather detailed, specific information about individuals' social networks, the most common approach is to ask individuals to identify their social network members, either in an interview or in a survey.

Early criticism of survey-based network research noted that respondents are not reliable sources of information about their own networks. Several early studies (e.g., Bernard & Killworth, 1979) compared respondents' reports of their network members with the researchers' observations of the people with whom respondents actually interacted. They found that the respondents' self-reports corresponded to the researchers' observed interactions only about half the time. What is the source of this disconnect? People sometimes inaccurately report or misremember patterns of social interaction, and people report the relationships that are most important to them.

It is often more useful to ask *respondents* about their social network ties because their personal impressions provide good information about durable patterns of social interaction that emerge over a long period of time (Freeman, Romney, & Freeman, 1987). In addition, even when respondents' perceptions of their social networks or resources are inaccurate or biased, those perceptions are often tied to individuals' actual observed patterns, because people act on their *perceptions* of reality (e.g., McDowell & Serovich, 2007; Wethington & Kessler, 1986). Thus, survey-based social network data—which derive from individuals' self-reports—are often considered more meaningful than data gathered using other methods. The remainder of this section explains how researchers collect valid social network data via surveys; it also shows how these data can address questions at the core of sociology.

Name Generators

The primary task in network research is to identify each respondent's social network members. The most common way to generate a list, or *roster*, of a respondent's social network members—especially in egocentric network studies—is to ask the respondent to list the names, nicknames, or initials of everyone in his or her social network. The questions that are used to elicit names of network members from respondents are called **name generators**. Table 13.1 provides a list of name generators that have been used in several influential egocentric social network studies.

name generator A question that is used to elicit names of network members from respondents.

TABLE 13.1 Examples of Name Generators Used in Surveys

Some Common Name Generators	Nationally Representative Data Source
"From time to time, most people discuss important matters with other people. [For example, these may include good or bad things that happen to you, problems you are having, or important concerns you may have.] Looking back over the last six months, who are the people with whom you discussed matters important to you? Just tell me their first names or initials."	General Social Survey (GSS); National Social Life, Health, and Aging Project (NSHAP)
"First, please tell me the names of your five best [male/female] friends, starting with your best [male/female] friend."	National Longitudinal Study of Adolescent to Adult Health (Add Health)
"Who are the people you really enjoy socializing with?"	Various regional and community studies
"If you need to borrow a large sum of money, say $1,000, whom would you ask for help?"	Various regional and community studies
"Suppose you need to borrow some small thing like a tool or a cup of sugar, from whom outside your household would you ask to borrow it?"	Various regional and community studies
"Please list anyone who is especially close to you whom you have not listed in one of the previous questions."	National Social Life, Health, and Aging Project

Boundary specification can be challenging in survey-based network research. For example, individuals can come into contact with thousands of people over a period of several months (Fu, 2005). Such an expansive contact network is relevant only in specific research contexts; for instance, in studies of the spread of diseases like influenza (e.g., Mikolajczyk & Kretzschmar, 2008). Likewise, a given individual is likely to "know" or be able to recognize thousands of people (Bernard et al., 1990). But only some of these people are important or relevant to the research question. To identify these people, it is important to use a name generator that helps respondents cut through the fog of everyday life and call to mind only the most pertinent network members.

The most widely used and empirically validated name generator asks respondents to name people with whom they "discuss [personal/important] matters," which combines interactive and emotional elements. This item first gained widespread exposure with its inclusion in the 1984 General Social Survey. It has since been used in hundreds of studies. Respondents are typically asked to name up to five network members in response to this question, which tends to elicit "core" or strong social network ties; that is, ties through which social influence and resources (like social support) are most likely to flow.

To construct the network of high school students featured in Figure 13.4, researchers asked students to identify up to three classmates with whom they had been involved in a *special romantic relationship* at some point during the past 18 months (Bearman, Moody, & Stovel, 2004). While many students named only one partner, and some students didn't name any, a large component of interconnected students nonetheless emerged. The result is a wealth of information about a network structure that had particular implications for the spread of disease in this setting. This case goes to show that simple name generators can reveal highly consequential social structures.

FIGURE 13.4 Network Diagram of Sexual Relationships at Jefferson High

This diagram first appeared in a study by Bearman, Moody, and Stovel (2004). It is based on data from a survey of high school students in the mid-1990s. The nodes represent the students, and the lines between them represent romantic/sexual relationships that occurred during the year of the survey. The structure shown here represents the most highly connected portion of the school's larger sexual/romantic network. It is a structure that has tremendous implications for the potential spread of sexually transmitted diseases.

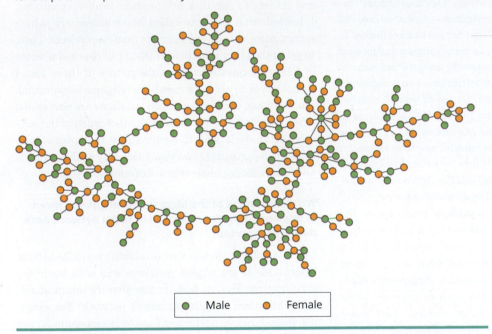

● Male   ● Female

Source: Bearman, Moody, & Stovel, 2004.

LIMITS ON THE NUMBER OF NAMES GENERATED

To keep data-collection costs down and to minimize respondent burden, survey researchers typically limit the number of names respondents can list in response to a name generator. The GSS allows respondents to list up to five people with whom they discuss important matters. The National Longitudinal Study of Adolescent to Adult Health (Add Health), which studies adolescents and young adults in the United States, limits the number of friends one can list at Wave 1 to five girls and five boys per respondent. The most common limit for the number of network members named hovers between four and ten.

An important question is whether a cap on the number of alters that can be named allows researchers to fully capture their respondents' networks. Some people have very large social networks and would list hundreds of network members if permitted. Researchers must strike a balance between allowing respondents to reach the boundaries of their full network and conducting a feasible and cost-effective study. Research shows that a cap of five alters is probably the most cost-effective number for gathering enough data to glean important information about the structure of individuals' strong-tie networks (Merluzzi & Burt, 2013).

EDWARD O. LAUMANN

In the middle of the twentieth century, social scientists' investigations of what we now call social networks *were limited to very small samples and focused primarily on how individuals' social ties were patterned within families, small groups, villages, and towns. With the advent of large-scale survey research and improvements in computer technology, researchers began to examine more complex social networks that provided insight into larger-scale social processes (such as urban inequality) and the diffusion of innovations, rumors, and diseases within a population.*

Edward O. Laumann, a sociology professor at the University of Chicago, was conducting his dissertation research at Harvard University during the early 1960s—a period when sociologists were just beginning to think about using social network analysis in larger-scale studies. He played a key role in the push to examine social networks using population-based surveys that cover larger areas, including entire cities and nations. Over the past half century, he has overseen dozens of social network data-collection efforts that have yielded data for hundreds of subsequent studies. We asked Professor Laumann about his experiences with social network analysis early in his career, during the method's formative period.

What was your earliest experience doing social network analysis?

It was in the early 1960s when I was conducting research for my dissertation at Harvard. Back then it wasn't called *social network analysis*, so I didn't really know I was doing it. I was motivated by the work of W. Lloyd Warner, a social anthropologist who viewed social classes as sets of overlapping, hierarchically arranged social circles. The idea was that this could be studied more concretely by looking at the extent to which people who had similar attributes (in particular, occupational status) were connected to each other.

My idea was to move this concept from small communities to large cities. I wanted to characterize the class structure of cities. I was interested in who were people's best friends, their next-door neighbors, parents, in-laws, and so on. To get this information from respondents, I devised what are now called *name generators*, which extract names of network contacts from respondents. Then, to get at the class structure of these ties, I asked a series of follow-up questions about the nature of these social contacts—each network member's religious background, ethnicity, and occupation. (Such questions are now called *name interpreters*.) The primary goal of much of the subsequent analysis was to demonstrate that people who belong to a particular class tend to identify as their friends and family those people who are of similar status.

What were some of the biggest challenges you faced in implementing the collection of social network data during that period?

The main challenge was that this hadn't really been done before. One of the biggest problems was with boundary specification. That is, how do you identify the most relevant members in a given person's network? For example, when I did my first study, I asked respondents for the names of three friends. Of course, not everyone has three friends—some people have fewer, some have more. So by asking things that way, our measure of network size was an artifact of how we phrased the name generator, which constrained people to a three-friendship circle. That was an early lesson in collecting network data through surveys. Later studies asked the question in a more open-ended way.

Another problem was with name interpreters. Following Warner's research, my earliest network studies were concerned in part with understanding the extent to which people of similar occupational statuses were interconnected. But in a society in which there are thousands of occupational titles, how do you ask people in the context of a survey what is the occupation of each of their network members? You can't present the respondent with a complete list. So, to classify the occupations of network members, we had to come up with a simpler classification, and we settled on a question that classified people in one of nine categories (reflecting, for example, skill level). This was an early exercise in the effort to come up with meaningful name interpreters.

What challenges did you face in analyzing the data you collected?

The key was that in those days, the computer was just beginning to appear. It was very hard to communicate with computers. As I recall, FORTRAN was the main language, and that was about it. You couldn't use any kind of automated program to record and classify respondents' answers to questions. You had to do coding manually. That was one thing. It took a lot of time and data entry.

The other thing was that we had to process each respondent's information using punch cards. You fed those into the machine one at a time. You had to count them and calculate statistics for them. And this cost something on the order of $750 per hour on the University of Michigan's computers, as I recall. And the calculation of network features, like centrality and distance, was very computationally intensive, involving matrix multiplication and so on. It was very expensive.

> " Only when you visually inspect the network you are studying can you begin to discern its structure. "

One of the most frustrating studies I conducted was during the early 1970s, and this frustration stemmed from computational issues. We had sociocentric network data for a sample of dozens of elites in a city in Germany. We wanted to know who was the most structurally prominent member of the elite network. We collected information about the elites' social, business-professional, and community affairs–based connections with each other. Cross-tabulating all of those reports and seeing a final network structure took several days. To see who held that structure together the most, we needed to see whose elimination from that network would result in the greatest amount of network-structural disintegration.

[For example, whose absence from the city would disrupt lines of communication within the city the most?] We had a theory about who that person was, so we wanted to re-generate all of our analyses both before and after eliminating that person from the network. Unfortunately, one of our assistants accidentally deleted that person's brother from the network instead. Once we discovered our error, we resubmitted all of the cards and re-ran the whole thing.

All things considered, the error cost us a week of analysis time, and a lot of money. Nowadays, that kind of analysis can be done in less than a minute. So, it was the advent of the modern computer, and the speed of the modern computer, that allowed network analysis to get off the ground. Before, we were confined to small samples, where it was practical to enter all of the punch cards and invert all of the matrices that were needed to process the network data.

What advice would you give to a student doing his or her first network study?

My main advice would be that you need to get your hands really dirty by seeing the network diagrams themselves. Look at the parts of the network you are studying in detail, the old-fashioned way. Only when you visually inspect the network you are studying can you begin to discern its structure. Otherwise, you are likely to come up with esoteric results that are not all that interesting. They may be elegant, and conform to some general expectation, but they won't help you understand what is going on.

The bigger point here is that you need to have a theory about the factors that are likely to explain the structure of your network. That is, you should have substantive intuitions about what undergirds/generates the nature of network organization well before the study begins—what sort of network patterns you should see, and why. Only once you get an intuition about this—the structuring principles that organize a social system—can you (1) identify the most appropriate network data collection and analysis strategies, and (2) speculate about the patterns that will emerge in the data that are collected. So, your method should always be guided by a theory.

MULTIPLE NAME GENERATORS

Some researchers use multiple name generators that encompass different types of ties in order to elicit a wider variety of social network members. Marin and Hampton (2007) compared the effectiveness of using single name generators and multiple name generators. They found that no single name generator provided as reliable an estimate of network size as multiple name generators used in combination, though the network measures based on "important matters" and a generator based on "socializing" were highly correlated with measures derived from the multiple name generators. In response to the "important matters" item, respondents are more likely to list people who are reliable but who may not be in contact with the respondent every day (for example, parents or old friends), while names listed in response to the "socializing" item are more likely to be people with whom the respondent is in daily contact but who may not have a strong emotional tie to the respondent (for example, a roommate). Thus, researchers often recommend using at least two (but preferably more) name generators to gain a more complete sense of individuals' social networks.

Free-Choice versus Fixed-Choice Generators

Before collecting network data, researchers must determine whether to set a limit on the number of network members respondents can list. In the **free-choice approach**, the researcher lets respondents list as many network members as they can (or want) in response to a name generator; researchers can also ask respondents to add names to an existing roster or create their own roster. In the **fixed-choice approach**, researchers restrict respondents' responses to some maximum number of network members or connections or cut respondents off once some other threshold has been reached (Wasserman & Faust, 1994). The practice of supplying participants with rosters of potential alters is a variant of the fixed-choice approach, because a respondent's network cannot exceed the size of the roster. This approach is more feasible, and useful, in contexts in which the researchers already know who the respondent's potential network members are; for example, in school or small community settings.

Both approaches have advantages and disadvantages. Free choice produces larger networks and therefore makes it possible to identify a wider range of potential network influences and resources of different types (for example, weak ties as well as strong ties). However, if the researcher wants to ask follow-up questions about each named network member, this approach can be costly and time-consuming. This approach may also encourage respondents to refrain from naming all of their network members, in order to shorten the length of the interview. Some researchers get around this challenge by letting respondents list as many network members as they like, but then asking follow-up questions about only a subset of the alters (usually the first ones who were named).

Some scholars argue that supplying respondents with a fixed roster, from which they identify their network members, is misleading because the roster prespecifies the boundaries of the network (which are not always clear from any official records that are available to the researcher). As a result, some potentially consequential network members who do not appear on the supplied roster will be ignored. For example, by presenting students with rosters of the other students who go to their school, as Add Health did, the researcher artificially limits each student's

free-choice approach An approach to collecting network data in which researchers allow respondents to list as many network members as they wish.

fixed-choice approach An approach to collecting network data in which researchers restrict respondents' responses to some predetermined set of potential network members, or where they cut respondents off once some maximum or threshold is reached.

friendship network to the school's roster. In other words, the roster does not allow students to name friends who do not go to their school. Thus, some researchers leave the task of identifying the most relevant network members to the respondent, whose subjective sense of who constitutes an important network tie may be more accurate than the researcher's (see Laumann, Marsden, & Prensky, 1983).

Visual Aids

Using respondents as network informants can introduce various forms of bias (for example, recall bias or inaccurate memories) into the network data. Some researchers therefore use visual aids to increase the accuracy of respondents' reports of their network members, how important each network member is, and how they are connected to each other (see McCarty et al., 2007). One approach is **hierarchical mapping** (Figure 13.5), in which the researcher presents respondents with four concentric circles, with the word "You" appearing in the center of the innermost circle (see Ajrouch, Antonucci, & Janevic, 2001). The respondent writes the first names, nicknames, or initials of their alters at various places in the diagram, placing people whom "it would be hard to imagine life without" in the innermost circle, other close contacts in the middle circle, and any additional (presumably less intimate) network members in the outermost circle. A variation on this approach is to construct a participant-aided network diagram, which depicts the individuals as circles (nodes) and the relationships between them as lines, during the course of the interview. Some researchers (e.g., McCarty et al., 2007) simply ask respondents to draw their own social networks.

Name Interpreters

The goal in many social network studies is to assess the associations among the attributes, behaviors, attitudes, or other characteristics of the members of a respondent's social network, on the one hand, and the respondent's own characteristics, on the other. Researchers also may be interested in respondents' relationships with their network members (tie strength). Therefore, lists of respondents' social network members are useful only insofar as a researcher also develops information about those network members and the respondents' relationships with them.

Many researchers collect information about the behaviors, attitudes, and experiences of the members of individuals' social networks because those attributes are thought to affect individuals in some way. For example, numerous studies have shown that people's health-related statuses and behaviors mirror those of their network members. Health statuses such as obesity and health-related behaviors such as smoking diffuse along network pathways through numerous subtle mechanisms of influence (e.g., see Christakis & Fowler 2007, 2008; Valente, 2010). One way to learn about respondents' environments is to ask them directly about their network members'

FIGURE 13.5 Hierarchical Mapping Techniques

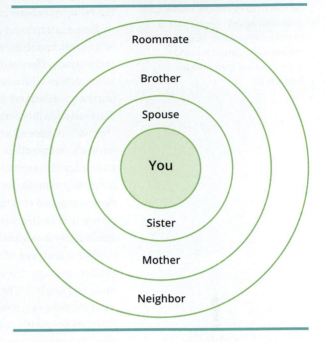

hierarchical mapping
An approach to simplifying the collection of network data in which the researcher presents respondents with a diagram containing concentric circles, and asks them to write down their closest contacts in the center and list weaker ties as they move outward from the innermost circle.

health-related attributes. This information is usually drawn out of respondents via follow-up questions called **name interpreters**.

Name interpreters develop information about network members' attributes, the nature of their relationships with network members (tie strength), network members' behaviors and attitudes (for example, health-related behaviors), and the nature of network members' relationships with one another. In egocentric designs, a common name interpreter following the use of a name generator is: "What is the nature of your relationship with [Name]?" This question is typically followed by a list of options, including "spouse/partner," "child," "friend," "neighbor," and "coworker." This name interpreter allows researchers to assess network composition (for example, the proportion of network members who are kin) and range (for example, number of roles played by the respondent). This information is extremely valuable for understanding the types of social influences to which the respondent is exposed and the resources to which he or she has access. For example, research shows that people who have few family members in their networks experience higher levels of psychological distress, including depression (Peek & Lin, 1999).

Other features of interest to researchers include network members' race, sex/gender, and age. These can be assessed with straightforward questions: "Is [NAME] male or female?" The information gleaned from such questions is indispensable for assessing the extent to which people have diverse social networks and how much they interact only with people who are similar to themselves. As it turns out, people disproportionately form relationships with people who are similar to them, resulting in highly segregated social networks.

CONCEPT CHECKS

1 | Give an example of a name generator.

2 | What is the difference between free-choice and fixed-choice network questions?

SOURCES OF BIAS IN SOCIAL NETWORK STUDIES

Researchers need to remain mindful of potential sources of bias when using informants to generate social network data. Careful selection and wording of name generators can prevent some forms of bias. Preventing other types of bias requires the careful training of interviewers.

Instrument Bias

The way a researcher words or formats the questions used to collect network data can lead to systematic bias. For example, asking respondents about their connectedness to a fixed set of different types of network members—for example, how many "friends, relatives, or acquaintances" they have—will result in a heavily skewed picture of network connectedness because it artificially reduces the apparent size of people's social networks. It prevents respondents from listing other, unnamed types of network members who may be more relevant to them.

A related problem is that different respondents may read and interpret questions such as name generator prompts in different ways. For example, some name generators (such as "Who are your closest friends?") create confusion for respondents because of the many meanings of the word *friend* (Marin & Hampton, 2007). These ambiguities may lead different groups of people—including those from different generations, those who have different levels of access to the Internet—to respond to the same question in different ways. Resulting estimates of friendship networks will be skewed for some groups (for example, younger people may appear to have more "friends"), not because of underlying differences in access to friends but because of the question that was used to assess friendship.

Another problem relates to name generators that focus on a specific action, such as "With whom do you discuss important matters?" or "Whom could you turn to for a loan if you needed it?" These questions are often unable to distinguish between respondents who have few such contacts from those who have not had the need or occasion to utilize such contacts within the time period being studied (Bearman & Parigi, 2004). Some researchers therefore recommend asking respondents about network members who come to mind relative to very specific social phenomena; for example, asking "With whom do you discuss health matters?" instead of "With whom do you discuss important matters?" (Perry & Pescosolido, 2010). In this regard, it is often advisable to use a name generator that is highly relevant to the particular phenomenon being studied.

Recall Bias

When responding to general name generators like the "important matters" item, some informants do not name the types of network members in whom researchers are most interested, even when respondents maintain such relationships. For example, when asked to provide names of close contacts or confidants, many respondents fail to mention their spouses (Bell, Belli-McQueen, & Haider, 2007). This **recall bias** can arise from memory or recall issues, time pressure, and other factors. Therefore, after the completion of a social network roster, it is advisable to ask one or two more questions to pick up additional contacts. For example, in the National Social Life, Health, and Aging Project (NSHAP) study, a multiwave study of older adults, respondents who do not name a spouse/partner in response to the "important matters" item are asked whether they have a spouse or partner. Notably, 23% of the respondents who had a spouse or partner did not name him or her until this follow-up question was asked.

As we noted earlier, some researchers use visual aids—such as the hierarchical mapping technique—to increase the accuracy of respondents' reports of who their network members are (e.g., Ajrouch, Antonucci, & Janevic, 2001; McCarty et al., 2007). Some research also suggests that using name generators that avoid imprecise concepts like "acquaintance" or "friend" can help reduce the risk of forgetting network members (Bell, Belli-McQueen, & Haider, 2007). Unless researchers use some kind of follow-up probe or visual aid, recall bias can lead to deflated estimates of network size.

Projection Bias

In some network designs, all of the data about network alters—including their attributes such as sex and race—are provided by informants. Researchers therefore must be mindful of issues relating to informant accuracy and bias. Name interpreters that

> **recall bias** In network data, a form of bias that occurs when informants do not name the most relevant network members due to memory or recall issues, time pressure, and other factors.

assess basic attributes (for example, "What is [NAME]'s sex?") are rarely problematic. In many studies, however, researchers are interested in the relationship between the ego's characteristics (for example, health-related behaviors) and the alters' characteristics. In egocentric designs, all of this information comes directly from respondents, which leads to **projection bias**: People often project their own attributes onto their network members (Goel, Mason, & Watts, 2010; Hogset & Barrett, 2010). In other words, we tend to assume that our friends and social contacts are like us, that they share our preferences and behaviors.

projection bias In network data, the type of bias that occurs when respondents project their own attributes onto their network members.

Projection may result from a number of factors, including the self-affirmation that comes with fitting in or the convenience of using oneself as a guide when guessing others' unknown attributes or behaviors. Regardless, this tendency to project inflates the association between respondents' reports and network members' actual attributes. The severity of this bias can be assessed only if the researcher has whole-network data or some other, more objective, source of information about alters' actual attributes (for example, archival information).

In some cases, projection bias can account for associations that might be otherwise interpreted as social-influence effects. In their analysis of farming practices among 120 households in Kenya, for example, Hogset and Barrett (2010) found that respondents' own farming practices correlated significantly with their reports of their network contacts' farming practices but did not correlate with those network contacts' actual farming practices. The researchers concluded that the respondents' reports of their network contacts' farming practices were influenced by their assumption that those individuals used similar practices. Similar results have been reported in studies of drug use and drinking among adolescents, the implication being that some adolescents perceive excessive substance abuse to be more normal than it actually is (e.g., Aseltine, 1995).

Projection bias likely varies according to the type of network characteristics being reported by respondents. Reports of important characteristics or behaviors are likely relatively accurate. But it is advisable to remain particularly cautious when working with respondents' reports about the extent to which network members engage in behaviors that carry some social stigma or about which the respondents themselves may have no direct knowledge (for example, smoking, drug use, or risky sex) unless you have some way to confirm or disconfirm the respondents' reports.

Respondent and Interviewer Fatigue

Respondent fatigue can affect the number of network members that respondents list when responding to a name generator. Some respondents learn through the course of an interview that providing long lists of items in response to a question can increase the number of follow-up questions. This *training effect* may induce some respondents to cut back on the number of network members they provide in response to a name generator (Marsden, 2003).

Interviewer fatigue may lead to variation in interviewers' efforts to probe for additional names in response to name generators (see Eagle & Proeschold-Bell, 2015). One study found that interviewer effects were so widespread in the 2004 General Social Survey that it produced a substantial (but artificial) reduction in the average size of respondents' confidant networks compared to the 1985 General Social Survey (Paik & Sanchagrin, 2013). Respondent fatigue and interviewer fatigue are good reasons to

IS DIVORCE CONTAGIOUS?

In December 2013, a published sociological study argued that divorce is "contagious" (McDermott, Fowler, & Christakis, 2013). The study found that a person is 75% more likely to get divorced if one of his or her network members was recently divorced. The study also found that a person is 33% more likely to get divorced if a friend's *friend* was recently divorced. The researchers argued that marriages are more stable in situations that reinforce and support marriage. When friends of friends get divorced, this lack of support can spread through networks like a virus.

The study's findings were based on longitudinal data from the Framingham Heart Study (FHS). The FHS began in 1948 as a long-term study of health. Researchers collected data from several hundred residents in Framingham, Massachusetts, seven times between 1948 and 2001. Each time the FHS personnel also asked respondents for the names of their family members and at least one close friend. Researchers later realized that they could use the data, in conjunction with archival information, to construct the larger social network of Framingham residents who participated in the study.

To understand whether divorce diffused through the community's social network, the researchers examined the association between respondents' likelihood of getting divorced at a given time point and whether their friends and/or their friends' friends were divorced by then. The researchers tested the association using time-series logistic regression analyses (discussed in Chapter 15), which allowed them to control for a number of other potential predictors of divorce, such as age and education.

This study is part of a series of similar studies conducted by two of the study's authors, sociologist Nicholas Christakis and political scientist James Fowler, using the FHS data (Christakis & Fowler, 2007, 2008; Fowler & Christakis, 2008). The first and most famous of these studies showed that obesity spreads through social networks in much the same way as communicable diseases. One of the explanations given for this apparent "contagion" effect is that obesity is a product of behaviors that are learned from and shaped by social contacts. If you spend enough time with someone, his or her behavior will eventually rub off on you.

Several critics have since argued that these FHS-based network studies suffer from important methodological limitations that undermine the overall contagion claim. One issue is the choice of study setting. Framingham's relatively small size may inflate the likelihood of contagion. Connected

Signs like this one serve as a caution that what looks like contagion might actually reflect local contextual effects.

subgroups are more likely to develop similar behaviors because they are exposed to similar local influences, like particular restaurants, grocery stores, or even doctors. It is unclear whether rates of contagion would be as high in large metropolises or in rural areas.

Others have criticized the nature of the network data. The FHS researchers did not design the study with social network analysis in mind and they collected respondents' ties only as a means of helping to locate respondents for future interviews. At that time, they asked each respondent for the name of at least one close friend.

Other critics have raised concerns about the analysis. One criticism of longitudinal analyses is that selection bias may arise from *attrition*; that is, from the fact that people who dropped out of the study were different from people who did not. Indeed, some people who dropped out had died, while others were institutionalized. Given that these things (including mortality) are more likely to occur among people who are poorly socially connected, the contagion analysis is, from wave to wave, progressively based on people who are more embedded in their networks and thus more susceptible to contagion.

The most serious challenge to these studies, though, is based on the concept of network *homophily*. People disproportionately form connections with others like them. If this is true, then the statistical association between respondents' obesity and their friends' obesity may simply reflect the fact that people who are likely to become obese select into relationships with one another. It is difficult to separate out the effects of contagion (for example, direct social influence) and homophily, even with longitudinal data.

minimize the number of network members that respondents are asked to provide information about and to ensure that interviewers are well trained. In addition, some studies have begun to collect social network rosters at the beginning of the interview, before respondent fatigue and interviewer fatigue set in (e.g., see Cornwell et al., 2009).

Selection Bias

selection bias A form of bias that occurs when certain types of people are "selected" into particular situations based on their personal characteristics.

Concerns about selection bias affect various aspects of social network research design. **Selection bias** means that certain types of people are "selected" into particular situations on the basis of their personal characteristics. Research suggests that the sample chosen for a network study can affect the resulting network data (e.g., see Entwisle et al., 2007; Fiori, Antonucci, & Akiyama, 2008). A given network survey can yield very different networks that have different properties when fielded in different neighborhoods, regions, or countries. This criticism is a frequent objection to data on electronic social networks, which are disproportionately collected from members of advantaged social groups (Boyd & Crawford, 2012). For example, research shows that more disadvantaged social groups (including people of low socioeconomic status and racial minorities) have less access to the Internet (Hargittai, 2010). Studies of electronic social networks are thus likely to be disproportionately populated by members of advantaged social groups, which could create misleading impressions regarding the benefits of electronic social network usage. It is important, therefore, to carefully choose the study site and sample so as to guard against selection bias.

Longitudinal studies provide considerable evidence that sample selection processes are themselves driven by social networks. A key problem is that, for a number of reasons, such as their access to social support, people who are well embedded within social networks tend to live longer than those who are not (Holt-Lunstad, Smith, & Layton, 2010). As such, successive waves in longitudinal studies will be disproportionately composed of well-connected subjects, because these subjects are more likely to survive and to have the good health necessary to participate in a survey interview. In other words, sample attrition is partly a result of subjects' lack of social network connectedness. Some advanced statistical methods (e.g., Austin, 2011) can be used to decrease—but cannot eliminate—the selection bias that arises from this network-related phenomenon.

CONCEPT CHECKS

1 In the context of social network analysis, how might instrument bias occur?

2 What is the hierarchical mapping technique? How can it reduce bias in network data collection?

3 Provide one example of how selection bias can affect a social network analysis.

PSEUDO-NETWORK DATA

Most network researchers collect detailed information on social networks using either a whole-network or egocentric design. But we can also infer some properties of individuals' networks without having to compile an entire roster and information about each alter who appears in it. These approaches, which are used in surveys, do not yield conventional network data, but they can provide insight into some aspects of social connectedness. In this section, we briefly describe two of these approaches.

Position and Resource Generators

Some researchers consider the name generator–name interpreter combination too cumbersome to administer in a survey, especially if the main goal is to measure individuals' access to resources or a variety of social contacts. To simplify the process, researchers have developed position generators (Hällsten, Edling, & Rydgren, 2015; Lin, Fu, & Hsung, 2001) and resource generators (Van Der Gaag & Snijders, 2005). These instruments do not elicit names of or information about specific alters. Instead, they focus on the types of alters to which one has access.

Position generators are a series of parallel questions that ask respondents if they know people who occupy various hierarchically ordered positions—usually occupations ("Do you know someone who is a [social worker/lawyer/doctor]?"). A researcher can then determine the occupational diversity and influence level of the different types of people in respondents' networks. For example, in a study of Canadians, Thomas (2011) found that foreign-born adults have significantly less occupational diversity among their social network members than do those who were born in Canada. One implication is that immigrants have fewer friends who possess certain skills or expertise (for example, carpenters or doctors) and fewer people to turn to when they need help in these areas.

Resource generators (also referred to as *exchange generators*) combine aspects of name generators–name interpreters and position generators. Respondents answer a series of questions about whether they know someone through whom they can access certain resources, such as specific types of social support, money, or information (for example, "Do you know anyone who can give you legal advice?"). Researchers who use resource generators typically ask about different types of positions/resources, and they sometimes ask follow-up questions about the strongest or most frequently accessed contact in each category, such as the specific nature of the respondent's relationship with that person. One study (see Kobayashi et al., 2013) found that people who report being well connected to others who in turn possess important resources are healthier than those who are not well connected, suggesting that even indirect access to valuable resources through networks can be personally beneficial.

One important goal of position and resource generators is to assess individuals' access to different forms of "social capital" (Lin, 2001), such as access to a doctor, lawyer, or a person who can lend money. Table 13.2 provides some examples of position and resources generators that may be relevant in health research. Position and resource generators often take less research time than name generators and interpreters. Unless combined with name generators, however, position and resource generators do not usually result in a list of network members. They also tend to overlook ties to people who do not occupy key positions (for example, retirees and students) and to people who do not possess many resources. When using resource generators in particular, researchers must be careful to distinguish between respondents who do not have any network members who possess certain resources and respondents who simply have not had to search for those resources.

position generators A series of parallel questions that ask respondents if they know people who occupy various hierarchically ordered positions—usually occupations.

resource generators Questions used to elicit network data that ask respondents about whether they know someone through whom they can access resources such as social support, money, or information. Also called *exchange generators*.

TABLE 13.2 Examples of Position and Resource Generators

Position Generators*	Resource Generators**
Do you know anyone who is a . . .	Do you know anyone who . . .
doctor?	owns a car?
lawyer?	has a professional degree?
professor?	can work with a personal computer?
social worker?	is handy repairing household equipment?
physical therapist?	has knowledge of literature?
psychologist or psychiatrist?	can help with small jobs around the house?
minister, priest, or rabbi?	can do your shopping when you (and your household members) are ill?
	has knowledge about financial matters (taxes, subsidies)?
	can loan you a large sum of money?
	owns a holiday home abroad?
	can watch your children for you at a moment's notice?
	you can rely on for help/support if you need it?

*Some of these items can be found in the position generator battery developed by Lin, Fu, and Hsung (2001).
**Some of these items are from the Survey on the Social Networks of the Dutch (SSND) and/or from Van Der Gaag and Snijders (2005).

Social Network Indices

social network index (SNI) A single composite measure that reflects generic information about a number of interrelated dimensions of one's social network.

Some researchers construct a **social network index (SNI)**, a single composite measure that reflects generic information about a number of interrelated dimensions of one's social network. Respondents answer a series of questions that assess their connectedness to different types of social network ties. For example, they may be asked if they are married, how many close friends and relatives they have, how many neighbors they know, and their level of involvement in church and community groups. The researcher then categorizes respondents according to the combination of ties they have, sometimes giving greater weight to relationship categories that contain more intimate types of contacts (see Cannuscio, Colditz, & Rimm, 2004; Cohen et al., 1997). The resulting measure reflects either an assessment of how socially connected the individual is ("not connected," "poorly connected," "moderately connected," or "well connected") or a straightforward sum of the number of different types of social network ties the individual has.

For example, if you have at least three friends and/or family members with whom you can talk about private matters on a regular basis, are involved with an organized group, and attend religious services, you would be scored as at least moderately well integrated. If you have few such contacts or if you have several contacts but interact with them only rarely, you would be scored as relatively socially isolated. SNIs vary with respect to the number and types of social ties that are included and how different types of ties are weighted. Regardless, most SNIs essentially measure the range of a given individual's active network in terms of the number of different social roles (for example, child, student, boyfriend/girlfriend) that the individual plays.

Social network indices are simple, require fewer items than combinations of name generators and interpreters, and often perform well in statistical analyses. However, SNIs predetermine which types of social ties are most important to ask about, and they therefore ignore variation in how individuals benefit from different types of relationships. More important, because SNIs combine numerous dimensions of social network connectedness into a single measure, they do not allow researchers to assess which aspects of a social network are most relevant to the analysis at hand. Exceptions are found in studies that separate network indices into subscales or multiple separate measures that capture different dimensions of social networks (York Cornwell & Waite, 2009). These studies suggest that different aspects of social networks are not always correlated with one another and are related in different ways to different types of phenomena. For example, Golden, Conroy, and Lawlor (2009) found that the extent to which older adults are involved with community and voluntary groups is negatively associated with their levels of depression, anxiety, cognitive impairment, and physical disability, but the extent to which they have contact with family is not associated with these health outcomes.

CONCEPT CHECKS

1 What is the difference between a position generator and a resource generator?

2 What is one advantage and one disadvantage of measuring networks using a social network index?

ASSESSING SOCIAL NETWORK CHANGE

Researchers are increasingly interested in the nature and extent of change within social networks, or *social network dynamics* (Snijders, 2011). Numerous aspects of social networks may change over time, including who is in the network (which may change because of turnover), the relationships among the members of the network, and the overall characteristics of network members at different time points. Research suggests that network changes (for example, the addition of new network members) can have important consequences (for example, health outcomes) for social actors regardless of the network features at baseline. For instance, one study (Cornwell & Laumann, 2015) suggests that older adults who expand their personal social networks by cultivating new ties have better health than those whose networks shrink or remain stable over time.

The analysis of social network change may also provide valuable clues about why social networks are so closely related to important outcomes such as individual health. As discussed in the "From the Field to the Front Page" feature in this chapter, there is considerable debate about this topic. For example, when scholars find that individuals' consequential behaviors, such as delinquency or smoking, tend to mirror those of their network members (e.g., see Weerman, 2011), critics ask: Do we observe this effect

Like obesity, divorce, and other social phenomena, smoking and related risky substance use behavior are common topics in social network research. This is partly because such behaviors are highly responsive to influence from one's social network members.

because people disproportionately form relationships with others who are already like them (homophily) or because network members actually influence or change the behavior of their contacts over time? The study of social network dynamics is becoming increasingly popular partly because it helps researchers determine the actual sequencing of these processes.

Studying social network change requires researchers to shift the focus from static measures of network properties at a single time point to the over-time processes through which social networks evolve. Data must therefore be collected at multiple time points. Computational social science methods, including analysis of electronic social networks and the collection of real-time data via mobile devices, make data collection at multiple time points more feasible and less burdensome for researchers and subjects alike. However, researchers have also developed new ways to collect data on network change in population-based survey research, such as by showing respondents the egocentric network rosters they had reported several years earlier and asking them to indicate where they match up with their current network rosters (e.g., Cornwell & Laumann, 2015).

The challenges of tracking social networks over time mirror those already discussed in Chapter 7, which addresses the challenges of longitudinal study designs. There are the usual concerns about recall when using retrospective designs, or studies that ask respondents to remember and report on experiences from the past. Likewise, studies using prospective designs are susceptible to problems with selection and attrition, as particular types of people may drop out of future waves of the study. There are also some unique issues when distinguishing between different sources of change in social networks. There are at least four sources of social network change: (1) changes with respect to which social actors compose a given network at different time points, (2) changes with respect to which social ties (relationships between the actors) are present in the network at different time points, (3) changes in the attributes of network members who are present at both time points, and (4) changes in the attributes of the ties that are present at both time points (see Feld, Suitor, & Hoegh, 2007).

These types of change have different implications for measuring network dynamics. For example, assume we are studying how much the cohesion of adolescents' friendship networks changes as they transition from high school to college. Assume further that we are using data on Facebook friend connections from a sample of adolescents, recorded in the last month of high school (time 1) and then again about 4 months later during the first month of college (time 2). We know exactly who is in each person's network at each of these two time points, and we also know which of them are "friends" with each other. We can measure network cohesion at each time point in terms of network density; that is, the proportion of network members who are friends with each other. We can then quantify the overall level of change in network cohesion during this transition by subtracting the former quantity from the latter. Positive values would reflect an increase in cohesion, while negative values would reflect a decrease.

Without knowing whether a given adolescent in this sample has the exact same set of friends at both time points, however, it is impossible to distinguish among several sources of change in cohesion. A change in cohesion may reflect (1) the addition of new friends at time 2, who perhaps do not yet know each other or the subject's old friends, (2) the loss of old friends who had some level of connectedness with the subject's other friends at time 1, or (3) changes in the nature of the ties that existed between the subject's old friends at time 1. Each of these three social scenarios is inherently different and involves different mechanisms. Thus, when designing an instrument to capture change in respondents' social networks over time, researchers must not only measure network properties at each time point; they must also track specific changes with respect to which actors compose the network at each time point. They can do so with either whole-network or egocentric designs. In the case of egocentric designs, researchers will need to have information about the network at the previous time point so that subjects can help researchers determine which network members were included at both time points, which were lost, and which were added.

CONCEPT CHECKS

1 | Name at least two sources of change within social networks.

2 | What is one of the challenges associated with collecting data on social network change?

CONCLUSION

People are connected to one another through a vast web, or network, of social relationships. The methods of social network analysis are essential for systematizing the study of social structure. There are advantages and disadvantages to each method, just as there are with all the other methods discussed in this book. As much as any other set of methods, social network analysis marries art and science, especially in the visualization of complex webs of social relationships. These methods require ongoing refinement, but they are already yielding important insights into the origins and consequences of social structure.

Thanks to social network analysis, scientists now know much more about how dangerous behaviors such as smoking and binge drinking spread, how quickly diseases such as HIV/AIDS can become epidemics, and how new ideas and innovations diffuse through society. The methods and concepts covered in this chapter have helped make it possible for analysts to explore such diverse questions as how segregated people's friendship networks are in terms of race and ethnicity, which aspects of social support networks are most necessary for reducing older adults' vulnerability to major health problems, how rapidly people's networks change in the wake of major life events, and just how small our social world really is. The overarching lesson is that regardless of whether we are separated by six degrees, fewer, or more—we are all interconnected, and we therefore shape each other's lives in many ways. Only with the powerful tools of network analysis can we begin to unlock the secrets of these relentless and fascinating social processes.

End-of-Chapter Review

Summary

Social network analysis (SNA) is the systematic study of the web of relationships that link people together in a given setting. SNA is not a single research method but a family of methods used to study our connections to others in a vast web of social relations and how these connections influence our behaviors and attitudes.

What Is a Social Network?

- Social networks include actors and the actors' relations with one another. Actors are nodes in a larger social structure. Ties are the links that connect the nodes.

Social Network Concepts

- The structural characteristics of networks include its overall size, the types of actors who compose it, and the actors' relationships to one another.
- Ties between actors within a network can be directed, meaning mutually acknowledged and reciprocated, or nondirected, meaning ties are not dependent on the members' acknowledgment.
- Cohesion refers to the level of interconnectedness among network actors.
- Centrality refers to the extent to which an actor can access other actors through few intermediaries. Betweenness and bridging focus on the ability of a given actor to connect other network members.
- Networks can also be characterized by the nature of its ties. Tie strength can be assessed by the intensity, frequency, or durability of actors' relationships. Tie valence considers whether the relations are positive or negative.

Social Network Study Design Issues

- Boundary specification is the process of determining the sampling frame for a social network study.
- Social network studies that consider an entire network structure are called sociocentric network designs. Egocentric study designs, by contrast, focus only on the local network of a given actor.
- Data for social network research are typically recorded and stored as a matrix.

Collecting Social Network Data

- Data can be collected using direct observation, archives, and surveys.
- Researchers using surveys ask respondents questions designed to elicit information about their social network.
- Online social networks are a unique type of social network. They are also a new source of social network data. Using social networking sites to collect data reduces respondent burden, but it also raises ethical concerns.

Respondents as Social Network Informants

- The most common way to produce a list of a respondent's social network members is to use a name generator. The most widely used name generator asks respondents to provide the names of people with whom they discuss personal/important matters.
- Researchers may use free-choice generators, for which respondents identify as many network members as they can, or fixed-choice generators, for which respondents are limited to a certain number of network members.
- Name interpreters are follow-up questions that researchers use to collect data about the behaviors and attitudes of individuals identified through name generators.

Sources of Bias in Social Network Studies

- Instrument bias occurs when the wording or format of the questions used to collect network data leads to systematic bias.
- Recall bias is the failure of respondents to mention network relationships that are significant due to memory issues, pressure, or other factors.
- Projection bias refers to the tendency of respondents to project their own attributes onto their network members.

- Respondent fatigue occurs when the respondents learn that providing a long list of network members will lead to a longer interview. Interviewer fatigue occurs when an interviewer fails to ask an appropriate number of follow-up questions.
- Selection bias refers to the fact that some respondents are more likely than others to be found in particular social networks, limiting generalizability.

Pseudo-Network Data

- Researchers can use position and resource generators to learn about individuals' access to certain resources, such as legal advice, or contacts, such as doctors.
- Social network indices (SNIs) are composite measures generated from respondents' responses to multiple questions about their network.

Assessing Social Network Change

- Researchers are increasingly interested in social network change, or *social network dynamics*, such as change in the actors that comprise a network.

Key Terms

Exercise

Think of 10 people you know. Or, if you have a Facebook or other online networking account, go to your page and choose the 10 contacts to whom you feel closest. Now, make a list of those people on a sheet of paper, with each name on a separate line. Next to the name of the first person on the list, write down how many of the other nine people on the list that first person knows. (If you are using a social networking site, you can do this by seeing how many of those other people are linked to that first person's page.) Next, divide that number by the maximum possible, which is nine. Write down the resulting number. Repeat this process for each of the other nine people on the list.

Using this information, respond to the following:

- Draw your network by hand on a piece of paper, using small circles to depict the individuals and lines to depict the relationships that exist between them.
- Who is the most *central* member of your social network (apart from you)?
- What is the *density* of your social network?
- To what extent do you sit on a *bridge* between other pairs of actors within your social network? Are there any members of your network (apart from you) who appear to sit on bridges between others?

Social researchers use quantitative data analysis to describe populations, such as how many people are unemployed. The unemployment rate is one of the nation's most important statistics.

14

UNIVARIATE AND BIVARIATE ANALYSIS OF QUANTITATIVE DATA

Every month, the U.S. government conducts the Current Population Survey (CPS) by contacting 60,000 households and asking people questions about their jobs. One of the most important questions is, "Are you currently working, and if not, are you looking for work (as opposed to being retired or discouraged in your job hunt)?" The answers are used to compute one of the nation's most important statistics: the unemployment rate.

Interviewing 60,000 people each month costs a lot of money, but it is money well spent. Policy makers use the unemployment rate to determine how the economy is doing. Changes in the unemployment rate indicate whether the economy is improving or worsening. Researchers also compare state unemployment rates to assess which states are hit hardest by economic downturns and need federal assistance. For example, in November 2016, Alaska had the nation's highest unemployment rate (6.8%), while the lowest rates were found in South Dakota (2.7%) and New Hampshire (2.7%) (Bureau of Labor Statistics, 2016).

Private businesses also use unemployment data. For example, financiers use the data to decide where and how to invest money. In fact, the unemployment rate is so important to investment decisions that it remains a closely guarded secret until it is announced on the first Friday of every month, at precisely 8:30 a.m. Knowing the unemployment rate before others do would give an investor an unfair advantage in the marketplace.

Imagine if the government did not use specific numbers to measure unemployment. Instead, imagine that it simply announced that unemployment was "high" or "low." These words are extremely imprecise. We would not know whether unemployment is getting better or worse or whether "high" unemployment in one place is the same as or different than "high" unemployment somewhere else. Let's move from this hypothetical example to a real one: After the terrorist attacks of September 11, 2001, the U.S. government implemented a color-coded "terror alert system." The estimated risk of an attack would fluctuate between yellow, indicating "elevated" risk, and orange, corresponding to a "high" risk. The system was widely criticized and was eventually abandoned because it did not specify the basis for changes from one color to another or how those changes should be interpreted.

STATISTICS AND QUANTITATIVE DATA ANALYSIS

Statistics are the primary means by which societies collect and process systematic information about themselves. As we have seen throughout this book, many methods of sociological research make little or no use of numbers, but for questions that involve the description of basic features of populations—such as "How much unemployment is there in the United States?" or "Is there more unemployment now than there was a year ago?"—there is no substitute for the precision and comparability that numbers provide.

quantitative data analysis
The process by which substantive findings are drawn from numerical data.

Quantitative data analysis is the process by which substantive findings are drawn from numerical data. Quantitative social research can usually be divided into three distinct phases: (1) project design, (2) data collection, and (3) data analysis. When analysts begin with flawed data, they can easily draw incorrect or misleading conclusions. In social research, high-quality data are the result of rigorous sampling (Chapter 6) and precise measurement (Chapter 4). We have already covered these topics, and we will not repeat that information here. But we cannot emphasize enough that the strength of quantitative sociological research depends *first* on good data being collected and *then* on analyzing those data.

univariate analysis An analysis of a single variable.

bivariate analysis An analysis of the relationship between two variables.

This chapter and the next provide an in-depth discussion of quantitative data analysis. In this chapter, we focus on the use of quantitative data to describe basic characteristics of populations. We begin with **univariate analysis**, or analysis of a single variable, such as how many people are unemployed or how much money the average person earns in a year. We then move to **bivariate analysis**, in which we look at the relationship between two variables. For example, we are conducting a bivariate analysis when we consider whether the unemployment rate is lower for college graduates than it is for people without high school diplomas (unemployment rate is one variable in this analysis, and educational attainment is the other). We end the chapter by briefly discussing a set of tools that will help you think more critically and sociologically about the statistics you encounter in your daily life.

UNIVARIATE ANALYSIS

Univariate analysis relies on an understanding of several key concepts: distributions, measures of central tendency, variation, and margin of error. We discuss each in turn.

Distributions

A **distribution** is the most fundamental concept in univariate analysis. The distribution of a variable provides information about the different values of the variable that have been observed and how common each value is.

distribution The set of different values of a variable that have been observed and how common each value is.

FREQUENCY AND RELATIVE DISTRIBUTIONS

Let's use a simple example to explain what a distribution is. Consider this question: "How confident are you that God exists?" Obviously, this question asks about a deeply personal and subjective matter. If a friend asked you this question, you might give a very long and complicated response. The nation's premier survey of social attitudes, the General Social Survey (GSS), asks about belief in God as part of its measures of religiousness. More specifically, GSS participants are handed a card containing six statements, and they respond by indicating which one comes closest to their own beliefs:

1. I don't believe in God.

2. I don't know whether there is a God and I don't believe there is any way to find out.

3. I don't believe in a personal God, but I do believe in a Higher Power of some kind.

4. I find myself believing in God some of the time, but not at others.

5. While I have doubts, I feel that I do believe in God.

6. I know God really exists and I have no doubts about it.

These six simple categories do not capture all the nuance and complexity of all Americans' religious or spiritual beliefs, but they do tell us something about Americans' general views about the existence of God. And, because the GSS is based on a representative sample of the U.S. population, having this question on the GSS provides reliable and valid information about the religious beliefs of the U.S. population.

A **frequency distribution** presents the possible values of a variable along with the number of observations for each value that was observed. Table 14.1 is a frequency distribution that summarizes the responses to the question about belief in God, as asked on the GSS between 1988 and 2014. Table 14.1 shows that a total of 19,498 people answered this question, and 12,099 of them said they have no doubts that God exists. We can also see that 62.05% of respondents say that they have no doubts that God exists, because 12,099 divided by 19,498 equals 0.6205. While the

frequency distribution A presentation of the possible values of a variable along with the number of observations for each value that was observed.

TABLE 14.1 Frequency Distribution: Categorical Variable

Confidence That God Exists?	Frequency	Percent
Don't believe in God	547	2.81
Don't know, no way to find out	922	4.73
No personal God but some Higher Power	1,929	9.89
Believe in God sometimes	800	4.10
Have doubts but do believe	3,201	16.42
Know God exists, have no doubts	12,099	62.05
Total	**19,498**	**100.00**

Source: General Social Survey, 1988–2014.

frequency The number of observations with a particular value of a variable.

relative frequency The percentage of observations with a particular value.

relative distribution A presentation of the possible values of a variable along with the percentage of observations for each value that was observed. Also referred to as a *percentage distribution*.

frequency is the *number* of observations with a particular value of a variable, the **relative frequency** is the *percentage* of observations with that particular value. Frequency distributions describe how often different values of a variable occur using actual counts, while **relative distributions** (sometimes called *percentage distributions*) use percentages instead. While the total number of observations in a frequency distribution will vary, the percentages always add up to 100.

Relative distributions are usually easier for audiences to follow, but they can sometimes be misleading if the total number of observations is very small. If a friend told you she had conducted her own survey and found that only 50% of respondents have no doubts that God exists, you would feel misled if you later found out that the survey had only four respondents. For this reason, tables of relative frequencies typically present the total number of observations somewhere, usually referred to by the abbreviation *N*. So, the results of your friend's survey should specify *N* = 4. Many frequency distributions, like the ones in this chapter, present both the frequency and relative frequency.

BAR GRAPHS AND HISTOGRAMS

When values are categories, like the answers to the belief-in-God question, it is easy to present the relative frequency distribution using a bar graph (Figure 14.1). When you present your data visually, your audience can use their intuitive sense of the size of the bars to understand the relative frequency. You also may see pie charts used in newspapers or websites. Although these charts are visually appealing, experts often avoid

FIGURE 14.1 Relative Frequency Distribution Presented as a Bar Graph

Relative frequency distributions use percentages to show how often different values of a variable occur. We can see that a large majority of Americans say that they "know God exists, have no doubts."

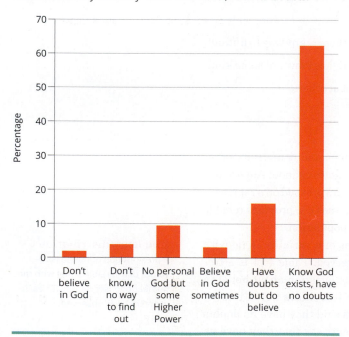

Source: General Social Survey, 1988–2014.

presenting data this way because differences between the sizes of the slices can be difficult to discern.

Belief in God is an example of a **categorical variable**; the values of categorical variables are categories. In contrast, the values of **continuous variables** are quantities such as dollars, years, pounds, or the number of times one had a particular experience (see Chapter 4 for a review of the different types of variables). Continuous variables are often counts of a particular attribute, asset, or experience. How many times someone has attended a religious service in the past year is an example of a continuous variable; a value of 2 would mean that the person has attended a religious service twice during the past year. Continuous variables are more complicated than categorical variables because each observation may have a different value, and the values may vary widely. For example, each of the 193 nations in the United Nations has a different value for its gross national product. Here, $N = 193$, and it is likely that no two of the values are exactly the same.

Even when researchers ask survey questions with responses that are continuous variables in principle, researchers typically do not expect that respondents can provide especially precise answers. For example, the GSS asks, "On the average day, about how many hours do you personally watch television?" The GSS requires a whole number as a response, so if a respondent tried to give an answer that is not a whole number (for example, 4.5 hours), the interviewer would ask the respondent which whole number would provide the best answer.

Even though the GSS does not allow fractional answers, over the history of the GSS all 25 possible answers between 0 hours and 24 hours have been given by at least one person. Listing 25 different categories typically results in a long, complicated frequency distribution. To simplify matters, the researcher may divide the frequency distribution of a continuous variable into categories, as in Table 14.2.

The researcher can use these same categories to create a bar graph or pie chart. By contrast, imagine a pie chart with 25 slices; it would be difficult to read and even more difficult to develop a sense of Americans' television viewing habits.

Another method of presenting data visually is a **histogram**, which depicts the frequency distribution of a continuous variable. Figure 14.2 is a histogram of how many hours a day GSS respondents say they watch television. A histogram looks a lot like a bar graph, only without any spaces between the bars. However, the bars in a bar graph are used to depict categories, whereas the bars in a histogram (called "bins") represent a range of values

categorical variable A variable that has a finite set of possible values that are fixed and distinct from one another with unknown differences between them.

continuous variable A variable that could have an infinite set of possible values that exist on a continuum from low to high with meaningful and identifiable differences between them.

TABLE 14.2 Frequency Distribution: Continuous Variable

How Much TV Do You Watch in a Typical Day?	Frequency	Percent
0–1 hours	8,844	24.90
2–3 hours	16,055	45.19
4–5 hours	7,049	19.84
6–7 hours	1,900	5.35
8 or more hours	1,676	4.72
Total	35,524	100.00

Source: General Social Survey, 1975–2014.

FIGURE 14.2 Number of Hours of TV U.S. Adults Report Watching per Day

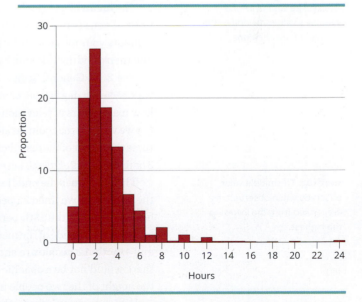

Source: General Social Survey, 1975–2014.

of a continuous variable. Because the bins in a histogram represent a range of values, it is not appropriate to draw histograms for categorical variables.

CONCEPT CHECKS

1   Give an example of a categorical variable and a continuous variable. What would be the best way to represent each variable visually?

2   What are the differences between a bar graph and a histogram?

Measures of Central Tendency

Rather than presenting an entire distribution, we often want to provide a simple summary. A single value that summarizes some feature of a distribution is called a **summary statistic**, and those that indicate the center of a distribution are called **measures of central tendency**. In this subsection, we discuss the three main measures of central tendency: average (or mean), median, and mode. Each provides slightly different information about the distribution.

The most common summary statistic is the average value of a variable. But what exactly is the average of a distribution? When we ask how much television the typical American watches, we are asking about an average. In essence, we are asking where the center of the distribution is. The method for determining the center differs slightly for continuous versus categorical measures.

AVERAGES FOR CONTINUOUS VARIABLES: MEAN AND MEDIAN

The number of hours of television watched in a day is an example of a continuous variable. There are two primary ways of computing the average for continuous variables: the mean and the median.

The **mean** of a variable is the sum of all its values divided by the number of observations. If you scored 95, 87, 85, and 81 on four sociology exams this semester, you would compute your mean score by adding the four scores together (95 + 87 + 85 + 81 = 348) and then dividing this sum by 4 (348 ÷ 4 = 87), giving you a mean of 87.

The 2014 General Social Survey found that the mean number of hours of television watched each day is 2.98, or very close to 3. (We could question the relationship between how many hours of television people *say* they watch and how much they *actually* watch, but we will put that point aside for now.) We might wonder how well the mean really captures the center of the distribution. In particular, about 70% of respondents say they watch 3 or fewer hours of television each day, while only 30% say they watch more than 3 hours.

The **median** is the middle value observed if we rank observations from the lowest to the highest. If we lined 25 people up from shortest to tallest, the median height would be the height of the 13th person in line, because the same number of people (12) are found on either side of the median. That is, exactly 12 people are taller than that person, and exactly 12 people are shorter than that person. If we had 26 people instead of 25, there would not be a specific middle value; instead, our median would be the mean of the height of the two people in the middle—the 13th person and the 14th person.

Which is more informative, the mean or the median? To answer this question, we need to clarify why the two differ, focusing on the *shape* of the distribution rather

histogram A visual representation of data that depicts the frequency distribution of a continuous variable.

summary statistic A single value that summarizes some feature of a distribution.

measure of central tendency A summary statistic that refers to the center of a distribution.

mean The sum of all of a variable's values divided by the number of observations.

median The middle value observed when observations are ranked from the lowest to the highest.

than just its center. If we look at the histogram for hours of television (repeated as Figure 14.3a), we see that the distribution has a single peak at a lower value and then a long tail to the right for high values. An unbalanced distribution is said to be **skewed**. Specifically, this distribution is skewed to the right, as the long tail is on the right side of the distribution.

In Chapter 4, you learned about **ratio variables**, which are interval variables that have a true zero. The number of hours of television someone typically watches in a day is an example of a ratio variable, because somebody who watches 2 hours of television a day watches twice as much television as somebody who watches 1 hour a day. Ratio variables are often skewed to the right. That is, more people are close to the lowest possible value than to the highest possible value. For television watching, nobody can watch fewer than zero hours a day, and the number of hours that most people *say* that they watch television is much closer to zero than to the maximum possible value of 24 hours.

The mean is more sensitive to extreme values than the median is. What do we mean by "more sensitive"? Imagine if we eliminated the extreme values in our GSS data by taking everyone who said they watched more than 4 hours of television a day and changed their answer to 4. The mean would drop from 2.98 to 2.48, because the total number of hours when all the responses are added together would be smaller. But the median would not change at all. As long as the number of cases above and below the

skewed An unbalanced distribution.

ratio variable A variable with a continuum of values with meaningful distances (or intervals) between them and a true zero.

FIGURE 14.3 Skewed Distributions, Mode, and Outliers

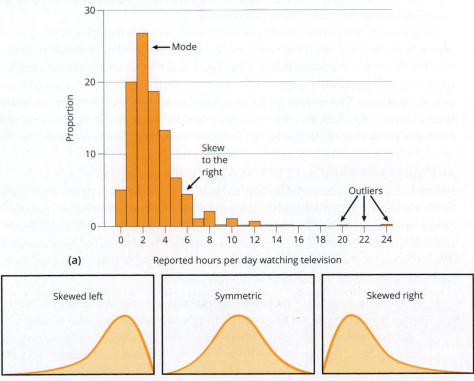

(a) Reported hours per day watching television

(b) Examples of distributions that are skewed to the left and skewed to the right, along with a distribution that is symmetric.

median remains the same, the median remains the same. The median is not affected by how far the other observations are above or below the median.

outlier An extreme value.

When a variable is skewed, the mean will be pulled more in the direction of the skew than the median. The mean is also more affected by **outliers**, or very extreme values. Earlier, we asked you to consider an example where your four sociology exams had a mean score of 87. Now let's say you completely missed the fifth exam and therefore got a grade of 0. The 0 would be an outlier, in that it is very different from the pattern of performance you established with your other scores. And it would change your mean score from 87 to just below 70 ($348 \div 5 = 69.6$), but your median score would drop only one point, from 86 to 85. In Figure 14.3a, the outliers are people who say they watch television 18 or more hours a day.

The mean is the measure of central tendency that most social researchers use, except for cases in which it is misleading because of skew or outliers, as is commonly the case with financial variables. Financial variables are often ratio variables that are skewed highly to the right. For example, government publications about "average household income" in a particular state or country typically report the median, not the mean. Why? While negative income is possible (when people spend more than they earn), it is uncommon and modest compared with the very large incomes that the wealthiest households make. Consequently, the mean household income is much higher than the median, so the mean can be deceptive if it is interpreted as the income of a typical U.S. household. Consider another example: If you lived in a dormitory building with 99 other students, and one of them won $100 million in a lottery last year, the mean income in your building would be at least $1 million, which would likely be a very misleading indicator of the typical income.

Even in cases where the median provides a more accurate depiction of the typical person than the mean, the mean can be more useful if our purpose is simply to detect whether the distribution is changing. Consider a situation where household incomes are largely staying the same (adjusted for inflation), but the incomes of the top 20% are expanding rapidly. This change would have no influence on the median, which would appropriately reflect that the typical person's income is not changing. However, the mean would increase, reflecting the fact that total household income is increasing.

AVERAGES FOR VARIABLES WITH CATEGORICAL VALUES?

Determining averages for variables with values that are categories is trickier than it is for continuous variables. We need to divide these variables into three types: (1) dichotomous variables, (2) ordinal variables, and (3) nominal variables. (Dichotomous variables are usually considered a type of nominal variable, but the advice about averages differs for nominal variables that are dichotomous and those that are not, so we've separated them out for the purposes of this discussion.)

dichotomous variable A variable with only two categories.

1. *Dichotomous variables.* A **dichotomous variable** has only two categories. With a dichotomous variable, we can assign each of the two categories a value of either 0 or 1. For example, we might assign female respondents a value of 1 and male respondents a value of 0. In the 2014 GSS, there were 1,397 female respondents and 1,141 male respondents, which means that 55.0% of 2014 GSS respondents were female:

$$\frac{1,397}{1,397 + 1,141} = 0.550 = 55.0\%$$

If we calculate the mean of the variable, it is also

$$\frac{1,141 \times 0 + 1,397 \times 1}{1,397 + 1,141} = \frac{1,397}{2,538} = 0.550 = 55.0\%$$

When we code a dichotomous variable with 0 and 1, the mean is just the proportion of whatever category is coded as 1. As a result, there is no logical problem with talking about the average of a dichotomous variable. In practice, however, it is clearer to state the information as a proportion. In this case, we would just say that 55.0% of respondents are female, and 45.0% are male.

2. *Ordinal variables.* As we learned in Chapter 4, an **ordinal variable** has categories that can be ordered in some way. These categories can be ranked from low to high, but the actual difference or distance between ranks cannot be known. That is, the numerical values assigned to the categories do not imply equal distances in a strict mathematical sense. The GSS question about belief in God that we have been considering is an example of an ordinal variable. The six response categories range in order from unequivocal nonbelief to unequivocal belief. However, there is no yardstick that would allow us to say that the difference between answering "I don't believe in God" and "I don't know whether there is a God" represents the same amount of change in confidence about God's existence as the difference between "I have doubts but do believe in God" and "God really exists and I have no doubts."

Is it technically appropriate to compute the mean of an ordinal variable? Strictly speaking, the answer is no. Computing the mean involves adding the values of the variable for different observations, but addition is justified only if the differences between values represent meaningful intervals. So, saying that the mean of confidence of belief in God is 5.19 does not offer any useful, valid, or reliable information.

Nevertheless, in practice, researchers do present the mean of ordinal variables quite often, and doing so can be useful, as long as the scale on which the mean is based is clear. For example, in the GSS, the mean of the belief variable is 4.8 for men and 5.3 for women, and 4.9 for whites and 5.6 for blacks. These results suggest that overall strength of belief in God is stronger for women than for men and stronger for blacks than for whites. However, a more straightforward way of reporting these conclusions would be to note that while 81% of black respondents and 67% of women report knowing that God exists with "no doubts," only 55% of white respondents and 51% of men report the same thing.

As we noted earlier, the median is based on the rank order of cases, and cases can be ranked by their order on the ordinal variable. In the GSS question we are considering, the median value is "no doubt in the existence in God," which is the response that a majority of respondents give. The problem is that this answer is the median regardless of whether we are talking about women or (by a slimmer margin) men, or blacks or (by a slimmer margin) whites. The differences we noticed when looking at the mean are not there when we look at the median, because the median is less sensitive to the value of each case. With ordinal variables, the median is often not sensitive enough to the differences we care about.

3. *Nominal variables.* Unlike an ordinal variable, a **nominal variable** indicates states or statuses that cannot be ranked or ordered. When numerical values are assigned to a nominal variable, those values simply indicate that observations with different values belong to different categories.

If a nominal variable is dichotomous, the advice we provided earlier about presenting the average of dichotomous variables as proportions applies. Apart from that, however, you should never present either the mean or the median for a nominal variable with more than two categories. To understand why, we can look at respondents' race/ethnicity in the GSS. While there are many different ways of categorizing race/ethnicity, here is the one we use:

1. Asian/Pacific Islander

2. Black, not Hispanic

3. Hispanic

4. Native American

5. White, not Hispanic

6. Other

Notice that the ordering has nothing to do with the substance of these categories. The order is simply alphabetic, with "Other" at the end. Race/ethnicity is a nominal variable because the numeric values are completely arbitrary and we could rearrange them however we wanted, as long as we keep using different values to indicate different categories. As a result, saying the "average" ethnicity is 3.5 is completely meaningless.

With nominal variables, the best approach is simply to present the frequency (and/or relative frequency) distribution when possible. Table 14.3 is the frequency distribution of this variable in the 2000–2014 GSS.

The closest thing to an "average" for nominal variables is the **mode**, which is the most common value of a variable. In Table 14.3, the mode is "White, not Hispanic" (68.4%). A variable does not have to be a nominal variable for us to

TABLE 14.3 Frequency Distribution: Race/Ethnicity

Respondent Race/Ethnicity	Frequency	Percent
Asian/Pacific Islander	370	3.2
Black, not Hispanic	1,638	14.2
Hispanic	1,481	12.9
Native American	116	1.0
White, not Hispanic	7,874	68.4
Other	33	0.3
Total	11,512	100.0

Source: General Social Survey, 2000–2014.

refer to the mode. With our ordinal variable example regarding belief in God, the mode is that one believes in God without any doubts (62.1%). We can also use mode to refer to the peak value in a histogram of a continuous variable. So, for example, the modal number of hours of television that respondents report watching is 2, as shown in Figure 14.3a.

The mode is sometimes characterized as a type of "average," like the mean or median. This characterization is misleading because an average measures the center of a distribution, and, with nominal variables, the values can be arranged in any order. For variables with a very large number of categories, such as the make of all cars purchased in the United States in a given year, the modal category does not tell us what the "typical" American is doing. Consider that the most popular car in the United States in 2014 was the Toyota Camry, but this model accounted for only 3% of all new automotive vehicle sales. The Camry is therefore the mode, but the percentage is so small that it would be misleading to say that the average new car was a Camry or (worse) that the average person drives a Camry. Whenever presenting a categorical variable as the mode, one should also indicate how common it is, so that the audience knows whether *most* observations belong to the modal category or only a few.

CONCEPT CHECKS

1. Imagine having data from a random sample of college students on the number of alcoholic drinks consumed in the previous month. Which would you expect to be a better measure of what is typical: the mean or the median? Would you expect this variable to be skewed? Why?

2. Give an example of a dichotomous variable, an ordinal variable, and a nominal variable. For each variable, state whether the mean, median, or mode would be most useful for comparing different populations.

Variation across Observations

Averages summarize a distribution by telling us what the central value is. However, averages tell us nothing about how much observations vary; that is, how much they differ from one another.

As an example, imagine that respondents are asked to rate, on a scale from 0 to 10, how much they like two different political candidates. Figure 14.4 shows the distribution of ratings for each candidate. Both candidates in this example have the same mean rating: 7.0. Yet we can see that simply saying the candidates have the same mean misses an important part of the story. Candidate A is positively regarded by most people but does not have many very strong supporters or very negative critics. In contrast, most people seem to either love or hate candidate B. If we look only at the averages in this example, we would miss the most sociologically interesting difference between these two distributions. Because many sociologists are interested in social

FIGURE 14.4 Histograms of Ratings for Two Political Candidates

While the candidates have the same mean rating (7.0), the ratings of candidate B vary more widely, with many more ratings of 0 or 10.

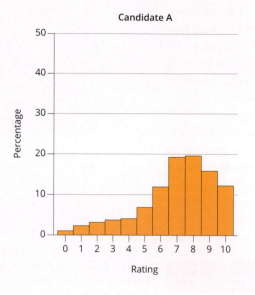

Candidate A

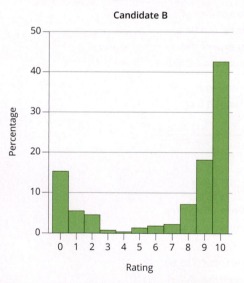

Candidate B

range The differences between the maximum and minimum values of a distribution.

inequalities—and inequalities are variation—sociologists often consider the amount of variation in a distribution to be just as telling as the average.

RANGE

The simplest way to summarize the variation in a variable is to present the **range** of a variable, which is just the difference between the maximum and minimum values of a distribution. For example, in 2015, gross domestic product (GDP) per capita varied from a low of $277 (Burundi) to a high of $163,026 (Monaco) (World Bank, 2016). The total range across all countries is therefore $162,749. In practice, instead of reporting the range, researchers will usually present just the minimum and maximum values.

The range is a simple and informative measure of variation, but it can be very misleading because it is extremely sensitive to outliers. In the case of GDP, Monaco is an outlier. It is a very small nation with just 40,000 residents. Situated on the French Riviera, it is home to the greatest number of millionaires and billionaires per capita in the world. If we recalculated our range including only countries with a population of at least a million people, the richest country by GDP per capita would be Switzerland ($80,945) and the range would decrease to $80,121. In other words, including the outlier of Monaco has a dramatic effect on the range.

STANDARD DEVIATION

While knowing the minimum and maximum values of a variable is often useful, we usually want a measure of variation that is not determined solely by the extreme values of a population. For this reason, the most commonly used measure of variation in sociology and other disciplines is the **standard deviation**. The precise definition of a standard deviation is not intuitive, but we show how it is calculated in Box 14.1. The larger the standard deviation of a variable, the more variation in the variable. Usually, the standard deviation ends up being fairly close to the average distance between the value of each observation and the overall mean.

In practice, the standard deviation is not a very effective way to convey variation to an audience that has not had formal statistical training. For this reason, we recommend describing variation in terms of percentiles rather than the standard deviation. **Percentiles** indicate values at or below which a certain percentage of values falls. For example, 50% of observations have a value at or below the median. That is, the median is the value of the 50th percentile.

According to a 2014 report by the U.S. Census Bureau, the 10th percentile of household income in the United States was $12,401 in 2013, the 50th percentile was $51,939, and the 95th percentile was $196,000. In other words, a household that had an income of $12,401 in 2013 had a higher income than only 10% of American households, whereas a household with an income of $196,000 had an income higher than 95% of households.

Percentiles provide a good sense of how values vary, and, in the case of inequality, they are also useful for showing how inequality is changing. In fact, many of the Occupy Wall Street protests that erupted in the 2010s and the protesters' rallying cry of "We are the 99 percent" were inspired by recognition of rising levels of income inequality in the United States.

On the basis of the numbers provided, the median household in 2013 earned 4.2 times what a household in the 10th percentile earned (51,939 / 12,401 = 4.2). In 1980, this ratio was 3.9, or nearly the same. However, in 2013, a household in the 95th percentile had income that was 3.8 times higher than the median household. In 1980, by contrast, the ratio between the 95th percentile and median household income was only 2.9. In other words, looking at percentiles allows us to see not only that income inequality in the United States increased between 1980 and 2013, but also that the increase was a result of high-earners pulling further away from middle- and low-income households, while differences between middle-income households and low-income households remained largely the same.

In 2015, the top 1% of U.S. families captured 22% of all income.

standard deviation The average distance between the value of each observation and the overall mean.

percentiles Values at or below which a certain percentage of values fall.

BOX 14.1 Calculating a Standard Deviation

A standard deviation is formally the square root of the average squared differences between the values of a distribution and the distribution's mean.

We can illustrate how the standard deviation is calculated with a simple example. Say a student has the following test scores in a class: 70, 80, 90, 100. The mean of these scores would be: (70 + 80 + 90 + 100) / 4 = 85.

1. Subtract the mean from each score. The differences are: –15, –5, 5, 15.

2. Square these differences: 225, 25, 25, 225.

3. Compute the average for these squares: (225 + 25 + 25 + 225 = 500) / 4 = 125.

4. Take the square root of this average: 11.18.

CONCEPT CHECKS

1 | Give an example of a question for which looking at the variation in a distribution would be more useful than looking at the average.

2 | Why is range not always a good measure of variation?

3 | What does it mean to say that the 10th percentile of height for 20-year-old women in the United States is 61 inches?

Margin of Error

The GSS is a high-quality survey that asks a wide range of questions about people's opinions and lives. Nevertheless, the GSS is still based on a sample in which the responses of a few thousand people are used to generate estimates to describe the entire population of U.S. adults. As we emphasized in Chapter 6, whenever a sample is used, there is *always* uncertainty about how well the results from the sample estimate the true parameters of the population. The great virtue of *probability samples*, in which individuals are randomly selected to participate, is that we can talk precisely about the uncertainty that results from using a sample instead of the entire population.

The **margin of error** accounts for the fact that the estimates generated from samples are likely to differ from the real population parameter by some amount just by random chance. The margin of error does not tell us precisely how much our estimate differs from the true parameter—which we can never know for sure—but it does tell us how confident we can be that the difference is not more than a specific amount. More precisely, we can be 95% confident that the estimate generated from a sample will differ from the true population parameter by no more than the margin of error, at least as a result of chance alone.

In 2014, GSS respondents reported watching television 2.98 hours a day on average. The margin of error was ± 0.12 hours. Consequently, we can be 95% confident that the population mean is somewhere between 2.86 hours per day and 3.10 hours per day, because $2.98 - 0.12 = 2.86$ and $2.98 + 0.12 = 3.10$.

The numbers 2.86 and 3.10 in this example compose the 95% confidence interval. If we took 100 different random samples from the population and the 95% confidence interval computed for each sample, we would expect 95% of the intervals to contain the population mean (and 5% of the intervals not to contain the population mean). In practice, we draw only one sample and do not know whether our interval includes the population mean or not, but we can be 95% confident that it does. The **confidence interval** gets wider as the margin of error gets larger.

The margin of error is important because it allows us to speak precisely about how much uncertainty we have about our estimates because they are based on a probability sample instead of the entire population. The size of the margin of error depends on two things: (1) the size of the sample and (2) the amount of variation in the variable. All else being equal, the larger our sample, the smaller our margin of error. The more variation in a variable, the larger the margin of error. For example, say researchers are trying to estimate the average income of workers with the same occupation, and they do not want a margin of error of more than $10,000. The researchers would have to survey more workers to achieve this for an occupation where workers' incomes vary widely than for an occupation in which incomes are similar.

margin of error The amount of uncertainty in an estimate; equal to the distance between the estimate and the boundary of the confidence interval.

confidence interval A range of possible estimates in which researchers can have a specific degree of confidence; includes the population parameter.

CONCEPT CHECKS

1   If the mean number of hours worked per week in a sample was 31 and the margin of error was 4, what would the 95% confidence interval be?

2   How could the GSS reduce the margin of error for the mean hours of television reported to be watched per day?

HOW TO USE STATISTICS TO ROOT OUT CHEATING

The headline of the *Atlanta Journal-Constitution* proclaimed "State to Examine Test-Score Surge" (Perry & Vogell, 2008). The reporters delved into a surprising yet potentially uplifting discovery: Some of Atlanta's public schools had documented pronounced improvements in students' standardized test scores. At one elementary school, about half of all fifth graders had received a failing score on the state's math competency exam. Consistent with state policy, these students were required to retake the test. When they retook the exam, not only did all 32 pass, but 26 of them passed *at the highest level*.

Certainly, students may improve in their math ability, but this leap struck some as too extreme to be believable.

So just how big was this improvement? The way that student scores typically change between the first test and a retest can be viewed as a distribution. As you have learned, the standard deviation is the most common way of describing variation in a distribution. The news story reported that the improvement shown by this school's students was 9 standard deviations above average. Under normal conditions, a change this big would be expected to happen fewer than once in a quadrillion times. If you are familiar with the Powerball lottery, one in a quadrillion is roughly the same as the odds of someone who buys a single ticket winning that lottery and then buying another ticket the next week and winning the lottery again.

This statistical result is not necessarily proof of cheating, but it certainly sends up a red flag. A technique that investigators use with standardized tests is to look at which answers are erased and changed. Students change their answers often, but, when they do, they change from a right answer to a wrong answer almost as often as they change from a wrong answer to a right one. However, when investigators looked at the Atlanta tests, they found that the number of times in which wrong answers were changed to correct answers vastly outnumbered the number of times correct answers were changed to wrong answers. One analyst compared this outcome to the probability that a sellout crowd at a football game would consist entirely of people more than 7 feet tall (Wheelan, 2013).

Widespread irregularities with changed answers provide strong evidence that the problem is not with students cheating, but with teachers or school principals cheating. Students take the test; afterward, teachers or administrators correct some answers. In the Atlanta case, the problem was not confined to just one classroom or even one school. Some teachers had even held "parties" where they got together to change answer sheets (Wheelan, 2013). In the end, well over 150 educators across 44 schools were accused of wrongdoing, and more than 35 were indicted.

FIGURE 14.5 Distribution of Midterm Grades

The two separate peaks indicate a bimodal distribution.

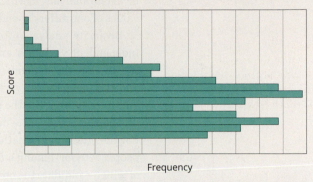

Score

Frequency

There is a larger debate about the value of standardized tests and the pressure they put on teachers. Here, we want to emphasize the role that quantitative data analysis plays in detecting cheating. So many students take standardized tests that the overall distribution of results is very predictable.

To give another example, in 2010 a video of an accounting professor accusing his class of widespread cheating went viral. The professor began to suspect that something was wrong when he noticed that the mean score on the midterm was substantially higher than it was in earlier semesters. Of course, a substantially higher mean could happen if the professor happened to have an unusually bright group of students or if he had made a dramatic improvement in how effectively he was teaching. However, when he looked at the shape of the distribution of test scores, he noticed that it was *bimodal*, meaning that it had two distinct peaks (Figure 14.5).

When a large number of students take a test, the scores almost always have just one mode. A bimodal distribution suggests that there are two separate groups in the class, each with its own typical score. In the case of the accounting exam, the lower peak was consistent with the peak in the distribution of scores in previous semesters. In other words, his class could be divided into two groups: one group that performed much like the students in previous semesters, and a second group that mysteriously performed much better. The professor discovered that about a third of the students had gained access to the bank of questions he used to write the test.

Quantitative analyses allow us to detect patterns too strong to be ignored. Of course, not all unusual situations result from misbehavior. However, widespread misbehavior tends to leave statistical traces.

BIVARIATE ANALYSIS

Up to now, this chapter has focused on univariate analysis, or describing a population with respect to a single variable. However, even when doing simple research, we often want to know whether a variable differs between groups. For example, we may want to know how men and women differ with respect to annual income or how people with and without college degrees differ in terms of whom they vote for. These questions involve bivariate analysis, in which we look at two variables simultaneously to determine if the values of one differ depending on the values of the other.

Bivariate analysis often, but not always, makes use of the distinction between independent variables and dependent variables that we introduced in Chapter 2. Recall that the dependent variable is the outcome we are seeking to understand, and the independent variable is a variable on which values of the dependent variable may depend. For the question of whether men and women have different annual incomes, income is the dependent variable and gender is the independent variable. For the question of whether having a college degree is associated with the candidate people vote for, having a college degree is the independent variable and the decision of which candidate to vote for is the dependent variable. Using the terms *independent variable* and *dependent variable* does not necessarily imply that we think differences in one variable cause differences in the other variable; however, when there is a causal connection between the two, the independent variable is the cause and the dependent variable is the effect.

In this section, we examine two kinds of bivariate analysis. First, we compare groups on a categorical variable using cross-tabulation. Second, we compare groups on a continuous variable by comparing their means. We then extend this example to describe how the means of a continuous variable differ depending on the values of another continuous variable. We conclude with a brief introduction to regression analysis, a very broad and important technique for assessing how variables relate to one another.

Cross-Tabulating Categorical Variables

A **cross-tabulation** is the simplest way of presenting a comparison between the groups that make up the categories in a categorical variable. Specifically, a cross-tabulation presents the categories of one variable as rows and the categories of the other variable as columns, with information about the frequency and/or relative frequency of the variable presented in the **cells** formed by the intersection of these rows and columns.

Throughout this chapter, we have been using an example from the GSS about belief in God. To compare responses for men and women, we could create a simple two-way or bivariate cross-tabulation between belief in God and one's gender. The cells in Table 14.4 represent the frequency for each group. For example, of the 547 people who said they do not believe in God, 367 were male and 180 were female.

The totals in the bottom row and right-most column of a table are called **marginal frequencies**, or simply *marginals*. They are overall frequency distributions of our focal measure that do not take into account differences among the subgroups. If we look at the marginal frequencies at the bottom of Table 14.4, we can see that there

cross-tabulation A presentation of distributions between two or more variables as a table.

cells The intersections of the rows and columns in a cross-tabulation.

marginal frequency The overall frequency distributions of a focal measure that do not take into account differences among the subgroups; the totals in the bottom row and rightmost column of a table. Also called *marginals*.

TABLE 14.4 Cross-Tabulation: Frequencies of Religious Beliefs by Gender

Confidence That God Exists?	Male	Female	Total
Don't believe in God	367	180	547
Don't know, no way to find out	590	332	922
No personal God but some Higher Power	1,037	892	1,929
Believe in God sometimes	418	382	800
Have doubts but do believe	1,588	1,613	3,201
Know God exists, have no doubts	4,560	7,539	12,099
Total	8,560	10,938	19,498

Note: Shaded areas are marginal frequencies.
Source: General Social Survey, 1988–2014.

are more female respondents than male respondents. What can we conclude from the data? Women are more likely than men to have no doubts that God exists, but substantially more women than men participated in the study.

Thus, when we compare groups on a categorical variable, we want to compare the *percentage* of members of one group who fall into the category of interest with the *percentage* of members of another group. In other words, we want to compare the percentage of women who say they have no doubts about the existence of God with the percentage of men who provide the same response. Table 14.5 presents these results; all the numbers shown are percentages. It shows that 68.92% of women said that they know God exists and have no doubts, compared with 53.27% of men. Using percentages instead of frequencies when comparing distributions across groups allows for clearer comparisons of groups of different sizes.

TABLE 14.5 Cross-Tabulation with Percentages

Confidence That God Exists?	Male	Female	Total
Don't believe in God	4.29	1.65	2.81
Don't know, no way to find out	6.89	3.04	4.73
No personal God but some Higher Power	12.11	8.16	9.89
Believe in God sometimes	4.88	3.49	4.10
Have doubts but do believe	18.55	14.75	16.42
Know God exists, have no doubts	53.27	68.92	62.05
Total	100.00	100.00	100.00

Source: General Social Survey, 1988–2014.

If we look down any of the last three columns of Table 14.5, we see that the percentages in each column sum to 100%. However, the percentages across the rows do not add up to 100. Whenever we create tables that include percentages, we need to choose which percentages add up to 100.

We have three options for doing so: (1) cell percentages, (2) column percentages, and (3) row percentages. To illustrate them, let's consider an example in which we tabulate the same two variables in each of the three ways. We will use two questions from the General Social Survey: whether respondents have a gun in their home, and whether a child under age 13 lives in the home. Table 14.6 provides three cross-tabulations of these two variables.

Table 14.6a provides **cell percentages**. The total of all of the cells is 100%. From the marginals on the bottom row, we learn that 21.5% of all households have a child under age 13 in the home. From the marginals on the right, we learn that 32.7% of all households have a gun in the home. We can also see that 6.0% of all households have both a gun and a child under 13 in the home.

TABLE 14.6 Three Cross-Tabulations

(a) Cross-Tabulation Using Cell Percentages (Sum of All Cells Is 100)

Has Gun in Home?	Child Under 13 in Home?		
	No	Yes	Total
No	51.8	15.5	67.3
Yes	26.7	6.0	32.7
Total	78.5	21.5	100.0

(b) Cross-Tabulation Using Column Percentages (Sum of Cells in Each Column Is 100)

Has Gun in Home?	Child Under 13 in Home?		
	No	Yes	Total
No	66.0	72.2	67.3
Yes	34.0	27.8	32.7
Total	100.0	100.0	100.0

(c) Cross-Tabulation Using Row Percentages (Sum of Cells in Each Row Is 100)

Has Gun in Home?	Child Under 13 in Home?		
	No	Yes	Total
No	77.0	23.0	100.0
Yes	81.7	18.3	100.0
Total	78.5	21.5	100.0

Source: General Social Survey, 2010–2014.

We may wonder whether households with a child under 13 in the home are less likely to have a gun than households without a child under 13 in the home. To answer this question, we want to compare the distribution of gun ownership among households *with* children under 13 to the distribution among households *without* children under 13. Because we are comparing households with and without children under 13, and because these categories are represented in the columns of the table, we use **column percentages**, as shown in Table 14.6b. With column percentages, the percentages in each column add up to 100.

From the column percentages, we can see that 27.8% of households with children under 13 in the home also have a gun in the home, compared to 34.0% of households without children under 13 in the home. Because we have computed the percentages within columns, we can compare percentages within the same row. The difference here is modest, only 6.2 percentage points. The overall conclusion we might draw is that households with and without children are fairly similar in their likelihood of having a gun in the home.

In Table 14.6c, we present **row percentages** instead of column percentages. The percentages in each row add to 100. Now, instead of comparing households with and without children, we are comparing households with and without guns. We can see that 18.3% of households with a gun have a child under 13, while 23.0% of households without a gun have a child under 13.

In this example, when we compute the percentages by whether households have children under 13, we are asking "Are households without children under 13 more likely or less likely to own a gun than households with children under 13?" When we compute percentages by gun ownership, we change the question to "Are households that own guns more likely or less likely to have children under 13 than households without guns?"

Whenever we compare groups, we want to use row percentages or column percentages instead of cell percentages. Specifically, if the groups we wish to compare are represented by the different rows of our table, we use row percentages. If the groups are represented by different columns, we use column percentages.

Comparing Conditional Means

Cross-tabulations are very useful when both variables are categorical. If we wanted to look at whether income (a continuous variable) differs for men and women, however, the number of different values of the variable may be very large, making the tabulation unwieldy or incomprehensible. If we want to make a table using a continuous variable, it is often helpful to convert the variable into a smaller number of categories ("high income," "medium income," "low income").

That said, we may be specifically interested in the question of whether the average income for men is higher than the average income for women and, if so, by how much. To find an answer, we may want to compare the **conditional means**. We use "conditional" here to refer to a statistic that is calculated only for observations that meet a particular condition rather than calculated for every observation. The average income for men and the average income for women are both conditional means, as opposed to the overall mean that includes the average income of both sexes.

column percentages For each cell in a table, the percentage of observations in that column of the table that are represented by that cell.

row percentages For each cell in a table, the percentage of observations in that row of the table that are represented by that cell.

conditional mean A statistic that is calculated only for observations that meet a particular condition rather than calculated for every observation.

TABLE 14.7 Mean Income for Men and Women, 2000–2014

Sex	Mean Income ($)	N
Male	68,612	4,987
Female	45,499	4,261

Source: General Social Survey, 2000–2014.

error bars A way of indicating the confidence interval for a statistic presented in a graph.

line graph A graph in which a line indicates how the conditional mean of the outcome changes as values of an explanatory variable change.

bivariate regression analysis A summary of a relationship between variables that describes how the conditional mean of the dependent variable changes as the independent variable changes.

We can generate a table in which the rows are the different values of the categorical variables and the cells in the table are the conditional means of the continuous variable within each category. For example, if we take respondents who reported being employed full-time in the 2000–2014 GSS, we can compare the mean income (adjusted for inflation) for men and women, as shown in Table 14.7.

As the table shows, the average income for women employed full-time is more than $23,000 less than the average income for men employed full-time ($68,612 compared to $45,499). When we make a table comparing conditional means, we also usually want to include the frequency of cases (N) so that our audience can see how many people the conditional means are based on. Table 14.7 shows that data are reported for more men than women (4,987 men compared to 4,261 women).

We can follow the same strategy if we have a variable with many categories, like race/ethnicity in the General Social Survey. We could make a table again (Table 14.8), but the information might be presented just as effectively in a bar graph, as shown in Figure 14.6. From the graph, we can see that Asian/Pacific Islanders and white respondents have substantially higher incomes than members of the other groups.

Figure 14.6 uses **error bars** to show the 95% confidence intervals for each of the means that we estimate. The graph illustrates how confidence intervals narrow as sample size increases. The confidence interval is narrowest for whites, which is the largest group in our sample (6,012 respondents). The interval is smallest for those classified as "Other," which is the smallest group (only 21 respondents). When confidence

TABLE 14.8 Mean Income by Race/Ethnicity, 2000–2014

Race/Ethnicity	Mean Income ($)	N
Asian/Pacific Islander	82,805	269
Black, non-Hispanic	43,740	1,156
Hispanic	40,360	1,006
Native American	39,859	68
White, non-Hispanic	63,472	6,012
Other	49,168	21

Source: General Social Survey, 2000–2014.

intervals between groups overlap, we have less confidence that the observed difference between groups represents a true difference as opposed to just a difference due to chance.

Regression Analysis

In the previous section, we looked at how average income changes over the categorical variables of respondent's sex and respondent's race/ethnicity. We might also ask if average income is higher for people with more education, which is a continuous variable when measured in terms of the highest year of education completed. Instead of a bar graph, we can make a **line graph** in which the horizontal, or x, axis indicates the number of years of education, and the vertical, or y, axis indicates the average income for people with each level of educational attainment. We show this graph in Figure 14.7, with dots used to depict each conditional mean and a line connecting them.

The line graph in Figure 14.7 shows a clear pattern in which each additional year of schooling is associated with higher average income. If we wanted to summarize this relationship mathematically, we could use a **bivariate regression analysis** to describe how the conditional mean of the dependent variable changes as the independent variable changes. In our case, bivariate regression analysis would allow us to present concisely how much average income tends to change as level of educational attainment increases.

Bivariate regression is similar to correlation, which we learned about in Chapter 2, but the two differ in one important way. Both bivariate regression and correlation tell us the strength of the association between two variables, such as schooling and income. In correlation, the association works in both directions: Measuring the correlation between schooling and income is the same as measuring the correlation between income and schooling. In contrast, the premise of regression is that differences in one variable are dependent on differences in the other. In our example, correlation tells us that education and income vary together, but regression is

FIGURE 14.6 Mean Income by Race/Ethnicity, 2000–2014

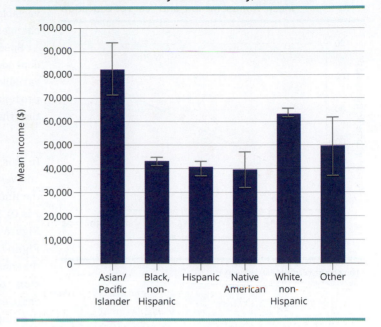

Source: General Social Survey, 2000–2014.

FIGURE 14.7 Income of Full-Time Workers (Conditional Mean) and Educational Attainment

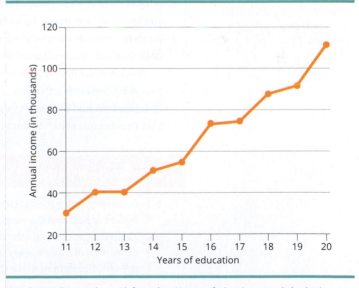

Note: For simplicity, workers with fewer than 11 years of education are coded as having 11 years.
Source: General Social Survey, 2000–2014.

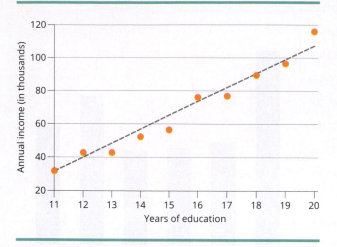

FIGURE 14.8 Bivariate Regression Analysis of Conditional Mean: Annual Income and Years of Education

Note: Annual income of full-time workers.
Source: General Social Survey, 2000–2014.

regression coefficient A value that indicates the expected change in our outcome that is associated with a one-unit increase in our explanatory variable.

based on the assumption that changes in the independent variable (education) may trigger, or at least be used to predict, changes in the dependent variable (income).

Specifically, bivariate regression analysis expresses the dependent variable as a simple function of the independent variable. If we use x to represent the independent variable and y to represent the conditional mean of the dependent variable, then this function is

$$y = a + bx$$

In this equation, x and y are values on the horizontal (x) and vertical (y) axes, respectively, b represents the slope of the line and a represents the intercept (the value of y when x is 0). Figure 14.8 contains the same conditional means as Figure 14.7, but instead of connecting the dots directly, Figure 14.8 draws the straight line that most closely fits the conditional mean. The slope of this line is called a **regression coefficient**, and it tells us how much average income changes as educational attainment changes by 1 year.

We use a computer and a statistical software package to estimate the best-fitting line. This is the resulting equation:

Average income = −62,181 + (8,283 × Years of education)

The regression coefficient is $8,283. This means that each additional year of education increases a full-time worker's average yearly income by a little more than $8,000. This equation also suggests that obtaining a 4-year college degree will increase one's average yearly income by more than $33,000 ($8,283 × 4 additional years of education). Also note that you can use this equation to estimate the annual income of a person on the basis of how many years he or she attended school. In short, bivariate regression analysis provides a useful way of summarizing how much the conditional mean of a dependent variable changes as an independent variable changes.

Regression analysis can be extended beyond two variables. Indeed, regression analysis provides such a flexible and powerful way of describing the relationship between independent and dependent variables that most published sociology research articles that involve quantitative data analysis use at least one form of regression analysis.

CONCEPT CHECKS

1   According to a national survey, the number of male respondents who do not believe in God is 307, and the number of female respondents who do not believe in God is 153. What additional information do you need in order to evaluate whether men or women are more likely to report that they do not believe in God? How could you present the data to make this comparison easier to see and understand?

2   Does the cross-tabulation in Table 14.5 (p. 477) use row or column percentages? What groups are being compared here?

DESCRIBING TRENDS

Sociologists are often interested in social and historical change. As we learned in Chapter 12, some sociologists rely on historical records to explore change, while others rely on survey data obtained at multiple points in time to explore the ways that attitudes have changed. These data sources provide a foundation for exploring **population trends**, or analyses showing how some characteristic of a population changes or remains stable over time. Trends are essentially bivariate patterns in which one of the variables is time. For example, over the past three decades, surveys have documented a steep increase in Americans' acceptance of gay and lesbian individuals.

Repeated Cross-Sectional Surveys and Panel Surveys

How steep has the increase in the acceptance of gay men and lesbians been? We can answer this question by looking at repeated cross-sectional surveys. As we learned in Chapter 7, a repeated cross-sectional survey is a survey in which a representative sample of a population is surveyed at different times. The General Social Survey is a repeated cross-sectional survey. It has been conducted every year or every 2 years since 1972. Each time it is conducted, a fresh representative sample is selected and interviewed.

The GSS asks a series of questions about sexual matters that are sometimes regarded as moral issues, such as premarital sex and extramarital sex. A similar question has been used to ask about gay and lesbian relationships: "What about sexual relations between two adults of the same sex—do you think it is always wrong, almost always wrong, wrong only sometimes, or not wrong at all?"

Figure 14.9 shows the trend in the proportion of respondents who responded "always wrong" to this question. The clearest way to display information about trends is with a line graph. In a line graph, the horizontal axis shows time, and the vertical axis shows the proportion or mean of the population characteristic we are studying.

From the line graph, we can see that three-quarters of respondents in the late 1980s responded "always wrong," but this proportion has dropped steadily. Since 2010, less than half of respondents have provided this response. The clear population trend here is toward a smaller proportion of people believing that same-sex relationships are wrong.

Population trends such as Americans' growing support of same-sex relationships can be thought of as bivariate patterns in which one variable is time.

population trends Analyses showing how some characteristic of a population changes or remains stable over time.

FIGURE 14.9 Proportion of People Who Believe Same-Sex Sexual Relationships Are "Always Wrong," 1985–2014

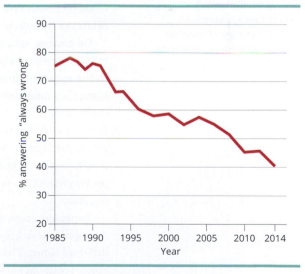

Source: General Social Survey, 2000–2014.

There are big differences among cohorts, but since 1985 each cohort has also become more tolerant toward gay people over time.

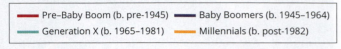

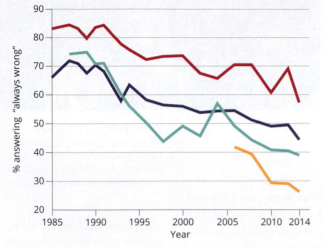

Source: General Social Survey, 1985–2014.

cohort replacement When the younger people who enter a survey population by becoming adults have systematically different attitudes from older adults who exit a population by death.

Looking at Figure 14.9, you might be tempted to conclude that many people have changed their minds over the years about same-sex relationships. However, this is not necessarily the case. Changes in the number of people who have a particular attitude in a population can occur without any particular individual changing his or her mind, because populations are always changing. Specifically, population trends can happen solely by **cohort replacement**, in which the younger people who enter a survey population by becoming adults have systematically different attitudes from older adults who exit a population by death. For example, the GSS samples persons over age 18. In each subsequent year, the oldest persons in a population will die out, taking with them the values and beliefs that may reflect an earlier era. Likewise, each year, a new generation of 18-year-olds becomes eligible for the sample, bringing with them ideas and attitudes that reflect a newer cultural and social period.

In Figure 14.10, we divide GSS respondents using the rough concept of "generations." Looking at this graph, we can see that, for most years, each generation has been less likely to say same-sex relationships are "always wrong" than the generation preceding it.

At the same time, when we look within a generation, we can also see that each generation shows a trend toward being more tolerant of same-sex relationships over time. In other words, changing population attitudes toward gay men and lesbians appear to reflect both cohort replacement and people who at one time thought same-sex relationships were "always wrong" later changing their minds.

Of course, whenever we talk about members of a population "changing their minds," presumably there are at least some individuals who changed their opinion in the opposite direction. Some people have undoubtedly become less tolerant over time; they answered "always wrong" on the survey when they would have answered differently if they had been asked at some earlier point in their lives. However, the data suggest that many more people have become more tolerant rather than less tolerant, perhaps a reaction to the changing legal landscape in which same-sex couples now have the right to marry in the United States or to prime-time television shows portraying same-sex married couples as no different than opposite-sex married couples.

Repeated cross-sectional surveys are sometimes confused with panel surveys. As we discussed in Chapter 7, in a panel survey, the same people are interviewed at different times. These surveys are used to study how *individuals* change. In a repeated cross-sectional survey such as the GSS, individuals are typically surveyed only once, and new representative samples with new people are surveyed in subsequent years. These surveys are used to study how *populations* change.

Age Effects and Period Effects

When sociologists describe broad tendencies about how individuals change their opinions (or other characteristics) over time, they typically distinguish between two major patterns of change. **Age effects** reveal how people change as they get older. Developmental psychologists and gerontologists, for example, have demonstrated nearly universal changes that happen in people as they mature. For instance, people's memory worsens from their late twenties onward.

Period effects, by contrast, are broad patterns in which all ages in a population exhibit a tendency toward change over the same historical period. For example, if people in general become more tolerant during a particular historical period compared to earlier periods, a period effect is at work. In contrast, an example of an age effect would be if people tend to become more tolerant as they get older across historical eras. While age effects are usually attributed to maturation, period effects are often attributed to a particular event or cultural/historical context that affects most people in a population.

Does the evidence that people have become more tolerant of same-sex relationships reflect an age effect or a period effect? To answer this question, we can look at the 10-year period prior to 1985. Figure 14.11 shows the GSS data for these years. Here, when we look at the pre–Baby Boom (born pre-1945) or Baby Boom (born 1945–1964) cohorts, we can see that there was no overall tendency for people to become more tolerant as they aged. Instead, since around 1985, a historical tendency of more tolerant attitudes toward same-sex relationships has been observed across age groups. In other words, there is no broad historical pattern of people becoming more tolerant toward same-sex relationships as they age. Instead, we are currently in a period in which tolerance toward same-sex relationships is increasing within all age groups. In other words, the higher tolerance for same-sex relationships is a period effect, not an age effect.

Researchers' ability to ascertain age versus period effects depends on data availability; to observe and define population trends accurately, they require data from a broad age range across many points in time. The GSS has been conducted regularly since 1972, it includes the full range of adults over the age of 18, and it has regularly asked the same question about attitudes toward same-sex relationships. A maxim for sociologists who study trends is, "If you want to measure change, don't change your measure." In other words, the easiest way to study change is to use data collected the

FIGURE 14.11 Differences between Pre–Baby Boom and Baby Boom Cohorts on Attitudes toward Same-Sex Relationships, 1976–1985

The graph shows a large cohort difference and no tendency during these years for cohorts to become more tolerant with age.

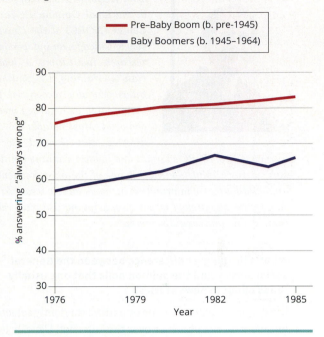

Source: General Social Survey, 1976–1985.

age effect How peoples' opinions or other characteristics change as they get older.

period effect A broad pattern in which all ages in a population exhibit a tendency toward change over the same historical period.

Conversations from the Front Lines

TOM W. SMITH

Tom W. Smith is a senior fellow at National Opinion Research Center (NORC) at the University of Chicago, an independent research institution. A historian by training, Dr. Smith is internationally recognized for his research as a survey methodologist. Most notably, he has directed the General Social Survey (GSS), NORC's largest and longest-running opinion survey, since 1980. The GSS is one of the most frequently analyzed sources of information in the social sciences, asking Americans about such issues as marijuana use, race relations, crime, and sexual behavior.

What's the biggest difference between the General Social Survey and the opinion polls that one usually reads about in news stories?

Most opinion polls are done by calling randomly selected numbers on the phone or over the Internet. Usually less than 10% of the people sampled agree to do the survey, and polls last about 10 minutes. GSS has response rates that are about ten times higher than phone surveys, and the GSS is about ten times longer. GSS asks many more questions and has much greater capacity to allow researchers to look at the relationships among different questions. Phone surveys underrepresent important sectors of the population, but GSS is a full probability sample and does interviews in English or Spanish. Also, many opinion polls are designed to measure current hot topics of interest and not to carefully monitor societal change.

How does the General Social Survey decide what households to interview?

General Social Survey is a multistage sample. In our case, this means that first we select a sample of areas (counties or metro areas), then a sample of segments (i.e., neighborhoods), and finally a sample of households within those blocks. The result of our procedure is that all members of the target population—adults who live in households and speak either English or Spanish—have an equal probability of being sampled.

When more than one person lives in a household, how do you decide which one to interview?

We use a Kish table, named after the late sampling statistician Leslie Kish. First we ask the person we contact to list everyone in the household. Then there is a pre-generated label that indicates which of the listed potential respondents will be the selected respondent. Take a household with three adults. One-third of the labels will say to take the first (oldest) respondent on the list, one-third will say to take the last (youngest), and the remaining third will say to take the middle.

same way over time. Of course, our ideas about the best way of measuring something also change over time, which creates a trade-off: Should we keep measuring the concept the old (and potentially outdated) way to be consistent or should we measure it the new way so that we have the best possible measure now? This brings us back to issues of reliability and validity, discussed in Chapter 5, and the trade-offs researchers are often confronted with when conducting actual research.

If someone says they don't want to be interviewed, what do you do?

We make every effort to persuade them of the value and importance of the GSS and change them from a nayer to a sayer.

> The result of our procedure is that all members of the target population—adults who live in households and speak either English or Spanish—have an equal probability of being sampled.

The General Social Survey interviews people in person whenever possible. What do you think is the biggest advantage of that versus doing the interview online or over the phone?

The evidence indicates that in-person interviews get higher response rates and higher-quality measurements. It also makes it much easier to integrate data from our survey with data from other sources, such as geographical information and data from the Census, which expands what researchers can do with our study.

The GSS asks people some very personal questions, such as about their sexual behavior. Do people ever get upset about being asked these questions? Do interviewers get embarrassed?

The most sensitive items are "asked" and answered on a self-administered questionnaire so that the interviewer does not see or hear their responses. For the less sensitive items people can demur to answer any question. Of course, some people do dislike some questions, but overall interviewers rate only about 0.4% of respondents as "hostile."

What's the biggest change that's taken place in surveys since the GSS began?

Surveying has gotten more difficult. It takes more time and effort to make contact and it is harder to persuade respondents to do the interview once they are contacted. As a result, while in the 1970s we were able to field the GSS over a period of 1–2 months, currently it takes 5–6 months.

One way to address this trade-off is to have at least a year or two in which the concept is measured both ways. The GSS used to measure a respondent's race by having interviewers record it unless they felt uncertain, in which case they asked a question with the response categories "White," "Black," and "Other." This approach has become increasingly out of step with the complexity of race in the United States. In 2000, the GSS began asking every respondent a question about his or her race with many more response options; it also allows respondents to select more than one category if they wish. At the same time, the GSS has also kept the old measure so that researchers who want to look at long-term trends can do so with the same measure.

PUTTING NUMBERS IN CONTEXT: WHICH STATISTICS SHOULD YOU BELIEVE?

As we noted at the beginning of this chapter, the U.S. government announces unemployment statistics on the first Friday of every month. In 2012, the final unemployment report prior to the Tuesday, November 6, presidential election was released in early October. These numbers were heavily anticipated, with some pundits breathlessly anticipating that the election's outcome could be determined by these data. If the numbers suggested that the economy was improving, the report would be good for then-incumbent President Barack Obama. If instead the numbers suggested that the economy was stagnant or worsening, the report would be good for his opponent, Mitt Romney.

When the numbers were announced, the national unemployment rate was 7.8%, the lowest since President Obama's first month in office and a surprising half-percentage point decline in just 2 months. This was great news for the Obama campaign. Meanwhile, a few high-visibility figures opposed to President Obama's reelection regarded the numbers as suspicious. Jack Welch, former CEO of General Electric, tweeted that the numbers were "unbelievable."

The episode might have attracted greater controversy if not for the credibility that the Bureau of Labor Statistics had built up with Democrats and Republicans alike over the years. (In the months after the election, the unemployment statistics were similar, which made it clear that the October 2012 numbers were not a fluke.) Nonetheless, this example demonstrates that the numbers generated to describe populations can have high stakes attached to them. In fact, numbers that cost a lot of money to produce typically have high stakes; otherwise, why go to the trouble?

It is also not unreasonable to imagine that government officials could mislead citizens about the state of their economy. Greek government officials concealed the size of Greece's budget deficit, which then became a major cause of the 2010 financial crisis that threatened to destabilize the European Union. Governments have a long history of producing misleading information about casualties and conditions of war, overstating progress and understating costs. In World War I, the British government and its major newspaper (the *London Times*) concealed the enormous casualties that its ally France suffered at the start of the war. The editor later stated that "British determination [would have] gravely weakened" if the actual losses had been published (Andreas & Greenhill, 2010, p. 14).

Sociologist Joel Best has written several books, one aptly titled *Damned Lies and Statistics*, in which he explains how the public should interpret the statistics reported in the media. His books are based on the assumption that many people accept numbers uncritically, without questioning where the numbers come from or what they mean. Best emphasizes that "all statistics, even the most authoritative, are created by people. This does not mean that they are inevitably flawed or wrong, but it does mean that we ought to ask ourselves just how the statistics we encounter were created" (Best, 2012, p. 12).

A healthy skepticism about statistics is particularly important in sociology and the other social sciences. The social problems that sociologists study have many stakeholders and competing viewpoints. People closely involved with a particular social problem may have a financial or emotional interest in conveying the great magnitude of the problem. Take the case of one advocate for aid to the African nation of Sudan. In terms of information about the Sudanese population, she says, "Sometimes it just isn't possible to get the 'right' number. So I just pick one that is large enough and shocking enough, as a way of assuring it gets attention" (Andreas & Greenhill, 2010, p. 271).

Social problems compete with one another for public attention. Just think about the many political and social interest groups with a presence on your campus: racial equality, animal rights, environmental issues, gender equity, LGBT issues, religious freedom. How do you determine which social issue best deserves your time and money? To gain your attention (and your donations, whether in time or money), advocates may try to use statistics, such as numbers about how many people are adversely affected by a particular social problem. These reports can create a cycle in the media where misleading numbers drive out accurate numbers. The numbers most likely to grab our attention are those that are the most surprising or alarming, and such numbers, upon closer scrutiny, are likely to be wrong. For example, in the 1980s, there was a sudden increase in concern about missing children, perhaps the result of an often-repeated claim that 50,000 children were kidnapped by strangers each year. The actual number of child kidnappings investigated each year by the FBI at the time was about 70 (Best, 2012). However, 70 missing children a year may not be sufficient to entice people to financially support organizations dedicated to finding missing children.

Advocates for causes often have the best intentions. They believe strongly in the importance of their issue and are trying to break through the often-cluttered news media to grab the national spotlight. However, picking

Images of missing children started to appear on milk cartons in the early 1980s.

and choosing numbers to gain support for one's cause undermines credibility in the long term. When members of the public conclude that numbers are only political, they then have an easy excuse for dismissing any numbers that call their current beliefs into question. Some people will always be closed-minded toward inconvenient facts, but presenting misleading statistics because they bolster an argument just promotes cynicism about statistics in the long run. Serious social problems deserve honest and accurate numbers. Sociologists can play an important role in providing the tools that people need to question misleading numbers and to figure out which numbers are accurate and why.

How should we evaluate the statistics that we read in the news media and on the web? There are no easy answers, but a key piece of advice is to *always consider the source*. When numbers are presented with no cited sources or without the names of the people and organization that collected and analyzed the data, there is cause for great suspicion. When the source seems to have a clear and biased interest in presenting positive or negative numbers, extra scrutiny of the source of the numbers and how they were generated is highly recommended.

The Internet is often described as a cesspool of misleading statistics. We can all provide plenty of examples of blatantly untrue reports that have circulated online. But, as the example of missing children from the 1980s shows, the circulation of ludicrous numbers precedes the Internet. While we were doing the research for this chapter, we looked up many different examples that have been cited in different books as examples of misleading statistics. For instance, we still often hear that half of all marriages end in divorce, but the actual probability that a new marriage will end in divorce is less than one in three, and may be as low as one in four (Miller, 2014). We were pleased by how often we could find more accurate numbers alongside the misleading ones, with clear information about the sources of the statistics. When you see an argument that includes a statistic that surprises you, some digging with a search engine can turn up a lot of information about the source of the statistic, what other people think of that source, and whether there is debate surrounding the statistic.

CONCLUSION

Statistics are the primary means by which researchers describe basic features of societies, how they are changing, and how they differ from other societies. This chapter has described some of the basic ways that sociologists can use quantitative data analysis to describe populations. We spent much of the chapter introducing ways to describe a single aspect of a population, such as its unemployment rate, its average income, or the average number of hours of television people watch. Central to all these examples is the concept of a distribution: knowing what values are possible and how often each of these values is observed. When we know the distribution of a variable such as income, we can talk about the average income in a population, as well as the amount of income inequality among its people.

Most of the time, our descriptions of a population are based on observing only a sample of its members. Whenever a sample is used, there is uncertainty about how well the estimates based on these samples describe the population. The great virtue of probability samples (such as the GSS) is that we can calculate confidence intervals to describe precisely the uncertainty that is due to chance differences between a sample and the population. This, however, is only one kind of uncertainty; another type of uncertainty is based on measurement. If the number of hours that people *report* watching television bears little relationship to how much television they truly watch, our results are misleading and inaccurate, no matter how large and carefully selected our sample is.

Often in social research we want to compare groups. We want to know not only the unemployment rate in the United States but also whether it is higher in California or Texas and whether it is higher for people with college degrees or for high school dropouts. The techniques we introduced in the second half of this chapter allow us to talk about these differences precisely by examining the ways that the values of one variable depend on the values of another variable. This precision allows us to ask deeper questions of numerical data. When we discussed trend analysis, for example, we showed how we can ask whether differences of opinion are actually due to people changing their minds or are simply the result of young adults having different opinions from older adults. In this way, what we learn about describing populations allows us to do more than describe a population; we can also begin to test hypotheses about social life. Analyzing numerical data in order to test hypotheses is the focus of the next chapter.

End-of-Chapter Review

Summary

Quantitative data analysis is the process of drawing substantive findings from numerical data. Social researchers can use quantitative analysis to describe populations, such as its unemployment rate, its average income, or the average number of hours of television people watch.

Statistics and Quantitative Data Analysis

- Univariate analyses involve one variable while bivariate analyses assess the relationship between two variables.

Univariate Analysis

- A distribution is the most fundamental concept in univariate analysis. The distribution of a variable refers to how common the different values of a variable are in the observed data.
- Frequency distributions provide actual counts, while relative distributions present values as percentages. Relative distributions are easier to interpret but can be misleading if the data are based on a very small sample.

- It is best to visually present the relative distribution of a categorical variable as a bar graph. For a continuous variable, a histogram is more appropriate.
- Measures of central tendency allow researchers to present simple, easy-to-interpret descriptions of data rather than entire distributions. The mean of a variable represents the sum of all its values divided by the number of observations, while the median is the middle value when observations are ranked from lowest to highest.
- When describing categorical variables, means must be interpreted differently. For dichotomous variables, each category is assigned a value of either 0 or 1, so the mean represents the proportion of the total number of cases that were assigned a value of 1 in the data. For ordinal variables, the mean is often transformed into percentages that can be compared across subgroups. The closest approximation of a mean for a nominal variable is the mode, which represents the most frequent value of a variable. In general, it is best to present a frequency distribution for nominal variables.
- Measures of central tendency cannot describe how much a distribution varies. The simplest measure of variation is the range, which represents the difference between the maximum and minimum values of a distribution. The range can be misleading because it is extremely sensitive to outliers. For this reason, the standard deviation is more often used.
- A margin of error accounts for the fact that statistics obtained from a sample are likely to differ from the real population parameter by some amount due to random chance. The size of a margin of error is influenced by the sample size and the amount of variation in a variable.

Bivariate Analysis

- Bivariate analysis is useful because social researchers often want to know about distinctions between subgroups of a population. This type of quantitative analysis often uses independent and dependent variables to describe relationships in the data.
- A cross-tabulation is a simple way of comparing groups on a categorical variable. Cross-tabulations present the categories of one variable as rows and the categories of another variable as columns, with information about the frequency of the variables presented in the intersections, or cells.
- Too many cells would be required to create a cross-tabulation with a continuous variable, so researchers instead use a conditional mean, or a statistic calculated only for observations that meet a particular condition in the data, such as men or women.
- Bivariate regression analysis is used to describe how the conditional mean of a dependent variable changes as an independent variable changes. Regression analysis differs from a correlation because the differences in one variable are presumed to be dependent on differences in another variable.

Describing Trends

- Population trends are analyses that show how populations change or remain stable over time.
- Repeated cross-sectional surveys collect data from a representative sample of a population at different time points to assess change in the overall population. A new sample is collected at every time point, so this survey design can only tell us how populations change, not individuals.

- Panel surveys, which collect data on the same sample at multiple time points, are used to assess individual change. There are two major patterns of change: Age effects refer to how people change as they get older, while period effects refer to broad patterns in which all members of a population change over a certain historical period.

Putting Numbers in Context: Which Statistics Should You Believe?

- It is important to have a healthy skepticism about statistics. The key to evaluating statistics is to always consider the source.

Key Terms

Exercise

Find competing statistics on an issue that you care about. By "competing statistics," we mean two numbers from different sources that either directly contradict each other or at least have contrary implications for what one thinks about the issue.

- First, consider the sources where you first found competing statistics. Do the sources have a stake in promoting some stance on the issue, and if so, what is it?

- Second, identify the original sources for the competing statistics. For each statistic, write a paragraph describing the original source and the research that was used to generate the statistic.

- On the basis of your investigations, does one statistic seem like it is based on better evidence than the other? If so, which one, and why? Does the statistic you regard as more credible coincide with what you already believed about the issue? If so, do you think that influenced your opinion?

Multivariate methods—methods of quantitative data analysis where at least three variables are considered—allow social researchers to consider complex relationships, such as the relationship between paternal incarceration and maternal health.

494

15

MULTIVARIATE AND ADVANCED QUANTITATIVE METHODS

In Chapter 14, we discussed how to use quantitative data to make descriptive statements about populations, such as "The majority of Americans have no doubts that God exists." Most social science research is not directed simply at describing a population, however, but instead tries to evaluate different ideas about how the social world operates. In these cases, researchers are interested in *understanding how and why different variables are related to one another*.

To understand the distinction between describing societies and asking "how" or "why" questions about them, we can return to the calculation of the unemployment rate, first discussed in Chapter 14. We emphasized the importance of accurately and precisely describing the amount of unemployment in the United States. Once we have accurate information about unemployment, we can start to ask more complex, interesting, and policy-relevant questions, such as "What causes the unemployment rate to change?" "Why are some people more likely to be unemployed than others?" And, "What are the consequences of unemployment for people's lives?"

Let's look more closely at the last of these questions: "What are the consequences of unemployment?" Here are some of the questions on this specific topic that sociologists have answered with quantitative data:

- How much does being unemployed affect people's levels of life satisfaction? Are the negative psychological consequences of being unemployed less acute when the unemployment rate is high—that is, when many other people are also out of work—than when the unemployment rate is low (Oesch & Lipps, 2013)?

- Do people have more negative attitudes toward immigration when unemployment rates are high? Does becoming unemployed lead people to view immigration more negatively (Chandler & Tsai, 2001; Wilkes, Guppy, & Farris, 2008)?

- When a married person becomes unemployed, does he or she respond by doing more housework? Upon losing a job, do husbands and wives adjust their housework duties (Gough & Killewald, 2011)?

This chapter explains how sociologists address questions like these by developing evidence for or against a hypothesis. First, we describe how sociologists address the possibility that apparent patterns in their data may arise simply due to chance. Second, we discuss the challenges of establishing that a cause-and-effect relationship exists between two variables. Third, we describe how researchers can strengthen the evidence about their theories by devising and testing hypotheses about conditions that modify the relationship between one variable and another. In doing so, we give much attention to understanding how the relationship between two concepts—especially the relationship between an independent variable and a dependent variable—can be enhanced by considering them alongside other variables. Methods of quantitative analysis where at least three variables are included are called **multivariate methods**.

multivariate methods
Methods of quantitative analysis where at least three variables are included.

SIGNIFICANCE TESTING

When we have numerical data that are relevant to a hypothesis, the first step in our analysis is to determine if the basic pattern in our data is consistent with our hypothesis. For example, we might hypothesize that enacting laws requiring minors to have parental consent in order to obtain birth control might lead to an increase in teenage pregnancy (Girma & Paton, 2013). To check our hypothesis, we may first want to look at our data to see whether teenage girls who live in places with parental consent laws are more likely to become pregnant than teenage girls living in other areas. Specifically, we want to look at the association between two variables.

Association (Correlation)

If some values of one variable in a data set are more likely to co-occur with certain values of another variable, we say that an **association**, or correlation, exists between the two variables. If teenage pregnancy rates are higher in places with parental consent laws, then an association exists between parental consent laws and teenage pregnancy. More precisely, the association is a **positive association**, in that higher teenage pregnancy rates co-occur with requirements for parental consent. When higher values of one variable occur with lower values of another variable, then a **negative association**, or inverse association, exists. For example, if lower incomes are associated with higher risk of teenage pregnancy, there would be a negative association between income and teenage pregnancy.

If we observe results consistent with our hypothesis, our next concern is assessing whether the pattern is strong enough for us to be confident that it reflects a true association in the population or is instead due to chance. A finding is **statistically significant** when we can be at least 95% confident that the observed association is too large to be the result of chance. We will explain how researchers determine how large is too large later in the chapter.

Let's consider an example that builds on our familiarity with the General Social Survey (GSS). In the GSS, adults are asked their opinion about government spending to help those living in poverty. More precisely, the GSS asks respondents whether they think the government spends too much, too little, or the right amount on welfare. In 2014, only 20% of respondents answered "too little." From this piece of data, one might conclude there is little public interest in spending more money to help the poor.

An alternative hypothesis is that many Americans have a particularly negative reaction to the word *welfare*. If we asked a similar question that avoids using the word *welfare*, people might be more supportive of additional public spending. Specifically, we might hypothesize that people will respond more favorably when we substitute the phrase "assistance to the poor" for "welfare."

The best way to test this hypothesis is to conduct an experiment. As it happens, the GSS regularly conducts such experiments. Some respondents are asked about "assistance to the poor," while others are asked about "welfare." Consistent with the principles of good experiments, which respondent receives which wording is determined randomly.

The results are striking. As noted, in 2014, only 20% of the GSS respondents who were asked about "welfare" said the government was spending too little. In contrast, 64% of those who were asked about "assistance to the poor" said the government was spending too little. This pattern of results is consistent with the hypothesis that U.S. adults have negative feelings about the word *welfare*. Before going further with our analysis, however, we want to confirm that the difference between groups in our experiment isn't simply the result of chance.

As discussed in Chapter 8, experiments use random assignment to eliminate *systematic* differences between treatment groups and control groups. However, random assignment does not eliminate the possibility of *chance* differences. If you divide a classroom randomly into two groups, the groups will not necessarily have exactly the same percentage of men or the same average height. The same observation is true of

association A relationship whereby some values of one variable in a data set are more likely to co-occur with certain values of another variable.

positive association An association in which higher values of one variable occur with higher values of another variable.

negative association An association in which higher values of one variable occur with lower values of another variable.

statistically significant An observed association that we are at least 95% confident is too large to be the result of chance.

experiments: Even if the experimental manipulation has no effect whatsoever on the dependent variable, we do not expect to observe exactly the same distribution of the dependent variable in the treatment and control groups.

On the face of it, the difference between 20% and 64% might seem too big to occur just by chance. Or, we might acknowledge that such a large difference might be the result of chance, but that such an outcome is extremely unlikely. Significance testing allows us to evaluate our hunches precisely and confidently.

The Null Hypothesis and *p*-Values

Significance testing is the process of evaluating whether a result is statistically significant. If this is the first time you have encountered the concept, be warned that the logic of significance testing seems backwards to many students at first. In significance testing, instead of testing our hypothesis, we test what is called the null hypothesis. The **null hypothesis** is that any observed difference between groups is simply the result of chance. In our case, we hypothesized that people will respond differently to a question about "assistance to the poor" than to one about "welfare." The null hypothesis, then, is that the wording of the question did *not* affect responses, such that any observed difference between the question's wording and the responses is simply the result of chance.

In significance testing, we assess the likelihood that we would observe a difference as large as the one we did (64% vs. 20%) if the null hypothesis is *true*; that is, the wording of the question in our example does not affect responses. How likely is it that we would see a difference of 44 percentage points simply by chance?

We can give a precise answer to this question. We can calculate the probability that we would observe a difference as large as the difference that we actually observed if the null hypothesis were true. This probability is called a **p-value** (the *p* stands for "probability"). In most cases, for a result to be considered statistically significant, the *p*-value needs to be lower than 5%. That is, for the result to be statistically significant, we must be 95% confident that we would not observe a difference as large as we observed simply due to chance.

We will explain how to calculate *p*-values in the next section. In the current example, the *p*-value turns out to be extraordinarily small (of the order 10^{-85}). Consequently, by any standard, our finding that people are more likely to support additional government spending when asked about "assistance to the poor" instead of "welfare" is statistically significant.

Statistical significance is very important in social research because findings are usually not regarded as evidence in favor of a hypothesis unless they are statistically significant. In other words, researchers may have an interesting hypothesis, but until they can provide evidence that the results of their hypothesis testing are not due to chance, they will likely be unable to publish their results or get much attention.

Importantly, the reverse is not the case: Statistically significant findings do not necessarily mean a hypothesis is true. Even when we are confident that our results do not simply reflect chance, our results might be weak evidence for our hypothesis for other reasons. Perhaps results are statistically significant because there are flaws in our study's design or perhaps the results can be explained by some other hypothesis

significance testing The process of evaluating whether a result is statistically significant.

null hypothesis A hypothesis that no relationship between concepts exists or no difference in the dependent variable between groups exists.

p-value The probability that we would observe a difference as large as the difference that we actually observed if the null hypothesis were true.

besides the one we tested. For these reasons, statistical significance in practice is usually considered necessary but far from sufficient for providing convincing evidence for a hypothesis.

Determining Statistical Significance

The process of figuring out if a result is statistically significant is called significance testing. In practice, significance testing usually consists of figuring out the *p*-value for the null hypothesis, and the result is statistically significant if it is less than 5%. We can calculate *p*-values in two different ways: with (1) a chi-square test or (2) a *t* test. We will not go into the mathematical details of either, but describing the basic logic will clarify how significance testing works.

THE CHI-SQUARE TEST

As we saw, the difference in how respondents react to "welfare" versus "assistance to the poor" is so large that the probability of such a result occurring by chance was essentially zero. Let's now extend our example. Only 6.1% of 2012 GSS respondents believe the government is spending too little on "assistance to other countries." Perhaps "other countries" has the same sort of negative connotations as "welfare," and if we simply asked about "foreign aid" instead, people would be more supportive.

Here the results are not so dramatic. Only 8.6% of 2012 GSS respondents said that the government was spending too little on foreign aid (Smith, 2015). This observation may be consistent with our hypothesis, but it is far less obvious whether the difference (6.1% for "other countries" vs. 8.6% for "foreign aid") is statistically significant.

To see if it is, we can do a **chi-square test**. A chi-square test is based on cross-tabulation, which we explained in Chapter 14. As with cross-tabulations, chi-square tests can be done only with categorical variables. Figure 15.2 shows the steps in conducting a chi-square test. The key principle is that we compare the cross-tabulation of the variables that we *actually observed* to the cross-tabulation that we would *expect under the null hypothesis*. We are able to do so by using the *marginal frequencies* from the table (also discussed in Chapter 14). As the final step, we calculate a quantity called the **chi-square statistic** that summarizes how much discrepancy there is between the observed frequency and the expected frequency.

Using probability theory, we can translate this chi-square statistic into a *p*-value. Figure 15.2 shows how chi-square statistics and *p*-values are related for a test in which two dichotomous variables are used (like the test in our example). The important principle is that the larger the discrepancy between the observed and expected frequencies, the larger the chi-square statistic. The larger the chi-square statistic, the smaller the *p*-value. The smaller the *p*-value, the less likely it is that we would have observed discrepancies as large as what we observed by chance alone.

chi-square test A way to calculate *p*-values that is based on cross-tabulation.

chi-square statistic A quantity that summarizes how much discrepancy there is between the observed frequency and the expected frequency.

FIGURE 15.1 *P*-Values and Chi-Square Statistics for a Test with Two Dichotomous Variables

For the *p*-value to be less than .05, the chi-square statistic must be more than 3.84.

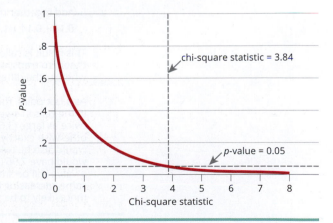

FIGURE 15.2 Steps in Conducting a Chi-Square Test

1. Generate a cross-tabulation of the observed frequencies of the independent variable and the dependent variable.

Variable	"Assistance to Other Countries"	"Foreign Aid"	Total
About right/too much	845	823	1,668
Too little	55	77	132
Total	900	900	1,800

2. Calculate the expected frequencies for each cell that we would expect to observe given the null hypothesis. To do so, we keep the marginal frequencies (row and column totals, highlighted in yellow) in the table exactly the same, and we calculate the cell values we would observe if the column percentages of people answering "too little" was exactly the same in both the "assistance to other countries" and "foreign aid" groups.

Variable	"Assistance to Other Countries"	"Foreign Aid"	Total
About right/too much	834	834	1,668
Too little	66	66	132
Total	900	900	1,800

3. Calculate the difference between the observed frequencies and the expected frequencies.

Variable	"Assistance to Other Countries"	"Foreign Aid"
About right/too much	−11	11
Too little	11	−11

4. For each cell, square the differences calculated in step 3 and divide the result by the expected frequency in step 2.

Variable	"Assistance to Other Countries"	"Foreign Aid"
About right/too much	0.14	0.14
Too little	1.85	1.85

5. Add together the result in each cell:

0.14 + 0.14 + 1.85 + 1.85 = 3.98

This result is called the *chi-square statistic*. We can then use probability theory to translate the chi-square statistic into a *p*-value and determine whether the difference we observe is statistically significant.

As a last point, think about what would happen if we double all the numbers in the cells in step 1. We would get these numbers if our sample size was twice as large (3,600 instead of 1,800) but the pattern of responses was otherwise exactly the same. In subsequent steps, all of the other numbers would also be twice as large. When we added up the results at the end, we would have 7.96 (3.98 × 2). When we convert this result into a *p*-value, the *p*-value will be smaller. If the association between two variables remains the same, increasing the sample size lowers the *p*-value, making the results more likely to be statistically significant.

As noted, for a result to be statistically significant by conventional standards in social science, the *p*-value needs to be below .05, which means that the chi-square statistically needs to be larger than 3.84. For our example in Figure 15.2, the chi-square statistic is 3.98. The *p*-value is thus lower than .05 (specifically, it is .037), meaning that our result is statistically significant. While the conclusion here is much less definitive than it is in our "welfare" example, we can still say that it is unlikely that we would have observed the difference we did between "assistance to other countries" and "foreign aid" simply due to chance.

THE *t* TEST

The other way to calculate the *p*-value is to do a *t* test. A ***t* test** is a method for testing whether the mean of the dependent variable differs depending on the value of the independent variable. Because *t* tests compare means, they are appropriate for continuous variables. In our "other countries"/"foreign aid" example, the variables are dichotomous, and we showed in Chapter 14 how a dichotomous variable coded so that its values are either 0 or 1 has a mean that is the same as the proportion of cases that are coded as 1. As a result, we can use either a *t* test or a chi-square test when our independent variable and dependent variable are both dichotomous.

In our example, the proportion of people who said the government was spending too little was 8.6% in the "foreign aid" group and 6.1% in the "assistance to other countries" group. Our difference in means is (0.086 − 0.061) = 0.025.

A *t* test is based on the distribution of the difference in means that we would expect if the null hypothesis is true. In other words, instead of looking at the distribution of the variable as we did in Chapter 14, we are now talking about the distribution of results we would expect if the null hypothesis is true and if we repeated the same experiment many times. We would expect the result of each experiment to be slightly different, but, in general, the results would cluster around the finding of zero difference, and large differences would be less likely than small differences.

We can calculate this distribution given information about the standard deviation and our sample size. Figure 15.3 shows this distribution. As you can see, it looks like a bell curve. As sample size gets larger, this bell curve converges to a particular form known as the **normal distribution**. For a difference to be statistically significant, it needs to be outside the middle 95% of this bell curve. Using a term introduced in Chapter 14, the difference between groups needs to be large enough that it falls outside the 95% confidence interval of this distribution.

In our case, the difference of 0.025 falls just barely outside the interval. As with the chi-square test, the *p*-value is .037 (the details of how this specific value is computed are outside the scope of this book). We can therefore say that respondents express higher support for increased government spending when asked about "foreign aid" than when asked about "assistance to other countries." However, we would not be

_t_ test A method for testing whether the mean of the dependent variable differs depending on the value of the independent variable.

normal distribution The random distribution of values in a bell-shaped curve.

FIGURE 15.3 Normal Distribution

The graph shows the expected distribution of the difference in support for "foreign aid" and "assistance to other countries" in repeated experiments in which the null hypothesis is true. For a difference to be statistically significant, it needs to fall outside the middle 95% of this distribution, demarcated by the dashed lines below.

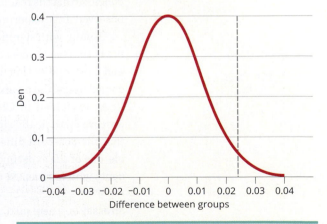

as confident that the difference could not be explained by chance as we were in the "welfare" versus "assistance to the poor" example.

Overall, the lower the p-value, the more confident we can be that an observed difference that is consistent with our hypothesis is not simply due to chance. Consequently, all else being equal, we want to design studies that provide the best opportunity for observing low p-values and statistically significant findings if our hypothesis is correct. **Statistical power** refers to a study's ability to detect statistically significant differences between groups if such differences exist.

Say we were interested in who shoplifts more: teenage boys or teenage girls. High statistical power means that if a difference between boys and girls really does exist, our study would have a high probability of yielding a statistically significant result. Low statistical power means that even when there is a real difference, our study results would not be statistically significant.

Two aspects of a study that are especially important for statistical power are (1) how large the sample is and (2) how big we expect the difference to be between groups. The larger the sample, the smaller the p-values will be for a given difference between groups. A study of 10,000 boys and girls would have a lot more power to detect differences than a study of 100. Likewise, the larger the actual difference that exists, the smaller the sample size necessary to be confident we can detect it. If the real difference between boys and girls was 30 percentage points, we would not need as large of a sample to detect that a difference existed than if the real difference was only 3 percentage points. The smaller the effect we expect, the larger the sample we will need.

Statistical Significance and Samples

The experiments described in the previous sections were conducted using the General Social Survey, a probability sample of U.S. adults. Experiments using probability samples are a good starting point for talking about statistical significance because they allow us to draw two separate conclusions from statistically significant results: (1) Because the studies are based on experiments with random assignment, statistically significant results imply that the differences we observe between groups were the result of the differences in wording. (2) Because a probability sample was used, we can conclude that the results provide a reasonably accurate estimate of what we would have observed if the experiment had been conducted on the entire population of U.S. adults.

Usually, with significance testing, the results speak to one question or the other, but not both. That is, most experimental studies are not conducted on probability samples, and most studies that use probability samples are not experiments. In this section, we consider how the meaning of significance testing differs for each of these cases.

As explained in Chapter 8, experiments offer high internal validity. When we observe statistically significant differences between groups, we have strong evidence that the observed differences are due to the experimental manipulation. For example, one of the experiments described in Chapter 8 found that Cornell University students who were asked to write an essay contemplating their own death subsequently reported a stronger belief in the existence of an afterlife than students asked to write an essay on a neutral topic (Willer, 2009). Because the writing topic was determined by random assignment, we can conclude that the observed difference in reported beliefs about an afterlife was somehow caused by the different essay topics.

At the same time, significance testing offers no information about whether what we observe among participants in an experiment resembles what we would see in an entire population. The result we saw among Cornell students is not necessarily the same result we would observe for the whole U.S. population. We may have theoretical reasons to expect the results of an experiment to generalize more broadly, but the statistical significance of experimental results does not speak to that issue. Here we are speaking about external validity, a topic we have discussed frequently in this book (see Chapter 5). Unless probability samples are used, significance testing in experiments simply determines whether differences between the treatment and control groups may be due to chance.

However, most research projects that use probability samples are not experiments. For example, we may be interested in whether adults who attended college tend to be happier than people who did not get a college degree. Using the GSS, we can cross-tabulate these variables, which we summarize in Table 15.1. As the table shows, more than 36% of college graduates rate themselves as "very happy" compared to less than 28% of those who did not graduate from college. When we do a chi-square test, we find that this difference is statistically significant, with a p-value of less than .001.

In this case, what does statistical significance tell us? We can be at least 95% confident that if we had surveyed the entire population instead of just this sample, we would find that respondents who graduated from college are more likely to report being "very happy" than respondents who did not get a college degree. We can be confident in this conclusion because our study is based on a probability sample.

Notably, statistical significance does not tell us whether completing college is what actually *causes* college graduates to be happier. For example, maybe people from wealthier families are more likely to go to college and are more likely to be happier regardless of whether they go to college. If that is the case, then perhaps the association between graduating college and happiness just reflects people's family background and says nothing about the effects of graduating from college. We will explore this idea in more detail shortly. For now, we want to emphasize that significance testing in probability samples allows us to be confident that sample differences reflect true

TABLE 15.1   Frequency Distribution: College Degrees and Happiness

Very Happy?	College Degree?		
	No	Yes	Total
No	8,960	2,891	11,851
	(72.2)	(63.2)	(69.7)
Yes	3,458	1,687	5,145
	(27.9)	(36.9)	(30.3)
Total	12,418	4,578	16,996
	(100.0)	(100.0)	(100.0)

Note: $N = 16,996$. Percentages are shown in parentheses.
Source: General Social Survey, 2000–2014.

population differences. Statistical significance, by itself, does nothing to explain why differences exist.

In Chapter 6, we emphasized the importance of randomness in sampling. Later, in Chapter 8, we emphasized the importance of using randomness in experiments. Perhaps the cases seemed quite different at the time, but we can now see that the underlying strength of randomization is the same. Randomization ensures that groups are comparable except for chance, allowing us to draw conclusions from cases in which differences occur that are larger than what we would expect by chance.

Statistical Significance versus Practical Significance

The "significance" part of the term *statistical significance* can be misleading. When a difference is statistically significant, it is large enough that it is unlikely to be due to chance. Statistical significance does *not* mean that a result is necessarily big, important, illuminating, or anything else we might associate with the word *significant*.

Sociologists distinguish between statistical significance and **practical significance** (also called *substantive significance*). Again, a statistically significant difference between groups just means we have evidence that it is too large to be simply the result of chance. Practical significance, in contrast, refers to whether a difference is large enough to be important for the purposes of our research or for social policies.

For example, in Chapter 14, we showed that while 27.8% of households with a child under 13 owned a gun, 34.0% of households without a child under 13 did. The p-value for this 6.2 percentage point difference is .006, so it is statistically significant. This difference seems large enough that we would imagine it also is practically significant. If the difference was only 1 or 2 percentage points, it might still be statistically significant if we had a large enough sample, but it would probably not be practically significant in terms of what it tells us about which households are more likely to have guns.

> **practical significance**
> Whether a difference is large enough to be important for the purposes of research or social policies. Also called *substantive significance*.

Concerns about Significance Testing

Traditionally, p-values have played an important role everywhere that statistics are used in the natural or social sciences. Yet p-values have also been the subject of considerable concern—especially in recent years—because of their potential for abuse.

When properly applied, $p < .05$ seems a reasonably strict standard: Results are large enough that the possibility of their being due to chance is only 1 in 20. But once a researcher starts to do multiple analyses, the chance that some result will have a p-value $< .05$ increases, and with enough analyses the likelihood becomes a certainty.

The web comic *xkcd* illustrated this problem with an example of scientists looking to see if the color of jelly beans caused acne (see https://xkcd.com/882/). The scientists tried 20 colors. Because they tried 20 colors, we would expect that, even if jelly bean color had no effect whatsoever on acne, one of them would be statistically significant with a $p < .05$. In the comic, the jelly beans with $p < .05$ were green, and the result was newspaper headlines announcing "Green Jelly Beans Linked to Acne!"

Enough concern has been raised that the American Statistical Association (2016) issued a statement about p-values. In its statement, the association noted that p-values can be properly interpreted only when researchers are fully transparent about the analyses they have done. In the *xkcd* case, the *p*-value below .05 for green jelly beans becomes much less impressive when one knows that they also tested 19 other jelly bean colors.

Significance testing has also been criticized for putting too much emphasis on whether *p* is above or below a particular value. Researchers sometimes report only whether a difference is statistically significant or not, which implies that the difference between a *p*-value of .049 (just below the cutoff) and .051 (just above the cutoff) is more meaningful than the difference between .00001 and .049 or between .051 and .9. Thus, researchers are strongly encouraged to present *p*-values explicitly or to provide enough information so that readers can calculate them.

CONCEPT CHECKS

1 Give an example of a variable that you believe is positively associated with how religious people are, and a variable that is negatively associated with how religious people are.

2 What does it mean to say that the *p*-value for the comparison between gun ownership in households with and without children is .006?

3 Suppose that a study based on a representative sample finds that children whose parents are divorced are more likely to have problems with antisocial behavior than children whose parents are not divorced, and the difference is statistically significant. What does statistical significance here allow us to tentatively conclude? What do statistically significant differences in well-conducted experiments allow us to conclude that we cannot conclude from this example?

4 What is the difference between statistical significance and practical significance?

CONFOUNDING FACTORS

On average, days with higher ice cream sales are also days on which more people drown. The drownings are not the result of people eating ice cream and then cramping up as they swim or to people reacting to the news of a drowning by buying a pint of rocky road. Instead, hot weather causes both more people to buy ice cream and more people to go swimming.

The problem of **confounding** occurs when two variables can be consistently associated with each other even when one does not cause the other (Figure 15.4). If two variables directly or indirectly share a common cause (for instance, the way that hot weather influences both ice cream sales and swimming), then the two variables will tend to be associated even if neither variable influences the other. When we hear the common warning that "correlation is not causation," we are hearing a warning about the possibility of confounding.

We can present the problem in visual terms using a **path diagram**, which depicts how variables influence one another by using arrows to indicate the direction of influence. The plus and minus signs in a path diagram indicate whether an independent

confounding When two variables can be consistently associated with each other even when one does not cause the other.

path diagram A depiction of how variables influence one another that uses arrows to indicate the direction of influence.

FIGURE 15.4 Spurious Correlations

An example of two variables that are correlated but do not cause one another: U.S. per capita cheese consumption and deaths from becoming tangled in one's bedsheets.

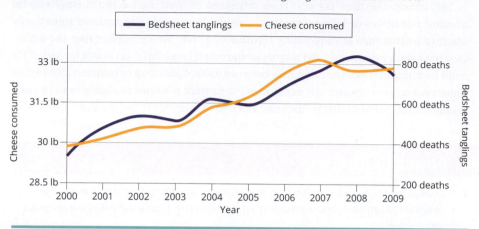

Source: http://tylervigen.com/spurious-correlations.

variable increases (+) or decreases (−) the level of the dependent variable. In Figure 15.5, our hypothesis is diagram (a): education influences happiness. A correlation between education and happiness is also consistent with diagram (b): family background influences both educational attainment and happiness.

Confounding makes sociological research much more challenging than it would be if correlation actually *was* causation. Many sociological hypotheses concern cause-and-effect relationships that cannot be readily or satisfactorily addressed using experiments. In these cases, we can show that two variables are associated with each other in the way our hypothesis predicts (for example, that people who have more education tend to report being happier). Using the statistical tools described earlier, we can also establish that the bivariate association is strong enough that it is unlikely due to chance. Yet, the possibility of confounding often presents alternative explanations to any given hypothesis.

For example, we suggested that the relationship between completing college and happiness might be confounded by family background. In this example, completing college is the independent variable, and happiness is the dependent variable. Family background is potentially a **confound** that produces an association between an independent variable and a dependent variable. For family background to be a confound, it would need to influence both whether people complete college and, separately, people's happiness. In that event, completing college and happiness would be associated with one another even if finishing college had no effect on happiness. Because family background differences could by themselves produce an association between college completion and happiness, we cannot infer from the association that finishing college leads people to be happier.

confound A third variable that is linked to two concepts in a way that makes them appear to be related even when they are not.

FIGURE 15.5 Path Diagram of Two Potential Scenarios

In this example, family background is a possible confound because it influences both whether people complete college and, separately, people's happiness.

(a) Hypothesis

(b) Example of confounding

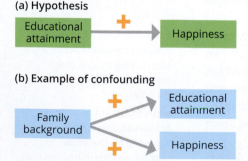

A longer example will help reinforce what confounding is and how we might begin to address it. Our dependent variable here is whether people report that they pray at least once per day. One hypothesis might be that working full-time leads people to pray less, either because full-time work takes up more time or because it diverts people's attention away from their religious commitments. If our hypothesis is true, and we compare people who work full-time to people who work part-time, we would expect that people who work full-time are less likely to pray every day.

When we cross-tabulate the variables, we find an association consistent with our hypothesis, as summarized in Table 15.2. While 58.2% of respondents who work part-time say that they pray every day, only 53.9% of those who work full-time do. In terms of statistical significance, the p-value for this difference is .001 (well under .05), meaning that it is very unlikely that chance alone would produce a difference as large as 4 percentage points.

Even though the relationship is statistically significant, we might still wonder whether the association is actually due to people's work status influencing how much they pray. For example, we might worry specifically that the relationship is confounded by gender.

Why gender? As noted earlier, a confounding variable must be associated with both our independent variable and, separately, our dependent variable. With respect to our independent variable, employed women in the United States are more likely to work part-time than are employed men, primarily because women are more likely to cut back their work hours so that they can care for their families. Among employed women in the GSS, 23% work part-time (instead of full-time), while only 12% of employed men work part-time. With respect to the dependent variable, women in the United States are more likely to pray every day than men, for reasons that have themselves been the subject of lively sociological debate (Freese & Montgomery, 2007; Stark, 2002). In the GSS, 69% of women report praying daily compared to only 46% of men.

TABLE 15.2 Frequency Distribution: Daily Prayer and Work Status

Pray Daily?	Work Status		
	Part-Time	Full-Time	Total
No	706	3,544	4,250
	(41.8)	(46.1)	(45.3)
Yes	983	4,146	5,129
	(58.2)	(53.9)	(54.7)
Total	1,689	7,690	9,379
	(100.0)	(100.0)	(100.0)

Note: N = 9,379. Percentages are shown in parentheses.
Source: General Social Survey, 2000–2014.

FIGURE 15.6 Path Diagrams of Hypothesis and an Alternative Scenario That Involves Confounding

(a) Hypothesis

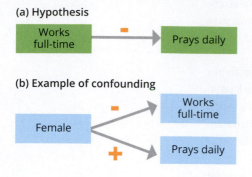

(b) Example of confounding

elaboration A cross-tabulation technique used to determine whether a confounding variable can account for the association between two categorical variables.

If women are more likely to pray every day and more likely to work part-time, then working part-time and praying every day might be associated with one another simply as a consequence of both activities being disproportionately female. In this case, gender is a confounding variable.

Figure 15.6 illustrates this example with a path diagram. As before, our hypothesis is shown in diagram (a). However, the association between work status and prayer that we observe is also consistent with diagram (b). In the next section, we explain how we incorporate information about respondents' gender to determine which of these two diagrams is more consistent with the data.

Using Elaboration to Address Confounding

We have reason to think that gender might confound the relationship we observe between working full-time and praying daily. How do we assess whether gender truly is a confounding variable? A simple strategy is **elaboration**, a cross-tabulation technique used to determine whether a confounding variable can account for the association between two categorical variables.

To do elaboration, we divide our sample into groups on the basis of the value of the potentially confounding variable—in this case, gender. Then, for each group, we construct a separate cross-tabulation of the independent variable and dependent variable. In our case, we make separate tables for men and for women of the relationship between work status and daily prayer. The logic here is that if working full-time reduces the extent to which people pray daily, then we would expect similar patterns to emerge regardless of gender. In other words, men who work full-time should be less likely to pray daily than men who work part-time. Likewise, women who work full-time should be less likely to pray daily than women who work part-time.

We present the separate tables in Table 15.3. When we look at women and men separately, we do not see any consistent association between work status and prayer. Men who work part-time are slightly more likely to pray daily, but the opposite is true for women: Women who work part-time are a bit more likely to pray every day. Both associations are weak and neither is statistically significant, and so these patterns may simply be due to chance.

In this case, elaboration provides strong reason to doubt our earlier hypothesis. The negative association we had observed between working part-time and praying daily appears to reflect confounding by gender.

We can do elaboration with a continuous dependent variable by using the means of this variable to fill the cells of the table. To stay with a similar example, let's continue using whether someone prays daily as our independent variable and look at the reported incomes of respondents who work full-time. As Table 15.4a shows, for full-time employees, the average income for those who pray daily is $8,000 per year lower (in 2014 dollars) than the average income of those who do not.

In Table 15.4b and Table 15.4c, we compute means separately for men and women. When we do, we see that the differences among men and the differences among women are substantially smaller than the overall difference, because women are both more likely to pray daily and to have lower average incomes.

TABLE 15.3 Elaboration

(a) Women (n = 4,682)

Pray Daily?	Work Status		
	Part-Time	**Full-Time**	**Total**
No	404	1,237	1,641
	(36.0)	(34.7)	(35.1)
Yes	717	2,324	3,041
	(64.0)	(65.3)	(65.0)
Total	1,121	3,561	4,682
	(100.0)	(100.0)	(100.0)

(b) Men (n = 4,697)

Pray Daily?	Work Status		
	Part-Time	**Full-Time**	**Total**
No	302	2,307	2,609
	(53.2)	(55.9)	(55.6)
Yes	266	1,822	2,088
	(46.8)	(44.1)	(44.5)
Total	568	4,129	4,697
	(100.0)	(100.0)	(100.0)

Percentages are shown in parentheses.
Source: General Social Survey, 2000–2014.

Elaboration is a good basic technique for determining whether the independent variable and dependent variable remain associated when the confounding variable is held constant. When conducting an elaboration, the researcher holds the confounding variable constant by examining separate bivariate analyses for each value of the confounding variable. If a hypothesis that the independent variable causes a change in the dependent variable is true, we would expect to still see the association between the variables when the confounding variable does not vary.

Using Regression Analysis with a Control Variable

In practice, elaboration is not often used because modern computing makes more sophisticated techniques easy to use. Rather than using elaboration, sociologists will typically use regression analysis, which we introduced in the previous chapter. Here, we will first show how regression analysis works for our prayer example, and then we will discuss the advantages of using regression analysis instead of elaboration.

Regression analysis is a way of describing precisely the relationship between an independent variable and the conditional mean of a categorical dependent variable. In our prayer example, because the dependent variable is dichotomous, we can think of the conditional mean as the probability of a person praying daily.

TABLE 15.4 Elaboration with a Continuous Dependent Variable

(a) Men and women combined (N = 6,609)

Pray Daily?	Mean Income (in Thousands of Dollars)	n
No	62.8	3,091
Yes	54.8	3,518

(b) Men (n = 3,569)

Pray Daily?	Mean Income (in Thousands of Dollars)	n
No	69.8	2,019
Yes	69.0	1,550

(c) Women (n = 3,040)

Pray Daily?	Mean Income (in Thousands of Dollars)	n
No	49.8	1,072
Yes	43.6	1,968

Source: General Social Survey (full-time employees only), 2000–2014.

(For technical reasons, sociologists would typically handle a dichotomous dependent variable a bit differently, albeit with similar results. We are taking some liberties here for the sake of simplicity in showing the connection between elaboration and regression analysis. We will show a different example that uses a continuous dependent variable shortly.)

In bivariate regression analysis, we use an equation in which the dependent variable is a function of the independent variable:

$$y = a + bx$$

Here, y is the dependent variable; x will be 1 if the respondent works full-time and 0 if the respondent works part-time. Also, if $x = 0$, then $bx = 0$, so $y = a$. So we can write our example as:

$$\text{Probability of praying daily} = a + b \text{ (works full-time)}$$

If $x = 0$, that is, somebody works part-time, then a is the probability of their praying daily. Table 15.2 showed that 58.2% of GSS respondents who worked part-time prayed daily compared to 53.9% of those who worked full-time. In terms of our regression equation:

$$\text{Probability of praying daily} = 0.582 - 0.043 \text{ (works full-time)}$$

The value of b, −0.043, is our regression coefficient, and it indicates the relationship between the independent variable and the conditional mean of the dependent variable. This means that people who work full-time are 4.3 percentage points less likely to pray daily than people who work part-time. The p-value for the regression coefficient is .001, so it is very unlikely that we would observe a coefficient this large by chance alone.

The way that we evaluate gender as a potential confounder in regression analysis is simply to add it to our equation:

$$\text{Probability of praying daily} = a + b \,(\text{works full-time}) + z \,(\text{gender})$$

We refer to gender here as a **control variable**, a potentially confounding variable that we add to our regression analysis to estimate the relationship between the independent variable and dependent variable after adjusting for its influence. Sociologists often say that control variables allow them to estimate relationships while "holding constant" or "controlling for" the control variable.

Because we have added a new variable, the values of a and b will change. In our example, when we estimate this equation using a statistical software package, we get the following result:

$$\text{Probability of praying daily} = 0.446 - 0.001 \,(\text{works full-time}) + 0.205 \,(\text{female})$$

The regression coefficient for working full-time is now almost zero ($b = -0.001$). Its p-value is .89, so it is not statistically significant. The regression analysis reveals that once we control for gender, there is no longer a statistically significant relationship between working full-time and daily prayer. In other words, the statistically significant association we observed earlier between work status and prayer is not actually consistent with the hypothesis that working full-time causes people to pray less; instead, the association appears to reflect confounding by gender.

To provide a different example in which the association between the independent variable and dependent variable is only partly due to confounding, let's change our independent variable from whether people pray daily to how much money they make. Table 15.5 shows mean incomes in the GSS. First, not surprisingly, people who work full-time have higher annual earnings than people who work part-time, as Table 15.5a

TABLE 15.5 Mean Incomes by Work Status and Income

	Mean Income (in Thousands of Dollars)	n
(a) By work status		
Full-time	55.2	9,248
Part-time	22.3	1,786
(b) By work status and gender		
Women, full-time	41.4	4,261
Men, full-time	66.9	4,987
Women, part-time	19.0	1,166
Men, part-time	28.7	620

Source: General Social Survey, 2000–2014.

FIGURE 15.7 An Example of Partial Confounding

As an example of partial confounding, gender accounts for some, but not all, of the association between working full-time (vs. part-time) and income.

(a) Hypothesis

(b) Example of confounding

(c) Example of partial confounding

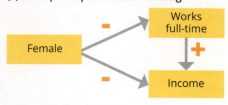

shows. Second, women who work full-time make less than men who work full-time, and women who work part-time make less than men who work part-time, as shown in Table 15.5b. As we noted earlier, women are also more likely than men to work part-time. As a result, part of the relationship between working full-time and earnings may be attributed to women being more likely to work part-time (Figure 15.7).

In regression analysis, the bivariate analysis would be written as follows:

$$y = a + xb$$
$$\text{Income} = a + b \text{ (works full-time)}$$

The result of running the regression analysis is:

$$\text{Income} = 22.3 + 32.9 \text{ (works full-time)}$$

We would interpret the regression coefficient 32.9 as meaning that people who work full-time make \$32,900 more per year than people who work part-time.

When we add gender to the equation, it looks like this:

$$\text{Income} = a + b \text{ (works full-time)} + z \text{ (female)}$$

Our statistical software package provides these results:

$$\text{Income} = 37.4 + 28.4 \text{ (works full-time)} - 23.1 \text{ (female)}$$

We interpret the regression coefficient 28.4 as follows: Controlling for gender, people who work full-time make \$28,400 more than people who work part-time. In other words, about \$4,500 (\$32,900 – \$28,400) of our original difference of \$32,900 was due to women being more likely to work part-time than men.

Regression analysis is a far more powerful approach than elaboration to address confounding, for several reasons. First, regression analysis allows researchers to consider potential confounding variables that are measured at the interval or ratio variables, such as number of years of schooling or age in years, in addition to nominal or ordinal variables, such as male/female. Second, as we will discuss in the next section, regression analysis allows researchers to evaluate many possibly confounding variables at once. In both cases, the power of regression analysis is its use of an equation to express the relationship between the dependent variable and many independent variables.

Regression Analysis with Many Control Variables

In the previous section, we showed that an observed statistical relationship between two variables (work status and daily prayer) could result from confounding by a third variable, gender. In practice, a relationship may be confounded by multiple variables, each of which accounts for only a small part of the observed association. To estimate the relationship between variables net of this confounding, we need to account for all these variables simultaneously. Regression analysis provides a method for doing so; we simply need to add more variables to our regression equation.

Controlling for many variables becomes important in situations where we can easily imagine many independent variables that might affect the dependent variable. One example comes from the literature on reducing alcohol and drug use among teenagers. Policy makers have suggested that a simple way parents can help is by making sure the family eats dinner together almost every night. The idea is that these dinners strengthen family relationships and help parents keep better track of their children's activities, which in turn reduces teenagers' risk of substance use.

In what ways do families that eat dinner together differ from families that don't?

Data do indicate that children from families who eat dinner together at least six times a week are less likely to use alcohol or drugs compared to those in families eating together fewer than six times a week. But does this relationship mean that family dinners actually *cause* the difference? Families that regularly have dinner together differ from other families in many ways. Yet, studies that examined relatively simple alternative explanations found that these other factors could not account for all of the observed association between family dinners and drug use. Such results lend credence to the hypothesis that dining together reduces teenagers' substance use.

Alternatively, sociologists John Hoffmann and Elizabeth Warnick (2013) proposed that previous research may have failed to account adequately for the many possible differences between families that eat together nightly and those that do not. Their analyses included controls for income, parents' education, family structure, race, whether the mother was working, parents' age, religiousness, and other activities the family did together besides eating dinner. When all these potential confounders were simultaneously taken into account, the relationship between family dinners and teenagers' substance-use behaviors was no longer statistically significant. In other words, even though the relationship cannot be explained by any single confounding variable, controlling for many variables simultaneously provides reason to question whether dining together lowers the risk of alcohol or drug use.

So far, our examples have illustrated how multiple regression analysis can explain away a bivariate association by taking confounding variables into account. However, variables may prove to not be confounding at all. As an example, we can consider the effects of a father going to prison on the well-being of his children's mother.

One might imagine that men who go to prison may not be the best fathers or romantic partners, and so it is possible that incarcerating these men might not have much of an effect on the mothers of their children. One could even imagine these women being better off when the father is in prison. However, research by Christopher Wildeman and colleagues (2012) showed a clear relationship in which women whose children's fathers had recently been incarcerated were more likely to have a major depressive episode than other mothers.

Because of the possibility of confounding, we must interpret this bivariate relationship accurately. Women who have children with men who later become incarcerated differ in systematic ways from mothers in general. Those differences might make women more prone to depressive episodes. Perhaps they are more likely to be poor or to live in unsafe, crime-ridden neighborhoods—both of which are well-documented correlates of depression.

Conversations from the Front Lines

DAVID GRUSKY

David Grusky is a professor of sociology at Stanford University and director of its Center for Poverty and Inequality. His research includes work on understanding trends in inequalities in the United States and elsewhere and patterns of social mobility between generations. He has also been heavily involved in trying to improve the data infrastructure that exists in the United States for tracking and studying social inequality.

You have been involved in research that has used tax records to study economic inequality. Why are tax records better than the way income is usually measured in social science studies?

It's not just that tax data are of very high quality. It's even more important that piecing together multiple administrative sources, like tax and census data, can build a true population frame. This allows us to overcome the increasingly troubling problems—such as nonresponse and attrition—that now plague many surveys. Because social processes are fundamentally selective processes, we have to worry about a methodology that's so vulnerable to selection. We should therefore reserve surveys for social science questions for which they're absolutely necessary and exploit administrative data whenever they're available. It goes without saying that much administrative data, like criminal justice data, are the direct product of highly selective processes, so it's immensely important to hang those data on a population frame (such as the census) that allows those selective processes to be exposed and analyzed.

Tax information is extremely sensitive. How is it that researchers are able to gain access to it?

Before the data are made available to researchers, names and other identifying information are always stripped away. Even afterward, the data are only analyzed in secure locations with a host of protections. We all know that if there's just one breach—just one—the country will pay a massive price in terms of its capacity to carry out evidence-based policy analysis. Hence, it's a matter of the highest priority to ensure that there never is a breach. (The private sector, which often deals in data that are even more sensitive, would be well-advised to adopt the same level of care.)

> " If ever social science research on inequality mattered in a deep and profound way, now would be the time. "

What do you think is the best way of summarizing the amount of inequality that exists in a society?

It is probably instinctive for a social scientist to rail against a question of this sort. That is, a standard-issue social scientist would not just insist that there are many types of inequality, such as gender inequality, race inequality, and income inequality, but also that within each of these types different measures would bring out different features of the inequality in question.

To consider the possibility of confounding, Wildeman and his colleagues conducted a regression analysis that included more than 30 different control variables to address various possible confounding variables. They found that the observed relationship between father's incarceration and mother's likelihood of a depressive episode decreased when control variables were added, but it remained statistically significant.

But I'm not going to rail in that way! Why not? Because in fact it seems that there's a grand sweep to history in which all of these measures tend to move together. This tendency for cross-trend contamination used to work in favor of the egalitarian commitment: In the not-so-distant past, we witnessed a grand decline in income inequality, in gender inequality, and in various types of racial and ethnic inequality. All at once. It's no wonder that postwar theorists like Daniel Bell or Talcott Parsons viewed the sweep of history in such optimistic terms.

Now we're seeing, in other words, a simultaneous increase in income inequality and wealth inequality, a stalling out of historic downward trends in poverty and gender inequality, and the rise of new forms of racial and religious conflict. It's a classic hell-in-a-handbasket story. But underlying that story is the larger tendency—in good times and bad—for trends to cross-fertilize and contaminate one another. That's a deep sociological dynamic that we need to better understand.

What do you think is the biggest misconception about social inequality in the United States?

I'll nominate two as standing out. First, it is sometimes assumed that tax cuts for the well-off are a main reason why income inequality in the United States took off. That's misguided. Tax cuts did play a role, but the distribution of pre-tax income has also become increasingly unequal and that accounts for much of the larger trend. The implication: The takeoff is largely driven by changes in the extent to which our labor market institutions generate paychecks of varying sizes.

Second (and closely related): The best or only way to redress rising inequality is through tax policy. Here again, tax policy would be immensely helpful, but a social scientist should also care about how inequality is baked into our institutions, in particular how our institutions give inequality a misleadingly meritocratic cast.

It's now well established, for example, that rising inequality is partly attributable to rising economic returns to schooling, a trend that comes off as very meritocratic. But it's not. Because access to high-quality schooling depends in large part on whether the stork dropped the child into a high-income family or neighborhood, the growth in returns to schooling is, in part, a deeply illegitimate form of "ascriptive inequality" that's only masquerading as merit-based inequality. This means that children who are so lucky as to be dropped into these high-income families and neighborhoods are protected against competition from other less fortunate children who were dropped into poor families and neighborhoods and hence don't have any meaningful access to high-quality schooling. What happens when one group is protected from competition coming from another group? It parlays that protection into higher returns.

What do you see as being the future of social science research on inequality?

To return to one of my earlier points, I think social scientists need to better understand the sources of what I've labeled "cross-trend contamination," the tendency for trends to move of a piece. If ever social science research on inequality mattered in a deep and profound way, now would be the time.

Confounding by these 30-plus variables explained about half of the association, but not all of it.

Thus, the Wildeman study strengthened the evidence for the idea that a father's incarceration tends to have negative effects on a mother's well-being. Even so, for reasons we will explain shortly, this evidence may still not persuade us that a causal relationship exists.

How Do Researchers Choose Control Variables?

Researchers use control variables to address the possibility that the association between two variables is due to confounding. We can get a better sense of the ways that researchers use control variables in practice by looking at some of the possibly confounding variables that Wildeman and colleagues (2012) used in their study.

First, the researchers considered the idea that the fathers exhibit behavioral traits that increase their likelihood of incarceration and also have negative mental-health effects on mothers. For example, they controlled for information about whether the father had committed domestic violence and whether the father had abused drugs or alcohol.

Second, it is also possible that the association between incarceration and depression reflects differences in families that already existed before the father's incarceration. For example, the researchers controlled for the mother's household income before the father was incarcerated and whether the mother had experienced particular economic hardships such as not being able to pay the rent or having to borrow money from friends to pay bills.

A third set of possibly confounding factors is different sociodemographic characteristics of the mothers and fathers. For example, Wildeman and his colleagues controlled for the mother's education. Lower education may lead to various stressors that increase the likelihood of depression for mothers. However, the mother's education does not explain whether the father is more likely to be incarcerated. Instead, the key point to keep in mind here is that characteristics of the mothers and fathers are likely correlated. That is, women with less education may be disproportionately likely (compared to women with college degrees) to have children with men who become incarcerated. Likewise, the researchers controlled for the father's education because less educated fathers could be more likely to partner with women at higher risk of depression. The association between the father's incarceration and the mother's depression remained after all these different control variables were taken into account.

Ultimately, when a measure is available to address a confounding scenario, researchers usually include it in their analysis. However, researchers sometimes encounter situations where no measure is available. Also, variables that occur after the independent variable—for example, the change in the mother's economic situation after the father is incarcerated—are sometimes included in a regression analysis. However, these are not control variables, but rather ways of trying to understand mechanisms by which the father's incarceration may affect the mother's depression.

suppressor variable A variable that hides or even reverses the direction of a true causal relationship between an independent variable and a dependent variable.

When studying the relationship between paternal incarceration and maternal health, Chris Wildeman and colleagues used control variables such as mother's and father's education to address the possibility of confounding.

Suppression

Adding control variables to a regression analysis may account for or reduce an association between two variables or the association may persist even after these confounding sources are taken into account. We might be tempted to conclude that when an association between two variables does not exist in a bivariate analysis, we can safely say that one variable does not cause the other. However, that conclusion would be incorrect because of the possibility of suppressor variables. A **suppressor variable** is a variable that hides or even reverses the direction of a true causal relationship between an independent variable and a dependent variable.

We can see how suppressor variables work by considering research inspired by the idea that doing volunteer work has positive effects on one's health (Cornwell, Laumann, & Schumm, 2008). A key potential suppressor variable in studying this relationship is age. Older adults—especially retired adults—spend more time doing volunteer work than younger adults do. Older adults also are more likely to have health problems for reasons that have nothing to do with whether they volunteer. Thus, even if volunteering itself is good for health, we might observe that volunteers have more health problems than those who do not, simply because volunteers are more likely to be older and thus have more health problems. Including age as a control variable in our regression analysis addresses this possibility.

We can see when we might have to worry about suppression by looking at a path diagram. Figure 15.8a presents the hypothesized relationships among age, volunteering, and health. We need to worry about suppression if *one of the three* arrows in the diagram hypothesizes a negative direction of influence or if *all three* do. In our example, we hypothesize that the suppressor variable (age) negatively influences health, but the other two hypothesized relationships are positive.

As a different example, as people get older, they also consume less junk food. Consequently, even though eating fatty or sugary foods may have negative effects on health, we might conclude the opposite if we failed to take age into account, because younger people are healthier than older people despite being more prone to eat junk food (not *because* of it). We can write this path diagram as Figure 15.8b. All three arrows are negative, and again we need to worry about suppression.

In sociology, suppression is rarer than confounding, in which not including a control variable causes us to exaggerate the relationship between an independent variable and a dependent variable. The relative rarity of suppression reflects the deeply patterned character of social life, as Figure 15.9 shows. When sociologists study beneficial events and positive outcomes (such as getting a college education and earning a high income), we can usually imagine broader social advantages that increase the odds of experiencing both. When we study adverse events and negative outcomes (such as one's partner being imprisoned and poor mental health), we can readily envision how broader advantages make it less likely that a person will experience both. That is, it is easier to imagine characteristics of people that make them more likely to go to college and more likely to earn a high income (regardless of whether they go to college) than it is to imagine characteristics of people that make them simultaneously more likely to have a partner in prison and more likely to have higher incomes.

FIGURE 15.8 Path Diagrams Implying the Possibility of Suppression

In these examples, the confounding influence of age may hide the true direction of the causal relationship.

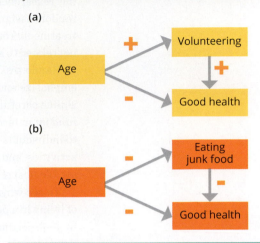

FIGURE 15.9 Path Diagrams Suggesting the Commonly Pervasive Influence of Social Advantages

Note that the diagrams have either 0 negative associations or 2 negative associations; suppression would occur if each diagram had either 1 or 3 negative associations.

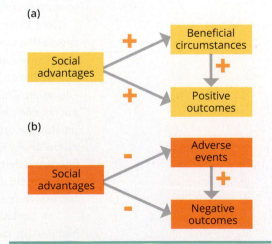

The Problem of Unmeasured and Incorrectly Measured Differences

In Chapter 8, we touted the strength of random assignment in experiments for allowing researchers to draw conclusions with strong internal validity. The benefit of random assignment is that participants have no influence over whether they are in the treatment group or control group. As a result, the group to which they are assigned is not related to any of their personal characteristics.

Random assignment works great in experiments, but at the same time we cannot emphasize enough that social life in the real world does not use random assignment! Unlike carefully controlled experiments, social experiences tend to be extremely *non-random* in terms of what happens to whom. Experiences are usually strongly related to individuals' characteristics. In other words, we are "selected" into particular roles, activities, and experiences on the basis of our preexisting characteristics. As a result, sociological research can be profoundly difficult.

To see why, consider that many sociologists are interested in studying the effects of living in a poor neighborhood. Certainly, researchers can show that people who live in poor neighborhoods experience many negative economic, health, and educational outcomes compared to people who live in less poor neighborhoods. At the same time, where people live is no accident. Many people spend a large portion of their income in their effort to move to a "better" neighborhood, and many people are financially or otherwise constrained from living exactly where they want. In other words, it is intrinsically difficult to disentangle the influence of neighborhoods from the influence of the individual characteristics of those who live in a neighborhood.

One might hope that multiple regression analysis would solve this problem, because regression allows us to use control variables to take differences among people into account. A key limitation of standard multiple regression analysis, however, is that it can account only for *measured* differences. That is, we can include control variables in our analysis only if we have measured them and if the variables are available in our data sets.

For example, if we wanted to study the effect of neighborhoods on academic achievement, we might consider two potential confounders to be differences in parental involvement and the learning environment in the home. If we do not have measures of these variables, we cannot control for them, and they will therefore be left unaddressed in our regression analysis.

Even more challenging, control variables can address confounding only to the degree that the confounding influence is measured completely and accurately. Suppose that we are concerned about parental involvement as a potential confounding variable, and we have a survey item that asks parents how involved they are in their children's education. This survey item is better than nothing, but we might imagine that parents are not completely unbiased reporters of their own involvement. We might also imagine that the categories of a survey question on parental involvement might not capture all the gradations or dimensions of parental involvement that differ across neighborhoods and that matter for achievement. To the extent that these differences in involvement remain unmeasured, they are possible confounders not addressed by a multiple regression analysis.

The problem of unmeasured differences underscores the value of data with high-quality measures of many variables. Even under the best circumstances, however, social scientists are usually very limited in what they can measure, especially when the unit of analysis is individual persons. Consequently, concerns about unmeasured differences mean that standard multiple regression analyses must be carefully conducted and cautiously interpreted. In the remainder of the chapter, we consider some other ways that researchers can strengthen the evidence about their hypotheses.

REVERSE CAUSALITY

In regression analysis, we specify which variable is independent and which is dependent. Often, we do regression analysis specifically because we are interested in estimating the effect of the independent variable on the dependent variable. In one of the examples we've been considering, the independent variable is paternal incarceration and the dependent variable is maternal mental health. For the moment, let's imagine that the study determined at a particular point in time whether a child's mother suffered from depression and whether the child's father was in prison. The study finds that the mother is more likely to suffer from depression if the father is incarcerated.

What if a woman's mental health influenced her choice of romantic partner (or her sexual behavior or her contraception practice)? What if, as a result, mental-health problems in one way or another made some women more likely to have children with men whose criminal behavior would later lead them to be incarcerated? In that case, the mother's mental health and father's incarceration would be associated with one another. We would observe this association even if the father's incarceration had no effect at all on the mother's mental health. In effect, we have our independent and dependent variables switched around: The mother's mental health should really be the independent variable, and the father's incarceration should be the dependent variable.

reverse causality The possibility that the dependent variable influences the independent variable.

lagged dependent variables Past values of the dependent variable.

reciprocal causality A situation where two variables are both a cause and an effect of each other.

exogenous variation Special circumstances that are like natural experiments, in which differences in the independent variable are induced by events that ostensibly have nothing to do with the characteristics of the individual.

The term **reverse causality** refers to the possibility that the dependent variable influences the independent variable. Reverse causality is a type of confounding in which the confounding variable is the dependent variable at an earlier point in time. In our scenario, a woman's past mental health influenced her romantic choices, and past mental health also influences current mental health.

Regression analysis assumes we have correctly designated which variable is independent and which is dependent. If we set up the equation incorrectly, regression analysis will misattribute any influence of a dependent variable on an independent variable to the influence of the independent variable on the dependent variable. Say we had data on how regularly people brushed their teeth and how white their teeth were. If we did a regression analysis in which tooth-brushing was our dependent variable and tooth-whiteness was our independent variable, we might mistakenly conclude that people brushed their teeth more because they had whiter teeth, rather than the other way around. Reverse causality can lead researchers to mistake the consequences of problems for their causes, which, in turn, can lead to recommended interventions that fail to address a problem's real causes.

One important strategy for addressing reverse causality is analysis of longitudinal data. Recall from Chapter 7 that *longitudinal data* have been collected from respondents at multiple points in time. If the dependent variable has been measured at several points in time, then the model can include past values of the dependent variable as control variables. These past values are sometimes called **lagged dependent variables**, because of the time lag between the measure we use as a control variable and the measure we use as our dependent variable.

The study of fathers' incarceration and mothers' mental health was based on longitudinal data. As a result, the researchers were able to specifically account for reverse causality by including a mother's earlier mental health as a control variable. The study's results demonstrate the importance of longitudinal data, because about 25% of the relationship between a father's incarceration and a mother's mental health appeared to be directly or indirectly the result of reverse causality. However, a statistically and practically significant relationship between a father's incarceration and a mother's mental health remained even after the lagged variable was taken into account, thus strengthening the hypothesis that a father's incarceration did have negative effects on a mother's mental health.

The use of longitudinal data is the most important approach to reverse causality, but it is not a perfect solution. The best longitudinal data contain high-quality measurements taken at many points in time that are relatively close together. Because longitudinal data are expensive to collect, the best available longitudinal data for many sociological research questions often fall short of this ideal.

To understand the limitations of longitudinal data, consider the question of whether becoming unemployed causes depression. We can easily imagine how losing one's job may cause someone to become depressed, but we can also easily imagine how depressive episodes may result in people quitting or losing their jobs. Sociologists often confront such examples of **reciprocal causality**, where two variables are both a cause and an effect of each other. If our longitudinal data sets are spaced many years apart, we may not be able to determine which changed first, job status or mental health.

In this situation, researchers can try to gain some leverage by looking for examples of exogenous variation in the independent variable. By **exogenous variation**, we mean special circumstances that are like natural experiments, in which differences in the

THE UNITED STATES: A LONELY SOCIETY?

The headline in *USA Today* lamented, "25% of Americans Have No One to Confide In." "The Lonely American Just Got Lonelier," announced the *New York Times*. Both headlines described a study that appeared to show an alarming increase in social isolation in the United States: While 10% of Americans in 1985 had reported not having any confidants, 25% did so in 2004 (McPherson, Smith-Lovin, & Brashears, 2006).

If true, the finding would represent a remarkably large change in social isolation over only two decades. Sociologists are usually very skeptical of dramatic claims of social changes, but this study had anticipated the most obvious concerns. For example, sometimes people claim evidence of social change on the basis of survey samples of low or varying quality. However, the McPherson et al. study was based on the GSS, which has used consistent, high-quality sampling methods over time. Also, sometimes when people have claimed that surveys reveal significant social change, it turns out that comparisons are impossible because of differences in the way questions were worded. The 1985 and 2004 GSS, however, used exactly the same questions to determine the size of people's social networks.

Nevertheless, some sociologists remained unconvinced. Berkeley sociologist Claude Fischer (2009) maintained that two methodological issues mentioned by the investigators presented more serious problems than they had proposed.

To understand the issue, we need to describe how "having no confidants" was measured. Respondents were asked to think back over the previous 6 months and to name people with whom they had discussed important matters. Interviewers recorded up to five people and asked some follow-up questions about each person. Fischer noted that even though the particular method and questions used to measure people's social networks were the same in 1985 and 2004, the questions that preceded them had changed. The 2004 questions came very late in the GSS interview, when respondents had already been answering questions for over an hour. Worse, perhaps, the social network questions followed a battery of questions about what social organizations the respondents belonged to. Fischer worried that some of the 2004 respondents were tired by this point and had surmised that any people they listed as confidants would prompt follow-up questions. In other words, he worried that some people had simply not listed any confidants in order to get the interview over with faster.

The GSS decided to conduct an experiment in its 2010 survey. Respondents were asked the same social network

A recent study based on GSS data found a dramatic rise in social isolation among U.S. adults.

questions used in 1985 and 2004. One group in the experiment was asked the network questions after the long series of questions about social organizations, just like in 2004. A different group was not asked the social organizations questions first. If the 2004 findings represented a true change in social isolation, we would not expect a difference between the two randomly assigned groups. Fischer predicted, however, that the percentage of people reporting no confidants would be much lower in the group that did not receive the social organizations questions first.

Fischer was right. In the 2010 experiment, 21% of the respondents who received the social organizations questions first reported no confidants, a result similar to what had been observed in 2004. However, only 5% of the respondents who did not receive the social organizations questions first reported no confidants. This number was not significantly different from the 1985 observation.

A subsequent twist was uncovered by two other sociologists. Anthony Paik and Kenneth Sanchagrin wondered whether the problem might be less about tired and uncooperative respondents than about weary survey interviewers.

To test their hypothesis, Paik and Sanchagrin (2013) looked at the set of surveys conducted by each interviewer. They found that some interviewers in the 2004 GSS had much higher rates of respondents reporting no confidants than what would be expected by chance. One interviewer did 28 interviews, and in 27 of them the respondent was recorded as having no confidants. In sum, the difference between the 1985 and 2004 surveys now seems very likely to have reflected differences in the conduct of the survey, and not any dramatic change in the true amount of social isolation among U.S. adults.

independent variable are induced by events that ostensibly have nothing to do with the characteristics of the individual. As we noted earlier, even when we adjust for measurable differences between individuals, we often have to worry about unmeasured differences. The point of searching for exogenous variation is to identify circumstances in which variation in the independent variable is likely uncorrelated even with these unmeasured differences.

For example, to isolate the effects of job loss on depression, researchers have studied cases where people have lost their jobs due to a business closing or moving elsewhere. The key advantage here is that, at least in comparison to people with similar jobs and similar businesses that did not happen to close or move, we would not presume in this circumstance that a worker's depression caused his or her job loss. So, in this special circumstance, we can rule out one side of an otherwise reciprocal relationship. Consequently, in this case, we can estimate the effect that job loss unrelated to one's personal characteristics has on depression.

CONCEPT CHECKS

1 | Draw a path diagram for the example concerning paternal incarceration and maternal mental health showing how to use longitudinal data to examine reverse causality. Label the lagged dependent variable.

2 | Living in a poor neighborhood is associated with many negative economic, health, and educational outcomes. Using living in a poor neighborhood as one variable, name a second variable that may show reciprocal causality. How could you test your hypothesis?

3 | Provide one reason why having higher income might have a positive influence on one's physical health and one reason why having better physical health may have positive consequences for one's income.

4 | Some research has tried to estimate the effect of income on health by comparing the health of state lottery winners several years after the win to the health of people who play the lottery regularly but have never won. How does this research use exogenous variation to address the problem of reciprocal causality?

MODERATORS AND MEDIATORS

Regression analysis allows us to estimate the relationship between an independent variable and a dependent variable and to see whether the relationship changes when possible confounding variables are added as control variables. However, simply showing that a relationship exists, even after taking control variables into account, still tells us little about *why* the two variables are related. Even if we are very confident that our evidence shows that the independent variable causes the dependent variable, we still do not know *why*.

To answer the "why" question, sociologists often develop specific hypotheses about moderating variables and mediating variables (Figure 15.10). *Moderating variables* help us determine "for whom" or "under what conditions" an independent variable affects a dependent variable. *Mediating variables* help us answer "why" and "how" an independent variable affects a dependent variable. We describe these two concepts in turn, illustrating each with examples from sociological research.

Moderating Variables

The "fatherhood wage premium" refers to the tendency for men to earn higher wages after they become a father. A good deal of research indicates that this change cannot be explained by confounding factors. That is, becoming a father really does appear to increase wages by prompting men either to work harder at their jobs or to pursue opportunities to raise their wages more aggressively. Why do men behave in this manner? Sociologist Alexandra Killewald (2013) hypothesized that becoming a father motivates new fathers to pursue higher wages.

If this particular explanation was correct, Killewald reasoned that there would be important differences in the size of the fatherhood wage premium for different fathers. She proposed that the relationship would be strongest when the man's social identity as a new father was least ambiguous. Specifically, she hypothesized that the premium would be highest when a man was the biological father of the child, when the father lived with the child, and when the father was married to the child's mother. Killewald's findings were consistent with this hypothesis. Indeed, in her data, she found no clear evidence of a fatherhood wage premium unless all three of these conditions were met. Moreover, for married fathers who lived with their children, the fatherhood premium was statistically significant only for men whose wives did not work full-time.

Killewald's study provides an excellent example of moderating variables. A **moderating variable** modifies or "moderates" the relationship between an independent variable and a dependent variable. In Killewald's study, the relationship between fatherhood and wages changed depending on several characteristics of the father's relationship to the child and mother. These characteristics are moderating variables. Moderators are sometimes called *interaction effects*, because the independent variable interacts with the moderating variable in its influence on the dependent variable. We show more specifically how moderating variables are included in regression analyses in Box 15.1.

As another example, let's consider sociological research on where people live in the United States after they are released from prison. Neighborhoods affect people's lives in many ways, and so incarceration may have lasting negative effects on people by leading them to live in worse neighborhoods than they otherwise would have. Blacks and Latinos who are released from prison are particularly likely to live in very poor neighborhoods. We might then imagine that race moderates the relationship between having been incarcerated and neighborhood of residence, so that the effect of incarceration on where people live is more pronounced for minorities than it is for whites.

Sociologist Mike Massoglia and colleagues (2013) showed that race does indeed moderate the association between incarceration and residence, but in precisely the opposite way. The key factor that needs to be taken into account here is where people lived *before* they went to prison. Minority ex-offenders disproportionately live in bad neighborhoods, but they lived in equally bad neighborhoods prior to incarceration. White ex-offenders, however, may live in somewhat better neighborhoods than their minority counterparts, but the white ex-offenders still live in worse neighborhoods

FIGURE 15.10 Moderating versus Mediating Variables

Moderating variable	For whom	An independent variable affects a dependent variable.
	Under what conditions	
Mediating variable	Why	
	How	

moderating variable
A variable that modifies or "moderates" the relationship between an independent variable and a dependent variable.

BOX 15.1   Regression Analysis with a Moderating Variable

To see how regression analysis includes moderators in practice, we can pose the hypothesis that the relationship between getting a college degree and income is stronger for men than it is for women. We could test this idea by conducting a regression analysis using this equation:

$$\text{Income} = a + b_1 \text{(college degree)} + b_2 \text{(female)} + b_3 \text{(college degree} \times \text{female)}$$

Table 15.6 shows the results we estimate using a statistical software package. For men, the difference in earnings for those who have a college degree versus those who do not have a college degree is given by the coefficient for college degree (b_1). That is, men with college degrees report earning, on average, $63,800 more each year than men without college degrees.

For women, the difference between those with and without college degrees is determined by adding together the college degree (b_1) and college degree × female (b_3) coefficients (63.8 – 30.4 = 33.4). Women with college degrees report earning, on average, $33,400 more each year than women without college degrees. As a result, the difference in earnings associated with a college degree is $30,400 ($63,800 – $33,400) higher among men than it is among women.

The combination of gender and education in our data mean there are four groups: men and women with and without college degrees. Table 15.7 shows how we can use these coefficients to calculate the conditional means for each group. For example, because we have coded the data such that female = 1 and college degree = 1, the values of the independent variables are 0 for men without college degrees, meaning that b_1, b_2, and b_3 all drop out of the equation because we are multiplying those by 0. The conditional mean for men without college degrees is therefore equal to $53,200. Meanwhile, for men with college degrees, b_1 stays in the equation (multiplied by 1), but b_2 and b_3 drop out, so the conditional mean is $a + b_1$ ($53,200 + $63,800 = $117,000).

TABLE 15.6   Regression Model with Income as Dependent Variable

	Coefficient (in Thousands of Dollars)
College degree (b_1)	63.8
Female (b_2)	–19.6
College degree × female (b_3)	–30.4
Intercept (a)	53.2

Source: General Social Survey, 2000–2014, full-time employees ages 30–65, with income scaled to 2014 dollars.

TABLE 15.7   How to Compute the Conditional Means for the Four Groups

Men without college degrees	a	53.2
Men with college degrees	$a + b_1$	53.2 + 63.8
Women without college degrees	$a + b_2$	53.2 – 19.6
Women with college degrees	$a + b_1 + b_2 + b_3$	53.2 + 63.8 – 19.6 – 30.4

than they did before they went to prison. In other words, white ex-offenders experience a larger drop in the quality of their neighborhoods after their time in prison. Massoglia and colleagues showed that incarceration appears to have no effect on neighborhood quality for minorities, but it has a substantial negative effect for whites.

Moderating variables are important for testing hypotheses because these hypotheses often imply that relationships should be stronger for some groups than for others. Earlier we described research on whether the incarceration of fathers had negative effects on the mental health of mothers. Even though the researchers used many control variables, one might still worry about unmeasured differences between mothers who have children with fathers who become incarcerated and other mothers.

In this research project, however, the researchers used a measure of whether the father had been incarcerated recently (within 2 years of when the mother's mental health was measured) or incarcerated further back. The reasoning was this: If paternal incarceration really was detrimental to mothers' mental health, then the relationship should be stronger for recent incarceration than for incarceration that had happened years earlier because the stress of the transition might fade over time. In other words, the researchers predicted that the recency of incarceration would moderate the relationship between paternal incarceration and maternal depression. The research confirmed this prediction, strengthening the evidence for the conclusion that incarceration has negative mental-health consequences for mothers, especially in the immediate term after the imprisonment happens.

Mediating Variables

About 30% of non-Hispanic white women are obese by conventional measurement standards; for African American women, the obesity rate is 54% (Ogden et al., 2006). While blacks have made considerable progress on a wide variety of economic and health disadvantages over the past half century, the obesity gap between white women and black women has actually increased (Johnston & Lee, 2011). The most immediate predictors of obesity are diet and exercise. While individuals vary a great deal on both, evidence indicates that, on average, black women consume more calories than white women, and black women also exercise less.

Researchers David Johnston and Wang-Shen Lee (2011) used regression analysis to evaluate the importance of diet and exercise for explaining the obesity gap between black women and white women. According to their findings, only about 10% of the gap could be explained by exercise differences, while about 40% could be explained by differences in diet. Their findings suggest that public health officials seeking to reduce obesity differences between blacks and whites would likely see more benefit from policies that focus on diet than from policies that focus on exercise.

In Johnston and Lee's study, diet and exercise are **mediating variables**, which measure some aspect of a mechanism by which an independent variable is hypothesized to influence a dependent variable. They are sometimes called *intervening variables* because they "intervene" between the independent variable and the dependent variable. In our example, racial differences in diet and exercise are hypothesized to account for part of the racial difference in obesity rates. By adding measures of diet and exercise to a regression model, we can evaluate how much of the association between

mediating variable
A variable that links the independent variable to the dependent variable.

race and obesity can be explained by these mediators. We show how mediating variables can be included in a regression analysis in Box 15.2.

Mediating variables allow us to evaluate the potential importance of different hypothesized mechanisms for how an independent variable affects a dependent variable. For example, we can look again at the study of fathers' incarceration and mothers' mental health. Because the study used longitudinal data, the researchers were able to look at recent changes in a woman's life as potential mediators. For example, the researchers proposed that the father's incarceration may have negative consequences for the mother's material well-being and that this variable, in turn, may increase her risk of depression. The results supported this hypothesis. Measures of financial well-being accounted for about 25% of the relationship between paternal incarceration and maternal mental health. That these mediating variables work as hypothesized gives us more confidence in the researchers' conclusion that paternal incarceration influences maternal mental health. It also adds credence to the researchers' hypotheses about the specific nature of this influence.

Mediation analyses can also help assess the potential influence of interventions. For example, if measures of financial well-being do account for about 25% of the relationship between paternal incarceration and maternal mental health, we might conclude that a social intervention designed to minimize the financial consequences of a father being incarcerated would partly, but not entirely or even mostly, reduce the mental-health consequences for a mother.

Mediation versus Confounding

Mediating variables can be easily confused with confounding variables. In both cases, we add new variables to our regression analysis and see how the relationship between the independent variable and the dependent variable changes. With confounding, we add variables that we hypothesize directly or indirectly affect both the independent variable and the dependent variable. We use confounding to determine if the relationship between the independent variable and the dependent variable could be due to the common influence of the confounding variable, instead of due to the independent variable causing the dependent variable. For example, in our earlier example of confounding, we showed that the negative relationship between working full-time and praying daily could be explained by the common influence of gender on both variables.

In the Johnston and Lee study, meanwhile, the point of adding diet and exercise to the regression analysis is not that we think people's diets somehow change their race. Instead, we are trying to explain why racial differences in obesity exist. Racial differences in diet and exercise are hypothesized to be possibilities, and Johnston and Lee's study compares the relative importance of each.

To make sure we are clear on the difference between confounding variables and mediating variables, we can use a new example: the long-debated question of whether having a large number of siblings has negative consequences for academic achievement. More siblings are certainly associated with lower achievement in the United States and many other countries (e.g., Blake, 1989). However, some researchers are skeptical that this association is due to additional siblings actually causing lower student achievement (Angrist, Lavy, & Schlosser, 2010).

BOX 15.2   Regression Analysis with a Mediating Variable

As an example of mediating variables in practice, let's consider differences between black Americans' average incomes and white Americans' average incomes. Compared to whites, blacks have lower average incomes and are also less likely to have a college degree. We can ask whether having a college degree mediates the relationship between race and income and, if so, how much of a difference it makes.

To do so, let's fit two regression models, summarized in Table 15.8. In model 1, the only independent variable is whether someone is black or white (we omit all other respondents in this analysis to keep things simple, and we look only at people who are working full-time). The –9.2 estimate for the coefficient for blacks in this model means that, on average, blacks who work full-time report making $9,200 per year less than whites.

In model 2, we add variables for the highest educational degree that the respondent has received. The coefficients are relative to someone who did not graduate from high school. The coefficient of 5.2 for high school means that someone who graduated from high school but received no higher degree makes $5,200 more on average than someone who did not graduate from high school. Meanwhile, the coefficient of 21.9 for bachelor's degree means that someone with a bachelor's degree makes $21,900 more on average than someone without a high school diploma. (Again, these numbers are only for people who work full-time, so they do not include the advantage that higher education provides in making it easier to get a full-time job.)

In model 2, the coefficient for blacks is –4.8. In other words, when we adjust for differences between blacks and whites in educational attainment, a $4,800 difference in average income remains. In other words, about $4,400 of the original $9,200 difference between blacks and whites (about 48%) is explained by differences in educational attainment. Thus, differences in educational attainment mediate about half of the difference, but we would need to look elsewhere to explain the rest of the difference.

TABLE 15.8   Regression Models with Respondents' Income* as Dependent Variable

	Model 1	Model 2
Blacks (compared to whites)	–9.2	–4.8
Education (compared to no high school diploma)		
High school		5.2
Junior college		16.4
Bachelor's degree		21.9
Degree above bachelor's degree (e.g., master's, PhD, MD)		41.3
Intercept	29.8	17.4
N	3,399	3,399

*In thousands of dollars.
Source: General Social Survey, 2000–2014. Income scaled to 2014 dollars. Analyses limited to GSS respondents who are identified either as black or white and who work full-time.

One alternative is that the relationship is confounded by the family's socioeconomic status (SES). Families with lower SES in the United States have more children, and, even for families with the same number of children, children from families with lower SES have lower academic achievement. So, even if siblings have no influence on academic achievement, we would still expect to see an association because of the confounding influence of SES on both the independent variable and dependent variable.

In contrast, a leading theory for why more siblings might negatively affect achievement is that siblings divert parental attention and resources away from one another (Downey, 1995). The idea here is that a larger number of siblings reduces parental investment. Here, we might treat a measure of parental investment as a mediating variable, asking how much of the relationship between number of siblings and academic achievement can be explained by this measure of parental investment.

We contrast the two scenarios with the path diagrams in Figure 15.11. In Figure 15.11a, a confounding variable (socioeconomic status) influences both the independent variable (number of siblings) and the dependent variable (academic achievement). As a result, confounding variables make it harder to determine if the independent variable actually causes or affects the dependent variable. A mediating variable also influences the dependent variable, but instead of influencing the independent variable, it is a consequence of the independent variable. We analyze mediating variables to try to account for how an independent variable influences a dependent variable.

In practice, the difference between mediating variables and confounding variables is not always clear-cut. Consider again the example we have used frequently in this chapter: how living in a bad neighborhood can negatively affect a child's well-being. Part of the problem here is that individual characteristics are strongly related to where one lives, so the effect of living in a bad neighborhood is hard to distinguish from the effect of growing up in a poor family. Regression analyses routinely control for parental income, treating it as a confounding variable.

As sociologists Patrick Sharkey and Felix Elwert (2011) have pointed out, however, bad neighborhoods may be partly responsible for parents' low income (for instance, by limiting nearby employment opportunities). Over the longer term, then, parental income may also be a mediating variable for how bad neighborhoods affect children, because families may live in bad neighborhoods for generations, and so bad neighborhoods could have negative effects on children by first having negative effects on parents' income. Sociologists are still trying to figure out how best to represent relationships of reciprocal causality between an independent variable (in our example, neighborhoods) and a confounding/mediating variable (parents' income). What is clear is that longitudinal data are absolutely vital, as such data provide the best way to see whether and how changes in one variable precede changes in another. When we start to

FIGURE 15.11 Distinction between a Confounding Variable and a Mediating Variable

Confounding variables obscure whether or not the independent variable causes the dependent variable, whereas mediating variables represent a possible path through which the independent variable causes the dependent variable.

(a) Example of socioeconomic status as confounding variable

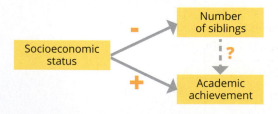

(b) Example of parental investment as mediating variable

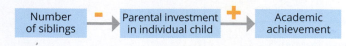

think about how reciprocal causality can unfold across generations, we see the value of longitudinal data that do not simply follow individuals over parts of their lives but rather follow families over much longer periods.

CONCLUSION

In this chapter, we explained how researchers use numerical data not only to describe societies but also to test ideas about how social life operates. The research techniques that use quantitative data typically take considerable advanced training to master. The range of techniques is so vast and ever-changing that researchers who do quantitative work acquire new technical skills throughout their careers. The information provided in this chapter is rudimentary; nevertheless, we have sought to provide a sampling of the challenges that researchers face in practice and the tools they have to address them.

In our discussions about confounding and reciprocal causality, we emphasized that it is difficult to draw conclusions about cause-and-effect relationships because many of the questions that sociologists study are not amenable to experiments. In closing, we should emphasize that for many research questions, no satisfactory solution is to be found in a single analysis using a single data source. Instead, many questions end up requiring multiple strategies and multiple different sources of data, and results may be published as a series of different articles by groups of researchers who are working either together or separately. Doing quantitative data analysis often requires the researcher to play the role of a detective, trying to figure out the solutions to the mysteries posed by a research question. Often, it also requires the researcher to play the role of a courtroom lawyer, attempting to figure out what types of analyses must be done in order to assemble the most persuasive case about a hypothesis.

End-of-Chapter Review

Summary

Social researchers use quantitative data analysis not only to describe populations but to test ideas about how social life operates. Multivariate methods are used to explore how three or more variables are related, enabling researchers to ask *how* and *why* questions.

Significance Testing

- When values of one variable are more likely to co-occur with values of another variable, there is an association, or correlation, between the variables. The association can be positive or negative.

- A finding is statistically significant when the pattern of association between variables is strong enough for researchers to be confident that it reflects a true association in the population. Social researchers conventionally aim to be 95% confident that observed associations in the data reflect true associations in the population.

- Significance testing refers to the process of assessing whether associations between variables are strong enough to reject the null hypothesis that there is no true association between variables in the population. A p-value refers to the probability that we would observe a difference as large as the difference that we actually observed if the null hypothesis were true. Social researchers typically consider findings to be statistically significant when the p-value they obtain is lower than 5%.

- Two methods for calculating p-values are chi-square tests and t tests. A chi-square test is used with cross-tabulations of categorical variables. A t test is used with continuous variables, and tests whether the mean of the dependent variable differs depending on the value of the independent variable.

- Statistical power refers to a study's ability to detect statistically significant differences between groups, which maximizes researchers' ability to obtain a low p-value. Two aspects of a study that are important for statistical power are how large the sample is and how big the differences between groups are expected to be.

- Statistically significant findings tell researchers how confident they can be that the associations they observe in their data reflect true associations in the population, but they do not indicate that the association between variables is causal.

Confounding Factors

- Confounding occurs when two variables are consistently associated with one another despite having no causal relationship.

- Elaboration is a strategy for assessing confounding and determining whether the independent variable and dependent variable remain associated when the confounding variable is held constant. Another way to assess confounding is by conducting regression analysis with a control variable.

- A suppressor variable hides or reverses the direction of a true causal relationship. Suppression is rarer than confounding in social research, because social life is patterned so that advantage begets advantage.

- A key limitation of multiple regression analysis is that it can only account for variables that are included in the data set and have been measured accurately.

Reverse Causality

- Reverse causality is the possibility that the dependent variable influences the independent variable.
- Using longitudinal data is an important strategy for assessing reverse causality. If the dependent variable has been measured at multiple points in time, the statistical model can include past values of the dependent variable as control variables.
- Reciprocal causality occurs when two variables are both a cause and effect of each other. This can be assessed by looking for circumstances in which differences in the independent variable are unrelated to the characteristics of the individual.

Moderators and Mediators

- Moderating variables can be used to assess "for whom" or "under what conditions" an independent variable affects a dependent variable. Mediating variables explain "why" and "how" an independent variable affects a dependent variable.
- Moderating variables modify the relationship between the independent and dependent variables. Moderators are important for hypothesis testing, because many social research hypotheses assume relationships should be stronger for some groups.
- Mediating variables allow researchers to understand *how* an independent variable affects a dependent variable.

Key Terms

association, **497**
chi-square statistic, **499**
chi-square test, **499**
confound, **506**
confounding, **505**
control variable, **511**
elaboration, **508**
exogenous variation, **520**
lagged dependent variables, **520**

mediating variable, **525**
moderating variable, **523**
multivariate methods, **496**
negative association, **497**
normal distribution, **501**
null hypothesis, **498**
path diagram, **505**
positive association, **497**
practical significance, **504**

p-value, **498**
reciprocal causality, **520**
reverse causality, **520**
significance testing, **498**
statistical power, **502**
statistically significant, **497**
suppressor variable, **516**
t test, **501**

Exercise

For this exercise, pick an activity that you enjoy doing. Now, say that you read a news story about a survey in which people who do the activity you identified reported being less happy than people who do not engage in that activity.

- First, propose an explanation for how the activity really could lead people to being less happy. Depending on the activity you've selected, the explanation may seem highly plausible or a bit fanciful.
- Second, propose a way in which the relationship between the activity and unhappiness could be confounding. Be specific.
- Third, suggest how researchers might be able to provide additional evidence about the relationship between the activity and unhappiness. That is, what specific research might help researchers understand the association?

Laurence Ralph conducted fieldwork in Chicago, focusing on the relations between black youth and the police. The process by which he transformed his field notes and other raw data into his ethnography *Renegade Dreams* is called qualitative data analysis.

ANALYSIS OF QUALITATIVE DATA

Anthropologist Laurence Ralph wrote the following field note at 10:11 p.m. on March 3, 2009:

This morning Mr. Otis tells me that the police are going to check the blue-light footage from his street, to try and figure out why the eighteen-year-old Eastwood boy was shot last week. Mr. Otis paces in front of me, gripping the community newspaper, the *Eastwood Gazette*, which features a photograph of the slain teenager. Glancing at the paper, then shaking his head, Mr. Otis tells me the part of the story that is not in the newspaper: "Police say the boy ran from them"—he says, still pacing—"ducked and dodged through an alleyway when he saw them right? When the officers cornered him, they say he pointed a gun at them, so they shot to kill. And believe me, they succeeded. But, get this, man: The kid was shot in the back. The boy's mama says he was scared stiff of the police. A couple days ago, before he was shot and all, she said some cops told the boy, 'We're gonna get you.' So, now she's trying to sue the city. She says the police planted the gun. She says the police wanna turn her son into a criminal, you know, justify the shooting—make it seem okay."

After I left Mr. Otis's stoop, I take the paper from him and read it. Mr. Otis is right. Both the city of Chicago and the family of the slain boy are waiting for footage from the blue-light video, waiting for the footage to prove that the boy was either a criminal or unjustifiably killed. But who's to say what the footage actually reveals? Does a blurry image of a teenage boy running from the police prove that he's guilty? Or does the frame capture a boy who knows he is always presumed to be guilty? And maybe that's why he's running. (Ralph, 2014, pp. 165–166)

Ralph was conducting ethnographic research for his PhD dissertation on gangs and violence in Chicago, which ultimately led to the publication of *Renegade Dreams: Living through Injury in Gangland Chicago* (Ralph, 2014). His fieldwork explored the cycle of violence in Chicago and the relations between the police and black urban youth. Since then, the shooting of unarmed black men by police has catapulted police brutality into the national spotlight and inspired the Black Lives Matter movement.

Ralph includes the snippet from his field notes in his book partly because he wanted to show readers the progression from the raw material he collected in the field to the polished narrative exposition in the book. The data-collection methods discussed in Chapters 10 and 11 often generate voluminous amounts of text. With so many conversation topics, ideas, and facts, how do researchers decide what is important? How do scholars like Laurence Ralph transform thousands of pages of field notes or hundreds of transcripts of in-depth interviews into a cohesive whole that puts forth a convincing theory or explanation? **Qualitative data analysis** is the process by which researchers draw substantive findings from qualitative data, such as text, audio, video, and photographs.

We begin this chapter by describing the challenges and different types of qualitative research. Next, we examine some of the debates regarding the purposes and scope of qualitative data analysis. Lastly, we describe the standard steps in qualitative data analysis, including the role of qualitative data analysis software.

qualitative data analysis
The process by which researchers draw substantive findings from qualitative data, such as text, audio, video, and photographs.

QUALITATIVE DATA ANALYSIS: PRODUCT AND PROCESS

It is easy for beginning researchers, and even seasoned researchers, to feel overwhelmed by the sheer volume of their notes. For example:

- One week in a field site can yield as many as 200 to 300 pages of field notes.

- Ethnographers sometimes spend years in the field, which often leads to thousands of pages of notes (Miles & Huberman, 1994, p. 56).

- In-depth interviews that last an hour can produce 80 pages of text. When researchers conduct hundreds of interviews, the result is thousands of pages of transcribed conversation.

Researchers use several metaphors to capture what the beginning of a large research project feels like: driving in the fog when you can only see a few yards ahead; climbing a mountain when you can only see the trail as it winds through the woods. The Chinese philosopher Lao Tzu said, "A journey of a thousand miles begins with a single step." This is the best approach to tackling a large amount of data—one step at a time.

Like all social science, qualitative analysis requires a mix of logic, theory, and systematic evidence about the social world. Qualitative data analysis is often described as "creative"—an art rather than a science. This description is accurate. Any kind of data analysis—quantitative or qualitative—requires creativity. However, the analysis of qualitative data can be less straightforward than the statistical analysis of quantitative data. There is less agreement about terminology, as well as the steps to be followed, in qualitative data analysis. Nonetheless, many qualitative researchers do follow a similar process, which we discuss later in this chapter.

All social science research—whether quantitative or qualitative—must meet three key criteria. It should be (1) transparent, (2) logical, and (3) rigorous. *Transparency* means providing enough information about the decisions made during the research and analysis so that readers can evaluate the researcher's conclusions. The *logic* and the *rigor* of the analysis are grounds for either supporting or challenging the conclusions of the research.

TYPES OF QUALITATIVE RESEARCH

Analysis of qualitative data rests on assumptions about the nature of social science, the goal of social science research, and philosophies of social science. The **positivist approach** assumes a reality external to the observer that can be objectively described and analyzed with scientific standards. In contrast, the **interpretivist approach** does not seek objective truth but rather a faithful rendering of the research subjects' interpretations of events, social movements, or any other phenomenon that the researcher is studying. The interpretivist approach is rooted in the anthropologist's quest to understand a specific culture, where culture means a communally defined subjective understanding. The anthropologist Clifford Geertz claimed that what we think of as facts or data cannot be truly objective because they are really "our own constructions of other

positivist approach An approach to research that assumes a reality external to the observer that can be objectively described and analyzed with scientific standards.

interpretivist approach An approach to research whereby the researcher does not seek objective truth but rather a faithful rendering of the subjects' interpretations of events, social movements, or any other phenomenon that the researcher is studying.

Newman sought to understand both why school shootings, such as the 1997 shooting at Health High School in Paducah, Kentucky, occur as well as how people in these communities interpret and explain them.

people's constructions of what they and their compatriots are up to" (qtd. in Roth & Mehta, 2002, p. 134).

Take, for example, sociologist Katherine Newman's study of school shootings in Paducah, Kentucky, and Jonesboro, Arkansas, documented in the book *Rampage: The Social Roots of School Shootings* (see Chapter 3; Newman, 2004). Newman and her team conducted participant observation research and in-depth interviews with 200 people in the two communities in 2001, after a high school student shot and killed two students and wounded five in a shooting at Heath High School in Paducah in December 1997 and two middle school students killed four students and injured ten in a middle school in Jonesboro in March 1998. They examined their in-depth interview data with witnesses to school shootings—parents, teachers, and community leaders— to answer the positivist question "Why do school shootings occur?" with the goal of preventing such shootings in the future.

They also used the data to explore the interpretivist question "How do people in these communities understand these school shootings, and what do their interpretations tell us about them?" (Roth & Mehta, 2002, p. 133). They described and explained differences and similarities in accounts of the shootings without necessarily presuming that one interpretation was more "correct" or true than another (Roth & Mehta, 2002). While these two approaches—the positivist and the interpretivist—represent two poles on a continuum, sociologists Wendy Roth and Jal Mehta (2002), members of Newman's team of researchers, argue that they can be combined. According to Roth and Mehta, some people in the two communities thought the shootings were the result of the pressure of standardized tests. Others thought that one of the shootings could be explained by the fact that one shooter was taking the drug Ritalin.

From a positivist position, the researchers had enough evidence to dismiss these explanations as incorrect. The shootings, they concluded, were partly a result of the failure to act on warnings the student shooters had made. They traced that failure to both the organizational structure of the schools, which impeded the sharing of information, as well as a reluctance in the small towns to talk about marginal or troubled children. Taking an interpretivist point of view, though, the researchers do not judge the veracity of the respondents' opinions. The people who blame the shootings on drugs or standardized testing were transmitting valuable information. These respondents were providing insights into their views of the world and using the experience of the school shootings to express their own fears and concerns about the societies they live in.

Another way of describing the distinction between a researcher's and a respondent's viewpoints is the distinction between emic and etic approaches. Researchers with an **emic focus** take on the respondent's viewpoint and use his or her language. Researchers with an **etic focus** maintain a distance from their respondents with the goal of achieving more scientific objectivity.

The positivist approach argues that qualitative researchers should follow the same general rules as quantitative researchers and answer the same kinds of questions that

emic focus An approach to research in which researchers take on the respondent's viewpoint and use his or her language.

etic focus An approach to research in which researchers maintain a distance from their respondents with the goal of achieving more scientific objectivity.

quantitative researchers address. Political scientists Gary King and his colleagues have argued that "the differences between the quantitative and qualitative traditions are only stylistic and are methodologically and substantively unimportant" (King, Keohane, & Verba, 1994, p. 4). Therefore, they argue, qualitative and quantitative research should be approached in the same way. The goal of analysis is to describe and explain the empirical world by following the rules of science and employing many of the criteria discussed earlier in this book, including replicability, statistical inference, validity, and reliability.

Other scholars believe there are profound differences between qualitative research and quantitative research. Gary Goertz and James Mahoney (2012) argue that while quantitative and qualitative researchers are both interested in causality, they generally approach their work in different ways. Quantitative scholars seek to discover and understand the **effects of causes**. They might ask, "What is the average effect of an independent variable X on a dependent variable Y?" In the case of school shootings, quantitative scholars might ask, "What is the effect of gender, psychological illness, social isolation, or gun ownership on the probability of being a school shooter?" In contrast, qualitative researchers adopt a **causes-of-effects** approach. They start with an outcome and ask, "What are the various X's that explain Y for a population of cases?" (Goertz & Mahoney, 2012, p. 43). In the case of school shootings, qualitative researchers might ask, "What are the various factors that caused the school shootings in Paducah and Jonesboro?"

In the effects-of-causes approach, the researcher would never sample on the dependent variable. In other words, the researcher would not look at school shooters and then ask if being socially isolated causes students to become shooters. Why? There may be many socially isolated students who would never shoot anyone. Likewise, many shooters are not socially isolated. Researchers would arrive at these conclusions only by comparing and contrasting. Thus, the correct sample would be all students, and researchers could examine whether being socially isolated increases or decreases the probability of being a shooter.

In the causes-of-effects approach, it does make sense to sample on the dependent variable. In this case, the researcher would look at all school shooters and try to identify what they have in common; that is, to identify the possible variables associated with becoming a school shooter. In the causes-of-effects approach, the researcher starts with the outcome and works backward to develop a causal model (Goertz & Mahoney, 2012, p. 43).

effects of causes An approach to establishing causality, generally associated with quantitative research, that tries to estimate the average effect of different independent variables on a particular outcome.

causes of effects An approach to establishing causality, generally associated with qualitative research, that starts with the outcome the researcher is trying to explain and works backwards to develop a causal model.

CONCEPT CHECKS

1 Contrast positivist and interpretivist approaches to qualitative research.

2 Some cultures do not eat pork. Give an etic and an emic reason for the taboo on eating pork.

3 A researcher tries to explain why some police officers shoot unarmed civilians by reading through thousands of pages of interviews with officers who have shot at unarmed civilians. Is this a causes-of-effects approach or an effects-of-causes approach? Explain your answer.

APPROACHES TO CAUSALITY IN QUALITATIVE ANALYSIS

A wide range of approaches are available for establishing causality in qualitative analysis. On one end of the spectrum, researchers who conduct qualitative comparative analysis (QCA) specifically set out to build causal models and use explicitly causal language. On the other end of the spectrum, researchers who focus on processes and mechanisms assume that qualitative analysis cannot establish causation; however, where a causal relationship does exist, qualitative research can be used to show how the causality operates. In other words, a QCA approach tries to isolate the combination of independent variables across cases that *causes* a given outcome, whereas a mechanism approach takes as a starting point the assertion that one group of variables causes a particular outcome and then tries to show the process by which those variables come together to cause that outcome. In between these two approaches, a great deal of qualitative research is more exploratory and suggestive—examining in an inductive way how events or characteristics might be related. This inductive research may suggest that a causal relationship exists but would rely on a different kind of sample or method to establish causality; for instance, an experiment or survey.

Qualitative Comparative Analysis

One important model that can guide researchers using the causes-of-effects approach is the QCA data analysis technique. Developed by Charles Ragin in the 1980s, this technique uses the rules of logic to establish causality in qualitative analysis (Ragin, 1987, 2008; Ragin & Amoroso, 2010). A simple example shows two of the most important elements of logical inference: necessary and sufficient causes. If you believe that a rain dance causes it to rain, logical inference can be used to assess this belief. Does it ever rain when the rain dance has not been performed? Then the rain dance cannot logically be the cause of the rain because it is not *necessary* for it to rain. Does it ever fail to rain after the rain dance is performed? Then the rain dance is not *sufficient* to create rain. It is possible to dance without rain and to rain without the dance. In this case, logic tells us that the rain dance is logically neither necessary nor sufficient for rain.

For QCA to work, you must identify a number of cases, some positive and some negative. *Positive* cases have the outcome you are interested in. *Negative* cases do not have the outcome. In our simplistic account, to logically look at the association between rain and rain dances we would need to look at many days, some positive cases where it rained, and some negative cases where it did not rain. Then we would check whether there was a rain dance on those days and look at the association.

An example from social science is, of course, more complicated. Most important, analysts are not just looking for the presence or absence of one variable; instead, they are often looking for the complex set of variables that are necessary and sufficient to explain a particular outcome. Suppose you are interested in comparing cities in the United States that passed sanctuary laws to protect undocumented immigrants from detention and

Why do some cities and not others become sanctuaries?

deportation. You want to know which factors make a city more likely to pass sanctuary laws. How would you proceed?

1. You would first do case studies of several cities—some with sanctuary laws and some without. Using these cases, you would then select important causal conditions that might influence the outcome; for example, the size of the immigrant population, the rapidity with which immigration has grown in the past 5 years, the political party affiliation of the mayor and the governor, the history of immigration to the city, and the city's unemployment rate. The choice of these variables is based on the researchers' deep knowledge of particular cases.

2. Next, you would make a **truth table**—a table that sorts cases by the presence or absence of these variables, some combination of which you believe provides a "recipe" that makes a city more likely to pass sanctuary laws.

3. You would then assess the consistency of the cases in each row with respect to the outcome. Are the rows consistent in the variables and outcome or is there inconsistency?

4. Finally, you would compare the rows to see what combinations of variables are associated with the outcome or the absence of the outcome.

Figure 16.1 is a truth table for our hypothetical sanctuary city study. Each row in the table is a combination of cases (cities) that have the same measurements for the causal conditions the researcher has identified on the basis of his or her knowledge of the cases. The eighth and ninth columns are the outcomes—are the cities sanctuaries or not? The last column is the consistency across the cases in the individual rows. There are 26 cities (or cases), and 13 have declared themselves sanctuaries and 13 have not. Four rows are consistent: They either all have declared themselves sanctuaries or all have declared themselves not to be sanctuaries. Two rows (row 2 and row 4) are not consistent. In row 2, half the cities with this set of characteristics are sanctuaries and half are not. In row 4, one city with these characteristics is a sanctuary and four are not. This outcome would lead the researcher to go back to the case studies of these cities to see what differentiates them. The four cities in row 2 are all the same on the variables in the table, so there must be at least one important variable that is not included in the analysis that differentiates them.

truth table A table, used in qualitative comparative analysis, that sorts cases by the presence or absence of certain variables.

FIGURE 16.1 Example of a Truth Table

This truth table is for a hypothetical study of factors associated with being an immigrant sanctuary city using qualitative comparative analysis.

Row	History of Immigration	Large Immigrant Population	Rapid Increase in Immigration	Democratic Mayor	Republican Governor	Low Unemployment	Cases with Sanctuary	Cases without Sanctuary	Consistency (% of cases with sanctuary)
1	0 (No)	1 (Yes)	1 (Yes)	1 (Yes)	1 (Yes)	1 (Yes)	0	5	100
2	0 (No)	0 (No)	1 (Yes)	0 (No)	1 (Yes)	0 (No)	2	2	50
3	1 (Yes)	0 (No)	0 (No)	1 (Yes)	0 (No)	0 (No)	3	0	100
4	1 (Yes)	1 (Yes)	0 (No)	1 (Yes)	0 (No)	1 (Yes)	1	4	25
5	1 (Yes)	1 (Yes)	1 (Yes)	1 (Yes)	0 (No)	0 (No)	0	2	100
6	1 (Yes)	1 (Yes)	0 (No)	0 (No)	1 (Yes)	1 (Yes)	7	0	100

The researcher should analyze these cases further to decide what other variable or variables might explain the outcome. One possible variable is the source country of the recent immigrants. All the cities in row 2 have experienced rapid recent immigration. Perhaps two of them have experienced immigration from Mexico, and the other two have experienced immigration from China. Could that be the source of the differences between them? A new truth table for those four cities might show that immigrants from China are more likely to lead to sanctuary cities than immigrants from Mexico, perhaps because of anti-Latino sentiment among natives. The goal of the reanalysis would be to identify variables that would result in a new truth table with no inconsistent rows. The "recipe" or combination of variables would lead to a consistent outcome across cities.

This analysis can get complicated fast, too complicated sometimes to be able to eyeball the table to determine what is happening. A computer program can aid in the analysis of the truth table, calculating the smallest number of combinations of variables that are associated with the outcome. In our sanctuary city example, a city's unemployment rate and population size do not matter (that is, they are not associated with a city's decision to become a sanctuary city). The factors that really matter may be having a history of immigration, a Democratic mayor, and a large undocumented population. In this hypothetical example, the logic of the truth table would lead to a plausible argument about the factors that drive particular cities to pass sanctuary laws.

Qualitative comparative analysis uses the language of causality: The goal of the method is not just to show an association between variables across cases but to use logic to identify necessary and sufficient causes of the outcome. Critiques of QCA include the difficulty of establishing causality and issues concerning measurement. QCA does not specify the mechanisms of causation—how the combination of variables leads to the outcome. The method also does not deal well with time and the effects of reverse causality. In our example of sanctuary cities, perhaps rapid recent immigration is not what causes cities to become sanctuaries but is rather an effect: Immigrants move to cities that are sanctuaries. Or perhaps there is a third variable that is unmeasured but may explain both rapid immigration and sanctuary status. In addition, qualitative comparative analysis operates on dichotomies—all the variables are measured as present or absent—hence measurement is not precise. What is the cutoff for high or low immigration or for low or high unemployment? These measurement decisions are in many ways arbitrary and can affect the reliability and validity of the measurements.

Processes and Mechanisms

Another important model that can guide researchers using the causes-of-effects approach to causality in qualitative research is the study of processes and mechanisms. Qualitative research can help us understand causality by showing us how one variable causes another. For instance, we know that education is associated with better health: The more education a person has, the better his or her health tends to be. But what is the mechanism through which education causes better health?

Diet is one mechanism through which education may affect health. Sociologist Caitlin Daniel (2016) wanted to understand how parents' behavior influences their children's food preferences. These preferences, she hypothesized, might be a mechanism through which social class affects health. Daniel studied how parents encourage their children to eat a wide variety of vegetables and other healthy foods. Previous studies had shown that children tend to refuse unfamiliar foods when they are first offered; children need to be offered these foods 8 to 15 times before they accept them. In her study of high-income and low-income parents and caregivers, Daniel found that the high-income parents repeatedly offered new foods to their children, even after the children refused the foods. In contrast, low-income parents were worried about the cost of buying food that their children would not eat. After a child rejected the food once, the parents stopped trying. Daniel proposed that a lack of concern about the cost of food could be one reason why higher-income people in general have wider tastes in food than lower-income people. The concern for cost may also partly explain the poorer-quality diets of lower-income people.

Because ethnography focuses on the "how" question, it is particularly well suited to showing how social processes unfold and the mechanisms that connect cause and effect (Small, 2009). How does income affect children's diets? How do young people decide which college to attend? How does the death of a parent affect his or her adult children (Umberson, 2003)? This concern with mechanisms, explaining exactly how X causes Y, is at the heart of analytical sociology, and it has helped us understand the interplay between micro and macro social phenomena: the ways that large social trends and influences shape the behavior of individuals (Hedstrom & Bearman, 2009).

Emerson, Fretz, and Shaw (1995, p. 146) outline the six questions that ethnographers use to uncover information about processes and mechanisms:

1. What are people doing? What are they trying to accomplish?

2. How exactly do they do this? What specific means or strategies do they use?

3. How do members talk about, characterize, and understand what is going on?

4. What assumptions are they making?

5. What do I see going on here? What did I learn from these notes?

6. Why did I include them?

Researchers operating under the mechanism approach to causality draw attention to social context, arguing that qualitative research is uniquely suited to unpacking the processes by which one variable influences another. For example, quantitative data may show that doctors do not tell terminally ill patients how much time they have left. But why do doctors resist making predictions when patients desire that information? What keeps doctors from sharing what they know about how terminal diseases progress? Nicholas Christakis, a sociologist and physician, interviewed physicians who care for the dying. His goal was to unpack their reluctance to share information with their patients, and he explained the ways in which their medical training and experiences with dying patients contributed to this reluctance (Christakis 1999).

Christakis found that doctors were not trained well in prognosis and tended to overestimate the survival of their patients. Doctors, he discovered, were unprepared for the emotional stress of conveying a negative

Nicholas Christakis's qualitative research can help us better understand why doctors avoid making prognoses for terminally ill patients.

prognosis and feared that it could act as a self-fulfilling prophesy: They were concerned that patients would change their behaviors in ways that might hasten their deaths. Doctors also feared that an inaccurate prognosis would be held against them. Christakis shows the harm in this reluctance to deliver critical health information: Patients are often not referred to hospice care early enough to reap all its benefits. Hospice care has been found to improve terminal patients' day-to-day lives through pain reduction and attention to their psychological and spiritual needs. In addition, those patients who prolong treatment when there is little or no chance of extending life often suffer through painful, unnecessary treatments.

CONCEPT CHECKS

1 | List three of the possible six questions that ethnographers should ask when studying explanatory processes and mechanisms.

2 | Give an example of a mechanism that explains how an independent variable of your choosing, *X*, causes a dependent variable of your choosing, *Y*.

INDUCTION, ABDUCTION, AND DEDUCTION

Qualitative research analysis generally can be characterized as using three types of reasoning: (1) inductive, (2) abductive, or (3) deductive. These terms, which were introduced in Chapter 2, refer to the relationship between data and generalization in scientific work.

Inductive research begins with the data and then generalizes or produces theoretical generalization from the data. It is a "bottom-up" approach, beginning at the bottom with the data and generalizing outward and upward from there. **Abductive research** attempts to build theory from "surprises" in empirical data. **Deductive research** is a "top-down" approach, where the theory or hypothesis drives the data-collection strategy and analysis. In this approach, the researcher develops a hypothesis rooted in theory and scholarly literature and then tests this hypothesis with the data. The deductive approach is much more common in quantitative research than in qualitative research, so we do not cover it in this chapter. More common in qualitative research is the extended case study approach, which begins with theory and uses case studies to test the theory.

Inductive Approaches: Grounded Theory

In 1967, sociologists Barney G. Glaser and Anselm L. Strauss published *The Discovery of Grounded Theory: Strategies for Qualitative Research*. Their book promoted a systematic, inductive approach to qualitative research called **grounded theory**, which suggests that qualitative researchers should extrapolate conceptual relationships from data rather than formulate testable hypotheses from existing theory. They labeled the approach *grounded theory* because concepts are built from the ground up through a line-by-line analysis of the field notes, interview notes, or transcripts. The term implies that the data speak for themselves, and theory will grow from the data (Charmaz, 2014). Note, however, that "grounded theory" is *not* a theory but rather a method of analyzing qualitative data inductively in order to generate theory.

inductive research Research that begins with the data and then generalizes or produces theoretical generalization from the data.

abductive research Research that attempts to build theory from "surprises" in empirical data.

deductive research Research that takes a "top-down" approach, where the theory or hypothesis drives the data-collection strategy and analysis.

grounded theory A systematic, inductive approach to qualitative research that suggests that researchers should extrapolate conceptual relationships from data rather than formulate testable hypotheses from existing theory.

Grounded theory has become almost synonymous with induction in many researchers' minds. Often, the authors of qualitative articles and books say very little about how they analyzed their data, simply stating, "We used grounded theory to analyze our data." This broad description is not sufficient because many varieties of grounded theory have been developed since 1967.

Why has grounded theory become so influential in qualitative research? Glaser and Strauss were the first to describe how careful, systematic qualitative research should be conducted. Thus, grounded theory offered a "scientific" approach to what quantitative researchers in the 1960s and 1970s had diagnosed as the biased, impressionistic, and anecdotal nature of qualitative research. The inductive approach of grounded theory begins with qualitative material and encourages the researcher to produce concepts and theory from it, which leads to theory *generation* rather than mere theory *testing*.

Grounded theory requires a good deal of scientific rigor. For example, Glaser and Strauss (1967) advocated for what they called "theoretical sampling," or **purposive sampling**, whereby cases are deliberately selected on the basis of features that distinguish them from other cases. In a strict grounded theory approach, sampling is not an event that occurs at one point in time. Instead, researchers select interview cases as the study proceeds, with the goal of building on emerging findings. This is referred to as sequential sampling, which you learned about in Chapter 6. As data are collected, the researcher reaches **saturation**: Sampling and data collection are considered complete when new data do not lead to new conceptual categories or theoretical refinements.

In practice, few qualitative researchers implement the unfolding data collection suggested by a grounded theory approach. Practical demands of modern academic life, which include adhering to the requirements of the institutional review board (IRB) and writing grants to secure research funding, can prevent the perfect implementation of grounded theory. Grant applications often require researchers to specify the amount of time they will spend in the field, the sample sizes for interviews, and how the research speaks to and builds on previous literature. Researchers cannot just state that they will be in the field for some unspecified amount of time until they reach saturation. The specific steps of grounded theory that current qualitative researchers use are those associated with coding and writing memos, which we describe later in this chapter.

Alternatives to Grounded Theory: Abductive Research and the Extended Case Study Approach

The inductive nature of grounded theory allows researchers to learn from their respondents and to remain open-minded regarding their field observations. It sometimes allows surprising results and phenomena to emerge. When Sudhir Venkatesh was a graduate student at the University of Chicago, his professor sent him into an inner-city housing project with a questionnaire that asked, "How does it feel to be black and poor?" Venkatesh inadvertently starting talking to members of the Black Kings gang. Through a long period of inductive research, he concluded that the gangs operating in the housing project were highly complex operations with intricate hierarchies, and that the gangs provided a surprising amount of social services to the population of the projects. Venkatesh did not enter the field with any preconceived theory of gangs, but over the course of many years with the gang, he developed an inductive model of

purposive sampling A sampling strategy in which cases are deliberately selected on the basis of features that distinguish them from other cases.

saturation When new materials (interviews, observations, survey responses) fail to yield new insights and simply reinforce what the researcher already knows.

Diane Vaughan found that the *Challenger* disaster was not the result of rule-breaking but rather a consequence of the rules themselves.

how the gangs functioned in the projects. This research yielded one of the best-selling, most widely read sociological studies in recent decades. Yet, this extreme inductive research is not that practical or common. Most social scientists enter the field with a deep knowledge of the literature on the subject they are researching and general expectations about what they will find.

Timmermans and Tavory (2012) suggest that the best qualitative researchers are *sensitized* by the previous research on a topic. At the same time, they urge researchers to remain open to surprising or unexpected findings rather than confining themselves to testing a specific hypothesis. This is the *abductive* approach we mentioned earlier: "an inferential creative process of producing new hypotheses and theories based on surprising research evidence. A researcher is led away from old to new theoretical insights" (Timmermans & Tavory, 2012, p. 170). In effect, Timmermans and Tavory suggest qualitative researchers use both a deductive approach (comparing their data with the results predicted by existing theories) and an inductive approach (focusing on unexpected or anomalous findings that need new explanations).

For example, Diane Vaughan (1996) studied the decision of NASA scientists to launch the *Challenger* space shuttle in January 1986. The *Challenger* exploded 73 seconds into its flight, killing all seven astronauts aboard. The launch took place in very cold weather, and the explosion was traced to the failure of an O-ring seal in the solid rocket booster. That ring had not been designed to function in cold weather. Vaughan, a sociologist who studies organizations, began her study with the idea that the engineers had violated NASA rules in the lead-up to the disaster. She writes that her knowledge of organizational theory led her to hypothesize that there was pressure on the engineers to go ahead with the launch. The original government inquiry into the disaster pointed to this theory, concluding that NASA managers took risks because of economic pressures.

But Vaughan's interviews and study of the process leading to the launch decision indicated that her original theory of misconduct was not accurate. She found no evidence of misconduct: The engineers did not cut corners or violate rules or protocols. Vaughan traced all the decisions made about the solid rocket boosters from 1977 to 1985, finding that there was a gradual shift in the culture at NASA. A commitment to secrecy in the organization and an acceptance of risk better explained why the engineers went ahead with the launch despite the knowledge that the rings were not designed for the weather that day. No one broke any rules; instead, the rules themselves were at fault, inhibiting the sharing of critical information that might have prevented the disaster. Vaughan's approach was abductive in that she began with a theory of misconduct and deviance, and when it did not fit the surprising empirical data she gathered, she constructed a new theoretical explanation—of an organizationally produced mistake—that better fit her findings.

In the **extended case study approach** which is specific to participant observation or ethnography, the goal is to produce broad theoretical knowledge. Developed by sociologist Michael Burawoy (1998), this method emphasizes going beyond a particular field site to develop a much more general theory about society. Burawoy worked in the personnel office of a copper company in the newly independent African country of Zambia in 1968. At one level, his study examined how one copper company assigned jobs to workers, but at another level, his work addressed much broader questions about Zambia's legacy of colonialism and sources of underdevelopment. Burawoy's approach

extended case study approach An approach to theory in qualitative research in which the researcher starts with an established theory and chooses a field site or case to improve upon or modify the existing theory.

is very different from grounded theory. Instead of "discovering" or "creating" theory in the field, he argues, researchers should begin with their "favorite theory" and refine it in the field by finding "refutations that inspire us to deepen that theory" (Burawoy, 1998, p. 11).

STEPS IN QUALITATIVE DATA ANALYSIS

Whether the researcher adopts an inductive, abductive, or extended case study approach to qualitative research reflects that researcher's approach to the data and the preexisting literature and theories on the subject. Regardless of the approach one adopts, qualitative data analysis always involves six main steps: (1) managing and preparing the data, (2) becoming familiar with and reducing the data, (3) coding data for purposes of sorting and retrieval, (4) writing memos, (5) building and testing models, and (6) writing the final report, article, or book. Although we describe these as ordered steps, researchers do not always move through this process in lockstep order. Qualitative research is often an iterative process in which the researcher moves back and forth from one step to another; for example, writing memos while reading transcripts or building a model before all coding is done.

Managing and Preparing the Data

The first step in qualitative data analysis is managing and preparing the data. The raw data generated during qualitative research most often take the form of text files. In-depth interviews result in extensive notes, recordings, and transcriptions. Field notes must be digitized if the investigator plans to use a computer to analyze the notes. Many ethnographers take notes throughout the day in notebooks or on bits of paper or they dictate notes onto phones or digital recorders. They often spend their nights typing up and organizing the notes and filling in critical details that they abbreviated as they rushed to get everything down on paper when they were in the field. This cleanup should be conducted as soon as possible, while the information is fresh in the researcher's mind.

Transcribing and cleaning up interviews can be a herculean task. Voice-recognition software can be useful, but only in certain situations. Voice-recognition software has to learn an individual's pronunciation patterns. With field notes, it is usually just the ethnographer speaking, so voice-recognition software can be trained to transcribe the notes with few errors. However, with interviews, voices are constantly changing, and it is usually not worth the time or effort to train voice-recognition software for each respondent.

Most researchers use either a transcribing machine or an app to transcribe in-depth interviews. The transcribing machine allows the researcher to play back a recording by pressing a foot pedal so that the hands can stay on the keyboard and the transcriber can use his or her foot to stop and continue the playback. Transcribing apps also allow the user to play back audio on their phones or tablets while typing and to pause, resume, and speed up or slow down the playback. Transcribing apps or machines also allow researchers to specify the amount of time that the recording will backtrack every time they press "stop," allowing them to pick up where they left off as they type.

An important part of data preparation is the process of **de-identification**, which protects each respondent's anonymity. A pseudonym should be chosen for each person mentioned, and identifying information provided during the interview (such as names, addresses, and phone numbers) should not be transcribed. The transcriber should also adopt and implement a series of rules about how to handle common elements of in-person interviews, such as interruptions, digressions, and expressions of emotions such as laughter or crying. Often, the spoken word can convey a tone (for example, sarcasm) that is not obvious when the words are written out, so the transcriber should note if the tone of voice is transmitting important information.

Using a qualitative data analysis (QDA) program for transcription can save a lot of time and facilitate analysis afterward. Many QDA programs, such as NVivo, allow you to import the raw audio or video of your interviews and interview transcripts. If you are transcribing the interviews yourself, you can do so within the QDA program. NVivo provides a transcribing function that allows you to play the audio, set the speed, pause, and rewind as you type, much as a transcribing machine does. NVivo also allows you to record your thoughts about an interview at the moment they occur and link them to the appropriate part of the interview you are transcribing through the process of memo writing, which we describe later. Transcribing within the program also allows you to synchronize audio or video files with the transcription.

Some further basic organization will make life easier when working with large numbers of interviews. Using a uniform naming convention for files can help reduce confusion and increase efficiency. If documents are named with respondent ID numbers, the major software programs will import the document name as an "anchor" to which you can attach respondent-level characteristics. If you use a respondent ID or pseudonym instead of "respondent" in transcripts, it will be easier to identify excerpted text during data analysis. And if the project has multiple interviewers, you can use the interviewer initials in the transcript, which will tell you who is talking. If you are interested in whether different interviewers elicit different kinds of responses, adding interviewer initials can also help facilitate an examination of **interviewer effects** (Lowe, Lustig, & Marrow, 2011).

In some studies, you will collect a variety of different types of data about your unit of analysis. In an interview study, for example, your unit of analysis is the person you interviewed. You might have interview transcripts, audio or video of the interviews, field notes from the interviewer, photos, maps, even quantitative survey responses if it is a mixed-methods study. In the field notes, the researcher might include information about the place of the interview, the respondent's appearance and demeanor, and the highlights and drawbacks of the interview; the researcher might also indicate whether the respondent seemed nervous or at ease, whether others were present for all

de-identification The process of protecting each respondent's anonymity by suppressing or changing identifying data.

interviewer effects The possibility that the mere presence of an interviewer, or that the interviewer's personal characteristics, may lead a respondent to answer questions in a particular way, potentially biasing the responses.

or part of the interview, and whether the respondent asked for the recorder to be turned off at any point during the interview. Figure 16.2 shows how NVivo will bundle all these different data sources together for a large qualitative interview project. QDA software allows you to bundle together many different types of data and associate them all with a "case" or unit of analysis, which in this example is a person, with the identification number P61. This facilitates an integrated analysis. While you are reading a transcript, you can decide to listen to a snippet of the audio of that interview to hear the tone of voice or you can decide to read the field notes to find out what the interviewer saw during the interview. You could click on a photo of the person or his or her house.

This network view of Person P61 is taken from Waters's study of Hurricane Katrina survivors (2016). This view of the case is generated by the software. It identifies the case (P61) in the middle, and then shows the different data associated with this person. Person P61 was interviewed three separate times, so three different transcripts are linked to the case, as well as a picture of his or her house; field notes from the interviewer, labeled "Helen notes"; and some attribute codes that have been assigned to all the different data points: This person is African American, employed full time, has health problems in their family, and has returned to New Orleans. It would also be possible to link the digital audio or video recording of the interview to the case.

When Waters is ready to write about a particular topic, such as storm damage, she can then summon all these pieces of evidence from each respondent. It is even possible to integrate PDFs of journal articles on this topic so that when the researcher is writing, she can summon not only all the evidence from her data on the topic of storm damage, but also everything she has read in the literature that touches on storm damage.

Becoming Familiar with and Reducing the Data

Transcribing is often considered an unskilled job, and many researchers outsource it to professional transcribers (if they have the money). Any researcher who has transcribed interviews or field notes will tell you that the process can be pure drudgery. Transcription can take up to 8 hours for every 1 hour of recorded interview. However, if you do the transcribing yourself, you may find that the drudgery leads to profound insights. When you listen to the interview again, you may begin to really hear what a respondent is saying. You may make connections and see similarities or sharp differences on particular topics across respondents. You can connect the interviews to theories or previous research on the topic. For these reasons, most researchers who

FIGURE 16.2 File Structure in NVivo

This is a network view of all of the data associated with one person (with the ID number 61) in Waters's Hurricane Katrina study. The data include interview transcripts, codes, field notes, and images.

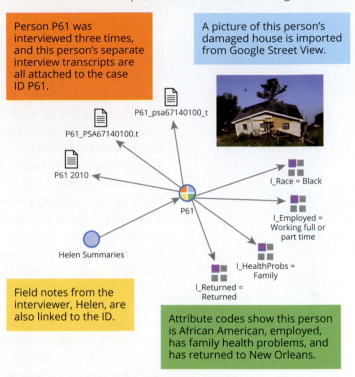

Person P61 was interviewed three times, and this person's separate interview transcripts are all attached to the case ID P61.

A picture of this person's damaged house is imported from Google Street View.

Field notes from the interviewer, Helen, are also linked to the ID.

Attribute codes show this person is African American, employed, has family health problems, and has returned to New Orleans.

transcribe their interviews keep an open notebook on their desk or an open Word file on their computer to record their ideas while they are transcribing. In fact, the act of transcribing an interview or a day of field notes is often the first step in a conceptual analysis of the data.

Transcribing recordings yourself is also a good way to reduce the data; that is, eliminate data that will not be useful to your analysis. For example, you can choose not to transcribe any digressions or interruptions (for example, a phone call) that you are confident will play no role in your analysis. If you do not transcribe your own interviews, you will need to spend time listening to or reading the interviews. At this point, you can reduce the data by noting digressions, interruptions, and sections of the interview that can safely be cut from further analysis. But the main goal of your reading is to begin thinking actively about what your interviews are telling you. In doing so, you may develop hunches about commonalities across interview respondents or you may identify surprising and unexpected things that respondents said.

For example, when Waters (1999) analyzed interviews with immigrants from the Caribbean for her study published as *Black Identities*, she found that one of her questions unearthed an important theme among Caribbean parents: "What surprised you the most about life in the United States?" She expected people to comment on the weather or Americans' manners, but instead many parents expressed their surprise that Americans did not beat their children to discipline them and that teenagers could report their parents to social services for child abuse. It was not until she reread all the interview transcripts that she realized the pervasiveness of this theme.

In addition to transcripts and field notes, researchers often prepare a summary of their interviews during the familiarization and data-reduction step. This summary provides the context for each interview that is so necessary to interpret each respondent's words as the analysis proceeds. Each summary, which should be about one or two pages long, should summarize the entire interview and should point to any unusual or representative sections of the interview that shed light on the themes or key insights of the study.

Coding the Data

coding The process of translating written or visual material into standardized categories. In qualitative data analysis, this involves tagging or labeling segments of data as an example of or related to a theoretical idea, wider theme, or concept.

codes Labels or tags for chunks of text.

Coding is the process of breaking down the qualitative data into parts and then noticing and creating conceptual links among the descriptive labels and abstract concepts. It is the actual work of analyzing qualitative data. **Codes** are labels or tags for chunks of text. The chunks can be words, sentences, paragraphs, or even many pages of text. For example, the part of an interview that deals with the respondent's neighborhood would be labeled "neighborhood." The discussion of crime would be labeled "crime." Eventually, the researcher might use codes that are more conceptual, such as "resistance to gentrification." To use the latter code, the researcher must define "gentrification" and "resistance," and if there are multiple coders, they would need to agree on the definitions.

Although coding is one of the most important parts of qualitative analysis, researchers rarely describe it in detail in publications. Often, researchers indicate only that they "coded the data using grounded theory techniques," that "data were transcribed and coded," or that they "coded the data with ATLAS.ti" (another widely used QDA program). Coding is the most laborious and time-consuming part of qualitative research, and it varies greatly across studies. There is no given set of codes to choose from; each researcher must choose and define the best codes for his or her project. For these reasons, it is not surprising that coding is the most mysterious part of the qualitative research cycle for many beginning researchers.

Three key challenges in coding are deciding (1) how to develop a list of codes, (2) how much material to assign to each code, and (3) how to determine whether codes should be combined or split as your analysis proceeds. In this section on coding, we present a coding procedure that reflects the power of QDA software but that also can be performed with paper and pen or with word-processing software such as Microsoft Word. This approach to coding provides for both deductive and inductive code development—a process that matches how most modern qualitative researchers do their work. Table 16.1 describes how coding tasks are done with three different tools: paper, pen, and scissors; word-processing programs; and QDA software.

GROUNDED THEORY AND THE ORIGINS OF CODING

Grounded theory provided the first systematic approach to coding. In this approach, the advice to researchers is clear: Begin by generating many codes that reflect only your data (Charmaz, 2014; Glaser & Strauss, 1967; Strauss & Corbin, 1998). Later, cull the list of codes by deleting some and combining others. The idea is that only in late stages should researchers allow the codes to reflect previous research, including theories and concepts from the preexisting literature. This approach to coding makes sense when you think about the technologies available when grounded theory was born. Transcripts were typed on typewriters, thus producing hard copy only; the codes were written in the margins of the transcripts; and the resulting categories were cut up with scissors into snippets of paper, taped onto index cards, and the index cards sorted into thematic piles.

Waters (1990) did an analysis of 60 in-depth interviews about ethnic identity with middle-class whites in suburbia using this paper-and-scissors method. In the first round of coding, she assigned codes to her interviews such as "ethnicity is fun," "Saint Patrick's Day," "loves Italian food," "people can't pronounce my name," "discrimination against Italians," and "Irish are seen as drunks." These codes were drawn directly from the data she was analyzing and covered very small pieces of the interviews. She cut up the interviews into these little snippets. Eventually, she sorted these into "positive aspects of ethnicity" and "negative aspects of ethnicity." Later, she linked the positive aspects of ethnicity to the idea of a "symbolic ethnicity," which had been theorized by Herbert Gans (1979). The small pieces of interview transcripts were sorted and re-sorted until Waters also came up with her own idea of "optional ethnicity." She realized that her respondents could claim an ethnic identity—as Irish or Italian or Polish—when they wanted to and not identify with any ethnicity when they did not want to. They had what she referred to as "ethnic options," which became the title of her book.

When grounded theory was developed, chopping up data into small pieces was a very time-consuming, physical process. After chopping up the data, researchers set aside material that was no longer needed, combining the small pieces into larger codes. An example would be taking a pile of pieces of text labeled "attitudes about senators,"

Waters came up with the idea of "optional ethnicity" while coding in-depth interview transcripts. She realized while going through the different codes that some groups, like Irish Americans, could choose where and when they identify with an ethnic group.

TABLE 16.1   Coding Tasks and Tools

Tasks	Paper, Pen, and Scissors	Word-Processing Programs	QDA Software
Data management	Paper copies of interviews, with at least one complete set for cutting up	Files in a project folder on your computer: One complete set of full transcripts and one set that can be cut and pasted into files containing all quotations on a particular topic	Files that keep together and associate all aspects of an individual transcript, such as transcripts, field notes, pictures, memos
Preparing quotations for coding	Cut out quotations or "chunks" of conversation into little pieces of paper	Take a quotation and copy it to a file, along with identifying information about what person said it, and put it in a file for that theme	Highlight a piece of text
Attaching codes	Write the code in the margin or on a Post-it note that is attached to the piece of paper	Label the file of quotations with the code you want to attach to them	Attach the code to the highlighted text
Storing codes	Put all the pieces of paper with the same code into a file folder labeled with that code	Save a document with all the quotations coded with the same code and label the file with the code	Store codes automatically by the software
Reading thematically	Open the file folder and read the quotations	Open the document and read all the quotations	Retrieve all the quotations by clicking on the code name; either just read the quotations or output them to another file
Merging codes	Take the material in two different file folders and put it together with a new name	Merge two documents and give the file a new name	Merge codes by providing the names of the codes and the new merged code name
Splitting codes	Use scissors to further cut up your quotations and then put them in different file folders	Take quotations and copy and paste them into different documents	Highlight text and attach a new code
Retrieving codes	Find the folder	Open the document	Click on the code
Doing Boolean ("and/or") searches, such as finding all the women who experienced discrimination and all the men who experienced discrimination	Create piles of quotations that meet the requirements	Look through the documents and create new documents	Write a simple command for a Boolean search and save the results
Figuring out your theoretical model or explanation	Draw on a blackboard a diagram of how your codes relate to one another or write the codes on index cards and lay them out on a table so you can rearrange them	Draw on a blackboard a diagram of how your codes relate to one another or write the codes on index cards and lay them out on a table so you can rearrange them	Use the modeling software to create a graphical model of how your concepts relate to one another

combining it with a pile of text labeled "attitudes about mayors," and then labeling the combined pile "attitudes about elected officials." The level of abstraction matters deeply. Let's say you began by cutting up your transcripts into pieces of text organized by broader categories—attitudes toward elected officials, for instance. If you then decided to compare attitudes about mayors to attitudes about senators, you would need to cut up the papers again. When you are working with paper and coding by hand, it makes more sense to start with tiny bits of text and many codes and then aggregate them than to start with big chunks of text. This approach is essentially inductive, matching the way qualitative researchers approach their projects.

The widespread development of word-processing programs in the early 1980s led to the development of QDA software soon after. Using word-processing programs or specialized QDA software allows for a more efficient and sensible approach to coding.

THE THREE TYPES OF CODES

There are three types of codes: attribute codes, index codes, and analytic codes. Attribute codes are like filing cabinet labels; they allow you to classify your cases by gender, age, race, location, and the like. Once you have applied them, you can query your data by asking, for example, to see all the respondents who are urban residents over age 50 and female. Index codes organize your interview transcripts according to your research questions, usually reflecting your interview schedule. In a life history interview, for example, you would apply codes for childhood, teen years, young adulthood, and so forth. Index codes are often used for each major question in your interview schedule, allowing you to query your data and ask to see everything every respondent said about their childhood.

Analytic codes link the material to your research question. So you might apply an analytic code of "unhappy experiences" to some descriptions of childhood and "happy experiences" to others. Analytic codes might arise from both surprising or unexpected comments from respondents and ideas and concepts from theory and other researchers. Once you have applied your analytic codes, you can begin to query your data in more complex ways, asking, for instance, whether men or women are more likely to have more unhappy experiences in childhood or in young adulthood. Each code has an important role to play in qualitative research. We discuss them each in depth in the following sections.

Attribute codes The **attribute codes** are the salient personal characteristics of the interviewees that played a role in the study design. These may be demographic variables (such as age, gender, race, occupation, socioeconomic status) or specific contextual data such as experimental group or control group, state, or neighborhood of residence. To use the language of variables, attributes are the demographic and structural independent variables that the researcher thinks may affect the topic (dependent variable) being studied.

For example, in the "Second Generation in New York" study, the authors sampled second-generation young adults whose parents had emigrated to New York City from five sending areas—China, the Dominican Republic, South America, the West Indies, and the former Soviet Union—along with white, black, and Puerto Rican young adults with native-born parents. In this study, ethnic and racial origins were attribute codes.

attribute codes Codes that represent the salient personal characteristics of the interviewees that played a role in the study design.

If you are working with mixed-methods data, attributes are the way to connect person-level data from surveys to the open-ended interview text. Sometimes in-depth interviews are conducted as a follow-up to a survey. The attribute codes from the survey might include not only demographic information but also answers to closed-ended survey questions. In a mixed-methods study of voting, for instance, survey responses about attitudes toward abortion could be assigned as attributes and then in-depth questions could be asked about why people got involved in politics. Later, the researcher could query on the attribute of whether an individual was antiabortion or supported abortion rights and then look at whether these individuals described different routes into politics. Attributes are not limited to person-level characteristics; other units of analysis are possible. For instance, if the project has multiple research sites, you could also designate each site as an attribute, allowing you to examine the transcripts for thematic differences among research sites.

Index codes The **index codes** represent large chunks of text, enabling data reduction and retrieval as you build your argument. Think of index codes as broad categories or topics. For example, in Waters's study of Hurricane Katrina survivors, index codes included topics such as "evacuation experiences" and "physical health" and "mental health" (Asad, 2015; Waters, 2016). Index codes for a study of immigration might include "migration experiences," "naturalization," and "American identity." As noted earlier, index codes for life history interviews would reference different parts of the life course, such as childhood, adolescence, and old age. Attaching index codes to the data familiarizes you with the data and makes subsequent rounds of reading more focused. It also takes advantage of the natural organization of the transcripts to help you easily find and retrieve content.

A logical starting place for index coding in an interview study is the interview protocol. Include an index code for each question on the interview schedule. If your interview protocol is organized with questions inside broader topics, you can aggregate question codes to the topic level as well. For example, in a life history interview, the protocol may begin by asking about childhood, then neighborhood, then schools; each section may have several questions or prompts. The index would have "childhood" as the major heading and would include answers to several specific questions in the protocol, each with its own code. The answers to the question "Tell me about the neighborhood you grew up in" would receive the index code "childhood—neighborhood." The question "Whom did you live with when you were growing up?" would receive the index code "childhood—household." These large topics likely include pages of text spanning several different questions in a given interview. You should aim to identify and link answers to broad content areas wherever these topics appeared during the conversation.

Given that most sociological interviews are only semi-structured, indexing is not as straightforward as it may seem at first. For example, to preserve conversational flow, the interviewer likely will not re-ask questions that were already answered in the natural course of the conversation. To make sure you have completely identified material for the index codes, features such as NVivo's "matrix coding query" or ATLAS.ti's "code-by-document matrix" are extremely helpful. These tools create a chart of all codes and transcripts, showing which transcripts appear to be missing information. Figure 16.3 is a code-by-document matrix created by NVivo for index codes for

index codes Codes that represent broad categories or topics related to a research question, enabling data reduction.

FIGURE 16.3 Code-by-Document Matrix for "Second Generation in New York" Study

This is a matrix, created in NVivo, showing how many times each code (the rows) is used for each respondent (columns).

	P1	P11	P21	P31	P41	P51	P65	P73	TOTALS
Childrencodes	22	19	13	11	6	4	25	15	115
Citizencodes	2	0	3	0	0	0	0	1	6
Employmentcodes	9	3	2	3	4	1	0	6	28
Ethnicrelationscodes	37	32	18	15	19	12	13	19	165
Fatherfigure	2	2	1	4	7	1	1	1	19
Highschoolcodes	3	4	4	2	0	1	0	1	15
Identitycodes	23	19	19	13	14	8	10	15	121
Motherfigure	2	5	5	2	11	1	12	1	39
Neighborhoodcodes	41	30	19	16	19	15	14	24	178
Parentfigure	4	7	6	6	16	2	13	2	56
Partnercodes	10	7	5	8	8	7	15	14	74
Politicscodes	10	15	9	11	3	5	9	11	73
Successcodes	7	7	6	6	2	2	3	3	36
TOTALS:	172	150	110	97	109	59	115	113	925

eight transcripts from the "Second Generation in New York" study. It looks like the questions on citizenship did not yield much material. Perhaps none of those questions were asked, or maybe they were coded under another topic—such as "politics." There are also a number of respondents who do not have any employment codes. Perhaps they are students who are not employed. After your first pass at indexing, if it appears that a respondent has not answered a question in the protocol, it's time to reread the interview to make sure the answer was not overlooked (and therefore not coded).

As you identify respondent attributes and read the text for indexing, you will begin to develop ideas about your transcripts. According to Small (2009, p. 169), it helps to think about qualitative interviews as a series of case studies. In reading each case, you will develop an idea of the important concepts and the linkages in the data—provisional answers to the "how" and "why" questions at the center of your research. You can document your insights in respondent-level memos, which we suggest you write for each interview you read. Whether you begin writing respondent memos immediately after you conduct the interview or begin analyzing cases upon completion of data transcription, cross-case analysis of respondent memos will produce several ideas about "the story" in the data.

Analytic codes The **analytic codes** begin to sort or characterize the data you have gathered. They reflect what the text signifies or means. Analytic codes include ideas that come from previous research and theorizing on the topic as well as ideas that arise from respondents themselves. Figure 16.4 includes examples of the three types of codes developed for the "Second Generation in New York" study. One of the questions prepared by the investigators concerned how young people think about getting ahead in life. As the fieldwork for the study was beginning, one of the research

analytic codes Codes that reflect what the text signifies or means, enabling the researcher to sort or characterize qualitative data.

Attribute codes

Age (years)	18–20, 21–23, 24–26, 27–29, 30–32
Gender	Male, female
Ethnic group	Black, Chinese, CEP, Dominican, Puerto Rican, Russian, White, West Indian, mixed ethnicity
Cohort	U.S. born, arrived 0–6, arrived 7–12, arrived over 12
Parents' background	One parent foreign born, both parents foreign born
Residence	New Yorker, moved to New York
Education	Less than high school, in-between, college graduate
Parents' education	Neither parent has high school/GED; at least one parent has high school/GED; at least one parent has some college; at least one parent has BA; at least one parent has more than BA
Employment	Working full time, working part time, in school—not working
Family status	Partnered, children, single parent
Politics	Voter, nonvoter
Crime	Arrested, not arrested

Index codes

EDUCATION	For whole section on schooling and discussion of education in other sections.
EMPLOYMENT	Whole section on employment and any discussion of employment in other sections. Includes military experience.
IDENTITY	Whole section on ethnic identity and other references, including identity based on class, religion, music, being a New Yorker, etc.
POLITICS	Whole section on politics and any other references; for example, to parents' experience of politics in home country.
RELIGION	Whole section on religion and other references; for example, when discussing choice of partner or school.
SUCCESS	Discussions about success anywhere in interview, including parents', respondent's (R's), and friends' ideas about what it takes to be successful in the United States, whether R thinks education is important, etc.

Analytic codes

Paths	Discussions of anything that seems to have affected R's life trajectory. This includes decisions about which school to attend, tracking at school, the influence of friends, involvement with or avoidance of drugs and crime, the existence or absence of role models, how R found employment, etc.
Role model	References to positive and negative role models (will probably also be coded "paths").
Sacrifices	Discussion of sacrifices made for R by parents, sibling, partner, etc. Any discussion of familial obligations. Also, sacrifices R made for them or for children.

Fine-grained analytic codes for success:
Conceptions of what success is and how to achieve it

Avoiding trouble (prison, pregnancy, drugs, crime)	Being famous
Being "free"	Being happy and content
Being a good person, strong values	Being healthy
Being confident, aggressive, ambitious	Being lucky
	Being married, in a relationship

FIGURE 16.4 Codebook for the "Second Generation in New York" Life History Interviews—cont'd

Being prepared to make sacrifices
Being respected
Being a shark, ready to step on people
Being smart, streetwise
Being the boss
Being yourself
Connections important for success
Connections not important for success
Decent job, high rank
Discrimination—a barrier to success
Discrimination—not a barrier to success
Discrimination is barrier but can be
    overcome with determination
Doing good for others, making the world
    a better place
Doing what you want to do, making a
    living with it
Education—ambivalent attitude
Education—necessary and desirable
Education—not associated with success
Family
Great quote
Hard work, doing your best
Having a job
Having children
Having close friends
Having free time for yourself
Having strong support network
Having your needs met

Income
Knowing how to behave, how to talk
Knowing yourself
Living in a good neighborhood
Minorities who stress education are
    selling out
Minorities who stress education are not
    selling out
Minorities selling out—heard it but reject it
Money—is important measure of success
Money, material goods not most
    important measure of success
Not being dependent
Not causing harm to others
Not having to work
Occupation—must be good, decent,
    higher position
Occupation—must be interesting, fun
Occupation—must be professional
Occupation—steady income enough
Other
Owning material goods
Reaching one's goals
Respect, prestige
Security
Selfishness
Something to be proud of, being the best
Surviving
Taking opportunities

assistants suggested that the researchers' view of success was "narrow," and she wondered whether young people would see the matter differently. So the researchers added a question: "How would you define success for someone your age?"

The entire section of the interview that addressed this question was coded "definition of success" (an index code), but the specific definitions of success functioned as analytic codes. Some of the researchers' initial analytic codes included "occupation—must be good, decent higher position," "education—necessary and desirable for success," and "income." These concepts came from sociological theory and from previous research. But other analytic codes came directly from the interview transcripts. For example, the study found striking differences across groups. The Chinese second-generation respondents defined success much as the researchers had—their top three answers were education, occupation, and income. In contrast, the South American second-generation respondents mentioned being married, achieving stability, and having material goods. The Dominican second-generation respondents were concerned with discrimination limiting their success and also defined success as staying out of trouble and even surviving. The high crime rate and murder rate among young men at the time strongly influenced this Dominican respondent:

Investigator: How would you define success for someone your age?

Respondent: Being able to say that you're alive.

Investigator: Why do you say that?

Respondent: Look at the news, you know. Look at the newspaper. You don't hear about too many twenty-five, twenty-six-year-old males, Hispanic, African

American, you know, doing anything with their lives other than dying or going to jail. (Kasinitz et al., 2008, p. 90)

In their analysis of the data, the authors reported the three most common analytic codes for each ethnic group, as well as any unique codes that appeared for only a specific ethnic group. For example, the Russian second-generation respondents were the only group that mentioned "being lucky" as a measure of success. Puerto Ricans were the only group that mentioned "having good relations with your family." Dominicans were the only group who mentioned "moving out of New York" as a measure of success.

The work of analytic coding is the heart of data analysis in qualitative research. Analytic codes can blend concepts from theory and previous research with concepts, behaviors, and beliefs that come from research subjects. Applying analytic codes is an ongoing process. Often, researchers will split analytic codes into subcodes or will combine analytic codes into broader codes as they further refine their ideas. QDA software facilitates this conceptual work, but in the end, it is the researcher's judgment and analysis that determines how these codes are generated, applied, and modified. Figure 16.5 shows a network view in ATLAS.ti of all the analytic codes created on a first pass through the discussions of success. There are many different types of codes representing a lot of different ways of thinking of success. An advantage of looking at the codes in the network view is that you can click on any code and it will bring up all the quotations that have been assigned that code across all the transcripts you are analyzing. Figure 16.6 shows how the quotations are linked to the codes, enabling you to easily see where the code came from.

FIGURE 16.5 Success Codes, Unsorted

Qualitative data analysis software can show you all the analytic codes you've created. This screenshot from the software program ATLAS.ti shows all the analytic codes related to conceptions of success.

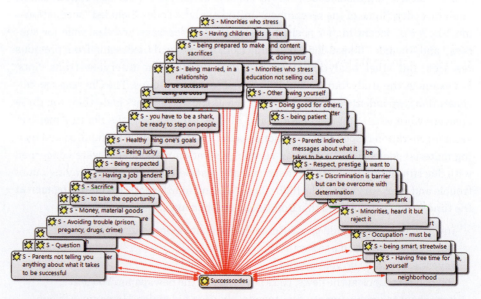

Figure 16.7 then shows a sorted network of success codes. There are codes that refer to family and social support as definitions of success; codes that focus on how people become successful; codes that reflect the idea that being successful is staying alive or staying out of trouble; codes about how success requires sacrifice and hard work; a single code that defines success as being lucky; codes that associate success with fame, money, and material goods; and codes that focus on education, occupation, and

FIGURE 16.6 Codes Linked to Quotations

The code "you have to be a shark, be ready to step on people," comes from the memorable quote to the left from a Russian second-generation respondent who has a very dark view of the competitiveness of New York City.

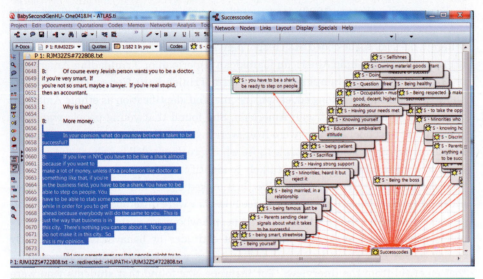

FIGURE 16.7 Network View of Success Codes, Sorted

Codes related to success are sorted by theme. Codes can then be assigned to a "parent" code, such as those in the lower-right-hand corner, which all relate to socioeconomic success.

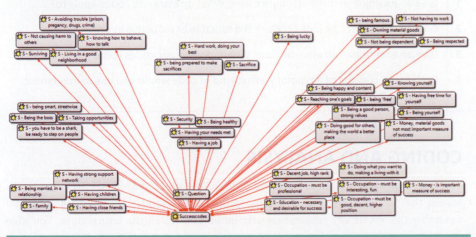

income as measures of success. After these codes are sorted, the researcher can merge the smaller codes into larger ones or create a "parent" code of "socioeconomic status," for example, that will include all the codes in the lower-right-hand corner of the figure (which will become "child codes").

Typologies: An analytic code that is also an attribute code Some analytic codes should be applied to the entire person, becoming attributes. This is especially true if you decide on a typology as a way to organize your data. A **typology** is a way of generalizing from concrete cases by defining a common core within a set of cases (Weiss, 1994, p. 173). This common core defines the specific way in which your cases cluster together. A typology is not a theory but rather a way of organizing data as a step toward producing a theory.

typology A way of generalizing from concrete cases by defining a common core within a set of cases.

For example, Waters (1999) constructed a typology of racial and ethnic identity among second-generation West Indian teens. On the basis of their responses to many different questions, she coded each respondent as (1) identifying as African American, (2) identifying as ethnic American (Jamaican American or Trinidadian American), or (3) identifying as an immigrant (Jamaican or Trinidadian). Her goal was to understand the relationship among education, income, and identification as ethnic American versus identification as African American. She found that young people who were doing worse in school and who were from working-class families were more likely to identify as African American, while those who were doing well in school and grew up in middle-class families were more likely to identify as Jamaican American or Trinidadian American (Waters, 1999). She then looked systematically across the three different types of West Indian teens to see how they were different, using these typology attribute codes to see whether young people who were assigned to these different typologies held systematically different attitudes or behaved very differently in day-to-day life. Those behaviors and attitudes were captured in analytic codes that emerged from the interviews. For instance, she found that students who were American-identified saw more racial discrimination in day-to-day life and did not do as well in school as those who were ethnic-identified.

CONCEPT CHECKS

1 Give an example of three attribute codes. What do attribute codes apply to?

2 Give an example of an index code. Is it deductive or inductive in origin?

3 Give an example of an analytic code. Where do analytic codes come from?

4 Explain the concept of a typology. What kind of code would you use to implement a typology?

CODING AND ANALYSIS

The best approach is a three-stage process for coding and analysis. In stage 1, you assess the "big picture," exploring and preparing the data. During this step, you assemble the set of key respondent attributes and index the transcripts. You also produce respondent-level and cross-case memos, beginning the analytic process by developing hypothesized relationships between the codes. In stage 2, you apply analytic codes to focused sections of the transcripts. Analytic codes represent the concepts you will explore in a paper, and they integrate your emergent findings with what is known from the literature. In stage 3, you use various software tools for querying the data, validating your concepts, model building, and testing and refining your data-based theory.

Throughout all stages of the coding process, you should take care to note chunks of text where respondents are particularly concise, articulate, or poignant. Include or make a separate code for snippets of text that trigger "aha" moments in your understanding of the data—either during your coding or when you were in the field—so that you can easily find these again later.

Stage 1: Preparing the Data with Attribute and Index Codes

Familiarizing yourself with your data can occur while listening to recordings, reading and rereading field notes or interviews, or transcribing handwritten notes or audio files. The important part is getting to know what you have collected very well. During this phase, you will start to notice common themes and begin developing ideas for the codes you will use to classify the data. You will also write memos and take detailed notes about your ideas. If you do not transcribe your own interviews, you will listen to or read the interviews, considering common themes that should be coded.

How will you recognize whether what you are seeing in your data is significant? One technique is to ask the "So what?" question. Sometimes as you are reading through your interviews or field notes, you will find particular passages very interesting or exciting and will highlight them. Asking the "So what?" question will help you pin down why you are so drawn to these passages and will push you to think about what your data are telling you (Dey, 1993, pp. 87–88).

When researchers studying Hurricane Katrina survivors began examining their in-depth interviews, a surprising theme emerged. Waters and her colleagues noticed that some respondents who had experienced severe trauma during the hurricane were describing the storm a year later as a blessing. These respondents described growing as a person through adversity and developing a new outlook on life. Waters found this interesting and exciting but wasn't sure exactly why. After asking herself the "So what?" question, she realized it was because this response to the storm was so unexpected and ran counter to her expectations. She was expecting to see the negative consequences of post-traumatic stress disorder. Instead, she was seeing personal growth and gratitude for the opportunity to change. She later found there was a whole literature in psychology on something called "post-traumatic

While studying the transcripts from their study of Hurricane Katrina survivors, Waters and her colleagues realized that some respondents viewed the storm as a positive force in their life.

growth"—the finding that for some people, going through trauma leads to personal growth and positive changes (Calhoun & Tedeschi, 2013). Her initial question about why she found certain passages from the interview transcripts interesting led to codes about positivity, which eventually led to codes about post-traumatic growth (Waters, 2016).

Before beginning to code, researchers also need to familiarize themselves with their field notes. Emerson, Fretz, and Shaw (1995) advise researchers to read through all their field notes in chronological order, with close, intensive reflection. In a multiyear study, it is not possible to read all the field notes before coding begins, but it's important to read a selection of notes across the time in the field. As you read the notes, you should see "how perceptions and relations change over time. You should approach the notes as if they were written by a stranger" (Emerson et al., 1995, pp. 145). Emerson and colleagues also advocate "a sensitivity to the practical concerns, conditions, and constraints that actors confront and deal with in their everyday lives and actions" (Emerson et al., 1995, p. 147). In short, reading interviews, field notes, and other relevant materials will suggest your first codes.

Why is it important to apply attribute codes before you conduct your analysis? Later in the process, you will be exploring relationships in your data by examining the *intersection* of codes, and attributes are codes that are applied to the *entire transcript.* Different software packages have different options for these analyses. However, they all allow you to query transcripts by selecting on attribute codes and then examining index and analytic codes across cases. In Figure 16.8 we show a query in

FIGURE 16.8 Using the Query Tool in ATLAS.ti

This screenshot from ATLAS.ti shows how you can search transcripts by first selecting an attribute code such as "Dominican" and then selecting certain index and analytic codes. The quotations in the lower right corner include every time a Dominican respondent talked about discrimination in reference to his or her career.

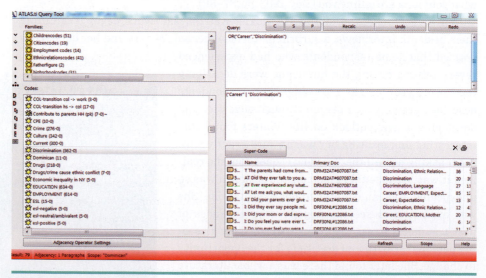

ATLAS.ti of the "Second Generation in New York" study. The command narrowed the scope to all transcripts with the attribute code "Dominican," and then asked for all quotations that were coded with both the index code "career" and with the analytic code "discrimination." The result is in the lower-right window and includes every example of a Dominican respondent speaking about discrimination in his or her career. The next query could ask for the same index and analytic codes but for the transcripts labeled "Chinese." The analyst could then compare how Chinese respondents versus Dominican respondents experience—or do not experience—discrimination in their careers.

Stage 2: Applying Analytic Codes

After you have indexed transcripts and applied attribute codes, you will have several ideas about questions you could pursue. The list will likely include your original research questions, along with other themes and research questions that emerged from your research. To keep yourself from becoming overwhelmed by possibilities, we suggest approaching the application of analytic codes one research question at a time, rather than trying to code every possible idea or concept that could be applied to your data. Your familiarity with the transcripts from the first reading means you will have a good idea of where to find the relevant chunks of the transcript for your research question.

Applying codes in a reliable manner is a major challenge in analysis of a large interview data set (Campbell et al., 2013). While team coding can help, you can also use software to ease your way. A word of warning: With QDA software, you can easily apply as many codes as you like. At the same time, software allows you to apply far too many codes to be either useful or reliable. For this reason, we suggest that you use your first read of the text for indexing the data; during the first read, the themes and theories are not yet ready to be applied in a reliable or valid way. Valid and reliable coding is necessary if you wish to take full advantage of your data (and the power of QDA software) in later stages of analysis. In your second, more focused, reading, you will be better able to apply analytic codes one research question at a time. Figure 16.9 shows a coded section of a transcript with all three codes, from a study of undocumented immigrants to the United States (Asad, 2017).

On your second reading, limit yourself to the relevant text, using the appropriate index code to select the relevant sections of the transcripts, and apply only one or two analytic codes at a time to this text. For instance, in a study examining multiple life-history interviews, you might begin by writing a paper on what factors lead to a happy childhood. In this case, you would focus your coding on the parts of the transcripts with index codes of "childhood."

For example, Nicole Deterding (2015) studied how community college students think about their education and how this thinking affected their persistence toward a degree. She began her analysis of 127 interviews with community college students by index coding the transcripts with large chunks covering "education history" and "successful adulthood." She then pulled all that text material and examined whether students were adopting an expressive or instrumental approach to their education. These two concepts—*expressive approach* and *instrumental approach*—served as

FIGURE 16.9 A Coded Transcript with Attribute, Index, and Analytic Codes

This entire manuscript is coded "Mexican" (attribute code) because the respondent is an immigrant from Mexico. The index code is for the section of the interview that asks "Do you consider yourself American?" The analytic code is "marriage" because the respondent believes that his marriage to an American could make him American if he has the right papers (Asad, 2017).

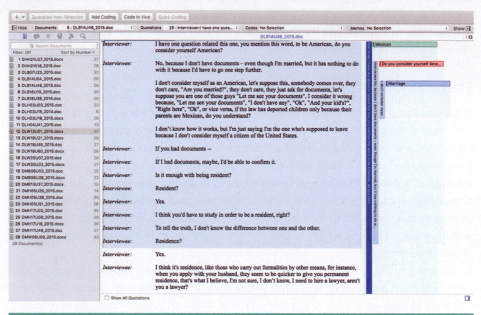

analytic codes. An *expressive* approach to education emphasizes the moral value of being a college student and attaining upward mobility. An *instrumental* approach stresses education as an avenue to better employment. By examining the sections of the transcripts that had the index codes "education history" and "successful adulthood," she only needed to read about 20% of the full transcripts to examine the information in which she was most interested. After reading the reduced interview excerpts, Deterding made a judgment about whether the *person* should be categorized as instrumental, expressive, or mixed on the basis of the textual evidence, and she added this information to the attribute file.

The application of analytic codes is the most creative part of any qualitative analysis. It requires close attention to the text you have gathered as well as a theoretical and substantive grounding in your subject area. While you develop the analytic codes, it is important to document your decision making by writing memos.

WRITING MEMOS

Memos are an integral part of qualitative data analysis. Memos are notes to yourself, and perhaps to your future readers. They can take many forms and cover many different topics, including why you decided on particular codes, what you found interesting about particular events or people, and how your interviews or field notes relate to your wider conceptual questions or to the literature on a particular topic. They can be written at any time during the research process—while you are in the field, while you are transcribing or reading, while you are coding, or while you are reading other published studies on your topic. They are relatively easy to write because they are musings—possible ideas to pursue further, your assumptions about the data, or puzzles that you do not understand yet. You should also use memos to document the steps you took in your research so that you can provide detailed information in the methodology section of your paper. QDA software allows you to write general memos that relate to your whole research project, respondent-level memos that refer to a particular interview, code memos that refer to a particular code, and model memos that refer to a model you have developed to explain your data.

Warren and Karner (2005, p. 209) suggest that you focus on three activities in writing memos:

- Making connections: How do codes and your knowledge of the literature relate to each other?

- Interpreting: Which sociological questions do the data answer?

- Validating: Are you sure about your conclusions? Does your evidence support your interpretations?

It is also important to create a **codebook**, especially for large projects with many different researchers and assistants. This codebook should explain each code used in the study, but it should include much more than frequencies and value labels. Figure 16.3 is an example of a codebook. Often, researchers include an example of a quotation for each code, and sometimes they provide cross-references with other codes.

Stage 3: Building and Testing Models

Once your data are coded, you can build and test a model that answers your research question. A **model** is a verbal or visual description of your argument. The model describes how you think the various variables fit together to tell a story about the empirical world. The model should combine a theoretical or conceptual insight with the empirical data you gathered. All the major QDA software packages have modules that help you draw these models. Sometimes you can link attribute and analytic codes, showing, for example, that men are more likely to report having happy childhoods than women. QDA software can compare across the attribute codes for gender and for whether the respondent had a happy childhood as analytic codes. But unlike quantitative software that gives you an answer once you have chosen a statistical model to run, qualitative software cannot tell you whether a finding is significant or whether it even is a finding. The model-building capability of these programs is only as good as the thinking of the scholar using them.

The primary way in which you explore your data once it is coded is through the query process. This can be a very simple query, such as telling the software to give you every part of every interview that references "childhood." Or it can be a more complex search that looks for intersections of codes or codes that overlap. For example, the researcher can ask for all young people who grew up with two parents and

codebook A system of organizing information about a data set, including the variables it contains, the possible values for each variable, coding schemes, and decision rules.

model A verbal or visual description of an argument.

who went to college and how they talk about their childhoods, and then compare that to all young people who grew up with two parents and who only graduated from high school and how they talk about their childhoods. By examining the frequency of "happy" versus "unhappy" childhoods, you might begin to build a model that posits that family structure and respondents' education are related to whether childhood is remembered fondly.

Suppose this relationship held. The real question then for the qualitative researcher would be *how* family structure and education affects how you view your childhood. Is it that education gives you rose-colored glasses, so you remember your childhood differently than do those with less education? Is it that social class structures childhood experiences in ways that make one happy or unhappy? Reading the transcripts and understanding what makes one happy or unhappy would be a crucial step in developing this explanation.

Researchers aim to construct an account of the data that achieves theoretical validity (Maxwell, 1992). A theoretically valid explanation is an explanation that has a strong base in the empirical data but that is abstract enough to be useful to explain other situations or events. As a social scientist, you are not just trying to explain one small piece of the social world, but rather are attempting to build a theory or explanation that is useful for other places and times (Silbey, 2009, p. 81). Software can aid you in the construction of a theoretically valid explanation by helping you identify trends across cases, investigate alternative explanations, and quickly locate negative cases that refine or limit your explanation. The key to building a good model is moving beyond a description of your data to a conceptual explanation or theory about your topic.

As you build and test your models, you will often use software commands that find and retrieve the data you need, which allows you to test your hypotheses by searching for co-occurrences of codes in your data. To see how this process works, let's use a study of gender dynamics that sought to identify and explain how spouses care for each other during serious illness. Previous research had examined only heterosexual couples and had found that women provide more emotional support and physical care for their husbands during an illness than husbands do when their wives are sick. Debra Umberson and her colleagues (2016) were interested in the dynamics of caregiving among same-sex couples. They conducted in-depth interviews with 45 married partners, including heterosexual couples, lesbian couples, and gay male couples (see "Conversations from the Front Lines").

The researchers developed codes that characterized the kinds of support the healthier spouses provided for the ill spouses, as well as codes that measured the ill spouses' expectations of what their partners should do for them. After applying all these codes, Umberson and her team systematically examined how straight, gay male, and lesbian couples talked about caregiving and expectations of caregiving. First, they looked at all the material coded on men caring for women in straight marriages, for women caring for men in straight marriages, for men caring for men in gay marriages, and for women caring for women in lesbian marriages. To conduct their analysis, the researchers used the following codes:

- Attribute codes: gender of the respondent, type of marriage (same-sex or opposite-sex)

- Index code: caring for a sick spouse
- Analytic codes: stress, perceptions of illness, and expectations of care

By comparing how spouses in different types of marriages talked about giving and receiving care, the researchers developed a model that answered their original question. The model they eventually formed from their data (and previous studies) can be summarized as: Perceptions of illness shape care work, and those perceptions also shape the unhealthy partner's expectations for care. The fit between one partner's expectations for care and the care provided by the other partner partly shapes illness-related stress. If both partners expect to minimize illness and let it interfere with their everyday lives as little as possible, or if both partners expect intense caregiving and lots of focus on the ill partner, stress is much reduced. It is when expectations do not match that stress is high. Because these expectations tend to be different among men and women, same-sex couples tended to approach illness with shared expectations about the role of the caregiver much more often than heterosexual couples (Umberson et al., 2016).

Once you have developed your model, you need to test it to see whether it is valid. You must check that your interpretation of the data is correct by examining the reliability of your coding and by searching for alternative explanations of the patterns you found. Umberson and her colleagues were able to determine whether stress was more common in certain types of marriages and also able to unpack the mechanisms leading to that stress; specifically, the different expectations that men and women bring to illness and the mismatch that results in opposite-sex marriages but not in same-sex marriages.

Examining unique cases that do not fit the conclusions is another important step in testing models. Umberson found some same-sex couples where the spouses had different perceptions of caregiving in illness—with one spouse minimizing the illness and the other considering it an all-encompassing experience. These couples suffered the same stress as the heterosexual couples with mismatched expectations. These unusual cases reinforced the researchers' conclusions that expectations were the mechanism leading to the different stress outcomes among the different types of marriages. In other words, the lower stress associated with caregiving in same-sex marriages was not about sexual orientation per se, but rather about the higher likelihood that same-sex spouses would have similar expectations regarding caregiving. When the members of the same-sex couples did not have the same expectations, they suffered just as much as opposite-sex couples.

PRESENTING DATA AND MODELS VISUALLY

Models can be described verbally or presented visually. Figure 16.10 is a visual representation of Umberson's model. Visual representations are particularly useful in our modern, visual age, but qualitative researchers have a long history of developing visual displays to explain

FIGURE 16.10 Visual Model of Spousal Caregiving Perceptions, Expectations, and Stress

This visual representation of Umberson's model illustrates how differing perceptions of and expectations of caregiving lead to stress.

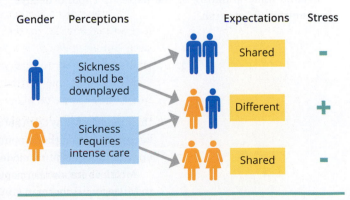

Conversations from the Front Lines

DEBRA UMBERSON

Debra Umberson is Centennial Professor of Sociology and director of the Population Research Center at the University of Texas at Austin. She studies social factors that influence health, with a particular emphasis on aging and life course change, marital and family ties, and gender and racial variation in health outcomes. Her early work helped to establish the strong link between social ties and mortality; in particular, a 1988 study she coauthored that was published in the journal Science *and was one of the first studies to establish that social support can lower the incidence of illness, reduce the risk of mortality from illness, and speed illness recovery. We started by asking Professor Umberson about her skills in both quantitative and qualitative methods.*

You were originally trained in quantitative methods. How did you come to use qualitative methods?

Before I went to graduate school in sociology, I got a master's degree in social work. Social work is all about in-depth assessment of individuals with attention to their social contexts. So you learn how to interview people in ways that reveal who they are and how they came to be the way they are. I really enjoyed doing this type of assessment, so it was quite natural for me to later return to in-depth interviewing as a way to expand understanding of the patterns I found in my quantitative research.

> " **Even though you may start with some ideas about major coding categories, the most interesting results usually come from the coding categories you did not expect.** "

When you are analyzing your qualitative data, what general steps do you follow?

First, I put a lot of thought into clarifying exactly what I want to know and then into figuring out the best sampling and interviewing strategies for getting that information. This is the most fun part of research methods for me. I love brainstorming about who should be in my in-depth interview sample and the best guiding questions to ask my interviewees. The easy way out is to generate a long list of questions to ask people. But the most rewarding and productive strategy is to identify a great and broad question that gets at exactly what you're looking for.

For example, in my research on how the death of a parent affects adults, I wanted to study the symbolic meaning of loss of a parent. This is a fairly vague concept, and there are lots of ways I could have approached this. But I found that one very general question generated rich data on the symbolic meaning of loss. I simply asked people, "What do you feel you lost with the death of your

their models. Many QDA software packages make it easy to prepare a visual model, but keep in mind that the computer does not build the model for you. Rather, you must come up with the conceptual model yourself; the computer only helps you sketch it.

Matrices are another popular way to display data and seek new insights. According to Miles and Huberman (1994), a matrix allows you to visualize all your major codes parent?" With this question, I could see a shift in people as they recognized what their parent symbolized to them. Equally important, the people I interviewed easily understood the question and had a lot to say in response.

Do you use a qualitative analysis software package? How did you choose it? Are there particular features you value?

I do use a software package, but I value it primarily as an organizing tool. Qualitative software makes it very easy to code excerpts from in-depth interviews and to create second-level codes and to cross-code.

What is the most difficult part of analyzing qualitative data?

The most difficult part is the daunting task of coding thousands of pages of transcribed interviews. Creating those initial codes is the hardest part. Even though you may start with some ideas about major coding categories, the most interesting results usually come from the coding categories you did not expect. You have to pay careful attention to your data because you certainly don't want to miss those novel findings.

Do you see value in a mixed-methods approach?

Absolutely! That's why I use both qualitative and quantitative methods. There is no substitute for quantitative methods when you want to establish population patterns and dynamics. For example, in my recent work, I showed that black Americans face many more family member deaths than do whites from childhood through later life. The only way to establish that pattern was to use

quantitative methods. But it was qualitative methods that led me to this research project in the first place. I had conducted in-depth interviews with equal numbers of black and white respondents to study how social relationships shape health habits throughout the life course. I did not set out to study race differences in the death of family members in this interview study, but that was the most striking theme that emerged from the qualitative data. And I will return to qualitative methods when I go further with this research topic—so that I can learn more about how premature and frequent exposure to death of family members shapes social, economic, and health experiences throughout the life course.

You were the editor of the *Journal of Health and Social Behavior*. Did you see systematic differences in how scholars reported on their qualitative analyses?

Different journals seem to have different norms for the reporting of qualitative findings. For *JHSB*, researchers are fairly consistent in clearly laying out the key themes that emerge from their qualitative research, finding some way of indicating the degree of group differences in those themes (this is often hard to do with qualitative research), and in presenting illustrations of those themes with their qualitative data.

What would improve a paper that used qualitative data in terms of providing transparency in the analysis?

One strategy is to have more than one person code the data and identify key themes in the data. Another important strategy is to clearly describe your methods and how the data were coded and decisions made.

and concepts across all your data simultaneously, helping you see how your variables correlate with one another. Matrices can be ordered by time, concepts, codes, respondents, or any other variables that the researcher thinks are important. Figure 16.11 is a matrix from Waters's Hurricane Katrina study. It lays out each respondent and provides information about household status, partner status, evacuation timing, current

FIGURE 16.11 Matrix of Responses in Hurricane Katrina Project

Matrices help researchers see how the different variables in a study are related to one another.

ID	Qual_ID	S0_...	L.c...	S...	L_PartnerS...	L_Part...	L_ResStat	L_ResSatNotes	L_Child...	L_EvacTiming	S3_residence	L_Health	HealthNotes
7	P10	1 1		No	No Partner	n/a	Household head, living with other adults	n/a	4	Pre-Katrina	New Orleans	Not a major issue	n/a
8	P11	3 3		No	No Partner	n/a	Household head, living with other adults	n/a	7	Pre-Katrina	Original Home	Major Issue	anxiety attacks
9	P12	1 1		No	Partner	n/a	Household head with partner, plus other adults	n/a	6	Pre-Katrina	Original Home	Major Issue	son has asthma, r has depression and stress
10	P13	2 2+pregnant		Pre	Partner	n/a	Household head with partner, plus other adults	n/a	>5	Pre-Katrina	Original Home	Major Issue	husband has stress probs, r currently on bedrest for pregnancy
11	P14	1 1		No	No Partner	n/a	Living with other adults, not household head	At mother's house with sibling and child	3	Pre-Katrina	New Orleans	Major Issue	physically exhausted
12	P15	3 5		Yes	Partner	Father of her children	Household head with partner, plus other adults	Family friends who come and go	5	Post-Katrina	New Orleans	Major Issue	1 son with asthma, children with evacuation-related stress, newborn has trauma related to evacuated stress
13	P16	5 5		No	Partner	n/a	Household head with partner, no other adults	n/a	11	Pre-Katrina	Houston Area	Major Issue	1 son with sickle cell anemia, r has been hospitalized with kidney problems, abused by her mother
14	P17	2 2		No	No Partner	n/a	Household head, no other adults	Father lives on other side of duplex	4	Post-Katrina	Original Home	Not a major issue	Children had rashes from water in evacuation, describes some pretty bad nightmares, but doesn't consider it a mental health issue
15	P18	3 4		Yes	Partner	n/a	Household head	n/a	6	Post-Katrina	Houston Area	Major Issue	pneumonia after previous child

Record 3 of 57

residence, and health status. The researcher can then read across to see whether any of the factors, such as whether the respondent has returned to New Orleans, are associated with health status.

The key to creating a useful matrix is laying out the relationships between two lists explicitly. For example, across the top of your matrix could be time in the field—with the four columns as the four seasons of the year you spent in the field. Across the rows you might include the friendships you established, the people you met, and how often you saw them. Looking at the matrix, you could begin to decipher seasonal patterns in the social relationships you formed, and you might notice something useful about how your friendships grew and waned during your time in the field.

ethnoarray A type of matrix used in qualitative research where the columns represent respondents and the rows represent domains and measures relevant to the research.

A specific type of matrix used in qualitative research is the **ethnoarray** (Abramson & Dohan, 2015). Arranging ethnographic data from fieldwork or interviews into an ethnoarray allows you to share your de-identified ethnographic data while preserving some of the context. The concept of an ethnoarray is adapted from arrays in biology, called *microarrays*, that are color-coded to show genes, markers, individuals, and populations (Abramson & Dohan, 2015, p. 281). According to Abramson and Dohan (2015, p. 300), the advantage of an ethnoarray is that it "helps readers see patterns, understand the analyst's interpretations, evaluate reliability, and gain a sense of an argument's scope and grounding."

Abramson and Dohan constructed an ethnoarray that displayed the results of an ethnographic and interview-based study of how cancer patients become involved in clinical trials (Figure 16.12). The columns in the array were patients they had studied, and the rows were domains and measures that were relevant to the decision to take part in a clinical trial. Each cell in the array reflects all the data that were relevant to each patient's domains and measures. The researchers color-coded the array to show whether a particular characteristic was present for each patient. The different colors in the ethnoarray indicate the degree to which a given characteristic is present. Orange means less than others, blue means typical or unremarkable among participants, and

FIGURE 16.12 Ethnoarray for Study of Cancer Patients and Involvement in Clinical Trials

This ethnoarray displays the results of a study of how cancer patients become involved in clinical trials. The patients are the columns. They were interviewed at two time periods (T1 and T2). The rows display factors associated with taking part in the trials. The colors indicate whether that patient experienced more or less of that factor: Orange means less than others, blue means typical, and green means more than others.

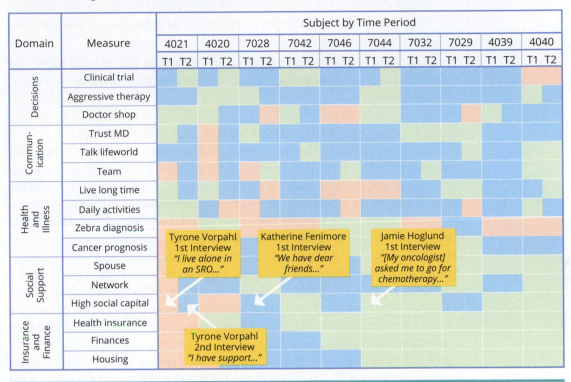

Source: Abramson and Dohan, 2015.

green indicates more than others. So, for example, for the rows of measures in the top-most domain, in clinical trials green means more consideration of taking part in a trial, and blue means little consideration of a trial. For aggressive therapy, green means more aggressive therapy, and orange means less aggressive. For doctor shop, green means more doctor shopping or change in doctor, and orange means relatively stable in doctor choice. The result is an array that can be "read" to see which domains and measures are associated with which outcomes among patients.

Abramson and Dohan suggest that this could be a way for ethnographers and interviewers to share data going forward in the future. This would work if the underlying data—interview quotations and field notes—were linked to the cells in the array: "If data are appropriately anonymized, they can be bundled with the array and shared so readers can examine the ethnographic evidence more directly and probe cell-to-data links" (Abramson & Dohan, 2015, p. 300).

Most QDA packages, including NVivo and ATLAS.ti, allow you to pull matrices directly from the coded transcripts using attribute codes and analytic codes. The link to the full transcript is preserved in the coding query, so it is possible to revisit the context easily. If you do not have access to QDA software or prefer a lower-tech approach, here are some suggestions for using simple tools to present your data and models visually:

- Miles and Huberman (1994) recommend diagrams on paper, with lines linking related issues, to display the conceptual framework.

- Becker (1998) suggests putting data and memos about the data on file cards that can then be spread on a large, flat surface and arranged and rearranged until they achieve a logical sequence.

- Agar (1991) suggests finding an empty classroom full of blackboards (or whiteboards) on which to draw maps of concepts and their interrelations (Weiss, 1994, p. 162).

RELIABILITY, COUNTERTHEMES, AND THE NULL HYPOTHESIS

Qualitative data analysis software makes it relatively simple to examine the cross-case *reliability* of the researcher's analytical coding. While some researchers have suggested using multiple coders to enhance reliability (see Campbell et al., 2013), another option is to query the intersection of analytic attributes and textual codes. For example, for each person-level categorization (instrumental/expressive), Deterding (2015, p. 289) output the text-level codes for instrumental and expressive logic. She did so to ensure that the textual evidence supported the distinct groups. The process of reducing data down from full transcripts, to indexed extracts, and finally to textual codes allowed her to assess whether she had applied uniform qualitative criteria across the sample, thus increasing the reliability of her results. As she examined the data in this reduced form, she realized that some respondents seemed misclassified. She then revised their classification, strengthening the validity of her analytic categories.

Researchers also need to double-check whether their models lead to counterthemes or disprove their hypothesis. As Howard Becker (1998) has noted, you need to evaluate the **null hypothesis**, which is the assumption that there is no relationship between two variables. According to Becker, once you think you know what the story is, you should assume that no relationships or patterns exist; for example, that instrumental or expressive identities do not determine persistence in community college or that ethnic background is unrelated to personal definitions of success. If you are not able to reject the null hypothesis, then you can have more confidence that your interpretation of your data is correct.

Let's consider a specific example of rejecting the null hypothesis. In their study of whether New York City young adults' perceptions of success vary by ethnic group, Kasinitz and colleagues (2008) cross-classified the most common codes in each transcript by ethnicity. They found that responses were very different *across* different ethnic groups and very similar *within* ethnic groups. But perhaps this association was due to some confounding factor, such as social class or neighborhood, rather than ethnicity. The researchers tested alternative explanations by checking whether gender or social class accounted for differences in ideas of success. They sorted the respondents' ideas of success by the social class of the respondents' parents and by the respondents' gender. Neither of those attributes created the large differences that sorting by ethnic group did. After testing these alternative explanations, Kasinitz and colleagues were more confident in their conclusion that ethnic groups differ in their cultural models of success.

null hypothesis A hypothesis that no relationship between concepts exists or no difference in the dependent variable between groups exists.

Examining the prevalence of codes across cases can also help researchers test and refine their theoretical explanations. There is considerable debate over the best methods for determining what counts as a robust finding in qualitative research. However, it seems clear that systematically evaluating alternative explanations and negative cases is an important part of creating a convincing theory. In doing so, you can refine your understanding of important relationships by examining (and interpreting) where your explanation does not work. Blee (2009, p. 148) suggests that model testing should take into account how data will be assessed "to ensure that (1) all data are considered, (2) spectacular/extraordinary events aren't overly stressed, [and] (3) data that diverge from the pattern are not discounted without a clear rationale to do so." Keep in mind that it is not the number of exceptions that is analytically important, but rather how the exceptions help refine the theory. The data-querying capacity of QDA software allows you to easily identify cases that are exceptions to trends and require further examination, helping you meet the "best practices" of research that require you to explicitly treat negative cases in your analysis.

If you apply your index and analytic codes reliably and your analytic codes are consistent, you can run text queries to document the interpretive validity of your findings (Maxwell, 1992, p. 48). For example, the analyst may want to make statements such as "N respondents demonstrated this logic." However, it is important to make sure that such statements are appropriate for the data (Small, 2011). For instance, if the interview protocol evolved over the course of the study and the same questions were not asked of everyone, it may not be appropriate to report coding counts. It may also be the case that you want to write about a topic that applies to only half your interviewees. By querying codes, you can identify how many transcripts include those codes, which might provide a more accurate number of interviews to report for your paper than would the full interview sample.

When building and testing models, researchers may merge (or lump) and split codes. For example, you may decide that the concept you have applied is too broad and that the concept has two qualitatively different dimensions to it. For example, in a study of gentrification, you may begin by just noting every time people describe gentrification positively. As you progress in your analysis, it may become clear that it is important to differentiate when people think gentrification is positive for all residents, when it is positive for old timers, and when it is positive just for newcomers. In this case, you would split the original code "gentrification—positive" into three new codes that note who the gentrification is positive for. Alternately, you may decide that multiple smaller concepts fall under a larger umbrella. QDA software makes it easy not only to split codes but also to aggregate them.

CONCEPT CHECKS

1. What is the purpose of writing memos? What might you write in a memo?

2. What is one technique for improving the reliability of coding?

3. Why would a researcher split or merge an analytic code?

WRITING THE FINAL REPORT

Writing the final report is not necessarily a completely separate stage of the process. The memos you have written along the way will compose a large chunk of your write-up, and the process of writing will no doubt lead to more analyzing of data, coding, retrieving of data, and elaborating or revising of models. A written qualitative report will follow many of the same conventions as a written quantitative or mixed-methods report (which we will describe in Chapter 17). However, several issues are unique to qualitative researchers.

A question that qualitative researchers often face in the writing process is how much of their raw material to include. It is important to resist the temptation to include too many quotes from your interviews or field notes. Sometimes, novice researchers will string together a long series of quotes on a topic to convince readers that it was the most common response. It is fine to include one or two illustrative quotes, noting whether this response was common. You should also avoid including a quote and then rephrasing it in the text. Quotes should stand on their own, and instead of repeating the material in your own words, you should explain to readers why this material is important.

You must also decide whether to include case studies, to focus on a holistic account of a few representative cases, or to organize the report thematically. For her book *Strangers in Their Own Land*, Arlie Hochschild (2016) conducted interviews with 60 people but organized her book around six characters, whom she fleshed out in great detail. Note that the final work is based on much wider work that does not make it into the write-up (see "From the Field to the Front Page"). Just as you do not report on every statistical model you run or every quantitative data set you create, you do not need to provide detailed information on every individual you interviewed. However, you *do* need to provide sufficient information about your methods and enough transparency about the decisions you made in sampling, coding, and building your model so that readers can entertain possible alternative explanations and decide whether your argument is convincing.

Finally, researchers who write using people's spoken words must decide how to portray spoken speech in written form. People do not speak as they would if they were writing. Laurence Ralph (2014, p. xviii) describes his interactions with one of the people he wrote about in his study in Chicago:

> Mrs. Pearl was speaking about how Tiko, a young gang-affiliated Eastwoodian, could help raise awareness about an upcoming rally at City Hall. What she said sounded to my ears like "Tiko can help us wit passing out dem flyers. He's always at our meetings, tryna figure out what he can do."
>
> When I showed Mrs. Pearl the transcript of the conversation, she changed "wit" to "with," "dem" to "them," and "tryna" to "trying to." Even though she agreed that my recounting of her dialogue accurately depicted what she actually said and how she actually sounded, she explained "Some things are just right" and what I had given her to read wasn't. To make matters worse, she chided me: "You're supposed to be educated, boy." She even shook her head.

The decision of whether to capture nonstandard English and whether to edit transcripts to delete "you know" and "like" differs among scholars. Some believe that you

THE FACES BEHIND TRUMP'S RISE

Donald **Trump's** meteoric rise from a reality TV star and real-estate developer to president of the United States seemed very improbable to many people, especially to liberal commentators on America's two coasts. In the aftermath of the 2016 election, newspapers and magazines scrambled to explain the Trump phenomenon (or "Trumpism"), interviewing people who attended his rallies, voted for him in the primaries and the general election, and saw him as a solution to problems they were facing in their own lives. People also turned to a book titled *Strangers in Their Own Land: Anger and Mourning on the American Right* by Berkeley sociologist Arlie Russell Hochschild (2016).

Hochschild began her research for the book in 2012, but the timing of its publication was fortuitous. The book, which examines the political beliefs of white conservatives, many of them Tea Party members, in rural Louisiana, burst on the national scene and quickly became a best seller. It was touted in major newspapers and magazines, and Hochschild appeared on radio and television talk shows to explain one group of Americans—white conservative rural Southerners—to other Americans, those who did not necessarily share or even understand their worldviews.

Hochschild began her research because she had grown concerned about political polarization in the United States. Living in the liberal bubble of Berkeley, California, she set out to understand how people with very different political views understood the world. She decided to concentrate on environmental issues and went to Lake Charles, Louisiana, to explore why people who lived in a very polluted part of the country were against regulating polluters—a political position that seemed incomprehensible to her. She started by holding four focus groups with local people and then conducted 60 in-depth interviews with Lake Charles residents. She attended political rallies and events, Tea Party and Republican gatherings, and toured the area. In the end, she had 4,000 pages of transcribed interviews as well as countless pages of field notes. She chose six people to profile in depth in her book and then conducted participant observation research, spending time at their homes, workplaces, churches, and in social activities.

Hochschild's book joined many analyses of the Trump candidacy. Even though she did not set out to understand him, many of the people she studied supported him, and her analysis of their thinking helps to explain some of his political support. Hochschild argues that the people she studied felt like they played by the rules and worked hard to get ahead, but they saw others—racial minorities and immigrants—getting ahead by receiving special favors from the government that sponsored their mobility. She uses the metaphor of the people she studied waiting in line and

Sociologist Arlie Hochschild's best-selling book *Strangers in Their Own Land* is based on qualitative research she conducted, including in-depth interviews, focus groups, and ethnography, of the white residents of Lake Charles, Louisiana.

the undeserving minorities and poor people cutting ahead in the line that leads to the American Dream while white working people fall further and further behind.

With so many journalists also trying to explain Trump's support, what makes Hochschild's book a work of social science? While some of the presentation of the data in Hochschild's book might seem similar to journalistic accounts, it is the design and, especially, the analysis of the data that sets this work apart. Hochschild set out with an inductive question of how to understand conservative voters in the rural South. She did not have a preconceived idea of what she would find, and she systematically talked to a wide range of people and participated in a great deal of social life. It was only after analyzing all her data that she began to craft the stories she tells in the book through the six people she profiles. While the book can be read as the story of six individuals, it is based on a wide-ranging and systematic study of an entire community.

A journalist, in contrast, would begin with the knowledge that he or she was going to write a story on the rise of Trump and would choose individuals who would articulate the points that the journalist already wanted to make on the basis of either poll data or the narrative the journalist had constructed. In other words, journalists set out to tell a story that they know matches what the experts on a topic have told them is going on. Hochschild *is the expert* on the thinking of these voters, and it is only after she entered the field with an open question and conducted a great deal of wide-ranging interviews and ethnography that she fashioned an explanation. Luckily for Hochschild, and for the American reading public, her basic research questions helped to address an urgent national debate centered on understanding the 2016 election results. Thanks to Hochschild, qualitative sociology has contributed to this national conversation.

should not change any words or edit quotations in any way. Most social scientists do edit spoken English to read more like written English, taking out verbal tics such as "um" and tightening the language to read better. However, these light edits should never change the meaning of what was said.

CONCLUSION

Qualitative data analysis is the rigorous process by which researchers systematically analyze textual data for the purpose of building or testing theory, providing an explanation for a social phenomenon, or generating hypotheses for further research. Using the steps outlined in this chapter, you move from an overwhelming mass of text to an ordered way of sorting and understanding what your data are saying. For QDA to contribute to social science, scholars must be transparent about their research process. This clear explication is essential and will help other researchers replicate key aspects of your study on their own populations or communities of interest.

Qualitative data analysis software can help the analyst in many ways: by keeping track of the codes; helping to organize the codebook that defines the codes; and helping analysts test their interpretations by looking at patterns in the data, finding negative cases, and summarizing the distribution of codes across cases. QDA software also improves the retrieval of information, allowing analysts to search their data and examine quotations within the context of the whole transcript. However, QDA software, unlike quantitative software, does not explain how two variables are related. Rather, it allows the analyst to define the variables and to examine the data.

The steps outlined in this chapter—managing and preparing the data, becoming familiar with and reducing the data, coding the data, writing memos, building and testing models, and writing the final report—are the steps that many qualitative researchers have followed and that have yielded order and insight from the chaos of thousands of pages of material. While there are no "cookbook" solutions to qualitative research analysis, there are many rewards to the creative hard work that goes into this task. Qualitative analysis helps us better understand our social world and yields new insights into human society.

End-of-Chapter Review

Summary

Qualitative data analysis refers to the process whereby researchers draw substantive findings from qualitative data such as text, audio, and images. Qualitative data analysis embodies both the "art" and "science" of social research because it requires creativity and methodological rigor.

Qualitative Data Analysis: Product and Process

- While qualitative data analysis does require creativity, many qualitative researchers follow a similar process.
- Whether qualitative or quantitative, all social science research should be transparent, logical, and rigorous.

Types of Qualitative Research

- The positivist approach to qualitative research assumes that there is an objective, external reality that can be described and analyzed with science, while the interpretivist approach focuses on research subjects' interpretations of the phenomena under study.
- Another way of distinguishing between the researchers' and the research subjects' perspectives is emic versus etic focus. An emic focus takes the respondent's viewpoint, while an etic focus maintains distance from the respondents in the interest of achieving scientific objectivity.
- Quantitative scholars seek to understand the effects of causes, or the effect of x on y. Qualitative scholars aim to assess the causes of effects, starting with an outcome and then working backward to identify the factors that influenced it.

Approaches to Causality in Qualitative Analysis

- Qualitative comparative analysis (QCA) is a model that guides the analysis of qualitative data for researchers using the causes-of-effects approach. It relies on rules of logic to distinguish necessary and sufficient causes of outcomes. One technique for making this distinction is constructing a truth table that sorts cases by the presence or absence of certain variables.
- The study of processes and mechanisms is another model that can guide qualitative researchers using the causes-of-effects approach. This model aims to show *how* one variable causes another.

Induction, Abduction, and Deduction

- Inductive research is a "bottom-up" approach; it begins with the data and then produces theoretical generalizations. Deductive research is a "top-down" approach; it begins with a theory or hypothesis and then collects and analyzes data to test the hypothesis. The deductive approach is more common in quantitative research.
- Grounded theory is a type of inductive analysis in which the qualitative researcher generates concepts and theories from a line-by-line analysis of the data. Researchers using this approach will use purposive sampling to select cases, then select additional cases based on emerging findings, and remain in the field until they reach saturation.

- The abductive approach, which attempts to build theory from "surprises" in the data, effectively combines deduction and induction.
- The extended case study approach, which is specific to ethnography, aims to produce broad theoretical knowledge. With this approach, researchers begin with a theory and then refine it in the field.

Steps in Qualitative Data Analysis

- Managing and preparing the data is the first step in qualitative data analysis. Recordings or notes taken during field work are digitized as text files, along with any impressions or ideas that the researcher had while in the field. The data should also be de-identified at this stage to protect research subjects' privacy.
- Becoming familiar with and reducing the data is the next step of qualitative data analysis, which involves eliminating any data from your interview transcripts or field notes that will not be useful for your analysis. At this point, researchers often prepare one- or two-page summaries of each of their interviews.
- The third step of qualitative data analysis is known as coding, which is the actual work of analyzing qualitative data. Coding involves breaking down the data into parts and identifying links among concepts.
- There are three types of codes: attribute codes, the salient personal characteristics of interviewees; index codes, or broad categories or topics; and analytic codes, which specify the meaning of significant portions of text.

Coding and Analysis

- Coding and analysis can be broken down into a three-stage process. The first stage involves preparing the data with attribute and index codes. Researchers should also familiarize themselves with their data and field notes at this stage.
- During the second stage of coding and analysis, researchers apply analytic codes to the data, typically by doing several, more progressively focused readings.
- Researchers should also write memos that explain why they created certain codes, highlight what they found interesting, and document the steps they took during their research. While writing memos is considered the fourth step in the qualitative data analysis process, it can occur at any point during the research process.
- Once coding is complete, the next step in the qualitative data analysis process involves building and testing models that answer the research question. The model, which can be described verbally or presented visually, should explain how the variables fit together to tell a story about the empirical world.
- After developing a model, researchers must test it to determine whether it is valid. This involves examining the reliability of the coding and searching for alternative explanations of patterns. Researchers will also evaluate the null hypothesis that there is no relationship between variables.

Writing the Final Report

- The last step in qualitative data analysis is writing the final report. When writing the report, it is important to avoid including too many direct quotations from interviews or field notes. Those quotes that are included should be able to stand on their own.

Rather than paraphrasing a quote, the researcher should explain to readers why the material is important.

- The researcher must also decide whether to structure the report thematically, by case study, or holistically.
- Lastly, the researcher must decide how to handle spoken speech. Some researchers believe you should not alter quotations in any way, while others make light edits so that the quotes read more like written English, removing verbal tics such as "um" and "you know."

Key Terms

abductive research, **542**

analytic codes, **553**

attribute codes, **551**

causes of effects, **537**

codebook, **563**

codes, **548**

coding, **548**

deductive research, **542**

de-identification, **546**

effects of causes, **537**

emic focus, **536**

ethnoarray, **568**

etic focus, **536**

extended case study approach, **544**

grounded theory, **542**

index codes, **552**

inductive research, **542**

interpretivist approach, **535**

interviewer effects, **546**

model, **563**

null hypothesis, **570**

positivist approach, **535**

purposive sampling, **543**

qualitative data analysis, **534**

saturation, **543**

truth table, **539**

typology, **558**

Exercise

The American Rhetoric website has a page that contains the text of 100 great American speeches (see http://www.americanrhetoric.com/top100speechesall.html). Choose three speeches that you think are related by topic, by speaker, or by some other theme. Read through the speeches and develop a coding scheme. Define at least 10 codes and apply them across the speeches. Define your codes. Using your coding scheme, write a short analysis comparing the speeches.

- How are the speeches you chose similar or different?
- What made it difficult to code the speeches?
- Did you code every part of every speech or only some parts?
- Do you have a hypothesis about why these are great speeches?
- Do the speeches you analyzed share anything in common?

In addition to writing and publishing research reports, social science researchers will often give oral presentations about their studies. The process of sharing scientific reports with others is known as dissemination.

17

COMMUNICATING SOCIAL SCIENCE RESEARCH FINDINGS

Sharing Your Results with Academic Audiences
Research Reports
Research Proposals
Posters
Oral Presentations

Beyond the Academy: Reaching Out to Broader Audiences
Evaluation Reports
Monographs
Government Reports
Policy Briefs
Editorials
Blogs

The Path to Publication: The Peer-Review Process
Step 1: The Author Decides Where to Send His or Her Work

Step 2: The Editor Decides whether to Send the Written Work Out for Peer Review

Step 3: Peer Reviewers, Selected by the Editor, Evaluate the Written Work

Step 4: The Author Revises and Resubmits the Work

Tips for Effective Writing
Getting Organized: Using Outlines Effectively

The Importance of Clarity, Precision, and Readability

Academic Integrity: Giving Credit Where Credit Is Due

Conclusion

Congratulations! You have learned the basics of sociological research methods and the fundamentals of carrying out quantitative and qualitative research. But carrying out your research project is just one part, albeit a major part, of the scientific process. Equally important is dissemination, or the process of sharing scientific results with others. This process involves writing up exactly what you did, why you did it, what you found, and how your findings shape our understanding of society. Precisely how you write up your research varies on the basis of your intended audience and your goal for communicating your discoveries. In this chapter, we describe the many different ways that social scientists disseminate their work and provide guidelines for effective and engaging communication.

We begin by describing the main elements of research reports and proposals, which are the primary vehicles through which academic researchers share their work. Chapter 16 provided in-depth guidelines for analyzing and presenting qualitative data, so we focus primarily on quantitative research reports in this chapter. We then discuss two alternative formats for disseminating your research: poster presentations and oral presentations. We then introduce approaches that researchers may use to communicate with nonacademic audiences, such as policy makers, journalists, and everyday people who care about human behavior but lack the specific knowledge necessary to read a technical research report.

We then describe the peer-review process, which refers to the intricate steps that research reports and books must go through before they can be published. It takes a village to produce science, as researchers rely on one another for feedback to help perfect their work. We conclude by sharing tips to help ensure that your writing is well organized, clear, and engaging, as well as rules for ethical writing. Citing others' work properly is a necessity, lest a writer be charged with plagiarism, or the intellectual theft of others' words or ideas. As you will see, writing can be challenging but is also one of the most rewarding and creative aspects of social research: Conveying our ideas clearly and convincingly is the first step in effecting social change.

SHARING YOUR RESULTS WITH ACADEMIC AUDIENCES

Think about the most recent paper you wrote for a sociology class. Let's say your grandparents or your 15-year-old cousin asked you, "So, what was your paper about?" You'd probably answer differently than you would if your professor asked the same question. Unless they are professional sociologists, you might avoid words like "convenience sample," "intersectionality," and "sociological imagination." Those phrases might draw blank stares or require extended explanations. Similarly, social science researchers tailor what they write and how they write it on the basis of the intended audience. We use different language, tone, and format when we are communicating to an academic audience of professors and fellow sociologists than when communicating to a nonacademic audience, which might include policy makers, the media, or people such as your grandparents and 15-year-old cousin. In this section, we focus on writing for academic audiences and describe research reports, research proposals, posters, and oral presentations.

Research Reports

Qualitative and quantitative sociologists alike write **research reports**, or formal written summaries of their research projects. Research reports follow a similar structure regardless of whether the work is quantitative or qualitative, although they differ slightly in how authors present their results and supporting materials such as tables or interview transcripts. Among professional social scientists, the most common form of research report is the peer-reviewed article in a **refereed journal**. Many of the studies that you read about in this book were published in journals such as *American Sociological Review, Journal of Health and Social Behavior*, or *Sociology of Education*. Studies published in a refereed journal are first evaluated by peer reviewers, or experts in the field, who provide substantive feedback that the author must incorporate before the study is ready for publication. As we will see later in this chapter, the peer-review process helps to uphold the quality and integrity of published research.

Research reports are different from other forms of writing you might have done, such as an essay, argument paper, or newspaper article. A research report, by definition, presents original research. The original research must be motivated by a theoretical puzzle and situated within a larger research context. The report also must answer the "So what?" question, conveying to readers why the research is important and what the results may mean for society. We describe the components of a research report in the following sections.

TITLE

The title should be concise, typically 10–15 words, and describe precisely what the study explores. Most quantitative researchers include in the report's title the name of the main independent and dependent variables; for example, "Racial Differences in Parental Responses to Children's Chronic Pain" (El-Behadi, Gansert, & Logan, 2017). This clearly conveys that the report will explore the effect of race (independent variable) on parental reactions to their children's chronic pain (dependent variable). Some authors elaborate by adding an amusing opening phrase to engage readers, such as "Your Face Is Your Fortune: Does Adolescent Attractiveness Predict Intimate Relationships Later in Life?" (Karraker, Sicinski, & Moynihan, 2017). The titles of qualitative research reports typically convey both the topic and site of the study, such as "Clubbing Masculinities and Crime: A Qualitative Study of Philadelphia Nightclub Scenes" (Anderson, Daly, & Rapp, 2009).

ABSTRACT

An **abstract** is a brief summary of the research report; it appears on the first page, just beneath the report's title and author names. Most abstracts range from 150 to 250 words, although the length and format differ slightly across journals and academic disciplines. Most sociology journals use an **unstructured abstract**, which has no subheadings and provides a brief synopsis of the work (Figure 17.1). Other journals, especially those in medicine, psychology, gerontology, and public health, have a **structured abstract**, which typically has four or five separate sections, such as background,

research report A formal written summary of a research project.

refereed journal A periodic publication in which all articles have gone successfully through the peer-review process.

abstract A brief description of the content of a scientific report.

unstructured abstract An abstract without subheadings that differentiate sections of the article.

structured abstract An abstract that typically has four or five separate and labeled sections, such as background, objectives, methods, results, and discussion.

FIGURE 17.1 Example of an Unstructured Abstract

American Sociological Association
Sociology of Education
2017, Vol. 90 (I) 89–108
© American Sociological Association 2017
DOI: 10.1 177/0038040716685873
journals.sagepub.com/home/soe

Into the Red and Back to the Nest?
Student Debt, College Completion, and Returning to the Parental Home among Young Adults

Jason N. Houle and Cody Warner

Abstract

Rising student debt has sparked concerns about its impact on the transition to adulthood. In this paper, we examine the claim that student debt is leading to a rise in "boomeranging," or returning home, using data from the National Longitudinal Survey of Youth 1997 Cohort and discrete time-event history models. We have four findings. First, student loan debt is not associated with boomeranging in the complete sample. However, we find that the association differs by race, such that the link between student debt and returning home is stronger for black than for white youth. Third, degree completion is a strong predictor of returning home, whereby those who fail to attain a degree have an increased risk of boomeranging. Fourth, young adult role transitions and socioeconomic well-being are associated with boomeranging. Findings suggest that rising debt has created new risks and may reproduce social inequalities in the transition to adulthood.

Source: Houle & Warner, 2017.

objectives, methods, results, and discussion (Figure 17.2). Regardless of the format, an abstract should tell readers the questions that are addressed by the research, why these questions are important, the data and methods used, the key findings, and the implications of the work for theoretical development, policy, or practice.

With abstracts, it is important to write as concisely as possible and to make every word count. As you can see in Figure 17.1, authors Jason Houle and Cody Warner (2017) briefly convey that student debt is a major social problem, and that they will explore the impact of student debt on young adults' ability to leave their parents' homes. They inform readers that they drew on data from the National Longitudinal Survey of Youth (NLSY) and then highlight the four key findings of their work. They conclude by alerting readers to the social and economic implications of student debt. There are no extraneous words: The abstract is clear and to the point.

While writing your abstract, keep in mind that it is the first impression a reader gets of a paper. Recall that when you have done literature reviews, you seldom saw an entire journal article online, but instead read its abstract. The abstract helps readers determine whether the article is relevant to their work, and whether they should track down the entire article. For this reason, the abstract must provide an accurate and clear synopsis of the full report.

INTRODUCTION

The introduction to a research report is similar to a movie trailer or the brief blurb on a novel's inside cover. Like a movie trailer, which offers a brief glimpse into the film's

FIGURE 17.2 Example of a Structured Abstract

The Gerontological Society of America

Journals of Gerontology: Social Sciences
cite as: *J Gerontol B Psychol Sci Soc Sci*, 2017, Vol. 72, No. 1, 187–199
DOI: 10.1093/geronb/gbv112
Advance Access publication December 11, 2015

Original Article
Your Face Is Your Fortune: Does Adolescent Attractiveness Predict Intimate Relationships Later in Life?

Amelia Karraker, Kamil Sicinski, and Donald Moynihan

Abstract

Objective: A growing literature documents the importance of physical attractiveness in young and middle adulthood for romantic, marital, and sexual relationships, but little is known about how attractiveness in adolescence matters to intimate relationships in later life. We ask: Does attractiveness early in life convey ongoing benefits late in life, or do such benefits erode over time?

Methods: We use multivariate regression models and more than 50 years of data from the Wisconsin Longitudinal Study to examine the connections between adolescent physical attractiveness and intimate relationships (i.e., sexual activity and access to potential sexual partners) in later life.

Results: We find that adolescent attractiveness facilitates sexual activity in later life. This relationship is largely driven by attractiveness increasing the probability of having access to potential sexual partners. However, attractiveness is not related to sexual activity among married couples, even after controlling for marital duration. Men, those in good health, and wealthier individuals are also more likely to engage in several facets of intimate relationships.

Discussion: These findings highlight the importance of relationship context for later life sexual activity and begin to explicate the pathways through which factors across the life course—particularly attractiveness—influence sexual activity in later life.

Source: Karraker, Sicinski, & Moynihan, 2017.

plot without giving away the ending, the introduction to a research report should pique readers' interest enough that they continue to read the entire report. But more important, the introduction should convey precisely what the report is about without giving away the results.

The introduction typically begins by conveying the importance of the study topic or the magnitude of the problem under investigation. Authors often begin by stating how many people are affected or by documenting that rising rates of people face the problem at hand. For instance, many sociologists study the causes and consequences of high body weight. To convince readers of the importance of this topic, they may begin their report by showing that obesity rates are high and rising and that more than 60% of Americans are now overweight. Another approach is to demonstrate the personal or financial costs of an issue, such as the toll that childhood poverty takes on children's health (Wimer et al., 2016) or the high cost to employers of worker absenteeism due to untreated depression (Fox, Smith, & Vogt, 2016).

After convincing readers of the importance of the study topic, the introduction should briefly establish the context for the study. This can be achieved with just one or two sentences summarizing what is already known about the topic and then highlighting the research gaps that motivated the project. The next sentences provide a road map of what follows, including a statement of the paper's goals and the methods used to achieve those goals. The introduction should convey how this paper makes a novel contribution to the literature on the study topic. Introductory remarks should be fairly brief, typically no more than two double-spaced pages.

LITERATURE REVIEW

All research reports, whether for a class assignment or an academic journal, include a review of the literature. (Revisit Chapter 2 for pointers on how to conduct a literature review.) The literature review included in your research report is distinct from the reviews you might write for a class. In a research report, you do not merely summarize the literature on your topic but rather synthesize it, critique it, and identify inconsistencies or limitations in prior studies. By highlighting deficiencies or gaps in prior work, you can demonstrate precisely what your study is doing that is new and different.

For instance, let's say as part of your literature review you read one article showing that women hold more liberal political attitudes than men do, another study that finds no gender differences, and a third reporting that men are more politically liberal than women. A good literature review would highlight potential reasons for these conflicting results, such as differences in the samples used in the three studies, the time periods of the studies, or the wording of the questions. A particularly effective literature review will use those discrepancies as a springboard for describing the research questions and analyses that follow.

During your literature search process, you should take detailed notes on each study that you will reference in your report. However, a literature review should not simply summarize individual studies one at a time, in a laundry-list fashion. Rather, the literature review should make general claims about what the literature shows, supporting those general claims with specific examples and references. As noted, the studies you cite may offer conflicting results, so it is important to make a generalized claim about what each group of studies shows, supporting each claim with references, and suggesting reasons for the discrepant findings. This discussion can be fleshed out by providing further detail on a few carefully selected studies that are most relevant to your own work (Patten, 2009). (To help you read, assess, and extract the key substantive and methodological points of the articles included in your literature review, we have included a guide in the Appendix.)

The literature review also should convey how your research questions developed from a larger theoretical or conceptual framework. A particularly good strategy is to organize the literature review around two or three competing conceptual models. Briefly describe each of the theoretical perspectives that guide the research puzzle, summarize empirical studies that offer support for each such perspective, and then articulate precisely how your own study will contribute to the literature.

For example, Rozario, Morrow-Howell, and Hinterlong (2004) explored how holding multiple social roles, such as worker or volunteer, affects the emotional well-being of older caregivers. In their literature review, the authors presented readers with two competing conceptual models: The first, *role strain theory*, proposes that holding multiple roles is stressful and emotionally exhausting, while the second, *role enhancement theory*, posits that multiple roles can increase emotional well-being because struggles in one area may be counterbalanced by joys in the others. The authors begin by making a general claim about each perspective and then provide specific details from past studies that support each theory. This approach is effective because it builds in some dramatic tension; readers will be curious to learn which of the two perspectives the research supports, and why. The authors explicitly state that their goal is to identify which framework best characterizes the experiences of older caregivers: "We address the question of whether or not multiple productive role occupancy has a positive or negative impact on older caregiver well-being" (Rozario et al., 2004, p. 416).

METHODS

The methods section of a research report conveys precisely what you did and how you did it. It is common to have subsections describing the sample, site, or population on which the study is based; the study's key measures; and the analytic technique used. The overall section typically begins with a description of the study population. If you collected your own data, you will describe your sampling strategy (see Chapter 6 for review) and other important pieces of information. For instance, if you carried out a survey study, you would provide information such as the response rate, number of persons in the overall sample and the number included in your own analysis, and possible sources of sample bias.

This section also describes how the data were collected, specifying whether the mode was a face-to-face interview, a telephone survey, a mail questionnaire, and so on. If you used a secondary data set, such as the General Social Survey (GSS), you would provide a brief summary of the study's sample and explain which participants were included in your study and why. For instance, if you are studying the attitudes of working-age adults toward Social Security, you would limit your analytic sample to persons ages 18–65.

Qualitative researchers provide slightly different information, such as the criteria for case selection (for example, did they choose typical cases? extreme cases? deviant cases?), what their sampling approach was, the number of persons interviewed, duration of time spent in the field, and whether saturation was used to determine the final sample size. For quantitative papers, the methods section also describes which variables were included in the analysis, and how they were measured. It is customary to describe the dependent variable(s) first, the key independent variable(s) second, purported pathway or mediator variables third, and control variables last.

The text also should describe precisely how the variables were conceptualized and operationalized. It is not sufficient to say that you include a measure of "parental status." A research report must clearly state whether "parental status" is a continuous measure indicating total number of children or a dichotomous variable where 1 = "yes, I have at least one child" and 0 = "no, I do not have any children," and so on. Readers cannot understand your study results or interpret the values presented in the paper's tables unless they know exactly what each variable represents. If the study includes indexes or scales, such as the Center for Epidemiologic Studies Depression Scale (CES-D; described in Chapter 5), it is customary to report the wording of all items composing the scale, the response categories used (for example, agree strongly to disagree strongly), how the total score was calculated (for example, all items were averaged), and some indicator of the scale's reliability, such as a Cronbach's alpha. Scales and instruments that are widely used, such as the CES-D, must be cited and included in the study's references list.

Qualitative researchers may provide a summary of the questions that they asked and may even include a copy of the semi-structured interview schedule as an appendix. They also may indicate where the interviews took place, how long they lasted, and any other details that may shape their results. Some also may provide details on how they gained access to the group they studied. (For further information on collecting and analyzing qualitative data, see Chapter 16.)

The final subsection of the methods section describes precisely how the data were analyzed; this is also called the *analytic plan*. Recall from Chapters 14 and 15 the types of quantitative data analysis techniques one might use, such as means comparisons or multivariate analyses such as ordinary least squares (OLS) regression. Authors should tell readers which method they used and why. Qualitative researchers will also describe precisely how they coded their data, providing information on the coding technique used, how they determined saturation, the software used to analyze the data (such as NVivo or ATLAS.ti), and other details of analysis, as described in Chapter 16.

Whether you are a qualitative or quantitative researcher, one golden rule should guide you as you write up your methods section: the goal of replicability. Methods sections should be sufficiently detailed so that a researcher reading your paper could replicate your study by following the steps that you laid out. Recall that replicability is a hallmark of good science: **Replicability** means that a study should produce the same results if repeated exactly.

replicability The capacity to be reproduced with similar results in different samples or populations.

RESULTS

The results section is often the most interesting and exciting part of a paper, because this is where the new research discoveries are presented. In general, results sections of quantitative reports are organized around the tables that present full results. We will say more in later sections about what goes into tables, how to format them, and how to order them. Think about each table as addressing a specific research aim, where the descriptive statistics table provides a statistical portrait of your sample or shows basic differences between the subpopulations you are comparing. The multivariate analysis tables, by contrast, demonstrate the effect of one variable on another, often revealing the pathways or mechanisms that link your key independent and dependent variables. Carefully structuring your tables will help you organize your results section. A results section typically begins by describing the sample composition, referring to the descriptive statistics table. It then focuses on simple associations between the key independent and dependent variables, such as the results from cross-tabulations or means tests. Finally, it summarizes the results of the multivariate analyses such as regression models.

Tables can be dense and contain highly detailed information. Researchers need not report every single result that emerged from their analysis. Rather, the results section should focus on answering the paper's main research questions or evaluating the study hypotheses. If a researcher is examining whether race and ethnicity affect one's college aspirations, he or she need not report the coefficients of every single control variable included in the statistical models. Rather, the results should focus on the size and significance of the variables capturing race and ethnicity and describe how these effects change when strategically selected control variables are entered into the model. Likewise, qualitative researchers need not report every interesting quote that emerged from their interviews or every observation they made in the field.

Specificity and precision are essential when writing up results. Always identify the unit of a measure, such as dollars, inches, or points on a standardized personality test. Specify the direction and magnitude of an association; that is, whether an association is positive or negative, and how large or small it is. Be precise when discussing correlation versus causation. If you cannot definitively ascertain causal ordering because you are using a cross-sectional study, it is best to use language of association rather than causation. For example, if a researcher uses cross-sectional data and discovers that obese high school students have lower self-esteem than their slender classmates, she cannot say "being obese causes teenagers to have low self-esteem." It would be more accurate to simply say "obese high school students reported lower self-esteem than their more slender classmates."

DISCUSSION

The discussion is the final section of the research report. It summarizes the study's key findings but goes beyond the information already presented in the results section. This section provides the author with an opportunity to step back from the numbers or quotes and interpret or contextualize these discoveries. It typically opens with a statement of the study's purpose, often repeating the main questions or hypotheses. Next, the author will summarize the key findings or answer the study's main questions. If the results do not support the paper's original hypotheses, the author should suggest both theoretical and methodological reasons for this departure. A good discussion will contrast or highlight consistencies (or inconsistencies) between the study findings and prior research and theory. The discussion section also must answer the question: What does this study add to our knowledge, and how does it build upon prior work?

In some subdisciplines of sociology, the discussion section will also highlight the implications of the findings for policy or practice. For example, Houle and Warner (2017) found that among blacks but not whites, student loan debt increases the chances that a young person will "boomerang" back to living in his or her parents' home. In their discussion section, the authors use these results as a springboard for evidence-based policy recommendations, writing, "Policies intended to alleviate debt hardship should be targeted toward particular vulnerable groups rather than universally" (p. 104). Authors are advised to tread lightly: The recommendations offered should be supported by the data and should not be personal opinions that stray beyond what the data can support.

One way to strengthen one's recommendations for policy or practice is to tackle head-on the issue of substantive or practical significance, which refers to whether a statistical effect is large enough to be meaningful in the "real world." Let's say you conducted an evaluation study testing whether a school system's new fourth-grade math curriculum increased students' scores on standardized math tests. Your results showed that 72% of students exposed to the new curriculum passed their standardized math test, compared to 67% of students who received the old curriculum. This difference was

Houle and Warner found that the link between student loan debt and boomeranging was stronger for black youth than white youth.

statistically significant at the $p < .001$ level. Would you then recommend that all school systems adopt the new curriculum? Here, you would want to explain to readers the magnitude of the difference and what it would mean in real-world costs. Miller (2004) suggests the following text, which honestly weighs whether the costs justify the benefits:

> Although the improvement in math test scores associated with the new math curriculum is highly statistically significant, the change is substantively inconsequential, especially when the costs are considered.... [This] increase in math scores corresponds to very few additional students achieving a passing score, or mastering important fourth-grade math skills such as multiplication or division. Spending the estimated $40 million needed to implement the new curriculum on reducing class sizes would likely yield greater improvements. (p. 50)

Discussion sections also include a limitations subsection. This subsection summarizes the methodological weaknesses of the study and suggests ways these limitations might have affected the study results. Quantitative and qualitative researchers note different types of limitations. Qualitative researchers often point out that findings from their particular study site or subpopulation may not be generalized to other contexts. For instance, in writing up the results of her ethnography of the ways that middle-class versus working-class parents raise their children, Annette Lareau (2003, p. 774) acknowledged that "ethnographies offer rich descriptive detail but typically focus on a single small group." Researchers may also acknowledge how their personal characteristics biased their interpretation of the results or shaped their interactions with research subjects. Sociologists often study hard-to-reach and disadvantaged populations such as homeless persons. As highly educated individuals, researchers should be sensitive to the implications of these status differentials.

In the limitations subsection, quantitative researchers tend to report on potential sources of sample bias and study attrition (see Chapter 7 for a review of different types of bias); a narrowly defined or nonrepresentative sample (for example, a study of whites only or college graduates only) or a small sample size with limited statistical power; poor-quality measures of key concepts; the use of cross-sectional data only, which limits one's ability to ascertain causal ordering; and lack of data on potentially important control variables. For instance, Houle and Warner (2017, p. 104) acknowledge "it is possible that young adults in our sample may not have been residentially independent long enough to observe an association between debt and boomeranging."

Rest assured that every study has limitations, and acknowledging them does not detract from the quality of your study. Rather, it is a sign of having a critical mind and a deep understanding of the research process. Most authors discuss their study limitations but then note ways that they might address these concerns in a larger or more rigorous study in the future. Researchers also tend to provide an honest appraisal of how much a limitation undermines their conclusions. For instance, in a study of the ways that marital quality affects older adults' emotional well-being, Carr, Cornman, and Freedman (2016) acknowledged that they could not definitively ascertain causal ordering because of their cross-sectional data. However, they put this limitation in perspective by noting that their "concerns are partly allayed by a recent meta-analysis showing that the association between marital quality and well-being was stronger when well-being was the dependent variable (Proulx et al., 2007)." In other words, although they used data from only a single point in time, prior studies suggest that the direction of association runs from marital quality to well-being, rather than well-being affecting marital appraisals.

REFERENCES

Scholarly writing always includes a **bibliography** (also referred to as a *references list* or *works cited*), which provides a full reference for every source cited in a report. In the report, sources are typically referenced using parenthetical citations, and every parenthetical cite is accompanied by a full entry in the bibliography, which appears at the end of the report. On rare occasions, sociologists will cite sources using endnotes or footnotes rather than parenthetical citations. Different academic disciplines and publications have different citation styles, but all bibliographies share one important characteristic: The sources are alphabetized on the basis of the first letter of the last name of the study's first author or, if the author is an organization (for instance, the American Medical Association), the first letter of the first word of the organization name.

Most sociologists abide by the *American Sociological Association Style Guide* (American Sociological Association, 2014). The guidelines are complex, with slightly different formats for journal articles, newspaper articles, books, unpublished reports, personal interviews, survey codebooks, and so on. Over the past decade or two, scholars have increasingly cited online documents, such as statistical reports from government organizations such as the U.S. Census Bureau. These reports also must be cited in full, and each of these sources in the references list should include the most recent date on which the web address of the document was accessed. Just as authors must double-check their references for accuracy, they should also check to see whether the web links they referenced are still "live" and accurate. When you think your paper is completely finished and ready to hand in, take a moment to do a final references check. This means that every work cited in the paper should be listed in the bibliography, and every work listed in the bibliography should be cited in the paper.

TABLES AND FIGURES

Tables, figures, and other appendices, such as a copy of the interview schedule used during one's in-depth interviews, are an essential part of any research report. In fact, many readers often flip to the tables before reading the paper! We can think about tables or interview transcripts as the raw material that forms the basis of one's paper, whereas the results section is a carefully constructed although incomplete synopsis of every finding generated in the analysis. Tables vary in their format and content, but most quantitative social scientists follow the same general sequence.

The first table of a report typically presents results from the univariate analysis. This includes descriptive statistics for the full sample, such as the mean, standard deviation, and range for continuous variables, and proportions for categorical variables. Some authors also include bivariate analyses, which entails presenting the descriptive statistics for the subgroups of interest and indicating which subgroup differences are statistically significant. The subgroups compared typically are the different categories that comprise a study's key independent variable. For instance, Figure 17.3 presents Table 1 from Houle and Warner's (2017) study of young adults who "boomerang," or return to live in their parents' home after college. In the table, the second column shows

bibliography A list that provides a full reference for every source cited in a research report.

FIGURE 17.3 Example of a Descriptive Statistics Table

Variable	Full Sample	Never Boomerang	Ever Boomerang	t Test
Ever boomerang	0.590			
Annual boomerang	0.093			
Student debt				
Proportion with debt	0.351	0.397	0.247	***
Debt among debtors (thousands of dollars)	17.57	18.42	14.50	***
	(21.73)	(21.91)	(20.73)	
Observations	31,731	21,767	9,964	

Data: National Longitudinal Study of Youth 1997. Analytic sample includes respondents who attended college.
Note: Standard deviations in parentheses. Significance tests denote difference of means between never and ever boomerang.
***$p < .001$.

Source: Houle & Warner, 2017.

descriptive statistics for the full sample, the third column describes those who have "never" boomeranged back to their parents' home, and the fourth column shows those who have "ever" returned to their parents' home. The last column indicates which subgroup differences are statistically significant. We can see that 35% of the total sample has debt, yet this proportion is significantly higher among those who have "never" (40%) versus "ever" (25%) boomeranged back to the parental home, a difference that is statistically significantly at the $p < .001$ level. That means that in the overall sample, before the authors control for any covariates, never-boomeranged versus ever-boomeranged young people differ significantly with respect to whether they have any debt.

The third table and higher of a report usually present the results from multivariate analyses, or the analyses that generated the report's main findings. Recall from Chapters 14 and 15 that analytic techniques such as regression tell us how our theoretically key independent variable affects our dependent variable, after adjusting for potential confounds. It is helpful for researchers to delineate the pathways through which the key independent variables affect the dependent variables: These pathways are called *mediators*. Researchers tend to arrange their models in a multivariate table so that readers can see whether unadjusted effects of the key predictor variable can be partially explained by each block of potential explanatory factors.

The regression table in Figure 17.4 shows whether a mother's ethnicity and immigration status affect the internalizing behaviors of her child, where internalizing behaviors include feeling sad, anxious, and fearful (Landale et al., 2015). This table presents the OLS regression coefficients. The key independent variables are entered in the first block (model 1) and are followed by subsequent blocks, including controls for child characteristics (model 2), mother and family characteristics (model 3), and perceived neighborhood characteristics (model 4). Model 1 shows that children of every "Ethnicity/mother's immigration status" group (except "Other Latino undocumented") have fewer mental health symptoms than do children of "Mexican undocumented" mothers. As the table shows, across all four models the coefficients for

FIGURE 17.4 Example of a Multivariate Analysis Table

Ordinary Least Squares Regression Analysis of Children's Internalizing Behavior Problems (Los Angeles Family and Neighborhood Survey, 2000–2002, *N* = 2,535).

Variable	Model 1	Model 2	Model 3	Model 4
Ethnicity/mother's immigration status				
Mexican undocumented	(reference)	(reference)	(reference)	(reference)
Mexican naturalized/documented	–1.20***	–.94**	–1.02***	–1.04***
Mexican U.S. born	–2.07***	–1.60**	–1.79***	–1.90***
Other Latino undocumented	–.21	–.22	–.49	–.45
Other Latino naturalized/documented	–1.10**	–.81*	–1.04**	–1.08**
Other Latino U.S. born	–2.58***	–2.19***	–2.33***	–2.43***
White naturalized/documented	–2.86***	–2.19***	–2.49***	–2.42***
White U.S. born	–2.28***	–1.64***	–1.84***	–1.82***
Black naturalized/documented	–2.52*	–2.82*	–2.66*	–2.75*
Black U.S. born	–1.93***	–1.63***	–1.84***	–1.87***
Asian naturalized/documented	–2.40***	–1.72***	–1.77***	–1.78***
Asian U.S. born	–2.57***	–1.99**	–2.09**	–2.16**
Child characteristics				
Female	.08	.06	.06	.06
Age	–.03	–.04[a]	–.04*	–.05**
Mother/family characteristics				
Mother's education < high school		.42[a]	.32	.29
Poor family		.55*	.51*	.48*
Single parent		.55**	.46*	.42*
Mother depressed			1.73***	1.71***
Family routines				–.04**
Perceived neighborhood characteristics				
Child-centered closure and control				–.03*

Note: Analysis based on weighted data.
[a]*p* < .10, *p < .05, **p < .01, ***p < .001 (two-tailed tests)

Source: Landale et al., 2015.

every measure of "Ethnicity/mother's immigration status" is statistically significant as indicated by the asterisks, except for children of "Other Latino undocumented" mothers, which have no asterisks. Children of "White U.S. born" mothers have 2.28 fewer mental health symptoms than do children of "Mexican undocumented" mothers, although this difference decreases considerably to –1.64 after family socioeconomic characteristics are controlled in model 2, suggesting that part of the advantage enjoyed by white U.S.-born children is due to their parents' higher education and lower rates of poverty.

A bar graph or line graph can be particularly effective in conveying complex results. Authors tend to use figures sparingly in research reports, relying on them more when presenting their research in posters or oral presentations, as we shall see later in the chapter. Bar graphs are helpful when conveying the results from interaction term

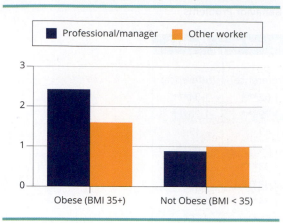

*Body mass index.
Source: Carr and Friedman, 2005.

analyses. Recall from Chapter 15 that moderating variables help us determine "for whom" or "under what conditions" an independent variable affects a dependent variable. Figure 17.5 summarizes moderation analyses showing that obese workers are more likely than their normal-weight counterparts to report workplace discrimination; however, these odds are highest for obese white-collar professional workers. They are nearly 2.5 times as likely as normal-weight workers in other professions to report such discrimination, whereas obese workers in nonprofessional jobs are only 1.5 times as likely as their more slender counterparts to report such mistreatment. These results suggest that the stigma of obesity is most pronounced in upper-middle-class social worlds (Carr & Friedman, 2005).

Tables and figures should be able to stand on their own. That means a reader should be able to make sense of this information without flipping back to the text for explanation. Thus, tables should include a clear and descriptive title, the rows and columns should be clearly labeled, the variable names should be written out in full, the metric such as the scale range should be clear, and the table notes should signify what kinds of statistical tests were performed; asterisks are often used to denote the level of statistical significance. In Figure 17.3, the descriptive statistics table tells us that the sample includes National Longitudinal Study of Youth 1997 cohort respondents who attend college, what each value represents, which differences are statistically significant, and other analytic details, such as whether missing data were imputed. Tables and figures tell a story that is as valuable as the prose presentation of results.

Research Proposals

The research report you write for your research methods class might inspire you to carry out a larger research project, such as a senior thesis. You might even consider applying for a small research grant from your university to help support this larger project. Before researchers launch a new and substantial research project, they often write a proposal to help guide them through the full project. Sometimes they will submit this proposal to an organization that could potentially fund their research study, such as the National Science Foundation. The proposal provides a road map for what you intend to do and includes sufficient detail such that if you follow it like a cookbook, you should have a successful research project.

A proposal has many of the same components as a research report, with two main differences: First, the proposal describes the method that one intends to follow, whereas the research report describes the method that the investigator already followed. Second, the proposal will not have a formal results section because the project has not yet been carried out. The most important goal of your proposal is to inspire confidence in your readers; they must be convinced that your project is important and well designed and that you are capable of carrying it out in a timely manner. Proposals vary in length and style on the basis of the type of research question and research methodology proposed. As a general rule, proposals include the following sections.

SPECIFIC AIMS

This brief (one- to two-page) section describes your specific research goals. You will state your main research questions, the method to be used, and a brief synopsis of the strengths and potential contributions of your proposed study. This section is similar to an abstract, as it captures the key points of the remaining sections. Most research projects have no more than five aims. You can think of each aim as a discrete research question to be explored, such as: "We intend to examine: (1) whether parents' level of education affects the political attitudes of young adults ages 18–24; (2) whether these effects differ for 18- to 24-years-olds who are attending college full-time versus those engaged in other activities; and (3) the extent to which the patterns explored in (1) and (2) differ by the young adult's gender."

BACKGROUND AND SIGNIFICANCE

This section will probably be the longest and most detailed, accounting for roughly half of the entire proposal. It is similar to the literature review in a research report. This synthesis and critique of prior work provides the springboard for conveying why your research is innovative and important. You also can describe how your research will make a contribution to sociological knowledge and, in some cases, public policy or practice.

PRELIMINARY STUDIES

The length of this section varies on the basis of how much preliminary work you have done. Advanced scholars describe their related research projects and highlight any remaining unanswered questions. This brief section might be a place where a junior scholar would report the results from a course paper and highlight those results that they will delve into more fully in a larger subsequent project. Researchers also may report the results of a **pilot study**, or a small preliminary study that is a "trial run" for the larger study. For instance, you might plan to do a content analysis of 50 issues each of three different young women's magazines to explore how messages about teen sex have changed over the past 50 years. Your pilot study might involve analyzing just two or three issues to demonstrate that you have developed a sampling and data-coding strategy that is appropriate for your research question.

pilot study A small preliminary study that is a "trial run" for the larger study.

PROPOSED METHODS

The length of the proposed methods section varies on the basis of how elaborate or well formulated one's research plans are. It should describe in as much detail as possible the data-collection procedures and whether the research method is ethnographic, experimental, survey, interview study, content analysis, or other method. If you are using secondary data, you should describe the data set and variables thoroughly. The choice of research method should be justified on scientific grounds: Is this the best method to explore your aims? If so, why? It's important to be honest and upfront about the limitations and challenges you anticipate and describe a clear plan for mitigating the effects of these limitations.

FIGURE 17.6 Sample Timeline for a Research Study

Project Activity	Sept.	Oct.	Nov.	Dec.	Jan.	Feb.	March	April	May
Write literature review	X	X							
Write and submit IRB form	X								
Identify magazine sampling frame	X	X							
Conduct content analysis		X	X	X	X				
Data analysis				X	X	X	X		
Write up results					X	X	X		
Write and submit final paper							X	X	X

TIMELINE

Some funding agencies (or your professors) may require that you provide a timeline for carrying out your proposed project. Here, you list the time period (month and year) when you expect to carry out each stage of the research. For example, the proposed timeline for your senior thesis project on magazines' coverage of teenage sex over the past 50 years might be shown in Figure 17.6.

HUMAN SUBJECTS OR ETHICS STATEMENT

Every proposal must include a brief summary of human subjects concerns and how you will address these concerns in an ethical manner. Although a content analysis of magazine images and articles does not involve human subjects, let's say you wanted to supplement that analysis with open-ended interviews with young female magazine readers. You might want to ask them how they felt reading articles about teen sex or whether these articles changed their minds about being sexually active. Although these questions might seem innocuous to you, they may conjure up troubling memories to a young woman who has been sexually assaulted. As you develop the human subjects or ethics statement of your proposal, please revisit the important lessons presented in Chapter 3.

REFERENCES

As with research reports, complete bibliographic information for all sources cited in the proposal should be included in a bibliography.

Posters

While walking the hallways of your academic department, you might have noticed large colorful posters with statistical tables and bar graphs brightening the walls. These posters are not merely decorative; they contain the results of original research. The poster format is a common way for researchers to present their work at professional conferences, science fairs, and research showcases, where sophisticated studies are presented in a concise, clear, and visually appealing way. Researchers often have a choice as to whether they will give a poster or oral presentation at a conference.

Posters, like all other forms of research dissemination, should be tailored to their audience. A poster at a university-wide research showcase or science fair attended by students and faculty from dozens of disciplines (and even parents) would be simpler and use less jargon than a poster presented at a specialized meeting, such as the annual meeting of the American Sociological Association or American Society of Criminology. At poster sessions, the author typically stands in front of his or her poster and answers questions as people come by to visit. Poster presentations are an excellent opportunity for junior scholars because they provide a venue for one-on-one conversations with conference attendees who may be known experts in the field.

A poster can be constructed using basic software such as PowerPoint. Researchers create 16–20 slides that summarize their work and then arrange those slides in a series of rows or columns to tell their story. Most posters are 4 feet by 8 feet, so authors often use a professional printing service to print them. Others print each slide on a separate piece of paper and then tack them up to a large corkboard. The substantive structure of a poster is similar to that of a research report, with sections focused on background, methods, results, and discussion. The main difference is that the poster presents only the minimal information one needs to understand the study. One of the most common mistakes that poster authors make is clutter: putting too much material on a single slide; using a small, hard-to-read font; and burying the key messages. While posters should aim to be visually appealing, substance is more important than form. The visual bells and whistles should not detract attention from the poster's results (Miller, 2007).

Figure 17.7 provides a general schematic for organizing your poster. Most posters have three or four wide columns, with the paper's title, author names, and author affiliations at the top. The columns would then include slides that present (1) the abstract; (2) theoretical background; (3) the overarching aims or objectives of the study; (4) study hypotheses or specific research questions; (5) a description of the data resource or site; (6) sample characteristics; (7) the study's variables, including independent, dependent, and control variables; (8) results; (9) discussion and implications; and (10) limitations. As noted earlier, most posters are made up of 16–20 individual slides, so an author may include multiple slides on a particular section, such as three results slides or several discussion slides, according to the complexity and design of the study. Before printing your poster, proofread it carefully to ensure the slides are presented in a sensible order that follows a logical progression (Miller, 2007).

Presenting a poster is an active, two-way experience. As we noted earlier, people who come to visit your poster may pepper you with questions. For that reason, it is

Research posters present the results of original studies in a concise and visually appealing way.

FIGURE 17.7 Guidelines for Preparing a Research Poster

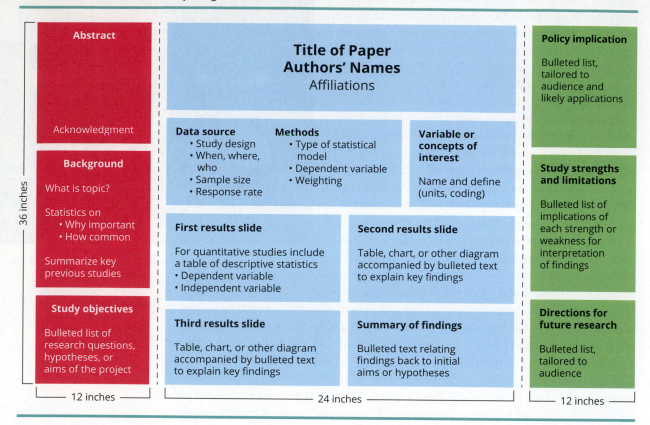

Source: Miller, 2007.

important to be well prepared. You might anticipate questions and then have a few brief responses rehearsed. You may also have printouts of your paper's abstract on-hand; you can then provide passersby with a brief summary of your research and your contact information. That will help to continue the conversation and may even lead to a new research partnership.

Oral Presentations

Comedian Jerry Seinfeld famously observed that public speaking is the No. 1 fear of American adults, even more common than fear of death. So, he reasoned, "To the average person, if you go to a funeral, you're better off in the casket than doing the eulogy." Jokes aside, oral presentations are one of the most effective and engaging ways for scientists to share their work. But an oral presentation doesn't mean just standing up and providing an improvisational riff on one's study; it requires the same careful preparation as a poster or a written research report. Even the most experienced presenters spend hours preparing their results for clear presentation in an oral presentation.

At professional academic meetings, such as American Sociological Association (ASA) meetings, a presenter will be one of four or five speakers on a topical panel. Sometimes speakers are invited; other times they submit a paper to a conference and are selected to speak on a panel with scholars studying similar topics. Each speaker is allotted 15–18 minutes, so those precious minutes must be used strategically. Most presenters use slides that resemble the content and style of slides displayed at a poster presentation. The content and order of these slides would generally mirror those in the poster. The slides should convey the research aims, a cursory review of the theoretical framework that motivated the project, data and methods, results, and discussion. Most experts estimate that speakers should have no more than one slide per minute, so a 15-minute talk should include no more than 15 slides. Audience members are most excited to hear new results, so the bulk of the talk should focus on methods and results, rather than the literature review.

Avoid slides that are too cluttered, and make sure to use a font big enough that people sitting in the back row of the audience can read it clearly. Tables should not be pasted in from your paper, although a small excerpt of a full table could be shown in large font. Use basic graphics such as bar graphs or line graphs to communicate your statistical results. Remember, the slides are not only for your audience; they also serve as a guide for you, the speaker. Although novice presenters will sometime write out a script and read it word for word, that approach is generally frowned upon. Notes can be helpful, but speakers who read off their paper are not very engaging. If their eyes are glued to their script, they may avoid eye contact with audience members or may not gesture to the screen to point out appropriate images. Worse yet, people who read off the page may lose their place, and then frantically try to get back on track. That's why it is so important to practice, practice, practice—both to ensure that you deliver a clear and engaging talk that accurately conveys your findings and to stay within the allotted time.

Oral presentations have another essential component: the question and answer (Q&A) period after the end of the formal presentation. The Q&A period can be challenging, but it is also an opportunity for the speaker to shine. Audience members may ask you to clarify methodological aspects of your work, speculate about the "real world" implications of your findings, or even imagine how you might have carried out your study differently if you had received a large research grant. It is a good idea to come to your talk prepared with answers to those questions you anticipate receiving. Your professor or classmates can help you develop such a list, especially if you do a practice presentation with them. Try to speak slowly, clearly, and to breathe. Practice makes perfect; new researchers are encouraged to do as many as three "dress rehearsals" in preparation of their formal oral presentation.

CONCEPT CHECKS

1 | Name each of the components of a research report.

2 | What is the main purpose of a research proposal?

3 | What are two similarities between poster and oral presentations?

4 | What are two differences between poster and oral presentations?

BEYOND THE ACADEMY: REACHING OUT TO BROADER AUDIENCES

Social scientists study topics that nearly everyone cares about in some way. Whether education, health, crime, the environment, or race relations, chances are that you are studying a topic that is of great concern to citizens of the United States and around the world. Our work also can help shape public policy and public opinion, provided the results are conveyed clearly and succinctly. Researchers have many platforms at their disposal for disseminating their work broadly. We describe several of these mechanisms and provide guidelines for effective communication with policy makers, corporate decision makers, and everyday citizens.

Evaluation Reports

evaluation research A type of research designed to determine whether a social intervention or policy, such as reducing class size or implementing a new workplace program, produces its intended effects.

Evaluation research, as we learned in Chapter 9, assesses whether an intervention, such as smaller class sizes or a workplace wellness program, produces its intended effects. Evaluation reports disseminate the results of an intervention study, with an eye toward communicating results to stakeholders, such as policy makers, practitioners, or corporate decision makers. They follow the same format as a research report, but they emphasize the practical rather than theoretical implications of the study findings. Evaluation reports should convey (1) whether the program or intervention was effective and (2) the extent to which the study findings might be applied to other settings (Centers for Disease Control and Prevention, 2013). For example, if a pregnancy prevention program is introduced in the New York City public school system to great success, might we expect a comparable program to generate the same results in the Atlanta public school system? A clear evaluation report can have far-reaching effects on social institutions such as schools, corporations, or the government (Centers for Disease Control and Prevention, 2013).

Monographs

A monograph is a book-length publication that focuses on a specific research question or research project. For most qualitative researchers, the monograph is the primary format used to describe a study's goals, methods, results, and the implications of those results. Monographs might also include illustrations and photographs, especially for researchers who want to provide glimpses into their fieldwork. Monographs are of interest to both academic and nonacademic audiences; for this reason, many are called "crossover" books, meaning they bridge the two different types of audiences. Many classic ethnographies in sociology, such as *Sidewalk* by Mitchell Duneier (1999) and *The Challenger Launch Decision: Risky Technology, Culture, and Deviance at NASA* by Diane Vaughan (1996), and observational and interview studies such as Annette Lareau's (2003) *Unequal Childhoods: Class, Race, and Family Life* and Arlie Hochschild's (2012) *The Second Shift: Working Families and the Revolution at Home*, are monographs.

Government Reports

State, federal, and local governments publish informative reports that describe the characteristics of a population, the results of a government study, or new trend data based on federally funded resources such as the Current Population Study. These reports do not have a literature review nor do they discuss sociological theories; rather, they focus on the questions of who, what, when, and why. Government reports have a brief and straightforward methods section, where they define the key terms or measures used. Some of the most common topics of these reports are population size and growth, marriage and family-formation patterns, education and employment statistics, health data, and shifts in the nation's population composition on the basis of age, race, or migration status.

The Census Bureau publishes concise, descriptive reports describing the characteristics of individuals, families, and households in the United States. For instance, in one such report, the Census Bureau described the prevalence and patterning of same-sex households in the United States on the basis of an analysis of 2010 American Community Survey data (Lofquist, 2011). The first page of these reports typically defines the terms and concepts used, such as explaining how same-sex households are measured. The statistics presented are straightforward, showing univariate and bivariate statistics only, and simple graphics and tables are used to help communicate the results. Sometimes maps are also used.

For instance, the report on same-sex marriages presents a color-coded map of the United States to show state-level differences in the prevalence of same-sex households. The map shows that same-sex households are more common on the East and West Coasts than in the Heartland and Deep South. Rural states like the Dakotas have particularly low rates of same-sex households. The reports are vetted internally before publication. Government reports are an excellent resource for ascertaining the prevalence and social patterning of a particular phenomenon and the level of change documented over time.

Policy Briefs

A **policy brief** is a short, impartial summary of what is known about a particular social or economic issue (Eisele, n.d.). Its main purpose is to facilitate and inform policy making. Policy makers often need to make important decisions under tight time constraints and require short briefs that provide clear and impartial evidence-based assessments of the policy options on the table. Policy briefs synthesize detailed information in a concise and jargon-free way so that stakeholders can understand the core issues and make informed decisions regarding the likely consequences of different policies. Briefs use straightforward tables and clear graphics to convey trends and facts and include a short list of references as well as suggestions for additional sources of background information.

Because the main audience for these reports is time-pressed policy makers or journalists writing about policy issues, the reports often begin with a one-page "executive summary." The executive summary distills the essential issues being debated, provides a brief statement about the importance of the issues at hand, and offers recommendations for action (Eisele, n.d.). Policy briefs are typically authored by researchers who work at nonacademic research organizations such as the Urban Institute, which focuses on urban and poverty issues, or think tanks such as the Brookings Institution, a centrist political research group. Figure 17.8 is an excerpt of a policy brief produced by researchers at Brookings; it examines reasons for and potential solutions to the steep rise in incarceration rates in the United States in recent decades. On the basis of their review of the research, the authors of this brief recommend shorter and less

policy brief A short, impartial summary of what is known about a particular social or economic issue; includes policy recommendations based on this evidence.

FIGURE 17.8 Excerpt of a Policy Brief by the Brookings Institution

Recommendations

- The resources currently dedicated to supporting long prison sentences should be reallocated to produce swifter, surer, but more moderate punishment. This approach includes hiring more police officers—we know now that chiefs using modern management techniques can make effective use of them.

- Increased alcohol excise taxes reduce not only alcohol abuse but also the associated crime at very little cost to anyone except the heaviest drinkers. Federal and state levies should be raised.

- Crime patterns and crime control are as much the result of private actions as public. The productivity of private-security efforts and private cooperation with law enforcement should be encouraged through government regulation and other incentives.

- While convicts typically lack work experience and skills, it has proven very difficult to increase the quality and quantity of their licit employment through job creation and traditional training, either before or after they become involved with criminal activity. More effective rehabilitation (and prevention) programs seek to develop non-academic ("social-cognitive") skills like self-control, planning, and empathy.

- Adding an element of coercion to social policy can also help reduce crime, including threatening probationers with swift, certain and mild punishments for illegal drug use, and compulsory schooling laws that force people to stay in school longer.

Source: Cook and Ludwig, 2011.

costly prison sentences and more effective job-training and rehabilitation programs in prisons (Cook & Ludwig, 2011).

A particular type of policy brief is an **amicus brief**, which a team of researchers may submit to an appellate court. Amicus briefs are legal documents filed in appellate court cases by nonlitigants with a strong interest or expertise in the subject matter. These briefs advise the court of relevant, additional information or arguments that they might wish to consider when making a ruling. In recent years, the American Sociological Association has submitted such briefs in cases where their expertise could inform decisions. One of the most famous of these is an amicus brief submitted to the U.S. Supreme Court in 2015 in support of same-sex marriage and marriage equality. The brief summarized extensive research showing that children of same-sex parents fare just as well as children of different-sex parents on a range of psychological, social, cognitive, and physical health outcomes (American Sociological Association, 2017).

amicus brief A legal document filed in an appellate court case by nonlitigants with a strong interest or expertise in the subject matter.

Editorials

Editorials, or "op-eds," are short opinion pieces (usually 500 to 1,000 words) that appear in newspapers and some magazines. This is a platform for writers to share their views on a particular topic, where their main thesis is supported by data, personal experiences, observations of other's experiences, or other evidence. Most editorials explicitly point out the policy implications of the social problem at hand. Unlike refereed journal articles, these essays are free of jargon and do not include citations. One of the most prestigious publishers of op-eds is *The New York Times*; the paper receives thousands of submissions a year and selects only the highest-quality editorials, many of which are written by professors or other experts with respected credentials. Sociologists sometimes appear in the editorial pages of *The New York Times*; this can be a rewarding forum because it has a very large readership and may be a way to shape public opinion and even public policy.

Sociologists Keith Robinson and Angel Harris (2014) recently published an op-ed in *The New York Times* titled "Parental Involvement Is Overrated." Their main thesis is that parental involvement in children's homework and activities isn't as beneficial as previously believed. They provide evidence for their thesis, drawing from the research they conducted for their 2014 book *The Broken Compass*. They also argue that recent educational initiatives, including President Barack Obama's Race to the Top and President George W. Bush's No Child Left Behind, are based on a faulty assumption. These policies promoted parental engagement as one solution for racial and socioeconomic gaps in children's academic performance. But as Robinson and Harris argue in their op-ed, "Most forms of parental involvement yielded no benefit to children's test scores or grades." They suggest that promoting pro-education values among children may be a better way to facilitate their academic success. The authors' takeaway message is that conventional wisdom is sometimes wrong, so public policy should be based on rigorous scientific research.

Blogs

Growing numbers of social scientists want to break away from what they consider the stifling format of standard academic platforms such as refereed journal articles and share their ideas with general audiences via blogs (Daniels & Gregory, 2016). A blog is a regularly updated website maintained by one individual or a small group of like-minded people, such as the sociologists who maintain the Conditionally Accepted and orgtheory.net blogs. If you've ever read (or written) a blog, you know that the tone is often conversational and at times edgy and even confrontational. The authors of blogs might have a political or social message that they would like to convey, and they can do so unfettered, as their work is not usually monitored by peer reviewers.

Sociology bloggers vary widely in their writings, with some leaning toward personal essays, such as the bloggers on Conditionally Accepted (described as "a space for scholars on the margins of academia"), who often write about their encounters with racism, sexism, and homophobia. Others focus more squarely on research, such as University of Maryland sociologist Philip Cohen's Family Inequality blog. He uses his blog as a forum to report on the findings of empirical studies that either he or other social scientists have carried out, and he uses everyday language to talk about the larger social or political implications of the data. In his June 2016 post titled "No, Black women are not the 'most educated' group in the U.S.," Cohen challenged the veracity of recent media headlines asserting that black women were more highly

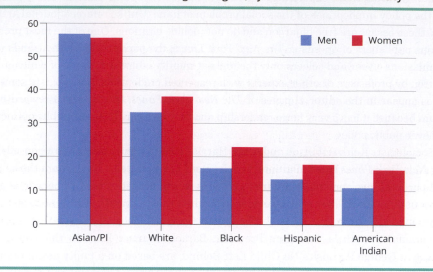

FIGURE 17.9 Percent with a BA or Higher Degree, by Gender and Race/Ethnicity*

*Ages 25–54, 2010–2014
Source: Cohen, 2016.

educated than their white or Latina counterparts. He then presented his own analysis of data from the American Community Survey to support his thesis, as shown in Figure 17.9. His analysis shows that 23% of black women ages 25–54 in the 2010–2014 period had a college degree, compared to 55% and 38% of Asian and white women, respectively.

Yet, like most bloggers, Cohen doesn't simply present the data to his readers: He offers his interpretation of the source of the misinformation about black women's educational attainment. In his full blog post, Cohen offered a harsh critique of journalism, noting that "our current information economy rewards speed and clickability.... Making good graphics and funny GIFs is a good skill, but it's a different skill than interpreting and presenting information.... [T]hose of us with the skills and training to track these things down should all pitch in and do some debunking once in a while." This and Cohen's other blog posts carry a consistent message: Professional sociologists should challenge and contest the "facts" that are bandied about by the media and should instead rely on rigorous data and science.

CONCEPT CHECKS

1   What are the main goals of an evaluation report?

2   How is a policy brief distinct from a regular research report?

3   Describe two characteristics of an op-ed.

4   How might blogs be an effective way to disseminate social science research?

THE PATH TO PUBLICATION: THE PEER-REVIEW PROCESS

At the beginning of this chapter, we mentioned that refereed research reports go through a lengthy process of review, critique, and revision before they are published in scholarly journals. But if the authors of these articles are highly respected PhDs and social scientists, why must their research be reviewed? The peer-review process ensures that the research is of the utmost quality, that it contributes something new to the field, and that it upholds ethical research practices.

The path to publication has twists and turns. It starts with a researcher writing a research report, but that is just the start of a multistep process. These steps vary a bit across disciplines and according to the prestige or competitiveness of the publisher, but most authors will experience a generally similar process. We focus primarily on the journal article review process, although we do note the specific case of book publishing as well. Every published study that you have read about in this book has proceeded through a similar process.

Step 1: The Author Decides Where to Send His or Her Work

After completing their research report or book, researchers must decide where they would like to publish it. Submitting one's work to an academic journal or book publisher is not a guarantee that the work will actually be published. Authors must go through an extensive process called **peer review**, the process whereby a manuscript is reviewed by a panel of experts for its originality, quality, accuracy, and scientific rigor. But first, scholars must identify a potential home for their work. Many sociologists read and publish in general-interest sociology journals, meaning that both the journal's readers and authors span a full range of sociological subfields from comparative historical to demography, from sociology of science to sociology of family. These general-interest journals also tend to feature research from all methodological approaches. Some of the most highly respected general-interest sociology journals include the *American Journal of Sociology*, *American Sociological Review*, and *Social Forces*.

Specialty journals, in contrast, are read by social scientists who focus on a particular subfield. Readers who would like to disseminate their work to readers who share similar interests would turn to a specialty journal rather than a general-interest journal. The American Sociological Association publishes journals that focus on medical sociology (*Journal of Health and Social Behavior*), social psychology (*Social Psychology Quarterly*), and urban sociology (*City & Community*). Because sociologists study such a broad range of topics, many also belong to other professional associations that publish their own scholarly journals. For example, many demographers are members of the Population Association of America and submit their papers to *Demography*. Similarly, family scholars often join the National Council on Family Relations and publish their work in the *Journal of Marriage and Family*.

When deciding where to submit their work, researchers often review their own report's bibliography and send their manuscript to the journal they cited most widely in their own work. Some researchers consider the prestige of the journal. Journals tend

peer review The process whereby a manuscript is evaluated by a panel of experts for its originality, quality, accuracy, and scientific rigor.

Lisa Wade's recent trade book *American Hookup* turns a sociological lens on the hookup culture that dominates today's college campuses.

to be ranked using metrics such as impact factor and other statistics that demonstrate how widely read and cited a journal's articles are. An **impact factor** is a numerical value that indicates the average number of times the articles published in a journal within the past two years have been cited in other articles. A higher value means that the journal's average article is cited more often than an article published at a journal with a lower impact factor. There is no single metric that is best for evaluating the quality or prestige of a journal, and many scholars disagree vehemently about the value of such statistics (Nederhof, 2006).

Authors should be strategic about where they submit their articles. According to professional ethics guidelines, such as those outlined by the Committee on Publishing Ethics (COPE), authors should submit their paper to only one journal at a time. If the paper is rejected from a journal, then the author is free to submit that paper to another venue. Most competitive journals accept only a small percentage of the manuscripts they receive, typically just 10% to 20%. Less competitive journals accept a considerably higher share. As a result, authors often choose a journal that fits their interests and also offers a reasonable chance of acceptance.

Most scholars publish their books with an academic or university press, which is a publishing house affiliated with a university or scholarly organization such as the American Psychological Association. These presses mainly publish books written by college and university faculty members. Smaller academic presses tend to specialize in a particular area. For instance, ILR Press, an arm of Cornell University Press, publishes books focused on workplace and employment issues, while University of Arizona Press is known for publishing books on the experiences of Native Americans and Latinos in the United States. By contrast, larger and highly prestigious university presses such as Oxford University Press or University of Chicago Press publish work from many fields, including books of interest to a more general audience. Authors submit their manuscript directly to an academic press, often sending it to the specific editor who works in their subfield, such as the social sciences editor.

Sometimes, though less often, a sociologist will write a book that appeals to a broad audience of nonacademics, and they may turn to a trade press, which publishes more copies of each book and markets them to a wider audience than does an academic press. Books such as Matthew Desmond's (2016) Pulitzer Prize–winning *Evicted: Poverty and Profit in the American City* or Lisa Wade's (2017) *American Hookup: The New Culture of Sex on Campus* are examples of successful trade books written by sociologists. Part of their popularity reflects the fact that they explore topics of great general interest, and they are written in a clear and straightforward way that does not require an advanced knowledge of social research methods.

Step 2: The Editor Decides whether to Send the Written Work Out for Peer Review

Before the peer-review process starts, the editor must decide whether the article is appropriate for the journal or whether the book is appropriate for the press. A sociological journal such as *Sociology of Education* might not be interested in publishing a paper about an on-the-job training program in a corporate workplace. The journal editor might do a **desk reject**, or immediate reject, in which the manuscript is

PREDATORY JOURNAL PUBLISHES "STUDY" BASED ON SITCOM

The peer-review process is at the core of high-quality social science. Yet, in recent years, a crisis has struck academic publishing: the flourishing of "predatory journals," or online journals that publish research with little or no real peer review and charge authors a hefty fee—often as much as $3,000. Some of the articles published in predatory journals appear to be scientific, but they offer questionable findings such as "eating cowpeas could play a vital role in managing diabetes" (Ryan & Vicini, 2016).

Predatory journals have existed quietly since the early 2000s, often taking advantage of vulnerable scholars who are desperate to succeed in the "publish or perish" environment of academia. As of 2016, an estimated 900 such journals existed (Ryan & Vicini, 2016). Predatory journals often have authentic-sounding titles that include terms such as "science" or "research." So-called editors of these journals aggressively e-mail scholars to try to entice them to submit their work, promising a quick turnaround time. Of course, this speed is something that legitimate peer-reviewed journals cannot promise, given how much time is dedicated to the review process.

In spring 2017, major newspapers and magazines started to blow the lid off predatory publishing. *The New York Times* reported that "A Scholarly Sting Operation Shines a Light on 'Predatory' Journals" (Kolata, 2017), while a headline in the journal *Nature* announced that "Predatory Journals Recruit Fake Editor" (Sorokowski et al., 2017). These articles recounted how legitimate scholars had devised an investigation to shed light on the questionable practices of predatory journals. A team of psychologists at the University of Sussex created a fake curriculum vitae (CV), the academic version of a job résumé, for a fictitious scholar named Dr. Anna O. Szust (*szust* is Polish for "fraudster"). They sent the CV to 360 randomly selected online journals and included a cover letter saying that Dr. Szust would like to volunteer to be a journal editor. However, her CV revealed that Dr. Szust had no experience as a journal editor and had barely published research herself (Burdick, 2017).

Despite her lean credentials, a remarkable 48 journals accepted Dr. Szust's request, and four named her as editor in chief. She received two additional offers to start her own journal and serve as its editor. Another journal responded with an e-mail saying, "It's our pleasure to add your name as our editor-in-chief for the journal with no responsibilities." The journals that rejected her application were legitimate peer-reviewed online journals. The University of Sussex researchers contacted every journal that offered "Dr. Fraud" a position to withdraw her application. But the journals would not let go so easily. Dr. Anna Szust remained on the list of editorial boards of at least 11 journals.

Recent articles in *The New York Times* and *Nature* have called attention to the questionable practices of certain online journals.

An even more incriminating set of news headlines announced that "'Study about Nothing' Highlights the Perils of Predatory Publishing" (*Science*, 2017) and "Hello . . . Newman: Yet Another Sting Pranks a Predatory Journal, Seinfeld-Style" (Retraction Watch, 2017). These articles recounted a ruse pulled off by science writer John McCool. He authored a fake study under the pseudonym Dr. Martin van Nostrand and submitted his article to the predatory journal *Urology & Nephrology Open Access*, where it was ultimately published. In the article, McCool wrote about a condition called "uromysitisis." He wrote that the condition, caused by a "prolonged failure to evacuate the contents of the bladder," could bring about psychological problems and infections. He did not write that the entire condition was made up by comedy writers for *Seinfeld*. In an episode of the 1990s sitcom, Jerry Seinfeld's character, after relieving himself in a mall's parking deck, was apprehended by a security guard. In an effort to evade punishment for public urination, Jerry tried to convince the guard that he had uromysitisis.

These stunts shed light on the important fact that many scholars are publishing poor-quality research in "journals" trying to pass themselves off as scientific, and the companies behind these predatory journals are profiting handsomely. Efforts are under way to monitor or even halt these practices. In 2016, the Federal Trade Commission (FTC) filed a lawsuit against a group of companies behind these journals. The lawsuit charges that each of the companies is "deceiving academics and researchers about the nature of its publications and hiding publication fees ranging from hundreds to thousands of dollars" (Straumscheim, 2016). The lawsuit could help restore a culture in which the science published in online journals is rigorous, reputable, and replicable.

promptly rejected without being reviewed by other scholars. However, the author would still receive a brief rejection letter encouraging him or her to submit the work to a more appropriate journal, such as *Work & Occupations*. However, if the editor believes the study's topic and method are appropriate, he or she would then initiate the peer-review process.

Step 3: Peer Reviewers, Selected by the Editor, Evaluate the Written Work

For journal editors, the first step of the peer-review process is identifying scholars who have expertise in the manuscript's topic or method. The editor then invites these scholars to serve as peer reviewers, which involves providing detailed and constructive feedback on the manuscript. Most articles and books have three peer reviewers, although that number varies slightly by journal or publisher. In sociology, the reviewers tend to be anonymous. Because reviewers may offer critical feedback, they want their identity protected. This anonymity frees them to offer more critical comments than they might otherwise share.

single-blind peer review A peer-review process in which the reviewers know who authored the manuscript, but the author does not know who the reviewers are.

double-blind peer review A peer-review process in which both the author of the manuscript and the reviewers are anonymous.

In the case of books, the process is typically **single-blind**, meaning reviewers know who authored the manuscript, but the author does not know who the reviewers are. In the case of journal articles, the process tends to be **double-blind**: Both the author and reviewers are anonymous. The reviewers receive a copy of the manuscript that is blinded: The author's name and any identifying information are removed. Likewise, the reviewers send their feedback confidentially: The editor knows who they are, but the author does not. Double-blind review upholds the integrity of the peer-review process. If a reviewer received a manuscript and saw that the author was an old classmate from graduate school or a former student, then it might be hard to be completely objective when reviewing the work.

After the reviewers send their feedback to the editor, the decision process unfolds. In the case of book manuscripts, the editor typically sends his or her own feedback to the author along with the reviewers' comments. The author is either invited to submit a revised manuscript that addresses the reviewers' concerns or is encouraged to take the book to another publisher. The criteria editors use when deciding whether to publish a book are much like the criteria used in the journal review process: the originality of the idea, methodological rigor, quality of writing, and importance of the contribution.

For academic journals, the process is more complex. Reviewers use a computer interface maintained by the journal, where they weigh in on a manuscript. First, reviewers provide written feedback and constructive criticism for the author, just as reviewers of books would do. This information is entered into a box labeled "Comments to Author." Reviewers are encouraged to use constructive, measured, and respectful language in their comments to the author. Rather than simply pointing out what's wrong, reviewers should provide guidance on how to address these problems.

Reviewers are then asked to provide confidential comments to the editor. These comments will not be seen by the author and are intended to help guide the editor's decision. Reviewers might offer forthright comments that they would not want the author to see, such as, "This is a competent and well-written analysis but it does not add anything new to our knowledge" or "The author cited some of my own work but did not cite it properly." The first comment might hurt the author's morale, whereas the second comment might unwittingly leak the anonymous reviewer's identity. The peer reviewers also are asked to make a recommendation to the editor regarding next steps—whether to reject, accept, or invite a revision of the manuscript. A reviewer may recommend accepting the paper as is or accepting it with minor changes ("conditional accept"). Likewise, the reviewer may recommend a minor or major revision. The editor reads the reviewers' comments to the author, comments to the editor, and recommendations, and then makes his or her own final decision of reject, revise and resubmit, or accept.

A manuscript is rarely accepted after the first review. A more common recommendation is **revise and resubmit**, or "R&R." It can be a "major" R&R, meaning that serious changes are required, or a "minor" R&R, meaning that the changes required are more straightforward and simple. The author receives a letter from the editor detailing the paper's major weaknesses and offering concrete suggestions for improvement. The letter also includes all the specific feedback and critiques provided by the peer reviewers. Most often, this feedback focuses on the strength and appropriateness of the paper's theoretical framework; the quality of the analysis, including the methods and measures; the clarity of the writing; and the originality of the contribution. Many reviewers and editors consider the latter to be the most important. A report may be well written with a thoughtful analysis, but if the findings are not new and do not contribute substantially to the literature, it will likely be rejected. This process is intended to enhance the quality and impact of published scholarship (Campanario, 1998).

At prestigious journals, the most common decision is reject. But even if a paper is rejected, all hope is not lost. The author receives a letter from the editor saying that the paper is rejected, along with all the feedback offered by the reviewers—just as occurs in the R&R scenario. The one difference is that those who get an R&R decision will resubmit the improved paper to the same journal. Those who receive a rejection are not allowed to resubmit their revised manuscript to the same journal and instead may send it to another journal. However, if the concerns raised by the reviewers and editor are insurmountable, the author may decide to go back to the drawing board and do a drastic overhaul.

revise and resubmit A decision made by a journal editor that allows an author to revise his or her originally submitted manuscript in accordance with reviewer feedback, and to resubmit the improved manuscript for possible publication.

Step 4: The Author Revises and Resubmits the Work

Authors who receive a revise and resubmit invitation do exactly that. They revise their manuscript in accordance with all the feedback provided by the reviewers and editor and write up a detailed memo that says exactly what changes they made. If the reviewers ask for a change that the author cannot make, then he or she must explain why. For instance, let's say a paper uses survey data to explore race and ethnic differences in high school students' career aspirations. A reviewer might ask that the author add a statistical control for the language the child speaks at home. The reviewer believes that the paper's finding that Latino youth are less likely to aspire to college may reflect the fact that they are less comfortable with and confident speaking English. If the survey did not include a measure of language spoken at home, then the author cannot make this suggested change. The author would acknowledge in the revision memo that the survey did not include language information and could speculate about why and how it would be important to include such a measure in a future study.

The author then resubmits to the journal editor the revised version of the manuscript, along with the detailed memo describing precisely what revisions were made and why. The editor shares these documents with the original reviewers, who again weigh in with feedback and with their recommendation as to whether to accept, reject, or offer another opportunity to revise and resubmit. In most cases, if the author has done a responsive and careful revision, the manuscript will be accepted conditional upon minor editorial changes. The author can then celebrate his or her acceptance, and in the coming months the manuscript will be published in a printed copy of the journal and/or online. Authors should be patient, though. Academic journals often have a backlog, or a large queue of papers that have been accepted but have not yet been published in printed copies of the journal. For this reason, some authors may have to wait anywhere from 18 to 24 months for their article to appear in a printed copy of the journal. However, the online or "early access" version posted on the journal's website is every bit as real.

Even for those who do not aspire to publish research, understanding the peer-review process is important because the process demonstrates why and how social research is so challenging, why social research is both an art and science, and what mechanisms are in place to ensure that the science we read has integrity. The peer-review process is complex, time consuming, and imperfect. Although reviewers should be fair and impartial, an occasional reviewer may not be. Others may lack the expertise to offer meaningful feedback. But on the whole, this process is the best method to date for ensuring that research is vetted carefully, with the goal of producing rigorous and high-quality science.

CONCEPT CHECKS

1 | Why is it important for science to be peer reviewed?

2 | What are the possible outcomes when a manuscript is submitted to a peer-reviewed journal?

3 | What are the main criteria an editor uses when deciding whether to publish an article?

4 | Describe the benefits of the double-blind peer-review process.

TIPS FOR EFFECTIVE WRITING

Now that you've learned how to disseminate your work, how to structure it for different audiences, and what to include in different types of presentations, it's time to write up your paper. Writing is a difficult task that requires countless revisions, edits, and rewrites. Think about what some of the world's most renowned writers have said about their craft. John Irving, the prolific novelist who wrote *The World According to Garp,* has acknowledged, "Half of my life is an act of revision." Even the Algonquin Roundtable founder Dorothy Parker, known for her off-the-cuff witticisms, admitted, "I can't write five words but that I change seven." Revision and practice are the tricks of the trade, and writers are made, not born. As novelist Ernest Hemingway noted, "It's none of their business that you have to learn to write. Let them think you were born that way" (Sikiru, 2014).

We provide a few general guidelines to help ensure that your writing is precise, clear, grammatically correct, and lively. Many books are dedicated to writing techniques in general (Strunk & White, 1999; Turabian, 2007; Zinsser, 2016) and to the social sciences specifically (Becker, 2010; Galvan, 2014; Smith-Lovin & Moskovitz, 2016). In this section, we outline three major goals that should guide your research: organization, clarity, and integrity (see "Conversations from the Front Lines").

Getting Organized: Using Outlines Effectively

Organization is often the hardest part of writing, and a well-thought-out outline can be helpful. While you shouldn't consider your outline as carved in stone, you should think carefully about the subsections of your paper, the subheadings that you will give to those subsections, and the order in which you will arrange those subsections. Outlines are most useful for the literature review and discussion sections of research reports, because the results section is already highly structured and systematic. We provide some general guidelines to help you create an outline, or the scaffolding that supports your work. Using both A-level headings and B-level subheadings can be helpful. A-level headings such as "Literature Review" and "Methods" are major sections of your paper, but you may use B-level subheadings within those sections to help further organize and group together material and ideas.

STEP 1: DETERMINE THE MAIN POINTS OF EACH MAJOR SECTION, AND CREATE SUBHEADINGS THAT CORRESPOND TO EACH POINT

What are the main points you'd like to convey to readers? You should select three or four main points, which will serve as the subheadings that organize your writing. Let's say you are doing a study of the impact of body weight on one's personal relationships and are particularly interested in whether being overweight makes it more difficult for young women to date than it does for young men. You have read widely on the consequences of body weight for young men and women and have decided that Erving Goffman's theory of stigma will provide the theoretical frame for your study. This theory proposes that some personal traits are highly devalued by others, but the extent to which they are devalued varies by social context. You might use the following subheadings in your literature review section:

I. Stigma Theory: A Brief Review

II. Obesity as Stigmatized Identity: Implications for Interpersonal Relationships

III. The Gendered Context of Obesity: Gender Differences in the Effects of Body Weight on Personal Relationships

One important organizational decision is whether to take a "top down" or "bottom up" approach. In the former, the literature review opens up with a broad theoretical exploration of stigma before moving into the specifics of body weight. In the latter, the author would begin with a specific discussion of empirical studies demonstrating the high premium placed on female slenderness, and then work up to a larger theoretical discussion of stigma. Social science papers tend to adopt a top-down approach, although you will want to consult with your instructor or research mentor in making this decision.

Conversations from the Front Lines

JANE E. MILLER

Jane E. Miller is a professor at the Edward J. Bloustein School of Planning and Public Policy and the Institute for Health, Health Care Policy, and Aging Research at Rutgers University. She received her PhD in demography at the University of Pennsylvania. Her research focuses on poverty and its implications for children's health and access to health care. She also is the director of Project L/Earn, a social science research training program for undergraduates. Dr. Miller is a nationally recognized expert on quantitative communication and statistical literacy. She has written several articles and books on this topic, including The Chicago Guide to Writing about Numbers *and* The Chicago Guide to Writing about Multivariate Analysis. *She has played a major role in helping social scientists communicate their research, especially quantitative research, as clearly and precisely as possible. Dr. Miller shares her insights and tips for becoming a skilled writer and communicator.*

What factors shaped your decision to write books about writing, specifically books focused on writing about numbers?

The idea to write a book on writing about numbers hatched when I was grading homework assignments for an undergraduate research methods course. The assignment asked students to do some simple calculations of death rates and write up the comparisons by age, gender, or race. I was getting extremely frustrated correcting the same kinds of mistakes over and over, when finally it dawned on me that the students had probably never been taught how to write about numbers. I decided to write some simple guidelines for them, such as stating "the W's" (who, what, when, where), identifying units, and specifying direction and magnitude of an association.

By using those guidelines, the students' work improved, and colleagues started asking me for my materials for teaching how to write about numbers, whether I would guest lecture in their classes, and whether I covered other common mistakes such as poor chart design or writing about "significance." The guidelines I wrote in response to their requests evolved into the 12 basic principles in *The Chicago Guide to Writing about Numbers*.

A second factor was one that several people throughout my career had pointed out: that I have the ability to break a writing issue into its component problems, articulate general principles to explain how to avoid those problems, and explain step-by-step approaches that others can apply to their work. That process morphed into the "poor/better/best" approach that I use in my books.

A third factor was that for most of my life I have gravitated toward numbers, starting with histograms of M&Ms by color in elementary school, math and science classes in high school, economics in college, demography in graduate school, and health services research as a professor. All along I have pursued hobbies like sports and cooking that involve lots of numbers. Those experiences gave me a wide range of examples to use when teaching others how to communicate numeric information. We all learn better when the initial examples are on familiar topics, so being able to cite diverse examples helps reach a broader audience. In the end, the combination of my interests, abilities, and opportunities as a college professor crystalized into my writing about numbers projects.

What are the most common problems that you see in papers written by social scientists?

One of my pet peeves, which is shared by many social scientists and statisticians, is when writers state that an association between two variables they are studying is "significant" but don't specify which kind of "significance" they are referring to. Often, the authors mean that a t test or regression model showed that the association was statistically significant at $p < .05$, but many readers will interpret "significant" to mean "important." This is especially true if those readers are not well versed in statistics, which includes many journalists, everyday citizens, and others interested in the topic but not the numeric methods. Instead, authors should discuss both the statistical significance and real-world importance of their numeric findings, using language that conveys which type of "significance" they are discussing in each of their paragraphs.

Another common problem is what I call "writing the word problem, not the answer," when writers report the numeric results of their calculations or statistics but don't interpret them in ways that answer the underlying substantive question. That leaves it up to readers to do their own calculations and comparisons, meaning that all but the most expert or persistent readers will lose the narrative line of the paper and won't learn the answer to the underlying question.

> ❝
> As geeky as it sounds, the best advice I received about writing up numeric results was 'always specify the direction and magnitude of an association.'
> ❞

What is the best piece of advice you ever received about writing? What piece of advice do you most commonly offer to student authors?

As geeky as it sounds, the best advice I received about writing up numeric results was "always specify the direction and magnitude of an association." Instead of writing that two variables are "correlated" or "associated" with one another (astonishingly common, even in top journals!), explain the shape of that pattern; for example, *which group* is bigger, faster, or smarter (direction)? *How much* bigger, faster, or smarter (magnitude)?

This principle is so universally helpful that I refer to it as the "money shot"—the one that will win the game for you if you use it right. I have had colleagues and students say to me that by using that principle to tweak their writing, they got a paper accepted to a journal or had people tell them how clear their research talk was.

The advice I offer to students is that good writers are made, not born. Expect to have to work at your writing.

Read guidelines, ask your professors to suggest examples of good writing, write a draft, obtain feedback, revise, repeat. In college, an economics professor told me my paper was so boring he had to put it down and come back to it twice, so I committed myself to working on my writing. Now, people tell me that my writing is not only clear, but that I can even be funny when talking about statistical concepts. Like any other skill, regular practice will help you improve.

What book or article in the social sciences do you think is an exemplar of high-quality writing? What three things make this publication so exemplary?

One of my favorite articles to teach from is by Tufts University researcher Rebecca Fauth and her colleagues (2004) about a study of the Moving to Opportunity (MTO) experiment. [Recall from Chapter 4 that MTO assessed whether giving families vouchers that enabled them to move from low-income to middle-class neighborhoods improved their outcomes.] It is an excellent example of several key principles for writing about numbers. First, it carries a clear story line through a research paper on an important social issue. From the introduction of the substantive question, to theory and empirical evidence on that issue, to a description of the experimental study design and statistical methods, the results (including well-designed tables), and the concluding section, every section of the paper keeps the reader oriented to the specific topic of the paper, not to generics like "independent and dependent variables."

Second, the methods of data collection and analysis are described using both the necessary technical terms and clear, precise explanations of what those terms mean for this specific data set and research question. Third, the paper conveys the direction and magnitude of differences in neighborhood and social outcomes between the two groups in the MTO experiment. The result is a paper that is both compelling and informative about the issue it sought to address, showing that moving out of high-poverty neighborhoods was associated with better housing and neighborhood outcomes for the participants.

STEP 2: PROVIDE SUPPORT FOR YOUR KEY POINTS

The next task is to provide supporting ideas or evidence for each of the main ideas presented in your subsections. The evidence you provide may be statistical data, findings from other empirical studies, or quotes from previously published open-ended interview studies. Your main goal is to present this supporting information in a logical order, where one point of support flows naturally into the next. At this step, it's not necessary to write in perfectly structured sentences. You may find it easier to use bullet points to help ensure that you have provided all the information you need to support your main ideas.

STEP 3: REVISE YOUR BULLET POINTS INTO COMPLETE SENTENCES

After you have incorporated your detailed facts and research summaries into the outline, your next step is to turn those notes into complete sentences. One sentence should flow logically into the next.

STEP 4: TRANSFORM YOUR SENTENCES INTO PARAGRAPHS

Each paragraph should capture a new idea, where the first sentence asserts the key point or thesis of the paragraph, and the subsequent sentences support the initial assertion. Transitional phrases can help one sentence or paragraph flow naturally to the next. As you craft your paragraphs, you should be mindful of redundancies. You can summarize many studies on the same topic concisely, without repeating the same finding. After reading and editing your paragraphs, you are well on your way to having a first draft of your paper (Galvan, 2014).

The Importance of Clarity, Precision, and Readability

Sociologist Deborah Carr, one of the coauthors of this book, recalls the best piece of writing advice she ever received: "Don't make your reader work so hard." Think back to a time when you were reading an article for a class, and you were so confused by obtuse language or meandering run-on sentences that you just thought, "Why bother reading. I don't understand this." Consider the following passage, written by the renowned and highly respected feminist scholar Judith Butler:

> The move from a structuralist account in which capital is understood to structure social relations in relatively homologous ways to a view of hegemony in which power relations are subject to repetition, convergence, and rearticulation brought the question of temporality into the thinking of structure, and marked a shift from a form of Althusserian theory that takes structural totalities as theoretical objects to one in which the insights into the contingent possibility of structure inaugurate a renewed conception of hegemony as bound up with the contingent sites and strategies of the rearticulation of power. (Butler, 1977)

Could you summarize the key point of this important statement about social relations? Probably not. This sentence was selected, somewhat tongue-in-cheek, by philosopher Denis Dutton (1999) as the winner of a "Bad Writing Contest" (Birkenstein, 2010). Why do you think the passage won this embarrassing "honor"? Your answer should provide obvious clues about how to be a good writer. We share a few pointers to help ensure that your writing is crystal clear.

1. *Define your key concepts the first time you mention them.* Your initial definition can be brief, because your study's focal concepts will be fleshed out more fully throughout the paper. Likewise, define acronyms in full on first mention. You might say that your study uses data from the General Social Survey (GSS), and then use the acronym GSS thereafter.

2. *Use the active voice whenever possible.* Which sentence do you find more engaging?
   (a) "Sociologists and economists find that college graduates tend to have more prestigious jobs and higher earnings than their peers who completed high school only."
   OR
   (b) "There is evidence that there are financial and occupational benefits associated with graduating college."
   Sentence (a) is clearly the better sentence because it uses the active voice. It reveals who has documented the positive consequences of a college education. It also clearly and precisely describes what those benefits are.

3. *Use first person.* It is better to say, "I explore media representations of the 2017 Women's March" as opposed to "this paper explores" or "media representations are explored."

4. *Avoid extraneous words.* Words like "indeed" or "interestingly" add nothing to your work. Writing experts also frown upon adverbs and adjectives unless absolutely necessary. Case in point: Is it necessary to say "she tip-toed quietly" when "tip-toed" already suggests a quiet step?

5. *Don't complicate things.* Simple and precise language is better than bloated prose. The phrase "Few studies have explored young Latinas' career aspirations" captures your point just as clearly as "there is a lacuna of scholarship on studies exploring the career aspirations of young Latina women." Sentences should not run on too long. A paragraph should convey one main idea in its opening sentence, and then no more than three or four sentences supporting and expanding on the thesis sentence.

6. *Say exactly what you mean.* Novice writers can be timid about stating their ideas and sometimes hide behind vague language. Direct language is best. If the purpose of your paper is to explore Latinas' career aspirations, state exactly that: "I examine the ways that family factors affect Latinas' aspirations." Also strive to use the most precise word possible to capture an idea; if you are at a loss, consult a thesaurus (Zinsser, 2016).

7. *Be engaging but not overly casual.* As the Judith Butler example makes clear, overly jargon-filled writing is off-putting to readers. At the same time, you should adopt a professional and respectful style. Slang and colloquialisms are not acceptable. While you might refer to people as "you guys" or your possessions as "stuff," those words and phrases should not seep into academic writing. Most

writing experts frown on the use of contractions. It is better to say, "I do not consider gender differences in this study" than "I don't consider gender differences in this study."

8. *Edit, edit, and edit again.* A final paper should be impeccable: free of typographical errors, run-on sentences, spelling errors, and the like. But no one is perfect the first time around. When you are in the earliest stages of writing, write freely and put your ideas down on paper as quickly as those ideas come into your mind. Try not to fear the blank screen and instead write as quickly as you can when your ideas are fresh. Once you have your first draft typed, that's when you can edit the spelling, grammar, and other details essential to high-quality work. Consider enlisting a friend or family member to provide feedback on your work. They do not need to be an expert in sociology or the topic of your paper. Rather, they can help you determine whether your work is clear, logical, and engaging.

Academic Integrity: Giving Credit Where Credit Is Due

Our research projects build upon the work of scholars who came before us. We must give credit where credit is due by citing those studies that inform our work. Failure to properly cite another author's words or ideas constitutes **plagiarism**. Defining plagiarism can be tricky. Directly quoting someone else's work without citing the original source is the most blatant form of plagiarism.

But plagiarism is seldom that blatant. Novice writers often don't understand that paraphrasing someone else's work without acknowledging the original source or doing a minor tweak of someone else's text also constitutes plagiarism (Johnson et al., 1998). Our advice is to err on the side of caution. A general rule is to cite the work of others if the information they convey is not considered part of our common knowledge. For instance, it is not necessary to provide a cite for a claim such as "High school students enjoy spending time with their friends" or "Most people marry for love." These kinds of claims would constitute common knowledge. However, if you wrote, "High school students with many close friendships are less likely to drop out of school," this would require a cite, such as a study by Carbonaro and Workman (2013) that found support for this hypothesis. A casual observer of high school students could not have made such a discovery, thus this specific claim requires citations. Likewise, if you were to say, "Most people marry for love today, although they did not in earlier centuries," you might cite a historical study showing that romantic love is a modern notion, and in the past people married for far-reaching reasons such as tradition or to cement economic or political ties between two families (Coontz, 2006).

Plagiarism can be a fuzzy concept, but these three general rules should be helpful:

- Do not use another author's exact words unless you use quotation marks, followed by a cite, including the author's name, publication date, and page number.

- Do not try to pass off another author's ideas as your own. If you extend their ideas in new directions, you should state this directly.

- Do not summarize, paraphrase, or lightly edit another author's words without citing them.

CONCLUSION

A methodologically rigorous, well-written sociological research study can reshape our understanding of society as well as public policies that affect our daily lives. Writing about sociological research is challenging yet extremely rewarding. After working on a research project for a semester or even for several years, we must disseminate our discoveries with other scientists in an effort to shape knowledge. We also want to share our results with our colleagues, the general public, journalists who can help change public opinion, and policy makers who can help change lives. To do so, we must write clearly, honestly, and critically, recognizing not only the limitations of others' work, but also the limitations of our own. We also need to convey the magnitude of what we have discovered, demonstrating the importance of our results both for theory and for the "real world." A critical mechanism in ensuring that our work is rigorous is the peer-review process: This is an essential check to uphold integrity in our science. Just as important is the process of revising our work. As we have shown, good writers are made, not born. We hope that we have inspired in you an appreciation of the importance of social research, the challenges of conducting high-quality, high-impact research, and the joys of knowing that research can make a difference in the world.

End-of-Chapter Review

Summary

Social researchers study topics that have wide appeal, so they must be prepared to communicate the findings of their research to diverse audiences. Well-written, peer-reviewed sociological research can contribute to the knowledge and practices that help improve daily life in our society.

Sharing Your Results with Academic Audiences

- Communicating social science research requires researchers to be able to tailor their writing to diverse audiences, varying the language, tone, and format as needed.
- Research reports are formal, written summaries of research projects. Reports should begin with a concise title, an abstract that summarizes the report, and an introduction.
- The report should also include a literature review and a methods section. Next, the report should summarize the results of the study, discuss how the study contributes to the state of knowledge on the topic, and finally end with a full list of references.
- Research proposals are written to help guide researchers though their project, and are often submitted to organizations that could potentially fund the research. A research proposal includes the specific aims of the proposed research, a critique of previous literature, and a review of any preliminary studies the researcher has done. Proposals will also include a section on intended research methods, a timeline, a brief section describing human subjects concerns, and a full references list.
- Posters are created by researchers to showcase their research to colleagues at professional conferences and other academic events. Researchers might also give an oral presentation, followed by a Q&A session.

Beyond the Academy: Reaching Out to Broader Audiences

- Researchers can use a variety of different platforms to disseminate their research to a broader audience, including evaluation reports, monographs, government reports, policy briefs, editorials, and blogs.

The Path to Publication: The Peer-Review Process

- After completing a report, a researcher decides which academic journal or book publisher to submit his or her manuscript for peer review. Researchers often consider the prestige and impact factor of different journals as well as their acceptance rates.
- The peer-review process involves the journal editor identifying scholars, typically three, to provide feedback on the manuscript. Based on the feedback from the reviewers, the editor then decides whether to accept the manuscript for publication. It is common for journals to invite authors to revise and resubmit (R&R) their manuscript.
- Authors who receive an R&R decision revise their manuscript to address the reviewers' feedback and then write a detailed memo describing the changes.
- The peer-review process is complex, time consuming, and imperfect, but it is also the best way to ensure that published research is of the highest quality.

Tips for Effective Writing

- Outlines are important tools for helping researchers organize the subsections of their paper. The first step is to determine the major points that will be included in each subsection, and then incorporate the supporting evidence for each major point. The next step is to transform the bullet points into complete sentences and then sentences into complete paragraphs.

- To keep your writing clear and concise, make sure to define key concepts the first time they are used, use active voice, avoid extraneous words, and use direct language.
- The main goal of a first draft should be to get your ideas down on paper quickly; careful editing for spelling, grammar, and word choice can be done in subsequent drafts.
- Failure to properly cite another author's words or ideas constitutes plagiarism. A general rule of thumb is to cite any ideas from other works that are not part of common knowledge.

Key Terms

abstract, **581**

amicus brief, **600**

bibliography, **589**

desk reject, **604**

double-blind peer review, **606**

evaluation research, **598**

impact factor, **604**

peer review, **603**

pilot study, **593**

plagiarism, **614**

policy brief, **599**

refereed journal, **581**

replicability, **586**

research report, **581**

revise and resubmit, **607**

single-blind peer review, **606**

structured abstract, **581**

unstructured abstract, **581**

Exercise

Demographer Jane Miller (see "Conversations from the Front Lines") has written an entire book that teaches quantitative social scientists to write their results as clearly as possible, and she offers concrete tips to show the difference between "poor," "better," and "best" writing in results sections. Miller chooses an amusing example to illustrate this point: the fact that people with white hair are more likely to die in a given year than people with other hair colors. She offers three different versions of a hypothetical results section (Miller 2004, p. 38).

Poor: "The effect of white hair on mortality was substantial, with five times the risk of any other hair color."

Better: "The whiter the hair, the higher the mortality rate."

Best: "People with white hair had considerably higher mortality rates than people with a different hair color. However, most people with white hair were over age 60—a high-mortality age group—so the association between white hair and high mortality is probably due to their mutual association with old age."

- Describe two problems with the "poor" example.
- Provide two reasons why the "better" text is superior to the "poor" example.
- Provide three reasons why the "best" example is the best of the three.
- Using the descriptive statistics presented in Figure 17.3, a page from the Houle and Warner (2017) article, write "poor," "better," and "best" versions of your summary of the Houle and Warner study results. Explain why your "best" version is superior.

Appendix A:
Sample Consent Form

HARVARD UNIVERSITY
John F. Kennedy School of Government

KATHERINE S. NEWMAN
Malcolm Wiener Professor of Urban Studies

79 John F. Kennedy Street
Cambridge, Massachusetts 02138

(614) XXX-XXXX
(617) XXX-XXXX
Fax (617) XXX-XXXX
KATHERINE_NEWMAN@HARVARD.EDU

Chair; Ph.D. Programs in Government/Sociology & Social Policy
Director, Multidisciplinary Program
in Inequality & Social Policy

CONSENT FORM #1
For Subjects of Majority Age

Introduction:
Many people are worried that more and more children and adults are being killed while they are studying or working at school. Researchers still know very little about why these tragedies happen. Through this study, we hope to learn more about why murders happen in schools. The Congress of the United States has asked us to help understand how the events that took place in Jonesboro in 1998 happened so that we can inform school officials, parents, and community leaders about efforts they can make that might help to prevent similar tragedy from occurring elsewhere.

Purpose of the Research:
In this study we want to learn as much as we can about your community, particularly the young people who live here. We want to understand as best we can what kinds of social activities and groups youth participate in, what kinds of community events (for example, sports or church activities) the young people, families, and adults participate in. We want to learn about the kinds of children who are active in clubs and school and those who tend not to get involved. We need this kind of background information to understand the context within which the tragedy developed.

We are going to be interviewing many people in the community—friends and acquaintances of those most directly involved in the violence, teachers and students familiar with the social relationships in the school, parents and community leaders (including law enforcement officials, school administrators, leaders of churches and community groups), and anyone else who can shed light on what happened. We are interested in learning as much as we can about their opinions and insights about the events that led up to and followed from the shooting. Some people have thought about this a great deal and others have not. We are not seeking your opinion because you are an "expert." Rather, we are interested in your perspective because you are a member of the community with your own point of view.

The National Academy of Sciences is sponsoring the same kind of study in several other American communities touched by similar tragedies. Our purpose is to try to understand what these events have in common and what might be done to help avert them.

Procedures:
If you agree to let us interview you, we will be asking you a series of questions that do not have simple answers. This interview is not a "test" with right or wrong answers. It is not a psychological assessment. It is a way of gathering your thoughts and opinions, which we would like to learn about in depth. For this reason, and because we want to listen while you speak (rather than scribble notes), we would like to tape record this interview. This tape will remain our confidential property. No one outside of the members of our research team will be allowed to hear it, ever.

This interview will be sent back to Harvard University where it will be transcribed and archived. It will become part of the record of this research project, which we expect will include hundreds of similar interviews by the time we are finished. We will be examining all of these interviews in order to see what common and divergent views members of the Jonesboro community have about the events in question. We will draw from these interviews a portrait of the community and the school prior to and after the shootings.

When we have finished this analysis, we will write a report for the National Academy of Sciences, the country's most prestigious and important scientific consulting organization. Congress specifically requested that the National Academy conduct this study and we, in turn, were asked by the Academy to complete it. The report we write will become part of the Academy's response to Congress. It will be published and disseminated widely, particularly to school administrators who are responsible for improving the climate of safety in the nation's schools. We also intend to publish the results of this study in professional journals and books so that other social scientists, educators, members of the legal community and the public at large can learn from this experience. It is important that you understand that these publications have as their purpose the widespread dissemination of our findings.

Risks:
We do not expect any harm to come to participants in this study as a result of their cooperation. Yet we realize that discussing events of this tragic a nature may raise painful memories and that it can be stressful to talk about them. We have already explained that you can stop the interview at any time if you would prefer not to continue and that you may refuse to answer any particular question you deem inappropriate or disquieting. We want to remind you of this right and be sure you understand that you can ask to stop recording any portion of the interview.

Because this was a traumatic event for the whole community, we recognize that sensitivities may be raised in recounting these events. Some people may feel embarrassed on behalf of the community or angry at some of its members. There is, then, a risk of discomfort. This is something you may want to consider before agreeing to participate.

For most of the people we interview, we anticipate that we will be successful in preserving their privacy. However, as you know, these events were widely publicized.

National newspapers, radio, and television carried extensive reports on the tragedy. As such many of the individuals involved—even only tangentially as observers—may have already been identified publicly. And in a small community, many know one another as friends and neighbors. Public figures, including school administrators, government officials, police officers, and those directly implicated as victims or offenders, have already been identified in the media.

Under these circumstances, we cannot in all honesty be certain that it would be impossible for your words to be identified by others who know you well or who might have seen or heard you in a media interview. Where possible, we will not identify the source of quotes that we use in our writings. For examples, we will say "a teacher" or "a student" in describing a source. However, in some instances the individuals involved are known to the public, especially in the local community, and it will not be possible to quote without attribution. We can only say that we will make the utmost effort to protect your privacy, because we know you value it and because we appreciate how important that promise is in encouraging you to provide your frank and honest opinion of these difficult events. However, we are honor bound to point out that despite our best efforts, there is a risk that your identity could be recognized.

While we hope very much that you will agree to participate, we want to be sure you understand that nothing bad will happen to you or your family if you decline.

We understand that thinking about what happened in your community may be hard for you. Thinking about these things may depress you, perhaps a great deal. If thinking about these things upsets you, you may need to see a doctor to help you cope. Upon your request, we will provide you with a list of counselors in the community who might be able to help you if you feel the need to talk to a professional. We cannot pay for these services, but we will make every effort to provide a list that includes local counselors who charge modest fees.

Benefits:
There will be no direct benefit for you, your family members, or for the school if you agree to help us with this study. But helping us do this study may tell us a lot about why shootings happen in schools. If so, that could be good for you or someone you know in the future.

We believe Congress asked for this study in pursuit of its obligation to make the country a safer place for children and families. The events we have come to your community to study are thankfully very rare. But when they happen, they cause tremendous grief. Anything we can do to shed light on why these tragedies occur and to make recommendations that might prevent them from happening elsewhere will only be possible because of your cooperation. For this reason, there is a benefit to your community and to the country as a whole that we hope you will consider.

Confidentiality:

Because sensitive information will be collected in this interview, the National Academy of Sciences has applied for an "assurance of confidentiality" for this project under the provisions of the Public Health Services Act, Section 301(d).

This certification has not yet been received and we do not know for certain whether we will be able to obtain it. If we are successful in receiving a Certification of Responsibility, this will insure that we cannot be forced to tell people who are not connected with the study about your participation. This includes the courts and the police.

We are legally obliged to inform you that there are circumstances that require us to disclose information, including evidence of "child abuse or threat of other potential violence" by the study participant to the participant of others. We do not expect information of this kind to be an issue in this study, however, we are bound to follow the rules if evidence of this kind comes to light in our interview.

To protect your privacy and your family members' privacy, we will keep all information under a code number instead of a name. We will keep the records in locked files and only study staff will be allowed to look at them. Names or any other facts that might point to you or your family members will be disguised to the best of our ability. We realize, again, that public figures who have already been identified in the media will be harder for us to disguise than citizens who have not been so identified. We retain the right to quote from our interviews and to provide our analysis based on all the interviews we collect to the National Academy, which will, in turn, publish the results. We also retain the right to publish scholarly articles in professional journals and in books, making use of this data. But we will retain control of the interview material ourselves and will not release it to anyone else.

Cost/Payment:

There is no cost for helping us with this study. You will not be paid for helping with this study.

Persons to Contact:

If you have any questions about how the study works, contact Dr. Katherine Newman at the Kennedy School of Government, the director of the study. You may call her at 617-XXX-XXXX. She will return your call as soon as possible.

If you have any questions about your rights in the study, contact Ms. Jane Calhoun, Research Officer for the Committee on the Use of Human Subjects, the Harvard University review board that approved this study. Her phone number is 617-XXX-XXXX. You may call her at any time and leave a message. Your call will be returned as soon as possible.

Your consent:

I have read this consent form. I have had my questions answered so that all parts of the study are clear to me now. I have received a copy of this consent form. I agree to participate in this interview under the terms outlined in this letter.

_____   _____
(Signature)   (Date)

I DO NOT wish to participate in this study.

_____   _____
(Signature)   (Date)

Appendix B: American Sociological Association Code of Ethics

INTRODUCTION

The American Sociological Association's (ASA's) Code of Ethics sets forth the principles and ethical standards that underlie sociologists' professional responsibilities and conduct. These principles and standards should be used as guidelines when examining everyday professional activities. They constitute normative statements for sociologists and provide guidance on issues that sociologists may encounter in their professional work.

ASA's Code of Ethics consists of an Introduction, a Preamble, five General Principles, and specific Ethical Standards. This Code is also accompanied by the Rules and Procedures of the ASA Committee on Professional Ethics which describe the procedures for filing, investigating, and resolving complaints of unethical conduct.

The Preamble and General Principles of the Code are aspirational goals to guide sociologists toward the highest ideals of sociology. Although the Preamble and General

Principles are not enforceable rules, they should be considered by sociologists in arriving at an ethical course of action and may be considered by ethics bodies in interpreting the Ethical Standards.

The Ethical Standards set forth enforceable rules for conduct by sociologists. Most of the Ethical Standards are written broadly in order to apply to sociologists in varied roles, and the application of an Ethical Standard may vary depending on the context. The Ethical Standards are not exhaustive. Any conduct that is not specifically addressed by this Code of Ethics is not necessarily ethical or unethical.

Membership in the ASA commits members to adhere to the ASA Code of Ethics and to the Policies and Procedures of the ASA Committee on Professional Ethics. Members are advised of this obligation upon joining the Association and that violations of the Code may lead to the imposition of sanctions, including termination of membership. ASA members subject to the Code of Ethics may be reviewed under these Ethical Standards only if the activity is part of or affects their work-related functions, or if the activity is sociological in nature. Personal activities having no connection to or effect on sociologists' performance of their professional roles are not subject to the Code of Ethics.

PREAMBLE

This Code of Ethics articulates a common set of values upon which sociologists build their professional and scientific work. The Code is intended to provide both the general principles and the rules to cover professional situations encountered by sociologists. It has as its primary goal the welfare and protection of the individuals and groups with whom sociologists work. It is the individual responsibility of each sociologist to aspire to the highest possible standards of conduct in research, teaching, practice, and service.

The development of a dynamic set of ethical standards for a sociologist's work-related conduct requires a personal commitment to a lifelong effort to act ethically; to encourage ethical behavior by students, supervisors, supervisees, employers, employees, and colleagues; and to consult with others as needed concerning ethical problems. Each sociologist supplements, but does not violate, the values and rules specified in the Code of Ethics based on guidance drawn from personal values, culture, and experience.

GENERAL PRINCIPLES

The following General Principles are aspirational and serve as a guide for sociologists in determining ethical courses of action in various contexts. They exemplify the highest ideals of professional conduct.

Principle A: Professional Competence

Sociologists strive to maintain the highest levels of competence in their work; they recognize the limitations of their expertise; and they undertake only those tasks for which they are qualified by education, training, or experience. They recognize the need for ongoing education in order to remain professionally competent; and they utilize the appropriate scientific, professional, technical, and administrative resources needed to ensure competence in their professional activities. They consult with other professionals when necessary for the benefit of their students, research participants, and clients.

Principle B: Integrity

Sociologists are honest, fair, and respectful of others in their professional activities—in research, teaching, practice, and service. Sociologists do not knowingly act in ways that jeopardize either their own or others' professional welfare. Sociologists conduct their affairs in ways that inspire trust and confidence; they do not knowingly make statements that are false, misleading, or deceptive.

Principle C: Professional and Scientific Responsibility

Sociologists adhere to the highest scientific and professional standards and accept responsibility for their work. Sociologists understand that they form a community and show respect for other sociologists even when they disagree on theoretical, methodological, or personal approaches to professional activities. Sociologists value the public trust in sociology and are concerned about their ethical behavior and that of other sociologists that might compromise that trust. While endeavoring always to be collegial, sociologists must never let the desire to be collegial outweigh their shared responsibility for ethical behavior. When appropriate, they consult with colleagues in order to prevent or avoid unethical conduct.

Principle D: Respect for People's Rights, Dignity, and Diversity

Sociologists respect the rights, dignity, and worth of all people. They strive to eliminate bias in their professional activities, and they do not tolerate any forms of discrimination based on age; gender; race; ethnicity; national origin; religion; sexual orientation; disability; health conditions; or marital, domestic, or parental status. They are sensitive to cultural, individual, and role differences in serving, teaching, and studying groups of people with distinctive characteristics. In all of their work-related activities, sociologists acknowledge the rights of others to hold values, attitudes, and opinions that differ from their own.

Principle E: Social Responsibility

Sociologists are aware of their professional and scientific responsibility to the communities and societies in which they live and work. They apply and make public their knowledge in order to contribute to the public good. When undertaking research, they strive to advance the science of sociology and to serve the public good.

Appendix C: Examples of Widely Used Survey Data Sets

Data Set	Website
American Community Survey (ACS)	https://www.census.gov/programs-surveys/acs/
American Time Use Survey (ATUS)	https://www.bls.gov/tus/
Fragile Families and Child Well-Being Study	http://www.fragilefamilies.princeton.edu/
Consumer Expenditure Survey (CES)	https://www.bls.gov/cex/
Current Population Survey (CPS)	https://www.census.gov/programs-surveys/cps.html
Early Childhood Longitudinal Program (ECLS)	https://nces.ed.gov/ecls/
General Social Survey (GSS)	http://www.gss.norc.org/
Health and Retirement Study (HRS)	http://hrsonline.isr.umich.edu/
High School and Beyond (HSB)	https://nces.ed.gov/surveys/hsb/
Longitudinal Study of Generations (LSOG)	https://www.census.gov/programs-surveys/cps/about.html
Midlife Development in the United States (MIDUS)	http://midus.wisc.edu/
National Health and Nutrition Examination Survey (NHANES)	https://www.cdc.gov/nchs/nhanes/index.htm
National Health and Aging Trends Study (NHATS)	http://www.nhats.org/
National Health Interview Survey (NHIS)	https://www.cdc.gov/nchs/nhis/index.htm
National Longitudinal Study of Adolescent to Adult Health (Add Health)	http://www.cpc.unc.edu/projects/addhealth
National Longitudinal Studies of Youth (NLSY1979, NLSY1997)	http://www.bls.gov/nls/
National Social Life, Health, and Aging Project (NSHAP)	http://www.norc.org/Research/Projects/Pages/national-social-life-health-and-aging-project.aspx
Panel Study of Income Dynamics (PSID)	http://psidonline.isr.umich.edu/
Wisconsin Longitudinal Study (WLS)	http://www.ssc.wisc.edu/wlsresearch/

Integrated Data Resources Containing Multiple Survey Studies from the United States and Beyond	
Gateway to Global Aging Data	https://g2aging.org/
Integrated Public Use Microdata Series (IPUMS)	https://www.ipums.org/
World Fertility Surveys (WFS)	http://wfs.dhsprogram.com/
World Values Surveys (WVS)	http://www.worldvaluessurvey.org/WVSContents.jsp

Appendix D:
Template for Reading, Summarizing, and Identifying Key Contributions of Research Articles

This chart can help you to take notes and organize important information on the research articles you read.

Component	Notes on Study
Title	
Authors	
Journal, date, pages	
Data used in study	
Theoretical or conceptual framework	
Most important previous studies mentioned in literature review	
Key contributions of previously named articles	
Guiding hypothesis or research question(s)	
Study design or method	
Sample size, characteristics, and selection procedures	
Dependent variable(s) or outcomes	
Primary independent variable(s)	
Important mediator variables	
Control variables	
Moderator variables (if any)	
Data analysis or statistical technique used	
Key findings	
Study limitations	
Study strengths and contributions	
Other important issues	

Appendix E: Influential Peer-Reviewed Journals in Sociology

Journal	Website
Administrative Science Quarterly	http://journals.sagepub.com/home/asq/#
American Journal of Sociology	http://www.journals.uchicago.edu/journals/ajs/about
American Sociological Review	http://journals.sagepub.com/home/asr
Annual Review of Sociology	http://www.annualreviews.org/journal/soc
Criminology	http://onlinelibrary.wiley.com/journal/10.1111/(ISSN)1745-9125
Demography	http://www.springer.com/social+sciences/population+studies/journal/13524
Journal of Health and Social Behavior	http://journals.sagepub.com/toc/hsbb/0/0
Journal of Marriage and Family	http://onlinelibrary.wiley.com/journal/10.1111/(ISSN)1741-3737
Law and Society Review	http://onlinelibrary.wiley.com/journal/10.1111/(ISSN)1540-5893
Public Opinion Quarterly	https://academic.oup.com/poq
Social Forces	https://academic.oup.com/sf/issue
Social Networks	https://www.journals.elsevier.com/social-networks/
Sociology of Education	http://journals.sagepub.com/home/soe
Social Psychology Quarterly	http://journals.sagepub.com/home/spq/
Sociological Theory	http://journals.sagepub.com/home/stx/

Appendix F: Random Numbers Table

19	10	11	08	17	88	75	89	47	99
71	02	09	14	98	46	02	61	30	22
00	40	21	03	30	50	17	16	92	65
18	61	85	12	77	10	83	91	41	18
13	01	36	31	74	17	64	75	68	90
96	25	66	69	87	06	96	52	83	19
57	94	83	63	24	41	42	39	49	20
06	20	79	04	02	33	40	46	30	78
07	93	62	27	32	71	26	35	62	82
22	48	23	97	49	92	90	44	08	42
15	23	72	23	45	33	68	62	06	48
95	80	73	95	28	56	98	74	92	37
27	84	88	50	89	99	15	95	56	73
74	71	80	25	38	52	10	35	34	65
72	77	61	09	39	24	94	59	63	03
58	67	93	87	53	79	28	29	81	97
21	76	13	73	20	54	04	55	76	64
00	67	11	80	00	12	04	27	59	88
03	05	24	69	59	16	19	82	94	31
47	26	87	78	79	76	86	57	70	84
15	67	66	96	77	82	66	14	70	29
25	90	68	08	89	72	98	18	85	84
60	60	13	29	53	07	45	05	51	86
09	86	81	70	05	99	43	11	32	43
36	58	91	93	34	37	55	01	64	21
51	14	26	63	78	58	19	10	11	08
17	88	75	89	47	99	71	02	09	14
98	46	02	61	30	22	00	40	21	03
30	50	17	16	92	65	18	61	85	12
77	10	83	91	41	18	13	01	36	31
74	17	64	75	68	90	96	25	66	69

87	06	96	52	83	19	57	94	83	63
24	41	42	39	49	20	06	20	79	04
02	33	40	46	30	78	07	93	62	27
32	71	26	35	62	82	22	48	23	97
49	92	90	44	08	42	15	23	72	23
45	33	68	62	06	48	95	80	73	95
28	56	98	74	92	37	27	84	88	50
89	99	15	95	56	73	74	71	80	25
38	52	10	35	34	65	72	77	61	09
39	24	94	59	63	03	58	67	93	87
53	79	28	29	81	97	21	76	13	73
20	54	04	55	76	64	00	67	11	80
00	12	04	27	59	88	03	05	24	69
59	16	19	82	94	31	47	26	87	78
79	76	86	57	70	84	15	67	66	96
77	82	66	14	70	29	25	90	68	08
89	72	98	18	85	84	60	60	13	29
53	07	45	05	51	86	09	86	81	70
05	99	43	11	32	43	36	58	91	93
34	37	55	01	64	21	51	14	26	63
78	58	19	10	11	08	17	88	75	89
47	99	71	02	09	14	98	46	02	61
30	22	00	40	21	03	30	50	17	16
92	65	18	61	85	12	77	10	83	91
41	18	13	01	36	31	74	17	64	75
68	90	96	25	66	69	87	06	96	52
83	19	57	94	83	63	24	41	42	39
49	20	06	20	79	04	02	33	40	46
30	78	07	93	62	27	32	71	26	35
62	82	22	48	23	97	49	92	90	44
08	42	15	23	72	23	45	33	68	62
06	48	95	80	73	95	28	56	98	74
92	37	27	84	88	50	89	99	15	95
56	73	74	71	80	25	38	52	10	35
34	65	72	77	61	09	39	24	94	59
63	03	58	67	93	87	53	79	28	29
81	97	21	76	13	73	20	54	04	55

Appendix G: Chi Square Table

In Chapter 15, we described chi-square tests. This table shows the minimum values of the chi-square test statistic for different levels of statistical significance. *df* is the degrees of freedom of the chi-square test.

df	$p < .10$	$p < .05$	$p < .01$	$p < .001$
1	2.706	3.841	6.635	10.828
2	4.605	5.991	9.210	13.816
3	6.251	7.815	11.345	16.266
4	7.779	9.488	13.277	18.467
5	9.236	11.07	15.086	20.515
6	10.645	12.592	16.812	22.458
7	12.017	14.067	18.475	24.322
8	13.362	15.507	20.090	26.124
9	14.684	16.919	21.666	27.877
10	15.987	18.307	23.209	29.588
11	17.275	19.675	24.725	31.264
12	18.549	21.026	26.217	32.909
13	19.812	22.362	27.688	34.528
14	21.064	23.685	29.141	36.123
15	22.307	24.996	30.578	37.697
16	23.542	26.296	32.000	39.252
17	24.769	27.587	33.409	40.790
18	25.989	28.869	34.805	42.312
19	27.204	30.144	36.191	43.820
20	28.412	31.410	37.566	45.315

Appendix H: Normal Distribution

In Chapter 15, we described the normal distribution. The table below provides the area under the normal curve that is equal to or greater than z or –z standard deviations away from the center of a normal distribution. The shaded area in the figure illustrates this for $z = 2$.

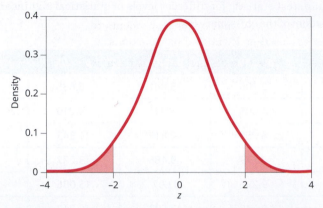

z	p	z	p	z	p	z	p
0	1	1	0.317	2	0.046	3	0.003
0.05	0.96	1.05	0.294	2.05	0.04	3.05	0.002
0.1	0.92	1.1	0.271	2.1	0.036	3.1	0.002
0.15	0.881	1.15	0.25	2.15	0.032	3.15	0.002
0.2	0.841	1.2	0.23	2.2	0.028	3.2	0.001
0.25	0.803	1.25	0.211	2.25	0.024	3.25	0.001
0.3	0.764	1.3	0.194	2.3	0.021	3.3	0.001
0.35	0.726	1.35	0.177	2.35	0.019	3.35	0.001
0.4	0.689	1.4	0.162	2.4	0.016	3.4	0.001
0.45	0.653	1.45	0.147	2.45	0.014	3.45	0.001
0.5	0.617	1.5	0.134	2.5	0.012	3.5	0
0.55	0.582	1.55	0.121	2.55	0.011	3.55	0
0.6	0.549	1.6	0.11	2.6	0.009	3.6	0
0.65	0.516	1.65	0.099	2.65	0.008	3.65	0
0.7	0.484	1.7	0.089	2.7	0.007	3.7	0
0.75	0.453	1.75	0.08	2.75	0.006	3.75	0
0.8	0.424	1.8	0.072	2.8	0.005	3.8	0
0.85	0.395	1.85	0.064	2.85	0.004	3.85	0
0.9	0.368	1.9	0.057	2.9	0.004	3.9	0
0.95	0.342	1.95	0.051	2.95	0.003	3.95	0

Glossary

abductive research • Research that attempts to build theory from "surprises" in empirical data.

abstract • A brief description of the content of a scientific report.

acquiescence bias • The tendency for respondents to answer "agree" to closed-ended attitudinal questions.

advocacy tale • A type of ethnographic writing, also known as *critical ethnographies*, that goes beyond reporting and observing to documenting a wrong and advocating for political change.

age effect • How peoples' opinions or other characteristics change as they get older.

agency • Our capacity to make our own choices and act autonomously.

aggregate data • Summary statistics, such as a group mean, describing people or organizations of a particular type or in a particular location.

aggregation • The process of counting or averaging individual-level data in some context to capture individual-level concepts at the group level.

alters • The other actors to whom one is connected within a given network.

amicus brief • A legal document filed in an appellate court case by nonlitigants with a strong interest or expertise in the subject matter.

analytic codes • Codes that reflect what the text signifies or means, enabling the researcher to sort or characterize qualitative data.

annotated bibliography • A list of cites with a short description of the content of the text as well as the reader's thoughts on the text.

anonymity • When no identifying information can be linked to respondents and even the researcher cannot identify them.

anthropology • The study of societies and cultures, often non-Western.

applied research • A form of research that seeks to answer a question or concrete problem in the real world or to evaluate a policy or program.

archive • A physical or web location where materials are brought together, organized by theme, preserved, and made available for inspection by scholars.

artifact count/assessment • The process of cataloging social artifacts and objects, qualitatively or quantitatively.

association • A relationship whereby some values of one variable in a data set are more likely to co-occur with certain values of another variable.

attitudinal measures • Self-reported responses of participants to questions about their attitudes, opinions, emotions, and beliefs.

attribute codes • Codes that represent the salient personal characteristics of the interviewees that played a role in the study design.

attrition • The loss of sample members over time, usually to death or dropout.

audio computer-assisted self-interview (ACASI) • An interview in which the respondent uses a laptop or tablet to listen to and answer prerecorded questions.

audit study • A type of experimental study that is used to assess whether characteristics such as gender, race, and sexual orientation lead to discrimination in real labor and housing markets.

basic research • A form of research that seeks to answer theoretically informed questions or to resolve a fundamental intellectual puzzle about social behavior.

behavioral measures • Measures collected by observing the overt and observable actions of participants.

beneficence • The principle that refers to the responsibility to do good and to protect subjects from harm in a research study.

betweenness centrality • The extent to which an actor serves as an intermediary on the shortest paths between other pairs of actors in the network.

between-subject design • A study design in which participants are randomly assigned to different levels of the independent variable, such as viewing résumés for a male or a female job applicant.

biased · When results either overstate or understate the true effect of an intervention.

bibliography · A list that provides a full reference for every source cited in a research report.

big data · Data sets with information on millions of individuals and their preferences, behaviors, or networks, often drawn from electronic traces.

bivariate analysis · An analysis of the relationship between two variables.

bivariate regression analysis · A summary of a relationship between variables that describes how the conditional mean of the dependent variable changes as the independent variable changes.

bridge · A tie that connects two (sets of) otherwise poorly connected (or unconnected) actors in a network. Bridges span structural holes.

case study logic · An approach to research in which the goal is to understand the case or person in depth, not as a representation of a wider population.

case-oriented research · Research in which social scientists immerse themselves in an enormous amount of detail about a small number of cases, or even just a single case.

categorical variables · Variables that have a finite set of possible values that are fixed and distinct from one another with unknown differences between them.

causal hypothesis · A statement that the relationship between two concepts is the result of cause and effect.

causal inference · The degree of confidence that an observation based on the test of a hypothesis is truly causal.

causality · A relationship where one factor or variable is dependent on another factor or variable.

causes of effects · An approach to establishing causality, generally associated with qualitative research, that starts with the outcome the researcher is trying to explain and works backwards to develop a causal model.

cell percentages · For each cell in a table, the percentage of all observations that are represented by that cell.

cells · The intersections of the rows and columns in a cross-tabulation.

census · A study that includes data on every member of a population, as opposed to only a sample.

centrality · The extent to which an actor plays an important role in connecting a large number of other actors in a network.

certificate of confidentiality · A certificate issued by the National Institutes of Health that allows researchers to protect participants from future requests for data disclosure.

chi-square statistic · A quantity that summarizes how much discrepancy there is between the observed frequency and the expected frequency.

chi-square test · A way to calculate p-values that is based on cross-tabulation.

clique · A subset of at least three actors who are all directly connected to one another.

closed-ended question · A focused interview question to which subjects can respond only in preset ways.

closeness centrality · The degree to which an actor can "reach" or access the other members of the network in a small number of steps.

cluster sampling · A probability sampling strategy in which researchers divide up the target population into groups, or "clusters," first selecting clusters randomly and then selecting individuals within those clusters.

codebook · A system of organizing information about a data set, including the variables it contains, the possible values for each variable, coding schemes, and decision rules.

codes · Labels or tags for chunks of text.

coding · The process of translating written or visual material into standardized categories. In qualitative data analysis, this involves tagging or labeling segments of data as an example of or related to a theoretical idea, wider theme, or concept.

coding scheme · A document that lists all the possible categories and outlines specific rules for how to apply those categories to the material.

cognitive dissonance · The unpleasant or distressing feeling we experience when we hold two discrepant beliefs, or we engage in a behavior that violates our beliefs.

cognitive interview · An interview with survey respondents to understand how they interpret particular questions and terms. Respondents "think out loud" as they answer the questions. Also called a *cognitive pretest*.

cohesion · The degree to which actors in a network are highly interconnected.

cohort design • A type of longitudinal study design in which data are collected from a particular cohort at multiple time points.

cohort replacement • When the younger people who enter a survey population by becoming adults have systematically different attitudes from older adults who exit a population by death.

column percentages • For each cell in a table, the percentage of observations in that column of the table that are represented by that cell.

community studies • Studies most related to the way anthropologists study whole villages, tribes, or towns or the way sociologists study neighborhoods or towns.

comparative research methods • Using materials to examine change across locations to answer questions about how and why social processes unfold in particular ways.

complete participant • One of the four roles a researcher can adopt when doing fieldwork; as complete participants, fieldworkers "go undercover," immersing themselves in a fieldwork site and keeping their identities as researchers a secret.

composite measure • A measure that combines multiple items, whether as a scale or an index, to create a single value that captures a multifaceted concept.

composite variable • A variable that averages a set of items (typically from a survey) to measure some concept.

computer-assisted personal interview (CAPI) • A face-to-face interview in which the researcher uses a laptop or tablet computer that is preprogrammed with all of the survey questions and response categories.

computer-assisted telephone interview (CATI) • A telephone interview in which the researcher uses a laptop or tablet computer that is preprogrammed with all of the survey questions and response categories.

concept • An idea that can be named, defined, and eventually measured in some way.

conceptualization • The process of precisely defining ideas and turning them into variables.

concurrent validity • A dimension of validity concerning how strongly a measure correlates with some preexisting measure of the construct that has already been deemed valid.

conditional mean • A statistic that is calculated only for observations that meet a particular condition rather than calculated for every observation.

confederates • Individuals who pretend to be study participants but who are instead trained to play a role in the experiment.

confessional tale • A type of ethnographic writing, also known as *postmodern ethnography*, in which the account of the field is very personalized and incorporates the researcher's thoughts and feelings throughout; often written in the first person.

confidence interval • A range of possible estimates in which researchers can have a specific degree of confidence; includes the population parameter.

confidence level • The probability that a confidence interval includes the population parameter.

confidentiality • When participants' identifying information is only accessible to the research team.

conflict of interest • If researchers' interests or loyalties compromise the way they design, conduct, or report their research.

confound • A third variable that is linked to two concepts in a way that makes them appear to be related even when they are not.

confounding • When two variables can be consistently associated with each other even when one does not cause the other.

construct validity • A dimension of validity concerning how well multiple indicators are connected to some underlying factor.

content validity • A dimension of validity concerning how well a measure encompasses the many different meanings of a single concept.

continuous variables • Variables that could have an infinite set of possible values that exist on a continuum from low to high with meaningful and identifiable differences between them.

control condition • A condition where the independent variable is not manipulated.

control group • The group that is not exposed to the manipulation of the independent variable.

control variable • A potentially confounding variable that we add to regression analysis to estimate the relationship between the independent variable and dependent variable net of its influence.

convenience sample • A sample that selects observations based on what is cheapest or easiest.

cost-benefit analysis • The process of comparing the estimated value of the intervention to the cost of the intervention.

counterfactuals • A thought exercise of imagining what might have happened but did not, which can be useful in case selection.

cover story • A false reason for participation in an experiment.

coverage error • A type of error that occurs when the sampling frame does not adequately capture all members of the target population, either by systematically omitting some or including others more than once.

covert observer • One of the four roles a researcher can adopt when doing fieldwork; as a covert observer, the researcher observes people who do not know they are being observed or studied.

criterion-related validity • A dimension of validity concerning how closely a measure is associated with some other factor.

critical content analysis • An interpretive analysis of media designed to uncover societal blind spots.

Cronbach's alpha (α) • A calculation that measures a specific kind of reliability for a composite variable.

cross-sectional study design • A study in which data are collected at only one time point.

cross-sectional survey • A survey in which data are collected at only one time point.

cross-tabulation • A presentation of distributions between two or more variables as a table.

cultural relativism • The principle whereby scholars refrain from making judgments about practices they observe and instead adopt the viewpoint of the communities being studied.

cyberethnography or netnography • A form of ethnography focused on the study of online life.

data swapping • A statistical technique for ensuring confidentiality in which data on households that have been matched on a set of key variables are swapped across blocks.

debriefing • The process of interviewing participants after the study and then informing them of the actual purpose of the experiment.

decision rule • Used in quantitative content analysis, a rule that clearly distinguishes mutually exclusive categories of a variable.

deconstruction • A critical interpretive approach to research that involves dissecting the content of some type of media to uncover hidden or alternative meanings.

deductive approach • The translation of general theory into specific empirical analysis.

deductive disclosure • The use of unique combinations of variables to identify specific individuals in data sets.

deductive research • Research that takes a "top-down" approach, where the theory or hypothesis drives the data-collection strategy and analysis.

degree centrality • The number of ties a given actor has.

de-identification • The process of protecting each respondent's anonymity by suppressing or changing identifying data.

demand characteristics • The process whereby research subjects, when they become aware of a study's hypothesis, behave in a way that confirms that hypothesis.

dense network • A network that has a large number of ties.

dependent variable • In a causal hypothesis, the variable that is acted upon; the outcome we are seeking to understand.

descriptive research • Research that documents or describes trends, variations, and patterns of social phenomena.

desk reject • A manuscript that is promptly rejected by a journal editor without being reviewed by other scholars. Also referred to as an *immediate reject*.

deviant case • A case that is unusual, unexpected, or hard to explain given what we currently understand.

dichotomous outcome • When only two options are available to a question, such as "yes" or "no."

dichotomous variable • A variable with only two categories.

diffusion • The communication or dissemination of information or resources among social actors through network ties over a period of time.

dimensions • Components of a concept that represent its different manifestations, angles, or units.

directed network tie • A link between two actors in a network that may or may not be mutual.

distribution • The set of different values of a variable that have been observed and how common each value is.

double-barreled question • A question that asks about two or more ideas or concepts in a single question.

double-blind peer review • A peer-review process in which both the author of the manuscript and the reviewers are anonymous.

double-blind study • A study where neither the researcher nor the participant is aware of which condition the participant is in.

ecological fallacy • A mistake that researchers make by drawing conclusions about the micro level based on some macro-level analysis.

effects of causes • An approach to establishing causality, generally associated with quantitative research, that tries to estimate the average effect of different independent variables on a particular outcome.

ego • A given individual in a network in whose perspective on a network a researcher is interested.

egocentric network approach • The study of a network from the perspective of individual actors within the setting.

elaboration • A cross-tabulation technique used to determine whether a confounding variable can account for the association between two categorical variables.

emic focus • An approach to research in which researchers take on the respondent's viewpoint and use his or her language.

empiricism • The idea that the world can be subjected to observation, or the use of the senses to gather data about social phenomena.

equivalence • Similarity between social actors with respect to the profile of ties they maintain with other actors in the network.

error bars • A way of indicating the confidence interval for a statistic presented in a graph.

ethics • The moral system that determines whether actions are right or wrong, good or bad.

ethnoarray • A type of matrix used in qualitative research where the columns represent respondents and the rows represent domains and measures relevant to the research.

etic focus • An approach to research in which researchers maintain a distance from their respondents with the goal of achieving more scientific objectivity.

evaluation research • A type of research designed to determine whether a social intervention or policy, such as reducing class size or implementing a new workplace program, produces its intended effects.

exhaustive • Preset response categories that give all subjects at least one accurate response.

exogenous variation • Special circumstances that are like natural experiments, in which differences in the independent variable are induced by events that ostensibly have nothing to do with the characteristics of the individual.

experiment • A research method where the researcher manipulates one or more independent variable(s) to determine the effect(s) on a dependent variable.

experimental condition • A condition in an experiment where the independent variable is manipulated.

experimental group • The group that is exposed to the experimental manipulation.

experimenter effects • When a researcher subtly or unconsciously affects the performance of a study participant.

explanatory research • Research that documents the causes and effects of social phenomena, thus addressing questions of why.

exploratory research • Research that tends to answer questions of how, with the goal of documenting precisely how particular processes and dynamics unfold.

extended case study approach • An approach to theory in qualitative research in which the researcher starts with an established theory and chooses a field site or case to improve upon or modify the existing theory.

external validity • A dimension of validity concerning the degree to which the results of a study can generalize beyond the study.

face validity • A dimension of validity concerning whether a measure looks valid.

factorial design experiment • An experiment that has two or more independent variables.

field experiment • An experiment that takes place in a natural or "real world" setting.

field notes • The data produced by a fieldworker, including observations, dialogue, and thoughts about what is experienced in the field.

first-person account • Primary evidence of what a person experienced, gleaned from interviews, diaries, or similar sources.

fixed-choice approach • An approach to collecting network data in which researchers restrict respondents' responses to some predetermined set of potential network members, or where they cut respondents off once some maximum or threshold is reached.

focus group • A group interview, led by a moderator, on a specific topic.

forced choice • Survey questions that do not offer choices like "neither agree nor disagree," therefore forcing the respondent to indicate their general leanings toward either agreement or disagreement.

formative research • A type of research where researchers collect qualitative data to help them design effective questions for their survey instrument.

free-choice approach • An approach to collecting network data in which researchers allow respondents to list as many network members as they wish.

frequency • The number of observations with a particular value of a variable.

frequency distribution • A presentation of the possible values of a variable along with the number of observations for each value that was observed.

gatekeeper • A person with the authority to allow outsiders into (or ban them from) a research setting.

generalizable • The extent to which results or conclusions based on one population can be applied to others.

geodesic distance • The fewest number of steps a given actor must take to "reach" another actor in the network. Also known as *path length*.

geographic information systems (GIS) • Statistical software that takes many bits of quantitative data and associates them with locations on maps to create visual images of how social phenomena are unfolding.

globalization • The development of worldwide social and economic relationships.

going native • The threat that fieldworkers who completely immerse themselves in the world of their subjects will lose their original identity and forget they are researchers.

grounded theory • A systematic, inductive approach to qualitative research that suggests that researchers should extrapolate conceptual relationships from data rather than formulate testable hypotheses from existing theory.

Hawthorne effect • Named after a study of factory workers, the phenomenon whereby merely being observed changes subjects' behavior.

hierarchical mapping • An approach to simplifying the collection of network data in which the researcher presents respondents with a diagram containing concentric circles, and asks them to write down their closest contacts in the center and list weaker ties as they move outward from the innermost circle.

histogram • A visual representation of data that depicts the frequency distribution of a continuous variable.

historical research methods • Examining change over time to answer questions about how and why social processes unfold in particular ways.

history • The study of past events, presidencies, social movements, or cultural patterns.

homogeneity • The principle that states that you should put people of similar social statuses or backgrounds together when constructing a focus group.

human subjects research • Any study of persons that is a systematic investigation designed to develop or contribute to generalizable knowledge.

hypothesis • A testable statement of a relationship between two concepts.

hypothesis of association • A statement that two variables will increase or decrease together, without an explicit specification of cause and effect.

hypothesis of difference • A testable statement about group differences in some concept.

impact factor • A numerical value that indicates the average number of times the articles published in a journal within the past two years have been cited in other articles.

independent variable • In a causal hypothesis, the concept purported to be the cause; the variable on which values of the dependent variable may depend.

in-depth interviewing • A qualitative method in which the researcher asks open-ended questions to elicit as much detail as possible about the interviewee's experiences, understandings, thoughts, feelings, and beliefs.

index • A composite measure that sums responses to survey items capturing key elements of a particular concept being measured.

index codes • Codes that represent broad categories or topics related to a research question, enabling data reduction.

indicators • The values assigned to a variable.

inductive approach • The process by which scientists draw a general understanding of some social phenomenon through specific empirical observations.

inductive research • Research that begins with the data and then generalizes or produces theoretical generalization from the data.

informant • A person who has special knowledge about a research question based on the person's social or professional position.

informed consent • The freedom to say yes or no to participating in a research study once all the possible risks and benefits have been properly explained.

institutional review board (IRB) • A committee located at an institution where research is done that is responsible for reviewing all research involving human subjects, with the goal of protecting the human subjects and preventing ethical violations in the research.

intercoder reliability • A type of reliability that reveals how much different coders or observers agree with one another when looking at the same data.

internal reliability • The degree to which the various items in a composite variable lead to a consistent response and, therefore, are tapping into the same concept.

internal validity • The degree to which a study establishes a causal effect of the independent variable on the dependent variable.

internal validity of a measure • The degree to which a measure truly and accurately measures the defined concepts.

interpretivist approach • An approach to research whereby the researcher does not seek objective truth but rather a faithful rendering of the subjects' interpretations of events, social movements, or any other phenomenon that the researcher is studying.

intersectionality • A theoretical tradition emphasizing that our overlapping identities and group memberships are critical to our life experiences.

interval variables • Variables with a continuum of values with meaningful distances (or intervals) between them but no true zero.

interview schedule • A prepared list of questions and follow-up prompts that the interviewer asks the respondent.

interviewer effects • The possibility that the mere presence of an interviewer, or that the interviewer's personal characteristics, may lead a respondent to answer questions in a particular way, potentially biasing the responses.

justice • The principle that research must be conducted in a fair manner with the potential risks and benefits distributed equally among participants.

key informant • A person who is usually quite central or popular in the research setting and who shares his or her knowledge with the researcher or a person with professional or special knowledge about the social setting.

laboratory experiment • An experiment that takes place in a laboratory.

lagged dependent variables • Past values of the dependent variable.

life course • The study of human development over the life span, taking into account how individual lives are socially patterned and affected by historical change.

life history interview • An in-depth interview used to understand how lives unfold over time, the timing and sequencing of important life events, and other turning points in individual lives.

Likert scale • A type of rating scale that captures the respondent's level of agreement or disagreement with a particular statement.

line graph • A graph in which a line indicates how the conditional mean of the outcome changes as values of an explanatory variable change.

literature review • A systematic reading of the body of theory and evidence to determine what has been done (and how) and what needs to be done.

longitudinal study design • A study in which data are collected at multiple time points.

longitudinal survey • A survey in which data are collected at multiple time points.

macro level • The broadest way of thinking about social life, focusing on the structure, composition, and processes of society.

macro-social phenomena • Social patterns or trends that are bigger than any individual, such as societal composition, structures, and processes.

macrosociology · The study of large-scale social systems and processes such as the political system or the economy.

manipulation · Something that is done to some subjects of an experiment but not others so that the outcomes of the two groups can be compared.

margin of error · The amount of uncertainty in an estimate; equal to the distance between the estimate and the boundary of the confidence interval.

marginal frequency · The overall frequency distributions of a focal measure that do not take into account differences among the subgroups; the totals in the bottom row and rightmost column of a table. Also called *marginals*.

matching procedure · A method of ensuring that treatment and control groups are as equivalent as possible. Researchers select pairs of participants who are identical on specific characteristics and split them up to form the treatment and control group.

materials · Preexisting information, such as expert analyses, reports, records, news media, other media, written accounts of events, maps, and preexisting data sets, or physical objects used as the basis for materials-based research.

materials-based methods · Sociological methods that involve analyzing existing materials rather than interviewing, surveying, or observing people.

matrix · A rectangular array of rows and columns (as in a spreadsheet) in which the actors in a network are listed in the headings and the ties between them are recorded in the corresponding cells.

mean · The sum of all of a variable's values divided by the number of observations.

measure of central tendency · A summary statistic that refers to the center of a distribution.

measurement error · A type of error that occurs when the approach used to measure a particular variable affects or biases the response provided.

media · Artifacts of popular culture, including paintings, novels, songs, television shows, movies, magazines, comic books, and blogs.

median · The middle value observed when observations are ranked from the lowest to the highest.

mediating variable · A variable that links the independent variable to the dependent variable.

mediation · The expected relation between two concepts is channeled through a third concept that links them to each other.

meso level · The middle ground way of thinking about social life, focusing on the physical settings and organizations that link individuals to the larger society.

micro data · Individual-level data.

micro level · The most intimate way of thinking about social life, focusing on face-to-face interaction and small-group processes.

microsociology · The study of personal concerns and interpersonal interactions.

mixed-methods approach · A general research approach that uses more than one method in a single study.

mode · The most common value of a variable.

mode effects · The ways that the mode of administration might affect respondents' answers.

mode of administration · The way the survey is administered, such as face to face, by phone or mail, or on the web.

model · A verbal or visual description of an argument.

moderating variable · A variable that modifies or "moderates" the relationship between an independent variable and a dependent variable.

moderation · The strength of the association between two variables is made weaker or stronger by a third variable.

moderator · A professionally trained person who leads the discussion in a focus group.

multiple time-series design · A type of reflexive control design in which the researcher compares the effect of an intervention over multiple times and locations.

multivariate methods · Methods of quantitative analysis where at least three variables are included.

mutually exclusive · Preset response categories that do not overlap with one another, ensuring that respondents select the single category that best captures their views.

name generator · A question that is used to elicit names of network members from respondents.

name interpreters · Follow-up questions posed to respondents to collect information about the behaviors, attitudes, and experiences of their network members.

natural experiment · An experiment in which the independent variable is manipulated by "nature," not by the experimenter.

negative association · An association in which higher values of one variable occur with lower values of another variable.

network density · The extent to which network members are connected to one another, quantified in terms of the proportion of possible connections in the set that are actually realized.

network size · The number of actors in the network.

nodes · The social network analysis term for the actors who appear in a network structure, especially when diagrammed.

nominal variables · Variables with states or statuses that are parallel and cannot be ranked or ordered.

nondirected network tie · A link between two actors that is by definition mutual, such as the link between siblings, or co-members of the same club.

nonequivalent comparison design · A study design in which treatment and control groups are formed by a procedure other than randomization.

nonprobability sample · A sample that is not drawn using a method of random selection.

normal distribution · The random distribution of values in a bell-shaped curve.

null hypothesis · A hypothesis that no relationship between concepts exists or no difference in the dependent variable between groups exists.

Nuremberg Code · A set of ethical principles for human subjects research, including the requirement of informed consent, developed in the wake of the Nuremberg Trials following World War II.

observation · The process of seeing, recording, and assessing social phenomena.

observer · One of the four roles a researcher can adopt when doing fieldwork; as an observer, the researcher tells people they are being observed but does not take part in the subjects' activities and lives.

one-mode network · A network that includes just one type of actor.

open-ended question · A broad interview question to which subjects are allowed to respond in their own words rather than in preset ways.

operationalization · The process of linking the conceptualized variables to a set of procedures for measuring them.

oral history · An unstructured or semi-structured interview in which people are asked to recall their experiences in a specific historical era or during a particular historical event.

order effects · When the order in which questions appear biases the responses.

ordinal variables · Variables with categories that can be ordered in some way but have unknowable differences between them.

ordinary least squares (OLS) regression · A statistical procedure that estimates how well changes in the independent variable predict changes in the dependent variable.

outlier · An extreme value.

oversample · A group that is deliberately sampled at a rate higher than its frequency in the population.

panel design · A type of longitudinal study in which data are collected on from the same subjects at multiple time points.

panel survey · A type of longitudinal survey in which data are collected from the same subjects at multiple time points.

paper-and-pencil interview (PAPI) · A survey interview in which the researcher asks questions and records the respondent's answers in a preprinted copy of the survey booklet.

paradata · Information about the process by which the survey data were collected.

paradigm · A broad set of taken-for-granted and often unacknowledged assumptions about how social reality is to be defined.

participant observation, or ethnography · A research method where researchers immerse themselves in the lives and social worlds of the people they want to understand.

participant observer · One of the four roles a researcher can adopt when doing fieldwork; as a participant observer, the researcher tells at least some of the people being studied about his or her real identity as a researcher.

path diagram · A depiction of how variables influence one another that uses arrows to indicate the direction of influence.

peer review • The process whereby a manuscript is evaluated by a panel of experts for its originality, quality, accuracy, and scientific rigor.

percentiles • Values at or below which a certain percentage of values fall.

period effect • A broad pattern in which all ages in a population exhibit a tendency toward change over the same historical period.

physiological measures • Biological responses to stimuli.

pilot study • A small preliminary study that is a "trial run" for the larger study.

pilot testing • The process of administering some measurement protocol to a small preliminary sample of subjects as a means of assessing how well the measure works.

plagiarism • The failure to properly cite another author's words or ideas.

policy brief • A short, impartial summary of what is known about a particular social or economic issue; includes policy recommendations based on this evidence.

poll • A very brief single-topic survey.

population parameter • A number that characterizes some quantitative aspect of a population.

population trends • Analyses showing how some characteristic of a population changes or remains stable over time.

population-based survey experiment • An experiment that relies on survey methods and is conducted on a representative sample of the population of interest.

position generators • A series of parallel questions that ask respondents if they know people who occupy various hierarchically ordered positions—usually occupations.

positive association • An association in which higher values of one variable occur with higher values of another variable.

positivism • The paradigm holding that all knowledge can be confirmed or refuted through empirical observation.

positivist approach • An approach to research that assumes a reality external to the observer that can be objectively described and analyzed with scientific standards.

postmodernism • A paradigm characterized by significant skepticism of claims about general truths, facts, or principles.

postsurvey weighting • When a sample is weighted to match known characteristics of the population from which it is drawn.

practical significance • Whether a difference is large enough to be important for the purposes of research or social policies. Also called *substantive significance*.

precision • A quality of measurement referring to how detailed and specific it is.

predictive validity • A dimension of validity concerning how strongly a measure correlates with a measure that it should predict.

pre-post design • A type of reflexive control design in which the researcher measures the outcome of interest once before the intervention, introduces the intervention, and then measures the outcome again.

primary data collection • When social scientists design and carry out their own data collection.

primary information • Researchers' direct observations.

priming effects • A type of order effects in which exposure to a particular image, word, or feeling shapes how respondents think and feel in the immediate aftermath.

privacy • Control over the extent, timing, and circumstances of sharing oneself with others.

probability sample • A sample in which (a) random chance is used to select participants for the sample, and (b) each individual has a probability of being selected that can be calculated.

projection bias • In network data, the type of bias that occurs when respondents project their own attributes onto their network members.

prospective design • A study that follows individuals forward over time.

psychology • The study of individual behavior, attitudes, and emotions, and their causes.

purposive sampling • A sampling strategy in which cases are deliberately selected on the basis of features that distinguish them from other cases.

p-value • The probability that we would observe a difference as large as the difference that we actually observed if the null hypothesis were true.

qualitative data analysis • The process by which researchers draw substantive findings from qualitative data, such as text, audio, video, and photographs.

qualitative methods • Research methods that collect and analyze data that enable rich description in words or images.

quantitative content analysis • Testing hypotheses through the systematic review of materials that have been converted into a quantitative data set.

quantitative data analysis • The process by which substantive findings are drawn from numerical data.

quantitative methods • Research methods that rely on data that can be represented by and summarized into numbers.

quasi-experimental methods • Experimental methods that lack random assignment of individuals to treatment and control groups.

random assignment • A process that ensures that participants have an equal likelihood of being assigned to experimental or control conditions in order to ensure that individual characteristics are randomly distributed across conditions.

randomized field experiment • An experiment that takes place in a natural setting and where participants are randomly assigned to the treatment or control condition.

range • The differences between the maximum and minimum values of a distribution.

ranking items • A type of closed-ended question that asks respondents to rank-order their priorities or preferences.

rapport • A close and harmonious relationship that allows people to understand one another and communicate effectively.

rating scale • A series of ordered categories.

ratio variables • Variables with a continuum of values with meaningful distances (or intervals) between them and a true zero.

reactivity • When the presence and actions of the researcher change the behaviors and beliefs of the research subjects.

realist tales • A type of ethnographic writing, also known as classical or mainstream ethnography, often written objectively, in the third person, with most discussion of methods and the ethnographer's role placed in the introduction or the appendix.

recall bias • In network data, a form of bias that occurs when informants do not name the most relevant network members due to memory or recall issues, time pressure, and other factors.

reciprocal causality • A situation where two variables are both a cause and an effect of each other.

reciprocity • The extent to which pairs of actors give and receive mutual emotions, information, support, and resources in generally equal and balanced ways.

reductionism • A mistake that researchers make by drawing conclusions about the macro-level unit based on analyses of micro-level data.

refereed journal • A periodic publication in which all articles have gone successfully through the peer-review process.

reflexive controls • A method for ensuring treatment and control groups are equivalent in which researchers compare measures of an outcome variable on participants before and after an intervention.

regression coefficient • A value that indicates the expected change in our outcome that is associated with a one-unit increase in our explanatory variable.

relative distribution • A presentation of the possible values of a variable along with the percentage of observations for each value that was observed. Also referred to as a *percentage distribution*.

relative frequency • The percentage of observations with a particular value.

reliability • A quality of a measure concerning how dependable it is.

repeated cross-sectional study design • A type of longitudinal study in which data are collected at multiple time points but from different subjects at each time point.

repeated cross-sectional survey • A type of longitudinal survey in which data are collected at multiple time points but from different subjects at each time point.

replicability • The capacity to be reproduced with similar results in different samples or populations.

reports • Direct feedback, written or verbal, from people.

research protocol • A description from the researcher of the intended methods and procedures, target population and recruitment methods, possible risks and benefits of the study, and major research questions.

research report • A formal written summary of a research project.

resource generators • Questions used to elicit network data that ask respondents about whether they know someone through whom they can access resources such as social support, money, or information. Also called *exchange generators*.

respect • The principle that people are to be treated as autonomous agents in research studies and that those with diminished autonomy receive protection.

respondent • The person who is interviewed. Also called an *interviewee*.

response categories • The preset answers to questions on a survey.

response set • The tendency to select the same answer to several sequential questions, perhaps out of boredom or a desire to quickly finish the survey.

reverse causality • The possibility that the dependent variable influences the independent variable.

revise and resubmit • A decision made by a journal editor that allows an author to revise his or her originally submitted manuscript in accordance with reviewer feedback, and to resubmit the improved manuscript for possible publication.

risk versus benefit analysis • An assessment in which the potential harms to research subjects are weighed against the potential benefits of the research.

robustness • A quality of an operational protocol referring to how well it works.

row percentages • For each cell in a table, the percentage of observations in that row of the table that are represented by that cell.

salience • When participants notice the experimental manipulation, such as noticing that a job applicant is female (or male).

sample • A subset of a population selected for a study.

sampling • The process of deciding what or whom to observe when you cannot observe and analyze everything or everyone.

sampling distribution • A set of estimates that would be observed from a large number of independent samples that are all the same size and drawn using the same method.

sampling error • The difference between the estimates from a sample and the true parameter that arise due to random chance.

sampling for range • A purposive sampling strategy in which researchers try to maximize respondents' range of experiences with the phenomena under study.

sampling frame • A list of population members from which a probability sample is drawn.

sampling weights • Values that are assigned to each case so that researchers can construct an overall representative sample; often found in secondary data sets.

saturation • When new materials (interviews, observations, survey responses) fail to yield new insights and simply reinforce what the researcher already knows.

scale • A composite measure that averages responses to a series of related items that capture a single concept or trait, such as depressive symptoms or self-esteem.

scientific method • The systematic process of asking and answering questions in a rigorous and unbiased way.

screener question • A question that serves as a gateway to (or detour around) a follow-up question; also called a *filter question*.

secondary data source • A resource collected by someone else.

secondary information • Indirect evidence of something; the researchers learn of it through at least one other person.

selection bias • A form of bias that occurs when certain types of people are "selected" into particular situations based on their personal characteristics; in experiments, selection bias occurs when the control and treatment groups differ on some characteristic prior to the intervention that affects the outcome of interest.

self-administered questionnaire (SAQ) • A survey completed directly by respondents through the mail or online.

semi-structured interview • A type of in-depth interview in which the researcher has prepared a list of questions and follow-up probes but is free to ask questions out of order, ask follow-up questions, and allow the conversation to unfold naturally.

sequential sampling • A flexible sampling strategy used in case-based research in which researchers make decisions about what additional data to collect based on their findings from data they've already collected.

showcard • A preprinted card that reminds the respondent of all the response options for a particular question or questions.

significance testing • The process of evaluating whether a result is statistically significant.

simple random sample • A type of probability sample in which each individual has the same probability of being selected and in which each pair of individuals has the same probability of being selected.

single-blind peer review • A peer-review process in which the reviewers know who authored the manuscript, but the author does not know who the reviewers are.

skewed • An unbalanced distribution.

skip pattern • A question or series of questions associated with a conditional response to a prior question.

snowball sampling • A sampling strategy in which the researcher starts with one respondent who meets the requirement for inclusion and asks him or her to recommend another person to contact (who also meets the requirement for inclusion).

social actors • The social network analysis term for individuals, families, organizations (such as firms), and other social entities.

social artifacts • Concrete aspects of social life that can be counted, such as newspaper articles, tombstones, or text messages.

social desirability bias • A type of bias that occurs when study participants report positively valued behaviors and attitudes rather than giving truthful responses.

social intervention • A policy implementation or change, such as introducing a new urban housing program, that is intended to modify the outcomes or behaviors of individuals or groups.

social network • A set (or sets) of actors and the relations that link them together.

social network analysis • The systematic study of the web of relationships that link actors in a given setting.

social network composition • The profile of the different types of actors who compose a network.

social network index (SNI) • A single composite measure that reflects generic information about a number of interrelated dimensions of one's social network.

social structures • The patterned social arrangements that may constrain (or facilitate) our choices and opportunities.

societal blind spots • A tendency of individuals to romanticize the past or to presume that certain things are true, even when the facts contradict them.

sociocentric network design • A study that is interested in an entire network structure that includes numerous actors who may or may not be directly connected to one another. Also called *whole-network design*.

sociological imagination • A distinctive viewpoint, originated by C. Wright Mills, recognizing that our personal experiences are powerfully shaped by macrosocial and historical forces.

sociology • The scientific study of the social lives of individuals, groups, and societies.

split-ballot design • A survey in which a randomly selected subset of respondents, typically 50% of those persons selected to participate in the survey, receives one topical module while the other 50% receives a different topical ballot.

split-half method • A method of testing robustness in which the similarity of results is assessed after administering one subset of an item to a sample and then another subset.

spuriousness • When an apparent relation between two concepts is actually the result of some third concept (confound) influencing both of them.

stakeholders • The various parties with interests in the outcomes of a social intervention.

standard deviation • The average distance between the value of each observation and the overall mean.

statistical controls • A statistical technique that adjusts for the effects of additional variables that may differ between treatment and control groups.

statistical power • A study's ability to detect statistically significant differences between groups if such differences exist.

statistical validity • A dimension of validity concerning the degree to which a study's statistical operations are in line with basic statistical laws and guidelines.

statistically significant • An observed association that we are at least 95% confident is too large to be the result of chance.

stem • The part of the survey question that presents the issue about which the question is asking.

strata • Subgroups that a population is divided into for the purposes of drawing a sample. Individuals are drawn from each stratum.

stratified sampling • A probability sampling strategy in which the population is divided into groups, or strata, and sample members are selected in strategic proportions from each group.

structural holes • The gaps that exist between (sets of) actors who are poorly connected or unconnected within a network.

structured abstract · An abstract that typically has four or five separate and labeled sections, such as background, objectives, methods, results, and discussion.

subculture · A group within a larger culture; a subset of people with beliefs and behaviors that differ from those of the larger culture.

summary statistic · A single value that summarizes some feature of a distribution.

suppression · A technique for ensuring confidentiality in which data are simply not shown.

suppressor variable · A variable that hides or even reverses the direction of a true causal relationship between an independent variable and a dependent variable.

survey · A social research method in which researchers ask a sample of individuals to answer a series of questions.

survey instrument · The types of questions asked, the response categories provided, and guidelines that help survey designers organize their questions.

systematic error · A flaw built into the design of the study that causes a sample estimate to diverge from the population parameter.

systematic observation · A method of observation in which the researcher follows a checklist and timeline for observing phenomena.

systematic sample · A probability sampling strategy in which sample members are selected by using a fixed interval, such as taking every fifth person on a list of everyone in the population.

_t_ test · A method for testing whether the mean of the dependent variable differs depending on the value of the independent variable.

target population · A group about which social scientists attempt to make generalizations.

team ethnography · An ethnography conducted by two or more scholars working together.

test-retest method · A method of testing robustness in which the similarity of results is assessed after administering a measure to the same sample at two different times.

theory · A sequential argument consisting of a series of logically related statements put forward to illuminate some element of social life.

tie strength · The extent to which a given tie is characterized by emotional closeness or intensity, frequent interaction, and durability or stability.

tie valence · The extent to which a tie is characterized by positive or negative sentiments or relations.

ties · The links that connect the nodes in a social network.

time-series design · A type of reflexive control design in which the researcher takes multiple measures of the outcome of interest over time.

translation · The process of implementing the components of an evaluation research project on a larger scale.

treatment condition · A condition in an experiment where the independent variable is manipulated.

treatment group · The group that receives the intervention.

triad · A set of three nodes that are at least indirectly connected to each other.

triangulation · The use of multiple research methods to study the same general research question and determine if different types of evidence and approaches lead to consistent findings.

truth table · A table, used in qualitative comparative analysis, that sorts cases by the presence or absence of certain variables.

two-mode network · A network that includes two different types of actors.

typical · When a case's features are similar in as many respects as possible to the average of the population it is supposed to represent, and when nothing makes it stand out as unusual.

typology · A way of generalizing from concrete cases by defining a common core within a set of cases.

unbiased · A sample estimate that is the same as the population parameter except for the difference caused by random chance.

unfolding question · A sequence of questions intended to elicit respondent estimates about topics such as income when respondents are uncertain of the answer; also called _unfolding brackets_.

unit of analysis · The level of social life about which we want to generalize.

univariate analysis · An analysis of a single variable.

unobtrusive methods · Term used to describe materials-based methods.

unstructured abstract · An abstract without subheadings that differentiate sections of the article.

unstructured interview · A highly flexible type of in-depth interview in which the researcher has a list of general topics he or she would like to cover but has control over all the questions and the flow of the interview.

validity · A quality of a measure concerning how accurate it is.

value-free · The goal of being objective and not biased by personal ideologies.

variable-oriented research · Research in which social scientists study a large number of cases, such as undergraduates or employment discrimination lawsuits, but only with information organized into variables about each case.

variables · Representations that capture the different dimensions, categories, or levels of a concept.

verstehen · A German word best translated as "empathetic understanding."

vignette · A short description of characters or situations that is presented to respondents in order to elicit a response.

visual ethnography · A form of ethnography that involves taking photos of and filming people in their everyday lives.

vulnerable population · A group of people who cannot give informed consent, including those who are underage or have diminished mental capacity.

weighted · Samples in which some cases should be counted more or less than others in producing estimates.

within-subject design · A study design in which participants receive all levels of the independent variable, such as viewing résumés for both male and female job applicants.

Bibliography

Abouharb, M. R., & Cingranelli, D. L. (2006). The human rights effects of World Bank structural adjustment, 1981–2000. *International Studies Quarterly, 50*(2), 233–262.

Abramson, C., & Dohan, D. (2015). Beyond text: Using arrays to represent and analyze ethnographic data. *Sociological Methodology, 45*(1), 272–319.

Acerbi, A., Lampos, V., Garnett, P., & Bentley, R. A. (2013). The expression of emotions in 20th century books. *PLoS One, 8*(3), e59030.

Achenbach, T. M. (1991). *Manual for the Teacher's Report Form and 1991 profile.* Burlington: Department of Psychiatry, University of Vermont, Burlington, VT.

Adams, J., & Light, R. (2015). Scientific parenting, the law, and same-sex parenting outcomes. *Social Science Research, 53,* 300–310.

Adler, P. A. (1985). *Wheeling and dealing: An ethnography of an upper-level drug dealing and smuggling community.* New York, NY: Columbia University Press.

Adler, P. A. & Adler, P. (2008). Of rhetoric and representation: The four faces of ethnography. *Sociological Quarterly, 49,* 1–30.

Adut, A. (2005). A theory of scandal: Victorians, homosexuality, and the fall of Oscar Wilde. *American Journal of Sociology, 111*(1), 213–248.

Agar, M. (1991). The right brain strikes back. In N. G. Fielding & R. M. Lee (Eds.), *Using computers in qualitative research* (pp. 195–199). Beverly Hills, CA: Sage.

Ainsworth-Darnell, J., & Downey, D. (1998). Assessing racial/ethnic differences in school performance. *American Sociological Review, 63,* 536–553.

Ajrouch, K. K., Antonucci, T. C., & Janevic, M. R. (2001). Social networks among blacks and whites: The interaction between race and age. *Journals of Gerontology Series B – Psychological Sciences and Social Sciences, 56,* S112–S118.

Alfred, R. (1976). The church of Satan. In C. Glock & R. Bellah (Eds.), *The new religious consciousness* (pp. 108–204). Los Angeles: University of California Press.

Allen, C. (1997). Spies like us: When sociologists deceive their subjects. *Lingua Franca, 7,* 31–37.

Allen, I. E., & Seaman, C. A. (2007). Likert scales and data analyses. *Quality Progress, 40*(7), 64.

Almeida, D. M., Davis, K. D., Lee, S., Lawson, K. M., Walter, K. N., & Moen, P. (2016). Supervisor support buffers daily psychological and physiological reactivity to work-to-family conflict. *Journal of Marriage and Family, 78,* 165–179.

Almeida, J., Johnson, R. M., Corliss, H. L., Molnar, B. E., & Azrael, D. (2009). Emotional distress among LGBT youth: The influence of perceived discrimination based on sexual orientation. *Journal of Youth and Adolescence, 38,* 1001–1014.

Altheide, D. L., & Johnson, J. M. (1998). Criteria for assessing interpretive validity in qualitative research. In N. Denzin & Y. Lincoln (Eds.), *Collecting and interpreting qualitative materials* (pp. 485–499). London, England: Sage.

Amdur, R. J., & Bankert, E. A. (2007). *Institutional review board member handbook.* Sudbury, MA: Jones & Bartlett.

Amenta, E., Caren, N., Olasky, S. J., & Stobaugh, J. E. (2009). All the movements fit to print: Who, what, when, where, and why SMO families appeared in the *New York Times* in the twentieth century. *American Sociological Review, 74*(4), 636–656.

American Association for Public Opinion Research (AAPOR). (2015). *Standard definitions: Final dispositions of case codes and outcome rates for surveys* (8th ed.). Oakbrook Terrace, IL: AAPOR.

American Educational Research Association. (2003). Research points. Significant benefits in reading from attending small classes [figure]. Retrieved from http://files.eric.ed.gov/fulltext/ED497644.pdf.

American Management Association. (2007). *Electronic monitoring & surveillance survey.* Retrieved from http://press.amanet.org/press-releases/177/2007-electronicmonitoring-surveillance-survey/.

American Sociological Association. (2014). *American Sociological Association style guide* (5th ed.). Washington, DC: ASA.

American Sociological Association. (2017). Amicus briefs. Retrieved from http://www.asanet.org/about-asa/how-asa-operates/amicus-briefs.

American Statistical Association. (2016). American Statistical Association releases statement on statistical significance and p-values. Retrieved from http://www.amstat.org/newsroom/pressreleases/P-Value Statement.pdf.

Aminzade, R. (1992). Historical sociology and time. *Sociological Methods and Research, 20*(4), 456–480.

Anderson, E. (2006). Jelly's place: An ethnographic memoir. In D. Hobbs & R. Wright (Eds.), *Handbook of fieldwork* (pp. 39–58). London, England: Sage.

Anderson, N. (1961). *The hobo: The sociology of the homeless man.* Chicago, IL: University of Chicago Press.

Anderson, T., Daly, K., & Rapp, L. (2009). Clubbing masculinities and crime: A qualitative study of Philadelphia nightclub scenes. *Feminist Criminology, 4,* 302–332.

Andreas, P., & Greenhill, K. M. (2010). *Sex, drugs, and body counts: The politics of numbers in global crime and conflict.* Ithaca, NY: Cornell University Press.

Angrist, J., Lavy, V., & Schlosser, A. (2010). Multiple experiments for the causal link between the quantity and quality of children. *Journal of Labor Economics, 28*(4), 773–824.

Anon. (2016). AidData 3.0. Open data for international development. Retrieved from http://aiddata.org.

Ante, S., & Edwards, C. (2006). The science of desire. *Bloomberg Business News.* Retrieved from https://www.bloomberg.com/news/articles/2006-06-04/the-science-of-desire.

Aral, S., Muchnik, L., & Sundararajan, A. (2009). Distinguishing influence-based contagion from homophily-driven diffusion in dynamic networks. *Proceedings of the National Academy of Sciences of the United States of America, 106*(51), 21544–21549.

Armstrong, E. A., & Hamilton, L. T. (2013). *Paying for the party: How college maintains inequality.* Cambridge, MA: Harvard University Press.

Arnett, J. J. (2014). *Adolescence and emerging adulthood.* New York, NY: Pearson Education.

Asad, A. (2015). Contexts of reception, post-disaster migration, and socioeconomic mobility. *Population and Environment, 36,* 279–310.

Asad, A. (2017). *From immigrant illegality to immigrant risk: Immigration law and enforcement as a total institution* (Unpublished doctoral dissertation). Department of Sociology, Harvard University, Cambridge, MA.

Asch, S. E. (1955). Options and social pressure. *Scientific American, 193,* 31–35.

Asch, S. E. (1956). Studies of independence and conformity: A minority of one against a unanimous majority. *Psychological Monographs, 70*(416).

Aseltine, R., Jr. (1995). A reconsideration of parental and peer influences on adolescent deviance. *Journal of Health and Social Behavior, 36,* 103–121.

Astone, N. M., & McLanahan, S. S. (1991). Family structure, parental practices and high school completion. *American Sociological Review,* 309–320.

Attewell, P., & Lavin, D. E. (2007). *Passing the torch: Does higher education for the disadvantaged pay off across the generations?* New York, NY: Russell Sage Foundation.

Austin, P. C. (2011). An introduction to propensity score methods for reducing the effects of confounding in observational studies. *Multivariate Behavioral Research, 46,* 399–424.

Auyero, J. & Berti, M. F. (2016). *In harm's way: The dynamics of urban violence.* Princeton, NJ: Princeton University Press.

Axinn, W. G., & Pearce, L. D. (2006). *Mixed method data collection strategies.* New York, NY: Cambridge University Press.

Backstrom, L., Boldi, P., Rosa, M., Ugander, J., & Vigna, S. (2012). Four degrees of separation. In *Proceedings of the 3rd Annual ACM Web Science Conference* (pp. 33–42).

Bandura, A. (2001). Social cognitive theory: An agentic perspective. *Annual Review of Psychology, 52*(1), 1–26.

Barker, E. (1984). *The making of a Moonie: Choice or brainwashing?* Oxford, England: Blackwell.

Barnes, J. A. (1954). Class and committees in a Norwegian island parish. *Human Relations, 7,* 39–58.

Batagelj, V., & Mrvar, A. (1998). Pajek—Program for large network analysis. *Connections, 21,* 47–57.

Bearman, P. (2005). *Doormen.* Chicago, IL: University of Chicago Press.

Bearman, P., & Parigi, P. (2004). Cloning headless frogs and other important matters: Conversation topics and network structure. *Social Forces, 83,* 535–557.

Becker, G. S. (1965). A theory of the allocation of time. *Economic Journal, 75,* 493–517.

Becker, H. (1953). Becoming a marijuana user. *American Journal of Sociology, 59*(3), 235–242.

Becker, H. (1963). *Outsiders: Studies in the sociology of deviance.* New York, NY: Free Press.

Becker, H. (1998). *Tricks of the trade: How to think about your research while you're doing it.* Chicago, IL: University of Chicago Press.

Becker, H. (2009). How to find out how to do qualitative research. *International Journal of Communication, 3,* 543–553.

Becker, H. S. (1951). The professional dance musician and his audience. *American Journal of Sociology, 57*(2), 136–144.

Becker, H. S. (2010). *Writing for social scientists: How to start and finish your thesis, book, or article.* ReadHowYouWant.com. Retrieved from http://www.read howyouwant.com/blog/post/2011/09/30/Writing-for-Social-Scientists-reviewed-by-Large-Print-Review.aspx.

Becker, H., Geer, B., Hughes, E. C., & Strauss, A. S. (1961). *Boys in white: Student culture in medical school.* Chicago, IL: University of Chicago Press.

Beilenson, J. (2004). Developing effective poster presentations. *Gerontology News, 32,* 6–9.

Bell, D. C., Belli-McQueen, B., & Haider, A. (2007). Partner naming and forgetting: Recall of network members. *Social Networks, 29,* 279–299.

Bellesiles, M. A. (2000). *Arming America: The origins of a national gun culture.* New York, NY: Alfred A. Knopf.

Belsky, J., Steinberg, L. D., Houts, R., Friedman, S., DeHart, G., Cauffman, E., . . . NICHD Early Child Care Network. (2007). Family rearing antecedents of pubertal timing. *Child Development, 78,* 1302–1321.

Bem, S. L. (1981). Gender schema theory: A cognitive account of sex typing. *Psychological Review, 88,* 354–364.

Benner, A. D. (2011). The transition to high school: Current knowledge, future directions. *Educational Psychology Review, 23,* 299–328.

Benner, A. D., & Graham, S. (2009). The transition to high school as a developmental process among multiethnic urban youth. *Child Development, 80,* 356–376.

Berg, B. L., & Klune, H. (2012). *Qualitative research methods for the social sciences.* Upper Saddle River, NJ: Pearson.

Berger, J., Wagner, D. G., & Webster, M. (2014). Expectation states theory: Growth, opportunities, and challenges. *Advances in Group Processes, 31,* 19–55.

Berk, R. A., & Rossi, P. H. (1999.) *Thinking about program evaluation 2.* Thousand Oaks, CA: Sage.

Berk, R., Campbell, A., Klap, R., & Western, B. (1992). The deterrent effect of arrest in incidents of domestic violence: A Bayesian analysis of four field experiments. *American Sociological Review, 57,* 698–708.

Berkinsky, A. J., Huber, G. A., & Lenz, G. S. (2012). Evaluating online labor markets for experimental research: Amazon.com's Mechanical Turk. *Political Analysis, 20*(3), 351–368.

Berkowitz, D., & Belgrave, L. L. (2010). "She works hard for the money": Drag queens and the management of their contradictory status of celebrity and marginality. *Journal of Contemporary Ethnography, 2010*(39), 159–186.

Bernard, H. R., & Killworth, P. D. (1979). Informant accuracy in social network data II. *Human Communication Research, 4,* 3–18.

Bernard, H. R., Johnsen, E. C., Killworth, P. D., McCarty, C., Shelley, G. A., & Robinson, S. (1990). Comparing four different methods for measuring personal social networks. *Social Networks, 12,* 179–215.

Best, J. (2012). *Damned lies and statistics: Untangling numbers from the media, politicians, and activists* (updated ed.). Berkeley: University of California Press.

Biernacki, P., & Waldorf, D. (1981). Snowball sampling: Problems and techniques of chain referral sampling. *Sociological Methods and Research, 102*(2), 141–163.

Bir, Al., Corwin, E., MacIlvain, B., Beard, A., Richburg, K., & Smith, K. (2012). *Impacts of community health marriage initiative* (OPRE Report No. 2102-34A). Washington, DC: Office of Planning, Research and Evaluation, Administration for Children and Families, Department of Health and Human Services. Retrieved from https://www.acf.hhs.gov/sites/default/files/opre/chmi_impactreport.pdf.

Birkenstein, C. (2010). We got the wrong gal: Rethinking the "bad" academic writing of Judith Butler. *College English, 72*(3), 269–283.

Birkland, T. A., & Lawrence, R. G. (2009). Media framing and policy change after Columbine. *American Behavioral Scientist, 52,* 1405–1425.

Bishop, G. F. (2004). *The illusion of public opinion: Fact and artifact in American public opinion polls.* Lanham, MD: Rowman & Littlefield.

Blackwell, L. S., Trzesniewski, K. H., & Dweck, C. S. (2007). Implicit theories of intelligences predict achievement across adolescent transition: A longitudinal study and an intervention. *Child Development, 78*(1), 246–263.

Blake, J. (1989). *Family size and achievement.* Berkeley: University of California Press.

Blee, K. (2009). Defining and communicating standards for systematic qualitative research. In M. Lamont & P. White (Eds.), *Workshop on interdisciplinary standards for systematic qualitative research.* Washington, DC: National Science Foundation.

Blumenthal, M. (2010). The Literary Digest poll. Retrieved from http://www.pollster.com/blogs/re_the_literary_digest_poll.php.

Boardman, J. D., Onge, J. M. S., Rogers, R. G., & Denney, J. T. (2005). Race differentials in obesity: The impact of place. *Journal of Health and Social Behavior, 46*(3), 229–243.

Boas, F. (1887). Museums of ethnology and their classification. *Science, 9,* 589.

Bodovski, K., & Farkas, G. (2008). "Concerted cultivation" and unequal achievement in elementary school. *Social Science Research, 37,* 903–919.

Bohrnstedt, G., & Stecher, B. M. (Eds.). (2002). *What we have learned about class size reduction in California.* CSR Research Consortium.

Bordo, S. (2003). *Unbearable weight: Feminism, Western culture and the body.* Berkeley: University of California Press.

Borgatti, S. P., & Everett, M. G. (1997). Network analysis of 2-mode data. *Social Networks, 19,* 243–269.

Borgatti, S. P., & Halgin, D. S. (2011). Analyzing affiliation networks. In P. Carrington & J. Scott (Eds.), *The Sage handbook of social network analysis* (pp. 417–433). Beverly Hills, CA: Sage.

Borgatti, S. P., Everett, M. G., & Freeman, L. C. (2002). *Ucinet for Windows: Software for social network analysis.* Lexington, KY: Analytic Technologies.

Bosk, C. (1979). *Forgive and remember: Managing medical failure.* Chicago, IL: University of Chicago Press.

Boslaugh, S. (2008). National Survey of Family Growth. In S. Boslaugh (Ed.), *Encyclopedia of epidemiology* (pp. 718–719). Thousand Oaks, CA: Sage.

Bourgeois, P. (1995). *In search of respect: Selling crack in El Barrio.* Cambridge, England: Cambridge University Press.

Bove, C. F., & Olson, C. M. (2006). Obesity in low-income rural women: Qualitative insights about physical activity and eating patterns. *Women & Health, 44*(1), 57–78.

Bowles, S., & Gintis, H. (1976). *Schooling in capitalist America: Educational reform and the contradictions of economic life.* New York, NY: Basic Books.

Bowling, A. (2005). Mode of questionnaire administration can have serious effects on data quality. *Journal of Public Health, 27,* 281–291.

Boyd, D., & Crawford, K. (2012). Critical questions for big data. *Information, Communication & Society, 15,* 662–679.

Boyle, E. H. (1998). Political frames and legal activity: The case of nuclear power in four countries. *Law and Society Review, 32,* 141–174.

Brace, I. (2008). *Questionnaire design: How to plan, structure and write survey material for effective market research.* London, England: Kogan Page.

Bradley, R. H., & Caldwell, B. M. (1979). Home Observation for Measurement of the Environment: A revision of the preschool scale. *American Journal of Mental Deficiency, 84,* 235–244.

Brannon, R. (1976). The male sex role: Our culture's blueprint for manhood, what it's done for us lately. In D. David & R. Brannon (Eds.), *The forty-nine percent: The male sex role* (pp. 1–49). Reading, MA: Addison-Wesley.

Brechwald, W. A., & Prinstein, M. J. (2011). Beyond homophily: A decade of advances in understanding peer influence processes. *Journal of Research on Adolescence, 21*(1), 166–179.

Brehm, H. N. (2014). *Conditions and courses of genocide* (Unpublished doctoral dissertation). Department of Sociology, University of Minnesota, Minneapolis, MN.

Brehm, H. N. (Forthcoming). Re-Examining Risk Factors of Genocide. *Journal of Genocide Research, 19,* 1–27.

Breiger, R. L. (1974). The duality of persons and groups. *Social Forces, 53,* 181–190.

Brenner, P. S. (2011). Exceptional behavior or exceptional identity? Overreporting of church attendance in the US. *Public Opinion Quarterly, 75,* 19–41.

Brines, J. (1994). Economic dependency, gender, and the division of labor at home. *American Journal of Sociology, 100*, 652–88.

Britt, C. L., & Gottfredson, M. R. (Eds.). (2011). *Control theories of crime and delinquency.* New Brunswick, NJ: Transaction Publishers.

Brody, G. H., Yu, T., Chen, Y. F., Kogan, S. M., Evans, G. W., Beach, S. R., . . . Philibert, R. A. (2013). Cumulative socioeconomic status risk, allostatic load, and adjustment: A prospective latent profile analysis with contextual and genetic protective factors. *Developmental Psychology, 49*(5), 913–927.

Brown, E., Hendrix, S., & Svrluga, S. (2015, June 14). Drinking is central to college culture—and to sexual assault. *Washington Post.* Retrieved from https://www.washingtonpost.com/local/education/beer-pong-body-shots-keg-stands-alcohol-central-to-college-and-assault/2015/06/14/7430e13c-04bb-11e5-a428-c984eb077d4e_story.html.

Browning, C. R., Leventhal, T., & Brooks-Gunn, J. (2005). Sexual initiation in early adolescence: The nexus of parental and community control. *American Sociological Review, 70*, 758–778.

Brumberg, Joan Jacobs. (2000). Fasting girls: The history of anorexia nervosa. New York: Vintage Books.

Bryan, C., Walton, G. M., Rogers, T., & Dweck, C. S. (2011). Motivating voter turnout by invoking the self. *Proceedings of the National Academy of Sciences of the United States of America, 108*(31), 12653–12656.

Buckley, C. (2010, December 8). To test housing program, some are denied aid. *New York Times.* Retrieved from www.nytimes.com/2010/12/09/nyregion/09placebo.html

Budig, M. J., & England, P. (2001). The wage penalty for motherhood. *American Sociological Review, 66*(2), 204–225.

Budig, M. J., & Hodges, M. J. (2010). Differences in disadvantage variation in the motherhood penalty across white women's earnings distribution. *American Sociological Review, 75*(5), 705–728.

Buhrmester, M., Kwang, T., & Gosling, S. D. (2011). Amazon's Mechanical Turk a new source of inexpensive, yet high-quality, data? *Perspectives on Psychological Science, 6*, 3–5.

Burawoy, M. (1979). *Manufacturing consent: Changes in the labor process under monopoly capitalism.* Chicago, IL: University of Chicago Press.

Burawoy, M. (1998). The extended case method. *Sociological Theory, 16*(1), 4–33.

Burawoy, M., Burton, A., Ferguson, A. A., Fox, K. J., Gamson, J., Gartrell, N., . . . Ui, S. (1991). *Ethnography unbound: Power and resistance in the modern metropolis.* Berkeley: University of California Press.

Burdick, A. (2017, March 22). "Paging Dr. Fraud": The fake publishers that are ruining science. *New Yorker.* Retrieved from http://www.newyorker.com/tech/elements/paging-dr-fraud-the-fake-publishers-that-are-ruining-science.

Bureau of Labor Statistics. (2016). Local area unemployment statistics. Retrieved from https://www.bls.gov/web/laus/laumstrk.htm.

Burke, M., Kraut, R., & Marlow, C. (2011). Social capital on Facebook: Differentiating uses and users. In *Proceedings of the 2011 Annual Conference on Human Factors in Computing Systems.* New York, NY: ACM.

Burt, R. S. (1992). *Structural holes: The social structure of competition.* Cambridge, MA: Harvard University Press.

Burt, R. S. (2005). *Brokerage and closure: An introduction to social capital.* Oxford, England: Oxford University Press.

Business Think. (2011). *The rise of ethnography: How market research has gone gonzo.* Sydney, Australia: USNW Australia Business School.

Butler, J. (1997). Reflections on conversations of our time. *Diacritics, 27*(1), 13–15.

Byrd, M. E. (1999). Questioning the quality of maternal caregiving during home visiting. *Journal of Nursing Scholarship, 31*(1), 27–32.

Caldwell, B. M., & Bradley, R. H. (2003). *Home Observation for Measurement of the Environment: Administration manual.* Tempe: Family & Human Dynamics Research Institute, Arizona State University.

Calhoun, L. G., & Tedeschi, R. G. (2013). *Posttraumatic growth in clinical practice.* New York, NY: Brunner Routledge.

Calvo, R., Rojas, V., & Waters, M. C. (2014). The effect of universal service delivery on the integration of Moroccan immigrants in Spain: A case study from an anti-oppressive perspective. *British Journal of Social Work, 44*(1), 123–139.

Campanario, J. M. (1998). Peer review for journals as it stands today—Part 1. *Science Communication, 19*, 181–211.

Campbell, J. L., Quincy, C., Osserman, J., & Pedersen, O. K. (2013). Coding in-depth semi-structured interviews: Problems of unitization and intercoder reliability and agreement. *Sociological Methods and Research, 42*(3), 294–320.

Cannuscio, C. C., Colditz, G. A., & Rimm, E. B. (2004). Employment status, social ties, and caregivers' mental health. *Social Science and Medicine, 58*, 1247–1256.

Carbonaro, W., & Workman, J. (2013). Dropping out of high school: Effects of close and distant friendships. *Social Science Research, 42*(5), 1254–1268.

Carey, B. (2010, May 23). Families' every hug and fuss, taped, analyzed and archived. *New York Times*, p. A1.

Carmichael, S. G. (2017, June 11). Employers are less likely to hire a woman wearing a headscarf. *Harvard Business Review*. Retrieved from https://hbr.org/2017/05/study-employers-are-less-likely-to-hire-a-woman-who-wears-a-headscarf.

Carr, D. (2012). "I don't want to die like that. . .": The impact of significant others' death quality on advance care planning. *Gerontologist, 52*(6), 770–781.

Carr, D., & Friedman, M. (2005). Is obesity stigmatizing? Body weight, perceived discrimination, and psychological well-being in the United States. *Journal of Health and Social Behavior, 46*, 244–259.

Carr, D., Cornman, J. C., & Freedman, V. A. (2016). Does marital quality protect against distress? Marital quality and momentary negative mood in later life. *Journal of Gerontology: Social Sciences, 71*, 177–187.

Carr, D., Jaffe, K. J., & Friedman, M. A. (2008). Perceived interpersonal mistreatment among obese Americans: Do race, class, and gender matter? *Obesity, 16*(S2), S60–S68.

Carr, P. J., & Kefalas, M. (2009). *Hollowing out the middle: The rural brain drain and what it means for America*. Boston, MA: Beacon Press.

Carter, P. (2006). *Keepin' it real: School success beyond black and white*. New York, NY: Oxford University Press.

Cavanagh, S. (2004). The sexual debut of girls in early adolescence: The intersection of race, pubertal timing, and friendship group dynamics. *Journal of Research on Adolescence, 14*, 285–312.

Center for American Progress. (2016). *Sexual orientation and gender identity data collection in the Behavioral Risk Factor Surveillance System*. Retrieved from https://www.americanprogress.org/issues/lgbt/report/2016/03/29/134182/sexual-orientation-and-gender-identity-data-collection-in-the-behavioral-risk-factor-surveillance-system.

Centers for Disease Control and Prevention. (2013). *Developing an effective evaluation report: Setting the course for effective program evaluation*. Atlanta, GA: Centers for Disease Control and Prevention, National Center for Chronic Disease Prevention and Health Promotion, Office on Smoking and Health, Division of Nutrition, Physical Activity and Obesity.

Centers for Disease Control and Prevention. (2016). *About behavioral risk factor surveillance system ACE data*. Retrieved from https://www.cdc.gov/violenceprevention/acestudy/ace_brfss.html.

Centola, D., & Macy, M. (2007). Complex contagions and the weakness of long ties. *American Journal of Sociology, 113*, 702–734.

Cha, M., Haddadi, H., Benevenuto, F., & Gummadi, K. (2010). Measuring user influence in Twitter: The million follower fallacy. In *Proceedings of the 4th International AAAI Conference on Weblogs and Social Media*. New York.

Chambliss, D. (1989). The mundanity of excellence: An ethnographic report on stratification and Olympic swimmers. *Sociological Theory, 7*(1), 70–86.

Chandler, C. R., & Tsai, Y-m. (2001). Social factors influencing immigration attitudes: An analysis of data from the General Social Survey. *Social Science Journal, 38*(2), 177–188.

Charmaz, K. (2006). *Constructing grounded theory: A practical guide through qualitative analysis*. London, England: Sage.

Charmaz, K. (2014). *Constructing grounded theory* (2nd ed.). Thousand Oaks, CA: Sage.

Chaves, M., & Anderson, S. L. (2014). Changing American congregations: Findings from the third wave of the National Congregations Study. *Journal for the Scientific Study of Religion, 53*, 676–686.

Chaves, M., & Eagle, A. J. (2015). *Religious congregations in 21st Century America: A report from the National Congregations Study*. Durham, NC: Department of Sociology, Duke University. Retrieved from http://www.soc.duke.edu/natcong/Docs/NCSIII_report_final.pdf.

Cheadle, J. E. (2008). Educational investment, family context, and children's math and reading growth from kindergarten through the third grade. *Sociology of Education, 81*, 1–31.

Cheng, S., & Powell, B. (2015). Measurement, methods, and divergent patterns: Reassessing the effects of same-sex parents. *Social Science Research, 52*, 615–626.

Chermack, K., Kelly, E. L., Moen, P., & Ammons, S. K. (2015). Implementing institutional change: Flexible work and team processes in a white collar organization. In S. K. Ammons & E. L. Kelly (Eds.), *Work and family in the new economy* (Research in the Sociology of Work, Vol. 26, pp. 331–359). Bingley, UK: Emerald Group Publishing.

Cheung, S., & Powell, B. (2015). Measurement, methods, and divergent patterns: Reassessing the effects of same-sex parents. *Social Science Research, 52*, 615–626.

Chien, N. C., & Mistry, R. S. (2013). Geographic variations in cost of living: Associations with family and child well-being. *Child Development, 84*(1), 209–225.

Child, B. (2016, January 28). Barack Obama on Oscars diversity: Are we giving everyone a fair shot? *Guardian.* Retrieved from https://www.theguardian.com/film/2016/jan/28/barack-obama-speaks-oscars-diversity-academy-awards-2016.

Christakis, N. (1999). *Death foretold: Prophesy and prognosis in medical care.* Chicago, IL: University of Chicago Press.

Christakis, N. A., & Fowler, J. H. (2007). The spread of obesity in a large social network over 32 years. *New England Journal of Medicine, 357*(4), 370–379.

Christakis, N. A., & Fowler, J. H. (2008). The collective dynamics of smoking in a large social network. *New England Journal of Medicine, 358*(21), 2249–2258.

Christakis, N. A., & Lamont, E. B. (2000). Extent and determinants of error in doctors' prognoses in terminally ill patients. *BMJ, 320*, 469–473.

Christensen, A. I., Ekholm, O., Glümer, C., & Juel, K. (2014). Effect of survey mode on response patterns: Comparison of face-to-face and self-administered modes in health surveys. *European Journal of Public Health, 24*, 327–332.

Chronister, M., Dew, C., MacArthur, C., Nunnally, B., & Yuda, J. (2016). Expectations and challenges: Informing the future of the Federal Front Door. Washington, DC: General Services Administration.

Church, A. H. (1993). Estimating the effect of incentives on mail survey response rates: A meta-analysis. *Public Opinion Quarterly, 57*(1), 62–79.

Cingranelli, D. L., Richards, D. L., & Clay, K. C. (2014). The CIRI Human Rights Dataset, version 2014.04.14. Retrieved from www.humanrightsdata.com.

Citro, C. F., & Michael, R. T. (Eds.). (1995). *Measuring poverty: A new approach.* Washington, DC: National Academy Press.

Clampet-Lundquist, S., Edin, K., Kling, J. R., & Duncan, G. J. (2006). *Moving at-risk youth out of high-risk neighborhoods: Why girls fare better than boys* (Princeton IRS Working Paper Series 509). Princeton, NJ: Princeton University.

Clampet-Lundquist, S., Edin, K., Kling, J. R., & Duncan, G. J. (2011). Moving teenagers out of high risk neighborhoods: How girls fare better than boys. *American Journal of Sociology, 116*(4), 1154–1189.

Clarke, A. Y. (2011). *The inequalities of love: College-educated black women and the barriers to romance and family.* Durham, NC: Duke University Press.

Clemetson, L. (2004, July 30). Homeland Security given data on Arab-Americans. *New York Times.* Retrieved from http://www.nytimes.com/2004/07/30/politics/30census.html.

Cohen, P. (2016, June 7). No, black women are not the "most educated" group in the US. Family Inequality [blog]. Retrieved from https://familyinequality.wordpress.com/2016/06/07/no-black-women-are-not-the-most-educated-group-in-the-us/.

Cohen, G. L., Garcia, J., Apfel, N., & Master, A. (2006). Reducing the racial achievement gap: A social-psychological intervention. *Science, 313*(5791), 1307–1310.

Cohen, S., Doyle, W. J., Skoner, D. P., Rabin, B. S., & Gwaltney, J. M., Jr. (1997). Social ties and susceptibility to the common cold. *Journal of the American Medical Association, 277*, 1940–1944.

Cohen-Cole, E., & Fletcher, J. M. 2008. Detecting implausible social network effects in acne, height, and headaches: Longitudinal analysis. *British Medical Journal, 337*, a2533.

Colditz, G. A., Manson, J. E., & Hankinson, S. E. (1997). The Nurses' Health Study: 20-year contribution to the understanding of health among women. *Journal of Women's Health, 6*(1), 49–62.

Cole, J., & Symes, C. (2015). *Western civilizations: Their history and their culture.* New York, NY: W. W. Norton.

Coleman, J. S. (1988). Social capital in the creation of human capital. *American Journal of Sociology, 94*, S95–S120.

Coleman, J. S., & Fararo, T. J. (Eds.). (1992). *Rational choice theory*. New York, NY: Sage.

Coley, R. L., Lombardi, C. M., Lynch, A. D., Mahalik, J. R., & Sims, J. (2013). Sexual partner accumulation from adolescence through early adulthood: The role of family, peer, and school social norms. *Journal of Adolescent Health, 53*(1), 91–97.

Collier, J. (1967). *Visual anthropology: Photography as a research method*. New York, NY: Holt, Rinehart & Winston.

Conger, R. D., Conger, K. J., & Martin, M. J. (2010). Socioeconomic status, family processes, and individual development. *Journal of Marriage and Family, 72*, 685–704.

Conley, D. (1999). *Being black, living in the red: Race, wealth, and social policy in America*. Berkeley: University of California Press.

Conron, K. J., Scott, G., Stowell, G. S., & Landers, S. J. (2012). Transgender health in Massachusetts: Results from a household probability sample of adults. *American Journal of Public Health 102*, 118–122.

Consumers Union. (2012, May 22). *Consumer Reports survey: Americans say fuel economy most important car buying factor*. Retrieved from http://consumersunion.org/news/consumer-reports-survey-americans-say-fuel-economy-most-important-car-buying-factor.

Contreras, R. (2012). *The stickup kids: Race, drugs, violence, and the American dream*. Berkeley: University of California Press.

Converse, P. E. (1970). Attitudes and non-attitudes: Continuation of a dialogue. *The Quantitative Analysis of Social Problems, 168*, 189.

Cook, P. J., & Ludwig, L. (2011, December). More prisoners versus more crime is the wrong question. *Brookings Institution Policy Brief, 185*. Retrieved from https://www.brookings.edu/wp-content/uploads/2016/06/12_prisons_cook_ludwig.pdf.

Cooley, C. H. (1902/1983). *Human nature and the social order*. New Brunswick, NJ: Transaction Publishers. (Reprint of original work)

Coontz, S. (1992). *The way we never were: American families and the nostalgia trap*. New York, NY: Basic Books.

Coontz, S. (2006). *Marriage, a history: How love conquered marriage*. New York, NY: Penguin.

Cornwell, B., & Laumann, E. (2015). The health benefits of network growth: New evidence from a national survey of older adults. *Social Science & Medicine, 125*, 94–106.

Cornwell, B., Laumann, E. O., & Schumm, L. P. (2008). The social connectedness of older adults: A national profile. *American Sociological Review, 73*(2), 185–203.

Cornwell, B., Laumann, E. O., Schumm, L. P., & Graber, J. (2009). Social networks in the NSHAP study: Rationale, measurement, and preliminary findings. *Journals of Gerontology, Series B: Social Sciences, 64B*(S1), i47–i55.

Correll, S. J., Benard, S., & Paik, I. (2007). Getting a job: Is there a motherhood penalty? *American Journal of Sociology, 112*(5), 1297–1338.

Correll, J., Park, B., Judd, C. M., & Wittenbrink, B. (2002). The police officer's dilemma: Using ethnicity to disambiguate potentially threatening individuals. *Journal of Personality and Social Psychology, 83*(6), 1314–1329.

Corsaro, W. A. (2003). *We're friends right? Inside kids' culture*. Washington, DC: Joseph Henry Press.

Couper, M., & Lyberg, L. (2005). The use of paradata in survey research. In *Proceedings of the 55th session of the International Statistical Institute*, Sydney, Australia.

Couper, M. P., & Miller, P. V. (2008). Web survey methods introduction. *Public Opinion Quarterly, 72*(5), 831–835.

Cowen, T. (2008, January 9). A dealer in the ivory tower. *New York Sun*. Retrieved from http://www.nysun.com/arts/dealer-in-the-ivory-tower/69223/.

Crenshaw, K. (1991). Mapping the margins: Intersectionality, identity politics, and violence against women of color. *Stanford Law Review*, 1241–1299.

Cressey, P. G. (1932/2008). *The taxi-dance hall: A sociological study in commercialized recreation and city life*. Chicago, IL: University of Chicago Press. (Reprint of original work)

Creswell, J. W., & Clark, V. L. P. (2007). *Designing and conducting mixed methods research*. Thousand Oaks, CA: Sage.

Cronbach, L. J. (1951). Coefficient alpha and the internal structure of tests. *Psychometrika, 16*, 297–334.

Crosnoe, R. (2011). *Fitting in, standing out: Navigating the social challenges of high school to get an education.* New York, NY: Cambridge University Press.

Crosnoe, R., & Trinitapoli, J. (2008). Shared family activities and the transition from childhood into adolescence. *Journal of Research on Adolescence, 18,* 23–48.

Crosnoe, R., Kendig, S., & Benner, A. (Forthcoming). Educational attainment and drinking trajectories from adolescence into adulthood. *Journal of Health and Social Behavior.*

Crosnoe, R., Morrison, F., Burchinal, M., Pianta, R., Keating, D., Friedman, S., Clarke-Stewart, A., & the NICHD Early Child Care Network. (2010). Instruction, teacher-student relations, and math achievement trajectories in elementary school. *Journal of Educational Psychology, 102,* 407–417.

Crowley, M. (2000). *Clearer than truth: Determining and preserving grand strategy: The evolution of American policy toward the People's Republic of China under Truman and Nixon* (Unpublished doctoral dissertation). Columbia University, New York, NY.

Cummings, H. A., & Vandewater, E. A. (2007). Relation of adolescent video game play to time spent in other activities. *Archives of Pediatric and Adolescent Medicine, 161*(7), 684–689. doi:10.1001/archpedi.161.7.684.

Daipha, P. (2015). *Masters of uncertainty: Weather forecasters and the quest for ground truth.* Chicago, IL: University of Chicago Press.

Dane County Youth Assessment. (2015). *2015 Dane County Youth Assessment.* Madison, WI: Dane County Youth Commission.

Daniel, C. (2016). Economic constraints on taste formation and the true cost of healthy eating. *Social Science & Medicine, 148,* 34–41.

Daniels, J., & Gregory, K. (Eds.). (2016). *Digital sociology in everyday life.* New York, NY: Policy Press.

David, C. (2005). Mode effects. In S. J. Best & B. F. Radcliff, (Eds.), *Polling America: An encyclopedia of public opinion* (pp. 453–457). Westport, CT: Greenwood Press.

Davis, D. W. (1997). Nonrandom measurement error and race of interviewer effects among African Americans. *Public Opinion Quarterly, 61,* 183–207.

Davis, A., Gardner, B. B., & Gardner, M. R. (1941). *Deep south: A social anthropological study of caste and class.* Chicago, IL: University of Chicago Press.

Dearden, L. (2016, August 9). German judges call for headscarf ban in court to show "neutrality." *Independent.* Retrieved from http://www.independent.co.uk/news/world/europe/german-judges-call-for-headscarf-hijab-ban-in-court-lawyers-to-show-neutrality-a7180591.html.

De Leeuw, E. D. (2005). To mix or not to mix data collection modes in surveys. *Journal of Official Statistics, 21,* 233–255.

Delaney, K. J. (2012). *Money at work: On the job with priests, poker players, and hedge fund traders.* New York, NY: New York University Press.

DeLuca, A., Das, S., Ortleib, M., Ion, I., & Laurie, B. (2016). Expert and non-expert attitudes towards (secure) instant messaging. In *Proceedings of the Twelfth Symposium on Usable Privacy and Security (SOUPS 2016).* Retrieved from https://www.usenix.org/system/files/conference/soups2016/soups2016-paper-de-luca.pdf.

DeNavas-Walt, C., & Proctor, B. D. (2014). Income and poverty in the United States: 2013. *Current population reports* (Report No. P60-249). Retrieved from https://www.census.gov/content/dam/Census/library/publications/2014/demo/p60-249.pdf.

Denny, G., Young, M., Rausch, S., & Spear, C. (2002). An evaluation of an abstinence education curriculum series: Sex can wait. *American Journal of Health Behavior, 26*(5), 366–377.

Denney, J. T., Wadsworth, T., Rogers, R. G., & Pampel, F. C. (2015). Suicide in the city: Do characteristics of place really influence risk? *Social Science Quarterly, 96,* 313–329.

Denzin, N. K. (1989). *The research act.* Englewood Cliffs, NJ: Prentice Hall.

Desilver, D. (2014, July 9). The politics of American generations: How age affects attitudes and voting behavior. Pew Research. Retrieved from http://www.pewresearch.org/fact-tank/2014/07/09/the-politics-of-american-generations-how-age-affects-attitudes-and-voting-behavior.

Desmond, M. (2007). *On the fireline: Living and dying with wildland firefighters.* Chicago, IL: University of Chicago Press.

Desmond, M. (2016). *Evicted: Poverty and profit in the American city.* New York, NY: Crown Publishers.

Deterding, N. (2015). Instrumental and expressive education: College planning in the face of poverty. *Sociology of Education.*

Dey, I. (1993). *Qualitative data analysis: A user friendly guide for social scientists*. New York, NY: Routledge.

Diamond, D. (2015, January 28). Want to save kids' brains? Then ban tackle football for preteens. *Forbes*. Retrieved from www.forbes.com/sites/dandiamond/2015/01/28/want-to-save-kids-brains-then-ban-tackle-football-for-ages-12-and-under/#2d98046b72b9.

Dickerson, S. S., & Kemeny, M. E. (2004). Acute stressors and cortisol responses: A theoretical integration and synthesis of laboratory research. *Psychological Bulletin, 130*(3), 355–391.

Dillman, D. A., & Parsons, N. L. (2008). *Self-administered paper questionnaire*. London, England: Sage.

Dillman, D. A., Smyth, J. D., & Christian, L. M. (2014). *Internet, phone, mail, and mixed-mode surveys: The tailored design method* (4th ed.). Hoboken, NJ: Wiley.

Dixon, T. L., & Linz, D. (2000). Overrepresentation and underrepresentation of African Americans and Latinos as lawbreakers on television news. *Journal of Communication, 50*(2), 131–154.

Doan, L., Hoehr, A., & Miller, L. R. (2014). Formal rights and informal privileges for same-sex couples: Evidence from a national survey experiment. *American Sociological Review, 79*(6), 1172–1195.

Dodds, P. S., Muhamad, R., & Watts, D. J. (2003). An experimental study of search in global social networks. *Science, 301*(5634), 827–829.

Dong, Y., & Peng, C. Y. J. (2013). Principled missing data methods for researchers. SpringerPlus. Retrieved from https://springerplus.springeropen.com/articles/10.1186/2193-1801-2-222.

Donoho, C. J., Seeman, T. E., Sloan, R. P. & Crimmins, E. M. (2015). Marital status, marital quality, and heart rate variability in the MIDUS cohort. *Journal of Family Psychology, 29*, 290–295.

Dordick, G. A. (1997). *Something left to lose: Personal relations and survival among New York's homeless*. Philadelphia, PA: Temple University Press.

Downey, D. B. (1995). When bigger is not better: Family size, parental resources, and children's educational performance. *American Sociological Review, 60*(5), 746–761.

Druckman, J. N., & Kam, C. D. (2011). Students as experimental participants: A defense of the "narrow data base." In J. N. Druckman, D. P. Green, J. H. Kuklinski, & A. Lupia (Eds.), *Handbook of experimental political science*. New York, NY: Cambridge University Press.

Du Bois, W. E .B. (1899/2010). *The Philadelphia Negro*. New York, NY: Cosmio. (Reprint of original work)

Duling v. Gristede's Operating Corp. (No. 06 CV 10197) (LTS) i [2006]

Duncan, G. J., Brooks-Gunn, J., Yeung, W. J., & Smith, J. R. (1998). How much does childhood poverty affect the life chances of children? *American Sociological Review, 63*, 406–423.

Duncan, G. J., Magnuson, K., Kalil, A., & Ziol-Guest, K. (2012). The importance of early childhood poverty. *Social Indicators Research, 108*, 87–98.

Duneier, M. (1999). *Sidewalk*. New York, NY: Farrar, Straus, and Giroux.

Duneier, M. (2011). How not to lie in ethnography. *Sociological Methodology, 41*(1), 1–11.

Duneier, M., & Carter, O. (1999). *Sidewalk*. New York, NY: Macmillan.

Duneier, M., Kasinitz, P., & Murphy, A. (Eds.). (2014). *The urban ethnography reader*. New York, NY: Oxford University Press.

Durkheim, E. (1951 [1897]). Suicide: A Study in Sociology. Trans. J.A. Spaulding and G. Simpson. New York: The Free Press.

Dutton, D. (1999, February 2). Language crimes: A lesson in how not to write, courtesy of the professors. *Wall Street Journal*. Retrieved from https://www.wsj.com/articles/SB918105259720869000.

Eagan, M. K., Stolzenberg, E. B., Ramirez, J. J., Aragon, M. C., Suchard, M. R., & Rios-Aguilar, C. (2016). *The American freshman: Fifty-year trends, 1966–2015*. Los Angeles, CA: Higher Education Research Institute, UCLA.

Eagle, D. E., & Proeschold-Bell, R. J. (2015). Methodological considerations in the use of name generators and interpreters. *Social Networks, 40*, 75–83.

Eagle, N., Pentland, A., & Lazer, D. (2009). Inferring friendship network structure by using mobile phone data. *Proceedings of the National Academy of Sciences of the United States of America, 106*, 15274.

Edin, K., & Kefalas, M. (2011). *Promises I can keep: Why poor women put motherhood before marriage*. Berkeley: University of California Press.

Edin, K., & Kissane, R. J. (2010). Poverty and the American family: A decade in review. *Journal of Marriage and Family, 72*(3), 460–479.

Edin, K., & Lein, L. (1997). *Making ends meet: How single mothers survive welfare and low-wage work*. New York, NY: Russell Sage Foundation.

Edin, K., & Nelson, T. J. (2013). *Doing the best I can: Fatherhood in the inner city*. Berkeley: University of California Press.

Eisele, F. (n.d.). Preparing a policy brief issue. Retrieved from https://www.courses.psu.edu/hpa/hpa301_fre1/IBInstructions_fa02.PDF.

Eisinga, R., Te Grotenhuis, M., Larsen, J. K., & Pelzer, B. (2012). Interviewer BMI effects on under- and over-reporting of restrained eating: Evidence from a national Dutch face-to-face survey and a postal follow-up. *International Journal of Public Health, 57*(3), 643–647.

El-Behadli, A. F., Gansert, P., & Logan, D. E. (2017). Racial differences in parental responses to children's chronic pain. *Clinical Journal of Pain*.

Elder, G. (1974). *Children of the Great Depression: Social change and life experience*: Chicago, IL: University of Chicago Press.

Elder, G. H., Shanahan, M. J., & Jennings, J. A. (2015). Human development in time and place. In R. M. Lerner (Series Ed.), *Handbook of child psychology and developmental science: Vol. 4. Ecological settings and processes in developmental systems* (pp. 6–54). New York, NY: Wiley.

Elder, K., Xirasagar, S., Miller, N., Bowen, S. A., Glover, S., & Piper, C. (2007). African Americans' decisions not to evacuate New Orleans before Hurricane Katrina: A qualitative study. *American Journal of Public Health, 97*(Suppl. 1), S124–S29.

Ellis, C. (1986). *Fisher folk: Two communities on Chesapeake Bay*. Lexington: University Press of Kentucky.

Ellison, N. B., & Boyd, D. (2013). Sociality through social network sites. In W. H. Dutton (Ed.), *The Oxford handbook of Internet studies* (pp. 151–172). Oxford, England: Oxford University Press.

Emerson, R. M. (1983). *Contemporary field research: A collection of readings*. Prospect Heights, IL: Waveland Press.

Emerson, R. M., Fretz, R. I., & Shaw, L. L. (1995). *Writing ethnographic fieldnotes*. Chicago, IL: University of Chicago Press.

Entwisle, B., Faust, K., Rindfuss, R. R., & Kaneda, T. (2007). Networks and contexts: Variation in the structure of social ties. *American Journal of Sociology, 112*, 1495–1533.

Euling, S. Y., Herman-Giddens, M. E., Lee, P. A., Selevan, S. G., Juul, A., Sørensen, T. I., & Swan, S. H. (2008). Examination of US puberty-timing data from 1940 to 1994 for secular trends: Panel findings. *Pediatrics, 121*, S172–S191.

Experientia. (2011, October 20). Google's ethnographic studies on device use [blog]. Retrieved from http://blog.experientia.com/googles-ethnographic-studies-on-device-use/.

Faigman, D. L., Dasgupta, N., & Ridgeway, C. L. (2008). A matter of fit: The law of discrimination and the science of implicit bias. *Hastings Law Journal, 59*, 1389–1390.

Fauth, R. C., Leventhal, T., & Brooks-Gunn, J. (2004). Short-term effects of moving from public housing in poor to middle-class neighborhoods on low-income, minority adults' outcomes. *Social Science and Medicine, 59*, 2271–2284.

Fazio, R. H. (1990). Multiple processes by which attitudes guide behavior: The MODE Model as an interactive framework. In M. P. Zanna (Ed.), *Advances in experimental and social psychology* (Vol. 23, pp. 75–109). San Diego, CA: Academic Press.

Feagin, J. R., & Hernan, V. (2000). *White racism: The basics*. New York, NY: Routledge.

Feld, S. L., Suitor, J. J., & Hoegh, J. G. (2007). Describing changes in personal networks over time. *Field Methods, 19*, 218–236.

Felitti, V. J., Anda, R. F., Nordenberg, D., Williamson, D. F., Spitz, A. M., Edwards, V., . . . Marks, J. S. (1998). Relationship of childhood abuse and household dysfunction to many of the leading causes of death in adults: The Adverse Childhood Experiences (ACE) Study. *American Journal of Preventive Medicine, 14*(4), 245–258.

Ferree, M. M. (2010). Filling the glass: Gender perspectives on families. *Journal of Marriage and Family, 72*, 420–439.

Ferreira, F. (2015). *The international poverty line has just been raised to $1.90 a day, but global poverty is basically unchanged. How is that even possible?* Washington, DC: World Bank.

Festinger, L., Riecken, H. W., & Schachter, S. (1956). *When prophecy fails*. Minneapolis: University of Minnesota Press.

Figlio, D., Guryan, J., Karbownik, K., & Roth, J. (2014). The effects of neonatal health on children's cognitive development. *American Economic Review, 104*(12), 3921–3955.

Fine, G. A. (1993). Ten lies of ethnography: Moral dilemmas of field research. *Journal of Contemporary Ethnography, 22,* 267–294.

Fink, J. S., & Kensicki, L. J. (2002). An imperceptible difference: Visual and textual constructions of femininity in *Sports Illustrated* and *Sports Illustrated for Women. Mass Communication & Society, 5*(3), 317–339.

Finkel, S. E., Guterbock, T. M., & Borg, M. J. (1991). Race-of-interviewer effects in a preelection poll Virginia 1989. *Public Opinion Quarterly, 55*(3), 313–330.

Fiori, K. L., Antonucci, T. C., & Akiyama, H. (2008). Profiles of social relations among older adults: A cross-cultural approach. *Ageing and Society, 28,* 203–231.

Fischer, C. S. (2009). The 2004 GSS finding of shrunken social networks: An artifact? *American Sociological Review, 74*(4), 657–669.

Fisher, T. D. (2009). The impact of socially conveyed norms on the reporting of sexual behavior and attitudes by men and women. *Journal of Experimental Social Psychology, 45,* 567–572.

Fitzgerald, F. S. (1926/1989). The rich boy. In F. S. Fitzgerald & M. J. Bruccoli (Eds.), *The short stories of F. Scott Fitzgerald* (p. 335). New York, NY: Harcourt. (Reprint of original work)

Fletcher, A. C., Steinberg, L. D., & Williams-Wheeler, M. (2004). Parental influences on adolescent problem behavior: Revisiting Stattin and Kerr. *Child Development, 75,* 781–796.

Flizik, A. (2008). Showcards. In P. J. Lavrakas (Ed.), *Encyclopedia of survey research methods* (pp. 818–819). Thousand Oaks, CA: Sage.

Florida Department of Health. (2016). Florida Healthy Beaches Program. Retrieved from www.floridahealth.gov/environmental-health/beach-water-quality/index.html.

Ford Media Center. (2013). Ford Archives, The Henry Ford to make more Ford history accessible online. Retrieved from https://media.ford.com/content/ford media-mobile/fna/us/en/news/2013/12/12/ford-archives—the-henry-ford-to-make-more-ford-history-accessib.html.

Foucault, M. (1970). *The order of things.* New York, NY: Vintage Books.

Fouts, J., Baker, D., Brown, C., & Riley, S. (2006). *Leading the conversion process: Lessons learned and recommendations for converting to small learning communities.* Seattle, WA: Bill & Melinda Gates Foundation.

Fowler, F. J., Jr. (2014). *Survey research methods.* Thousand Oaks, CA: Sage.

Fowler, J. H., & Christakis, N. A. (2008). Dynamic spread of happiness in a large social network: Longitudinal analysis over 20 years in the Framingham Heart Study. *British Medical Journal, 337,* A2338.

Fox, A. B., Smith, B. N., & Vogt, D. (2016). The relationship between anticipated stigma and work functioning for individuals with depression. *Journal of Social and Clinical Psychology, 35,* 883–897.

Fox, L., Wimer, C., Garfinkel, I., Kaushal, N., & Waldfogel, J. (2015). Waging war on poverty: Poverty trends using a historical supplemental poverty measure. *Journal of Policy Analysis and Management, 34,* 567–592.

France, L. R. (2016). Hollywood: A town divided when it comes to race. CNN. Retrieved from www.cnn.com/2016/02/26/entertainment/hollywood-oscars-race-feat/.

Franzen, A., & Hangartner, D. (2006). Social networks and labour market outcomes: The non-monetary benefits of social capital. *European Sociological Review, 22*(4), 353–368.

Freeman, L. C. (1979). Centrality in social networks: Conceptual clarification. *Social Networks, 1,* 215–239.

Freeman, L. C., Romney, A. K., & Freeman, S. C. (1987). Cognitive structure and informant accuracy. *American Anthropologist, 89,* 310–325.

Freese, J., & Montgomery, J. D. (2007). The devil made her do it? Evaluating risk preference as an explanation of sex differences in religiousness. In S. J. Correll (Ed.), *Advances in group processes* (Vol. 24, pp. 187–229). Bingley, UK: Emerald Group Publishing.

Friedman, H. L. (2013). *Playing to win: Raising children in a competitive culture.* Berkeley: University of California Press.

Friemel, T. N. (2016). The digital divide has grown old: Determinants of a digital divide among seniors. *New Media & Society, 18,* 313–331.

Fu, Y. (2005). Measuring personal networks with daily contacts: A single-item survey question and the contact diary. *Social Networks, 27,* 169–186.

Fu, H., Darroch, J. E., Henshaw, S. K., & Kolb, E. (1998). Measuring the extent of abortion underreporting in the 1995 National Survey of Family Growth. *Family Planning Perspectives, 30,* 128–138.

Fujimoto, K., & Valente, T. W. (2012). Decomposing the components of friendship and friends' influence on adolescent drinking and smoking. *Journal of Adolescent Health, 51,* 136–143.

Furr, M. (2011). Scale construction and psychometrics for social and personality psychology. Thousand Oaks, CA: Sage.

Furstenberg, F. (2016). Social class and development in early adulthood: Some unsettled issues. *Emerging Adulthood, 4*(4), 236–238.

Furstenberg, F. F., Jr., Cook, T. D., Eccles, J., Elder, G. H., & Sameroff, A. (1999). *Managing to make it: Urban families and adolescent success.* Chicago, IL: University of Chicago Press.

Galaskiewicz, J. (1985). *Social organization of an urban grants economy.* New York, NY: Academic Press.

Galinsky, A. D., Magee, J. C., Ena Inesi, M., & Gruenfeld, D. H. (2006). Power and perspectives not taken. *Association for Psychological Science, 17*(12), 1068–1074.

Galliher, J. F., Brekhus, W., & Keys, D. P. (2004). *Laud Humphreys: Prophet of homosexuality and sociology.* Madison: University of Wisconsin Press.

Gallucci, M. (2017, March 6). How social media use might leave us feeling #ForeverAlone. *Mashable.* Retrieved from http://mashable.com/2017/03/06/social-media-mental-health-study/#ng6ZDAZTKaqY.

Galvan, J. L. (2014). *Writing literature reviews: A guide for students of the social and behavioral sciences* (6th ed.). New York, NY: Routledge.

Gans, H. (1967). *The Levittowners: Ways of life and politics in a new suburban community.* New York, NY: Columbia University Press.

Gans, H. J. (1962). *The urban villagers: Group and class in the life of Italian Americans.* Glencoe, IL: Free Press.

Gans, H. J. (1979). Symbolic ethnicity: Future of ethnic groups and cultures in America. *Ethnic and Racial Studies, 2*(1), 1–20.

Gans, H. J. (1999). Participant observation in the era of "ethnography." *Journal of Contemporary Ethnography, 28*(5), 540–548.

Gates, G. J. (2011). *How many people are lesbian, gay, bisexual, and transgender?* Los Angeles, CA: The Williams Institute. Retrieved from http://williams institute.law.ucla.edu/wp-content/uploads/Gates-How-Many-People-LGBT-Apr-2011.pdf.

Geertz, C. (1973). *The interpretation of cultures.* New York, NY: Basic Books.

Geleta, S. B., Briand, C. H., Folkoff, M. E., & Zaprowski, B. J. (2014). Cemeteries as indicators of post-settle ment anthropogenic soil degradation on the Atlantic coastal plain. *Human Ecology, 42*(4), 625–635.

Gerson, K. (1986). *Hard choices: How women decide about work, career, and motherhood.* Berkeley: University of California Press.

Gerson, K. (2011). *The unfinished revolution: How a new generation is reshaping family, work, and gender in America.* New York, NY: Oxford University Press.

Gerson, K., & Horowitz, R. (2002). Observation and interviewing: Options and choices. In T. May (Ed.), *Qualitative research in action* (pp. 200–225). Thousand Oaks, CA: Sage.

Gillborn, D. (2005). Education policy as an act of white supremacy: Whiteness, critical race theory and education reform. *Journal of Education Policy, 20*(4), 485–505.

Giordano, P. C., Cernkovich, S. A., & Rudolph, J. L. (2002). Gender, crime, and desistance: Toward a theory of cognitive transformation. *American Journal of Sociology, 107,* 990–1064.

Giordano, P. C., Longmore, M. A., & Manning, W. D. (2006). Gender and the meanings of adolescent romantic relationships: A focus on boys. *American Sociological Review, 71,* 260–287.

Girma, S., & Paton, D. (2013). Does parental consent for birth control affect underage pregnancy rates? The case of Texas. *Demography, 50*(6), 1–24.

Glaeser, A. (1999). *Divided in unity: Identity, Germany, and the Berlin police.* Chicago, IL: University of Chicago Press.

Glaser, B. G., & Strauss, A. S. (1967). *The discovery of grounded theory: Strategies for qualitative research.* New Brunswick, NJ: Aldine Transaction.

Gleitman, H., Gross. J., & Reisberg, D. (2010). *Psychology* (8th Ed.). New York, NY: W. W. Norton.

Glenn,D.(2007,March23).Patrioticorunethical?Anthropologists debate whether to help U.S. security agencies. *Chronicle of Higher Education.* Retrieved from http://chronicle.com.ezp-prod1.hul.harvard.edu/article/Patriotic-or-Unethical-/34785/?otd=Y2xpY2t0aHJ1Ojo6c293aWRnZXQ6OjpjpaGFubmVsOmZhY3VsdHksYXJ0aWNsZTTptaWxpdGFyyXplZC1zb2NpYWwtc2NpZW5jZS10aGUtZGViYXRlLWWNvbnRpbnVlczo6Om5oYW5uZWw6cmVzZWFyY2gsYXJ0aWNsZTTpwwYXRyaW90aWMtaMtb3ItdW5ldGhpY2FsLWFudGhyb3BvbG9naXN0cy1kZWJhdGUtd2hldGhlci10by1oZWxwLXVzLXNlY3VyaXR5LWFnZW5jaWVz.

Glenn, D. (2009, December 3). Military's Human Terrain Program might be ethical, philosopher says. *Chronicle of Higher Education.* Retrieved from http://chronicle.com.ezp-prod1.hul.harvard.edu/article/Militarys-Human-Terrain/49345.

Glueck, S., & Glueck, E. (1950). *Unraveling juvenile delinquency.* Cambridge, MA: Harvard University Press.

Glueck, S., & Glueck, E. (1968). *Delinquents and nondelinquents in perspective.* Cambridge, MA: Harvard University Press.

Goel, S., Mason, W., & Watts, D. J. (2010). Real and perceived attitude agreement in social networks. *Journal of Personality and Social Psychology, 99,* 611–621.

Goertz, G., & Mahoney, J. (2012). *A tale of two cultures: Qualitative and quantitative research in the social sciences.* Princeton, NJ: Princeton University Press.

Goffman, A. (2009). On the run: Wanted men in a Philadelphia ghetto. *American Sociological Review, 74*(3), 339–357.

Goffman, A. (2014). *On the run: Fugitive life in an American city.* Chicago, IL: University of Chicago Press.

Goffman, E. (1961). *Asylums: Essays on the social situation of mental patients and other inmates.* New York, NY: Anchor Books.

Goffman, E. (1979). *Gender advertisements.* Cambridge, MA: Harvard University Press.

Goffman, E. (1989). One fieldwork. *Journal of Contemporary Ethnography, 18,* 123–132.

Golash-Boza, T. (2015). *Deported: Immigrant policing, disposable labor, and global capitalism.* New York, NY: New York University Press.

Gold, R. L. (1958). Roles in sociological field observations. *Social Forces, 36,* 217–223.

Goldin, C., & Katz, L. F. (2008). *The race between technology and education.* Cambridge, MA: Harvard University Press.

Goldin, C., & Rouse, C. (2000). Orchestrating impartiality: The impact of "blind" auditions on female musicians. *American Economic Review, 90*(4), 715–741.

Golden, J., Conroy, R. M., & Lawlor, B. A. (2009). Social support network structure in older people: Underlying dimensions and association with psychological and physical health. *Psychology, Health & Medicine, 14,* 280–290.

Gonzales, R. G. (2015). *Lives in limbo: Undocumented and coming of age in America.* Berkeley: University of California Press.

Gonzalez, R. J. (2007). Towards mercenary anthropology? *Anthropology Today, 23*(3), 14–19.

Goode, W. J. (1997). Rational choice theory. *American Sociologist, 28,* 22–41.

Goodwin, D. K. (2009). *Team of rivals: The political genius of Abraham Lincoln.* London, England: Penguin UK.

Gordon, R. (2010). *Regression analysis for the social sciences.* New York, NY: Routledge.

Gordon, M. S., & Cui, M., (2012). The effect of school-specific parenting processes on academic achievement in adolescence and young adulthood. *Family Relations, 61*(5), 728–741.

Gough, M., & Killewald, A. (2011). Unemployment in families: The case of housework. *Journal of Marriage and Family, 73*(5), 1085–1100.

Gould, R. V., & Fernandez, R. M. (1989). Structures of mediation: A formal approach to brokerage in transaction networks. *Sociological Methodology, 19,* 89–126.

Gouldner, A. W. (1960). The norm of reciprocity: A preliminary statement. *American Sociological Review, 25,* 161–178.

Gourlay, A., Mshana, G., Birdthistle, I., Bulugu, G., Zaba, B., & Urassa, M. (2014). Using vignettes in qualitative research to explore barriers and facilitating factors to the uptake of prevention of mother-to-child transmission services in rural Tanzania: A critical analysis. *BMC Medical Research Methodology,* 14–21.

Granovetter, M. S. (1973). The strength of weak ties. *American Journal of Sociology, 78*(6), 1360–1380.

Retrieved from http://links.jstor.org/sici?sici=0002-9602%28197305%2978%3A6%3C1360%3ATSOWT%3E2.0.CO%3B2-E.

Grazian, D. (2003). *Blue Chicago: The search for authenticity in urban blues clubs*. Chicago, IL: University of Chicago Press.

Grazian, D. (2008). *On the make: The hustle of urban nightlife*. Chicago, IL: University of Chicago Press.

Grazian, D. (2015). *American zoo: A sociological safari*. Princeton, NJ: Princeton University Press.

Greely, H. (1998). Legal, ethical, and social issues in human genome research. *Annual Reviews in Anthropology, 27*, 747–769.

Grissmer, D. W., Flanagan, A., Kawata, J. H., & Williamson, S. (2000). *Improving student achievement: What state NAEP test scores tell us*. Santa Monica, CA: RAND Corporation. Retrieved from www.rand.org/pubs/monograph_reports/MR924.

Groves, R. M., & Fultz, N. H. (1985). Gender effects among telephone interviewers in a survey of economic attitudes. *Sociological Methods & Research, 14*, 31–52.

Groves, R. M., Fowler, F. J., Jr., Couper, M. P., Lepkowski, J. M., Singer, E., & Tourangeau, R. (2011). *Survey methodology* (Vol. 561). Hoboken, NJ: John Wiley & Sons.

Grow, K. (2015, November 16). Spike Lee blasts academy's lack of diversity in Oscar speech. *Rolling Stone*. Retrieved from www.rollingstone.com/movies/news/spike-lee-blasts-academys-lack-of-diversity-in-oscar-speech-20151116.

Gunnell, J. (2010). Value-free social science. In M. Bevir (Ed.), *Encyclopedia of political theory* (Vol. 3, pp. 1412–1398). Thousand Oaks, CA: Sage.

Guo, G., Roettger, M., & Cai, T. (2008). The integration of genetic propensities into social control models of delinquency and violence among male youths. *American Sociological Review, 73*, 543–568.

Haas, A. P., Rodgers, P. L., & Herman, J. (2014). *Suicide attempts among transgender and gender nonconforming adults: Findings of the National Transgender Discrimination Survey*. American Foundation for Suicide Prevention and the Williams Institute. Retrieved from http://williamsinstitute.law.ucla.edu/wp-content/uploads/AFSP-Williams-Suicide-Report-Final.pdf.

Haight, M., Quan-Haase, A., & Corbett, B. A. (2014). Revisiting the digital divide in Canada: The impact of demographic factors on access to the Internet, level of online activity, and social networking site usage. *Information, Communication & Society, 17*, 503–519.

Haines, V. A., Hurlbert, J. S., & Beggs, J. J. (1996). Exploring the determinants of support provision: Provider characteristics, personal networks, community contexts, and support following life events. *Journal of Health and Social Behavior, 37*, 252–264.

Hällsten, M., Edling, C., & Rydgren, J. (2015). The effects of specific occupations in position generator measures of social capital. *Social Networks, 40*, 55–63.

Halpern-Meekin, S., Edin, K., Tach, L., & Sykes, J. (2015). *It's not like I'm poor: How working families make ends meet in a post-welfare world*. Berkeley: University of California Press.

Hamermesh, D. (2011). *Beauty pays: Why attractive people are more successful*. Princeton, NJ: Princeton University Press.

Hamilton, L., and Armstrong, E. A. (2009). Gendered sexuality in young adulthood: Double binds and flawed options. *Gender & Society, 23*, 589–616.

Harding, D. J., Fox, C., & Mehta, J. D. (2002). Studying rare events through qualitative case studies: Lessons from a study of rampage school shootings. *Sociological Methods and Research, 31*(2), 174–217.

Hargittai, E. (2010). Digital na(t)ives? Variation in Internet skills and uses among members of the "net generation." *Sociological Inquiry, 80*, 92–113.

Harper, D. (1994). On the authority of the image: Visual methods at the crossroads. In N. K. Denzin & Y. S. Lincoln (Eds.), *The handbook of qualitative research* (pp. 403–412). Thousand Oaks, CA: Sage.

Harrington Meyer, M., & Herd, P. (2010). *Market friendly or family friendly? The state and gender inequality in old age*. New York, NY: Russell Sage.

Harris, A. (2006). I (don't) hate school: Revisiting oppositional culture theory of blacks' resistance to schooling. *Social Forces, 85*, 797–833.

Harris, K. M., Halpern, C. T., Whitsel, E., Hussey, J., Tabor, J., Entzel, P., & Udry, J. R. (2009). *The National Longitudinal Study of Adolescent to Adult Health: Research design*. Chapel Hill: Carolina Population Center, University of North Carolina. Retrieved from http://www.cpc.unc.edu/projects/addhealth/design.

Harwood, J., & Anderson, K. (2002). The presence and portrayal of social groups on prime-time television. *Communication Reports, 15*(2), 81–97.

Hasan, Y., Bègue, L., Scharkow, M., & Bushman, B. J. (2013). The more you play, the more aggressive you become: A long-term experimental study of cumulative violent video game effects on hostile expectations and aggressive behavior. *Journal of Experimental Social Psychology, 49*(2), 224–227.

Haviland, W. A., Prins, H. E. L., McBride, B., & Walrath, D. (2010). Cultural anthropology: The human challenge (13th ed.). Belmont, CA: Cengage Learning.

Haynie, D. (2001). Delinquent peers revisited: Does network structure matter? *American Journal of Sociology, 106,* 1013–1057.

Haynie, D. L. (2003). Contexts of risk? Explaining the link between girls' pubertal development and their delinquency involvement. *Social Forces, 82,* 355–397.

Hedstrom, P., & Bearman, P. S. (2009). What is analytical sociology about? An introductory essay. In P. Hedstrom & P. S. Bearman (Eds.), *The Oxford handbook of analytical sociology* (pp. 1–24). New York, NY: Oxford University Press.

Heller, S. B., Shah, A. K., Guryan, J., Ludwig, J., Mullainathan, S., & Pollack, H. A. (2016). Thinking, fast and slow? Some field experiments to reduce crime and dropout in Chicago. *Quarterly Journal of Economics.*

Henderson, G. E. (2008). Introducing social and ethical perspectives on gene-environment research. *Sociological Methods and Research, 37*(2), 251–276.

Hijmans, R. (2015). GADM database of global administrative areas. Retrieved from www.gadm.org/home.

Hitsch, G. J., Hortacsu, A. L., & Ariely, D. (2010). Matching and sorting in online dating. *American Economic Review, 100,* 130–163.

Ho, K. (2009). *Liquidated: An ethnography of Wall Street.* Durham, NC: Duke University Press.

Hoang, K. K. (2015). *Dealing in desire: Asian ascendancy, Western decline, and the hidden currencies of global sex work.* Berkeley: University of California Press.

Hobson, K. (2017, March 6). Feeling lonely? Too much time on social media may be why. *National Public Radio.* Retrieved from http://www.npr.org/sections/health-shots/2017/03/06/518362255/feeling-lonely-too-much-time-on-social-media-may-be-why.

Hochschild, A. (1983). *The managed heart: Commercialization of human feeling.* Berkeley: University of California Press.

Hochschild, A. (2012). *The second shift: Working parents and the revolution at home.* New York, NY: Viking.

Hochschild, A. R. (1997). *The time bind: When work becomes home and home becomes work.* New York, NY: Henry Holt and Company.

Hochschild, A. R. (2016). *Strangers in their own land: Anger and mourning on the American Right.* New York, NY: The New Press.

Hoffman, J. (2016). As attention grows, transgender children's numbers are elusive. *New York Times.* Retrieved from http://www.nytimes.com/2016/05/18/science/transgender-children.html?_r=0.

Hoffmann, J. P., & Warnick, E. (2013). Do family dinners reduce the risk for early adolescent substance use? A propensity score analysis. *Journal of Health and Social Behavior, 54*(3), 335–352.

Hogset, H., & Barrett, C. B. (2010). Social learning, social influence, and projection bias: A caution on inferences based on proxy reporting of peer behavior. *Economic Development and Cultural Change, 58,* 563–589.

Holt-Lunstad, J., Smith, T. B., & Layton, J. B. (2010). Social relationships and mortality risk: A meta-analytic review. *PLoS Medicine, 7.7,* e1000316.

Horowitz, R. (1983). *Honor and the American dream: Culture and identity in a Chicano community.* New Brunswick, NJ: Rutgers University Press.

Houle, J. N., & Warner, C. (2017). Into the red and back to the nest? Student debt, college completion, and returning to the parental home among young adults. *Sociology of Education, 90,* 89–108.

House, J. S., Landis, K. R., & Umberson, D. (1988). Social relationships and health. *Science, 241*(4865), 540–545.

Howe, N., & Strauss, W. (2009). *Millennials rising: The next great generation.* New York, NY: Vintage.

Hristova, D., Musolesi, M., & Mascolo, C. (2014). Keep your friends close and your Facebook friends closer: A multiplex network approach to the analysis of offline and online social ties. arXiv preprint arXiv:1403.8034.

Huff Post Lifestyle. (2017, March 6). Social media is increasing loneliness among adults, say psychologists. Is it time to log out? *Huffington Post UK.* Retrieved from http://www.huffingtonpost.co.uk/entry/social-media-making-adults-feel-lonely-study_uk_58bd26c9e4b05cf0f4016e11.

Hughey, M. (2012). *White bound: Nationalists, antiracists, and the shared meanings of race*. Palo Alto, CA: Stanford University Press.

Humphreys, L. (1970). *Tearoom trade: A study of homosexual encounters in public places*. London, England: Duckworth.

Hunt, J. (2010). *Seven shots: An NYPD raid on a terrorist cell and its aftermath*. Chicago, IL: University of Chicago Press.

Hunt, D., & Ramón, A. (2015). 2015 Hollywood diversity report: Flipping the script. Retrieved from https://www.google.com/url?sa=t&rct=j&q=&esrc=s&source=web&cd=1&cad=rja&uact=8&ved=0ahUKEwimzO_F5KTLAhVrx4MKHan1DBwQFggdMAA&url=http%3A%2F%2Fwww.bunchecenter.ucla.edu%2Fwp-content%2Fuploads%2F2015%2F02%2F2015-Hollywood-Diversity-Report-2-25-15.pdf&usg=AFQjCNEBr6-OnbUos77Rq0Unx-MZM9Ab0A&sig2=newi9pmllHoSQcGCGrKVFQ.

Hunt, D., Ramón, A, & Price, Z. (2014). 2014 Hollywood diversity report: Making sense of the disconnect. Retrieved from https://www.google.com/url?sa=t&rct=j&q=&esrc=s&source=web&cd=1&cad=rja&uact=8&ved=0ahUKEwiH856x5aTLAhWrtIMKHQetDCAQFggdMAA&url=http%3A%2F%2Fwww.bunchecenter.ucla.edu%2Fwp-content%2Fuploads%2F2014%2F02%2F2014-Hollywood-Diversity-Report-2-12-14.pdf&usg=AFQjCNHSazw3sZcjsTKz_ODko2ePAn4Psw&sig2=WZXVHv17aI9Lp4S8dWhAIg.

Hwang, J., & Sampson, R. (2014). Divergent pathways of gentrification: Racial inequality and the social order of renewal in Chicago neighborhoods. *American Sociological Review, 79*(4), 726–751.

Ikegami, E. (2013.). Visualizing networked self: Agency, reflexivity, and the social life of avatars" *Social Research*, Winter, 1155.

Internet World Stats. (2015). *Internet users in the world by region, 2015*. Retrieved from http://www.internetworldstats.com/stats.htm

Investigative Committee in the Matter of Professor Michael Bellesiles. (2002, July 10). *The Emory University report of the Investigative Committee in the matter of Professor Michael Bellesiles*. Retrieved from www.emory.edu/news/Releases/bellesiles1035563546.html.

Inwood, K., Oxley, L., & Roberts, E. (2016). "Tall, active and well made"? Māori stature and health in New Zealand (Unpublished manuscript). University of Minnesota, Minneapolis, MN.

Israel, M., & Hay, I. (2006). *Research ethics for social scientists*. London, England: Sage.

Jackman, M. (2002). Violence in social life. *Annual Review of Sociology, 28*, 387–415.

Jaffe, K. (2008). *Forming fat identities* (Unpublished doctoral dissertation). Department of Sociology, Rutgers University, New Brunswick, NJ.

Jerolmack, C., & Khan, S. (2014). Talk is cheap: Ethnography and the attitudinal fallacy. *Sociological Methods and Research, 43*(2), 178–209.

Jimenez, T. (2010). *Replenished ethnicity: Mexican Americans, immigration, and identity*. Berkeley: University of California Press.

John, O. P., Naumann, L. P., & Soto, C. J. (2008). Paradigm Shift to the Integrative Big Five Trait Taxonomy. In O. P. John, R. W. Robins, & L. A. Pervin (Eds.), *Handbook of personality: Theory and research* (3rd ed., pp. 114–158). New York, NY: Guilford Publishing.

Johnson, D. S., & Smeeding, T. M. (2012). A consumer's guide to interpreting various U.S. poverty measures. *Fast Focus*, No. 14-2012.

Johnson, W. A., Jr., Rettig, R. P., Scott, G. M., & Garrison, S.M. (1998). *The sociology student writer's manual*. Upper Saddle River, NJ: Prentice Hall.

Johnson-Hanks, J. (2008). Demographic transitions and modernity. *Annual Review of Anthropology, 37*, 301–315.

Johnston, D. W., & Lee, W-S. (2011). Explaining the female black-white obesity gap: A decomposition analysis of proximal causes. *Demography, 48*(4), 1429–1450.

Johnston, L. D., O'Malley, P. M., Bachman, J. G., & Schulenberg, J. E. (2010). *Monitoring the future: National survey results on drug use, 1975-2009. Volume I: Secondary school students* (National Institutes of Health Publication No. 10-7584). Retrieved from http://monitoringthefuture.org/pubs/monographs/vol1_2009.pdf.

Jones, J. H. (1993). *Bad blood: The Tuskegee syphilis experiment*. New York, NY: Free Press.

Jost, J. T., Rudman, L. A., Blair, I. V., Carney, D. R., Dasgupta, N., Glaser, J., & Hardin, C. D. (2009). The existence of implicit bias is beyond reasonable doubt: A refutation of ideological and methodological objections and executive summary of ten studies that no manager should ignore. *Research in Organizational Behavior, 29,* 39–69.

Joyner, K., Manning, W., & Bogle, R. (2014). Social context and the stability of same-sex and different sex relationships. Poster presented at the annual meeting of the Population Association of America, Boston, MA.

Junker, B. H. (1960). *Field work.* Chicago, IL: University of Chicago Press.

Kaczynski, A., Massie, C., & McDermot, N. (2017). Trump aide Monica Crowley plagiarized thousands of words in Ph.D. dissertation. *CNN Money.* Retrieved from http://money.cnn.com/interactive/news/kfile-monica-crowley-dissertation-plagiarism/.

Kalaian, S. A., & Kasim, R. M. (2008). External validity. In P. J. Lavrakas (Ed.), *Encyclopedia of survey research methods* (pp. 255–258). Thousand Oaks, CA: Sage.

Kalev, A., Dobbin, F., & Kelly, E. (2006). Best practices or best guesses? Assessing the efficacy of corporate affirmative action and diversity policies. *American Sociological Review, 71*(4), 589–617.

Kane, E. W., & Macaulay, L. J. (1993). Interviewer gender and gender attitudes. *Public Opinion Quarterly, 57*(1), 1–28.

Kapferer, B. (1972). *Strategy and transaction in an African factory.* Manchester, England: Manchester University Press.

Kaplowitz, M. D., Hadlock, T. D., & Levine, R. (2004). A comparison of web and mail survey response rates. *Public Opinion Quarterly, 68,* 94–101.

Karabel, J. (2005). *The chosen: The hidden history of admission and exclusion at Harvard, Yale, and Princeton.* New York, NY: Houghton Mifflin.

Karraker, A., Sicinski, K., & Moynihan, D. (2017). Your face is your fortune: Does adolescent attractiveness predict intimate relationships later in life? *Journals of Gerontology Series B: Psychological Sciences and Social Sciences, 72*(1), 187–199.

Kasinitz, P., Mollenkopf, J. H., & Waters, M. C. (Eds.). (2004). *Becoming New Yorkers: Ethnographies of the new second generation.* New York, NY: Russell Sage.

Kasinitz, P., Mollenkopf, J. H., Waters, M. C., & Holdaway, J. (2008). *Inheriting the city: The children of immigrants come of age.* Cambridge, MA, and New York, NY: Harvard University Press and Russell Sage Foundation.

Katz, J. (2007). Toward a natural history of ethical censorship. *Law and Society Review, 41*(1), 797–810.

Kellogg, K. C. (2009). Operating room: Relational spaces and micro-institutional change in surgery. *American Journal of Sociology, 115*(3), 657–711.

Kelly, J. (2008). Computer-assisted telephone interviewing (CATI). In P. J. Lavrakas (Ed.), *Encyclopedia of survey research methods* (pp. 123–125). Thousand Oaks, CA: Sage.

Kelly, E. L., Moen, P., & Tranby, E. (2011). Changing workplaces to reduce work-family conflict: Schedule control in a white-collar organization. *American Sociological Review, 76,* 265–290.

Kelly, E. L., Ammons, S. K., Chermack, K., & Moen, P. (2010). Gendered challenge, gendered response: Confronting the ideal worker norm in a white-collar organization. *Gender & Society, 24,* 281–303.

Kelly, E. L., Moen, P., Oakes, J. M., Fan, W., Okechukwu, C., Davis, K. D., . . . Casper, L. M. (2014). Changing work and work-family conflict: Evidence from the Work, Family, and Health Network. *American Sociological Review, 79*(3), 485–516.

Khan, S. R. (2011). *Privilege: The making of an adolescent elite at St. Paul's School.* Princeton, NJ: Princeton University Press. (Hardcover)

Khan, S. (2012). *Privilege: The making of an adolescent elite at St. Paul's School* Princeton, NJ: Princeton University Press. (Paperback)

Killewald, A. (2013). A reconsideration of the fatherhood premium: Marriage, coresidence, biology, and fathers' wages. *American Sociological Review, 78*(1), 96–116.

Kimbro, R. T., Bzostek, S., Goldman, N., & Rodríguez, G. (2008). Race, ethnicity, and the education gradient in health. *Health Affairs, 27*(2), 361–372.

King, G., Keohane, R. O., & Verba, S. (1994). *Designing social inquiry: Scientific inference in qualitative research.* Princeton, NJ: Princeton University Press.

Kinney, D. A. (1999). From "headbangers" to "hippies": Delineating adolescents' active attempts to form an alternative peer culture. *New Directions for Child and Adolescent Development, 1999*(84), 21–35.

Kirby, D. B. (2008). The impact of abstinence and comprehensive sex and STD/HIV education programs on adolescent sexual behavior. *Sexuality Research and Social Policy, 5*(3), 18–27.

Klinenberg, E. (2002). *Heat wave: A social autopsy of disaster in Chicago*. Chicago, IL: University of Chicago Press.

Kling, J. R., Liebman, J. B., & Katz, L. F. (2007). Experimental analysis of neighborhood effects. *Econometrica, 75*, 83–119.

Knodel, J., Chamratrithirong, A., & Debavalya, N. (1987). *Thailand's reproductive revolution: Rapid fertility decline in a third-world setting*. Madison: University of Wisconsin Press.

Knorr-Cetina, K. (1999). *Epistemic cultures: How the sciences make knowledge*. Cambridge, MA: Harvard University Press.

Kobayashi, T., Kawachi, I., Iwase, T., Suzuki, E., & Takao, S. (2013). Individual-level social capital and self-rated health in Japan: An application of the Resource Generator. *Social Science & Medicine, 85*, 32–37.

Kolata, G. (2017, March 22). A scholarly sting operation shines a light on "predatory" journals. *New York Times*. Retrieved from https://www.nytimes.com/2017/03/22/science/open-access-journals.html?_r=0.

Komarovsky, M. (1967). *Blue collar marriage*. New York, NY: Vintage Books.

Kozinets, R. V. (2015). *Netnography: Redefined*. London, England: Sage.

Kramer, A. D. I., Guillory, J. E., & Hancock, J. T. (2014). Experimental evidence of massive-scale emotional contagion through social networks. *Proceedings of the National Academy of Sciences of the United States of America, 111*(24).

Kreager, D. A., and Haynie, D. L. (2011). Dangerous liaisons? Dating and drinking diffusion in adolescent peer networks. *American Sociological Review, 76*, 737–763.

Kreager, D. A., & Staff, J. (2009). The sexual double standard and adolescent peer acceptance. *Social Psychology Quarterly, 72*, 143–164.

Kroeber, A. L. (1925). *Handbook of the Indians of California*. Washington, DC: U.S. Government Printing Office.

Kuhn, T. S. (1962). *The structure of scientific revolutions*. Chicago, IL: University of Chicago Press.

Kurzman, C. (1991). Convincing sociologists: Values and interests in the sociology of knowledge. In M. Burawoy (Ed.), *Ethnography unbound: Power and resistance in the modern metropolis* (pp. 250–268). Berkeley: University of California Press.

Kwak, H., Lee, C., Park, H., & Moon, S. (2010). What is twitter, a social network or a news media? In *Proceedings of the 19th International Conference on the World Wide Web*. New York.

Lacy, K. (2007). *Blue-chip black: Race, class, and status in the new black middle class*. Berkeley: University of California Press.

Ladson-Billings, G., & Tate, W. F. (1995). Toward a critical race theory of education. *Teachers College Record, 97*(1), 47–68.

Landale, N. S., Hardie, J. H., Oropesa, R. S., & Hillemeier, M. H. (2015). Behavioral functioning among Mexican-origin children does parental legal status matter? *Journal of Health and Social Behavior, 56*(1), 2–18.

Langenkamp, A. G. (2009). Following different pathways: Social integration, achievement, and the transition to high school. *American Journal of Education, 116*(1), 69–97.

Langlois, J. H., Kalakanis, L., Rubenstein, A. J., Larson, A., Hallam, M., & Smoot, M. (2000). Maxims or myths of beauty? A meta-analytic and theoretical review. *Psychological Bulletin, 126*, 390–423.

Lantz, P. M., House, J. S., Lepkowski, J. M., Williams, D. R., Mero, R. P., & Chen, J. (1998). Socioeconomic factors, health behaviors, and mortality: Results from a nationally representative prospective study of US adults. *JAMA, 279*(21), 1703–1708.

Lareau, A. (2003). *Unequal childhoods: Class, race, and family life*. Berkeley: University of California Press.

Lareau, A. (2012). Using the terms *hypothesis* and *variable* for qualitative work: A critical reflection. *Journal of Marriage and the Family, 74*(4), 671–677.

Laub, J., & Sampson, R. (2003). *Shared beginnings, divergent lives: Delinquent boys to age 70*. Cambridge, MA: Harvard University Press.

Laumann, E. O., Marsden, P. V., & Prensky, D. (1983). The boundary specification problem in network analysis. In R. S. Burt & M. J. Minor (Eds.), *Applied network analysis: A methodological introduction* (pp. 18–34). Beverly Hills, CA: Sage.

Lavrakas, P. ed (2008). Encyclopedia of Survey Research Methods. Thousand Oaks, CA: Sage Publications.

Lawrence, R. G., & Birkland, T. A. (2004). Guns, Hollywood, and school safety: Defining the school-shooting problem across public arenas. *Social Science Quarterly, 85,* 1193–1207.

Lawrence-Lightfoot, S. (1983). *The good high school: Portraits of character and culture.* New York, NY: Basic Books.

Lazarsfeld, P. F. (1944). The controversy over detailed interviews—an offer for negotiation. *Public Opinion Quarterly, 8*(1), 38–60.

Lazer, D., Pentland, A., Adamic, L., Aral, S., Barabasi, A. L., Brewer, D. . . . & Van Alstyne, M. (2009). Life in the network: The coming age of computational social science. *Science, 323*(5915), 721–723.

Lee, R. M. (1993). *Doing research on sensitive topics.* Thousand Oaks, CA: Sage.

Lee, J., & Zhou, M. (2014). The success frame and achievement paradox: The costs and consequences for Asian Americans. *Race and Social Problems, 6*(1), 38–55.

Lee, H. J., Park, N., & Hwang, Y. (2015). A new dimension of the digital divide: Exploring the relationship between broadband connection, smartphone use, and communication competence. *Telematics and Informatics, 32,* 45–56.

Leidner, R. (1993). *Fast food, fast talk: Service work and the routinization of everyday life.* Berkeley: University of California Press.

Levey, H. (2009). Pageant princesses and math whizzes: Understanding children's activities as a form of children's work. *Childhood, 16,* 195–212.

Levine, J. (2013). *Ain't no trust: How bosses, boyfriends, and bureaucrats fail low-income mothers and why it matters.* Berkeley: University of California Press.

Lewis, K., Gonzalez, M., & Kaufman, J. (2012). Social selection and peer influence in an online social network. *Proceedings of the National Academy of Sciences of the United States of America, 109,* 68–72.

Lewis, K., Kaufman, J., Gonzalez, M., Wimmer, A., & Christakis, N. (2008). Tastes, ties, and time: A new social network dataset using Facebook.com. *Social Networks, 30*(4), 330–342.

Liebow, E. (1967). *Tally's corner: A study of Negro streetcorner men* (Legacies of social thought series). Lanham, MD: Rowman & Littlefield.

Liebow, E. (1993). *Tell them who I am: The lives of homeless women.* New York, NY: Penguin Books.

Lin, A. C. (1998). Bridging positivist and interpretivist approaches to qualitative methods. *Policy Studies Journal, 26*(1), 162–180.

Lin, N. (2001). *Social capital: A theory of social structure and action.* New York, NY: Cambridge University Press.

Lin, N., Fu, Y., & Hsung, R. (2001). The position generator: Measurement techniques for social capital. In N. Lin, K. Cook, & R. S. Burt (Eds.), *Social capital: Theory and research* (pp. 57–84). New York, NY: Aldine De Gruyter.

Lincoln, Y. S., & Guba, E. G. (1985). *Naturalistic Inquiry.* Newbury Park, CA: Sage.

Lipset, S. M., Trow, M. A., & Coleman, J. S. (1956). *Union democracy: The internal politics of the International Typographical Union.* New York, NY: Free Press.

Liu, K., King, M., & Bearman, P. S. (2010). Social influence and the autism epidemic. *American Journal of Sociology, 115,* 1387–1434.

Lofland, J. (1971). *Analyzing social settings: A guide to qualitative observations and analyses.* Belmont, CA: Wadsworth.

Lofland, J., & Stark, R. (1965). Becoming a world saver: A theory of conversion to a deviant perspective. *American Sociological Review, 30,* 862–875.

Lofquist, K. (2011). *Same-sex couple households: American Community Survey briefs.* Washington, DC: U.S. Census Bureau. Retrieved from https://www.census.gov/prod/2011pubs/acsbr10-03.pdf.

Lorrain, F., & White, H. C. (1971). Structural equivalence of individuals in social networks. *Journal of Mathematical Sociology, 1,* 49–80.

Love, S. R., & Park, S.-M. (2013). Images of gender twenty years later: A content analysis of images in introductory criminal justice and criminology textbooks. *Feminist Criminology, 8*(4), 320–340.

Lowe, S. R., Lustig, K., & Marrow, H. B. (2011). African American women's reports of racism during Hurricane Katrina: Variation by interviewer race. *New School Psychology Bulletin, 8*(2), 46–57.

Luker, K. (2008). *Salsa dancing into the social sciences: Research in an age of info-glut.* Cambridge, MA: Harvard University Press.

Luscombe, B. (2012). Do children of same-sex parents really fare worse? Retrieved from http://healthland.

time.com/2012/06/11/do-children-of-same-sex-parents-really-fare-worse/.

Lynd, R. S., & Lynd, H. M. (1929). *Middletown: A study in contemporary American culture.* New York, NY: Harcourt, Brace, and Company.

Maass, A., Cadinu, M., Guarnieri, G., & Grasselli, A. (2003). Sexual harassment under social identity threat: The computer harassment paradigm. *Journal of Personality and Social Psychology, 85*(5), 853–870.

MacLeod, J. (1995). *Ain't no makin' it: Aspirations and attainment in a low income neighborhood.* Boulder, CO: Westview Press.

Makambi, K. H., Williams, C. D., Taylor, T. R., Rosenberg, L., & Adams-Campbell, L. L. (2009). An assessment of the CES-D scale factor structure in black women: The Black Women's Health Study. *Psychiatry Research, 168,* 163–170.

Malcolm, H., & Davidson, P. (2015, February 20). Walmart employees to get raises. *USA Today.* Retrieved from http://www.usatoday.com/story/money/2015/02/19/walmart-employees-raises/23666047.

Marin, A., & Hampton, K. (2007). Simplifying the personal network name generator: Alternatives to traditional multiple and single name generators. *Field Methods, 19,* 163–193.

Markus, H., Uchida, Y., Omoregie, H., Townsend, S., & Kitayama, S. (2006). Going for the Gold: Models of agency in Japanese and American contexts. *Psychological Sciences, 17,* 103–112.

Marsden, P. V. (2003). Interviewer effects in measuring network size using a single name generator. *Social Networks, 25,* 1–16.

Marsden, P. V. (Ed.). (2012). *Social trends in American life: Findings from the General Social Survey since 1972.* Princeton, NJ: Princeton University Press.

Marsh, H., & Hau, K. T. (2003). Big-fish-little-pond effect on academic self-concept. A cross-cultural (26 country) test of the negative effects of academically selective schools. *American Psychologist, 58,* 364–376.

Marshall, W. A., & Tanner, J. M. (1969). Variations in pattern of pubertal changes in girls. *Archives of Disease in Childhood, 44,* 291–303.

Martin, S. P., Astone, N. M., & Peters, H. E. (2014). *Fewer marriages, more divergence: Marriage projections for Millennials to age 40.* Washington, DC: Urban Institute.

Masci, D., Brown, A., & Kiley, J. (2017). *5 facts about same-sex marriage.* Pew Research Center. Retrieved from http://www.pewresearch.org/fact-tank/2017/06/26/same-sex-marriage/.

Massoglia, M., Firebaugh, G., & Warner, C. (2013). Racial variation in the effect of incarceration on neighborhood attainment. *American Sociological Review, 78*(1), 142–165.

Matthews, S. H. (2005). Crafting qualitative research articles on marriages and families. *Journal of Marriage and the Family, 67*(4), 799–808.

Matthews, T., Liao, K., Turner, A., Berkovich, M., Reeder, R., & Consolvo, S. (2016). She'll just grab any device that's closer: A study of everyday device and account sharing in households. In *Proceedings of the ACM Conference on Human Factors in Computing Systems.* Retrieved from https://static.googleusercontent.com/media/research.google.com/en//pubs/archive/44670.pdf.

Maxwell, J. (1992). Understanding and validity in qualitative research. *Harvard Educational Review, 62*(3), 279–301.

McAdam, D., McCarthy, J., Olzak, S., & Soule, S. (2009). Dynamics of collective action data. Retrieved from http://web.stanford.edu/group/collectiveaction/cgi-bin/drupal/.

McCabe, J., Fairchild, E., Grauerholz, L., Pescosolido, B. A., & Tope, D. (2011). Gender in twentieth-century children's books: Patterns of disparity in titles and central characters. *Gender & Society, 25*(2), 197–226.

McCall, G. J., & Simmons, J. L. (Eds.). (1969). *Issues in participant observation: A text and reader.* New York, NY: Newbury Award Records.

McCarty, C., Molina, J. L., Aguilar, C., & Rota, L. (2007). A comparison of social network mapping and personal network visualization. *Field Methods, 19,* 145–162.

McDavid, J. C., & Hawthorn, L. R. L. (2006). *Program evaluation & performance measurement: An introduction to practice.* Thousand Oaks, CA: Sage.

McDermott, M. (2006). *Working class white: The making and unmaking of race relations.* Berkeley: University of California Press.

McDermott, R., Fowler, J. H., & Christakis, N. A. (2013). Breaking up is hard to do, unless everyone else is doing it too: Social network effects on divorce in a longitudinal sample. *Social Forces, 92*(2), 491–519.

McDowell, T. L., & Serovich, J. M. (2007). The effect of perceived and actual social support on the mental health of HIV-positive persons. *AIDS Care, 19,* 1223–1229.

McGeeney, K., Kennedy, C., & Weisel, R. (2015, November 18). *Advances in telephone survey sampling.* Washington, DC: Pew Research Center. Retrieved from http://www.pewresearch.org/2015/11/18/advances-in-telephone-survey-sampling/.

McIntyre, L. (2013). *The practical skeptic: Core concepts in sociology.* New York, NY: McGraw-Hill Higher Education.

McPherson, M., Smith-Lovin, L., & Brashears, M. E. (2006). Social isolation in America: Changes in core discussion networks over two decades. *American Sociological Review, 71*(3), 353–375.

McPherson, M., Smith-Lovin, L., & Cook, J. M. (2001). Birds of a feather: Homophily in social networks. *Annual Review of Sociology, 27,* 415–444.

Mears, A. (2011). *Pricing beauty: The making of a fashion model.* Berkeley: University of California Press.

Merluzzi, J., & Burt, R. S. (2013). How many names are enough? Identifying network effects with the least set of listed contacts. *Social Networks, 35,* 331–337.

Merton, R. K. (1972). Insiders and outsiders: A chapter in the sociology of knowledge. *American Journal of Sociology, 78*(1), 9–47.

Merton, R. K., & Kendall, P. K. (1946). The focused interview. *American Journal of Sociology, 51,* 541–557.

Meyer, J. W. (2010). World society, institutional theories, and the actor. *Annual Review of Sociology, 36,* 1–20.

Michels, R. (1915). *Political parties: A sociological study of the oligarchical tendencies of modern democracy.* New York, NY: Dover.

Miech, R., Patrick, M. E., O'Malley, P. M., & Johnston, L. D. (2016a). What are kids vaping? Results from a national survey of US adolescents. *Tobacco Control.*

Miech, R. A., Johnston, L. D., O'Malley, P. M., Bachman, J. G., & Schulenberg, J. E. (2016b). *Monitoring future National Survey results on drug use 1975–2015. Volume 1, secondary school students.* Retrieved from http://www.monitoringthefuture.org//pubs/monographs/mtf-vol1_2015.pdf.

Mikolajczyk, R. T., & Kretzschmar, M. (2008). Collecting social contact data in the context of disease transmission: Prospective and retrospective study designs. *Social Networks, 30,* 127–135.

Miles, M. B., & Huberman, A. M. (1994). *Qualitative data analysis* (2nd ed.). Thousand Oaks, CA: Sage.

Milgram, S. (1967). The small-world problem. *Psychology Today, 1,* 61–67.

Milgram, S. (1974). *Obedience to authority: An experimental view.* New York, NY: Harper and Row.

Milgram, S. (1977). Ethical issues in the study of obedience. In S. Milgram (Ed.), *The individual in a social world* (pp. 188–199). Reading, MA: Addison-Wesley.

Miller, A. (2016). Obama weights in on Oscars diversity debate, Super Bowl. *USA Today.* Retrieved from http://abcnews.go.com/Politics/obama-weighs-oscar-diversity-debate-super-bowl/story?id=36555716.

Miller, C. C. (2014, December 2). The divorce surge is over, but the myth lives on. *New York Times.* Retrieved from http://www.nytimes.com/2014/12/02/upshot/the-divorce-surge-is-over-but-the-myth-lives-on.html?smid=tw-share&abt=0002&abg=0&_r=2.

Miller, J. E. (2004). *The Chicago guide to writing about numbers.* Chicago, IL: University of Chicago Press.

Miller, J. E. (2007). Preparing and presenting effective research posters. *Health Services Research , 42,* 311–328.

Miller, J. E. (2015). *The Chicago guide to writing about numbers* (2nd ed.) (Chicago guides to writing, editing, and publishing). Chicago, IL: University of Chicago Press.

Mills, C. W. (1959). *The sociological imagination.* New York, NY: Oxford University Press.

Minkel, J. R. (2007, March 13). Confirmed: The U.S. Census Bureau gave up names of Japanese Americans in World War II. *Scientific American.* https://www.scientificamerican.com/article/confirmed-the-us-census-b/

Miranda–Diaz, M., & Corcoran, K. (2012). "All my friends are doing it": The impact of the perception of peer sexuality on adolescents' intent to have sex. *Journal of Evidence-Based Social Work, 9*(3), 260–264.

Mirowsky, J., & Ross, C. E. (2003a). *Education, social status, and health.* New York, NY: Aldine de Gruyter.

Mirowsky, J., & Ross, C. E. (2003b). *Social causes of psychological distress* (2nd ed.). New York: Aldine de Gruyter.

Mislove, A., Koppula, H. S., Gummadi, K. P., Druschel, P., & Bhattacharjee, B. (2008). Growth of the Flickr social network. In *Proceedings of the First Workshop on Online Social Networks - WOSP '08* (pp. 25–30). Seattle, WA: Association for Computing Machinery.

Mize, T. & B. Minago. (n.d.). *Precarious sexuality: How men and women are differentially categorized and evaluated for similar sexual behavior* (Unpublished manuscript).

Moen, P., Kelly, E. L., Fan, W., Lee, S. R., Almeida, D., Kossek, E. E., & Buxton, O. M. (2016). Does a flexibility/support organizational initiative improve high-tech employees' well-being? Evidence from the work, family, and health network. *American Sociological Review, 81*(1), 134–164.

Moen, P., Kelly, E. L., Tranby, E., & Huang, Q. (2011). Changing work, changing health: Can real work-time flexibility promote health behaviors and well-being? *Journal of Health and Social Behavior, 52,* 404–429.

Moffitt, R. A. (2015). The deserving poor, the family, and the U.S. welfare system. *Demography, 52,* 729–749.

Moisander, J., & Valtonen, A. (2012). Interpretive marketing research: Using ethnography in strategic market development. In L. Penaloza, N. Toulouse, & L. M. Visconti (Eds.), *Marketing management: A cultural perspective* (pp. 246–261). New York, NY: Routledge.

Moore, T. (2010, October 2). Mayor Bloomberg goes to bat for program that studied homeless people. *New York Daily News.* Retrieved from http://articles.nydailynews.com/2010-10-02/local/27076978_1_homebase-homeless-services-study.

Moore, M. R., & Stambolis-Ruhstorfer, M. (2013). LGBT sexuality and families at the start of the twenty-first century. *Annual Review of Sociology, 39,* 491–507.

Moore, S. R., Harden, K. P., & Mendle, J. (2014). Pubertal timing and adolescent sexual behavior in girls. *Developmental Psychology, 50*(6), 1734–1745.

Morenoff, J. D., Sampson, R. J., & Raudenbush, S. W. (2001). Neighborhood inequality, collective efficacy, and the spatial dynamics of urban violence. *Criminology, 39*(3), 517–558.

Morgan, D. L. (1996). Focus groups. *Annual Review of Sociology, 22,* 129–152.

Morgan, D. L. (1997). *Focus groups as qualitative research: Planning and research design for focus groups.* Thousand Oaks, CA: Sage.

Morgan, D. L., & Krueger, R. A. (1993). When to use focus groups and why. In D. L. Morgan (Ed.), *Successful focus groups: Advancing the state of the art* (pp. 3–20). Thousand Oaks, CA: Sage.

Morgan, S. L. (2001). Counterfactuals, causal effect heterogeneity, and the Catholic school effect on learning. *Sociology of Education, 74,* 341–374.

Morris, A. (2015). *The scholar denied: W. E. B. Du Bois and the birth of modern sociology.* Berkeley: University of California Press.

Moskos, P. (2008). *Cop in the hood: My year policing Baltimore's eastern district.* Princeton, NJ: Princeton University Press.

Mosteller, F. (1995). The Tennessee study of class size in the early grades. *Future of Children: Critical Issues for Children and Youth 5*(2), 113–127.

Mouw, T., & Verdery, A. (2012). Network sampling with memory: A proposal for more efficient sampling from social networks. *Sociological Methodology, 42,* 206–256.

Mroczek, D. K., & Kolarz, C. M. (1998). The effect of age on positive and negative affect: A developmental perspective on happiness. *Journal of Personality and Social Psychology, 75*(5), 1333–1349.

Murray, C. (2016). *In our hands: A plan to replace the welfare state.* New York, NY: Rowman & Littlefield.

Mutz, D. C. (2011). *Population-based survey experiments.* Princeton, NJ: Princeton University Press.

Nathan, R. (2006). *My freshman year: What a professor learned by becoming a student.* Ithaca, NY: Cornell University Press.

National Center for Education Statistics. (2016a). *Digest of education statistics, 2015.* Washington, DC: NCES. Retrieved from https://nces.ed.gov/programs/digest/d15/.

National Center for Education Statistics. (2016b). *Total fall enrollment in degree-granting postsecondary institutions, by attendance status, sex, and age: Selected years, 1970 through 2025.* Retrieved from https://nces.ed.gov/programs/digest/d15/tables/dt15_303.40.asp.

National Commission for the Protection of Human Subjects of Biomedical and Behavioral Research.

(1979). *Belmont report: Ethical principles and guidelines for the protection of human subjects of research.* Retrieved from http://ohsr.od.nih.gov/guidelines/belmont.html.

Nederhof, A. J. (1985). Methods of coping with social desirability bias: A review. *European Journal of Social Psychology, 15*(3), 263–280.

Nederhof, A. J. (2006). Bibliometric monitoring of research performance in the social sciences and the humanities: A review. *Scientometrics, 66*(1), 81–100.

Neidig, H. (2016, May 19). Poll: Americans split over transgender bathroom debate. *The Hill.* Retrieved from http://thehill.com/blogs/blog-briefing-room/news/280509-poll-americans-split-over-transgender-bathroom-debate.

Nesse, R. M., Wortman, C., House, J., Kessler, R., & Lepkowski, J. (2003). *Changing lives of older couples (CLOC): A study of spousal bereavement in the Detroit Area, 1987–1993.* ICPSR03370-v1. Ann Arbor, MI: Inter-university Consortium for Political and Social Research [distributor]. Retrieved from http://doi.org/10.3886/ICPSR03370.v1.

Newman, K. (2004). *Rampage: The social roots of school shootings.* New York, NY: Basic Books.

Newman, K. (2004). *Rampage: The social roots of school shootings.* New York, NY: Basic Books.

New York Times. (2017, January 6). Inside a killer drug epidemic: A look at America's opioid crisis. *New York Times.* Retrieved from https://www.nytimes.com/2017/01/06/us/opioid-crisis-epidemic.html?_r=0.

NICHD Early Child Care Research Network. (2005). *Child care and child development: Results from the NICHD Study of Early Child Care and Youth Development.* New York, NY: Guilford.

Nielsen, L. B., Nelson, R. L., & Lancaster, R. (2010). Individual justice or collective legal mobilization? Employment discrimination litigation in the post-civil rights United States. *Journal of Empirical Legal Studies, 7,* 175–201.

Nolen-Hoeksema, S. (2001). Gender differences in depression. *Current Directions in Psychological Science, 10,* 173–176.

O'Brien, L. T., et al. (2009). Understanding white Americans' perceptions of racism in Hurricane Katrina-related events. *Group Processes & Intergroup Relations, 12*(4), 431–444.

O'Leary, R. (2003). Social surveys. In R. L. Miller & J. D. Brewer (Eds.), *The A-Z of social research* (pp. 301–304). Thousand Oaks, CA: Sage Research Methods.

O'Neil, M., Kendall-Taylor, N., & Nall Bales, S. (2014). Finish the story on immigration: A FrameWorks message memo. FrameWorks Institute. Retrieved from www.frameworksinstitute.org/pubs/mm/immigration/index.html.

Oesch, D., & Lipps, O. (2013). Does unemployment hurt less if there is more of it around? A panel analysis of life satisfaction in Germany and Switzerland. *European Sociological Review, 29*(5), 955–967.

Office of Management and Budget (OMB). (1995). *Standards for the classification of federal data on race and ethnicity.* Retrieved from https://www.whitehouse.gov/omb/fedreg_race-ethnicity/.

Ogbu, J. U. (1997). African American education: A cultural-ecological perspective. In H. P. McAdoo (Ed.), *Black families* (pp. 234–250). Thousand Oaks, CA: Sage.

Ogden, C., Carroll, M., Curtin, L., McDowell, M., Tabak, C., & Flegal, K. (2006). Prevalence of overweight and obesity in the United States, 1999–2004. *Journal of the American Medical Association, 295,* 1549–1555.

Oldendick, R. (2008). Question order effects. *Encyclopedia of Survey Research Methods,* 664–666. Thousand Oaks, CA: Sage.

Oloritun, R. O., Madan, A., Pentland, A., & Khayal, I. (2013). Identifying close friendships in a sensed social network. *Procedia-Social and Behavioral Sciences, 79,* 18–26.

Olsen, W. (2004). Triangulation in social research: Qualitative and quantitative methods can really be mixed. *Developments in Sociology, 20,* 103–118.

Olsen, R., & Sheets, C. (2008). Computer-assisted personal interviewing (CAPI). In P. J. Lavrakas (Ed.), *Encyclopedia of survey research methods* (pp. 118–120). Thousand Oaks, CA: Sage.

Olson, K. (2008). Double-barreled question. In P. J. Lavrakas (Ed.), *Encyclopedia of survey research methods* (pp. 119–121). Thousand Oaks, CA: Sage.

Olzak, S. (2015). Ethnic collective action in contemporary urban United States—data on conflicts and protests, 1954-1992. ICPSR. Retrieved from www.icpsr.umich.edu/icpsrweb/ICPSR/studies/34341.

Olzak, S., & Shanahan, S. (2003). Racial policy and racial conflict in the urban United States, 1869–1924. *Social Forces, 82*(2), 481–517.

Oppenheimer, M. (2012, October 12). Sociologist's paper raises questions about the role of faith in scholarship. *New York Times,* p. A16.

Osgood, D. W., Ragan, D. T., Wallace, L., Gest, S. D., Feinberg, M. E., & Moody, J. (2013). Peers and the emergence of alcohol use: Influence and selection processes in adolescent friendship networks. *Journal of Research on Adolescence, 23,* 500–512.

Padgett, J. F., & Ansell, C. K. (1993). Robust action and the rise of the Medici, 1400-1434. *American Journal of Sociology, 98,* 1259–1319.

Pager, D. (2003). The mark of a criminal record. *American Journal of Sociology, 108*(5), 937–975.

Pager, D., & Quillian, L. G. (2005). Walking the talk? What employers say versus what they do. *American Sociological Review, 70,* 335–380.

Pager, D., Western, B., & Bonikowski, B. (2009). Discrimination in a low wage labor market: A field experiment. *American Sociological Review, 74*(5), 777–799.

Paik, A., & Sanchagrin, K. (2013). Social isolation in America: An artifact. *American Sociological Review, 78,* 339–360.

Palmer, B. (2010, June 7). Mein data: Did any useful science come out of the Nazi concentration camps? *Slate.* Retrieved from http://www.slate.com/articles/news_and_politics/explainer/2010/06/mein_data.html.

Palmore, E. (1978). When can age, period, and cohort be separated? *Social Forces, 57*(1), 282–295.

Papapostolou, A. (2016). Exclusive: Paul Sorvino says there's no racism in Hollywood [video]. Retrieved from http://hollywood.greekreporter.com/2016/03/02/exclusive-paul-sorvino-says-theres-no-racism-in-hollywood-video.

Park, R. (1950). *Race and culture.* New York, NY: Free Press.

Parry, M. (2011, July 10). Harvard researchers accused of breaching students' privacy. *Chronicle of Higher Education.* Retrieved from http://www.chronicle.com/article/Harvards-Privacy-Meltdown/128166.

Pascoe, C. J. (2007). *Dude, you're a fag: Masculinity and sexuality in high school.* Berkeley: University of California Press.

Patrick, R. (2016, October 25). Lawsuit by Muslim woman from St. Louis County claims employment discrimination. *St. Louis Post-Dispatch.* Retrieved from http://www.stltoday.com/news/local/crime-and-courts/lawsuit-by-muslim-woman-from-st-louis-county-claims-employment/article_8e8bf443-60fc-50e5-8b0c-31e5c4139f9e.html.

Patten, M. L. (2009). *Understanding research methods: An overview of the essentials* (7th ed.). Glendale, CA.: Pyrczak Publishing.

Paxton, P., Green, J., & Hughes, M. M. (2008). Women in Parliament Dataset, 1893–2003. [computer file]. ICPSR24340-v1. Ann Arbor, MI: ICPSR.

Pearce, N. C., & Parks, R. A. (Eds.). (2011). *User's guide, Wisconsin Longitudinal Study instrumentation: 1957 to 2010.* Madison: University of Wisconsin-Madison.

Peek, M. K., & Lin, N. (1999). Age differences in the effects of network composition on psychological distress. *Social Science & Medicine, 49,* 621–636.

Penner, A., & Saperstein, A. (2008). How social status shapes race. *Proceedings of the National Academy of Sciences of the United States of America, 105,* 19628–19630.

Perreira, K., Deeb-Sossa, N., Harris, K. M., & Bollen, K. (2005). What are we measuring? An evaluation of the CES-D across race/ethnicity and immigrant generation. *Social Forces, 83,* 1567–1601.

Perrin, A., & Duggan, M. (2015, June 26). *Americans' Internet access: 2000-2015.* Pew Internet. Retrieved from http://www.pewinternet.org/2015/06/26/americans-internet-access-2000-2015.

Perry, B. L., & Pescosolido, B. A. (2010). Functional specificity in discussion networks: The influence of general and problem-specific networks on health outcomes. *Social Networks, 32,* 345–357.

Perry, J., & Vogell, H. (2008, December 14). Surge in CRCT results raises "big red flag." *Atlanta Journal-Constitution.* Retrieved from http://www.ajc.com/news/news/local/surge-in-crct-results-raises-big-red-flag-1/nQSXD/.

Pescosolido, B. A., & Georgianna, S. (1989). Durkheim, suicide, and religion: Toward a network theory of suicide. *American Sociological Review, 33–48.*

Petersen, T. (2008). Split ballots as an experimental approach to public opinion research. In W. Donsbach & M. W. Traugott (Eds.), *The SAGE handbook of public opinion research* (pp. 322–329). Thousand Oaks, CA: Sage.

Pew Research Center. (2016, April 26). *A wider ideological gap between more and less educated adults.* Retrieved from http://www.people-press.org/2016/04/26/a-wider-ideological-gap-between-more-and-less-educated-adults.

Pfeffer, R. (1979). *Working for capitalism.* New York, NY: Columbia University Press.

Pianta, R., La Paro, K., & Hamre, B. (2007). *Classroom Assessment Scoring System (CLASS).* Baltimore, MD: Brookes.

Pianta, R. C., Belsky, J., Houts, R., Morrison, F., & the NICHD Early Child Care Research Network. (2007). Opportunities to learn in America's elementary classrooms. *Science, 315*(5820), 1795–1796.

Pierce, J. (1996). *Gender trials: Emotional lives in contemporary law firms.* Berkeley: University of California Press.

Pleis, J. R., Dahlhamer, J. M., & Meyer, P. S. (2007). Unfolding the answers? Income nonresponse and income brackets in the National Health Interview Survey. In *Proceedings of the 2006 Joint Statistical Meetings* [CD–ROM] (pp. 3540–3547). Alexandria, VA: American Statistical Association. Retrieved from http://www.amstat.org/Sections/Srms/Proceedings/y2006/Files/JSM2006-000277.pdf.

Popenoe, R. (2012). *Feeding desire: Fatness, beauty and sexuality among a Saharan people.* New York, NY: Routledge.

Primack, B. A., Shensa, A., Sidani, J. E., Whaite, E. O., Lin, L. Y., Rosen, D., Colditz, J. B., Radovic, A., & Miller, E. (2017). Social media use and perceived social isolation among young adults in the U.S. *American Journal of Preventive Medicine.*

Proulx, C. M., Helms, H. M., & Buehler, C. (2007). Marital quality and personal well-being: A meta-analysis. *Journal of Marriage and Family, 69,* 576–593.

Public Health Service Act, 42 U.S.C. §241d, §301(d).

Pugh, A. J. (2013). What good are interviews for thinking about culture? Demystifying interpretive analysis. *American Journal of Cultural Sociology, 1*(1), 42–68.

Pugh, A. J. (2014). The divining rod of talk: Emotions, contradictions and the limits of research. *American Journal of Cultural Sociology, 2,* 159–163.

Quinnipiac Poll. (2017, February 23). Republicans out of step with U.S. voters on key issues, Quinnipiac University national poll finds; most voters support legalized marijuana. Retrieved from https://poll.qu.edu/images/polling/us/us02232017_U68mdxwa.pdf/.

Radloff, L. S. (1977). The CES-D scale: A self-report depression scale for research in the general population. *Applied Psychological Measurement, 1*(3), 385–401.

Radloff, L. S., & Locke, B. S. (1986). The community mental health assessment survey and the CES-D scale. In M. M. Weissman, J. K. Meyers, & C. E. Ross (Eds.), *Community surveys of psychiatric disorders* (pp. 177–189). New Brunswick, NJ: Rutgers University Press.

Ragan, D. T., Osgood, D. W., & Feinberg, M. E. (2014). Friends as a bridge to parental influence: Implications for adolescent alcohol use. *Social Forces, 92,* 1061–1085.

Ragin, C. (1987). *The comparative method: Moving beyond qualitative and quantitative methods.* Berkeley: University of California Press.

Ragin, C. (2008). *Redesigning social inquiry: Fuzzy sets and beyond.* Chicago, IL: University of Chicago Press.

Ragin, C., & Amoroso, L. M. (2010). *Constructing social research: The Unity and diversity of method.* Newbury Park, CA: Pine Forge Press.

Ragusa, A. T. (2005). Social change and the corporate construction of gay markets in the *New York Times'* advertising business news. *Media, Culture & Society, 27*(5), 653–676.

Ralph, L. (2014). *Renegade dreams: Living through injury in gangland Chicago.* Chicago, IL: University of Chicago Press.

Rasic, D. T., Belik, S. L., Elias, B., Katz, L. Y., Enns, M., Sareen, J., & Team, S. C. S. P. (2009). Spirituality, religion and suicidal behavior in a nationally representative sample. *Journal of Affective Disorders, 114*(1), 32–40.

Ratcliffe, C., & McKernan, S. (2010). *Childhood poverty persistence: Facts and consequences.* Washington, DC: The Urban Institute.

Rea, L. M., & Parker, R. (2014). *Designing and conducting survey research: A comprehensive guide* (4th ed.). San Francisco, CA: Jossey-Bass.

Reeves, A., Stuckler, D., McKee, M., Gunnell, D., Chang, S. S., & Basu, S. (2012). Increase in state suicide rates in the USA during economic recession. *Lancet, 380*(9856), 1813–1814.

Regnerus, M. (2012a). How different are the adult children of parents who have same-sex relationships? Findings from the New Family Structures Study. *Social Science Research, 41*(4), 752–770.

Regnerus, M. (2012b). The gay parents study. *Slate.* Retrieved from http://www.slate.com/articles/double_x/doublex/features/2012/gay_parents_study/gay_parents_study_mark_regnerus_and_william_saletan_debate_new_research_.html.

Reskin, B. F., & McBrier, D. B. (2000). Why not ascription? Organizations' employment of male and female managers. *American Sociological Review, 65,* 210–233.

Retraction Watch. (2017, April 6). Hello . . . Newman: Yet another sting pranks a predatory journal, Seinfeld-style. Retrieved from http://retractionwatch.com/2017/04/06/hello-newman-yet-another-sting-pranks-a-predatory-journal-seinfeld-style/.

Rhodes, J., Chan, C., Paxson, C., Rouse, C. E., Waters, M. C., & Fussell, E. (2010). The impact of Hurricane Katrina on the mental and physical health of low-income parents in New Orleans. *American Journal of Orthopsychiatry, 80,* 233–243.

Ridgeway, C. (1991). The social construction of status value: Gender and other nominal characteristics. *Social Forces, 70,* 367–386.

Ridgeway, C., Boyle, E., Kuipers, K., & Robinson, D. (1998). How do status beliefs develop? The role of resources and interaction. *American Sociological Review, 63,* 331–350.

Rivera, L. (2015). *Pedigree: How elite students get elite jobs.* Princeton, NJ: Princeton University Press.

Robison, K. K. (2010). Unpacking the social origins of terrorism: The role of women's empowerment in reducing terrorism. *Studies in Conflict & Terrorism, 33*(8), 735–756.

Robinson, K., & Harris, A. (2014). *The broken compass.* Cambridge, MA: Harvard University Press.

Robinson, K., & Harris, A. (2014, April 12). Parental involvement is overrated. *New York Times.* Retrieved from https://opinionator.blogs.nytimes.com/2014/04/12/parental-involvement-is-overrated/#more-152776.

Rogers, E. M. (1995). *Diffusion of innovations.* New York, NY: Free Press.

Rohde, D. (2007, October 5). Army enlists anthropology in war zones. *New York Times.* Retrieved from http://www.nytimes.com/2007/10/05/worldasia/05afghan.html.

Roscigno, V. J., Mong, S., Byron, R., & Tester, G. (2007). Age discrimination, social closure and employment. *Social Forces, 86*(1), 313–334.

Rosenberg, M. (1965). *Society and the adolescent self-image.* Princeton, NJ: Princeton. University Press.

Rosenberg, M. (1986). *Conceiving the self.* Malabar, FL: R. E. Krieger.

Rosenfeld, M. J. (2010). Nontraditional families and childhood progress through school. *Demography, 47*(3), 755–775.

Rosman, K. (2013, April 9). Test-marketing a modern princess. *Wall Street Journal.* Retrieved from www.wsj.com/articles/SB10001424127887324050304578412771510068366.

Rossi, P. H., Berk, R. A. & Lenihan, K. J. (1980). *Money, work and crime: Experimental evidence.* New York, NY: Academic Press.

Rossi, P. H., Lipsey, M. W., & Freeman, H. E. (2004). *Evaluation: A systematic approach* (7th ed.). Thousand Oaks, CA: Sage.

Rossman, G., Esparza, N., & Bonacich P. (2010). I'd like to thank the academy, team spillovers, and network centrality. *American Sociological Review, 75,* 31–51.

Roth, W. (2012). *Race migrations: Latinos and the cultural transformation of race.* Stanford, CA: Stanford University Press.

Roth, W., & Mehta, J. D. (2002). The Rashomon effect: Combining positivist and interpretivist approaches in the analysis of contested events. *Sociological Methods and Research, 31,* 131–173.

Roy, D. (1952). Quota restriction and goldbricking in a machine shop. *American Journal of Sociology, 57,* 427–442.

Rozario, P. A., Morrow-Howell, N., & Hinterlong, J. E. (2004). Role enhancement or role strain: Assessing the impact of multiple productive roles on older caregiver well-being. *Research on Aging, 26*(4), 413–428.

Rudd, R. A. (2016). Increases in drug and opioid-involved overdose deaths—United States, 2010–2015. *MMWR. Morbidity and Mortality Weekly Report, 65.* Retrieved from https://www.cdc.gov/mmwr/preview/mmwrhtml/mm6450a3.htm.

Ruggles, P. (1997). *Drawing the line: Alternative poverty measures and their implications for public policy.* Washington, DC: Urban Institute Press.

Russell, D. M. (2015). Research skills matter: How to teach them. In E. Wojcicki, L. Izumi, & A. Chang. *Moonshots in education: Launching blended learning in the classroom.* San Francisco, CA: Pacific Research Institute.

Ryan, P. (2016). #OscarsSoWhite controversy: What you need to know. *USA Today.* Retrieved from www.usatoday.com/story/life/movies/2016/02/02/oscars-academy-award-nominations-diversity/79645542/.

Ryan, C., & Vicini, J. (2016, June 30). Why you should avoid predatory journals, welcome rigorous review. *Forbes.* Retrieved from https://www.forbes.com/sites/gmoanswers/2016/06/30/predatory-journals/#230dff9a55d6.

Salganik, M. J., & Heckathorn, D. D. (2004). Sampling and estimation in hidden populations using respondent-driven sampling. *Sociological Methodology, 34*(1), 193–239.

Sallaz, J. J. (2009). *The labor of luck: Casino capitalism in the United States and South Africa.* Berkeley: University of California Press.

Sampson, R., & Laub, J. (1993). *Crime in the making: Pathways and turning points through life.* Cambridge, MA: Harvard University Press.

Sampson, R., & Raudenbush, S. W. (1999). Systematic social observation of public spaces: A new look at disorder in urban neighborhoods. *American Journal of Sociology, 105,* 603–651.

Scarce, R. (1999). Good faith, bad ethics: When scholars go the distance and scholarly associations do not. *Law and Social Inquiry, 24*(4), 977–986.

Schaeffer, N. C. (1980). Evaluating race-of-interviewer effects in a national survey. *Sociological Methods & Research, 8,* 400–419.

Schafer, M. H. (2011). Health and network centrality in a continuing care retirement community. *Journals of Gerontology B: Psychological and Social Sciences, 66B,* 795–803.

Schalet, A., Hunt, G., & Joe-Laidler, K. (2003). Respectability and autonomy: The articulation and meaning of sexuality among girls in the gang. *Journal of Contemporary Ethnography, 32*(1), 108–143.

Scharf, D. M., Martino, S. C., Setodji, C. M., Staplefoote, B. L., & Shadel, W. G. (2013). Middle and high school students' exposure to alcohol-and smoking-related media: A pilot study using ecological momentary assessment. *Psychology of Addictive Behaviors, 27,* 1201–1206.

Scheper-Hughes, N. (2001). *Saints, scholars and schizophrenics: Mental illness in rural Ireland.* Berkeley: University of California Press.

Schiller, K. S. (1999). Effects of feeder patterns on students' transition to high school. *Sociology of Education, 72,* 216–233.

Schmidt, B. (2015). Gendered language in teacher reviews: Interactive chart. Retrieved from http://benschmidt.org/profGender.

Schulenberg, J., O'Malley, P. M., Bachman, J. G., Wadsworth, K. N., & Johnston, L. D. (1996). Getting drunk and growing up: Trajectories of frequent binge drinking during the transition to young adulthood. *Journal of Studies on Alcohol, 57*(3), 289–304.

Schuman, H., & Bobo, L. (1988). Survey-based experiments on white racial attitudes toward residential integration. *American Journal of Sociology, 94,* 273–299.

Schwartz, B. (2003). *Abraham Lincoln and the forge of national memory.* Chicago, IL: University of Chicago Press.

Schwarz, N., & Bless, H. (1992). Scandals and the public's trust in politicians: Assimilation and contrast effects. *Personality and Social Psychology Bulletin, 18,* 574–574.

Schworm, P. (2014, May 6). BC will return its interviews on Ireland: A bid to protect participants. *Boston Globe.* Retrieved from http://www.bostonglobe.com/metro/2014/05/06/boston-college-says-interviewees-northern-ireland-troubles-oral-history-project-can-get-their-tapes-back/cRgXf2Th3My0H3zqOq1q6H/story.html.

Science. (2017). "Study about nothing" highlights the perils of predatory publishing. Retrieved from http://www.sciencemag.org/news/sifter/study-about-nothing-highlights-perils-predatory-publishing.

Scieszka, J., & Smith, L. (1992). *The Stinky Cheese Man and other fairly stupid tales.* New York, NY: Viking.

Shalizi, C. R., & Thomas, A. C. (2011). Homophily and contagion are generically confounded in observational social network studies. *Sociological Methods & Research, 40*(2), 211–239.

Sharkey, P. (2013). *Stuck in place: Urban neighborhoods and the end of progress toward racial equality*. Chicago, IL: University of Chicago Press.

Sharkey, P., & Elwert, F. (2011). The legacy of disadvantage: Multigenerational neighborhood effects on cognitive ability. *American Journal of Sociology, 116*(6), 1934–1981.

Shiffman, S. (2009). How many cigarettes did you smoke? Assessing cigarette consumption by global report, time-line follow-back, and ecological momentary assessment. *Health Psychology, 28*, 519–526.

Shiffman, S., Stone, A. A., & Hufford, M. R. (2008). Ecological momentary assessment. *Annual Review of Clinical Psychology, 4*, 1–32.

Shively, J. E. (1992). Cowboys and Indians: Perceptions of Western films among American Indians and Anglos. *American Sociological Review, 57*, 725–734.

Shushan, D, & Marcoux, C. (2011). The rise (and decline?) of Arab aid: Generosity and allocation in the oil era. *World Development, 39*(11), 1969–1980.

Sieber, J. E. (1992). *Planning ethically responsible research*. Newbury Park, CA: Sage.

Sikiru, S. (2014). *Quotes about writing: 1000+ quotes about writing by great and successful writers to inspire and motivate you in your writing journey*. Amazon Digital Services. Retrieved from https://www.amazon.com/Quotes-about-Writing-Successful-Motivate-ebook/dp/B00I2WYG9Y/ref=sr_1_5?s=digital-text&ie=UTF8&qid=1502724992&sr=1-5.

Silbey, S. (2009). In search of social science. In M. Lamont & P. White (Eds.), *Workshop on interdisciplinary standards for qualitative research*. Washington, DC: National Science Foundation.

Silent Spring Institute. (2016). Cape Cod breast cancer and environment study. Retrieved from http://silentspring.org/research-area/cape-cod-breast-cancer-and-environment-study.

Simmel, G. (1922/1971). Conflict. In D. N. Levine (Ed.), *On individuality and social forms* (pp. 70–95). Chicago, IL: University of Chicago Press. (Reprint of original work)

Simmel, G. (1950). The triad. In K. H. Wolff (Ed.), *The sociology of Georg Simmel* (pp. 145–169). New York, NY: Free Press.

Skenazy, L. (2015, January 16). I let my 9 year old ride the subway alone. I got labeled the "world's worst mom." *Washington Post*. Retrieved from https://www.washingtonpost.com/posteverything/wp/2015/01/16/i-let-my-9-year-old-ride-the-subway-alone-i-got-labeled-the-worlds-worst-mom/?utm_term=.051b29125dbc.

Skocpol, T. (1979). *States and social revolution: A comparative study of France, Russia, and China*. Cambridge, England: Cambridge University Press.

Small, M. L. (2008). Lost in translation: How not to make qualitative research more scientific. In M. Lamont & P. White (Eds.), *Workshop on interdisciplinary standards for systematic qualitative research*. Washington, DC: National Science Foundation.

Small, M. L. (2009). "How many cases do I need?" On science and the logic of case selection in field-based research. *Ethnography, 10*(1), 5–38.

Small, M. L. (2011). How to conduct a mixed method study: Recent trends in a rapidly growing literature. *Annual Review of Sociology, 37*, 55–84.

Small, M. L. (2014). Causal thinking and ethnographic research. *American Journal of Sociology, 119*(3), 597–601.

Smirnova, M., & Scanlon, P. (2013). *2013 Census test cognitive interview report*. Washington, DC: Center for Survey Measurement Research and Methodology Directorate, U.S. Census Bureau.

Smith, A. (2016, February 11). *15 percent of American adults have used online dating sites or mobile dating apps*. Washington, DC: Pew.

Smith, C. (2016, December). How Jon Stewart took over the *Daily Show* and revolutionized late-night TV: An oral history. *Vanity Fair*. Retrieved from http://www.vanityfair.com/hollywood/2016/11/how-jon-stewart-took-over-the-daily-show-late-night-tv.

Smith, T. (2011). *Public attitudes towards climate change & other environmental issues across time and countries, 1993-2010*. Chicago, IL: National Opinion Research Center (NORC). Retrieved from http://www.norc.org/PDFs/Public_Attitudes_Climate_Change.pdf.

Smith, T. (2015). *General Social Survey final report: Trends in national spending priorities, 1973–2014*. Chicago, IL: National Opinion Research Center. Retrieved from http://www.norc.org/PDFs/GSS%20Reports/GSS_Trends%20in%20Spending_1973-2014.pdf.

Smith, K. P., & Christakis, N. A. (2008). Social networks and health. *Annual Review of Sociology, 34*, 405–429.

Smith, J. A., McPherson, M., & Smith-Lovin, L. (2014). Social distance in the United States: Sex, race, religion, age, and education homophily among confidants, 1985 to 2004. *American Sociological Review, 79,* 432–456.

Smith, T. W., Marsden, P., Hout, M., & Kim, J. (2016). *General Social Surveys,* 1972–2014 [machine-readable data file]. Principal investigator, T. W. Smith; co-principal investigator, P. V. Marsden; co-principal investigator, M. Hout. National Opinion Research Center (Ed.). Sponsored by the National Science Foundation. Chicago, IL: NORC at the University of Chicago [producer and distributor].

Smith-Lovin, L. & Moscovitz, C. (2016). *Writing in sociology: A brief guide* (1st ed.). New York, NY: Oxford University Press.

Snijders, T. A. B. (2011). Network dynamics. In J. Scott & P. J. Carrington (Eds.), *The SAGE handbook of social network analysis* (pp. 501–513). London, England: Sage.

Snow, D., & Anderson, L. (1993). *Down on their luck: A study of homeless street people.* Berkeley: University of California Press.

Snowdon, D. A., Kemper, S. J., Mortimer, J. A., Greiner, L. H., Wekstein, D. R., and Markesbery, W. R. (1996). Linguistic ability in early life and cognitive function and Alzheimer's disease in late life: Findings from the Nun Study. *JAMA, 275*(7), 528–532.

Sorkowski, P., Kulczycki, E., Sorokowska, A., & Pisanski, K. (2017, March 22). Predatory journals recruit fake editor. *Nature.* Retrieved from http://www.nature.com/news/predatory-journals-recruit-fake-editor-1.21662.

Sowińska, A. (2013). A critical discourse approach to the analysis of values in political discourse: The example of freedom in President Bush's State of the Union addresses (2001–2008). *Discourse & Society,* 957926513486214.

Spencer, S. J., Steele, C. M., & Quinn, D. M. (1999). Stereotype threat and women's math performance. *Journal of Experimental Social Psychology, 35,* 4–28.

Springer, K. W., & Mouzon, D. M. (2011). "Macho men" and preventive healthcare: Implications for older men in different social classes. *Journal of Health and Social Behavior, 52*(2): 212–227.

Stack, C. (1974). *All our kin: Strategies for survival in a black community.* New York, NY: Harper and Row.

Stanovich, K. (2007). *How to think straight about psychology* (8th ed.). Boston, MA: Allyn & Bacon.

Stark, R. (2002). Physiology and faith: Addressing the "universal" gender difference in religious commitment. *Journal for the Scientific Study of Religion, 41*(3), 495–507.

Stattin, H., & Kerr, M. (2000). Parental monitoring: A reinterpretation. *Child Development, 71,* 1070–1083.

Steeh, C., & Piekarski, L. (2007). Accommodating new technologies: Mobile and VoIP communication. In J. M. Lepkowski, C. Tucker, J. M. Brick, E. D. d. Leeuw, L. Japec, P. J. Lavrakas, …R. L. Sangster (Eds.), *Advances in telephone survey methodology* (pp. 423–446). Hoboken, NJ: Wiley.

Steele, C. M., Spencer, S. J., & Aronson, J. (2002). Contending with the group image: The psychology of stereotype and social identity threat. In M. P. Zanna (Ed.), *Advances in experimental and social psychology* (Vol. 37, pp. 397–407). San Diego, CA: Academic Press.

Steglich, C., Snijders, T. A. B., & Pearson, M. (2010). Dynamic networks and behavior: Separating selection from influence. *Sociological Methodology, 40*(1), 329–393.

Stein, J. (2013, May 20). Millennials: The me me me generation. *Time* magazine. Retrieved from http://time.com/247/millennials-the-me-me-me-generation/.

Steinpreis, R. E., Anders, K. A., & Ritzke, D. (1999). The impact of gender on the review of the curricula vitae of job applicants and tenure candidates: A national empirical study. *Sex Roles, 41*(718), 509–528.

Sternberg, R. J. (1986). A triangular theory of love. *Psychological Review, 93,* 119–135.

Stone, J., Lynch, C., Sjomeling, M., & Darley, J. (1999). Stereotype threat effects on black and white athletic performance. *Journal of Personality and Social Psychology, 77,* 1213–1227.

Straumscheim, C. (2016, August 29). Feds target "predatory" publishers. *Inside Higher Ed.* Retrieved from https://www.insidehighered.com/news/2016/08/29/federal-trade-commission-begins-crack-down-predatory-publishers.

Strauss, A. S., & Corbin, J. (1998). *Basics of qualitative research: Techniques and procedures for developing grounded theory* (2nd ed.). London, England: Sage.

Streib, J. (2013). Class origin and college graduates' parenting beliefs. *Sociological Quarterly, 54,* 670–693.

Strunk, William, Jr.; White, E. B. (1999) [1959]. The Elements of Style (4th ed.). Boston: Pearson.

Suls, J., & Wheeler, L. (2012). Social comparison theory. In P. Van Lange, A. Kruglanski, & E. T. Higgins (Eds.), Handbook of theories of social psychology (Vol. 1, pp. 460–482). Thousand Oaks, CA: Sage.

Sutherland, E. H., Cressey, D. R., & Luckenbill, D. (1995). The theory of differential association. In N. Herman (Ed.), Deviance: A symbolic interactionist approach (pp. 64–68). Lanham, MD: General Hall.

Swim, J., Borgida, E., Maruyama, G., & Myers, D. (1989). McKay vs. McKay: Is there a case for gender biased evaluations? Psychological Bulletin, 105, 409–429.

Takhteyev, Y., Gruzd, A., & Wellman, B. (2012). Geography of Twitter networks. Social Networks, 34, 73–81.

Terkel, S. (1970). Hard times: An oral history of the Great Depression: New York, NY: The New Press.

Terkel, S. (1984). The good war: An oral history of World War II. New York, NY: The New Press.

Texas Education Agency. (2011). Testing and accountability. Retrieved from http://www.tea.state.tx.us.

Thomas, D. (2011). Personal networks and the economic adjustment of immigrants. Canadian Social Trends. No. 92. Statistics Canada Catalogue no. 11-008-X.

Thompson, R., & Lee, C. (2011). Sooner or later? Young Australian men's perspectives on timing of parenthood. Journal of Health Psychology 16, 807–818.

Thorne, B. (1993). Gender play: Girls and boys in school. New Brunswick, NJ: Rutgers University Press.

Timmermans, S., & Tavory, I. (2012). Theory construction in qualitative research: From grounded theory to abductive analysis. Sociological Theory, 30(3), 167–186.

Traugott, M. W. (2008). The uses and misuses of polls. In W. Donsbach & M. W. Traugott (Eds.), The SAGE handbook of public opinion research (pp. 232–240). Thousand Oaks, CA: Sage.

Trenholm, C., Devaney, B., Fortson, K., Quay, L., Wheeler, J., & Clark, M. (2007). Impacts of four Title V, Section 510 abstinence education programs. Princeton, NJ: Mathematica Policy Research, Inc. Retrieved from https://aspe.hhs.gov/sites/default/files/pdf/74961/report.pdf.

Turabian, K. L. (2007). A manual for writers of research papers, theses, and dissertations, revised by W. C. Booth, G. G. Colomb, J. M. Williams, and the University of Chicago Press Editorial Staff.

Turgeman-Goldschmidt, O. (2005). Hackers' accounts: Hacking as a social entertainment. Social Science Computer Review, 23(1), 8–23.

Turner, M. L., & LaMacchia, R. A. (1999). The U.S. Census, redistricting, and technology: A 30-year perspective. Social Science Computer Review 17(1), 16–26.

Tyson, K., Darity, W., & Castellino, D. R. (2005). It's not a 'black thing': Understanding the burden of acting white and other dilemmas of high achievement. American Sociological Review, 70, 582–605.

Udry, J. R. (1988). Biological predispositions and social control in adolescent sexual behavior. American Sociological Review, 53, 709–722.

Uhlmann, E. L., & Cohen, G. L. (2005). Constructed criteria: Redefining merit to justify discrimination. Psychological Science, 16, 474–480.

Umberson, D. (2003). Death of a parent: Transition to a new adult identity. New York, NY: Cambridge University Press.

Umberson, D., Thomeer, M. B., Reczek, C., & Donnelly, R. (2016). Physical illness in gay, lesbian and heterosexual marriages: Gendered dyadic experiences. Journal of Health and Social Behavior, 57(4), 517–531.

U.S. Census Bureau. (2010). Explore the form. Retrieved from http://www.census.gov/2010census/about/interactive-form.php

U.S. Census Bureau. (2009, March 17). Confidentiality. Retrieved from http://factfinder.census.gov/jsp/saff/SAFFInfo.jsp?_pageId=su5_confidentiality.

U.S. Census Bureau. (2011). Number, timing, and duration of marriages and divorces: 2009. Figure 1b. Percentage of women never married by age, race and Hispanic origin: 2009. Retrieved from https://www.census.gov/prod/2011pubs/p70-125.pdf.

U.S. Census Bureau. (2016). Marital status. Figure MS-2: Median age at first marriage: 1890 to present. Retrieved from https://www.census.gov/hhes/families/data/marital.html.

U.S. Department of Education. (2001). The No Child Left Behind Act of 2001. Washington, DC: Author.

U.S. Department of Health and Human Services. (2011). HHS poverty guidelines. Retrieved from http://aspe.hhs.gov/poverty/09poverty.shtml.

U.S. Department of Health and Human Services. (2014). *Prior HHS poverty guidelines and Federal Register references.* Retrieved from http://aspe.hhs.gov/poverty/figures-fed-reg.cfm.

U.S. Department of Housing and Urban Development. (2013). *Data collection and analysis plan: Family Options Study.* Retrieved from www.huduser.org/portal/publications/pdf/HUD_501_family_options_Data_Collection_Analysis_Plan.pdf.

Vaisey, S. (2009). Motivation and justification: A dual process model of culture in action. *American Journal of Sociology, 114*(6), 1675–1715.

Vaisey, S. (2014). Is interviewing compatible with the dual-process model of culture? *American Journal of Cultural Sociology, 2,* 150–158.

Valente, T. W. (2010). *Social networks and health.* Oxford, England: Oxford University Press.

Van Der Gaag, M., & Snijders, T. A. B. (2005). The resource generator: Social capital quantification with concrete items. *Social Networks, 27,* 1–29.

Van Maanen, J. (1978). The asshole. In P. K. Manning & J. Van Maanen (Eds.), *Policing: A view from the street* (pp. 221–237). New York, NJ: Random House.

Van Maanen, J. (2011). *Tales of the field: On writing ethnography* (2nd ed.). Chicago, IL: University of Chicago Press.

VanderWeele, T. J. (2011). Sensitivity analysis for contagion effects in social networks. *Sociological Methods & Research, 40*(2), 240–255.

Vaughan, D. (1996). *The Challenger launch decision: Risky technology, culture and deviance at NASA.* Chicago, IL: University of Chicago Press.

Vaughan, D. (2005). Organizational rituals of risk and error. In B. Hutter & M. Power (Eds.), *Organizational encounters with risk* (pp. 33–66). Cambridge, England: Cambridge University Press.

Venkatesh, S. (2000). *American project: The rise and fall of a modern ghetto.* Cambridge, MA: Harvard University Press.

Venkatesh, S. (2002). Doin' the hustle: Constructing the ethnographer in the American ghetto. *Ethnography, 3*(1), 91–111.

Venkatesh, S. (2008). *Gang leader for a day: A rogue sociologist takes to the streets.* New York, NY: Penguin.

Verbrugge, L. M. (1979). Multiplexity in adult friendships. *Social Forces, 57,* 1286–1309.

Wade, L. (2015, June 9). Energy drinks and violent masculinity. The Society Pages. Retrieved from http://thesocietypages.org/socimages/2015/06/19/energy-drinks-and-violent-masculinity.

Wade, L. (2017). *American hookup: The new culture of sex on campus.* New York, NY: W. W. Norton.

Wang, Y., & Rodgers, S. (2014). Reporting on health to ethnic populations: A content analysis of local health news in ethnic versus mainstream newspapers. *Howard Journal of Communications, 24*(3).

Warner, W. L., & Lunt, P. S. (1941). *The social life of a modern community.* New Haven, CT: Yale University Press.

Warr, M. (2002). *Companions in crime: The social aspects of criminal conduct.* Cambridge, England: Cambridge University Press.

Warren, C. A. B. (2002). Qualitative interviewing. In J. F. Gubrium & J. A. Holstein (Eds.), *Handbook of interview research: Context and method* (pp. 83–102). Thousand Oaks, CA: Sage.

Warren, C. A. B., & Karner, T. X. (2005). *Discovering qualitative methods: Field research, interviews, and analysis.* Los Angeles, CA: Roxbury Publishing.

Wasserman, S., & Faust, K. (1994). *Social network analysis: Methods and applications.* Cambridge, England: Cambridge University Press.

Waters, M. C. (1990). *Ethnic options: Choosing identities in America.* Berkeley: University of California Press.

Waters, M. C. (1999). *Black identities: West Indian immigrant dreams and American realities.* Cambridge, MA: Harvard University Press.

Waters, M. C. (2016). Life after Hurricane Katrina: The resilience in survivors of Katrina (RISK) project. *Sociological Forum, 31,* 750–769.

Waters, M. C., & Sykes, J. (2009). Spare the rod, spoil the child?: First and second generation West Indian child rearing practices. In N. Foner (Ed.), *Across generations: Immigrant families in America* (pp. 72–97). New York, NY: New York University Press.

Waters, M. C., Carr, P. J., Kefalas, M., & Holdaway, J. (Eds.). (2011). *Coming of age in America: The transition to adulthood in the twenty-first century.* Berkeley: University of California Press.

Watts, D. J., & Strogatz, S. H. (1998). Collective dynamics of "small-world" networks. *Nature, 393*(6684), 440–442.

Wax, R. (1971). *Doing fieldwork: Warnings and advice.* Chicago, IL: University of Chicago Press.

Weerman, F. M. (2011). Delinquent peers in context: A longitudinal network analysis of selection and influence effects. *Criminology, 49,* 253–286.

Weiss, R. S. (1994). *Learning from strangers: The art and method of qualitative interview studies.* New York, NY: Free Press.

Weitzer, R., & Kubrin, C. (2009). Misogyny in rap music: A content analysis of prevalence and meanings. *Men and Masculinities, 12*(1), 3–29.

Wellman, B. (2001). Physical place and cyberplace: The rise of personalized networking. *International Journal of Urban and Regional Research, 25,* 227–252.

Wellman, B., Salaff, J., Dimitrova, D., Garton, L., Gulia, M., & Haythornthwaite, C. (1996). Computer networks as social networks: Collaborative work, telework, and virtual community. *Annual Review of Sociology, 22,* 213–238.

West, B. T. (2013). Paradata in survey research. *Survey Practice 4*(4). Retrieved from http://surveypractice. org/index.php/SurveyPractice/article/view/112/html.

Wethington, E., & Kessler, R. C. (1986). Perceived support, received support, and adjustment to stressful life events. *Journal of Health and Social Behavior, 27,* 78–89.

Wheelan, C. (2013). *Naked statistics: Stripping the dread from the data.* New York: W. W. Norton.

White, P., & Selwyn, N. (2013). Moving on-line? An analysis of patterns of adult Internet use in the UK, 2002-2010. *Information, Communication & Society, 16*(1), 1–27.

White, H. C., Boorman, S. A., & Breiger, R. L. (1976). Social structure from multiple networks. I. Block-models of roles and positions. *American Journal of Sociology, 81,* 730–780.

Whyte, W. F. (1943/1955). *Street corner society.* Chicago, IL: University of Chicago Press. (Reprint of original work)

Wildeman, C., Schnittker, J., & Turney, K. (2012). Despair by association? The mental health of mothers with children by recently incarcerated fathers. *American Sociological Review, 77*(2), 216–243.

Wilkes, R., Guppy, N., & Farris, L. (2008). No thanks, we're full: Individual characteristics, national context, and changing attitudes toward immigration. *International Migration Review, 42*(2), 302–329.

Willer, R. (2009). No atheists in foxholes: Motivated reasoning and religious ideology. In A. C. Kay, J. T. Jost, & H. Thorisdottir (Eds.), *Social and psychological bases of ideology and system justification* (pp. 241–266). Oxford, England: Oxford University Press.

Williams, C. L. (1989). *Gender differences at work: Women and men in nontraditional occupations.* Berkeley: University of California Press.

Williams, C. L. (1991). *Gender differences at work: Women and men in non-traditional occupations.* Berkeley: University of California Press.

Williams, C. L. (1995). *Still a man's world: Men who do women's work.* Berkeley: University of California Press.

Williams, C. L. (2006). *Inside toyland: Working, shopping, and social inequality.* Berkeley: University of California Press.

Willis, G. B. (2015). *Analysis of the cognitive interview in questionnaire design.* Oxford, England: Oxford University Press.

Willis, P. (1977). *Learning to labour: How working class kids get working class jobs.* New York, NY: Columbia University Press.

Wilson, W. J. (1987). *The truly disadvantaged: The inner city, the underclass, and public policy.* Chicago, IL: University of Chicago Press.

Wilson, W. J. (2012). *The truly disadvantaged: The inner city, the underclass, and public policy.* Chicago, IL: University of Chicago Press.

Wilson, S. P., & Peterson, L. C. (2002). The anthropology of online communities. *Annual Review of Anthropology 31,* 449–467.

Wimer, C., Nam, J. H., Waldfogel, J., & Fox, L. (2016). Trends in child poverty using an improved measure of poverty. *Academic Pediatrics, 16*(3), S60–S66.

Wimmer, A., & Lewis, K. (2010). Beyond and below racial homophily: ERG models of a friendship network documented on Facebook. *American Journal of Sociology, 116,* 583–642.

Wisconsin Longitudinal Study (WLS). (1957–2012). Version 13.03 [machine-readable data file]. R. M. Hauser, W. H. Sewell, & P. Herd (principal investigators). Madison: University of Wisconsin-Madison [distributor]. Retrieved from http://www.ssc.wisc. edu/wlsresearch/documentation/.

Wolch, J., Wilson, J. P., & Fehrenbach, J. (2005). Parks and park funding in Los Angeles: An equity-mapping analysis. *Urban Geography, 26*(1), 4–35.

Wolcott, H. F. (1990). *Writing up qualitative research.* Newbury Park, CA: Sage.

Word, E., Johnston, J., Bain, H. P., Fulton, B. D., Zaharias, J. B., Achilles, C. M., . . . Breda, C. (1990). *The state of Tennessee's Student/Teacher Achievement Ratio (STAR) Project, final summary report 1985-1990.* Nashville: Tennessee State Department of Education.

World Bank. (2016). *World development indicators: GDP per capita (current U.S. $).* Retrieved from http://databank.worldbank.org/data/reports.aspx?source=world-development-indicators.

Wraga, M., Helt, M., Jacobs, E., & Sullivan, K. (2006). Neural basis of stereotype-induced shifts in women's mental rotation performance. *Social Cognitive and Affective Neuroscience, 2*(1), 12–19. doi:10.1093/scan/nsl041.

Wright, J. (2010). Just what is an archives, anyway? Smithsonian Institution Archives. Retrieved from http://siarchives.si.edu/blog/just-what-archives-anyway.

Wright, J. D., & Marsden, P. V. (Eds.). (2010). *Handbook of survey research* (2nd ed.). Bingley, England: Emerald Group Publishing.

Yakubovich, V. (2005). Weak ties, information, and influence: How workers find jobs in a local Russian labor market. *American Sociological Review, 70,* 408–421.

Yavorsky, J. E., Kamp-Dush, C. M., & Schoppe-Sullivan, S. J. (2015). The production of inequality: The gender division of labor across the transition to parenthood. *Journal of Marriage and Family, 77,* 662–679.

Yeager, D. S., Krosnick, J. A., Chang, L., Javitz, H. S., Levendusky, M. S., Simpser, A., & Wang, R. (2011). Comparing the accuracy of RDD telephone surveys and Internet surveys conducted with probability and non-probability samples. *Public Opinion Quarterly, 75*(4), 709–747.

Yeung, K. T. & Martin, J. L. (2003). The looking glass self: An empirical test and elaboration. *Social Forces, 81,* 843–879.

Yin, R. K. (2002). *Case study research design and methods.* Los Angeles, CA: Sage.

York, E., & Cornwell, B. (2006). Status on trial: Social characteristics and influence in the jury room. *Social Forces, 85,* 455–477.

York Cornwell, E., & Cornwell, B. (2008). Access to expertise as a form of social capital: An examination of race-and class-based disparities in network ties to experts. *Sociological Perspectives, 51,* 853–876.

York Cornwell, E., & Waite, L. J. (2009). Social disconnectedness, perceived isolation, and health among older adults. *Journal of Health and Social Behavior, 50,* 31–48.

Yoshikawa, H., Aber, J. L., & Beardslee, W. R. (2012). The effects of poverty on the mental, emotional, and behavioral health of children and youth: Implications for prevention. *American Psychologist, 67*(4), 272.

Zaller, J., & Feldman, S. (1992). A simple theory of the survey response: Answering questions versus revealing preferences. *American Journal of Political Science,* 579–616.

Zimbardo, P. G. (2007). *The Lucifer effect: Understanding how good people turn evil.* New York, NY: Random House.

Zimbardo, P. G., Maslach, C., & Haney, C. (1999). Reflections on the Stanford Prison Experiment: Genesis, transformations, consequences. In T. Blass (Ed.), *Obedience to authority: Current perspectives on the Milgram paradigm* (pp. 193–237). Mahwah, NJ: Erlbaum.

Zimmer, M. (2010). "But the data is already public": On the ethics of research on Facebook. *Ethics of Information Technology, 12,* 313–325.

Zimmerman, G. M., & Messner, S. F. (2010). Neighborhood context and the gender gap in adolescent violent crime. *American Sociological Review, 75*(6), 958–980.

Zinsser, W. (2016). *On writing well: The classic guide to writing nonfiction* (30th anniversary ed.). New York, NY: Harper Perennial.

Zogby, J. (2009, July 22). The Baby Boomer legacy. *Forbes.* Retrieved from https://www.forbes.com/2009/07/22/baby-boomer-legacy-change-consumer-opinions-columnists-john-zogby.html.

Zuberi, D. (2006). *Differences that matter: Social policy and the working poor in the United States and Canada.* Ithaca, NY: Cornell University Press.

Zuckerman, M. (1979). Attribution of success and failure revisited, or: the motivational bias is alive and well in attribution theory. *Journal of Personality, 47*(2), 245–287.

Credits

Chapter 15 Pages 494-495: ELIJAH NOUVELAGE/REUTERS/Newscom; p. 513: Steve Skjold/Alamy Stock Photo; p. 514: Steve Gladfelter; p. 516: REUTERS/Mario Anzuoni/Newscom; p. 521: Hero Images/Getty Images.

Chapter 16 Pages 532-533: Tim Boyle/Staff/Getty Images; p. 536: AP Photo/The Paducah Sun/Steve Nagy; p. 538: Kevin Sullivan/The Orange County Register via AP; p. 541: Comstock Images/Getty Images; p. 544: NASA; p. 547: Ann Johansson/Contributor/Getty Images; p. 549: David Grossman/Alamy Stock Photo; p. 559: Robert Gauthier/Contributor/Getty Images; p. 566: The University of Texas at Austin; p. 572: ZUMA Press Inc/Alamy Stock Photo.

Chapter 17 Pages 578-579: Hero Images/Getty Images; p. 587: Damon Casarez; p. 595: Courtesy of College of Idaho; p. 604: W. W. Norton & Company, Inc. and Gregg Kulick; p. 605: Marcelo Horn/Getty Images; p. 610: Larry Levanti Photography.

TEXT CREDITS

Fig. 3.1: Philip G. Zimbardo, Prisoner Consent Form, "The Stanford Prison Experiment: 40 Years Later." Reprinted by permission of Philip G. Zimbardo, Inc.

Fig. 3.2: Arts and Sciences IRB New Brunswick, Office of Research Regulatory Affairs, Rutgers, the State University of New Jersey, "Informed Consent Form For Confidential Data Collection With Audio/Visual Recording Addendum (General Use)." Reprinted with permission.

Fig. 5.2: From Lenore Sawyer Radloff, "The CES-D Scale A Self-Report Depression Scale for Research in the General Population," *Applied Psychological Measurement*, Vol. 1, No. 3, Summer 1977, pp. 385-401. Copyright © 1977, © SAGE Publications. Reprinted by Permission of SAGE Publications, Inc.

Fig. 8.2: From Devah Pager, "The Mark of a Criminal Record," *American Journal of Sociology*, Volume 108, Number 5 (March 2003), pp. 937-975. Copyright © 2003, The University of Chicago Press. Reprinted with permission.

Fig. 9.1: Figure from Claudia Goldin and Cecilia Rouse, "Orchestrating Impartiality: The Impact of "Blind" Auditions on Female Musicians," *American Economic Review*, Vol. 90, No. 4 (Sept. 2000), pp. 715-741. Reprinted with permission of the American Economic Association and the authors.

Fig. 9.2: From Phyllis Moen, Erin Kelly, Eric Tranby, Qinlei Huang, *Journal of Health & Social Behavior Policy Brief*, Vol. 52, No. 4 (Dec. 2011), p. 403, by American Sociological Association. Reproduced with permission of SAGE Publications, Inc. in the format Book via Copyright Clearance Center.

Fig. 9.3: From "Class Size: Counting Students Can Count," Research Points, Vol. 1, Issue 2 (Fall 2003). Copyright 2003 by American Educational Research Association. Used with Permission.

Fig. 12.1: From Jennifer Wolch, John P. Wilson, and Jed Fehrenbach, "Parks and park funding in Los Angeles: An equity-mapping analysis." Reprinted with permission from Center for Sustainable Cities, Sol Price School of Public Policy, University of Southern California.

Fig. 12.2: From http://benschmidt.org/profGender. Reprinted with permission.

Fig. 12.3: Global Initiative to End All Corporal Punishment of Children, www.endcorporalpunishment.org, April 2017. Reprinted with permission.

Fig. 13.2: From Mark S. Granovetter, "The Strength of Weak Ties," *The American Journal of Sociology*, Vol. 78, No. 6 (May 1973), pp. 1360-1380. Copyright © 1973, The University of Chicago. Reprinted with permission.

Fig. 13.4: From Peter S. Bearman, James Moody, and Katherine Stovel, "Chains of Affection," *American Journal of Sociology*, Vol. 110, No. 1 (July 2004), pp. 44-91. Copyright © 2004, The University of Chicago Press. Reprinted with permission.

Fig. 15.4: Tyler Vigen, "Per capita cheese consumption correlates with Number of people who died by becoming tangled in their bedsheets," http://www.tylervigen.com/spurious-correlations. Reprinted with permission.

Fig. 16.12: Republished with permission of SAGE Publications, Inc., from "Beyond Text: Using Arrays to Represent and Analyze Ethnographic Data," Corey M. Abramson and Daniel Dohan, *Sociological Methodology*, Vol. 45, No. 1 (April 2015), pp. 272-319, by American Sociological Association; permission conveyed through Copyright Clearance Center, Inc.

Fig. 17.3: Republished with permission of SAGE Publications, Inc., from "Into the Red and Back to the Nest? Student Debt, College Completion, and Returning to the Parental Home among Young Adults," Jason N. Houle and Cody Warner, *Sociology of Education*, Vol. 90, No. 1 (January 2017), pp. 89-108, by American Sociological Association; permission conveyed through Copyright Clearance Center, Inc.

Fig. 17.4: Republished with permission of SAGE Publications, Inc., from "Behavioral Functioning among Mexican-Origin Children Does Parental Legal Status Matter?," Nancy S. Landale, Jessica Halliday Hardie, R. S. Oropesa, Marianne M. Hillemeier, *Journal of Health & Social Behavior*, Vol. 56, No. 1 (Feb. 2015), pp. 2-18, by American Sociological Association; permission conveyed through Copyright Clearance Center, Inc.

Fig. 17.7: Republished with permission of John Wiley and Sons, from "Preparing and Presenting Effective Research Posters," Jane E. Miller, *Health Services Research*, Volume 42, Issue 1 (Feb. 2007), Copyright © 2006, John Wiley and Sons; permission conveyed through Copyright Clearance Center, Inc.

Fig. 17.8: Philip J. Cook and Jens Ludwig, "More Prisoners Versus More Crime is the Wrong Question," Brookings Institution Policy Brief, No. 185 (December 2011), Copyright © 2011 the Brookings Institution. Reprinted with permission.

Fig. 17.9: Philip N. Cohen, "No Black women are not the 'most educated' group in the US," *Family Inequality* (blog), June 7, 2016. Reprinted with permission of the author.

Appendix A: Katherine S. Newman, "Consent Form #1 For Subjects of Majority Age." Reprinted with permission of the author.

Appendix B: American Sociological Association, "ASA Code of Ethics," www.asanet.org. Copyright © 1999 by the American Sociological Association. Reprinted with permission.

Index

causal hypothesis, 55–56
    variables in, 61
causality, 19, 27, 236, 239–40, 278
    in qualitative analysis, 538–42
cause-and-effect relationships, 173,
    174, 176, 236, 506
causes, necessary and sufficient, 538
causes-of-effects, 537, 538
CBCL, 143
cell percentages, 478
cells, 476
census, 160–62, 348, 393–94
    confidentiality and, 89–90
Census Bureau. *See* U.S. Census Bureau
Center for Epidemiologic Studies
    Depression scale (CES-D), 138,
    139, 140–41, 220
Centers for Disease Control and
    Prevention (CDC), 210
centrality of a network actor, 429
certificate of confidentiality, 85
CES-D, 138, 139, 140–41, 220
Challenger disaster, 544
The Challenger Launch Decisions:
    Risky Technology, Culture,
    and Deviance at NASA
    (Vaughan), 598
Chambliss, Don, 312
Chamratrithirong, 370
chance differences, 497–98
Changing Lives of Older Couples
    (CLOC), 203, 222
Charmaz, Kathy, 317
cheating detected by statistics, 475
chemical exposure, testing for, 171–72
Cherlin, Andrew, 47
Chicago, 314, 532–34
The Chicago Guide to Writing about
    Numbers (Miller), 610
Chicago heat wave of 1995, 181
Chicago School, 305, 306
Chicago Tribune, 159
childbearing, 3, 47, 200
Child Behavior Checklist (CBCL), 143
childless women and wage differences
    between mothers, 240, 259, 260,
    262, 268
child-rearing, 48, 335
children
    creating culture through play, 36, 37
    extracurricular activities, 369–70
    food preferences influenced by
        parents' behavior, 540–41
    impact of neighborhood on, 528
    internalizing behaviors, 590–91

parents' involvement in their
    education, 41, 44
of same-sex parents, 175
Children of the Great Depression
    (Elder), 347
Children's Catalog, 404, 405
children's literature and portrayal of
    boys and girls, 404
China, 379
chi-square statistic, 499
chi-square test, 499–501
Chosen, The (Karabel), 179–80
Christakis, Nicholas, 451, 541–42
church attendance, 204
churches and key informants, 195
CIRI Human Rights Data, 389
Civil Rights History Project, 346, 387
class, social, 8
class-action employment discrimina-
    tion lawsuits, 242
classical ethnography, 332
CLASS protocol, 124–25, 137, 138, 140, 147
Classroom Assessment Scoring System
    (CLASS) protocol, 124–25, 137,
    138, 140, 147
classroom quality
    academic dimensions of, 147
    conceptualization of, 142
    socioemotional dimensions of, 147
    validity and, 147
classroom size, 274, 275, 277, 289
    Tennessee class-size experiment,
    290–93
class-size reduction (CSR), 290–93
Clinton, Hiliary, 409
clip-on directional microphone, 363
cliques, 428
closed-ended questions, 122, 195,
    215–17
closed triad, 427
closeness centrality, 429–30
clustering, 165
clustering coefficient, 428
clusters, 167
cluster sampling, 167–68, 169
coat closet approach to theory, 43
coauthor, 19, 308, 612
codebook, 222, 408, 415, 562
Code of Ethics of the American
    Anthropological Association,
    307, 308
codes, 548
    analytic, 551, 553–58, 561–62
    attribute, 551–52, 554, 558
    index, 551, 552–53, 554

intersection of, 560
    types of, 551–58
codes of ethics, 84–92
    American Sociological Association
        Code of Ethics, 94
coding, 406–7, 548–62
    analysis and, 558–71
    automated, 408–9
    origins of, 549–51
    tasks and tools, 550
coding scheme, 406–7
cognitive dissonance, 309
cognitive interviewing, 227
cognitive interviews, 348
cognitive pretest, 227
Cohen, Philip, 601–2
cohesion, 428, 457
cohort designs, 19
cohort replacement, 484
collective memory, 399
college
    attending, 27–28
    choosing, 341–42, 355
    gender and income, 524
    happiness and attending college,
        503, 506
    life at, 319
    sexual assault and misconduct at, 311
college students
    complete participant and, 307–8
    as research subjects, 173–74
Columbine High School shootings,
    109, 117
column percentages, 479
Committee on Publishing Ethics
    (COPE), 604
communicating research findings,
    578–617
    to academic audiences, 580–97
    academic integrity in, 614–15
    beyond academic audiences, 598–602
    oral presentations, 596–97
    posters, 594–96
    research proposals, 592–94
    research report, 581–92
    summary, 616–17
    tips for effective writing, 608–15
communication, 50
Community Healthy Marriage
    Initiative, 281–82
community studies, 314
companionate love, 108
comparative research methods, 397
competitive kid capital, 369
complete participant, 307–9

expert analyses, 383–84
expert sample, 349
explanatory research, 27
explanatory theory, 37
exploratory research, 27
exploratory theory, 37–38
expressive approach to education,
    561–62
extended case study approach, 317,
    544–45
external markets of status, 34
external validity, 148–49, 150, 245–46,
    247, 252, 254, 278, 319, 503
    linking to internal validity, 149, 151
extremity, 178–79
Exxon Valdez oil spill, 85

F

Fab Five basketball team, 113
Facebook, 188, 333, 424, 434, 438,
    439–40
    study, 68–69
face-to-face interviews, 50, 202–5, 229
    limitations of, 204–5
    strengths of, 204
face validity, 146
factorial design experiment, 248
factory workers, 317, 325
falsifiable theories, 40
falsification, 55
Family Inequality blog, 601–2
family process model, 39, 54
fashion modeling, 180
fast-food restaurant, 10, 330
fatherhood wage premium, 523
Fauth, Rebecca, 611
feasibility, 23, 26
Federal Front Door, 334
federal poverty line (FPL), 103, 134–35
Federal Trade Commission (FTO), 605
felons and financial support to, 298
female. *See* women
female circumcision laws, 14–15
female Marines, 351
female self-denial, 11
femininity, 350–51
feminist theory, 8, 34, 49
Festinger, Leon, 309
fictional interviewees, 359
field experiments, 247–48
    randomized, 279
    strengths and weaknesses, 249, 255
field notes, 328–30, 365, 560
field of study, 117–18

field research, 16
field study, ethnographic, 320–33
fieldwork, 306, 314–15, 317–18
    complete participant, 307–9
    virtual, 306
figures in a research report, 589–92
filter question, 203
financial support to felons, 298
Fine, Gary Alan, 43
first-person accounts, 387
first person in writing, 613
Fischer, Claude, 521
Fisher Folk (Ellis), 331
Fitzgerald, F. Scott, 316
fixed-choice name generator, 446–47
fixed response options, 199
fixed trait, 247
Flickr, 439
flight attendants, 179
Florida Healthy Beaches Program, 387
focus group, 342, 370–72
    running and analyzing, 371–72
    sampling for, 371
follow-up questions, 360–61
forced choice, 216
Ford Motor Company, 394
foreign aid, 497–501
formative research, 285
formulating the evaluation
    question, 276
FORTRAN, 445
Foucault, Michel, 410
Fowler, James, 451
Fragile Families study, 90
FrameWorks Institute, 343
Framingham Heart Study (FHS), 451
free-choice name generator, 446–47
Freedom of Information Act (FOIA),
    378, 394–95
Free-Range Kids, 369
Freese, Jeremy, 25
free will being eroded by television, 150
freezing experiments with humans, 72
French Revolution, 379
frequency, 222, 464
frequency distribution, 227, 230,
    463–64, 470
frequency response category, 123
Friedman, Hiliary Levey, 369
friends' data accessed without
    permission, 68–69
functional magnetic resonance imaging
    (fMRI), 263
fundamental cause perspective on
    health inequalities, 25

G

GADM database, 389
Gallup polls, 163, 164, 165
Game of Death, The (documentary), 150
Gang Leader for a Day (Venkatesh), 69,
    328, 332
gangs, 315
Gans, Herbert, 306, 315, 326, 549
Garfunkel, Art, 345
gatekeepers, 325
gay and lesbian couples, attitudes
    towards by heterosexuals,
    250–51
Geertz, Clifford, 304, 535
gender, 8, 34
    college degree and income, 524
    different roles in U.S. and Papua New
        Guinea, 304
    impacting experiments, 238
    impacting happiness, 14
    power and, 49
    prayer and, 507–9
    status beliefs and, 244–45
gender-affirming condition, 237
gender discrimination, 241, 242–43
    hiring of orchestra musicians,
        253, 283
gender gap in violent crime, 176
gender identity, 350–51
gender segregation, 242
gender stereotypes, 242–43, 263
gender theory, 325
gene-environment studies, 92
generalizability, 150, 200
    nonrepresentative samples and,
        173–76
generalizable knowledge, 5, 40, 77
General Mills, 334
General Social Survey (GSS), 165, 171,
    197–98, 199, 202, 222, 381, 416,
    432–33, 436, 442, 443, 450,
    463–65, 469, 474, 483–88, 497
general theory of crime, 37, 53, 57
Generation X and projected marriage
    rate, 9
genetic material and confidentiality,
    90, 92
genocides, 411–14
geodesic distance, 428
geographic information system
    (GIS), 389
geography and suicide, 21
Georgianna, 21
Germany, 402
Giordano, Peggy, 51, 121

Office for Human Research Protection (OHRP), 78
Office of Strategic Services (OSS), 70
off-line, 425, 428, 440
oligarchy, 180
Olympic coverage, 45
Olzak, Susan, 386, 392
omnibus surveys, 197–98
one-mode networks, 435
online community, 336
online dating site, 193
online social networks, 438–40
online surveys, 212–13
onset of puberty, 107, 108, 109–10
    as dimension of puberty, 115
    as individual-level factor, 110
    measurement of, 116–17, 123–24
On the Fireline: Living and Dying with Wildland Firefighters (Desmond), 324
On the Run (Goffman), 321, 322
op-ed, 600–1
open-ended questions, 122, 195, 217–19
Open Government Initiative, 395
open triad, 427
operationalization, 57, 116–28, 406
    definition, 102
    field of study, 117–18
    measurement, 119–24
    mismatches between units of analysis, 118–19
    of poverty, 103–4
    progressed from conceptualization, 104–6
    steps of, 116
oppositional culture, 40, 113
optional ethnicity, 549
Oracle of Bacon, 425
oral histories, 77–78, 345–46
Oral History Association, 77
oral presentations, 578, 580, 596–97
orchestra musicians and gender discrimination, 253, 283
order effects in surveys, 225–26
Order of Things, The (Foucault), 410
ordinal response category, 123
ordinal variables, 112, 469
ordinary least squares (OLS) regression, 151–52
organization as unit of analysis, 109
organizations for materials for materials-based methods, 395–96
original questions, 223
Oscar nominees and ethnicity, 382
other-report, 119

out-group, 411
outliers, 180, 468, 472
outlines in writing, 609
outsiders, 321, 324–25
oversample, 169
Oxford Bibliographies (database), 383
Oxford University Press, 604

P

Paducah, Kentucky, 536
Pager, Devah, 83, 93, 248–49, 252, 255, 259, 261, 266
Paik, Anthony, 521
panel design, 18, 127
panel study, 126, 207
Panel Study of Income Dynamics (PSID), 105–6, 222
panel surveys, 196–97, 484–85
paper-and-pencil interview (PAPI), 202–3
paradata, 202, 209
paradigms, 45–46
    clashing of, 47
    scientific, 46
    sociological, 48–51
parental monitoring, 107, 108, 117–18
    reducing juvenile delinquency, 118
parents
    behavior influencing children's food preferences, 540–41
    children's education and, 41, 44
    educational attainment influencing children's, 141–42
    education of, 143
Park, Robert, 305, 386
Parker, Dorothy, 608
parks
    racial inequality in access to, 388
    used in materials-based methods, 388–89
Parsons, Talcott, 48
partial confounding, 512
participant observation, 304, 306
participant observer, 310–12
participants being randomly assigned, 237–38
party culture at college campuses, 310, 311
past experience, 182–83
path diagram, 505–6, 508, 517, 528
path length in a network, 428
Patient-Reported Outcomes Measurement Information System (PROMIS), 20

Pavalko, Eliza, 42–43
Paxton, Pamela, 396
Paying for the Party (Armstrong & Hamilton), 310, 311
peer-review
    predatory journals and, 605
    process, 580, 603–8
peer reviewed journals, 59
peer reviewers, 606–7
people in occupations studied by observers, 312–13
percentage distribution, 464
percentages in cross-tabulation, 477–79
percentiles, 472, 473
perception of success and ethnicity, 570
perceptions of reality, 441
period effects, 485
Perreira, Krista, 140
personal experiences, 4, 7
personal response style, 244
personal troubles versus public issues, 7, 8
perspective-taking experiment, 261
Pew Charitable Trusts, 60
Pew Research Center, 171, 193, 217
Pfeffer, Ric, 93
Phelps, Michael, 45
Philadelphia, 314, 322
Philadelphia Negro, The (Du Bois), 314
photographs, 386
    in interviews, 361–62
physical attractiveness, 34, 136
physical materials used in materials-based methods, 387
physiological measures, 262–63, 264
Picou, Steven, 85
pie charts, 464
pilot study, 593
pilot testing, 145
plagiarism, 614
play and children creating culture, 36, 37
Playing to Win: Raising Children in a Competitive Culture (Friedman), 369
police and black youth, 532–34
police shooting bias, 267–68
police work, 316
policy briefs, 599–600
policy makers, 79, 87, 104, 267, 288–89, 292, 295, 298–99
political exit polls, 167
politically charged contexts, 274–75
political views in the U.S., 199–200
politics of evaluation research, 298–99

research methods, 300
  mixed, 5
  qualitative, 4, 5, 9, 11, 16–17, 37, 38, 41, 54
  quantitative, 4, 5, 9, 11, 16–17, 27, 38, 41, 54
  used in evaluation research, 278–88
research process
  asking questions, 23, 26
  choosing a question and setting goals, 22–28
  completing, 128–29
research proposals, 592–94
research protocol, 78–79
research question, 414
research reports, 581–92
residential integration, 250, 262
re-socialized, 326
re-sort, 402, 549
resource generators, 453–54
respect for subjects, 71
respondent fatigue, 209, 450
respondents, 194, 349
  paying, 364
  as social network informants, 441–48
response categories, 122–23
response rate, 201, 211, 214
response set, 224–25
Ressler, Cali, 286–87
results in a research report, 586–87
Results-Only Work Environment (ROWE), 284, 286–87
résumé, 93, 238, 240, 258, 259, 268, 605
"returners" from rural America, 354
reverse causality, 519–22
revise and submit in the publication process, 607
revolutions and their occurrence, 379
Rice, Ray, 62, 398
Ridgeway, Cecilia, 241, 244, 246
Riecken, Henry, 309
risks and benefits assessed by institutional review board, 79–82
risk versus benefit analysis, 72
Rivera, Lauren, 316
Robert Taylor Homes, 69
Robinson, Keith, 601
Robison, Kristopher, 397
robocalls, 207
robustness
  definition, 143
  testing for, 143–45
Rodger, Shelly, 392
role enhancement theory, 584

role strain theory, 584
romantic love, 108
Romney, Mitt, 488
Roosevelt, Franklin D., 91, 159
Roscigno, Vincent, 17
Rose, Jalen, 113
Rosenberg self-esteem scale, 225
Rosenfeld, Michael, 175
roster, 441, 446
Roth, Wendy, 361–62, 536
ROWE, 284, 286–87
row percentages, 479
rural America, growing up in, 354
Russian Revolution (1917), 379
Rwanda, 411–14

S

Saint Elizabeth's Hospital, 93
Saints, Scholars, and Schizophrenics (Scheper-Hughes), 327–28
salience, 246
Sallaz, Jeffrey, 183
same-sex marriage, 18, 599, 600
same-sex parenting, 175
same-sex relationships, 483, 484, 485
  dynamics of, 564–65
sample for range, 350
samples
  cluster, 169
  definition, 158
  random choice of, 159–60
  representativeness of, 187–88
  statistical significance and, 502–4
sampling, 28–29, 128, 156–91, 404–6
  advantages of probability sampling, 162–63
  in case-oriented research, 176–88
  cluster, 167–68
  convenience sample, 162
  definition, 158
  to describe populations, 158–65
  for focus groups, 371
  hidden populations, 187–88
  margin of error, 163–65
  nonprobability, 162, 170–71
  nonrepresentative samples usefulness, 171–76, 190
  probability, 160, 165–71, 190
  purposive, 177, 400, 404, 543
  random, 177, 404
  sequential, 183, 186
  simple random, 166–67, 169
  stratified, 168–69
  summary, 190–91

  theoretical, 543
  weighting, 169–71
sampling distribution, 164
sampling error, 163, 164, 201
sampling for an interview, 349–56
  mixed-methods samples, 355–56
  purposive, 349–50
  snowball sampling, 351
sampling for range, 186
sampling frame, 166
sampling weights, 415
Sampson, Robert, 313, 347
Sanchagrin, Kenneth, 521
sanctuary cities, 538–40
SAS, 441
Satanists, 307
saturation, 186–87, 331, 354, 402, 543
Saturday Night Live, 345
scale, 220
Scarce, Rik, 85
Schachter, Stanley, 309
schema theory, 34
Scheper-Hughes, Nancy, 327–28
Schmidt, Benjamin, 390
Schneider, Barbara, 42
school
  quality, 107, 108, 111, 137
  size as a ratio variable, 114
schooling and poverty, 105
school sector as nominal variable, 112
school shootings, 536
School Sisters of Notre Dame, 172–73
Schuman, Howard, 250
Schwartz, Barry, 398–99
science's relationship with media, 47
scientific method, 22–23, 35
  steps of, 35
  theory within, 34–44
scientific paradigms, 46
scientific relevance, 23, 26
screener question, 203
search engines, 59, 383–84, 386
Seattle, 182
secondary data source, 194
secondary quantitative data sets, 414–16
secondary versus primary information, 391–93
"Second Generation in New York" study, 551, 553–54, 560–61
Second Life, 336
Second Shift: Working Families and the Revolution at Home (Hochschild), 598
Secure Sockets Layer (SSL) protocol, 88
"seekers" from rural America, 354

segregation by gender, 242
Seinfeld, Jerry, 596
selection bias, 280, 452
self-administered questionnaires
    (SAQs), 195, 209
self-esteem, 29
self-interest, 50
self-reports, 116, 119, 252, 277, 441
semenarche, 115
semi-structured interview, 344
semi-structured questions, 217–19
sentences into paragraphs, 612
sequential sampling, 183, 186
service-sector workers, 179
setting in a laboratory experiment,
    256–57
Seventh Ward of Philadelphia, 314
Sewell, William H., 228
*Sex and Temperament in Three
    Primitive Societies* (Mead), 304
sexual assault and misconduct at
    college campuses, 311
sexual behavior, 294
sexual harassment, 261
    as result to threats to masculinity,
        236–37, 258, 259
sexuality, 221
    perceptions of men's and women's, 174
sexual knowledge, 294
sexual relationships network
    diagram, 443
sex work, 325
Shanahan, Suzanne, 386
Sharkey, Patrick, 528
short-answer questions, 343
showcard, 202, 203
siblings, number of, and academic
    achievement, 526, 528
Sidewalk (Duneier), 328, 598
significance testing, 496–505
    concerns about, 504–5
    definition, 498
Silent Spring Institute, 387
Simmel, Georg, 431
simple random sample, 166
simple random sampling, 166–67, 169
simulated experiments, 74–76
single-blind peer review, 606
singlehood, 9
single item questions, 219–20
single mothers, 9
single name generator, 446
single-observation survey, 195
Sinn Fein political party, 78
six degrees of separation, 423, 425, 429

Skenazy, Lenore, 369
skewed, 467
Skidmore, 342
skip pattern, 203
Skocpol, Theda, 379, 383
Slick, Grace, 345
Small, Cathy, 307–8, 354
Small, Mario, 186
small-group processes, 39
smartphones for data collection,
    437–38
Smith, Tom W., 486
Snow, David, 315
snowball sample, 186, 187
snowball sampling, 351
Snowdon, David, 172
social actors, 425, 426, 429, 431–32
    characteristics, 429–30
social artifacts, 109
social capital, 453
social causes of death rates, 181
social change, 199–200
social class, 8, 34
    differences and involvement in
        children's education, 41, 44
    health and, 540–41
    shaping identities of immigrants, 350
    in Southern Society, 435
social cognitive theory, 62
social comparison, 39
social construction of reality, 36
social context, 51
    of poverty, 104
social desirability bias, 204–5,
        262, 277
social differences, 8–9
social elites and privilege, 177
Social Forces, 603
social hierarchies, 8
social importance, 23
social inequality, 514–15
social influence on humans, 150
social institutions, surveying, 194–95
social intervention, 274
    implementation, 277–78
social isolation
    social media use by young adults
        and, 20
    in the U.S., 521
social life, level of, 39–40, 109
socially disadvantaged older adults, 15
social media use of youth adults and
    social isolation, 20
social movements and media coverage,
    160–61

social network
    analysis, 29
    concepts, 425–31
    definition, 424–25
    online, 438–40
    respondents as informants, 441–48
    stability of, 15
social network analysis, 423–59
    assessing social network change,
        455–57
    automating, 445
    collecting data, 436–41
    data organization, 434
    definition, 424
    design issues, 431–35
    identifying members, 441–48
    pseudo-network data, 452–55
    software, 440–41
    sources of bias, 448–52
    summary, 458–59
    visual aids for, 447, 449
social network composition, 426
social network dynamics, 455–57
social network index (SNI), 454–55
social psychology, 10, 39
Social Psychology Quarterly (journal), 43
social reality, 45
social research ethics, 150
social roles, 379
    well-being of older caregivers and,
        584–85
social science research
    ethics in, 67–98
    shedding light on social differences,
        8–9
    types of, 12–22
social sciences, 9–12
social science theory, 45–52
social scientists, 316
social security number, 84, 85–86, 160,
        228, 585
social structures, 6, 10
social ties, 425
    mortality and, 566
societal blind spots, 380
societal structures, 379
society as unit of analysis, 109
society containing competing
    interests, 49
sociocentric network designs, 432–34
sociodemographic, 10, 516
socioeconomic status (SES) and
    academic achievement, 528
socioemotional, 107, 111, 124
Sociological Abstracts (database), 59, 383

sociological analysis, 330
Sociological Images blog, 410
sociological imagination, 4
    adopting, 6–8
sociological paradigms, 48–51
    conflict, 49, 51–52
    rational choice, 50, 52
    structural functionalism, 48–49, 51
    symbolic interactionism, 50–51, 52
sociological perspectives, 6–12
Sociological Theory, 59
sociologist, 4, 5, 304–6, 318, 398–99
    becoming a, 14, 15, 24, 25
sociology
    as an art and a science, 5
    answering questions, 4
    definition, 4
    differences from other social
        sciences, 9–12
    in relation to anthropology, 304–5
    as a science, 4
    themes, 4
Sociology of Education (journal),
        42, 59
Sorvino, Paul, 381
South Africa, 183
Southern society and social network
        analysis, 435
South Lawndale, 181
"So what?" question, 559
specific aims of research proposal, 593
speech to text, 366
spirituality and desistance from
        crime, 121
split-ballot design, 198
split-half method, 143–44
Sports Illustrated, 404
spousal caregiving perceptions,
        564–65
Springer, Kristen, 223
spurious correlations, 506
spuriousness, 54–55, 239–40
St. Louis, 281
St. Paul's School, 177
stability, 135
stakeholders, 274
standard deviation, 472–73
Stanford prison experiment, 74–76
Stanford University, 311
STAR study, 290–93, 295–96, 298
Stata, 441
STATcompiler tool, 394
statistical controls, 282
statistically significant, 497
statistical power, 502

statistical significance
    determination, 499–502
    versus practical significance, 504
    samples and, 502–4
statistical validity, 151–52
statistics, 462–63
    detecting cheating, 475
    misleading, 488–90
statnet, 440
status and external markers, 34
status attainment process, 141
status beliefs and their formation, 241,
        244–45
status characteristics theory, 34, 35,
        42–43
"stayers" from rural America, 354
stem, 215
stereotypes
    gender, 242–43
    threat, 238–39, 261, 262–63
Sternberg, Robert, 108
Stickup Kids: Race, Drugs, Violence,
        and the American Dream, The
        (Contreras), 324
Stormfront, 384
StoryCorps, 346
Strangers in Their Own Land
        (Hochschild), 572, 573
strata, 168
stratification, 165
stratified sampling, 168–69
Strauss, Anselm, 306, 355, 542, 543
Street Corner Society (Whyte), 314
Streib, Jesse, 47
Stringer, Scott, 297
strong ties, 430–31
structural functionalism, 48–49, 51
structural holes, 429
structured abstract, 581–82, 583
structured interviews, 344
structured survey interview, 195
students
    changing their intelligence, 247–48
    white benefiting more than
        non-whites, 49
Student/Teacher Achievement
        Ratio (START) Project, 290–93,
        295–96, 298
Studio System, 382
study execution, 128
Study of Early Child Care and
        Youth Development (NICHD),
        116, 119
subculture, 305
subject fatigue, 21

subjects
    interacting with them, 326–28
    relationship with researcher, 326–27
subnetwork, 428
substantive significance, 504
success codes, 557
Sudan, 411, 412, 489
suicide
    predictors, 21
    religious affiliation and, 119
Suicide (Durkheim), 119
summary statistic, 466
supplemental line, 134–35
supplemental poverty measure, 103
suppression, 90
    of variables, 517–18
suppressor variable, 517
survey data sites available on the
        Internet, 222
survey experiments
    strengths and weaknesses of,
        252–53, 255
    web-based, 250
survey instrument, 214
SurveyMonkey, 212
survey research, 29, 193–233
    ethical concerns in, 230–31, 233
surveys, 5, 13, 16, 117, 119, 184–85, 192,
        193–94, 343–44, 367, 437–38,
        441–43
    avoiding monotony and response set,
        224–25
    avoiding order effects, 225–26
    breath of topics, 197–98
    challenges of, 200–1
    closed-ended questions, 215–17
    conducting, 226–30, 232
    content, 214–26, 232
    cross-sectional, 195–96
    definition, 194
    errors in, 200–1
    establishing trust and rapport, 224
    face-to-face interviews, 202–5, 229
    format, 195
    generalizability, 200
    Internet-based surveys, 212–13
    longitudinal, 196, 228–29
    mail, 209, 211
    mixed-mode approaches, 213–14
    omnibus, 197–98
    panel, 196
    population-based, 444
    preliminary data analysis, 227, 230
    pretesting, 226–27
    repeated cross-sectional, 196